DIAMOND INSIGHTS 2018

Charting the Ongoing Evolution of Baseball and Its Players

Edited by Geoff Young

David Brown, Russell A. Carleton, Dennis Cleary, Mary Craig, Zach Crizer, Patrick Dubuque, Mike Gianella, Craig Goldstein, Bryan Grosnick, Jonathan Judge, Jeff Long, Rob Mains, Kate Morrison, Rob Neyer, John Paschal, Harry Pavlidis, Dave Pease, Jarrett Seidler, Holly M. Wendt

Dave Pease, Consultant Editor
Harry Pavlidis and Rob McQuown, Statistics Editors

Baseball Prospectus LLC

Library of Congress Cataloging-in-Publication Data:
paperback
ISBN-10: 1979885370
ISBN-13: 978-1979885379

Project Credits
Cover Design: Karen Sitras
Interior Design and Production: Jeff Pease, Dave Pease
Layout: Jeff Pease, Dave Pease

Cover Photos
Front Cover: Zack Greinke. © Bill Mitchell
Back Cover: Topps® trading cards used courtesy of The Topps
Company, Inc.

Baseball icon courtesy of Uberux, from https://www.shareicon.net/
author/uberux

Manufactured in the United States of America
10 9 8 7 6 5 4 3 2 1

Table of Contents

Part 3: Player Analysis

Preface

by Dave Pease

I used to play Dungeons and Dragons, and one of the things I loved about the game books was how they worked in concert with one another, providing complementary material to increase knowledge of the game without ever being duplicative or boring. Our goal with *Diamond Insights 2018* is to provide a useful supplement for our flagship publication, *Baseball Prospectus 2018*, augmenting without repeating. Think of the book you now hold in your hands as the *Unearthed Arcana* to the *Annual*'s *Dungeon Master's Guide*.

Such comparisons aside, how did we get here? It's a good question. *Diamond Insights* came out of our early editor's meetings for *Baseball Prospectus 2018*. As has become our tradition, the editors get on the phone mid-year and start preparation for next year's Annual. One of the very first topics we cover is what we can add to the book.

On the one hand, we expect that after all these years, there aren't a mass of obvious improvements to the general formula for the book. My former boss used to refer to this as a "target-rich environment," a situation where easily improvable circumstances are everywhere in a process flow. We hope that isn't where we're at with the design of the *Annual* at this point. On the other hand, Baseball Prospectus as an organization has changed a lot over time, and the types of things we can do have changed in lockstep.

We walk a fine line on changes for other reasons, too. The *Annual* always clocks in at around 600 pages, and we don't get a lot of complaints from readers that it's too short. With a return to the nicer 60# paper a couple of years back, the book got even more unwieldy. We've heard from people who claim to have thrown out their back by keeping their copy of the *Annual* in their backpacks, and we *think* they're kidding.

During our meetings, we talked about original essays (the Fungoes from the early *Annuals*), and it became immediately apparent that we had a lot of good material to explore and a long list of authors we wanted to work with. This is great but presents certain logistical challenges. *Baseball Prospectus 2018* includes unique profiles of the Korea Baseball Organization and Nippon Professional Baseball, and while we're proud of those, their inclusion left us without room to pursue any of those other ideas we'd identified.

⚾   ⚾   ⚾

Hopefully, you are aware of our Baseball Prospectus Premium subscription and the articles our hardworking staff publishes every weekday at BaseballProspectus.com. (Actually, since I'm hoping for things, hopefully you are a subscriber.) For years, we'd wanted to run some of our favorite work over the previous year in the *Annual*. Ever since Ben Lindbergh and I produced the *Best of Baseball Prospectus* books in 2011, we'd been aware that there are limits to our ability to reproduce web-published content in book format. Some of our most popular and most shared articles over the years don't work at all on paper, and it just gets worse as time goes on and videos, figures, and images that don't translate to print find greater inroads into the content our authors and editors produce. But even in embed-happy 2017, we knew that left dozens upon dozens of articles that we'd love to see presented on the printed page, if only we had the space.

We always discuss the features we can provide on a per-player basis during these meetings. We'll usually swap in a stat or two in the blocks of stats that accompany each player comment, and we ended up adding Harry Pavlidis and team's top-line pitching metrics as columns in *Baseball Prospectus 2018*. We knew we could do a lot more with Harry's data: He has been doing some amazing things visualizing it that we're excited for you to see in this book. I'd also been spending a lot of time lately thinking about Nate Silver's original PECOTA card projection graphs and other ways we could help visualize the statistics.

Also, Stephen Reichert had worked with the good people at Topps to get us clearance to include their baseball cards in our books; we were eager to take them up on that and increase the visual interest in the player sections. But we are limited by scope with what we can do in the *Annual*, which featured 2,070 (!) players this year. Two problems present themselves: Topps doesn't run near that many cards in a season, so we'd be missing a ton of them. More problematic, even adding a postage-stamp-sized depiction of a baseball card across hundreds of players would inflate the page count significantly, and any graph we'd add would need to have a larger footprint than that to be legible. We'd have to cut something or size something else smaller to make the space. Again, we felt like we had something more to offer, and again we couldn't justify cutting something to include it. We were out of room to reclaim and wouldn't be able to fit any of these elements in the *Annual*.

⚾   ⚾   ⚾

Those are the features we wanted to fit into *Baseball Prospectus 2018* but couldn't: some brand-new standalone essays, a selection of the best articles published on the website in 2017, and an arrangement of player-specific charts, graphs, and other information. Under normal circumstances, we would give an emo sigh, consider a happier world where we can publish a 3,000 page book without making reasonable people unhappy, and move on to other things.

Last year's editor meetings weren't exactly normal circumstances, though, because we had decided after years of mulling it over to take the entire book production process in-house and handle the processing from editors' hands to printable PDF ourselves. Thanks to a cloud of tech buzzwords (github, d3js, symfony, Prince XML) that read like the menu at Nerd Christmas dinner maturing and stabilizing over the years, we were now at the point where we could pull these technologies together into an automated process that would give us a fully baked printable file in minutes.

Since we already need to have that in time for *Baseball Prospectus 2018*, or we're in tons of trouble already, the thinking went, let's just count on it being available, take all that great stuff that wouldn't fit, and make another book out of it. (Or, as an organizer of the spectacularly failed Fyre Festival put it, "Let's just do it and be legends, man.")

If you're reading this, it worked.

We're thrilled to be able to present this additional material to you. And we're confident that you'll find it more useful and entertaining in an *Unearthed Arcana* kind of way, and less in a Fyre Festival ripped-tent-on-a-windswept-beach kind of way. Welcome to *Diamond Insights 2018*. Enjoy your book. ▓

Introduction

by Geoff Young

To study baseball is to study life. Well, that's probably an overstatement, although for those of us caught in the game's web of delight it's often hard to tell the difference. Our curiosity gets the best of us as we pursue greater knowledge, sometimes as a means to an end, other times as an end in itself.

Baseball. Life. Whatever.

At this point, as you read these words, you may find yourself wondering why Baseball Prospectus has decided to publish a third yearly book, *Diamond Insights*. The *Annual* has established itself as a perennial favorite for commentary on teams and their players. The *Futures Guide* provides a closer look at the baseball stars of tomorrow. So why this book? Why now?

The short answer is that we are no more immune to curiosity than you are. There are questions worth answering and so we seek to find those answers. At the very least, we hope to learn something of interest and share it with you.

The long answer is, well, long. But hey, it's the offseason, we have time. Right?

It all began with a desire to show you some very cool things. Who among us wouldn't want to stare at mesmerizing charts that help add context to an individual's performance in a given season or throughout his career? With this book, now you can do that. You will learn something and like it!

We've chosen 300 of the most interesting players in baseball to do a deeper visual dive than you'll find anywhere else. A select few among them will also include brief profiles geared toward fantasy players to help guide you to your next championship.

Beyond pictures that tell a compelling story we had other things to share. For example, words that also tell a compelling story. Herein you will find six original essays as well as 24 examples of the best work that appeared at BaseballProspectus.com in 2017. (All of it is good, of course, but we can't very well reprint the entire website.)

Recycling is good. Besides, these 24 articles deserve a permanent home as part of a larger collection that seeks to illuminate and entertain. Among them are cutting-edge research on pitch tunneling, meditations on time travel and baseball cards, inquiries into social concerns (baseball does not exist in a vacuum, although what would happen to knuckleballs if it did?), questions of literal life and death, the evolution of bullpens, and the ubiquitous and unstoppable so much more.

The original essays are no less fascinating. Harry Pavlidis, Jeff Long, and Kate Morrison walk us through the pitching data presented in this book. John Paschal takes a closer look at the youngest players in each major league from 1871 to now. Rob Neyer examines the late-season streaks of the Dodgers and the Indians in a historical context. Dennis Cleary talks with Baseball Prospectus cofounder Gary Huckabay and other BP alumni about statistics, analytics, and the gradual acceptance of both within mainstream circles. Finally, Russell A. Carleton peers into the crystal baseball and offers some thoughts on what the sport might look like 20 years hence.

⚾   ⚾   ⚾

We started with a simple premise: Using a combination of original graphics, in-depth analysis of key players, and thoughtful essays from today's top writers, *Diamond Insights* provides a unique look at baseball and its ongoing evolution.

We ended with a surprisingly diverse collection that promises to satisfy those late-night cravings through the winter and also serve as a reusable resource that can be referenced and enjoyed well into the future. Especially in 2038, when you can make fun of Russell for getting everything wrong.

Baseball is hard to predict. So is life. But then, isn't that the beauty of it?

Part 1: Featured Articles

Baseball's Youngest Players from Season to Season, Part 1: 1871-1940

by John Paschal

On the afternoon of May 8, 1890, in Cleveland, Ohio, Willie "Kid" McGill honored the spirit of his nickname by stepping to the mound at Brotherhood Park and delivering his first major-league pitch—indeed, his first *professional* pitch—at the remarkably tender age of 16 years, 179 days.

On the afternoon of May 25, 2008, in Los Angeles, California, Clayton "Kid K" Kershaw honored the spirit of his nickname by stepping to the mound at Dodger Stadium and, at the slightly less remarkable but nonetheless tender age of 20 years, 67 days, striking out the first batter he faced in a major-league regular-season game, Cardinals leadoff hitter Skip Schumaker.

What Kid and Kid K had in common, aside from the rudiment of a nickname and the keen ability to pitch a baseball left-handed and well, is the distinction of being the youngest player in his respective league that season, McGill in the fledgling Players' League and Kershaw in the National League. Of course, the two Kids are hardly the only kids, relatively speaking, to have made their major-league debuts as the youngest players in their circuits. In fact, in the 147-year history of Major League Baseball, nearly 250 players have served as the uppercase Youngest Players—each hereafter termed the YP—in their respective league and season. Some went on to Hall of Fame careers. Some faded away. Others never played another professional game.

What follows, for young and old alike, is an examination of history's YPs—a deep dive into the patterns, trends, and origins associated with an often overlooked aspect of the old ballgame.

Early Pitchers (1872-1899)

Clichés are cliché for a reason. They bear a lot of truth. Case in point: "You can never have too much pitching." The facts of history have carried its weight. Nearly half of baseball's YPs—118 of 249, or 47 percent—have been pitchers.

"But wait!" I hear you shouting. "That means more than half—precisely 53 percent!—have been nonpitchers! Doesn't this imply, contrary to the popular platitude, that you can never have too much position playing?"

Au contraire, my exceptionally wordy shouter. What it means is that more emphasis is placed on the pitcher position than on any of the other eight spots on the field, and that in efforts to satisfy this premium, teams have often reached to teenagers, especially in the early years of MLB.

It began in 1872, when the Brooklyn Atlantics turned to 16-year-old Jim Britt and basically told him, "Hey, young'n, stop inspecting the progress of your peach fuzz and come pitch this baseball."

Boy, did he.

Not only did the boy take the mound, he took it in each of the team's 37 games. The following year, when, at 17, he was still the youngest player in MLB, he took the mound in each of the team's 54 games. Child labor laws, anyone?

Granted, pitchers of the 1870s did throw underhanded, but baseball wasn't exactly your great-grandpappy's beanbag toss. Pitchers snapped fastballs and curveballs. And Jim Britt, just 5-foot-6, snapped thousands.

But wait, there's more. Not only did Britt take the mound in each game for two years, he started each game. And not only did he start each game, he finished all but three. You read that correctly: Across two seasons, a teenager started 91 games and finished 88. In 1873, at 17, he led the league with 51—fifty-one!—complete games. He tossed 480 2/3 innings that year after throwing 336 as a 16-year-old.

And that was it for young Jim Britt. After 1873, perhaps with his arm in a sling, he vanished from the game.

The lesson is this: You really can have too much pitching, especially on one arm and particularly a young one. Despite the obvious signs—namely, Jim Britt looking for work at age 18—it took baseball a couple decades to learn the lesson. From 1883 through 1891, no fewer than four teenaged YPs suffered the burden of too many innings. Pitching for the

Indianapolis Hoosiers in 1884, 18-year-old Larry McKeon logged 512 innings and 59 complete games. After tossing 460 innings across the next two campaigns, McKeon left professional baseball before his 22nd birthday.

In 1885, when National League pitchers could throw from any arm angle while American Association pitchers were limited to deliveries below the shoulder, 18-year-old YP Ed Seward logged six innings, all scoreless, for the AA Providence Grays. Call it a good start. But in 1887, after a season in the minors, he posted 52 complete games and 470 2/3 innings. As if that weren't enough, he posted 57 complete games and 518 2/3 innings a year later, in his age-21 season. He would last three more seasons.

In his final season, at age 24, he pitched 16 1/3 innings. Call it a bad finish.

The 1886 season saw a pair of 17-year-old YPs make their mound debuts, Nat Hudson in the AA and Ed Fuller in the NL. Hudson pitched well, and often, posting a 3.03 ERA and 16-10 record while logging 234 1/3 innings. The following season he started just nine games and finished seven, logging only 67 innings. Sore arm? In lieu of a reliable seance and a talk with Hudson's ghost, we guess yes.

Hudson rebounded the following year, going 25-10 with a 2.54 ERA, but his 333 innings might've been too much. In 1889 he threw just 60 innings and never played again after that.

Meanwhile, in the NL, Fuller personified the other end of the 1880s young-pitcher spectrum by logging just 13 innings and a 6.92 ERA before disappearing from baseball at the age of a high-school senior. Balanced against the overusage trend, this diametric trend—young pitchers completely out of their depth—would continue for several seasons.

In 1887, 19-year-old YP John Roach made his mound debut for the New York Giants by yielding 17 runs—10 earned—in an eight-inning loss. For Roach, it was all she wrote. Though he would go on to pitch in the minor leagues through age 41, the righty had just compiled his career major-league stat line.

Each of the next three seasons produced a similar scenario. Teenagers Mike Kilroy, Andy Dunning, and Charlie Heard all made their mound debuts as the youngest players in baseball, and each would be gone from the big leagues without posting a win. Their combined MLB record: 0-12.

At the same time Heard was posting an 8.39 ERA for the Pittsburgh Alleghenys, the appropriately named Kid McGill was pitching to a respectable 4.12 ERA—again, at age 16—for the appropriately named Cleveland Infants. After logging 183 2/3 innings that season, McGill increased his load to 298 innings. The following season, at 18, he pitched just 17 innings. We can guess why. He returned in 1893 to post more than 300 innings, but in the three subsequent seasons he took the mound less and less often, finishing with just 79 2/3 innings in his final season at 22. He continued pitching in the minors through 1905, but the man known as Kid would never be the same.

Nat Hudson

This dual trend—young pitchers either too good for their own good or way way WAY too bad—would continue through the 1890s. The prevailing likelihood, though, was that a teenage pitcher just wasn't ready, and never would be, for the big time.

In 1883, 19-year-old YP Seth Sigsby managed to compile his major-league career stat line in one crummy inning for New York Giants: one hit, four walks, one hit batsman, and three earned runs. Slow to get the hint, Sigsby would leave the sport after three seasons in the minors.

In 1894, 18-year-old YP Andy Sommerville also compiled his lifetime line in just one game: 1/3 inning, five walks, one hit, one wild pitch, and six earned runs for a 162 ERA. He would never pitch again at any level.

As for 1898 YP Bert Conn, his lifetime MLB stats—0-3 record, 7.77 ERA, 24 1/3 innings—don't tell the full story. After being declared ineligible to play for his prep team because he had played semipro ball, the 18-year-old made his major-league debut for the hometown Phillies on September 16 and promptly yielded a home run to the first batter he faced. After a year in the minors, he made one start in 1900 and took the loss. He would never pitch in the majors again. One

John Roach

Then in 1881, a year after Bond's workload decreased from 551 1/3 innings to a comparatively paltry 493 1/3, something big occurred in baseball: the NL lengthened the pitching distance from 45 feet to 50 feet. Already suffering from overwork, Bond struggled, pitching just 37 2/3 innings in the next two seasons before calling it quits at 26. After a year away from the game, he returned—with a new arm angle—in 1884, but no new angle could save him. The damage was done. After throwing 232 innings, Bond was gone. Tommy John and his namesake surgery were still a century away.

The close of the century gave us the most interesting outlier of all. Like Cy Young and Honus Wagner, 19-year-old Eddie Kolb posted a big-league stat line during that fin de siècle season. Unlike them, he did it in just one game—the final game of the Cleveland Spiders' final season in the National League. Kolb, a cigar boy at the hotel where the woeful Spiders stayed during trips to Cincinnati, had become acquainted with Cleveland manager Patsy Tebeau during a season that had seen the Spiders lose more than 130 games while playing a majority of those games on the road.[1]

Before the season-ending doubleheader, the cigar boy convinced Tebeau to let him start the season finale. And he did, yielding 17 runs while pitching to a complete-game loss for a team that included players named Crazy Schmitt and Highball Wilson. The youngest player in baseball would retire with a lifetime ERA of 10.13. But, hey, the cigar boy—and we do mean boy—did manage to score a run, too.

Early Position Players (1871-1899)

By 1875, a trend had begun to establish itself: YP position players would enjoy longer major-league careers than their YP pitching counterparts. It's harder to ruin an arm with throws from, say, second base.

Though not absolute, and not determinable until many years later, the trend began with baseball's first YP, Joe Battin, an infielder who made his MLB debut at age 17 in 1871 and went on to a decade-long career. In 1875, 17-year-old YP Jim Keenan debuted at catcher and went on to an 11-year major-league career. The following season, by contrast, 16-year-old YP Frank Pearce pitched four innings for the Louisville Grays and then—poof!—vanished from baseball.

Though exceptions abounded, position players would continue to enjoy longer careers than Pearce. In 1880, outfielder Dan Stearns made his YP debut at 18 and then became an early journeyman, playing for six teams in his seven seasons. He never became the star his teenaged start might have suggested, but he did achieve what Ty Cobb never could: He led the league in walks, in 1883.

Also in 1883, 16-year-old YP Piggy Ward made his debut for the Philadelphia Quakers, going 1-for-5 in his lone contest. Ward wouldn't return to the majors until 1889, at age 22, but upon his return he played half a dozen seasons and

reason: he had pitched for two semipro teams—under an assumed name—while on the Phillies roster. It wasn't overuse at the big-league level that got him, but overuse nonetheless. Arm injured, Conn would continue as a minor-league position player through age 33.

As in any field of endeavor, there were exceptions and outliers. In 1874, 18-year-old YP Tommy Bond debuted for the Brooklyn Atlantics by posting a 2.03 ERA in 497 innings. Though just 5-foot-7, baseball's first Irishman did not break down. The righty averaged 477 innings and 51 complete games across the next six seasons, winning 40 or more games in three consecutive seasons and twice finishing with a league-leading ERA—2.11 in 1877 and 1.96 in 1879. As if that weren't enough, he played in the field on his days away from the mound, posting 23 lifetime assists from the outfield. That's a lot of arm work.

---

1. http://sabr.org/bioproj/person/373985e9

established a major-league record along the way. From June 16 to June 19, 1893, Piggy reached base in a record 17 straight plate appearances, notching eight hits, eight walks, and one hit by pitch. Ward still shares the record with Earl Averill Jr.

In 1889, 19-year-old YP Jack Doyle debuted at catcher for the Columbus Solons and played 11 games as a rookie. He then went on to play a total of 1,569 games for 10 teams across 17 big-league seasons before retiring with a .299 batting average and one awesome nickname: Dirty Jack.

A player named Sammy Strang debuted at age 19 for the Louisville Colonels in 1896, but he wasn't born Sammy Strang. He was born Samuel Nicklin.[2] To shield his identity from his parents, who believed baseball to be a disreputable career for their college-educated son, he would take on a series of pseudonyms while playing minor-league baseball for several seasons following his major-league debut. After

Jim Keenan

playing in 14 games as a rookie, he returned to the major leagues in 1900 and finished his 10-year career with a World Series ring he earned with the New York Giants in 1905.

⚾   ⚾   ⚾

Exceptions to long careers, like Doyle's and Strang's, were many and not so far between. Like Sammy Strang, the player named Leonidas Lee was born with a different name: Leonidas Pyrrhus Funkhouser. If looking to name your crunkcore band, look no more.

Like Strang, Lee was college-educated: in his case, Princeton. Unlike Strang, Lee played just four major-league games, at age 16 in 1877, going 5-for-18 while failing to tally an RBI or a run scored. He would become a physician.

Like Lee, Bill White attended an Ivy League school: in his case, Brown. Also like Lee, he failed to tally an RBI. Unlike Lee, he played just one big-league game, in 1879 at age 18—baseball's YP. Today he is this to us: Bats: Unknown. Throws: Unknown.

History can yield facts with a sifter—slowly, barely. Indeed, what happened to Tom Hess? After making his professional debut at age 14, for a minor-league team, the 16-year-old catcher made his MLB debut in 1892 for the Baltimore Orioles. He then returned to the minors, playing from age 17 through age 35 without ever returning to the big leagues. His career major-league batting average: .000.

As for John Montgomery Ward, he personified a pair of trends by forging a lengthy career as a position player after succumbing to overuse on the mound. Upon joining the Providence Grays in 1878, the 18-year-old became the NL's YP and went on to post a league-leading 1.51 ERA in 334 innings. The following year he posted a league-best 47 victories while pitching 58 complete games and 587 innings. In 1880, he increased his workload to 597 innings and hurled the circuit's second perfect game.

Overworked, Ward pitched an average of "just" 238 innings across the next four seasons, finishing with a career-low 60 2/3 in 1884 before turning himself into an everyday player. First as an outfielder and then as a middle infielder, Ward registered 1,624 hits across the next 11 seasons. After 17 seasons of a prolonged career, Ward retired with 164 wins and 2,107 hits. All in all, it wasn't too shabby for a guy who burned out on the mound at 24. Ward was voted into the Hall of Fame in 1964.

Early 20th-Century Players (1900-1940)

The first year of the new century provided the latest YP, after John Montgomery Ward, to fashion a Hall of Fame career. Early signs weren't so promising, though. Debuting at 19 for the Giants, the lanky right-hander pitched to a 5.08 ERA and 0-3 record across the six games of his rookie season. Then in

2. http://sabr.org/bioproj/person/09c30bed

his first full season, at 20, he hurled a no-hitter and finished 20-17 with a 2.41 ERA. Born Christopher Mathewson, he would finish his career as the era's most popular and accomplished pitcher, becoming one of the game's first celebrity endorsers while registering a career record of 373-188.

But if 1900 provided the century's first YP success story, 1901 provided its first YP tragedy—in fact, tragedies. As the NL's YP, 18-year-old pitcher Dick Scott started two games for the Cincinnati Reds. Both came against Christy Mathewson and his Giants. Scott would finish the year—and his career—with an 0-2 record. After pitching in 40 games for a minor-league team the following year, Scott vanished. Then in July 1911, he committed suicide by slashing his throat with a pocketknife.

Christy Mathewson

John Montgomery Ward

As the AL's YP, 19-year-old Ed Cermak played one game in 1901, striking out in each of four at-bats. He would play six more seasons in the minors before trading his spikes for umpiring gear. In 1911—the same year Scott committed suicide—a ball struck the ump in the throat. Cermak lost his ability to speak. He died later that year.

In hindsight, the century's first two years supplied a primer for the existential dichotomies to follow, those dualities of the human condition—success and failure, triumph and tragedy. And the human condition is the baseball condition.

On September 8, 1902, 20-year-old YP Jimmy Sebring stroked his first major-league hit—off future Hall of Famer Joe McGinnity—in a game against the Giants. Sebring would go on to bat .325 in the 19 games of his rookie season. Impressed, team owner Barney Dreyfuss said Sebring "is as good as they make them in the rough."[3] In 1903, Sebring

---

3. http://sabr.org/bioproj/person/77650ebd

batted .277 in 506 at-bats and became the first player in World Series history to homer. Just six years after the homer, Sebring died at 27 of Bright??s disease.

A year after Sebring's debut, 19-year-old righty Chief Bender made his first MLB start. On the heels of 16 seasons and 212 wins, Bender would see his Hall of Fame induction a year before his death, at 70.

The year 1903 not only marked Bender's debut, it marked the beginning of a long run of YPs who would go on to Hall of Fame careers. Naturally, it also launched a run of disparities—stark divisions between those who went on to remarkable careers and those who debuted as YPs in the same season but slowly faded or quickly vanished.

The year 1905, for example, marked the debuts of an 18-year-old YP in the AL and a 19-year-old YP in the AL. Ty Cobb would notch 4,189 hits, Bill McCarthy precisely 4,188 fewer. The 1906 season marked the introductions of two 19-year-old YPs: Eddie Collins in the AL, Henry Mathewson in the NL. Collins would post 3,315 hits and earn a place in the Hall of Fame. Mathewson, known otherwise as Christy Mathewson's younger brother, would sputter to a career pitching record of 0-1. In 1917, a year when Collins slumped to 163 hits and a batting average of .289, Mathewson died of tuberculosis.

Similar starts, divergent ends: though not to such poignant results, the theme would continue. In 1907, pitcher Bill Bailey debuted at 19 for the Browns and went on to a respectable 11-year career. Debuting in the NL, meanwhile, was an 18-year-old catcher who, at 19, would make his mark in infamy. It took the name Merkle's Boner, the Fred Merkle base-running gaffe that cost the Giants the 1908 pennant. A lone moment would overshadow a 16-year career.

In 1912, a 17-year-old catcher and an 18-year-old pitcher made their YP debuts for different teams in the same city, one for the NL's Phillies and the other for the AL's Athletics. Similar starts, divergent ends: catcher Mike Loan would play one game in the major leagues and two sporadic seasons in the minors before disappearing from the sport. Herb Pennock would pitch for 22 seasons, picking up 241 wins and three World Series rings en route to the Hall of Fame.

The disparities wouldn't end with Loan and Pennock. In fact, 1917 also marked the beginning of a quarter century of great YP turnouts: Nine YPs who debuted in years from 1917 through 1940 would reach the Hall of Fame. Of course, not every player can be a Hall of Famer. In 1922, Travis Jackson, at 18, debuted at shortstop for the Giants in 1922 and went on to a Hall of Fame career, while pitcher Jim Brillheart, also 18, debuted for the Senators but managed only an 8-9 record across four big-league seasons. He then pitched in the minors through age 47, finishing at Class B Tacoma. Facts can support conjecture: Brillheart must've loved the game. Unfortunately, love doesn't always square with talent.

COBB, DETROIT

Ty Cobb

The 1924 season saw the NL debut of Big Ed Clough, who would post a .105/.105/.105 line in 11 career games, and the AL debut of 19-year-old Red Ruffing, who would finish at age 42 and land in the Hall. Ruffing, one supposes, also loved the game.

In 1936, a pair of pitchers got their starts. In the NL, 19-year-old Elmer Burkart debuted by yielding just two earned runs—though walking eight—in six innings against the Pirates. In the AL, a 17-year-old Iowan also displayed control problems in his lone inning, walking two of the five batters he faced. In his next outing, Burkart walked four in 1 2/3 innings. In his, Bob Feller issued zero walks in two. Burkart would never control his control problems and faded from the game. Feller? Sure, he led the league in walks in four seasons, but he also led in strikeouts in seven. He went on to 266 wins and a place in the Hall.

A Trend Toward Improving Pitchers

In the 29-season period from 1871 through 1899, 11 YP pitchers (not including cigar boy Kolb) failed to stick in the majors for more than two years. In the 41-season period from 1900 through 1940, just eight YP pitchers failed to last for the same duration. The conclusion is that people in positions of power—managers, coaches, scouts, owners—had become a bit more judicious in eyeballing young talent and determining the best way to develop it. That conclusion is further supported when we evaluate the diametric ends of the pitcher spectrum. On one end are the pitchers who burned out from overuse. On the other are those who went on to lengthy and even Hall of Fame careers.

From 1871 through 1899, five YP pitchers succumbed to severe overuse. From 1900 through 1940, only one YP pitcher—Pete Schneider, in 1914—appears to have suffered from overwork. Upon debuting at age 18 with the Reds, Schneider averaged 257 innings in his first four seasons, topping out at 333 2/3 in 1917 at age 21, two years after starting both games of a doubleheader. In 1918 he dropped to 217 innings and in 1919 just 16. And then he was gone from the bigs. He played four more seasons in the minors, but mostly as an outfielder (he even once hit five homers in a 1923 contest). You could argue that control problems caused his demise—Schneider led the league in walks in his final two full-time seasons, with 117 each time—but it's just as likely that arm trouble contributed to the wildness. Still, compare his four-year average of 257 innings to John Montgomery Ward's 401.5-inning average across his first six seasons. Granted, Ward pitched from a shorter distance, but it still appears that baseball people were increasingly aware of overuse. It hadn't ended, mind you, but it had decreased.

This sensitivity to overuse, combined with a keener sophistication in discerning talent, might have been the primary factor in the increase of quality YP pitchers from 1900 to 1940. Not only did six YP hurlers from that era reach the Hall, but several others crafted long and impressive careers. In 1908, Smoky Joe Wood debuted at 18 and went on to post a combined 1.98 ERA across his first four seasons while averaging just 164 innings. In his fifth season, at 22, he solidified himself as an ace by posting a 1.91 ERA, 34 wins, an .872 win percentage, 35 complete games, and 10 shutouts, each a league-leading mark. His 344 innings might have contributed to his steady fade in the next few years, but, according to anecdotes from the era, a series of freak injuries more likely derailed what could have been a Hall of Fame career for a man about whom Walter Johnson said, "Listen, mister, no man alive can throw any harder."[4]

In 1925, Jumbo Brown debuted as the NL YP and went on to pitch a dozen MLB seasons. A year later, 19-year-old Wes Ferrell began a career that would include four consecutive

Smokey Joe Wood

20-win seasons, six overall, and 193 wins. The following season, 18-year-old Mel Harder began a 20-year career that produced 223 victories. And in 1931, Van Lingle Mungo debuted with a complete game shutout and went on to average 16 wins per season from 1932 through 1936 while leading the NL in strikeouts in 1936. He did pitch 311 innings or more in each of two seasons, but, per the archives, it was a spring training injury that led to his fade. But hey, at least he got a song written about him.[5]

Simply put, the kind of talented pitchers who a generation earlier might have been overused were now allowed to ease into the big leagues, learning their craft first in the minors and polishing it in "The Show." The result: a group of men who fashioned good, long careers on the mound.

4. http://sabr.org/bioproj/person/9f244666
5. https://www.youtube.com/watch?v=nKzobTlF8fM

Exceptions—Always the Exceptions

Of course, for every Jumbo Brown, there was a Jake Hehl. And for every Van Mungo, there were two Harry Kanes.

On June 20, 1918, the 18-year-old Hehl made his MLB debut for the Brooklyn Robins against former YP Ross Youngs and his Giants by relieving in the ninth inning of an eventual 8-6 loss. In his lone frame, Hehl held the Giants hitless and scoreless but did hit a batter. His victim: Jim Thorpe. And that was it. Despite pitching eight more seasons in the minor leagues, Hehl would never return to the majors.

If he was good enough for the Robins at 18, why wasn't he at 26? One word: war. By June 1918, the Robins had lost 13 players to military service in World War I. Desperate for help, they signed Hehl out of Brooklyn Prep High School on June 17, and three days later the teen was on the mound at Ebbets Field. After the war ended in November 1918, the players returned stateside in time for the 1919 season.

In 1902, Harry Kane debuted at 18 for the Browns and played his final big-league game four years later. Having compiled a 2-7 record and 4.81 ERA across four sporadic MLB seasons, the man born Harry Cohen ended his pro career pitching for the Class D Wichita Falls Drillers.

All told, Kane pitched seven no-hitters in the minor leagues, including a 13-inning affair that he lost, 1-0. The man had talent. But it goes without saying that minor-league hitters aren't major-league hitters, and the scrap heap is full of guys whose best stuff came in the sticks.

Kane and Hehl were just two of the many 1900-1940 YP pitchers who failed to gain a foothold in the majors. The fact gives rise to a question, asked once more: How could a pitcher with enough talent to debut as a teenager manage to peter out so rapidly? You'd think a hurler who debuts at 18 or 19 would last until 35 or 36 and finish with triple-digit wins.

There are several reasons, each applicable to position players, too:

1. War, in many of its modern iterations, created major leaguers out of players who weren't yet or never would be ready for the major leagues.

2. In the early years of baseball, and particularly before the advent of large scouting departments and modern tools such as video, teams were always on the lookout for talent. Injuries and/or suspensions meant that big-league teams, which weren't yet affiliated with their own farm systems, had to scour the obscure reaches of the minor, semipro, and even amateur leagues for a warm body. The result: a player who wasn't anywhere close to major-league ready got to play in the major leagues.

3. Long before massive TV contracts and a players union that made sure its members got a chunk of that change, a player could often earn more money in a trade than he could on the professional ball field. Why labor on the mounds of Burlington and Harrisburg or even New York when you could earn a good living back home? In all likelihood, everyday big leaguers would never give up their gig for a shot at plumbing or welding, but a fringe player who didn't quite have the goods? Sure, why not.

4. The September call-up: from 1871 through 1919, when modern roster rules were not yet in place, 24 of the 75 YPs debuted in September or October. In large part, those youngsters were auditioning for next year's squad when the team was out of contention. Contrast this with 1920 through 1940, when 17 of the 33 YPs debuted in September or October. Why? Beginning in 1920, roster rules were changed to increase the player limit to 25 and to permit a tryout period beginning on September 1, when younger players could impress the honchos—or not!—by matching their skills against major-league competition. The rules also allowed an early tryout period spanning from Opening Day to May 15. The result: eight YPs from 1920 through 1940 debuted before May 15. For example, 17-year-old catcher Jimmie Foxx debuted on May 1, 1925, before heading back to the minors.

   All told, 25 of the 33 YPs from 1920 through 1940—75 percent—debuted during one of the two tryout periods. Then in 1968, baseball eliminated the early tryout period. The result: just two of next 25 YPs debuted in April, while 16—64 percent—debuted in either September or October. Of course, whatever the era, a September look-see has often become a September *I've-seen-enough*. Down goes player, never to be seen again.

5. Injury, says Captain Obvious: Dr. Jobe was decades away.

6. Baseball is a fickle business. It is, in a word, unpredictable. What divides a 10-year vet from a one-game vet is often the ability to throw a full-count curve.

The 1910 season yielded two YP pitchers who failed, albeit in different ways, to leave much of a major-league impression: Bunny Hearn and Dave Skeels. Hearn debuted at 19 for the Cardinals and pitched to a 13-24 record across six scattered campaigns. Perhaps his biggest contribution to baseball came during his participation in John McGraw's world baseball tour of 1913, when, according to Hearn himself, he showed King George V of the United Kingdom how to throw a curveball.[6]

Skeels pitched his first—and, as it turned out, last—major-league game for the Tigers at age 18, yielding eight earned runs in six frames before leaving pro ball after two minor-league seasons at 19. What happened? Granted, he hadn't performed well in his lone shot in the majors, but he had managed a 10-5 mark while pitching for the Class B Seattle Giants in 1911. Where did he go, and why did he leave?

Skeels, a one-quarter Native American, experienced chronic arm trouble and retired to a life of farming on the Colville Reservation in Washington. Though no longer a full-time pro, he would continue to play for semipro teams in Washington before his death from tuberculosis in a sanitorium at 34.[7]

The 1918 season also produced a pair of failed YPs: In addition to the aforementioned Hehl there was William Pierson. Across the eight games of his rookie season, Pierson pitched to an 0-1 record—the same mark with which he would depart MLB following his age-25 season. In the intervening years, Pierson had thrown 250-plus innings in each of two minor-league seasons and hadn't pitched at all at ages 23 and 24. What happened? Were the innings too much for his developing arm? Or did he simply decide to leave baseball for a steadier and better-paying vocation?

The answer remains a mystery. What is known is that Pierson pitched his final professional game in a big-league uniform, that of Connie Mack's Athletics, yielding one run in 2 2/3 innings against the Red Sox.

On June 11, 1931—three days past his 19th birthday—Lew Krausse debuted by yielding two earned runs in 2 1/3 innings before going on to post a 4-1 mark through his age-20 season. He then spent the next 11 seasons in the minors while failing to make it back to the bigs. In 1942, while pitching to a 2.93 ERA for Boston's Class A team, he fathered Lew Krausse Jr., who, in 1961, would become the youngest player in the American League upon debuting at 18 for the Kansas City Athletics. Like father, like son. The difference? Junior would pitch 12 seasons in the bigs.

As for Al Epperly, the 19-year-old Cubs pitcher made his debut by inheriting two runners with two outs in the bottom of the fifth inning of a 1938 game against Pittsburgh. After an error loaded the bases, Epperly walked in a run before striking out catcher Ray Berres to end the inning with the bases full. Not bad! He would finish his rookie season with a 2-0 record and a respectable 3.67 ERA. High hopes!

Alas, he wouldn't return to the majors until 12 years later, in 1950, at age 32, having spent 10 years in the minors and two in the US Army during World War II. In sum, he would spend 17 years in the minors and two years in the military to throw 27 innings in the big leagues. Of course, Epperly isn't the only fringe major leaguer to have spent several seasons in the minors and lost time to military service, but we'll talk about that in Part 2. ▨

---

6. http://www.milb.com/milb/history/top100.jsp?idx=57

7. Cary Rosenbaum, "The Ghost: How the Epic Story of One Colville Indian Died with Him," *Tribal Tribune*, September 16, 2016.

Streaky

by Rob Neyer

In the comic books, Superman has a dog. Krypto.

Now, you might find this silly. Yes, sillier even than a creature from another galaxy who somehow looks exactly like an Earthling, but is able to fly and see through stuff and toss anvils around because his home planet was illuminated by a different sort of star than ours. Sillier than that, even. See, Krypto was a product of the 1950s, when Lois Lane *and* Jimmy Olsen (Jimmy Olsen?) both graced their very own titles for years, and an imp named Bat-Mite routinely vexed the Caped Crusader.

Krypto first appeared in '55, in the pages of a Superboy story. Thirty years later, the super-pet was essentially disappeared ... but in the comics, of course, nobody's dead forever. As I write these words, Krypto serves as the loyal, flying, super-strong canine companion of Superman, not to mention his wife Lois Lane and their young (super-powered) son Jon.

Okay. Enough about Krypto. What I really want to talk about is Streaky.

You know. Supergirl's cat.

I thought about Streaky a lot last fall. Radio and TV broadcasters love to talk about *streaky* players and teams. As if, you know, that's a thing. Players, mostly. But last fall at almost exactly the same time, two of Major League Baseball's best teams were bizarrely, historically, news-rattlingly streaky.

Beginning on August 24, the Cleveland Indians—at the time, nursing a semi-comfortable (if surprisingly small) 4 1/2 game lead over the second-place Twins—ran off a streak of 22 wins, breaking the Oakland A's American League record, famously set 15 years earlier.

Two days after the Tribe opened their streak, the Los Angeles Dodgers—at the time on pace for 116 wins, which would have tied the all-time MLB record—lost to Milwaukee, beginning a stretch in which they dropped five straight, then beat the Padres, then lost another 11 straight. Even losing 16 of 17 games didn't come close to costing them first place, but it did put the kibosh on most of the Superteam talk (and left the ghosts of the 2001 Mariners to fight another day; no word on whether or not they broke open the bubbly).

I do want to talk about the Dodgers. But first I want to talk about the Indians and the A's and the 1935 Chicago Cubs and the 1916 New York Giants. Those four teams are the only four since 1884 to win at least 20 straight games. (I'm using 1884 because in 1884, *two* teams racked up 20-game winning streaks: the pennant-winning St. Louis Maroons and the pennant-winning Providence Grays. The Grays dominated the weak National League, and the Maroons *really* dominated the *really* weak Union Association; the latter was a major league of sorts in name only, and one of these days some of the smart people who run statistics websites will finally decertify the UA, and the Maroons' winning streak will finally fall from the list. Anyway, "major league" baseball was so unbalanced in 1884 that it would be surprising if some team *didn't* win 20 straight. So let us speak of the Maroons and the Grays no more.)

So, those four teams. I asked BP's Rob McQuown to run some pretty rudimentary numbers for me: the odds of each of those four teams putting together their winning streaks, considering only their run differentials for the season. We did *not* look at the qualities of their competition, or whether their games during the streaks were played at home or on the road. But as (my long-ago STATS, Inc. colleague) Rob noted, even if we did consider those factors, it's unlikely that the results would change much.

Did you know the 1935 Cubs won 21 straight? I didn't. Nobody *ever* mentions this for a pretty simple reason: The Cubs, unlike the other clubs, never held any sort of record. They weren't *said* to hold the record, anyway (more on that soon). When the Cubs won—on their way to the National League pennant—21 straight in '35, they were said to have fallen five games short of the '16 Giants' record: 26 straight.

But while we're (of course) going to forget them in about five minutes, let's just take a *moment* to recognize those '35 Cubs. More than anyone else on the list, the Cubs' streak *mattered*. When it began on September 4, they were in third place, 2 1/2 games behind the first-place Cardinals and also a hair behind the Giants. But when their streak ended—the final wins coming on September 27, with a doubleheader sweep of the Cardinals—the Cubs were 6 games ahead of second-place St. Louis. With only two games left in the season. Both of which the Cubs lost, narrowly. Still their 21-game streak must also certainly rank, by definition, as the greatest stretch run in major-league history. Except nobody remembers it, because of a) the aforementioned '16 Giants, and b) the Cubs losing the '35 World Series to the Tigers.

But (almost) everybody remembers the 2002 Athletics' streak, because its climax serves as the pivotal event in a mega-bestselling book *and* the Oscar-nominated movie of the same name. As you'll (almost certainly) recall, the A's set an American League record with 20 straight wins. Like all our other streaks, this one came fairly late in the season. Like the '35 Cubs, the '02 A's were sitting in third place when they started winning: 4 1/2 games behind the Mariners, 2 1/2 behind the Angels. That was before their game on August 13. But that night they beat the Blue Jays in Oakland. And after winning their 20th straight on August 4, they were 3 1/2 games ahead of the second-place Angels.

It's not the streak we remember so much, as the last game in the streak. For one thing, that's the game that gave the A's the American League record, previously coheld by the 1906 "Hitless Wonder" White Sox and the 1947 "Bevens' Boys" New York Yankees. For another, it's that last game in which the A's took an 11-0 lead in the third inning, then *blew the lead* ... before winning on Scott Hatteberg's pinch-hit homer in the bottom of the ninth. So what would Michael Lewis have done without the winning streak?

"Or if Scott Hatteberg, of all people, hadn't hit that home run," Lewis told me via email. "I was counting on them winning more than they should have but nothing more than that. I assumed that the season would offer me a narrative of some sort. The winning streak solved the problem."

Lewis did have another narrative thread in mind, absent the streak and the crazy-dramatic home run. He's just not telling what it was. Considering Lewis's history, we might assume that *Moneyball* would have been an entertaining bestseller even if Scott Hatteberg had never been born. It's more difficult to imagine what the movie would have looked like, since every sports movie—unlike every book—needs a *moment* ... and without that one, would the filmmakers have simply invented one? Like how the guys who made *42* invented a pennant-clinching homer for Jackie Robinson?

Hey, they're just selling popcorn. But the great thing about *Moneyball* (the movie) was they didn't have to make up the best part. Hatteberg hit the home run. The A's won 20 straight. Art Howe really was—actually, Art Howe really was *not* like that. Gotta sell that popcorn.

Are you ready for a statistical interlude, courtesy of Rob McQuown? Considering just their run differential in 2002—they ultimately scored 800 on the nose, gave up 654—the A's had a 0.4 percent chance of running off a 20-game winning streak that season. Which is actually higher than I would have guessed.

But not nearly as high as the 2017 Indians' chances of winning 22 straight. By virtue of their tremendous, MLB-best 818-564 differential, the Indians actually had a 1.8 percent chance of topping the A's record, but topping it by two wins rather than just one. But surprisingly (to me) the '35 Cubs chances of winning 21 straight were even higher: 2.2 percent, according to McQuown's figures.

So what gets you more excited? The length of the streak? The estimated likelihood/unlikelihood of the streak? Chris Pratt taking Jason Grimsley deep?

Or do you simply prefer *that thing you just saw*? Recency Bias is a well-known and -studied thing, and I couldn't help thinking about that when so many of our Internet Friends seemed to take so much pleasure in questioning the legitimacy of the 1916 Giants' 26-game winning streak. Because if we could somehow decertify that one, then the Indians streak, *the one we just saw*, would be the greatest winning streak in major-league history. And might not that make, by extension, *us* the greatest too?

The questions about the Giants' streak are predicated upon this notion: The Giants actually did *not* win 26 straight games.

Beginning on September 7, the Giants won a dozen straight (yes, yet another late-season streak; there's probably something there, but I'm not smart enough to figure out what it is). They won their 12th straight on September 18, in the first game of a doubleheader against the Pirates. The second game was stopped because of rain, after eight innings with the score 1-1. People describe this game as a tie, and thus *not a win. Streak over.*

Here's the thing, though: There's no tying in baseball. It's not soccer or hockey or American football, and if you don't believe me, just look at the standings. Yes, the players' statistics counted. But the game itself did. Not. Count. As. Anything.

The next day, the Giants and Pirates made up that game, and of course the Giants won, and would win 13 other games after the nontie, which is how you get to 26 and still the all-time champion winning streak in baseball's biggest leagues.

Apologies, modernists. If it's any consolation at all—or rather, if you need a different reason to embrace the real record—*the Giants weren't all that good.*[1] At least not that season. The very next season, they would win the National League pennant. But in 1916, they were in fourth place when the streak began, and fourth place when it ended. They finished with a good-but-hardly-great 597-504 run differential. Which is why McQuown rates their chances of winning 26 straight as just 0.007 percent.

Not 7 percent. Not 0.7 percent. Their chances were 70 in a million.

Okay, that does overstate the case some. The Giants were playing at home throughout the streak. The whole thing. But winning 26 straight with hardly any great players ... that's not nothing. I'm okay with keeping it. Celebrating it, even.

---

1. They actually had a losing record when the streak started.

And speaking of 70 in a million, that's (improbably enough!) the same estimated chance of the Dodgers losing 16 of 17 games in 2017, despite their tremendous (770-580) run differential. I find the utter unlikelihood of the 2017 Dodgers far more appealing than the relative likelihood of the 2017 Indians. Purely in terms of raw, unadulterated, devil-may-care *appeal*, I'd go like this: '16 Giants, '17 Dodgers, '02 Athletics, '17 Indians, '35 Cubs, and then whatever that was that happened when Chester Arthur was running the country.

But that's just me. I like weird shit.

If you take two things away from this essay, I hope it's these things: Krypto lives, and in 1916 the Giants wore plaid purple uniforms. But if you've somehow got room for three things, I hope the third is this: We're all entitled to our own opinions and preferences, but we don't get to ret-con baseball history. You might not like it because you weren't around to see it, but the Giants did win 26 straight, which was the record and remains the record and probably always will be the record.

Besides, the Indians had their chance. After their streak was busted with a 4-3 loss to the Royals on September 15, they won another five straight. If they'd really wanted the Giants' record, they would have tried just a little bit harder.

Revolution to Evolution: Statistics, Analytics, and Baseball Prospectus

by Dennis Cleary

It was a situation George Springer had probably dreamed about as a kid. The Houston Astros' 28-year-old outfielder strode confidently to the plate, stared down Dodgers pitcher Brandon McCarthy, and dug in. Game 2 of the 2017 World Series had gone into extra innings, and as the Astros' batting order turned over, their leadoff hitter readied himself. Springer's strong 2017 campaign ranked 43rd among hitters by BWARP—Batter Wins Above Replacement Player.

Springer was an unorthodox leadoff hitter. Classic baseball lineup construction dictated a speedy slap hitter should bat first. The old-school baseball world saw Springer as a power hitter—he had banged out 63 extra-base hits, including 36 home runs, during the regular season—better suited to hitting lower in the order, where he could take advantage of RBI opportunities. To make matters worse, Springer was an indifferent baserunner who stole only 5 bases in 12 attempts all year. And yet, here he was, in a high-leverage moment, ready to bring all his on-base and slugging skills to bear.

Springer's manager, A.J. Hinch, watched intently from the dugout. A Stanford graduate and former MLB catcher, Hinch was drafted by the Oakland A's and played during General Manager Billy Beane's "Moneyball" tenure. Hinch both understood and utilized modern statistics to inform his decisions; batting Springer higher in the order gave him more at-bats, and thus more chances to make a significant impact, especially late in the game—like right now.

Indeed, Springer made a significant impact when he knocked McCarthy's 2-1 pitch into the cheap seats for a two-run homer that gave the Astros a lead they would not relinquish. The unorthodox leadoff hitter had come through for Hinch, and it never would have happened without Hinch's current GM, Jeff Luhnow. A sabermetrically minded executive in the mold of Branch Rickey, Luhnow knew that baseball was a game of percentages, and he wanted the percentages to add up in his favor.

Building a Champion Through Analytics

Hired in December 2011 to turn around a flailing franchise, Luhnow was empowered by new owner Jim Crane to remake the organization. In addition to bringing on former Astros greats Craig Biggio, Roger Clemens, and Enos Cabell to advise him, Luhnow repeatedly plucked talent from a new source of competitive advantage: Baseball Prospectus.

Kevin Goldstein was recruited directly from Baseball Prospectus, and then promoted after he demonstrated his analytical chops. In November 2013, Luhnow added Colin Wyers to the Astros' team of five research and development analysts. Led by another BP alum, Mike Fast, this team of analysts "sets the vision for the application of information within baseball operations."[1] Luhnow was stacking the deck, and reaping the rewards.

It wasn't always that way, though. In 2007, the Astros forfeited their first-round pick in the amateur draft to sign free agent outfielder Carlos Lee. They went 82-80 in 2006, finishing 1 1/2 games back of the eventual world champion St. Louis Cardinals for the division crown. Adding a hitter of Lee's caliber was a time-tested way to immediately improve the club's short-term results.

Lee's first year with Houston was productive: He played 162 games, hitting .303/.354/.528, but Houston won only 73 games and finished 12 games back of the Cubs. The next year, an injured Lee played in only 115 games, hitting .314/.368/.569 as the Astros won 86 games, finishing 4 games back of Milwaukee in the wild-card standings.

Lee continued to offer sporadic production, but having a middling thirty-something corner outfielder on a losing team didn't make a lot of sense. Even though Blake Beavan—whom the Rangers drafted as compensation for losing Lee—never amounted to much, this was not the sort of move the Astros could afford to make.

---

1. http://houston.astros.mlb.com/hou/team/exec_bios/fast_mike.html

They started to free fall, losing 100+ games three years in a row, cratering at 51-111 in 2013. To the untrained eye, the franchise's future looked bleak. For Luhnow and his team, however, the opportunity to build a world champion was within their grasp, if they acted smartly.

In exchange for that awful run of bad baseball, the Astros were rewarded with high draft picks. In 2011, with the 11th pick, they selected the aforementioned Springer from the University of Connecticut. In 2012, with the first overall pick, they selected shortstop Carlos Correa from the Puerto Rico Baseball Academy. In 2015, with the second pick, they grabbed third baseman Alex Bregman. All three were in the starting lineup last October and had been major contributors to the Astros' success in reaching the World Series.

In addition to drafting well (they also popped Lance McCullers in 2012), Luhnow and the Astros made astute signings such as Yuli Gurriel (international free agent, Cuba) Josh Reddick (free agent), as well as shrewd trades (for Ken Giles, Chris Devenski, Brian McCann, and Game 2 starter Justin Verlander). Inheriting Marwin Gonzalez and Jose Altuve from the previous regime didn't hurt.

Even though the Astros had seen a steep increase from their $13 million payroll in 2013—on Opening Day 2017, their salary ranked 19th among 30 MLB teams at $112,437,541—they had to make every dollar work for them. Their World Series opponent, the Los Angeles Dodgers, ranked first at $242,065,828. By comparison, when the "Moneyball" Oakland A's famously faced off against the powerhouse New York Yankees in the 2001 AL Divisional Series, the free-spending Yankees led the league at $109,791,893. Even if they wanted to, the Astros were not financially able to spend themselves into contention. They had to be smarter than their opponent, who wielded payroll like a club.

So when Springer launched his dramatic Game 2 home run, it not only gave the Astros a much-needed victory, it also represented the culmination of over a century of analytical and statistical work. Like Branch Rickey, Earl Weaver, and Davey Johnson before them, A.J. Hinch and Jeff Luhnow understood that there's far more to winning baseball games than playing—and spending—by the book.

Five games later, sabermetrics and sabermetricians everywhere had hit a proverbial grand slam: a statistically oriented world champion. And Baseball Prospectus, conceived by cofounder Gary Huckabay as "a training ground—almost like a college—for young front office executives," had played no small part. But how did we get here?

A Brief History of Baseball Statistics and Analytics

> To be relevant, sabermetrics must inform a decision: data for data's sake is not useful. Bill James once defined sabermetrics as the search for objective knowledge about baseball. While this is still true, it doesn't cut to the heart of the matter.[2]
>
> —Keith Woolner

The universe of possible baseball questions is infinite. Like Hercules battling the Hydra of Greek myth, answering one question only spawns three more. Since 1856, generations of curious baseball fans have studied the game, created (and discarded) statistics to measure the performance of players and teams, and debated each other vigorously. Beginning in 1860, publishers have produced statistical compendiums that sold thousands of copies. For most of that time, MLB largely ignored analytics and what we now know as the sabermetric community.

Original Statheads

Henry Chadwick, the "Father of Baseball," was a cricket reporter for the *New York Times* on that fateful day in 1856 when he covered his first baseball game. Though the game he witnessed varied from the modern game we enjoy—pitchers delivered the ball underhand from a pitchers' "box," there were no balls called, and fielders did not wear gloves—the excitement and speed of the game caught his attention, and baseball became his lifelong fascination.

Chadwick was one of baseball's earliest promoters. Sometimes referred to as "the moral compass of the game," Chadwick was a sports writer and editor, wielding considerable influence over the game even as he developed (and often discarded) statistics to measure and compare player performance. Foreshadowing the path analytics would one day forge, he was interested in using statistics not only to describe the game, but also to determine which players were most valuable in winning games. In 1861, Chadwick (then editor of *Beadle's Dime Base-Ball Player* baseball annual) wrote, "In order to obtain an accurate estimate of a player's skill, an analysis, both of his play at the bat and in the field, should be made, inclusive of the way he was put out."[3]

In 1859, Chadwick developed the modern box score, which allowed fans to quickly see the performance of their favorite team and players, and compare their performance to that of hated foes. Over time, his contributions to baseball statistics included inventing the modern scoring method and ERA

2. Keith Woolner, "Baseball's Hilbert Problems," in *Baseball Prospectus 2000* (Washington, DC: Brassey's, 2000), 479-483.

3. Alan Schwarz, *The Numbers Game* (New York: Thomas Dunne Books, 2004), 6.

(including differentiating earned and unearned runs), as well as promoting batting average (first proposed by H.A. Dobson in 1872) as a means to judge hitting skill. Unhappy with the National League's fielding percentage as a way to measure defense, Chadwick proposed a version of range factor more than 100 years before Bill James rediscovered it, noting that "the best player in a nine is he who makes the most good plays in a match, not the one who commits the fewest errors."[4]

From the beginning, baseball fans loved their statistics, and publishers moved to satisfy this newly found need. The 1860 edition of *Beadle's Dime Base-Ball Player* sold 50,000 copies. In the 1890s, Chadwick edited *Spalding's Official Baseball Guide*, an annual that competed against rivals by Beadle, Reach, and DeWitt for the attention of baseball's early fans. Each tome claimed it had the most complete, most reliable stats for any true fan.

A generation of baseball fans grew up reading Chadwick's work and poring over box scores, the greatest among them being Ernie Lanigan. Too sick as a boy to play competitively, Lanigan fell in love with the numbers of baseball. He started his career as a copy boy for *The Sporting News*, and in 1907 the *New York Press* named him baseball editor. The original stathead, Lanigan was clear on where his love of baseball came from: "I really don't care much about baseball, or looking at ball games, major or minor. All my interest in baseball is in its statistics."[5]

Seeking to give credit for "clutch" hitting, Lanigan was an early champion of the RBI, and in 1907 began printing that statistic in the daily box scores. Noting the importance of baserunning in the offense-depressed early 1900s, Lanigan tracked both caught stealing and its defensive counterpart, thrown out by catcher.

Lanigan saw his RBI stat officially adopted in 1920. In 1922 he published the *Baseball Cyclopedia*, whose title page proudly exclaimed:

> Comprises a review of Professional Baseball, the history of all Major League Clubs, playing records and unique events, the batting, pitching and base running champions, World's Series' statistics and a carefully arranged alphabetical list of the records of more than 3500 Major League ball players, a feature never before attempted in print.

The *Cyclopedia* published 12 supplements. In 1946, Lanigan was named curator (and later, first historian) of the Baseball Hall of Fame, a position he maintained until his retirement in 1959.

⚾   ⚾   ⚾

John Heydler, who recognized early the importance of keeping accurate statistics, was hired in 1903 to be the National League secretary, and unofficial stat keeper. Heydler, previously a sports writer who compiled his own statistics by hand to inform his columns, worked his way through the baseball hierarchy: NL umpire to secretary, to secretary-treasurer and eventually NL president from 1918 to 1934. Heydler made two important contributions to modern statistics: developing the current ERA formula that allowed for increased reliever usage (prorating to earned runs per 9 innings pitched), and hiring the Elias Sports Bureau to keep statistics for the league.

But it wasn't just journalists and league executives who loved baseball and its numbers; increasingly, amateur statisticians would make their mark on the game. In 1912, when John Lawres walked into the Manhattan office of *Baseball Magazine*, he was the most important baseball statistician no one had ever heard of.

A fan of the 1889 New York Giants, Lawres kept stats by hand simply to win arguments with his friends. Starting with a little book of "argument settlers," over the years Lawres' work found its way into larger and larger ledgers. For the next 20 years, he spent 2-4 hours a day (on average) compiling stats on 52 leagues and over 22,000 ballplayers, noting that "the labor that was begun as a diversion has become little short of slavery, but I feel in my own little way that it is a pleasure to accomplish unknown a work that, in its creation, may please thousands who know neither my face, name, nor even existence."[6]

Lawres' work became the 1912 edition of *Who's Who In Baseball*, an annual that was published (after an initial 3-year hiatus) continually until 2016. What made *Who's Who* different was its completeness: Lawres assembled a compilation of stats and records for MLB that had never been seen before in one place.

While the 1912 edition had only games, batting average, and fielding average for batters (nothing for pitchers), by the 1916 edition it had added at-bats, runs, hits, and steals for batters, as well as nine stats for pitchers: games, innings pitched, wins, losses, win/loss percentage, strikeouts, walks, hits allowed, and earned runs. Oddly enough, home runs weren't added until 1940, 5 years after Babe Ruth's final at-bat.

⚾   ⚾   ⚾

---

4. Ibid., 10.
5. Ibid., 23.
6. Ibid., 30-31.

Ferdinand Cole Lane, a Boston University-trained biologist, was another baseball fan who lived vicariously through the numbers. He worked for *Baseball Magazine*, a monthly publication, starting in 1910 and quickly rising to Editor-In-Chief in 1912. He wrote hundreds of articles that deconstructed the game, trying to figure out which stats were useful and which were not. Batting average, he wrote, was "worse than worthless," as it ignored the importance of bases on balls and the value of doubles, triples, and home runs.[7] Pitching and fielding numbers were similarly flawed, and so Lane sought to fix them.

Starting from the premise that "simply because a problem is hard to solve, is no excuse for failing to make the attempt," Lane worked to develop the relative value of individual events, expressed in expected runs scored.[8] Scoring enough major-league games to add up 1,000 hits, Lane determined that singles were worth 0.3 runs, doubles 0.6, triples 0.9, and home runs 1.15. Over time, he refined the results: singles, he figured, were worth 0.457 runs, doubles 0.786, triples 1.15, home runs 1.55, and bases on balls 0.164. He now had a way to directly compare the contributions of diverse players, and show that high-average hitters were relatively overvalued, while less flashy hitters could carry the day based on consistent results.

In 1913, Lane encouraged his readers to become active participants. Thus *Baseball Magazine* was the first to attempt to create an interlinked community of baseball outsiders. The letters poured in, Lane wrote nearly 1,000 articles over the years, and no one in MLB paid him any notice.

The Next Wave

Allan Roth was the first full-time statistician ever hired by a major-league club, Branch Rickey's Brooklyn Dodgers. Debuting the same year as Jackie Robinson, 1947, Roth sat behind home plate, charting every one of the season's 40,000+ pitches, analyzing results, and finding small advantages. As he noted, "baseball is a game of percentages. I try to find the actual percentage."[9]

Roth looked where no one had thought to look before. He charted batting averages in every ball-strike count, as well as batting results against right- and left-handed pitchers. Detail-oriented and tireless, Roth charted the results of each at-bat, including where each hit landed. After the game, he would spend hours analyzing, looking for anything that could help the Dodgers win.

Roth's observations sometimes led to significant baseball decisions. For example, Roth noticed in 1947 that right fielder Dixie Walker wasn't pulling the ball, an indication that his bat was slowing. Even though the All-Star hit .306 that year (his lifetime batting average), Rickey—who believed in trading away a player a year too soon, rather than a year too late—shipped Walker to Pittsburgh for Preacher Roe and Billy Cox. Two years later, Walker was out of baseball, while Roe and Cox were mainstays for the Dodgers.

In another case, Roth recommended moving Robinson from leadoff to the fourth spot in the lineup. Despite the fact that Robinson's 1948 power numbers—.296 batting average, 12 home runs, and 85 RBI—were unimpressive at first glance, Roth knew that he had converted the most RBI opportunities that year. Robinson responded with 124 RBI in an MVP season; the Dodgers won 97 games and the world championship.

When Rickey left the Dodgers to run the Pittsburgh Pirates in 1950, Roth lost much of his influence. He even lost his place behind the plate, and was moved to the press box, where he assisted young announcer Vin Scully. Roth's statistical work informed broadcasters and sportswriters, and later in life he would assist in All-Star and World Series broadcasts.

In 1954, Roth's name was again prominent due to a *Life* magazine article on Branch Rickey, "Goodby to Some Old Baseball Ideas." The article pictured Rickey at a blackboard, pointing to a mathematical formula developed by Roth that Rickey declared "the most disconcerting and at the same time most constructive thing to come into baseball in my memory."[10] The complicated formula combined early versions of on-base percentage, isolated power, and baserunning prowess, as well as fielding and pitching results, generating One True Number for ranking ballplayers. While there's no evidence that anyone in baseball ever used the formula to make any baseball decisions, Roth's place among ambitious statisticians was forever etched in public memory.

His work eventually gained influence within the Dodgers hierarchy again, especially after Walter Alston became manager in 1954. When the Dodgers moved to Los Angeles, Roth began attending spring training. He had individual meetings with players and their coaches, discussing their statistical record and recommending areas where improvement was possible. Sandy Koufax credited Roth with impressing on him the importance of first-pitch strikes and changing speeds.

Roth was let go by the Dodgers after the 1964 season, and soon began working for newspapers and TV networks. He consulted for 20 major-league teams, and did not retire until his late 80s. Roth died in 1992, and was elected to the Baseball Hall of Fame in 2010. The Los Angeles chapter of the Society for American Baseball Research still bears his name.

---

7. Ibid., 34.
8. Ibid., 35.
9. Ibid., 55.
10. Ibid., 58.

ⓧ   ⓧ   ⓧ

Amateur statisticians continued to love and evaluate the game, while being virtually ignored by major-league front offices. Charles and George Lindsey scored hundreds of games by hand, laboriously entering the results into a charting system they invented.

Military operations officers by training, they were determined to examine the efficacy of "The Book," baseball's unwritten strategy guide. Over the years, the father-and-son team used actual play-by-play results to create both an expected runs table and an early win expectancy chart.

They found that platooning works (it increases batting average by 32 points, on average), bunting is in general a bad idea (while it can sometimes help you score one run, in general it costs you runs and therefore victories), and the stolen base didn't provide much in the way of actual run production. Published in periodicals like *Operations Research* and the *Journal of the American Statistical Association*, their groundbreaking work was ignored by the very men who needed it the most.

ⓧ   ⓧ   ⓧ

In 1963, *Sports Illustrated* featured an article titled, "Baseball Is Played All Wrong." Statistician Earnshaw Cook, churning out numbers on his Friden STW Mechanical Calculator (later donated to the Baseball Hall of Fame), had found that major-league managers were not very good at their jobs.

"There are two primary objects in baseball," he wrote. "The first is to score runs. And the second is *not* to make outs."[11] Expanding on his work in 1964's *Percentage Baseball*, Cook claimed that platooning was a waste of time (managers should bat their best eight every game); that the best hitter should bat first to maximize how many times he came to bat; and that games should be started by a relief pitcher, who would be pinch-hit for as soon as possible. He also claimed that he could turn any .500 club into an instant playoff contender, if they would throw out the book and use his tactics instead.

While most of baseball ignored Cook, a young Davey Johnson was interested enough to strike up a lifelong friendship with the author. Johnson, who holds a mathematics degree from Trinity University, was later known for his innovative techniques as manager of the Mets, Reds, Orioles, and Dodgers. Johnson was part of a movement of baseball minds that had been brought up thinking differently about the game.

Bill James

By far the most popular baseball outsider was Bill James. Described as "the most influential baseball writer of the 20th century," James had a love for baseball, and a love for numbers.[12] Naturally curious, he liked to ask questions and then gather the data to find the real answer.

By the time James started his job as a night security watchmen for Stokely-Van Camp's pork and beans cannery (where he claimed to spend about 5 minutes of every hour ensuring the boilers didn't explode, the rest working on his baseball stats), he held three undergraduate degrees from the University of Kansas: English, economics, and education. After a 2-year stint in the Army, he enrolled in a graduate program but quit when an advisor warned him that even a Ph.D. wouldn't guarantee a teaching position.

James knew that he wasn't alone in his love of baseball statistics, and he felt he might be able to earn a living writing to and for the mathematically inclined baseball fan. In the 1977 offseason he self-published the first *Baseball Abstract*. Advertised only in a 3 1/2-inch classified ad in *The Sporting News*, it claimed to offer "statistical information you just can't find anywhere else." James was right, there was an audience. Seventy-five people purchased that booklet, and for all his hard work he profited the tidy sum of $93.77.

This was encouraging enough that James started early on the 1978 version, expanding his commentary to all 26 teams and key players for each team. The second *Abstract* sold better, and caught the eye of *Sports Illustrated* writer Dan Okrent.

Okrent's 1981 article "He Does It By the Numbers" catapulted James into the public consciousness. Self-published no more, James received a $40,000 advance from Ballantine, and subsequent sales of the *Baseball Abstract* pushed the book as high as number 4 on the *New York Times* bestseller list.

James constantly challenged "The Book." Bunting, baserunning, player development ... there wasn't a sacred cow that he wouldn't slaughter on the altar of data. But more than that, he was the consummate outsider, the rare talent who could both crunch the numbers and present his findings in an intelligent, understandable manner. James made baseball analysis accessible to a wider audience.

He deconstructed the game, creating metrics such as Runs Created that sought to illuminate which parts of offense were the most valuable. He railed against front offices that underestimated the impact each out had on scoring and overestimated the flash of the stolen base.

James hated fielding percentage, which undervalued range, and created range factor as the best way to evaluate defense and compare players. He used his own Pythagorean Formula to predict a team's winning percentage, developed

---

11. Ibid., 80.
12. http://www.baseballamerica.com/majors/25-for-25-don-fehr-peter-gammons-pat-gillick-bo-jackson-bill-james-1957/

the Plexiglass Principle to predict a team's rise (and fall) after a surprising season, and invented a predictive system he named Brock2 for career projections. One of James' most popular inventions was the "favorite toy" for determining a player's chance to reach certain career milestones (3,000 hits, 300 wins, 500 home runs, etc.).

He relied on data and rigorous methods. When common wisdom said a player's best years were 28-32, he checked and found to his own surprise that 25-29 was a typical player's peak. One implication of this finding was that free agents were aging out of their prime (if they weren't past prime already), and the vast majority were a bad risk. James understood that teams were likely paying for past performance, not future.

He also took ballpark effects, another poorly understood concept at the time, into account when he wrote his player comments, and correctly predicted that Fenway Park would help Carney Lansford. Not only was James right, he could explain the methodology that underpinned his predictions. He took away the mystique of the "baseball man" who knew things based on long years of experience. He made baseball decisions accessible.

James soon determined that box scores weren't granular enough for his needs. Knowing what happened was important; knowing the sequence of events, even more so. He needed play-by-play data. Only one company, Elias Sports Bureau, kept that information. Rebuffed again and again, James created a crowdsourced solution: Project Scoresheet. Initially, he had over 100 volunteers who personally scored games and provided the data to James for his analysis.

James continued to publish the *Abstract* until 1987. An entire generation of baseball executives such as Billy Beane, Dan Duquette, and Theo Epstein credited him with fueling their passion for the business of baseball.

Baseball Prospectus Is Born

With the end of the *Abstracts* came a void waiting to be filled, but as James later noted, there was a problem:

> Look, the problem with Earnshaw Cook, and with the other pre-1970s baseball statistics guys, excepting Allan Roth, is that **none of them ever did one damn thing toward the creation of a sabermetric community**. They didn't do that because they didn't have any concept of this being a field of knowledge that was bigger than themselves. They weren't interested in having a million little debates with others who were into the same topics. They weren't interested in creating a community.[13]

Fortunately, the advent of the Internet gave the sabermetric community a way to connect. It started in universities and government institutions, and accelerated in a little group on Usenet—the precursor to Internet forums—called rec.sport.baseball.

From this little group, in the fall of 1995, Baseball Prospectus launched. A small team of amateur baseball researchers and writers led by Gary Huckabay collaborated on a revolutionary "new" project. The original team consisted of five like-minded individuals: Huckabay, Clay Davenport, Rany Jazayerli, Chris Kahrl, and writer/editor Joe Sheehan.

Changing Perceptions

From the start, Huckabay and the team had lofty goals:

> We wanted to get people to stop paying attention to stats that were potentially misleading. Runs batted in, for example, where you get individual credit for basically stuff that other people did. We wanted on-base percentage and walks to be well understood and appreciated.
>
> There were specific, measurable goals we wanted to [achieve]. One of them was, instead of batting average, home runs, and RBI being reported, we wanted batting average, OBP, and slugging [percentage]. I think that trifecta, even before park adjustments, even before getting it perfect ... gives you a great idea of what a player's offensive shape looks like. It tells you a lot more in a very parsimonious fashion. I think it's great management. If you have bad metrics that you're using to measure things, you're going to have bad management practices. Not too surprising.
>
> Rickey Henderson is a good example of where things kept coming back to BP. People think Rickey Henderson is Rickey Henderson because of the stolen bases. No, stolen bases were only one aspect of his game. Rickey's game was drawing walks and hitting for power.

As F.C. Lane, Bill James, and others had previously shown, drawing walks and hitting for power were important—far more so than conventional wisdom cared to admit. But, Huckabay adds, offense wasn't the only area that had room for improvement:

> Next, defensive reporting needed to change dramatically. Fielding percentage is an awful way to measure defense; it's just horrible. It was so prevalent, and so dominant in terms of reporting,

---

13. https://www.billjamesonline.com/article1597/

that it really was holding a lot of clubs back and individuals back from appreciating the contributions of someone like Ozzie Smith.

Henry Chadwick would doubtless agree. Huckabay continues:

> [Many] things were not appreciated because of park effects and the media's focus on the highly visible and not on things that are not perceived as being exciting. So, we wanted to make those changes to the media. And from there, we would expect that to change the baseball zeitgeist (or whatever term you want to use) … then the clubs would start to pay attention.
>
> MLB clubs are as affected by the media as much as anyone else. We would start down the road of change the media, then you change the perception of the whole game, and then coverage will be better. And I think by and large we have seen that.

Shaping the Discussion

Huckabay was a college student in the late 1980s, working as a computer consultant at the University of California, Davis. In between helping students unlock the mysteries of cut-and-paste and deciding on just the right font for their anthropology paper, he discovered Usenet and, more specifically, rec.sport.baseball.

"I started actually looking forward to coming to work," he says. "I could spend a lot of the university's time and money on my own edification and entertainment."

Rec.sport.baseball revealed a world of like-minded baseball fans:

> I didn't connect the dots in terms of what Bill James was writing, and in terms of what it actually meant on the ball field I don't think until much later. It took some of rec.sport.baseball and Sherri Nichols to kind of bring a lot of that home. These theories and this information has a direct causal link to winning. That didn't really come home to me until I ran into people on the pre-web that knew this stuff better than I did.

For a baseball fan who grew up listening to Oakland A's radio broadcasts and Hall of Fame baseball announcer Bill King, Huckabay learned about Bill James early:

> I don't know what year exactly, but Bill King would start interjecting stuff from [James] that was contrary to conventional wisdom, like by and large bunting doesn't make a lot of sense. And [King] would refer back to Bill James, some of the

studies in the *Abstracts*, some of the early writings. It was really kind of insightful, something you didn't hear from anybody.

When Huckabay received a copy of Bill James' *Player Ratings* as a gift, he was hooked:

> It was great writing, above all else. I didn't know that much about the depth of the quality of the research; I wasn't really in a position to make an informed assessment about that. But, I did know that I'd start reading something, and then I'd look up and I would have read 100 pages. It was above all else entertaining and engaging.

Rec.sport.baseball exposed Huckabay to the thoughts of super fans like Dave and Sherri Nichols, David Tate, and Clay Davenport:

> Those were kind of the biggest influences. There really were multiple factions in terms of what was going on at the time. There were the statheads, who were derided by the more mainstream fans. But they were the ones that were writing most of the stuff that was really engaging and compelling. The quality of the writing was extremely high from the folks I was interested in seeing. It was young enough at that point, so there wasn't an overload of stuff. There wasn't the volume there is today.

Later in his UC Davis career, while completing his MBA, Huckabay would hurry through his campus job, completing 8 hours of work in 2-4 hours, so he could indulge his real love.

"You would go and refresh the articles every once in a while," he recalls, "and you might find three new articles in rec.sport.baseball instead of the 10 million Twitter blasts you get today. It was kind of a habit to sit there and refresh. Compulsively."

As Huckabay notes, rec.sport.baseball became a laboratory for fledgling analytics:

> We were trying to figure out a different way to put together a winning ballclub. If you think about it, it pretty much was open source free management consulting for clubs that could get into it that early. But even the earliest adopters—the A's and the Red Sox—they weren't there yet.

For Huckabay, an entrepreneur by nature who had started two successful businesses by age 21, the opportunity was obvious. Rec.sport.baseball would become the genesis of a sports consulting business, run by passionate outsiders who would change how the game was portrayed by the media, and how clubs were run.

The idea I had was you do a few things. One was to put together a book I wanted to read. At the time, Bill James had just wrapped up his *Player Ratings* books. He wasn't going to do those anymore. I loved those. I thought they were a lot of fun. It was something I looked forward to in terms of reading throughout the baseball season.

Two, I wanted to move the needle on the media. Start focusing more on things like on-base percentage, paying attention to pitcher abuse, and really leverage a lot of these ideas to connect those dots between a winning team on the field and then the analysis that you do behind making those player decisions. It's really decision science.

Mining New Talent

In the process, Huckabay also turned an open forum on baseball into the minor leagues for his next business project.

"So, on rec.sport.baseball," he recalls, "what you basically got was free scouting. You got to see people write; you got to see people research. And then you could easily pick out those people."

Just as he would later try to pick out the future stars of baseball while they toiled in relative obscurity in the minor leagues, here he looked for undiscovered analytical talent:

I would look for writings by Rany Jazayerli, Joe Sheehan, and Chris Kahrl. I really loved Clay Davenport's Davenport Translations, which I thought were really key to being able to really understand the player performance aspect because I thought that park effects and hitting effects were much bigger than people thought. Clay was translating minor-league and major-league numbers to a neutral park, neutral league.

Pre-Colorado I don't think people understood the amplitude of the effect a ballpark could have. At the time, before the reconfiguration of Oakland Coliseum (i.e., the "Mount Davis" remodel), I was used to seeing ballgames in Oakland where it was the opposite of Coors. There's this expansive foul territory, the batter's eye was effectively gray, and I remember thinking "How come no A's hitter ever hits .300?" Part of the reason is ... they give up 20-30 outs a year that end up being out of play in other parks. And also, the Coliseum is at -9 feet sea level, as opposed to +5,000 feet at Coors.

As Huckabay identified potential collaborators, he reached out via the relatively new technology of email.

"I can't remember if I reached out to Rany or Joe first," he says, "but one of them referred me to the other."

The team grew, and in the fall of 1995 the first *Baseball Prospectus* was produced. It was a bootstrap operation. Jazayerli, a self-proclaimed math geek from his earliest memories, remembers that time:

One of the first things I did when I went to university was scour every used bookstore until I completed my collection of Bill James books. I was writing Pitching Organizational Reports for rec.sport.baseball, something Clay wasn't publishing translations for yet, and I had been writing player comments for the Kansas City Royals for a couple years.

I got this email from Gary, asking if I was interested in working on a book, and I was thrilled. I told him about Joe Sheehan, a guy I knew from Strat-O-Matic. Joe had a degree in journalism from USC, and I recall Gary saying, "Well, we won't hold that against him." I gave Joe's number to Gary, and by that night we were both in.

Wiping Clean the Baseball Publishing Landscape

It's hard to remember now, but in the fall of 1994 MLB was in real trouble, both financially and within its fan base. Labor strife ruled the headlines: Facing a looming deadline to renegotiate the soon-to-expire Collective Bargaining Agreement, and unable to come to an agreement with owners on a proposed salary cap and revenue sharing, the Major League Baseball Players Association struck on August 12.

The move was calculated to provide maximum negotiating leverage; with playoff baseball and its associated revenues looming, the owners would surely be motivated to capitulate to the players' demands. Seven times before, the MLBPA's resolve had proven stronger than the owners'; seven times before, the MLBPA had played chicken with the owners, and the owners had blinked. This time, though, the MLBPA miscalculated.

The breaking of the reserve clause in 1975 had caused a dramatic rise in baseball salaries. Arbitration and free agency had raised the average baseball salary from $44,676 in 1975 to nearly $1.2 million by the time of this CBA negotiation. Owners, who steadfastly refused to open their books to union scrutiny, claimed 19 of 28 teams had lost money the year before. "How much is enough?" they asked Donald Fehr during the negotiations. He wanted it all, as much as the market would bear.

The strike continued; on September 14, Acting Commissioner Bud Selig announced the cancellation of the World Series. For the first time in nearly 90 Octobers, there was no playoff baseball. Not even the casual fan could deny that the realities of doing business had forcefully collided with the anachronism of baseball.

The strike—and its perceived public backlash—had wiped clean the publishing landscape for baseball books. Undaunted, Huckabay and his team decided to the write the book that they wanted to read:

> We wanted to do this book. We had Clay Davenport's Translations from the last 3-4 years. I had a forecasting system that I had put together. So you'd have the translations, which were translated stats for the last 3 or 4 years, a forecast for what they were going to do this coming year, a little blurb about the players, kind of like what the Bill James *Player Ratings* book had. Then we also wanted to do little blurbs on the teams. We divided the major leagues up into basically five groups and started writing.
>
> The first year you had to basically send a blank check to Joe Sheehan, that we were advertising through our (dot) signature lines on rec.sport.baseball. I can't remember where we printed them out; it was a local Copymat-type place that would do the binding and the books. But we had to wait until we had all the money before we could do that. And that was in 1995; the first book was 1996.

As if to prove they really were human, the original *Baseball Prospectus* left out the 62-81 St. Louis Cardinals.

Recalls Christina Kahrl, "I still view the white label *Prospectus* as the ultimate act of hubris. Our arrogance was so great that it didn't matter that our first book was terrible. We didn't let it discourage us, no matter what."

"It was a very idealistic project," remembers Jazayerli. "We were going to change how MLB teams were run. It's hard to believe we thought we would have an impact, but looking back now we accomplished everything we set out to do."

Growing the Business

According to Huckabay, there was enough interest for the project to continue for at least one more year:

> We did the 1997 book, and I think we sold 3,000 that year, or a little over 3,000. That's when I knew we had something. It was really going to be a question of constraints in terms of time and generating enough revenue to keep people happy enough to keep going. I saw right away that was going to be one of the major challenges we were going to face ... we basically had to grow our way out of any problems we were running into. It's tough to do that with an annual book being your main thing.
>
> That's why we started the website in ... late 1996. In the beginning, everything was free content. We wanted to keep people plugged in

and hooked up with us all year, and familiar with the brand, so that when the book came out they purchased it. And it worked.

Kahrl, now a senior editor for ESPN, recalls the experience:

> We thought we should have a website, that it would be good as a year-long advertisement for the book. Now, of course, the web is bigger, more important than print. Back then, though, it was an actual debate. It was such an interesting, dynamic-changing, Wild West situation for the whole concept: What kind of content do people want, where do they want it, and what medium do they want it? And we were kind of making it up as we went along.

As the scope of coverage expanded, Huckabay recalls that "there were a lot of contributors at this time that were doing more and more stuff, really, really good work. Michael Wolverton doesn't get enough credit; neither does Dave Pease. It's about this time that we started doing significant growth."

It became immediately obvious that they needed more people. The problem was, they couldn't afford to pay them:

> The first business meeting didn't really happen until well after we were already down the road. We had some specific business meetings on an annual basis, either at a hotel or a law firm or whatever the appropriate place was. We'd get everybody together and try to do a year review, and then a plan for what's coming up next. The constraints were always so severe in terms of the number of people we had, and the amount of stuff we wanted to do, that it really became a question of triage.
>
> The book was the major source of revenue at this point. I think we were making a few thousand bucks, low five figures of cash. Even though it wasn't very much, all the revenue came from there, so that had to take a big part in what was going on. We would spend an inordinate amount of time making sure the book was done as best we could given all the constraints, get it out the door.
>
> It put us behind the eight-ball in terms of people we had left to work on projects, work on the web, original research, and such. That's when we really started to expand, [started] to get into the intern program. A big part of our success was because of the fantastic interns we were able to get.
>
> The Baseball Prospectus intern program turned out to be one of the biggest successes. If you take a look around baseball right now there [are a lot

of] former interns and former BP staff members who were here and are either now currently involved ... or have been involved with clubs, or agents or agencies. I think that's where ultimately the biggest impact will be. People now know that if you're not ... a former player, then [after] going to BP ... as an intern or a research assistant ... you will have some skills that are valuable.

Creating the "Saturday Night Live of Sabermetrics"

Kahrl has seen the world of MLB as both an outsider at Baseball Prospectus, and an insider at ESPN.

It has been an interesting development to see how many people work at BP, maybe only for a couple of years, before moving on. That ends up being a platform for them to get launched in a front office job, kind of a "Dream Factory." For those like Jonah Keri, Keith Law, and those working in front offices, it became a magnificent opportunity.

We were sort of the *Saturday Night Live* of sabermetrics; there was always a rotating cast. BP was the start of something wonderful for so many different people that makes the company itself and the brand something we should always love and treasure because of what it made possible for so many of us.

As of Opening Day 2017, 45 of these interns and collaborators worked in various MLB offices, as well as for popular media and sporting agencies. In addition to the Astros' contingent, notable BP alumni include Jason Parks (Diamondbacks) and Keith Woolner (Indians), who have important front office positions and considerable influence on decisions. Mainstream names such as Nate Silver (fivethirtyeight.com), Keith Law (ESPN), Jonah Keri (CBS, Sports Illustrated), and many others did significant work in their time at Baseball Prospectus.

Their success comes as no surprise to Huckabay:

When you're talking about the type of contracts we see now in baseball where the top five guys make $30 million a year or so, it's going to make sense having five or six guys in your front office (that you didn't used to have) that are not going to cost very much money, relatively speaking, and they're going to be able to add a lot of value in terms of saying, "Hey! Here's where we want to spend our dollars, here's where we don't. Here are the players we want to chase down, here are the ones we don't." I saw that coming a long time ago; but I think a lot of people did.

Working for BP for a while, then moving onto a paid position within a major-league club or sports representation agency, that was the career path that made coming to BP appealing. Although it made it very challenging to keep people in an ongoing business concern.

You end up with the circumstance of me and a couple other people running the business side, and us not wanting to do that. Taking a lot of time for that meant less time for research, less time to write, and there was so much people wrangling and so much management that needed to be done that it really turned into a very negative time sink for me, personally. But it was one of those things where no one else was going to do this, but it needs to be done.

Even though Huckabay had a limited amount of time to contribute, contribute he did. With articles such as "There Is No Such Thing As A Pitching Prospect (TINSTAAP)" and "Kenny Williams, A's Fan" he pushed the conversation away from the anti-intellectual "by the book" media, while keeping the appropriate tone.

Huckabay and his team challenged popular baseball culture to reexamine its view of everything, including the sport's biggest stars. For example, popular opinion held that Ken Griffey Jr. and Derek Jeter were excellent defenders. The numbers said they were not, and Baseball Prospectus boldly stated that fact.

Challenging Received Wisdom

Huckabay defends such boldness, which became a hallmark of BP:

Those kind[s] of statements were things that drew attention and we wanted to draw attention because this stuff is supposed to be fun. Baseball is fun; talking about baseball is fun. Watching, *playing*, is the most fun you can possibly ever get. If we got criticism for some of those comments, I was fine with that.

We tried not to get into hyperbole but, I had no problem [making] sensational statements. They draw attention, and also there were enough things out there where perception was so different from reality that it made people at least think about things, for at least a minute even just to gainsay it.

Consider, as Huckabay clearly has, Carney Lansford:

As an A's fan, I don't know how many times I got into a conversation with people about Carney Lansford's defense. Lansford's defense was poor, no doubt about that. In terms of, just looking at the numbers. And also, if you actually watched him play at the time.... Once you understood the numbers, it gave an entire new lens to watching him play. He would fall down. People called it diving, it was borderline diving. He'd play in tight, and balls were getting by him left and right that were not getting by other third basemen. Yet, he was receiving a lot of accolades because he made a lot of diving stops.

People's perception about defense [is] tough because humans tend to remember the exceptional rather than the generic. People remember Ken Griffey Jr. making the great leaping catch. Sure, he makes those catches. One thing that was always telling—I was talking to Mark Wolfson, who produced the A's broadcasts on local television for a number of years—one thing that struck us both in terms of observation was that, when they were televising Mariners games, whether it was [in] Oakland, LA, or wherever they were playing, the producer could always switch the camera to Griffey (when the ball was hit to him) before Griffey moved. There was always a question of who was better getting a break on the ball, the TV producer or Griffey?

People [also] tend to conflate offense and defense. For example, I have no idea why people ever thought Derek Jeter could play shortstop. I really don't. Sure, he played 20 years there, and had a great career and has some rings, therefore he must be a great shortstop defensively. Um, no! Sorry. That's simply not the case.

Striving to Improve

Huckabay's graduation from UC Davis marked a new beginning for Baseball Prospectus:

I got a job at a Big 6 consulting firm with the idea of forming a sports consulting practice. I put together a brief on what kind of analysis needed to be done, and how clubs could benefit, and basically how could any small business (which is what these clubs were at the time) not want to save $10 million in player costs and still have a better team at same time?

I sent a copy of *BP '97* to several people in the Oakland front office to try and say, "Let me come down and talk to you about this. I think we can help you put together a better team on the field and save money at the same time." I never got a response back until a year or so later when Billy Beane became the general manager of the A's. He called me on the phone.

While many at Baseball Prospectus aspired to be general managers, Huckabay had a different goal:

I realized pretty quickly that I wasn't going to be a GM because I was too old when I started, so instead I changed my focus a little bit. I had a sit-down with a GM of a club, and I had been doing some work for him, and I wanted to join his staff. So they sat down with me and said, we're more interested in you on the consulting side because we don't want to bloat up our front office staff. And that's when I realized that a GM job probably wasn't going to be coming my way.

So I focused instead on trying to become an owner of a club. Statistically, my chances of making enough money to do that are better than becoming a GM. As a fail-safe, if I don't make the hundreds of millions necessary to do that, maybe I'll do well enough to have a comfortable existence.

Even after 20+ years, there are still aspects of media coverage and the sport that command Huckabay's attention, for example, the reliance on ex-players to comment on games. Instead, he would like to see a true meritocracy, where reporters have a mix of in-game knowledge and statistical chops:

The training for explaining something may not be the same thing as actually doing it.... I'm sure there's probably some kid out there at age 13 or whatever who started to love baseball, went through high school and college, and ... would be a fantastic commentator who could really bring a lot of insight and entertainment to the game. But he just simply never had the opportunity.

Standing the Test of Time

On a more positive note, Huckabay notes that some sabermetric discoveries have aged quite gracefully, although the nature of those discoveries may surprise some:

Scouting pitchers has stood up, and will continue to stand up. Even though the language was not there for communication between stats and scouts. (I'm bifurcating people into stats and scouts, even though that's a false dichotomy. For these purposes, it's illustrative.)

If you think about what we've learned from statistical analysis and pitching: we like guys that strike people out, we like guys that don't get hurt, and we know that if we abuse the hell out of their arms they get hurt. Well, in a way, that's always what scouting has been about. They look for guys with great stuff (presumably to miss bats); they wanted guys who had a mechanical delivery that made a lot of sense, that didn't have a lot of extra motion or torque (on things that shouldn't receive torque). Durability has been the Holy Grail for pitching for as long ... as there's been pitchers.

So I think that those two things—the stats side, the scouting side—were always very close but they were always talking past each other because of language, by and large. But I think that's what stood up best.

The framework for thinking about baseball in a different way and challenging conventional wisdom has also held up well. In another venture, Jazayerli teamed with Bill James intern and early Baseball Prospectus supporter Rob Neyer to produce *Rob and Rany on the Royals*, a blog that allowed them to vent their frustrations with team management to the world. Remembers Jazayerli:

The success of the *Rob and Rany on the Royals* blog surprised us. There were so many non-Royals fan who read us; we never expected that.

Sabermetrics gave us a framework to assess baseball. From 2000 to 2010, there really was no reason why teams made decisions other than randomness. Case in point, 2002 Jermaine Dye for Neifi Perez. Terrible trade! And it played out that way.

By 2010 and beyond there really was a methodology to how teams made decisions. When the Royals traded Wil Myers for James Shields, I thought it was a horrible deal, and I said so. It felt good to be wrong; the Royals did well in the trade, and Wil Myers, while a good ballplayer, never realized the potential we thought he had.

For Kahrl, some things have changed since that initial act of hubris:

As a University of Chicago grad, I figure everything is worthy of investigation (and doubt). In the beginning, we had a semi-antagonning relationship with Major League Baseball. We've come so far in the [last] 20+ years, to get a place in the conversation, and not talk past one another [stats and scouts] but talk with one another about the different things we all have to contribute in evaluating the game, and evaluating players and teams.

If anything, it's way more fun now than it was then when we were just making fun of so-called dumb people in baseball. Some instances—such as catcher defense, pitch framing, for example—it was something people in the game understood, they just didn't have the language to describe it. When Earl Weaver played Rick Dempsey over Earl Williams, even though he was a worse hitter, it was the right choice. Baseball managers like Weaver knew there was real value in what they were doing; they weren't making [stuff] up, they just didn't have the math to explain it. We have the math now.

Whatever our background, in the end we're all just talking baseball. Sabermetrics is invited to the table—BP obviously helped earn us that place—but it's nothing but magic now that we're here. It's a wonderful thing about the baseball industry but it says a wonderful thing about sabermetrics and knowing the kind of information it can give us. Baseball is fun! It's a treat, but it's also a privilege.

As baseball caught Henry Chadwick's attention and became his lifelong fascination more than 160 years ago, so it continues to captivate members of the current generation. We persist in our pursuit of elusive answers to the infinite number of questions this seemingly simple sport has spawned.

Though we may never find the entire truth, we will never stop looking. And we will doubtless be surprised by what those who follow us may yet discover, even as the past greats on whose shoulders we now stand would gaze at us with wonder.

A treat and a privilege, indeed. ▨

Baseball's Youngest Players from Season to Season, Part 2: 1941-2017

by John Paschal

On October 2,1938, 19-year-old Cubs reliever Al Epperly—the youngest player in the National League—coaxed a bases-loaded strikeout to end his first inning of work in the major leagues. On July 7, 1950, the now 32-year-old Dodgers reliever coaxed a bases-empty fly-ball out from Dick Sisler to end in his *last* inning of work in the major leagues. Contrary to appearance, however, Epperly's major-league career hadn't lasted 13 seasons. It had lasted two. In the seasons between his debut and denouement, Epperly had spent 11 years in the minor leagues and two in military service during World War II. Of course, Epperly wasn't the first Youngest Player (YP) to falter in the big leagues, nor was he the last to lose time to war.

The War Years (1941-1945, 1950-1953)

Upon reading "The War Years," you arrive at a logical conclusion: that 1941-1945 and 1950-1953 generated player shortages due to the military enlistment of everyday big leaguers, and that the shortage allowed openings for replacement players who otherwise might never have played in the big leagues. And some of those players, it stands to reason, surely included young players—indeed, YPs. That conclusion, however, is only partly correct.

When we consider the correlation of baseball and war, we typically think of the superstar—Ted Williams, Joe DiMaggio—who lost prime years to his military service. What we often fail to consider, however, is not only the midlevel player who lost time to war but also the fringe player, one whose talent pushed him against the hard margin between minor- and major-league baseball.

Here is the reality: Many players never had a chance to become stars or even everyday big leaguers because they lost developmental years to Uncle Sam and his timely belligerence. The years they could have spent in the minor leagues, getting the necessary repetitions, were spent instead in theaters of war. And upon their stateside return—if in fact they did return physically, mentally, and emotionally sound—they often found their baseball skills had stagnated or eroded due to their time away. Just as harmfully, they had gotten two or three or four years older.

In 1941, 17-year-old first baseman Vern Freiburger made his MLB debut in the back end of the Indians' September 6 doubleheader against the Tigers and finished 0-for-4 against ace Al Benton. True, it hadn't been the best debut, but Freiburger could have been forgiven his 0-fer: At the time, he was supposed to have been a high schooler. He had skipped his senior year to pursue a career in professional baseball.

Nine days later, Freiburger went 1-for-4 with an RBI against eventual Hall of Famer Lefty Gomez in Yankee Stadium. The future had to have looked rosy for the 6-foot-1 teenager. Sadly, it would be his final major-league contest.

In 1943, after posting a .301/.421/.721 line with Cleveland's 1942 Cedar Rapids affiliate and being slated for a major-league roster spot due to the retirement of Indians first baseman Hal Trosky, Freiburger instead was called upon him to serve in the US Navy. He would spend three years in the war effort. He returned to baseball in 1946 at age 23 but never made it above Class B. His career MLB line: .125/.125/.125, posted at 17.

Like Freiburger, 18-year-old Ted Sepkowski was still in high school when he made his MLB debut—also for the Indians—on September 9, 1942, going 1-for-5 and booting two balls at second base. Though hitless in his five additional at-bats that season, the kid whom International League president Frank J. Shaughnessy called "the greatest 18-year-old player I have ever seen" remained solidly in the Indians' plans.[1]

---

1. http://sabr.org/bioproj/person/b9e4b4f7

But in August of 1943, while playing for the Indians' Double-A affiliate, Sepkowski received a notice from Uncle Sam and spent the next three years in the US Coast Guard. He returned to pro ball in 1946 but never made good on the promise he had shown as a "$50,000 prospect," notching just 14 more big-league games.

It is disingenuous, however, to pin Sepkowski's failure solely on his military service. While in the Coast Guard, Sepkowski played ball for the Curtis Bay Station Cutters and matched his talents against those of several other big leaguers. Did he really miss out on prime development time? It's hard to say.

What is not hard to say is that after his two games with the Yankees in 1947—he served as a pinch-runner in each—he played eight more seasons in the minors and never made it back to the bigs. Perhaps his baseball career, had it not been for his military career, would have been different. Perhaps it would not have. All we can say with certainty is that Sepkowski, like Freiburger, was a high-school big leaguer.

So, too, were Carl Scheib and Joe Nuxhall. In 1942 and 1943, with the manpower drain at its most active, each skipped out of high school to take a big-league mound, Scheib as a 16-year-old for the Athletics and Nuxhall as a 15-year-old for the Reds. After beginning his career as a batting-practice pitcher for Connie Mack's Philadelphia team, Scheib got his first game action on September 6, 1943, when he pitched two-thirds of an inning against the Yankees and yielded one earned run in an 11-4 Athletics' loss. Nuxhall likewise pitched two-thirds of an inning in his 1944 debut, yielding five earned runs in an 18-0 Reds loss to the Cardinals. Scheib and Nuxhall both owed their starts—their early starts—to the war. In the end, perhaps they owed their careers to the fact that, unlike Sepkowski and Freiburger, they were never forced to serve in it. Permitted development time—Scheib in the majors, Nuxhall in the minors—each forged a long major-league career, Scheib's 11 years and Nuxhall's 15.

Harry Chiti wasn't so lucky. In 1953, three years after becoming the NL's YP, the 20-year-old catcher got the call from Uncle Sam. The Korean War had to have him. In his three partial seasons as a teen, Chiti had slashed .293/.325/.440 in 44 games and seemed a player on the upswing. Now he had to fight in a war 6,000 miles away. Upon his return he played seven partial seasons in the major leagues, becoming most famous, in 1962, for being the first player traded for himself.

Would he have wanted to trade places with Scheib or Nuxhall? Perhaps. Would he have wanted to trade places with Joe Kirrene? Probably not.

In 1950, Kirrene became the AL's YP when, at 18, he debuted at third base for the White Sox in their season finale against the Browns. Batting sixth in the lineup, he went 1-for-4 and performed flawlessly in the field. Before the 1951 season, however, Uncle Sam tapped him on the shoulder.

Joe Nuxhall

He would lose three seasons to the Korean War, a teenager rapidly becoming a man. Upon his return in 1954, he led the Class A Western League with a .343 batting average and in September received another trial run with the parent club, slashing .304/.448/.348 in 23 at-bats. And that was it: big-league career kaput.

In his final game, as in his first, Kirrene, now 22, went 1-for-4 and played flawlessly in the field. He would play two more years in the minor leagues before leaving the sport for good. Would his career have gone differently had Korea not called? Some questions remain unanswerable.

The Bonus Babies (1947-1957)

On the afternoon of September 28, 1947, in East Coast cities about 140 miles apart, a pair of 18-year-olds stepped to their respective mounds to face men decidedly more seasoned. In Washington DC, left-hander Chuck Stobbs began the fourth appearance of his professional career by replacing Red Sox starter Earl Johnson in the bottom of the third inning and facing the Senators' second-place hitter, 24-year-old Ed Lyons. To this point of his young career, Stobbs had pitched four big-league innings, all in September, and yielded three earned runs for an ERA of 6.75. The teenager was about to add to that mark. Following a Lyons single, Stobbs issued a walk to 25-year-old right fielder Gil Coan. Next, 29-year-old All-Star Mickey Vernon slapped a double to score Lyons and Coan and ignite a three-run inning.

Meanwhile, in Philadelphia, 18-year-old Curt Simmons stepped to the Shibe Park mound to make his first MLB start—indeed, his debut—against the New York Giants. The first batter he faced: 34-year-old All-Star slugger Johnny Mize, whom Giants manager (and former YP) Mel Ott had slotted into the leadoff position. A cross-firing lefty, Simmons coaxed a groundout—to another former YP, shortstop Granny Hamner—from Mize en route to a complete-game 3-1 win. The final batter he retired: Johnny Mize.

Curt Simmons

What Stobbs and Simmons had in common, aside from age and handedness, is that both had signed as Bonus Babies before making their debuts as YPs, Stobbs in the AL and Simmons in the NL. The Bonus Rule had been implemented earlier in the year to prevent the wealthiest teams from doing what they'd been doing for decades: signing the best players by offering the most money and then stashing those players in their farm systems, thus preventing them from playing for other teams. In short, the rule was designed to limit the dominance of rich teams—read: Yankees—and give poorer teams a chance.

As originally implemented, the Bonus Rule stipulated that when a franchise signed a player to a contract in excess of $4,000, the major-league team had to keep that player on the 40-man roster for two seasons or otherwise lose the rights to the player's contract. Before its abolition in 1965, the rule would go through several iterations, but in 1947, in contrast to later years, the rule allowed players a season in the minors before advancing to the parent club.

The time in the minors, however brief, appears to have benefitted both Stobbs and Simmons. After signing out of high school, Stobbs had gone to the Class B Lynn Red Sox and posted a 1.74 ERA and a 9-2 record in 174 innings. Simmons had gone to Class B Wilmington and notched a 2.69 ERA and a 13-5 record in 174 innings. In 1948 and 1949, the Bonus Rule required that their respective teams keep them on the active roster, and both suffered the consequences. Stobbs, watching mostly from the bullpen, pitched just seven innings in 1948, to a 6.43 ERA. Simmons, pitching in 31 games, couldn't recapture the magic of his debut, stumbling to a 4.87 ERA and a 7-13 record.

Still, each had experienced sufficient refinement in the minors, and learned sufficient lessons in the majors, to craft long and productive careers. Stobbs would pitch 15 years in the majors, posting 107 wins and 19 saves, and Simmons 20, notching 193 wins and a World Series ring.

Other Bonus Babies—and Bonus Baby YPs—weren't as fortunate. On September 30, 1956, in the season finale for the White Sox, 6-foot-3 lefty Jim Derrington took the mound in Kansas City to make his big-league debut in a start against the 51-win, last-place Athletics. What stood out was not his nickname, Blackie. It was his age, 16.

Jim Derrington

Signed from a California high school under the Bonus Rule, Derrington had been required to spend the entire season with the parent club, without benefit of time in the minors. And there he had sat, on the bench, watching like a spectator the first 153 games. Now here he was, barely old enough to drive and facing All-Star leadoff hitter Vic Power. Power would be the last man Derrington retired for some time.

Following Power's fly-ball out, the inexperienced Derrington went single, single, double, error, walk, balk, and lineout. Indeed, two of the three outs had come by way of a runner thrown out at third base and a hard-hit liner. All told, the teen would go six innings that day, yielding five earned runs on nine hits and six walks. Two of the hits were homers.

Still under the dictates of the Bonus Rule, Derrington had to remain on the White Sox roster in 1957 as well. And though he did pitch more often, he mostly stagnated again. The 17-year-old pitched just 37 innings, to a 4.86 ERA. Granted, a 4.86 ERA is pretty impressive for a kid who might otherwise be a high-school junior, but the fact remained that across his first two seasons as a pro, Derrington had pitched just 43 innings of game action, and, in essence, only because of the Bonus Rule.

At last allowed time in the minors, Derrington pitched for Chicago's Triple- and Single-A affiliates but staggered to a combined 7.06 ERA. Four years later, at 22, Derrington was out of baseball, a wasted talent.

Similar beginnings, divergent ends: the precept still held true, even for, or especially for, BBYPs—Bonus Baby Youngest Players. In 1953, both YPs—pitcher Joey Jay in the NL and pitcher Bob Miller in the AL—were also BBs, Jay having signed for $40,000 and Miller for $60,000. And each went directly from the high-school diamond to the big-league mound at age 17. Yet though both pitched sporadically if decently across their first two seasons, when by rule they had to remain on the parent club, only Jay managed a good career. He earned 99 victories in 13 seasons. Miller would notch just six in five.

Of course, Jay had found his footing only after spending two seasons in the minors, at 20 and 21, following three limited seasons in the bigs. Miller? His minor-league seasons came too late, you could argue. He spent his age-22 through -26 seasons in Double- and Triple-A, at last getting the work he might have gotten earlier had it not been for the Bonus Rule. His final pitch in the majors, resulting in a late-September groundout, lowered his season ERA to 10.17. He was pitching for the 40-win Mets.

⚾   ⚾   ⚾

Though other BBYP pitchers—Mike McCormick (134 MLB wins), Dick Ellsworth (115 MLB wins), Mike Lee (one MLB win)—came and went with varying degrees of success, the Bonus Babies weren't limited to the pitching position. Several Bonus Babies, and several BBYPs, were position players. And like their mound counterparts, they forged careers that ran the spectrum from tragic to Hall of Fame triumphant.

After signing with the Senators out of high school and, by rule, going directly to the big club, 18-year-old Harmon Killebrew made his MLB debut by pinch-running for Clyde Vollmer in the first inning of a June game. (Vollmer had pinch-hit for none other than former YP Chuck Stobbs.) Killebrew would play in just eight more games that year and in only 38 the following year, posting a combined .215/.298/.355 line.

Harmon Killebrew

But Killebrew, by spending parts of the next three seasons in Charlotte, Chattanooga, and Indianapolis, overcame his compromised start. In 142 games at Chattanooga in 1957, the big third baseman slammed 29 home runs. It made for good practice: He would hit 564 more in the bigs.

By contrast, Fred Van Dusen would go on to hit zero homers in the majors. Required by the Bonus Rule to remain on the Phillies' 40-man roster in 1955, the 17-year-old outfielder stepped to the plate in a pinch-hitting role during a late-September game against the Braves for his first big-league at-bat. It would also be his last. On an 0-2 count, starter Humberto Robinson hit Van Dusen in the head with a fastball. Careers are forged by talent, of course, but also by fortune good or bad.

⚾   ⚾   ⚾

At times, talent does conquer rotten luck—or what might seem rotten. In 1948, 18-year-old BBYP Johnny Antonelli spent most of his rookie season watching his Boston Braves teammates from the bench. The left-handed pitcher appeared in only four games that season, tossing just four innings.

After finally getting more work across the next two seasons, Antonelli had entered preparations for 1951 spring training when Uncle Sam got him. The war that had taken Joe Kirrene had now taken him.

Based at Fort Meyer, Antonelli joined the Army baseball team and used the time to refine his mound skills by getting the regular starts he had missed. Across his two years on the Army team, Antonelli fashioned a record of 42-2.

Instead of ruining his career, the war had helped it. Following his discharge in 1953, Antonelli went on to post a 12-year MLB career that included a pair of 20-win seasons. Baseball had been unpredictable again.

The Lambs (1961-1973)

On June 16, 1961—exactly 30 years and five days after the major-league debut of his father—Lew Krausse Jr. stepped to the mound before the largest crowd at Kansas City's Municipal Stadium that season and tossed his first major-league pitch. Precisely two hours and 14 minutes later, the 18-year-old Krausse coaxed a pop fly out from the Angels' Lee Thomas to complete a three-hit shutout in front of 25,869 suddenly optimistic A's fans.

Having failed to win a pennant in the three decades since the debut of Lew Krausse Sr., the A's had turned Lew Jr. into a $125,000 Bonus Baby by signing him out of a Pennsylvania high school in the hope that the right-hander could revive the beleaguered franchise. Not only had the A's failed to win a pennant since 1931, they'd fashioned just five winning seasons in that span.

In addition, per-game attendance at Municipal Stadium had fallen from 12,515 in 1959 to 9,999 in 1960. It marked the first time the A's had averaged in the four figures since moving from Philadelphia in 1955.

Ever the salesman, owner Charlie O. Finley needed a marketing hook for the disheartened fan base, and found it in a kid who had thrown 18 no-hitters in amateur play. Though the Bonus Rule no longer required players to remain on the active roster for two years, Finley and Lew Krausse Sr., who functioned as his son's agent, had placed in Lew Jr.'s contract a stipulation that he be permitted to pitch for the parent club in his rookie year. Suddenly, it looked like a winning idea.

Lew Krausse Jr.

Not only had Junior won the game in impressive fashion, he had helped to triple attendance. The $125,000 bonus payment appeared a wise investment. Later in the season, Charlie O. told the press that "[w]e packed the park the first four times [Krausse Jr.] pitched and probably got our money back."[2]

The statement might have been accurate, but it ignored a key point. True, Junior had attracted 26,304 fans to his second game, and true, he had attracted more than 10,000 fans to each of his next two home starts, but for his fifth home start, in the back end of a September doubleheader, he had attracted just 4,692.

Why? Perhaps because his star had begun to fall. Entering the game, Krausse had seen his ERA rise to 4.99. The culprit: control. In the excitement surrounding his first start, people had focused on the zero runs and three hits and ignored the five walks. Bad idea. In his second start, the teen had walked eight batters in seven innings. Indeed, in the seven games between his second home start and his fifth, he had walked 25 batters in 23 2/3 innings. As for that fifth start, he would issue seven more walks in just five innings while surrendering six earned runs.

---

2. http://sabr.org/bioproj/person/e423e439

The A's would go on to lose 100 games that season while averaging just 8,442 fans. And Krausse would spend the next three seasons in the minors before returning to the big leagues in 1964 to resume a mediocre 12-year career. Had the early start been worth the price? Would Krausse have been better served, along with his franchise, had he not debuted as the AL's youngest player? A counterfactual history might have seen him go on to a Hall of Fame career. It might not have. We can't really know.

What we can know is that David Clyde, the AL's YP in 1973, saved a franchise and ruined his career in the process. Touted as the next Sandy Koufax, Clyde had been the first overall pick of the 1973 first-year player draft—instituted, in 1965, to end the abuses of the Bonus Rule—when the Rangers took him out of a Houston high school, where the lefty had gone 18-0 with a 0.18 ERA in his senior season.

David Clyde

Just a year after their move from Washington DC, the financially strapped Rangers were already in danger of handing the franchise to the American League. Owner Bob Short, in desperate need of cash, hatched a plan: Clyde, 18, would make two home starts and then go to the minors for development.

On June 27, just 18 days after receiving his high-school diploma, Clyde took the mound at Arlington Stadium before a sellout crowd of 35,698. They had come to see the home-state kid, just 66 days removed from his 18th birthday, take on two-time AL batting champ Rod Carew and the Twins.

Anxious, the teenager walked Jerry Terrell and Carew to begin the game but then settled in to strike out the next three batters. The massive crowd erupted. The crowd erupted again when the teenager left the mound at the conclusion of a scoreless fifth inning. Finished for the night, Clyde had allowed just one hit and two runs in his madly promoted debut. For the last-place Rangers, he must have seemed a godsend.

Following Clyde's next start, when he yielded just one earned run in six frames while attracting another sellout crowd, Short changed the plan. Not only had the teen attracted consecutive sellouts for a team averaging just 6,000 fans, he had also pitched a 2.45 ERA in his two starts. Clyde, Short decided, would finish the season with the big club.

And he did, though not well. Following his September 29 loss to the Royals—his eighth loss against four wins—Clyde would end the season with an ugly 5.01 ERA. Lost in the fervor of that June 27 debut had been one incriminating inning: In addition to yielding a two-run homer in the second frame that night, Clyde had surrendered four walks. The only reason he'd escaped with two runs allowed was that catcher Ken Suarez had gunned down two runners on stolen-base attempts, including Carew to end the inning. The teenager would finish the season with a ghastly 5.2 BB/9.

That mark would increase to a 7.7 BB/9 two years later. Six years after that, Clyde would be gone from the sport. The Rangers would still be in Arlington. Unwittingly, Clyde had sacrificed his career to save his employer. Aside from the attendance of 22,114 for their season opener, the Rangers had drawn 19,000 fans or more only seven times that season—the first seven starts of David Clyde's rookie campaign.

On August 7, 1979, at Fenway Park, 31,204 fans watched 24-year-old Indians starter David Clyde hit Carl Yastrzemski with the final pitch of his MLB career.

⚾   ⚾   ⚾

As the Colt .45s entered the final series of their second season, the team conceived a radical idea. Having seen average attendance drop from 11,413 in 1962 to 8,883 in 1963, the Houston franchise would boost gate receipts in the series opener versus the expansion Mets by doing what had never been done in baseball: field a starting lineup composed entirely of rookies.

- At second base: Joe Morgan
- In center field: Jim Wynn
- At first base: Rusty Staub

- On the mound: Larry Yellen

Before the game, however, the team had to reshuffle the pitching slate. Due to his observance of a religious holiday, Yellen would be unavailable for the September 27 opener. In his stead, the team inserted Jay Dahl. A 17-year-old southpaw, Dahl had pitched to a 5-1 record and a 1.33 ERA with the team's Single- and Double-A affiliates.

Early on, his stuff appeared to translate to the big-league level. He retired the side in the first inning. In the second, however, the 50-win Mets began to figure him out, scoring three runs on three singles, a wild pitch, and an error. Then in the third, they exploded for five runs and drove Dahl from the mound. All told, the YP had yielded seven runs—five earned—in 2 2/3 frames.

But had the plan worked? Well, yes—to a degree. The previous night, for a game against Pittsburgh, the Colt .45s had drawn 2,782 to Colt Stadium. The following night, for the second game against the Mets, they would draw 2,566. But on this night—the night of Dahl's debut—they drew 5,802.

The game would also mark Dahl's major-league denouement. Two years later, just hours after pitching his Class-A Salisbury Astros into first place with a 7-3 victory over the Gastonia Pirates, Dahl was killed in a car accident.

The Roaring 20s (1981-2017)

From 1942 through 1980, only two YPs—pitcher Fred Holdsworth in 1972 and pitcher Rick Sutcliffe in 1976—had reached their 20th birthdays at the time of their big-league debuts. The other 66 YPs in that span—eight had *repeated* as YPs—were still teenagers when they debuted.

Some were products of the war years, others of the Bonus Rule. Some, like Mickey Mantle, Bert Blyleven, Robin "The Kid" Yount, and Tim Raines, were exceptionally gifted and proved it by fashioning Hall of Fame careers. Others were nearly as gifted, even equally gifted, but due to injury or the vagaries of baseball managed great careers that fell short of Cooperstown's standards. Put Gary Nolan, Cesar Cedeño, Alan Trammell, and Jack Clark in that category.

Several, like Tim McCarver, Joe Coleman, and Darrell Porter, managed long and productive careers. Each accrued at least 15 years' service time and a WARP of 23.5 or greater. Others, like Art Houtteman, Ed Kirkpatrick, Ed Kranepool, Dave Duncan, Willie Montanez, Ken Brett, Larry Christenson, and Alfredo Griffin, became longtime veterans whose back-of-the-baseball-card numbers might not have vindicated their early debuts but who nonetheless had recognizable front-of-the-card photos.

Others, like Jim Waugh and Jimmy McMath, flamed out after a year or two.

Still others, like 16-year-old Alex George, were talented prospects who served as warm bodies near season's end and never made it back to the majors. George, who had just enrolled at the University of Kansas on a basketball

Alan Trammell

scholarship, was sitting in his fraternity house on the night of September 15, 1955, when he received a call from his hometown Athletics.

They needed a shortstop, and needed him now. The following morning at Kansas City's Municipal Stadium, George signed a $4,000 contract, spread across two years to skirt the provisions of the Bonus Rule, and donned an Athletics jersey (no. 2) that evening. One night hence, in an eighth-inning pinch-hitting appearance, George received the first of his 10 career big-league at-bats. He whiffed.

All told, the YPs from 1942 through 1980 included a lot of teenagers (the following counts both years of the eight repeated YPs):

Age	No.
15	1
16	4
17	17
18	32
19	22

But the trend toward teenagers began to change, and change dramatically, in 1981, a year after Fernando Valenzuela zoomed to stardom in LA and Ricky Seilheimer plummeted to obscurity in Chicago. Both Valenzuela and Seilheimer were 19. By contrast, the year 1981 began a four-decade stretch when 40 YPs were aged 20 or 21. In that same time frame, only 28 teenagers debuted, none younger than 18. In fact, only one 18-year-old—Alex Rodriguez—has debuted in that 37-year span. The last 17-year-old to debut: Larry Dierker, in 1964. The last 16-year-old: Jim Derrington in 1956, one year after George debuted.

Adrian Beltre

Fernando Valenzuela

By contrast, in the 109 years of MLB prior to 1981, only ten 20-year-olds—and zero 21-year-olds—had served as YPs. In comparison, nine of the past ten YPs have been 20 years old. When Chris Sale debuted as the AL YP in 2010, he was 21, as was Lastings Milledge in 2006.

Simply put, as development costs have increased and baseball acumen has advanced, franchise executives of the past four decades have been a little more cautious about the ages at which they promote prospects to the majors. And for the most part, the prospects have returned the favor with respectable if not tremendous careers. Following his debut at age 20 in 1981, Cardinals outfielder David Green (once part of a trade for former YP Jack Clark) flamed out after six partial seasons due to chronic alcohol problems, but among the remaining 34 YPs from 1981 through 2000, 22 fashioned major-league careers of a decade or longer. Four enjoyed careers of two decades or longer. All told, the average major-league career of those 34 players is 11.7 years ... and counting, because the 1998 NL YP, Adrian Beltre, isn't finished.

By contrast, the 33 YPs in a separate 20-year stretch—from 1941 through 1960—averaged an MLB career of 9.1 years. Twelve had careers that lasted three years or fewer, whereas from 1981 through 2000, only two YPs—Ed Correa and Miguel Garcia—had MLB careers of three years or fewer.

Of the 28 YPs from 2001 through 2016, only six failed to see major-league action in 2017. Among the other 22 are several superstars: CC Sabathia, Francisco Rodriguez, Felix Hernandez, Clayton Kershaw, Madison Bumgarner, Chris Sale, Mike Trout, and Bryce Harper; a few other All-Stars in Matt Cain, Justin Upton, Starlin Castro, Julio Teheran, and Roberto Osuna; plus a Cy Young winner in Rick Porcello. We'll wait and see about Jurickson Profar, Rougned Odor, Raul Mondesi, Rafael Devers, and others.

In short, YPs are starting later and enjoying longer and better careers. The obvious reason is the evolution of scouting and development, coupled with the abolition of the Bonus Rule and the increased unwillingness among executives to promote a prospect to the majors only to let him watch from the bench. If he's up, he's playing. If not, he's down in the boondocks, developing.

Further evidence that recent YPs are better prepared for big league action is this: Of the 25 most recent YPs, just four—Bumgarner, Profar, Mondesi, and Victor Robles—have debuted after the September 1 roster expansion. (And Mondesi, of course, debuted in the 2015 World Series.) In

Mike Trout

Americans served as YPs, while from 1871 through 1939, only one Latin American—Cuban Merito Acosta, in 1923—served as the YP.

Baseball, indeed, is changing, just as it has always changed. Which brings us to another reason for the shift toward older and better YPs: Everybody's watching. When Joe Nuxhall debuted, in 1944, 3,510 spectators saw it happen. When Harmon Killebrew debuted, in 1954, 7,234 fans watched. Indeed, major-league attendance figures from past decades simply don't stand up to the sepia-toned nostalgia their custodians give us. When the Giants and Dodgers left New York following the 1957 season, they did so because fewer than 15,000 people, on average, had come to see them play. By contrast, MLB attendance in 2017 averaged 30,023.

What's more, in 1963, people were watching *Gunsmoke* on TV. They sure weren't watching the Colt .45s. These days, roughly 2.5 million people watch about three hours of MLB each night of the regular season. Over the course of said season, viewers watch roughly one billion hours of baseball.

Add those eyeballs to the ones focused on baseball websites, team blogs, MLB Network, ESPN, and Twitter, and you've got a lot of people paying attention. No general manager is going to risk his vocational neck to bring up an untested teenager for a gimmicky start. Too many dollars are at stake—dollars that far exceed what one night's gate receipts can produce. No team is going to put a 16-year-old frat boy, however gifted, at shortstop or even pinch-hitter. And no manager is going to concede to a cigar boy's dreams. You, and millions of others, will see a Roberto Osuna, not an Eddie Kolb. Which raises another question: Will we ever see another 18-year-old YP? It's possible, sure, but not bloody likely.

Indeed, the greatest player of the 21st century debuted 30 days shy of his 20th birthday. That's right: even the 2011 AL YP had to spend his age-17 and -18 seasons, and part of his age-19 season, down in the boondocks where he belonged. He certainly doesn't belong there now. Mike Trout, notwithstanding the nickname "Kiiiiid," is a grown man.

brief, recent YPs are being promoted when they can help the team and not just so managers and executives can evaluate them.

The shift toward older and more polished YPs has also coincided with an increased focus on the scouting and development of Latin American players. In fact, of the past ten YPs, nine are Latin American. Of the past 20, 12 have hailed from Latin American backgrounds. And of the past 65 YPs, 38 were born in Latin American countries. Contrast this to the fact that from 1940 through 1979, only four Latin

What Will Baseball Look Like in 2038?

by Russell A. Carleton

The writing prompt itself is a trap. Writing about what baseball will look like in 20 years is an invitation for someone to pick up this book in the future, read it, and laugh about how wrong I was about everything. That's not even the part where they hide the trap. The trap waiting for anyone who wants to take on such a project is that it's easy to fall into analyzing a few trend lines that have presented themselves in the past few years and assuming that they will continue. The rest is projecting that baseball will become a dark and dystopian world as a result.

We now return you to 2014, in a bleak time when the average team scored 4.07 runs per game, the lowest scoring rate since 1976. Scoring had been on the decline for the past eight seasons. The home-run rate had dipped below one per team per game, and the league OBP was .314, lowest since 1972. Offense was dead. Strikeouts were on the increase. But the American League Champion Kansas City Royals seemed to have it all figured out. In a world where everyone was striking out because they kept swinging and missing, the Royals had built a high-contact offense (and a shutdown bullpen). We all reasoned that if there was a way out of this mess, it was going to be the Royals' approach of slapping at the ball and putting it in play. The Royal counterrevolution was on!

After only a couple of years, that sort of thinking about "the future of baseball" looks silly. The Royals did make it back to the World Series in 2015, but none of the rest of what we thought might happen actually did. The game did not descend into a bog of constant 2-1 games. By 2017, MLB teams were scoring 4.65 runs per game and had the *highest* home-run rate in history. Contact wasn't the new trend; strikeouts continued to surge. And suddenly, the ball was flying over the fence.

By this point, most readers will be familiar with the idea that the ball is (don't say "juiced," don't say "juiced," don't say "juiced") clearly performing differently than it used to. MLB has repeatedly denied that they've conspired to tamper with the ball, and they wouldn't necessarily have to. Every baseball is going to be a little different, but MLB regularly tests the balls to make sure they are within an acceptable standard, and the league found no evidence that any nonconforming balls were being used. But they really wouldn't need a conspiracy for the ball to get ... juicy. For one, upon further inspection, the balls may have fit into MLB's specifications, but the latitude allowed by those specifications was so wide as to allow balls that could be vastly different from one another. A ball that is slightly smaller or has slightly lower seams—even if the difference isn't visible to the naked eye—hit with the same force and at the same angle against the same speed can travel several feet further. Over a few thousand fly balls, that extra few feet is the difference between a fly out to the warning track and the scoreboard shooting off some fireworks.

During the 2017 season, researcher Rob Arthur found that by using PITCHf/x data back to 2008, he could calculate how much air resistance the ball had by looking at how it performed while it was being thrown toward home plate.[1] What he found was that starting around 2015, although the ball wasn't substantially different than it had been in the past, there was now greater consistency from ball to ball. In earlier years, the air resistance of the ball was *more variable*, meaning that in a crate of 50 game balls, it used to be there were a few that had more drag on them and some that had less. During the home-run spike, that gap narrowed, with the balls becoming *more uniform* ... but bunching together on the juicy side of the spectrum. The juiced balls were always in the box, but there used to be a few more balls that were more loathe to leave the field.

MLB might do something about the ball, although they might not be in a hurry to do it. People like home runs, and even if MLB didn't juice the ball themselves, they probably like the results. However, I bring up the tale of the ball not to prognosticate on whether MLB will decide to deflate the home-run bubble or to let it go, but rather to provide a lesson in how baseball can change in ways that no one expects. A seismic shift in the way the game is played took place in the space of three years, and the cause of it wasn't something that a player or a manager or a general manager did, or even

---

1. https://fivethirtyeight.com/features/in-mlbs-new-home-run-era-its-the-baseballs-that-are-juicing/

some greater movement among players, managers, and general managers. It may very well have happened because some middle manager at Rawlings decided to install some new piece of equipment or changed some component of the process in making the balls, all in the name of making them more uniform. Among all the things that we normally would assume would be "game changers," who would ever suspect the middle manager?

If the sabermetric enterprise has succeeded, I'd argue that it's not so much in illuminating things that no one knew about as in putting things into their proper order of magnitude. Even the field's greatest moments, the catcher framing revolution, for example, were things that had been talked about for years. "He's a good receiver of pitches" has been part of the scouting lexicon for ages. Everyone knew that defense was important, but we didn't realize how much until we had the data to put a number on it. Clutch hitting might actually be "a thing," but the numbers tell us that even if it is, the effect size isn't all that impressive. Yes, it's great to have a hitter who is particularly adept at stealing bases, if the alternative is a guy who has lead feet. It's also better to have a hitter who is good at getting on base than one who makes a bunch of outs. But those talents are not equally valuable. It turns out that while both provide value, getting on base is much more important. As a result, we see more leadoff hitters who aren't speed demons, but who don't need a GPS to get to first base.

There are changes happening all the time in baseball, and some of the time, we can even see them coming. What we're really bad at is guessing how big that change is going to be. Three years ago, how could we have predicted the differences in the ball? Even if we could have, would we have guessed how much it would end up affecting the game?

⚾   ⚾   ⚾

It's worth looking back over how the game has changed in the *last 20(ish)* years before we start looking ahead. Actually, to get the full picture, I want to go back 25 years to 1992, when something happened that changed the game, probably more than any other force in the last 20 years, including (allegedly) steroids. Baseball went global.

It's not fair to say that baseball wasn't already a global game in the early 1990s. Despite an (inexcusable) past in which owners took racism pills for the first half of the 20th century, MLB had become a much more welcoming and open place. Part of that was pragmatism. If you find a kid who can throw 96 with a crackerjack curveball, it doesn't matter where he's from. Players from countries such as the Dominican Republic and Venezuela were already playing key roles in MLB in 1992, but it was around then that the trend line really shifted upward. Here are the percentage of players in MLB each year who were born outside the United States, starting from 1992.

Year	Percentage of Players Born Outside USA
1992	15.0%
1997	22.0%
2002	25.9%
2007	27.2%
2012	27.1%
2017	28.9%

Prior to 1992, the line was fairly flat with the number of players from outside the USA around 12 percent (about three players on a 25-man roster). In 2017, the average MLB 25-man roster contained seven players who were born on distant shores. Some of the growth was probably due to changes in technology. I'm old enough to remember—as late as those mid-1990s—when the question that people asked was "Do you have an email address?" Now, someone on a back field somewhere in South America can take video of an international prospect with his phone and upload it to a team server in minutes. If there is a kid who has a chance at a major-league career, it has become easier to get him into "the system." Another factor was that as prices for free agents rose, teams realized it might be cheaper to bring young talent into the system and so they naturally went to places where there was already a vibrant baseball culture and young kids who grew up playing the game. As the infrastructure surrounding the game developed further (and as teams began writing bigger checks), more talent made its way into the MLB pipeline.

It's hard to know whether those four "extra" players born in other countries are the superstars or the bit players. For example, would Miguel Cabrera have been discovered in Venezuela if he had been born 20 years earlier? The answer in his case is probably yes. A kid who has the clear potential to be a star will probably get some eyeballs thrust upon him no matter what. But what about the kid who no one thought highly of as a 16-year-old but who turned out to be a really nice player? What about the kid who might have gone into another sport 20 years earlier, but now has plenty of incentive to go into baseball?

Consider for a moment what we would be left with if MLB's international push had never happened. There'd likely still be baseball, but there would be fewer players born outside the United States in the game. Not all teams would be equally impacted, but on average, four of their current players on their 25-man roster would never have made it to MLB. We can assume that a few of the "missing" players would be stars and a few would be scrubs, but someone would take their place. Teams would make do likely with American-born guys who are currently in AAA and the precise definition of replacement-level talent. If we assume that, on average, the players who would go missing are currently worth about 1 WARP each to their teams (usually the value of a second-division starter), then baseball's international push over the last 25 years has raised the quality of play, across the board, by four wins per team.

The good news for MLB is that there are plenty of other countries out there and MLB is already in a few of them. In 2011, Alex Liddi debuted for the Seattle Mariners, becoming the first player from MLB's European Academy to make it all the way to "The Show." In 2017, Pittsburgh Pirates second baseman Gift Ngope became the first player born on the continent of Africa to play in the majors. The development of these new talent markets is not a process that's going to happen overnight. Indeed, it took a quarter century for the ones in the Caribbean, Central America, and South America to mature as much as they have. But in 20 years, the thing that might be different about MLB is that you'll hear more languages being spoken in the clubhouse.

⚾   ⚾   ⚾

Since we're trafficking in 20-year increments, it's worth pointing out how special the previous 20 years of baseball history have been. There hasn't been a labor stoppage, either a strike or a lockout since that one in 1994-1995. That one was at the time (and remains) the longest strike in MLB history, by far. Prior to 1994, there had been work stoppages in 1972, 1973, 1976, 1980, 1981, 1985, and 1990. Most of them were in spring training and didn't end up affecting the regular season, but they happened. Baseball has an unfortunate history of solving its labor problems by not doing any labor, and most of the time, that "labor problem" centered around a rather sticky issue. How is it that teams in "small markets" can compete with—can we just skip the code word and say "the Yankees"—and not have it affect the salary structure for players in MLB?

Over the last 20 years, though, it's not like the market size problem has gone away; New York City is still much bigger than Cincinnati, and the "solutions" MLB has cycled through—especially to address the issue of free agents leaving small market teams for bigger paydays (a competitive balance draft, Type A/B free agent compensation, and the qualifying offer system)—haven't really worked either. And yet, baseball has managed to avoid a work stoppage. Can it continue?

Some of the credit for the *pax baseballis* goes to good old-fashioned economics. Some of that labor strife went back to the age-old question of how owners and players were going to split the large pile of money in the middle of the room. Over the past 20 years, MLB has seen its revenues grow, with more money coming in through national broadcasting contracts and the development of MLB Advanced Media (MLBAM), which was so successful in building a streaming platform for its games that when the NHL wanted to do something similar for its games, they called MLB. Then HBO came along and did the same.

When the pile of money in the middle of the room is particularly large, it makes things easier. That pile of money will probably draw the interest of other investors, who are hoping to get a piece of the action through an expansion franchise. Expansion, whatever else it does to the game, is incredibly lucrative to the existing owners. The more they can sell another seat at the table for, the more they all split the proceeds. In 20 years, it's not unreasonable to think there might be two new teams in the game for that reason. There are several cities that support a "major" league franchise in another sport, but have no MLB team, to go with cities like Montreal who lost Les Expos after 2004 and Mexico City, whose addition to the league might bring another entire country into the MLB fanbase.

However, there's still the question of what is politely called "competitive balance." There's a widely held cultural belief in the United States that success in something should be the result of intelligence mixed with hard work despite a mountain of evidence that this is not even remotely true, whether in baseball or the rest of life. For MLB, it's not just a cultural issue, but a marketing one.

In English soccer, where the free market reigns in terms of player acquisitions (player rights are directly bought and sold between teams), only five teams have won the Premiership in the last 20 years (Arsenal, Chelsea, Manchester City, Manchester United, and improbably, Leicester City.) More than that, in the past 20 years, the top three spots in the league (60 spots total) have been held by Arsenal, Chelsea, Manchester City, Manchester United, and Liverpool a total of 55 times. In Dutch soccer, the Eredivise has been won by one of four teams (Ajax, AZ, Feyenoord, and PSV Eindhoven) every year back into the 1960s. That sort of hegemony might fly over in Europe, but in the United States, it probably wouldn't. Fans know that their team won't compete every year, but every few years, it's nice to think that the team has some chance. Imagine if you grew up cheering for a team like Everton, who always find themselves in the middle of the pack. What if the only surprise at the beginning of the year was whether the team would finish in 8th place or 12th in a 20-team league?

On the flip side, the NFL, NBA, and NHL have embraced the idea of a salary cap. In those leagues, teams can't outspend each other, and yet, strangely, MLB has had more of its teams win championships (13) in the last 20 years than the NBA (9) or the NHL (11) and as many as the NFL (13). Part of that magic is that MLB is not as much of a free market as one might wish to believe. Compared to the days of the reserve clause—before free agency—it is, but baseball isn't nearly the haven of capitalism that it might appear.

For readers not familiar with the reserve clause, players used to sign contracts of a specific length (for example, a two-year contract), but at the end of those two years, the player was not a free agent. His original team would have to give its blessing for him to hop to a different team. The "good old days" in which players played their whole career with one team were less about loyalty and more about the fact that they had no other options. It was also a really good way to keep salaries down. A player could walk away from the game, if he believed that he wasn't being paid enough, but he was not free to offer his services to the other teams in the game. With only one bidder, players were often told how much they would receive. Once a market system opened up, salaries went up as well, and some teams simply had deeper pockets than others and could afford more expensive players. Baseball has struggled with that tension ever since.

It's not correct to say that the reserve clause has been abandoned. Baseball still uses a drafting system for players born in the United States, Canada, and Puerto Rico, and high school and college baseball players are selected by a team that then has exclusive negotiating rights. Players in their first three years generally make the league minimum salary and have no recourse to challenge that salary. In their fourth through sixth years in the league, salaries are largely governed by an arbitration system that is widely known to underpay players what they might otherwise get on the open market. Baseball players don't reach free agency eligibility until their seventh year in MLB.

This weird hybrid system produces a double-edged set of opportunities for sense to better cents. A team that can put together a suite of good, young players can benefit from the exclusive control and below-market salaries it can pay. The fact that MLB players reach free agency around the time they turn 30 (and statistically, are past what are, on average, their prime years) encourages teams to take big-dollar, long-term risks on players who are likely on the decline. Add that to the inherent randomness in the game, and perhaps MLB has found the magical middle of the road in competitive balance.

Still, with free agency, they haven't quite gotten it right. After the 2015 season, the Kansas City Royals, fresh off of a World Series championship, tendered a qualifying offer to their homegrown star, Alex Gordon. Gordon had been drafted and developed by the Royals, and played his entire career in Kansas City, and it would have been a shame to see him wander away. But that same qualifying offer system was used by the Dodgers to effectively keep Howie Kendrick around, even though Kendrick had been drafted and developed by the Angels, and all the Dodgers really did with him was have him be a part-time quasi-utility player, and then dump him in the offseason in a trade. It's not like Kendrick was part of Dodger lore. The Dodgers seemed to do it just because they could.

Still, baseball seems to have enough competitive balance to keep things interesting, despite the fact that its system for dealing with the inequalities of life is a mishmosh of policy mixed with a healthy dose of randomness. In 20 years, it's likely that there will still be a conversation about the outsized influence of big money in the game and perhaps a new system for "dealing with it" that doesn't really work. We'll swear we haven't solved "competitive balance" and yet, we will likely still have something that is very close to it.

Ah, but we haven't talked about what the game will look like on the field in 20 years. We, of course, have no way of knowing who the stars will be then. The 27-year-old MVP of tomorrow is currently in first grade. The 22-year-old rookie phenom is just learning to run and throw a ball. But we can see where the game is evolving and perhaps what those players are likely to do once they reach "The Show."

First, let's look backward at the buildup of a trend that plenty of people have complained about, but that's honestly been building for a number of years. Below are the average number of the three (and a half) "true" outcomes—home runs, walks, and strikeouts (and their cousin, hit by pitches)—recorded by each team in a game.

Year	PA	HR	BB	SO	HBP	TTO Pct
2017	38.13	1.26	3.26	8.25	0.36	34.43%
2007	38.80	1.02	3.31	6.62	0.36	29.15%
1997	38.73	1.02	3.46	6.61	0.32	29.46%
1987	38.46	1.06	3.42	5.96	0.20	27.67%
1977	38.41	0.87	3.27	5.16	0.19	24.71%
1967	37.61	0.71	2.98	5.99	0.23	26.35%
1957	38.62	0.89	3.31	4.84	0.21	23.95%
1947	38.37	0.63	3.71	3.68	0.13	21.24%
1937	38.81	0.58	3.41	3.63	0.13	19.97%
1927	38.67	0.37	3.01	2.79	0.19	16.45%
1917	37.18	0.13	2.77	3.48	0.23	17.78%

The game of baseball has been trending toward a higher strikeout, higher home-run environment since its earliest days, with some lesser growth in walks and HBP. The increase in strikeouts means that the defensive players who aren't the pitcher have become less important. You can't defend walks or strikeouts or home runs, and the frequency of those outcomes has nearly doubled over the past 100 years. Players are swinging and missing more, but connecting for more home runs. That's not all that surprising when you start looking at another set of numbers. These are the average body mass index (BMI) figures. BMI, an indicator of how "big" someone is adjusting for height, is a person's weight in kilograms divided by the square of their height in meters.

Year	BMI
1917	24.2
1927	24.4
1937	24.7
1947	24.8
1957	24.7
1967	24.6
1977	24.5
1987	24.5
1997	25.1
2007	26.9
2017	27.2

Players have gotten much bigger. While bigger players means more muscle to hit the ball over the wall, it also means bigger pitchers, and the data confirm that in the last 15 years (since these records have been kept) the average fastball has gotten 3 mph faster. But what's more important is that the mound is still the same distance from the plate that it's always been.

It takes a ball traveling at 90 mph over 55 feet (yes, the mound is 60 feet, 6 inches away, but the 6-foot-tall pitcher steps forward and extends his arm toward the plate before letting the pitch go) a mere 417 milliseconds to reach its destination. The human brain, even on its best days, needs 200 milliseconds to react to *anything*, leaving the batter a little more than two-tenths of a second to first decide whether or not to swing and then actually start his swing. An increase of 3 mph in velocity takes away 13 of those milliseconds, or roughly 6 percent of what reaction time he used to have.

This means that on a few more pitches, our brave hitter has to guess a little bit. There's less incentive to wait on the ball when it's coming in that fast. Even though you might pick up on more of the movement and have a better idea of where in the strike zone it's going, because it's coming in so fast, even if you hit the ball, you're more likely to be behind on the swing. Sometimes, you have to sit on one specific pitch and if you get it, wail on it. If you're doing that, you might as well swing real hard in case you hit it, because if you're not going to make contact very often, why think "single" if you do? In fact, it's almost better if you swing and miss, because you get two more swings, and frankly, a strikeout isn't all that different from a grounder to second.

Faster fastballs haven't sapped *all* of the reaction time from our hitters, but with pitchers throwing faster, the incentives to use the high-risk "swing real hard" strategy become more lucrative. So do the incentives to develop big hitters who can hit those home runs. It's not like anyone's putting the ball into play anymore, so finding him a spot on defense becomes less of an issue. The system starts to feed on itself.

There's probably a natural maximum for how far the strikeouts-and-dingers game can go. Eventually, a new type of player with lightning-quick reaction time but not much power might feast on slapping singles through the forest of big guys who are mostly there to hit home runs, but it's not like we're going to run low on big guys anytime in the next 20 years.

⚾ ⚾ ⚾

And yes, they're finally going to put the DH in the National League, but not for the reason that you might think. In 1973, the DH was introduced in the American League as a way of stimulating scoring. (It worked!) Traditionalists (and National League fans) have long decried the move, although—as my father often points out—the NL teams still use the DH when they play an interleague game at an AL park. But the DH rule also does something else. It protects the pitcher from having to hit, not in the sense that he's probably a .120 hitter at best, but in the sense that he doesn't have to face 95-mph fastballs coming at *him*.

As the game begins to be overtaken more and more by outcomes that don't involve the fielders, the pitcher's role in the game becomes ever-so-much-more important. This means teams will feel a greater need to protect their pitchers. Thankfully there's already a mechanism for that which someone dreamed up in the early 1970s, and we already know that it works and did not make the game explode. Just some sportswriters. ▩

Part 2: Best Of BP 2017

Introducing Pitch Tunnels

by Jeff Long, Jonathan Judge, and Harry Pavlidis

Seeking to better understand the mysteries of pitching, Jeff Long, Jonathan Judge, and Harry Pavlidis have created a framework for evaluating hurlers that takes into account pitch sequencing, movement and velocity, command and control, and various other factors. – Geoff Y.

One day I sat a dozen feet behind Maddux's catcher as three Braves pitchers, all in a row, did their throwing sessions side-by-side. Lefty Steve Avery made his catcher's glove explode with noise from his 95-mph fastball. His curve looked like it broke a foot-and-a-half. He was terrifying. Yet I could barely tell the difference between Greg's pitches. Was that a slider, a changeup, a two-seam or four-seam fastball? Maddux certainly looked better than most college pitchers, but not much. Nothing was scary.

Afterward, I asked him how it went, how he felt, everything except "Is your arm okay?" He picked up the tone. With a cocked grin, like a Mad Dog whose table scrap doesn't taste quite right, he said, "That's all I got."

Then he explained that I couldn't tell his pitches apart because his goal was late quick break, not big impressive break. The bigger the break, the sooner the ball must start to swerve and the more milliseconds the hitter has to react; the later the break, the less reaction time. Deny the batter as much information—speed or type of last-instant deviation—until it is almost too late.

—Thomas Boswell[1]

Greg Maddux may have known about the concept of pitch tunnels. He may not have. Regardless, he knew how to put the concept into practice, and really that's the important part. Maddux:

[My] main goal was to make all of my pitches look like a column of milk coming toward home plate. Every pitch should look as close to every other as possible, all part of that 'column of milk'.

What we've set out to do is start quantifying pitch tunnels. To do that we've looked at how pitch tunnels intersect with things like pitch sequencing, movement and velocity, command and control, and many other things. This new pitch tunnels data should be another valuable tool in our toolbox when we set out to analyze pitcher performance.

How We're Doing It

You're probably wondering how exactly we've gone about measuring something like pitch tunnels. The beauty of PITCHf/x (and Trackman) data is that it allows for a full reconstruction of the entire likely flight of the pitch. Using the Pitch Info database, we can calculate the probable position of each pitch at any point on its flight from the release point to home plate.

The first step in quantifying tunnels is to forget everything we think we know about pitchers. The first step is to think like a hitter.

There are three types of hitters with regard to pitch recognition:

- Those who attempt to predict the next offering, using scouting reports and their gut and the sequence of pitches they've seen in the current plate appearance.
- Those who simply read and react, going into each pitch with a clear mind looking for any and all cues that allow them to properly identify the pitch and likely location.
- Those who do a little bit of both—maybe eliminating certain pitches or looking for a particular pitch based on the available intel before reacting to the next offering.

Regardless of the approach taken by the hitter, there's one thing they all have in common: They're limited by their human brains.

---

1. Thomas Boswell, "Greg Maddux Used Methodical Approach to Get to Cooperstown," *Washington Post*, January 7, 2014.

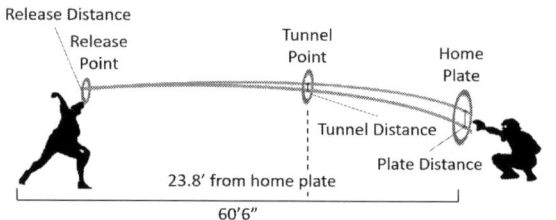

It takes about 400 milliseconds for a 90-mph fastball to reach home plate. One hundred seventy-five milliseconds before contact, the batter must have decided whether or not to swing and where it is he wants to swing.[2] One hundred seventy-five milliseconds after the pitcher releases the ball, the hitter must start deciding whether swinging is in the cards. It all comes down to those 50 milliseconds in the middle that remain—that's the decision point.

The point of no return, except for check swings, ends up being roughly 24 feet from home plate.[3] That's not a hard and fast number, as distance is actually variable depending on pitch speed, but 23.8 feet is the decision-making point based on 175 milliseconds and a league-average fastball. It's a complicated concept, but an excellent video from Business Insider helps explain it exceptionally well.[4]

First we have to define the point during the pitch trajectory that is most important. The point we've identified—the one 23.8 feet from home plate where the batter must decide whether or not to swing and where he wants to swing—we call that the Tunnel Point. It's here that we capture the differential between pitches, because it's here that a pitcher's mastery of tunneling makes all the difference. We're then going to pair that data with readily available information from the pitcher's Release Point and where pitches end up at the plate.

To capture the differential between pitches at each point we recreate the trajectory of each and every pitch in three dimensions. Once these trajectories are established, we can measure the difference between any two pitches at any point along their flight path. We of course focus only on the three key points we detailed above.

From there we calculate and add key pieces of information including total flight time, movement between release and the Tunnel Point, movement between the Tunnel Point and home plate, and some ratios of the average movement at various points along the flight path.

The next piece that builds onto what we've established above is pitch sequencing. Each pitch is viewed in the context of the one thrown before it, so we've worked to identify all pitch pairs—for example fastball-fastball or sinker-curveball or slider-changeup—for each pitcher. Data from the full season has been aggregated for each pitch-type pairing, allowing us to create rolled-up averages for each pitcher, as well as data for each individual pitch-type pairing by pitcher.[5]

Here are some terms you'll need to know as we work through this data:

Background

This project started as an effort to tie pitch break areas (i.e., the amount of space in square inches that a pitch thrown at a given point could move based on a pitcher's repertoire) together with pitch usage rates. Shortly after we set off down this path Jon Roegele released his own research on a similar topic. Roegele's work confirmed our suspicions and spurred our search for ways to measure and calculate the relevant differentials between subsequent pitches.

Indeed, Roegele's work was a critical precursor that fundamentally changed the way we approached our own research. The conclusion he reached became the target we aimed for over the subsequent months (bolded emphasis our own):

> **Through this study I've convinced myself that there is value for pitchers in being able to throw back-to-back pitches of different types that have almost identical trajectories during the initial stage of flight up to the point where the batter must make a decision of whether to commit to a swing.** In both seasons studied, consecutive pitches that were close to overlapping at the swing commit point but that crossed the plate in relatively different spots generated consistently higher rates of swings and misses. In addition, the closer consecutive pitches in a plate appearance are to overlapping at the swing commit point of the trajectory, the closer they can be as they arrive to home plate and still generate these additional swings and misses.
>
> —Jon Roegele[6]

Our goal quickly became clear. While Roegele had shown that there was some performance merit to the concept, we had yet to measure the space between sequential pitches. We hoped to do just that; measuring the differential between pitches at the hitter's decision-making point (**tunnels**) and on back-to-back pitches (**sequencing**), while incorporating

---

2. Based on a 90-mph pitch.

3. 23.8 feet or 23 feet, 9.6 inches to be exact.

4. https://www.youtube.com/watch?v=RENLMum5wz4

5. Bartolo Colon, for example, threw 21 pitch type pairings in 2015. They were: CH>CH, CH>FA, CH>SI, CH>SL, FA>CH, FA>FA, FA>FC, FA>SI, FA>SL, FC>CA, FC>FC, FC>SI, SI>CH, SI>FA, SI>FC, SI>SI, SI>SL, SL>CH, SL>FA, SL>SI, SL>SL.

6. Jon Roegele, "The Effects of Pitch Sequencing," The Hardball Times, November 24, 2014.

additional details like break/location (**tunnels, again**) and velocity (**speed changes**). Today we're finally able to roll out our findings.

The Data

To do this, we're introducing a few new statistics that might need a bit of explaining. There are two ways to look at this data, and each has its own pros and cons. We calculate the differential between every pair of pitches thrown, and then aggregate them into distinct pitch sequences. This means we have average differentials between each sequence every pitcher uses (e.g., there are 21 (!) entries for Bartolo Colon[7]).

We've also aggregated that same data by pitcher, so you can see how all of their various pitch pairings work together to create a singular profile for the pitcher in question.

To gather this data, we've applied a series of proprietary and open-source calculations to the raw data, allowing us to identify the location of the pitch in three dimensions at any point along its flight path. This involves leveraging trajectory insights, including drag correction, from Alan Nathan and applying some basic equations of motion.

In what follows we've provided a brief list of the data produced, along with a description of how one might interpret the resulting data. Also, it's worth nothing that this data can be reviewed on both a sequential level (i.e., for distinct pitch pairings) and as an overall number for each pitcher:

Tunnel Differential

This statistic tells you how far apart two pitches are at the Tunnel Point—the point during their flight when the hitter must make a decision about whether to swing or not (roughly 175 milliseconds before contact).

Example: Jon Lester's pitches average 9.8 inches of separation 23.8 feet in front of home plate. The average in our sample (min 1,000 pairs, n = 162) is 10.0 inches.

Data: This is found in the column "diffattunnel" on our stats pages.

Plate Differential

This statistic shows how far apart back-to-back pitches end up at home plate, roughly where the batter would contact the ball. This includes differentiation generated by pitch break and trajectory of the ball (which includes factors like gravity, arm angle at release, etc.).

Example: On average, Jon Lester's pitches end up roughly 19.1 inches apart at the plate. The average in our sample is 18.7 inches.

Data: This is found in the column "diffatplate" on our stats pages.

Break Differential

This stat tells us how much each spin-induced movement is generated on each pitch between the tunnel point and home plate. Think of this as PITCHf/x pitch movement, except that it is only tracking the time between the Tunnel Point and home plate.

Example: Jon Lester's pitches move, on average, an additional 2.8 inches in the final 23.8 feet to home plate, roughly the diameter of a baseball (baseballs range from 2.88 to 2.94 inches in diameter). The average in our sample is 2.6 inches.

Data: This is found in the column "posttunnelbreak" on our stats pages.

Speed Changes

This is the average difference, in seconds, between back-to-back pitches.

Example: Jon Lester's pitches have an average flight time difference of 0.028 seconds, or 28 precious milliseconds if you're a hitter. The average in our sample is 0.026 seconds or 26 milliseconds.

Data: This is found in the column "flighttimediff" on our stats pages.

Release Differential

When analyzing pitchers, we often talk about consistency in their release point, pointing to scatter plots to see if things look effectively bunched or not. This stat measures the average variation between back-to-back pitches at release.

Example: Jon Lester's average release point varies by just 1.2 inches, best in our sample. The league average in our sample is 2.4 inches.

Data: This is found in the column "diffatrelease" on our stats pages.

Break:Tunnel Ratio

This stat shows us the ratio of post-tunnel break to the differential of pitches at the Tunnel Point. The idea here is that having a large ratio between pitches means the pitches are either tightly clustered at the hitter's decision-making point or the pitches are separating a lot after the hitter has selected a location to swing at. Either way a pitcher's ratio can be large.

Example: Jon Lester's Break:Tunnel Ratio is 28.3 percent. The average in our sample is 27.6 percent.

Data: This is found in the column "breaktotunnelratio" on our stats pages.

---

7. Jon Roegele, "The Effects of Pitch Sequencing," The Hardball Times, November 24, 2014.

Release:Tunnel Ratio

This stat shows us the ratio of a pitcher's release differential to his tunnel differential. Pitchers with smaller Release:Tunnel Ratios have smaller differentiation between pitches through the tunnel point, making it more difficult for opposing hitters to distinguish them in theory.

Example: Jon Lester's Release:Tunnel Ratio is 13.6 percent, the best mark in our sample. The average ratio in sample is 23.7 percent.

Data: This is found in the column "releasetotunnelratio" on our stats pages.

The Potential

The value in creating these new statistics is largely rooted in their ability to inform us on opportunities for improvement and other such practical applications. In that spirit, we've started by listing some of the ways that we envision teams leveraging pitch tunnels data to improve their pitchers.

Adding a Pitch

Let's assume a pitcher is working on a new experimental pitch in spring training. By pulling the relevant data about average tunnel areas for pitchers with that same pitch and the pitcher in question's other pitches we can quickly get an idea of how adding said pitch might impact his tunnel and break differentials. The data could also help identify the optimal sequence(s) for the new pitch that would maximize its likelihood of success, diversifying the pitcher's repertoire and enabling him to be more successful.

Better yet, any team could replicate this methodology and apply actual data from any given pitcher during bullpen sessions, making the hypothetical adding of a pitch more concrete. In this way the pitcher in question isn't looking at the leaguewide average for a new pitch, but rather specific data for his own arsenal. All it takes is relevant data from the new pitch to be added, which can then be compared/contrasted with his existing repertoire and data. One way to show that a pitch may be ready for ??prime time" is when it generates a favorable tunneling profile.

Changing Sequences

Here's a solution that's even simpler than our first hypothetical. Simply mixing pitches differently can produce different results. For example, using a slider and curveball back-to-back could produce better results for a pitcher than his typical fastball > curveball sequence. Looking through the data can help identify underutilized pitch combinations, allowing a pitcher to enhance the effects of his existing offerings.

This solution could quickly and easily be implemented by every pitcher in baseball without the pesky need to tinker with new pitches, grips, etc.

Tweaking Pitches

Let's suppose that a hypothetical pitcher, we'll call him Pitcher A, throws a curveball. Through analysis of Pitcher A's tunnel and break differentials his team discovers that his favorite sequence of fourseam > curveball produces a relatively small tunnel window, but also a small break differential. Through tweaking of this pitch in accordance with spin axis and spin rate data, the team could help Pitcher A adjust his grip and change the shape of the curve. This new curveball shape could then produce a more optimal ratio of tunnel differential to break differential, thus enhancing that sequence.

This same process could be replicated by any team and any pitcher for any pitch. Perhaps it's a fastball that needs to be adjusted. Maybe it's a slider or a changeup. Each pitcher will be able to identify which of his offerings could be easily tweaked to produce a better ratio, enhancing his ability to keep hitters guessing. ▓

So many people were a huge help in pulling this project together, but we'd be remiss if we didn't mention Dan Brooks, Sam Miller, Alan Nathan, Bret Sayre, R.J. Anderson, Craig Goldstein, and the entire BP Stats team specifically.

Relevant Previous Research

We've worked on this project for over two years and gone through many iterations of the data you now see on our stats pages. Along the way, we've found inspiration, assistance, and insight in a variety of places. Many of those works are listed below. If you really enjoyed this introduction to Pitch Tunnels, we recommend you explore the many pieces of research that got us here:

1. http://www.sbnation.com/longform/2014/6/18/5818380/effective-velocity-pitching-theory-profile-perry-husband
2. http://www.hardballtimes.com/the-effects-of-pitch-sequencing/
3. http://www.baseballprospectus.com/article.php?articleid=24862
4. http://www.beyondtheboxscore.com/2013/7/26/4558940/strikeout-pitch-sequences-pitchfx-sabermetrics
5. http://www.beyondtheboxscore.com/2013/8/9/4599550/strikeout-pitch-sequences-by-location-pitchfx-sabermetrics
6. http://www.beyondtheboxscore.com/2011/3/31/2068855/pitch-fx-primer
7. http://grantland.com/the-triangle/2015-mlb-actual-versus-perceived-velocity-statcast-pitcher-data-carter-capps/
8. http://www.beyondtheboxscore.com/2016/4/12/11401508/statcast-data-perceived-velocity-vs-actual-velocity
9. https://www.drivelinebaseball.com/2014/03/protect-curveball/
10. http://www.hardballtimes.com/tht-live/trevor-bauers-pitch-design/
11. http://www.fangraphs.com/blogs/qa-trevor-bauer-pitching-genius/
12. https://www.oatesspecialties.com/wordpress/trevor-bauer-and-pitch-trajectory-drills/
13. http://www.espn.com/mlb/insider/news/story?id=6630630
14. http://www.fangraphs.com/community/babipfx-a-predictive-pitch-based-model/
15. http://www.baseballprospectus.com/article.php?articleid=10803
16. http://ericcressey.com/troubleshooting-baseball-hitting-timing-is-not-always-the-problem
17. https://vimeo.com/39177797
18. http://www.baseballprospectus.com/article.php?articleid=28193
19. http://www.baseballprospectus.com/article.php?articleid=26195
20. https://www.drivelinebaseball.com/2012/05/choosing-the-correct-pitch-sequences-data-driven-decisions/
21. http://www.sloansportsconference.com/wp-content/uploads/2016/02/1479-Testing_Pitch-Recognition-to-Improve-Ta
22. http://www.sloansportsconference.com/wp-content/uploads/2016/02/1482-Baseball.pdf
23. http://www.baseballprospectus.com/article.php?articleid=14572
24. http://sonsofsamhorn.com/baseball/hitting/hitting-visual-analysis/how-do-hitters-perform-with-their-eyes-wide-shut/
25. http://journals.plos.org/plosone/article?id=10.1371/journal.pone.0148498
26. http://ftw.usatoday.com/2016/03/houston-astros-spin-rates-statcast-mccullers-mchugh-keuchel-mlb
27. https://tartansportsanalytics.com/2016/03/02/a-new-method-for-clustering-pitchers/
28. https://www.amazon.com/Downright-Filthy-Pitching-Book-Effective-ebook/dp/B00EDP3GN
29. https://www.amazon.com/Art-Science-Pitching-Tom-House/dp/158518960X
30. https://www.amazon.com/Picture-Perfect-Pitcher-Tom-House/dp/1585186023
31. http://www.hardballtimes.com/recasting-pitchfx-data-in-two-dimensions/
32. http://www.fangraphs.com/blogs/what-can-hitters-actually-see-out-of-a-pitchers-hand/
33. http://www.sfgate.com/sports/article/The-art-and-science-of-Barry-Ball-Reflexes-2781677.php#photo-2202106

34. https://mglbaseball.com/2013/10/08/do-ex-pitchers-understand-how-to-pitch/
35. http://makenolittleplans.net/a-new-view-on-pitch-sequencing/
36. http://lokeshdhakar.com/baseball-pitches-illustrated/
37. http://baseball.physics.illinois.edu/trajectory-calculator-new.html
38. http://baseball.physics.illinois.edu/spindown.pdf
39. http://www.hardballtimes.com/dissecting-a-mystery-pitch/
40. http://www.baseballprospectus.com/a/23864
41. http://baseball.physics.illinois.edu/trackman/SpinParametersSportsBallPatent.pdf
42. http://baseball.physics.illinois.edu/trackman/SportsBallTrajectoryPatent.pdf
43. http://baseball.physics.illinois.edu/FastPFXGuide.pdf
44. http://baseball.physics.illinois.edu/Movement.pdf
45. http://www.fangraphs.com/community/estimating-pitcher-release-point-distance-from-pitchfx-data/
46. http://www.baseballprospectus.com/article.php?articleid=13109
47. http://www.baseballprospectus.com/article.php?articleid=12965
48. http://www.baseballprospectus.com/article.php?articleid=14098
49. http://www.hardballtimes.com/yes-we-actually-classified-every-pitch/
50. https://www.washingtonpost.com/sports/nationals/greg-maddux-a-hall-of-fame-approach-that-carried-an-average-arm-to-cooperstown/2014/01/07/fdd7ae82-77d3-11e3-af7f-13bf0e9965f6_story.html
51. http://spiff.rit.edu/richmond/baseball/traj/traj.html
52. http://baseball.physics.illinois.edu/Magnus.pdf
53. https://www.nytimes.com/video/sports/1247468158551/how-mariano-rivera-dominates-hitters.html
54. http://www.baseballprospectus.com/article.php?articleid=19994
55. http://baseball.physics.illinois.edu/KaganPitchfx.pdf
56. http://baseball.physics.illinois.edu/AJPFeb08.pdf
57. http://baseball.physics.illinois.edu/Template-for-drag-and-spin.xls
58. http://catfishstew.baseballtoaster.com/archives/576977.html

Command and Control

by Jeff Long, Jonathan Judge, and Harry Pavlidis

Jeff Long, Jonathan Judge, and Harry Pavlidis examine the likelihood of a pitch being called a strike based on a variety of factors, as well as the ability of players to influence that likelihood. – Geoff Y.

In January 2016, Baseball Prospectus revealed a suite of catching stats that formed the basis for our industry-leading valuation of catchers. These new stats would shape how we perceived and discussed catcher value, but they also opened the door to better understanding the performance of pitchers.

Two key statistics—CSAA and CS Prob—serve as the basis for the pitch framing portion of our catching metrics. Today, we'll show how those same statistics can tell us a great deal about pitching as well. CS Prob was initially introduced in 2014 with Harry Pavlidis and Dan Brooks' first catcher framing model.[1] Early the next year, Jonathan Judge joined the effort and the team introduced CSAA, officially moving our framing models beyond WOWY.[2]

Of the two, CS Prob—short for Called Strike Probability—is the more straightforward: the likelihood of a given pitch being a strike. CS Prob goes beyond what the strike zone *ought to be* and instead reflects *what it is*: a set of probabilities that depend on batter and pitcher handedness, pitch location, pitch type, and count. Good pitchers understand that while the strike zone is a dynamic construct, it nonetheless has some consistencies depending on which combinations of these factors are present. We calculate CS Prob for every pitch regardless of the eventual outcome.

The other statistic, CSAA, stands for Called Strikes Above Average, a measure of how many called strikes the player in question creates for his team. In the case of catchers, we isolate the effects of the pitcher, umpire, and other situational factors, which allows us to identify how many additional called strikes the catcher is generating, above or below average. For catchers, this skill is commonly described as "framing" or, in more polite company, "presentation."

For pitchers, we can apply a similar methodology—controlling for the catcher, umpire, etc.—to identify the additional called strikes created by the pitcher. CSAA is calculated only on taken pitches, an important nuance. A pitch must be taken to be eligible to be called a strike by the umpire, so while CS Prob looks at all pitches, CSAA only takes into account pitches where the outcome is left up to the umpire.

What can these two statistics tell us about pitcher performance and skill? First, we should define a couple important things:

Control The ability to keep the ball in the strike zone, though not necessarily in any particular location within that zone

Command The ability to precisely locate pitches, in or out of the zone, with the goal of keeping each pitch out of the heart of the plate

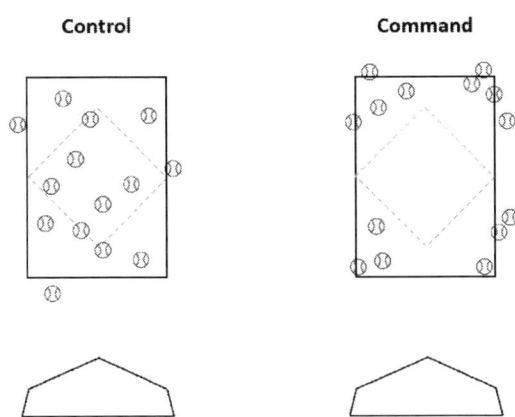

Control   Command

Control

At its core, CS Prob tells us the likelihood that each pitch is going to be called a strike. Having a high CS Prob is an indication that the pitcher in question is throwing a lot of strikes and largely keeping the ball around the strike zone. CS Prob fundamentally tells us which pitchers pound the strike zone, regardless of the quality of those offerings.

---

1. http://www.baseballprospectus.com/article.php?articleid=22934
2. http://www.baseballprospectus.com/article.php?articleid=25514

Take, for example, this graphic that showcases, from the catcher's perspective, some rough zones for called strike probabilities for a right-handed pitcher facing a right-handed hitter in an 0-0 count:

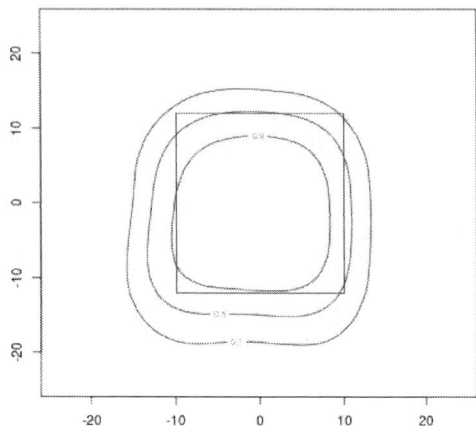

For the 2016 season, the innermost circle represents pitches that are called strikes 90 percent of the time. The larger second circle, which stretches from the top of the strike zone to below the bottom of it, includes pitches that are called a strike roughly half the time. Finally, the largest third circle, which stretches almost entirely outside the zone itself, represents pitches that go for a strike about 10 percent of the time. The reference strike zone is reflected by the black square, allowing you to see the difference between where the strike zone was supposed to be versus where it ended up being called.

These zones change and shift based on the count, the handedness of the batter or pitcher, and even the pitch in question. Overall, though, pitchers who have a high average CS Prob are clearly working within the confines of the strike zone.

There is a clear and obvious connection between the concept of control and CS Prob. Think of pitchers who pound the strike zone. Among pitchers with at least 100 innings, Bartolo Colon led the league with a 52.1 percent CS Prob. That is, any given pitch thrown by Colon has more than a 50 percent chance of being called a strike. The following table showcases the top 10 pitchers in the major leagues for 2016:

Player	CS Prob
Bartolo Colon	52.1%
Rich Hill	50.9%
Jimmy Nelson	50.7%
Steven Matz	50.4%
James Paxton	50.4%
Mike Foltynewicz	50.3%
Hisashi Iwakuma	50.1%
Max Scherzer	50.0%
Shelby Miller	49.9%
Clayton Kershaw	49.7%

CS Prob is an important piece particularly as distinguished from the rulebook strike zone. Take the CS Prob champion, Bartolo Colon: During the 2016 season, Colon led the majors with a 52 percent CS Prob. As we've established, that means that more than five out of every 10 pitches from Colon is likely to be called a strike. If Colon were subject to robot umps calling the rulebook strike zone, his Zone% tells us he would get strikes on 50 percent of his pitches. That means Colon is getting two extra strikes per 100 pitches simply because the strike zone that is called isn't the one the rulebook lays out. Rich Hill, on the other hand, actually gets penalized, as his Zone% of 52.6 percent is higher than his CS Prob.

Generally speaking, CS Prob and Zone% should correspond with each other because the called strike zone is generally pretty close to what the rulebook defines as the zone. Still, a few percentage points one way or another leads to a few more or a few less strikes over the course of a game. That could mean a few dozen strikes going the other way over the course of a season, and the value of a strike is sometimes really significant.

Throwing pitches in the strike zone as defined by the rulebook isn't necessarily a ticket to success; much like real estate it's all about location, location, location.

Command

Now that we've established that CS Prob is a proxy for *control*, we can build on it. After extensive review, we've concluded that CSAA substantially reflects a pitcher's ability to *command* his pitches. It's important to make the connection between what CSAA does and the popular definition of command.

Traditionally command is understood as the ability to "hit your spots"—having the ball end up where you intend it to. Over the years this has been studied in numerous ways—most notably by attempting to determine how much the catcher moves his glove to receive a pitch. This is flawed because the catcher's glove isn't always the target, and we can't know where the pitcher is truly intending the pitch to go.

What we can do is come at command from a different angle. A pitcher with good command should be more predictable for the catcher—his pitches often end up in the locations, and with the movement, that the catcher expects. This skill results in easier receiving for catchers, and additional called strikes for the pitcher. Once we aggregate the data across thousands of pitches, CSAA can tell us whether a pitcher is reliably hitting his spots.

CS Prob is actually covariate in the model for CSAA, which is a fancy way of saying that CSAA measures the extent to which a participant tends to affect the likelihood of a strike being called, notwithstanding its final location. As such, CSAA controls for all of the same things as CS Prob and adds in the umpire and catcher for good measure.

So what does accumulating CSAA look like? It's not as easy as it sounds. Sure, you could throw a ton of pitches in the middle of the zone and basically guarantee that you'll wrack up called strikes on the pitches hitters don't offer at. The downside to that approach is that pitches in the center of the plate get crushed.

The best command pitchers actually have a somewhat interesting approach. They tend to work further outside the edge of the strike zone than you might think, trying to pick up extra strikes in the 20 percent or 30 percent bands for CS Prob. When working within the zone, they avoid the center of the plate—the 90 percent zone—and focus on something in the 75 percent range. The very best command pitchers—guys who are one standard deviation or more above the mean—also have a high propensity to throw pitches in the sub-10 percent band as well. When these guys are trying to work out of the zone, they *really* work out of the zone. That means spiked curveballs, down-and-out sliders, and eye-high fastballs.

You can see in the following chart the density of offerings between the best and worst command pitchers and where they tend to concentrate their pitches along the spectrum of called strike probability:

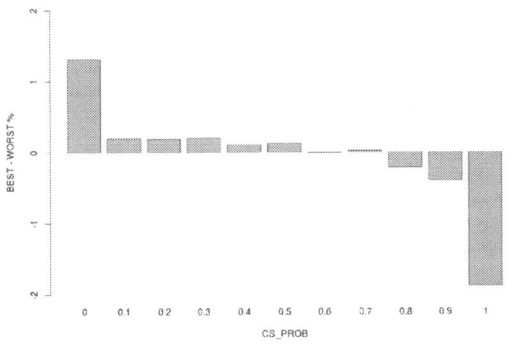

You'll notice that most of the positive values are located in the bottom half of the CS Prob range: 0 percent to 50 percent. This means that the best command pitchers actually work outside the effective strike zone—especially in the 0 percent

to 9.99 percent range—as compared to the worst CSAA performers. Simply put, if you have good command, you don't have to throw as many strikes.

Command thus differs from control because pounding the zone doesn't necessarily mean that you're hitting your spots. A guy like Clayton Kershaw can get away with having a high CS Prob (99th percentile) and an all right CSAA (69th percentile) because his raw stuff is so impressive. For someone like Colon, however, elite command (top six percent in CSAA) is critical to his success. Luis Perdomo combines throwing a lot of strikes with poor command (59th percentile CSAA) to disastrous results—nearly 1.5 home runs per nine innings.

As such, command is something you don't *need*, provided you are blessed with dynamic stuff. Most pitchers, though, need to work the edges of the zone effectively, gathering up extra strikes as much as possible to be successful.

The best command/CSAA pitchers tend to be guys who produce good results despite seemingly lackluster or otherwise inconsistent stuff. The top 10 pitchers with a minimum 500 chances in 2016 are listed in the following table (note: percentages here indicate how many more strikes the pitcher got than CS Prob would otherwise indicate).

Player	CS Prob
Zach Davies	3.5%
Josh Tomlin	2.8%
Kyle Hendricks	2.5%
Ryan Vogelsong	2.5%
Mike Leake	2.3%
Zack Greinke	2.1%
Wily Peralta	2.0%
A.J. Ramos	1.9%
Jon Lester	1.9%
Chris Young	1.9%

A pitcher like Davies—a righty whose fastball barely broke the 90-mph barrier—needs to work those edges to be successful at the highest level of baseball. Throughout much of his career as a prospect Davies seemed destined to be a Quadruple-A player because of his unimpressive stuff, but the Brewers are now reaping the rewards of Davies' command: His pitches are 3.5 percent more likely to be called a strike than the average pitcher.

Command can be a powerful tool. For Davies, it converts a seemingly fringe prospect into a three-win pitcher. A decline in command also corresponds to the difference between Jered Weaver being a league-average pitcher a few years ago to whatever it is he was in 2016. Take a look at how his CSAA and WARP have changed over the past three seasons:

Year	CS Prob	CS Prob Rank	CSAA	MLB Rank	Max FB Velo	HR/ 9	WARP
2014	65.3%	73rd	2.1%	2nd	89.7	1.1	0.4
2015	66.2%	12th	1.5%	7th	87.2	1.4	-1.7
2016	62.7%	33rd	0.6%	57th	86.2	1.9	-5.3

Suffice it to say that the margin for error for a pitcher with a mid-80s fastball is razor thin—maybe even less than 1.5 percentage points, if the preceding table is any indication. It's not enough to simply look at Weaver's declining CSAA and say that losing an extra strike or two per game hurt him so badly. His declining CSAA points to overall diminishing command. The result? More pitches over the middle and Weaver's home-run rate has soared, while his value has plunged in the other direction.

⚾   ⚾   ⚾

There is one special case that's worth pointing out and discussing at some length. Tom Glavine's 2008 season doesn't seem overly special when you look at raw CSAA. His 5.3 percent mark is certainly impressive, but ranks just 120th among all seasons since 1988.

Glavine's season really shines when you control for the era and seasonal factors. Creating Z-scores allows us to compare each pitcher to his peers, helping us better understand how they are performing compared to their peers that season. This is important because as PITCHf/x began being utilized by major-league teams and the league office, umpires started calling games differently. Specifically, they got a lot better and more consistent.

That's why Glavine's 2008 season is so remarkable. His 5.3 percent CSAA is barely half of Greg Maddux's best-ever mark, but that 5.3 percent was more than seven (!!!) standard deviations better than the mean for the 2008 season. By 2008 umpires had really improved in terms of calling the strike zone, but Glavine was still working like it was 1995.

We would also be remiss if we didn't mention the sheer dominance of Maddux, who from 1995 to 1997 was getting a strike bonus of 8–10 percent on every pitch he threw. That is, put bluntly, absurd.

⚾   ⚾   ⚾

There are, of course, two ways to analyze and understand pitcher performance. Let's use pitch movement as an example. We can look at PITCHf/x data and see that a pitch dropped 10 inches horizontally and traveled at 73.7 mph. We can also look and see that against that particular pitch opposing hitters swung and missed 15.4 percent of the time, hit groundballs 10.7 percent of the time, and were charged a strike (either via a called strike, a whiff, or a foul ball) 26.6 percent of the time.

For the pitcher, the measurements are a means to an end. The most important thing is that the pitch delivers positive outcomes and/or helps set up other pitches to have positive outcomes. Having the best stuff in baseball doesn't mean anything if you can't get hitters out.

Our approach to understanding command and control is rooted in the latter, as we look to describe the outcomes and intent related to pitch location. We can do this by using CS Prob and CSAA to isolate the performance of the pitcher from all other influencing factors, and to establish an idea of how an ability to locate the ball—either in the zone, or precisely outside of the zone if need be—impacts the intended outcome. This is unlike COMMANDf/x, a methodology that uses glove movement to measure precision. Catcher movement can be helpful, but it can also be misleading.

Being able to look at command and control through the lens of strikes is critical, because that is the currency in which pitchers trade throughout an at-bat. With CSAA and CS Prob, we believe that we've identified the tools to do just that. ▪

Fire Up the Time Machine

by Russell A. Carleton

Inspired by a reader question, Russell A. Carleton considers how far back in time a current team of average players would have to travel to become the team to beat. – Geoff Y.

The *Effectively Wild* Facebook group can be a fun place. In May 2017, member Adam Dyck posed a fun question. "How far back in time would you have to send a team of modern-day replacement-level players before they would be the greatest baseball team on the planet?" For those who aren't regular listeners to the show, it's a quintessential example of the sort of question that gets bantered about. It's one part baseball, one part science-fiction script idea. It's unanswerable, but it hints at a larger question that's worth discussing. How has baseball changed over its history?

In the field of psychometry, there's a concept known as "the Flynn Effect," named after researcher James Flynn, who noted that over several decades, scores on standardized intelligence tests have crept slowly upward. It's not entirely clear why this is. It's possible that humans are getting smarter (if you believe that intelligence tests actually measure smarts). It's also possible that humans have gotten better about designing intelligence tests that flatter themselves more thoroughly. (Comedian Emo Philips is noted for remarking: "I used to think that the brain was the most wonderful organ in my body. Then I realized who was telling me this.")

It's not unreasonable to think that humans are better off in some ways than they once were. Life expectancy has increased. Technology has improved life at least in some ways. Perhaps the pitchers and hitters of today, when compared to each other, aren't any better or worse than pitchers and hitters of the past, but what would happen if we introduced a time machine into the equation? If a team of hitters from the present day were sent to 1927, would they keep Babe Ruth company at the top of the home-run leaderboard? Would they blow past him?

I somehow doubt that a team of players who are replacement level today—a team that, depending on who you talk to, would win somewhere around 40 or 50 games out of 162—could raise that projection by the 50 or so games it would take to be the undisputed "best team in baseball," but I would frame the question in a slightly different way. How far back might we need to send a team of average players before they became the team that everyone feared?

Warning! Gory Mathematical Details Ahead!

This question has a bit of a hitch in it, and it has nothing to do with temporal paradoxes. It's widely known that the past few years have seen a spike in home-run rate. Is this spike the result of batters getting better? Is it that pitchers are getting worse? Is there some unseen other cause? The root cause is going to be important for this question. For example, if the cause of the spike was that all teams moved into stadiums that had fences 250 feet away, then transporting our players back into an era where they had real fences wouldn't make them better home-run hitters in that era.

But more than that, baseball's double-accounting system makes these sorts of cross-era comparisons difficult. A home run hit by the batter is a home run given up by the pitcher. We could say that our time-traveling hitters would hit more home runs in the past, but would the pitching staff arriving from the bullpen in a DeLorean be more likely to *give up* a bomb? We're going to have to tread very carefully.

So let's set up some parameters for answering the question. We assume that we're taking an average team back to the past. They will set down in whatever year we program the time machine for and quietly infiltrate and replace one of the already existing teams in the league. No one will notice or think it's weird. In other words, this is the baseball video game model where for some reason the 2017 Yankees have replaced the 1927 Yankees. Or vice versa.

I believe that the key question that we really need to answer is *what would they be allowed to take with them*? This question is often asked in the reverse form of "how would Babe Ruth perform if magically transported from 1927 into 2017?" versus "how would Babe Ruth perform if he had been born in 1982, benefited from all of modern medicine and science as he was growing up, and then played in 2017 as a 32-year-old (as he was in 1927)?" It's a way of asking the question of how much modern science and medicine really matter. It's an unanswerable question, which makes it interesting to discuss.

They Can Take Their Physical Bodies with Them

What if our time-traveling team could only take their physical bodies with them? If we set them down in 1977, they would believe that they had always lived in the world of disco and that Jimmy Carter had always been president and that wearing polyester uniforms was a good idea. One thing our time travelers would notice is that they were much bigger than most of the other players in the league.

This is a graph of the median (50th percentile), 70th percentile, and 90th percentile Body-Mass Index (BMI) of all players who appeared in the majors from 1900-2016, based on their "listed" height and weight in the Lahman database. This assumes that players kept the same weight through their careers and that teams were telling the truth, which are both bogus assumptions, but the aggregate should wash away a lot of those sins.

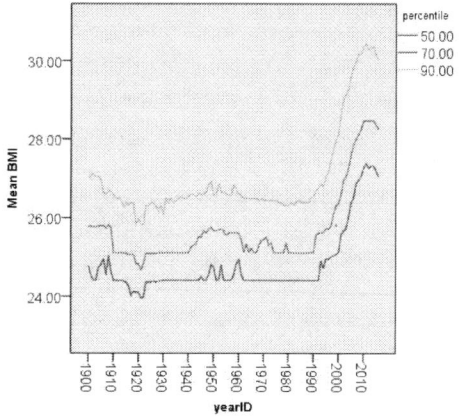

We see that in the mid-'90s, something (*cough*something*cough*) happened that caused an inflection point in MLB. After most of a century of the same body types, players started getting bigger. Mostly, they got heavier, although players today are also taller than they had been. The median player in MLB right now would be larger (in terms of BMI) than 90 percent of players who played in any year before the 1990s. To put that another way, while there were certain big guys playing in the 1960s and 1970s, it would seem that our temporally transported team had half their roster that were as big as or bigger than the biggest guys on any of the other teams.

That size came with a cost. Here's a graph over time from 1950-2016 of triples / (doubles + triples), again leaguewide.

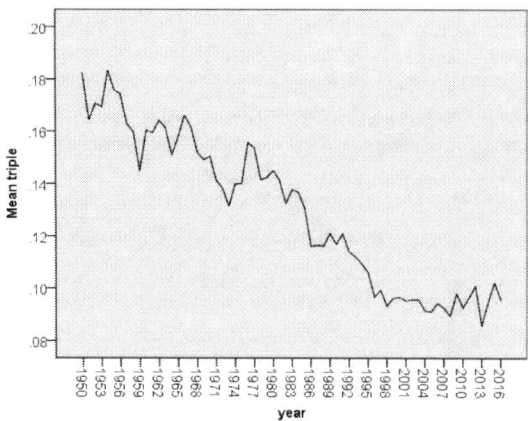

Here's another graph of the rate at which baserunners took an "extra" base on a hit, such as going from first to third on a single, or first to home on a double.

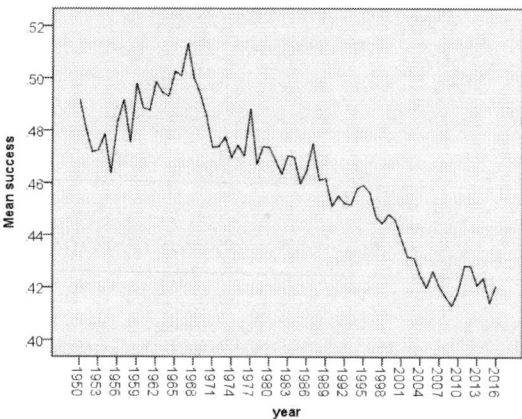

As time has gone along, baseball players have gotten slower. (Or is it that they've gotten less aggressive? Or the parks have gotten smaller? Or outfield arms are just more dangerous now?) There's also evidence that players have become poorer defenders over the years, potentially because teams have prioritized size and power over mobility. Here's a graph of leaguewide BABIP since 1950.

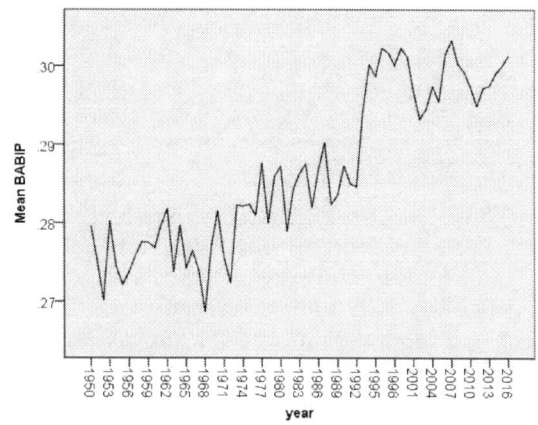

There's that mid-'90s inflection point again. Prior to 1992, BABIP leaguewide had been consistently in the high .280s. In 1992, it was .285. In 1993, it jumped to .294, and then again in 1994 to .300, and it has been stuck around .300 ever since. (No, it is not a Coors Field effect. I checked.) So, it seems that the mid-'90s, which some have referred to by another name (*cough*something*cough*), ushered in a radically different era in baseball. Players are less mobile than they used to be. But, my oh my, can they hit the ball further now.

Here's a graph, again since 1950, of home runs per fly ball*. I put an asterisk next to fly balls, because it's not really fly balls. We don't have batted ball-type data back into the '50s, so I improvised. That's actually HR / (HR + 2B + 3B + air outs caught by outfielders).

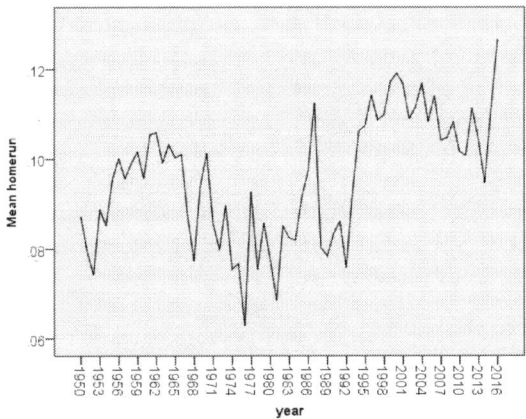

We can see that there was yet another inflection point in the 1990s. I ran a similar set of analyses for doubles and triples [(2B + 3B) / (HR + 2B + 3B + OF air outs)] and got a very similar graph (not shown). The bigger hitters that invaded the game in the 1990s ushered in an era of extra-base hits.

We know from modern research that while batters and pitchers combine to create a fly ball, once the ball is in the air, how hard it is hit and how far it goes and whether it goes over the fence is largely a function of the batter's talent. So, we can credit the increase in bigger fly balls mostly to the batters and likely to their increased size.

𝕏   𝕏   𝕏

In 2016, the average MLB team had 304 doubles and/or triples, had 462 opportunities for extra advancement on hits, and faced 4,107 balls in play that they needed to field. We've established that in these cases, the team of today is worse than teams of old. However, they do hit more home runs and extra-base hits on their fly balls. How many runs does that actually buy (or lose) them over what players used to be able to do?

Event	Chances	Relative (Dis)advantage	Additional Events	Value (in runs)	2016 Players Additional Value
Triple Instead of Double	304	4%	12	.25	-3.0
Advance an Extra Base on a Base Hit	462	5%	23	.20	-4.6
Make an Out on a Ball in Play	4,107	1.5%	62	.80	-49.6
Hit a 2B/3B on a "Fly Ball"	1,477	2%	30	1.1	33.0
Hit a HR on a "Fly Ball"	1,477	2%	30	1.7	51.0
Total					26.8

(Note: I'm using some very quick-and-dirty eyeball estimates for relative (dis)advantage and some "good enough" thumbnail run values for these events.)

If a team of (smaller) players from yesteryear showed up in today's environment, they would be better defenders, and they'd get some value from their better baserunning abilities, but they'd lose a lot of value from their relative lack of ability to hit for as much power as the current players, leading to a two- or three-win (again, I'm using some very slapdash math) advantage for our modern-day monsters.

But hang on a second. In the preceding table, we're talking about the differences between a team of old-school players (smaller, but more mobile) and today's bigger players *as if they were playing the same style of baseball played in 2016*. Today, there simply aren't as many balls hit into play. A modern team going backward in time would face off against a team that was more likely to put the ball into play, and therefore, our less mobile modern-day players and their somewhat questionable defensive abilities would be forced to make more plays in the field, and probably have more balls skip past them.

Let me repopulate that table, but use the rates from 1976.

Event	Chances	Relative (Dis)advantage	Additional Events	Value (in runs)	2016 Players Additional Value
Triple Instead of Double	258	4%	10	.25	-2.5
Advance an Extra Base on a Base Hit	505	5%	25	.20	-5.0
Make an Out on a Ball in Play	4,730	1.5%	71	.80	-56.8
Hit a 2B/3B on a "Fly Ball"	1,483	2%	30	1.1	33.0
Hit a HR on a "Fly Ball"	1,483	2%	30	1.7	51.0
Total					19.7

We see that our modern-day hitters (and fielders) going back in time would still have an advantage because of their larger size, even playing 1970s baseball, but that the effect would be worth about two wins, give or take.

They Can Take Modern Roster Construction with Them (and Velocity)

We know that prior to the late 1980s, the single-inning reliever wasn't "a thing." Up until 1992, the plurality of relief appearances lasted more than one inning. Once teams realized that the one-inning model worked and could cover most of their bullpen needs, there was a shift toward velocity in the game, especially in the bullpen. If a pitcher only needed to get three outs, he could air it out during that inning. More to the point, if there was a pitcher kicking around who had electric stuff that would short out after an inning or so, he finally had someone offering him a job.

Data is only available back to 2002 on velocity, but pitchers now throw about 4 mph faster than they did 15 years ago. There were guys who threw 95 back in the 1980s, and they were a rare find. Now, each team has a few. It's interesting to wonder if those guys who could hit 95 were always there, but since there was no job description for a guy who could only throw one inning at a time, they were simply passed over.

Our time-traveling team would be going back to a time in which they wouldn't face quite as much velocity as they do now. Their opponents would constantly be facing what they had previously known as "the hardest-throwing guy in the league." It's hard to model exactly what would happen if hitters from the 1960s or 1970s were constantly facing off against modern-day velocity. We can only guess that their performance would suffer, but what would happen to our present-day hitters as they entered a world where a 92-mph fastball was something worth noting?

I took all fastballs from 2016 and binned them into 1-mph segments. Here's how often players (in 2016) made contact when they swung.

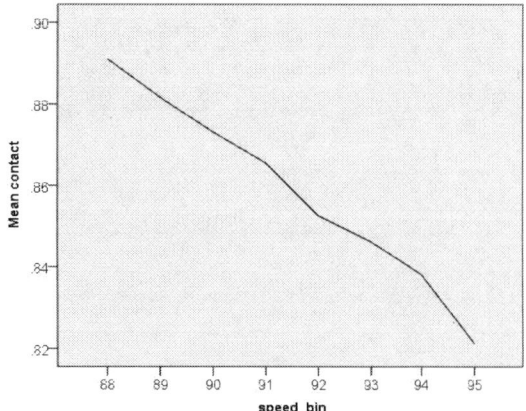

Dropping 4 mph, at least on fastballs, means that hitters had a 4 or 5 percent greater chance of making contact with the ball. It's worth noting that over the past 15 years, leaguewide contact rate and leaguewide strikeout rate have correlated at -.71 (more contact leads to fewer strikeouts for obvious reasons), and every additional percentage point of contact rate lowers the strikeout rate by 1.25 percentage points. If you multiply all of that together, it's a 5 percentage point drop in the strikeout rate.

In 2016, hitters struck out 21.1 percent of the time, and a drop to 16.1 percent would bring things back to strikeout levels last seen in the mid-'90s. Go back further and our time travelers would still strike out more than the average team, though not by as much. (This also assumes that velocity would be the only thing driving making contact and that contact is the only thing driving the strikeout rate.)

Hitters might make better contact off of lesser velocity, but does that mean getting more out of the balls that they do hit? Here's slugging percentage on contact, again, paneled by velocity bins for 2016 hitters, fastballs only.

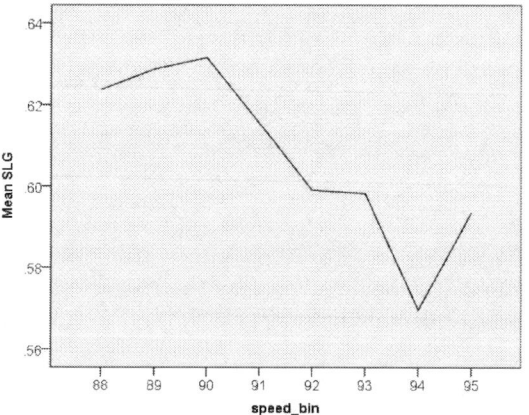

Well then ...

A drop of 4 mph in average fastball speed seems to be worth something like 40 points worth of slugging! Again, there may be other factors at work here, but as some point of comparison, in 2016 the league slugging percentage was .417. A jump of half of that (20 points) would put SLG level with the highest recorded league slugging percentage *ever* (.437 in 2000), when the average team scored in excess of five runs per game.

We are setting up a world where our modern-day players aren't going to strike out as much as they do now, and are probably going to be able to hit the ball more effectively, and we haven't yet accounted for what the effects of all that big-time velocity would be *against* the hitters of the 1960s and 1970s. Back then, competing *against their own contemporaries*, teams put up a mere 4.2 or 4.3 runs per game. Even assuming that ye olde offenses would see no ill effects of the bigger, harder-throwing modern-day pitchers, a team that was capable of putting up 5.0 runs per game playing against a bunch of teams that averaged 4.3 runs per game would have a Pythagorean record of 93-69.

Maybe the velocity of the modern game wouldn't play out exactly that way after the time machine landed, but clearly it's going to make a huge difference. This alone could turn an 81-win team into a surefire playoff team.

They Can Take Modern Medicine With Them?

This one is harder to do since we don't have reliable historical injury or disabled list data. It seems like this one would be a (pardon the mixed metaphor) slam dunk for the present-day players, but proving it is harder. Life expectancy in general has risen in the United States over the past century, and I guess that's as sure a sign of medical advancement as any. But does that filter down into baseball?

In the absence of disabled list data, I tried a couple of workarounds, including a trick I've used previously where I look for pitchers who go more than 21 days between major-league appearances. This is a *very* rough proxy for injury, because the reason for the time off might have been that a pitcher lost effectiveness and was sent to the minors for a few weeks. It might also just be strategic roster churn, but here's a graph from 1950 to 2016 on how often those "mysterious disappearances" happened per team. (The spike in the middle is 1981 when there was a work stoppage in the middle of the season and everyone took a couple of months off.)

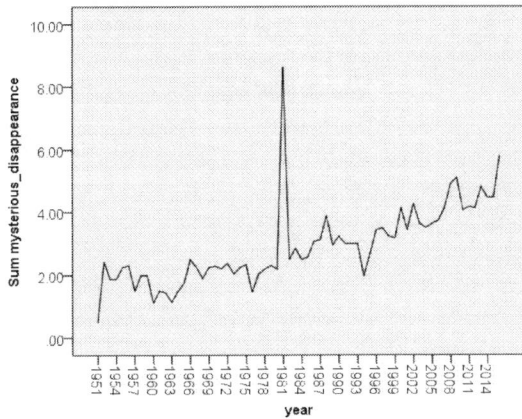

This graph is notable for the fact that it's not pointing downward. That's not necessarily evidence that there are now more injuries (it could just be more roster moves), and even if it shows more "injuries" it might be that modern medical technology just allows teams to see injuries that previously would have gone undiagnosed.

I also looked to see whether modern medicine allowed players to cheat "death" in baseball. I looked for pitchers who were on the wrong side of 30, and had posted a two-win season. I then looked to see how many more years they had left until they had their final two-win season. Perhaps modern medicine might keep older players going longer? (I

stopped the sample in 2006, because we don't know what's going to become of the "still pretty good" players over 30 from last year.)

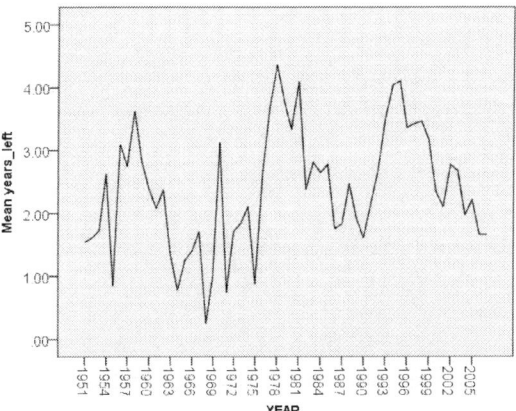

We see that there's plenty of noise in this one, but that the trend line is generally upward. If you shoot a line through that graph, the regression says that the line is significantly different from zero, so older players are able to stick around longer, but the effect size is about an extra tenth of a year every decade. Score a victory for modern medicine. A very small victory. (The graph for batters has the same form.)

There are probably some places where modern medicine is helping around the edges in baseball, but a torn rotator cuff is a torn rotator cuff, no matter what year it is. I think even if our time travelers are able to take all of their magical medical devices with them, it's not the huge advantage that we might think it is.

They Can Take ... The World Baseball Classic With Them?

And now what I think is the most interesting graph in the bunch.

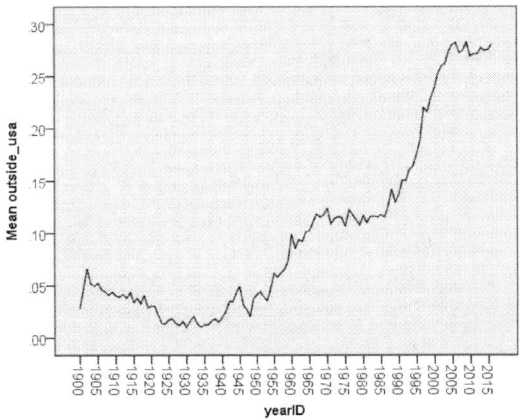

This is the percentage of players appearing in each season who were born outside of the United States. We see that it hovers below five percent until the 1950s, around the time when teams began to delete the (horrifically evil) color line that had kept African-Americans out of the game for so long. It grew until it plateaued around the late '80s/early '90s to about 15 percent. In the early 1990s, something happened. Teams started making heavy investments in the international market and began exploring new markets (Cuba, Japan, Brazil). Now, nearly 30 percent of players were born somewhere other than the United States. The existence of the World Baseball Classic is a tribute to that global expansion.

Once again, we see an inflection point in the early '90s. How would this affect our time travelers? Well, let me frame the question in a different way. Suppose that today, in 2017, Major League Baseball were to pass a rule saying that no more than 15 percent of a team's roster could be composed of players who were born outside the United States. The average team would have to cut roughly 15 percent of its roster, which is 3-4 players.

As insane a proposal as this would be, teams would do the only logical thing that they could, which would be to replace the four players they had to cast off with lesser guys from Triple-A or the waiver wire: in other words, (American) players who were functioning at or below replacement level. (If the players were better than replacement level, they'd probably all be in the majors.) Some teams would be more affected than others, but all of the teams would have less talent than they started with.

Here's the thing: Going back in time, our average team from today would be entering a world where this rule has effectively been put into place. It's not that in the early '90s there was some sort of agreement to keep players from outside the United States out of MLB, it's that those investments hadn't fully come to fruition yet. It's possible (and likely) that had MLB invested earlier, we would have seen more players come from other countries earlier.

We don't really have a way of knowing whether the marginal players that MLB attracted were stars or scrubs. MLB has long had at least *some* presence in a country like the Dominican Republic, and perhaps the guys people thought were future All-Stars made it, while the ones left behind might have been roster filler anyway. It's possible that the investments teams made drew in players who had talent, but who previously had no way to get in front of MLB scouts.

On average, one roster spot produces 1.3 wins. If we assume that the players who have to be let go were selected at random by the league office, each team would lose something like five wins worth of value (again, on average). If we assume that teams could make their own cuts, they would pick the least talented players and the damage might only be a win or two of value. We have to assume that because teams of today get to take advantage of those global

investments of yesteryear, a team going back in time would find an inferior product on the field because they hadn't been scouring (and scouting) the earth enough to find the very best players in the world.

It's possible that some of the effects that we saw earlier can also be tied to this global expansion. Perhaps velocity is up specifically because teams now have access to further reaches of the globe, and with a bigger pool of people to draw from, they are simply able to find more humans who are capable of throwing a ball 95 mph or who are big enough to hit home runs, but athletic enough that whatever mistakes they make on the field, they can outhit.

How Far Back?

If there's a theme that kept coming up over and over again, it's that baseball changed (for better or worse) starting around the early 1990s. And it changed a lot, at a pace that overwhelmed most of the changes that had come before it in the century before that. The game now is a different one than it was.

There was the obvious (*cough*something*cough*) issue in the 1990s, and that gets all the headlines, but even if we assume that the entirety of the growth in player size was attributable to the growth in the use of steroids, the effects weren't as large as we might think. Players got bigger and hit more home runs, but they also got slower. It looks like it was a net positive, but there was good and bad to it. What was interesting to me is that the numbers suggest that the global expansion of baseball has done more to affect the game than the expanding biceps of the players.

The revolution that few talk about is the velocity surge. It seems that baseball has been stuck in a quiet battle in which pitchers throw ever faster and the hitters that come into the league are probably being selected for the ability to hit that velocity or for an approach that works against velocity. It seems that once teams got past the idea that one pitcher must endure all nine innings, or at least must go multiple innings, it freed them up to pursue hard stuff.

Pitchers and batters have largely kept pace with each other (with some fits and starts here and there), but a look backward shows how far both sides have come. While they may have played each other to a stalemate, imagining these new hitters being unleashed on a major-league environment that was not ready for it is terrifying.

What's pretty clear, though, is that a present-day team of average players wouldn't have to travel more than a couple of decades into the past before they were the dominant force in Major League Baseball. ■

A Meditation on a Mess of Baseball Cards

by Holly M. Wendt

While sifting through a slew of old baseball cards, Holly Wendt rediscovers forgotten players as well as forgotten truths. – Geoff Y.

The collection has been housed in a leather valise, harder than glove-leather, dry with age, the colors of infield dirt before and after the dampening spray. It looks like it's going somewhere, waiting for its steamer-trunk sticker. The rusting clasp features a small lock, though key and case have long parted ways. Under the flipped lid, an imbroglio of cardboard and plastic—cards and sleeves tumbled loose, some correctly paired, everything shaken free of even the suggestion of stacks. Here and there, snap-closure plastic cases separate 15 or 20 cards from the rest: whole or partial sets of things, or maybe the lone pack of a certain brand or special release.

The empty sleeves distract, and the first thing I do is pull them out. Without someone's face between their translucent skins, the soft ones look like trash, like cigarette-box wrappers. The rigid ones tinge yellow, age and maybe smoke getting the better of them. I wouldn't want to put new cards in them, or anything I think has value.

I wish value wasn't the first thing I thought about when I lifted the lid, but that's what baseball cards seemed to mean most in the 1990s. That's why my brother collected them, going to shows and crowded road-side shops and that one table at the weekly farmers' market, and why he bought those hefty newsprint guides that told you what you—your collection—was worth.

The decade seemed to be full of people celebrating or lamenting found and lost cards—here the joy of a childhood trove unearthed from 30 years before, rich and ripe with DiMaggios and Williamses and maybe cards older, better, rarer; there the collective agony of "My mom threw them away when she cleaned the attic." Or the clarity knowledge brings: My dad told stories of how they played with their cards, carrying them everywhere, threading them through their bike-tire spokes to show them off and to enjoy the sounds they made straining against pedaled wind.

The collection boom loomed especially large in those years. The comic book industry ran rampant with it—variant covers, foil covers, renumberings, and special editions—and the practice of buying one copy to read and one copy to never, ever touch trickled even into my little cows-and-coal school district, a place where it was impossible for many of the kids to even get the cable television stations showing the cartoon series that spawned some of those comics.

It was equally difficult to actually watch televised baseball there. Baseball cards were one way to learn the faces of the people who showed up in newspaper box scores, to feel connected to a smirk, a stance, the pitch of the eyes. There were magazines, too, and some people could go to games, but for those of us in the middle of nowhere with no checkbooks of our own, stripping away the crinkling wrapping on a new pack of cards brought us as close to the players as we'd ever been.

⚾   ⚾   ⚾

There were people we knew—knew of—on baseball cards, too. Inside this leather case, there are six cards of pitcher Randy Martz, who spent three of his four seasons with the Cubs. On the outside of one of the card-sleeves, there's a handwritten masking tape label indicating the card's 25 cent price and a note: "Went to Upper Dauphin."

I don't know whose handwriting that is, whether the card is marked because it was bought that way or because someone tried to sell it. But Upper Dauphin is the next school district over from home, and Brad Hassinger, who graduated from there, too, came to talk to my fifth-grade class. Before the 1993 season started, Hassinger had pitched for High-A Clearwater, and he would peak in Double-A the following year. Somewhere in my parents' house is a little stack of white notebook paper squares, paper-clipped together, all bearing his signature because he was drafted by the Phillies. Ten-year-old me thought it would be important to have them.

Part of aging is learning where one was right, where one was wrong. I was right to keep all of my old softball mitts, wrong to sell back my college geology textbook. And until I wrote the previous paragraph, I would have said I was wrong to have kept that ridiculous pile of signatures—not even on cards, not even in an autograph book, but on two-by-four-inch slips of cheap wide-rule—but I'm glad now to have done it, glad now for its remembering, and that the memory is all mine. The collecting of cards was never really my own.

Maybe it was because my luck was bad—I don't remember ever plucking anything good from a pack's shallow sea—but I didn't have any passion for it. Cards' stats-printed backs didn't take long enough to read, didn't tell me enough of the story, and I wasn't allowed to make anything out of them. What if Rockies rookie pitcher Mo Sanford got good in a few years? One never knew. The cautious uncertainty was part of the appeal of it: The collectors who were careful, the ones who cased and bindered their cards against dust and bent corners, might find themselves good fortune. I wanted to carry them around, make them team-colored borders and frames, and hang them in my locker. It wasn't like slapping them on a bicycle, but at the time, it might as well have been.

So I picked books instead, borrowing without asking the baseball biographies on my dad's shelves: the lives of Hank Aaron and Bob Feller and Jackie Robinson and Sandy Koufax. In sixth grade, I was reading *I Had a Hammer: The Hank Aaron Story*, and I read the things people said to Aaron, the death threats he received. It was the first time I'd encountered the n-word in print, but I knew what it was, knew its ugliness thanks to a fifth-grade teacher who taught Civil War history with due gravity and specificity and its still-live weight. I knew—as much as a white adolescent from rural Pennsylvania could know—that racism hadn't ended after Jackie Robinson stole home.

In mid-August 2017, white supremacists, carrying Nazi insignias, marched in Charlottesville, Virginia, and shouted, beside anti-Semitic chants, the slur that had startled me so much 20 years ago that I turned around in my middle school desk to show the boy sitting in front of me. Back then, I never asked anyone for more information about what I'd read, didn't know who to ask, and didn't really want to know why the boy sitting in front of me had said something like, "So?"

This week, I opened this box and looked at baseball cards when I couldn't look at the news any more, but I found the news inside, anyway: on cards with rough-rounded corners and grainy photos, the phrase "Military Service" where a string of numbers usually sat, 1943-1945. 1944-1945. When I'd first learned about Ted Williams and Joe DiMaggio leaving baseball for three years and was so sheltered by youth and geography and a culture of not talking about anything unpleasant or nuanced, it was these gaps that told me how serious that war was: The greatest hitters of their age stopped playing baseball to join the war effort, not because they were forced to go, but because they thought it that important.

No longer a child, I recognize complexities and complicities in that historical moment—the gaps on these cards all post-1941, despite what the world knew about Hitler's Germany years earlier and America's own anti-Semitism, not to mention its legacies of slavery and genocide on home soil. When World War II ended and baseball returned to its own status quo, baseball and America were still segregated. To be looking at these cards this week has been to remember that there is no escaping our own pasts.

ⓧ   ⓧ   ⓧ

Between the more venerable Stan Musials and Mickey Mantles and Roberto Clementes, there is a whole set of Bo Knows cards, featuring the eponymous Mr. Jackson in everything from hockey pads to jockey silks because, well, Bo knows all. Two ridiculous specimens from a 1991 Fleer set figure Jose Canseco and Roger Clemens in near-mythological trappings, literal lightning charging Canseco's bat and mystic fire on Clemens's ball; pasting Marvel's Thor over Canseco's face wouldn't look out of place. There are replicas of the 1910 Honus Wagner tobacco card and the 1933 Goudey Gum Nap Lajoie card, distributed by special request to complete a 240-card set mistakenly released without card #106.

Randy Johnson, Tony Gwynn, and Pedro Martinez all stand between plastic sheathing, often twinned—two of the same cards, or at least the same player, posed back-to-back. Incomplete parades of Topps and Upper Deck hopefuls scatter loose between the rest, the cards a little warped, some of them cleaving fast to each other due to humidity, a suspect glossing agent, or simply a lonesome despair in this leather coffer.

The collection isn't mine, and I'm not keeping it. I only asked to borrow it, to look for a while, and I'll send it back a little neater if I can. But a box isn't like a binder; my efforts are temporary, and I keep changing my mind. I've piled things by date and by team, by the little price stickers still stuck to some and that I've resisted peeling off. Here, tonight, my only goal was to make them all of equal height, to confine the unruly empty sleeves against the edges. It's a small effort to make sure that whoever opens the box next can clearly see what's there, understand what this history is really worth. ▨

Oh, The People You'll Meet

by Jarrett Seidler

Jarrett Seidler recalls his ballpark visits with the late Gene "Stick" Michael, who always made time for baseball conversation and ice cream. – Geoff Y.

On September 7, 2017, Gene Michael, universally known in the baseball world as "Stick," passed away of a heart attack. He was 79, and perhaps the most universally beloved person in baseball amongst people who work in the game.

I can't tell you anything you won't see written better elsewhere about Stick's role in building the 1990s Yankee dynasty. I can't tell you about his relationship with George Steinbrenner, or his mentorship of Brian Cashman. I can't tell you whether he belongs in the Hall of Fame or not. I'm sure there are many obituaries that adequately cover his great impact on the Yankees from his playing days through the present day. That's just not the column I can write.

What I can do is talk about the Stick Michael I knew and admired, the generous man who frequently hung around the Trenton ballpark in his semi-retirement in recent years. Earlier this year I talked about the types of people you run into at the ballpark who you can glean information from. Something I didn't explicitly mention in that piece, but which is relevant here, is that I often take team executives and even scouts with a huge grain of salt when discussing their own team. My natural assumption is that they're working me; I'm media, after all, and baseball men have been working the media about their own players as long as there have been baseball men and media.

I ran into Stick every now and then in Trenton, in the press box or scout section. I don't exactly remember when the first time we met was other than "earlier this decade," but I remember he just appeared in the row behind me at a game and inserted himself into a conversation about whether 65 was a legitimate grade to give a player on speed. (The answer: yes, if the player is consistently right below 4.1 from the left or 4.2 from the right, but not scraping 4.0/4.1.)

We would talk about baseball and Yankees prospects and the weather and ballpark food, not because I was anyone special but because Stick would move around the park and talk to literally everyone about those things. Well, mostly he'd talk and I'd shut the hell up and listen, because a large chunk of what he said was absolute gold—the type of baseball education you can only get from someone like Stick Michael, even if only a few minutes at a time. Never once did I get the feeling that he was working me to hype a Yankee, and never once did he give me information on a player that did not verify. A few times he pointed me in a direction that ended up being way ahead of the curve, by showing me something that a player was or was not doing such that it sharpened my ability to spot similar in the future. If you've read and enjoyed my thoughts about prospects and baseball over the two seasons I've been writing at BP, know that they were greatly informed by talking to Stick out at the park.

When I'm asked about how to learn how to develop an eye for baseball, my response is usually "watch a lot of baseball at different levels from behind the plate, and talk about it all with a lot of people smarter than you." If there's a smarter person about baseball scouting than Stick Michael in this world, I've yet to meet them, and I've met an awful lot of incredibly smart baseball folks. And he'd hold court in a section for a few innings or a round of batting practice or even just a couple minutes in the press box, and then he'd move on to the next cluster of scouts, writers, and assorted other well-wishers. It once hit me that Stick couldn't possibly have known everyone who he talked to at these games, and I suspect he couldn't have picked me out of a police lineup outside of the ballpark. But he treated everyone like a friend, as generous with his time as any major figure in the game I've ever interacted with.

I hadn't seen Stick in a few months, because his minor-league haunt was Trenton and I was mostly covering Lakewood during the second half of the 2017 season. Trenton lost most of its top prospects by July to promotion or trade, whereas Lakewood picked up Arquimedes Gamboa and Adam Haseley, and frankly we've had more coverage needs late in the season at BP for the South Atlantic League than the Eastern League. Lakewood's season ended on Sunday, though, and Trenton comes home for the EL playoffs today. I'll be attending as much of Trenton's playoff run as I can, and just a few days ago I remarked to a friend that I was hoping to see Stick out at the park this weekend. Instead I expect I'll be watching a tribute to him.

In that weird way that you associate people with small stories, I will always associate Stick Michael with Mini Melts ice cream—you know, the little flash-frozen ice cream balls/

Dippin' Dots knock-off mostly consumed by small children for an immediate sugar high. Stick absolutely loved the Mini Melts at the Trenton ballpark. He would often skip a half-inning to go get a cup, and more than a couple times, he offered to buy me and whomever else was around a cup. I never took him up on it, and I always chuckled at the thought of a legitimate Hall of Fame candidate scout and executive being so excited for, of all things, a Dippin' Dots clone. But that was Stick Michael.

Farewell, Stick, and thanks for all the lessons and tips. The next cup of Mini Melts is on me. ▩

The Best of All Possible Jeffrey Leonards

by Patrick Dubuque

> *Jeffrey Leonard once went 1-for-3 in a single at-bat, raising the troublesome question asked by Patrick Dubuque: Did Leonard bat once or three times?* – Geoff Y.

Consider all the things you know about former All-Star and Rookie of the Year runner-up Jeffrey Leonard. Conjure his heavy-lidded frown into your mind. Remember his pejorative, self-accepted nicknames, HacMan and Penitentiary Face; summon the mental GIF of him loping around the bases on a solo home run, one flap down. Remember a man who spent 14 years in the major leagues and battled it to a draw.

Consider all this, and then consider that Jeffrey Leonard holds a forgotten and potentially unbreakable baseball record, one that you will never find in Cooperstown, or Baseball Reference, or even his own SABR biography. The only place you might find it, if you were so inclined, is on page 117 of the paperback *Official Baseball Guide of 1980*, published by The Sporting News.

Jeffrey Leonard is the only baseball player in recorded history to go 1-for-3 in a single at-bat.

⚾   ⚾   ⚾

The situation: August 21, 1979. Bottom of the ninth inning, Astros down 5-0 to the Mets, bases empty, two outs. Garbage time, except for Pete Falcone, who was working on a shutout. Leonard lifted a lazy fly to center field; Lee Mazzilli caught it with two hands, and the ballgame was over.

The remaining fans stood and filed out, the familiar postgame music sang from tinny speakers, the players headed toward their dugouts. Only, it wasn't over. Before the pitch, Mets shortstop Frank Taveras, seeing a pebble on the infield or a loose shoelace or a glint underneath the eyelids of Jeff Leonard, called time, and the third-base umpire had granted it. So the music stopped, the fielders were called back out of the dugout, and thousands of departing fans were left wondering why baseball was still being played.

Yet play they did, and this time our hero redeemed himself by singling to left. As he rounded first, both teams made a sudden discovery: There was no one there. First baseman Ed Kranepool was in the tunnel, wondering where all his teammates were. This time the Mets appealed, and Leonard was forced to bat yet again, with first base manned. He went to left again, but this time with too much air. The catch was made, and this time the game really was over.

Only, again, it wasn't. The Giants protested the game, and the league found in their favor; Kranepool was given his notice, teams were instructed to play ball, and the Mets willingly pitched. So they had to restart the game the next night, already in progress, with Leonard back at first and the tying run still a batter away from being in the hole. Jose Cruz immediately grounded out and the game was over, truly. It was a matter of two minutes. The only victim was Falcone, who couldn't finish his own start 24 hours later, and was denied the shutout.

⚾   ⚾   ⚾

Did Leonard have one at-bat or three? The answer is both, really. Only one at-bat is official, but the other two happened, and not only happened but did so under the most realistic possible circumstances, with every player on the field thinking that they were just as real.

It's an interesting thing. No other sport willingly discards its actual history the way baseball does. Phil Bradley hit the first night homer at Wrigley Field, until it rained in the fourth and suddenly he hadn't anymore. Mitch Moreland was probably given the ball after his first grand slam in 2011; one wonders what he did with it after his achievement got nullified. Extra innings are counted despite the fact that they aren't equal opportunity, and many records are set or lost based on that randomized extra opportunity. It's even more dramatic in football and basketball, where single-game numbers are more constant and the extra time of play skews numbers past generally recognized benchmarks.

It seems a little strange that we allow one but not the other, rare as the latter is. Sure, I get it. We don't count aborted games because we never have, and baseball is nothing if not bound by its past. It'd be impossible to go back and reestablish statistics based on hearsay and newspaper accounts, and it'd be a nightmare if doing so actually changed something, altered a batting title or a tiny fraction of legacy.

I always think about the opposite situation, however. Imagine a 43-year-old Rickey Henderson, starting in left field on the final day of the 2001 season. It's unclear whether he has a job next year, or ever; he has a 102 wRC+ with the Padres that year, but unfortunately for him wRC+ hasn't been invented yet, and batting average has. Henderson leads off the bottom of the first the same way, a flare near the right-field line 30 feet behind first for a double. The team pours out and crowds around him, Henderson hoists the plaque. And then it rains. And rains. There's no makeup game; the TV schedule for the playoffs has been set. Henderson heads to Newark with 2,999 hits, and waits for a call that never comes.

It's a drastic example, an almost impossible one. But this is the problem with a game so often built on soft rules: They always get tested, in the moments when we suddenly, desperately care about the milliseconds and millimeters.

As baseball's knowledge, its tools, and its computing power expand, the primary limit to the granularity of baseball data is what we bother to count. It still drives me a little crazy that we don't discern between pickoffs and caught stealing, and incorporate the former into a pitcher's sum defensive contribution. It's strange that we count fouls on a granular level but that there's no easily searchable Foul% statistic. We don't even track skypoints. We have enough people who enjoy baseball that we could create a modern Project Scoresheet for skypointing.

There's a good reason we don't have these: because counting statistics is demanding, exhausting work. It's something that needs to be paid for, and so we generally get numbers for things that are worth money, i.e.. wins. But maybe, at least for Jeffrey Leonard, it's time to reconsider. Back in 1980, statistics were largely descriptive, and very concerned with officiality. Now, in the era of evaluative statistics, Leonard's two outs, made under perfect baseball-like conditions, are every bit as meaningful as the single he gets credit for. If Billy Hamilton somehow hits a 480-foot home run in the first inning of a rained-out game, that feat should absolutely be factored into projecting his future performance; it'd be insane not to.

You could claim that this is trivial, and it is. But when it comes to history, I tend to mistrust the single monopolistic voice. If Phil Bradley tells me he hit 79 home runs instead of 78, I'm not going to argue with him. ▪

Reliably Stable (You Keep Using That Word)

by Russell A. Carleton

Russell A. Carleton revisits one of his old studies that showed the point at which player statistics stabilize within a season and urges people to avoid reaching faulty conclusions based on misunderstandings of said study. – Geoff Y.

It's been a surprising season for (name of player) so far. The (team) (position) has put up (adjective) numbers so far and is one of the reasons his team is (record). In the offseason, (name) worked with (name of famous trainer) on (new trick). "I made it a point in spring training to really work on (new trick) and to (action) (adverb)."

The early results have been (breathless adjective). As of last night, (name) has put up a (numbers) stat line and the question that everyone in (city) is wondering is whether he can keep it up. Are we seeing a new (name)?

There's evidence that the answer is yes! Ten years ago a pseudonymous Internet hack who called himself (auxiliary kitchen utensil) wrote an article which detailed the point at which certain statistics "stabilize."[1] We're not at the point in the season where things like OBP or ERA are stable, but there are certain indicators about a player that are reaching that stability point.

(Name) has a (stat) of (number) percent compared to his (number) rate from last year, and *that* statistic tends to stabilize more quickly than other stats. In fact (auxiliary kitchen utensil) work suggests that it's *enough* to say that he really is a changed man from last year. So (team) fans, the outlook is (adjective) for this year going forward, at least for (name). I'm not saying print the World Series tickets now, but do get the printer warming up.

⚾ ⚾ ⚾

Ahem.

YOU
ARE
DOING
IT
ALL
WRONG.
(Don't worry. I have too.)

Warning! Gory Mathematical Details Ahead!

We need to talk about what "stabilize" means, and the details are *really* important. You keep using that word, but I don't think it means what you think it means.

When I wrote that original article 10 (!) years ago, I wanted to answer a specific question. If I wanted to see, for example, whether walk rate was correlated with something else over some period of time, I obviously couldn't have batters in my sample with five plate appearances. I needed some empirical way to set my filter for PA > X. Reliability analysis is perfect for that sort of thing.

Reliability analysis answers the question *I see that Smith has had 100 PA this year and a walk rate of X. If I were to go back in time and give Smith another 100 PA **in the same basic circumstances**, how confident would I be that he would reproduce the same performance?*

We express that level of confidence in the language of a correlation. Now, I can't really go back in time and have a batter repeat the same set of circumstances, but I can do the next best thing. I can take a sample of 200 PA that he really did have and split it into two equal parts. Perhaps I can take the even-numbered and odd-numbered PA in that sample, so that I can get some PA from the same day or against the same pitcher in each basket. (Mathematically, I can do something even better using a technique known as Cronbach's alpha, but the idea is pretty much the same.)

I looked for the point where the reliability estimate/correlation crossed .70, because at that point, the R-squared is (just shy of) 50 percent. We have accounted for 50 percent of the variance just by keeping the batter and the

---

1. https://statspeakmvn.wordpress.com/2007/11/14/525600-minutes-how-do-you-measure-a-player-in-a-year/

circumstances (roughly) the same. That's helpful, because it allows me to say "within that timeframe, I can have pretty good confidence that Smith's performance really *was* (past tense) consistent with his true talent level."

There's nothing magical about .70. Any line between "reliable" and "not reliable" has a bit of arbitrariness to it. The only thing that .70 has going for it is that it's the point where the majority of the R-squared is accounted for by factors that are "endogenous." It's not a perfect method, but it's the best that we're going to do without a time machine. And I'm fresh out of time machines, because honestly, if I had one, I would go back and tell myself not to hit "publish" on that article.

Five years ago, I published another article in which I said this:[2]

> The generally accepted "stability numbers" chart is a good chart for researchers who are doing retrospective research. I think it's also a good one to look at in terms of understanding which stats stabilize more quickly relative to others, which I think can show us some interesting truths about the game. However, I would kindly point out that they are not nearly as powerful in predicting future performance as people seem to believe that they are.

The problem with using that chart as some sort of indicator of *future* performance is that it's asking something of the chart that it was never intended to do.

In that same article, I looked at strikeout rate, which "stabilizes" (according to the chart) at 60 PA. The problem is that most people use the 60 PA threshold in a way that fundamentally changes the question that's being asked. Instead of asking "what would happen if I gave a batter 60 more PA in the same basic circumstances?" it becomes "what would happen if I gave him 60 more PA in a **completely different set of circumstances**?" He's older than he was in the first 60. He??s facing a different set of pitchers. He may have made a change in his approach or maybe he has a nagging injury now that he didn't have back then (or maybe he has healed a bit since those last 60).

It turns out that when you look at *sequential* blocks of 60 PA for strikeout rate, you get correlations around .50 (which means an R-squared of 25 percent). That's not a horrible correlation, but let's put that in context. Using the split-half method, where the two baskets of plate appearances were drawn from the same games, I was able to get a correlation of .70 (and R-squared of 50 percent). By using a method where we kept the batter the same, but can't assume that the circumstances of those plate appearances were the same,

we lost half of our R-squared from when we were keeping the circumstances (roughly) the same. That means that the circumstances are *as important as the batter's talent level.*

If the question that you want to know is "how good is Smith, going forward, and how well does his performance to date predict his future performance?" then you can't use the old chart, at least if you plan on using my arbitrary cutoff of .70 for when the reliability coefficient hits "stability."

We could do the sort of analysis where we look at sequential blocks of plate appearances and look to see how long it takes to get back to a reliability estimate (this time, we can use straight up Pearson correlation) of .70. For strikeouts, it happens a little bit after 150 PA, rather than the 60 PA on the original chart. So, to feel safe that a player's performance is stable, you either have to wait longer into the season or you have to live with a lower threshold for "reliable." Your pick.

But even then, we need to deal with a couple of other issues. There are two major assumptions that go along with "he's been good in his first X plate appearances (and X is "enough!"), therefore, we can expect this from him the rest of the way!" One is that his body of work in April is still going to hold in September. If a batter has struck out 20 percent of the time in his first 60 PA, it's reasonable to assume (knowing nothing else) that in his 61st PA, he has a 20 percent chance of striking out, but would that hold in his 461st?

I again used strikeout rate as my bellwether, looking at all player seasons from 2012 to 2016 that had a minimum of 480 PA in them. The reason for 480 was that I created eight sequential blocks of 60 PA (that is, PAs 1-60, 61-120, 121-180, etc.) I then looked to see how well strikeout rate in those first 60 PA correlated with strikeout rate in the next set of 60 PA. And then how well the first and *third* sets correlated. And then first and fourth, and on down the line.

The answer, in a bit of a surprise, is that all of the blocks correlated with the early-season block at a correlation around .50 (not exactly, of course, but it was within .48 to .52 each time.) I ran a second batch of the same analyses, this time with walks, and found the same basic thing. Early-season performance is correlated with performance through the rest of the season at roughly the same rate. So, we've at least cleared that hurdle.

But there's another assumption lurking in all of this that we need to call out. Past performance is a good predictor of future performance … until it isn't. In fact, when these early-season "no really, it's stable!" articles are written, they're usually written about players who have had conspicuous changes in their performance. No one bothers to write the article that "Mike Trout is having an amazing season so far and, well, that's basically what he's done for the last five

---

2. http://www.baseballprospectus.com/article.php?articleid=17742

years, so we're not surprised, but hey, we've reached the point of stability, so we're pretty sure Mike Trout is still awesome."

Why do people write articles about a player who has clearly made some sort of big change, and then assume that because we've hit some magical point in the season, he will never change again? Sure, if it's working, he'll probably want to keep his new approach, but people backslide into bad habits all the time. Maybe some other change will come along and undo all the good that the first change did.

There's a fascination with stats that "stabilize quickly" because there's not a lot to write about numbers-wise early in the season without sounding silly. Quick-stabilizing stats offer a chance to talk about the numbers without having to hear the dreaded "but it's a small sample size" comment. Usually, the stats that stabilize most quickly are the ones that are more tightly in the control of the player himself. Swing rate is a good one, because the batter is the one who decides whether he will swing or not. (What happens when he does swing involves a complicated series of bounces, which may or may not go his way.)

Well, that sword cuts two ways. If the batter is more fully in charge of the decision that the statistic represents, there is a danger that he will simply start making different decisions tomorrow, which will render false our idea that we now have enough information to know deep secrets of his soul. People are constantly growing and changing. We don't live in a steady-state universe.

We also need to ask whether X PA, even once we adjust for all of the aforementioned issues, is a good cutoff for *all* hitters (or pitchers). For example, are older hitters more likely to show inconsistency over time? Are low-contact hitters more likely to show variance in their strikeout rate? We know that certain players tend to show marked variations in their abilities over the course of a season.[3] Maybe there are certain types of players who are just more given to change over time. That particular area has gone largely unstudied (oddly enough, outside of aging curves, which have plenty of work done on them).

All Statistics Face Backwards

A statistic is a reflection of what a player has done in the past. It is an assumption that he will continue to do the same in the future. It might not even be a bad assumption, but it's an assumption and as we've seen today, a methodologically shaky one. Sometimes players really do change for the better (or the worse), but if we're going to do real research, we need a more solid approach to the question.

I get the love for "quick-stabilizing" stats, and maybe we'll eventually find that some of them really do stabilize quickly, or we'll find some mark which portends stability, but I think that for 10 years, this chart and this idea of quick-stabilizing stats and the assumptions that the idea implies have gone critically unexamined. That's a problem.

Please, in the season's first few weeks, resist the urge to pull out that 10-year-old table (or the updates I made to it five years ago) and write the Mad-Lib article at the beginning of this column. You keep using that word, "stabilize." I don't think it means what you think it means. ▨

---

3. http://www.baseballprospectus.com/article.php?articleid=22831

Welcoming Instructional Design Into Player Development

by Bryan Grosnick

Bryan Grosnick wonders why we don't use the same data-driven approach to player development that we use in analyzing and improving other parts of the game, and offers suggestions on how we might start to do so. – Geoff Y.

The things that we, the public, know about baseball in 2017 are truly staggering. With Statcast we can measure launch angle and exit velocity. With PITCHf/x and Brooks Baseball we can figure out which slider has the most break, who repeats their release point the best, and nearly every tiny data point about the flight of a pitch. With Baseball Prospectus, Baseball-Reference, FanGraphs, Retrosheet, and more we have the most comprehensive dataset of player performance and statistical analysis in the history of athletic endeavor.

But what do we *really* know about how a player like Matt Carpenter goes from 13th-round pick to superstar, why a talent like Brandon Wood never succeeds, or how a leg kick and a change of mind transform some players into superstars while others see no shift at all? I'm not certain there's any part of baseball that's less understood in the public sphere than player development. Each franchise employs a dedicated, highly trained staff to assist players in reaching their potential and improving their skills. From coaching in instructs all the way up to the majors, conditioning and training specialists, and even psychological and "mental skills" assistance, teams are putting a huge amount of effort into transforming potential into performance.

When it comes to specifics, that's where things get kind of foggy.

What we in the public sphere don't know much of is exactly *how* teams attempt to do this. Team "ways" are codified in little red books, coaches talk about particular drills from time to time, but player development has hardly the same data available for us to study the way major-league performance or amateur scouting reports do. Some might say player development does not lend itself to "hard" data the same way other facets of the game do, and the unstructured information gets lost out in the ether even when it does slip past a team's web of silence.

As a result, when Josh Donaldson becomes an MVP or Domonic Brown becomes a washout, most of the credit or blame falls to the player himself and his work ethic or makeup. Occasionally the player development apparatus receives a shoutout, but more often than not we'll chalk it up to the luck of the draw. After all, it's incredibly difficult to separate the work of the player from that of the organization in one-on-one cases, isn't it?

While some teams gain reputations as player development hotbeds—the Cardinals and Giants and, um, ... well, I'm sure there's someone else!—player development comes across as a bit of a black box in terms of what works and what doesn't, what teams do and what they don't, and how to measure success other than World Series championships.

I think we can start to fix that.

In November 2015 Russell A. Carleton wrote a call to start looking deeper at player development from an analytical standpoint.[1] It was a great article in which he asked why folks don't apply the same rigor and data-driven research to the world of player development that they do to major-league performance, or scouting, or the other parts of the game.

I don't exactly picture myself riding in on a white horse to answer these questions, but I do think that I have a unique perspective on how this can and should be done. In addition to being interested in (read: obsessed with) baseball and sabermetrics, it so happens that in my day job I'm what's called an "instructional designer." And instructional designers could be a bridge between player development and the systematic approaches that made sabermetrics so valuable.

Instructional designers like myself specialize in learning, and how people learn. Some of us came up from training and HR backgrounds and fell face-first into the field looking

---

1. http://www.baseballprospectus.com/article.php?articleid=27855

for answers. Others carry advanced degrees in "Instructional Systems" or "Instructional Technology"—degrees that come with a background in educational psychology, systems thinking, and business.

Our jobs are, usually, to create training that does what it's supposed to do. Instructional designers design training programs and implement them, usually in business, higher education, or military fields. We use our backgrounds in educational psychology, adult learning, and communication to facilitate the acquisition of knowledge, skills, and attitudes (k/s/a for short) in learners. That certainly includes skills that apply to baseball, from physical skills like throwing motions to cognitive skills like knowing how enormous of a lead to take on Jon Lester.[2]

Instructional designers facilitate learning systematically, accounting for as many of the variables as we can that go into something as opaque as learning—trust me, there are a lot of them. But by designing instruction in a way that's systematic, formal, and based on best practices, we can develop interventions that work, that are repeatable, and that allow the measurement of success.

Training and learning without instructional design is like baking a cake without a recipe. Sometimes you try it and everything turns out fine. Sometimes you're left with a giant pile of scrambled eggs and sugar, wondering what the hell just happened.

A good instructional designer does a few things that separate him or her from your average coach or teacher—the "design" aspect of the job description. A great instructional designer works in concert with subject-matter experts like the top-tier coaches and analysts that teams already employ, and they allow for those people's wisdom and experience to be used in the best, most efficient possible way. This allows for structure, repeatability, and reliability.

Instructional design concepts are many, and far too involved to discuss in depth in a short article. But there are a couple to discuss on a broad scale that could apply some real value to the worlds of player development and/or coaching.

Objective-Based Design

More than anything else in training design, I believe in the power of structured, defined, performance-based objectives. It is quite a bit harder to reach your end goal when you're not sure what that goal is, or when you set a goal that is out of your control. A budding young outfielder may say, "I want to become a better baseball player." A number 3 starter might say, "I want to pitch well enough to get Cy Young votes."

Those are wonderful, admirable goals but not useful learning objectives. There are three major qualities that make for a good learning objective: It must be *specific*, *measurable*, and *observable*. By creating objectives that meet these three criteria, you train to an endpoint, rather than entering the world of guesswork. A player stating his desire to raise his batting average by 20 points is terrific, but even that's not a true performance goal. It relies too much on the work of others, and doesn't demonstrate a specific behavior in the same way another objective might.

Saying that you want to know when to swing at fastballs is good, too, but you can't observe that the learner has acquired that skill. On the other hand, stating that a player wants to lower his swing rate by 10 percent on pitches that are below the strike zone or decrease his throwing errors by 20 percent in the upcoming season can be effective high-level performance objectives. Those are things that you can observe and measure, and that are specific enough to judge success or failure.

Terminal vs. Enabling Objectives

The next step is taking those high-level objectives and turning them into smaller, more manageable steps. In the business, we call those smaller steps *enabling objectives* that help build toward our final goal or *terminal objective*. Without them, learning can look a lot like the old South Park joke about the elves that steal underwear:

1. Steal underwear
2. ???
3. Profit!!

As we all know, the middle stuff matters. Nevertheless, without design, that's how some people approach training or performance gaps. They start with an end goal "get better at baseball" and then try to get there without really breaking down what that means—systematically—into the smallest possible units.

Over at Statistically Speaking, Carleton went about this process from a mathematical perspective back in 2009.[3] It's the right idea, but done in a different way than I would do it. I'd start from an instructional design perspective. Let's say our end goal is a good one: Gonny Jomes wants to be a better defender by improving his range in left field—and he wants to record more putouts as proof. How could we break that down into manageable parts to help him achieve this objective?

It requires a lot of research, but the quick-and-dirty answer is that you spend a lot of time doing task analysis on what the aspects of range are. You may be able to improve your range by running faster, but you may be able to improve your range by taking a more direct path to a hit ball. You may be able

---

2. If you're wondering just how many and how varied baseball skills are, here's a piece documenting just how many types of baseball learning exist: http://www.baseballprospectus.com/article.php?articleid=29599

3. https://statspeakmvn.wordpress.com/2009/02/03/the_measure_of_a_man_or_10_things_i_didnt_know_about_you/

to improve your range by getting a better jump on the ball. So right there, you have three enabling objectives that tie to your terminal objective.

But that's not enough either. Let's look at the "run faster" objective, which we can make a good performance objective by restating as "increase my running speed when running toward a ball in play in left field." There are a couple of ways that this can be addressed. You can increase acceleration, and get up to a top speed faster. You can increase top speed, so that once you do accelerate your overall speed is better.

It may take some time, but I'd drill down to the smallest possible unit of behavior that you can test ... one of them in this case might be something like "given the crack of the bat, take a first step in the appropriate direction 95 percent of the time" or "given the crack of the bat, take a first step in under one second 90 percent of the time." Then we build from there.

Of course, it's important to keep in mind that some aspects of physical skill building can't be broken down into teachable skills. At some point, physical talents and limitations come into play—we can't just insist that Jeff Mathis swing the bat as hard as Bryce Harper does. So part of the overall process is separating the things we can train from the things we can't, and focusing on the former. But there's more that we can change than you might think! There are also costs and opportunities to training initiatives, so there's a complex set of circumstances in place. The goal is to find and train the ones with the biggest and best returns. And data can help us do that.

Instructional design is just one way that we can try to apply principles from the worlds of business or science to sports. And judging from what I've heard from league sources, teams *are* beginning to move in this direction with psychology specialists working on mental skills and performance enhancement. Beyond instructional design, there are other outsider, quasi-analytical concepts that lend themselves to player development: human performance technology, design theory, and human resources. By casting an analytical eye on what goes into player development, new avenues of success could open up. Finally cracking just a piece of the player development code—can we find a systematic way to improve player skills across a significant sample?—could be a very big thing, especially for the first team to find a way to make it work.

Special thanks to Russell A. Carleton and Rob Neyer for assistance with this piece.

TIDES Report: Gender and Race in MLB

by Kate Morrison

> *Kate Morrison reports that Major League Baseball hasn't been great at hiring women and people of color, which ultimately hurts the sport, as the best candidates for a job are often overlooked.* – Geoff Y.

In April, The Institute for Diversity and Ethics in Sport (TIDES) released its 2017 report card for Major League Baseball's hiring and employment practices regarding racial and gender diversity. When grading MLB, TIDES looks at a variety of positions at the league level, the team level, and the organization itself, including the makeup of on-field or field-related staff as well as executives.

Its findings were not surprising to anyone who has been following the recent news cycles around hiring within Major League Baseball. While the league itself (specifically, the commissioner's office, MLB Advanced Mecia, and MLB Network) scored the highest in both racial and gender diversity, the gender diversity number specifically dropped from 2016. On a team level, the gender diversity situation was even worse, with senior team administration receiving a D+ and professional administration a C-.

If we break these numbers down further, and look at how many of the women filling 27 percent of the "team senior administration" and 28.1 percent of the "team professional administration" roles are in positions that are—while incredibly important to the health of the team as a business—not related to the product on the field, the world is even bleaker. TIDES provides a breakdown of every woman and person of color in these senior roles, and the list of women only has six out of 82 women in roles that could be considered to have an impact on-field (athletic trainers, coaches, or scouts), and two of these are general "vice president" positions, with two others being "general partner" roles.[1]

When we look at the 28 percent of women employed in "professional administration roles," we have to take into account that TIDES includes specialists, technicians, analysts, engineers, and programmers alongside "assistant managers, coordinators, supervisors, and administrators in business operations such as marketing, promotions, publications, and various other departments." When restricted to, again, roles that directly impact the product on the field, that 28 percent is almost certainly much lower.

While MLB overall scored a B for racially diverse hiring practices in 2017, this again represented a falling off from its score in 2016—somehow, in a single year, the league lost 8.5 points off its TIDES-given score. People of color fill 44.3 percent of coaching roles, but as we know, only three current MLB managers are men of color. The league office employs the next-highest level of people of color in all positions, at 28.1 percent, with the teams falling off steeply from that—only 11.7 percent of vice president or equivalent positions.

What Does This All Mean?

If you're still with us after the preceding stats textbook case study, how does this affect the baseball community, down to individual blogs? After all, the report only states what we already knew, just in greater detail. Baseball in general is terrible at the hiring and promoting of women and people of color.

Recently, R.J. Anderson of CBS Sports wrote about "baseball's next Moneyball," which he considers to be the hiring of front-office personnel (specifically, scouts) from various public-facing websites such as BaseballProspectus.com.[2] A notable presence missing from

---

1. The last thing I want to do is imply that the other 78 women employed in vice president or equivalent roles are not important to their clubs. Their work is vital to the success of baseball—but Baseball Prospectus is not AdAge, a law review, or Fast Company. We deal with the game itself, for the most part.

his piece?[3] Women. If, as Anderson's piece suggests, public evaluation and analysis sites are being used as a kind of development system for front offices to pluck from, then the overwhelming white maleness of our websites is part of the root of the problem, not just a symptom of it.

The Baseball Prospectus article "The Perils of MLB's Sorting System" dove deep into this problem, and found that a great deal of the lack of diversity can be related back to the traditional entry points into the front office—the internship system, which creates a need for both financial security and in-league connections.[4] Now that baseball writing, or public-facing evaluation, seems to be something that teams are attempting to use as a development system for their future hirees, it would seem that more doors are open—and yet the numbers have gotten worse across the board.

This is due to the lack of women and people of color writing in an analytics or evaluation capacity for mainstream sites. The question, then, is: How do we more effectively reach a broader base with opportunities for mentorship, exposure, and potential advancement in the world of baseball? A lot of baseball writers come out of team-specific communities. How can we reach into these communities and find talented people there? How can we encourage an environment where these people will flourish?

This particular point is made more difficult by the fact that a good number of team-based communities are either indifferent or actively hostile toward their female fans, in particular, and this part of the culture is not limited to those communities. It's hard to find women writing about baseball when those women are inherently treated as something lesser—when the default is to assume that they don't know those jobs.

The only way any of this will be solved—the lack of inclusion of both women and people of color—is through concerted effort. Both the league and these outside sites must find, hire, and develop anyone with an interest. This isn't easy. It takes actual effort to find people, instead of just relying on the hundreds of résumés that pour in for every hiring call, but it's a much-needed effort. MLB's nascent support of women's baseball is a step in the right direction for increasing the gender diversity of its on-field staff, but these girls are at most 16 years old, meaning that we can't expect to truly see the results of these experiments for nearly a decade.

Both sides of the equation are playing chicken, seeing who will "solve" diversity—particularly gender diversity—first. Women don't write about baseball (in general) because they don't grow up playing it, or when they try, they are excluded and discouraged from roles that men are welcomed into with mentors and open arms. If there were more women in baseball decision-making roles, perhaps there would be more women writing about them. If there were more women writing about baseball decisions, perhaps there'd be more women in those important roles.[5] Too many people don't know that a front-office career path is something they could even consider, or are pushed away from baseball before they can make that discovery.

It's 2017. It's time to do better. After all of this, one thing is clear. All the report cards in the world are only so much finger wagging if MLB, and the community in general, doesn't actually make an effort to change things. If we do make this effort, it will only be for the best. The highest quality work comes out of having a wide pool of viewpoints, experiences, and opinions from which to draw, and baseball as a whole will only benefit from the highest quality work possible. ▨

---

2. http://www.cbssports.com/mlb/news/baseballs-next-moneyball-concept-turning-internet-writers-into-prospect-scouts/

3. This isn't to say that Anderson excluded women deliberately, but that there are few to include.

4. http://www.baseballprospectus.com/article.php?articleid=29576

5. This also goes for more writers of color, especially women writers of color. Baseball has a lot of problems it's not really open to discussing.

Graveman Comes to Grip with His Destiny

by David Brown

David Brown talks to Kendall Graveman about his nasty sinker and the coach who taught him how to throw it when he was an eighth-grade kid at baseball camp. – Geoff Y.

KANSAS CITY, Missouri — Kendall Graveman struggled at first to remember the name of the man who taught him the grip for his best pitch, a sinking fastball. It's kind of a funny story, learning to grip what has become one of the most effective pitches in the majors, from a man who today coaches the hitters for a junior-college softball team, who also in part learned about the importance of finger strength from conversations with a national-champion arm wrestler. It all sounds so over the top, but it's true: You just never know how wisdom will get passed along between generations.

About the coach's name. After being given a moment to think, does Graveman remember?

"I do …" Graveman said, his face grimacing as the mental wheels turned. "I don't. It was at Central Alabama Community College. Heck, he may still be there. It's a junior college in my hometown.

"We didn't have a lot of connections in Alexander City."

Sometimes, one good connection is all you need. At 13 years old, Graveman had little clue when his dad enrolled him at a baseball camp run by CACC that it would lead to the first big break of Graveman's baseball career. Regardless, being a polite and thoughtful kid, Graveman paid attention to the instructors in the event he might learn something.

Boy, did he.

"We were just messing around in the outfield," Graveman said. "I was in the eighth grade. It was me and a bunch of my friends. We were just having a good time, and he's teaching us to do a few things and he says, 'Hey, throw it like this. Grip it.' He has us all in a group and he says, 'This is how you can throw a sinker.'

"So I said, 'OK,' and I started doing it. I believed him. And I just continued to throw it and, naturally, you throw it enough that it starts to feel comfortable. Now, being able to repeat that grip and repeat that delivery is something that has come in handy."

Now 26, Graveman has been repeating himself a lot lately for the Athletics, who traded slugger Josh Donaldson to the Blue Jays to acquire him, infielder Brett Lawrie, top prospect Franklin Barreto, and another player after the 2014 season. So far, it has been a deal most analysts prefer for the Jays, who have gotten two dominant seasons from Donaldson and, not coincidentally, two playoff berths. Ever since the middle of 2016, the A's have been encouraged by Graveman's progress, but now he's showing indications of being able to dominate. And it's because of his sinker.

In his second start of 2017, Graveman took a no-hitter against the Rangers into the seventh inning. Of the 85 pitches he threw Saturday night, Brooks Baseball reports that 93 percent of them were the same kind—a fastball thrown with a modified two-seam grip that makes the ball sink. But 93 percent? Who throws the same pitch 93 percent of the time and survives? Mariano Rivera and his cut fastball are retired and waiting for induction to Cooperstown. Even Bartolo Colon thoroughly mixes his mostly fastball regimen with two-seamers and four-seamers.

Less so with Graveman. Much less. In his first start of the season, which came with Opening Day honors, he threw sinkers 84 percent of the time. That sinking feeling is definitely a trend. It's also been a long time coming. Graveman has known ever since the baseball camp 13 years ago that the sinker was his best pitch. He just didn't always remember to use what coach Steve Lewis taught him.

Something clicked in Graveman's brain and his eyes opened wide.

"Oh, Lew!" Graveman burst out. "His name was Lew. Coach Lew. I told you I'd remember!"

Steve Lewis also remembers Graveman, whom he later tried to recruit for Central Alabama knowing that he'd probably take a better offer, which he got—from Mississippi State, pretty much the gold standard in college baseball.

Toronto drafted Graveman in the eighth round in 2013 and promoted him late the following season, just before the trade.

As Graveman intuited, Lewis still works for CACC, only he's not the baseball team's pitching coach any longer after 15 seasons. He's in his first season as the batting coach for the softball team, which is working on a 30-win season. Lewis said that switching sports was inspired, in part, by having a 9-year-old daughter who plays softball. CCAC baseball, now run by Larry Thomas, won the NJCAA national championship in 2013, and had a number of All-American pitchers with Lewis as an assistant. But he coaches hitters now?

"I couldn't tell anyone the first thing about softball pitching," Lewis said in a phone interview.

Lewis, 50, might not have seemed like much of a baseball connection to Graveman when he was an adolescent, but his résumé—even pre-Central Alabama—tells another story. Lewis coached in Australia in 1998 through MLB's International Envoy Program after coaching at various colleges and high schools. A decade before, he was on the staff of the Braves' Double-A team in Greenville, Sout Carolina.

Those teams in 1989-1990 included the likes of future major leaguers Steve Avery, Mike Stanton, Turk Wendell, and Mark Wohlers. Greenville's pitching coach was Bill Slack, now a Canadian Baseball Hall of Famer. Lewis recalls going to spring training and learning from the Triple-A pitching coach at the time, Leo Mazzone. Lewis' professional influences were nonpareil, as they were in college.

Lewis tried to walk on the Auburn baseball team as a freshman, but after he got cut coach Hal Baird made him a student assistant for four years. Auburn's rosters included Bo Jackson and Frank Thomas, to drop a couple of names. Lewis calls Baird the best pitching mind he's ever been around, recalling that Baird taught the same Graveman two-seamer grip to Scott Sullivan, who went on to pitch in the majors (mostly for the Reds) for parts of 10 seasons.

Lewis, as a coach at Auburn High, also remembers picking the brain of Tim Hudson when he attended Auburn University in the mid-'90s. At CACC, he also coached former major leaguer Brandon Dickson, who now pitches in Japan. Lewis taught him the sinker grip, too.

"If you're a good coach and good educator, you don't stop learning along the way," Lewis said. "I asked a lot of questions, because finding different ways to beat an opponent can only help when you're trying to teach players how to win and do their best."

Lewis didn't want to take credit for Graveman's sinker, but did say he was glad that Graveman remembered him.

"What I added to it was probably very minor," Lewis said. "What's interesting is, guys learn grips and they hold on to 'em, and they bring 'em back out when things aren't going well sometimes."

That was Graveman's issue in mid-2016. The way Graveman remembers it, he was in a jam at Target Field on the Fourth of July. Making his 42nd career major-league start and 16th for the A's that season, he came in with a 4.84 ERA, not the results hoped for. Graveman was doing all right against the Twins in a scoreless game, but they had loaded the bases on a Miguel Sano walk in the fourth inning, putting Max Kepler in position to put up a crooked number.

The count was 1-0, and catcher Stephen Vogt called for time, went to the mound, and told Graveman to stop shaking him off and to start throwing his best pitch. Like, exclusively.

"He said, 'I'm gonna set up in the middle of the plate and you just throw the sinker,' because it had such good movement," Graveman recalled. So he did.

Graveman's first offering was up and caught too much of the plate. A's television analyst Ray Fosse noted that Graveman was lucky Kepler merely fouled it back. Vogt set up again where he said he would and Graveman, who had come in tied for the AL lead in ground-ball double plays, responded with a better pitch—a 93-mph sinker with late movement that Kepler chopped toward second. The A's couldn't turn a double play and the Twins scored to take the lead, but a light bulb illuminated Graveman's world. He started throwing sinkers. A lot of sinkers. At one point, the Twins made nine straight outs on grounders, and they didn't score any more runs that day. With the help of run support and reliever Ryan Dull, who wriggled from another jam later on, the A's won 3-1.

Graveman recalled telling A's ace Sonny Gray afterward, "I was just throwing it down the middle."

Gray, nudging his young teammate along mentally, replied: "Yeah, you should realize that your sinker is good enough to get people out."

Those were enough hints, Graveman thought. From then on, it's been (almost) nothing but sinkers.

"We were like, 'Hey, let's take it to the next game,'" Graveman said of Vogt's tactical shift. "Trust in Vogter."

A's pitching coach Curt Young had been trying to get Graveman to throw more sinkers, to use his best pitch more often. Ultimately, it's something the pitcher just had to realize himself.

"The pitch was so head-and-shoulders above his other stuff," Young said. "There were times in games when he was getting beat with his cutter, really for no reason. He's learned about himself, he's learned what works here. Locating the way he does, with the movement that he has, he understands how hard [the sinker] is to hit. He saw the good results he was getting from this pitch. The pitch works in any situation. He's not going to get beat with another pitch. He's going to get beat with his best."

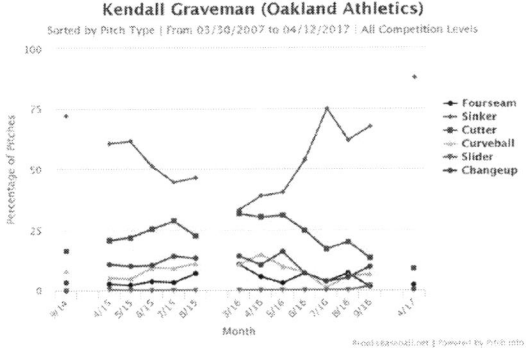

Kendall Graveman (Oakland Athletics)
Sorted by Pitch Type | From 03/30/2007 to 04/12/2017 | All Competition Levels

A pitch he had been throwing 30 or 40 percent of the time became one he was using 60 percent of the time, 70 percent, 80 percent. Results improved. Over the next 12 starts through September 4 (to arbitrarily pick an end point) Graveman posted a 2.82 ERA with a 604 OPS against. He wasn't getting a lot of strikeouts, but he also wasn't letting in runs.

So, can Graveman keep throwing sinkers that often and not only get away with it, but consistently dominate? Manager Bob Melvin, a former catcher, says he can.

"At the big-league level, it's difficult to throw any one pitch as much as Graveman does," Melvin said. "I think everyone tries to rely on their best pitch, but for the most part you can't just throw one pitch and get away with it at the big-league level. He's pretty unique in being able to do that."

Vogt, who caught Colon with the A's in 2012-2013 and is usually behind the plate for Graveman, said Graveman's sinker has a chance to be as good as or better than that of Colon, who is still chucking as he nears age 44. Vogt likes Graveman's other pitches, too; they include a cutter, a changeup, and a curve, all of which were abandoned against the Rangers. Graveman says he's continuing to work on them in bullpen side sessions.

"Yeah, there's a danger [when] you don't change speeds," Graveman said. "We always say that hitting is timing, and that pitching is disrupting timing. That's one thing I'm not doing—disrupting timing—but I'm a firm believer in, no matter what pitch you throw, if you throw it in a good location, you can still get outs. So if you can locate that pitch, then what's the point in throwing another one you can't locate as well? So that's the point I'm at now in my career."

Greg Maddux famously said something like: The best pitch in baseball is a well-placed fastball. He meant that it goes for just about any major-league fastball. Those around Graveman say that his sinker is better than most typical pitches.

"His sinker is one of the best in baseball," Vogt said. "You don't really need much more than that—other than to keep the hitters off it. Everybody in the ballpark knows that a fastball is coming, but when you put it in the right spot, it's tough to square up. I think he could end up being someone in that conversation, with Colon and Rivera, as being someone who has just one plus-plus-plus pitch."

That's a lot of plusses.

Why does Graveman's sinker work so well? What makes it move the way it does? Why do hitters have so much trouble with it when it's right?

"I'm not a scientist by any means, but when the ball is boring down on you in the right place as it crosses the zone, you can't get underneath it as a hitter," Vogt said. "The only way you're going to drive a sinker is if the pitcher makes a mistake."

Melvin said Graveman's sinker can be manipulated into different variations that keep hitters guessing.

"It's a good one pitch," Melvin said. "And it's a sinker that, even if you know it's coming and it's down, it's tough to get any air. But again, it's not just 'one' pitch. To get him off that pitch, you're going to have to make him throw something else. There's uniqueness to different sinkers. If you could teach Kendall's sinker to somebody, if I could tell you exactly what it is, everybody would want to throw it. It's a combination of everything—his arm slot, his leg drive, he's got good lower-half leg drive."

Graveman said the transition to professional baseball has given his time to work on his body and increase the strength in his legs. College pitchers usually throw year-round, he said. Pro baseball players get an opportunity to go 2-3 months without playing games. Using that time to work the weights has given Graveman more endurance, and added a few mph to his fastball.

In 2015, Graveman averaged 91.9 mph on his two-seamer. These days, he throws about 94.6 mph, and his strikeout rate is rising relative to his earlier results. When he throws a sinker, Graveman said he pronates with his hand—bending it forward at the wrist, which he believes helps create movement. In addition to the wrist and the legs, Lewis says Graveman has unusual power somewhere else that gives the sinker more movement: his ring and pinkie fingers.

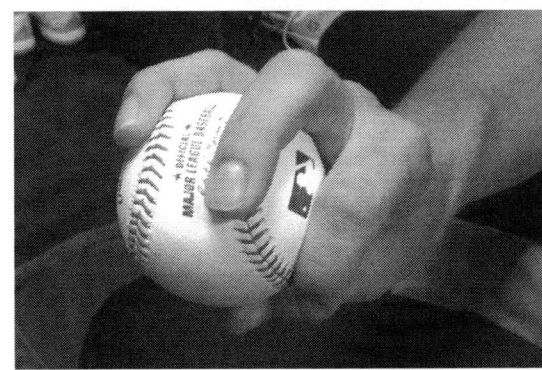

"When you look at that grip he uses, you've got to have strength not only in the first three fingers, in the front half of your hand, but you've got to have a lot of strength in your ring finger and your pinkie finger in the back half of your hand, which is uncommon," Lewis said. "Most people don't have any strength in the back half of their hands, so they can't dominate the ball with the back half of their hand."

How did Lewis come to realize this was important, and that most pitchers are different? From conversations with a national-champion arm wrestler named Tony Bishop, who happens to come from Alexander City, Alabama, like Graveman, and has a daughter on the CACC softball squad. "We got to talking about arm wrestling, what it takes to win there, and he said strength in the other fingers is essential. I realized, 'Hey, it's like he's talking about throwing a changeup'.

"Kendall's two-seam grip that he showed you, he kind of splits the ball with his third and fourth finger, and then he has an equal amount of strength with the other fingers, or at least he has enough, to dominate the ball," Lewis said.

Graveman would like to dominate the league—for more than just a start or two, or for more than a half-season. He might be on his way.

"We had a chance to have Bartolo Colon here, and he basically threw all fastballs," Young said. "And I'd say that formula works when the ball moves as much as Bartolo's did,

and when the ball moves as much as Kendall's does on the same pitch. I think he's learned it's what his strength is, and he's going to stay with it."

Lewis has stayed with Graveman from afar, rooting for the hometown kid who came to his baseball camp, and pleased that he remembers a lesson from long ago.

"It's like, 'Who taught Michael Jordan to dunk?'" Lewis said. "Someone else might get credit for helping him learn, but it's Michael Jordan who did all of the work, who had all of the ability. Kendall has amazing lower-body strength and lower-body explosiveness. And the grips? You just play around with stuff until something comes out of your hand with some movement. It's something we messed around with when he was 13. I might have said to him: 'One day, this might work for you.'"

It's working. And the report from Alexander City on Graveman goes like this:

"Alex City is just abuzz everyday, with him being in the big leagues, and being the Opening Day starter, and everything," Lewis said. "He's in the daily conversation."

Yep. And Graveman's in the conversation with Mariano, Bartolo, and Maddux, too. ▨

Let's Assume the Ball Isn't Juiced

by Russell A. Carleton

> *Recent upward trends in home-run rates have led to some interesting theories, but Russell A. Carleton wonders if maybe hitters are just swinging harder nowadays. – Geoff Y.*

Let's begin by assuming that the ball isn't juiced. Over the past two years, we've seen a rather obvious spike in the home-run rate, such that suddenly Ryan Schimpf and Yonder Alonso are getting mentions in articles about home runs. In 2014, runs scored per game (4.07) had dipped to their *lowest* rate since 1980, and the game, according to people who watch it for a living, had become unwatchable.

In 2017, thanks in large part to the aforementioned spike in the home-run rate—they're being hit at a rate around the all-time high set in 2000—runs are back in fashion. The 2016 season featured a home-run rate that was just off the all-time record set in 2000, and as of the time I write this, if the 2017 rate to date holds, it would best 2000. Not bad considering that in 2014, home runs were at their *lowest* rate since 1992.

Thus was born the great juiced baseball conspiracy. With other forms of juicing now being tested for via blood and urine, perhaps MLB was quietly altering the ball ever so slightly. Not to the point where 100-foot popups would suddenly become 500-foot moonshots, but just enough to encourage a few more balls to go over the right-field wall rather than into the right fielder's glove. It wouldn't take much to put a thumb on the scale. Even the increase from 2014 to 2016 rates going from record lows over the past 25 years to record highs only represents an extra home run every three games for each team.

Like most conspiracies, it consisted of leveling a charge at someone that they at least would have had motive and opportunity to do, while having no definitive proof that they actually did it, but demanding that they prove that they had not done it. In May 2017, MLB proved it. They provided a document to Ben Lindbergh of The Ringer (and my former

boss here at BP) that detailed the regular testing done by the league to ensure its game balls are indeed meeting their standards.[1] Lindbergh was not allowed to release the report, but was allowed to release one graph and a summary of what the report said.

According to Lindbergh, the message over and over again was that the balls showed little change over time on any physical specification imaginable and were always well within the official guidelines. I suppose that the conspiracy theorist's response would be to point out that MLB did the testing itself and provided the report, and could have (theoretically) doctored the data. (Here we are back to leveling a charge and demanding proof of a negative!) While it's possible that MLB went to the trouble to fake some data, perhaps it's possible that the ball hasn't really changed?

Let's assume the ball isn't juiced. The problem is we still have to explain this:

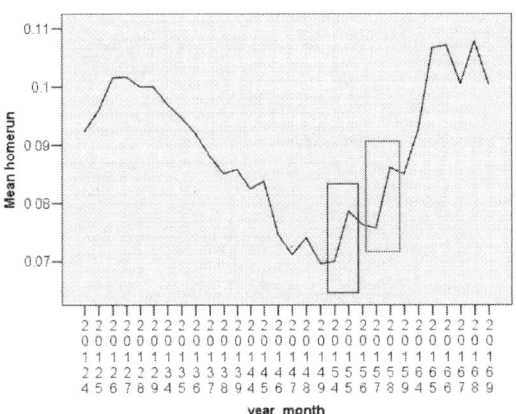

That's HR/FB, by month, over the last five full seasons (2012-2016). A good amount of the speculation about the ball was initially started by an article written by Lindbergh and BP alumnus Rob Arthur in which they noted that exit velocity jumped at the All-Star break in 2015, and the HR/FB chart shows a big jump from July to August of that year.[2] The

---

1. https://www.theringer.com/2017/5/9/16040456/2017-mlb-home-run-rate-is-the-ball-juiced-report-results-6e1dd0233203

2. https://fivethirtyeight.com/features/a-baseball-mystery-the-home-run-is-back-and-no-one-knows-why/; https://fivethirtyeight.com/features/are-juiced-balls-the-new-steroids/

thing is, there was an almost identical jump from September 2014 to April 2015. Maybe teams and players came to spring training looking to try something new out?

Perhaps there's a perfectly logical, nonconspiratorial reason that home runs have spiked?

Warning! Gory Mathematical Details Ahead!

Before we get into the home runs, we need to first talk about strikeouts, because they hold the key to all of this. Much has been made about the strikeout epidemic in baseball, and the numbers show that despite the increase in home runs, strikeouts have continued to climb, unabated over the past few years.[3]

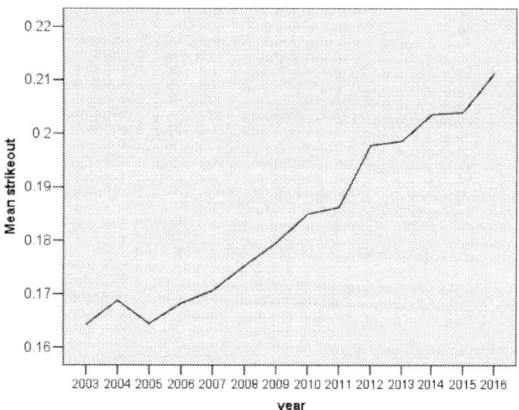

There's another trend that's been reborn of late as well. In the latter part of the last decade, teams began to develop a strategy in which they baited the starter into 14 pitch at-bats, seeing that most starters came into the game with a 100-pitch limit anyway. Well …

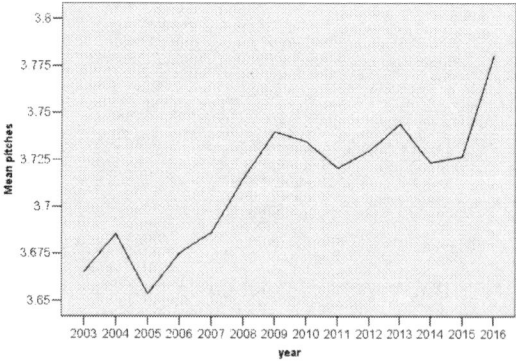

As shown above, the upward trend in pitches per plate appearance is back, but for a different reason than in the past. In the past, swing rates on the first pitch of a plate appearance had been very low, with batters effectively saying to pitchers, "I'm not going to swing until you throw me a strike." Pitchers eventually figured this out and responded with a collective, "OK, if you insist." After 2013, that changed.

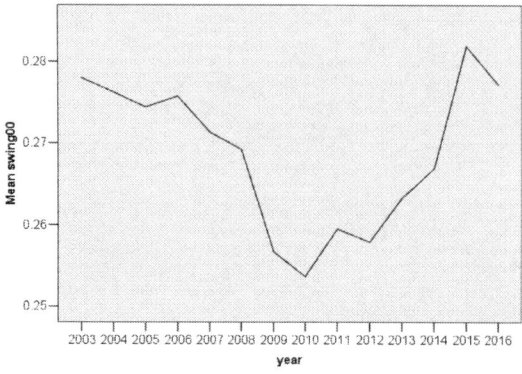

But here's the thing: While batters were willing to swing a little more early in the count, they weren't exactly hitting it more. In fact, contact rate on those swings fell.

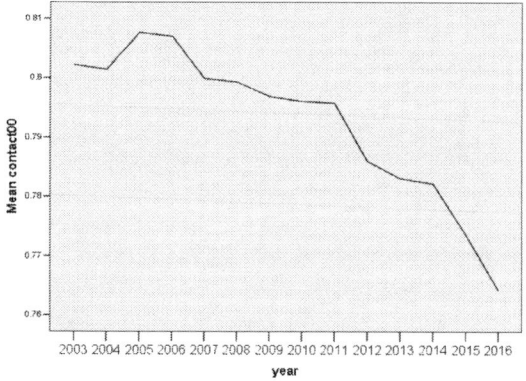

And it isn't just the first pitch of a plate appearance either. While overall swing rates haven't changed all that much over the past decade, rates of swinging and missing have steadily crept upward. The hot new thing to do isn't to take pitches, it's to swing and miss. In some sense, it's perfectly logical. If you're willing to accept a strike, why not swing really hard in case you hit it? If you miss, two-thirds of the time, they just throw you another pitch.

Engaging in behavior that leads to strikeouts might seem counterintuitive, but maybe there's a strategy behind it. It's generally accepted that there's a trade-off to be made between power and contact.[4] It's not the same trade-off for every hitter, but the harder you swing, the more likely it is

---

3. http://www.foxsports.com/mlb/story/there-s-gotta-be-a-reason-for-the-strikeout-epidemic-right-052714

4. https://www.fangraphs.com/tht/quantifying-the-trade-off-between-power-and-contact/

that you will miss, but also the more likely that the ball will go farther, and the home-run numbers suggest that when batters do hit the ball, it *is* going farther.

What's interesting is that fly-ball rates haven't been particularly high during the spike, so despite all of the discussion of launch angles, batters (as a whole) aren't hitting the ball upward more often. Just harder. Fly balls aren't increasing, but HR/FB sure has been. It's worth saying that there are cases where individual players seem to be fine-tuning the whole launch-angle thing, but leaguewide it seems that the big idea has been hitters getting *more out of the fly balls that they were already hitting*.

But ... those strikeouts.

Let's consider strikeouts for a moment, not as we often do instinctively from a moral perspective (a strikeout gets its own line in the box score with an implied tsk tsk at the end, but no one counts 4-3 groundouts or fly outs to left), but for what they functionally do. If a batter is going to make an out, in a lot of cases, it really doesn't matter whether it's a strikeout or a groundout.

If there are two outs or there are no runners on base, then functionally, a strikeout does the same thing as a grounder to second. In 2016, that described nearly three-quarters of plate appearances leaguewide. In addition, it's rare for an out to actually move a runner up. In 2016, when there was a runner on and fewer than two outs and a ball was put into play, it only resulted in the runner moving up about 20 percent of the time. Yes, strikeouts have the disadvantage of giving no chance to provide a ???productive" out, but it's not really common that grounders to second do either. Plus, strikeouts have the advantage of avoiding double plays.

So, let's trade some contact for power. Assume for a moment that in this trade-off, we could maintain a steady on-base percentage (i.e., the same number of outs), we just change the shape of those outs. Changing to a strikeout isn't going to be *that* big a penalty, and anything we pull out of the single or double or walk basket to put into the home-run basket is going to be very valuable. It's enough that even if we have to give back some OBP, it might actually be worth it.

It might not be great baseball to watch, but it makes sense.

Ⓧ   Ⓧ   Ⓧ

Now that we can justify the extra strikeouts, the patterns we're seeing make sense, but they're not quite enough to explain all that's happening. There's another chart worth seeing. This is the percentage of balls hit into play (or over the fence) that were fastballs.

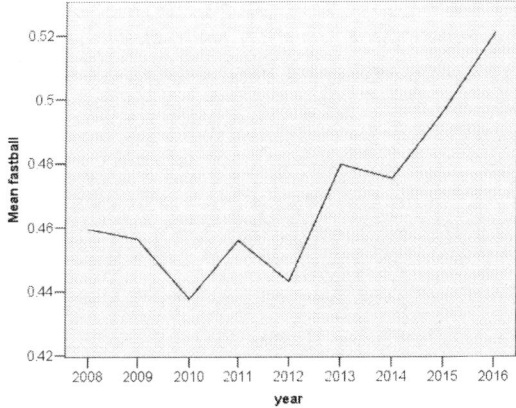

Here's another showing the percentage of home runs hit that were hit on fastballs.

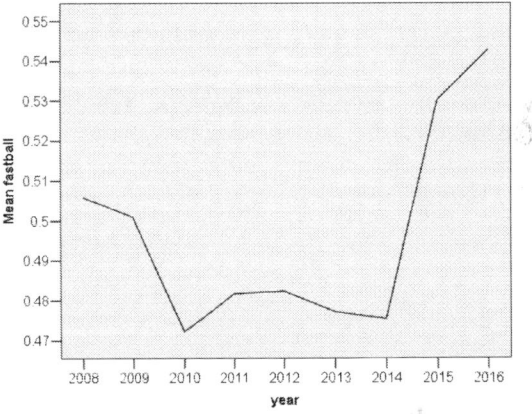

Starting in 2015, around the time of the current power spike, hitters seemed to be sitting fastball more. And why not? Even though fastball usage has actually declined among pitchers, it still accounts for more than half of all pitches. As a batter, you know you're eventually going to get one. So, why not wait for one and swing really hard? You might miss and eventually you might strike out, but if you do, so what?

Sit Fastball, Swing Hard, Strikeouts Don't Matter

It's not surprising that we've seen a big jump in home runs, and we don't need a juiced ball to explain it. We've got evidence that the game is just evolving toward an approach that favors a lot of home runs. There's no grand conspiracy other than evolution.

Consider the lament that started 10 years ago. Baseball was being overrun by pitchers, relievers especially, who threw really fast fastballs. Well, if you know that a lot of the pitchers you will be facing are going to be throwing heat, you might as well sit on the heat. You're probably also going to be brought to the majors more quickly if you show some ability to hit that heat. This is not rocket science.

There's always been an incentive to hit the ball hard in the game, and in this case Statcast just confirmed what was long known: that harder hit balls were better hit balls. The advantage that Statcast has wrought might not even be in its measurement, but in that it brought words like exit velocity and launch angle into the baseball vernacular. Players now talk with the media and perhaps with each other about these concepts, and sometimes having a word to call something is the missing ingredient in changing it.

Being able to say "I can change my launch angle" or "I can focus on adding more exit velocity" might be what gives a player the mental space to actually change his swing in a way that he wouldn't have been able to before. It may also be that Statcast and other radar and tracking technologies allow players to do work in the batting cages where they can see in real time what the effects of a little tweak here and there are in a nice, quantifiable way. You don't need a juiced ball if you swing harder.

And finally, there's been an embrace of the strikeout in baseball. The game has been trending toward more strikeouts since Chester Arthur was president, but lately the pace has been accelerating a bit more. There will always be some base level of strikeouts in the game, but at some point players stopped asking how to avoid striking out and instead focused on the best approach to generate value for the team. If living with an increased chance of a strikeout buys you something even more valuable, then it's worth living with the increased chance of a strikeout. This again is not rocket science. It's algebra.

It doesn't have to be every hitter in every plate appearance. In fact, if you look at the graphs, you see that the changes I'm pointing out are on the order of a couple of percentage points. But that's all it takes. It's a couple of guys a game picking a pitch or two that they're just gonna sit fastball on and decide that if they see it, they're gonna swing real hard in case they hit it. It might not be obvious in the moment what's going on or that there's anything different going on. It???s the sort of thing that you only see in the aggregate data, and as I pointed out earlier, we're talking about one of the greatest home-run spikes in baseball history, and it's really only a couple of extra home runs per week for a team.

It's entirely possible that my theory here isn't the *whole* story. There may be other things going on that are contributing, but I think that there are perfectly reasonable explanations for what's going on that don't involve shadowy plans made in the dead of the night. ▨

Shadows Stretching Across the Field

by Patrick Dubuque

Using the act of suicide as an unlikely yet effective backdrop, Patrick Dubuque considers baseball's enduring ability to unite people, even—especially—those who might otherwise feel alone in the world. – Geoff Y.

Like so many Japanese men of his generation, Shingo Furuya was a company man. Fresh out of college with an economics degree, he joined the Hanshin Electric Railway Company and devoted his life to it: worked ridiculous hours, floated through reorganizations and sideways promotions. It's how he became the manager of one of Hanshin's corporate subsidiaries: the Koshien baseball stadium. At 56, after one more business dinner, he became the general manager of the Hanshin Tigers.

At first blush, it seems like a strange progression. Furuya didn't know baseball; Japanese general managers rarely did in his time, 1988. The field manager was responsible for the team roster, and the owners for the financial decisions. Furuya's position was mediator, negotiating with both sides, and with the players themselves, trying to keep everyone happy. It was not, at that moment, an easy job. Champions a few years earlier, the Tigers had slipped into last place. Their hometown hero, Masayuki Kakefu, was seeing his glorious career wind down early as he struggled with injuries. He'd made public his intentions to retire; Furuya was busy trying to talk him out of it. And then there was Randy Bass.

Japanese teams had long struggled with their *gaijin* players in the '70s and '80s; the allure of talent always seemed to be undone by underperformance, miscommunication, alienation, and expectations. Bass, a busted first-base prospect in the majors, proved different. He became the league's MVP and its finest foreign player to date, and was equally on good terms with Japan and his employers. They, in turn, loved him back.

But even that happy story couldn't last. In early 1988, Bass learned that his young son back home, Zachary, needed treatments for brain cancer. Bass asked for, and received, two weeks leave to be there for the treatment, a laudable corporate act by Western standards, shockingly generous by Eastern ones. When the two weeks were up, Bass did not return. There were complications, attorneys, a conspicuous losing streak. The Tigers ultimately responded by cutting their star and waiving their responsibility to pay for medical bills as per his contract.

Bass claimed that he had been given permission by phone to continue to stay by his son's side. The team declared it a lie. Bass produced an audio recording of the conversation. The man on the other end of the telephone was Shingo Furuya. He knew Bass well, had met his family. He made a promise he had no power to keep. It was true of all his promises.

Furuya traveled to Tokyo to meet with the Hanshin owners in the aftermath. He called his wife that evening, after the stories broke, as he always did when he was on the road. Instead of "sleep well," he said "goodbye." Then he stepped onto the external stairwell of his hotel room, eight stories up. Two-and-a-half seconds later, Shingo Furuya died in the garden below.

⚉   ⚉   ⚉

It's almost difficult to believe in baseball ever being worth taking one's own life. And in a casual glance, the connection between baseball and self-harm is a fleeting one, punctuated by the psychotic rage of Marty Bergen, the acute despondency of Willard Hershberger, or the alcohol-soaked despair of Hideki Irabu. There are conditions within the game, a self-selection process, which would appear to build some mild immunity to the urge toward self-harm: the dogmatic, myopic positivity of the modern athlete, and the dilution of failure across an endless stream of games.

There are exceptions like Hershberger, players who were directly rebuffed by their failures, and who killed themselves out of despair. Generally, they are pitchers with arm problems, men whose loss of purpose was both abrupt and tangible. Reds starter Benny Frey, in 1937, was sent to the minors after his arm gave out, and he refused the assignment. When his arm failed to heal, he connected a hose from the exhaust pipe to the backseat of his car in his sister's garage. Pea Ridge Day, after spending tens of thousands of 1933 dollars at the Mayo Clinic to revive his own career, slit his throat with a hunting knife.

But even in these extreme cases, there are other factors. The philosopher-poet Jennifer Michael Hecht, in a work to be discussed in detail, notes:[1]

> In the Great Depression of the 1930s many individuals took their lives, either when they lost all their money in the stock market crash or during the period afterward, with its grinding unemployment. When we think of it now it seems surprising that people could take these widespread hardships so personally, but this seems to be how the mind works—all misfortune feels local.

So it was with Furuya, who shared the same problems as many middle managers in similar situations. He also shared many of their fates.

⚾   ⚾   ⚾

I spent my early twenties as a lost undergraduate student, failing my useless liberal arts classes and my parents. I missed classes and then grew too anxious to attend classes, anxious that I would be confronted over my truancy. After being put on academic probation, I toyed with the notion of suicide, though never seriously. My lack of ambition proved both my demon and my angel. Lying in bed in the empty midmorning, I envisioned joining the military and throwing my body against imaginary Cossacks. Instead, I sent myself into exile for a time, taught overseas, and the darkness slowly passed.

Recently I finished reading Hecht's *Stay*, the philosophical history of suicide and its pros and cons. (Her *Doubt*, a similar treatise on skepticism through the ages, is one of my favorite books.) I was surprised to discover it weighing me down, despite the fact that its message is intended to perform the opposite. The thesis is strongly antisuicide without resorting to the usual tactics of organized religion, shame, and hellfire. It is meant to be positive and constructive.

If you were to ask me directly if I were for or against suicide, as a liberty, I would probably say for. I do not mean dying with dignity in the hands of an incurable and painful illness, and neither does Hecht; that is a separate matter. But for the person who is in anguish, who seeks control over his or her own existence and identity, who simply does not want to live: instinctually, I would allow them the choice not to.

Hecht (and others, as she details in her history) would not. The counterpoint: Because it is a lonely act, it is by nature a selfish one, not because it necessarily willfully ignores or betrays the feelings of others, but because the signal between them is severed. She does make the argument, for completeness, that suicide is a crime against the future self because its desire may only be passing and its results permanent; the fact that some people who make the attempt come to regret doing so seems proof enough. Ernie Lombardi is an example of this. But to Hecht, the primary drive toward taking one's own life is alienation.

What makes suicide wrong, she argues, is that we owe our lives to the people around us, those who love us and depend on us. We owe it to our society, the shared strength of which is diminished by our decision to opt out. When it comes to existence, we are not allowed to vote with our feet; our decisions touch others no matter how isolated we feel (or want to be). We cannot remove ourselves from the world.

I sympathize with this sentiment, and yet as I slowly took it in, it chafed at me. The timing, personally, is poor. I currently possess two children, ages three and one, who are convinced they will disappear if I am not looking at them. The yoke is heavy enough. And as far as the social contract, it's perhaps not the best time to argue for the indebtedness of the individual to the government, at a time when the latter is in the business of consolidating power. If we live to serve a society, it'd be nice to see that society hold up its side of the bargain a little better.

But I understand that these are means to an end. Society has for nearly two millennia sought ways to dissuade suicide: rendering it illegal, sinful, shameful. Bodies of the voluntarily departed were publicly defaced, inheritances denied, barred from heaven, all in an effort to make the act as unappealing as possible for the survivors. And for good reason: Sociologists in the 20th century discovered that suicide does, in fact, have a snowballing effect in society, either through popular culture (*The Sorrows of Young Werther* set off an epidemic upon publishing) or by an infectious despair at the loss of a friend or relative. Hershberger in particular was surrounded by suicide his entire life. It was a constant reality to him.

Ianthe Brautigan, daughter of the counterculture author Richard Brautigan, explains in the preface to her own memoir, a work entirely about her relationship to her father:[2]

> This is not a book about therapy, nor is it a self-help tome about suicide and grief. I threw away all my books on both subjects long ago … Although I don't have any answers, I firmly believe there is no right or wrong way to navigate the suicide of a loved one, except to make sure you do. I don't pretend to be put back to rights. I just wanted to help break the silence that exists concerning suicide, so I broke mine.

---

1. Jennifer Michael Hecht, *Stay: A History of Suicide and the Arguments Against It* (New Haven: Yale University Press, 2013).
2. Ianthe Brautigan: *You Can't Catch Death* (New York: St. Martin's Press, 2001).

⚾ ⚾ ⚾

People outside of Baltimore might not remember Mike Flanagan. He won the AL Cy Young award for the pennant-winning Orioles of 1979, and made the All-Star team the following year, but after that he was a quiet and constant presence in the middle of Baltimore's rotation for a decade. He threw the final home pitch at Memorial Stadium in 1991, by then a middle reliever, facing two Tigers and striking them both out. After retirement he stayed with the team, moved up to vice president during the franchise's lean years in the late '90s, when the Yankees dominated all. The losing built up, and Flanagan found himself relocated to the broadcast booth, doing color for MASN.

Flanagan was a quiet, thoughtful man, constantly reflective, always trying to find something to tweak or improve. He was the quintessential crafty lefty, employing study and technique in place of raw talent. He took that same work ethic into the front office, where he toiled to improve the club despite few positive results. In public, he was polite, nonconfrontational, amiable, and silent. In private, the frustrations of every loss, every setback boiled within him.

"He used to talk about shadows," his wife Alex told reporter Dan Rodricks in 2012. "He would say, 'Sometimes there's this shadow that comes into my life,' and he wouldn't see anything good, just these shadows. ... He would see the world in black and white, without color."[3]

Stung by criticism in the press and online, struggling to make ends meet with inconsistent work, unable to find value in himself, Flanagan began to drink: at first, openly, and then after a heart-to-heart with Alex, in secret. He took a shotgun and shot at woodchucks on the property as therapy. When Alex traveled to be with her ailing mother, one day, Flanagan turned the weapon on himself.

Alex commented that she still felt guilt, still searched for other pathways that might have led out of the darkness. It's natural, and tragic. The family knew, they supported, cajoled, and cared. They searched for a way to connect, to show him how valuable he was. They couldn't reach him.

⚾ ⚾ ⚾

At the end of his book, *The Conquest of Happiness*, the philosopher Bertrand Russell caps off 200 pages of what makes people unhappy, and finds in conclusion:[4]

The whole antithesis between self and the rest of the world, which is implied in the doctrine of self-denial, disappears as soon as we have any genuine interest in persons or things outside ourselves. Through such interests a man comes to feel himself part of the stream of life.

Though he lived to a ripe 99 years old, Russell grew up in the Victorian era of Britain, a time when appearances and repression dominated culture. He rejected these things and, late in life, threw himself into the noisy, active, living democracies of the American 1960s. Going with the flow didn't mean avoiding conflict, or not making waves: It meant immersing one's self in the current of the times, to feel a part of something. To avoid feeling alone.

As an introvert, I don't find the prospect particularly thrilling. I find it difficult to reconcile my own preference for personal, local democracy and my desire, at all times, to be left alone in my room with a nice book. But in terms of living, the grand search for meaning, it's indisputable: The key is to immerse, to live in whatever way you choose, as long as it's not in silence.

And that brings us back, finally, to baseball. Sometimes I joke that I got into baseball to have a way to avoid talking about real things to strangers. But at the same time, there's something real in this. In a social network that feels increasingly isolated, baseball offers an increasingly rare opportunity to feel connected with other people, a model for taking disparate individuals and creating a working team. It is instant camaraderie.

A baseball team is, among its other properties, an excellent microcosm for a small society: specialized people banding together to achieve a common goal, dependent on each other's skills, stuck with each other's personalities. Thomas More would be proud. As with every collective, there are problems, differences in direction and ability, inequality, and unfairness. Regardless, each is its own nation. Any member leaving the arrangement would have an obvious effect on the welfare of the whole. Any member being left behind loses a piece of themselves.

Ballplayers do still harbor their private problems, hide injuries from their trainers, grouse about management in hallways, and suffer anxiety and depression despite a fan base that expects nothing less than 100 percent performance, even the day a man's child is born. Similarly, we should strive to destroy these barriers, allow the life of a ballplayer to be as natural as we would want our own. We should strive for openness, for understanding, just as we would a suffering friend. We should all make a baseball team with our baseball teams.

⚾ ⚾ ⚾

---

3. Dan Rodricks, "Death of Mike Flanagan, Orioles Great, Leaves Shadows of Doubt," *Baltimore Sun*, August 18, 2012.
4. Bertrand Russell, *The Conquest of Happiness* (London: George Allen and Unwin, 1930).

When they ran tests on the brain of Ryan Freel, former utility man for the Reds, they found evidence of second-stage CTE, the first such discovery in a baseball player. Long known to be an issue with football players, its discovery within a player in a relatively low-impact sport renewed awareness that brain trauma was, in fact, a problem in professional sports. Freel himself once estimated he suffered "nine or ten" concussions. An outfield collision that sent him off the field in a stretcher derailed his career, and a pickoff throw that tore off his helmet effectively ended it.

Freel made a comeback attempt, did some youth coaching, but as with Flanagan he found stability a difficult thing to maintain. He, too, struggled with alcohol, though he seemed to have bested it. When the tests confirmed to his family his erratic behavior, the mood swings and headaches and attention span problems, it was in one way a relief.

"Oh yes [it's helpful], especially for the girls," Freel's mother, Norma Vargas, said of his three children, speaking of the study to the *Jacksonville Times-Union*. "We adults can understand a little better. It's a closure for the girls who loved their dad so much, and they knew how much their dad loved them. It could help them understand why he did what he did. Maybe not now, but one day they will."[5]

Freel's stepfather saw the other side of the coin. "It's a release in that there was a physical reason for what he did," Clark Vargas was quoted. "On the other side, for me, Ryan fell through the cracks." Whether by medical ignorance or indifference, baseball, in a way, had failed one of its own.

⚾   ⚾   ⚾

In Roman times and before, suicide was generally considered at least neutral and potentially noble: Socrates drinking the hemlock, Samson pulling down the temple. It transformed, over the centuries, along with other mental illness, into something secret, shameful, something to disguise. We are only now beginning to understand how deadly that private shame has been. Men like Hershberger, Flanagan, and Freel ended up alone, in pain, amongst their friends and family. It may not always be possible to solve the divide—depression is as deep as it is obfuscated—but reversing the stigma of self-pain is the best way forward.

Baseball did not save Shingo Furuya; in fact, the entire structure of his existence, the powerlessness and the responsibility, the societal norms concerning corporate honor and expectations, appear to have driven him to his act. I wish it had been otherwise. Japan has struggled to overcome its culture of suicide, which appeared to be improving until the economic downturn of the late '90s drove it up again.

Furuya's fate was sealed as he stepped out of the owner's meeting that evening, because at that point, there was only one path left that he could see. If he had been honest with his wife, if he had called Bass, if he could have rejected the code of honor baked into his sensibilities, there may have been another way. There is almost always another way, when one is rational. It is difficult to be rational, when the shadows appear.

In the end, I guess my issue with *Stay* is not its message but the restrictions of its historical perspective, naturally oriented on the decision, and liberty, of the individual: the idea that eliminating suicide and failure is their responsibility or service toward society, rather than the other way around. In my mind, preventing alienation is the job of the community, not the individual, and suicide is a symptom of the failure of a society to tend to the health of its citizens.

Even those philosophers who fight for the sake of liberty in suicide aren't rooting for it; no one wants people to die. The ideal outcome is for everyone to have that choice, and choose to reject that outcome, to find their value in living. That is the difficult thing, the important thing. But in the face of shadows, expecting rationality and utilitarian calculus out of those suffering feels lofty, dispassionate. Instead of rejecting death, we should be defending life.

Fortunately, we have tools for this, for creating a sense of value and community in existence. There are so many to choose from: We have art, we have philosophy and religion, we have charity, and we have baseball.

One clear virtue in baseball: that if suicidal behavior is contagious, the opposite is equally true. As models for the human struggle, athletes who were able to break through their silence and share their stories can create a positive culture. Men like R.A. Dickey, Evan Gattis, and Aubrey Huff (among others) have come forward to talk about their own battles against depression, doing their part to open cultural dialogue on the subject in the face of the stereotype of the athlete as infallible and monomaniacal.

It's easy and cynical to treat baseball as a sort of postmodern nationalism, to see in it the usual gerrymandering and division of people by geography and demographics. But it also combines. It gives us a reason to talk to and care about each other, to share experience, to create memories. As much as the language of baseball shouldn't replace actual language, there is something in it, a code by which we can all relate to the people next to us, to feel part of something. Even if it's a placeholder for more meaningful conversation, for an avenue toward help, it's still better than silence. Anything is better than silence. ▪

---

5. Justin Barney, "Family: Ryan Freel Was Suffering from Brain Disease CTE," *Jacksonville Times-Union*, December 15, 2013.

The Strategic Argument Against the Designated Hitter

by Rob Mains

In his investigation of the designated hitter rule, Rob Mains discovers that key objections to it are no longer valid thanks to changes in the way baseball is played and the types of in-game decisions a manager must now make. – Geoff Y.

In March 2017 I attended the SABR Analytics Conference in Phoenix. The Society for American Baseball Research, as I assume you know, is dedicated to researching the game. Many of you are SABR members, as am I. This isn't an advertisement (though it is a great organization!); I just wanted to provide the background.

The Analytics Conference, as its name implies, is analytically focused. It's more for baseball numbers nerds than general baseball nerds. That being said, everybody there's a baseball fan and baseball fans have opinions.

One of their strongest is about the designated hitter. The DH was adopted by the American League in 1973, after a season in which scoring fell to 3.47 runs per game, the fourth-lowest in league history (3.41 in 1968, 3.441 in 1908, 3.443 in 1909). The intent of the DH was primarily to improve scoring, since the changes adopted in 1969 (lowered pitchers' mound, smaller strike zone) proved to be only a temporary fix.

I don't need to tell you that the DH has been controversial in each of its 44 years to date. Pro tip: If you're giving an address to a SABR gathering, or pretty much any group of longtime baseball fans, any riff on "get rid of the DH" is likely to be a crowd-pleaser. Those of us who are okay with it are, in my experience, generally not all that passionate. That's not always true of the anti-DH crowd.

I'm not here to litigate the DH. That's not going to get us anywhere. But I do want to point out the trajectory of one of the arguments against it.

There's the traditionalist argument: nine players to a side, each plays offense and defense. Making the pitcher a one-way player violates that simplicity. While the slippery-slope-toward-offensive-and-defensive-platoons fear can probably be put to rest, it's undoubtedly true that pitcher batting skills, never all that good in the first place, have atrophied:

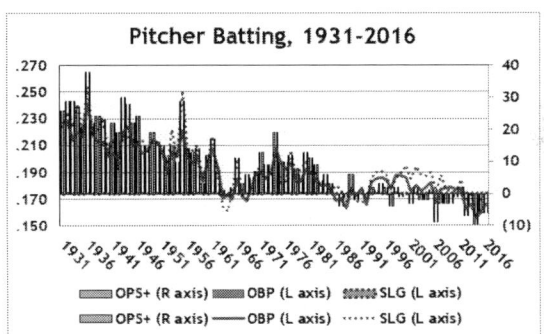

I know, there's a lot going on there. The key takeaway is that everything's sloping down.

In a way, this sort of buttresses the pro-DH argument, doesn't it? I mean, yeah, Bartolo Colon in 2016, but the pitcher's spot in the lineup has become more or less an automatic out (or, with runners on base, an automatic bunt attempt). There's not a lot of drama in that.

But that's not the argument I want to address. I want to talk about strategy.

The DH, it's argued, robs the game of strategy. Pinch-hitting, double-switches, and everything else that the pitcher's spot in the order may entail are, while interesting, pretty rote in most cases. But National League managers face a decision that their American League counterparts don't: whether to pull a pitcher who's doing well for a pinch-hitter when tied or trailing.

Take April 14 in the first year of the DH, 1973. In the American League that day two starters, Bert Blyleven and Wilbur Wood, pitched well. Blyleven allowed two runs, eight hits, no walks, and struck out eight while pitching a complete game. Wood also went the distance, allowing three runs (all unearned) on three hits and two walks, with six strikeouts. But both of them took the loss, because Blyleven's Twins scored only one run against the A's and Wood's White Sox scored none against the Royals.

Ah, but over in the DH-less National League, on April 24 of that same season, the Cubs were trailing the Giants 2-1 in the bottom of the seventh inning. Chicago manager Whitey Lockman had to make the tough decision to pull starter Rick Reuschel for a pinch-hitter with two outs and a runner on second. Reuschel had pitched well, allowing two runs and striking out 12 over seven innings, but the team needed to get back into the game. The strategy ultimately failed, as the pinch-hitter, Gene Hiser, flied out. And while the Cubs tied the game in the bottom of the ninth on a Ron Santo home run, Reuschel's replacement on the mound, Bob Locker, gave up the winning run in the 10th.

If that game had been played in the American League, Reuschel could have stayed in the game and the Cubs may have won. But the desire to keep a successful pitcher on the mound was outweighed by the need to get runs on the board. That's a decision that American League managers are spared. Ergo, less strategy.

But note that in the preceding examples from 1973, two of the pitchers went nine innings and the other went seven. In 1973, 54 percent of starting pitchers went seven innings or more. In 2016, that figure was only 23 percent. The decision whether to pinch-hit for a starter in the late innings of a game is a lot easier when the starter's not in the game anymore! So maybe that aspect of strategy has fallen by the wayside.

Let's check for that. The following graph shows the innings pitched per starter by league from the beginning of divisional play in 1969. The solid black line is 1973, the year the DH was implemented. (And yes, I realize, these numbers are somewhat polluted by interleague play, but with each team playing only 10 games per season with the other league's DH rules, it's not a big effect.)

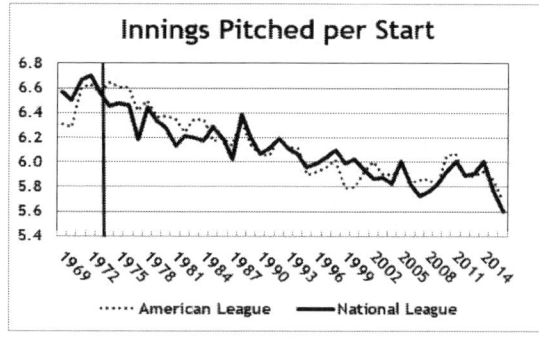

Innings Pitched per Start

As you can see, when the DH first came in American League starters did, in fact, stay in games longer than their National League counterparts. Since National League pitchers had lasted longer in the years heading into the DH, we can pretty safely say that the DH allowed AL managers to stick with starters longer. They didn't have to face the pinch-hitting conundrum when trailing or tied in late innings. DH = less strategy.

But as starting pitchers have yielded to relievers earlier and earlier, the spread has not only declined, it has vanished. Despite the DH, which in theory allows American League managers to leave pitchers in longer, National League starters have lasted longer in four of the last eight seasons and 11 of the 21 since the 1994-1995 strike. With starters lasting, on average, about 5 2/3 innings, the question of pinch-hitting for the starter in the seventh or eighth inning has become moot.

How moot? Well, as the following chart illustrates, AL starters lasted at least a tenth of an inning longer than their NL counterparts in nine of the 14 years beginning in 1974, the year after the DH was established. It has happened only four times in the subsequent 29 seasons.

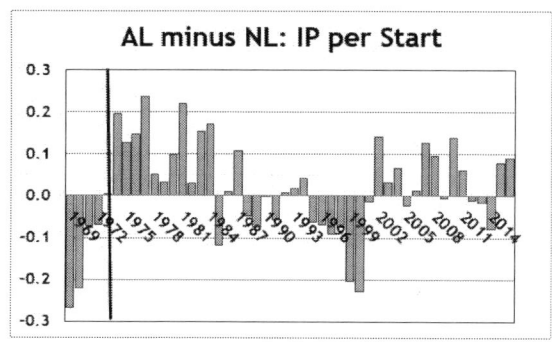

AL minus NL: IP per Start

But the DH doesn't create, at least in theory, a strategic difference between the leagues in only starter usage. It affects bullpens as well. Just as a National League manager is more likely than an American League manager to pull a starter (for a pinch-hitter) in the seventh inning of a game his team's losing by a run, so too is the NL manager more likely to bring in a pinch-hitter in the late innings to replace an effective reliever.

In fact, the difference between the leagues in reliever usage was starker, post-DH, than starter usage. In 1972, before the DH, American League relievers averaged 1.59 innings per appearance. National League relievers averaged an almost identical 1.62. In 1973, the first year of the DH, NL relievers pitched an average of 1.54 innings per appearance, but AL reliever innings per appearance zoomed all the way up to 2.06, *the highest level since World War II.*

American League relievers stayed in games at least a tenth of an inning longer, on average, than their National League counterparts every year through 1988. That year, Dennis Eckersley recorded 21 one-inning saves under Tony La Russa's American League champion A's, and the trend to one-inning relievers was ignited. Have shorter relief outings yielded less of a difference between the leagues? Yes, they have:

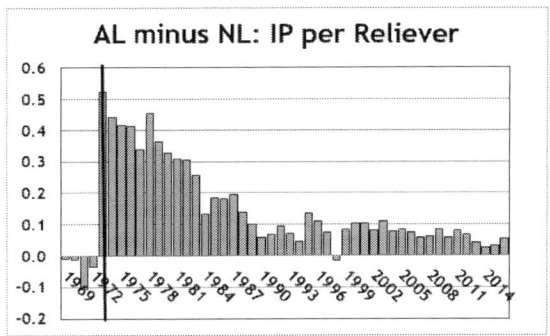

American League relievers still stay in games a little longer than National League relievers, but the difference hasn't exceeded a tenth of an inning pitched since 2003, as the following graph illustrates.

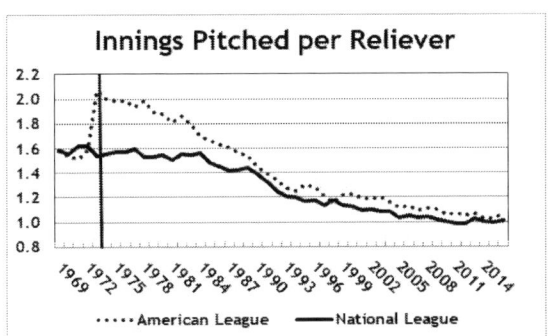

If you don't like the DH because you think the two leagues should play by the same rules, fine. If you think everybody on the field should play on offense and defense, that's okay. If you think it's fun to see Bartolo Colon hit, you're entitled to your opinion (as well as his .085/.093/.108 career line).

But if your objection is that the DH robs the game of strategy, you're fighting an outdated battle. The complaints about modern pitching staffs—starters who can't pitch deep into games, a parade of relievers who last only an inning at a time—have all but eliminated the decision National League managers used to face about keeping a pitcher in the game or pulling him for a pinch-hitter. In today's game, the pinch-hitter's going to bat regardless, because the pitcher he's replacing is done for the day. The strategic decision's not on the table the way it was in 1973. ▨

The Marketing of Baseball

by Kate Morrison

As Major League Baseball struggles to attract and retain new fans, Kate Morrison offers suggestions for increasing the sport's lasting appeal among younger generations. – Geoff Y.

For an industry with no direct competitors, a brighter inside future than ever, and a very owner-and-league-friendly system of dispensing with profits, Major League Baseball sure seems convinced that it's dying. And for a company publicly despairing, it doesn't seem to have any understanding of what little things it could do to make life easier on itself. Nowhere is this more apparent than in MLB's seeming inability to move its marketing efforts into the 21st century.

No matter what kind of organization you run, from a small start-up to a multinational telecom,[1] the fundamentals of the game are the same:

- How do you determine who you want to communicate with?
- What image of yourself, and what message, do you want to communicate?
- How do you communicate that message to the audience you've selected?

These three questions are what it all boils down to. It is extremely easy to get lost in the day-to-day of marketing, in the buzz of new ideas and what's "hot" at the moment. It's more difficult to refine down to the fundamentals.

How do you determine who you want to communicate with?

In various media availabilities since he became commissioner, Rob Manfred has defined MLB's marketing focus as wanting to reach out to a younger base, and make baseball more appealing to the coveted "millennial" group. Per market research firm Luntz Global, that's not a bad place to begin—baseball's fans are "older, whiter, and more male-dominated than any other sport."[2]

As the Luntz article continues, baseball turned to a mix of traditional storytelling and nostalgia, and the league was able to reap the benefits of social media and their cheaper options to digitally stream the games—for those without cable subscriptions or TVs. Baseball has clearly determined that the only way forward is to reach a wider mix of a younger group, and instill that nostalgia (false or not, rose-colored or not) in this group before they become enamored with a niche sport like curling or, heaven forbid, the NBA.

So far, this is well and good. Most companies, whether or not they're a sports organization, are looking to get younger. That bastion of New York jewelry, Tiffany & Co., is going through upheaval in its own search for a younger client base, one it can nurse through all stages of life.[3]

What image of yourself, and what message, do you want to communicate?

This is where we begin to run into serious problems with the public way Major League Baseball markets itself. If we had access to its internal memos, there's a decent chance we'd find an electronic piece of paper with an overall directive on how to present Major League Baseball across all platforms and to any and all demographics. Unfortunately for whoever is responsible for executing that memo, that doesn't show up to us out here in the wild.

---

1. I've worked with and for both types of organizations in my day job as a digital and social media marketing specialist, and these are the questions that, in my opinion, it all boils down to. While I do not have a marketing degree, and therefore my approach is slightly unorthodox, I've found it serves my clients and myself equally well, and that having this outsider's view has resulted in innovative campaign development. In this piece, I've hoped to apply my experience to the sport I love productively, instead of just ranting on Twitter.

2. http://www.luntzglobal.com/news/major-league-baseball-marketing/

3. Chavie Lieber, "The New Tiffany & Co. Needs Women," *Racked,* February 5, 2017.

If you were asked to describe the image of the NBA, or even of the NFL, in five or fewer words, it would be easy. The Olympics, as a group? The same. For those three—and probably the NHL, as well—your five words would likely be similar to the five words developed in conference rooms of varying sizes. For MLB, though, it's hard to imagine that their creative brief matches their coveted demographic's five words.

In an ad hoc market research Twitter[4] poll, words like "stodgy," "old-fashioned," and "nostalgic" dominated what one could call a negative axis, while "earnest," "traditional," and "beautiful" exemplified the positive.[5] While not confining to the five words, one person commented that "they've spent more time promoting Tim Tebow than Mike Trout." And from another user: "We can't market our stars." For a sport that seems desperate to be of the now, even this straw poll doesn't have inspiring results.[6]

The league seems to be aware of this, if not fully aware. In February 2017, Rob Manfred was quoted in the *Chicago Tribune* as saying, "Our fans, both avid fans and casual fans, want us to respond to and manage the change going on in the game."[7] Unfortunately, the fans and the league seem to have reached different conclusions on that change—again, damaging for that all-important image.

How do you communicate that message to the audience you've selected?

Right now, MLB is sending out a muddled message. It claims it wants to bring in more viewers, and retain a younger clientele, but its social media presence is stilted and antiquated, with more emphasis on not allowing the best parts of the game to be spread naturally than on facilitating a relationship. MLB has vocally recognized the need to market its stars but hasn't been able to consistently find the bandwidth to do so. It has been at the leading edge of streaming technology but shown no aptitude for capitalizing on that, simply relying on what the service will bring in without effort.

Instead, though, the 2016-2017 offseason was focused on "shortening the game," something that any person given five minutes and an average game's layout will tell you is impossible to do on any sort of meaningful level. Removing the four-pitch intentional walk is not going to make people buy commemorative cups, and encouraging owners to build fairy-castles dedicated to the sport is not going to bring a group with a diminished discretionary income flocking to the (metal-detector-clad) gates.

The easiest first step for the league to make in bringing eyeballs to the game would be to allow outside GIF creation. The NBA, and on a more limited level, the NHL, understands this. To make new fans in this current environment, one has to make the best parts of the game bite-sized and mobile. Videos are clumsy and hard to watch while, say, at the office or in a classroom. GIFs are shareable. They're retweetable, they're easy to lean over with a phone and say, "Dude, look at this," and they're getting better in quality every day.

The league has tried to fill the gap, with individual team accounts creating GIFs and posting them, but these GIFs are often lower in quality than what the freelancers can make and may be posted anywhere from 10 minutes to an hour after the play in question has occurred—because those social media managers are tasked with other duties.

Along with freeing the GIF, the league must promote the stars, and in service to both the league and the stars, not just the league. While Manfred is saying the right things about promoting the incredible wealth of young talent that has emerged over the last few years, the reality is that the league is struggling to put those thoughts into actions. In 2015, MLB retained the services of the major creative agency Anomaly, which helped develop the "#this" campaign that has been seen sporadically across the last two seasons. Here is a good idea—one with ties to social media and a simple, clean style, that has been poorly leveraged by a limited rollout and little-to-no cross-media usage.

A current prime example of MLB failing to understand where it needs to go, and instead retreading what has been, is the aggressive spring training marketing of Tim Tebow. While an interesting—if vaguely confusing—story, Tebow is not a superstar in the making. One could be forgiven for thinking otherwise, though, after a brief browse of various MLB-affiliated platforms.

In some ways, Tebow is a self-inflicted problem. He carries a large following with him from his past turns as an SEC presenter and a mediocre NFL starter, as well as a Heisman-winning SEC quarterback. He's good for clicks, for shirseys, for autograph seekers, and for pure exposure. That following, though, is unlikely to retain a loyalty to the sport itself once Tebow washes out, whether it be at Low-A or Double-A. In hitching the horse to Tebow, MLB is revealing how desperate for raw results it is, rather than long-term conversions.

These particular criticisms would be mitigated if MLB had shown any adeptness at marketing its currently young long-term stars. Even a player like Mike Trout (who is, admittedly, bland) can be marketed. His one well-documented personality quirk is being a weather nerd, and it would be

---

4. Caveat: The author's Twitter presence skews toward the knowledgeable fan, but Twitter and sites similar are where one can find quick results from a decent variety of people.

5. Baseball Prospectus author Patrick Dubuque: "A rather pleasant looking elm."

6. For more complete results, see http://unlikelyfanatic.blogspot.com/p/major-league-baseball-image-twitter.html

7. Paul Sullivan, "Kris Bryant Believes Baseball's Fine Just the Way It Is," *Chicago Tribune*, February 22, 2017.

shockingly easy to link that up with one of the bigger personalities in the game, Noah Syndergaard, to create a fun, memorable commercial and social media campaign.

By allowing its young stars to be themselves, and creating an easy and quick pathway for their accomplishments to be spread, the league could buy itself a respectable amount of time to figure out what comes next.

⚾   ⚾   ⚾

Of course, this piece has really only looked at how MLB should be marketing toward the millennial piece of the pie, in the predominantly English-speaking American market. There are many other markets out there that MLB touches, and services with varying brands of marketing. Additionally, the diminishing American fan base has roots in issues far more complicated than simple marketing. Baseball is now an expensive sport at nearly every level, and while the league has made a start with attempting to counteract this problem, there are still fewer children playing it from a young age and building the lifelong love of the game through participation.

If Major League Baseball is truly concerned about reaching this particular audience, though, it's clear that something has to change, and arbitrarily changing the rules of the fundamental game isn't the right answer. Baseball needs to understand what it is, before it tries to make revisions. ▨

Bring Back Ball Four

by Russell A. Carleton

One way Major League Baseball has tried to improve its product is by speeding up the game, but as Russell A. Carleton notes, eliminating the four-pitch intentional walk disrupts the narrative pacing that helps people identify the most important parts of a story. – Geoff Y.

Strangely, my defense of the "classic" intentional walk—the one where you have to actually throw four balls—begins with the center fielder. In fact, I'd argue that the guy standing out there waiting for a ball to come his way is *the* reason baseball needs to bring back ball four.

But first, we need to meditate on the absurdity of the center fielder. There are no other major sports that routinely place a defensive player 300 feet from the spot where the action is. Three hundred feet marks off the distance from end zone to end zone in football. Three hundred feet can fit the length of three basketball courts and one-and-a-half hockey rinks. In most other sports, it isn't even physically possible to have a defender that far away. In fact, a 300-foot fly ball in baseball is rather pedestrian. Three hundred feet might get you to the center fielder's starting point, but there's even more real estate out there beyond him.

Funny enough, most of the time that defender doesn't actually *do* anything. In 2016, during 59.8 percent of the half-innings played the center fielder never touched a ball, even if it was to simply pick up a single that had rolled through the middle infield and throw it back in. Yet when you have a small ball that is not launched by the human arm or leg, but rather an extended lever, the physics of propelling a ball 300 feet become easier. However, the rules also say that those balls can be harvested and traded in for outs, so it makes sense to have a worker out there ready to grab something that may never come.

A baseball field is a very large place.

That has a few consequences. Because the game requires building something that can contain a missile launched 400 feet, a good number of the seats in the ballpark are also several hundred feet away from the place where the ball is launched. Unlike a game such as soccer or basketball, where the location of the action moves around the playing surface—which means that at different times, seats will be closer to or further away from the game action—the batter's box doesn't move.

In fact, baseball is a game that likes its boxes. The batter must stand in one. The pitcher once had a box, too, but that was reduced to a small slab of rubber that simply made his cage even smaller. But combined, it means that the two most important people in any at-bat—the pitcher and the batter—are confined to only a few square feet worth of space, 60 feet, 6 inches apart, and 500 feet away from the guy who paid $12 to sit in the center-field bleachers.

⚾   ⚾   ⚾

Baseball is a game that looks very different when watched at close range. I remember clearly the first time that, as a teenager, my friends ~~and I~~ snuck down into the lower reserve section at Jacobs Field and watched half an inning from the first row behind the backstop before a nice usher politely asked my friends ~~and me~~ to kindly remove ~~ourselves~~ themselves from that area, lest ~~we~~ they kindly be removed from the park. (My friends described it to me in such vivid detail that it was almost as if I had been there myself.) The pitches *moved*. It wasn't video game movement. They still obeyed those laws of physics that we had been learning about, but they *moved*. And the batter muttered. And the pitcher danced. Calls were on the corners. There was emotion coming from all of the participants after each of those pitches.

For most of my life, when I had gone to a baseball game, I had sat in those $12 seats. I knew that the outcome of a pitch, whether ball or strike, was important, but I experienced it as the ball being tossed down the chute and the umpire making a call. In fact, I mostly considered it important because I knew that a strike brought the batter closer to a strikeout and a ball brought the batter closer to a walk. I didn't think about how it changed the 2-1 pitch that was about to come (or how that would have been different from the 1-2 pitch that would have happened if the call had gone the other way.)

There's a lot of action that goes on between the pitcher and hitter on all of the pitches. I knew of this action, because I watched the games on television, and the center-field camera gives a decent perspective on the ball's movement and I could see the body language of the pitcher and batter.

It isn't the whole picture, but it's part of the picture. There once was a time when baseball games were not shown on television. That means baseball spent a great deal of its existence where there were only two ways to experience the game. One was on the radio and the other was in person, probably sitting a few hundred feet from the batter's box, watching the white ball be fired in the direction of home plate and the umpire yelling something. A little further back, and the radio wasn't even consistently an option either.

Baseball is a game played in two parts. There's the delicate dance of the batter and pitcher, and then there's what happens at the end when the batter hits the ball or the batter fails to hit the ball or the pitcher hits the batter. Much of the first part of that dance is played out in the realm of inches. Plenty of pitchers live either just on the corner or just off of it. The difference between a "good" slider and a bad one might be a couple inches of break. It's the sort of resolution that even the best human eye can't get from a few hundred feet away, often off-set at an angle. From that distance, they all look the same. But a fly ball hit in the air 300 feet from the batter's box? That was easy enough to see.

That, too, had consequences. In baseball's formative years, a language grew up around the end of the dance. Hitters "singled" or "grounded to third" or "flied out to center field." A quasi-mathematical notation was invented so that 8-year-olds could document these events and learn about matrices. From these events, there came forth numbers, numbers that came to be culturally important, and almost all of them based on summarizing what had happened at the end of a player's turn in the box. Consider baseball's best known statistics. Batting average summarizes the outcome of a hitter's at-bats. On-base percentage summarizes the outcome of a hitter's plate appearances. Home runs are a specific outcome that can end a turn at the dish. So are strikeouts.

Baseball culture grew to speak of its heroes in terms of how their plate appearances *ended*. There's nothing wrong with that. That is eventually the object of the game, but what would have happened if baseball had built all of its ballparks with all of its seats behind home plate, close enough to watch the dance of the slider and batter? What if a language had developed where we were not unaware of the fact that Babe Ruth hit a lot of home runs, but that one of the reasons he hit those home runs was that he was able to lay off pitches just off the corner?

But alas, that never happened. The physics of the game called for a center fielder and seats that were too far away to fully appreciate that batter-pitcher tango. By the time radio and television were widespread, baseball already had an entire language, poetic and numerical, that it used to talk about itself and a set of cultural norms that went with it.

And the fundamental assumption of that language was that what happened at the end of the at-bat was what mattered, with special preference given to things that the fans could see from the stands. (This is the same culture that pretended walks had no value until the turn of the millennium.)

Television might be able to show the movement of the pitches and the emotions on the players' faces, but by this point the announcers didn't dwell on that as much. There were few words, and the fans watching at home didn't grow up speaking them. There has always been plenty of movement in the game. Each pitch unravels yards of strategic adjustment. And if you're lucky, the color commentator might mention that once in a while.

⚾ ⚾ ⚾

Year	K per game	BB per game	HBP per game	PA per game	NIP percentage	Minutes per game
2016	8.03	3.11	0.34	38.01	30.2%	184.77
2006	6.52	3.26	0.37	38.71	26.2%	171.91
1996	6.46	3.55	0.31	39.10	26.3%	175.77
1986	5.87	3.38	0.19	38.24	24.7%	168.99
1976	4.83	3.20	0.18	38.06	21.6%	149.17
Data mostly courtesy of Baseball Reference, values are per team.						

Baseball has decided that it has a problem. It just hasn't figured out what problem that it thinks it has, and in this case the words matter. Writing in *Sports Illustrated*, Tom Verducci put the case succinctly: "Baseball does not have a time of game problem. It has a pace of action problem."[1]

We can see that the games have gotten longer, by more than half an hour over the course of 40 years, despite the fact that patrons still get to see almost the exact same number of hitters come to the plate. But there's another trend that has walked alongside that increase. Driven almost entirely by strikeouts, hitters are putting the ball in play a lot less than they used to.[2] In the past 40 years, the number of plate appearances ending with a "not in play" event has jumped by almost 10 percent.

These are separate, though related, problems, and baseball has never really been clear on which one it's trying to solve. Maybe the answer is "both." The game has grown up with a clear cultural preference for the ball being hit into play, but the game has quickly evolved past seeing strikeouts as a moral failing (karma did not punish for Casey for his hubris by having him ground to third). Instead, strikeouts are now seen as more of an unfortunate, though bearable, side effect for behaviors that teams do like. But they're hard to appreciate from 500 feet away, and even though television

1. http://www.si.com/mlb/2017/02/13/raising-strike-zone-pace-action
2. http://www.foxsports.com/mlb/story/there-s-gotta-be-a-reason-for-the-strikeout-epidemic-right-052714

can show the anguished face of the batter after he flails at the forbidden candy that he shouldn't have chased, we are still programmed to associate "action" with "hitting the ball."

This leaves baseball in a weird position. They can't command teams to strike out less. They can't command teams to stop valuing a skill that might win them more games, but it's boring. The league knows that even though they are tempted to make rule changes, they have to do so gingerly. The idea of raising the bottom of the strike zone to the top, rather than the hollow of the knee, has been discussed as a way to encourage more balls in a hittable part of the zone,[3] but tinkering with the rules too much runs the risk of alienating the crowd that believes You Can't Change Baseball.

So, if MLB can't make players put the ball in play more, at least it can cut down on the time between balls by instituting "suggestions" like the "keep one foot in the batter's box" rule and its cousin lurking in the background, the pitch clock.[4] The oddity is that the solutions to the pace-of-action problem are actually more solutions geared toward the time of game. Baseball apparently believes that the game needs a more hyperfrenetic pace so that the lacunae between batted balls don't feel so lonely.

It might be worth asking why baseball has become a game of dawdling to begin with. There are plenty of suggestions that would knock off a minute here or 30 seconds there from a game, but they mostly boil down to, "c'mon guys, let's get this over with." That might end up being counterproductive.

⓪　　⓪　　⓪

The psychologist in me sympathizes with the gentlemen who are on the field, maybe taking an extra moment before stepping into place. More to the point, the father of five who has played more Candy Land than I care to mention understands. Baseball is a game of sustained attention in a low-stimulation environment under conditions of sleep deprivation. In English, baseball is a game where most of the time nothing happens, but you have to pay close attention anyway because when something does happen, you have to react quickly.

Using PITCHf/x data, we can look at a simple metric of dawdling, which is the average time between pitches. We'll panel it by inning. I removed all first pitches of an at-bat (because they come after the previous hitter did something, which may have involved running around the bases for days on end) and limited the sample to those where no runners were on, so that pitchers and baserunners looking longingly at one another were taken out of the equation.

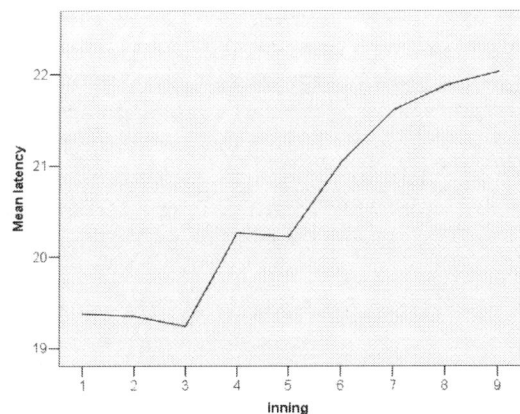

As the game wears on, things start taking just a bit longer. And that makes sense. Neurologically, it's hard to sustain attention for several hours, even for someone who does not have an attention problem. When people in laboratory settings are asked to perform a sustained attention task without rest, their reaction time slows and they have more lapses in attention. It's not surprising if hitters take an extra moment to reset their focus before climbing into the batter's box to face a 98-mph fastball that could kill them. MLB could legislate that they not take those extra moments, but they'd be legislating against the realities of neuropsychology. The consequence of that would be players who are more likely to be just a bit off their game.

And here we need to ask whether the cure is worse than the disease. Yes, the games could be shorter, but there also wouldn't be quite as much thrill from seeing some of the hemisphere's best athletes playing a game at the highest possible level that it can be played. There are going to be days when the score is 8-3 and the actual outcome of the game isn't much of a mystery. But in any one plate appearance a player can make a highlight-reel-worthy catch or hit a home run that breaks the tape measure. Even if the game is a dud, the fans can at least go home talking about *that*. Take away those little extra pauses and you take away some of the player's abilities to generate *those* moments. It's like cutting a few minutes off *Swan Lake* by sending in the junior varsity ballet dancers, because they pirouette a little faster.

Instead, may I suggest looking at this problem from a different camera angle than the one that inspires most baseball video games to have a "one-pitch" mode?

⓪　　⓪　　⓪

It's always important to listen to the words that people use to describe their problems. When I worked as a therapist, it was important to understand not only the problem a person

---

3. https://www.baseballprospectus.com/news/article/29358/baseball-therapy-the-knee/
4. https://www.baseballprospectus.com/news/article/25603/baseball-therapy-the-clock-is-ticking/

was bringing to the therapy room but also why they believed it was a problem. In baseball's case, they have identified the clock as the problem, but the reason behind that is a fear. For a business that makes its money by selling an entertainment product, it's a perfectly reasonable fear, but it's a fear of being "boring." Like anything else, "boring" is in the eye of the beholder, though MLB has a business interest in making sure that as many eyes as possible are beholding the game.

I rather like spending three-and-a-half hours at the ballpark, but even I can recognize a dud of a game when I see one. An 8-3 snoozer is no one's idea of a good time. And yet, while baseball complains about long games and extended pauses, they sure do sell the hell out of those moments when it suits them. Watch the television feed of a close game and you are guaranteed to see extended close-ups of a reliever as sweat drips down his face and he takes a deep breath before shaking off his catcher. The batter takes an extra moment before stepping in and has a determinedly placid look on his face as he wiggles his bat a little bit. Back to the pitcher who comes set as the crowd noise swells behind them both and then, the batter calls time. Baseball can be such a tease.

But suddenly, in a close game, the very issue baseball had declared as the reason for "boredom" is now a *dramatic moment*, despite the fact that "nothing" is happening. Now the pause is a reason to love the game. It's a reason to luxuriate in the fact that the game is in the balance and might be won by the heroes or the villains, and we have no idea who. It's an invitation to become emotionally invested. It's the setup for what is often called a "Hollywood ending."

I'd argue that baseball doesn't have a time-of-game problem or even a pace-of-action problem, as Verducci suggests. It has a narrative pacing problem. It wants to tell a good story, but the game sometimes gets in the way. To solve it, maybe baseball can take a few lessons from another art form: film. Not in the sense that baseball games should more resemble movies, but instead baseball can learn from the ways in which good filmmakers can take two hours and make them engaging and compelling, while bad filmmakers can make you demand a refund at the box office for the fact that you will never get those 120 minutes back.

Filmmakers don't tell a story in the most efficient way possible, because humans don't perceive stories in terms of efficiency. Instead, film uses a complicated visual language all its own that we often don't even recognize, but one that conforms to the way that people actually absorb narratives. When a scene opens, the filmmaker rarely jumps right to the action, but instead leaves a small "establishing shot" on the screen for a few seconds. If the characters will be interacting at a diner, the screen will show that diner from the outside. The establishing shot doesn't actually move the plot along,

but the brain needs a moment to transition from the last scene where they were in a laundromat. Or a spaceship. Or Mount Rushmore.

Filmmakers also play around with time in their composition. It's a standard film technique to use slow-motion footage during a particularly important moment in the film. Efficiency would be showing the event at full speed, which is how things actually proceed, but it's not how humans experience big events. When people experience crisis moments in real life, they will often recall the event by saying, "It's as if time slowed down." It didn't, but there's a very real cognitive reason it seems that way. During normal operations, the human brain has millions of pieces of information that it could pay attention to. The problem is bandwidth and capacity. To pay attention to every single detail all the time would be maddening.

Instead, the brain is predisposed to pay attention to certain bits of information, process others on autopilot, and ignore others. But in a crisis situation, the brain is cued to realize that this is an important moment and it begins collecting as much data as it can for this short burst. We are used to a certain amount of information representing a certain amount of time, but the brain's short-term information-gathering binge messes with that ratio. Filmmakers have learned to use that to their advantage, mirroring the brain's natural tendency to "slow things down" as a signal to the viewer. *Pay attention. This scene is really important.*

⚉   ⚉   ⚉

The intentional walk (you were wondering when I was going to back around to that, weren't you?) is a counterintuitive strategy. The pitcher is not supposed to want the batter to reach base, and yet there he is doing something that he could easily not do that will guarantee the batter first base. The whole process used to take a minute or so in the good old days when you actually had to throw the pitches, and now we can shave most of that minute off the game. But at what cost?

Using data from 1993 to 2016, I found that the average Leverage Index for a non-eighth-spot-in-the-lineup (to get to the pitcher) intentional walk is 1.4. For those unfamiliar with the Leverage Index, it was created by researcher Tom Tango and is a mathematical representation of how important a situation is to an individual baseball game.[5] Situations where the game is in the balance have high leverage values. Those where it doesn't matter have low values. An "average" situation has a value of 1.0, and so the intentional walk is generally pulled out of the manager's back pocket during a situation that is 1.4 times more important than a garden-variety situation in a baseball game.

---

5. https://www.fangraphs.com/tht/crucial-situations/

Whether by accident or design, the intentional walk is most often placed at an important juncture in the game, and like a good filmmaker who is trying to set a good narrative pace, the IBB slows the game down and allows a bit of time for baseball's version of an establishing shot (as we watch two grown men play catch exactly four times). And yes, we could get rid of that establishing shot and it would cut a little bit of time off of the movie, but would the movie actually be better for it?

I think we need to keep the "classic" intentional walk around. Not for the occasional giggle-inducing moments that it spawns when someone reaches out and hits one of the four pitches or the pitcher throws one of them away. Instead, we need those four pitches because they are part of the unspoken, visual language of the game. As the narrative of the game unfolds, the seconds that those four sham pitches consume actually serve a purpose in making the game fit with how humans process information, and by that measure, more engaging and interesting.

⚾   ⚾   ⚾

I think we need to accept something about baseball. It is not realistic to expect that a nonobsessed fan will watch every pitch of a game, especially one that isn't all that interesting. It might even be a little much to ask the obsessed ones to do it. The rules of basketball and football provide for "action"—with action being defined as people moving around in 10-yard increments—on a regular and predictable basis. Baseball suffers from an unpredictability in that sense. It's entirely possible to get through a half-inning without anyone hitting the ball into play and it's possible that any pitch might be the one that sets everyone running. To be a baseball fan, or a baseball watcher, is to have no idea when the next bit of "action" might be.

The fact that "action" in a baseball game is defined so narrowly turns out to be a historical accident that followed from the physics of the game. When you need a space so cavernous that it involves a center fielder and yet you do not allow the origin point for launch of the ball to move, you create a fan base that is largely ignorant of the great deal of action that goes on in the exchange of pitcher and batter as they negotiate the five pitches *before* the batter grounds out to second. When you create a long game that requires sustained attention *and* quick response times, you create a game where dawdling will happen. In some sense, I feel bad for Rob Manfred in his fight against the clock. He is actually fighting a two-front war against physics and the human brain. That's a hard battle to win.

I don't object to the idea of trying to shorten games, but if baseball believes that the reason it teeters on boring is the fact that there aren't enough balls in play per hour to satisfy people's craving for stimulation, it should make changes that work on the numerator in that ratio, rather than the denominator. Viewing the exercise through a simple lens of the ends (a few seconds saved) justifying the means is short-sighted. Sometimes the rituals we take for granted have deep functions that we don't appreciate until they're gone. I think the intentional walk, as silly as it may seem, is this sort of ritual.

It serves a purpose in making a game that can be hard to watch a little easier to watch, because it calls out to the viewer, "Hey, if you've checked out of the game mentally, you might want to check back in. We're about to do something important!" It gives the viewer a little time to readjust and reengage in the narrative. It even gives the announcers a chance to set the stage for what's going to happen next.

So I say bring back ball four. Make the pitcher actually issue an intentional walk, rather than just point the batter to first. Leave alone the language that baseball has evolved for itself to work around some of its limitations. Yes, they might seem like four useless lobs, but they do a job that's much more important than just allowing the batter a free pass to first. And they're worth the 45 seconds that it takes to make them happen. ▇

How Computers Killed a Sport

by Patrick Dubuque

While some may worry that baseball's ever-increasing reliance on data and use of analytics could lead to the sport's ultimate demise, Patrick Dubuque reminds us that similar concerns about chess have thus far been unfounded. – Geoff Y.

I was first introduced to the concepts behind sabermetrics in 1984. I was in first grade. My mother was taking classes to become a library technician at the local community college and a research project drew her, and me in tow, to the school library. On a bottom shelf I remember seeing an oversized book in striking Cooper Bold font with the title: *Every Great Chess Player Was Once A Beginner*. The book had colorful, easy-to-visualize diagrams explaining how the pieces moved, with gigantic cartoons of smug bishops with daggers tucked in vests, operatic queens in platemail dresses, and portly kings with spindly legs.

I enjoyed the pictures but was immediately drawn to the diagrams, which presented this plain-looking board game as an intricate puzzle. The back of the book contained full games, complete with annotations, which described how the game got from a symmetrical beginning to total victory and defeat. We checked out the book each week until my parents finally gave up and bought me my own. I didn't have anyone to play chess with—my parents had no interest—so I did what I did with so many other games as an only child in the early '80s: played against myself, transcribing the games on looseleaf paper. Until the next summer, when my father brought home a brand new Atari 400 and a cartridge: *Computer Chess*. I had no idea that I was witnessing what appeared to be the death of a sport.

In a sense it's amazing that anyone still plays chess. The game has been around for more than a millennium, and more than five centuries in its modern incarnation. People were playing chess before they'd invented the thermometer, the telescope, and the equals sign. And yet somehow it hasn't been worn out. Checkers has been solved: The game will always be drawn, if played correctly (ed. note: In an earlier draft of this piece, the author incorrectly stated that checkers was solved as won, not drawn). Connect Four took a couple of decades. Go has been broken on smaller boards;

the full-size version is vastly more complex, and still doomed. Meanwhile, a chess game after three moves on each side contains more than 9,000,000 possible configurations. It's as close to infinity as the human mind can approach, systematically.

Until the computers arrived, and then infinity didn't seem like such a big number. And in that arrival, and its repercussions, chess proved to be somewhat of a foreshadowing of baseball.

Part 1: The Eighth Century

The earliest form of chess, Shatranj, arrived from India and swept into Europe with the Muslims. It was as similar to modern chess as 1860s baseball is to the game today. Many of the pieces moved differently, more limited in their powers; the queen, not yet liberated, moved a single square. Because of this, opening games were slow, shuffling affairs, with pieces moving out slowly, cautiously; the early game lacked a sense of competition, as both sides casually rearranged their troops behind their lines.

This is also true of baseball: Pitchers weren't agents but only catalysts, and batters could ask for specific types of pitches to hit, high or low. The true combat was delayed until the ball entered play. In both games, this idea of delayed competition seems utterly foreign, pastoral.

Part 2: The Nineteenth Century

Fast forward a thousand years or so: Chess has moved from parlors to restaurants to having world champions. Games are transcribed in the newspapers. The style of the day is unscientific, reckless, romantic. It is the era of the Evergreen Game. Sacrifices are offered without careful thought, and gambits are accepted out of a sense of decorum. It's a time of swashbuckling and brilliant finishes, not because the game is played better but because it's so rare for anyone to see through the fog of the future, calculate more than a few moves ahead. The great attackers, like Morphy and Spielmann, have a sort of intuition of when to strike, but many games are about broken sieges as crippling blows.

So too, with baseball in the postdeadball, premodern era, with its golden age of heroes. It's managing, and strategy like bunting and hit-and-runs that are performed out of a sense of noble duty. It was an exciting time because it seemed limitless; there were patterns and rules, but we didn't see them. Instead the arm injuries and the breakout stars and the clutch moments seemed like magic.

Part 3: Modern Day

The "fall" of chess didn't come with computers, really. It began nearly a hundred years ago with a Danish master named Aron Nimzowitsch. Never a champion himself, he however built a philosophy that changed chess forever: He saw in the pieces their potential energy, rather than their kinetic energy. A piece was as powerful as the things it could do. Threats, not attacks, won chess games.

At first this created an exciting new era for chess, just as Bill James and Michael Lewis uncovered new possibilities in how to evaluate baseball. Hypermodern openings concentrated not on dominating the center by overrunning it but by controlling it from long range, remaining flexible, luring opponents into overadvancement and vulnerability. But as the full implications of this thinking played out, the game transformed. Positional chess caught up to tactical, attacking chess. No longer was a position just favored by the stronger side: There were these fractions of temporary values, initiative and space, that were just as important.

Chess became defensive, plodding, careful. Champions like Botvinnik and especially Petrosian won through iron-tight defenses and methodical, constrictive approaches focused on converting small advantages into definitive victories. Chess of this era perhaps most closely aligns with the early, precomputer era of sabermetric understanding: Pete Palmer, Earl Weaver, and the three-run home run. It was a time of rejecting, very slowly (because baseball, unlike chess, involves far more than just the will of its leader), the customary demands of a practiced game, an understanding that the aesthetic ideal of a sport and the truest path to victory are rarely aligned.

Part 4: Postmodern Day

Then, everyone's Ataris arrived, and everything changed.

Even before the IBM-constructed Deep Blue faced off against world chess champion Garry Kasparov and won, computers made their mark on the game. What they lacked in style and improvisational ability, they made up for in brute processing power. A chess program could take a position and play it a million different ways before settling on one with an outcome it liked. Openings were hit particularly hard by this: Any last vestiges of calm formality in the early moves were replaced by a thirst for any advantage. Memorization of openings went 10, sometimes 20 moves deep, and the decision of when to go "off book" became a major, often game-altering action.

This was supposed to be the end. The computers were supposed to whittle the dozens of tournament-acceptable openings down to one, openings would swallow up the midgame as the book grew longer, as more and more exchanges grew formulaic. Computers were supposed to suck the soul out of chess, then salt the earth by luring the next potential generation of players away with console video games and free-to-play apps.

So it will be with baseball, the purists often whisper. More and more of the game will be played on paper, decided before the games actually begin. They worry about the game but also about their ownership of the game, the way baseball is prepared and consumed and processed. It isn't so much luddism or a fear of change as a fear of the loss of magic: that we'll understand too much, lose the ability to be surprised. This isn't antiscience, because science provides invaluable results; baseball has no such virtuous purpose.

Part 5: The Future

A funny thing happened to chess in its death throes: It didn't die. Though it may never earn its due as the original e-sport, the game is more popular worldwide than ever. Technology has made the game not only easier to play, but easier to play against people thousands of miles away; the nascent AI of my own childhood is already obsolete in the days of Internet connectivity.

On the master scene, computers also played a funny trick: By uncovering interesting, undiscovered twists, openings display more variety than ever.

And by escaping stodgy, well-worn openings, midgame conflict became more sharp, more daring. It's almost as if the romantic era of chess never really died, it just found its footing.

What does this say about baseball? Computers have changed baseball since before the day Steve Boros plugged in his Apple IIe, and every change has in it a death. But if the fear is that the data of modern baseball will someday replace or reduce the feats of the human beings on the field, chess has proven such ideas unfounded. Deep Blue may have ultimately beaten Kasparov, but it did not take the game from him. Instead, the computers just supplied chess with another layer, just as the underrated aspects of physical endurance and psychological combat (witness the mastery of Bobby Fischer) that already complicated and enriched the game of chess.

So too will it be with baseball. Like chess, baseball has always had its data; the sport becomes more interesting as we understand how that data is recognized and manipulated. We have emerged from the era of the organization and moved into the era when the data is being used by the players themselves. What we'll have in the end is the same drama, the same prowess, but with a greater understanding of the how and why of what happens before our eyes. There will still be the unexpected, the magical: It'll just be at the subatomic level, the preparation and the practice.

Deep Blue didn't kill chess because the next step was to create teams: human and computer together, there to shore up each other's weaknesses. The computer was able to calculate probabilities of minute advantage; the human there to prevent predictability, instill an all-important element of creativity. This is another element where baseball has aligned with chess. While *Moneyball* championed the idea of the single visionary, the genius CEO model, teams are now growing outward, not upward.

Teams have brought in specialists of different realms: It's not just an army of Python-wielding interns anymore, but doctors and psychologists and translators. They're creating a neural network greater than any one person, or machine.

And that's why, even in a post-heroic GM era, fans will still probably continue to take a team-centric attitude toward sports: because of the creativity, the artistry that weaving a team together requires. Not that athletic performance doesn't share that same humanity; it's just that, in the instant of the ball crossing the plate, it's so much harder to see.

Until the data pulls back the fog from this, too, and we grow to understand the crucial actions that happen while we're blinking. Or at least until e-sports swallow up physical endeavor, and championships are played out through Twitch via *MLB The Show 46*. But even then, we'll still have people at the controls. It won't be so bad. ▨

The Best Failure in Baseball

by Zach Crizer

Mike Trout is great at many things, but as Zach Crizer observes, his best skill might be the ability to forget his lesser moments and stay relentlessly focused on pursuing further success at levels few can ever hope to achieve. – Geoff Y.

In August 2017, Mike Trout again etched his name atop one of those *through age 20-something* leaderboards—swallowing up another distinction like baseball prodigy kudzu. This one, though, isn't going on his eventual Hall of Fame plaque. He racked up his 856th strikeout, which surpassed Justin Upton for the most by any hitter through his age-25 season.

Even while posting perhaps the most successful out-of-the-chute baseball career ever, Trout has experienced much failure. The circumstances of his existence—reaching and dominating the majors before his 20th birthday, being the obvious best player on the field, being fast, hitting for power in the 2010s—have conspired in such a way that the strikeouts have piled up despite his rates being below the contemporary league average.

In the larger sense, Trout is succeeding, to put it mildly. He is playing as well as anyone ever has, but in baseball that only means failures make up a somewhat smaller majority of the events in his play log. Elite talent allows the best players to get to the majors earlier, get more plate appearances, and accrue more statistics. As a weird sort of collateral damage, they also accrue more failures. Albert Pujols has grounded into more double plays than anyone, ever. The all-time strikeout record has been passed directly from Babe Ruth to Mickey Mantle to Willie Stargell to Reggie Jackson.

Leading one of those lists, then, doesn't reveal a flaw so much as a choice. When every trip to the plate has a 60 percent chance of ending poorly, how do elite competitors want to go down, if they must—Pujols, for instance, ramps up his already startling ability to put the ball in play when men are on base. He has a 9.4 percent career strikeout rate with runners on—like Dustin Pedroia but with a .565 slugging percentage.

Failure is a construct of each individual mind. Because Trout is perpetually, wordlessly Trout, we don't have many (read: any) ruminations on the subject, but evidence surfaced early in his career that suggested his failures just ... escape him.[1] Poof. Now that Trout has overtaken this particular list, it's time we consider how the best player in the world grapples with the game's most ubiquitous experience, or whether he grapples with it at all.

⚾   ⚾   ⚾

It seems ludicrous. *Of course* Trout remembers his mistakes and his bad swings and the times he got fooled by an off-speed pitch. But let's think for just a second about the benefits of forgetting. Assuming you're among the athletically ungifted majority, try to envision—nay, try to *feel*—what it would be like to throw a baseball 95 mph. Release it at warp speed from your puny hand. Try to mind zap yourself into a YouTube clip where your bat collides with a major-league pitch just so, and sends the booming, emphatic announcer of your mind's eye (crossing my fingers for Gary Thorne) into hysterics over the extreme trajectory and distance of your incredible home run. Go on. I'll try, too.

Closes eyes tightly ... (Long, hissing exhale)

Didn't work. I merely summoned my recent attempt to hit a wiffle ball in the middle of my office. A playing-it-cool attempt at a Nomar Garciaparra stance unwound into a halting check swing, the handle merely clipping the bottom of the ball as it whizzed by at a speed of, oh, you know, 25 mph? Come to think of it, all my mental moments of potential baseball glory end with some version of me getting jammed and popping up. Gary Thorne's bellowing baritone doesn't materialize.

Trout's positive visualization warehouse is better stocked, but any major leaguer also has those teeth-clenching memories of frustration: silence-inducing whiffs with two

---

1. http://www.espn.com/mlb/story/_/id/8392192/los-angeles-angels-centerfielder-mike-trout-phenom-last-espn-magazine

runners on base in the bottom of the ninth inning, that last turn against the dominant reliever who spun him around with a slider in the dirt. Those things don't just vanish.

Unless we consider the tale Pedro Moura relayed in May.[2] For the sake of dramatic irony, let's get this out of the way: The Astros and Angels played a four-game set. On Monday, Astros relief weapon Chris Devenski whiffed Trout on three pitches. On Thursday, Trout took his devastating changeup out of the park. But by the time he reaches the clubhouse after the homer, Trout can't recall the earlier battle, the one he lost. We don't have anything to prove he ever dedicated it to memory at all.

In that Monday tilt, the first of a four-game series against the Astros, Trout faced Devenski in the seventh inning. None on, two outs. And Devenski came right at him, his strategy—you'd think!—shaped by his two times facing Trout in 2016, when he got to two strikes both times but failed to convince his otherworldly opponent to chase one of his out pitches.

Fastball for a strike. Slider fouled off. Fastball on the same low, outside corner as the slider, foul tipped into the mitt. Trout's 798th career strikeout, accomplished in three pitches.

Now, what happened then? Did he look into a Neuralyzer?

Thursday. Here comes Trout. Devenski is ready, maybe remembering Monday's triumph, thinking he has that little foothold in Trout's head. He doesn't know about the Neuralyzer, naturally.

Fastball, fouled off. Fastball, fouled off. Trout's down 0-2 again—which is a little failure in itself. It overwhelmingly portends larger failure against major-league pitching. Usually. Over the past two seasons, Trout's line in plate appearances that go to two-strike counts overall (.239/.380/.434) roughly mirrors 2017 Matt Carpenter. In those dreaded 0-2 counts, his line (.267/.337/.480) has approximated 2017 Yasiel Puig, while most hitters flail like above-average pitchers.

And this is where fantasy inches closer to something like magical realism. Devenski turns to that changeup, traveling a full 10 mph slower than either of the first two pitches. He hasn't thrown Trout the changeup since September 24, 2016. Trout has never had occasion to swing at Devenski's changeup. Even if he had, we've established that he didn't know he had faced this guy three days earlier.

Out goes the baseball.

⚾   ⚾   ⚾

This is, alas, also a data point that can be used to disprove the negative-event-mindwipe theory.

We knew that Trout would get to that 856th strikeout and take his place atop that aforementioned leaderboard, destined to be taken out of context by and for dumb people wherever silly sports arguments are found. But he's striking out less frequently than he was in 2016, when he struck out less frequently than in 2015, when he struck out less frequently than in 2014.

That 2014 season was the peak of Trout's struggles with the "hole" in his swing that made him susceptible to high fastballs. In 2015, Trout changed something and before long it became evident that the up-and-in fastball was no longer a way to make him human. It was 2016, however, when everything came together. Up until then, Trout had never been truly Trout-ian on two-strike heaters and off-speed pitches at the same time. Whether because of a focus on one or the other, or a natural tendency in his approach, he'd always displayed a preference when his back was against the wall.

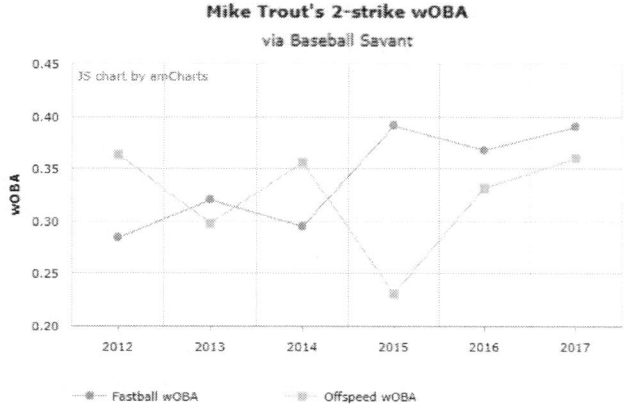

Now, though? Come one, come all, Trout will obliterate your two-strike offerings at any speed.

It's hard to take that as anything but learning. Dig deep enough into the tidbits of information that the beat writers get out of him, and you'll find that Trout's other changes mostly come with logical reasons, also, and of his own volition. Like his arm. He asked Kole Calhoun to throw with him to strengthen that part of his game. Since he asked the question, he presumably had to recall a time his arm let him down.

So, most likely, it's not that Trout forgets his lesser moments. He is just better at letting them be beaten down by the next moment, the next homer, the next question about tomorrow. Instead of allowing those moments to activate the sweat glands in his palms, or push him toward natural but counterproductive means of compensating for a weakness, he up and decides he should be the best at that thing, too—as if he'd simply never thought of it before.

2. Pedro Moura, "Angels? Mike Trout Should Never Be Counted Out, Regardless of the Count," *Los Angeles Times*, May 1, 2017.

Maybe, in addition to everything else, Trout is the best player in baseball at failing. Life's not fair.

⚾ ⚾ ⚾

Speaking of which, if we are to believe a rare candid-seeming conversation with Derek Jeter, the longtime Yankees shortstop did not shake off failures quickly: "The goal is to win. If I don't win, then I'm not fun to be around."[3] Quite the opposite, it sounds more like he was one flick of a butterfly's wing away from turning Pepcid AC into Microsoft (it was the '90s, people).

That's not aimed at comparing how a different great player dealt with the minefield of the majors, but to ask how Trout's experience thus far might shape the rest of his career. In addition to employing what sabermetrically inclined fans might see as a higher-risk, higher-reward approach to hitting, and the additional small disappointments that could bring, Trout has dealt with far, far more team-level failure. Saddled with poorly conceived veteran contracts, the Angels have mustered only one truly good team in Trout's time, and it was dispatched quickly by the Royals.

We could hypothesize that this type of early career path would have driven Jeter to drink, or worse. But it's also possible he would have turned out a somewhat different player. If his defense had declined as it did *before* he won a ring, or even before he won his second, or third, would he have been willing to make way for a young, spry replacement? Will Trout handle things differently if his center-field coverage drops below his standards?

If Trout's time in the relative limbo of this Angels team proves anything, it's that Jeter's stress is misplaced, if admirable—that it's probably best put out of mind when possible. It's an individual game of maximizing performance, played simultaneously by 25 people who share a clubhouse and an airplane. We're still discovering new ways of achieving those highest levels, and Trout is climbing faster than anyone.

Zoom out, and it's astounding how many of the sport's recent strategic shifts addressed habits are born of failure avoidance. Or, really, the need to dodge the *feeling* of abject defeat. If you sacrifice your at-bat to move a runner, your out can't be totally futile. Right? If you don't challenge that close play, you can't lose. If you don't shift, your shift can't be beaten. If you don't swing for the fences, you (probably) can't strike out 30 percent of the time. Even the teardown rebuilding trend could be seen as an outcrop of this broader, Trout-like philosophy.

Recent developments say the hell with hedging your bets. Be liberated from the quotidian pangs of your fifth-inning strikeout, that two-out single your pitcher allowed because your third baseman was in shallow right field, or the cellar-dwelling season that got you that draft pick. Think not of the elevated heart rate you experienced navigating the highway. Rejoice in your record time and superb gas mileage.

There is an unmistakable optimism in letting go.

Failing a lot is a product of trying a lot, and when you're as gifted as Mike Trout, it's rapidly replaced in the collective record by more highlights, more numbers, more greatness. With every double-speed wave of his bat and every pounding step, Trout is trying to be the best baseball player *ever*. The fruit of his efforts, Jeter would agree, won't be found in those details along the way that put the outcome in doubt. It will be in the hulking, smiling bundle of muscle standing there at the end, unburdened by the bumps in the road. ▨

---

3. https://twitter.com/BaseballKing/status/894921535852609536

Almost Always Counts (Emotionally)

by Craig Goldstein

In the wake of a no-hit bid broken up by a bunt single, Craig Goldstein wonders whether we should simply lament losing the opportunity to experience something remarkable rather than blame the batter for doing his job as best he can. – Geoff Y.

The date is June 21, 2017, and Justin Verlander has just struck out Mitch Haniger for the first out of the fifth inning. It was his 10th strikeout of the game, and if it wasn't vintage Verlander that's only because he didn't throw his (once) devastating changeup, instead relying on a curveball with more drop than a Tiesto banger to play off his riding, mid-90s heater.

He then worked a 1-1 count to Jarrod Dyson before the speedster pushed a bunt just out of Verlander's outstretched glove, into the Bermuda Triangle between the pitcher, first baseman, and second baseman, ultimately arriving at first base without a throw.

There's nothing particularly notable about this sequence of events, excepting Verlander's exceptional strikeout rate in this outing. Dyson isn't much of a hitter and his wheels are his best asset, so bunting for a hit is well within his game. But people got upset, as people do, because Verlander was in the midst of a perfect game at the time. The Detroit television announcers asked the question that was on the minds of many at the time:

> Mario Impemba: Here's a question: In strict terms of "baseball rules," when is it too late to bunt for a base hit in a no-hitter?

His broadcast partner, Kirk Gibson, opined that there's nothing cheap about Dyson's play and remarked that it's actually pretty smart, since swinging away wasn't working at all.

> Impemba: But there does come a time in the game where that's frowned upon, I would ... I would submit.
> Gibson: I would say if it was 6-0 right now, I don't know, maybe borderline.
> Impemba: So you're saying it's more the score than the inn—
> Gibson: Score and the innings.

There's no need to delve into the unwritten rules of when it is okay to bunt for a base hit during a no-hitter/perfect game again, especially when Grant Brisbee does it better than anyone.[1] Suffice to say that some people find it cheap, while others think the cheap thing is to not take every at-bat seriously and try to set your team up for a win. It's interesting to see noted hardass Kirk Gibson admire the play by Dyson—but then again, trying to win no matter what is very Kirk Gibson, too.

No, rather than pass judgment on whether it's acceptable, cheap, acceptably cheap, or otherwise, I wonder why we care at all. Why does our investment in Justin Verlander's attempt at greatness hinge on the score? The inning? The score *and* the inning?

It turns out others far smarter than myself have tackled these questions, if not specifically about baseball. Daniel Kahneman and Amos Tversky were mathematical psychologists who essentially founded the field of behavioral economics. Michael Lewis's recent book, *The Undoing Project*, covers their lives, and in it lies a scenario that hints at what is taking place when we argue about the etiquette of when it is acceptable to bunt for a base hit:[2]

> You have participated in a lottery at a fair, and have bought a single, expensive ticket in the hope of winning the single large prize that is offered. The ticket was drawn blindly from a large urn, and

---

1. http://www.sbnation.com/mlb/2014/9/16/6231827/bunting-to-break-up-a-no-hitter-domonic-brown-andrew-cashner
2. Michael Lewis, *The Undoing Project: A Friendship That Changed Our Minds* (New York: W. W. Norton & Company, 2016).

its number is 107358. The results of the lottery are now announced, and it turns out that the winning number is 107359.

They ran this scenario with three different groups. One was exactly as you see above. The others had the winning number as "207358" (Group 2) and "618379" (Group 3), and in each iteration they asked their subjects to rate their unhappiness on a 1-20 scale. The first group, the one in the prompt above, reported the greatest unhappiness. Group 2 was also more unhappy than Group 3. Indeed, as Lewis writes:

> [T]he further the winning number was from the number on a person's lottery ticket, the less regret they felt. 'In defiance of logic, there is a definite sense that one comes closer to winning the lottery when one's ticket number is similar to the number that won,' [Kahneman] wrote in a memo to [Tversky], summarizing their data. In another memo he added that 'the general point is that the same state of affairs (objectively) can be experienced with very different degrees of misery,' depending on how easy it is to imagine that things might have turned out differently.

And that is the crux of our case with no-hitters, perfect games, bunting for hits, and baseball etiquette. Knowing that we have the capacity to feel unhappiness over not winning a raffle by one number in a hypothetical context, it makes sense that we'd feel an intense disappointment at watching potential history evaporate in front of us. Each of us buys a nine-numbered lottery ticket with every baseball game that we take in. Our cost is not always in dollars, but in time and allegiance, in emotional investment.

Each game, each lottery ticket, is an assumed loss; that first-inning hit hardly registers as a disappointment, because we were unlikely to see that perfect game anyway. Even in the third inning, it's just so far away as to seem abstract. It's a bridge to be crossed when we arrive at it. By the fifth inning/number, you start to believe. It gains form and despite knowing it's not likely, you can *see* it. The sixth is when that feeling settles in. You know everyone knows what is at stake, when you unconsciously realize how many other possible results have been eliminated, so that even though you know there's a ways to go, it feels closer than you'd have ever assumed. The further a pitcher goes in a potentially historic outing—the closer and closer our lottery ticket gets to the winning number—the harder it gets to avoid disappointment in not getting there.

That's really what this is about. The etiquette, the method in which our disappointment is served to us, is mostly inconsequential. It's just a thing through which we can channel our regret, because without this *thing*, especially such a dinky thing as a bunt, we might have experienced transcendence. As Kahneman says later:

> The pain that is experienced when the loss is caused by an act that modified the status quo is significantly greater than the pain that is experienced when the decision led to the retention of the status quo.

In this light, we understand why there was a significantly smaller sense of loss (if any) when John Lackey allowed a leadoff double before retiring 27 straight in 2006. (Well, that and it was John Lackey who did it.) Still, there's clarity on why a decision to bunt—itself a departure from the status quo of swinging away—causes additional pain on top of its removal of the status quo of the game (no-hitter or perfect).

Understanding this process about ourselves probably won't alter our behavior. Knowing that being one number off winning the lottery is no different than having every number be wrong in terms of odds. It feels worse no matter what. But what we can do is change how we understand and act toward other fans. Perhaps the next time a no-hitter or perfect game is lost via a bunt or some other weird happening, rather than argue about whether that happening is justifiable, just nod and say, "It sucks to lose out on that experience." It does. ▨

The Case of the Missing Fireman

by Russell A. Carleton

> *Should we blame Tony La Russa for introducing the one-inning closer or, as Russell A. Carleton suggests, appreciate him for discovering a bullpen model better suited to the modern game?* – Geoff Y.

What if Goose Gossage showed up at a team's spring training camp. Not the 66-year-old, still fabulously mustachioed version of Goose Gossage. Imagine if Gossage stepped out of a time machine from, oh, let's just say 1978, and reported with the rest of the pitchers and catchers on a February day. The Gossage who was quite happy to work multiple innings to pick up a save. And he was pretty good at it. He is, after all, in the Hall of Fame.

Let's for a moment mute the arguments about whether he should be in The Hall and whether WAR properly captures his value.[1] Let's also mute Gossage's own well-publicized views on whether he should be in The Hall and whether WAR properly captures his value.[2] He was really good at being a relief pitcher, but he filled a role that doesn't really exist anymore. Gossage was a prototypical "fireman." And he was one of the best.

Whatever else one thinks of the "fireman" role, there's no question that the ability to pitch multiple innings of nonembarrassing relief is a *very* valuable skill to have in a bullpen. Why is it, then, that if Gossage were plunked into the middle of a current team's camp, he wouldn't be allowed to do the thing he was undeniably good at? There aren't any more firemen in MLB. I have a hard time believing that it's because there aren't pitchers who *could* do it. I think that MLB has simply foreclosed on the role itself.

Today's Goose Gossage would likely either be stretched out as a starter or be put into a one-inning relief role. It seems a strange misuse of his talents. If a pitcher can pitch well enough to handle high-leverage moments *and* can pick up *both* the eighth and ninth innings, why not let him? Where

are the missing firemen? It makes very little sense to take a job that could be done while only sacrificing one roster spot and make *two* pitchers do it.

According to legend, we are supposed to blame Tony La Russa and Dennis Eckersley, as Eckersley became the prototypical one-inning closer and La Russa designed a bullpen around the one-inning reliever model in Oakland. Your honor, I think Tony La Russa was framed for this kidnapping.

Warning! Gory Mathematical Details Ahead!

First, let's lament the graph that shows the downfall of the fireman closer. The graph shows the average number of outs recorded by pitchers who were awarded a save in a game. We see that in the 1950s and 1960s, the average save consisted of a pitcher getting about five outs. Today, the number is barely above three, and the bottom seems to have dropped out in the late 1980s, consistent with the emergence of Eck and the copycats that followed him.

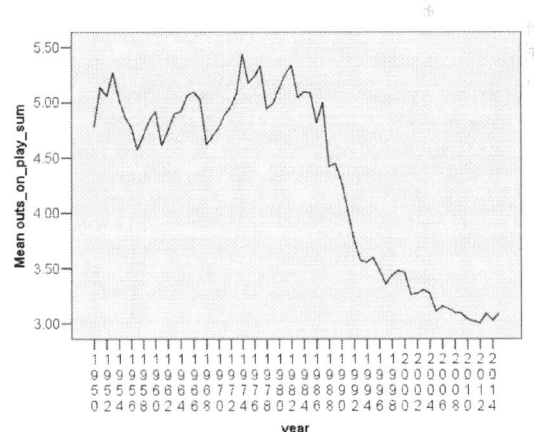

Small leads in the late innings are now usually handled by multiple hands, rather than one fireman, but as has been pointed out before, teams aren't actually getting better results than they used to in protecting those leads. The following graph shows all "save-worthy" (i.e., three runs or

---

1. https://www.baseballprospectus.com/news/article/30256/baseball-therapy-lets-see-if-we-can-get-a-handle-on-zach-brittons-cy-young-case/
2. http://m.mlb.com/news/article/216442236/goose-gossage-states-case-vs-modern-closers/

fewer) leads that teams were able to preserve in the seventh inning. (In these cases, the team entered the inning with the lead and emerged from that inning with the lead intact.)

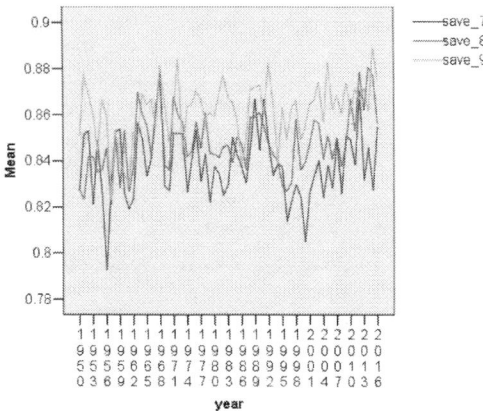

This graph is a little noisy, but we're not seeing the shift from a two-inning closer to a one-inning closer making much difference in whether teams actually protected their leads. There was an uptick in lead protection, especially in the eighth inning, but that happened within the last decade, well after the shift from the fireman closer to the one-inning closer.

I want to be careful making that claim, though. The shift to the one-inning closer model happened right before the 1990s, when offense went berserk. It's possible that there was a positive effect from the one-inning closer model, but there was a countervailing force from the increased offense in the atmosphere that made holding any sort of small lead a lot harder to do. To check this, I present to you a graph with three lines. The top line is runs per inning in *all* first innings within that season. This gives us a baseline from which to work. The other two lines are the average runs per inning in eighth- and ninth-inning situations in which the pitching team entered with a save-worthy lead.

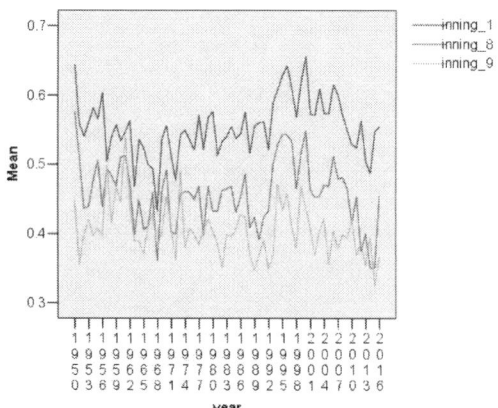

This graph turns out to be a pretty interesting one. It shows that in the early part of our timeframe (the 1950s and 1960s), the number of runs given up in late-inning, high-leverage situations ran a lot more closely together with the runs allowed rate for starters in the first inning, until the two groups got some separation in the *early 1970s*. But the odd thing is that the separation between those two lines didn't get wider as baseball experimented with the fireman and then the one-inning closer.

The following graph shows the difference between the first-inning line and the eighth-inning/high-leverage situation runs allowed lines. (The first-ninth inning graph shows the same pattern.)

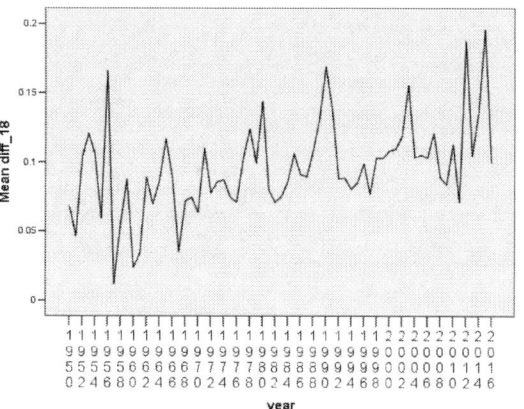

Teams generally give up fewer late-game/high-leverage situation runs than first-inning runs, but the magnitude of that difference hasn't really changed much through either the fireman era or the one-inning reliever era. Teams haven't really gotten better results through changing their strategy.

⚾   ⚾   ⚾

I think we need to back up for a moment. The following graph is another that shows that things may have started changing before we think they did. This is strikeout percentage (K/PA) for starters versus relievers. Again, we see that relievers and starters were tracking each other fairly closely until the early 1970s, when we begin to see some separation.

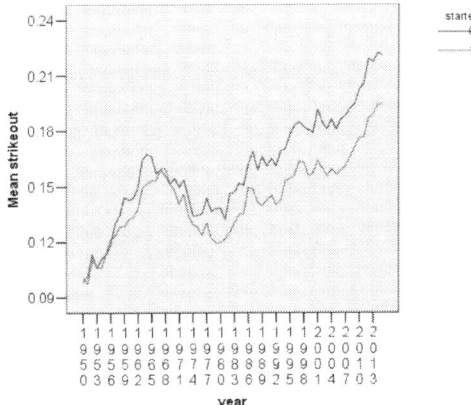

I'd argue that this is the result of another development in baseball that had been building up until the 1970s, which is the development of the relief specialist. By that, I mean baseball began to see more and more pitchers who were exclusively assigned to be relievers, and not just starters. Here's a graph of all pitchers within a year who pitched at least 70 innings in relief. Some of them were swingmen/long relievers who also picked up a few starts here and there. Some were exclusively relievers. But watch the proportion change over time.

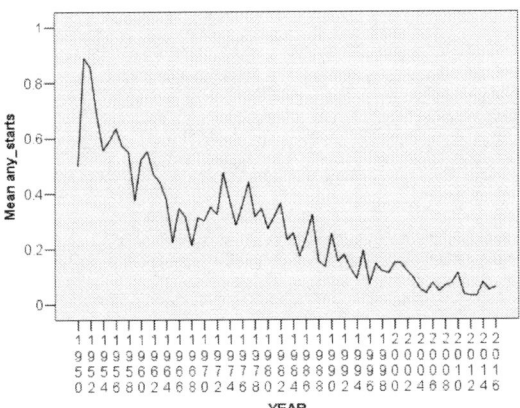

There's a major drop from 1950s into the late 1960s, and it tails off further to the present day. But it's worth noting that in the 1950s and 1960s, relievers were often called on to make starts on a consistent basis. During that time, we see that pitchers throwing in relief seem to get results consistent with starters. It seems that the late 1960s and early 1970s was the real birth of the "relief pitcher" as its own species. There had always been pitchers who had come into relieve the starter, but now the wall between the two groups had grown a little thicker.

⚾   ⚾   ⚾

The data shows very clearly that there have been two eras in high-leverage reliever usage. The following graph shows the evolution of how long a reliever remained in the game (measured by the number of outs he recorded) in games that he entered in the seventh, eighth, or ninth innings, and where his team held a "save-worthy" lead when he entered.

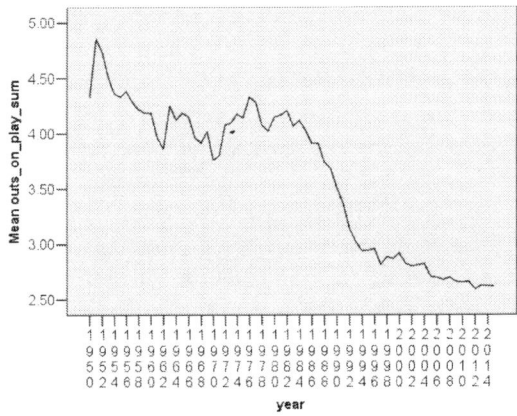

The standard story that we've been told is that this was a conscious decision to favor short-duration, max-effort outings. This had the twin benefits of allowing the relievers to throw really hard and also to come back the next night, if needed, because throwing one inning didn't build up as much of a pitch count. We've seen earlier in this article that the results that teams got overall weren't necessarily better, but perhaps the idea of using Eckersley on back-to-back nights was more appealing than using Gossage for 2 1/3 innings and not having him available for a day or two.

The evidence tells a different story. The following graph, separated out by decades, shows the average number of days a reliever "rested" after an appearance in which he recorded X outs. (I censored all values above 10, because that probably means he got sent to the minors or designated for assignment or something like that.)

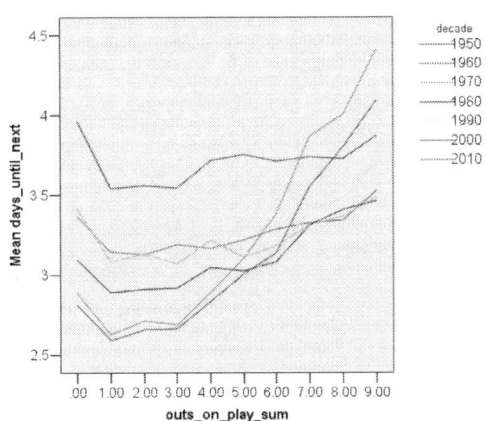

The immediate way to interpret this graph is to note that beginning in either the 1980s or 1990s, teams began looking at relief outings in two separate categories. There were outings that lasted three or fewer outs, and then there were multi-inning outings. If a pitcher had gone into a second frame, he was given more rest. In the 1950s through the 1970s, the line for rest is fairly flat. A relief outing was a relief outing. There seemed to be a set number of days that one rested after such an outing. I think that's the wrong way to interpret the preceding graph.

Let me draw your attention to the fact that in the 1950s, we see that no matter how long a reliever went (up to the three-inning mark, anyway), he got about 3.6 days off until his next appearance. In the 1960s and 1970s, that dropped to 3.4 or so, but it was still a flat line. I'd submit that the 1950s through 1970s are the oddity here. Consider for a moment: Why is it that a pitcher who was *soooooooo* much tougher back during the "good old days" needed three or four days to "recover" from an outing where he only got an out or two? Why are today's pitchers able to get back on the mound in two or three days? The "recovery" time for pitchers who pitch into a second frame in the 2000s and 2010s is in line with historical norms. What's really happening is that modern-day pitchers are coming back much more quickly after a *short* outing.

(Well, that's a little deceptive. We'll talk about why in a minute.)

The evidence also shows that the idea of modern pitchers as not able to be shut down by multiple outings isn't really true. The following graph shows all appearances in which a reliever entered the game in the seventh, eighth, or ninth innings, with his team holding a save-worthy lead. He pitched and recorded at least four outs. The graph shows the percentage of time that pitcher came back to pitch on the next calendar day (or in the event of a doubleheader, later that day).

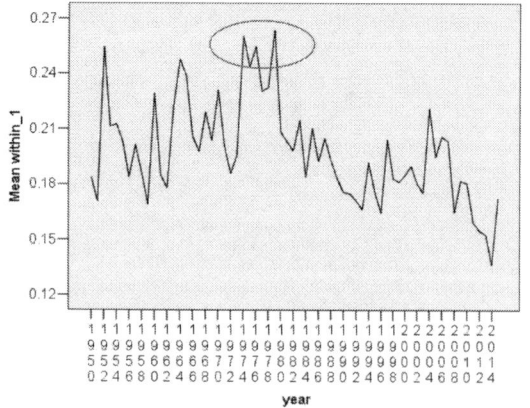

We see that it was never very common for a pitcher to do a multi-inning job and then come back the next night. Rates of this sort of reappearance have declined over the past few years, but note that the outlier seems to be a local maximum that just happens to coincide with the fireman's cultural heyday. If we look at how often that same group of pitchers came back within the next *two* days, we see that today's pitchers are no more or less able to handle coming back after a longer outing.

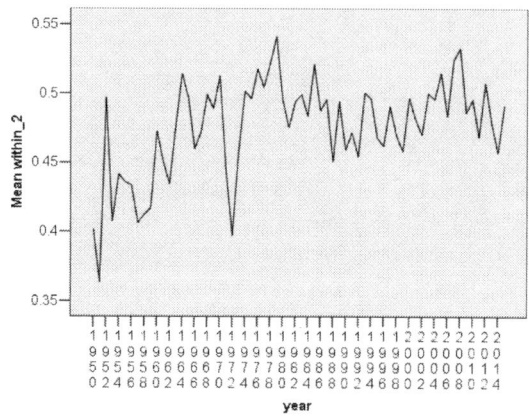

Before we go any further on that line of argument, there's something important that we need to say. Just because a pitcher didn't pitch in a game, it doesn't mean he wasn't available. It might mean he wasn't needed. Keep that in mind as we go forward.

⚾   ⚾   ⚾

I think I know who really kidnapped the fireman. We see that modern-day pitchers appear to be physically able to handle the role, and that the one-inning closer model isn't any better or worse than the fireman model in terms of protecting leads. I've speculated before that maybe the problem is that even an elite reliever gets a little worse in his second inning of work, and there may simply come a point at which there's another, better arm in the bullpen to take his place.[3] But surely there have got to be teams, or at least days, when a two-inning save makes sense. And if you have a pitcher who can do that, why not let him? Why has the idea of the fireman disappeared so completely from the game?

To answer this, I'd like to present two more graphs. One is the percentage of MLB starts in which the pitcher recorded 27 outs.

---

3. https://www.baseballprospectus.com/news/article/30615/baseball-therapy-stop-miller-time/

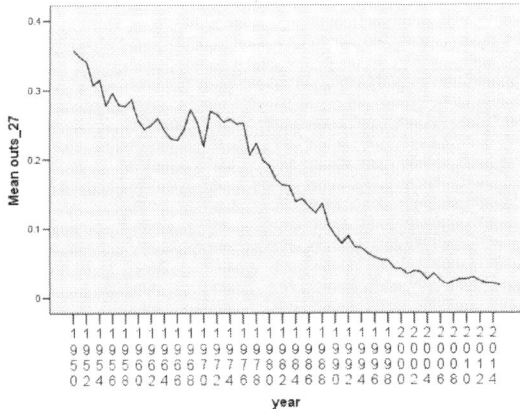

We know that the complete game is an endangered species and that rates of game completion have been slowly sliding downward for decades.[4] Part of that is the fact that relievers have gotten better, but part of it seems cultural. The following graph shows all situations in which the pitching team was entering the ninth inning with a save-worthy lead, and the percentage of the time it was the *starter* who was on the hill.

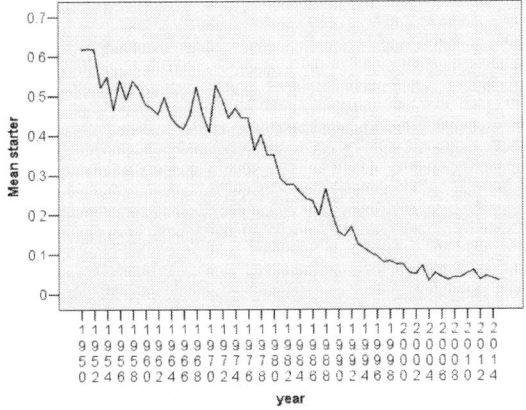

Up until the mid-1970s, half the time there was a situation that would now call for the closer, the starter was still out there! Rates were, of course, higher in the eighth and seventh innings. Now, it's very rare. It might be that teams are now a little more wary of what high-pitch-count games can do to a

pitcher's arm, but whatever the reasons, the question in the 1970s was not who would close out the game, but whether there would be a reliever in the game at all.

Now consider for a moment what this means for a manager's bullpen strategy. If he faces a situation in the seventh inning that might call for a fireman, he could put that guy in for an eight-out save. In any era, it probably means burning him for a day or two. But when you live in an era where tomorrow, you have a reasonable expectation that your starter will go nine innings—so you aren't as likely to need warm bodies to fill innings *and* you're used to having your starter essentially act as his own fireman—it's not a big deal to let a guy go for eight outs. The reality was that the demand for reliever workload in general was less than it is today.

But over time, as complete-game rates started to fall, relievers became more specialized and managers started to feel less comfortable riding their starters with small leads in the late innings, the fireman model didn't make as much sense. By the 1990s, a manager faced much less certainty that his pitcher would throw nine innings the next day. That means he wasn't going to farm out the fireman's job to the starter the next day. It also means a manager had to think about the distinct possibility of having to fill two or three innings tomorrow. He also has to think about the fact that tomorrow might be a close game. So, if a manager uses his really good reliever now for two innings, it might lead him to be hung out to dry for the next couple of days if a close game should come along.

The one-inning model represented a way to hedge that risk. A manager might not be able to have his ace reliever go two innings in this game, but tomorrow he could probably still come back. In fact, with the near extinction of the complete game, the short-burst model allowed a manager to think of his relievers as tactical weapons, useful for specific, short-range purposes (LOOGY, ROOGY, setup guy, mop-up guy, closer), and using them in shorter bursts meant that whatever situation the game presented the next day, he would always have his full complement of relievers (or at least close to it) from which to choose. It was a compromise that fit the new realities of how *starters* were pitching.

Tony La Russa just hit on a model that actually worked. ▦

---

4. https://www.baseballprospectus.com/news/article/22378/baseball-therapy-what-happened-to-the-complete-game/

A Monumental Decision

by Patrick Dubuque

Patrick Dubuque ponders the not entirely tangible value stadiums provide a city and its people. – Geoff Y.

It's not often that you have a philosophical question that hasn't been beaten to death; what with science and astronomy and politics getting their own fields, philosophy doesn't have much ground left to cover anymore. But there's a topic that's been dogging me for a long time now, never pressing enough to answer, but always around. The question: Are monuments ethical?

By monuments, I don't mean the ones that have been in the news lately, the statues of non-Americans that some Americans feel protective of. I mean monuments in the grander sense: the colossal civic projects, forged by mystical inspiration or whips or both, to create a lasting thing, a representation of the people who lived there. The Pyramids and the Taj Mahal—or even on a local level, the St. Louis Arch and the Golden Gate Bridge—are iconic constructions that inspire and memorialize, the last connections to the obelisks of an ancient age that spurred mankind toward revelation.

Monument-building has slowed down in the modern age, however, mostly because fewer people are getting whipped to build things. What we generally consider the wonders of the world are a product of despotism or, in the best of scenarios, the benefaction only possible through extreme wealth; they are not democratic things. In democracies, when we're about to gild the ceilings of our cathedrals and throw fortunes into construction, there are people to remind us that there are folks down the street who are starving. Or at least that we could build a mass transit system for them to get to the cathedral.

Monuments are tricky things because they create a shared good, in both the tangible present and the intangible future. The Space Needle doesn't really do anything, per se, except attract some tourism funds from people who like to eat from a height while rotating slowly. But it's a permanent feature of the Seattle skyline, a source of civic individuality at a time when that's difficult to find. But can they be justified when people are hungry and homeless? It's not an easy question to answer, but there's an easy follow-up while we mull: what about our modern cathedrals, the stadiums?

⚾ ⚾ ⚾

In 1949, Bertrand Russell gave a series of lectures, which were collected into a short volume entitled *Authority and the Individual*. Then a spritely 77-year-old, the Lord Russell had long completed his conversion from logic-based mathematician to reason-based social philosopher and humanitarian, and the speeches are packed with occasionally diverted arguments founded on common sense. His target, for so long dated and recently undated: the rise of government control, both in the communist and capitalist spheres, and the conflict of man versus society.

One of the primary failings of modern democracy, Russell finds, is rooted not in corruption or power-grasping, but in simple logistics: Governments are too big because nations are too big. Even in America's original 13-state condition, the Founding Fathers had to make some compromises on the original democratic blueprint of the Greek city-state: The town hall wasn't going to cut it. We needed the results of those town halls to collect into bigger town halls, which would head to a town hall at the nation's capital. The same expansiveness that defined the nation and provided its resources also handicapped its ability to represent its people, since every stage of growth only supplied an extra layer of difficulty and distance.

By 1949, Russell saw this remoteness between government and its civil service, and the people it was supposed to represent, and prophesied that the people would lose more and more of their power. In this sense, he was correct, though he could not see the completeness of the loss, the gerrymandering and campaign spending, or the destruction of local politics through television and Internet media. Today, paradoxically, Washington DC feels farther than ever, and yet at the same time we can never escape its noise. Russell was hardly a small-c conservative; he was a major proponent of a world government, and saw it as the only alternative to nuclear war. But he also recognized that it wasn't just about creating governments, it was about maintaining them.

And it's not just that government is actively distancing itself from its electors to avoid responsibility or repercussions; it's also just a natural aspect of the shared workload of the community. The individual, he says, is born with a spirit of adventure and primitive ferocity that is at odds with, and often stifled completely by, the drive toward efficiency and equality in society. Most people can get by with cooperating for the most part, employing vacations or trampolining to get their thrill-seeking out of their system. Artists and writers, who need to be apart from society to thrive, whose main purpose is to make their audience see something specifically outside of accepted truth, have it harder.

But the main goal is to channel that warlike instinct in all of us toward helping each other, often at our own cost. For most of history governments have employed that warlike nature into actual war, seizing fortune and property to the benefit of all, while constructing an Other to rally against. In the nuclear age, however, war grew expensive (though obviously not too expensive) and enemies became more dangerous to create (though obviously not too dangerous).

Still, a substitute is needed, and Russell provides his solution alongside his solution for democracy as a whole in the form of local government. "It would be a good thing," he says, "if cities could develop an artistic pride leading them to mutual rivalry, and if each had its own school of music and painting, not without a vigorous contempt for the school of the next city. But such local patriotisms do not readily flourish in a world of empires and free mobility." Or franchised business, or the Internet, two more forces that would have only hardened the philosopher's determination.

I cannot cite figures, and certainly position myself for criticism with an opinion, but it would appear that Russell's fears of homogenization of culture have proved worse than he could have imagined. On the small scale, we see it in the ripples of the death of the newspaper, and local news in general. Globally, languages and traditions wither before us. Advances in social and physical mobility have improved trade, shared ideas, created incredible efficiencies leading to the increased wealth of all; we can eat grapes in the winter, take in the works of master artists overseas. But the increased wealth has also led to increased sameness; cities are no longer as distinct, physically or culturally, as they once were. You can drink Starbucks in Seoul, eat Subway sandwiches in Stockholm.

Russell continues:

> In those who might have worthy ambitions, the effect of centralization is to bring them into competition with too large a number of rivals, and into a subjection to an unduly uniform standard of taste. If you wish to be a painter you will not be content to pit yourself against the men with similar desires in your own town; you will go to some school of painting in a metropolis where you will probably conclude that you are mediocre, and having come to this conclusion you may be so discouraged that you are tempted to throw away your paintbrushes and take to money-making or to drink, for a certain degree of self-confidence is essential to achievement.

We've already seen this effect in baseball through the dissolution of the spirit of the minor leagues, subservient to the demands of efficiency by their major-league overlords. Denied an identity through the baseball they play, these teams are forced to the creativity of *Game of Thrones* promotions and emblazoning their jerseys with pictures of tacos. Specialization of future athletes has become so vital that children are forced to channel their entire lives into the pursuit of a single dream, and forsake others. Sports cease being a diversion, cease to fulfill their original purpose of combat substitute, and become just another caste, unavailable to almost everyone except in vicarious form.

⚾   ⚾   ⚾

So where do we stand? America's largest cities, in an era of economic inequality and crumbling infrastructure, pour hundreds of millions of dollars into buildings where millionaires play for the profit of billionaires. With few exceptions, those cities that refuse to pay the ransom lose their teams to the highest bidder. Some of the deals work out better than others, but it's inevitably a sad Faustian bargain. But the evils of public financing for private stadiums is hardly a new, or interesting, argument.

Though it's difficult to quantify, and thus difficult to budget, sports teams do offer value to their cities beyond the fictional economic stimulus owners pretend they bring to their surroundings. Having survived the cookie-cutter dome era, the modern stadium is a rare display of uniqueness in modern America: individual foods, aesthetics, even individual playing dimensions.

It may make the arts critics shudder, but professional sports are one of the key components of American culture: They create shared experience, supply catharsis, provide avatars to act out our own quiet struggles and concerns. Not only has the playing of baseball become a form of expression, but even the act of watching baseball has become just that: an active verb, the foundation for mathematics, art, and discussion. It would be wonderful if Americans were still reading and arguing over poetry, or engaging in discussions at the local *salon*. But that's not the way of our culture in this efficient century; sports are, for whatever other value they offer, a better fit. And it's unquestionable that something is lost when a sports team leaves a city—perhaps not for every individual, but for the whole.

So how to solve the basic conflict between the private and the public good? How do we justify the baseball stadium? One solution, the capitalist solution: All public funding is withheld, and stadiums and teams become vanity projects at best and oversized theaters at worst. The minor/independent leagues become the model of baseball, a collection of informal pleasure and shoestring budgets, of players paid minimum wage (we'll at least give them that, in this utopia) while they play for the love of the game. The minor leagues, no longer bound to their masters, would regain relative independence and local presence, selling players when necessary to survive.

It wouldn't be a terrible way to conduct the game, as long as there weren't the parent clubs there to suck all of the value and currency out of the leagues for their own ends. It's the way baseball used to be, in the Class-D era of the game, reflecting a 19th-century feel for America. We can't return to the romanticism and comfort and tumult of local baseball; once you leave the small pond, you can't really go back.

I suppose the ideal solution for this problem would be nationalization; baseball's antitrust laws already make it a poor example of the capitalist ethic. In such a scenario, a baseball team's management would be itself a representative democracy, elected to terms, responsible for budgets. Meanwhile, the civics of baseball fandom would translate into a more active citizenship in the local arena, the ugly and necessary work of figuring out bike lanes and zoning laws, the actual teamwork that democracy demands. It would finally allow fans to earn that possessive first-person plural so unavoidable in sports: *We* won the World Series last year.

Is this rank naïveté, another example of paper-thin socialist idealism? Certainly. It's also the baseball I see when I close my eyes. It's a disservice to repeat the joke that the fan roots for laundry in the age of free agency—what they root for is a sense of place. Sports teams aren't defined by their ownership or their players; they're defined by the fans, the thousands of people who assemble and join together in that rarest of modern phenomena: a common cause. Sports belong to them. Each city, each town should have its own Hall of Fame, the way each school has its display case of trophies. Stadiums already do this, with wings and displays celebrating team history (or, in the case of the Mets, other teams). But they should advance even further and create museums, and tourist-fans should make pilgrimages to each.

Jim Bouton once said of Seattle, when the Pilots fled to Milwaukee between the completion and the publishing of *Ball Four*, that "a city that seems to care more for its art museums than its ballpark can't be all bad." There would be, it was eventually proven, room for both. ▨

Lew Fonseca and the Myth of Democratic Baseball

by Mary Craig

Mary Craig examines a short film from the 1950s that purports to present a brief history of baseball but that turns out to be mostly propaganda. – Geoff Y.

Baseball has a storied and deliberate history of being connected to American politics, from its roots in the Civil War to presidents throwing opening day first pitches to the widespread belief during World War II that baseball made America more peaceful than Europe. Though it is correct that these connections have in some ways produced an American baseball synonymous with American politics, these efforts have perpetuated the dangerous belief that the mere existence of American democracy safeguards people from suffering and persecution.

These issues were on full display in a 1951 Lew Fonseca short film titled *The Democracy of Baseball*. The film was packaged as a celebration of the game on behalf of the National League's 75th anniversary and the American League's 50th. The 17-minute film was shown to baseball writers, Boy Scouts, and young baseball players, among many others, as a means of educating them on the sport's history. However, the heavy-handed American democratic and militaristic ties to the sport on display in the film present a superficial account of the game that, in service of specific political goals, omits the real, full nature of baseball's American-ness.

In case the title did not do so, the film immediately makes clear its purpose by featuring an introductory screen that reads:

> This motion picture is dedicated to a nation of free people who have found in sport and in sports competition an undying exemplification of those principles of justice and liberty and democracy which point to a better world.

Switching immediately to the game itself, the film features a grandfather telling his two grandsons about the history of baseball. They eagerly listen ("Say, will you tell us all about it when we get home, Gramp? We wanna know how it started and all the rest!"), captivated by his stories of Abner Doubleday and the sport's invention; Candy Cummings' introduction of the curveball; and the careers of greats such as Babe Ruth, Ty Cobb, Cy Young, Lou Gehrig, Mel Ott, Ted Williams, and Connie Mack. Enveloping these images are the messages of baseball's democratic nature and its importance to America.

The long list of players noted in this film have all "lived and fought and played the game the American way," eventually becoming American heroes. Precipitating this rise to heroism is baseball's guiding principle, "fair play," which promotes a constant level of equality throughout the majors. If, according to Connie Mack, you have "physical ability, brains, courage, and good habits," you can find success in the game, regardless of your color or creed.

Baseball is open to everyone, so long as they have talent. Accompanying these remarks are scenes of fans at various baseball stadiums, which the *Galveston Daily News* summarizes thusly: "Shop-girls, kids, truck drivers, law clerks and celebrities carry out the democracy theme as they shoulder through turnstiles to watch performers in a game which has lowered its last racial barriers."[1]

In line with much of American history, the film itself features three white characters who tell the predominantly white history of the game. The only non-white person featured is Jackie Robinson, in a short clip of him fielding a ball. Fonseca presents the All-Star Game as the starkest example of democracy: Fans by the millions vote for the most deserving players. There is no mention of the grassroots democratic effort of a number of groups to end segregation. Indeed, there is no mention of black players, period. Not even Jackie Robinson gets called by name.

---

1. *Galveston Daily News*, January 5, 1952, p. 10.

Desegregation is merely the final note on a checklist. It would perhaps seem unfair to chastise a 17-minute film for glossing over the complexities of desegregation were it an anomaly and not an active component of erasing the struggle of black ballplayers. Although the color barrier was broken in 1947, by 1951 only seven of 18 teams had integrated, and it would be another eight years before the final team, the Red Sox, followed suit. It took 14 more years for baseball to have a black manager, and three years after that for a black general manager. Black players had to live up to much higher standards as many clubs looked for reasons to bench or demote them.

Jackie Robinson achieved massive success and became a fan favorite, but he still received death threats from vocal racists, and nonvocal ones used him as a measuring stick for all other black athletes. The labeling of desegregation as a tidy democratic triumph after only a handful of black players made the majors—and had to massively outperform white players to do so—enabled MLB to dictate its pace, impeding its progress. This made it difficult for black and Latino players to assert themselves as both legitimate baseball players and rights-bearing human beings.

This democratic facade manifests itself in class distinctions, as well, as it asserts that the only barrier to success is hard work. In 1952, Robert L. Finch, PR director for the National Association of Professional Baseball Leagues, spoke at a fundraising event about the meaning of democratic baseball. He heralded the game as being truly American in that both enable a boy "to go as far as he wants to." However, this democracy is threatened by the bonus rule, which forces clubs to "spend themselves out of existence" and counters the chief lesson of baseball, "how to sacrifice in a democracy."[2]

At a point in America at which appearing in any way to be antidemocratic meant being treasonous, sentiments like Finch's are mechanisms of control. They ensure obedience through using Red Scare language to achieve full financial control of players. It monetizes "effort," leaving players in a position in which they are forced to play for very little (the average annual salary was $14,000) on the grounds they have not yet earned otherwise.[3] Unsurprisingly, this left black players at the bottom of the payroll.

The latter part of the film links the sport to militarism. Accompanying clips of army and navy officers, Fonseca states that baseball has "kept step with Uncle Sam." Because the sport develops "strong bodies, keen minds, quick, decisive action, cooperation, and fair play," it is the perfect game for servicemen to play. Enthralled by the game, servicemen bring it with them everywhere, thus, "wherever Old Glory flies, this heartfelt voice of America proclaims the eternal brotherhood of the game.??

Fonseca's final words are "there will be no end to the democracy of baseball." These last remarks parrot those made by A.G. Spalding in his 1911 baseball history book, "Base Ball has 'followed the flag.' ... wherever a ship floating the Stars and Stripes finds anchorage to-day; somewhere on nearby shore the American National Game is in progress."[4]

Though baseball has always been linked to American military efforts, the 1950s provided a unique opportunity to make it the focal point of the sport. American isolationism ended when the country entered World War II, and the resulting conflict with the Soviet Union changed the landscape of American international relations for decades to come. By 1950, the Red Scare occupied much of American politics, as a select powerful few feared Communism would overtake democracy and bring ruin to America. Resulting from this fear was an extreme push to sell loyalty to America and insert "American values" into all aspects of life.

Fonseca's film was the most prominent anti-Communism display of baseball, but it was not alone. Throughout the country, various politicians and baseball officials gave speeches to American youths, urging them to take up baseball as a means of combating Communism. In November 1951, Yankees sportscaster Mel Allen gave a speech at the first annual Little League banquet in which he espoused the virtues of baseball as a "powerful bulwark against ... the threat of Communism." The game teaches young boys "that persons of all races, creeds and colors can play on the same team ... and learn to respect others in the true spirit of Christian brotherhood."[5]

This view migrated outward with the work of Dr. C Guyer Kelly, an American who began establishing baseball teams in Tunisia in the 1930s. He increased his efforts in the early 1950s, believing "the good old American game of baseball, played in sandlots across the world, is more likely to teach democracy, create international understanding, and route Communism than is all the displays of silk-hatted ambassadors."[6] The American Legion had also been combating Communism since the 1930s, but it took a more militaristic approach to the matter. Its Junior League, one of

---

2. *Daily Courier*, June 6, 1952, p. 7.

3. James Quirk and Rodney D. Fort, *Pay Dirt: The Business of Professional Team Sports* (Princeton: Princeton University Press, 1992), 210.

4. A.G. Spalding, *America's National Game: Historic Facts Concerning the Beginning, Evolution, Development and Popularity of Base Ball, with Personal Reminiscences of Its Vicissitudes, Its Victories and Its Votaries* (New York: American Sports Publishing Company, 1911), 14.

5. *Kingston Daily Freeman*, November 14, 1951, p. 18.

6. *Delta Democrat-Times*, March 9, 1951, p. 16.

the most fruitful development leagues for MLB, instilled in its youth a militaristic dedication to Americanism they were not to question.

Ford Frick maintained close ties with the American Legion and adapted its rhetoric to Major League Baseball. Frick, famous for eliminating All-Star Game fan voting, gave numerous speeches to college and high school students wherein he reaffirmed baseball's democratic ties. Baseball offers the antidote to "Communism, Fascism, and all other isms" because it houses "four freedoms guaranteed by the Constitution—assembly, religion, opportunity, and speech."[7] In combination with competition and discipline, these freedoms exemplify the American way.

Baseball became so quickly entwined with the Cold War that in 1950, cartoonist John Churchill Chase depicted Stalin as a baseball player, deciding between a number of bats labeled as various countries, as the world, holding a glove, looks on.[8] The connection was strengthened through numerous efforts to use the game as a stand-in for American values in countries vulnerable to Communism. Various ambassadors to South American countries, such as Venezuela and Colombia, championed baseball, helping establish several American baseball leagues in each country.

Many of these countries had well-established baseball leagues, but they did not play the American way, and so the ambassadors refused to recognize their legitimacy. In 1950, the San Francisco Seals toured Japan in an effort to expel the Communist encroachments on the country. Recalls Seals coach Del Young: "When we got there the Communists were on the soap boxes on almost every street corner. But we hadn't been there long before they disappeared in the crowds. I don't think they'll get far now."[9] When employed in a militaristic fashion, baseball was believed to be an effective means of repelling Communism.

The final scene of the short film is the grandfather telling his grandsons, "This great game of baseball will go on forever. But our story comes to an end." In just 17 minutes, this grandfather has laid out the entirety of baseball's history. In 17 minutes, this old man, sitting comfortably on his couch, erased the uncomfortable and real account of baseball from history. His grandchildren will not know of its past racism and they are not meant to perceive it in its present state. They are only supposed to associate baseball—and America—with what is right. To them, baseball has no story outside of the American story.

Though there is much to admire about baseball, and it has undeniably become entwined with American history, the version transmitted in *The Democracy of Baseball* serves as nothing but propaganda for an increasingly fragile democratic America. In doing justice to the game, it is necessary to tell its complete story in the hope of instilling in new fans a desire to address its deficiencies and push it toward actual democracy rather than the manufactured product sold in the 1950s.

7. *Alburquerque Journal*, February 2, 1953, p. 13.
8. https://www.loc.gov/item/2016679626/
9. Ron Briley, "Baseball and the Cold War: An Examination of Values," *OAH Magazine of History* 2, no. 1 (Summer, 1986): 16.

The Boring Index

by Rob Mains

Rob Mains has devised a formula to determine the least interesting players and teams in baseball, shedding light on historical performances from 2017 in the process. – Geoff Y.

One of the concerns about contemporary baseball is that it's becoming boring. The Three True Outcomes[1]—walks, strikeouts, and home runs—have accounted for more than a third of all plate appearances as of the 2017 All-Star break, an all-time high.

That means less action on the field. We're not just talking about, for example, fewer hit-and-runs; we're talking less running altogether. Byron Buxton sprinting first-to-third, Jarrod Dyson chasing down a liner to the gap, Yasiel Puig throwing out a runner—that's exciting. Players walking to and from the dugout, trotting around the bases, or taking first base on a walk—not so much. On a related note, 42 percent of runs so far this year have scored on homers, the highest percentage ever.

That being said, if you're a fan, the Three True Outcomes aren't necessarily boring. A Red Sox fan doesn't think Chris Sale strikeouts are boring. A Reds fan knows the mayhem that can follow a walk to Billy Hamilton. Yankees fans watch Aaron Judge at-bats hoping for a home run. The Three True Outcomes are boring only if your team is the victim, not if it's the perpetrator.

So let's try to quantify boredom from the perspective of the batter, or of the fan watching the batter. A strikeout, if not fascist, is boring. Watching your team's batters carry their bats back to the dugout isn't exciting. And you know what's an underrated play for being boring? Popups. Popups are pretty much like strikeouts: automatic outs, no chance of advancing baserunners. (Well, like dropped third strikes, hardly ever.)

We'll start our Boring Index by adding a batter's strikeouts and popups. At the All-Star break, the strikeout leader was Miguel Sano with 120, and the popup leader was Mookie Betts with 48, believe it or not. But nobody's going to call Sano or Betts boring. We need to adjust boring strikeouts and popups with excitement.

Total bases are exciting! That way we give Sano and Betts credit for what they do when not striking out or hitting popups. I'm proposing this formula: SO + POP - 0.55 x TB.

Why that factor of 0.55? Because accumulating every plate appearance since 1950 (the first year for which we have popup data), that formula gives us a value close to zero. If a player's SO + POP - 0.55 x TB is greater than zero, he leans boring. If it's less than zero, he leans nonboring. And rather than go with raw numbers, let's make this a rate stat by dividing it by plate appearances.

For example, this year Sano has 120 strikeouts, 11 popups, 162 total bases, and 345 plate appearances. (120 + 11 - 0.55 x 162) / 345 = .121. For Betts, it's (33 + 48 – 0.55 x 173) / 399 = -.035. He's been wholly nonboring. Let's call this the Boring Index. The Boring Index, expressed like a batting average, is strikeouts plus popups minus 0.55 times total bases, all divided by plate appearances.

Here is the all-time leaderboard among batters with 250 or more plate appearances in a season:

Player	Year	PA	SO	POP	TB	Boring Index
Adam Dunn	2011	496	177	31	115	.292
Jon Singleton	2014	362	134	23	104	.276
Mike Olt	2014	258	100	13	80	.267
Mike Zunino	2015	386	132	28	105	.265
Jeff Mathis	2008	328	90	44	90	.258
Rob Deer	1991	539	175	58	173	.256
Jeff Mathis	2011	281	75	30	64	.248
Curtis Casali	2016	256	82	23	76	.247
B.J. Upton	2013	446	151	21	113	.246
Cody Ransom	2012	282	109	15	101	.243

Or, if you prefer, batting title qualifiers:

---

1. Dave Pease notes that Christina Kahrl coined the term Three True Outcomes in an email exchange between them discussing what would soon become the now-defunct Rob Deer Fan Club. Kahrl goes into additional detail here: http://www.foxsports.com/mlb/just-a-bit-outside/story/appreciating-new-baseball-lingo-tootblan-maddux-three-true-outcomes-062915

Player	Year	PA	SO	POP	TB	Boring Index
Rob Deer	1991	539	175	58	173	.256
Rob Deer	1993	532	169	52	180	.229
Mark Reynolds	2010	596	211	43	216	.227
Dan Uggla	2013	537	171	33	162	.214
Chris Carter	2013	585	212	35	228	.208
Carlos Pena	2012	600	182	37	176	.204
Rob Deer	1990	511	147	61	190	.203
Drew Stubbs	2012	544	166	31	164	.196
Rob Deer	1989	532	158	55	198	.196
Mickey Tettleton	1990	559	160	42	169	.195

Basically Rob Deer and some other guys.

As a reality check, I looked at the least-boring players since 1950. I think this passes the sniff test:

Player	Year	PA	SO	POP	TB	Boring Index
George Brett	1980	515	22	12	298	-.252
Ted Kluszewski	1954	659	35	6	368	-.245
Ted Williams	1955	417	24	0	225	-.239
Don Mattingly	1986	742	35	2	388	-.238
Carl Furillo	1953	518	32	0	278	-.233
Ted Williams	1950	416	21	4	216	-.225
Yogi Berra	1950	656	12	15	318	-.225
Don Mattingly	1985	727	41	0	370	-.224
Stan Musial	1951	678	40	6	355	-.220
Don Mattingly	1984	662	33	0	324	-.219

No, I don't entirely trust those popup numbers from years past, either. But that's a good list, isn't it? George Brett in 1980 played only 117 games due to injuries but hit .390/.454/.664. His TAv was .392. He had 10.3 WARP and was an easy choice for MVP. And he struck out in only *four percent* of his plate appearances. You know who's struck out that infrequently this season? *Nobody.*

So who's The Most Boring Man in the World this year? Is anyone challenging Dunn's single-season record, or Deer's as a batting title qualifier? Here's where we stood at the break, minimum 125 plate appearances:

Player	PA	SO	POP	TB	Boring Index
Danny Espinosa	254	91	15	63	.281
Ryan Schimpf	197	70	19	70	.256
Chris Carter	208	76	13	68	.248
Mike Zunino	222	87	17	92	.241
Trevor Story	284	100	20	101	.227
Byron Buxton	283	87	19	78	.223
Joey Gallo	291	112	18	126	.209
Tyler Saladino	128	35	7	30	.199
Matt Davidson	257	106	12	124	.194
Cameron Rupp	197	66	7	64	.192

Espinosa, with his .162/.237/.276 slash line, is in rarefied territory, but he seems likely to fall short of Dunn's all-time record, and after being cut by the Angels over the weekend he's not on pace to accumulate enough plate appearances to challenge Deer's record for batting title qualifiers. Story and Buxton are on track to finish in the top 10 all time among batting title qualifiers, but not at the top of the list.[2] So for all of the legitimate complaints about the way baseball is being played in 2017, nobody's as boring as some of the players in the recent past.

But how about teams? Are there clubs that are threatening to set a new standard for being boring? Here are the all-time top 10:

Team	Year	PA	SO	POP	TB	Boring Index
Astros	2013	6,020	1,535	250	2,049	.109
Cubs	2014	6,102	1,477	330	2,118	.105
Padres	2016	6,000	1,500	293	2,115	.105
Astros	2014	6,055	1,442	304	2,084	.099
Mariners	2011	5,972	1,280	335	1,887	.097
Diamondbacks	2010	6,183	1,529	316	2,275	.096
Brewers	2016	6,061	1,543	231	2,168	.096
Cubs	2015	6,200	1,518	272	2,186	.095
Astros	2012	6,014	1,365	304	2,008	.094
Mets	2013	6,207	1,384	317	2,035	.094

It probably won't surprise you that, rebuild project done, this year's Astros are the only team in the majors with a negative Boring Index. Might anyone challenge the 2013 version of the club?

Team	PA	SO	POP	TB	Boring Index
Padres	3,219	840	201	1,108	.134
Athletics	3,337	852	177	1,256	.101
Rangers	3,319	819	188	1,269	.093
Rays	3,465	874	175	1,369	.085
Phillies	3,259	751	145	1,168	.078
Orioles	3,341	779	192	1,303	.076
Brewers	3,477	874	138	1,399	.070
Cubs	3,373	743	171	1,236	.069
Twins	3,386	735	176	1,238	.068
Giants	3,447	665	192	1,162	.063

Why, yes, someone might. The Padres, who appear to be running some sort of weird personnel experiment this year, are on pace to shatter the team Boring Index record.[3] So far they're fourth in strikeouts, third in popups, and last in total bases. They're slashing .243/.303/.374, which, among the 30 teams, equates to last/last/last. There may be no player on pace to take over as the all-time Most Boring Man in the World, but the Padres may be The Most Boring Team in the World, Ever. ▪

---

2. For the record, Espinosa did overtake Dunn, finishing at .293 thanks to two miserable eight-game stints in Seattle and Tampa Bay. Story and Buxton, on the other hand, failed to maintain their pace, finishing at .168 and .147, respectively.—Ed.

3. The Padres became somewhat less boring as the season progressed but still managed to shatter the record, finishing at .120.—Ed.

The Bullpen of My Dreams

by Russell A. Carleton

> *Using the best relievers at the most important point in a game sounds great in theory, but as Russell A. Carleton points out, it's difficult or even impossible to identify that point until well after the fact. – Geoff Y.*

"Doc, I had that dream again."

"The one about the bullpen?"

"Yeah, I'm walking out of the dugout to go get my starter. We're up 3-2 in the seventh and I'm waving for Andrew Miller."

"I see ..."

"The door opens up out in right field, but this time they start playing 'Dark Star' by the Grateful Dead and Harry Pavlidis starts jogging out from the bullpen."

"Who is Harr ..."

"He's not even left-handed, Doc! He's not even left-handed!"

"OK ..."

"And I'm yelling at the scoreboard operator guy to play something else, as if that will get Miller to come out of the 'pen."

"How are you feeling at this point?"

"Panicked. I spent all this time calculating the proper way to have a leveraged bullpen and all of a sudden, it's undone because they send the wrong guy out. And I'm standing in front of 40,000 people in the middle of the ballpark and they're all laughing at me."

"That sounds unsettling."

"What do you think it means, Doc?"

"Well, was Miller warmed up this time?"

"Beg pardon?"

"Was Miller warmed up?"

"Well, I don't know, the dream started with me walking out to the mound. I mean if I'm waving for him, it makes sense that I would have warmed him."

"Tell me what happened this time."

"Well, Doc, Harry Pavlidis comes in and throws some warmup pitches and then on the first pitch, he gets the batter to roll the ball to the second baseman and we get out of the inning."

"So, despite your stress, it all worked out."

"Yeah, I guess."

"What do you think the dream is trying to tell you?"

"Well, it's not finished, Doc."

"Oh?"

"After the groundout to second, I went down the dugout stairs and I just *had* to figure out what was going on. I meant to go to my office, but I ended up walking and walking down this dark hallway. And I was trying to talk myself through it. How did I mess up the leveraged bullpen thing?"

"Did you figure it out?"

"No, Doc. I walked down the hallway a while, and I came to a door that had a sign on it."

"Interesting. Could you read the sign?"

"Yes, which is weird for me. I don't usually read things in dreams. It said ..."

Warning! Gory Mathematical Details Ahead!

This has puzzled sabermetricians for years. Why don't managers use their bullpens more optimally? We know how to quantify game leverage. We know that runners at second and third with two outs in the seventh inning with a one-run lead is a more important spot than a clean three-run lead at the start of the ninth inning, so why doesn't the closer (or whoever is the bullpen's best reliever) come into the tight spot in the seventh?

Modern bullpen strategy has tended to be inning-based.[1] There's a closer for those ninth-inning close games. There's a setup guy for the eighth. There are guys who pitch in the sixth and seventh. And there's the LOOGY. During the playoffs, managers tend to get a little more creative, mostly borne of the fact that they start mistrusting everyone but two or three guys and they just ask those three guys to pitch all of the time.

---

1. https://www.baseballprospectus.com/news/article/18835/baseball-therapy-in-praise-of-the-modern-bullpen/

But why not make a change? When it's getting hairy, why not bring in the closer? Managers have embraced the shift. They are making better lineups. They've stopped bunting so much.[2] Is it really too much to ask them to do this?

I think the leveraged bullpen is a fantastic theory. It makes mathematical sense. What I've come to realize is that it's a perfect example of something that works great in a video game and not in reality. And frankly, I blame the video games. They never make you warm the pitcher up! (And the ones that do usually have that option turned off as the default.)

But before we get to that, let's ponder another problem. Time is linear. The seventh inning unfolds before the eighth inning presents itself, which is in turn followed by the ninth inning (and if necessary, the tenth). We want the closer to come into the point of highest leverage, but this whole linearity thing presents a problem.

I looked for the highest leverage index point that happened in the seventh inning for each team in all games from 2012 to 2016, with the criteria that it needed to be above 1.5. Any games that were already blowouts were discarded. If a leverage index value of at least 1.5 appears in the seventh inning, I found that this was also the highest leverage point in the game (from that point forward) in 53 percent of cases. So, yes, our manager could bring his closer in here to pitch the seventh inning, but if he did and the goal is to try to get him into the highest leverage point of the game, there's a 47 percent chance that this isn't it.

So, if our manager hits the "closer" button now, he very much runs the risk of having a bunch of people like me whining that he hit it too soon. If he gets into the eighth inning without using the closer and then a situation with a leverage of 1.5 or greater appears, there's still a 40 percent chance that yet another moment will appear in a later inning (either in the ninth or in extras) that will be a greater inflection point.

Should the manager bring in the closer at the first sign of trouble because the game might be won or lost *right here* or should he hold off a bit and maybe bring in his third-best reliever (if he's not already out there)? The data points to the fact that this is essentially a coin flip decision. You could make the case that probabilitstically, the managers should favor pushing the "closer button" more quickly because in the seventh inning, he'd be right 53 percent of the time, but he's going to be wrong *a lot*.

Plus, this kinda assumes that our manager has psychic powers. We're assuming that the manager *could* hit the "insert closer" button at this point. When I do a retrospective look at what the highest leverage point was in the seventh inning, I have the advantage of hindsight to know that a relatively big moment happened. In other words, I can whine because I get to know what happened after the decision was/wasn't made. I gotta say, all managers should manage that way. They'd be so much better at their jobs.

The problem is that when the seventh inning dawns in these games that eventually feature that high-leverage point in the seventh, there's no way to tell that it's anything other than a pedestrian medium-leverage seventh inning. But if our manager wants to have the "closer button" ready for pushing, that's when he has to make the decision to get the closer warming up. Let's prove that.

Warmup time varies from pitcher to pitcher. Some guys need more time than others, but for our purposes, we're going to assume that our reliever needs three batters of lead time to get fully ready. (And yes, I know that at-bats are not a unit of time.) I looked at all cases in which the seventh inning ended up holding the highest point of leverage in the game for a team and where that point had a leverage index over 1.5. I then looked back in time to see what the leverage index was three batters earlier. In 47 percent of cases, the leverage index was below 1.0 at that decision point, and in 60 percent, it was below 1.2. There are a bunch of these seventh-inning, tight-spot scenarios in which the manager couldn't reasonably have seen it coming.

Running that analysis the other way, I looked at all cases where, at the beginning of the seventh inning, the leverage index was somewhere between 0.8 and 1.2. Three batters *later*, I looked at the leverage index. In more than three-quarters of the cases, the leverage index was still below 1.5.

At the time a manager needs to make the decision to have his closer ready (i.e., tell him to warm up), we're talking about a 75 percent chance that there's not going to be a particularly high-leverage spot for him to work by the time he's ready. Even if one appears, it's a 50-50 shot as to whether that's *the one* spot in the game where we want him to be.

So yeah, our manager could have his closer warming at the beginning of the seventh inning if it looks like it might get a little hairy. And maybe he'll be right one of those times, but most of the time the data tell us that he'll be wrong. And if he's wrong, he has a closer who has gotten up and has to either be sat back down or perhaps be brought into the eighth inning of a game that isn't all that much in dispute, which is funny because the reason we started yelling at the manager in the first place was that he was bringing his closer into a situation that wasn't all that important.

Why The Modern Bullpen Will Persist

Using a bullpen strategy based on pitchers being assigned certain innings is tremendously inefficient and should be gotten rid of, except for the fact that the alternative is even more horribly inefficient and should be avoided at all costs. The leveraged bullpen is a great dream, but dreams don't

---

2. https://www.baseballprospectus.com/news/article/30503/flu-like-symptoms-five-things-you-probably-didnt-know-about-the-2016-season/

always come true. There will be times when our valiant manager will sense that something vile might be happening and have a high-leverage guy ready in a spot where he normally doesn't have a high-leverage guy ready. That's great on the day it happens, and I'm sure we'll all take it as evidence that he's surely capable of such feats (so why doesn't he do it regularly!).

The reason inning-based or matchup-based strategies persist is that managers have a pretty good idea of when the eighth inning is going to happen. If you want to play matchups, there is a handy, reliable guide on the dugout wall that details who is coming up to bat and when. There

are some smaller tweaks that managers could make to the prevailing strategy that are still inning-based, including using the closer in tie games on the road (or tie games in general), and bringing him into the eighth *or* ninth inning, depending on what matchups might present themselves. However, when you do the #GoryMath, they actually wouldn't add very much value.

Instead, I think we need a small rethink on how we evaluate managers and their bullpen usage. We're holding them to an ideal that isn't really achievable. It's time to put the idea of a leverage-based bullpen strategy to bed. ▪

The Natural Conclusion of Baseball Statistics

by Patrick Dubuque

> Statistics tell a story that contextualizes what we perceive, and as Patrick Dubuque reminds us, we need the right statistics—and an understanding of how they work—to tell the right story. – Geoff Y.

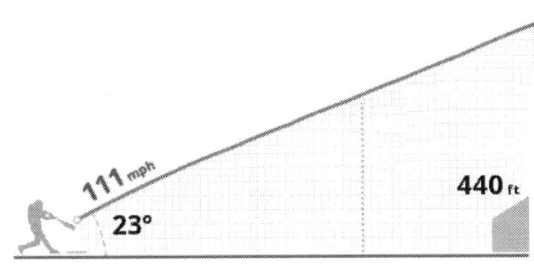

There was a once a time, not so terribly long ago, when a person interested in scientific pursuits might require little more than a (quill) pen and paper, bottles, a net, and a magnifying glass. Undiscovered wisdom was everywhere, on every beach and every country stroll, and people of different vocations would devote their weekends and evenings to the collection and collation of all sorts of data. This pursuit was dubbed "natural history," and societies sprang up to further combine and organize this knowledge into shared productivity. Clergymen and merchants would meet to compare notes, distinguish between different type of insects, occasionally argue about the names.

After the intellectual stagnation of the medieval era, this scientific revolution was an awakening of creativity and curiosity. Not all branches were equally accessible: Fields like optics, anatomy, and chemistry required specialized equipment and education. But others, particularly biology and agriculture, laid secrets for anyone to find given sufficient ingenuity. An abbot named Mendel discovered genetics in the peapods of his garden; Darwin and his associates flung themselves across the globe, seeking new species and new habitats.

There's something of the Wild West to this era of science, an open frontier with few restrictions and guidelines. It's a culture of infinite potential, of endless possibility and disappointment, that corresponds well to the early days of baseball research. The ideas were there for anyone to find, if they knew how to look.

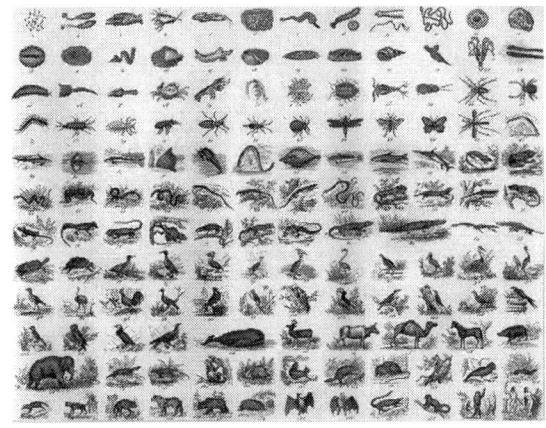

(The rudimentary beginnings of the WAR leaderboard.)

Science, around the turn of the 20th century, began to change, relocating from the fields to the laboratory. Astronomy created uncountable numbers; doctors created complicated tests to verify our growing knowledge of the human body. As our knowledge in physics and biology grew, it drove people to look closer, exploring under stronger and stronger microscopes to understand the realm of bacteria and atoms. Training and formal education became necessary, measurement grew increasingly expensive. These progressions were neither good nor bad; they were a simple evolution, the next step.

⚾   ⚾   ⚾

Since its unveiling at the MIT Sloan Sports Analytics Conference three short years ago, Statcast has transformed the nature and scope of baseball data. The sum of the immeasurable now measurable is dizzying: exit speed, launch angle, running speed, leadoff distance, spin rate, transfer speed on catch-and-throws. The secrets of these new veins of research are extracted and refined in 30 different laboratories, and measurement of players has already been altered. It's no longer batting average, it's batting velocity.

As with science, this is only the latest step in the natural progression of baseball analytics, a miniaturization of exploitable advantage. Just as secondary average and Win Shares pioneered the ability to accurately measure what a player had accomplished, fielding-independent metrics and BABIP drove us to think about not what happened, but what *should* have—that there was a talent level separate from production, something that existed on a separate plane. In one sense, such a shift in thought was liberating; finally, every discussion of a player didn't have to end in "how many rings/All-Star berths/MVPs did the guy get?" But in another way, the complexity and aethereality of modern statistics could portend an unhappy future.

⚾   ⚾   ⚾

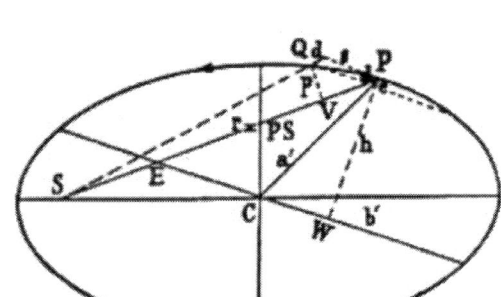

How many baseball diamonds can you spot in the picture above?

Science, like baseball, does not progress in a steady motion; it jumps forward in fits and starts, swept clean and rebuilt by ideas sprung from great minds. Idealists like Aristotle, Newton, and Bill James transformed the landscape in their fields, but ironically, these upheavals are often followed by lulls. It's difficult to exist under such great shadows, to pick through and understand the aftermath of their thought.

In a way, we're still recovering from Newton all this time later; we still think in his terms, despite the fact that in reality—the reality that exists beyond the scope of the naked eye—his most famous tenets don't really apply. It's hard to shrug off the ideas that we were taught as children, ideas that, in our everyday lives, appear so intuitive. And so we as laymen have taken on a split personality in science:

understanding the real, and the practical. So much of what we "know," in the theoretical sense, is no longer attached to our own experiential learning.

It's this, I believe, and not just a political movement of anti-intellectualism or conservative religious thought, that has created the recent pushback against science. The problem is exacerbated in an educational system that has slowly distanced itself from critical thinking, and emphasized testing and memorization. Once teaching is an authoritative act, a forceful transfer of knowledge and value robs the student of the ability to trust or mistrust, and then verify. Skepticism is replaced by cynicism. It results in a loss of ownership, a perceived disenfranchisement over what is considered "truth," that leads people to believe in flat earths and vaccination-autism links. Such beliefs, as ridiculous as they are from a scientific standpoint, are at least in formulation a creative act.

⚾   ⚾   ⚾

Batting average is not an intuitive stat. Neither is earned run average. Both of these statistics are considered meaningful because baseball has grown to love them over the course of a century and a half. BP's own True Average is what it is because people know what a "good" or a "bad" batting average looks like. The internalization has come slowly, and if baseball were to start over there's no way we arrive at the same numbers; they were forged through arguments and power shifts. But they're what we have, what our grandparents gave us.

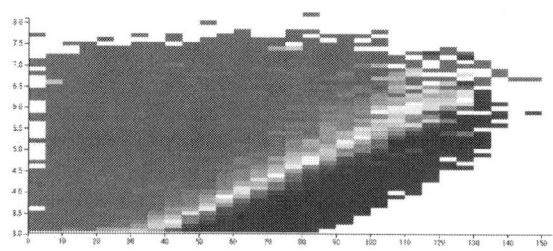

(Fig. 3: some data)

One of the points of contention in the sabermetric era was the inclusion of advanced statistics in popular baseball culture: getting broadcasters and talking heads to employ, or even correctly describe when debunking, "complicated" stats like OPS and WPA. It seems (and seemed) like a rather silly political battle, but it was political. Often the argument was that the statistics hadn't been internalized, that explaining these newfangled numbers would alienate viewers, disrupt the flow of the game. The vicious circle: The stats required explanation because the average fan didn't know them; they didn't know them because they never got taught.

A decade later, pockets of resistance still hold their ground, but the landscape has mostly transformed. Statcast's in-house sponsorship will allow it to avoid that awkward phase and beam straight into homes at full power. The tools now available to describe and analyze are almost unfathomably expansive and specific. But they also arrive at a time when caution is equally necessary.

It won't be an easy task, and it's not necessarily a problem of Statcast's making. As with the advancement of science, current baseball knowledge has reached a level of granularity that goes beyond our level of intuition. It's a tricky balance: We do want information that challenges preconceived notions, that pushes the audience closer to a concept of truth. As Sam Miller noted recently, a game without statistics, one in which intuition is given free reign, is an uncomfortable place. Both halves of the game feed off of each other.[1]

So much of modern analytics dwells in the realm of probability, a concept that can come off as unintuitive to the point of meaningless at best, and insulting at worst. The value of probability study is to provide context on exactly what isn't intuitive, that the reality we experience isn't predestined, but one possible result. In a society that values results, has bronzed its own national bootstraps and glamorized the concept of glamour, it's a difficult sell. It's also a vital one. Probability gives us an opportunity to move past the golden-era flawless hero to an imperfect, fortunate, and human one. It gives us an opportunity to find nobility and honor not just in triumph, but also in failure.

Unlike the Project Scoresheet and PITCHf/x revolutions of the past, which began as underground movements, Statcast is a top-down enterprise; while it's to be commended for how much data it has freely provided, its authority puts it at an immediate disadvantage. The advantage of not having to fight for its place is actually a disadvantage, because denying that conversation and debate is also denying a learning curve. It's not enough to just give the people statistics, quote barrels and launch angles without context and without meaning. It's not even enough to try to give them the context.

The masses will have to build that value themselves, take apart the pieces and look at them and argue about them and slowly understand them. It'll be messy, and it may not be a pleasure to watch in real time on Twitter. The turmoil over the usefulness of WAR, and its less creditable components, is a fine example. But it's vital if these numbers are to become more than incidental fun facts, or arbitrary judgments. The average fan will need to be able to see those statistics and not just know them but *feel* them, take them in as just as much of the game as the hue of the grass and the sound of the crowd and the arc of the left-hander's swing. Otherwise, baseball runs the risk of watching its fans reject them entirely, and go back to what they've always done: make up their own stories. ▨

---

1. http://www.espn.com/mlb/story/_/id/18683274/in-world-stats-baseball-best-player

Part 3: Player Analysis

Statistical Introduction

We tried to design the Player Profile pages to give a good selection of descriptive data for each player.

It was important to us that the information in *Diamond Insights 2018* not usurp or duplicate anything in *Baseball Prospectus 2018*. Beyond the biographical information and basic stat line, all player-based information is unique to the book in which it appears.

We cover 305 players in *Diamond Insights 2018*. We had to allocate a page per player, and we didn't want the book to get too long, big, or unwieldy. We chose the players to cover pseudo-scientifically, by starting with all position players with a 2.0 or better WARP and all pitchers with a 1.5 or better WARP in 2017. (WARP, Wins Above Replacement Player, is Baseball Prospectus' total value statistic and is discussed in more detail below.) This left a few open spots, so we took the most popular players not already included based on number of views of their player card at the Baseball Prospectus website and then manually selected a few final players to round out the roster.

Offense

The core of our offense measurements is **True Average (TAv)**, which attempts to quantify everything a player does at the plate—hitting for power, taking walks, striking out, and even making "productive" outs—and scale it to batting average. A player with a TAv of .260 is average, .300 exceptional, .200 awful.

True Average also accounts for the context a player performs in. That means we adjust it based on the mix of parks a player plays in. Also, rather than use a blanket park adjustment for every player on a team, we make adjustments so that a player who plays a disproportionate number of his games at home will see that reflected in his numbers. We also adjust based on league quality: The average player in the American League is better than the average player in the National League, and True Average accounts for this. Finally, TAv is year-adjusted so that the average is roughly .260 every year.

Because hitting isn't the entirety of scoring runs, we also look at a player's **Baserunning Runs (BRR)**, which accounts for the value of a player's ability to steal bases as well as his ability to go first to third on a single or advance on a fly ball.

Defense

Defense is a much thornier issue. The general move in the sabermetric community has been toward stats based on zone data, where human stringers record the type of batted ball (grounder, liner, fly ball) and its presumed landing location. That data is used to compile expected outs for comparing a fielder's actual performance.

The trouble with zone data is twofold. First, unlike the data we use in the calculation of the statistics you see in this book, zone data wasn't made publicly available; it was recorded by commercial providers who kept the raw data private, only disclosing it to a select few who paid for it. Second, as we've seen the field of zone-based defensive analysis open up—more data and more metrics based upon that data coming to light—we see that the conclusions of zone-based defensive metrics don't hold up to outside scrutiny. Different data providers can come to very different conclusions about the same events. Even two metrics based on the same data set can come to radically different conclusions based on their starting assumptions (which haven't been tested), using methods that can't be duplicated or verified by outside analysts. The quality of the fielder can bias the data: Zone-based fielding metrics will tend to attribute more expected outs to good fielders than bad fielders, irrespective of the distribution of batted balls. Scorers who work in parks with high press boxes will tend to score more line drives than scorers who work in parks with low press boxes.

Our **Fielding Runs Above Average (FRAA)** incorporates play-by-play data, allowing us to study the issue of defense at a granular level without resorting to the sorts of subjective data used in some other fielding metrics. We count how many plays a player made, as well as expected plays for the average player at that position based on a pitcher's estimated ground-ball tendencies and the handedness of the batter. There are also adjustments for park and base-out situations.

In addition, catchers have different defensive responsibilities than other defensive players, in particular framing pitches to make umpires more likely to call them strikes and blocking errant pitches. We incorporate PITCHf/x data, where available, and adjust for the pitcher, umpire, batter (including handedness), and home-field advantage using a mixed-model approach to determine how many strikes a catcher is adding to or subtracting from his pitchers' ledgers, and then convert those extra or lost strikes to runs using simple linear weights. We use a similar approach to determine how much better or worse than average a catcher is at letting errant pitches past him (regardless of whether the official scorer labels it a passed ball or a wild pitch)—PITCHf/x is a particularly powerful tool in this regard because we can tell which pitches end up in the dirt (and at what angle and speed) even though basic play-by-play data simply records the pitch as a ball or a swinging strike because the catcher successfully blocked it.

These metrics, as well as the catcher's abilities to prevent steals, are incorporated into catchers' FRAA along with their ball-in-play fielding (e.g., popups and bunts near home plate).

Pitching

Of course, how we measure fielding influences how we measure pitching. Most sabermetric analysis of pitching has been inspired by Voros McCracken, who stated, "There is little if any difference among major-league pitchers in their ability to prevent hits on balls hit in the field of play." When first published, this statement was extremely controversial, but later research has, by and large, validated it. McCracken (and others) went forth from that finding to create a variety of defense-independent pitching measures. One that you'll see in the book is **FIP, Fielding Independent Pitching**, which accounts for walks, strikeouts, hit-by-pitches, and homers accumulated by a pitcher and puts them into one number on an ERA scale. Another is **cFIP**, which takes those FIP inputs, makes a variety of adjustments (including, as appropriate, the batter, catcher, umpire, stadium, home-field advantage, and handedness), and puts the whole thing on a "100 minus" scale in which the lower the number the better. The standard deviation of cFIP is forced to 15, so you know that a 56 cFIP is nearly three standard deviations from the mean.

The trouble is that many efforts to separate pitching from fielding have ended up separating pitching from pitching—looking at only a handful of variables in isolation from the situation in which they occurred. What we've done instead is take a pitcher's actual results, event by event, and adjust each event based on the environment in which it occurred, including, as appropriate, park factor, batter, catcher, umpire, base-out situation, run differential, inning, defense, home-field advantage, whether the pitcher is a starter or reliever, and game-time temperature. We also consider the pitcher's effect on basestealing (both in terms of likelihood of stealing and likelihood of success) and the pitcher's effect on passed balls and wild pitches. Out of all this comes **Deserved Run Average (DRA)**, our core pitching metric. It is the rate stat on which pitcher WARP is determined.

One key point to note is that DRA is set on the same scale as runs allowed per nine innings, not ERA. Looking only at earned runs tends to overrate three kinds of pitchers:

1. Pitchers who play in parks where scorers hand out more errors. Looking at error rates between parks tells us scorers differ significantly in how likely they are to score any given play as an error (as opposed to an infield hit);

2. Ground-ball pitchers, because a substantial proportion of errors occur on groundballs; and

3. Pitchers who aren't very good. Good pitchers tend to allow fewer unearned runs than bad pitchers, because good pitchers have more ways to get out of jams than bad pitchers. They're more likely to get a strikeout to end the inning and less likely to give up a home run.

Player Profile Header

The Player Profile page header includes the player's name, primary position, current team as of mid-January 2018, and any icons that might apply to the player. The icons are allocated as follows:

Icon	Description
🏆	Top 3% of eligible players by 2017 WARP
💣	Bottom 10% of eligible players by 2017 WARP
⚡	Top 3% of eligible players by 2017 ISO
⊘	Bottom 10% of eligible players by 2017 ISO
🛡	Top 3% of eligible players by 2017 DWARP
🗑	Bottom 10% of eligible players by 2017 DWARP
⚓	Top 3% of 2017 PA for hitters or IP for pitchers
🔧	Position players: 40 games at two defensive positions, or 15 games at three positions, or five games at four positions, or two games at five positions; pitchers: three starts and six relief appearances.
👁	Top 3% of eligible players by 2017 (BB-IBB)/PA
👁̸	Bottom 10% of eligible players by 2017 (BB-IBB)/PA
⏩	Top 3% of eligible players by 2017 BRR/PA
⏪	Bottom 10% of eligible players by 2017 BRR/PA
🔥	Top 3% of eligible hitters by 2017 OWARP/PA, and eligible pitchers by PWARP/IP
❄	Bottom 10% of eligible hitters by 2017 OWARP/PA, and eligible pitchers by PWARP/IP
🚑	Appeared on the DL in 2017

The pool of eligible players for the icons includes anyone with 25 games started for a hitter, or 5 games started or 10 appearances as a pitcher.

The next row begins with the 2017 Topps baseball card image for a player (if he had one), courtesy of our friends at Topps.

Justin Bour (Player Pace Chart)

PACE
18th of 155
88°
Very Fast

Below the card image is the player's **Pace**. For both hitters and pitchers, Pace is defined as the number of seconds between pitches. The Pace graph is filled, and percentiles are assigned, based on the concept that faster is better—players who are quickest between pitches will have their graphs close to full. Players with high numbers here might constantly adjust their batting gloves or frequently shake off their catcher.

Daily Value Graph

Justin Bour (Batting Daily Value Graph)

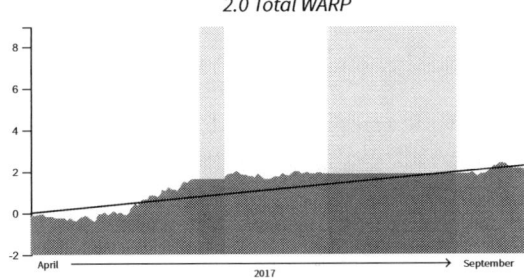

2017 Daily WARP Profile
2.0 Total WARP

Game 56: DL (ankle contusion), **Game 98:** DL (oblique strain)

Gio Gonzalez (Pitching Daily Value Graph)

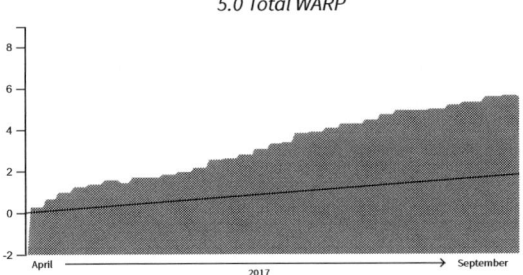

2017 Daily WARP Profile
5.0 Total WARP

Daily Value Graph

In the center of the page is the Daily Value graph, which describes the shape of the player's contributions throughout the year. The area under the graph displays the player's cumulative WARP across the entire season on a game-by-game basis.

- The best WARP day for a hitter in 2017 was 0.706, for J.D. Martinez's monstrous four-homer game against the Dodgers on September 4.
- The best WARP day for a pitcher in 2017 was 0.559, for Ervin Santana's complete-game two-hit shutout of the Orioles on May 23.
- The worst WARP day for a hitter in 2017 was -0.287, for Andrew McCutchen's 0-for-5 with two GIDP performance against the Braves, also on May 23.
- The worst WARP day for a pitcher in 2017 was -0.911, when Mike Foltynewicz allowed seven earned runs to the Cardinals across four innings on May 5.

POS	Avg WARP/game	Avg TAv/game
C	0.0114	.251
1B	0.0139	.286
2B	0.0110	.260
3B	0.0170	.274
SS	0.0153	.257
LF	0.0126	.270
CF	0.0163	.268
RF	0.0129	.273
DH	-0.0004	.254

POS	Avg WARP/game	Avg DRA/game
SP	0.0555	4.66
RP	0.0084	4.43

If a player missed time due to disabled list or minors stints, the Daily Value graphs will have a shaded region and a note explaining the absence.

Both daily and cumulative value graphs have a line for positional average production.

Fantasy Values and Comments

To the right of the page are the player's Fantasy Values. These values were supplied by Baseball Prospectus fantasy expert Mike Gianella and represent his final 2017 dollar value and his projected 2018 dollar value for each player.

In the shaded area on the next row you will see the player's 2017 statistic line (or lines, if he played for multiple teams). More than half the Player Profiles have a fantasy-oriented comment also courtesy of Mike Gianella directly beneath the stat block.

Mitch Haniger (Hitter Stat Line)

YEAR	TEAM	LVL	AGE	PA	R	2B	3B	HR	RBI	BB	K	SB	AVG/OBP/SLG	TAv	VORP	BABIP	WARP
2017	SEA	MLB	26	410	58	25	2	16	47	31	93	5	.282/.352/.491	.284	16.8	.338	2.2

Matt Garza (Pitcher Stat Line)

YEAR	TEAM	LVL	AGE	W	L	SV	G	GS	IP	H	HR	BB/9	K/9	K	GB%	BABIP	WHIP	ERA	DRA	WARP	MPH 95
2017	MIL	MLB	33	6	9	0	24	22	114.2	121	17	3.5	6.2	79	42%	.287	1.45	4.94	5.46	0.1	93.8

Hitter Statistics

The column headers begin with standard information like year, team, level (majors or level of minors), age, and the raw, untranslated tallies found on the back of a baseball card: PA (plate appearances), R (runs), 2B (doubles), 3B (triples), HR (home runs), RBI (runs batted in), BB (walks), K (strikeouts), and SB (stolen bases).

Following those are untranslated "slash" statistics: batting average (AVG), on-base percentage (OBP), and slugging percentage (SLG). The slash line is followed by True Average (TAv), which, as described above, rolls all those things and more into one easy-to-digest number.

One of our oldest active metrics, **Value Over Replacement Player (VORP)**, considers offensive production, position, and plate appearances. More specifically, it is the number of runs contributed beyond what a replacement-level player at the same position would contribute if given the same percentage of team plate appearances. VORP scores do not consider the quality of a player's defense or his contributions on the basepaths.

BABIP stands for **Batting Average on Balls in Play** and is what it sounds like: How often did a ball put in play by the hitter fall for a hit? An especially low or high BABIP may mean a hitter was especially lucky or unlucky. However, hitters who hit the ball hard tend to have especially high BABIPs from season to season; so do speedy hitters who can beat out more grounders for base hits.

The last column is **Wins Above Replacement Player. WARP** is our total-value stat that, for a hitter, combines a player's batting runs above average (derived from True Average), BRR, FRAA, an adjustment for positions played, and a credit for plate appearances based upon the difference between the "replacement level" (derived by looking at the quality of players added to a team's roster after the start of the season) and the league average.

Pitcher Statistics

The first line and the YEAR, TEAM, LVL, and AGE columns are the same as in the hitters example above. The next set of columns—W (wins), L (losses), SV (saves), G (games pitched), GS (games started), IP (innings pitched), H (hits), HR (home runs), BB/9 (walks per nine innings), K/9 (strikeouts per nine innings), and K (strikeouts)—are the actual, unadjusted stats compiled by the pitcher during each season.

Next is GB%, which is the percentage of all batted balls that were hit on the ground, including both outs and hits. As mentioned above, this is based on observation by human stringers and can be skewed based upon a number of factors. We've included the number as a guide, but please approach it skeptically.

BABIP is the same statistic as for batters, but often tells you more in the case of pitchers, because most major-league pitchers have little control over their batting average on balls in play. A high BABIP is often due to a poor defense or bad luck rather than a pitcher's own abilities and may be a good indicator of a potential rebound. A typical league-average BABIP is around .290–.300.

WHIP and ERA are common to most fans: The former measures the number of walks and hits allowed on a per-inning basis, while the latter prorates earned runs allowed on a nine-innings basis. Neither is translated or adjusted in any way.

FIP was discussed above: It puts onto an ERA scale a measurement of how the pitcher performed on the events that do not involve the fielders behind him.

Deserved Run Average (DRA) was also described above. It is the basis of pitcher WARP and measures how many runs (not earned runs) the pitcher "deserved" to allow per nine innings. One important point about minor leaguers is that because there's no minor-league PITCHf/x data, some of the precision in major-league DRA is forfeited. Because, as has been true of BP's pitching metrics in the past, neither DRA nor the conversion from DRA to WARP contains a "leverage" multiplier, WARP for relief pitchers (especially closers) may seem lower than you might see elsewhere and may conflict with how we feel about relief aces coming in and "saving" the game. This is by design: Saves give extra credit to the closer for what his teammates did to put him in a save spot to begin with; WARP is incapable of feeling excitement over a successful save and judges them dispassionately. Furthermore, DRA controls for players who have the benefit of pitching in short durations and at maximum ability.

cFIP, described above, adjusts FIP for a variety of factors and scales it on the familiar 100 scale; because these are pitchers preventing runs, below 100 is good and above 100 is bad.

MPH is the pitcher's 95th percentile velocity for that season—the goal is to give you a sense of the pitcher's peak fastball velocity, not his average. This comes from PITCHf/x data and thus is not publicly available for minor leaguers.

Player Profile

Josh Harrison Batting Profile

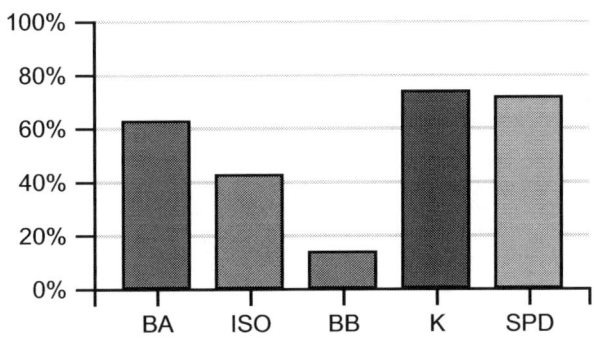

Rich Hill Pitching Profile

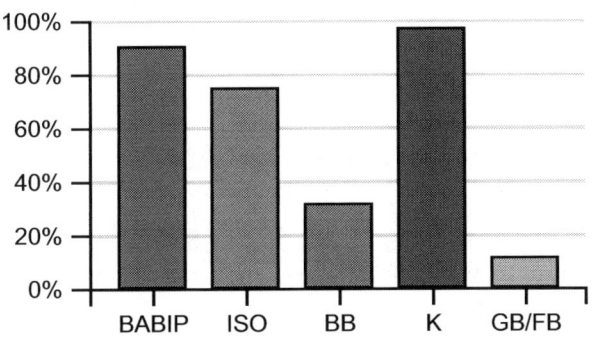

The Player Profile is a chart that evaluates a given hitter's primary production metrics (batting average, isolated power, unintentional walk rate, strikeout rate, and speed score) as a percentile compared to all major-league hitters; or a given pitcher's performance in five categories: strikeout rate, walk rate, opponents' isolated power (e.g., home-run rate), hit rate on balls in play, and groundball-to-flyball ratio. For example, a player with an isolated power rating of 75% is superior in this category to three-quarters of all major leaguers. The player profile is based on the player's three previous seasons of performance, rather than his projection.

Note that for pitchers, the denominator for strikeout rate and walk rate as presented in the Player Profile is not innings pitched, but batters faced. This calculation is somewhat more accurate, as pitchers differ in the number of batters they face per inning based on their on-base average allowed.

Note also that the percentiles take into account whether the pitcher threw in a starting or relief role, as most pitchers post substantially better numbers in relief.

DRA/TAv Distribution

Gary Sanchez Batting PECOTA Percentiles

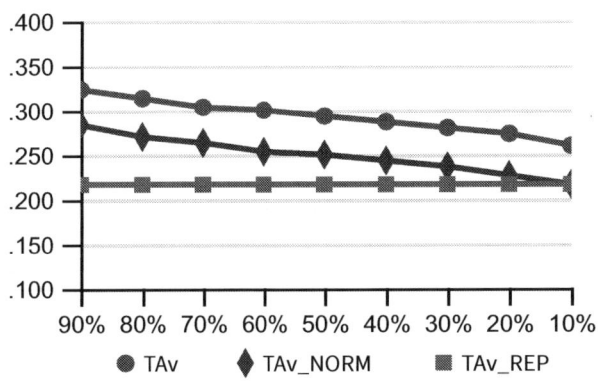

Kyle Hendricks Pitching PECOTA Percentiles

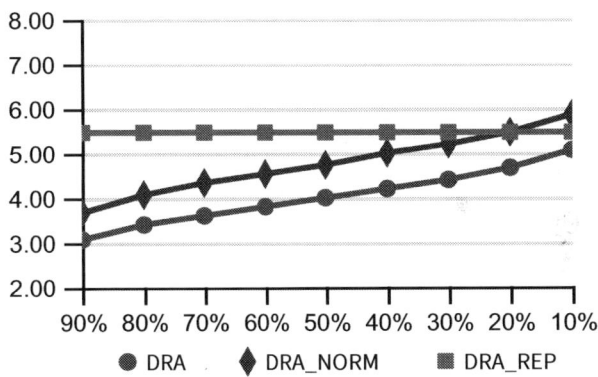

PECOTA, initially developed by Nate Silver (who has moved on to greater fame as a political analyst), consists of three parts:

1. Major-league equivalencies, to allow us to use minor-league stats to project how a player will perform in the majors;

2. Baseline forecasts, which use weighted averages and regression to the mean to produce an estimate of a player's true talent level; and

3. A career-path adjustment, which incorporates information on how comparable players' stats changed over time.

A full PECOTA projection for each player for the next two years is available in *Baseball Prospectus 2018*, but the Distribution chart displays a pitcher's DRA forecast or hitter's

TAv forecast at various levels of probability. It progresses in sequential intervals of five percentage points, ranging from a pitcher's 95th percentile forecast on the left to his 5th percentile forecast on the right.

In addition to the probability distribution for a given player, the chart also includes a normal distribution on DRA or TAv for all players in the league, as adjusted to the player's current park and league context ("NORM"), and a third line representing the performance of a replacement level pitcher ("REP").

Batting/Pitching WARP History

Mark Reynolds Batting WARP History

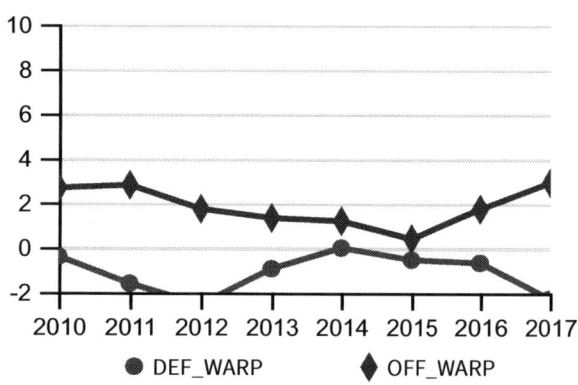

Rick Porcello Pitching WARP History

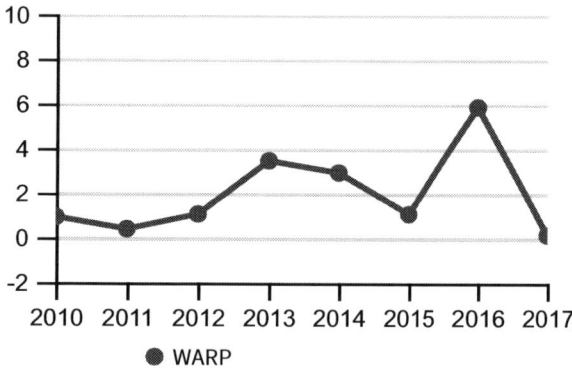

For batters, the WARP History chart displays defensive WARP per season (DEF_WARP) and offensive WARP per season (OFF_WARP) for all years a player has completed in the majors. For pitchers, the chart displays a single line for overall WARP. This graph is not presented for players without multiple years of experience and displays data from 2010 forward.

Baserunning Runs (BRR)

Tommy Pham BRR (Relative to Position)

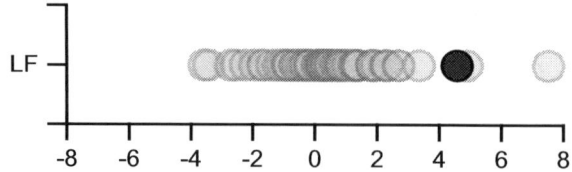

Rank		Player	BRR
1	97°	Delino DeShields	7.56
2	95°	Ben Revere	4.94
3	92°	**Tommy Pham**	**4.62**
4	90°	Starling Marte	3.40
5	88°	Gregor Blanco	2.75

Tommy Pham BRR (Relative to Team)

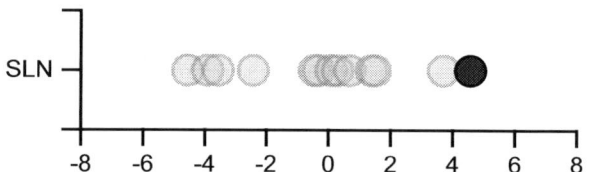

Rank		Player	BRR
1	77°	**Tommy Pham**	**4.62**
2	72°	Greg Garcia	3.75
3	64°	Kolten Wong	1.56
4	56°	Dexter Fowler	1.44
5	55°	Carson Kelly	0.74

Baserunning Runs (BRR), as mentioned earlier, covers all sorts of base-running accomplishments, not just stolen bases, and is intended to encapsulate the value a player is providing with his legs. We present BRR in several contexts. The Relative to Position and Relative to Team charts are based on the format of Baseball Savant's outstanding Sprint Speed charts[1], and show the 2017 BRR of the player relative to others in the grouping. Below each chart the player's BRR percentile and rank are listed, along with his nearest neighbors in the population. Note that the league-average BRR is 0.

---

1. Available at https://baseballsavant.mlb.com/sprint_speed_leaderboard.

Baserunning Components

Wil Myers Baserunning Components

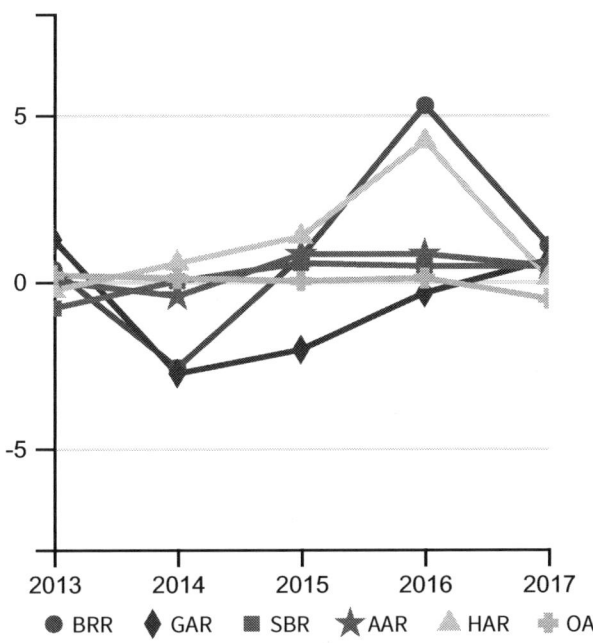

This chart displays a player's Baserunning Runs (BRR) and component values from 2010 onward. BRR was defined earlier and is calculated as the sum of various base-running components: Ground Advancement Runs (GAR), Stolen Base Runs (SBR), Air Advancement Runs (AAR), Hit Advancement Runs (HAR), and Other Advancement Runs (OAR).

Top-Line Pitcher Charts and Tables

The Tunnel vs LHH, Tunnel vs RHH, Pitch Types, Pitch Tunnel, and PI Scores sections of a pitcher Player Profile are covered in their own introduction, following this one.

Pitching Metrics Introduction

by Harry Pavlidis, Jeff Long, and Kate Morrison

While there is no shortage of metrics that purport to describe how "good" or "bad" a pitcher really is, there has been less focus on metrics that describe how a pitcher gets to his results. This, then, is the goal of the metrics introduced here: to provide as comprehensive a picture of a pitcher as possible, to be used as quantitative illustrations with his results. We are happy to introduce three new "top-line" pitching metrics. Our pitcher pages in this book will also include some other important aspects of "describing" a pitcher. Let's find out what these are, new and old.

Power Score

Chris Sale

POWER
56th of 150

Kenley Jansen

POWER
5th of 150

What is a "power pitcher"? We hear the term a lot, usually in reference to someone like Justin Verlander, but it's never been an exact term, for all that it seems to apply to the same general set of characteristics. As part of developing a new suite of pitching metrics and diving deeper into the ways we break down the art of throwing a ball very hard, we're taking a look at "power pitching" and quantifying exactly what it means to be a "power pitcher."

Luckily for us, the pieces to measure whether or not someone is quantifiably a "power pitcher" already exist, it's just deciding how best to put them together. Clearly, velocity is a large part of the equation, as the "power" part of the description, and we weight peak fastball velocity the heaviest when constructing these rankings.

Power pitchers use their fastballs a lot, as well, as it tends to be their highest-graded pitch and the one they feel most comfortable leaning on in stress situations. Other determining factors include median off-speed velocity—power pitchers tend to rely on harder off-speed pitches, so sliders over curveballs. The classic example here is Verlander, with his hard, biting power slider. This also points to the fact that the power pitcher isn't utterly relying on pitch velocity differential, but on something closer to pure

velocity. Differential and deception are obviously useful components, but for the power pitcher, they're of less concern.

As of right now, our Power Score is composed of these three identifiable parts: fastball velocity (three parts), fastball percentage (two parts), and the velocity of all off-speed pitches (one part). There are some other factors that we considered when developing this metric, such as the tendency to work up in the zone and to lean on fastballs in putaway counts, but the current version of this metric only includes the three main components discussed above. From there, we can elaborate: a pitcher who relies on his high-velocity fastball in a two-strike count, to "throw the ball past the batter." How, though, do we take those words and turn them into actionable numbers? How do we accurately define what is seemingly nebulous? We'll work on that for future versions.

Stamina Score

Chris Sale

STAMINA
3rd of 150

Kenley Jansen

STAMINA
140th of 150

As with all of these metrics, our measure of stamina, alone, has nothing to do with how "good" or "bad" a pitcher is; it is simply an objective measurement of how much of a workload any pitcher is capable of carrying. Since workload exists beyond Major League Baseball, we also included any of a pitcher's regular-season minor-league efforts in calculating Stamina.

To calculate Stamina Score, we looked at different ways of valuing days of rest, numbers of pitches, and batters faced per game. What we found most effective is a model that combines calculating the daily number of pitches thrown from a six-day moving average, with the straight average of batters faced per game against the square root of the mean of the days of rest between games. Not every pitcher at the top of these rankings is good, as sometimes teams carry a pitcher who can throw a large number of pitches but is only really good for games that are either already out of hand or in desperate numbers of innings. However, through selection, pitchers who see worse results tend to see fewer innings at a time, and more days between innings, for relievers. Bad starters also tend to see fewer pitches per outing over time, influencing their positioning on these rankings. This simplistic score is sufficient for the first generation of this metric. Future editions might benefit from in-game measurements (sustaining fastball velocity deep into outings, or back-to-back games).

Command Score

Chris Sale

COMMAND
128th of 150

Kenley Jansen

COMMAND
18th of 150

One of the most challenging aspects of pitching to quantify, command indicates that a pitcher can throw the ball where he intends to. Our Command Score builds on Called Strikes Above Average (CSAA), which is the pitcher's component of our framing model. To build on that we've identified target points in each corner of the zone using the likelihood of a pitch to be called a strike and quantified the pitcher's ability to hit that spot consistently. Pitchers are penalized for missing spots by a significant amount—either getting too much of the plate or missing off of it—to highlight their ability to effectively work the edges of the zone.

Command Score provides a new heuristic for understanding the ability of a pitcher to command his pitches. Command Score is a composite statistic that includes CSAA in addition to other factors that we believe reflect a pitcher's ability to command his pitches.

We've also broken down the strike zone into quadrants that highlight a pitcher's ability to miss the most dangerous part of the zone. These quadrants are mapped against called strike probability[1] (CSProb) contours to identify the ideal target in each section of the zone.

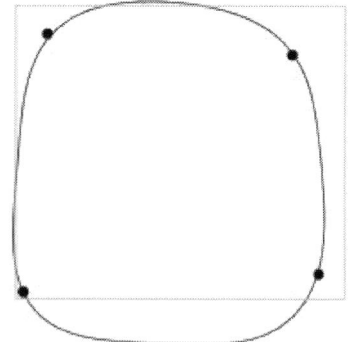

Using CSProb we can identify an appropriate target area in each quadrant and assess a pitcher's ability to hit that target with a pitch. Every pitch is mapped to the nearest quadrant, and the pitcher is penalized based on how much he misses that target. Pitches that miss the target toward the middle of the zone are penalized at a lower rate than those that miss outside the zone because, generally speaking, strikes are better than balls. Of course, we'd be remiss if we didn't acknowledge that pitches catching too much of the zone can be and often are hit for home runs, but pitchers with better command typically throw more strikes than those without.

Once all pitches are aggregated, each pitcher is compared to his peers to identify their relative ability to command their pitches. We recognize there are myriad additional elements to command, but we've found this version to provide a meaningful guide into the command skill, and perhaps style, of pitchers.

Pitch Types

In addition to our new metrics, our pitcher profiles also include a table with pitch type, velocity, and movement information. **Pitch Type** and **Usage %** are familiar, but we've beefed up the raw information with **Index** numbers—that is, we've given each pitcher's velocity, horizontal movement, and vertical movement context within the league. Each index is normalized to 100, and the higher or lower a number is, the more or less velocity or movement than the average it displays. As for **HMov (Horizontal Movement)** and **VMov (Vertical Movement)**, these numbers are the average, in inches, that the pitch moves as it comes in toward the plate, as caused by the spin put on the ball when the pitch is released. We measure a pitch over the **long flight** of the ball, that is, an additional ten feet of flight time than sources such as MLBAM, FanGraphs, and MLB's GameDay interface. This, along with our inclusion of gravity into the **VMov** calculation, allows us to have a much more realistic representation of what a pitch *actually* does, as opposed to how it performs in a hypothetical environment.

FA	Fastball; primarily four-seam
SI	Two-seam fastballs and/or sinkers
FC	Cutters, sometimes further split into "hard" (more like a cut fastball) or "soft" (more like a hard slider)
CH	Change-ups, splitters mostly excluded
FS	Split fingered-pitches, forkballs, and some split-changes
SL	Sliders and slurves
CU	Curveballs, including spike- and knuckle-curves; some slurvy curves, too
CS	Slow curves, or eephus pitches

---

1. Called strike probability indicates the likelihood that a particular pitch will be called a strike. CSProb controls for a number of factors including batter handedness, count, pitcher, and more.

KN Knuckleball

SB Screwball (rarely appears in MLB)

Chris Sale Pitch Types

Type	Freq	Velo	H Mov	V Mov
CH	16.6%	86.9 [107]	17.2 [67]	-28.3 [97]
FA	37.4%	95 [108]	13.9 [68]	-16.2 [97]
SI	13.1%	93.1 [104]	17.5 [64]	-23.7 [86]
SL	32.9%	80 [81]	-10 [124]	-41.7 [74]

DRA

While Earned Run Average (ERA) as it exists tells us what runs were assigned to a pitcher following a certain set of rules, averaged over 9 innings, **Deserved Run Average (DRA)** is our way of calculating what runs a pitcher most likely deserved to give up, independent of defense, but allowing for a pitcher's own defense and effect on batted-ball outcomes. First introduced in 2015, DRA has been refined each off-season and is a valuable resource for understanding the most likely contributions of a pitcher. Like defense-independent metric FIP, DRA is on a runs allowed per 9 innings scale, although unlike FIP, it is scaled to match RA9 rather than ERA. DRA attempts to control for, among other things, stadium effects, catcher framing, pitch classifications, game temperature, and other components, creating a well-rounded portrait of how a pitcher most likely performed.

2017 Top Starters (min. 162 IP)

Name	IP	DRA	ERA	FIP
Corey Kluber	203.2	2.05	2.25	2.47
Max Scherzer	200.2	2.26	2.51	2.91
Chris Sale	214.1	2.37	2.90	2.43

2017 Top Relievers (min. 50 IP)

Name	IP	DRA	ERA	FIP
Craig Kimbrel	69	1.89	1.43	1.39
Darren O'Day	60.1	1.94	3.43	3.68
Roberto Osuna	64	2.19	3.38	1.71

Release Points

Pitchers throw from all over the place—moving sides of the rubber sometimes, or dropping down from time-to-time (or all the time). Instead of providing a seemingly abstract pair of coordinates representing release point, we've decided to plot the average arm angle for each pitcher in the combined plots (see below).

In the diagram, the line from which the pitches originate represents the pitcher's average arm path, estimated by the Lentzner Axis.[2] This will show how the pitcher is delivering pitches, not just where. Submariners and side-armers will look funny, which is probably accurate. Guys with multiple

arm angles just get one Lentzner Axis; we'll try to make that better in the future. Generally, we think these will help you picture a pitcher, even with that limitation.

Tunneling

The concept of pitch tunnels—that a pitcher can be more effective by making his pitches more difficult to distinguish from one another—isn't a new one, though being able to quantify it certainly is. Not only have we included the traditional pitch tunnels data that was introduced in January 2017, but we've also included a new way to look at and think about pitch tunnels.

The pitch tunnels table includes the same tunnel metrics that were introduced in early 2017 and also includes an indexed version of each individual statistic for each pitcher. These indices (centered on 100) tell you quickly how much smaller or larger a pitcher's tunnels (or speed mixing) are than those of the average major-league pitcher. These indices are a different way to look at pitch tunnels, especially considering the fact that tunneling is but one of the many ways a pitcher can be successful (along with having really good stuff, throwing the ball by people, having excellent command, etc.).

The metrics included in the tables for each pitcher are:

Release Differential When analyzing pitchers, we often talk about consistency in their release point, pointing to scatter plots to see whether things look effectively bunched or not. This stat measures the average variation between back-to-back pitches at release.

Tunnel Differential This statistic tells you how far apart two pitches are at the Tunnel Point—the point during their flight when the hitter must make a decision about whether to swing or not (roughly 175 milliseconds before contact).

Plate Differential This statistic shows how far apart back-to-back pitches end up at home plate, roughly where the batter would contact the ball. This includes differentiation generated by pitch break and trajectory of the ball (which includes factors like gravity, arm angle at release, etc.).

Speed Changes This is the average difference, in seconds of flight time, between back-to-back pitches.

In addition to these tables, we've also included some new visualizations of the tunneling phenomenon to better showcase how it works for different pitchers. In the introduction to the new data we said, "The first step in quantifying tunnels is to forget everything we think we know about pitchers. The first step is to think like a hitter." Unfortunately, we largely ignored this advice when it came

---

2. https://www.fangraphs.com/tht/a-pitching-model-playing-the-slots1/

to the actual quantification and visualization of tunneling. As with most everything else done with pitching, we looked at things from the catcher's point of view.

Catchers aren't the ones trying to hit the ball, however. To truly understand the impact of pitch tunnels, it was critical that we look at things from a hitter's POV, and that includes mimicking the viewpoint of both a left-handed and a right-handed hitter. This isn't a novel concept either, as World Series champion and BP alum Mike Fast did so nearly a decade ago.[3]

This new perspective provides a completely new way of looking at and understanding the concept of pitch tunnels—not to mention helping to crystallize the *why* behind platoon splits among hitters.

Each chart includes the release of the ball, the flight path, and the average destination at the plate, identified by the pitch type indicator. The pitch type indicators are repeated roughly 0.25 seconds after release, and of course at the plate. In between, gray dots show the flight path of the ball, with each dot indicating a 0.01 second interval. The visuals include the mound (the black bar) and home plate for visual reference. To take things a step further, we've also included zone contour maps, indicating the range of locations that each pitcher typically works in. These are often different for right-handed and left-handed hitters, as pitchers mix up their

targets and pitch mix to get opposing hitters out. As a result, these contours highlight the areas that a hitter on each side of the plate will see pitches against a particular pitcher. Each chart includes a small legend indicating which pitch is represented by each icon.

Carlos Carrasco Tunnel vs RHH

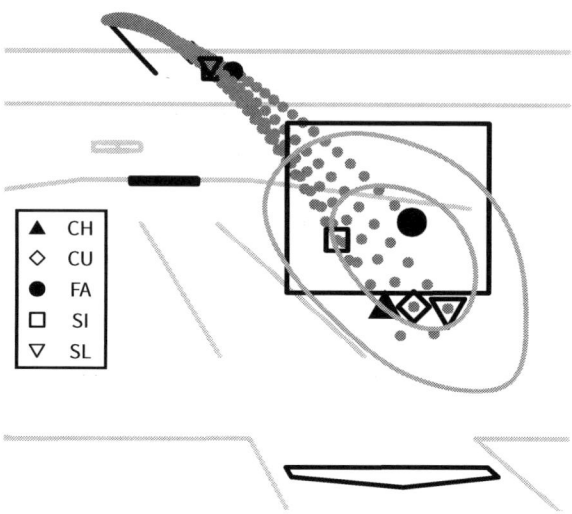

▲	CH
◇	CU
●	FA
□	SI
▽	SL

3. https://fastballs.wordpress.com/2008/06/15/view-from-the-batters-box/

Jose Abreu   1B   Chicago White Sox

Born: 1/29/1987   **Age:** 31   **Bats:** R   **Throws:** R   **Height:** 6'3"   **Weight:** 255 lbs   **Draft Info:** International Free Agent, 2013

22 Sec/Pit

PACE
99th of 155
36°
Slow

2017 Daily WARP Profile
3.9 Total WARP

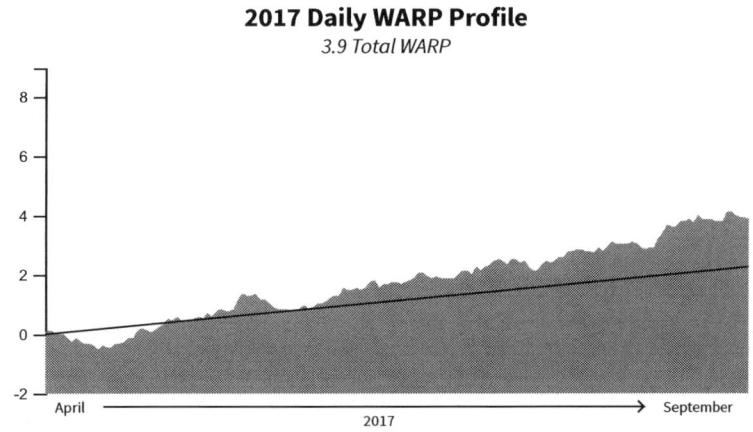

Fantasy Values

2017	2018
$27.69	**$26.00**

YEAR	TEAM	LVL	AGE	PA	R	2B	3B	HR	RBI	BB	K	SB	AVG/OBP/SLG	TAv	VORP	BABIP	WARP
2017	CHA	MLB	30	675	95	43	6	33	102	35	119	3	.304/.354/.552	.295	33.0	.330	3.9

Viewed as a disappointment in some circles because he has never come close to duplicating his stellar 2014 major-league debut, Abreu quietly posted a Top 10 season in AL-only and returned second-round value in mixed formats. While it may seem Abreu's value has dipped because everyone hits for power while he has stood still, the batting average puts him a cut above the Johnny-come-latelies at the position. — Mike G.

2017 Batting Percentages

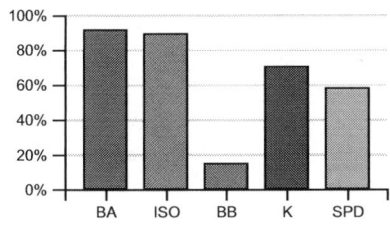

Batting PECOTA Percentiles

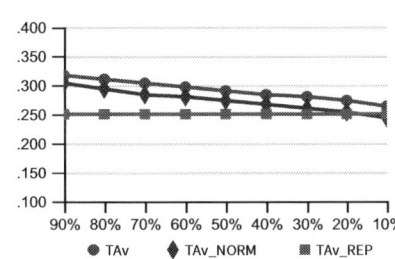

Batting WARP History

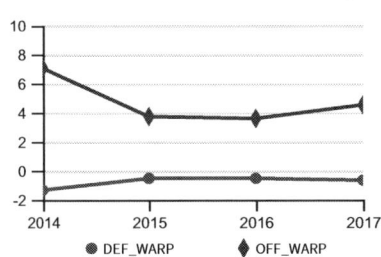

BRR (Relative to Position)

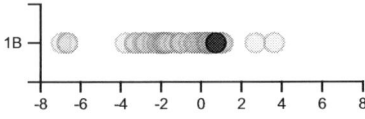

Rank		Player	BRR
4	89°	Wil Myers	1.08
5	89°	Ryder Jones	1.00
6	86°	**Jose Abreu**	**0.78**
7	85°	Efren Navarro	0.63
8	82°	Justin Smoak	0.60

BRR (Relative to Team)

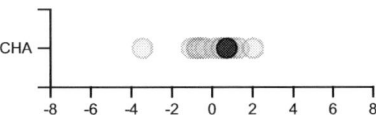

Rank		Player	BRR
4	57°	Yolmer Sanchez	0.86
5	53°	Nick Delmonico	0.85
6	44°	**Jose Abreu**	**0.78**
7	38°	Kevan Smith	0.55
8	33°	Leury Garcia	0.50

Base Running Components

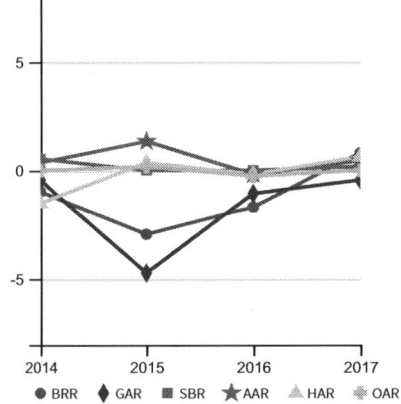

Aaron Altherr   OF   Philadelphia Phillies

Born: 1/14/1991   **Age:** 27   **Bats:** R   **Throws:** R   **Height:** 6' 5"   **Weight:** 215 lbs   **Draft Info:** Round 9, 2009 Draft (#287 overall)

2017 Daily WARP Profile
3.1 Total WARP

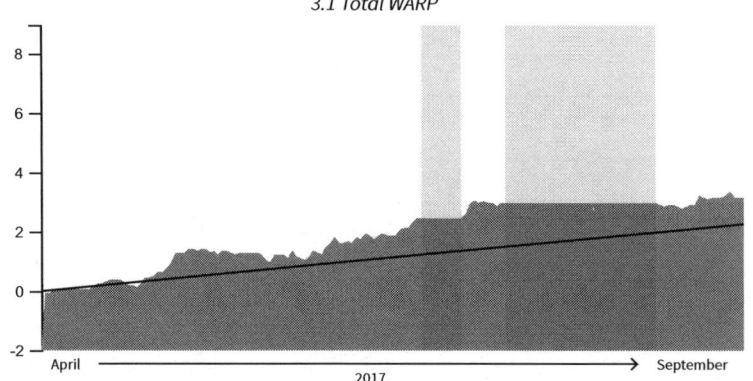

PACE
20 Sec/Pit
18th of 155
88°
Very Fast

Game 89: DL (hamstring strain), **Game 108:** DL (hamstring strain)

Fantasy Values
2017 *2018*
$15.26 **$18.00**

YEAR	TEAM	LVL	AGE	PA	R	2B	3B	HR	RBI	BB	K	SB	AVG/OBP/SLG	TAv	VORP	BABIP	WARP
2017	PHI	MLB	26	412	58	24	5	19	65	32	104	5	.272/.340/.516	.292	23.3	.328	3.1

A wrist injury and a poor performance in 2016 pushed Altherr's draft value down in 2017 and made him a sleeper in every format. By the end of the season, Altherr had emerged as a viable option in a suddenly rejuvenated Phillies offense. Altherr could return $20-25 in NL-only if he plays full-time, but the acquisition of Carlos Santana clouds his short-term prognosis. — Mike G.

2017 Batting Percentages

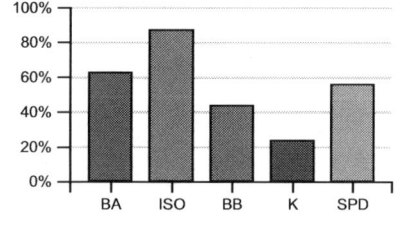

Batting PECOTA Percentiles

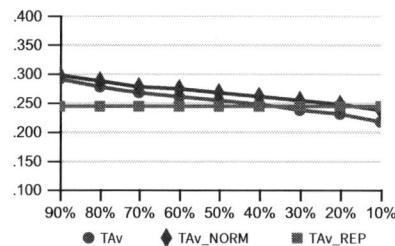

Batting WARP History

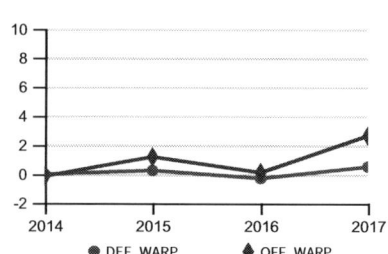

BRR (Relative to Position)

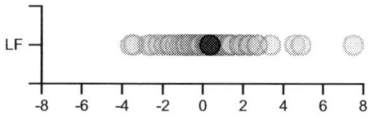

Rank		Player	BRR
33	47°	Chris Heisey	0.44
34	46°	Allen Cordoba	0.40
35	45°	**Aaron Altherr**	**0.40**
36	44°	Orlando Calixte	0.31
37	43°	Peter Bourjos	0.30

BRR (Relative to Team)

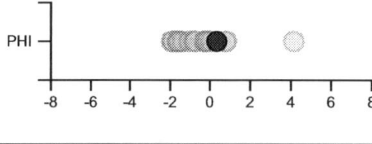

Rank		Player	BRR
2	81°	Ty Kelly	0.88
3	80°	Eric Fryer	0.84
4	73°	**Aaron Altherr**	**0.40**
5	69°	Andrew Knapp	0.11
6	66°	Adam Rosales	-0.07

Base Running Components

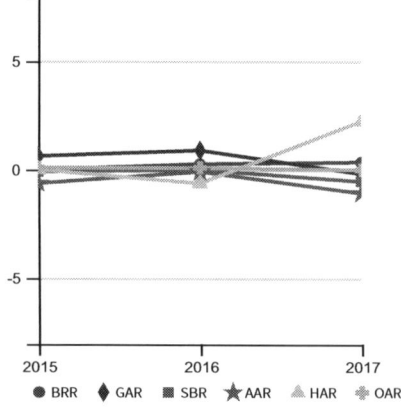

Jose Altuve 2B Houston Astros

Born: 5/6/1990 **Age:** 28 **Bats:** R **Throws:** R **Height:** 5' 6" **Weight:** 165 lbs **Draft Info:** International Free Agent, 2007

PACE
99th of 155
36°
Slow

22 Sec/Pit

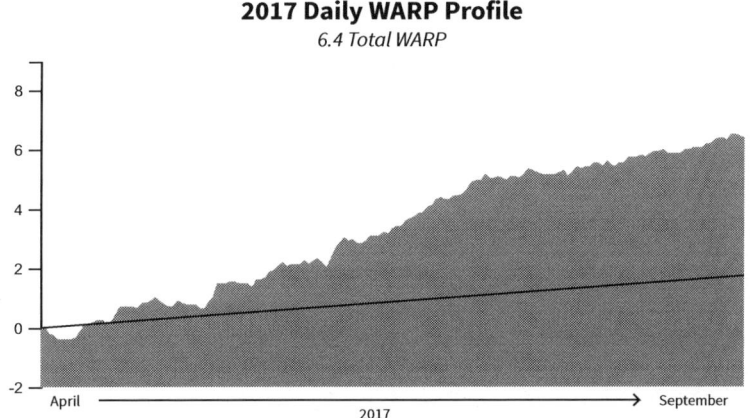

2017 Daily WARP Profile
6.4 Total WARP

Fantasy Values
2017	2018
$41.52	**$42.00**

YEAR	TEAM	LVL	AGE	PA	R	2B	3B	HR	RBI	BB	K	SB	AVG/OBP/SLG	TAv	VORP	BABIP	WARP
2017	HOU	MLB	27	662	112	39	4	24	81	58	84	32	.346/.410/.547	.322	64.0	.370	6.4

Although it might not be reflected in drafts yet again this year, Altuve has replaced Mike Trout as the best fantasy player on the planet, thanks to a spike in home runs to go along with his sixth consecutive season with at least 30 stolen bases and a batting average that carries fantasy teams in the category. Altuve is an automatic first-round pick and no one would look askance if you drafted him first overall. In auction formats, Altuve is one of the rare players where you can bid comfortably in to the $40s knowing that you will get most of your investment back even if he has a down year. — Mike G.

2017 Batting Percentages

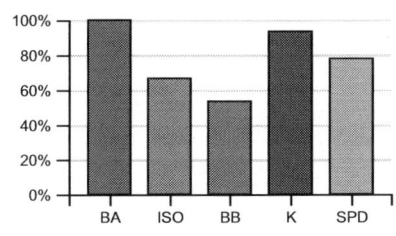

Batting PECOTA Percentiles

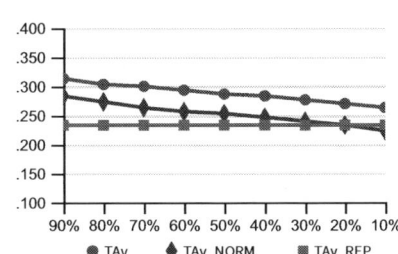

Batting WARP History

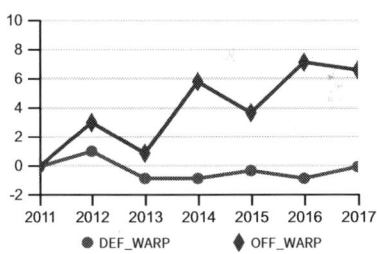

BRR (Relative to Position)

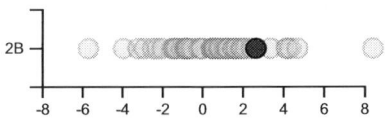

BRR (Relative to Team)

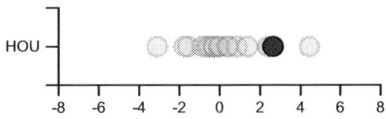

Base Running Components

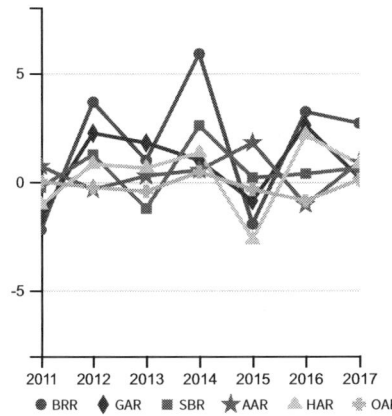

Rank		Player	BRR
5	84°	Cesar Hernandez	4.20
6	81°	DJ LeMahieu	3.38
7	77°	**Jose Altuve**	**2.68**
8	74°	Brandon Phillips	2.46
9	71°	Brian Dozier	2.17

Rank		Player	BRR
1	95°	Cameron Maybin	4.50
2	82°	**Jose Altuve**	**2.68**
3	73°	Josh Reddick	2.45
4	69°	Jake Marisnick	1.44
5	68°	Tony Kemp	0.90

Chase Anderson RHP Milwaukee Brewers

Born: 11/30/1987 **Age:** 30 **Bats:** R **Throws:** R **Height:** 6' 1" **Weight:** 200 lbs **Draft Info:** Round 9, 2009 Draft (#276 overall)

2017 Daily WARP Profile
2.4 Total WARP

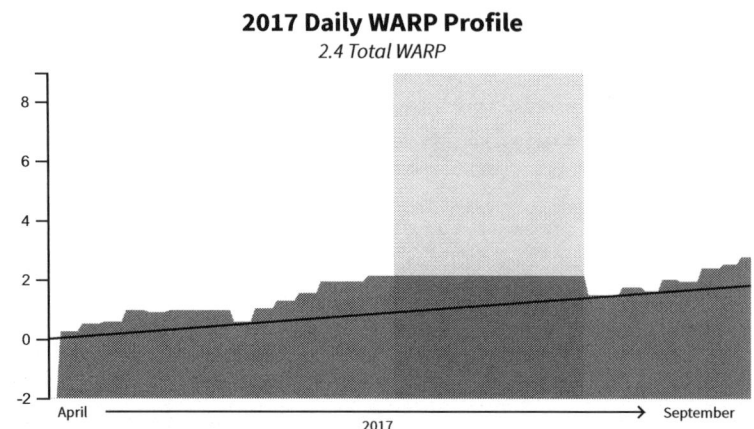

Game 81: DL (oblique strain)

POWER 45 PWR — 73rd of 150

STAMINA 61 STM — 100th of 150

COMMAND 59 CMD — 43rd of 150

PACE 21 Sec/Pit — 81st of 150 — 46° — Average

Fantasy Values

2017	2018
$22.16	$14.00

YEAR	TEAM	LVL	AGE	W	L	SV	G	GS	IP	H	HR	BB/9	K/9	K	GB%	BABIP	WHIP	ERA	DRA	WARP	MPH 95
2017	MIL	MLB	29	12	4	0	25	25	141.1	113	14	2.6	8.5	133	41%	.265	1.09	2.74	4.05	2.4	94.9

 *Anderson morphed from a back-end starting pitcher to an SP2, thanks to a 2-mph increase in velocity along with the development of a cutter that allowed him to attack hitters and challenge them more on the outer half of the strike zone. The combination of newfound stuff and the ability to use it makes Anderson a legitimate target in any fantasy format. He isn't likely to repeat and put up another sub-3.00 ERA, but something around 3.50 with a solid WHIP is achievable for the improved Brewers hurler. — Mike G.*

2017 Pitching Percentages

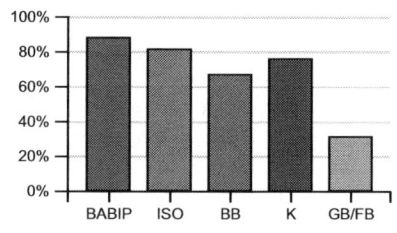

Pitching PECOTA Percentiles

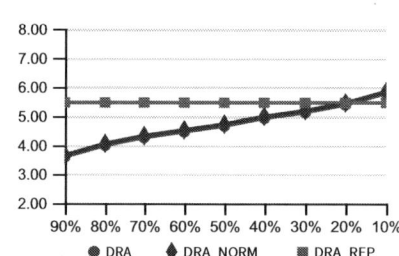

Pitching WARP History

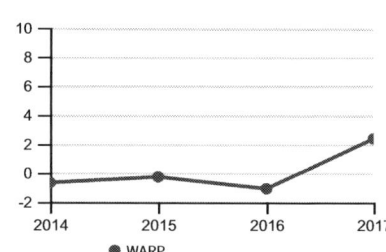

Tunnel vs LHH

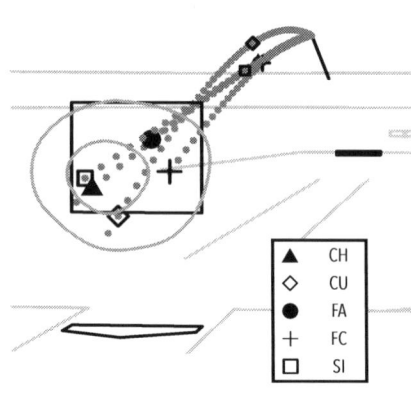

	CH
▲	CH
◇	CU
●	FA
+	FC
□	SI

Pitch Types

Type	Freq	Velo	H Mov	V Mov
CH	16.1%	84 [96]	-14.5 [81]	-23.3 [111]
CU	18.3%	78.5 [101]	6.1 [93]	-49.3 [97]
FA	32.2%	93.7 [104]	-5.4 [108]	-11.7 [111]
FC	13.1%	89.8 [108]	2.8 [106]	-19.7 [116]
SI	20.3%	93.1 [104]	-11.5 [107]	-15.1 [118]

Pitch Tunnel

Pairs	Release Diff	Tunnel Diff	Plate Diff	Speed Changes
1680	29.3	117.4	227.6	0.033

PI Scores

Year	Pitch Ct	Pwr	Cmd	Stm
2014	1886	41	44	62
2015	2439	44	48	63
2016	2630	42	59	67
2017	2252	45	59	61

Tunnel vs RHH

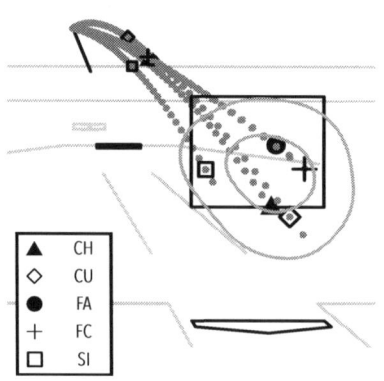

	CH
▲	CH
◇	CU
●	FA
+	FC
□	SI

Elvis Andrus SS Texas Rangers

Born: 8/26/1988 **Age:** 29 **Bats:** R **Throws:** R **Height:** 6' 0" **Weight:** 200 lbs **Draft Info:** International Free Agent, 2005

2017 Daily WARP Profile
5.4 Total WARP

PACE
21 Sec/Pit
45th of 155
71°
Fast

Fantasy Values
2017	2018
$31.41	$25.00

YEAR	TEAM	LVL	AGE	PA	R	2B	3B	HR	RBI	BB	K	SB	AVG/OBP/SLG	TAv	VORP	BABIP	WARP
2017	TEX	MLB	28	689	100	44	4	20	88	38	101	25	.297/.337/.471	.268	37.8	.325	5.4

One of the biggest beneficiaries of the "juiced" baseball, Andrus not only reached double digits in home runs for the first time in his career but got all the way to 20, mixing in his usual solid contributions in steals for a 20/20 season. Andrus was one of only nine hitters in baseball to reach this mark in 2017. While the home runs are great, Andrus has always been a strong fantasy contributor, as he was a $26 hitter in AL-only in 2016 even without the dingers. In a world where "everyone" hits home runs, Andrus' contributions in steals will make him worth a top pick in 2018. — Mike G.

2017 Batting Percentages

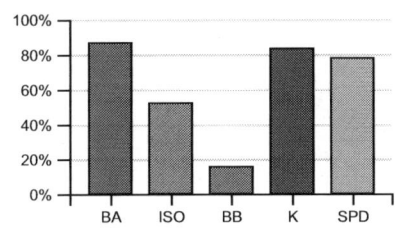

Batting PECOTA Percentiles

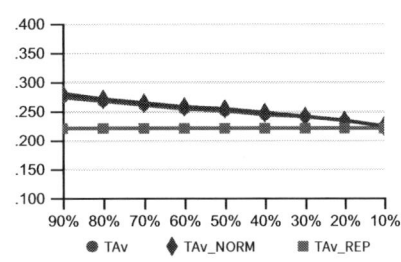

Batting WARP History

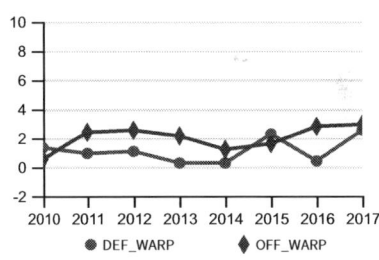

BRR (Relative to Position)

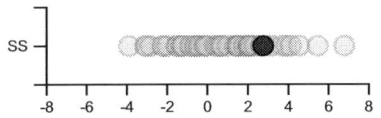

Rank		Player	BRR
6	83°	Jose Iglesias	3.72
7	81°	Dansby Swanson	3.19
8	77°	**Elvis Andrus**	**2.81**
9	75°	Jose Reyes	2.71
10	71°	Andrelton Simmons	2.71

BRR (Relative to Team)

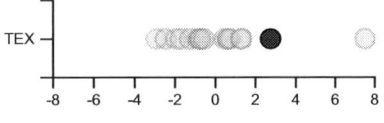

Rank		Player	BRR
1	90°	Delino DeShields	7.56
2	79°	**Elvis Andrus**	**2.81**
3	77°	Jared Hoying	1.36
4	69°	Rougned Odor	1.32
5	68°	Jurickson Profar	0.79

Base Running Components

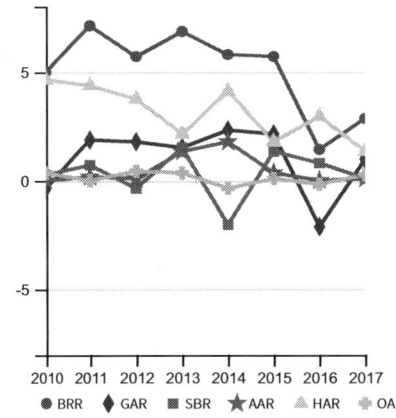

Chris Archer   RHP   Tampa Bay Rays

Born: 9/26/1988   **Age:** 29   **Bats:** R   **Throws:** R   **Height:** 6' 2"   **Weight:** 195 lbs   **Draft Info:** Round 5, 2006 Draft (#161 overall)

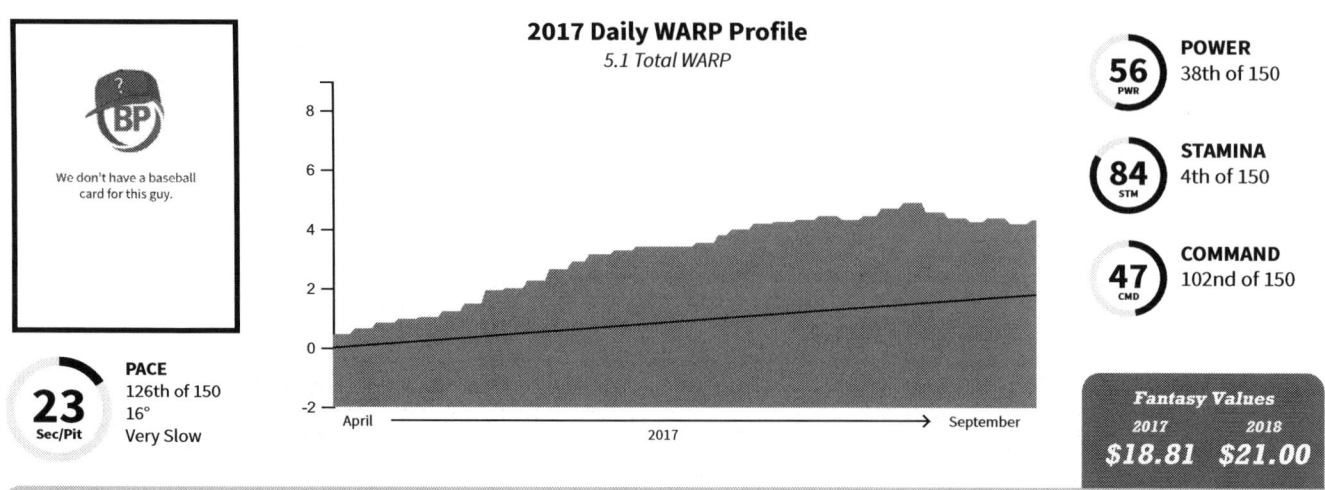

2017 Daily WARP Profile
5.1 Total WARP

POWER 56 PWR — 38th of 150

STAMINA 84 STM — 4th of 150

COMMAND 47 CMD — 102nd of 150

PACE 23 Sec/Pit — 126th of 150 / 16° / Very Slow

Fantasy Values
2017	2018
$18.81	$21.00

YEAR	TEAM	LVL	AGE	W	L	SV	G	GS	IP	H	HR	BB/9	K/9	K	GB%	BABIP	WHIP	ERA	DRA	WARP	MPH 95
2017	TBA	MLB	28	10	12	0	34	34	201	193	27	2.7	11.1	249	43%	.325	1.26	4.07	3.30	5.1	97.4

The differential between Archer's ERA and DRA is a headscratcher and something that keeps his fantasy owners awake nights. It can't even be explained by his performance in "clutch" situations, as most of the home runs Archer surrendered in 2017 were with the bases empty, and his numbers with men in scoring position were stellar. The hope if you buy Archer is that the raw numbers finally match the peripherals, but even if they don't you're still locking in 200+ strikeouts and a durable, reliable arm who has been a borderline Top 10 starter in AL-only. — Mike G.

2017 Pitching Percentages

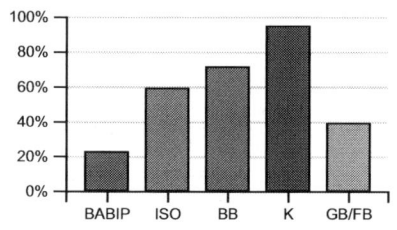

Pitching PECOTA Percentiles

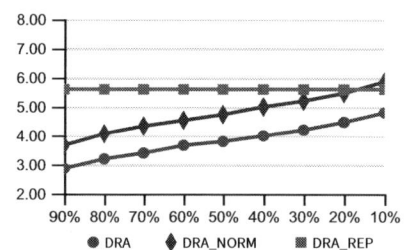

Pitching WARP History

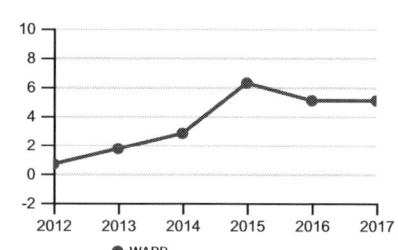

Tunnel vs LHH

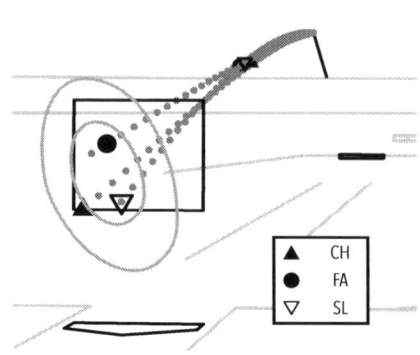

Pitch Types

Type	Freq	Velo	H Mov	V Mov
CH	8.0%	86.2 [104]	-11.2 [99]	-26.1 [103]
FA	47.3%	95.8 [111]	-4.4 [113]	-11 [113]
SI	0.2%	95.3 [117]	-12.3 [101]	-13.8 [123]
SL	44.5%	89.1 [121]	4.3 [99]	-30.1 [107]

Pitch Tunnel

Pairs	Release Diff	Tunnel Diff	Plate Diff	Speed Changes
2607	24.9	121.7	230.0	0.019

PI Scores

Year	Pitch Ct	Pwr	Cmd	Stm
2013	2092	63	38	72
2014	3151	67	38	78
2015	3448	62	38	81
2016	3390	51	38	85
2017	3384	56	47	84

Tunnel vs RHH

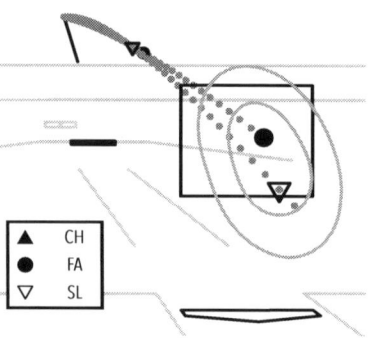

Orlando Arcia   SS   Milwaukee Brewers

Born: 8/4/1994   **Age:** 23   **Bats:** R   **Throws:** R   **Height:** 6' 0"   **Weight:** 165 lbs   **Draft Info:** International Free Agent, 2010

PACE
20 Sec/Pit
18th of 155
88°
Very Fast

2017 Daily WARP Profile
3.4 Total WARP

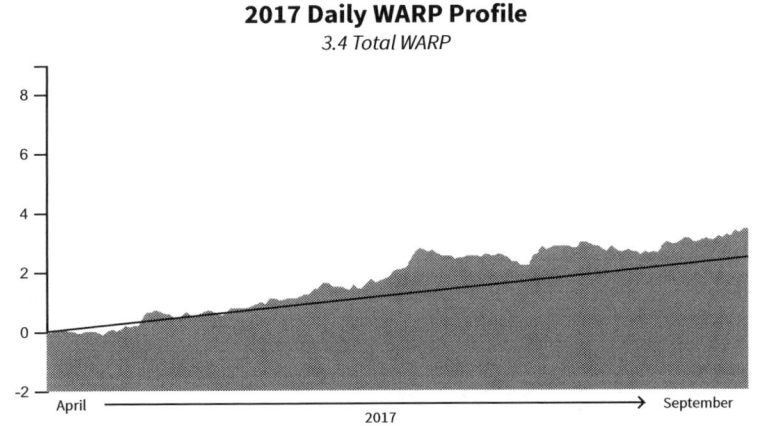

Fantasy Values
2017	2018
$17.35	$15.00

YEAR	TEAM	LVL	AGE	PA	R	2B	3B	HR	RBI	BB	K	SB	AVG/OBP/SLG	TAv	VORP	BABIP	WARP
2017	MIL	MLB	22	548	56	17	2	15	53	36	100	14	.277/.324/.407	.262	26.8	.317	3.4

Arcia was one of those "better in fantasy than real life" guys in 2017, posting 15 home runs and 14 stolen bases despite a .262 TAv that was middle-of-the-pack for shortstops. Arcia is young enough to see significant improvement in the coming years, but even if he stands still the double-digit home run/steal combo makes him playable as a third middle infielder in 12-team mixed and a solid shortstop just about everywhere else. — Mike G.

2017 Batting Percentages
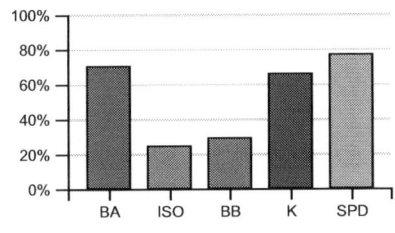

Batting PECOTA Percentiles
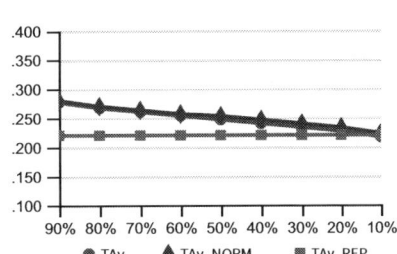

Batting WARP History
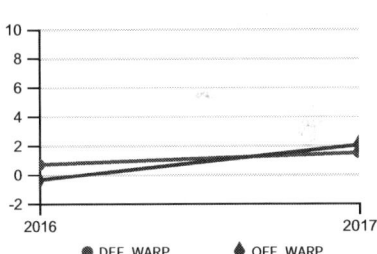

BRR (Relative to Position)
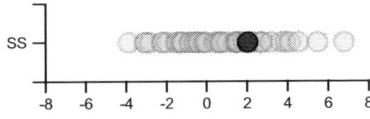

Rank	Player	BRR
13	62° Francisco Lindor	2.14
14	58° Jean Segura	2.09
15	55° **Orlando Arcia**	**2.07**
16	52° Tim Anderson	2.06
17	50° Didi Gregorius	1.87

BRR (Relative to Team)
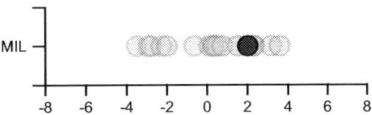

Rank	Player	BRR
3	96° Lorenzo Cain	2.36
4	89° Hernan Perez	2.36
5	80° **Orlando Arcia**	**2.07**
6	72° Jonathan Villar	1.59
7	60° Christian Yelich	0.81

Base Running Components
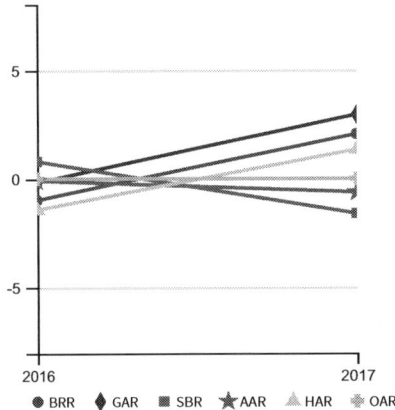

Nolan Arenado 3B Colorado Rockies

Born: 4/16/1991 **Age:** 27 **Bats:** R **Throws:** R **Height:** 6' 2" **Weight:** 205 lbs **Draft Info:** Round 2, 2009 Draft (#59 overall)

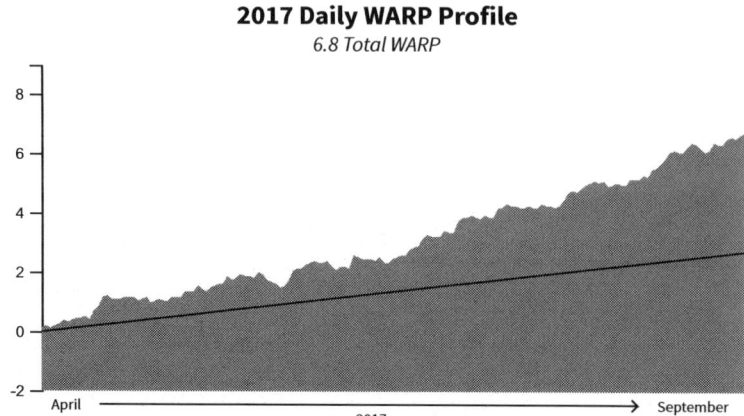

2017 Daily WARP Profile
6.8 Total WARP

PACE
22 Sec/Pit
99th of 155
36°
Slow

Fantasy Values
2017 **$31.88**
2018 **$33.00**

YEAR	TEAM	LVL	AGE	PA	R	2B	3B	HR	RBI	BB	K	SB	AVG/OBP/SLG	TAv	VORP	BABIP	WARP
2017	COL	MLB	26	680	100	43	7	37	130	62	106	3	.309/.373/.586	.317	63.0	.320	6.8

Domo arigato, Nolan Arenado, for taking my fantasy team just where it needed to (go). Arenado gets some flak in analytic circles for playing half his games at Coors Field, but in fantasy that's a feature, not a bug. Arenado hit at least 37 home runs, scored 100 runs, and drove in 130 for the third consecutive season. The cherry on the sundae was a batting average above .300 for the first time in his career. Arenado is an automatic first-round pick on draft day and an argument could be made that he should be the first third baseman off the board. — Mike G.

2017 Batting Percentages

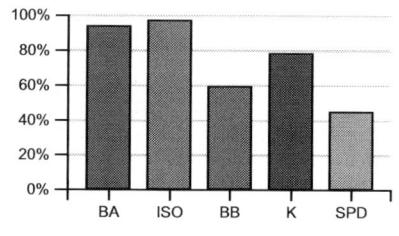

Batting PECOTA Percentiles

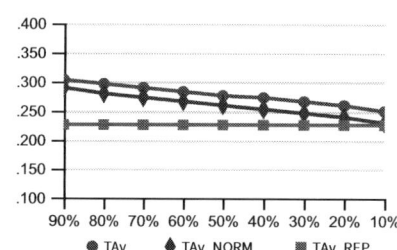

Batting WARP History

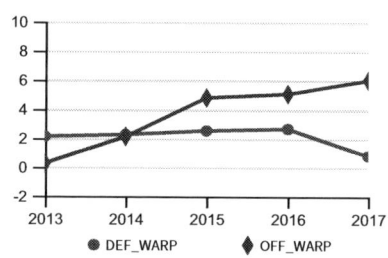

BRR (Relative to Position)

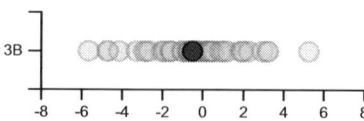

Rank		Player	BRR
31	49°	Jedd Gyorko	-0.40
32	48°	Giovanny Urshela	-0.46
33	45°	**Nolan Arenado**	**-0.47**
34	42°	Chase Headley	-0.50
35	41°	Wilmer Flores	-0.61

BRR (Relative to Team)

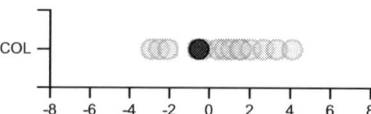

Rank		Player	BRR
9	32°	Tony Wolters	0.50
10	31°	Ryan Hanigan	-0.24
11	21°	**Nolan Arenado**	**-0.47**
12	21°	Michael Tauchman	-0.53
13	17°	Chris Iannetta	-2.02

Base Running Components

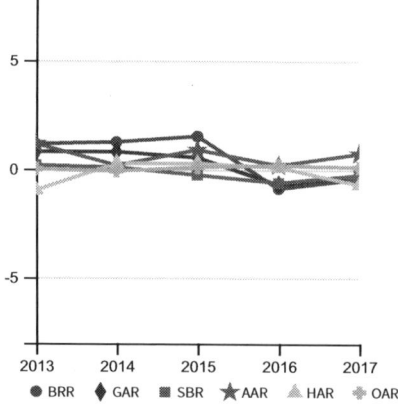

Jake Arrieta   RHP   Chicago Cubs

Born: 3/6/1986   **Age:** 32   **Bats:** R   **Throws:** R   **Height:** 6' 4"   **Weight:** 225 lbs   **Draft Info:** Round 5, 2007 Draft (#159 overall)

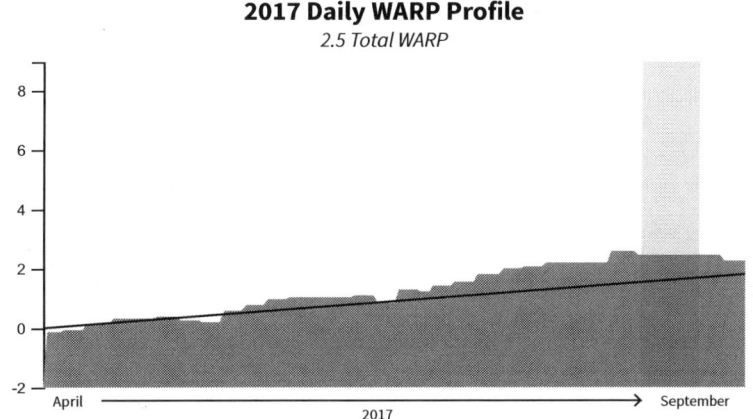

2017 Daily WARP Profile
2.5 Total WARP

Game 138: hamstring strain

PACE
21 Sec/Pit
81st of 150
46°
Average

POWER
51 PWR
56th of 150

STAMINA
72 STM
59th of 150

COMMAND
35 CMD
147th of 150

Fantasy Values

2017	2018
$19.98	$18.00

YEAR	TEAM	LVL	AGE	W	L	SV	G	GS	IP	H	HR	BB/9	K/9	K	GB%	BABIP	WHIP	ERA	DRA	WARP	MPH 95
2017	CHN	MLB	31	14	10	0	30	30	168.1	150	23	2.9	8.7	163	46%	.279	1.22	3.53	4.24	2.5	93.8

For the second consecutive season, Arrieta took a step back. No one expected him to replicate his banner 2015, but there were times when Arrieta's command eluded him, leading to higher pitch counts and difficulty pushing himself past the sixth inning. When he was on, Arrieta showed flashes of the high-quality ace he had been during his peak year, but it is fair to wonder if all those innings he put up in 2015 have taken their toll. Arrieta still is capable of pitching like an ace, but he isn't worth paying top dollar or drafting with a second- or third-round pick to find out if he can do it all season long. — Mike G.

2017 Pitching Percentages

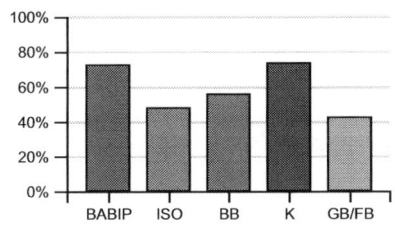

Pitching PECOTA Percentiles

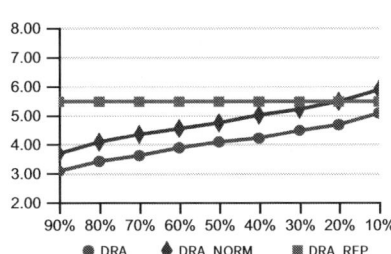

● DRA   ◆ DRA_NORM   ■ DRA_REP

Pitching WARP History

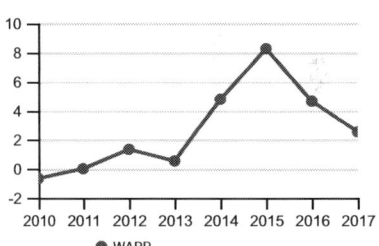

● WARP

Tunnel vs LHH

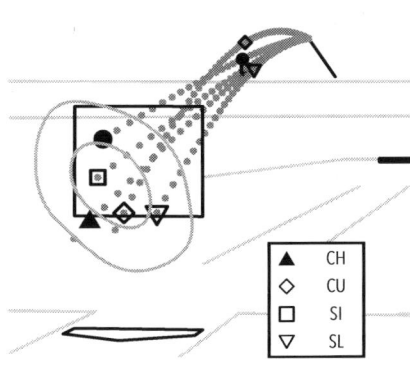

▲ CH
◇ CU
□ SI
▽ SL

Pitch Types

Type	Freq	Velo	H Mov	V Mov
CH	7.4%	87.5 [110]	-11.6 [98]	-29.8 [92]
CU	14.4%	79.1 [103]	13.6 [123]	-50.8 [94]
FA	3.5%	92.6 [99]	-5.4 [108]	-15.6 [99]
SI	60.8%	92.4 [101]	-11.6 [107]	-19.6 [101]
SL	14.0%	88.2 [117]	6 [106]	-27.5 [115]

Pitch Tunnel

Pairs	Release Diff	Tunnel Diff	Plate Diff	Speed Changes
1994	25.2	129.4	232.2	0.024

PI Scores

Year	Pitch Ct	Pwr	Cmd	Stm
2013	1261	63	38	66
2014	2403	52	36	68
2015	3425	56	39	82
2016	3115	60	34	79
2017	2701	51	35	72

Tunnel vs RHH

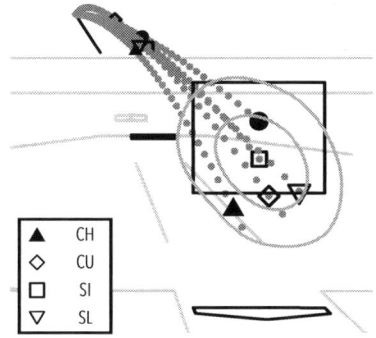

▲ CH
◇ CU
□ SI
▽ SL

Javier Baez   INF   Chicago Cubs

Born: 12/1/1992   **Age:** 25   **Bats:** R   **Throws:** R   **Height:** 6' 0"   **Weight:** 190 lbs   **Draft Info:** Round 1, 2011 Draft (#9 overall)

PACE
99th of 155
36°
Slow

22 Sec/Pit

2017 Daily WARP Profile
2.3 Total WARP

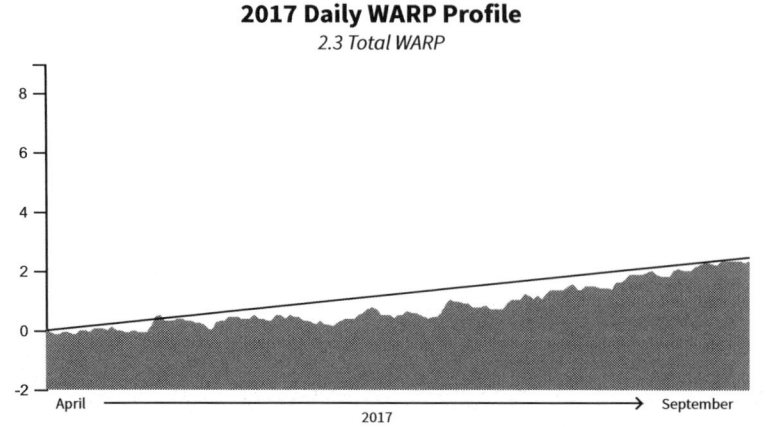

Fantasy Values

2017	2018
$20.11	**$24.00**

YEAR	TEAM	LVL	AGE	PA	R	2B	3B	HR	RBI	BB	K	SB	AVG/OBP/SLG	TAv	VORP	BABIP	WARP
2017	CHN	MLB	24	508	75	24	2	23	75	30	144	10	.273/.317/.480	.274	30.0	.345	2.3

After a second consecutive season of average offensive production, some believe that Baez was overrated as a prospect and will never live up to the hype. There's a buying opportunity here if most of your league feels this way. 2018 will be Baez's age 24 season and there were signs last year that a breakout could be on the way. Baez's ISO, walk rate, and batting average all improved in the second half. While cherry-picking split-season stats can be a fool's errand, even if you bet on the potential for growth and fail, you'll purchase a 20/10 hitter whose good defense will keep him in the lineup no matter what the strikeout rate looks like. — Mike G.

2017 Batting Percentages

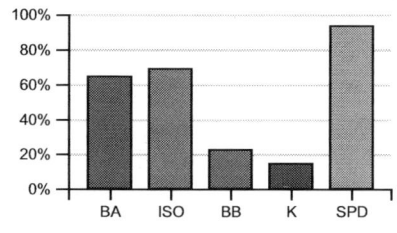

Batting PECOTA Percentiles

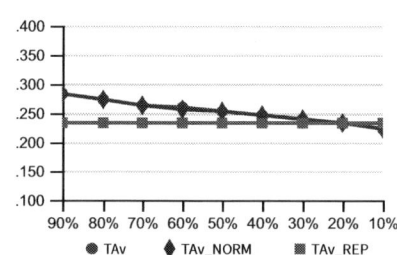

Batting WARP History

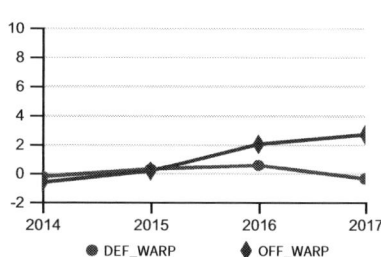

BRR (Relative to Position)

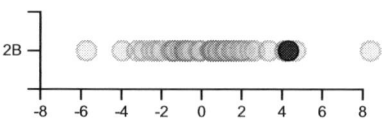

Rank		Player	BRR
1	95°	Dee Gordon	8.44
2	93°	Ian Kinsler	4.72
3	90°	**Javier Baez**	**4.36**
4	88°	Jonathan Schoop	4.21
5	84°	Cesar Hernandez	4.20

BRR (Relative to Team)

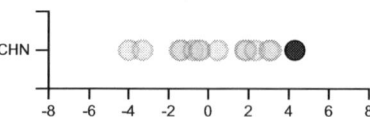

Rank		Player	BRR
1	89°	**Javier Baez**	**4.36**
2	83°	Albert Almora	3.17
3	77°	Ian Happ	3.07
4	68°	Jon Jay	2.37
5	59°	Jason Heyward	1.93

Base Running Components

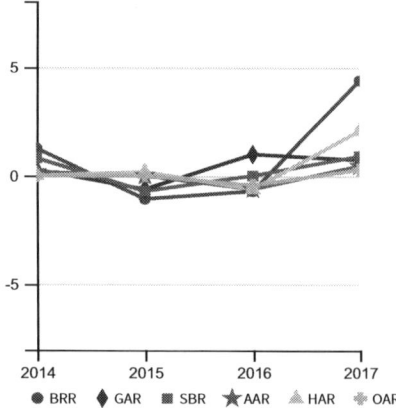

Homer Bailey RHP Cincinnati Reds

Born: 5/3/1986 **Age:** 32 **Bats:** R **Throws:** R **Height:** 6' 4" **Weight:** 223 lbs **Draft Info:** Round 1, 2004 Draft (#7 overall)

2017 Daily WARP Profile
-2.2 Total WARP

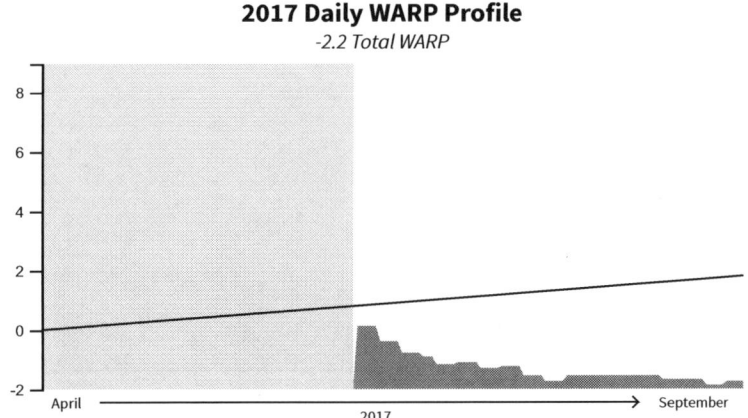

2017

April — September

Game 1: DL (tendon tear)

POWER
53 PWR 49th of 150

STAMINA
62 STM 94th of 150

COMMAND
42 CMD 128th of 150

PACE
22 Sec/Pit 108th of 150
28°
Slow

Fantasy Values
2017	2018
$-4.33	$1.00

YEAR	TEAM	LVL	AGE	W	L	SV	G	GS	IP	H	HR	BB/9	K/9	K	GB%	BABIP	WHIP	ERA	DRA	WARP	MPH 95
2017	CIN	MLB	31	6	9	0	18	18	91	112	11	4.2	6.6	67	46%	.346	1.69	6.43	7.72	-2.2	95.4

2017 Pitching Percentages

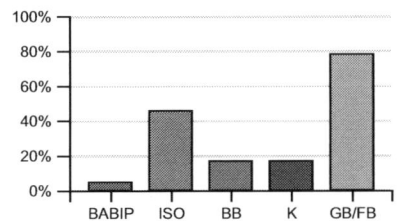

Pitching PECOTA Percentiles

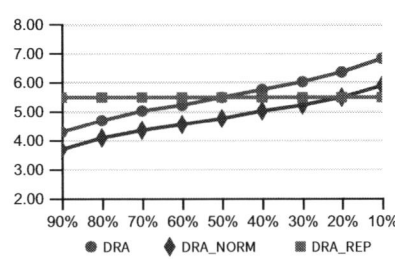

● DRA ◆ DRA_NORM ■ DRA_REP

Pitching WARP History

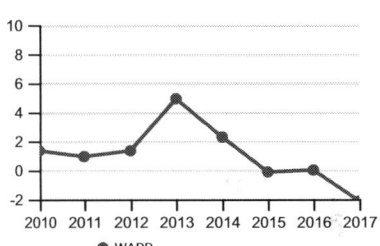

● WARP

Tunnel vs LHH

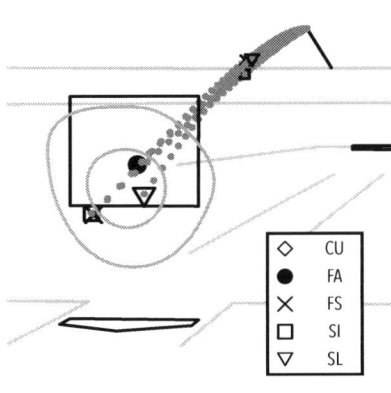

◇ CU
● FA
✕ FS
□ SI
▽ SL

Pitch Types

Type	Freq	Velo	H Mov	V Mov
CU	4.4%	78.5 [101]	10.7 [111]	-47.2 [102]
FA	48.7%	93.9 [104]	-6.5 [103]	-15.4 [99]
FS	17.8%	86.3 [106]	-6.2 [107]	-28.3 [105]
SI	8.3%	93.1 [105]	-13 [96]	-18.5 [106]
SL	20.9%	87.8 [115]	2.9 [92]	-26.8 [117]

Pitch Tunnel

Pairs	Release Diff	Tunnel Diff	Plate Diff	Speed Changes
1160	26.0	121.6	230.8	0.023

PI Scores

Year	Pitch Ct	Pwr	Cmd	Stm
2012	3318	58	48	78
2013	3280	62	56	81
2014	2260	60	44	68
2016	458	51	51	22
2017	1573	53	42	62

Tunnel vs RHH

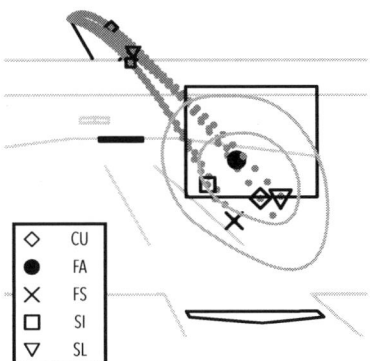

◇ CU
● FA
✕ FS
□ SI
▽ SL

Austin Barnes   C   Los Angeles Dodgers

Born: 12/28/1989   **Age:** 28   **Bats:** R   **Throws:** R   **Height:** 5' 10"   **Weight:** 190 lbs   **Draft Info:** Round 9, 2011 Draft (#283 overall)

We don't have a baseball card for this guy.

22 Sec/Pit

PACE
99th of 155
36°
Slow

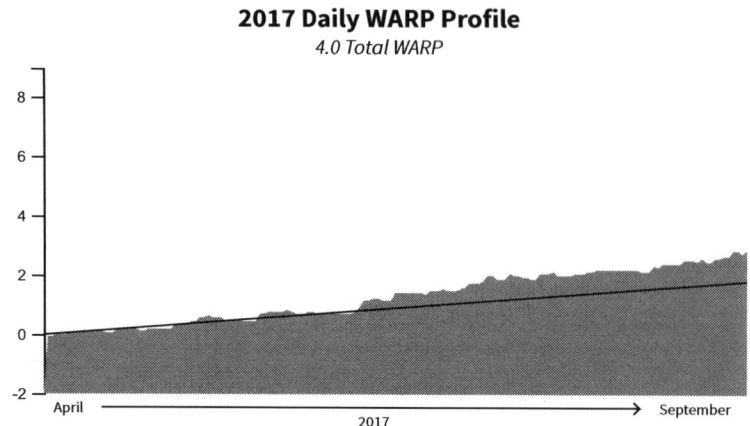

2017 Daily WARP Profile
4.0 Total WARP

Fantasy Values

2017	2018
$9.71	$12.00

YEAR	TEAM	LVL	AGE	PA	R	2B	3B	HR	RBI	BB	K	SB	AVG/OBP/SLG	TAv	VORP	BABIP	WARP
2017	LAN	MLB	27	262	35	15	2	8	38	39	43	4	.289/.408/.486	.325	29.5	.329	4.0

A deep sleeper among more than a few BP Fantasy staffers in February, Barnes wrested the starting job from Yasmani Grandal in the postseason and is likely to start for the Dodgers again this year. Barnes' raw numbers look underwhelming, but if he gets 400-450 plate appearances he has the potential to be a Top 10 catcher at a weak position. In leagues that use OBP, Barnes' value gets a considerable boost. He could be a poor man's J.T. Realmuto if everything breaks right. — Mike G.

2017 Batting Percentages

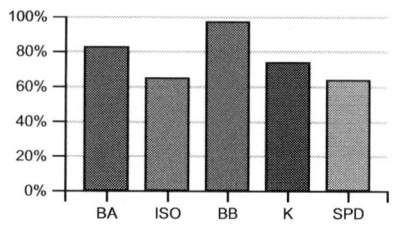

Batting PECOTA Percentiles

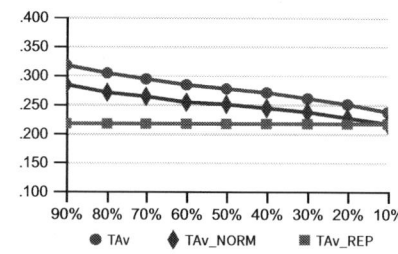

Batting WARP History

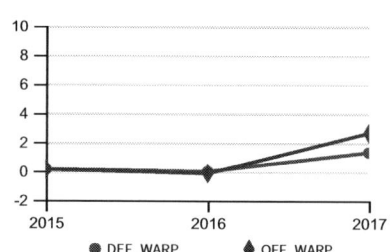

BRR (Relative to Position)

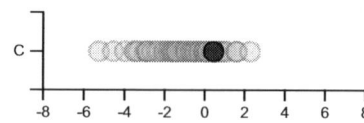

Rank		Player	BRR
15	81°	Tony Wolters	0.50
16	80°	Dustin Garneau	0.49
17	79°	**Austin Barnes**	**0.49**
18	79°	Stuart Turner	0.48
19	78°	Jeff Mathis	0.43

BRR (Relative to Team)

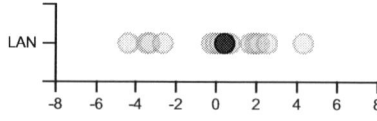

Rank		Player	BRR
6	55°	Franklin Gutierrez	0.76
7	48°	Logan Forsythe	0.50
8	43°	**Austin Barnes**	**0.49**
9	40°	Andrew Toles	0.22
10	40°	Travis Taijeron	0.03

Base Running Components

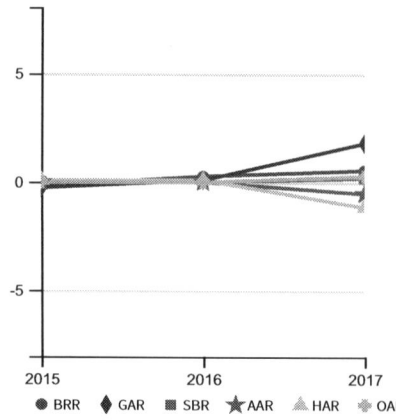

Matt Barnes RHP Boston Red Sox

Born: 6/17/1990 **Age:** 27 **Bats:** R **Throws:** R **Height:** 6' 4" **Weight:** 210 lbs **Draft Info:** Round 1, 2011 Draft (#19 overall)

We don't have a baseball card for this guy.

2017 Daily WARP Profile
1.5 Total WARP

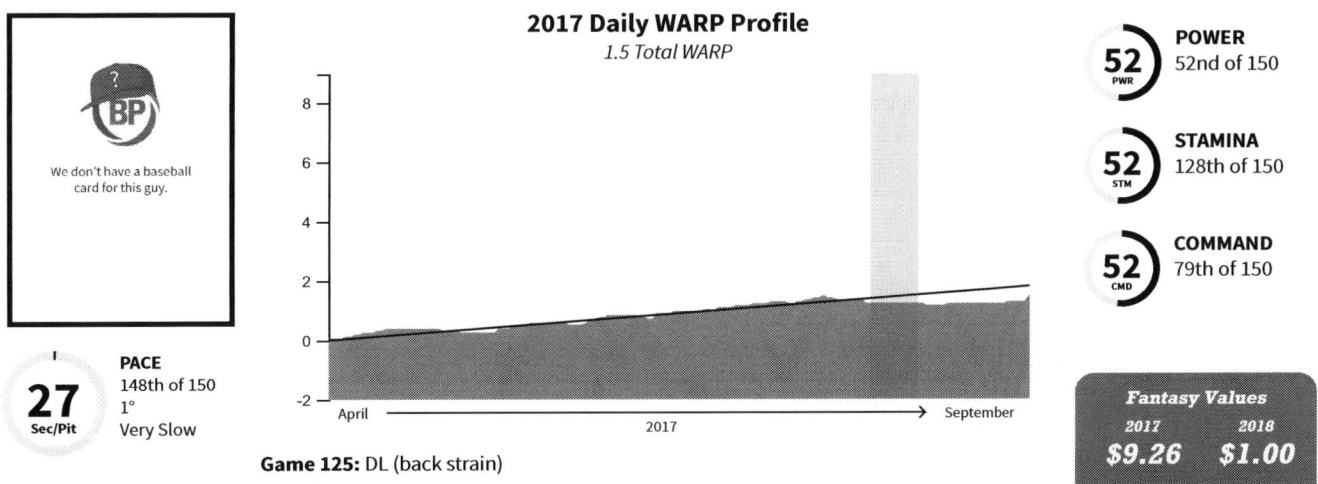

Game 125: DL (back strain)

PACE	
27 Sec/Pit	148th of 150 1° Very Slow

POWER — **52** PWR — 52nd of 150

STAMINA — **52** STM — 128th of 150

COMMAND — **52** CMD — 79th of 150

Fantasy Values

2017	2018
$9.26	$1.00

YEAR	TEAM	LVL	AGE	W	L	SV	G	GS	IP	H	HR	BB/9	K/9	K	GB%	BABIP	WHIP	ERA	DRA	WARP	MPH 95
2017	BOS	MLB	27	7	3	1	70	0	69.2	57	7	3.6	10.7	83	50%	.298	1.22	3.88	3.22	1.5	96.8

2017 Pitching Percentages

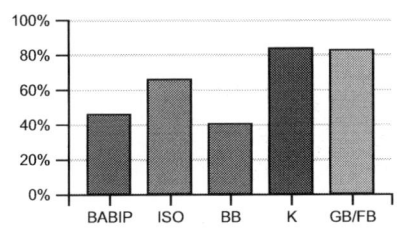

Pitching PECOTA Percentiles

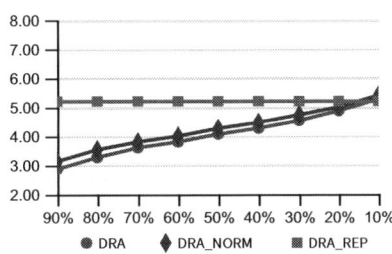

Pitching WARP History

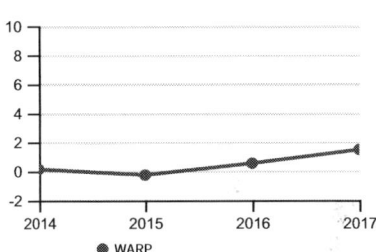

Tunnel vs LHH

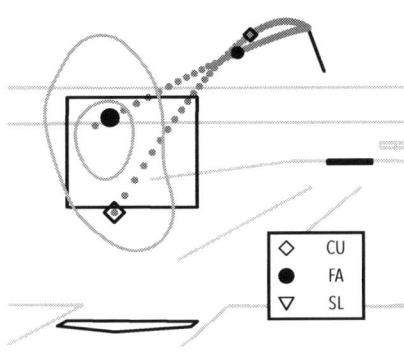

Pitch Types

Type	Freq	Velo	H Mov	V Mov
CU	31.4%	81.2 [111]	3 [81]	-49.2 [97]
FA	55.0%	95.6 [110]	-5.7 [107]	-10.4 [115]
SL	13.6%	88.3 [117]	3.8 [97]	-24.5 [123]

Pitch Tunnel

Pairs	Release Diff	Tunnel Diff	Plate Diff	Speed Changes
912	19.9	130.8	259.5	0.030

PI Scores

Year	Pitch Ct	Pwr	Cmd	Stm
2015	790	60	45	51
2016	1189	60	42	49
2017	1201	52	52	52

Tunnel vs RHH

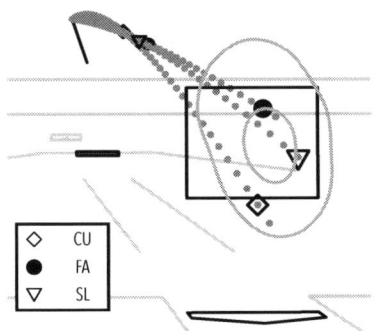

Trevor Bauer   RHP   Cleveland Indians

Born: 1/17/1991   **Age:** 27   **Bats:** R   **Throws:** R   **Height:** 6' 1"   **Weight:** 190 lbs   **Draft Info:** Round 1, 2011 Draft (#3 overall)

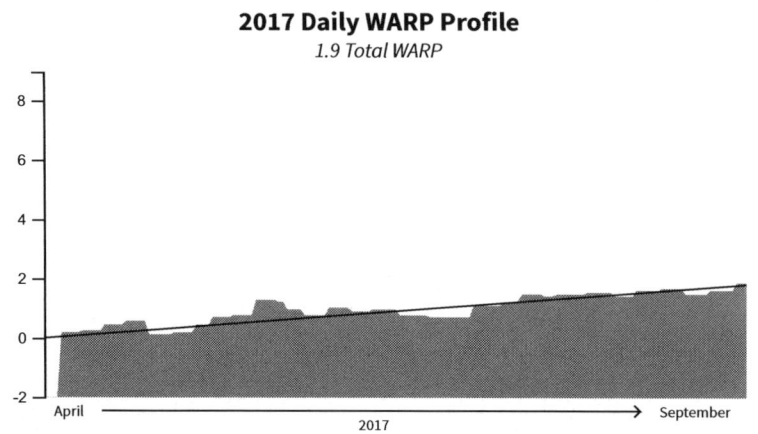

2017 Daily WARP Profile
1.9 Total WARP

April — 2017 — September

POWER 44 PWR — 80th of 150

STAMINA 77 STM — 32nd of 150

COMMAND 61 CMD — 30th of 150

PACE 20 Sec/Pit — 37th of 150 / 75° / Fast

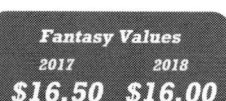
Fantasy Values
2017	2018
$16.50	$16.00

YEAR	TEAM	LVL	AGE	W	L	SV	G	GS	IP	H	HR	BB/9	K/9	K	GB%	BABIP	WHIP	ERA	DRA	WARP	MPH 95
2017	CLE	MLB	26	17	9	0	32	31	176.1	181	25	3.1	10.0	196	47%	.337	1.37	4.19	4.58	1.9	96.1

After starting the season with a 6.30 ERA, Bauer found his groove, adding more curveballs to his repertoire and pushing his ERA down and strikeouts up in the process. Bauer isn't exactly a sleeper, but if your leaguemates only pay attention to his full-season numbers, he could be a slight bargain. If there's anything to be wary about with Bauer it is that we have seen this story play out with him before, but the smart money should bet on the changes being legitimate and the emergence of a potential ace in the making. — Mike G.

2017 Pitching Percentages

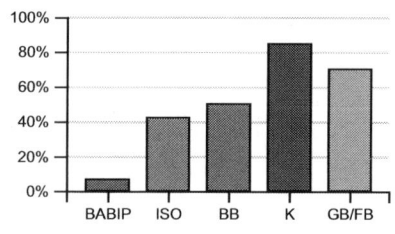

Pitching PECOTA Percentiles

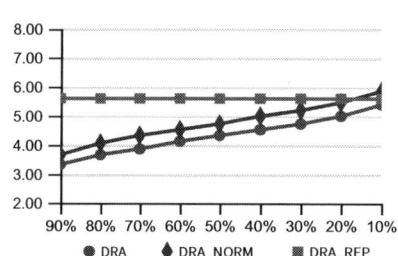

Pitching WARP History

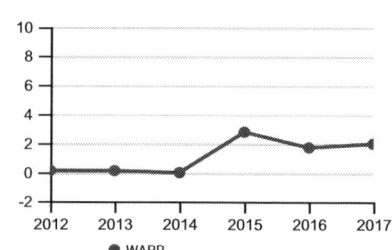

Tunnel vs LHH

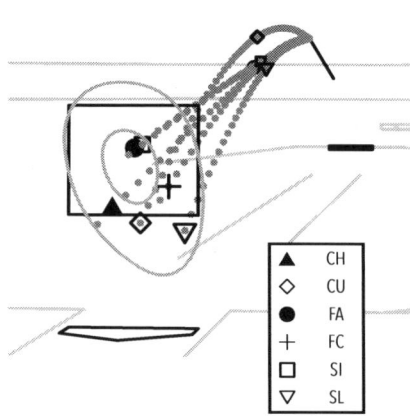

Pitch Types

Type	Freq	Velo	H Mov	V Mov
CH	6.5%	87.4 [109]	-12.3 [93]	-26.3 [102]
CU	29.8%	78.8 [102]	8.1 [101]	-56.2 [82]
FA	39.7%	94.3 [106]	-8.1 [95]	-12.8 [108]
FC	7.8%	87.9 [97]	4 [113]	-26.3 [90]
FS	1.1%	85.6 [103]	-8.8 [97]	-28.2 [105]
SI	9.6%	93.8 [109]	-13.3 [94]	-17.1 [111]
SL	5.6%	84.7 [101]	5.3 [103]	-35.1 [93]

Pitch Tunnel

Pairs	Release Diff	Tunnel Diff	Plate Diff	Speed Changes
2391	29.1	129.9	234.4	0.037

PI Scores

Year	Pitch Ct	Pwr	Cmd	Stm
2013	350	43	38	68
2014	2566	50	53	82
2015	2860	49	59	71
2016	2997	48	51	78
2017	3141	44	61	77

Tunnel vs RHH

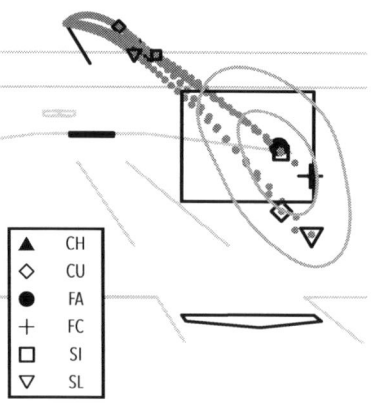

Jose Bautista   RF   Toronto Blue Jays   ⚓

Born: 10/19/1980   **Age:** 37   **Bats:** R   **Throws:** R   **Height:** 6' 0"   **Weight:** 205 lbs   **Draft Info:** Round 20, 2000 Draft (#599 overall)

2017 Daily WARP Profile
1.0 Total WARP

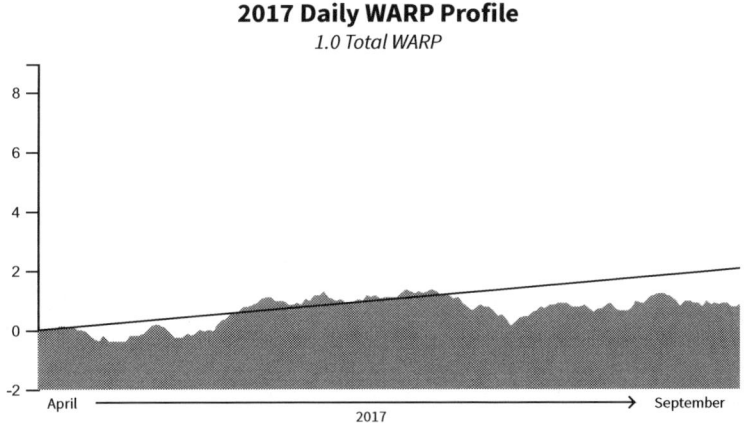

PACE
20 Sec/Pit
18th of 155
88°
Very Fast

Fantasy Values
2017	2018
$9.29	$4.00

YEAR	TEAM	LVL	AGE	PA	R	2B	3B	HR	RBI	BB	K	SB	AVG/OBP/SLG	TAv	VORP	BABIP	WARP
2017	TOR	MLB	36	686	92	27	0	23	65	84	170	6	.203/.308/.366	.237	-4.4	.239	1.0

2017 was likely the end of the line for Bautista, or at least the beginning of the end. The batting eye remained, and Bautista still had the ability to deposit a cookie into the left-field seats at Rogers Centre, but on most days Joey Bats looked more like Joey Toothpicks. If he does latch on somewhere, he is a back-end reserve pick in mixed at best and an $8-10 buy in AL-only assuming he has an everyday job. — Mike G.

2017 Batting Percentages

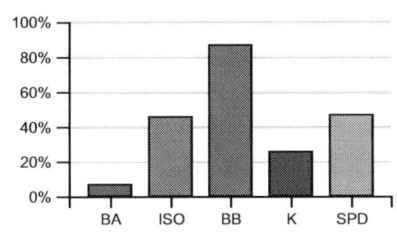

Batting PECOTA Percentiles

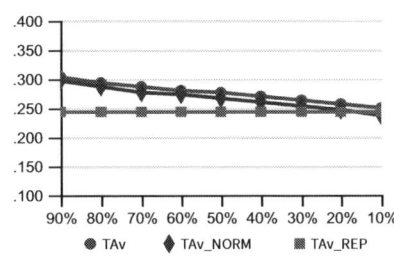

Batting WARP History

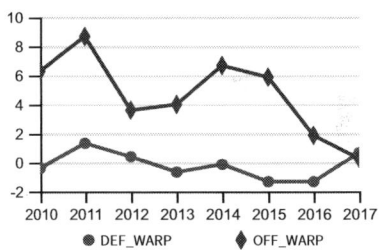

BRR (Relative to Position)

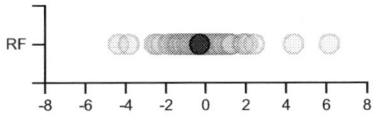

Rank		Player	BRR
28	49°	Giancarlo Stanton	-0.14
29	46°	Scott Schebler	-0.22
30	43°	**Jose Bautista**	**-0.25**
31	42°	Jorge Soler	-0.28
32	42°	Willy Garcia	-0.30

BRR (Relative to Team)

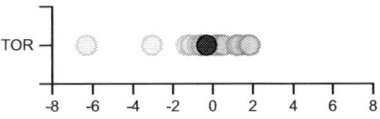

Rank		Player	BRR
13	59°	Luke Maile	0.20
14	53°	Russell Martin	0.17
15	41°	**Jose Bautista**	**-0.25**
16	37°	Miguel Montero	-0.49
17	31°	Ryan Goins	-0.54

Base Running Components

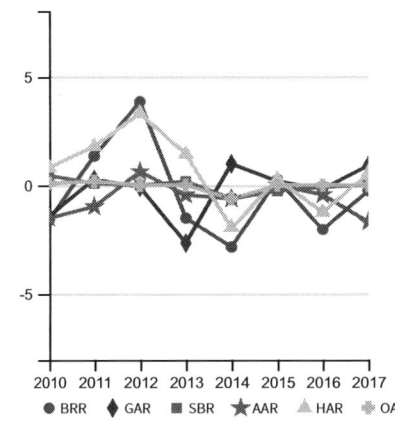

Tim Beckham   SS   Baltimore Orioles

Born: 1/27/1990   **Age:** 28   **Bats:** R   **Throws:** R   **Height:** 6' 1"   **Weight:** 205 lbs   **Draft Info:** Round 1, 2008 Draft (#1 overall)

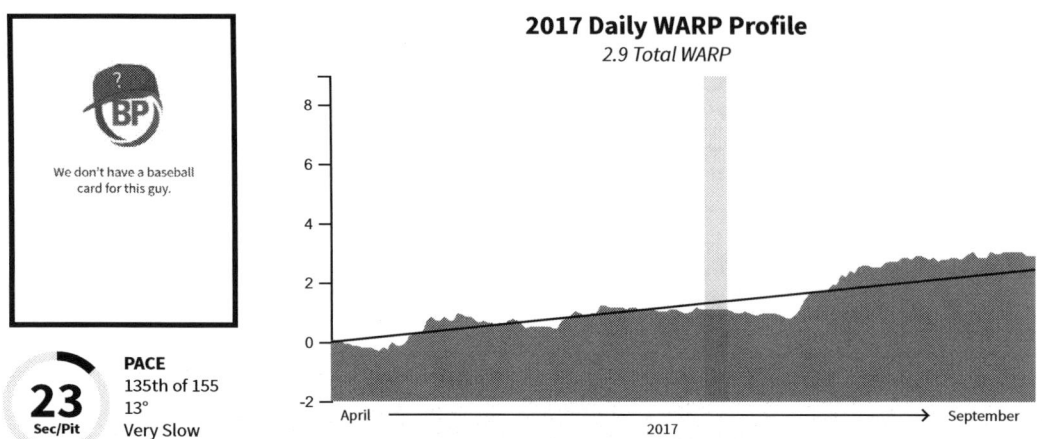

2017 Daily WARP Profile
2.9 Total WARP

PACE
23 Sec/Pit
135th of 155
13°
Very Slow

Game 87: DL (ankle sprain)

Fantasy Values
2017	2018
$17.57	**$15.00**

YEAR	TEAM	LVL	AGE	PA	R	2B	3B	HR	RBI	BB	K	SB	AVG/OBP/SLG	TAv	VORP	BABIP	WARP
2017	TBA	MLB	27	345	31	5	3	12	36	24	110	5	.259/.314/.407	.254	11.0	.357	.8
2017	BAL	MLB	27	230	36	13	2	10	26	12	57	1	.306/.348/.523	.292	18.2	.376	2.1

Perhaps all Beckham needed was an opportunity to play full time, although injuries certainly played a factor in his pre-2017 struggles as well. Whatever the reason, the former no. 1 overall pick went from draft bust to major-league contributor with a solid season first in Tampa Bay and then with Baltimore. Beckham was streaky, so in deeper formats you'll have to ride out the bad times, but the power should be there again this year even if the batting average and BABIP normalize. — Mike G.

2017 Batting Percentages

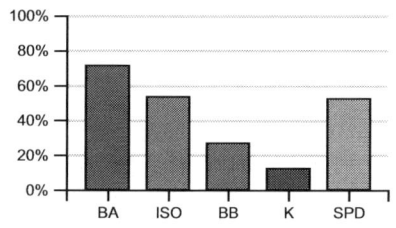

Batting PECOTA Percentiles

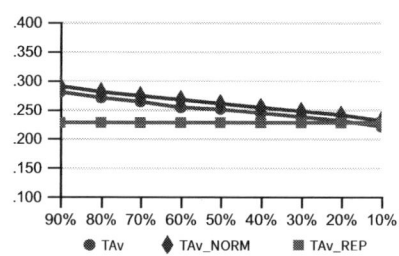

Batting WARP History

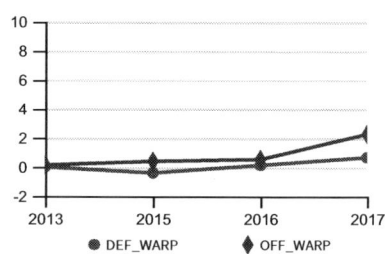

BRR (Relative to Position)

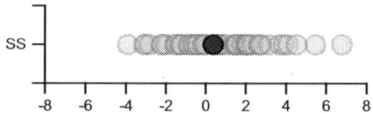

Rank		Player	BRR
26	38°	Franklin Barreto	0.68
27	35°	Alcides Escobar	0.55
28	32°	**Tim Beckham**	**0.41**
29	32°	Dusty Coleman	0.02
30	31°	Adam Rosales	-0.07

BRR (Relative to Team)

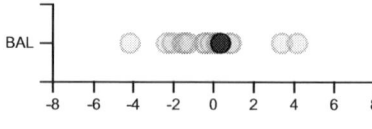

Rank		Player	BRR
3	69°	Trey Mancini	0.95
4	63°	Joey Rickard	0.88
5	53°	**Tim Beckham**	**0.41**
6	50°	Craig Gentry	0.30
7	46°	Caleb Joseph	0.21

Base Running Components

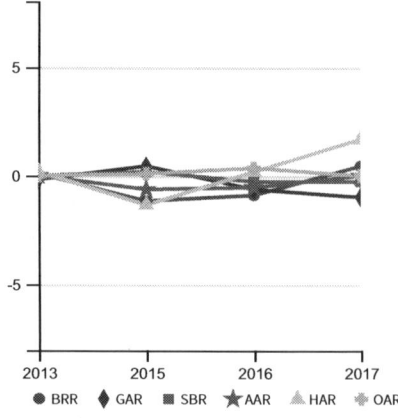

Josh Bell 1B Pittsburgh Pirates

Born: 8/14/1992 **Age:** 25 **Bats:** B **Throws:** R **Height:** 6' 2" **Weight:** 230 lbs **Draft Info:** Round 2, 2011 Draft (#61 overall)

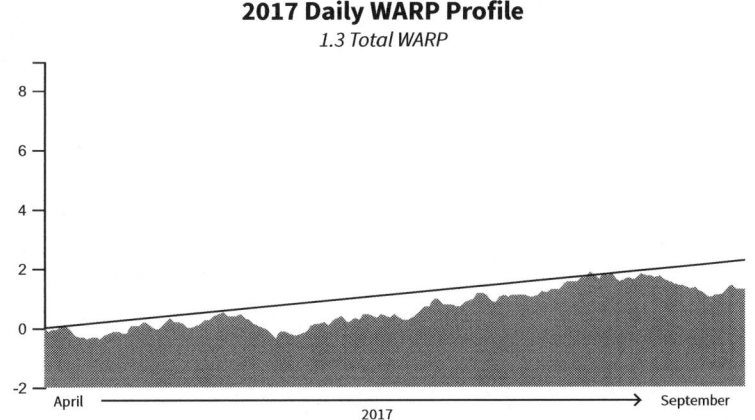

2017 Daily WARP Profile
1.3 Total WARP

20 Sec/Pit

PACE
18th of 155
88°
Very Fast

Fantasy Values
2017	2018
$16.75	**$17.00**

YEAR	TEAM	LVL	AGE	PA	R	2B	3B	HR	RBI	BB	K	SB	AVG/OBP/SLG	TAv	VORP	BABIP	WARP
2017	PIT	MLB	24	620	75	26	6	26	90	66	117	2	.255/.334/.466	.285	19.1	.278	1.3

Expected to be a high batting average hitter with only a smattering of power, Bell instead nearly doubled his prior career high in home runs as a professional while seeing his batting average dip. Bell held his own in his first full season, although in a climate where everyone is hitting home runs, a .300 batting average with 15-20 home runs would be more valuable. Bell was tied for 17th in home runs among first basemen in 2017. There's nothing wrong with that, but in the current context Bell's contributions make him solid and not special. — Mike G.

2017 Batting Percentages

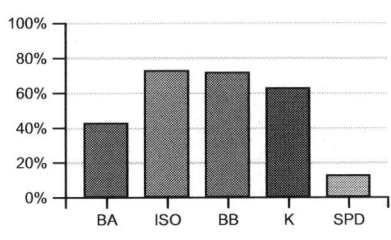

Batting PECOTA Percentiles

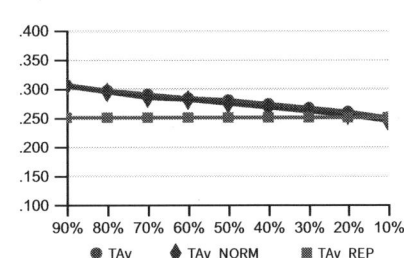

Batting WARP History

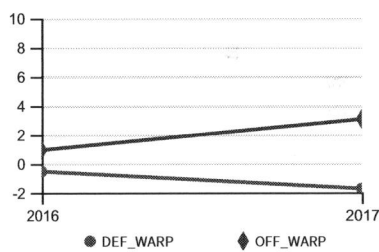

BRR (Relative to Position)

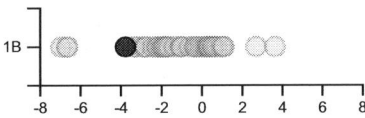

Rank		Player	BRR
40	16°	Anthony Rizzo	-3.23
41	14°	Lucas Duda	-3.26
42	11°	**Josh Bell**	**-3.73**
43	9°	Miguel Cabrera	-6.61
44	4°	Joe Mauer	-6.63

BRR (Relative to Team)

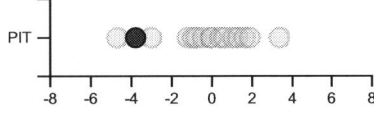

Rank		Player	BRR
12	33°	Elias Diaz	-0.89
13	23°	Jordy Mercer	-1.17
14	17°	Francisco Cervelli	-2.94
15	8°	**Josh Bell**	**-3.73**
16	0°	David Freese	-4.66

Base Running Components

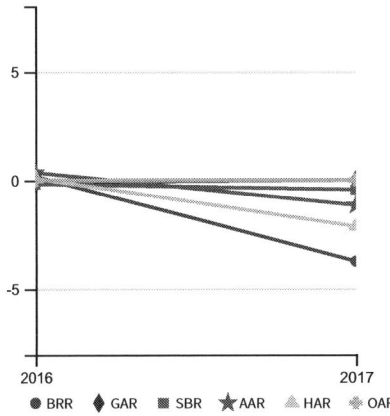

Cody Bellinger 1B Los Angeles Dodgers

Born: 7/13/1995 **Age:** 22 **Bats:** L **Throws:** L **Height:** 6' 4" **Weight:** 210 lbs **Draft Info:** Round 4, 2013 Draft (#124 overall)

21 Sec/Pit

PACE
45th of 155
71°
Fast

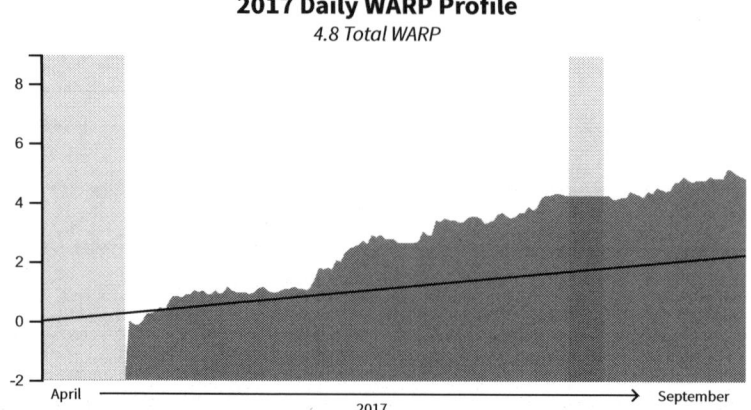

2017 Daily WARP Profile
4.8 Total WARP

April ← 2017 → September

Game 1: minors, **Game 122:** DL (ankle sprain)

Fantasy Values

2017	2018
$25.27	**$28.00**

YEAR	TEAM	LVL	AGE	PA	R	2B	3B	HR	RBI	BB	K	SB	AVG/OBP/SLG	TAv	VORP	BABIP	WARP
2017	LAN	MLB	21	548	87	26	4	39	97	64	146	10	.267/.352/.581	.331	48.6	.299	4.8

Bellinger was eventually expected to be a solid contributor in the majors, but "eventually" wasn't supposed to be early 2017. Bellinger found his way to the majors in late April and never looked back, mashing more taters than grandma used to on Christmas Day. Bellinger did cool off from his prodigious first half pace but even if he "only" manages to replicate his second half in 2018 he will still be a top-flight first baseman in every format. While the home-run rate dropped in the second half, the whiff rate did as well, suggesting that Bellinger will continue to adjust. Bet on the talent and let the stats come. — Mike G.

2017 Batting Percentages

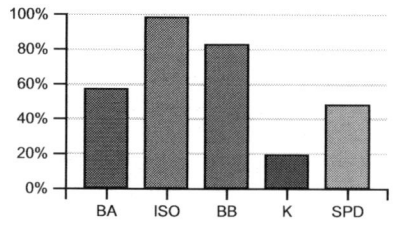

Batting PECOTA Percentiles

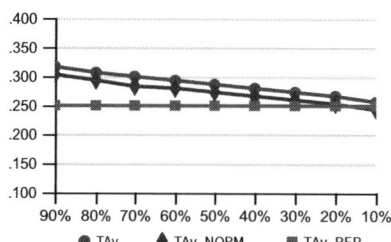

BRR (Relative to Position)

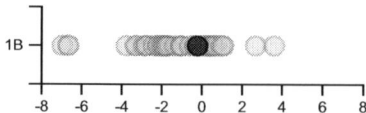

BRR (Relative to Team)

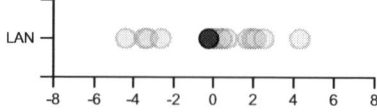

Rank		Player	BRR
16	72°	Jose Martinez	0.14
17	71°	Chris Carter	-0.01
18	69°	**Cody Bellinger**	**-0.17**
19	66°	Yonder Alonso	-0.29
20	64°	Ryan Zimmerman	-0.29

Rank		Player	BRR
9	40°	Andrew Toles	0.22
10	40°	Travis Taijeron	0.03
11	31°	**Cody Bellinger**	**-0.17**
12	25°	Yasmani Grandal	-2.58
13	16°	Justin Turner	-3.24

Brandon Belt 1B San Francisco Giants

Born: 4/20/1988 **Age:** 30 **Bats:** L **Throws:** L **Height:** 6' 5" **Weight:** 220 lbs **Draft Info:** Round 5, 2009 Draft (#147 overall)

21 Sec/Pit

PACE
45th of 155
71°
Fast

2017 Daily WARP Profile
3.4 Total WARP

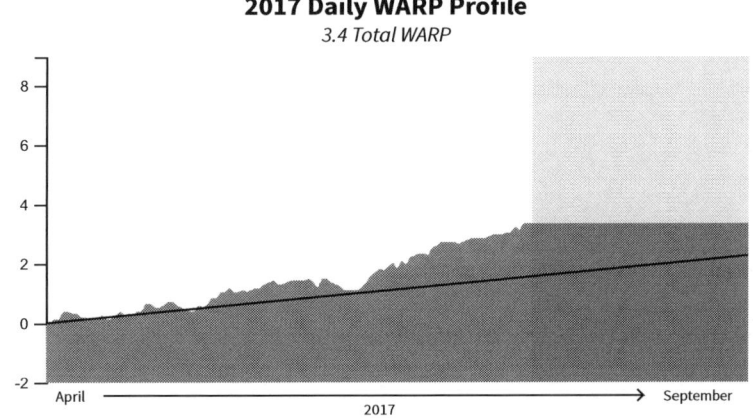

Game 112: DL (concussion)

Fantasy Values
2017	2018
$10.74	**$14.00**

YEAR	TEAM	LVL	AGE	PA	R	2B	3B	HR	RBI	BB	K	SB	AVG/OBP/SLG	TAv	VORP	BABIP	WARP
2017	SFN	MLB	29	451	63	27	3	18	51	66	104	3	.241/.355/.469	.302	25.6	.284	3.4

Belt was part of the dinger party in 2017, but it was hard to notice thanks to a concussion he suffered in early August that sidelined him for the rest of the season. The combination of a pitcher-friendly home venue at AT&T Park and the concussions make Belt difficult to recommend in 2018, particularly since so many first basemen can hit 20 home runs simply by showing up. If you draft Belt in a shallower format, try to stash a capable replacement; Belt has played more than 140 games only once since 2014. — Mike G.

2017 Batting Percentages

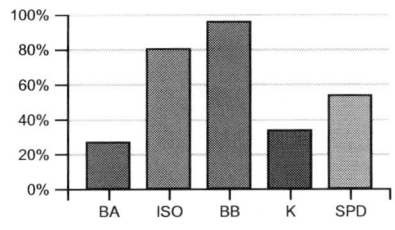

Batting PECOTA Percentiles

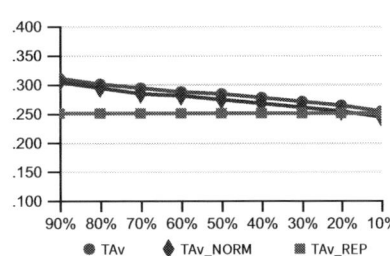

Batting WARP History

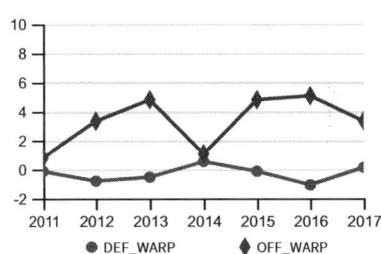

BRR (Relative to Position)

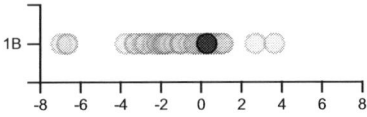

Rank	Player	BRR
12	78° Jesus Aguilar	0.39
13	78° Dominic Smith	0.35
14	75° **Brandon Belt**	**0.33**
15	74° Matt Olson	0.26
16	72° Jose Martinez	0.14

BRR (Relative to Team)

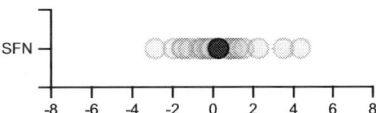

Rank	Player	BRR
9	60° Joe Panik	0.85
10	55° Alen Hanson	0.78
11	47° **Brandon Belt**	**0.33**
12	46° Orlando Calixte	0.31
13	45° Conor Gillaspie	0.30

Base Running Components

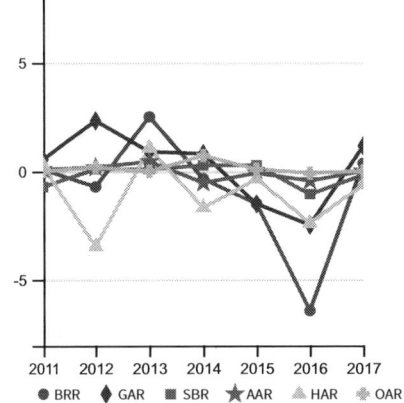

Adrian Beltre 3B Texas Rangers

Born: 4/7/1979 **Age:** 39 **Bats:** R **Throws:** R **Height:** 5' 11" **Weight:** 220 lbs **Draft Info:** International Free Agent, 1994

2017 Daily WARP Profile
3.1 Total WARP

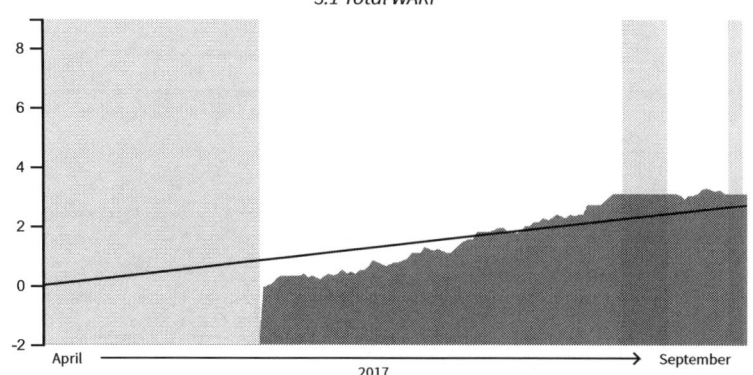

Game 1: DL (calf tightness), **Game 134:** DL (hamstring strain), **Game 158:** hamstring strain

PACE
21 Sec/Pit
45th of 155
71°
Fast

Fantasy Values
2017	2018
$16.25	$18.00

YEAR	TEAM	LVL	AGE	PA	R	2B	3B	HR	RBI	BB	K	SB	AVG/OBP/SLG	TAv	VORP	BABIP	WARP
2017	TEX	MLB	38	389	47	22	1	17	71	39	52	1	.312/.383/.532	.299	23.6	.321	3.1

On a per at-bat basis, Beltre was his usual self, posting his seventh season in the last eight with a TAv of .297 or higher. In fantasy terms, this typically means 30 home run power and a .300 batting average. The problem is that Beltre suffered the most serious injury of his career, playing under 100 games for the first time since his rookie campaign way back in 1998. It would be unwise to bet against Beltre, but at age 39 it makes sense to lop of a couple of bucks off his fantasy price just in case Father Time finally decides to tap the future Hall of Famer on the shoulder. — Mike G.

2017 Batting Percentages
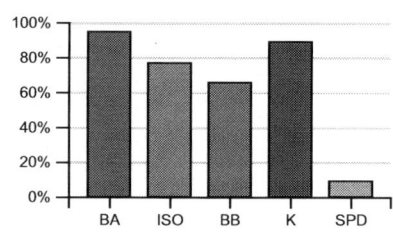

Batting PECOTA Percentiles
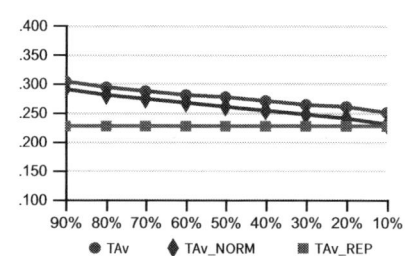

Batting WARP History
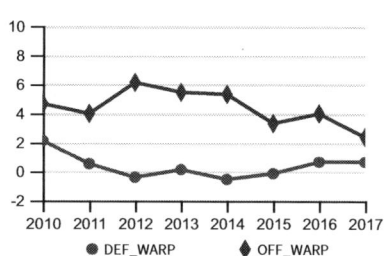

BRR (Relative to Position)
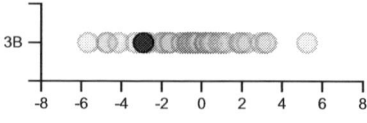

Rank		Player	BRR
49	16°	Nick Castellanos	-2.63
50	15°	Christian Arroyo	-2.77
51	13°	**Adrian Beltre**	**-2.87**
52	11°	Justin Turner	-3.24
53	8°	Manny Machado	-4.10

BRR (Relative to Team)
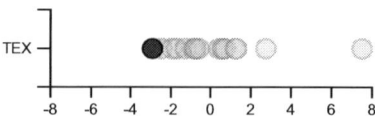

Rank		Player	BRR
13	27°	Brett Nicholas	-1.22
14	21°	Robinson Chirinos	-1.67
15	14°	Mike Napoli	-1.90
16	6°	Nomar Mazara	-2.41
17	0°	**Adrian Beltre**	**-2.87**

Base Running Components
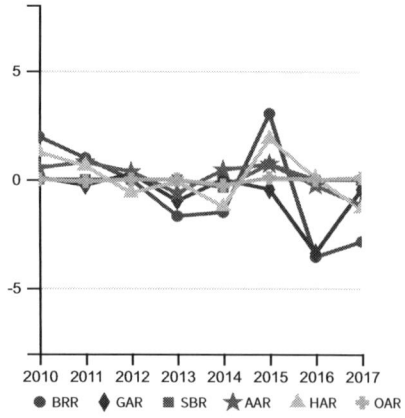

Andrew Benintendi   LF   Boston Red Sox

Born: 7/6/1994 **Age:** 23 **Bats:** L **Throws:** L **Height:** 5' 10" **Weight:** 170 lbs **Draft Info:** Round 1, 2015 Draft (#7 overall)

PACE
21 Sec/Pit
45th of 155
71°
Fast

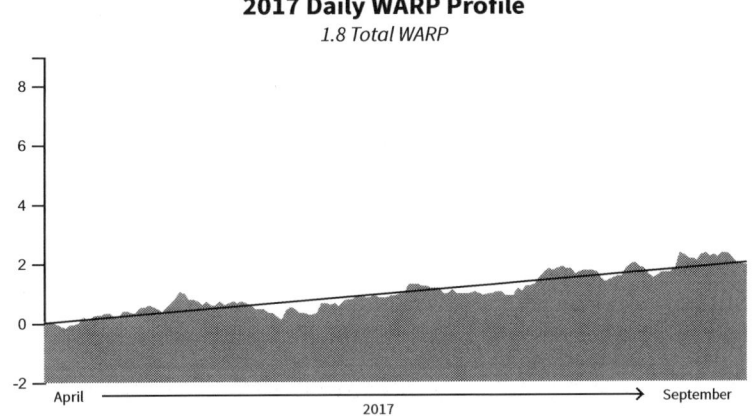

2017 Daily WARP Profile
1.8 Total WARP

Fantasy Values
2017	2018
$24.45	**$23.00**

YEAR	TEAM	LVL	AGE	PA	R	2B	3B	HR	RBI	BB	K	SB	AVG/OBP/SLG	TAv	VORP	BABIP	WARP
2017	BOS	MLB	22	658	84	26	1	20	90	70	112	20	.271/.352/.424	.262	18.5	.301	1.8

The preseason shoo-in for Rookie of the Year before Aaron Judge showed up and spoiled the party, Benintendi nevertheless lived up to fantasy expectations, and even parlayed his speed into 20 steals, something he never did in the minors. The 20/20 campaign made him plenty valuable, even though the batting average—something that was supposed to be automatic—slipped. Benintendi's value is cemented by his high floor. Even if he never becomes a 40-home-run hitter or a batting title contender, Benintendi's broad base of skills makes him a relatively safe pick in every format. — Mike G.

2017 Batting Percentages

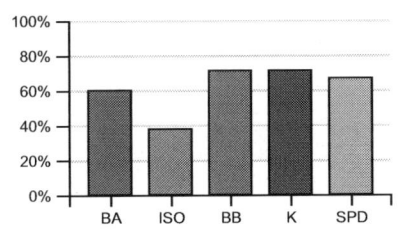

Batting PECOTA Percentiles

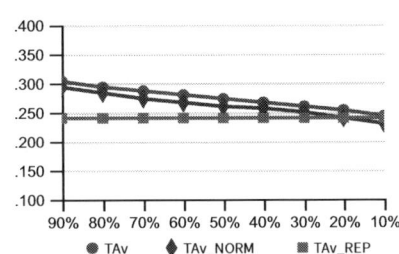

Batting WARP History

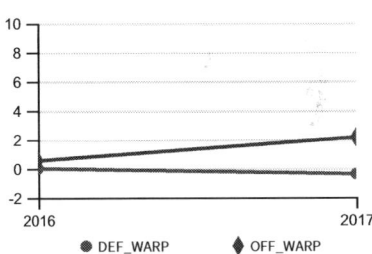

BRR (Relative to Position)

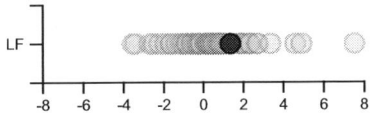

Rank	Player	BRR
14	Brett Gardner	1.44
15	Jace Peterson	1.44
16	**Andrew Benintendi**	**1.41**
17	Michael Conforto	1.39
18	Adam Frazier	1.34

BRR (Relative to Team)

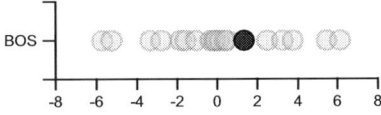

Rank	Player	BRR
4	Eduardo Nunez	3.28
5	Rajai Davis	2.55
6	**Andrew Benintendi**	**1.41**
7	Brock Holt	0.55
8	Deven Marrero	0.44

Base Running Components

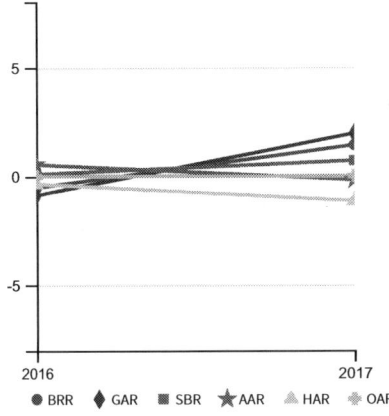

Jose Berrios   RHP   Minnesota Twins

Born: 5/27/1994   **Age:** 24   **Bats:** R   **Throws:** R   **Height:** 6' 0"   **Weight:** 185 lbs   **Draft Info:** Round 1, 2012 Draft (#32 overall)

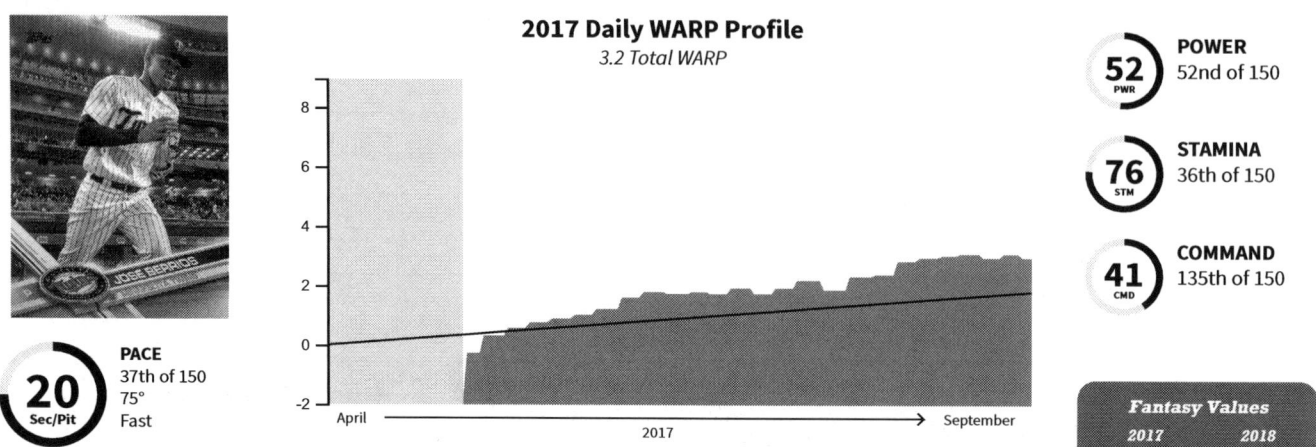

2017 Daily WARP Profile
3.2 Total WARP

Game 1: minors

	POWER
52 PWR	52nd of 150
76 STM	**STAMINA** 36th of 150
41 CMD	**COMMAND** 135th of 150
20 Sec/Pit	**PACE** 37th of 150 — 75° — Fast

Fantasy Values

2017	2018
$16.27	$14.00

YEAR	TEAM	LVL	AGE	W	L	SV	G	GS	IP	H	HR	BB/9	K/9	K	GB%	BABIP	WHIP	ERA	DRA	WARP	MPH 95
2017	MIN	MLB	23	14	8	0	26	25	145.2	131	15	3.0	8.6	139	41%	.289	1.23	3.89	3.62	3.2	95.9

Berrios took a significant step forward in his first full season, particularly with finding the command that had eluded him in 2016. There were some bumps in the road, but this is to be expected with nearly any young arm. When he was on his game, Berrios was as difficult to hit as any pitcher, but there were times when he left too many balls in the zone and suffered as a result. The doubts about Berrios' major-league future have been erased, but whether he will turn into an ace or merely a solid number 3 starter remains to be seen. — Mike G.

2017 Pitching Percentages

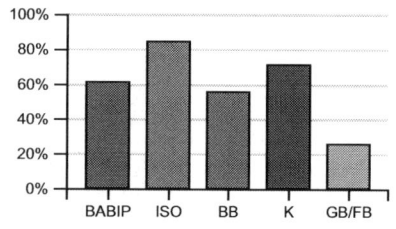

Pitching PECOTA Percentiles

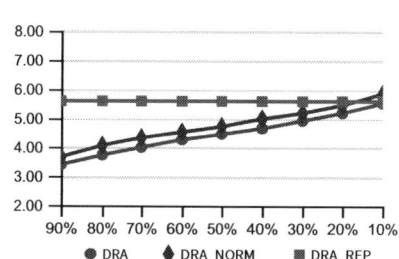

Pitching WARP History

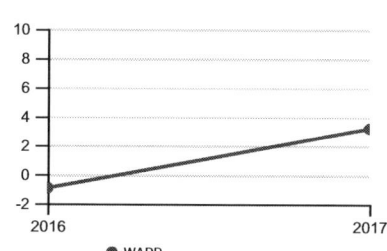

Tunnel vs LHH

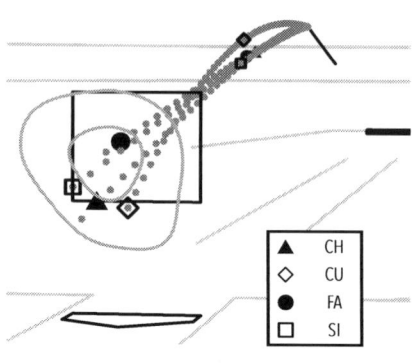

Pitch Types

Type	Freq	Velo	H Mov	V Mov
CH	8.7%	83.8 [95]	-12.4 [93]	-29.9 [92]
CU	29.9%	81.6 [112]	14 [124]	-41.3 [114]
FA	35.7%	94 [105]	-7.8 [97]	-13.8 [104]
SI	25.8%	93.5 [107]	-14.3 [87]	-19.1 [104]

Pitch Tunnel

Pairs	Release Diff	Tunnel Diff	Plate Diff	Speed Changes
1764	25.4	120.0	229.7	0.030

PI Scores

Year	Pitch Ct	Pwr	Cmd	Stm
2016	1207	52	46	69
2017	2380	52	41	76

Tunnel vs RHH

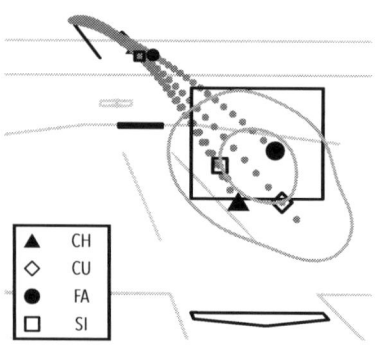

Mookie Betts   RF   Boston Red Sox

Born: 10/7/1992   **Age:** 25   **Bats:** R   **Throws:** R   **Height:** 5' 9"   **Weight:** 180 lbs   **Draft Info:** Round 5, 2011 Draft (#172 overall)

2017 Daily WARP Profile
5.6 Total WARP

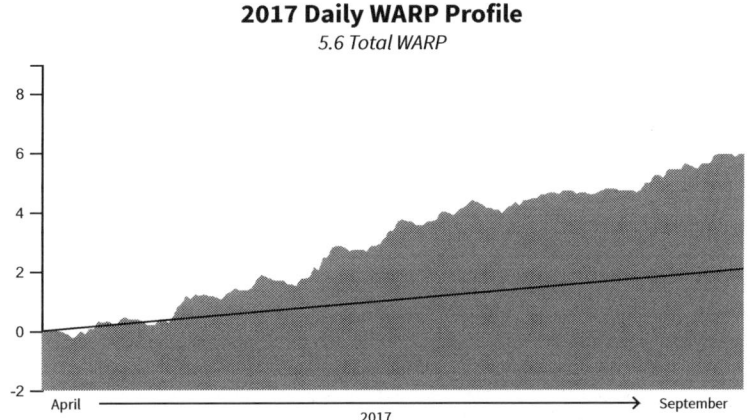

PACE
18th of 155
88°
Very Fast

20 Sec/Pit

Fantasy Values
2017	2018
$28.56	$35.00

YEAR	TEAM	LVL	AGE	PA	R	2B	3B	HR	RBI	BB	K	SB	AVG/OBP/SLG	TAv	VORP	BABIP	WARP
2017	BOS	MLB	24	712	101	46	2	24	102	77	79	26	.264/.344/.459	.276	31.5	.268	5.6

There are few players in fantasy for whom a 20/20 season with 100 runs and 100 RBI could be deemed a disappointment, but thanks to a sharp drop in batting average and a high ADP that's what 2017 was for Betts. While we've evolved past simply blaming BABIP, it is probable that Betts' batting average bounces back at least somewhat in 2018 and that he is an elite fantasy player once again. Betts should be taken late in the first round in mixers and is a mid-$30 buy in AL-only at a minimum. You should Betts on the bounce back. — Mike G.

2017 Batting Percentages

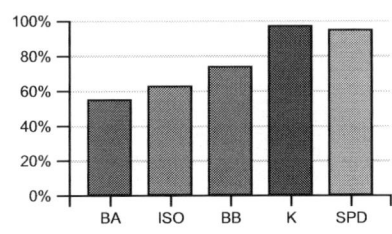

Batting PECOTA Percentiles

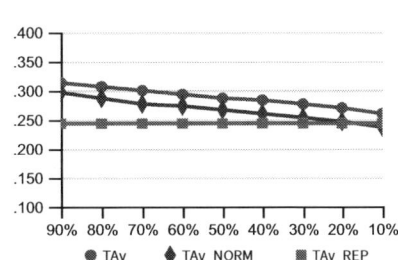

Batting WARP History

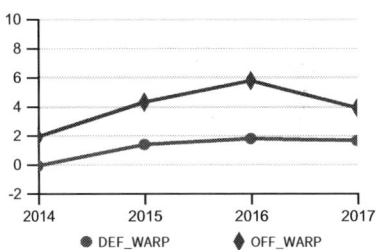

BRR (Relative to Position)

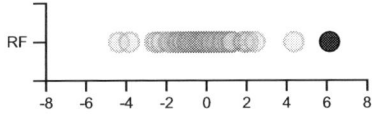

Rank		Player	BRR
1	96°	**Mookie Betts**	6.19
2	93°	Hunter Pence	4.40
3	90°	Josh Reddick	2.45
4	87°	Nick Markakis	2.12
5	85°	Jason Heyward	1.93

BRR (Relative to Team)

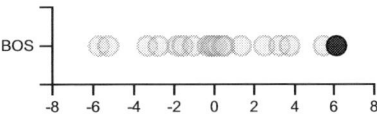

Rank		Player	BRR
1	98°	**Mookie Betts**	6.19
2	88°	Xander Bogaerts	5.51
3	81°	Jackie Bradley	3.79
4	72°	Eduardo Nunez	3.28
5	65°	Rajai Davis	2.55

Base Running Components

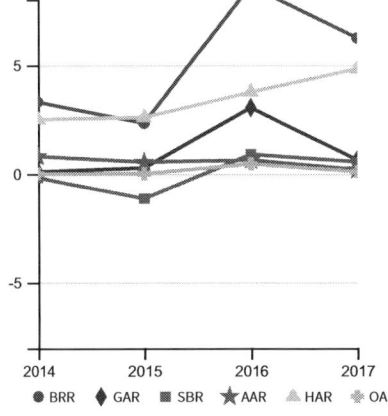

Ty Blach　LHP　San Francisco Giants

Born: 10/20/1990　**Age:** 27　**Bats:** R　**Throws:** L　**Height:** 6' 2"　**Weight:** 200 lbs　**Draft Info:** Round 5, 2012 Draft (#178 overall)

2017 Daily WARP Profile
-1.8 Total WARP

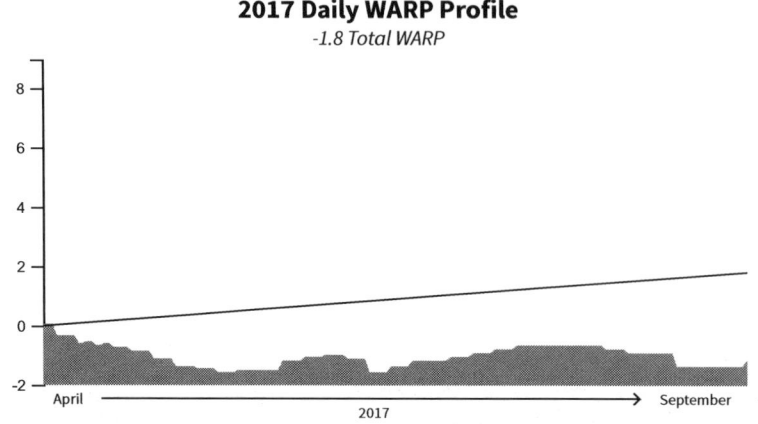

POWER
34 PWR
120th of 150

STAMINA
67 STM
82nd of 150

COMMAND
49 CMD
91st of 150

PACE
18 Sec/Pit
5th of 150
97°
Very Fast

Fantasy Values
2017	2018
$3.64	$2.00

YEAR	TEAM	LVL	AGE	W	L	SV	G	GS	IP	H	HR	BB/9	K/9	K	GB%	BABIP	WHIP	ERA	DRA	WARP	MPH 95
2017	SFN	MLB	26	8	12	0	34	24	163.2	179	17	2.4	4.0	73	48%	.290	1.36	4.78	6.55	-1.8	91.5

2017 Pitching Percentages

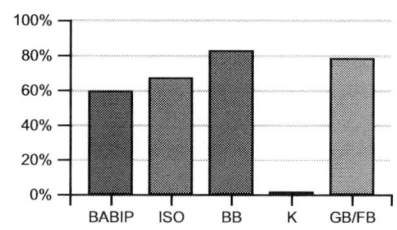

Pitching PECOTA Percentiles

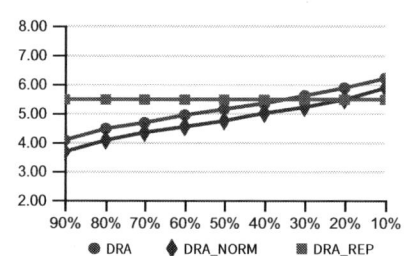

Pitching WARP History

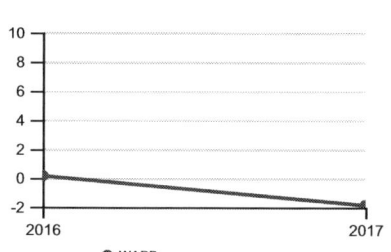

Tunnel vs LHH

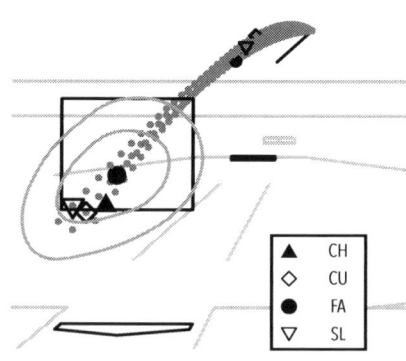

▲	CH
◇	CU
●	FA
▽	SL

Pitch Types

Type	Freq	Velo	H Mov	V Mov
CH	23.7%	80.5 [82]	13.7 [86]	-29.7 [92]
CU	11.0%	76.8 [94]	-4.7 [88]	-50.1 [95]
FA	60.1%	90.3 [91]	11.9 [78]	-18.9 [88]
SL	5.2%	79.8 [80]	-2.5 [91]	-39.6 [80]

Pitch Tunnel

Pairs	Release Diff	Tunnel Diff	Plate Diff	Speed Changes
1667	24.5	123.0	218.5	0.031

PI Scores

Year	Pitch Ct	Pwr	Cmd	Stm
2016	239	44	70	68
2017	2490	34	49	67

Tunnel vs RHH

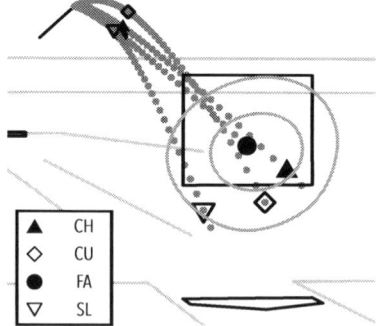

▲	CH
◇	CU
●	FA
▽	SL

Charlie Blackmon   CF   Colorado Rockies

Born: 7/1/1986   **Age:** 31   **Bats:** L   **Throws:** L   **Height:** 6' 3"   **Weight:** 210 lbs   **Draft Info:** Round 2, 2008 Draft (#72 overall)

2017 Daily WARP Profile
7.9 Total WARP

PACE
21 Sec/Pit
45th of 155
71°
Fast

Fantasy Values
2017	2018
$40.26	$37.00

YEAR	TEAM	LVL	AGE	PA	R	2B	3B	HR	RBI	BB	K	SB	AVG/OBP/SLG	TAv	VORP	BABIP	WARP
2017	COL	MLB	30	725	137	35	14	37	104	65	135	14	.331/.399/.601	.332	79.2	.371	7.9

Blackmon has pulled off the rare fantasy feat: increasing his fantasy value despite dropping off significantly in stolen bases. Some of this is due to the Coors factor, but those games count just as much for your fantasy team as any other contests. Blackmon is also a hard worker who has improved his game and taken advantage of both Coors and the overall offensive environment to adjust his swing and push for more power. Barring a trade, Blackmon is a first-round pick in every format, the only downside coming if the Rockies move him down in the lineup and reduce his opportunities to run even more. — Mike G.

2017 Batting Percentages

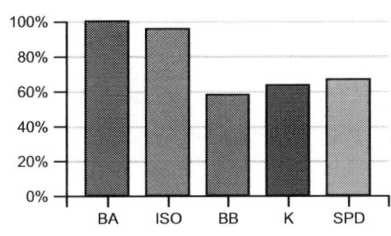

Batting PECOTA Percentiles

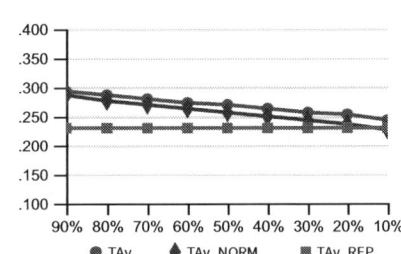

Batting WARP History

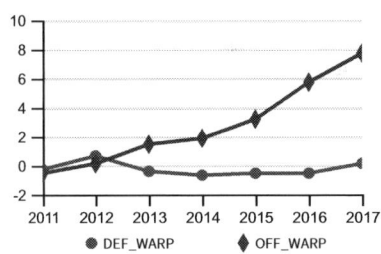

BRR (Relative to Position)

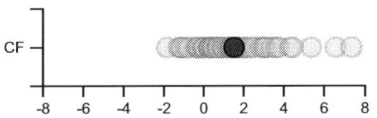

Rank		Player	BRR
22	52°	Bradley Zimmer	1.62
23	51°	Austin Jackson	1.58
24	46°	**Charlie Blackmon**	**1.57**
25	44°	Dexter Fowler	1.44
26	43°	Jake Marisnick	1.44

BRR (Relative to Team)

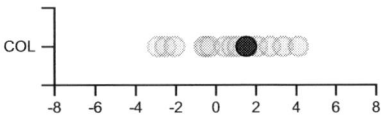

Rank		Player	BRR
4	74°	Patrick Valaika	2.11
5	70°	Raimel Tapia	1.62
6	53°	**Charlie Blackmon**	**1.57**
7	44°	Carlos Gonzalez	1.14
8	37°	Jonathan Lucroy	0.84

Base Running Components

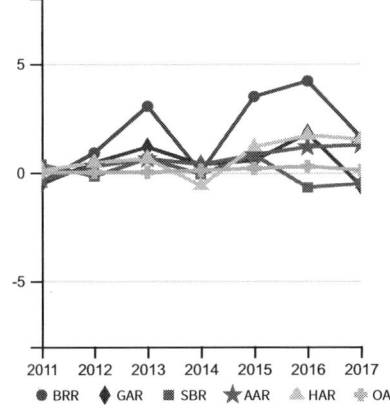

Xander Bogaerts   SS   Boston Red Sox

Born: 10/1/1992   **Age:** 25   **Bats:** R   **Throws:** R   **Height:** 6' 1"   **Weight:** 210 lbs   **Draft Info:** International Free Agent, 2009

PACE
21 Sec/Pit
45th of 155
71°
Fast

2017 Daily WARP Profile
2.3 Total WARP

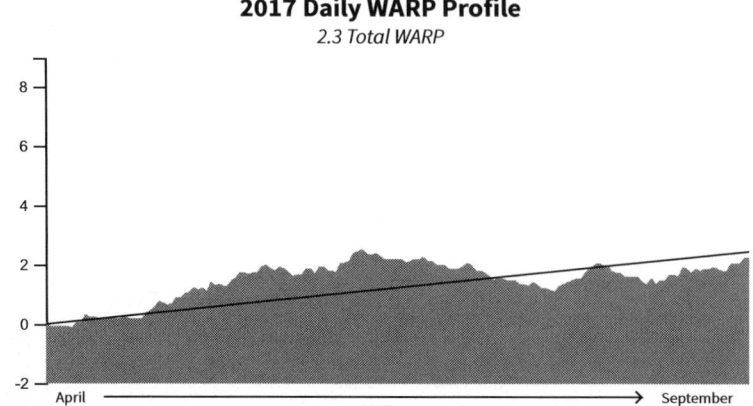

April → September
2017

Fantasy Values
2017	2018
$19.83	$21.00

YEAR	TEAM	LVL	AGE	PA	R	2B	3B	HR	RBI	BB	K	SB	AVG/OBP/SLG	TAv	VORP	BABIP	WARP
2017	BOS	MLB	24	635	94	32	6	10	62	56	116	15	.273/.343/.403	.259	31.9	.327	2.3

Those who ignored Bogaerts' high-ground-ball batted-ball profile paid the price last year, as the Boston shortstop saw his home runs drop from 21 in 2016 to 10, while the batting average slipped for the second consecutive season. The talent in real life is legitimate, but it is fair to wonder if Bogaerts' 2016 was an anomaly and if the heavy ground-ball approach limits his ceiling. Perhaps Bogaerts will become the next beneficiary of the launch-angle/fly-ball revolution, but I wouldn't bet my Topps' 1974 Rick Burleson rookie card on it. — Mike G.

2017 Batting Percentages

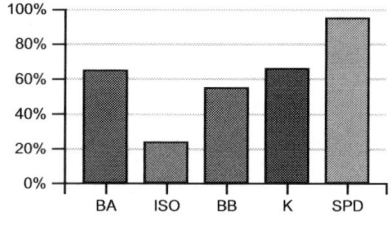

Batting PECOTA Percentiles

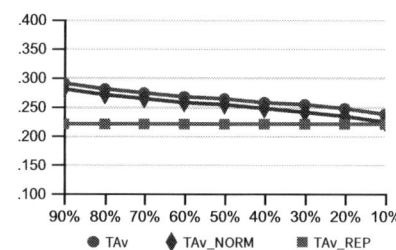

● TAv   ◆ TAv_NORM   ■ TAv_REP

Batting WARP History

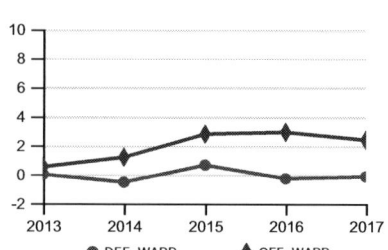

● DEF_WARP   ◆ OFF_WARP

BRR (Relative to Position)

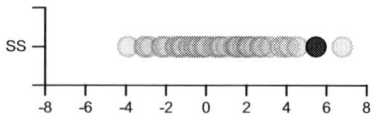

Rank		Player	BRR
1	96°	Trea Turner	6.83
2	93°	**Xander Bogaerts**	**5.51**
3	91°	Miguel Rojas	4.57
4	88°	Trevor Story	4.16
5	86°	Marcus Semien	3.94

BRR (Relative to Team)

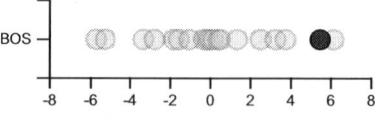

Rank		Player	BRR
1	98°	Mookie Betts	6.19
2	88°	**Xander Bogaerts**	**5.51**
3	81°	Jackie Bradley	3.79
4	72°	Eduardo Nunez	3.28
5	65°	Rajai Davis	2.55

Base Running Components

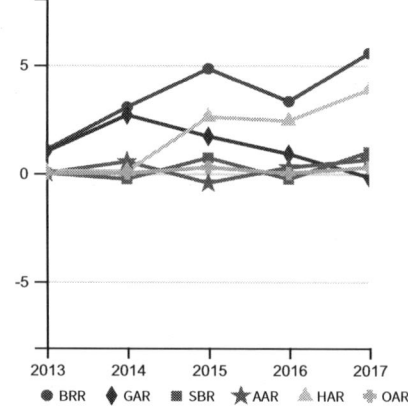

● BRR   ◆ GAR   ■ SBR   ★ AAR   ▲ HAR   ◈ OAR

Justin Bour 1B Miami Marlins

Born: 5/28/1988 **Age:** 30 **Bats:** L **Throws:** R **Height:** 6' 3" **Weight:** 265 lbs **Draft Info:** Round 25, 2009 Draft (#770 overall)

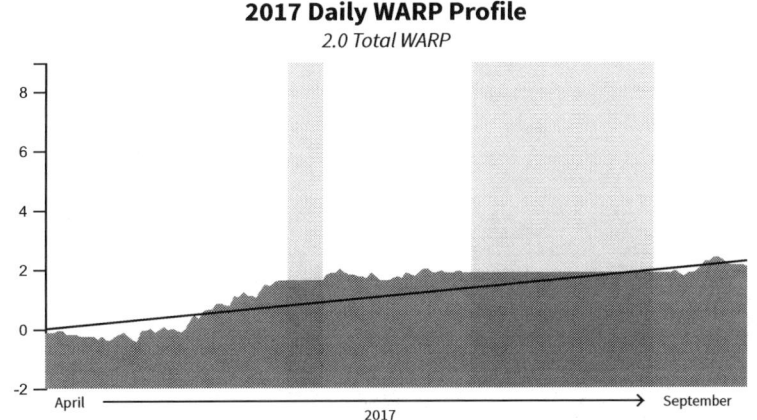

2017 Daily WARP Profile
2.0 Total WARP

Game 56: DL (ankle contusion), **Game 98:** DL (oblique strain)

PACE
20 Sec/Pit
18th of 155
88°
Very Fast

Fantasy Values
2017   *2018*
$17.68 $21.00

YEAR	TEAM	LVL	AGE	PA	R	2B	3B	HR	RBI	BB	K	SB	AVG/OBP/SLG	TAv	VORP	BABIP	WARP
2017	MIA	MLB	29	429	52	18	0	25	83	47	95	1	.289/.366/.536	.321	30.2	.322	2.0

Blocked by Anthony Rizzo for years in Chicago, Bour has flourished since the Cubs traded him to the Marlins ... when he has been able to stay on the field, that is. Bour would have hit 38 home runs had he played 162 games, but injuries limited him to 108 and cut his season short for the second consecutive year. There's certainly sleeper potential with Bour, but with so many first basemen capable of hitting for power Bour is a high-risk/high-reward pick in mixed leagues. In NL-only, Bour is worth the gamble even if you're stuck with 50-60 games of nothing at one of your corner infield slots. — Mike G.

2017 Batting Percentages

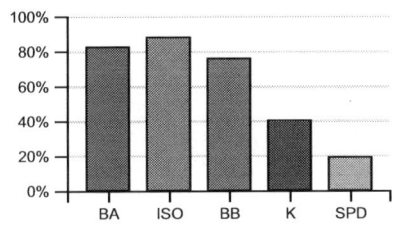

Batting PECOTA Percentiles

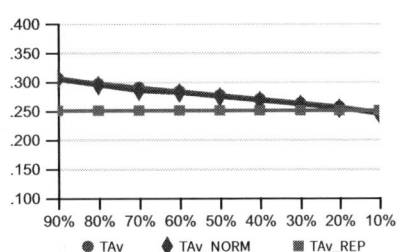

Batting WARP History

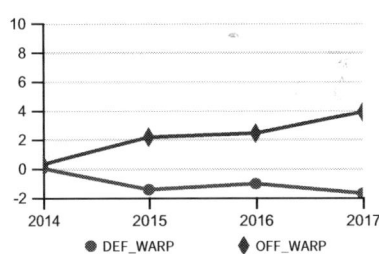

BRR (Relative to Position)

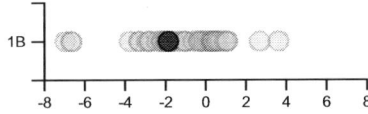

Rank		Player	BRR
28	48°	Yulieski Gurriel	-1.72
29	47°	Adrian Gonzalez	-1.82
30	44°	**Justin Bour**	**-1.82**
31	41°	Carlos Santana	-1.88
32	38°	Mike Napoli	-1.90

BRR (Relative to Team)

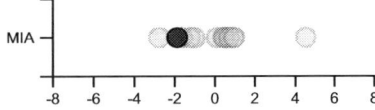

Rank		Player	BRR
10	13°	Martin Prado	-0.96
11	12°	Mike Aviles	-1.19
12	10°	A.J. Ellis	-1.59
13	4°	**Justin Bour**	**-1.82**
14	0°	Ichiro Suzuki	-2.71

Base Running Components

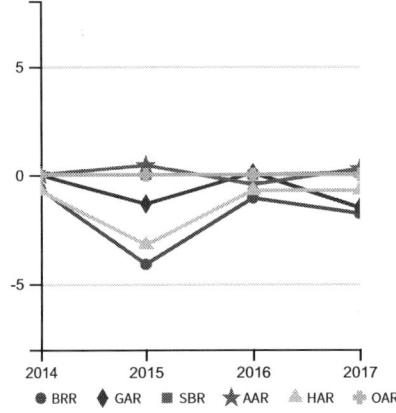

Matt Boyd   LHP   Detroit Tigers

Born: 2/2/1991   **Age:** 27   **Bats:** L   **Throws:** L   **Height:** 6' 3"   **Weight:** 215 lbs   **Draft Info:** Round 6, 2013 Draft (#175 overall)

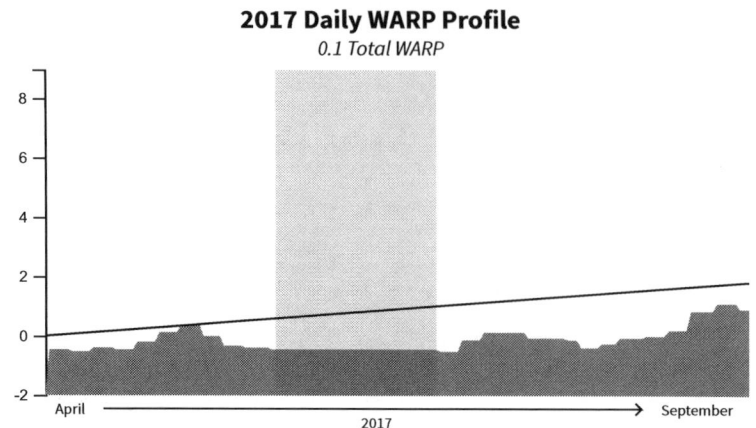

2017 Daily WARP Profile
0.1 Total WARP

April → September
2017

Game 54: minors

POWER 39 PWR — 100th of 150

STAMINA 79 STM — 17th of 150

COMMAND 38 CMD — 139th of 150

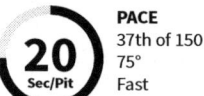
PACE 20 Sec/Pit — 37th of 150 / 75° / Fast

Fantasy Values

2017	2018
$-0.59	$5.00

YEAR	TEAM	LVL	AGE	W	L	SV	G	GS	IP	H	HR	BB/9	K/9	K	GB%	BABIP	WHIP	ERA	DRA	WARP	MPH 95
2017	DET	MLB	26	6	11	0	26	25	135	157	18	3.5	7.3	110	40%	.330	1.56	5.27	5.50	0.1	94.3

2017 Pitching Percentages

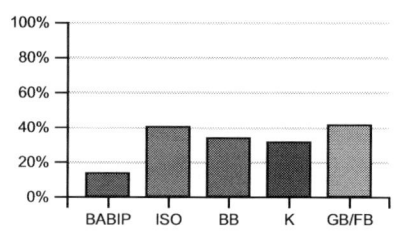

Pitching PECOTA Percentiles

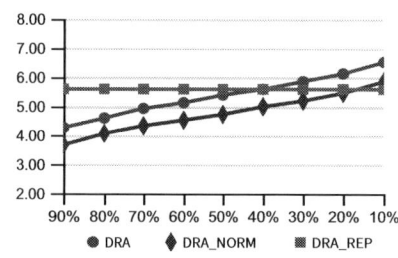

● DRA   ◆ DRA_NORM   ■ DRA_REP

Pitching WARP History

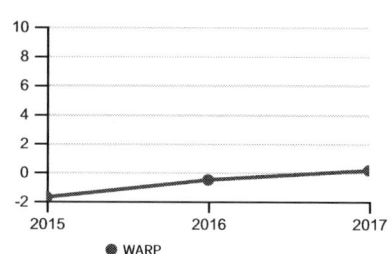

● WARP

Tunnel vs LHH

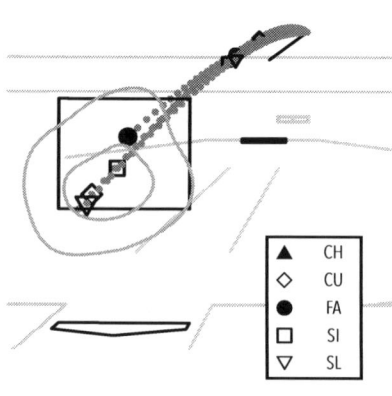

▲ CH
◇ CU
● FA
□ SI
▽ SL

Pitch Types

Type	Freq	Velo	H Mov	V Mov
CH	20.9%	81.4 [85]	12.6 [92]	-28.1 [97]
CU	18.1%	75 [88]	-10.1 [109]	-43.7 [109]
FA	32.1%	92.9 [101]	10.3 [85]	-15.2 [100]
SI	18.6%	91.4 [95]	14.2 [88]	-20.2 [100]
SL	10.3%	86.6 [110]	3 [66]	-27.5 [115]

Pitch Tunnel

Pairs	Release Diff	Tunnel Diff	Plate Diff	Speed Changes
1734	39.6	128.8	224.8	0.039

PI Scores

Year	Pitch Ct	Pwr	Cmd	Stm
2015	1003	39	46	68
2016	1683	43	50	70
2017	2335	39	38	79

Tunnel vs RHH

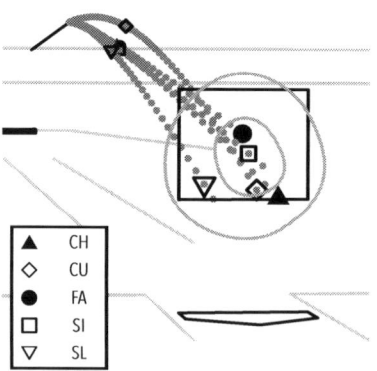

▲ CH
◇ CU
● FA
□ SI
▽ SL

Jackie Bradley   CF   Boston Red Sox

Born: 4/19/1990   **Age:** 28   **Bats:** L   **Throws:** R   **Height:** 5' 10"   **Weight:** 200 lbs   **Draft Info:** Round 1, 2011 Draft (#40 overall)

PACE
45th of 155
71°
Fast

21 Sec/Pit

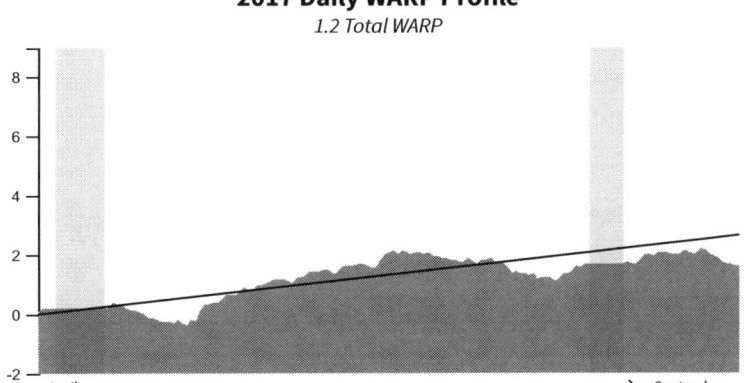

2017 Daily WARP Profile
1.2 Total WARP

Game 5: DL (knee sprain), **Game 127:** DL (thumb sprain)

Fantasy Values
2017   2018
$12.68 $16.00

YEAR	TEAM	LVL	AGE	PA	R	2B	3B	HR	RBI	BB	K	SB	AVG/OBP/SLG	TAv	VORP	BABIP	WARP
2017	BOS	MLB	27	541	58	19	3	17	63	48	124	8	.245/.323/.402	.257	19.3	.294	1.2

It was a frustrating year for Bradley buyers, as the Boston outfielder failed to build on his 2016 campaign and in fact took a step back. The defense will keep Bradley on the field when he's healthy, but his poor approach at the plate leads to long periods where he disappears and does nothing but hurt your squad. The potential remains tantalizing, but the time for hoping that Bradley will grow into his offensive profile is past. Let someone else bet on the upside in mixed leagues. — Mike G.

2017 Batting Percentages

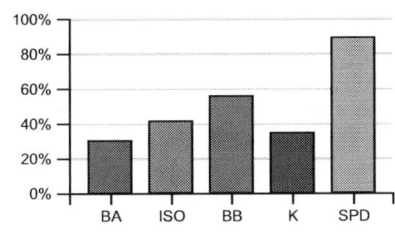

Batting PECOTA Percentiles

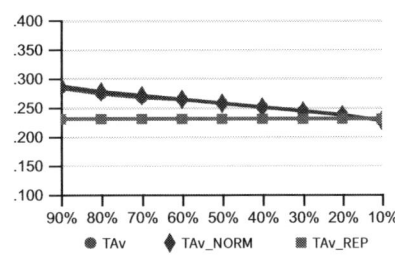

Batting WARP History

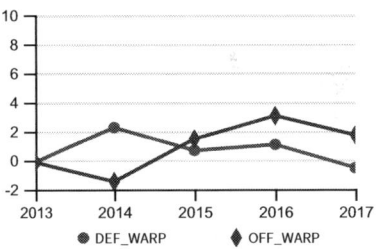

BRR (Relative to Position)

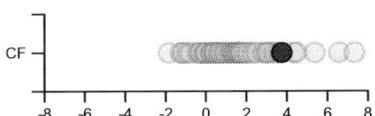

Rank		Player	BRR
4	87°	Cameron Maybin	4.50
5	84°	Chris Taylor	4.37
6	82°	**Jackie Bradley**	**3.79**
7	80°	Keon Broxton	3.64
8	78°	Adam Jones	3.43

BRR (Relative to Team)

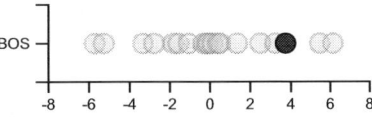

Rank		Player	BRR
1	98°	Mookie Betts	6.19
2	88°	Xander Bogaerts	5.51
3	81°	**Jackie Bradley**	**3.79**
4	72°	Eduardo Nunez	3.28
5	65°	Rajai Davis	2.55

Base Running Components

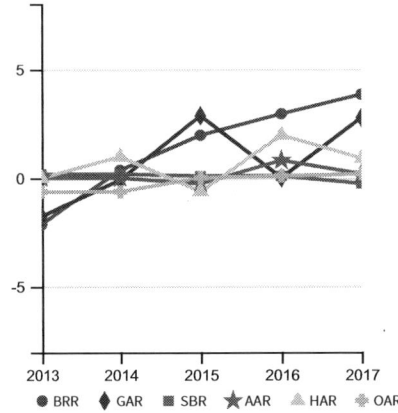

Alex Bregman 3B Houston Astros

Born: 3/30/1994 **Age:** 24 **Bats:** R **Throws:** R **Height:** 6' 0" **Weight:** 180 lbs **Draft Info:** Round 1, 2015 Draft (#2 overall)

PACE
45th of 155
71°
Fast

21 Sec/Pit

2017 Daily WARP Profile
4.1 Total WARP

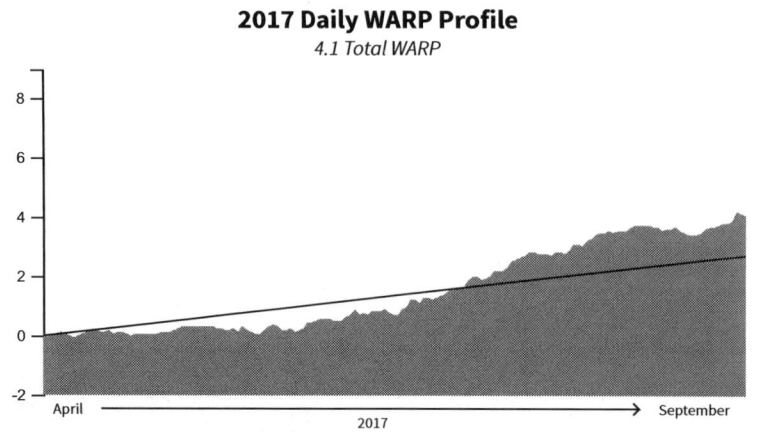

Fantasy Values
2017 *2018*
$23.94 **$23.00**

YEAR	TEAM	LVL	AGE	PA	R	2B	3B	HR	RBI	BB	K	SB	AVG/OBP/SLG	TAv	VORP	BABIP	WARP
2017	HOU	MLB	23	626	88	39	5	19	71	55	97	17	.284/.352/.475	.282	34.8	.311	4.1

The 17 steals were not only a nice surprise for Bregman but necessary to boost his fantasy value in a year when his power was okay but not great. At 23 years of age, there is a lot more good than bad to bet on in Bregman's profile, including growth in his overall game and perhaps 25-30 home runs to go along with a solid batting average. Bregman's appearance in the fall classic means he won't come cheap, but it's okay to stretch your bid and hope that the best is yet to come. — Mike G.

2017 Batting Percentages

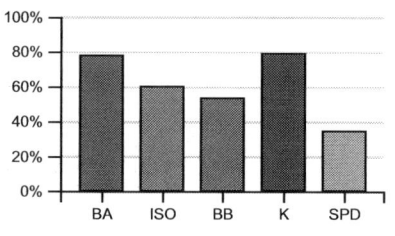

Batting PECOTA Percentiles

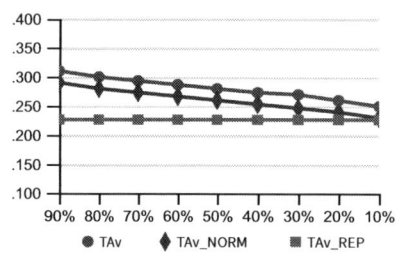

Batting WARP History

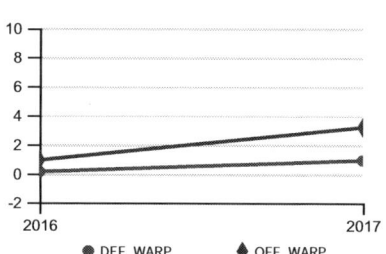

BRR (Relative to Position)

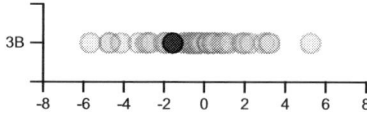

Rank		Player	BRR
41	34°	Martin Prado	-0.96
42	33°	Matt Chapman	-0.97
43	29°	**Alex Bregman**	**-1.52**
44	28°	Jhonny Peralta	-1.53
45	26°	Mike Moustakas	-1.59

BRR (Relative to Team)

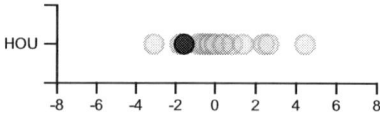

Rank		Player	BRR
13	35°	Carlos Beltran	-0.60
14	27°	Marwin Gonzalez	-0.81
15	16°	**Alex Bregman**	**-1.52**
16	7°	Yulieski Gurriel	-1.72
17	0°	Carlos Correa	-3.04

Base Running Components

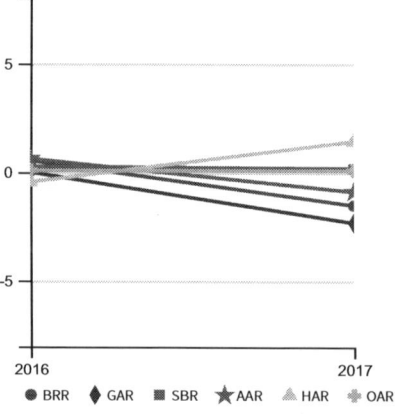

Jay Bruce RF New York Mets

Born: 4/3/1987 **Age:** 31 **Bats:** L **Throws:** L **Height:** 6' 3" **Weight:** 225 lbs **Draft Info:** Round 1, 2005 Draft (#12 overall)

21 Sec/Pit

PACE
45th of 155
71°
Fast

2017 Daily WARP Profile
3.2 Total WARP

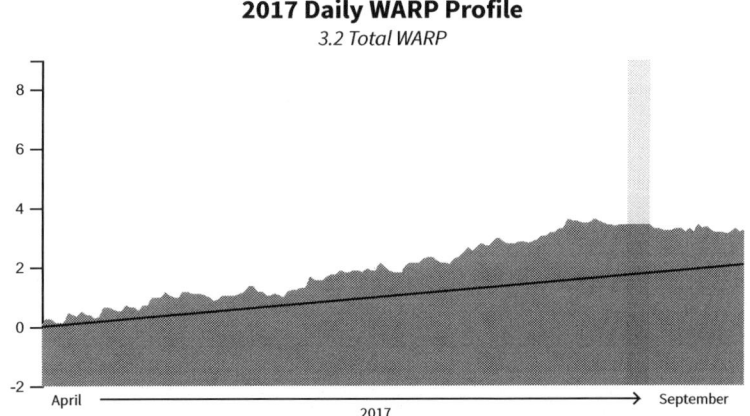

Game 135: neck stiffness

Fantasy Values

2017	2018
$4.51	**$18.00**

YEAR	TEAM	LVL	AGE	PA	R	2B	3B	HR	RBI	BB	K	SB	AVG/OBP/SLG	TAv	VORP	BABIP	WARP
2017	NYN	MLB	30	448	61	20	0	29	75	39	102	0	.256/.321/.520	.297	25.5	.271	2.8
2017	CLE	MLB	30	169	21	9	2	7	26	18	37	1	.248/.331/.477	.277	6.6	.283	.4

It took a couple years, but the nagging knee injury that hampered Bruce's performance in 2014-2015 is a thing of the past. What you see now is what you get: a reliable 30+ home-run hitter who will slightly hurt your batting average. Bruce isn't anywhere near elite, but that's okay; you need players like this to fill out the back end of your lineup in mixed and as essential contributors in deeper leagues. Hitters with this profile don't age well, but Bruce is still young enough where this won't matter for another two or three years. The Mets brought him back into the fold with a three-year, $39 million deal in January. — Mike G.

2017 Batting Percentages

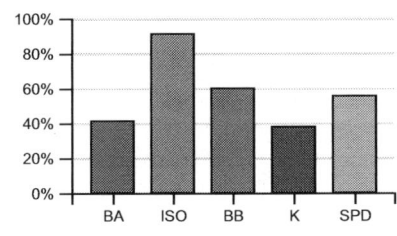

Batting PECOTA Percentiles

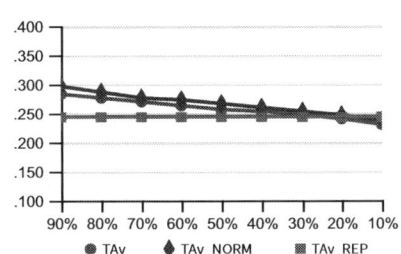

Batting WARP History

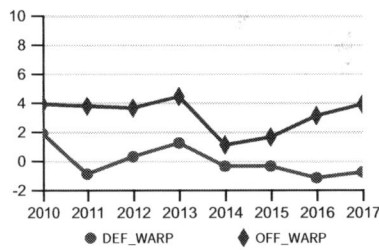

BRR (Relative to Position)

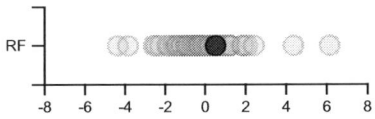

Rank		Player	BRR
15	73°	Magneuris Sierra	0.78
16	69°	Shin-Soo Choo	0.67
17	66°	**Jay Bruce**	**0.57**
18	66°	Andrew Stevenson	0.49
19	64°	Gregory Polanco	0.45

BRR (Relative to Team)

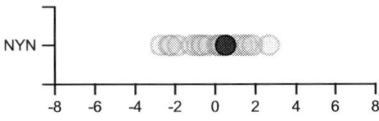

Rank		Player	BRR
5	61°	Amed Rosario	1.05
6	60°	Gavin Cecchini	0.58
7	51°	**Jay Bruce**	**0.57**
8	49°	Dominic Smith	0.35
9	48°	Phillip Evans	0.28

Base Running Components

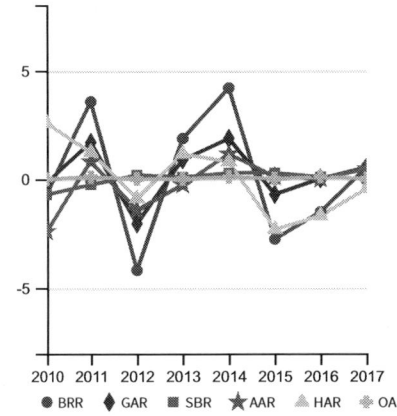

Kris Bryant   3B   Chicago Cubs

Born: 1/4/1992   **Age:** 26   **Bats:** R   **Throws:** R   **Height:** 6' 5"   **Weight:** 230 lbs   **Draft Info:** Round 1, 2013 Draft (#2 overall)

2017 Daily WARP Profile
6.6 Total WARP

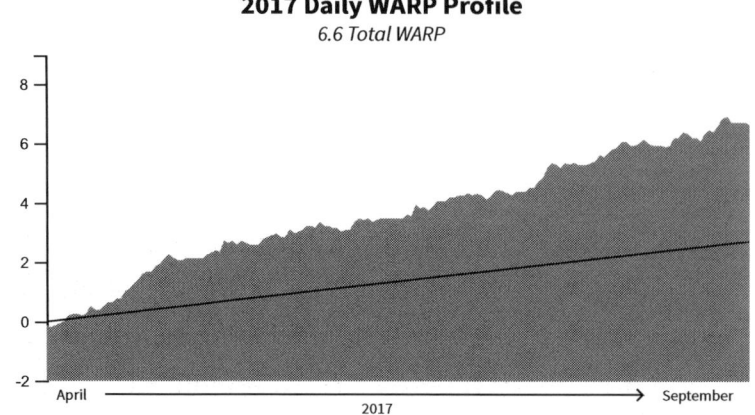

22 Sec/Pit

PACE
99th of 155
36°
Slow

Fantasy Values
2017	2018
$25.82	$31.00

YEAR	TEAM	LVL	AGE	PA	R	2B	3B	HR	RBI	BB	K	SB	AVG/OBP/SLG	TAv	VORP	BABIP	WARP
2017	CHN	MLB	25	665	111	38	4	29	73	95	128	7	.295/.409/.537	.326	69.6	.334	6.6

Bryant's fantasy earnings slipped, but this was mostly due to subpar numbers with RISP that impacted his RBI and a led to a slight drop in home runs. Bryant was the same elite hitter he was in 2016, even though it didn't show up in the box score. Bet on a 30-35 home run, .290 batting average in 2018 from a top-tier third baseman; in other words, pay the elite first-round premium. The floor is extremely high, and it is difficult to believe that 2016 was the most Bryant is capable of. — Mike G.

2017 Batting Percentages

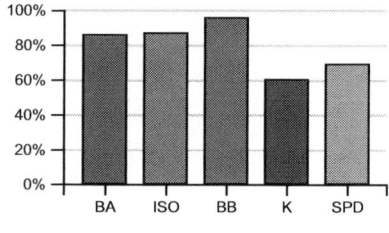

Batting PECOTA Percentiles

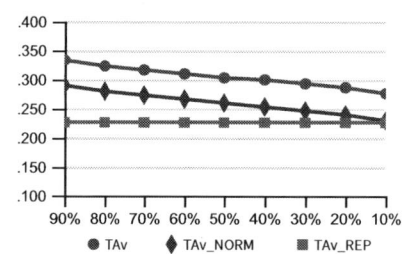

Batting WARP History

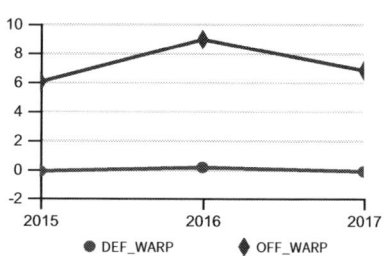

BRR (Relative to Position)

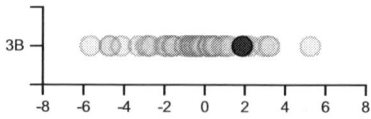

Rank		Player	BRR
6	84°	Anthony Rendon	2.04
7	81°	Jake Lamb	1.96
8	77°	**Kris Bryant**	**1.90**
9	75°	Josh Donaldson	1.27
10	75°	Sean Rodriguez	1.11

BRR (Relative to Team)

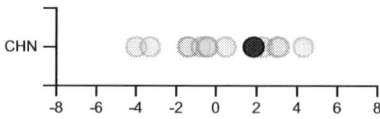

Rank		Player	BRR
4	68°	Jon Jay	2.37
5	59°	Jason Heyward	1.93
6	47°	**Kris Bryant**	**1.90**
7	40°	Kyle Schwarber	0.55
8	34°	Addison Russell	-0.35

Base Running Components

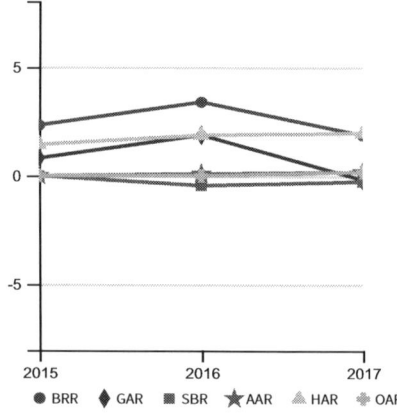

Madison Bumgarner   LHP   San Francisco Giants

Born: 8/1/1989 **Age:** 28 **Bats:** R **Throws:** L **Height:** 6' 5" **Weight:** 250 lbs **Draft Info:** Round 1, 2007 Draft (#10 overall)

PACE
20 Sec/Pit
37th of 150
75°
Fast

2017 Daily WARP Profile
1.8 Total WARP

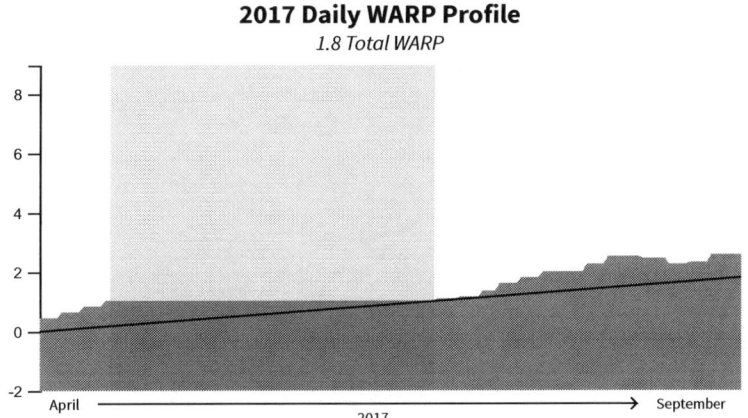

April — 2017 — September

Game 17: DL (shoulder sprain)

POWER
36 PWR
113th of 150

STAMINA
53 STM
121st of 150

COMMAND
53 CMD
72nd of 150

Fantasy Values
2017	2018
$12.85	**$25.00**

YEAR	TEAM	LVL	AGE	W	L	SV	G	GS	IP	H	HR	BB/9	K/9	K	GB%	BABIP	WHIP	ERA	DRA	WARP	MPH 95
2017	SFN	MLB	27	4	9	0	17	17	111	101	17	1.6	8.2	101	42%	.272	1.09	3.32	4.12	1.8	92.7

Bumgarner has always been one of the most durable starting pitchers in the game, so of course a freakish motorbike accident knocked him out of commission for weeks and limited him to under 120 innings. His numbers slipped even when he did return to full health, but given Bum's track record it is safe to write off 2017 as a lost season and assume a return to ace level for the former postseason hero. Bumgarner isn't quite in the Clayton Kershaw/Max Scherzer/Corey Kluber stratosphere, but he isn't all that far removed from it either. — Mike G.

2017 Pitching Percentages

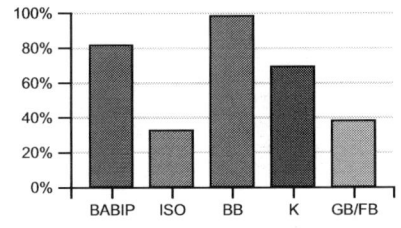

Pitching PECOTA Percentiles

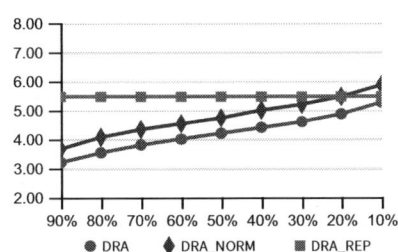

Pitching WARP History

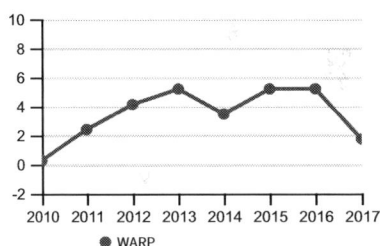

Tunnel vs LHH

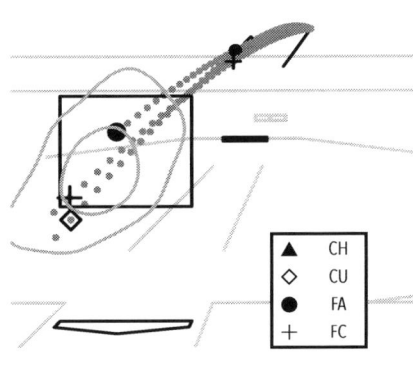

	CH
◇	CU
●	FA
+	FC

Pitch Types

Type	Freq	Velo	H Mov	V Mov
CH	5.5%	83.2 [92]	12.4 [93]	-30.3 [91]
CU	15.6%	78.3 [100]	-7.6 [99]	-44.6 [107]
FA	43.1%	91.4 [95]	8.3 [95]	-16.1 [97]
FC	35.7%	87.1 [93]	-1.7 [101]	-24.7 [96]

Pitch Tunnel

Pairs	Release Diff	Tunnel Diff	Plate Diff	Speed Changes
1213	25.1	123.3	232.9	0.026

PI Scores

Year	Pitch Ct	Pwr	Cmd	Stm
2013	3183	37	46	80
2014	3362	41	59	84
2015	3298	42	57	81
2016	3546	41	62	88
2017	1656	36	53	53

Tunnel vs RHH

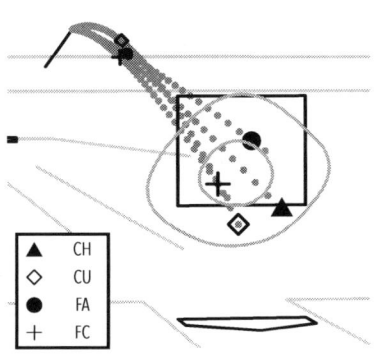

▲	CH
◇	CU
●	FA
+	FC

Dylan Bundy   RHP   Baltimore Orioles

Born: 11/15/1992   **Age:** 25   **Bats:** B   **Throws:** R   **Height:** 6' 1"   **Weight:** 200 lbs   **Draft Info:** Round 1, 2011 Draft (#4 overall)

2017 Daily WARP Profile
3.6 Total WARP

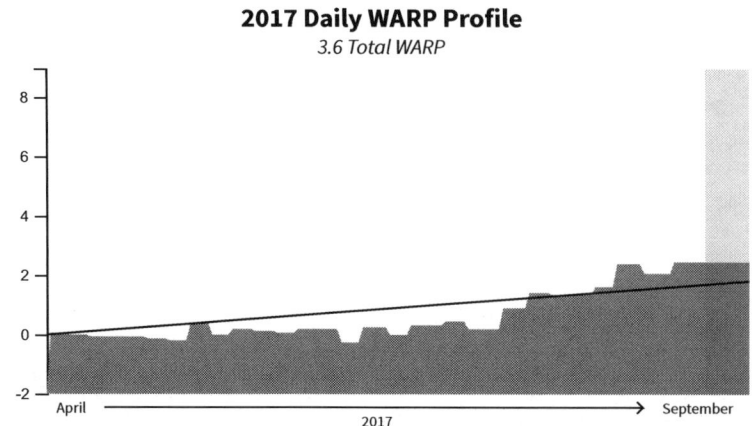

Game 152: hamstring strain

POWER
42 PWR
86th of 150

STAMINA
74 STM
44th of 150

COMMAND
45 CMD
117th of 150

PACE
20 Sec/Pit
37th of 150
75°
Fast

Fantasy Values
2017	2018
$15.97	$10.00

YEAR	TEAM	LVL	AGE	W	L	SV	G	GS	IP	H	HR	BB/9	K/9	K	GB%	BABIP	WHIP	ERA	DRA	WARP	MPH 95
2017	BAL	MLB	24	13	9	0	28	28	169.2	152	26	2.7	8.1	152	33%	.273	1.20	4.24	3.67	3.6	94.0

After years of battling injuries it was a mixed bag for Bundy in his first healthy season as a starter. At times he showed flashes of the brilliance that made him a top prospect, but during others he looked quite hittable. A drop in velocity and an increase in sliders kept him on the field but also limited his effectiveness at times, particularly when the slider wasn't working. Assuming health Bundy can be a solid, mid-tier fantasy contributor, but don't pay the former prospect premium unless he proves he can consistently perform at a high level on more than a start-to-start or even an inning-to-inning basis. — Mike G.

2017 Pitching Percentages

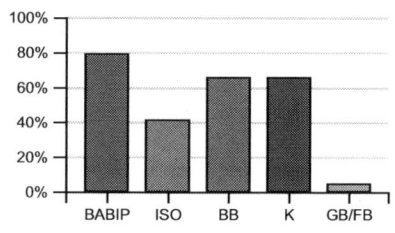

Pitching PECOTA Percentiles

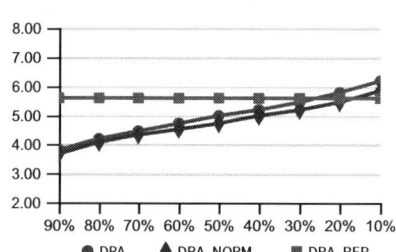

Pitching WARP History

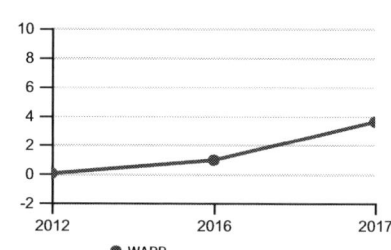

Tunnel vs LHH

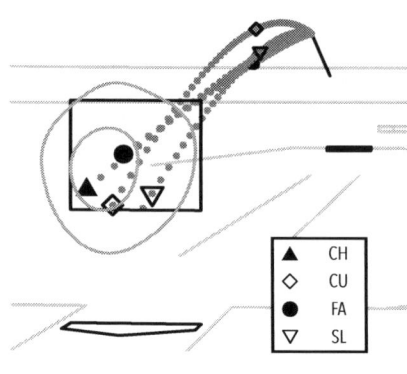

	CH
◇	CU
●	FA
▽	SL

Pitch Types

Type	Freq	Velo	H Mov	V Mov
CH	13.7%	84 [96]	-11 [100]	-25 [106]
CU	10.4%	74.9 [87]	7 [97]	-54.8 [85]
FA	53.8%	92.4 [99]	-7 [101]	-12.1 [110]
SL	22.1%	83.4 [96]	4 [97]	-33.7 [97]

Pitch Tunnel

Pairs	Release Diff	Tunnel Diff	Plate Diff	Speed Changes
2067	28.2	122.7	230.3	0.033

PI Scores

Year	Pitch Ct	Pwr	Cmd	Stm
2016	1843	53	43	54
2017	2751	42	45	74

Tunnel vs RHH

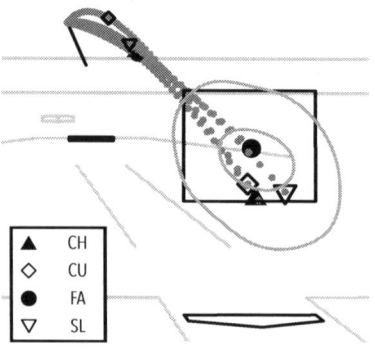

	CH
◇	CU
●	FA
▽	SL

Byron Buxton   CF   Minnesota Twins

Born: 12/18/1993   **Age:** 24   **Bats:** R   **Throws:** R   **Height:** 6'2"   **Weight:** 190 lbs   **Draft Info:** Round 1, 2012 Draft (#2 overall)

PACE
21 Sec/Pit
45th of 155
71°
Fast

2017 Daily WARP Profile
4.3 Total WARP

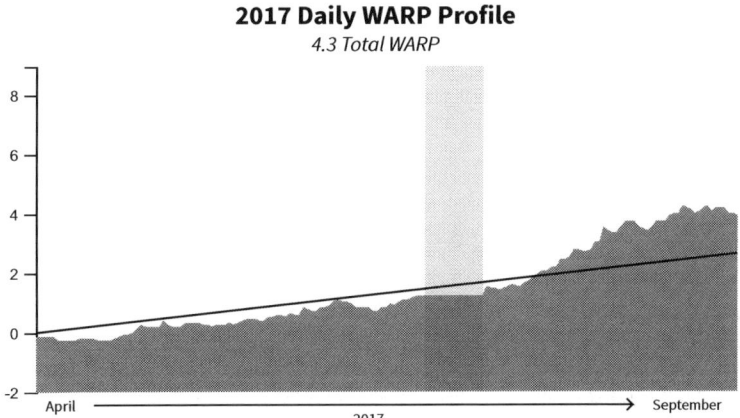

Game 90: DL (groin strain)

Fantasy Values
2017	2018
$20.88	$28.00

YEAR	TEAM	LVL	AGE	PA	R	2B	3B	HR	RBI	BB	K	SB	AVG/OBP/SLG	TAv	VORP	BABIP	WARP
2017	MIN	MLB	23	511	69	14	6	16	51	38	150	29	.253/.314/.413	.247	17.0	.339	4.3

Did Buxton figure something out or did a hot, two-month streak buoy his overall line? For the second consecutive season, this is the question fantasy managers were left asking themselves. Buxton appeared to have finally "solved" major-league pitching in the second half before coming down to earth with an okay September. Even if Buxton is "only" an average major-league hitter going forward, the stolen-base potential makes him a fantasy commodity. He's only 24 years old; at a minimum the days of Buxton scuffling to hit major-league pitching are behind him. His defense will keep him in the lineup no matter what his bat looks like, and a 15/30 season with a .250 batting average is a reasonable expectation as a baseline. It might finally be time for the excitement about his ceiling to translate into results. — Mike G.

2017 Batting Percentages

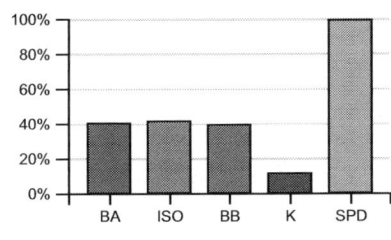

Batting PECOTA Percentiles

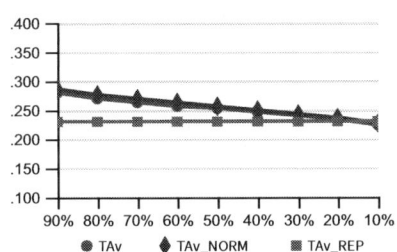

Batting WARP History

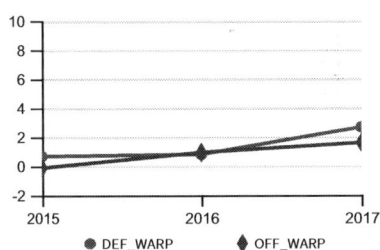

BRR (Relative to Position)

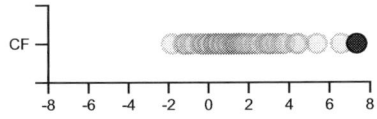

Rank		Player	BRR
1	98°	**Byron Buxton**	7.39
2	94°	Billy Hamilton	6.60
3	90°	Ender Inciarte	5.41
4	87°	Cameron Maybin	4.50
5	84°	Chris Taylor	4.37

BRR (Relative to Team)

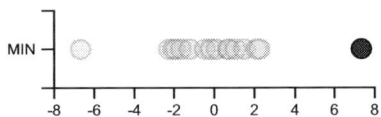

Rank		Player	BRR
1	90°	**Byron Buxton**	7.39
2	84°	Eduardo Escobar	2.30
3	71°	Brian Dozier	2.17
4	67°	Ehire Adrianza	1.55
5	64°	Kennys Vargas	1.12

Base Running Components

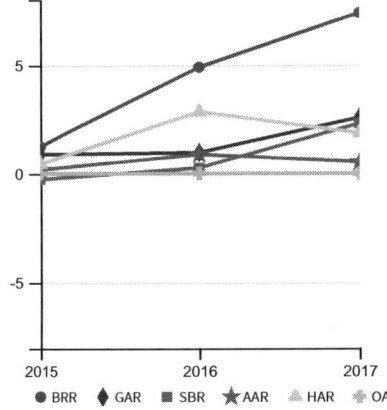

Asdrubal Cabrera   INF   New York Mets

Born: 11/13/1985   **Age:** 32   **Bats:** B   **Throws:** R   **Height:** 6' 0"   **Weight:** 205 lbs   **Draft Info:** International Free Agent, 2002

We don't have a baseball card for this guy.

PACE
22 Sec/Pit
99th of 155
36°
Slow

2017 Daily WARP Profile
2.8 Total WARP

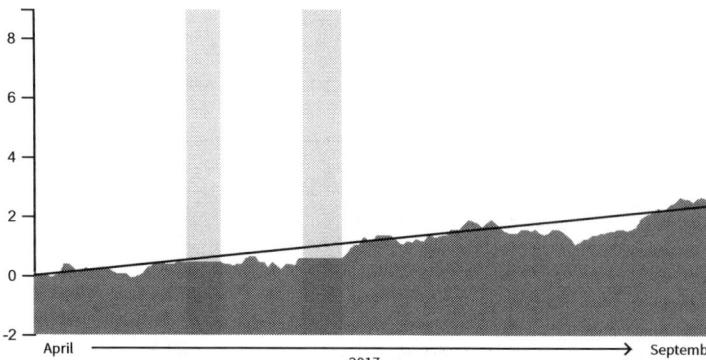

April ————————————— 2017 ————————————→ September

Game 36: DL (thumb sprain), **Game 63:** DL (thumb sprain)

Fantasy Values
2017	2018
$14.71	$13.00

YEAR	TEAM	LVL	AGE	PA	R	2B	3B	HR	RBI	BB	K	SB	AVG/OBP/SLG	TAv	VORP	BABIP	WARP
2017	NYN	MLB	31	540	66	32	0	14	59	50	83	3	.280/.351/.434	.285	31.1	.310	2.8

A swing adjustment in the second half of 2016 combined with a boost in power led some to believe that Asdrubal could be v2.0 of Daniel Murphy minus the batting average. Instead, Cabrera fell back to his previous levels, slipping significantly in power. Cabrera had a better season than you might think; his TAv was third among qualifying shortstops, but unless you're in a TAv league this won't help you in fantasy. The Mets picked up Cabrera's $8.5 million option for 2018, ensuring that he should get regular at-bats assuming full health. — Mike G.

2017 Batting Percentages

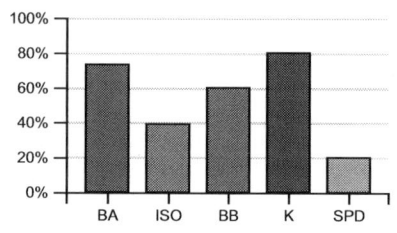

Batting PECOTA Percentiles

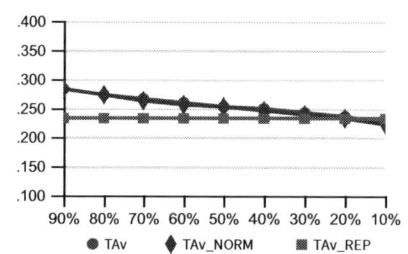

● TAv   ◆ TAv_NORM   ■ TAv_REP

Batting WARP History

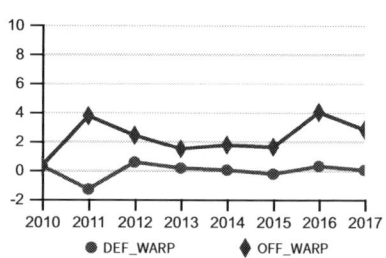

● DEF_WARP   ◆ OFF_WARP

BRR (Relative to Position)

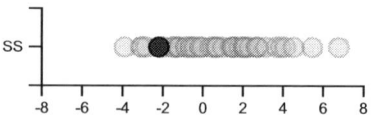

Rank		Player	BRR
42	13°	J.J. Hardy	-1.50
43	12°	Dixon Machado	-1.96
44	9°	**Asdrubal Cabrera**	**-2.16**
45	8°	Adeiny Hechavarria	-2.18
46	5°	Zack Cozart	-2.78

BRR (Relative to Team)

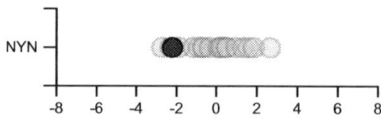

Rank		Player	BRR
16	26°	Yoenis Cespedes	-1.12
17	23°	Adrian Gonzalez	-1.82
18	12°	**Asdrubal Cabrera**	**-2.16**
19	8°	Travis d'Arnaud	-2.25
20	0°	Nori Aoki	-2.67

Base Running Components

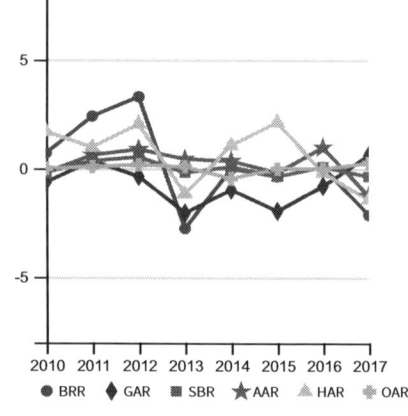

● BRR   ◆ GAR   ■ SBR   ★ AAR   ▲ HAR   ✦ OAR

Miguel Cabrera 1B Detroit Tigers

Born: 4/18/1983 **Age:** 35 **Bats:** R **Throws:** R **Height:** 6' 4" **Weight:** 240 lbs **Draft Info:** International Free Agent, 1999

23 Sec/Pit

PACE
135th of 155
13°
Very Slow

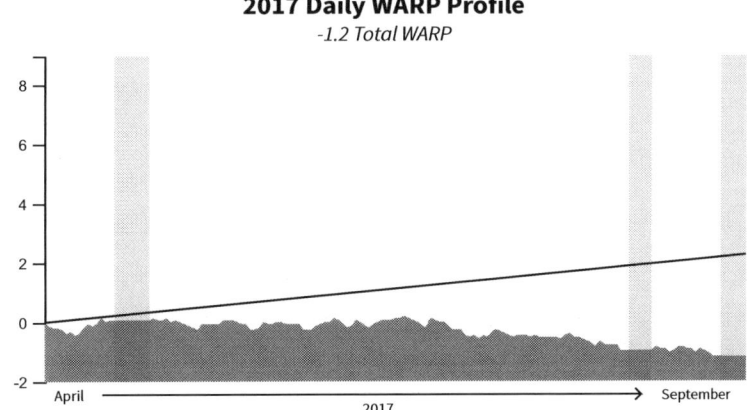

2017 Daily WARP Profile
-1.2 Total WARP

Game 17: DL (groin strain), **Game 135:** suspension, **Game 156:** herniated disks

Fantasy Values
2017	2018
$9.47	$19.00

YEAR	TEAM	LVL	AGE	PA	R	2B	3B	HR	RBI	BB	K	SB	AVG/OBP/SLG	TAv	VORP	BABIP	WARP
2017	DET	MLB	34	529	50	22	0	16	60	54	110	0	.249/.329/.399	.243	-1.2	.292	-1.2

Everything we love eventually crumbles to dust. Cabrera put up the worst season of his storied career and it wasn't particularly close. An MRI in September revealed that Miggy had played a good chunk of the season with two herniated disks in his back. If he's completely healthy in 2018, Miggy can certainly rebound and deliver an elite performance. It's fine to discount him, however, as he is approaching the point of his career where decline is likely if not inevitable and there are so many power hitters at first base who can offer 25+ home-run production without nearly the same level of risk. — Mike G.

2017 Batting Percentages
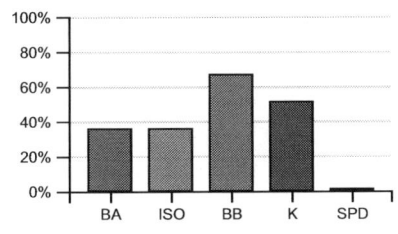

Batting PECOTA Percentiles
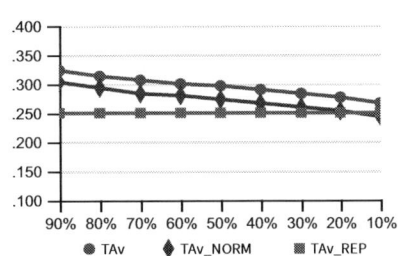

Batting WARP History
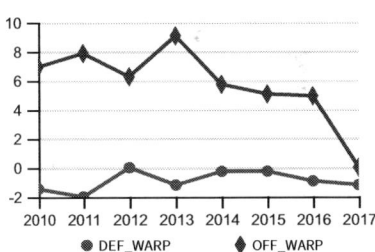

BRR (Relative to Position)
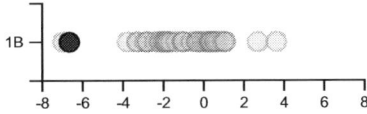

Rank		Player	BRR
41	14°	Lucas Duda	-3.26
42	11°	Josh Bell	-3.73
43	9°	**Miguel Cabrera**	**-6.61**
44	4°	Joe Mauer	-6.63
45	0°	Joey Votto	-6.92

BRR (Relative to Team)
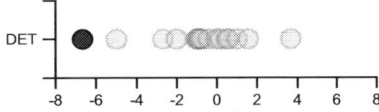

Rank		Player	BRR
15	26°	John Hicks	-0.97
16	22°	Dixon Machado	-1.96
17	14°	Nick Castellanos	-2.63
18	7°	Victor Martinez	-4.94
19	0°	**Miguel Cabrera**	**-6.61**

Base Running Components
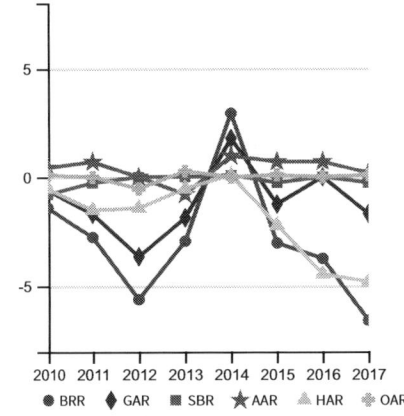

Trevor Cahill   RHP   Kansas City Royals

Born: 3/1/1988   **Age:** 30   **Bats:** R   **Throws:** R   **Height:** 6' 4"   **Weight:** 240 lbs   **Draft Info:** Round 2, 2006 Draft (#66 overall)

We don't have a baseball card for this guy.

2017 Daily WARP Profile
1.2 Total WARP

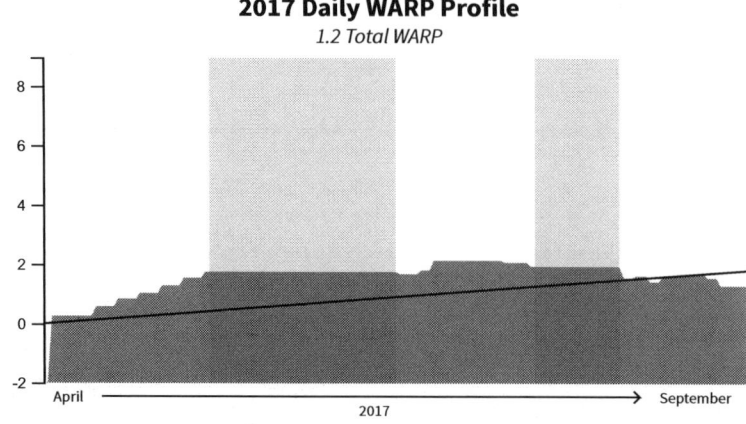

PACE
19 Sec/Pit
16th of 150
89°
Very Fast

POWER
34 PWR
120th of 150

STAMINA
44 STM
147th of 150

COMMAND
38 CMD
139th of 150

Game 39: DL (shoulder strain), **Game 114:** DL (shoulder impingement)

Fantasy Values

2017	2018
$-5.71	$3.00

YEAR	TEAM	LVL	AGE	W	L	SV	G	GS	IP	H	HR	BB/9	K/9	K	GB%	BABIP	WHIP	ERA	DRA	WARP	MPH 95
2017	SDN	MLB	29	4	3	0	11	11	61	58	6	3.5	10.6	72	58%	.329	1.34	3.69	3.84	1.1	93.1
2017	KCA	MLB	29	0	0	0	10	3	23	33	10	8.2	5.9	15	54%	.319	2.35	8.22	5.32	0.1	93.3

2017 Pitching Percentages

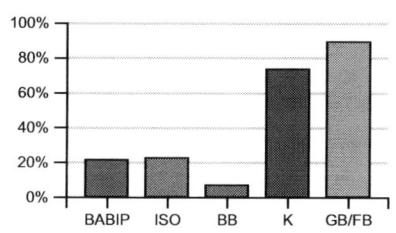

Pitching PECOTA Percentiles

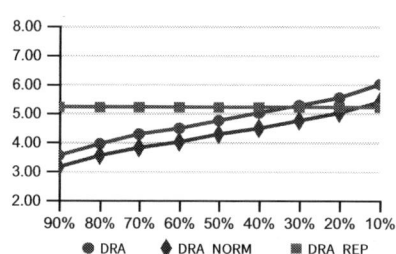

Pitching WARP History

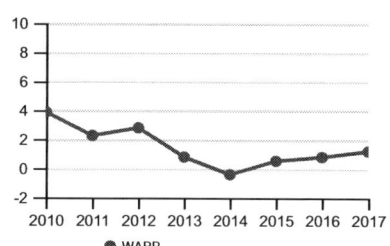

Tunnel vs LHH

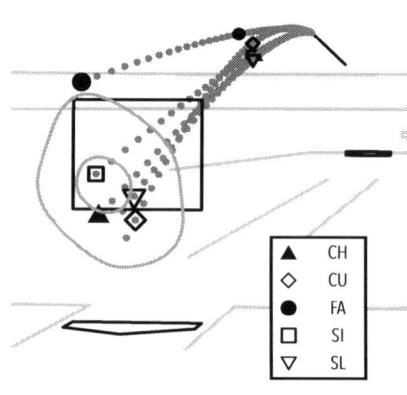

Pitch Types

Type	Freq	Velo	H Mov	V Mov
CH	22.4%	84.2 [96]	-9.7 [107]	-33.3 [82]
CU	21.7%	79.8 [106]	10.2 [109]	-49.3 [97]
FA	7.3%	92.3 [99]	-8 [96]	-16.6 [95]
SI	39.7%	91.1 [93]	-12.6 [99]	-24.3 [84]
SL	8.8%	85.9 [107]	0.7 [83]	-32 [102]

Pitch Tunnel

Pairs	Release Diff	Tunnel Diff	Plate Diff	Speed Changes
1135	50.9	137.7	259.0	0.030

PI Scores

Year	Pitch Ct	Pwr	Cmd	Stm
2013	2362	41	40	68
2014	1825	41	38	62
2015	672	44	47	46
2016	1151	44	35	53
2017	1515	34	38	44

Tunnel vs RHH

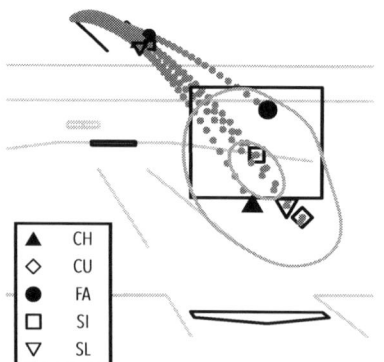

Lorenzo Cain   CF   Milwaukee Brewers

Born: 4/13/1986   **Age:** 32   **Bats:** R   **Throws:** R   **Height:** 6' 2"   **Weight:** 205 lbs   **Draft Info:** Round 17, 2004 Draft (#496 overall)

PACE
18th of 155
88°
Very Fast

20 Sec/Pit

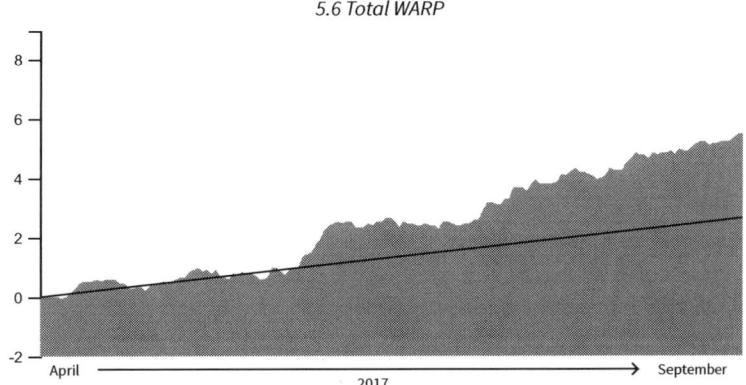

2017 Daily WARP Profile
5.6 Total WARP

Fantasy Values
2017	2018
$26.99	**$25.00**

YEAR	TEAM	LVL	AGE	PA	R	2B	3B	HR	RBI	BB	K	SB	AVG/OBP/SLG	TAv	VORP	BABIP	WARP
2017	KCA	MLB	31	645	86	27	5	15	49	54	100	26	.300/.363/.440	.280	36.6	.340	5.6

While Cain didn't quite repeat his 2015 career year, he did enough in fantasy that nearly no one noticed. Cain is a fantasy force when he is on the field, good for close to 15 home runs, 30 stolen bases, and a .300 batting average. Given his health profile, his age does make him a risk and it's tough to justify paying the full price even though stolen bases are at a premium. Cain delivered third-round value in 12-team mixed leagues, but you'll want to push him back a round or two to be on the safe side, and that might not nab him in most drafts. — Mike G.

2017 Batting Percentages

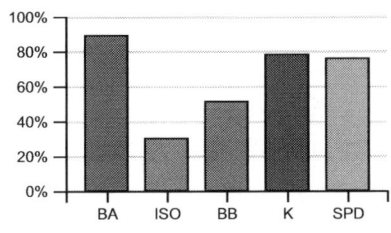

Batting PECOTA Percentiles

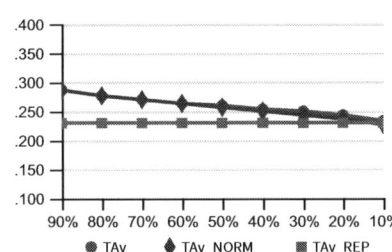

Batting WARP History

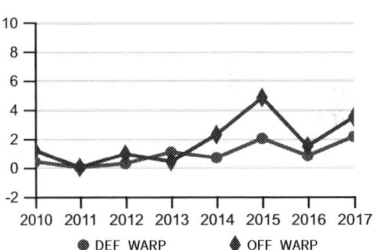

BRR (Relative to Position)

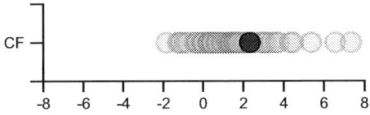

BRR (Relative to Team)

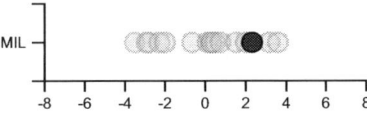

Base Running Components

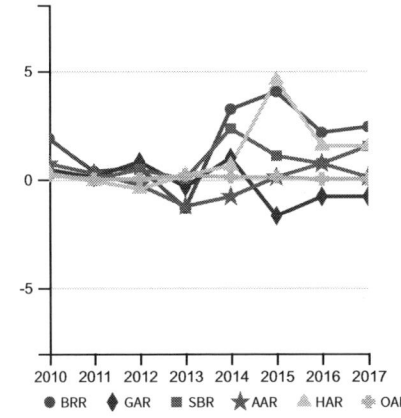

Rank		Player	BRR
12	71°	Kevin Kiermaier	2.89
13	69°	Rajai Davis	2.55
14	65°	**Lorenzo Cain**	**2.36**
15	63°	Mallex Smith	2.15
16	62°	Aaron Hicks	2.05

Rank		Player	BRR
1	100°	Keon Broxton	3.64
2	100°	Travis Shaw	3.21
3	96°	**Lorenzo Cain**	2.36
4	89°	Hernan Perez	2.36
5	80°	Orlando Arcia	2.07

Robinson Cano   2B   Seattle Mariners

Born: 10/22/1982   **Age:** 35   **Bats:** L   **Throws:** R   **Height:** 6' 0"   **Weight:** 210 lbs   **Draft Info:** International Free Agent, 2001

25 Sec/Pit

PACE
151st of 155
3°
Very Slow

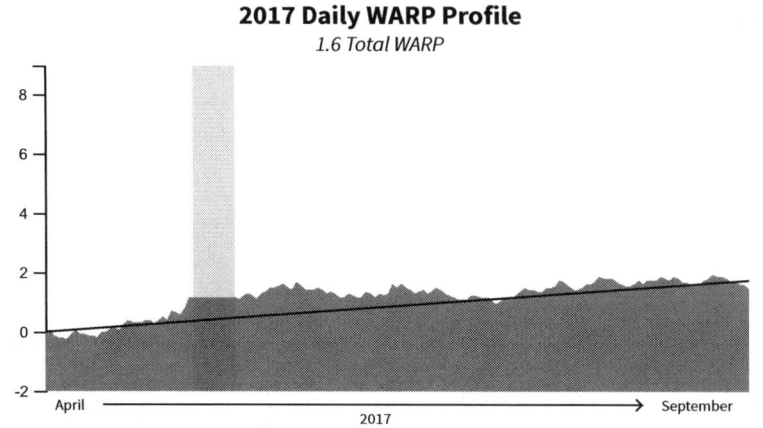

2017 Daily WARP Profile
1.6 Total WARP

April — 2017 — September

Game 35: DL (quad strain)

Fantasy Values

2017	2018
$19.90	**$21.00**

YEAR	TEAM	LVL	AGE	PA	R	2B	3B	HR	RBI	BB	K	SB	AVG/OBP/SLG	TAv	VORP	BABIP	WARP
2017	SEA	MLB	34	648	79	33	0	23	97	49	85	1	.280/.338/.453	.270	23.2	.294	1.6

Cano is far from cooked, but he has reached the point of his career where betting on what he did in his prime is a bad idea. He's not bad by any stretch of the imagination, but where you once were hoping for 30 home runs and a .300 batting average, 20 and .280 is now a far more reasonable expectation. Cano is a good get in the sixth or seventh round, but it's likely that at least one person in your league will reach and pay for the name and reputation. Go for the generic, younger versions of Cano in your drafts and auctions if you can. — Mike G.

2017 Batting Percentages

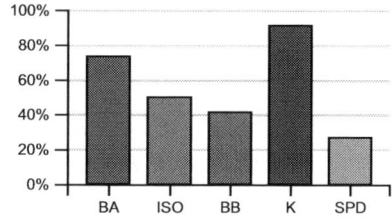

Batting PECOTA Percentiles

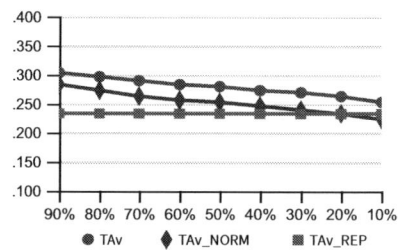

Batting WARP History

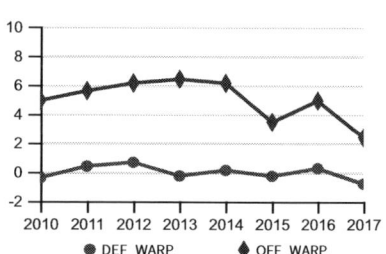

BRR (Relative to Position)

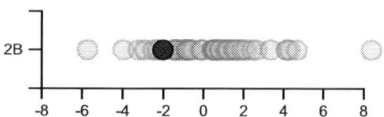

Rank		Player	BRR
48	15°	Raul Mondesi	-1.41
49	14°	Carlos Asuaje	-1.48
50	12°	**Robinson Cano**	**-1.98**
51	10°	Neil Walker	-2.22
52	7°	Jed Lowrie	-2.45

BRR (Relative to Team)

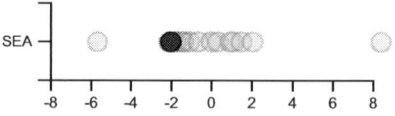

Rank		Player	BRR
12	35°	Danny Valencia	-1.71
13	25°	Nelson Cruz	-1.78
14	17°	**Robinson Cano**	**-1.98**
15	9°	Ryon Healy	-2.05
16	0°	Kyle Seager	-5.62

Base Running Components

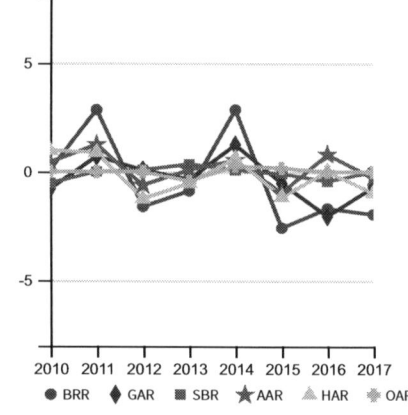

Matt Carpenter   1B   St. Louis Cardinals

Born: 11/26/1985   **Age:** 32   **Bats:** L   **Throws:** R   **Height:** 6' 3"   **Weight:** 205 lbs   **Draft Info:** Round 13, 2009 Draft (#399 overall)

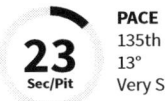

PACE
23 Sec/Pit
135th of 155
13°
Very Slow

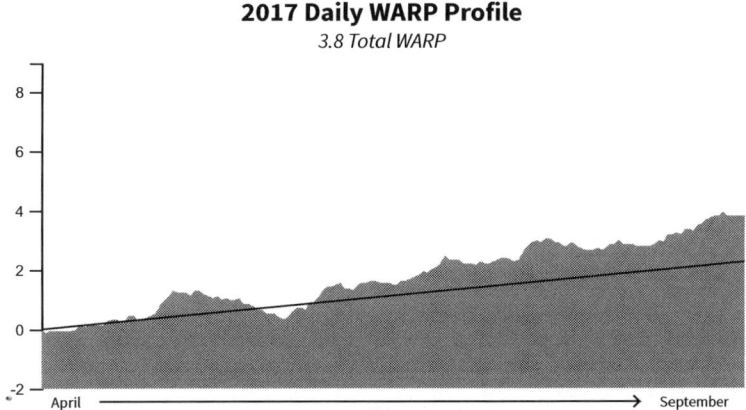

2017 Daily WARP Profile
3.8 Total WARP

Fantasy Values
2017	2018
$14.19	$18.00

YEAR	TEAM	LVL	AGE	PA	R	2B	3B	HR	RBI	BB	K	SB	AVG/OBP/SLG	TAv	VORP	BABIP	WARP
2017	SLN	MLB	31	622	91	31	2	23	69	109	125	2	.241/.384/.451	.302	34.2	.274	3.8

Carpenter has morphed into a consistent mainstay: a guy whose 20-home-run and .370 OBP contributions you can write in ink. The problem is most leagues don't use OBP, the batting average plummeted last year, and in league context Carpenter stood still while some hitters jumped past him in home runs. Carpenter will only have first-base eligibility in most leagues in 2018, further limiting his value. There's certainly a place for Carpenter on your roster, but there is no reason to stretch to add him to your squad. — Mike G.

2017 Batting Percentages

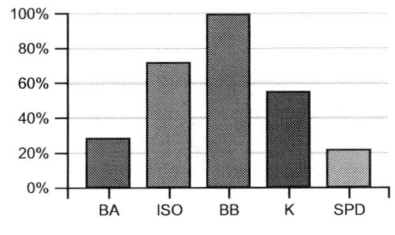

Batting PECOTA Percentiles

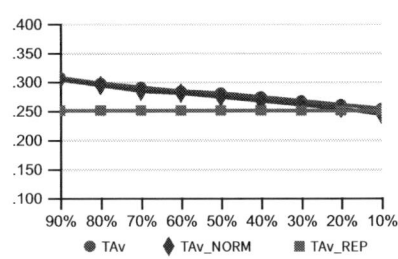

Batting WARP History

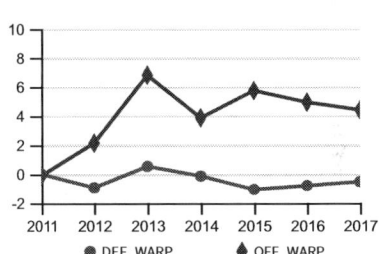

BRR (Relative to Position)

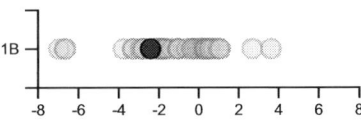

Rank	Player	BRR
34	35° Jefry Marte	-2.13
35	33° C.J. Cron	-2.15
36	29° **Matt Carpenter**	**-2.37**
37	26° Mitch Moreland	-2.72
38	23° Eric Thames	-2.73

BRR (Relative to Team)

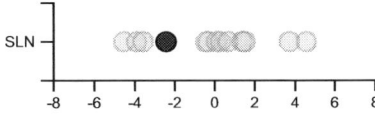

Rank	Player	BRR
8	46° Luke Voit	-0.27
9	38° Jedd Gyorko	-0.40
10	25° **Matt Carpenter**	**-2.37**
11	14° Marcell Ozuna	-3.52
12	8° Paul DeJong	-3.86

Base Running Components

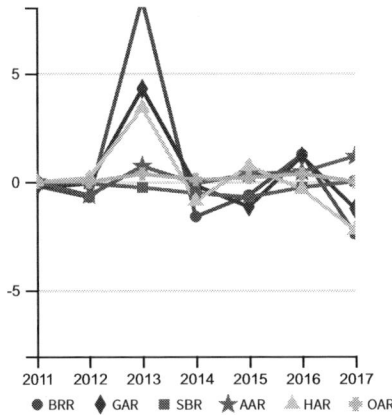

Carlos Carrasco   RHP   Cleveland Indians

Born: 3/21/1987   **Age:** 31   **Bats:** R   **Throws:** R   **Height:** 6' 3"   **Weight:** 212 lbs   **Draft Info:** International Free Agent, 2003

2017 Daily WARP Profile
4.9 Total WARP

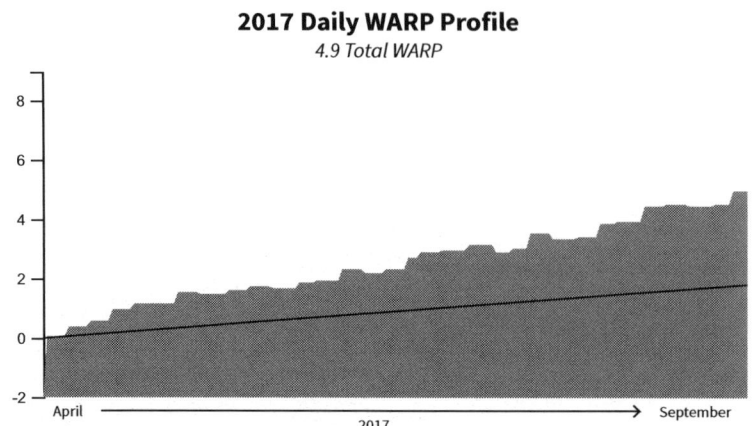

April — 2017 — September

PACE
22 Sec/Pit
108th of 150
28°
Slow

POWER **50** PWR 59th of 150

STAMINA **78** STM 25th of 150

COMMAND **47** CMD 102nd of 150

Fantasy Values
2017	2018
$30.08	$24.00

YEAR	TEAM	LVL	AGE	W	L	SV	G	GS	IP	H	HR	BB/9	K/9	K	GB%	BABIP	WHIP	ERA	DRA	WARP	MPH 95
2017	CLE	MLB	30	18	6	0	32	32	200	173	21	2.1	10.2	226	47%	.307	1.10	3.29	3.36	4.9	96.3

Finally liberated from years of mostly non-arm injuries limiting his innings, Carrasco reached 200 innings for the first time in his career and maintained his high level of performance that had tantalized fantasy managers for years. There's no reason to believe Carrasco can't do it again and it's possible that he could even take his performance to the next level in 2018. Carrasco should be one of the first 10 pitchers off the board in 2018 and in AL-only warrants a bid somewhere in the mid-$20s. — Mike G.

2017 Pitching Percentages
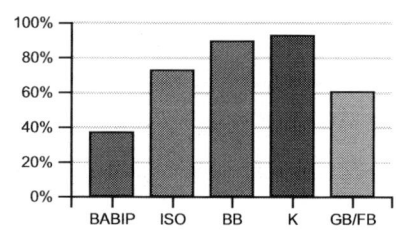

Pitching PECOTA Percentiles
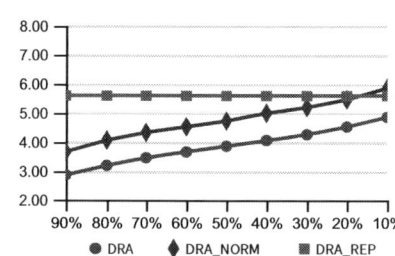

Pitching WARP History
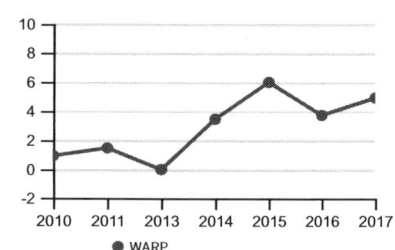

Tunnel vs LHH
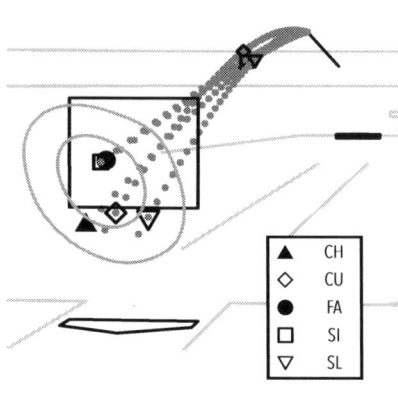

Pitch Types
Type	Freq	Velo	H Mov	V Mov
CH	16.1%	88.8 [115]	-10.4 [104]	-30.2 [91]
CU	14.1%	83.4 [119]	6.1 [94]	-39.8 [117]
FA	36.5%	94.8 [107]	-10.7 [83]	-15 [101]
SI	12.4%	93.8 [108]	-13.9 [90]	-20.5 [98]
SL	20.9%	85.6 [105]	2.3 [90]	-32.8 [99]

Pitch Tunnel
Pairs	Release Diff	Tunnel Diff	Plate Diff	Speed Changes
2265	27.4	119.5	226.2	0.025

PI Scores
Year	Pitch Ct	Pwr	Cmd	Stm
2013	779	65	46	52
2014	1947	65	50	55
2015	2765	61	50	70
2016	2229	53	53	63
2017	3027	50	47	78

Tunnel vs RHH
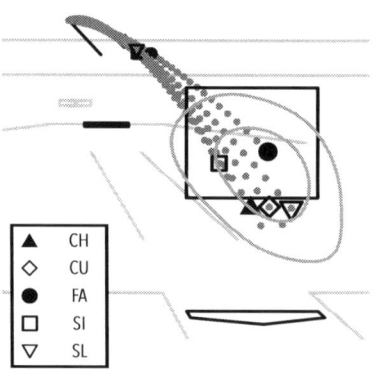

Andrew Cashner   RHP   Texas Rangers

Born: 9/11/1986   **Age:** 31   **Bats:** R   **Throws:** R   **Height:** 6'6"   **Weight:** 235 lbs   **Draft Info:** Round 1, 2008 Draft (#19 overall)

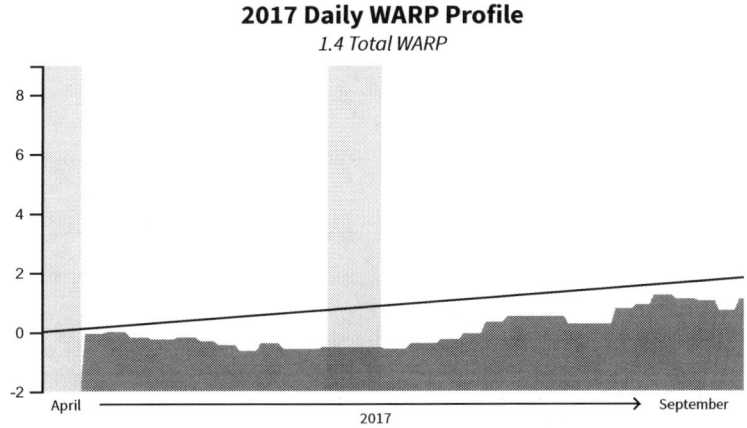

2017 Daily WARP Profile
1.4 Total WARP

Game 1: DL (biceps soreness), **Game 66:** DL (oblique strain)

POWER 59 PWR — 27th of 150

STAMINA 70 STM — 67th of 150

COMMAND 55 CMD — 62nd of 150

PACE 20 Sec/Pit — 37th of 150 / 75° / Fast

Fantasy Values
2017	2018
$11.94	$3.00

YEAR	TEAM	LVL	AGE	W	L	SV	G	GS	IP	H	HR	BB/9	K/9	K	GB%	BABIP	WHIP	ERA	DRA	WARP	MPH 95
2017	TEX	MLB	30	11	11	0	28	28	166.2	156	15	3.5	4.6	86	49%	.266	1.32	3.40	4.81	1.4	96.0

If you have any idea how Andrew Cashner managed a 3.40 ERA despite a 4.6 K/9 rate let me know. Seriously, does anyone know? Cashner did show a little more movement on his pitches, but his repertoire hardly changed, yet he still had the best ERA of his career since 2014. There's no reason to believe that last year is repeatable, and Cashner remains a spot starter in only despite results that were much better than that last year. — Mike G.

2017 Pitching Percentages

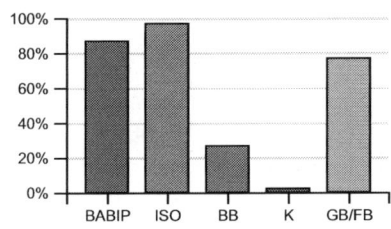

Pitching PECOTA Percentiles

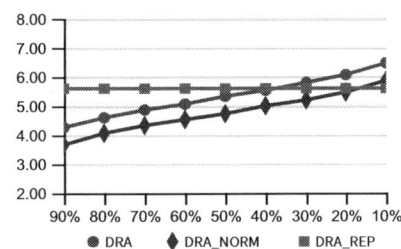

● DRA   ◆ DRA_NORM   ■ DRA_REP

Pitching WARP History

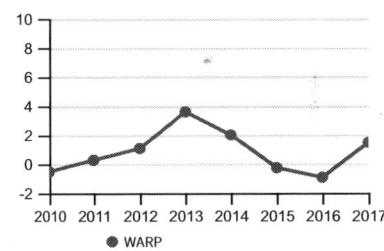

● WARP

Tunnel vs LHH

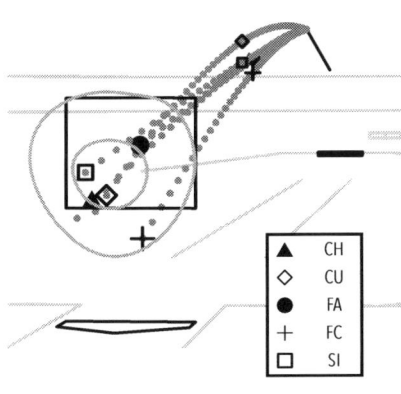

▲	CH
◇	CU
●	FA
+	FC
□	SI

Pitch Types

Type	Freq	Velo	H Mov	V Mov
CH	14.3%	85.3 [101]	-11.1 [100]	-26.2 [102]
CU	8.0%	82 [114]	6.3 [94]	-41.3 [114]
FA	25.3%	94.2 [105]	-8.3 [95]	-13.1 [107]
FC	12.2%	88.7 [101]	0.4 [94]	-25 [95]
SI	39.7%	93.2 [105]	-12.7 [99]	-17.1 [111]
SL	0.4%	82.7 [93]	5.3 [103]	-37.3 [87]

Pitch Tunnel

Pairs	Release Diff	Tunnel Diff	Plate Diff	Speed Changes
1923	27.2	119.8	221.1	0.021

PI Scores

Year	Pitch Ct	Pwr	Cmd	Stm
2013	2673	66	48	69
2014	1781	69	49	45
2015	3167	68	55	76
2016	2352	60	56	61
2017	2629	59	55	70

Tunnel vs RHH

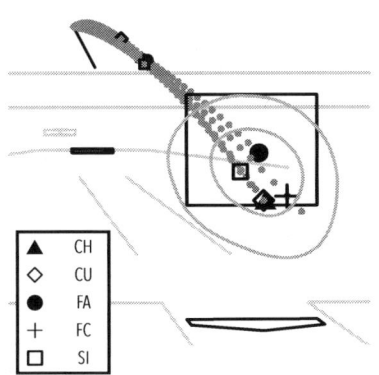

▲	CH
◇	CU
●	FA
+	FC
□	SI

Nick Castellanos 3B Detroit Tigers

Born: 3/4/1992 **Age:** 26 **Bats:** R **Throws:** R **Height:** 6' 4" **Weight:** 210 lbs **Draft Info:** Round 1, 2010 Draft (#44 overall)

2017 Daily WARP Profile
0.9 Total WARP

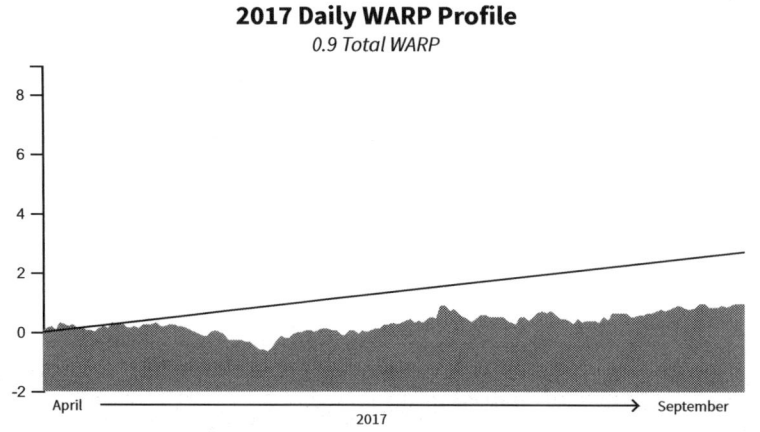

24
Sec/Pit

PACE
146th of 155
6°
Very Slow

Fantasy Values

2017	2018
$20.26	**$17.00**

YEAR	TEAM	LVL	AGE	PA	R	2B	3B	HR	RBI	BB	K	SB	AVG/OBP/SLG	TAv	VORP	BABIP	WARP
2017	DET	MLB	25	665	73	36	10	26	101	41	142	4	.272/.320/.490	.267	22.5	.313	.9

By simply staying healthy, Castellanos boosted his fantasy value, easily setting career highs in home runs, runs, and RBI. However, he hasn't delivered on the upside his many believers keep touting, and at age 26 Castellanos is no longer young enough to simply rely on the upside. Castellanos will keep his third-base eligibility for at least one more season, but with midseason acquisition Jeimer Candelario in the picture, Castellanos could be an OF-only starting in 2019. Twenty-five home runs at third base plays, but the smart money will bet on what Castellanos can do, not on what he might do. — Mike G.

2017 Batting Percentages

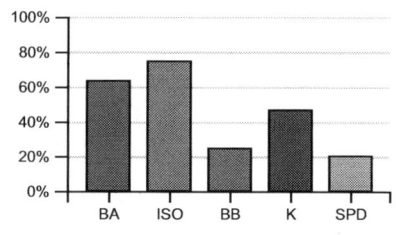

Batting PECOTA Percentiles

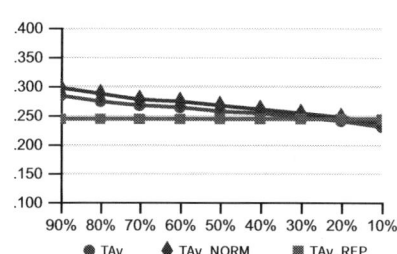

Batting WARP History

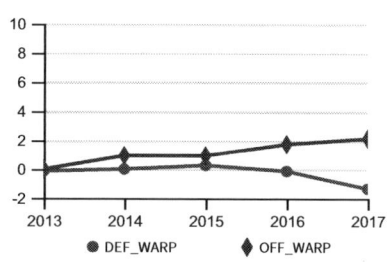

BRR (Relative to Position)

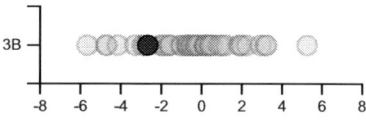

Rank		Player	BRR
47	20°	Evan Longoria	-1.90
48	18°	Miguel Sano	-1.98
49	16°	**Nick Castellanos**	**-2.63**
50	15°	Christian Arroyo	-2.77
51	13°	Adrian Beltre	-2.87

BRR (Relative to Team)

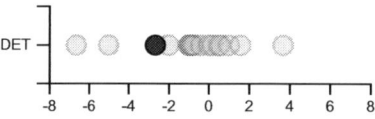

Rank		Player	BRR
15	26°	John Hicks	-0.97
16	22°	Dixon Machado	-1.96
17	14°	**Nick Castellanos**	**-2.63**
18	7°	Victor Martinez	-4.94
19	0°	Miguel Cabrera	-6.61

Base Running Components

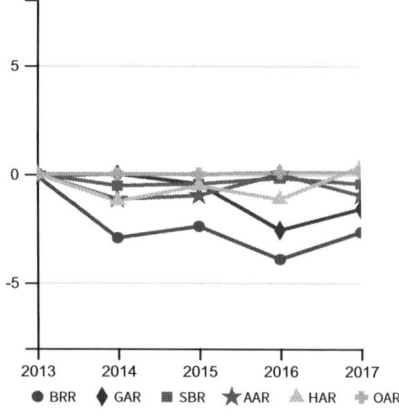

Luis Castillo   RHP   Cincinnati Reds

Born: 12/12/1992   **Age:** 25   **Bats:** R   **Throws:** R   **Height:** 6' 2"   **Weight:** 190 lbs   **Draft Info:** International Free Agent, 2012

We don't have a baseball card for this guy.

PACE
19
Sec/Pit
16th of 150
89°
Very Fast

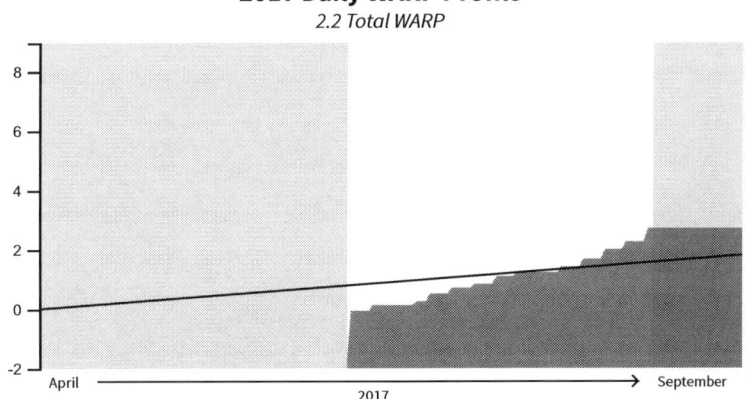

2017 Daily WARP Profile
2.2 Total WARP

April — 2017 — September

Game 1: minors, **Game 141:** innings limit

POWER
69 PWR
8th of 150

STAMINA
74 STM
44th of 150

COMMAND
48 CMD
97th of 150

Fantasy Values
2017 | 2018
$11.87 | **$14.00**

YEAR	TEAM	LVL	AGE	W	L	SV	G	GS	IP	H	HR	BB/9	K/9	K	GB%	BABIP	WHIP	ERA	DRA	WARP	MPH 95
2017	CIN	MLB	24	3	7	0	15	15	89.1	64	11	3.2	9.9	98	60%	.247	1.07	3.12	3.36	2.2	98.7

The raw stuff is no joke. Castillo throws a fastball in the upper 90s and complements it with a high-80s slider. Both pitches give hitters fits and are difficult to square up against due to their speed and movement. If there's a problem with Castillo it is that the hype is going to push his market price close to his ceiling and there is always plenty of margin for error with young starting pitchers. Paying $15 or so for Castillo's upside in NL-only makes sense, but there's a good chance someone will chase him to the low-$20s. The talent is unquestionable, but the risk with young starters is always something to consider. — Mike G.

2017 Pitching Percentages

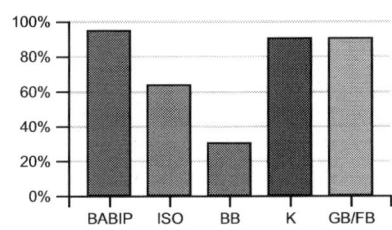

Pitching PECOTA Percentiles

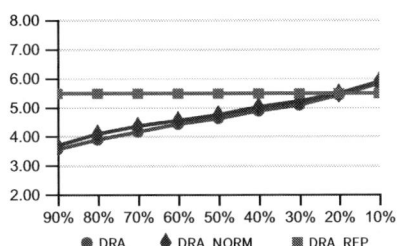

● DRA   ◆ DRA_NORM   ■ DRA_REP

Tunnel vs LHH

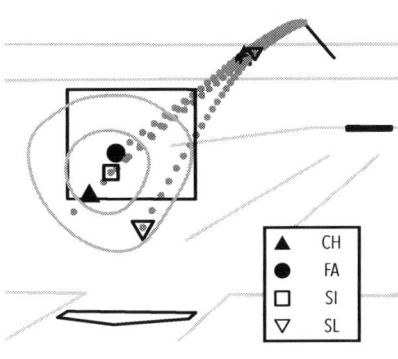

▲ CH
● FA
□ SI
▽ SL

Pitch Types

Type	Freq	Velo	H Mov	V Mov
CH	22.7%	87.6 [110]	-12.2 [94]	-29.1 [94]
FA	50.4%	97.7 [118]	-9.2 [90]	-12.9 [107]
SI	11.7%	97 [128]	-15.2 [80]	-19.4 [103]
SL	15.2%	85.2 [104]	0.7 [83]	-33.7 [97]

Pitch Tunnel

Pairs	Release Diff	Tunnel Diff	Plate Diff	Speed Changes
1042	32.1	113.2	215.6	0.024

PI Scores

Year	Pitch Ct	Pwr	Cmd	Stm
2017	1472	69	48	74

Tunnel vs RHH

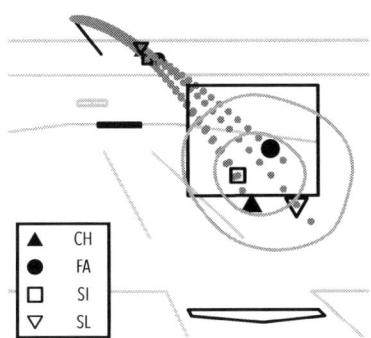

▲ CH
● FA
□ SI
▽ SL

Welington Castillo   C   Chicago White Sox

Born: 4/24/1987   **Age:** 31   **Bats:** R   **Throws:** R   **Height:** 5' 10"   **Weight:** 220 lbs   **Draft Info:** International Free Agent, 2004

PACE
45th of 155
71°
Fast

21 Sec/Pit

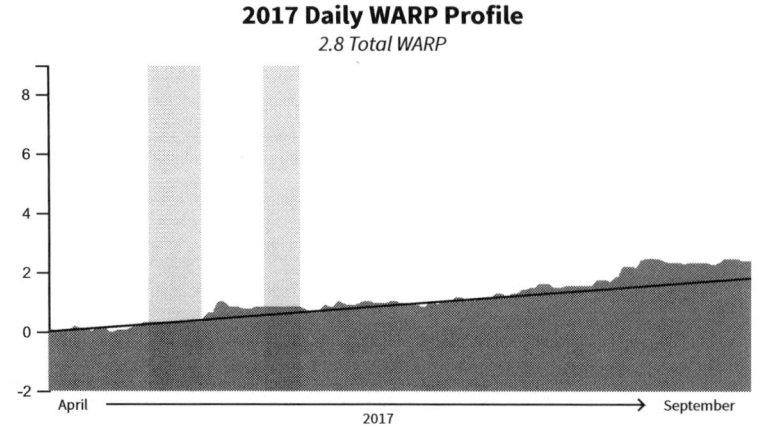

2017 Daily WARP Profile
2.8 Total WARP

Game 24: DL (shoulder tendinitis), **Game 51:** DL (groin contusion)

Fantasy Values

2017	2018
$12.42	$10.00

YEAR	TEAM	LVL	AGE	PA	R	2B	3B	HR	RBI	BB	K	SB	AVG/OBP/SLG	TAv	VORP	BABIP	WARP
2017	BAL	MLB	30	365	44	11	0	20	53	22	97	0	.282/.323/.490	.272	20.3	.336	2.8

Despite playing only 96 games, "Beef" set a career high with 20 home runs. The power has always enticed, but until last year Castillo was a below-average defensive catcher, which limited his opportunities. A two-year, $15 million deal with the White Sox locks in Castillo as a starter and secures his value in nearly every format. — Mike G.

2017 Batting Percentages

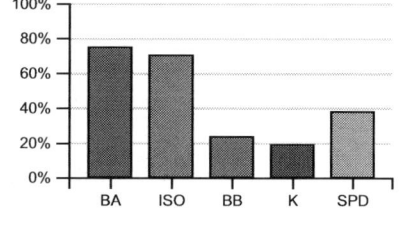

Batting PECOTA Percentiles

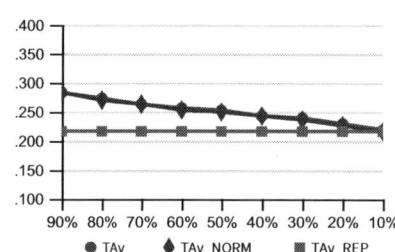

Batting WARP History

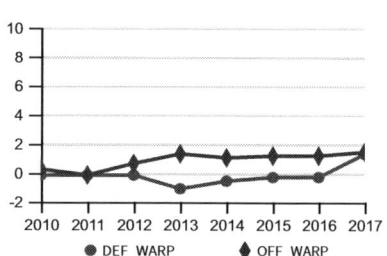

BRR (Relative to Position)

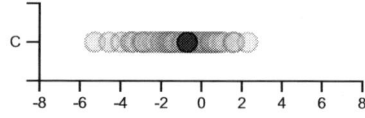

Rank		Player	BRR
40	56°	Manny Pina	-0.60
41	55°	Roberto Perez	-0.62
42	53°	**Welington Castillo**	**-0.67**
43	52°	Derek Norris	-0.72
44	52°	Devin Mesoraco	-0.82

BRR (Relative to Team)

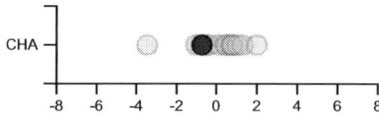

Rank		Player	BRR
10	30°	Willy Garcia	-0.30
11	21°	Avisail Garcia	-0.50
12	15°	**Welington Castillo**	**-0.67**
13	11°	Yoan Moncada	-0.72
14	5°	Omar Narvaez	-0.98

Base Running Components

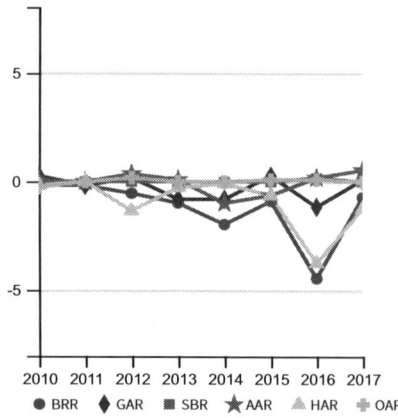

Yoenis Cespedes   LF   New York Mets

Born: 10/18/1985   **Age:** 32   **Bats:** R   **Throws:** R   **Height:** 5' 10"   **Weight:** 220 lbs   **Draft Info:** International Free Agent, 2012

PACE
45th of 155
71°
Fast

21
Sec/Pit

2017 Daily WARP Profile
2.7 Total WARP

Game 22: DL (hamstring strain), **Game 128:** DL (hamstring strain)

Fantasy Values
2017	2018
$11.91	**$23.00**

YEAR	TEAM	LVL	AGE	PA	R	2B	3B	HR	RBI	BB	K	SB	AVG/OBP/SLG	TAv	VORP	BABIP	WARP
2017	NYN	MLB	31	321	46	17	2	17	42	26	61	0	.292/.352/.540	.313	23.9	.316	2.7

When he was on the field, Cespedes was nearly identical to the hitter he was in 2016 during the first season of his $110 million, four-year contract with the Mets. However, a nagging hamstring injury that required multiple trips to the DL was (surprise!) mismanaged by the Mets, and limited the slugger to 81 games. Cespedes has the potential to blast 35-40 home runs, but it remains to be seen if the offseason regimen that he implemented to keep his legs healthy will have an impact. The bat flips are fun but don't count in fantasy. — Mike G.

2017 Batting Percentages

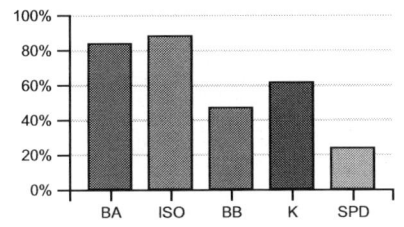

Batting PECOTA Percentiles

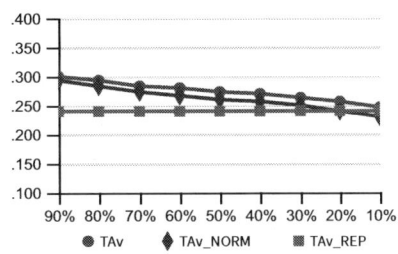

Batting WARP History

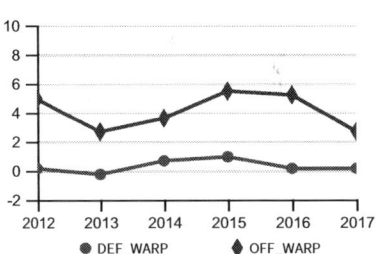

BRR (Relative to Position)

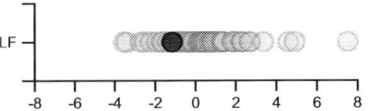

BRR (Relative to Team)

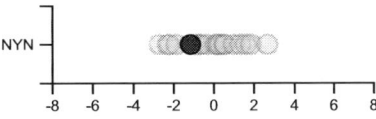

Base Running Components

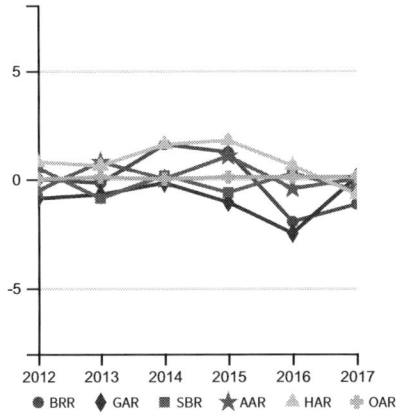

Rank		Player	BRR
55	22°	Brandon Nimmo	-0.85
56	21°	Daniel Nava	-1.01
57	20°	**Yoenis Cespedes**	**-1.12**
58	19°	Hyun-Soo Kim	-1.33
59	16°	Eddie Rosario	-1.60

Rank		Player	BRR
14	34°	T.J. Rivera	-0.64
15	31°	Brandon Nimmo	-0.85
16	26°	**Yoenis Cespedes**	**-1.12**
17	23°	Adrian Gonzalez	-1.82
18	12°	Asdrubal Cabrera	-2.16

Jhoulys Chacin   RHP   Milwaukee Brewers

Born: 1/7/1988   **Age:** 30   **Bats:** R   **Throws:** R   **Height:** 6' 3"   **Weight:** 215 lbs   **Draft Info:** International Free Agent, 2004

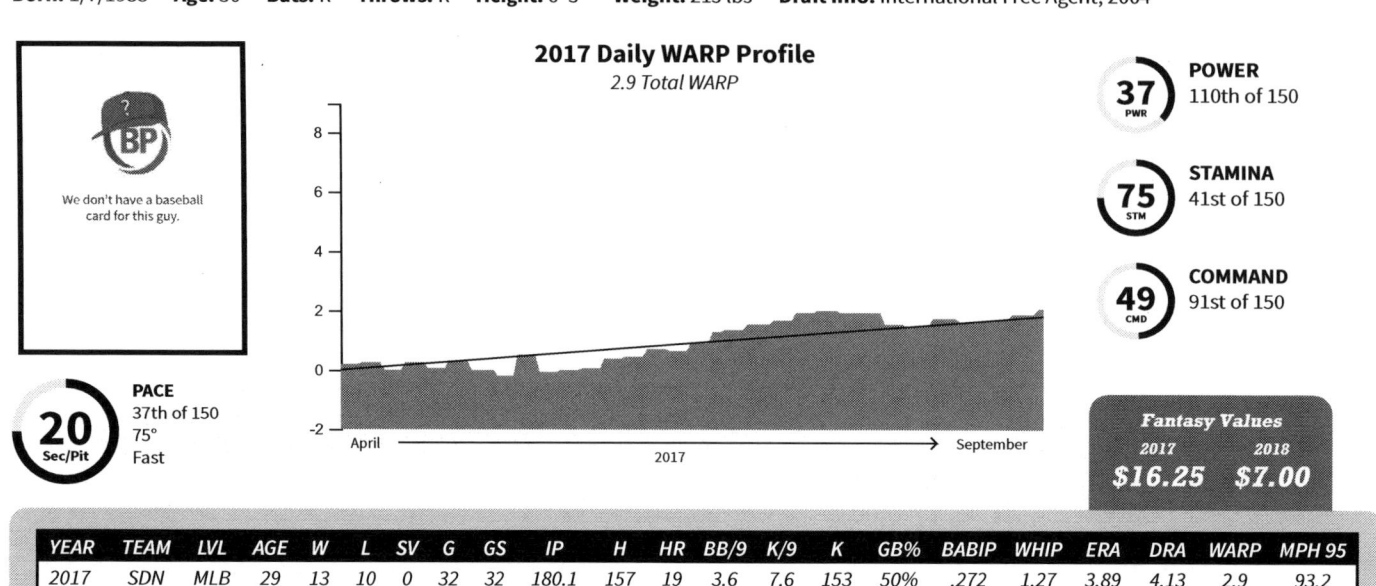

2017 Daily WARP Profile
2.9 Total WARP

	POWER
37 PWR	110th of 150
75 STM	STAMINA 41st of 150
49 CMD	COMMAND 91st of 150

PACE
20 Sec/Pit
37th of 150
75°
Fast

Fantasy Values
2017	2018
$16.25	$7.00

YEAR	TEAM	LVL	AGE	W	L	SV	G	GS	IP	H	HR	BB/9	K/9	K	GB%	BABIP	WHIP	ERA	DRA	WARP	MPH 95
2017	SDN	MLB	29	13	10	0	32	32	180.1	157	19	3.6	7.6	153	50%	.272	1.27	3.89	4.13	2.9	93.2

2017 Pitching Percentages

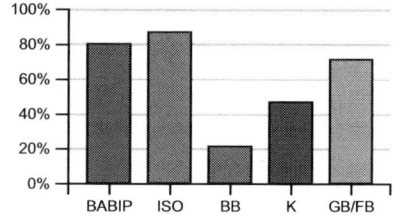

Pitching PECOTA Percentiles

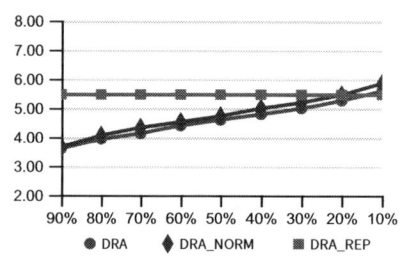

● DRA   ◆ DRA_NORM   ■ DRA_REP

Pitching WARP History

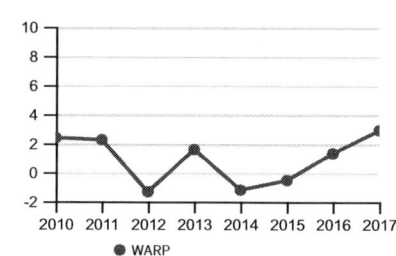

● WARP

Tunnel vs LHH

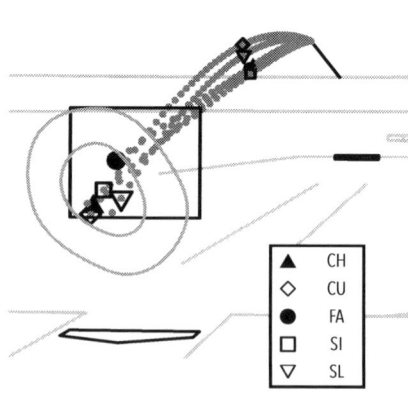

▲ CH
◇ CU
● FA
□ SI
▽ SL

Pitch Types

Type	Freq	Velo	H Mov	V Mov
CH	6.0%	83.8 [95]	-8.4 [114]	-28.3 [96]
CU	6.8%	77.6 [97]	14.4 [126]	-44.1 [108]
FA	14.9%	91.9 [97]	-7.1 [100]	-15.9 [98]
FC	0.5%	89.2 [105]	-0.3 [90]	-24.2 [98]
SI	39.2%	91.5 [95]	-13.7 [91]	-21.5 [95]
SL	32.7%	80.5 [83]	14.7 [145]	-34.8 [94]

Pitch Tunnel

Pairs	Release Diff	Tunnel Diff	Plate Diff	Speed Changes
2144	35.6	123.5	208.6	0.029

PI Scores

Year	Pitch Ct	Pwr	Cmd	Stm
2013	2947	44	45	76
2014	1020	29	54	54
2015	426	23	46	68
2016	2375	41	46	65
2017	2904	37	49	75

Tunnel vs RHH

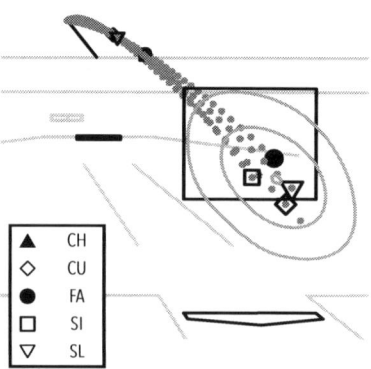

▲ CH
◇ CU
● FA
□ SI
▽ SL

Matt Chapman   3B   Oakland Athletics

Born: 4/28/1993   **Age:** 25   **Bats:** R   **Throws:** R   **Height:** 6' 0"   **Weight:** 210 lbs   **Draft Info:** Round 1, 2014 Draft (#25 overall)

20 Sec/Pit

PACE
18th of 155
88°
Very Fast

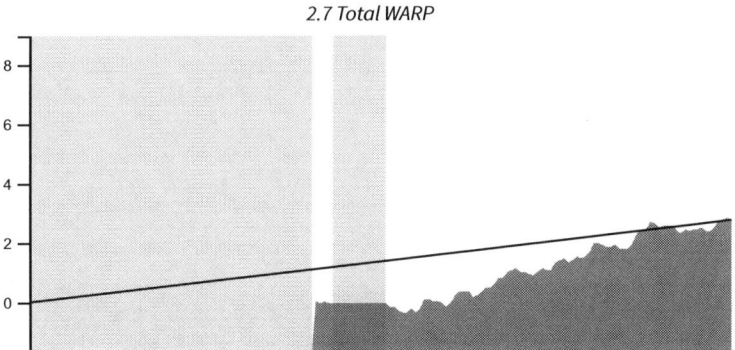

2017 Daily WARP Profile
2.7 Total WARP

Game 1: minors, **Game 70:** DL (knee cellulitis)

Fantasy Values

2017	2018
$6.29	**$13.00**

YEAR	TEAM	LVL	AGE	PA	R	2B	3B	HR	RBI	BB	K	SB	AVG/OBP/SLG	TAv	VORP	BABIP	WARP
2017	OAK	MLB	24	326	39	23	2	14	40	32	92	0	.234/.313/.472	.272	14.1	.290	2.7

Chapman's exemplary defense will keep him employed as a major-league third baseman for years to come, but will his bat provide fantasy value? The power is there, but once the book was out on Chapman's swing-happy approach pitchers stopped challenging him and the numbers predictably fell. Chapman adjusted in September, making it possible that his sophomore season will be successful for more than his amazing glove. — Mike G.

2017 Batting Percentages

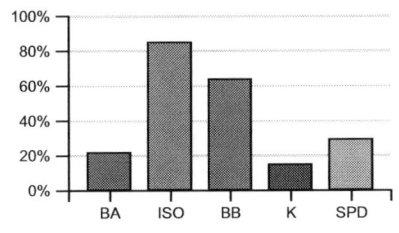

Batting PECOTA Percentiles

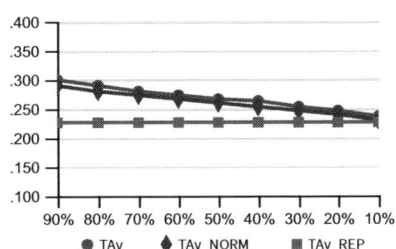

BRR (Relative to Position)

Rank		Player	BRR
40	35°	Yunel Escobar	-0.75
41	34°	Martin Prado	-0.96
42	33°	**Matt Chapman**	**-0.97**
43	29°	Alex Bregman	-1.52
44	28°	Jhonny Peralta	-1.53

BRR (Relative to Team)

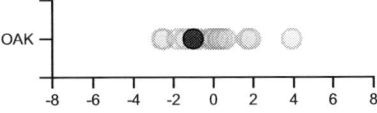

Rank		Player	BRR
10	39°	Khris Davis	-0.22
11	34°	Brandon Moss	-0.69
12	29°	**Matt Chapman**	**-0.97**
13	24°	Bruce Maxwell	-1.37
14	19°	Chad Pinder	-1.76

Shin-Soo Choo   RF   Texas Rangers

Born: 7/13/1982   **Age:** 35   **Bats:** L   **Throws:** L   **Height:** 5' 11"   **Weight:** 210 lbs   **Draft Info:** International Free Agent, 2000

2017 Daily WARP Profile
1.0 Total WARP

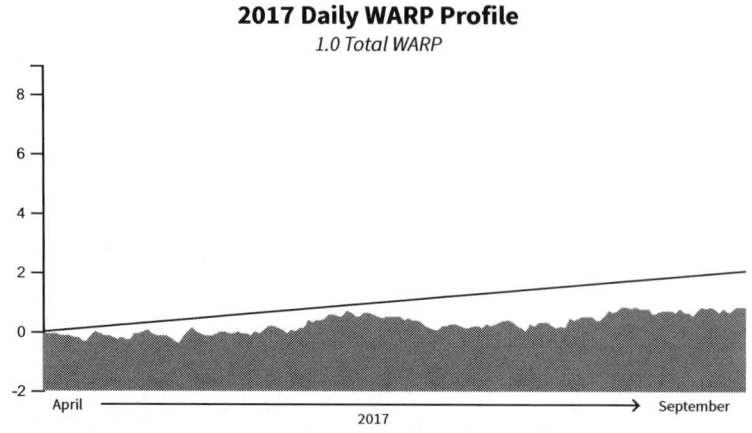

PACE
18th of 155
88°
Very Fast

20 Sec/Pit

Fantasy Values
2017	2018
$20.67	**$15.00**

YEAR	TEAM	LVL	AGE	PA	R	2B	3B	HR	RBI	BB	K	SB	AVG/OBP/SLG	TAv	VORP	BABIP	WARP
2017	TEX	MLB	34	636	96	20	1	22	78	77	134	12	.261/.357/.423	.261	11.1	.305	1.0

After a 2016 lost to injuries, Choo bounced back, posting nearly identical power numbers to his 2015 campaign and stealing in double digits for the first time since 2013. Choo is best cast as a back-end outfielder in mixed leagues or a reliable mainstay in AL-only. The days of elite performances are long gone, but with three years and $62 million left on his contract, the Rangers will roll Choo out there even if he is only an average real-life hitter. — Mike G.

2017 Batting Percentages

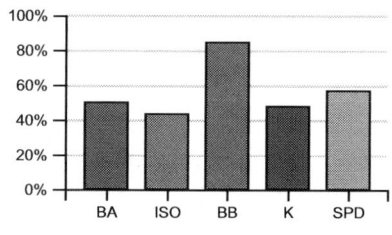

Batting PECOTA Percentiles

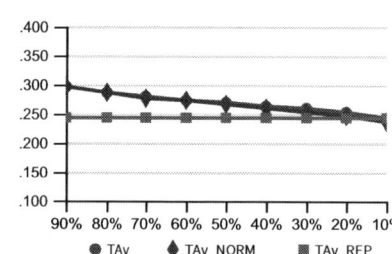

Batting WARP History

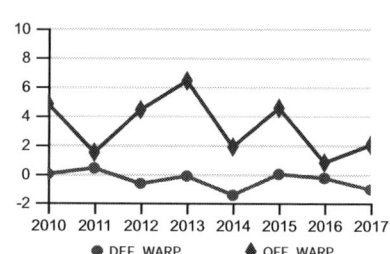

BRR (Relative to Position)

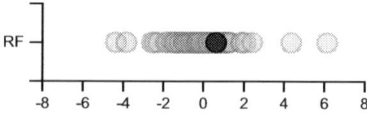

Rank		Player	BRR
14	74°	Jabari Blash	0.83
15	73°	Magneuris Sierra	0.78
16	69°	**Shin-Soo Choo**	**0.67**
17	66°	Jay Bruce	0.57
18	66°	Andrew Stevenson	0.49

BRR (Relative to Team)

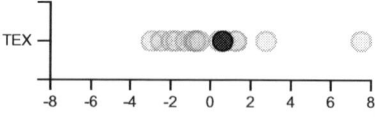

Rank		Player	BRR
5	68°	Jurickson Profar	0.79
6	65°	Ryan Rua	0.69
7	51°	**Shin-Soo Choo**	**0.67**
8	44°	Joey Gallo	0.49
9	43°	Juan Centeno	-0.52

Base Running Components

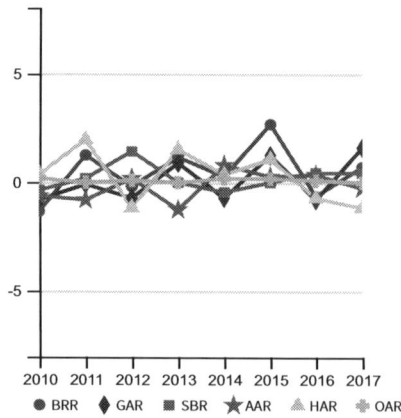

Alex Claudio　　LHP　　Texas Rangers

Born: 1/31/1992　**Age:** 26　**Bats:** L　**Throws:** L　**Height:** 6' 3"　**Weight:** 180 lbs　**Draft Info:** Round 27, 2010 Draft (#826 overall)

We don't have a baseball card for this guy.

2017 Daily WARP Profile
2.6 Total WARP

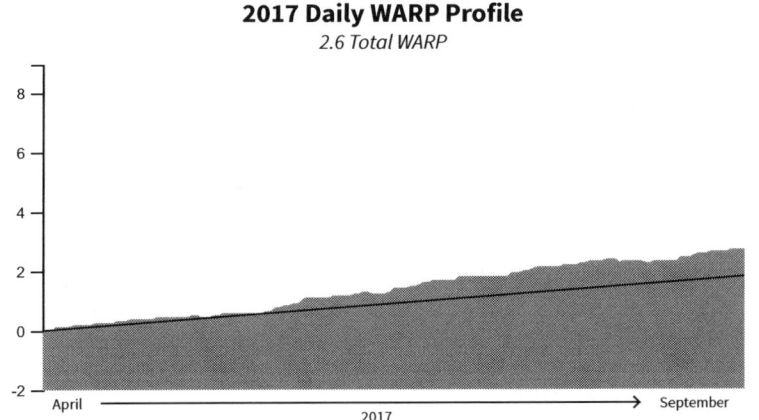

PACE
21 Sec/Pit
81st of 150
46°
Average

POWER
10 PWR
147th of 150

STAMINA
52 STM
128th of 150

COMMAND
66 CMD
16th of 150

Fantasy Values
2017	2018
$14.34	$2.00

YEAR	TEAM	LVL	AGE	W	L	SV	G	GS	IP	H	HR	BB/9	K/9	K	GB%	BABIP	WHIP	ERA	DRA	WARP	MPH 95
2017	TEX	MLB	25	4	2	11	70	1	82.2	71	5	1.6	6.1	56	68%	.269	1.04	2.50	2.41	2.6	88.0

2017 Pitching Percentages

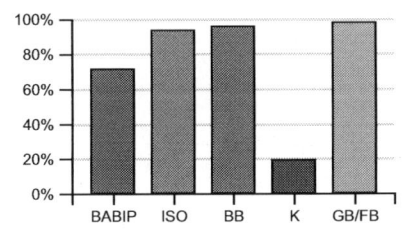

Pitching PECOTA Percentiles

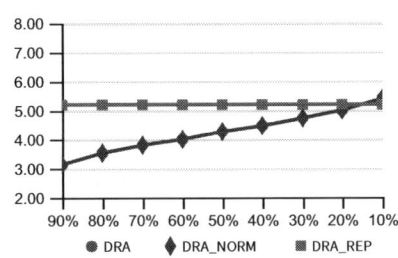

DRA　DRA_NORM　DRA_REP

Pitching WARP History

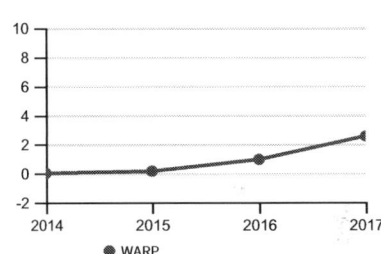

WARP

Tunnel vs LHH

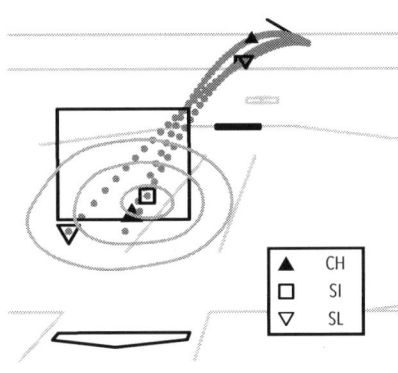

▲ CH
☐ SI
▽ SL

Pitch Types

Type	Freq	Velo	H Mov	V Mov
CH	29.4%	71.4 [45]	18.1 [62]	-51.2 [31]
CU	0.7%	71.2 [74]	16.8 [4]	-50.6 [94]
SI	56.6%	87 [69]	16.2 [73]	-36.4 [40]
SL	13.3%	77.3 [69]	-2.7 [91]	-37.5 [86]

Pitch Tunnel

Pairs	Release Diff	Tunnel Diff	Plate Diff	Speed Changes
789	31.3	104.5	189.4	0.042

PI Scores

Year	Pitch Ct	Pwr	Cmd	Stm
2014	208	0	49	43
2015	238	0	62	46
2016	788	18	68	40
2017	1127	10	66	52

Tunnel vs RHH

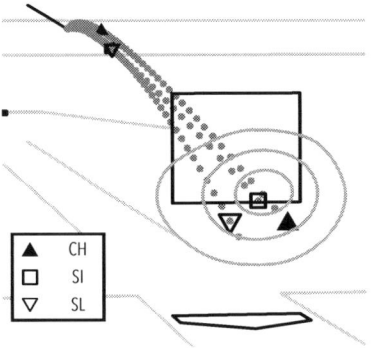

▲ CH
☐ SI
▽ SL

Mike Clevinger   RHP   Cleveland Indians

Born: 12/21/1990   **Age:** 27   **Bats:** R   **Throws:** R   **Height:** 6' 4"   **Weight:** 210 lbs   **Draft Info:** Round 4, 2011 Draft (#135 overall)

2017 Daily WARP Profile
2.3 Total WARP

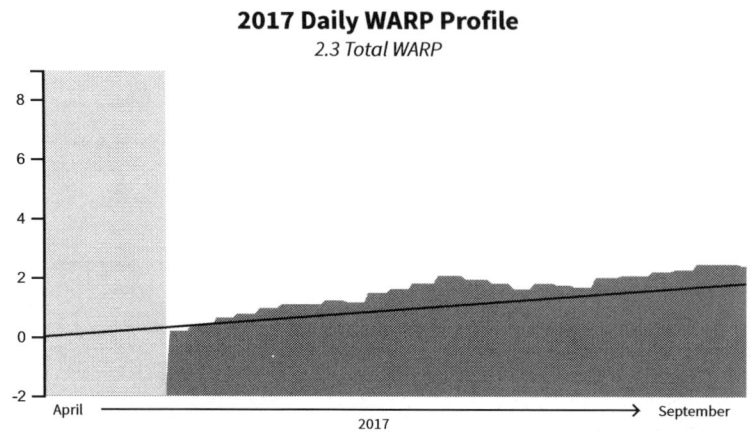

April — 2017 — September

Game 1: minors

POWER
42 PWR
86th of 150

STAMINA
69 STM
73rd of 150

COMMAND
54 CMD
70th of 150

PACE
20 Sec/Pit
37th of 150
75°
Fast

Fantasy Values
2017	2018
$16.95	$13.00

YEAR	TEAM	LVL	AGE	W	L	SV	G	GS	IP	H	HR	BB/9	K/9	K	GB%	BABIP	WHIP	ERA	DRA	WARP	MPH 95
2017	CLE	MLB	26	12	6	0	27	21	121.2	92	13	4.4	10.1	137	40%	.274	1.25	3.11	3.88	2.3	94.4

Cleveland seems to conjure pitchers out of thin air. The latest quality find is Clevinger, a former back-end starter who relied more heavily on a curve to give hitters more looks and resulted in a spike in his swinging strike rate. Clevinger is still a work in progress, as he has lapses in control and is hittable against lefties, but the overall package suggests that the gains last year were legitimate and he should be a mid-tier fantasy arm or better in 2018. — Mike G.

2017 Pitching Percentages

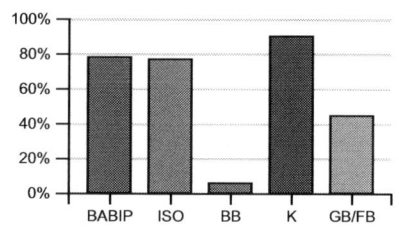

Pitching PECOTA Percentiles

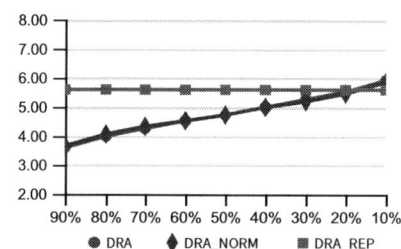

Pitching WARP History

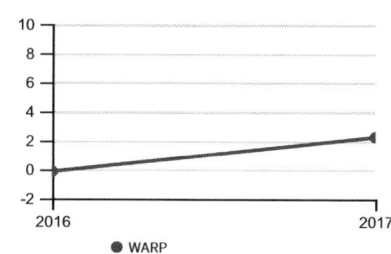

Tunnel vs LHH

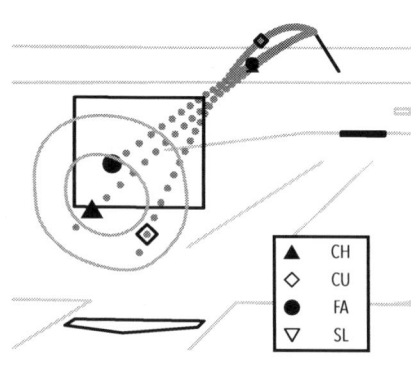

Pitch Types

Type	Freq	Velo	H Mov	V Mov
CH	15.8%	87.3 [109]	-11.6 [97]	-24.8 [106]
CU	11.5%	75.7 [90]	11.1 [113]	-51 [93]
FA	53.5%	92.8 [100]	-8.1 [96]	-14.6 [102]
SL	19.1%	81.6 [88]	12 [133]	-30.6 [106]

Pitch Tunnel

Pairs	Release Diff	Tunnel Diff	Plate Diff	Speed Changes
1660	38.0	117.6	229.0	0.036

PI Scores

Year	Pitch Ct	Pwr	Cmd	Stm
2016	951	53	44	64
2017	2100	42	54	69

Tunnel vs RHH

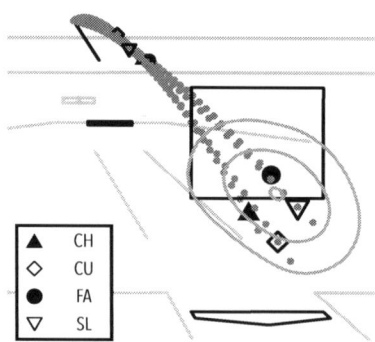

Alex Cobb   RHP   Tampa Bay Rays

Born: 10/7/1987   **Age:** 30   **Bats:** R   **Throws:** R   **Height:** 6'3"   **Weight:** 205 lbs   **Draft Info:** Round 4, 2006 Draft (#109 overall)

22 Sec/Pit — **PACE** 108th of 150, 28° Slow

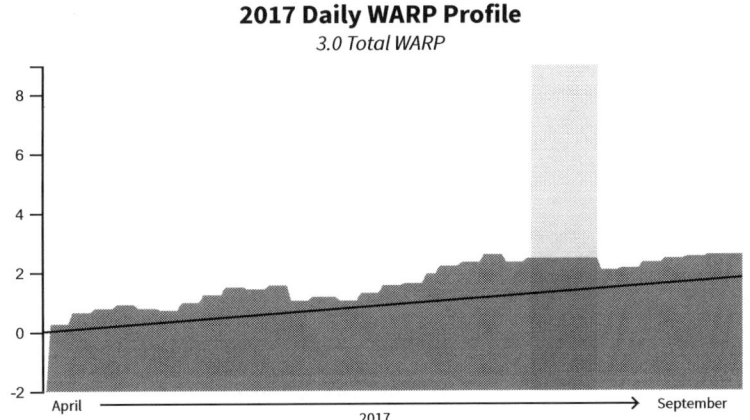

2017 Daily WARP Profile
3.0 Total WARP

April — 2017 — September

Game 113: DL (turf toe)

35 PWR — **POWER** 117th of 150

75 STM — **STAMINA** 41st of 150

63 CMD — **COMMAND** 20th of 150

Fantasy Values
2017	2018
$16.13	$9.00

YEAR	TEAM	LVL	AGE	W	L	SV	G	GS	IP	H	HR	BB/9	K/9	K	GB%	BABIP	WHIP	ERA	DRA	WARP	MPH 95
2017	TBA	MLB	29	12	10	0	29	29	179.1	175	22	2.2	6.4	128	49%	.282	1.22	3.66	4.06	3.0	93.0

Cobb's first full season back from Tommy John surgery was a success, but from a fantasy perspective the results were underwhelming. Cobb's pitch-to-contact approach led to a decent ERA but a low strikeout total in an era when a strikeout-per-inning is par for the course makes Cobb a lower end fantasy option. There is likely to be further improvement in Cobb's second full season back from the procedure but given that he was never a big strikeout guy, he's better used as a matchup play in standard mixed and a mid-tier option in mono leagues. — Mike G.

2017 Pitching Percentages
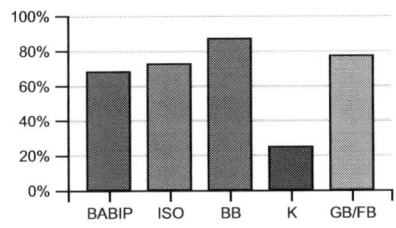

Pitching PECOTA Percentiles
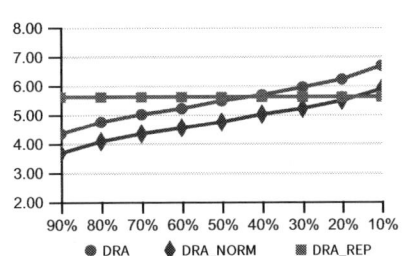

Pitching WARP History
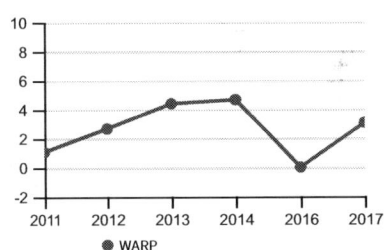

Tunnel vs LHH
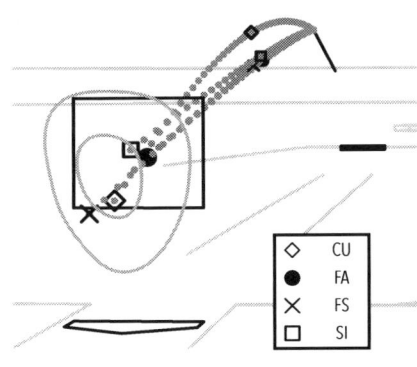

	CU
◇	CU
●	FA
✕	FS
□	SI

Pitch Types

Type	Freq	Velo	H Mov	V Mov
CU	34.1%	80.9 [110]	5.7 [92]	-51.6 [92]
FA	6.0%	92 [97]	-8.7 [93]	-14.7 [101]
FS	14.3%	85.9 [104]	-11.5 [87]	-23.9 [119]
SI	45.7%	92 [98]	-12 [104]	-16.5 [113]

Pitch Tunnel

Pairs	Release Diff	Tunnel Diff	Plate Diff	Speed Changes
2106	21.4	133.3	221.0	0.030

PI Scores

Year	Pitch Ct	Pwr	Cmd	Stm
2012	2164	34	52	68
2013	2198	34	48	56
2014	2555	39	65	64
2016	386	37	45	31
2017	2847	35	63	75

Tunnel vs RHH
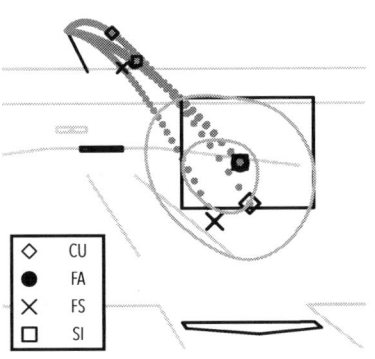

◇	CU
●	FA
✕	FS
□	SI

Gerrit Cole   RHP   Houston Astros

Born: 9/8/1990   **Age:** 27   **Bats:** R   **Throws:** R   **Height:** 6' 4"   **Weight:** 225 lbs   **Draft Info:** Round 1, 2011 Draft (#1 overall)

2017 Daily WARP Profile
3.2 Total WARP

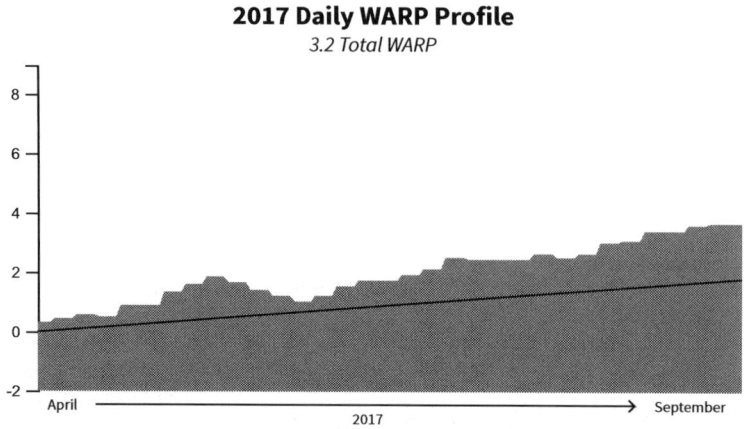

POWER
65
PWR
12th of 150

STAMINA
82
STM
7th of 150

COMMAND
63
CMD
20th of 150

PACE
19
Sec/Pit
16th of 150
89°
Very Fast

Fantasy Values
2017	2018
$16.92	**$18.00**

YEAR	TEAM	LVL	AGE	W	L	SV	G	GS	IP	H	HR	BB/9	K/9	K	GB%	BABIP	WHIP	ERA	DRA	WARP	MPH 95
2017	PIT	MLB	26	12	12	0	33	33	203	199	31	2.4	8.7	196	47%	.298	1.25	4.26	4.15	3.2	98.0

Endurance was Cole's biggest problem in 2017. Most pitchers' numbers slip their third time through the batting order, but for Cole those splits were extreme. The result was a spike in home runs that led to a subsequent jump in ERA. His raw velocity and movement remained strong, but it has now been a season and a half of an ERA around four for the former Pirates' ace. Traded to Houston, Cole remains a solid option but no longer the top-tier arm he once was. — Mike G.

2017 Pitching Percentages

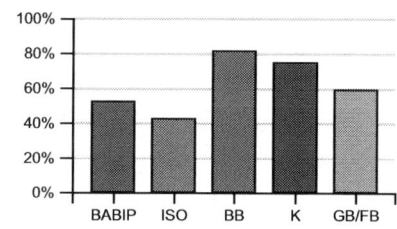

Pitching PECOTA Percentiles

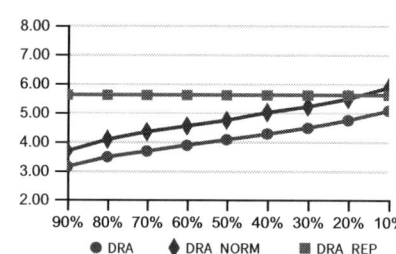

Pitching WARP History

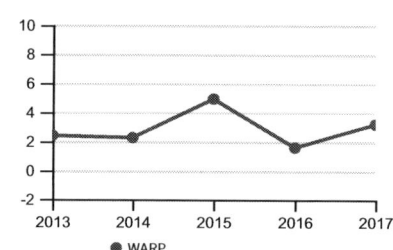

Tunnel vs LHH

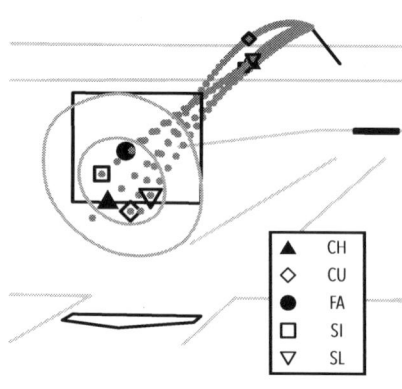

▲	CH
◇	CU
●	FA
□	SI
▽	SL

Pitch Types

Type	Freq	Velo	H Mov	V Mov
CH	10.4%	89.1 [116]	-13.1 [89]	-24.2 [108]
CU	12.3%	80.8 [110]	12.2 [117]	-44.9 [106]
FA	41.9%	96.4 [113]	-10.3 [85]	-13 [107]
SI	18.1%	96 [122]	-13.8 [90]	-17.2 [110]
SL	17.3%	88.5 [118]	4.1 [98]	-28.7 [111]

Pitch Tunnel

Pairs	Release Diff	Tunnel Diff	Plate Diff	Speed Changes
2337	26.7	117.7	220.1	0.027

PI Scores

Year	Pitch Ct	Pwr	Cmd	Stm
2013	1721	73	46	71
2014	2192	70	49	60
2015	3227	70	42	79
2016	1912	63	49	56
2017	3269	65	63	82

Tunnel vs RHH

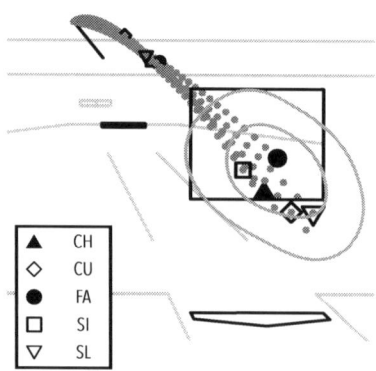

▲	CH
◇	CU
●	FA
□	SI
▽	SL

Bartolo Colon   RHP   Texas Rangers

Born: 5/24/1973   **Age:** 45   **Bats:** R   **Throws:** R   **Height:** 5' 11"   **Weight:** 285 lbs   **Draft Info:** International Free Agent, 1993

2017 Daily WARP Profile
-1.3 Total WARP

Game 56: DL (oblique strain), **Game 78:** free agent, minors

	POWER
49 PWR	64th of 150

	STAMINA
64 STM	89th of 150

	COMMAND
73 CMD	7th of 150

	PACE
20 Sec/Pit	37th of 150 / 75° / Fast

Fantasy Values
2017	2018
$0.81	$1.00

YEAR	TEAM	LVL	AGE	W	L	SV	G	GS	IP	H	HR	BB/9	K/9	K	GB%	BABIP	WHIP	ERA	DRA	WARP	MPH 95
2017	ATL	MLB	44	2	8	0	13	13	63	92	11	2.9	6.0	42	48%	.360	1.78	8.14	6.04	-0.3	91.5
2017	MIN	MLB	44	5	6	0	15	15	80	100	17	1.7	5.3	47	42%	.307	1.44	5.18	6.65	-1.0	91.3

2017 Pitching Percentages

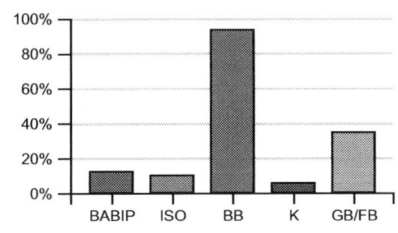

Pitching PECOTA Percentiles

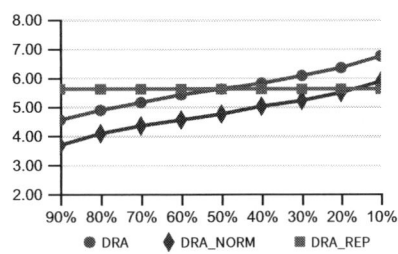

● DRA   ◆ DRA_NORM   ■ DRA_REP

Pitching WARP History

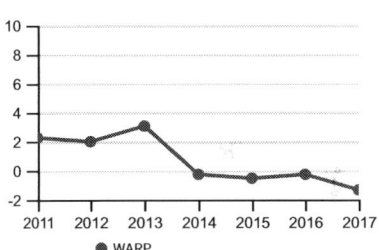

● WARP

Tunnel vs LHH

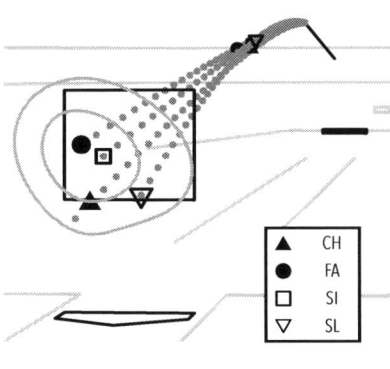

▲	CH
●	FA
□	SI
▽	SL

Pitch Types

Type	Freq	Velo	H Mov	V Mov
CH	10.0%	81.7 [86]	-11.6 [97]	-30.2 [91]
FA	20.2%	90.4 [92]	-6.9 [101]	-15.8 [98]
FC	0.6%	85.9 [86]	-1.1 [87]	-22.5 [105]
SI	61.9%	87.4 [72]	-13.5 [93]	-24.6 [83]
SL	7.2%	81.8 [89]	3.7 [96]	-32.9 [99]

Pitch Tunnel

Pairs	Release Diff	Tunnel Diff	Plate Diff	Speed Changes
1533	37.5	107.2	198.6	0.013

PI Scores

Year	Pitch Ct	Pwr	Cmd	Stm
2013	2777	66	61	71
2014	2993	54	64	76
2015	2681	53	66	72
2016	2840	59	70	74
2017	2270	49	73	64

Tunnel vs RHH

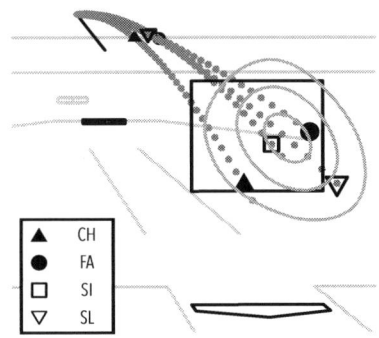

▲	CH
●	FA
□	SI
▽	SL

Michael Conforto LF New York Mets

Born: 3/1/1993 **Age:** 25 **Bats:** L **Throws:** R **Height:** 6' 1" **Weight:** 215 lbs **Draft Info:** Round 1, 2014 Draft (#10 overall)

21 Sec/Pit

PACE
45th of 155
71°
Fast

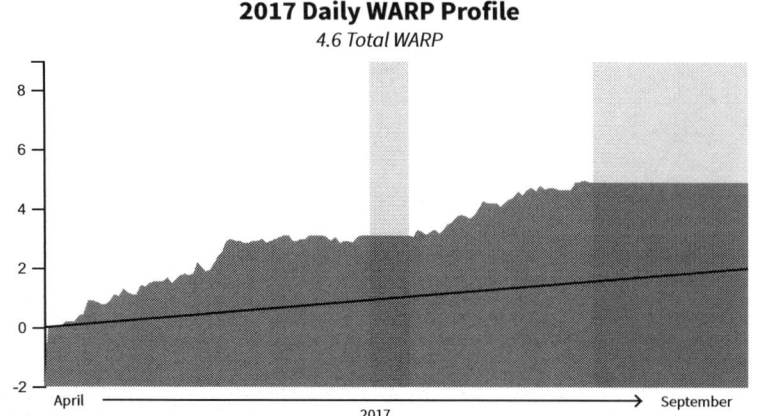

2017 Daily WARP Profile
4.6 Total WARP

Game 76: DL (shoulder dislocation), **Game 127:** DL (shoulder dislocation)

Fantasy Values

2017	2018
$17.80	$14.00

YEAR	TEAM	LVL	AGE	PA	R	2B	3B	HR	RBI	BB	K	SB	AVG/OBP/SLG	TAv	VORP	BABIP	WARP
2017	NYN	MLB	24	440	72	20	1	27	68	57	113	2	.279/.384/.555	.336	47.8	.328	4.6

Conforto was putting up near-elite real-life and strong fantasy numbers before a freakish shoulder injury incurred midswing ended his season and put both his 2018 and long-term effectiveness in doubt. Conforto is questionable for Opening Day and no one knows what he'll look like when he does return. In redraft leagues the risk is considerable and even in keeper formats you're better off shaving a few bucks off his price rather than paying for the ceiling. — Mike G.

2017 Batting Percentages

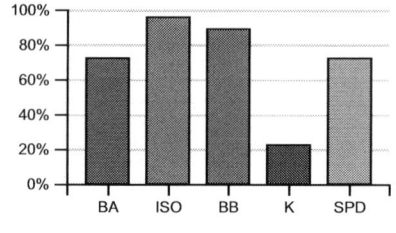

Batting PECOTA Percentiles

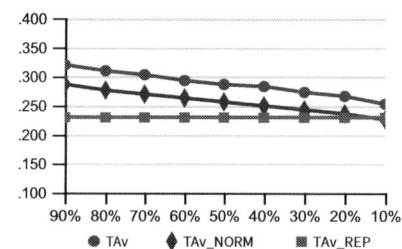

Batting WARP History

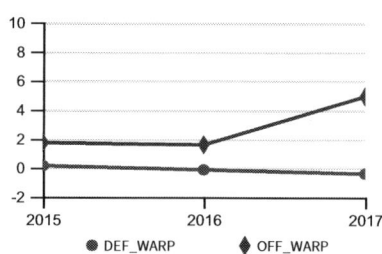

BRR (Relative to Position)

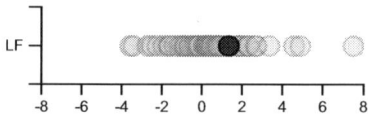

Rank		Player	BRR
15	71°	Jace Peterson	1.44
16	69°	Andrew Benintendi	1.41
17	66°	**Michael Conforto**	**1.39**
18	64°	Adam Frazier	1.34
19	63°	Jarrett Parker	1.31

BRR (Relative to Team)

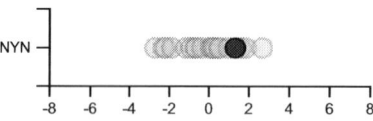

Rank		Player	BRR
2	76°	Juan Lagares	1.90
3	74°	Jose Lobaton	1.65
4	64°	**Michael Conforto**	**1.39**
5	61°	Amed Rosario	1.05
6	60°	Gavin Cecchini	0.58

Base Running Components

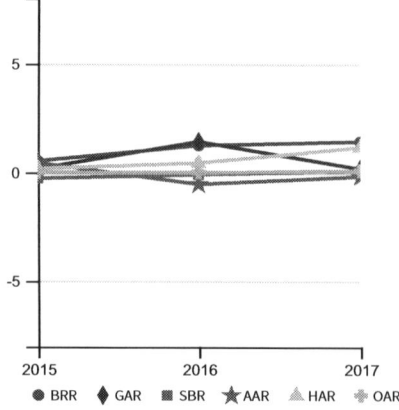

Adam Conley   LHP   Miami Marlins

Born: 5/24/1990   **Age:** 28   **Bats:** L   **Throws:** L   **Height:** 6' 3"   **Weight:** 200 lbs   **Draft Info:** Round 2, 2011 Draft (#72 overall)

2017 Daily WARP Profile
-1.4 Total WARP

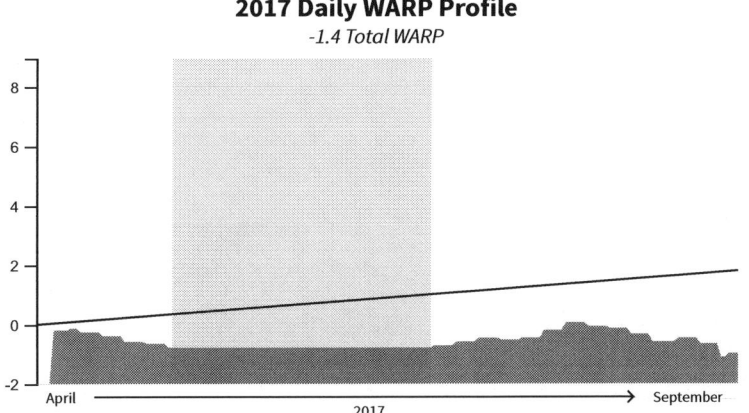

Game 32: minors

POWER
41 PWR   93rd of 150

STAMINA
74 STM   44th of 150

COMMAND
42 CMD   128th of 150

16 Sec/Pit   **PACE**
1st of 150
99°
Very Fast

Fantasy Values
2017	2018
$-0.92	$4.00

YEAR	TEAM	LVL	AGE	W	L	SV	G	GS	IP	H	HR	BB/9	K/9	K	GB%	BABIP	WHIP	ERA	DRA	WARP	MPH 95
2017	MIA	MLB	27	8	8	0	22	20	102.2	114	19	3.7	6.3	72	42%	.295	1.52	6.14	6.76	-1.4	91.9

2017 Pitching Percentages

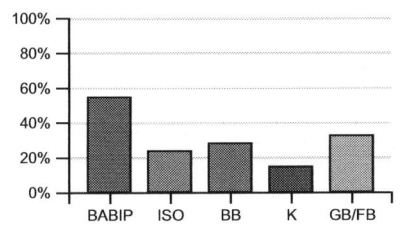

Pitching PECOTA Percentiles

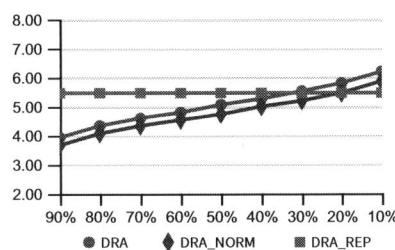

● DRA   ◆ DRA_NORM   ■ DRA_REP

Pitching WARP History

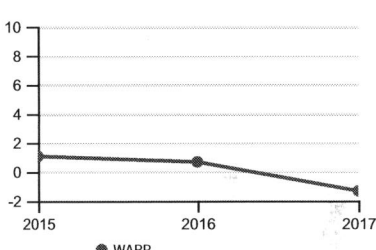

● WARP

Tunnel vs LHH

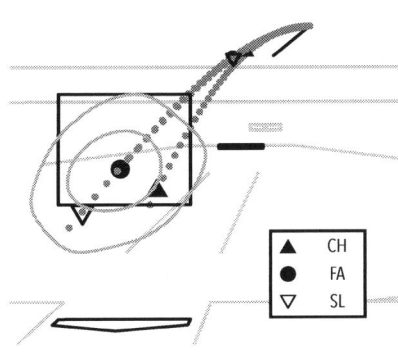

▲ CH
● FA
▽ SL

Tunnel vs RHH

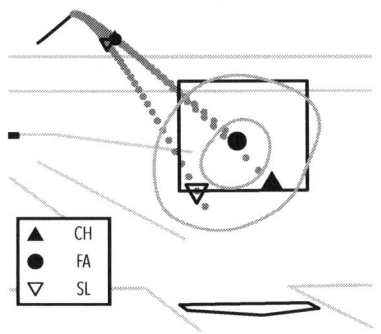

▲ CH
● FA
▽ SL

Pitch Types

Type	Freq	Velo	H Mov	V Mov
CH	18.1%	82.8 [91]	16.6 [70]	-27.8 [98]
CU	1.4%	79.5 [104]	-0.5 [71]	-39.9 [117]
FA	64.4%	89.9 [90]	13.2 [72]	-18.8 [88]
SL	16.1%	85.2 [103]	4.3 [61]	-29.7 [109]

Pitch Tunnel

Pairs	Release Diff	Tunnel Diff	Plate Diff	Speed Changes
1167	23.0	117.5	227.8	0.018

PI Scores

Year	Pitch Ct	Pwr	Cmd	Stm
2015	1100	49	54	69
2016	2241	52	57	58
2017	1700	41	42	74

Willson Contreras   C   Chicago Cubs

Born: 5/13/1992   **Age:** 26   **Bats:** R   **Throws:** R   **Height:** 6' 1"   **Weight:** 210 lbs   **Draft Info:** International Free Agent, 2009

22 Sec/Pit

PACE
99th of 155
36°
Slow

2017 Daily WARP Profile
3.1 Total WARP

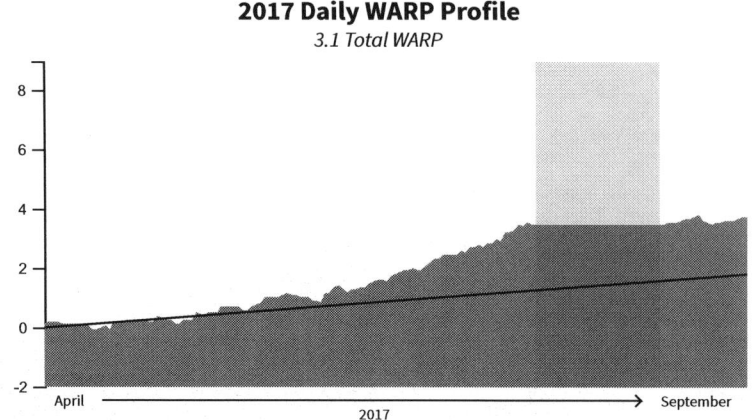

April   2017   September

Game 114: DL (hamstring strain)

Fantasy Values

2017	2018
$16.19	**$17.00**

YEAR	TEAM	LVL	AGE	PA	R	2B	3B	HR	RBI	BB	K	SB	AVG/OBP/SLG	TAv	VORP	BABIP	WARP
2017	CHN	MLB	25	428	50	21	0	21	74	45	98	5	.276/.356/.499	.302	34.2	.319	3.1

Contreras' bat is the genuine article, but questions about his defense and especially his game calling made it unclear if his future would be as a catcher or at another position. Contreras put those concerns to rest in 2017, working diligently to elevate his game and keep his bat in the lineup enough to make him a fantasy asset. In an era where many catchers are employed primarily for their defense and framing, Contreras' contributions with the bat could elevate him to the best fantasy catcher this side of Gary Sanchez. — Mike G.

2017 Batting Percentages

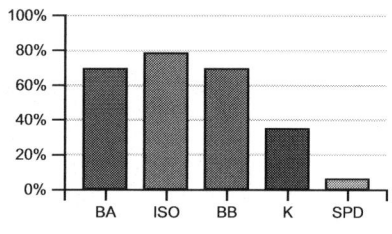

Batting PECOTA Percentiles

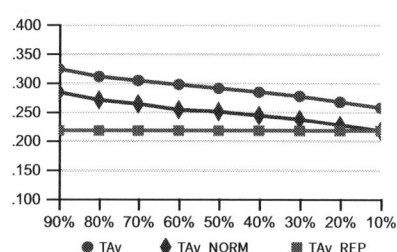

Batting WARP History

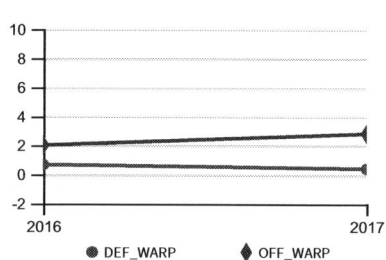

BRR (Relative to Position)

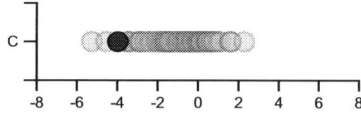

Rank		Player	BRR
72	8°	Wilson Ramos	-3.42
73	7°	Stephen Vogt	-3.45
74	4°	**Willson Contreras**	**-3.93**
75	2°	Yadier Molina	-4.51
76	0°	Sandy Leon	-5.21

BRR (Relative to Team)

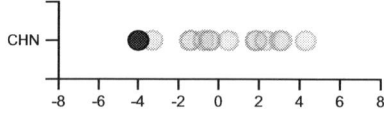

Rank		Player	BRR
10	30°	Tommy La Stella	-0.70
11	22°	Ben Zobrist	-1.32
12	18°	Chris Gimenez	-1.39
13	7°	Anthony Rizzo	-3.23
14	0°	**Willson Contreras**	**-3.93**

Base Running Components

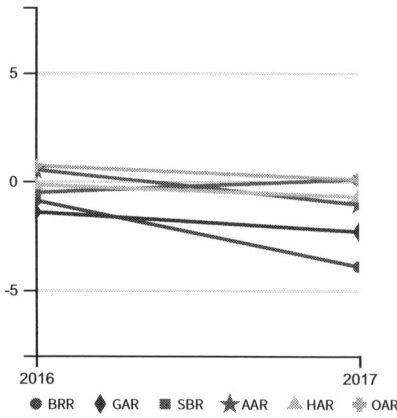

Patrick Corbin   LHP   Arizona Diamondbacks

Born: 7/19/1989   **Age:** 28   **Bats:** L   **Throws:** L   **Height:** 6'3"   **Weight:** 210 lbs   **Draft Info:** Round 2, 2009 Draft (#80 overall)

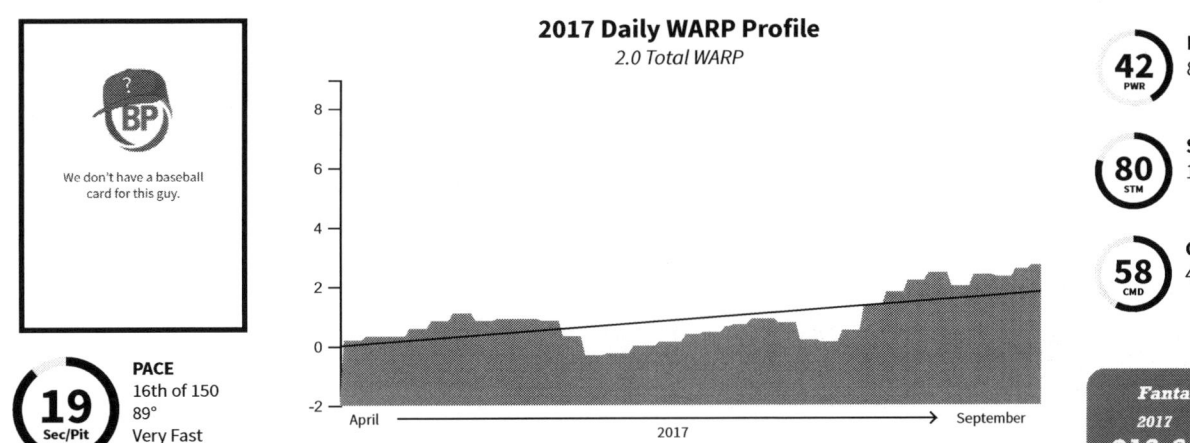

2017 Daily WARP Profile
2.0 Total WARP

POWER 42 PWR — 86th of 150

STAMINA 80 STM — 14th of 150

COMMAND 58 CMD — 49th of 150

PACE 19 Sec/Pit — 16th of 150 · 89° · Very Fast

Fantasy Values
2017	2018
$13.64	$7.00

YEAR	TEAM	LVL	AGE	W	L	SV	G	GS	IP	H	HR	BB/9	K/9	K	GB%	BABIP	WHIP	ERA	DRA	WARP	MPH 95
2017	ARI	MLB	27	14	13	0	33	32	189.2	208	26	2.9	8.4	178	52%	.326	1.42	4.03	4.60	2.0	94.3

2017 Pitching Percentages

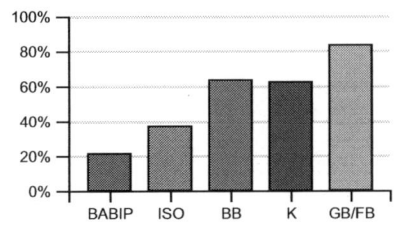

Pitching PECOTA Percentiles

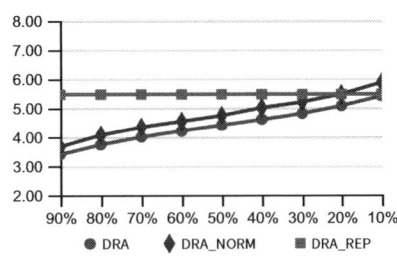

● DRA   ◆ DRA_NORM   ■ DRA_REP

Pitching WARP History

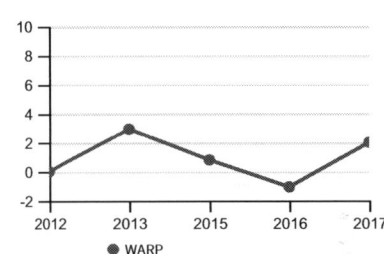

● WARP

Tunnel vs LHH

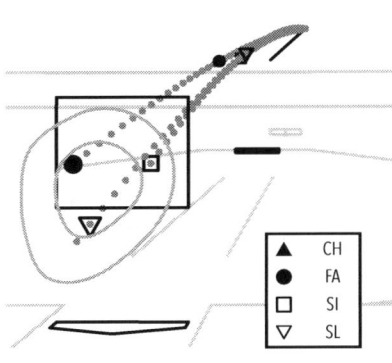

▲ CH
● FA
□ SI
▽ SL

Pitch Types

Type	Freq	Velo	H Mov	V Mov
CH	8.6%	83.8 [95]	11.4 [99]	-24.9 [106]
FA	30.2%	92.8 [100]	7.4 [99]	-15.1 [100]
FC	0.1%	87.8 [97]	0.5 [89]	-23.3 [102]
SI	23.1%	92.5 [101]	12.3 [102]	-18.7 [105]
SL	38.0%	81.3 [87]	-4.1 [98]	-38 [85]

Pitch Tunnel

Pairs	Release Diff	Tunnel Diff	Plate Diff	Speed Changes
2179	24.7	114.3	224.1	0.030

PI Scores

Year	Pitch Ct	Pwr	Cmd	Stm
2012	1588	49	47	69
2013	3081	52	41	79
2015	1253	49	45	52
2016	2531	49	48	68
2017	3087	42	58	80

Tunnel vs RHH

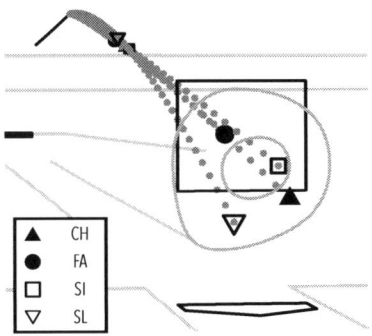

▲ CH
● FA
□ SI
▽ SL

Carlos Correa   SS   Houston Astros

Born: 9/22/1994   **Age:** 23   **Bats:** R   **Throws:** R   **Height:** 6' 4"   **Weight:** 215 lbs   **Draft Info:** Round 1, 2012 Draft (#1 overall)

2017 Daily WARP Profile
4.6 Total WARP

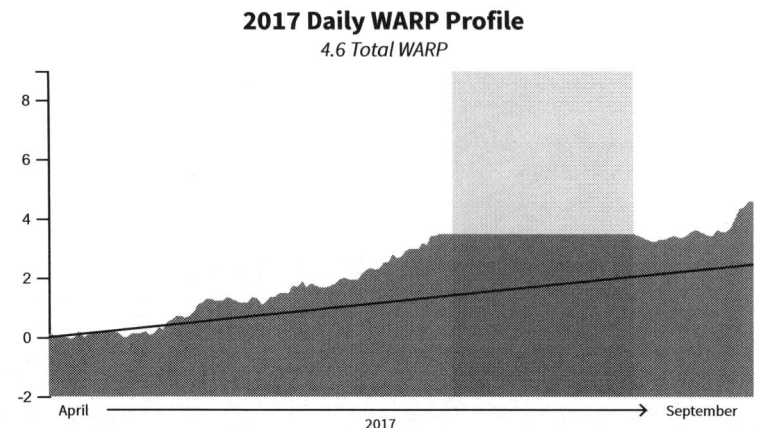

PACE
22 Sec/Pit
99th of 155
36°
Slow

Game 94: DL (thumb ligament tear)

Fantasy Values
2017	2018
$22.63	$30.00

YEAR	TEAM	LVL	AGE	PA	R	2B	3B	HR	RBI	BB	K	SB	AVG/OBP/SLG	TAv	VORP	BABIP	WARP
2017	HOU	MLB	22	481	82	25	1	24	84	53	92	2	.315/.391/.550	.320	47.4	.352	4.6

An injury and a drop in steals pushed Correa's fantasy value down and masked the emergence of a young and exciting superstar. Correa's numbers extrapolated to a full season would have been 36 home runs, 122 RBI, 125 runs, and a .315 batting average. Even if the steals don't return, Correa offers an excellent buying opportunity in every format, particularly in leagues where fantasy managers have soured on him for being a "disappointment." — Mike G.

2017 Batting Percentages

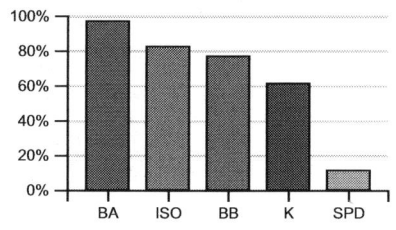

Batting PECOTA Percentiles

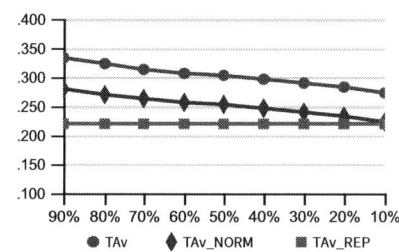

Batting WARP History

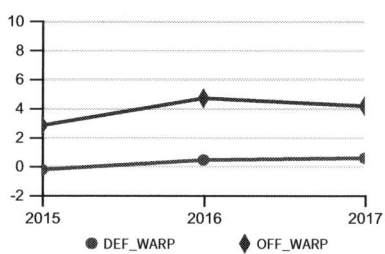

BRR (Relative to Position)

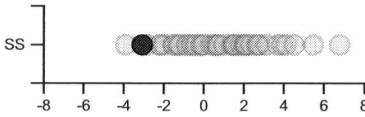

Rank		Player	BRR
45	8°	Adeiny Hechavarria	-2.18
46	5°	Zack Cozart	-2.78
47	4°	Troy Tulowitzki	-3.01
48	2°	**Carlos Correa**	**-3.04**
49	0°	Paul DeJong	-3.86

BRR (Relative to Team)

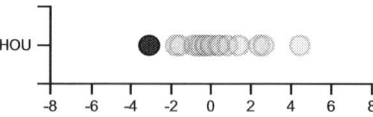

Rank		Player	BRR
13	35°	Carlos Beltran	-0.60
14	27°	Marwin Gonzalez	-0.81
15	16°	Alex Bregman	-1.52
16	7°	Yulieski Gurriel	-1.72
17	0°	**Carlos Correa**	**-3.04**

Base Running Components

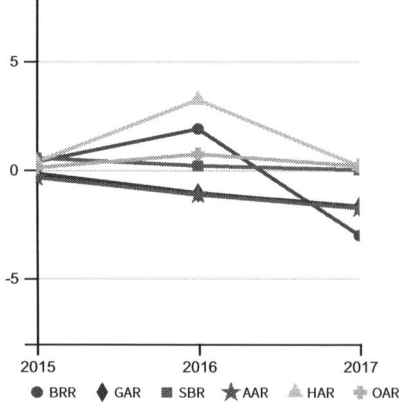

Zack Cozart   SS   Los Angeles Angels

Born: 8/12/1985 **Age:** 32 **Bats:** R **Throws:** R **Height:** 6' 0" **Weight:** 204 lbs **Draft Info:** Round 2, 2007 Draft (#79 overall)

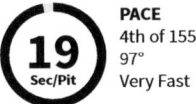

19 Sec/Pit

PACE
4th of 155
97°
Very Fast

2017 Daily WARP Profile
5.3 Total WARP

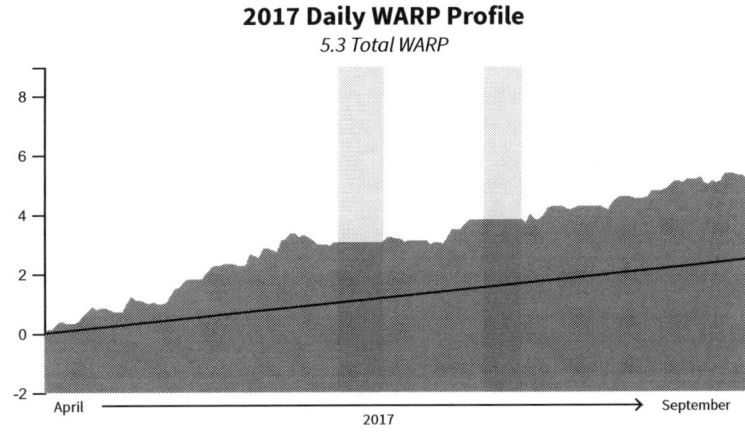

Game 68: DL (quad strain), **Game 101:** DL (quad soreness)

Fantasy Values
| 2017 | 2018 |
| $19.85 | $17.00 |

YEAR	TEAM	LVL	AGE	PA	R	2B	3B	HR	RBI	BB	K	SB	AVG/OBP/SLG	TAv	VORP	BABIP	WARP
2017	CIN	MLB	31	507	80	24	7	24	63	62	78	3	.297/.385/.548	.321	51.1	.312	5.3

If you weren't the best shortstop in baseball in 2017, take one step back. Not so fast, Zack Cozart. While Corey Seager and Elvis Andrus both had a higher WARP, on a game-by-game basis no one was better than Cozart. How this translates to fantasy this year is an open question. Although Cozart's improvements are legitimate, paying for a repeat of a career year at age 31 typically doesn't end well. The safe money won't bet on a repeat, but then, safe money seldom wins fantasy championships. Cozart will pick up third base eligibility this season, but in most leagues teams will continue to use him at short. — Mike G.

2017 Batting Percentages

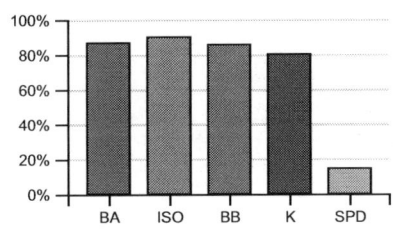

Batting PECOTA Percentiles

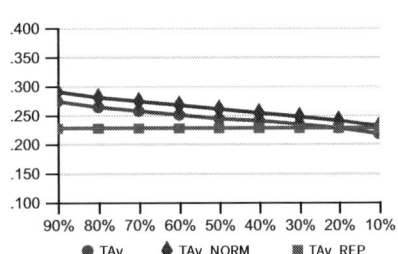

Batting WARP History

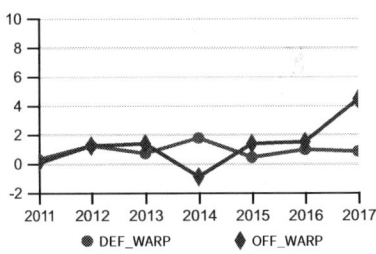

BRR (Relative to Position)

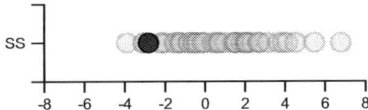

Rank		Player	BRR
44	9°	Asdrubal Cabrera	-2.16
45	8°	Adeiny Hechavarria	-2.18
46	5°	**Zack Cozart**	**-2.78**
47	4°	Troy Tulowitzki	-3.01
48	2°	Carlos Correa	-3.04

BRR (Relative to Team)

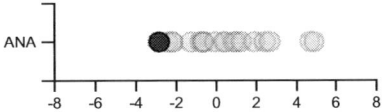

Rank		Player	BRR
17	24°	Jefry Marte	-2.13
18	19°	C.J. Cron	-2.15
19	12°	Martin Maldonado	-2.37
20	3°	**Zack Cozart**	**-2.78**
21	0°	Rene Rivera	-2.83

Base Running Components

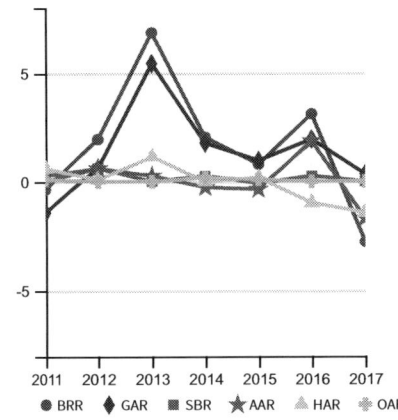

Brandon Crawford   SS   San Francisco Giants

Born: 1/21/1987   **Age:** 31   **Bats:** L   **Throws:** R   **Height:** 6' 2"   **Weight:** 215 lbs   **Draft Info:** Round 4, 2008 Draft (#117 overall)

PACE
22 Sec/Pit
99th of 155
36°
Slow

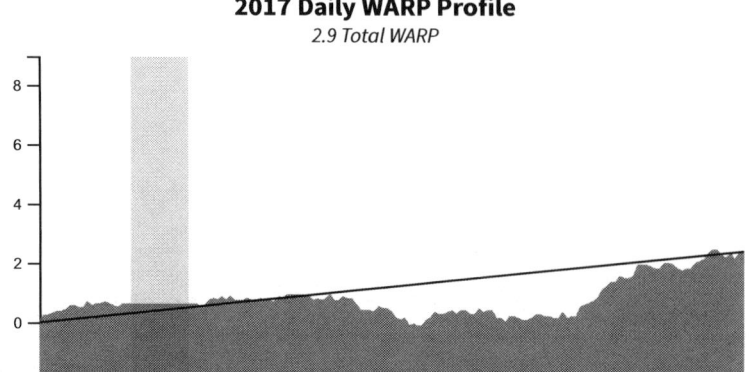

2017 Daily WARP Profile
2.9 Total WARP

Game 22: DL (groin strain)

Fantasy Values
2017	2018
$12.19	**$14.00**

YEAR	TEAM	LVL	AGE	PA	R	2B	3B	HR	RBI	BB	K	SB	AVG/OBP/SLG	TAv	VORP	BABIP	WARP
2017	SFN	MLB	30	570	58	34	1	14	77	42	113	3	.253/.305/.403	.263	24.5	.293	2.9

The Giants didn't lock Crawford up with a long-term deal for his offense. The slick-fielding San Francisco shortstop slipped a little bit with the bat in 2017, but if Crawford is picking it at short he'll have a place in the Giants' lineup. Crawford's value comes in deep leagues as an everyday contributor who is guaranteed playing time. In mixed leagues, you are better off pushing for offensive upside and drafting Crawford to plug in as a reserve if things go badly with your starter. — Mike G.

2017 Batting Percentages

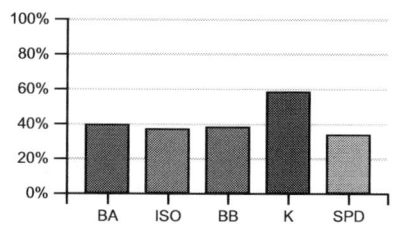

Batting PECOTA Percentiles

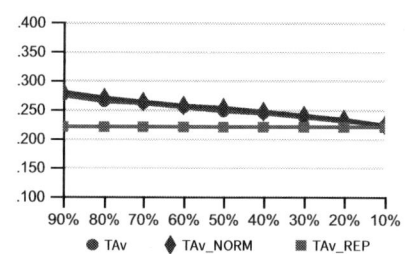

Batting WARP History

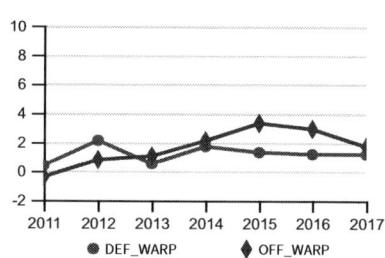

BRR (Relative to Position)

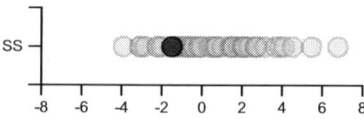

Rank		Player	BRR
39	18°	Mike Aviles	-1.19
40	17°	Aledmys Diaz	-1.27
41	14°	**Brandon Crawford**	**-1.44**
42	13°	J.J. Hardy	-1.50
43	12°	Dixon Machado	-1.96

BRR (Relative to Team)

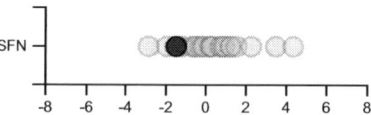

Rank		Player	BRR
20	32°	Pablo Sandoval	-0.65
21	31°	Justin Ruggiano	-1.14
22	22°	**Brandon Crawford**	**-1.44**
23	12°	Buster Posey	-1.49
24	4°	Evan Longoria	-1.90

Base Running Components

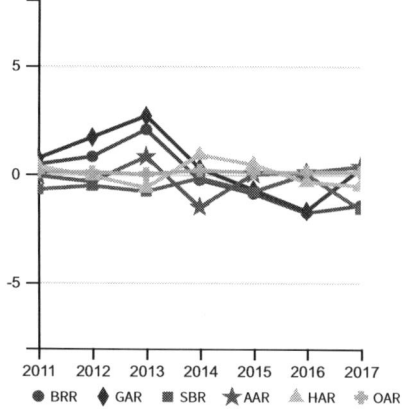

Nelson Cruz   DH   Seattle Mariners

Born: 7/1/1980   **Age:** 37   **Bats:** R   **Throws:** R   **Height:** 6' 2"   **Weight:** 230 lbs   **Draft Info:** International Free Agent, 1998

21
Sec/Pit

PACE
45th of 155
71°
Fast

2017 Daily WARP Profile
4.0 Total WARP

April — 2017 — September

Fantasy Values
2017	2018
$26.21	**$24.00**

YEAR	TEAM	LVL	AGE	PA	R	2B	3B	HR	RBI	BB	K	SB	AVG/OBP/SLG	TAv	VORP	BABIP	WARP
2017	SEA	MLB	36	645	91	28	0	39	119	70	140	1	.288/.375/.549	.312	40.4	.315	4.0

Thirty-seven-year-old power hitters aren't supposed to continue defying the age curve and providing an automatic 40 home runs, 90 runs, 100 RBI, and a .285 batting average, but this is exactly what Cruz has done since signing with Seattle. Cruz obviously won't do this forever, but there's no reason to discount him until his performance dictates otherwise. He's a DH-only in 2018, but this won't impact his draft or auction value. — Mike G.

2017 Batting Percentages

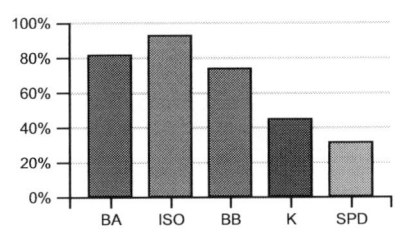

Batting PECOTA Percentiles

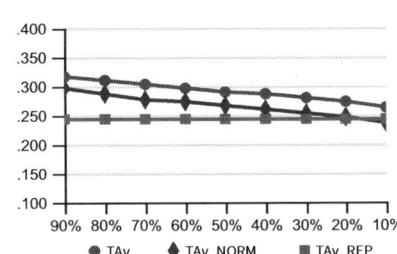

Batting WARP History

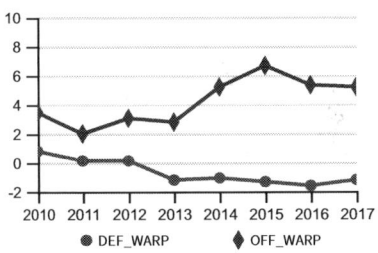

BRR (Relative to Position)

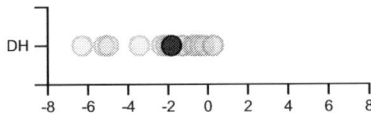

Rank		Player	BRR
8	73°	Matt Holliday	-1.27
9	65°	Hanley Ramirez	-1.78
10	55°	**Nelson Cruz**	**-1.78**
11	48°	Robbie Grossman	-1.86
12	40°	Ryon Healy	-2.05

BRR (Relative to Team)

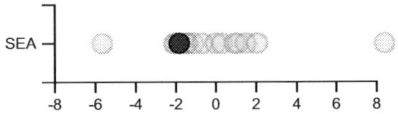

Rank		Player	BRR
11	42°	Mitch Haniger	-1.40
12	35°	Danny Valencia	-1.71
13	25°	**Nelson Cruz**	**-1.78**
14	17°	Robinson Cano	-1.98
15	9°	Ryon Healy	-2.05

Base Running Components

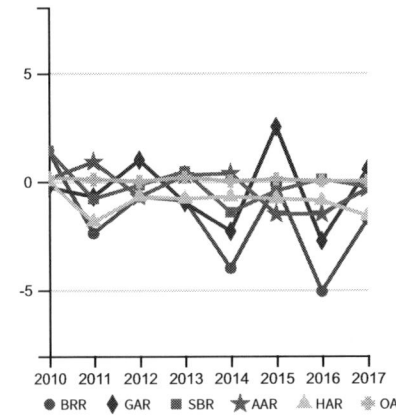

Johnny Cueto   RHP   San Francisco Giants

Born: 2/15/1986   **Age:** 32   **Bats:** R   **Throws:** R   **Height:** 5' 11"   **Weight:** 220 lbs   **Draft Info:** International Free Agent, 2004

PACE
19 Sec/Pit
16th of 150
89°
Very Fast

2017 Daily WARP Profile
0.8 Total WARP

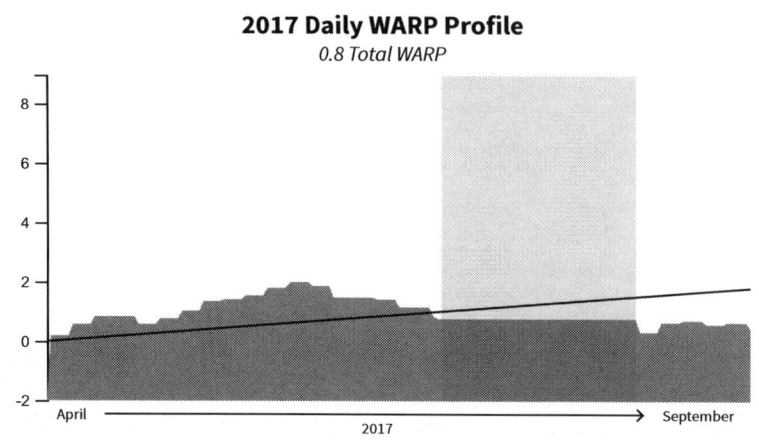

April ——————→ September
2017

Game 92: DL (finger blister)

POWER
39 PWR
100th of 150

STAMINA
69 STM
73rd of 150

COMMAND
60 CMD
37th of 150

Fantasy Values

2017	2018
$6.52	$11.00

YEAR	TEAM	LVL	AGE	W	L	SV	G	GS	IP	H	HR	BB/9	K/9	K	GB%	BABIP	WHIP	ERA	DRA	WARP	MPH 95
2017	SFN	MLB	31	8	8	0	25	25	147.1	160	22	3.2	8.3	136	41%	.322	1.45	4.52	5.07	0.8	93.1

Cueto's second full season with the Giants was a huge drop-off from his first. The right-hander's deceptive delivery didn't fool nearly as many hitters as it customarily did, and he would seem to have an inning in almost every game where he had nothing and was just hoping to make it out of the frame in one piece. Cueto's velocity has dropped in three consecutive seasons. While some pitchers adjust to a diminished heater, Cueto's price needs to drop below the ace premium he has been paid previously. — Mike G.

2017 Pitching Percentages

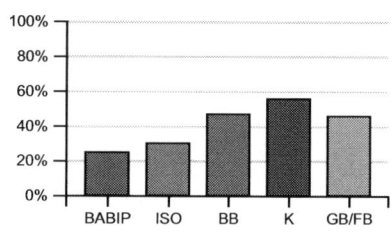

Pitching PECOTA Percentiles

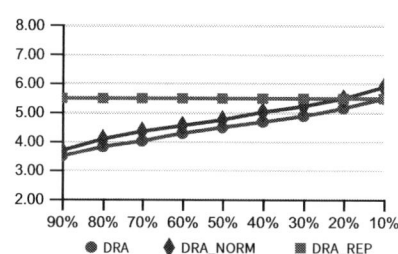

● DRA   ◆ DRA_NORM   ■ DRA_REP

Pitching WARP History

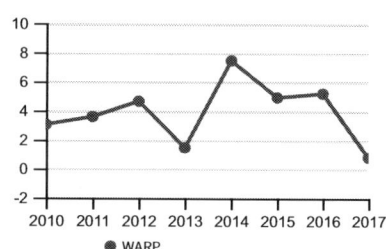

● WARP

Tunnel vs LHH

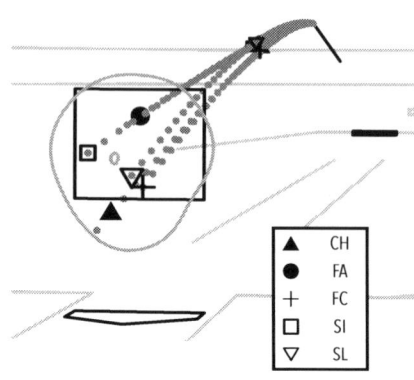

▲ CH
● FA
+ FC
□ SI
▽ SL

Pitch Types

Type	Freq	Velo	H Mov	V Mov
CH	19.5%	82 [88]	-10.5 [103]	-34.2 [80]
CU	0.2%	80.1 [107]	4.2 [86]	-39.4 [118]
FA	35.1%	91.6 [96]	-8.2 [95]	-15.7 [98]
FC	21.6%	85.7 [85]	1.3 [99]	-26.2 [90]
SI	16.2%	91.3 [94]	-13.1 [96]	-20.4 [99]
SL	7.3%	83.5 [96]	2.8 [92]	-30.8 [105]

Pitch Tunnel

Pairs	Release Diff	Tunnel Diff	Plate Diff	Speed Changes
1866	32.8	118.7	232.8	0.022

PI Scores

Year	Pitch Ct	Pwr	Cmd	Stm
2013	947	47	51	6
2014	3614	50	73	89
2015	3258	47	68	79
2016	3289	42	62	84
2017	2517	39	60	69

Tunnel vs RHH

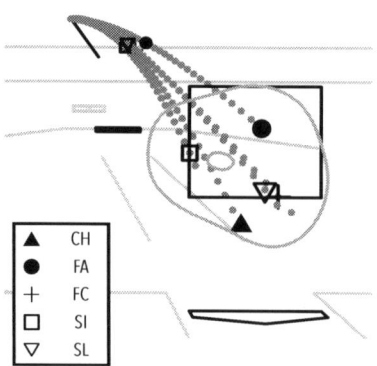

▲ CH
● FA
+ FC
□ SI
▽ SL

Yu Darvish   RHP   Los Angeles Dodgers

Born: 8/16/1986   **Age:** 31   **Bats:** R   **Throws:** R   **Height:** 6' 5"   **Weight:** 220 lbs   **Draft Info:** International Free Agent, 2012

We don't have a baseball card for this guy.

2017 Daily WARP Profile
5.2 Total WARP

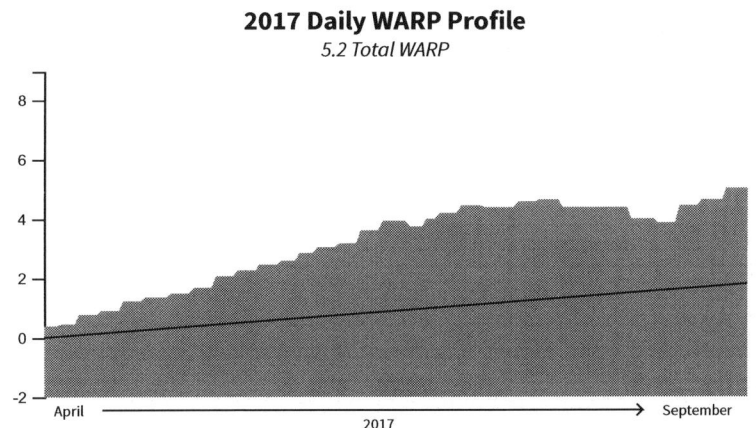

POWER
59 PWR
27th of 150

STAMINA
78 STM
25th of 150

COMMAND
42 CMD
128th of 150

23 Sec/Pit
PACE
126th of 150
16°
Very Slow

Fantasy Values
2017 $13.27   2018 $19.00

YEAR	TEAM	LVL	AGE	W	L	SV	G	GS	IP	H	HR	BB/9	K/9	K	GB%	BABIP	WHIP	ERA	DRA	WARP	MPH 95
2017	TEX	MLB	30	6	9	0	22	22	137	115	20	3.0	9.7	148	42%	.275	1.17	4.01	3.02	3.9	96.5
2017	LAN	MLB	30	4	3	0	9	9	49.2	44	7	2.4	11.1	61	45%	.308	1.15	3.44	3.24	1.3	96.4

All many will remember from Darvish's 2017 is a brutal World Series, but outside of a miserable July Darvish added yet another solid fantasy season to his résumé. It's easy to forget that 2017 was Darvish's first full year back from Tommy John surgery, and while he did pitch 100 1/3 innings in 2016 fatigue might have played a factor for him in the postseason. Darvish is a near-ace even when he isn't at his best, and while he will put up the occasional clunker he still is a top-tier arm who should be priced in or near the Top 10 — Mike G.

2017 Pitching Percentages

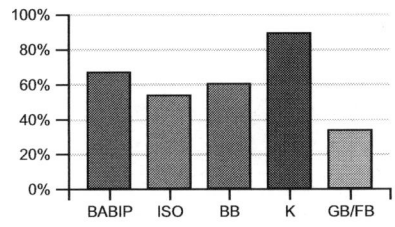

Pitching PECOTA Percentiles

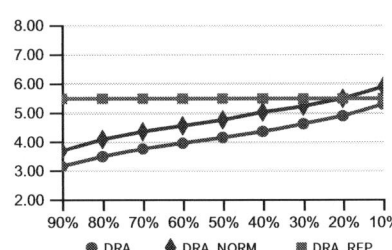

Pitching WARP History

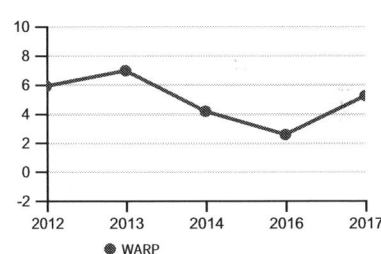

Tunnel vs LHH

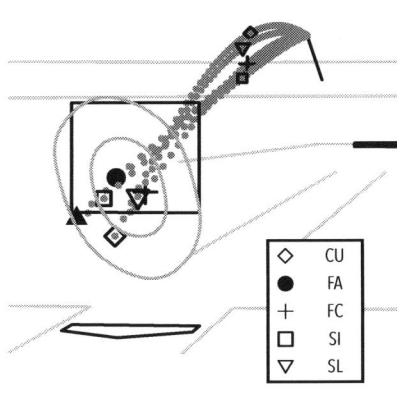

◇	CU
●	FA
+	FC
☐	SI
▽	SL

Pitch Types

Type	Freq	Velo	H Mov	V Mov
CH	1.7%	88.5 [114]	-9.1 [111]	-23 [111]
CS	1.0%	71 [107]	12.7 [108]	-64.9 [100]
CU	5.1%	73.9 [84]	11 [113]	-59.9 [75]
FA	35.4%	94.7 [107]	-2.9 [119]	-12.3 [109]
FC	15.4%	89 [103]	5.6 [120]	-27.2 [87]
FS	0.5%	88.5 [118]	-5 [111]	-26.6 [111]
SI	16.3%	93.9 [109]	-10.5 [115]	-18.3 [106]
SL	24.6%	82.8 [93]	15.6 [149]	-38.7 [83]

Pitch Tunnel

Pairs	Release Diff	Tunnel Diff	Plate Diff	Speed Changes
2265	27.9	128.4	226.7	0.036

PI Scores

Year	Pitch Ct	Pwr	Cmd	Stm
2012	3155	56	41	74
2013	3445	49	41	82
2014	2224	52	39	69
2016	1574	56	38	55
2017	3022	59	42	78

Tunnel vs RHH

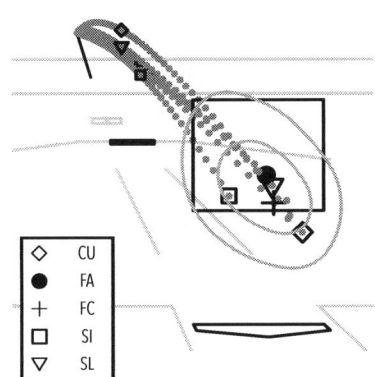

◇	CU
●	FA
+	FC
☐	SI
▽	SL

Zach Davies   RHP   Milwaukee Brewers

Born: 2/7/1993   **Age:** 25   **Bats:** R   **Throws:** R   **Height:** 6' 0"   **Weight:** 155 lbs   **Draft Info:** Round 26, 2011 Draft (#785 overall)

2017 Daily WARP Profile
3.4 Total WARP

April — 2017 — September

POWER
31 PWR 131st of 150

STAMINA
80 STM 14th of 150

COMMAND
73 CMD 7th of 150

19 Sec/Pit   **PACE**
16th of 150
89°
Very Fast

Fantasy Values

2017	2018
$14.59	$9.00

YEAR	TEAM	LVL	AGE	W	L	SV	G	GS	IP	H	HR	BB/9	K/9	K	GB%	BABIP	WHIP	ERA	DRA	WARP	MPH 95
2017	MIL	MLB	24	17	9	0	33	33	191.1	204	20	2.6	5.8	124	51%	.302	1.35	3.90	4.00	3.4	91.2

In his first full season as a starter, Davies' performance held up. His changeup keeps hitters off balance, and while it's unlikely that Davies will ever be a strikeout pitcher his DRA speaks to a lack of quality contact from opposing batters. The bad news in fantasy is that the low strikeout totals do hurt and while Davies' 17 wins were impressive it's a fool's errand to rely on wins as a constant from year to year. Davies is an okay mid-level starter in mixed, but if you roster him make sure you get enough strikeouts elsewhere. — Mike G.

2017 Pitching Percentages

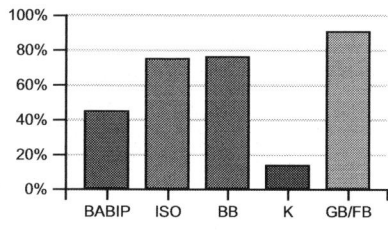

Pitching PECOTA Percentiles

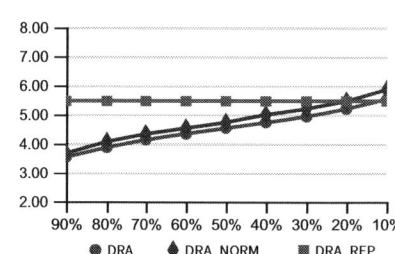

Pitching WARP History

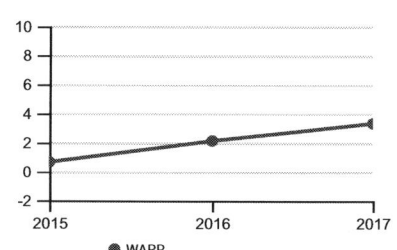

Tunnel vs LHH

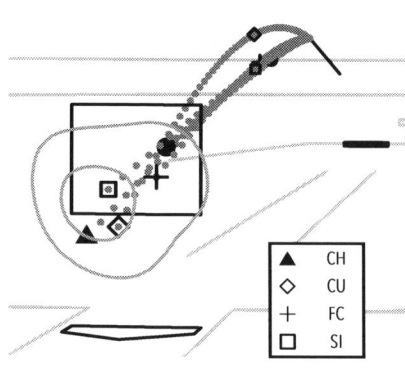

Pitch Types

Type	Freq	Velo	H Mov	V Mov
CH	13.9%	79.9 [79]	-13.2 [89]	-31.8 [86]
CU	15.4%	73.8 [83]	10.1 [109]	-58.1 [78]
FA	3.0%	90.1 [91]	-10.7 [83]	-15.5 [99]
FC	12.9%	86.9 [91]	1.3 [99]	-24.3 [98]
SI	54.7%	90.2 [87]	-14.2 [88]	-21.4 [95]

Pitch Tunnel

Pairs	Release Diff	Tunnel Diff	Plate Diff	Speed Changes
2169	27.9	121.1	212.6	0.037

PI Scores

Year	Pitch Ct	Pwr	Cmd	Stm
2015	539	29	61	67
2016	2586	35	81	72
2017	3060	31	73	80

Tunnel vs RHH

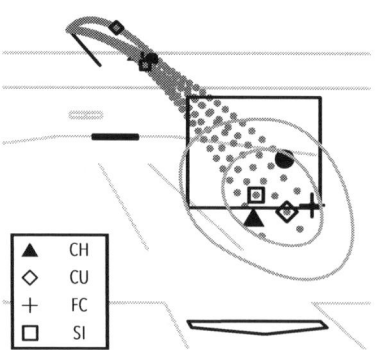

Chris Davis   1B   Baltimore Orioles

Born: 3/17/1986   **Age:** 32   **Bats:** L   **Throws:** R   **Height:** 6' 3"   **Weight:** 230 lbs   **Draft Info:** Round 5, 2006 Draft (#148 overall)

20 Sec/Pit

PACE
18th of 155
88°
Very Fast

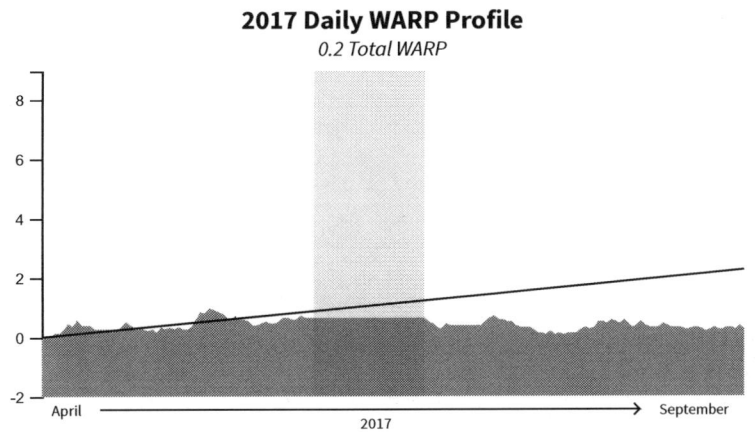

2017 Daily WARP Profile
0.2 Total WARP

Game 63: DL (oblique strain)

Fantasy Values	
2017	*2018*
$9.02	**$14.00**

YEAR	TEAM	LVL	AGE	PA	R	2B	3B	HR	RBI	BB	K	SB	AVG/OBP/SLG	TAv	VORP	BABIP	WARP
2017	BAL	MLB	31	524	65	15	1	26	61	61	195	1	.215/.309/.423	.250	-2.0	.301	.2

As recently as 2-3 years ago, fantasy teams could tolerate a terrible batting average if it was attached to herculean amounts of power. In 2017, this formula was a recipe for disaster. Davis can still launch one out of the park in any given at-bat, but so can nearly every other first baseman in the majors. While Davis has the potential to launch 50 bombs in any given season, his lousy batting averages make him a poor bet in anything outside of AL-only. — Mike G.

2017 Batting Percentages

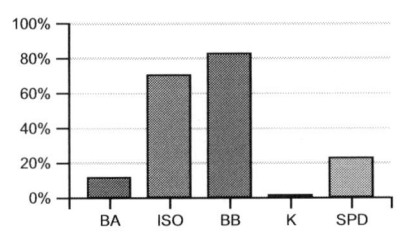

Batting PECOTA Percentiles

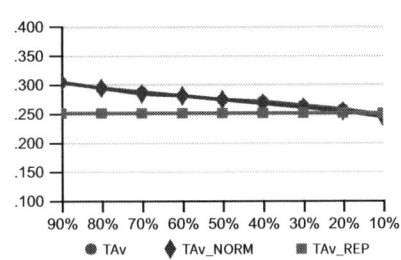

Batting WARP History

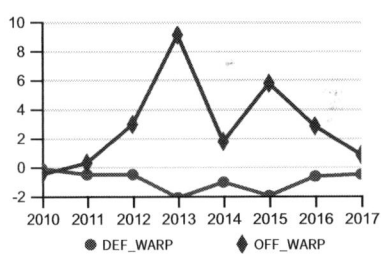

BRR (Relative to Position)

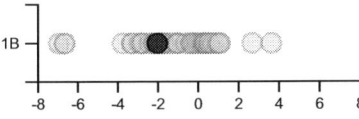

Rank		Player	BRR
31	41°	Carlos Santana	-1.88
32	38°	Mike Napoli	-1.90
33	36°	**Chris Davis**	**-1.98**
34	35°	Jefry Marte	-2.13
35	33°	C.J. Cron	-2.15

BRR (Relative to Team)

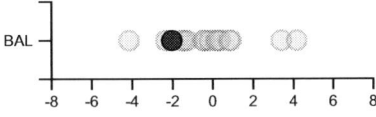

Rank		Player	BRR
12	32°	Seth Smith	-1.39
13	28°	J.J. Hardy	-1.50
14	21°	**Chris Davis**	**-1.98**
15	10°	Mark Trumbo	-2.28
16	0°	Manny Machado	-4.10

Base Running Components

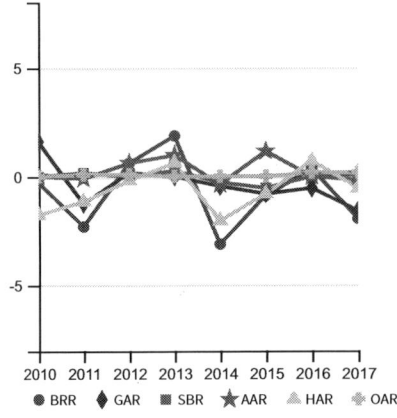

Khris Davis   LF   Oakland Athletics

Born: 12/21/1987   **Age:** 30   **Bats:** R   **Throws:** R   **Height:** 5' 10"   **Weight:** 195 lbs   **Draft Info:** Round 7, 2009 Draft (#226 overall)

2017 Daily WARP Profile
2.4 Total WARP

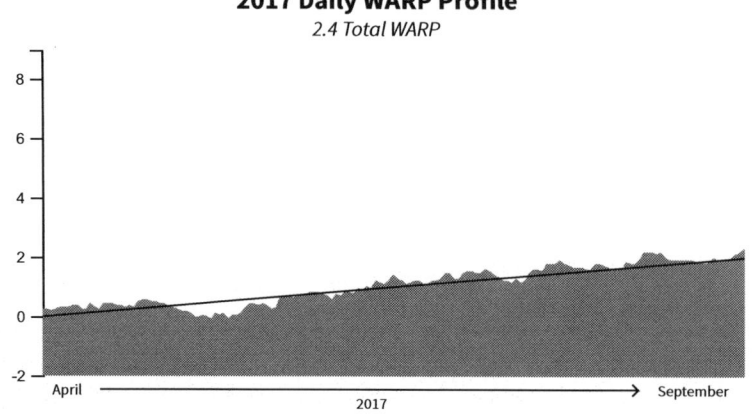

PACE
22 Sec/Pit
99th of 155
36°
Slow

Fantasy Values
2017	2018
$21.93	$22.00

YEAR	TEAM	LVL	AGE	PA	R	2B	3B	HR	RBI	BB	K	SB	AVG/OBP/SLG	TAv	VORP	BABIP	WARP
2017	OAK	MLB	29	652	91	28	1	43	110	73	195	4	.247/.336/.528	.289	32.3	.290	2.4

Consistency, thy name is Khris Davis. The overall package doesn't make him an elite hitter, but even though few believe in him, Davis has been a lock for 40 home runs with 100 RBI in a tough hitters' park. The average isn't pretty, but it isn't awful enough that it is a significant detriment to your squad. He has about as much business being in left field as the idiot who scaled the fence in the bottom of the sixth, but since defense doesn't count in fantasy be glad he's not limited to DH-only. — Mike G.

2017 Batting Percentages

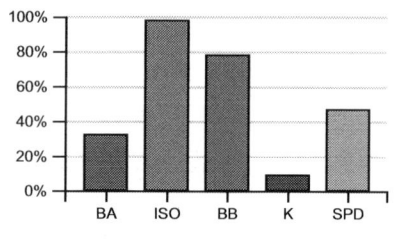

Batting PECOTA Percentiles

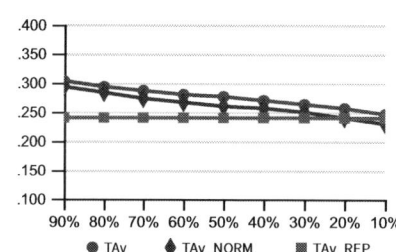

Batting WARP History

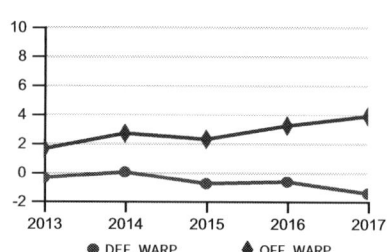

BRR (Relative to Position)

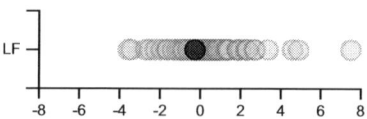

Rank		Player	BRR
45	36°	Rhys Hoskins	-0.11
46	35°	Chris Young	-0.11
47	32°	**Khris Davis**	**-0.22**
48	30°	Alex Gordon	-0.24
49	29°	Yasmany Tomas	-0.35

BRR (Relative to Team)

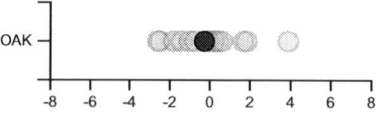

Rank		Player	BRR
8	52°	Josh Phegley	0.02
9	49°	Chris Carter	-0.01
10	39°	**Khris Davis**	**-0.22**
11	34°	Brandon Moss	-0.69
12	29°	Matt Chapman	-0.97

Base Running Components

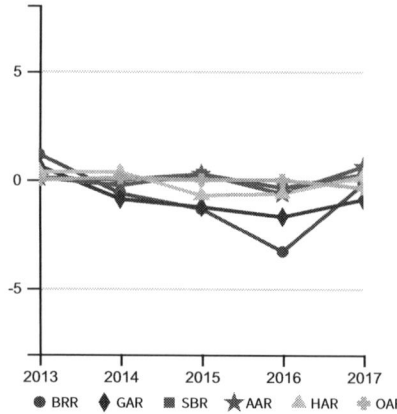

Jacob deGrom   RHP   New York Mets

Born: 6/19/1988 **Age:** 29 **Bats:** L **Throws:** R **Height:** 6' 4" **Weight:** 180 lbs **Draft Info:** Round 9, 2010 Draft (#272 overall)

2017 Daily WARP Profile
5.9 Total WARP

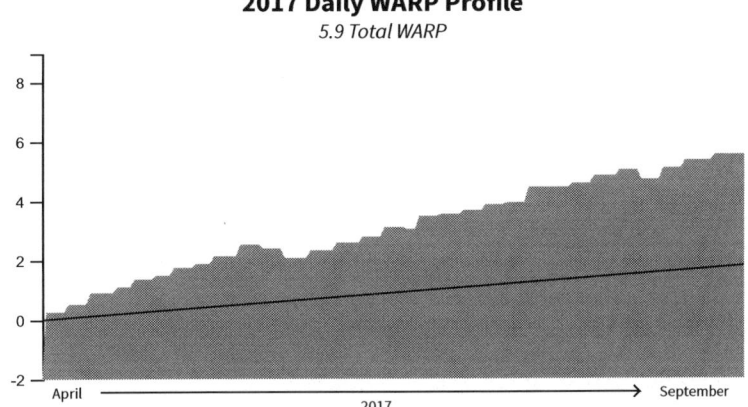

April — 2017 — September

PACE
20 Sec/Pit
37th of 150
75°
Fast

61 PWR **POWER** 23rd of 150

82 STM **STAMINA** 7th of 150

60 CMD **COMMAND** 37th of 150

Fantasy Values
2017	2018
$26.08	**$23.00**

YEAR	TEAM	LVL	AGE	W	L	SV	G	GS	IP	H	HR	BB/9	K/9	K	GB%	BABIP	WHIP	ERA	DRA	WARP	MPH 95
2017	NYN	MLB	29	15	10	0	31	31	201.1	180	28	2.6	10.7	239	48%	.305	1.19	3.53	2.92	5.9	97.2

On a team where every pitcher around him got hurt, deGrom was a constant. He reached 200 regular-season innings for the first time in his career and outside of a bumpy May was his usual reliable self. When he's at his best, deGrom's darting upper-90s fastball makes him virtually unhittable, but even on the days when the heater lacks movement he has enough confidence in his other pitches to keep himself and the Mets in the game. Betting on continued health from a Met seems risky, but deGrom is as a safe a bet on the Mets as you can find. — Mike G.

2017 Pitching Percentages

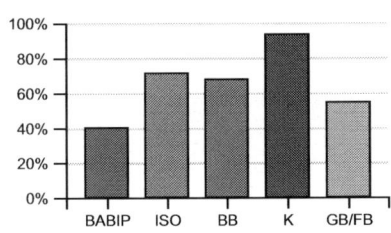

BABIP ISO BB K GB/FB

Pitching PECOTA Percentiles

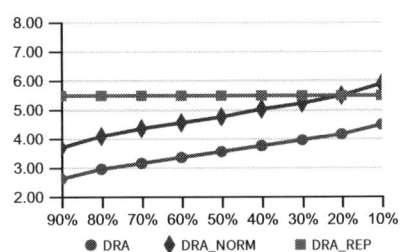

● DRA ◆ DRA_NORM ■ DRA_REP

Pitching WARP History

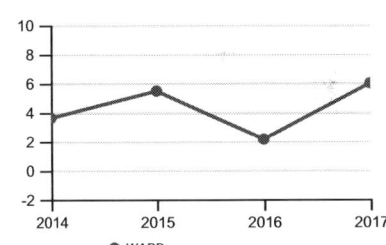

● WARP

Tunnel vs LHH

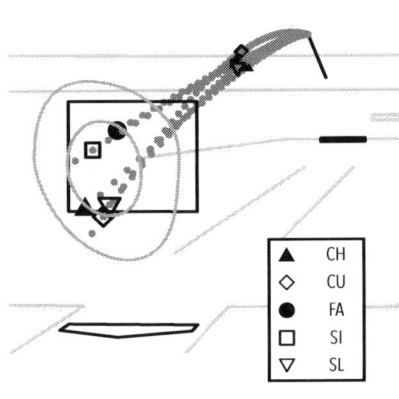

▲ CH
◇ CU
● FA
□ SI
▽ SL

Pitch Types

Type	Freq	Velo	H Mov	V Mov
CH	12.2%	88.2 [113]	-11.8 [96]	-25.1 [106]
CU	9.5%	81.8 [113]	6.8 [96]	-40.2 [116]
FA	38.7%	95.8 [111]	-4.8 [111]	-11.7 [111]
SI	16.8%	95.4 [118]	-11.9 [104]	-16.1 [114]
SL	22.8%	89.9 [124]	3.9 [97]	-25.6 [120]

Pitch Tunnel

Pairs	Release Diff	Tunnel Diff	Plate Diff	Speed Changes
2332	24.9	105.4	201.9	0.021

PI Scores

Year	Pitch Ct	Pwr	Cmd	Stm
2014	2223	57	64	72
2015	2963	62	62	72
2016	2350	54	58	66
2017	3158	61	60	82

Tunnel vs RHH

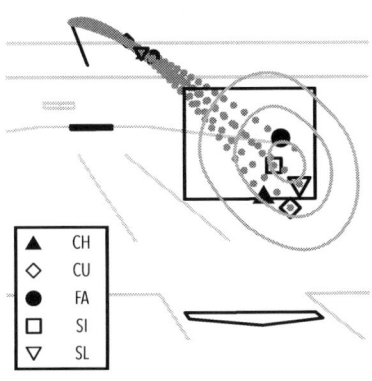

▲ CH
◇ CU
● FA
□ SI
▽ SL

Paul DeJong   SS   St. Louis Cardinals

Born: 8/2/1993   **Age:** 24   **Bats:** R   **Throws:** R   **Height:** 6' 1"   **Weight:** 195 lbs   **Draft Info:** Round 4, 2015 Draft (#131 overall)

21 Sec/Pit

PACE
45th of 155
71°
Fast

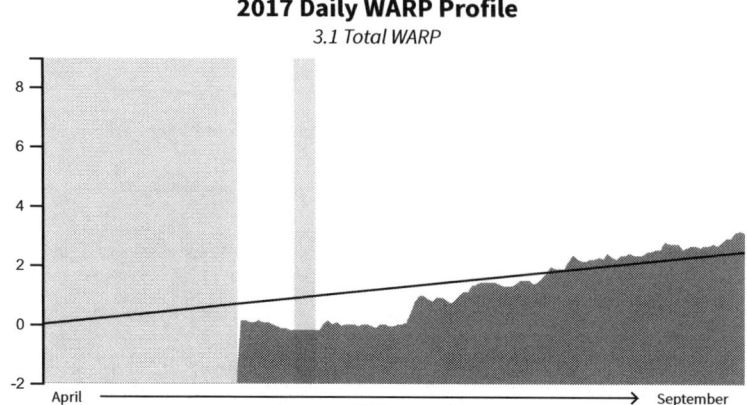

2017 Daily WARP Profile
3.1 Total WARP

2017   April → September

Game 1: minors, **Game 59:** minors

Fantasy Values
2017	2018
$16.37	**$18.00**

YEAR	TEAM	LVL	AGE	PA	R	2B	3B	HR	RBI	BB	K	SB	AVG/OBP/SLG	TAv	VORP	BABIP	WARP
2017	SLN	MLB	23	443	55	26	1	25	65	21	124	1	.285/.325/.532	.300	32.4	.349	3.1

Overlooked as a prospect because he was classified as future bench bat, DeJong emerged as a force, swatting a combined 38 home runs between Triple-A and St. Louis. While the BB/K rate does raise concerns about his batting average in the long term, DeJong's power is legitimate, so even if he slips in 2018 he should provide 20-25 home runs with eligibility at both shortstop and second base. — Mike G.

2017 Batting Percentages

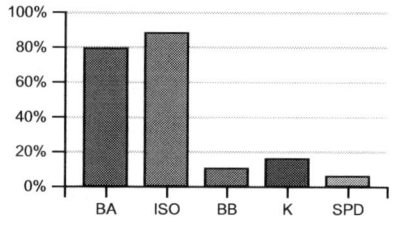

Batting PECOTA Percentiles

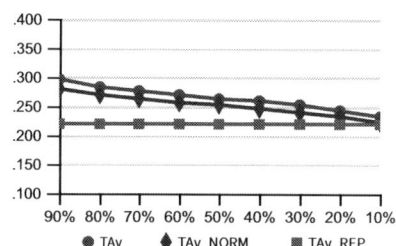

BRR (Relative to Position)

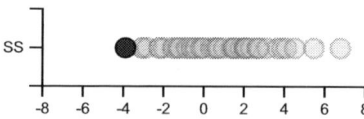

BRR (Relative to Team)

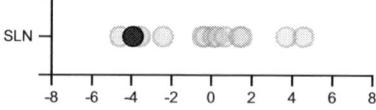

Rank		Player	BRR
45	8°	Adeiny Hechavarria	-2.18
46	5°	Zack Cozart	-2.78
47	4°	Troy Tulowitzki	-3.01
48	2°	Carlos Correa	-3.04
49	0°	**Paul DeJong**	**-3.86**

Rank		Player	BRR
9	38°	Jedd Gyorko	-0.40
10	25°	Matt Carpenter	-2.37
11	14°	Marcell Ozuna	-3.52
12	8°	**Paul DeJong**	**-3.86**
13	0°	Yadier Molina	-4.51

Chris Devenski   RHP   Houston Astros

Born: 11/13/1990   **Age:** 27   **Bats:** R   **Throws:** R   **Height:** 6' 3"   **Weight:** 210 lbs   **Draft Info:** Round 25, 2011 Draft (#771 overall)

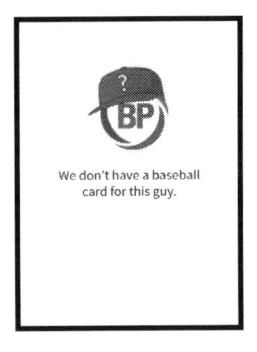

We don't have a baseball card for this guy.

2017 Daily WARP Profile
1.6 Total WARP

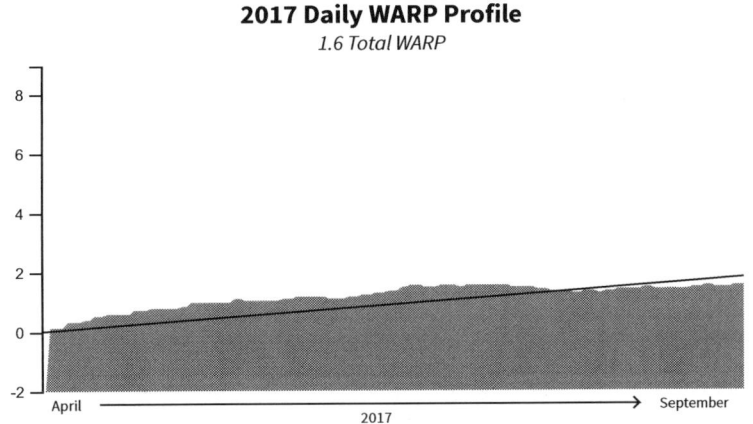

	POWER
39 PWR	100th of 150

	STAMINA
52 STM	128th of 150

	COMMAND
51 CMD	84th of 150

	PACE
20 Sec/Pit	37th of 150 75° Fast

Fantasy Values

2017	2018
$17.54	**$8.00**

YEAR	TEAM	LVL	AGE	W	L	SV	G	GS	IP	H	HR	BB/9	K/9	K	GB%	BABIP	WHIP	ERA	DRA	WARP	MPH 95
2017	HOU	MLB	26	8	5	4	62	0	80.2	50	11	2.9	11.2	100	41%	.220	0.94	2.68	3.40	1.6	95.5

The Astros committed to using Devenski as a multi-inning reliever and were rewarded with a terrific season from the 27-year-old right-hander. In fantasy, noncloser relievers are tough to properly value, but Devenski's high strikeout totals and ability to vulture wins on a team that uses its bullpen liberally make him an asset in any format. — Mike G.

2017 Pitching Percentages

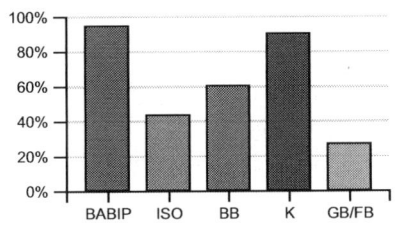

Pitching PECOTA Percentiles

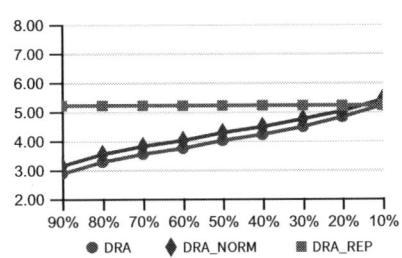

● DRA   ◆ DRA_NORM   ■ DRA_REP

Pitching WARP History

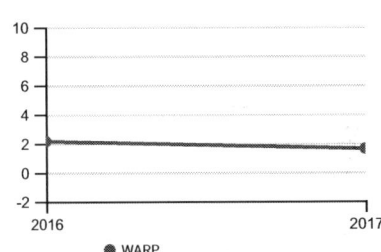

● WARP

Tunnel vs LHH

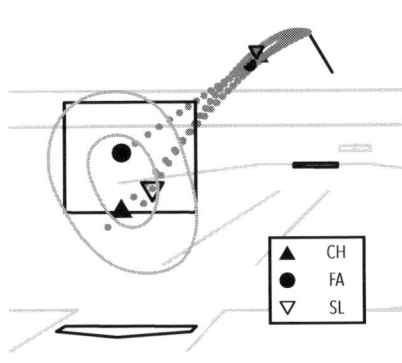

▲ CH
● FA
▽ SL

Pitch Types

Type	Freq	Velo	H Mov	V Mov
CH	38.2%	83.4 [93]	-11.5 [98]	-31.2 [88]
CU	0.2%	81.5 [112]	4.2 [86]	-40.6 [116]
FA	39.6%	94.3 [106]	-10 [87]	-11.8 [111]
SL	22.1%	83.1 [94]	5.2 [103]	-32.8 [100]

Pitch Tunnel

Pairs	Release Diff	Tunnel Diff	Plate Diff	Speed Changes
936	25.7	119.2	222.3	0.026

PI Scores

Year	Pitch Ct	Pwr	Cmd	Stm
2016	1576	39	56	53
2017	1263	39	51	52

Tunnel vs RHH

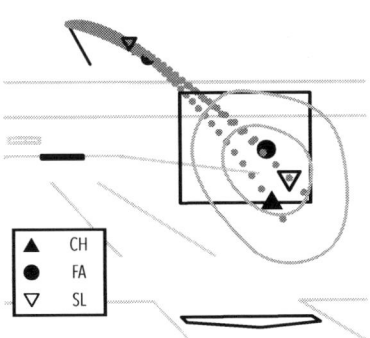

▲ CH
● FA
▽ SL

Corey Dickerson LF Tampa Bay Rays

Born: 5/22/1989 **Age:** 29 **Bats:** L **Throws:** R **Height:** 6' 1" **Weight:** 200 lbs **Draft Info:** Round 8, 2010 Draft (#260 overall)

2017 Daily WARP Profile
3.9 Total WARP

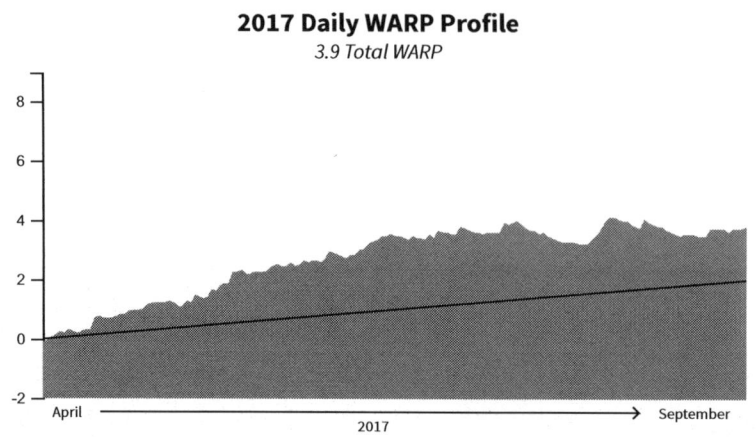

24 Sec/Pit

PACE
146th of 155
6°
Very Slow

Fantasy Values

2017	2018
$19.87	$16.00

YEAR	TEAM	LVL	AGE	PA	R	2B	3B	HR	RBI	BB	K	SB	AVG/OBP/SLG	TAv	VORP	BABIP	WARP
2017	TBA	MLB	28	629	84	33	4	27	62	35	152	4	.282/.325/.490	.284	24.9	.338	3.9

It was a tale of two seasons for Dickerson, who hit like he was back at Coors Field in the first half but then fell off the cliff in the second. He wasn't injured, and his overall numbers looked very similar to his 2016 line when all was said and done, so it is possible that Dickerson was fine, and his swoon was simply regression to the mean. Dickerson is a solid play in deeper formats, but until he can string two strong halves together he is more of a back-end option in mixed than a top-tier outfielder. — Mike G.

2017 Batting Percentages

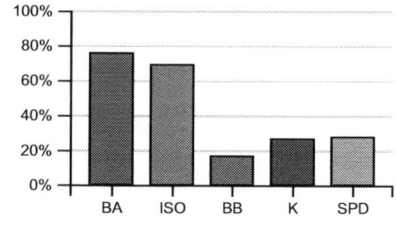

Batting PECOTA Percentiles

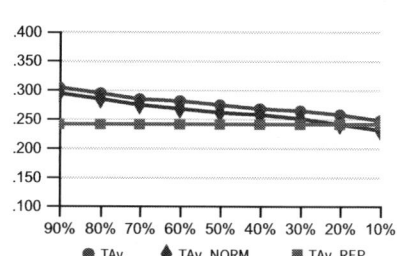

Batting WARP History

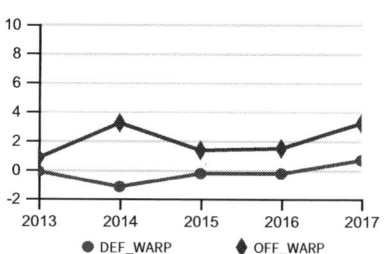

BRR (Relative to Position)

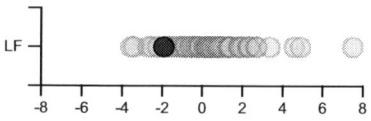

Rank		Player	BRR
59	16°	Eddie Rosario	-1.60
60	13°	Melky Cabrera	-1.60
61	10°	**Corey Dickerson**	**-1.88**
62	8°	Adam Duvall	-2.18
63	6°	Gerardo Parra	-2.47

BRR (Relative to Team)

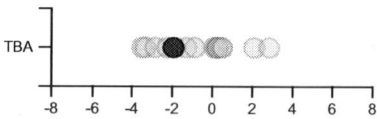

Rank		Player	BRR
12	41°	Brad Miller	-1.26
13	29°	Steven Souza	-1.85
14	18°	**Corey Dickerson**	**-1.88**
15	13°	Adeiny Hechavarria	-2.18
16	11°	Christian Arroyo	-2.77

Base Running Components

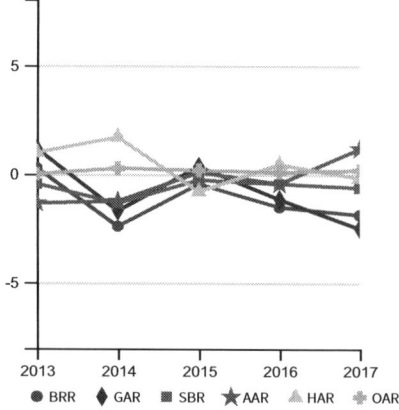

R.A. Dickey   RHP   Atlanta Braves

Born: 10/29/1974   **Age:** 43   **Bats:** R   **Throws:** R   **Height:** 6' 3"   **Weight:** 215 lbs   **Draft Info:** Round 1, 1996 Draft (#18 overall)

2017 Daily WARP Profile
2.0 Total WARP

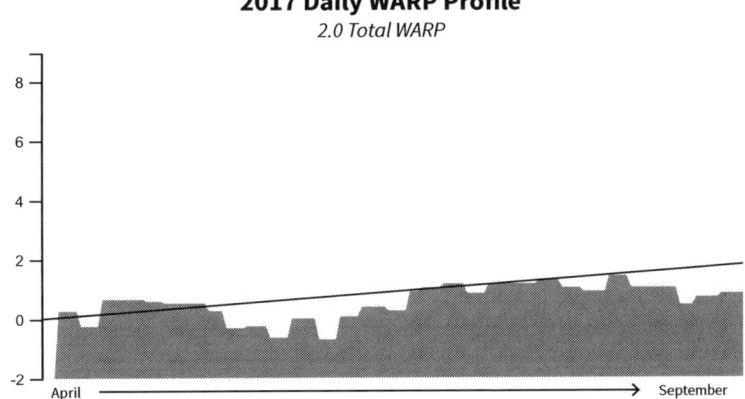

POWER
0 PWR
149th of 150

STAMINA
78 STM
25th of 150

COMMAND
69 CMD
12th of 150

PACE
18 Sec/Pit
5th of 150
97°
Very Fast

Fantasy Values
2017	2018
$9.53	$2.00

YEAR	TEAM	LVL	AGE	W	L	SV	G	GS	IP	H	HR	BB/9	K/9	K	GB%	BABIP	WHIP	ERA	DRA	WARP	MPH 95
2017	ATL	MLB	42	10	10	0	31	31	190	193	26	3.2	6.4	136	48%	.290	1.37	4.26	4.65	2.0	85.4

2017 Pitching Percentages

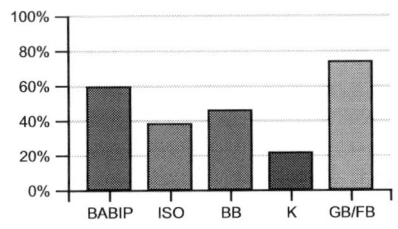

Pitching PECOTA Percentiles

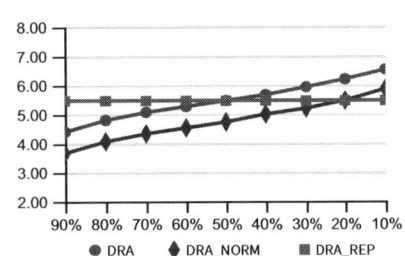

Pitching WARP History

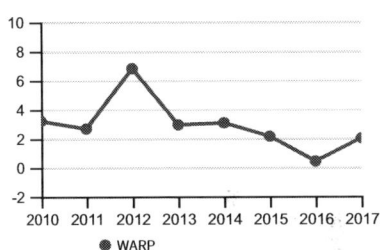

Tunnel vs LHH

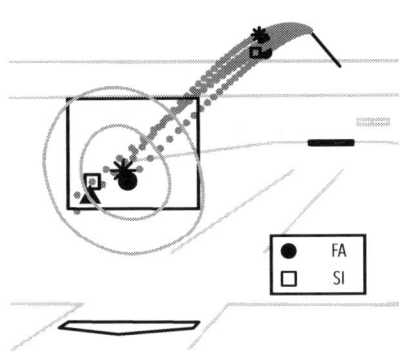

	FA
●	
□	SI

Pitch Types

Type	Freq	Velo	H Mov	V Mov
CH	3.7%	72.3 [49]	-12.4 [93]	-38.8 [66]
CU	0.1%	70.7 [72]	7.6 [99]	-53.1 [89]
FA	7.1%	83.9 [68]	-9.2 [90]	-22.4 [77]
KN	77.8%	77.7 [113]	1 [96]	-38.3 [115]
SI	11.3%	83.8 [50]	-13.7 [91]	-26.8 [75]
SL	0.1%	78.9 [76]	5.1 [102]	-30.8 [105]

Pitch Tunnel

Pairs	Release Diff	Tunnel Diff	Plate Diff	Speed Changes
1983	27.3	106.3	211.9	0.025

PI Scores

Year	Pitch Ct	Pwr	Cmd	Stm
2013	3503	0	70	87
2014	3498	0	70	85
2015	3257	0	51	81
2016	2727	0	57	73
2017	2859	0	69	78

Tunnel vs RHH

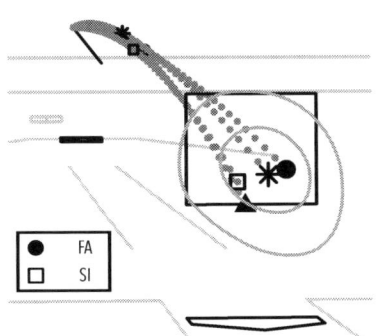

	FA
●	
□	SI

Josh Donaldson   3B   Toronto Blue Jays

Born: 12/8/1985   **Age:** 32   **Bats:** R   **Throws:** R   **Height:** 6' 1"   **Weight:** 210 lbs   **Draft Info:** Round 1, 2007 Draft (#48 overall)

PACE
99th of 155
36°
Slow

22
Sec/Pit

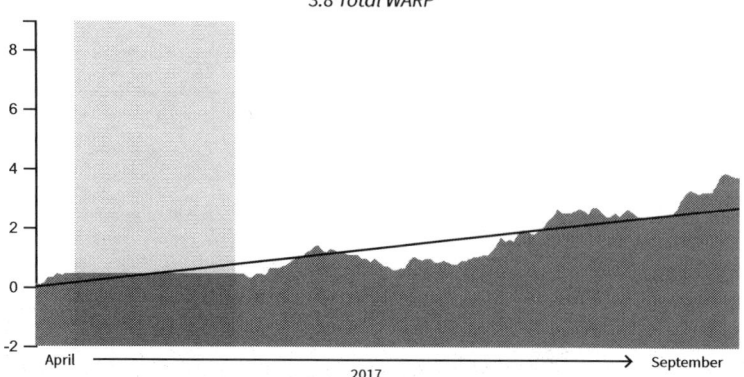

2017 Daily WARP Profile
3.8 Total WARP

Game 10: DL (calf soreness)

Fantasy Values
2017	2018
$18.02	$31.00

YEAR	TEAM	LVL	AGE	PA	R	2B	3B	HR	RBI	BB	K	SB	AVG/OBP/SLG	TAv	VORP	BABIP	WARP
2017	TOR	MLB	31	496	65	21	0	33	78	76	111	2	.270/.385/.559	.311	43.9	.289	3.8

Between a strained calf that knocked him out of commission for six weeks and a tepid first half, 2017 looked like a lost year for Donaldson before he went on a ridiculous tear, smacking 22 home runs in his final 50 games. Donaldson finished with his typically robust numbers despite the lousy first half. Assuming complete health in 2018, Donaldson should once again be a late-first-round player in mixers and a low $30s one in AL-only. — Mike G.

2017 Batting Percentages

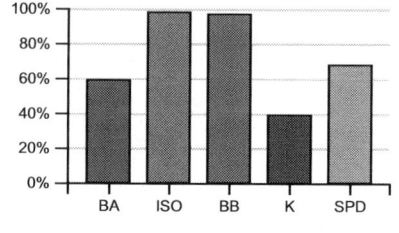

Batting PECOTA Percentiles

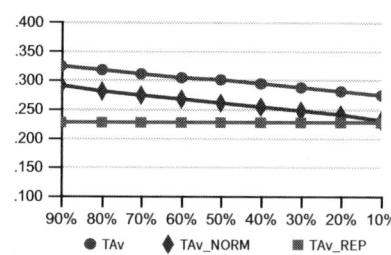

Batting WARP History

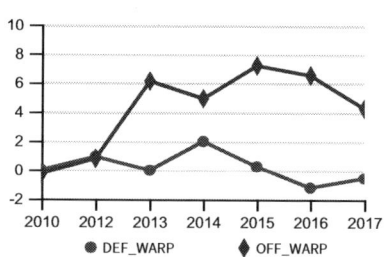

BRR (Relative to Position)

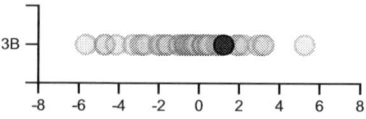

Rank		Player	BRR
7	81°	Jake Lamb	1.96
8	77°	Kris Bryant	1.90
9	75°	**Josh Donaldson**	**1.27**
10	75°	Sean Rodriguez	1.11
11	74°	Brian Anderson	0.98

BRR (Relative to Team)

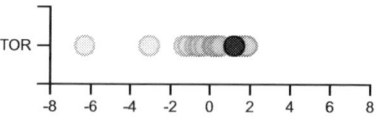

Rank		Player	BRR
5	97°	Richard Urena	1.43
6	95°	Michael Saunders	1.29
7	88°	**Josh Donaldson**	**1.27**
8	84°	Devon Travis	1.23
9	74°	Justin Smoak	0.60

Base Running Components

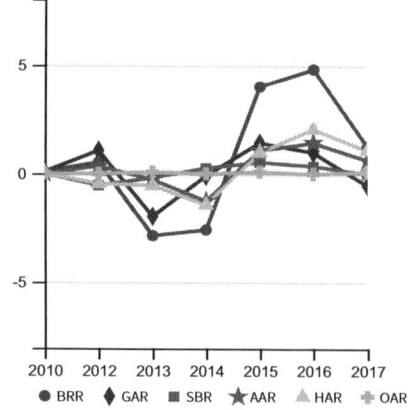

Brian Dozier   2B   Minnesota Twins

Born: 5/15/1987   **Age:** 31   **Bats:** R   **Throws:** R   **Height:** 5' 11"   **Weight:** 200 lbs   **Draft Info:** Round 8, 2009 Draft (#252 overall)

PACE
21 Sec/Pit
45th of 155
71°
Fast

2017 Daily WARP Profile
4.7 Total WARP

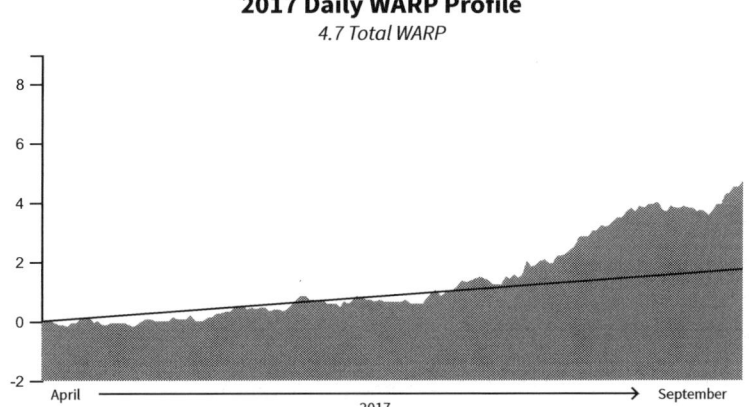

Fantasy Values
2017	2018
$27.35	$30.00

YEAR	TEAM	LVL	AGE	PA	R	2B	3B	HR	RBI	BB	K	SB	AVG/OBP/SLG	TAv	VORP	BABIP	WARP
2017	MIN	MLB	30	705	106	30	4	34	93	78	141	16	.271/.359/.498	.280	37.0	.300	4.7

While Dozier's encore wasn't quite as impressive as his 2016 breakout campaign, his 34 home runs and 16 steals were almost as good and made Dozier a Top 25 player for the second year running. Dozier repeated his pattern of a slow start followed by a fast finish, so if you draft Dozier patience is the watchword. The batting average prevents Dozier from being an elite pick, but after the Joses (Altuve and Ramirez) are off the board, Dozier is the obvious call. — Mike G.

2017 Batting Percentages

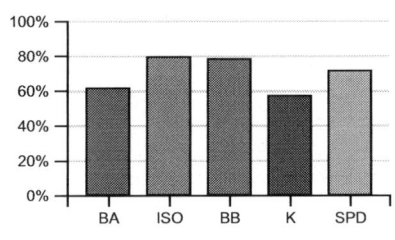

Batting PECOTA Percentiles

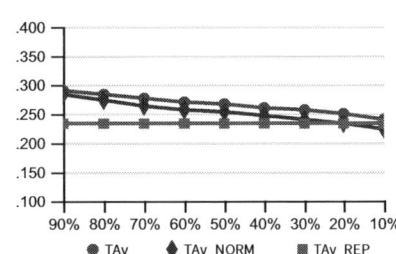

Batting WARP History

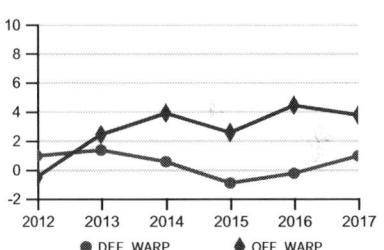

BRR (Relative to Position)

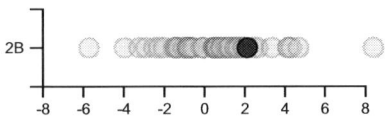

Rank		Player	BRR
7	77°	Jose Altuve	2.68
8	74°	Brandon Phillips	2.46
9	71°	**Brian Dozier**	**2.17**
10	69°	Chase Utley	2.02
11	68°	Cliff Pennington	1.95

BRR (Relative to Team)

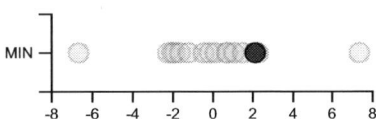

Rank		Player	BRR
1	90°	Byron Buxton	7.39
2	84°	Eduardo Escobar	2.30
3	71°	**Brian Dozier**	**2.17**
4	67°	Ehire Adrianza	1.55
5	64°	Kennys Vargas	1.12

Base Running Components

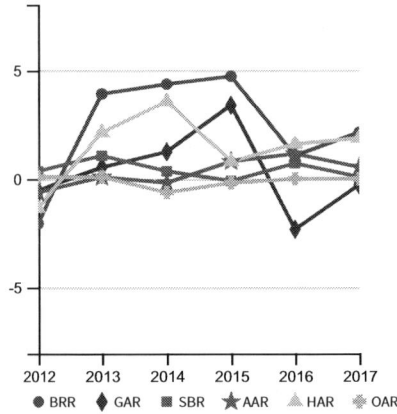

Danny Duffy   LHP   Kansas City Royals

Born: 12/21/1988   **Age:** 29   **Bats:** L   **Throws:** L   **Height:** 6' 3"   **Weight:** 205 lbs   **Draft Info:** Round 3, 2007 Draft (#96 overall)

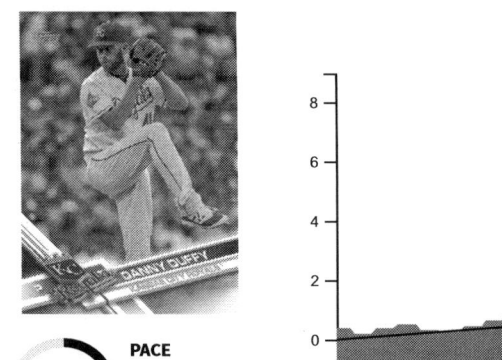

2017 Daily WARP Profile
2.8 Total WARP

April — 2017 — September

POWER 42 PWR — 86th of 150

STAMINA 64 STM — 89th of 150

COMMAND 47 CMD — 102nd of 150

PACE 21 Sec/Pit — 81st of 150 — 46° — Average

Game 50: DL (oblique strain), **Game 125:** DL (elbow impingement)

Fantasy Values
2017	2018
$12.86	$14.00

YEAR	TEAM	LVL	AGE	W	L	SV	G	GS	IP	H	HR	BB/9	K/9	K	GB%	BABIP	WHIP	ERA	DRA	WARP	MPH 95
2017	KCA	MLB	28	9	10	0	24	24	146.1	143	13	2.5	8.0	130	41%	.309	1.26	3.81	3.85	2.8	94.8

For the second consecutive season, Duffy started the year looking like an ace-in-the-making before his numbers faded down the stretch. In 2016 this was chalked up to fatigue, but last year he was diagnosed with loose bodies in his elbow that had to be surgically removed in October. If he's healthy, Duffy is a borderline ace with electric stuff, but durability and resiliency down the stretch has always been a question and does tamp down his fantasy value somewhat. — Mike G.

2017 Pitching Percentages

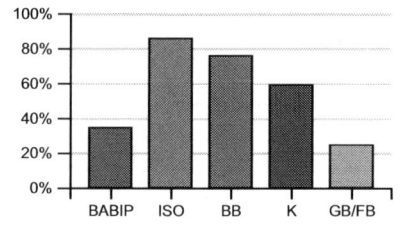

Pitching PECOTA Percentiles

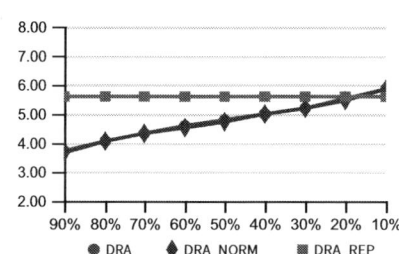

Pitching WARP History

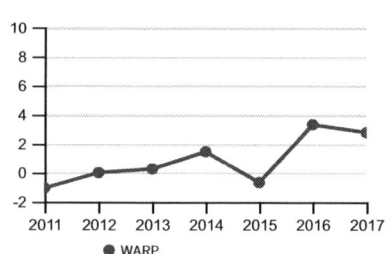

Tunnel vs LHH

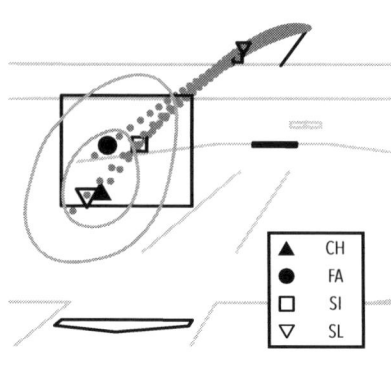

Pitch Types

Type	Freq	Velo	H Mov	V Mov
CH	22.8%	84.2 [96]	13.7 [86]	-23.6 [110]
CU	0.9%	75.2 [89]	-7.4 [99]	-54.4 [86]
FA	28.0%	93.4 [102]	5.7 [106]	-11.4 [112]
SI	19.3%	93.2 [105]	10.6 [114]	-14.1 [122]
SL	28.9%	83.5 [96]	-3.4 [95]	-35.7 [91]

Pitch Tunnel

Pairs	Release Diff	Tunnel Diff	Plate Diff	Speed Changes
1729	29.0	110.1	211.3	0.027

PI Scores

Year	Pitch Ct	Pwr	Cmd	Stm
2013	467	59	42	55
2014	2300	58	47	62
2015	2358	57	40	63
2016	2706	55	49	72
2017	2271	42	47	64

Tunnel vs RHH

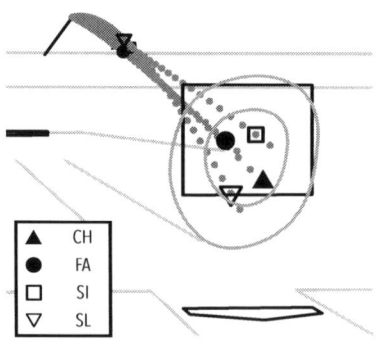

Adam Duvall   LF   Cincinnati Reds

Born: 9/4/1988   **Age:** 29   **Bats:** R   **Throws:** R   **Height:** 6' 1"   **Weight:** 215 lbs   **Draft Info:** Round 11, 2010 Draft (#348 overall)

PACE
23
Sec/Pit
135th of 155
13°
Very Slow

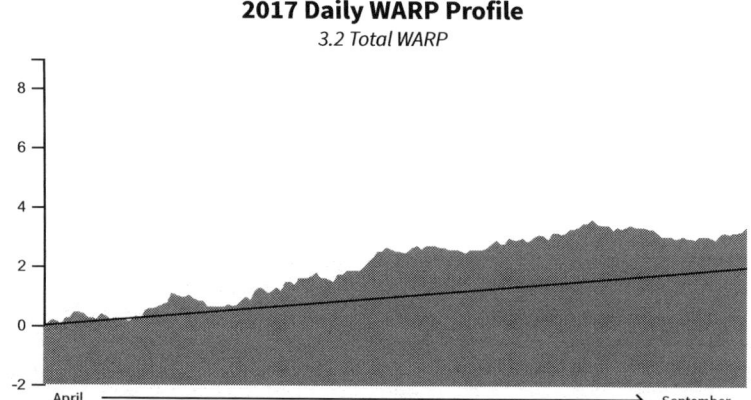

2017 Daily WARP Profile
3.2 Total WARP

Fantasy Values

	2017	2018
	$18.77	**$15.00**

YEAR	TEAM	LVL	AGE	PA	R	2B	3B	HR	RBI	BB	K	SB	AVG/OBP/SLG	TAv	VORP	BABIP	WARP
2017	CIN	MLB	28	647	78	37	3	31	99	39	170	5	.249/.301/.480	.279	25.0	.290	3.2

A popular bust pick entering the season due to a poor second half in 2016, Duvall followed up with a near carbon copy of his 2016 breakout. Duvall disproved the doubters with a sizzling 20 home runs in the first half but then gave them credence with a collapse in the second. His 81/18 K/BB ratio in 292 plate appearances after the All-Star break was particularly troubling, and his .212 batting average made him unplayable in mixers. Duvall's power makes him worth owning everywhere, but the risk is higher than it is for most 30+ home-run hitters. — Mike G.

2017 Batting Percentages

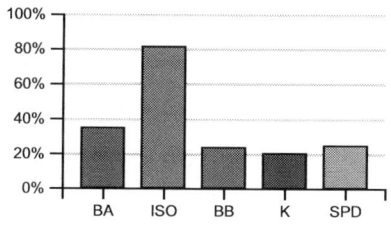

Batting PECOTA Percentiles

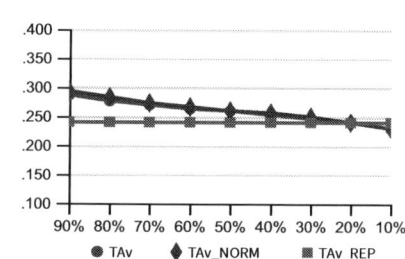

Batting WARP History

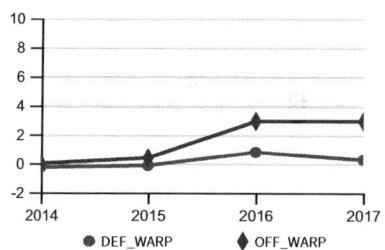

BRR (Relative to Position)

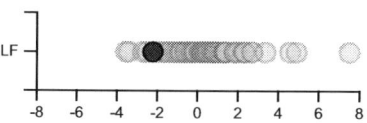

Rank		Player	BRR
60	13°	Melky Cabrera	-1.60
61	10°	Corey Dickerson	-1.88
62	8°	**Adam Duvall**	**-2.18**
63	6°	Gerardo Parra	-2.47
64	4°	Nori Aoki	-2.67

BRR (Relative to Team)

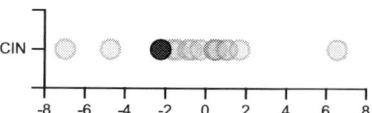

Rank		Player	BRR
12	37°	Scooter Gennett	-1.36
13	31°	Tucker Barnhart	-1.63
14	23°	**Adam Duvall**	**-2.18**
15	13°	Eugenio Suarez	-4.67
16	0°	Joey Votto	-6.92

Base Running Components

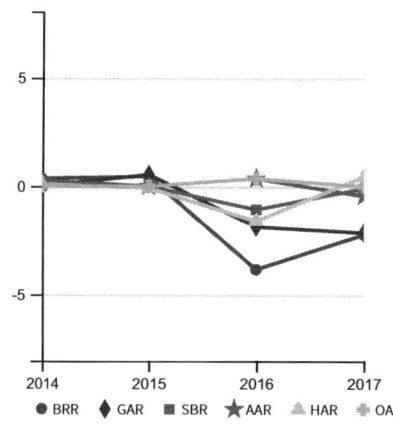

Carl Edwards Jr.   RHP   Chicago Cubs

Born: 9/3/1991   **Age:** 26   **Bats:** R   **Throws:** R   **Height:** 6'3"   **Weight:** 170 lbs   **Draft Info:** Round 48, 2011 Draft (#1464 overall)

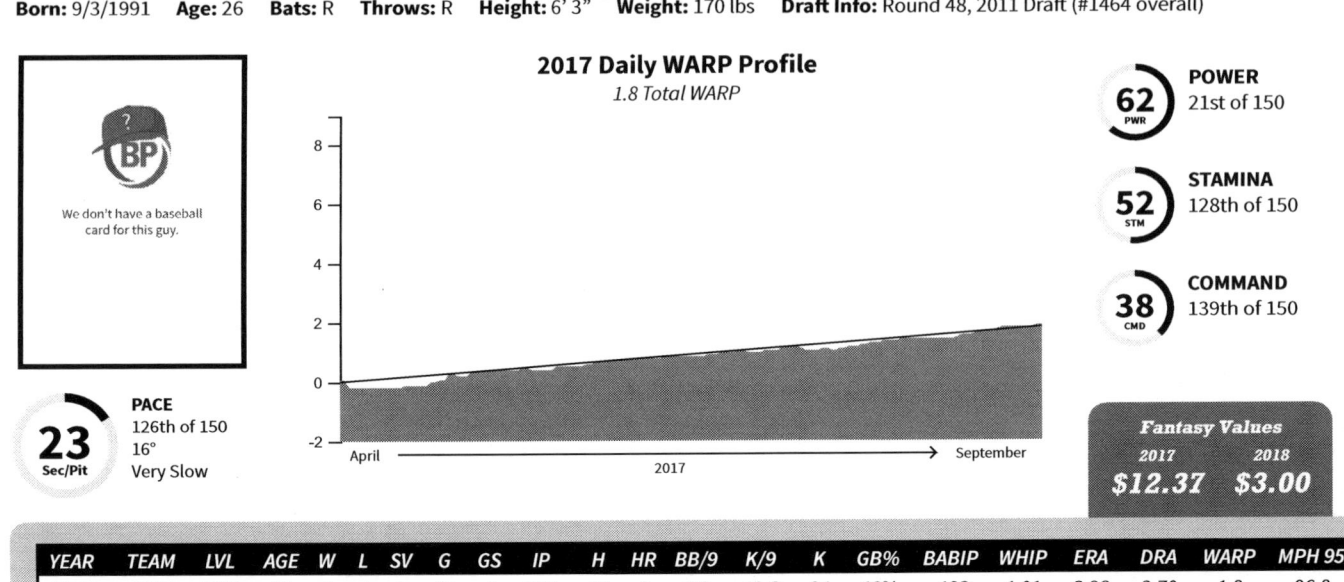

2017 Daily WARP Profile
1.8 Total WARP

62 PWR — **POWER** — 21st of 150

52 STM — **STAMINA** — 128th of 150

38 CMD — **COMMAND** — 139th of 150

23 Sec/Pit — **PACE** — 126th of 150 / 16° / Very Slow

Fantasy Values

2017	2018
$12.37	$3.00

YEAR	TEAM	LVL	AGE	W	L	SV	G	GS	IP	H	HR	BB/9	K/9	K	GB%	BABIP	WHIP	ERA	DRA	WARP	MPH 95
2017	CHN	MLB	25	5	4	0	73	0	66.1	29	6	5.2	12.8	94	46%	.193	1.01	2.98	2.70	1.8	96.8

2017 Pitching Percentages

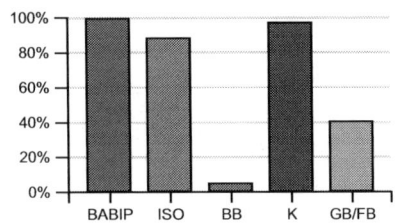

Pitching PECOTA Percentiles

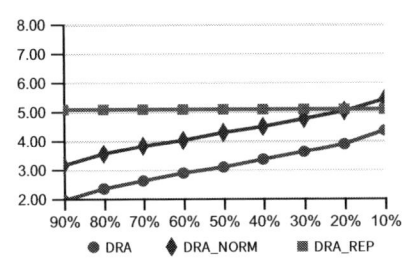

Pitching WARP History

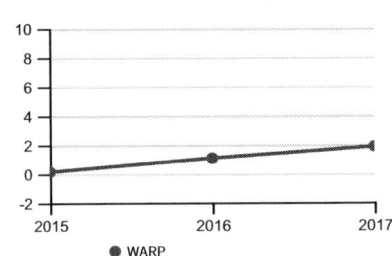

Tunnel vs LHH

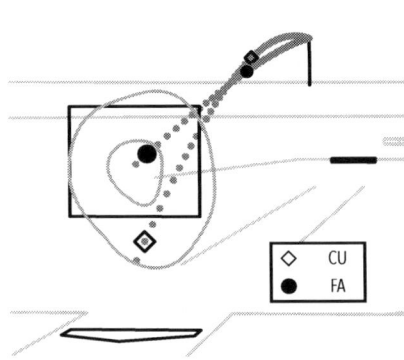

Pitch Types

Type	Freq	Velo	H Mov	V Mov
CH	0.1%	91.4 [125]	-10.8 [102]	-23.7 [109]
CU	29.9%	81.7 [113]	9.7 [108]	-46.2 [104]
FA	70.0%	95.5 [110]	0.7 [136]	-12.1 [110]

Pitch Tunnel

Pairs	Release Diff	Tunnel Diff	Plate Diff	Speed Changes
870	26.0	121.7	237.8	0.027

PI Scores

Year	Pitch Ct	Pwr	Cmd	Stm
2016	622	59	48	46
2017	1128	62	38	52

Tunnel vs RHH

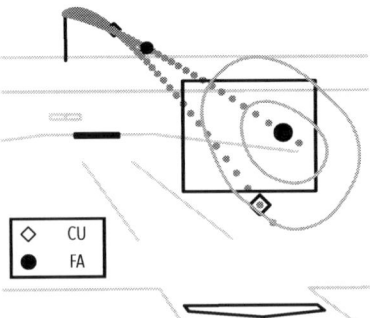

Edwin Encarnacion   1B   Cleveland Indians

Born: 1/7/1983   **Age:** 35   **Bats:** R   **Throws:** R   **Height:** 6' 1"   **Weight:** 230 lbs   **Draft Info:** Round 9, 2000 Draft (#274 overall)

PACE
20 Sec/Pit
18th of 155
88°
Very Fast

2017 Daily WARP Profile
2.7 Total WARP

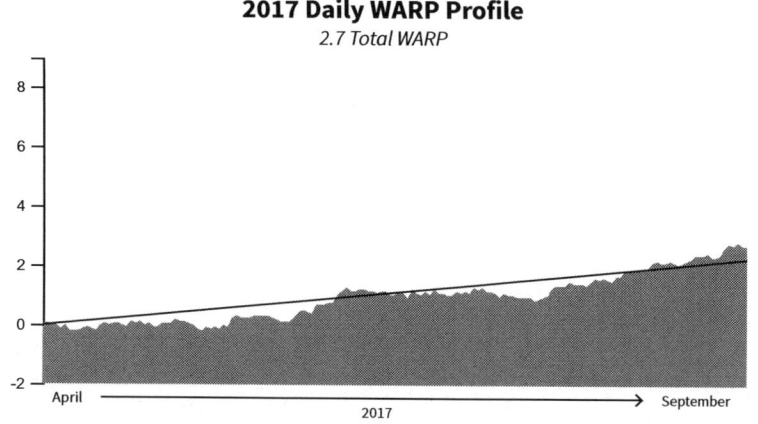

Fantasy Values
2017   2018
$21.87 $25.00

YEAR	TEAM	LVL	AGE	PA	R	2B	3B	HR	RBI	BB	K	SB	AVG/OBP/SLG	TAv	VORP	BABIP	WARP
2017	CLE	MLB	34	669	96	20	1	38	107	104	133	2	.258/.377/.504	.297	27.6	.271	2.7

A slow start led to whispers about whether Encarnacion was going to be a free agent bust, but the veteran first sacker quickly cast the doubts aside and finished with yet another strong season. When the dust settled, Encarnacion had his third consecutive season with at least 38 home runs, 94 runs, and 107 RBI. Despite his advancing age, Encarnacion is money in the bank, and remains a solid fourth- or fifth-round investment despite the altered home-run context dragging his overall value down ever so slightly. — Mike G.

2017 Batting Percentages

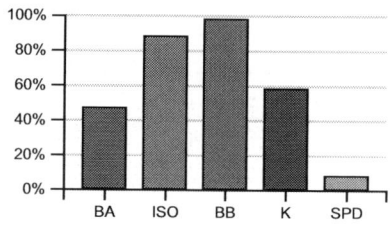

Batting PECOTA Percentiles

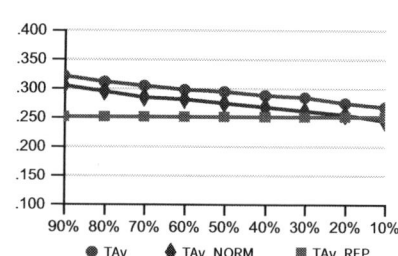

Batting WARP History

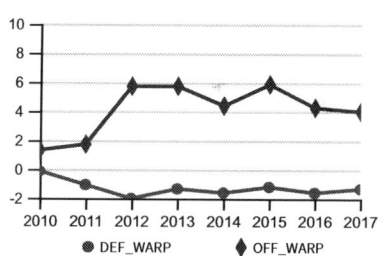

BRR (Relative to Position)

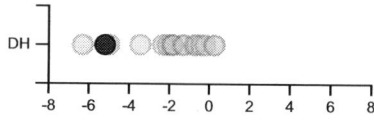

Rank		Player	BRR
13	30°	Mark Trumbo	-2.28
14	25°	Matt Davidson	-3.40
15	19°	Victor Martinez	-4.94
16	8°	**Edwin Encarnacion**	**-5.16**
17	0°	Kendrys Morales	-6.26

BRR (Relative to Team)

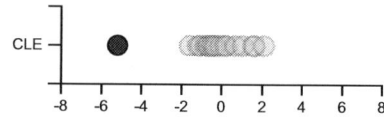

Rank		Player	BRR
15	18°	Jason Kipnis	-0.75
16	16°	Erik Gonzalez	-1.01
17	14°	Daniel Robertson	-1.13
18	10°	Lonnie Chisenhall	-1.55
19	0°	**Edwin Encarnacion**	**-5.16**

Base Running Components

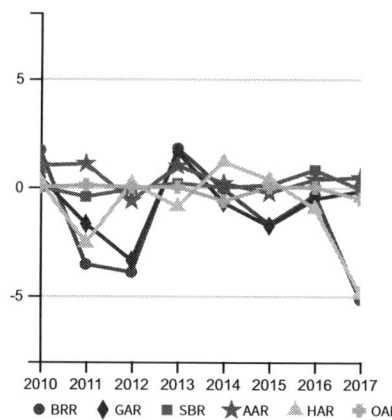

Marco Estrada   RHP   Toronto Blue Jays

Born: 7/5/1983   **Age:** 34   **Bats:** R   **Throws:** R   **Height:** 6' 0"   **Weight:** 180 lbs   **Draft Info:** Round 6, 2005 Draft (#174 overall)

2017 Daily WARP Profile
0.2 Total WARP

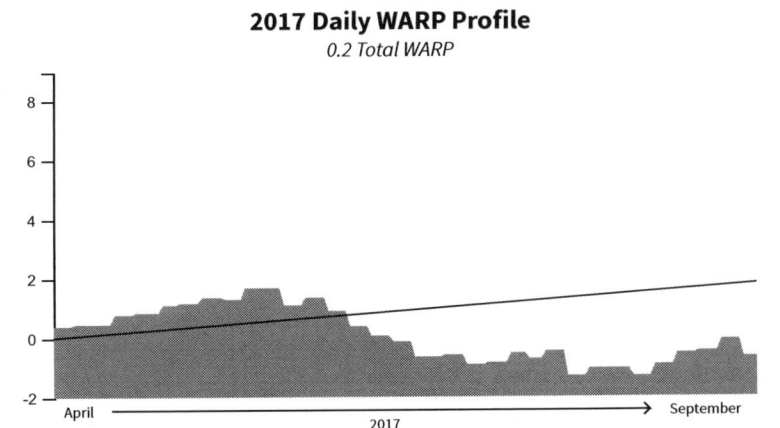

POWER
26 PWR
139th of 150

STAMINA
81 STM
11th of 150

COMMAND
60 CMD
37th of 150

PACE
20 Sec/Pit
37th of 150
75°
Fast

Fantasy Values
2017	2018
$7.64	$9.00

YEAR	TEAM	LVL	AGE	W	L	SV	G	GS	IP	H	HR	BB/9	K/9	K	GB%	BABIP	WHIP	ERA	DRA	WARP	MPH 95
2017	TOR	MLB	33	10	9	0	33	33	186	186	31	3.4	8.5	176	31%	.295	1.38	4.98	5.47	0.2	91.0

2017 Pitching Percentages

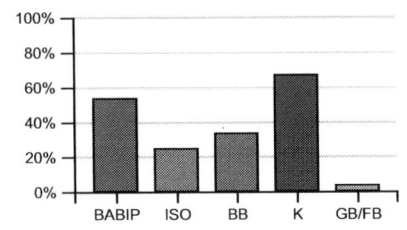

Pitching PECOTA Percentiles

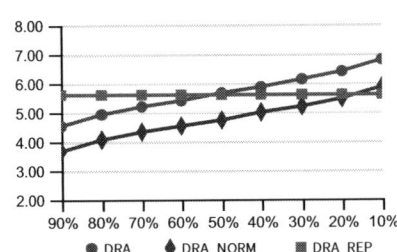

- ● DRA   ◆ DRA_NORM   ■ DRA_REP

Pitching WARP History

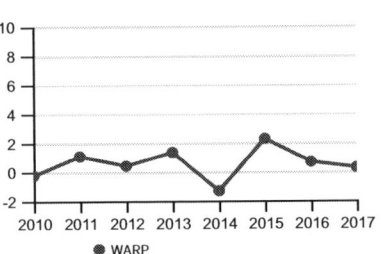

- ● WARP

Tunnel vs LHH

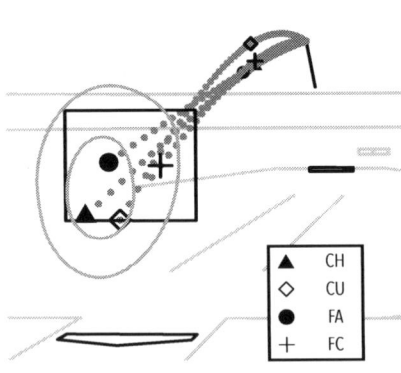

▲	CH
◇	CU
●	FA
+	FC

Pitch Types

Type	Freq	Velo	H Mov	V Mov
CH	31.8%	77.8 [71]	-8.3 [115]	-24.4 [108]
CU	7.7%	77.8 [98]	5.7 [92]	-50.6 [94]
FA	53.8%	90 [90]	-3.6 [117]	-10.7 [114]
FC	6.6%	86.7 [90]	4 [113]	-23.2 [102]

Pitch Tunnel

Pairs	Release Diff	Tunnel Diff	Plate Diff	Speed Changes
2364	29.5	121.4	225.7	0.033

PI Scores

Year	Pitch Ct	Pwr	Cmd	Stm
2013	1990	30	61	50
2014	2472	26	52	66
2015	2889	26	53	71
2016	2833	27	53	71
2017	3257	26	60	81

Tunnel vs RHH

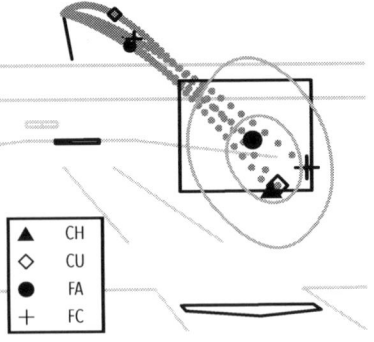

▲	CH
◇	CU
●	FA
+	FC

Jacob Faria RHP Tampa Bay Rays

Born: 7/30/1993 **Age:** 24 **Bats:** R **Throws:** R **Height:** 6' 4" **Weight:** 235 lbs **Draft Info:** Round 10, 2011 Draft (#330 overall)

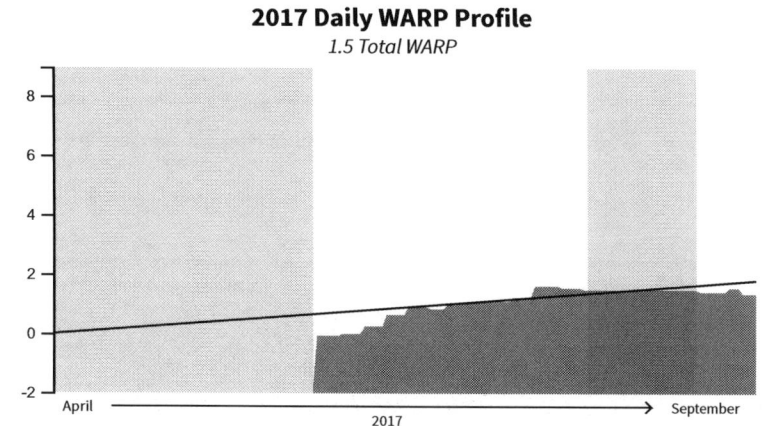

2017 Daily WARP Profile
1.5 Total WARP

Game 1: minors, **Game 123:** DL (abdominal strain)

POWER 39 PWR 100th of 150

STAMINA 63 STM 92nd of 150

COMMAND 45 CMD 117th of 150

PACE 22 Sec/Pit 108th of 150 28° Slow

Fantasy Values
2017 **$-2.45** 2018 **$9.00**

YEAR	TEAM	LVL	AGE	W	L	SV	G	GS	IP	H	HR	BB/9	K/9	K	GB%	BABIP	WHIP	ERA	DRA	WARP	MPH 95
2017	TBA	MLB	23	5	4	0	16	14	86.2	71	11	3.2	8.7	84	39%	.265	1.18	3.43	4.04	1.5	93.1

Faria dominated hitters in Triple-A prior to his promotion and at first did the same in the majors before tiring down the stretch and then getting placed on the DL with an abdominal strain. When he's on, Faria mixes up a low-90s fastball with a good change and a couple of show-me secondary offerings. He is the kind of pitcher who should be a quality major-league arm but might not be able to translate the high whiff rates in Triple-A to the majors because of the lack of a truly dominant pitch. — Mike G.

2017 Pitching Percentages

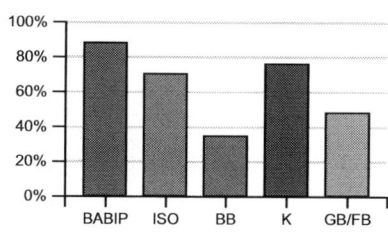

Pitching PECOTA Percentiles

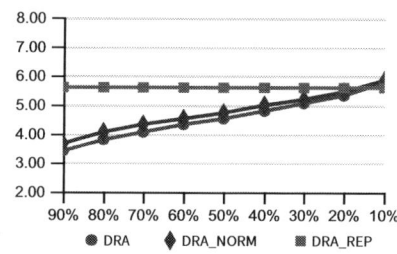

Tunnel vs LHH

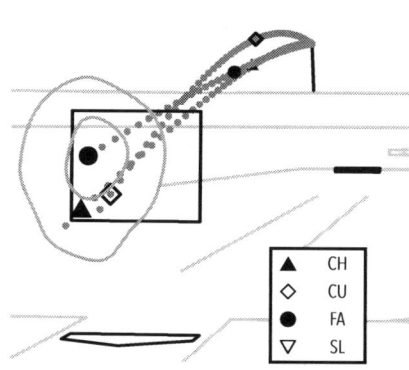

Pitch Types

Type	Freq	Velo	H Mov	V Mov
CH	17.0%	81.7 [86]	-8.1 [116]	-30.6 [90]
CU	4.5%	75.6 [90]	4.7 [88]	-51 [93]
FA	54.5%	92 [98]	-0.3 [132]	-11.8 [111]
SL	23.9%	83.6 [97]	4.4 [99]	-31.2 [104]

Pitch Tunnel

Pairs	Release Diff	Tunnel Diff	Plate Diff	Speed Changes
1052	32.3	129.7	244.2	0.029

PI Scores

Year	Pitch Ct	Pwr	Cmd	Stm
2017	1403	39	45	63

Tunnel vs RHH

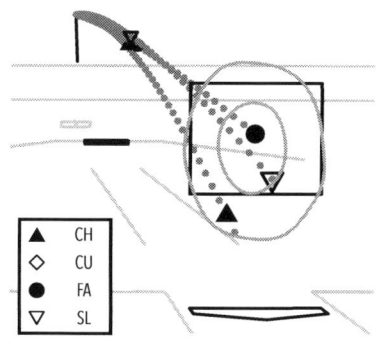

Mike Fiers RHP Detroit Tigers

Born: 6/15/1985 **Age:** 32 **Bats:** R **Throws:** R **Height:** 6' 2" **Weight:** 200 lbs **Draft Info:** Round 22, 2009 Draft (#676 overall)

PACE
21 81st of 150
Sec/Pit 46°
Average

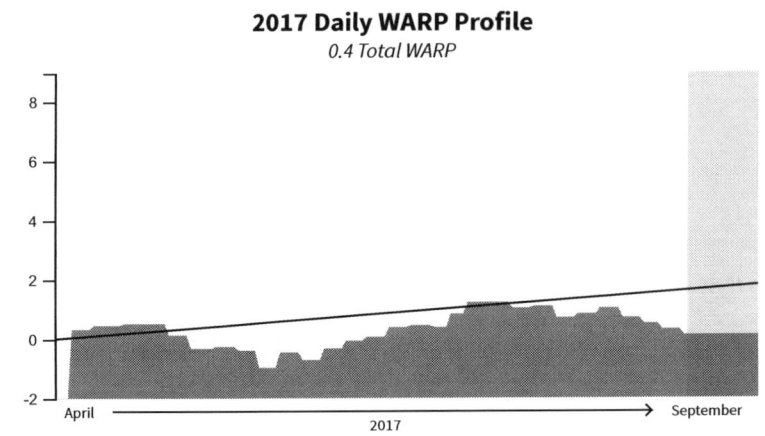

2017 Daily WARP Profile
0.4 Total WARP

Game 146: minors

POWER
28 136th of 150
PWR

STAMINA
71 63rd of 150
STM

COMMAND
55 62nd of 150
CMD

Fantasy Values
2017	2018
$4.15	**$2.00**

YEAR	TEAM	LVL	AGE	W	L	SV	G	GS	IP	H	HR	BB/9	K/9	K	GB%	BABIP	WHIP	ERA	DRA	WARP	MPH 95
2017	HOU	MLB	32	8	10	0	29	28	153.1	157	32	3.6	8.6	146	43%	.300	1.43	5.22	5.32	0.4	91.4

2017 Pitching Percentages

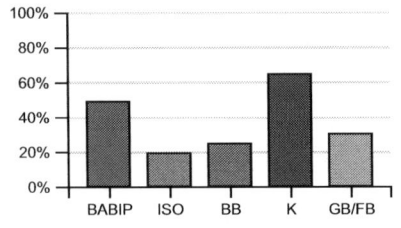

Pitching PECOTA Percentiles

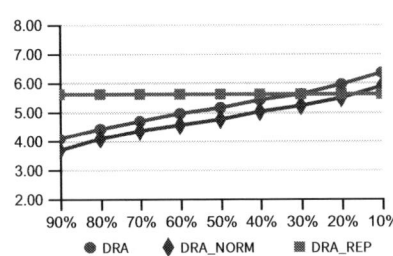

● DRA ◆ DRA_NORM ■ DRA_REP

Pitching WARP History

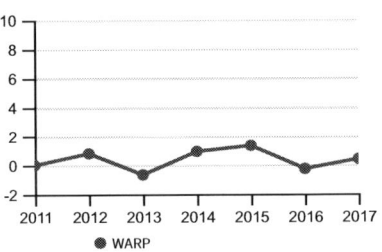

● WARP

Tunnel vs LHH

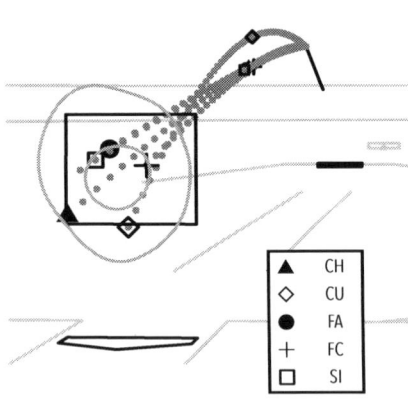

▲	CH
◇	CU
●	FA
+	FC
□	SI

Pitch Types

Type	Freq	Velo	H Mov	V Mov
CH	18.3%	82.8 [91]	-12.5 [93]	-30 [91]
CU	19.3%	74.3 [85]	11.5 [115]	-61.7 [71]
FA	30.6%	90.2 [91]	-6.4 [103]	-13.5 [105]
FC	11.1%	87.2 [93]	2 [102]	-20.5 [113]
SI	17.0%	89.8 [86]	-10.9 [112]	-16.7 [112]
SL	3.8%	82.1 [90]	5.2 [103]	-32.4 [101]

Pitch Tunnel

Pairs	Release Diff	Tunnel Diff	Plate Diff	Speed Changes
1951	42.3	131.4	242.1	0.036

PI Scores

Year	Pitch Ct	Pwr	Cmd	Stm
2013	402	27	47	44
2014	1114	35	43	66
2015	3020	33	43	74
2016	2766	30	42	72
2017	2625	28	55	71

Tunnel vs RHH

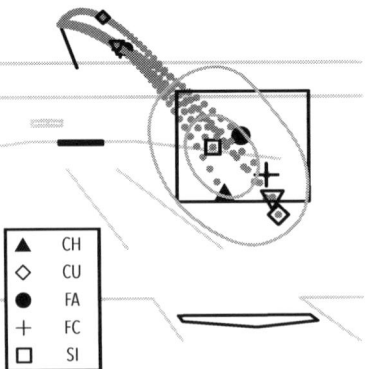

▲	CH
◇	CU
●	FA
+	FC
□	SI

Doug Fister   RHP   Texas Rangers

Born: 2/4/1984   **Age:** 34   **Bats:** L   **Throws:** R   **Height:** 6' 8"   **Weight:** 210 lbs   **Draft Info:** Round 7, 2006 Draft (#201 overall)

PACE
17 2nd of 150
Sec/Pit 99°
Very Fast

2017 Daily WARP Profile
0.9 Total WARP

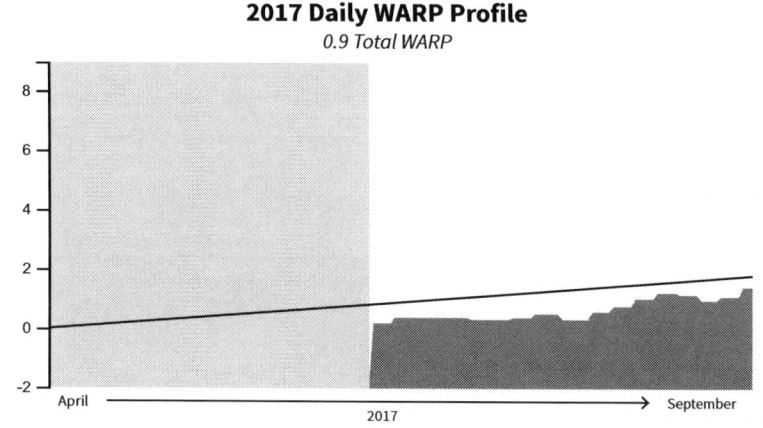

2017
April ———————————————→ September

Game 1: free agent, minors

POWER
36 113th of 150
PWR

STAMINA
59 106th of 150
STM

COMMAND
50 86th of 150
CMD

Fantasy Values
2017   *2018*
$3.61   **$2.00**

YEAR	TEAM	LVL	AGE	W	L	SV	G	GS	IP	H	HR	BB/9	K/9	K	GB%	BABIP	WHIP	ERA	DRA	WARP	MPH 95
2017	BOS	MLB	33	5	9	0	18	15	90.1	87	9	3.8	8.3	83	53%	.301	1.38	4.88	4.66	0.9	91.7

2017 Pitching Percentages

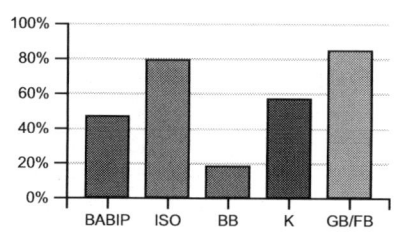

Pitching PECOTA Percentiles

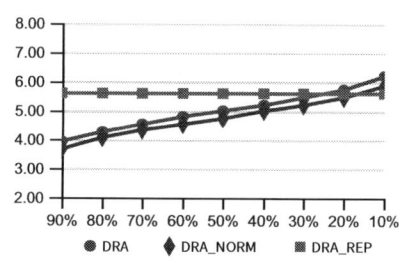

● DRA   ◆ DRA_NORM   ■ DRA_REP

Pitching WARP History

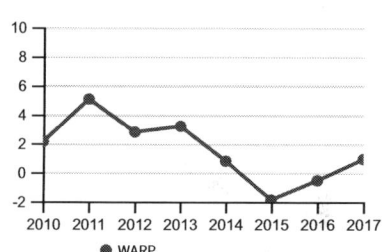

● WARP

Tunnel vs LHH

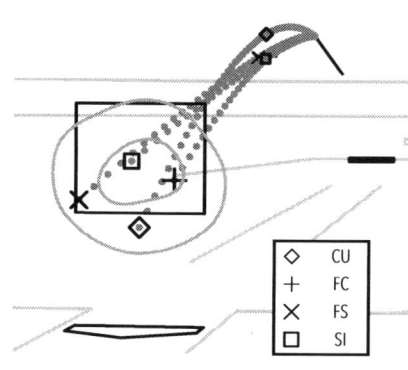

◇	CU
+	FC
✕	FS
▢	SI

Pitch Types

Type	Freq	Velo	H Mov	V Mov
CU	16.8%	73.7 [83]	7.5 [99]	-56.6 [82]
FA	1.2%	89.7 [89]	-7.6 [98]	-15.8 [98]
FC	16.7%	85.3 [83]	3.1 [108]	-28 [83]
FS	6.9%	82.9 [88]	-12.3 [85]	-28.7 [104]
SI	58.4%	90 [87]	-12.8 [98]	-21 [97]

Pitch Tunnel

Pairs	Release Diff	Tunnel Diff	Plate Diff	Speed Changes
1134	33.5	124.9	228.4	0.031

PI Scores

Year	Pitch Ct	Pwr	Cmd	Stm
2013	3341	28	48	83
2014	2454	31	54	70
2015	1644	27	57	50
2016	2995	36	61	77
2017	1526	36	50	59

Tunnel vs RHH

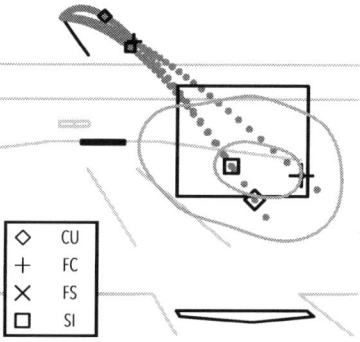

◇	CU
+	FC
✕	FS
▢	SI

Tyler Flowers C Atlanta Braves

Born: 1/24/1986 **Age:** 32 **Bats:** R **Throws:** R **Height:** 6' 4" **Weight:** 260 lbs **Draft Info:** Round 33, 2005 Draft (#1007 overall)

22 Sec/Pit

PACE
99th of 155
36°
Slow

2017 Daily WARP Profile
5.9 Total WARP

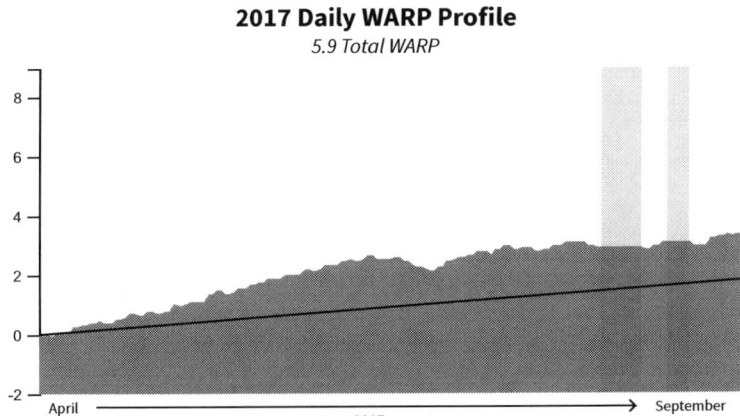

Game 130: DL (wrist contusion), **Game 145:** wrist contusion

Fantasy Values	
2017	2018
$10.27	**$8.00**

YEAR	TEAM	LVL	AGE	PA	R	2B	3B	HR	RBI	BB	K	SB	AVG/OBP/SLG	TAv	VORP	BABIP	WARP
2017	ATL	MLB	31	370	41	16	0	12	49	31	82	0	.281/.378/.445	.309	35.8	.342	5.9

Flowers experienced an unlikely breakout season at age 31 ... behind the plate. His framing metrics made him nearly a six-win player despite the fact he only played 99 games with 370 plate appearances. Flowers did have the best offensive season of his career, but that isn't saying much. He was one of the top 12 catchers in fantasy, which means that he should be in your lineup, but don't be surprised if the bat slips somewhat, particularly in batting average. — Mike G.

2017 Batting Percentages

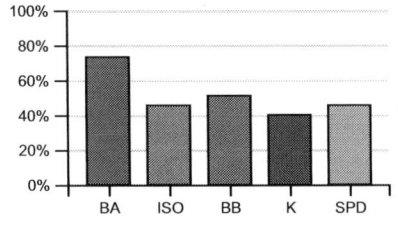

Batting PECOTA Percentiles

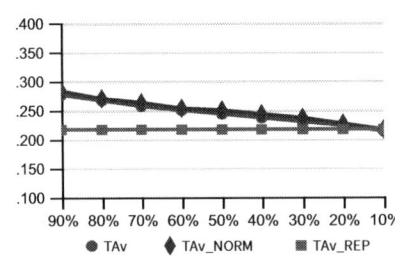

Batting WARP History

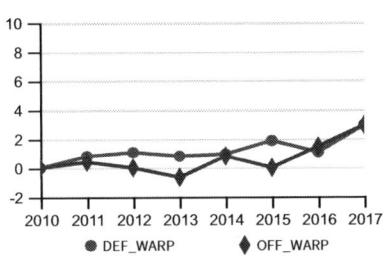

BRR (Relative to Position)

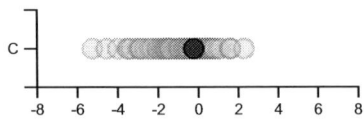

Rank		Player	BRR
30	68°	Chris Stewart	-0.00
31	67°	Drew Butera	-0.06
32	65°	**Tyler Flowers**	**-0.18**
33	63°	Brian McCann	-0.24
34	62°	Ryan Hanigan	-0.24

BRR (Relative to Team)

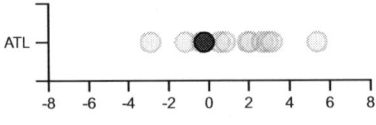

Rank		Player	BRR
7	23°	Rio Ruiz	0.89
8	18°	Ozhaino Albies	0.61
9	11°	**Tyler Flowers**	**-0.18**
10	8°	Adonis Garcia	-0.21
11	5°	Lane Adams	-0.29

Base Running Components

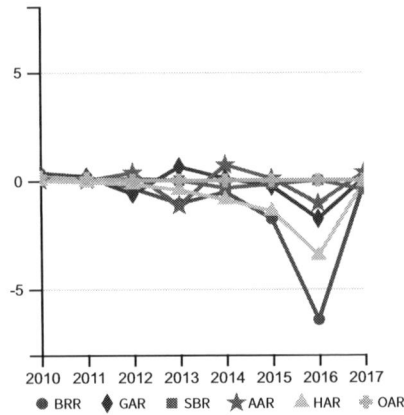

Mike Foltynewicz   RHP   Atlanta Braves

Born: 10/7/1991   **Age:** 26   **Bats:** R   **Throws:** R   **Height:** 6' 4"   **Weight:** 220 lbs   **Draft Info:** Round 1, 2010 Draft (#19 overall)

2017 Daily WARP Profile
-0.4 Total WARP

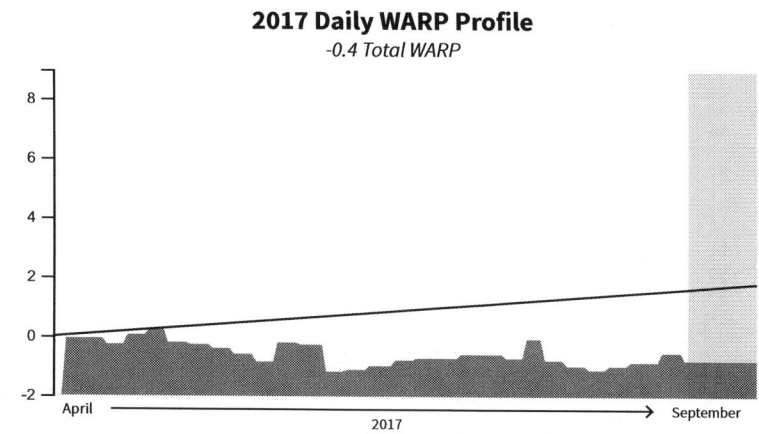

April — 2017 — September

Game 146: finger laceration

POWER 16th of 150 — 63 PWR

STAMINA 44th of 150 — 74 STM

COMMAND 49th of 150 — 58 CMD

PACE 18 Sec/Pit — 5th of 150 — 97° — Very Fast

Fantasy Values
2017	2018
$5.94	$4.00

YEAR	TEAM	LVL	AGE	W	L	SV	G	GS	IP	H	HR	BB/9	K/9	K	GB%	BABIP	WHIP	ERA	DRA	WARP	MPH 95
2017	ATL	MLB	25	10	13	0	29	28	154	169	20	3.4	8.4	143	42%	.324	1.48	4.79	5.83	-0.4	97.9

It's still more potential and promise than results for Folty, who at times did look like he had taken a big step forward before falling back on his inconsistent ways. Foltynewicz's throws a hard mid-90s fastball, but the pitch doesn't always have the movement it needs and when that happens it gets hit a long way. The potential and ceiling do entice, but until the results match up it's difficult to see him as more than a matchup play in mixed and primarily an NL-only arm. — Mike G.

2017 Pitching Percentages

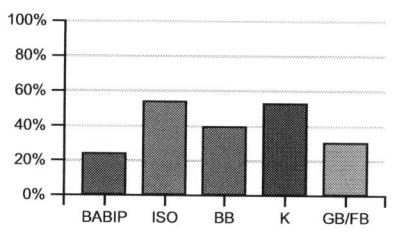

Pitching PECOTA Percentiles

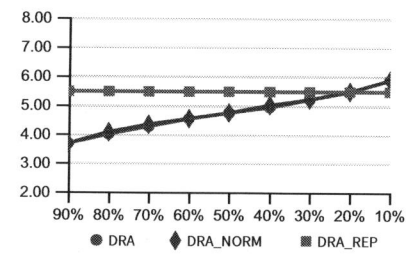

● DRA   ◆ DRA_NORM   ■ DRA_REP

Pitching WARP History

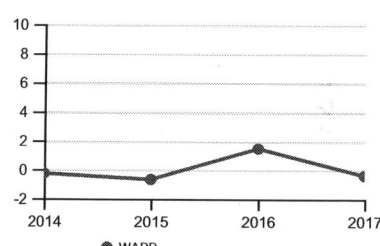

● WARP

Tunnel vs LHH

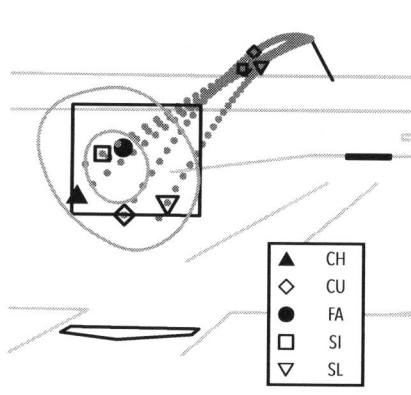

▲ CH
◇ CU
● FA
□ SI
▽ SL

Pitch Types

Type	Freq	Velo	H Mov	V Mov
CH	5.7%	86.7 [106]	-12 [95]	-22.8 [112]
CU	12.3%	80.3 [107]	4.8 [88]	-41.2 [114]
FA	33.7%	95.7 [111]	-6.5 [103]	-11.4 [112]
SI	27.0%	95.7 [120]	-12.6 [99]	-16 [115]
SL	21.2%	86.5 [109]	4.2 [98]	-29.3 [110]

Pitch Tunnel

Pairs	Release Diff	Tunnel Diff	Plate Diff	Speed Changes
2066	36.9	121.8	231.8	0.028

PI Scores

Year	Pitch Ct	Pwr	Cmd	Stm
2014	325	75	49	56
2015	1478	69	43	70
2016	2111	59	49	64
2017	2756	63	58	74

Tunnel vs RHH

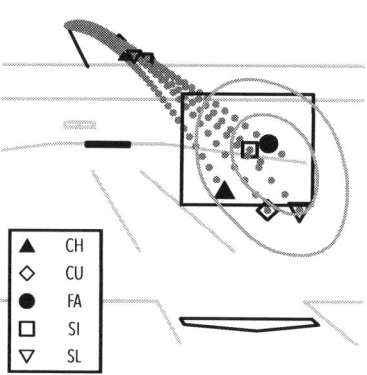

▲ CH
◇ CU
● FA
□ SI
▽ SL

DIAMOND INSIGHTS 2018

Dexter Fowler CF St. Louis Cardinals

Born: 3/22/1986 **Age:** 32 **Bats:** B **Throws:** R **Height:** 6' 5" **Weight:** 195 lbs **Draft Info:** Round 14, 2004 Draft (#410 overall)

2017 Daily WARP Profile
2.7 Total WARP

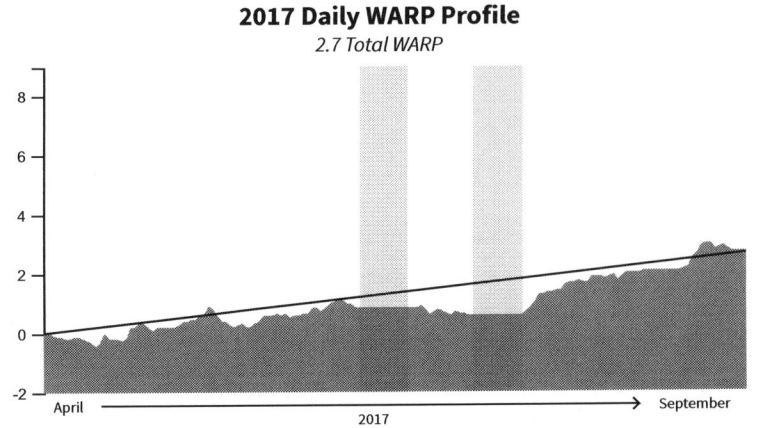

PACE
18th of 155
88°
Very Fast
20 Sec/Pit

Game 74: DL (heel spur), **Game 100:** DL (wrist strain)

Fantasy Values
2017	2018
$15.70	$17.00

YEAR	TEAM	LVL	AGE	PA	R	2B	3B	HR	RBI	BB	K	SB	AVG/OBP/SLG	TAv	VORP	BABIP	WARP
2017	SLN	MLB	31	491	68	22	9	18	64	63	101	7	.264/.363/.488	.298	36.9	.305	2.7

When he was on the field, Fowler was his usual productive self, albeit with the first single-digit stolen-base effort of his career. Fowler injured his heel in June and while he did return quickly, the aftereffects of the injury lingered all season. Fowler traded power for contact in the second half, and found himself resting frequently to get up to speed. If he's 100 percent in spring training, Fowler is a quality third outfielder in mixed formats, although if you do draft him note that he has only played more than 125 games once in the last five years. — Mike G.

2017 Batting Percentages

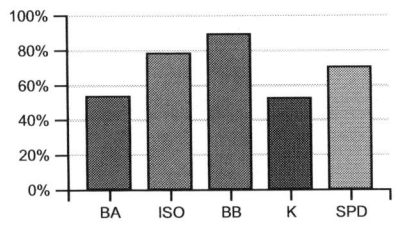

Batting PECOTA Percentiles

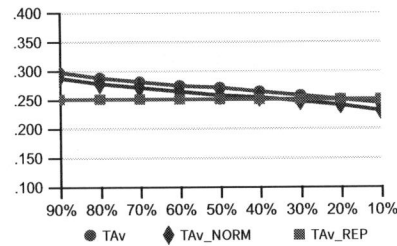

Batting WARP History

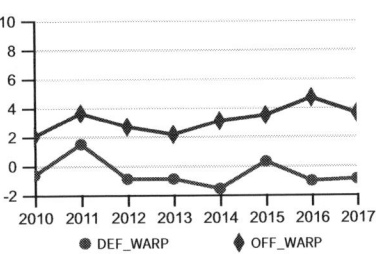

BRR (Relative to Position)

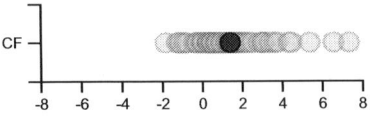

Rank		Player	BRR
23	51°	Austin Jackson	1.58
24	46°	Charlie Blackmon	1.57
25	44°	**Dexter Fowler**	**1.44**
26	43°	Jake Marisnick	1.44
27	41°	Jacoby Ellsbury	1.43

BRR (Relative to Team)

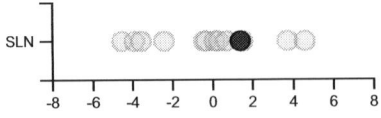

Rank		Player	BRR
2	72°	Greg Garcia	3.75
3	64°	Kolten Wong	1.56
4	56°	**Dexter Fowler**	**1.44**
5	55°	Carson Kelly	0.74
6	53°	Harrison Bader	0.34

Base Running Components

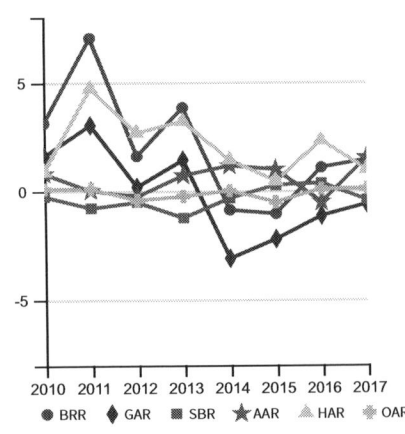

240 - Fowler, Dexter

Todd Frazier   3B   New York Yankees

Born: 2/12/1986   **Age:** 32   **Bats:** R   **Throws:** R   **Height:** 6' 3"   **Weight:** 220 lbs   **Draft Info:** Round 1, 2007 Draft (#34 overall)

2017 Daily WARP Profile
2.6 Total WARP

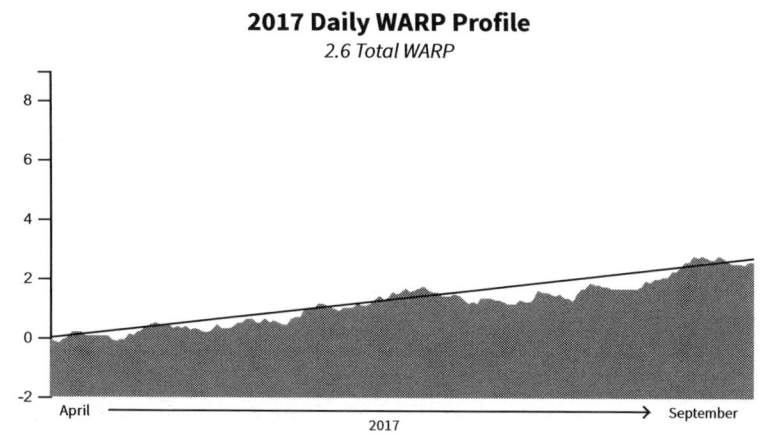

PACE
21 Sec/Pit
45th of 155
71°
Fast

Fantasy Values
2017	2018
$11.55	$14.00

YEAR	TEAM	LVL	AGE	PA	R	2B	3B	HR	RBI	BB	K	SB	AVG/OBP/SLG	TAv	VORP	BABIP	WARP
2017	CHA	MLB	31	335	41	15	0	16	44	48	71	4	.207/.328/.432	.267	12.0	.214	1.5
2017	NYA	MLB	31	241	33	4	1	11	32	35	54	0	.222/.365/.423	.268	10.2	.244	1.1

Always a risky fantasy proposition due to the ghastly batting average, the "Toddfather" saw his value take a hit primarily because he stopped running. Metrics-wise he had a comparable season to 2016, but the jump in walks, while better for Frazier in real life, limited his RBI opportunities in fantasy. Part of what hurt Frazier was his trade to the Yankees; he lost at-bats as part of the Yankees 1B/3B/DH rotation and finished with fewer than 600 plate appearances for the first time since 2012. If he gets a full-time gig the playing time should come back, but if the steals don't, Frazier's value is somewhat limited. — Mike G.

2017 Batting Percentages

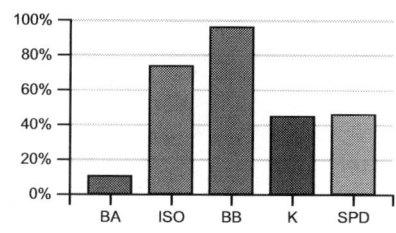

Batting PECOTA Percentiles

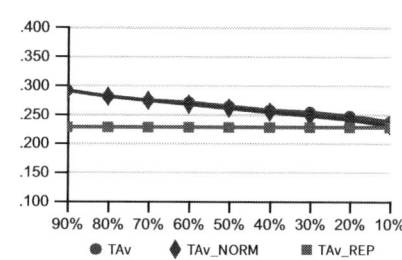

Batting WARP History

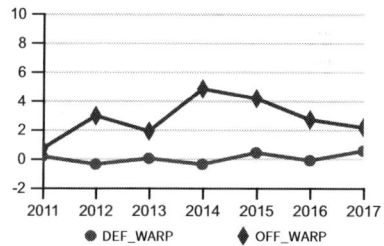

BRR (Relative to Position)

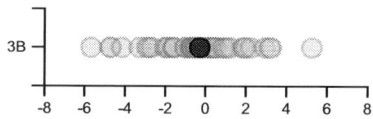

Rank		Player	BRR
25	58°	J.P. Crawford	-0.18
26	57°	Adonis Garcia	-0.21
27	54°	**Todd Frazier**	**-0.24**
28	54°	J.D. Davis	-0.24
29	53°	Marco Hernandez	-0.29

BRR (Relative to Team)

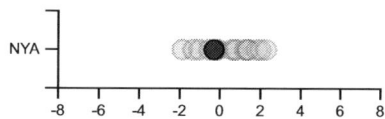

Rank		Player	BRR
11	34°	Aaron Judge	-0.06
12	22°	Giancarlo Stanton	-0.14
13	13°	**Todd Frazier**	**-0.24**
14	10°	Danny Espinosa	-0.48
15	9°	Greg Bird	-0.98

Base Running Components

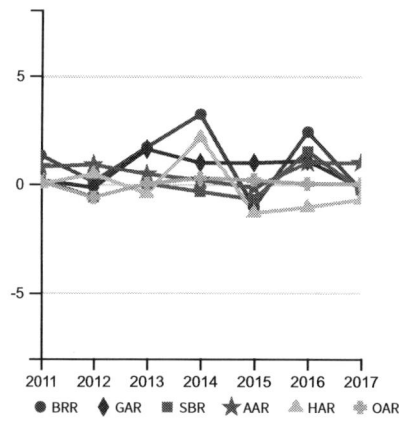

Freddie Freeman   1B   Atlanta Braves

Born: 9/12/1989   **Age:** 28   **Bats:** L   **Throws:** R   **Height:** 6' 5"   **Weight:** 220 lbs   **Draft Info:** Round 2, 2007 Draft (#78 overall)

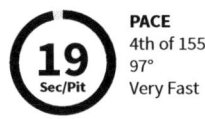

PACE
19 Sec/Pit
4th of 155
97°
Very Fast

2017 Daily WARP Profile
5.0 Total WARP

Game 38: DL (wrist fracture)

Fantasy Values
2017	2018
$24.46	$29.00

YEAR	TEAM	LVL	AGE	PA	R	2B	3B	HR	RBI	BB	K	SB	AVG/OBP/SLG	TAv	VORP	BABIP	WARP
2017	ATL	MLB	27	514	84	35	2	28	71	65	95	8	.307/.403/.586	.341	53.6	.335	5.0

Freeman appeared to be on his way to a career year when a fractured wrist in May put him on the shelf for six weeks. When he returned, he admitted he wasn't quite at full strength. This impacted his power somewhat and turned what would have been a breakout campaign into merely a very good one. The Braves experimented with Freeman at third base long enough to give him eligibility in some leagues. Regardless of his position, Freeman's power and batting average make him a second-round pick in drafts this spring. — Mike G.

2017 Batting Percentages

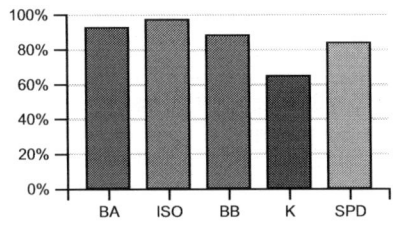

Batting PECOTA Percentiles

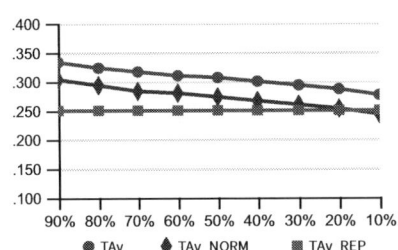

Batting WARP History

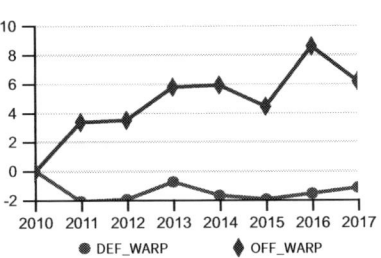

BRR (Relative to Position)

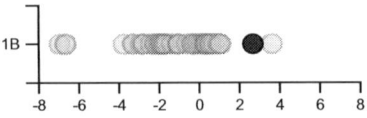

Rank	Player	BRR
1	97° Paul Goldschmidt	3.66
2	**94° Freddie Freeman**	**2.72**
3	93° Kennys Vargas	1.12
4	89° Wil Myers	1.08
5	89° Ryder Jones	1.00

BRR (Relative to Team)

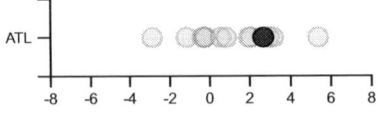

Rank	Player	BRR
2	52° Dansby Swanson	3.19
3	47° Johan Camargo	2.97
4	**39° Freddie Freeman**	**2.72**
5	28° Nick Markakis	2.12
6	26° Danny Santana	2.02

Base Running Components

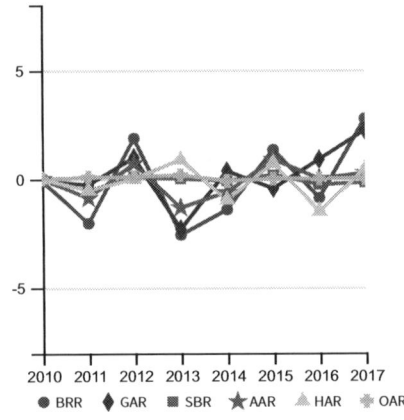

Michael Fulmer   RHP   Detroit Tigers

Born: 3/15/1993   **Age:** 25   **Bats:** R   **Throws:** R   **Height:** 6' 3"   **Weight:** 210 lbs   **Draft Info:** Round 1, 2011 Draft (#44 overall)

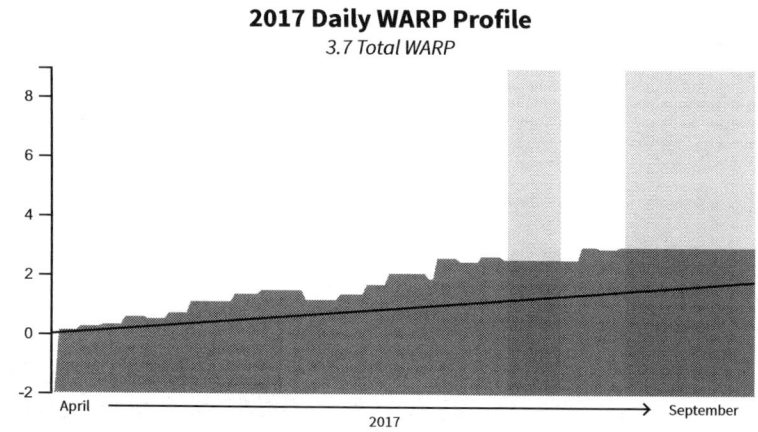

2017 Daily WARP Profile
3.7 Total WARP

Game 105: DL (elbow ulnar neuritis), **Game 132:** DL (elbow ulnar neuritis)

POWER
66 11th of 150

STAMINA
73 53rd of 150

COMMAND
57 53rd of 150

PACE
21 81st of 150
Sec/Pit   46°
Average

Fantasy Values
2017	2018
$15.02	$9.00

YEAR	TEAM	LVL	AGE	W	L	SV	G	GS	IP	H	HR	BB/9	K/9	K	GB%	BABIP	WHIP	ERA	DRA	WARP	MPH 95
2017	DET	MLB	24	10	12	0	25	25	164.2	150	13	2.2	6.2	114	51%	.273	1.15	3.83	3.56	3.7	97.7

Fulmer came out of the gate strong and initially put to rest the idea that his Rookie of the Year campaign was a fluke. Then he started to struggle. At first, it seemed like a case of the league catching up to him, but then he was diagnosed with an elbow injury that led to ulnar transposition surgery in September. Fulmer should be ready by Opening Day, and while the skills remain legitimate, the Tigers' rebuild isn't going to do any favors for a pitcher who relies on defense as much as Fulmer does. — Mike G.

2017 Pitching Percentages

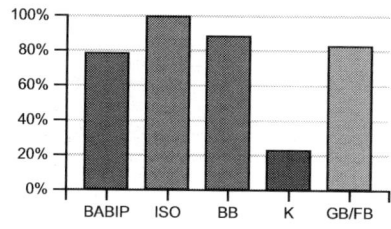

Pitching PECOTA Percentiles

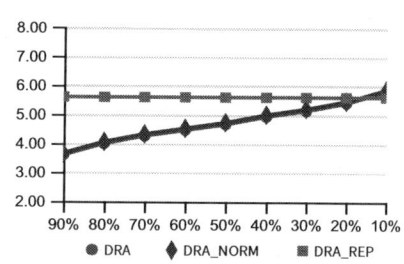

Pitching WARP History

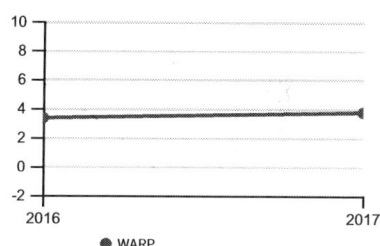

Tunnel vs LHH

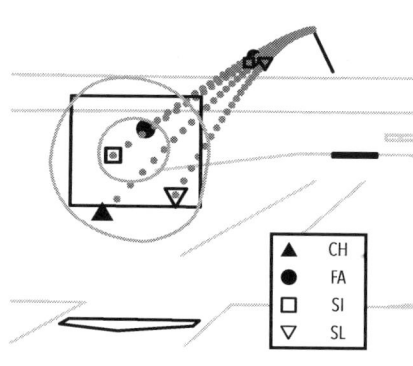

Tunnel vs RHH

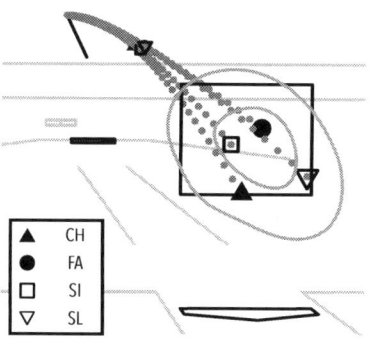

Pitch Types

Type	Freq	Velo	H Mov	V Mov
CH	18.7%	88.3 [113]	-10.7 [102]	-27.8 [98]
CU	0.5%	78.9 [102]	12 [116]	-46.5 [103]
FA	21.5%	96.2 [113]	-4 [115]	-12.5 [108]
SI	37.9%	96.4 [124]	-11.9 [104]	-15.4 [117]
SL	21.3%	89.7 [124]	2.8 [92]	-24.7 [123]

Pitch Tunnel

Pairs	Release Diff	Tunnel Diff	Plate Diff	Speed Changes
1636	41.4	115.4	219.9	0.016

PI Scores

Year	Pitch Ct	Pwr	Cmd	Stm
2016	2467	56	54	71
2017	2433	66	57	73

Joey Gallo   3B   Texas Rangers

Born: 11/19/1993   **Age:** 24   **Bats:** L   **Throws:** R   **Height:** 6' 5"   **Weight:** 235 lbs   **Draft Info:** Round 1, 2012 Draft (#39 overall)

2017 Daily WARP Profile

2.9 Total WARP

21 Sec/Pit

PACE
45th of 155
71°
Fast

Game 124: DL (concussion)

Fantasy Values

2017	2018
$16.22	$19.00

YEAR	TEAM	LVL	AGE	PA	R	2B	3B	HR	RBI	BB	K	SB	AVG/OBP/SLG	TAv	VORP	BABIP	WARP
2017	TEX	MLB	23	532	85	18	3	41	80	75	196	7	.209/.333/.537	.286	27.5	.250	2.9

Traditionalists will wince at the overall line, but Gallo's first full season in the bigs proved that he is a viable major leaguer, bad batting average or no. Unfortunately, bad batting average counts in traditional fantasy leagues, capping his value considerably no matter how much he walks. Putting Gallo's bad batting average into context, Ryon Healy was worth slightly more than Gallo despite 16 fewer home runs, 19 fewer runs, and seven fewer stolen bases. Gallo obviously must be owned in every format, but unless you're tanking in batting average, take care to value him appropriately. — Mike G.

2017 Batting Percentages

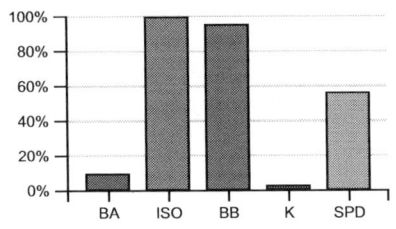

Batting PECOTA Percentiles

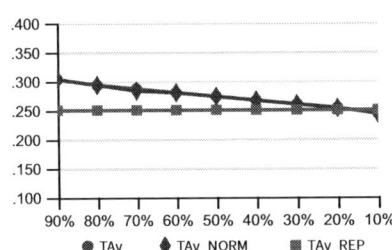

Batting WARP History

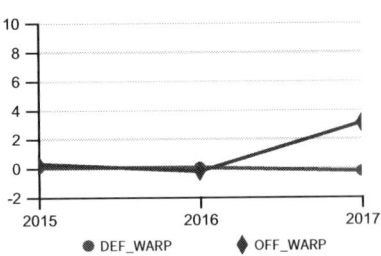

BRR (Relative to Position)

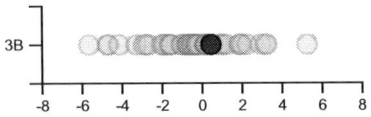

Rank		Player	BRR
12	73°	Rio Ruiz	0.89
13	73°	Ryan Schimpf	0.57
14	70°	**Joey Gallo**	**0.49**
15	68°	Derek Dietrich	0.49
16	68°	Chris Coghlan	0.44

BRR (Relative to Team)

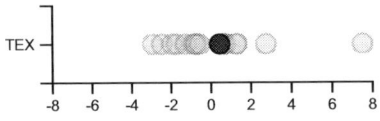

Rank		Player	BRR
6	65°	Ryan Rua	0.69
7	51°	Shin-Soo Choo	0.67
8	44°	**Joey Gallo**	**0.49**
9	43°	Juan Centeno	-0.52
10	42°	Drew Robinson	-0.69

Base Running Components

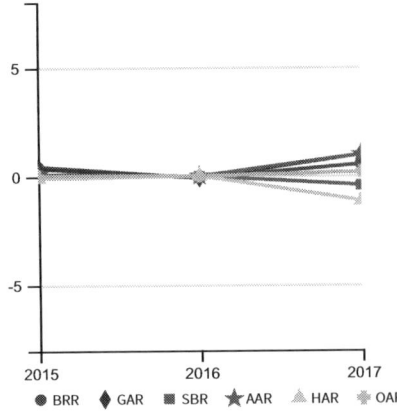

Freddy Galvis   SS   San Diego Padres

Born: 11/14/1989   **Age:** 28   **Bats:** B   **Throws:** R   **Height:** 5' 10"   **Weight:** 185 lbs   **Draft Info:** International Free Agent, 2006

2017 Daily WARP Profile
2.9 Total WARP

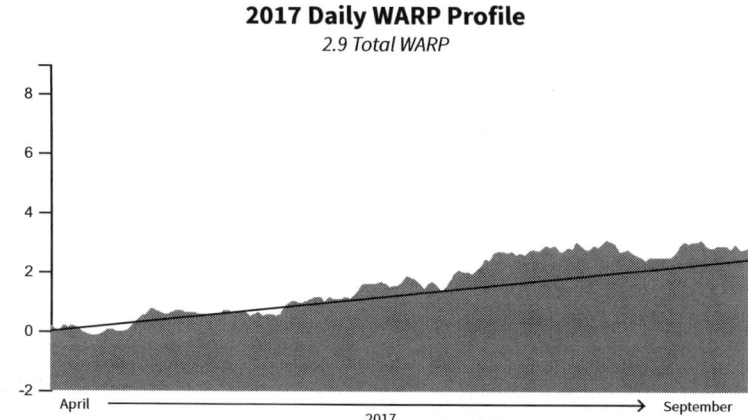

PACE
19 Sec/Pit
4th of 155
97°
Very Fast

Fantasy Values
2017 **$15.44**   2018 **$3.00**

YEAR	TEAM	LVL	AGE	PA	R	2B	3B	HR	RBI	BB	K	SB	AVG/OBP/SLG	TAv	VORP	BABIP	WARP
2017	PHI	MLB	27	663	71	29	6	12	61	45	111	14	.255/.309/.382	.256	27.4	.292	2.9

Cast as a utility player early in his career, Galvis has exceeded expectations as a starting shortstop for the perennial also-ran Phillies, mostly thanks to his defense. Despite well-below-average offensive contributions Galvis has parlayed his skills into a useful fantasy package thanks to moderate speed and the ability to capitalize on his cozy home park. Traded to the Padres, Galvis will be guaranteed at least another year of playing time and is a low-end deep leaue and NL-only option. — Mike G.

2017 Batting Percentages
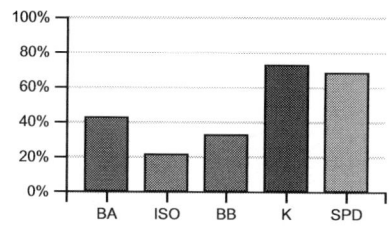

Batting PECOTA Percentiles
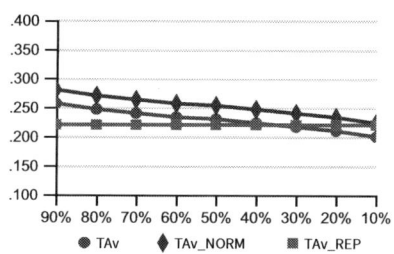

Batting WARP History
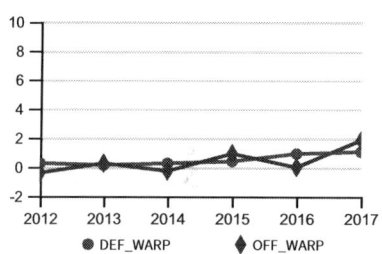

BRR (Relative to Position)
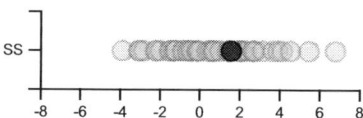

Rank		Player	BRR
16	52°	Tim Anderson	2.06
17	50°	Didi Gregorius	1.87
18	47°	**Freddy Galvis**	**1.62**
19	46°	Ehire Adrianza	1.55
20	45°	Taylor Motter	1.54

BRR (Relative to Team)
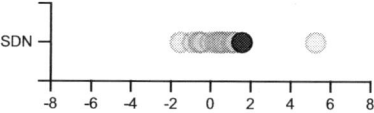

Rank		Player	BRR
1	98°	Cory Spangenberg	5.29
2	87°	**Freddy Galvis**	**1.62**
3	75°	Manuel Margot	1.26
4	73°	Franchy Cordero	1.24
5	71°	Luis Torrens	1.14

Base Running Components
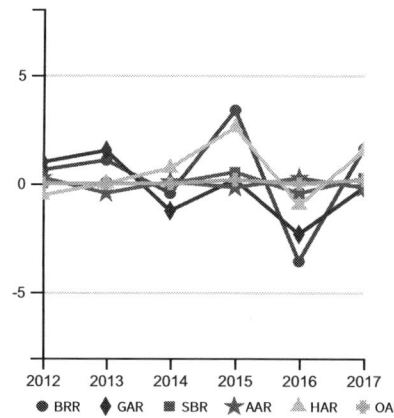

Avisail Garcia   RF   Chicago White Sox

Born: 6/12/1991 **Age:** 27 **Bats:** R **Throws:** R **Height:** 6' 4" **Weight:** 240 lbs **Draft Info:** International Free Agent, 2007

PACE

23 Sec/Pit

135th of 155
13°
Very Slow

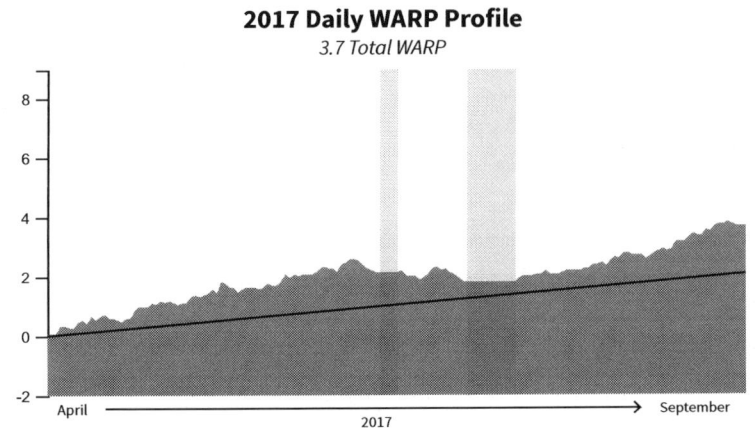

2017 Daily WARP Profile
3.7 Total WARP

Game 78: knee soreness, **Game 98:** DL (thumb sprain)

Fantasy Values
2017	2018
$24.84	$15.00

YEAR	TEAM	LVL	AGE	PA	R	2B	3B	HR	RBI	BB	K	SB	AVG/OBP/SLG	TAv	VORP	BABIP	WARP
2017	CHA	MLB	26	561	75	27	5	18	80	33	111	5	.330/.380/.506	.293	29.1	.392	3.7

While Garcia's gains are legitimate, it would be foolish to bet on any nonelite hitter repeating a .392 BABIP. Garcia profiles similarly to former teammate Melky Cabrera. He has an opportunity to be a mainstay for years, but his value will mostly come in deeper mixed and mono leagues thanks to steady production across the board and not top-tier production in any category. The batting average should settle in somewhere between .280 and .300, which is very good, but no one should pay Garcia expecting a repeat performance in 2018. — Mike G.

2017 Batting Percentages

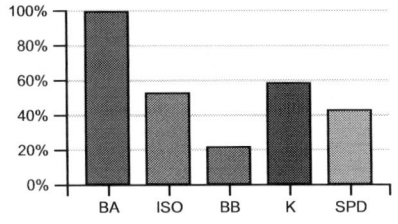

Batting PECOTA Percentiles

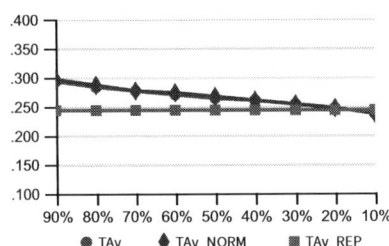

Batting WARP History

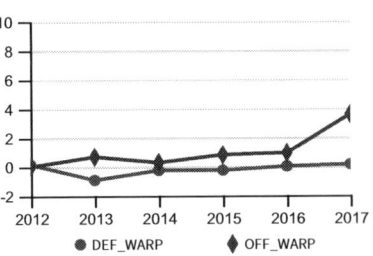

BRR (Relative to Position)

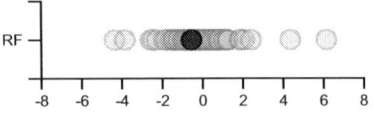

Rank		Player	BRR
33	41°	Jordan Luplow	-0.40
34	41°	Austin Hays	-0.42
35	38°	**Avisail Garcia**	**-0.50**
36	35°	Kole Calhoun	-0.59
37	34°	Jesse Winker	-0.63

BRR (Relative to Team)

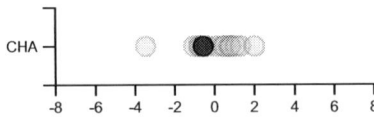

Rank		Player	BRR
9	32°	Rymer Liriano	0.17
10	30°	Willy Garcia	-0.30
11	21°	**Avisail Garcia**	**-0.50**
12	15°	Welington Castillo	-0.67
13	11°	Yoan Moncada	-0.72

Base Running Components

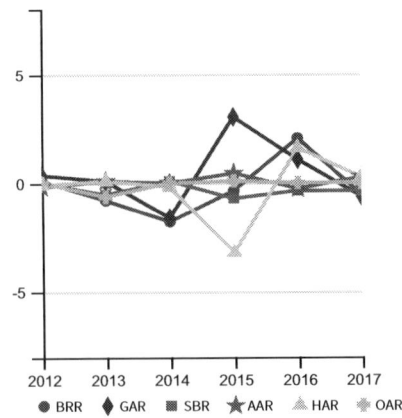

Brett Gardner   LF   New York Yankees   ⚓

Born: 8/24/1983   **Age:** 34   **Bats:** L   **Throws:** L   **Height:** 5' 11"   **Weight:** 195 lbs   **Draft Info:** Round 3, 2005 Draft (#109 overall)

2017 Daily WARP Profile
3.8 Total WARP

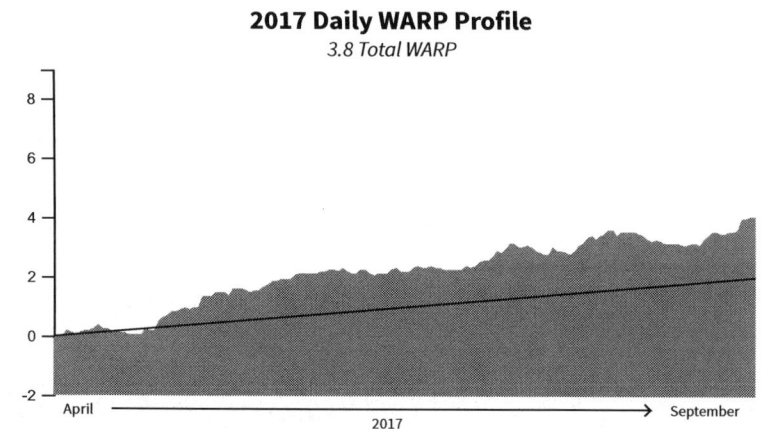

PACE
22 Sec/Pit
99th of 155
36°
Slow

Fantasy Values
2017	2018
$23.79	$19.00

YEAR	TEAM	LVL	AGE	PA	R	2B	3B	HR	RBI	BB	K	SB	AVG/OBP/SLG	TAv	VORP	BABIP	WARP
2017	NYA	MLB	33	682	96	26	4	21	63	72	122	23	.264/.350/.428	.271	25.4	.300	3.8

After a 2016 that saw diminished power and looked like the beginning of his swan song, Gardner bounced back to his usual levels of solid production and even swatted 20+ home runs for the first time in his career. The days of Gardner stealing 45+ bases are long gone, but there is enough speed in the profile for Gardner to deliver stats across the board despite a batting average that isn't anything special. — Mike G.

2017 Batting Percentages

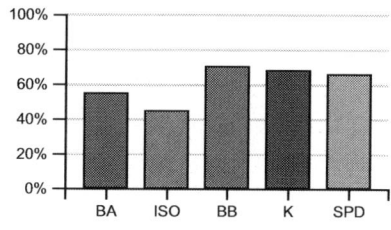

Batting PECOTA Percentiles

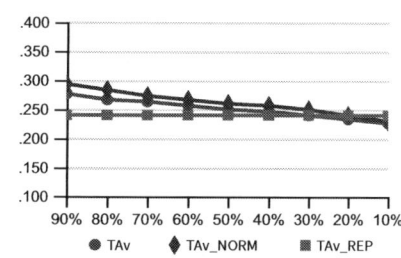

Batting WARP History

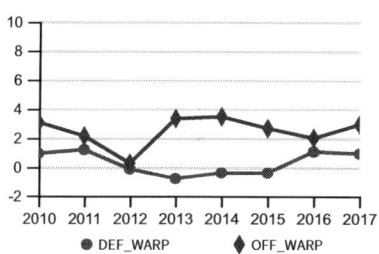

BRR (Relative to Position)

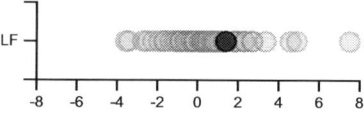

Rank		Player	BRR
12	76°	Ezequiel Carrera	1.88
13	76°	Teoscar Hernandez	1.88
14	72°	**Brett Gardner**	**1.44**
15	71°	Jace Peterson	1.44
16	69°	Andrew Benintendi	1.41

BRR (Relative to Team)

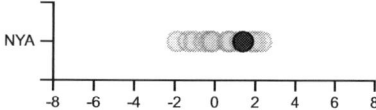

Rank		Player	BRR
2	92°	Aaron Hicks	2.05
3	85°	Didi Gregorius	1.87
4	70°	**Brett Gardner**	**1.44**
5	67°	Jace Peterson	1.44
6	58°	Jacoby Ellsbury	1.43

Base Running Components

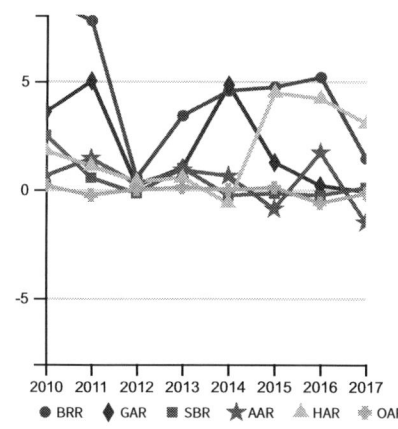

Matt Garza   RHP   Milwaukee Brewers

Born: 11/26/1983   **Age:** 34   **Bats:** R   **Throws:** R   **Height:** 6' 4"   **Weight:** 220 lbs   **Draft Info:** Round 1, 2005 Draft (#25 overall)

2017 Daily WARP Profile
0.1 Total WARP

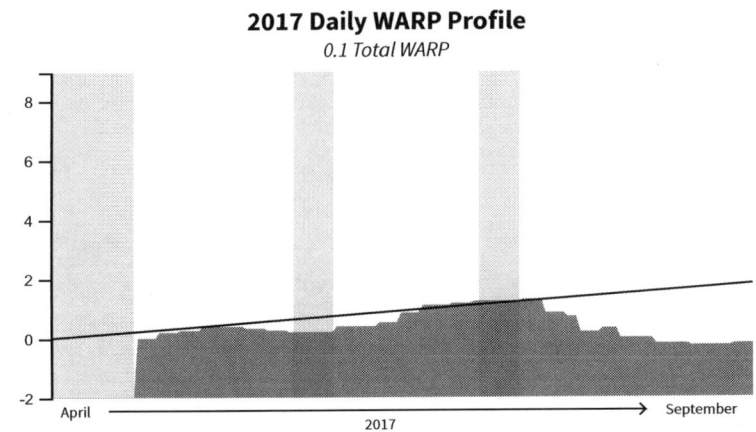

Game 1: DL (groin strain), **Game 57:** DL (chest contusion), **Game 100:** DL (leg strain)

POWER 45 PWR 73rd of 150

STAMINA 57 STM 111th of 150

COMMAND 53 CMD 72nd of 150

PACE 24 Sec/Pit 140th of 150 7° Very Slow

Fantasy Values
| 2017 | 2018 |
| $2.14 | $1.00 |

YEAR	TEAM	LVL	AGE	W	L	SV	G	GS	IP	H	HR	BB/9	K/9	K	GB%	BABIP	WHIP	ERA	DRA	WARP	MPH 95
2017	MIL	MLB	33	6	9	0	24	22	114.2	121	17	3.5	6.2	79	42%	.287	1.45	4.94	5.46	0.1	93.8

2017 Pitching Percentages

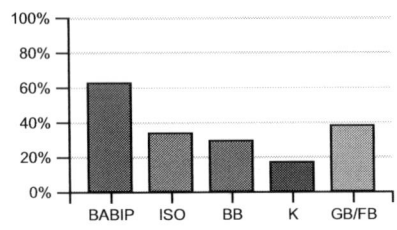

Pitching PECOTA Percentiles

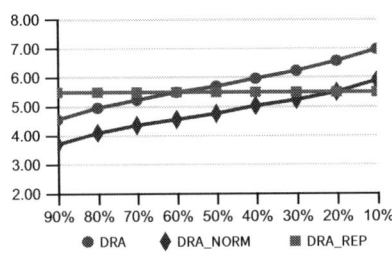

Pitching WARP History

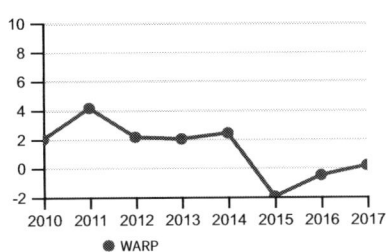

Tunnel vs LHH

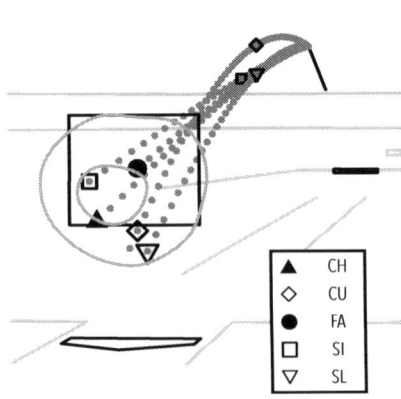

Pitch Types

Type	Freq	Velo	H Mov	V Mov
CH	6.6%	84.4 [97]	-7 [122]	-22.3 [114]
CU	10.3%	74.2 [85]	9.6 [107]	-56.6 [82]
FA	36.4%	92.5 [99]	-5.2 [109]	-13.9 [104]
SI	24.3%	92.2 [99]	-10.3 [116]	-15.7 [116]
SL	22.4%	82.8 [93]	5.1 [102]	-34.5 [95]

Pitch Tunnel

Pairs	Release Diff	Tunnel Diff	Plate Diff	Speed Changes
1403	30.7	127.4	245.0	0.035

PI Scores

Year	Pitch Ct	Pwr	Cmd	Stm
2013	2413	56	58	72
2014	2445	55	58	65
2015	2375	49	53	67
2016	1701	53	52	61
2017	1905	45	53	57

Tunnel vs RHH

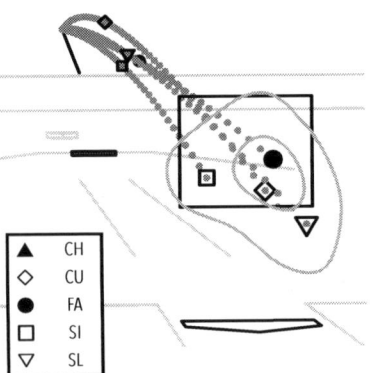

Kevin Gausman   RHP   Baltimore Orioles

Born: 1/6/1991   **Age:** 27   **Bats:** L   **Throws:** R   **Height:** 6' 3"   **Weight:** 190 lbs   **Draft Info:** Round 1, 2012 Draft (#4 overall)

2017 Daily WARP Profile
2.1 Total WARP

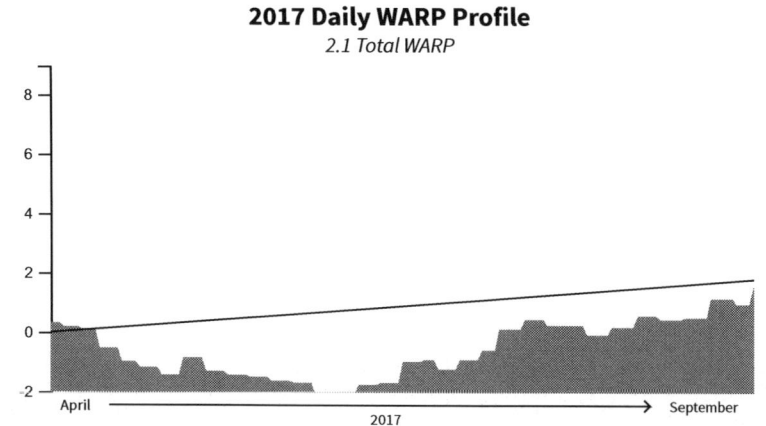

POWER 63 PWR — 16th of 150

STAMINA 81 STM — 11th of 150

COMMAND 52 CMD — 79th of 150

PACE 20 Sec/Pit — 37th of 150 — 75° — Fast

Fantasy Values
2017	2018
$6.77	$9.00

YEAR	TEAM	LVL	AGE	W	L	SV	G	GS	IP	H	HR	BB/9	K/9	K	GB%	BABIP	WHIP	ERA	DRA	WARP	MPH 95
2017	BAL	MLB	26	11	12	0	34	34	186.2	208	29	3.4	8.6	179	44%	.336	1.49	4.68	4.57	2.1	97.4

2017 Pitching Percentages

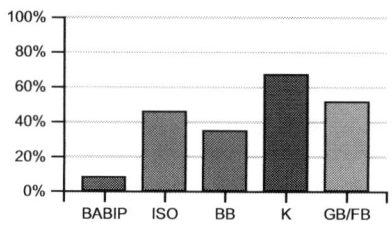

Pitching PECOTA Percentiles

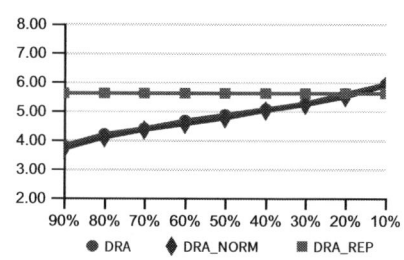

DRA   DRA_NORM   DRA_REP

Pitching WARP History

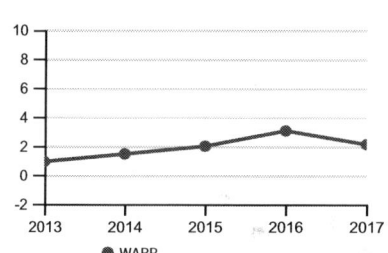

WARP

Tunnel vs LHH

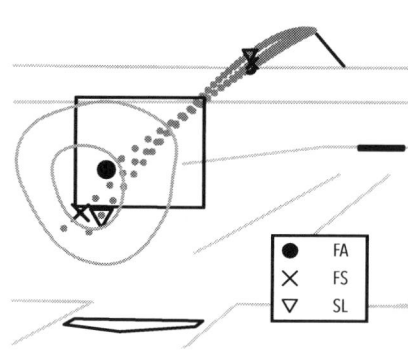

FA — FS — SL

Pitch Types

Type	Freq	Velo	H Mov	V Mov
CH	0.3%	88.3 [113]	-16 [74]	-22 [114]
FA	64.3%	95.3 [110]	-11.7 [79]	-12.9 [107]
FS	20.5%	85.4 [102]	-13.2 [81]	-28 [106]
SL	14.9%	83.1 [94]	1.3 [86]	-34.3 [95]

Pitch Tunnel

Pairs	Release Diff	Tunnel Diff	Plate Diff	Speed Changes
2472	26.3	115.2	222.5	0.026

PI Scores

Year	Pitch Ct	Pwr	Cmd	Stm
2013	788	72	53	55
2014	1951	68	47	67
2015	1872	69	50	58
2016	3111	59	47	80
2017	3339	63	52	81

Tunnel vs RHH

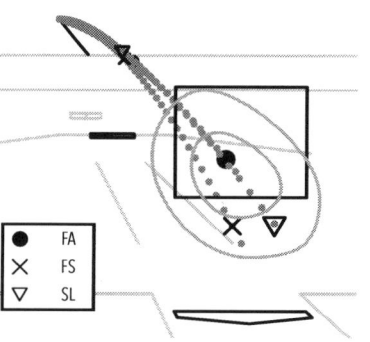

FA — FS — SL

Scooter Gennett 2B Cincinnati Reds

Born: 5/1/1990 **Age:** 28 **Bats:** L **Throws:** R **Height:** 5' 10" **Weight:** 185 lbs **Draft Info:** Round 16, 2009 Draft (#496 overall)

2017 Daily WARP Profile
2.1 Total WARP

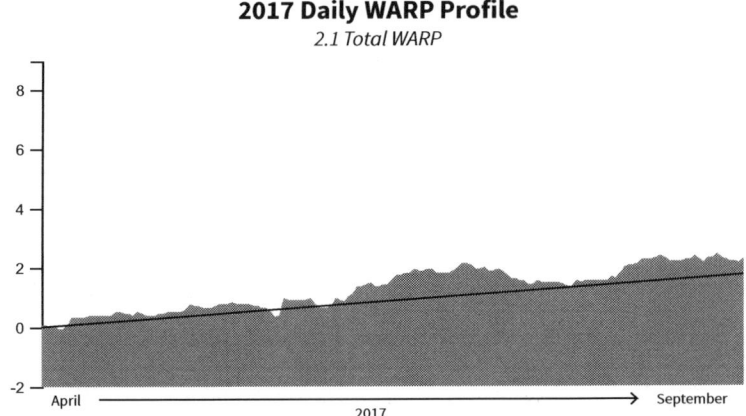

22 Sec/Pit

PACE
99th of 155
36°
Slow

Fantasy Values
2017	2018
$22.98	$17.00

YEAR	TEAM	LVL	AGE	PA	R	2B	3B	HR	RBI	BB	K	SB	AVG/OBP/SLG	TAv	VORP	BABIP	WARP
2017	CIN	MLB	27	497	80	22	3	27	97	30	114	3	.295/.342/.531	.299	32.7	.339	2.1

Even after a four-home-run game on June 6 against the Cardinals, Gennett was still viewed as a marginal player: someone who had a lucky day and wasn't going to be a fantasy mainstay. He proved the detractors wrong with a 27-home-run season, shattering his previous career high and casting himself as a starter once again. Even if there is some slippage baked into Gennett's projection, the power is legitimate and Gennett should be viewed as a 20+ home-run middle infielder going forward. — Mike G.

2017 Batting Percentages

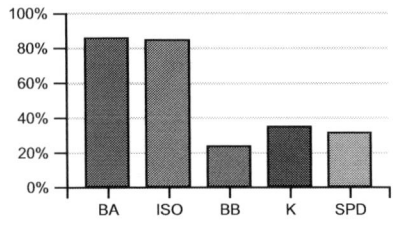

Batting PECOTA Percentiles

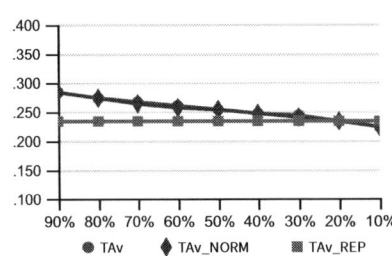

Batting WARP History

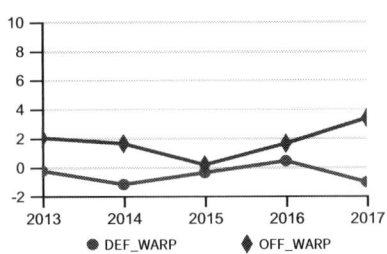

BRR (Relative to Position)

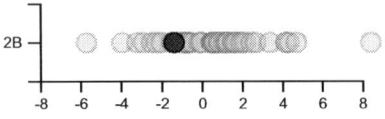

Rank		Player	BRR
45	20°	Brad Miller	-1.26
46	18°	Ben Zobrist	-1.32
47	16°	**Scooter Gennett**	**-1.36**
48	15°	Raul Mondesi	-1.41
49	14°	Carlos Asuaje	-1.48

BRR (Relative to Team)

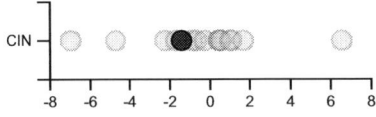

Rank		Player	BRR
10	48°	Jesse Winker	-0.63
11	45°	Devin Mesoraco	-0.82
12	37°	**Scooter Gennett**	**-1.36**
13	31°	Tucker Barnhart	-1.63
14	23°	Adam Duvall	-2.18

Base Running Components

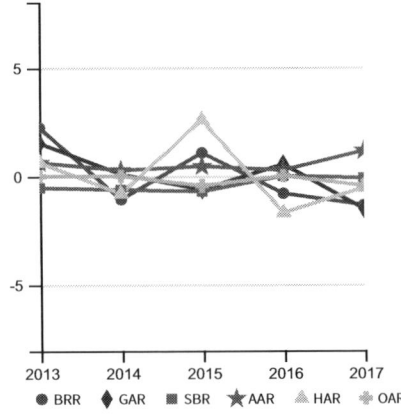

Lucas Giolito RHP Chicago White Sox

Born: 7/14/1994 **Age:** 23 **Bats:** R **Throws:** R **Height:** 6' 6" **Weight:** 255 lbs **Draft Info:** Round 1, 2012 Draft (#16 overall)

PACE
21 81st of 150
Sec/Pit 46°
Average

2017 Daily WARP Profile
0.2 Total WARP

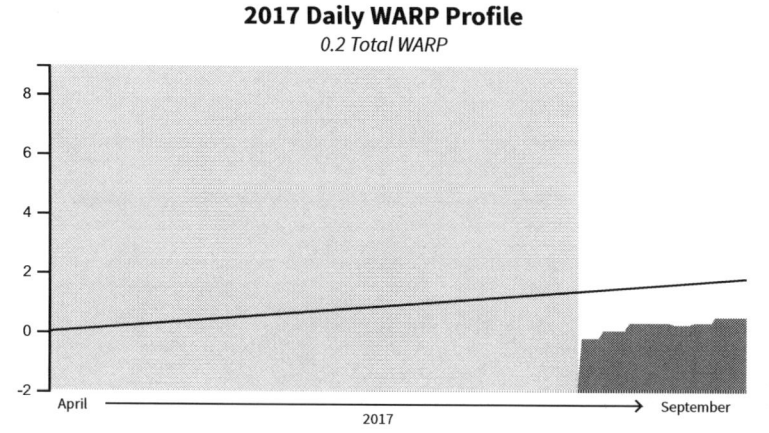

Game 1: minors

POWER
45 73rd of 150
PWR

STAMINA
75 41st of 150
STM

COMMAND
46 111th of 150
CMD

Fantasy Values
2017	2018
$7.70	**$5.00**

YEAR	TEAM	LVL	AGE	W	L	SV	G	GS	IP	H	HR	BB/9	K/9	K	GB%	BABIP	WHIP	ERA	DRA	WARP	MPH 95
2017	CHA	MLB	22	3	3	0	7	7	45.1	31	8	2.4	6.8	34	47%	.189	0.95	2.38	5.28	0.2	94.1

You never want to write off a 22-year-old phenom, but Giolito's stock fell as rapidly as his velocity did, and it didn't look like he'd ever recapture the ceiling he had in the low minors with the Nationals. Giolito was promoted to the White Sox in August and the raw results were good, but his 5.28 DRA and sub-.200 BABIP suggest that it was more fluke than fact. Despite the brand name, Giolito is an endgame flier, and in redraft leagues it's okay to pass on him for someone more established. — Mike G.

2017 Pitching Percentages

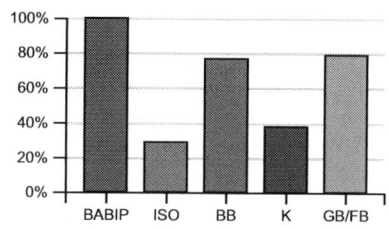

Pitching PECOTA Percentiles

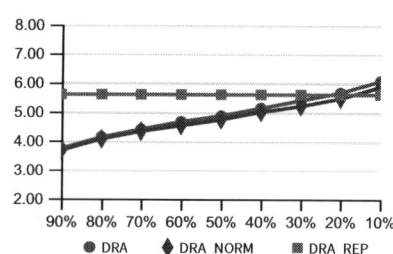

Pitching WARP History

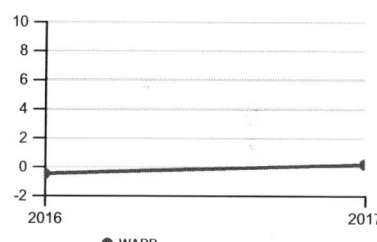

Tunnel vs LHH

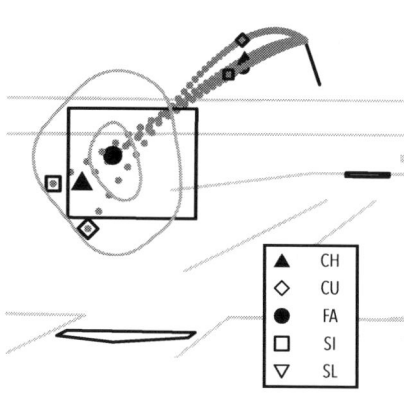

Pitch Types

Type	Freq	Velo	H Mov	V Mov
CH	16.1%	81.9 [87]	-4.6 [135]	-26.2 [103]
CU	11.0%	78.6 [101]	6.1 [93]	-56.1 [83]
FA	50.1%	92.7 [100]	-4.4 [113]	-13.2 [106]
SI	9.7%	92.1 [98]	-11.2 [110]	-17 [111]
SL	13.1%	84 [99]	3.8 [97]	-34.2 [95]

Pitch Tunnel

Pairs	Release Diff	Tunnel Diff	Plate Diff	Speed Changes
522	18.0	130.3	258.1	0.031

PI Scores

Year	Pitch Ct	Pwr	Cmd	Stm
2016	398	55	46	61
2017	701	45	46	75

Tunnel vs RHH

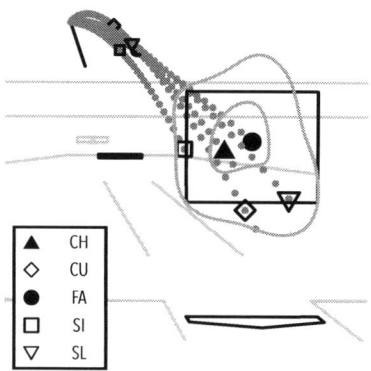

Mychal Givens RHP Baltimore Orioles

Born: 5/13/1990 **Age:** 28 **Bats:** R **Throws:** R **Height:** 6' 0" **Weight:** 210 lbs **Draft Info:** Round 2, 2009 Draft (#54 overall)

We don't have a baseball card for this guy.

PACE
20 37th of 150
Sec/Pit 75°
Fast

2017 Daily WARP Profile
2.0 Total WARP

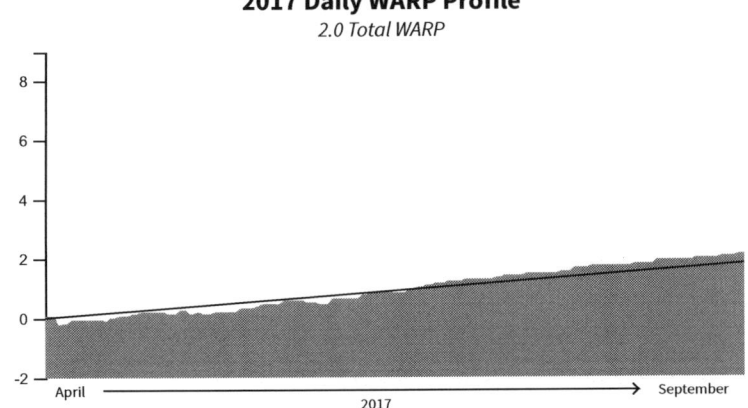

April ———————————— September
2017

POWER
72 6th of 150
PWR

STAMINA
54 118th of 150
STM

COMMAND
42 128th of 150
CMD

Fantasy Values
2017	2018
$14.32	$2.00

YEAR	TEAM	LVL	AGE	W	L	SV	G	GS	IP	H	HR	BB/9	K/9	K	GB%	BABIP	WHIP	ERA	DRA	WARP	MPH 95
2017	BAL	MLB	27	8	1	0	69	0	78.2	57	10	2.9	10.1	88	43%	.251	1.04	2.75	2.85	2.0	97.8

2017 Pitching Percentages

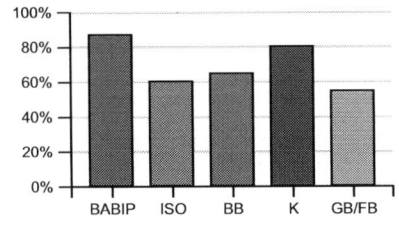

Pitching PECOTA Percentiles

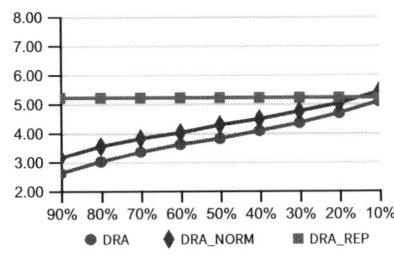

● DRA ◆ DRA_NORM ■ DRA_REP

Pitching WARP History

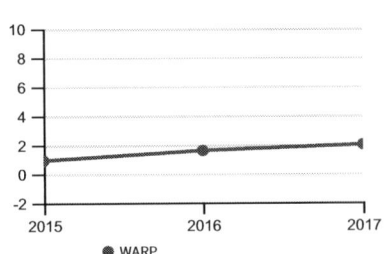

● WARP

Tunnel vs LHH

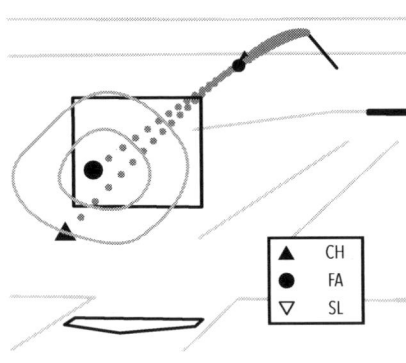

▲ CH
● FA
▽ SL

Pitch Types

Type	Freq	Velo	H Mov	V Mov
CH	8.4%	85.7 [103]	-10.7 [102]	-36.1 [74]
FA	72.2%	95.8 [111]	-7.7 [97]	-16 [97]
SL	19.4%	87.7 [115]	4.6 [100]	-29.3 [110]

Pitch Tunnel

Pairs	Release Diff	Tunnel Diff	Plate Diff	Speed Changes
978	37.7	111.3	207.4	0.016

PI Scores

Year	Pitch Ct	Pwr	Cmd	Stm
2015	466	61	60	52
2016	1298	59	43	52
2017	1321	72	42	54

Tunnel vs RHH

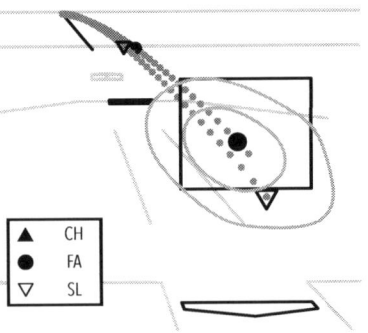

▲ CH
● FA
▽ SL

Zack Godley RHP Arizona Diamondbacks

Born: 4/21/1990 **Age:** 28 **Bats:** R **Throws:** R **Height:** 6' 3" **Weight:** 240 lbs **Draft Info:** Round 10, 2013 Draft (#288 overall)

PACE
20 Sec/Pit
37th of 150
75°
Fast

2017 Daily WARP Profile
4.2 Total WARP

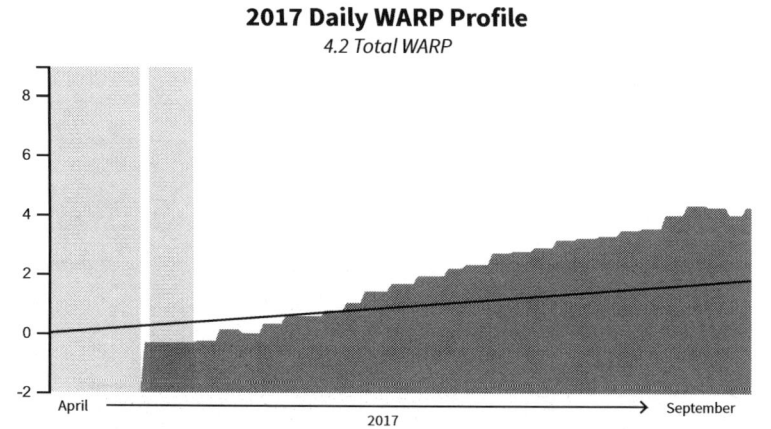

April — 2017 — September

Game 1: minors, **Game 24:** minors

POWER
26 PWR
139th of 150

STAMINA
73 STM
53rd of 150

COMMAND
23 CMD
150th of 150

Fantasy Values
2017	2018
$18.95	$11.00

YEAR	TEAM	LVL	AGE	W	L	SV	G	GS	IP	H	HR	BB/9	K/9	K	GB%	BABIP	WHIP	ERA	DRA	WARP	MPH 95
2017	ARI	MLB	27	8	9	0	26	25	155	124	15	3.1	9.6	165	58%	.280	1.14	3.37	3.14	4.2	93.0

A borderline major leaguer for most of his career, Godley adjusted and took a big step forward in 2017, doing a much better job of mixing up his arsenal and keeping hitters off balance despite the lack of a dominant pitch. The key was increased curveball usage and the reliance on a sinker that kept the ball on the ground. Godley isn't going to be a sleeper in anything but the shallowest leagues, but even with the increased price tag it's okay to take a shot on him as an SP3 and see if the gains are sustainable. — Mike G.

2017 Pitching Percentages

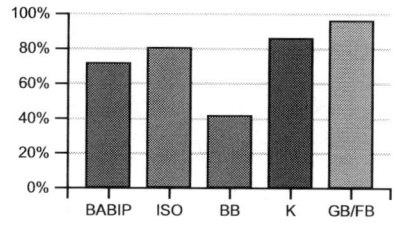

Pitching PECOTA Percentiles

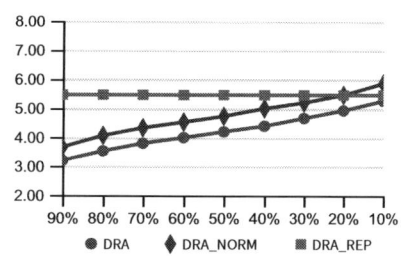

● DRA ◆ DRA_NORM ■ DRA_REP

Pitching WARP History

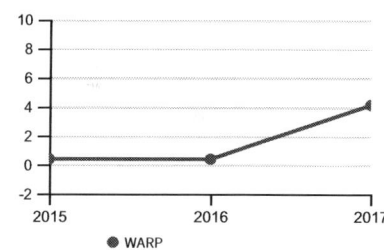

● WARP

Tunnel vs LHH

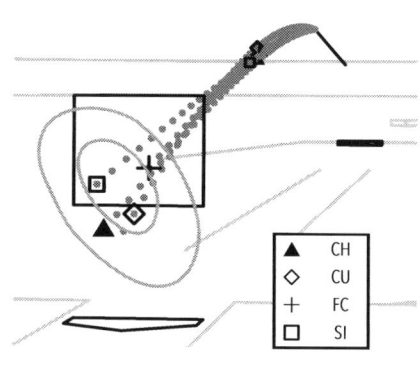

▲	CH
◇	CU
+	FC
□	SI

Pitch Types

Type	Freq	Velo	H Mov	V Mov
CH	7.5%	84.2 [96]	-6.7 [124]	-31.9 [86]
CU	35.6%	83.4 [119]	3.3 [83]	-42.8 [111]
FC	24.7%	90 [109]	0.9 [97]	-22.3 [106]
SI	32.2%	92 [98]	-11 [111]	-22.6 [90]

Pitch Tunnel

Pairs	Release Diff	Tunnel Diff	Plate Diff	Speed Changes
1792	35.7	124.8	230.3	0.020

PI Scores

Year	Pitch Ct	Pwr	Cmd	Stm
2015	570	27	46	50
2016	1136	28	30	68
2017	2419	26	23	73

Tunnel vs RHH

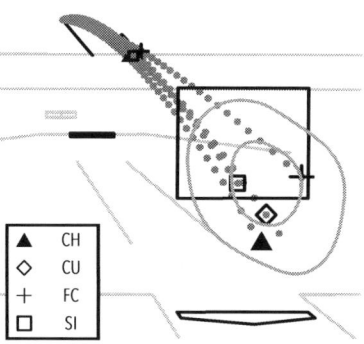

▲	CH
◇	CU
+	FC
□	SI

Paul Goldschmidt 1B Arizona Diamondbacks

Born: 9/10/1987 **Age:** 30 **Bats:** R **Throws:** R **Height:** 6' 3" **Weight:** 225 lbs **Draft Info:** Round 8, 2009 Draft (#246 overall)

22 Sec/Pit

PACE
99th of 155
36°
Slow

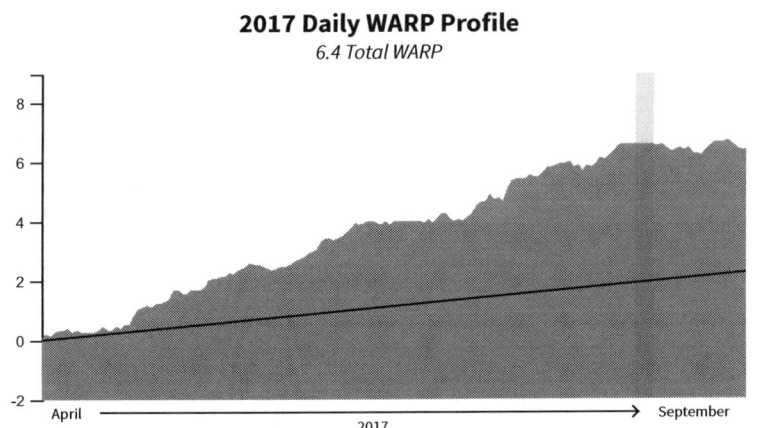

2017 Daily WARP Profile
6.4 Total WARP

Game 137: elbow inflammation

Fantasy Values

2017	2018
$35.53	$38.00

YEAR	TEAM	LVL	AGE	PA	R	2B	3B	HR	RBI	BB	K	SB	AVG/OBP/SLG	TAv	VORP	BABIP	WARP
2017	ARI	MLB	29	665	117	34	3	36	120	94	147	18	.297/.404/.563	.328	58.0	.343	6.4

In real life, Goldschmidt pales in comparison at first base to Joey Votto, but in fantasy Goldy is the guy you want. Jose Altuve, Charlie Blackmon, and Goldy are the only hitters to finish in the Top 10 for three consecutive seasons and there is no reason to expect him not to be an elite inner-circle player again. Someday the steals will disappear, but until they do keep paying close to $40 for Goldy in NL-only and don't be afraid to take him with one of the top three or four picks in draft formats. — Mike G.

2017 Batting Percentages

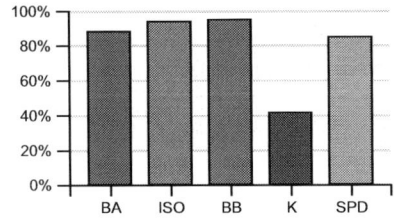

Batting PECOTA Percentiles

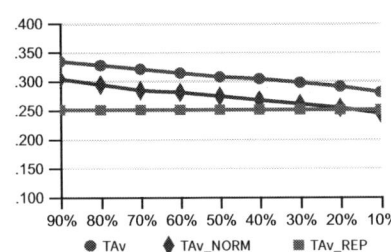

Batting WARP History

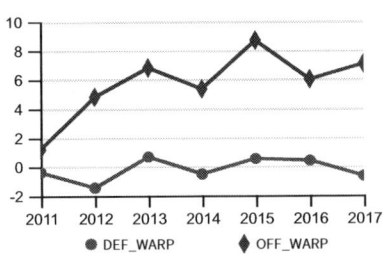

BRR (Relative to Position)

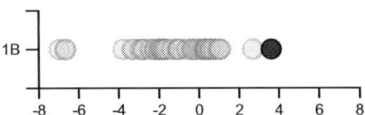

Rank		Player	BRR
1	97°	**Paul Goldschmidt**	**3.66**
2	94°	Freddie Freeman	2.72
3	93°	Kennys Vargas	1.12
4	89°	Wil Myers	1.08
5	89°	Ryder Jones	1.00

BRR (Relative to Team)

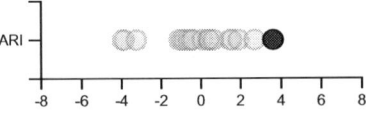

Rank		Player	BRR
1	91°	**Paul Goldschmidt**	**3.66**
2	84°	Gregor Blanco	2.75
3	74°	Jake Lamb	1.96
4	70°	Chris Herrmann	1.62
5	65°	Ketel Marte	1.53

Base Running Components

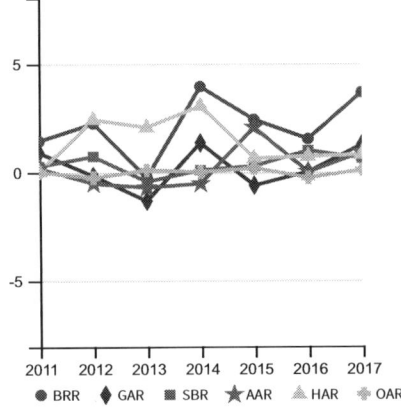

Carlos Gonzalez   RF   Colorado Rockies

Born: 10/17/1985   **Age:** 32   **Bats:** L   **Throws:** L   **Height:** 6' 1"   **Weight:** 220 lbs   **Draft Info:** International Free Agent, 2002

2017 Daily WARP Profile
0.6 Total WARP

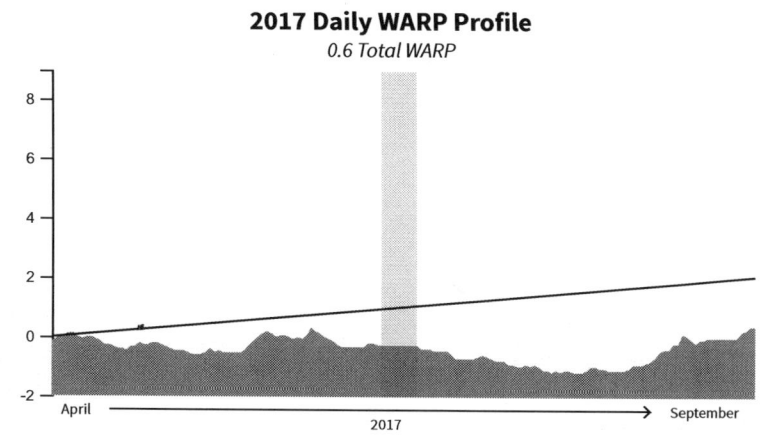

PACE
21 Sec/Pit
45th of 155
71°
Fast

Game 76: DL (shoulder strain)

Fantasy Values
2017	2018
$12.88	$9.00

YEAR	TEAM	LVL	AGE	PA	R	2B	3B	HR	RBI	BB	K	SB	AVG/OBP/SLG	TAv	VORP	BABIP	WARP
2017	COL	MLB	31	534	72	34	0	14	57	56	119	3	.262/.339/.423	.260	10.8	.318	.6

Always a product of his home environment, Gonzalez saw his numbers collapse away from Coors last year, making him unplayable in mixed and a pedestrian option in NL-only. Even Gonzalez's home stats, while solid, were missing the home runs that permitted his fantasy owners to look the other way at his below-average road performances in years past. Even if he finds a home somewhere as a starter, Gonzalez will be a risky fantasy bet in 2018 regardless of where he plays — Mike G.

2017 Batting Percentages

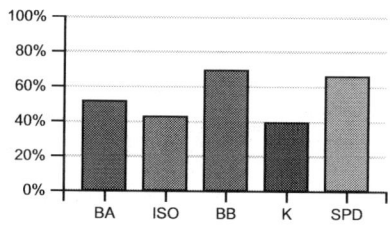

Batting PECOTA Percentiles

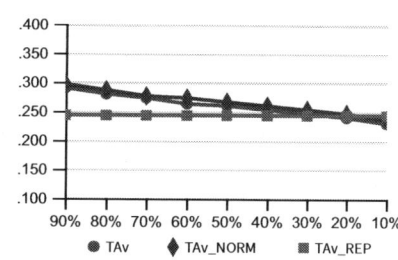

Batting WARP History

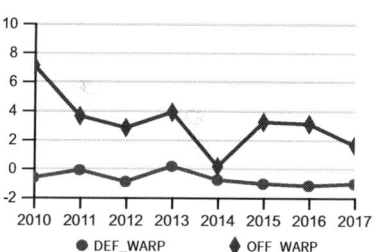

BRR (Relative to Position)

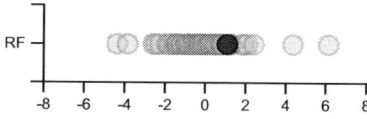

Rank		Player	BRR
8	81°	Mac Williamson	1.30
9	81°	Michael Saunders	1.29
10	78°	**Carlos Gonzalez**	**1.14**
11	77°	Abraham Almonte	1.10
12	76°	Paulo Orlando	0.93

BRR (Relative to Team)

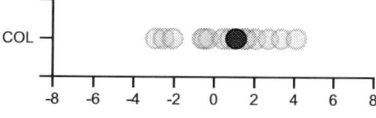

Rank		Player	BRR
5	70°	Raimel Tapia	1.62
6	53°	Charlie Blackmon	1.57
7	44°	**Carlos Gonzalez**	**1.14**
8	37°	Jonathan Lucroy	0.84
9	32°	Tony Wolters	0.50

Base Running Components

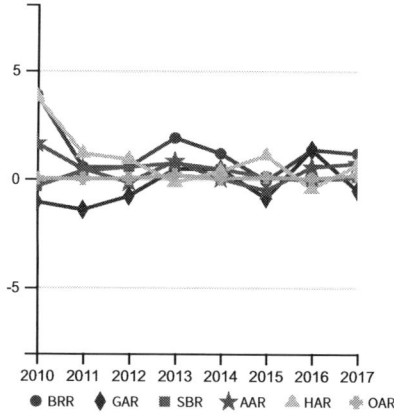

Gio Gonzalez LHP Washington Nationals ⚓

Born: 9/19/1985 **Age:** 32 **Bats:** R **Throws:** L **Height:** 6' 0" **Weight:** 205 lbs **Draft Info:** Round 1, 2004 Draft (#38 overall)

POWER
28 136th of 150
PWR

STAMINA
82 7th of 150
STM

COMMAND
62 24th of 150
CMD

2017 Daily WARP Profile
5.0 Total WARP

PACE
19 16th of 150
Sec/Pit
89°
Very Fast

Fantasy Values
2017 *2018*
$26.32 $14.00

YEAR	TEAM	LVL	AGE	W	L	SV	G	GS	IP	H	HR	BB/9	K/9	K	GB%	BABIP	WHIP	ERA	DRA	WARP	MPH 95
2017	WAS	MLB	31	15	9	0	32	32	201	158	21	3.5	8.4	188	48%	.258	1.18	2.96	3.35	5.0	91.4

After a few seasons where it appeared Gonzalez was more of a mid-tier starter than the near-ace he once was, he bounced back with one of the best years of his career. Gio went back to relying on the curve like he did in the good old days. While the pitch wasn't the loopy offering with wacky movement it once was, it kept hitters off balance and complemented his other pitches well. Gonzalez isn't likely to repeat a sub-3.00 ERA, but he should be able to keep it somewhere in the mid-3.00s while striking out enough batters to be a decent SP3 in mixed leagues. — Mike G.

2017 Pitching Percentages

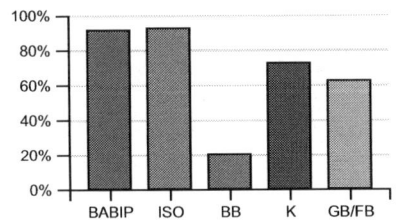

Pitching PECOTA Percentiles

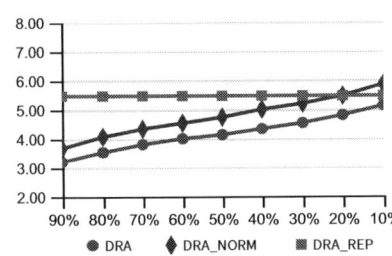

Pitching WARP History

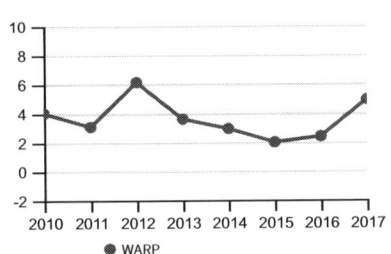

Tunnel vs LHH

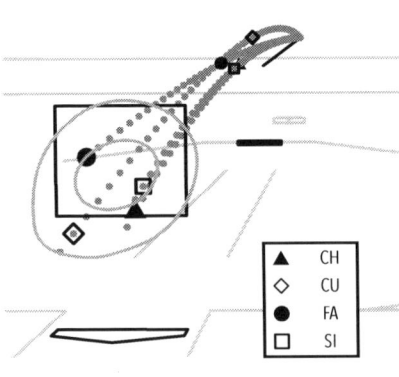

Pitch Types

Type	Freq	Velo	H Mov	V Mov
CH	18.5%	83.4 [93]	11.8 [96]	-28.2 [97]
CU	24.7%	75.1 [88]	-10.8 [112]	-57.9 [79]
FA	31.9%	90.4 [92]	8.6 [93]	-15.9 [98]
SI	24.9%	89.5 [83]	14.4 [86]	-21.8 [94]

Pitch Tunnel

Pairs	Release Diff	Tunnel Diff	Plate Diff	Speed Changes
2526	31.8	123.5	234.6	0.037

PI Scores

Year	Pitch Ct	Pwr	Cmd	Stm
2013	3307	52	58	81
2014	2613	49	58	67
2015	2955	48	68	72
2016	3100	46	63	78
2017	3352	28	62	82

Tunnel vs RHH

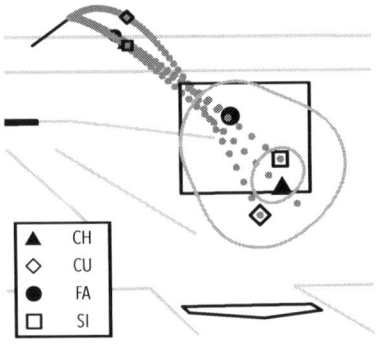

Marwin Gonzalez   UT   Houston Astros

Born: 3/14/1989 **Age:** 29 **Bats:** B **Throws:** R **Height:** 6' 1" **Weight:** 205 lbs **Draft Info:** International Free Agent, 2005

2017 Daily WARP Profile
3.1 Total WARP

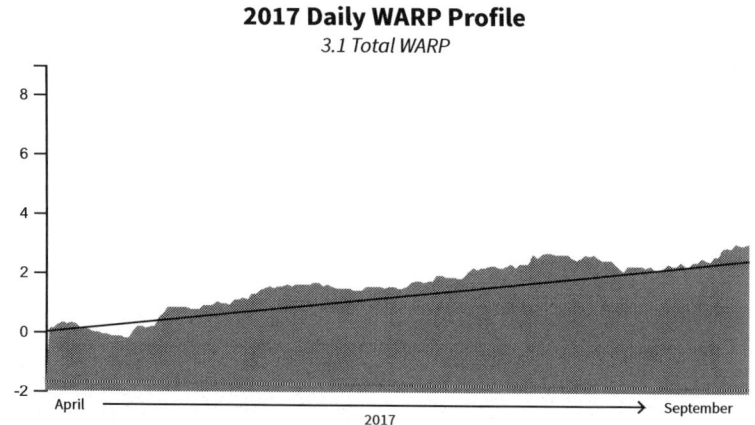

26 Sec/Pit

PACE
155th of 155
0°
Very Slow

Fantasy Values

2017	2018
$23.03	**$19.00**

YEAR	TEAM	LVL	AGE	PA	R	2B	3B	HR	RBI	BB	K	SB	AVG/OBP/SLG	TAv	VORP	BABIP	WARP
2017	HOU	MLB	28	515	67	34	0	23	90	49	99	8	.303/.377/.530	.303	36.5	.343	3.1

Underrated for years in fantasy, Gonzalez emerged as a force in 2017, pushing well past career highs in home runs and RBI and blowing away his prior TAv. It is rare to find the super-utility player who can adjust to moving around the diamond without suffering at the plate, but Gonzalez thrived in his role, hitting well regardless of where he was in the field on any given night. Whether the Astros decide to give him a regular job at one position or continue to move him around the diamond, Gonzalez will play and should once again accrue significant fantasy value. — Mike G.

2017 Batting Percentages

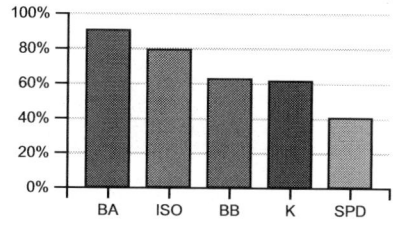

Batting PECOTA Percentiles

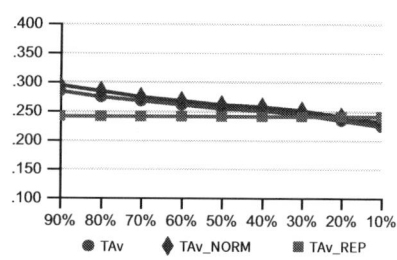

Batting WARP History

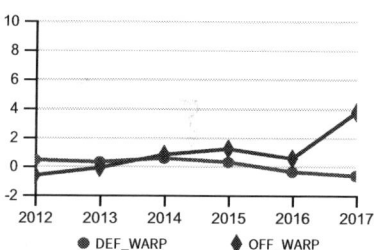

BRR (Relative to Position)

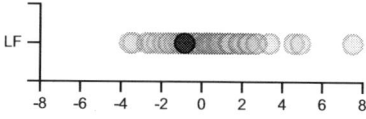

BRR (Relative to Team)

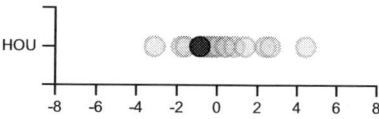

Base Running Components

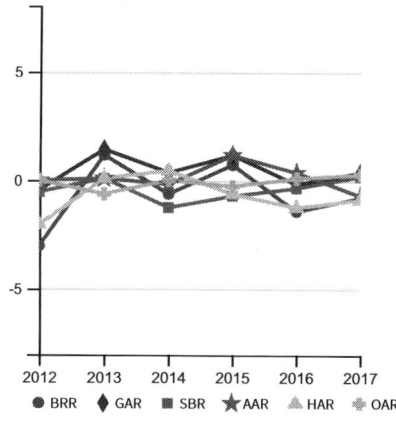

Rank		Player	BRR
52	26°	Michael Brantley	-0.59
53	25°	Jayson Werth	-0.79
54	23°	**Marwin Gonzalez**	**-0.81**
55	22°	Brandon Nimmo	-0.85
56	21°	Daniel Nava	-1.01

Rank		Player	BRR
12	41°	Derek Fisher	-0.47
13	35°	Carlos Beltran	-0.60
14	27°	**Marwin Gonzalez**	**-0.81**
15	16°	Alex Bregman	-1.52
16	7°	Yulieski Gurriel	-1.72

Miguel Gonzalez RHP Chicago White Sox

Born: 5/27/1984 **Age:** 34 **Bats:** R **Throws:** R **Height:** 6' 1" **Weight:** 170 lbs **Draft Info:** International Free Agent, 2004

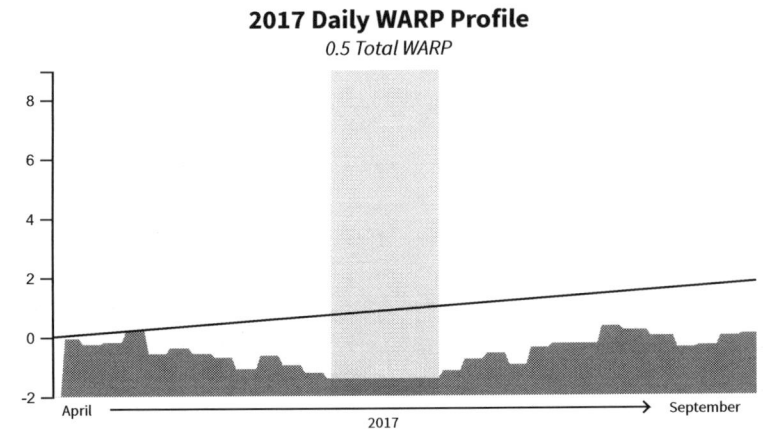

2017 Daily WARP Profile
0.5 Total WARP

Game 65: DL (AC joint inflammation)

POWER
36 113th of 150
PWR

STAMINA
71 63rd of 150
STM

COMMAND
57 53rd of 150
CMD

PACE
22 108th of 150
Sec/Pit 28°
Slow

Fantasy Values
2017	2018
$4.05	$2.00

YEAR	TEAM	LVL	AGE	W	L	SV	G	GS	IP	H	HR	BB/9	K/9	K	GB%	BABIP	WHIP	ERA	DRA	WARP	MPH 95
2017	CHA	MLB	33	7	10	0	22	22	133.2	145	16	3.2	5.7	85	38%	.296	1.44	4.31	4.95	0.9	92.6
2017	TEX	MLB	33	1	3	0	5	5	22.1	22	6	3.2	6.0	15	32%	.246	1.34	6.45	7.17	-0.4	93.1

2017 Pitching Percentages

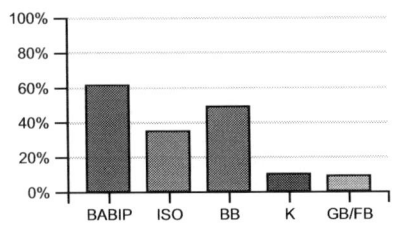

Pitching PECOTA Percentiles

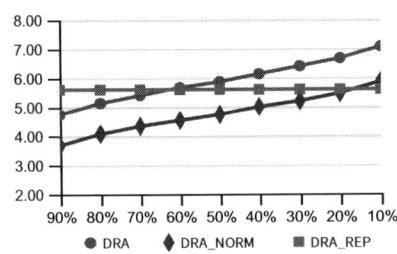

● DRA ◆ DRA_NORM ■ DRA_REP

Pitching WARP History

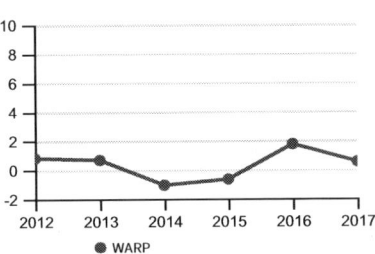

● WARP

Tunnel vs LHH

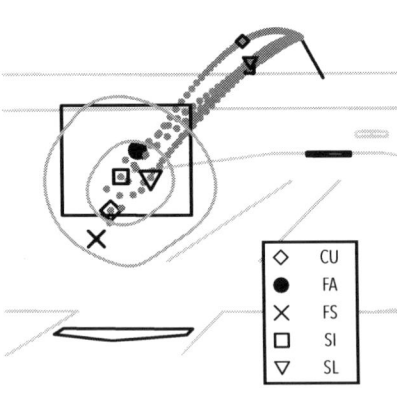

◇ CU
● FA
✕ FS
□ SI
▽ SL

Pitch Types

Type	Freq	Velo	H Mov	V Mov
CH	0.5%	85 [99]	-10.1 [106]	-31.6 [87]
CU	16.8%	77.7 [98]	8.1 [101]	-47.8 [100]
FA	26.9%	91.2 [94]	-6.8 [102]	-13.8 [104]
FS	12.2%	84.7 [98]	-9.5 [95]	-30.5 [98]
SI	22.9%	91.4 [94]	-13.4 [94]	-18.6 [105]
SL	20.7%	86.8 [111]	2 [88]	-24.7 [123]

Pitch Tunnel

Pairs	Release Diff	Tunnel Diff	Plate Diff	Speed Changes
1755	37.3	118.7	216.0	0.028

PI Scores

Year	Pitch Ct	Pwr	Cmd	Stm
2013	2704	47	49	68
2014	2535	42	47	68
2015	2433	45	54	63
2016	2087	40	52	65
2017	2506	36	57	71

Tunnel vs RHH

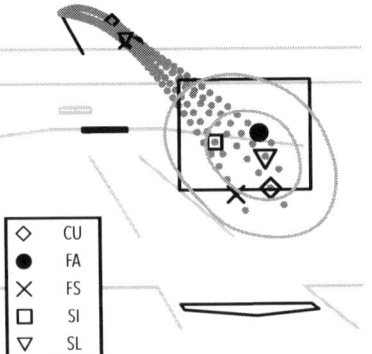

◇ CU
● FA
✕ FS
□ SI
▽ SL

Dee Gordon 2B Seattle Mariners

Born: 4/22/1988　**Age:** 30　**Bats:** L　**Throws:** R　**Height:** 5' 11"　**Weight:** 170 lbs　**Draft Info:** Round 4, 2008 Draft (#127 overall)

2017 Daily WARP Profile
2.6 Total WARP

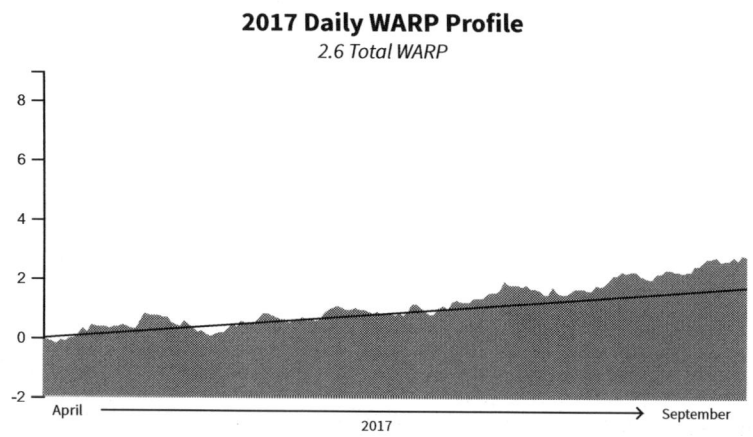

PACE
18 Sec/Pit
1st of 155
99°
Very Fast

Fantasy Values
2017	2018
$38.77	$32.00

YEAR	TEAM	LVL	AGE	PA	R	2B	3B	HR	RBI	BB	K	SB	AVG/OBP/SLG	TAv	VORP	BABIP	WARP
2017	MIA	MLB	29	695	114	20	9	2	33	25	93	60	.308/.341/.375	.258	26.8	.354	2.6

After missing 80 games due to a PED suspension in 2016, Gordon put to rest concerns about his durability with a solid season, reaching a career high in games played and his first season with 60 or more stolen bases since 2014. The TAv dropped from his career high in 2015, but in fantasy all that really matters for Gordon is that he stays on the field and racks up the swipes. Gordon will be undervalued in nearly every format because he has no power, but there's nothing wrong with taking Gordon in the second or third round and making him a category anchor. In 2018, Gordon will add outfield eligibility. — Mike G.

2017 Batting Percentages

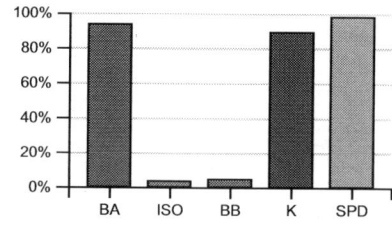

Batting PECOTA Percentiles

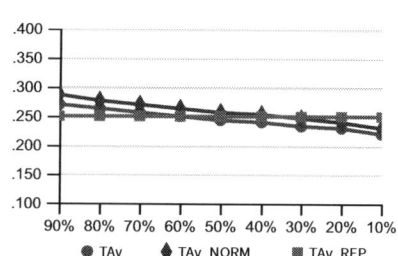

Batting WARP History

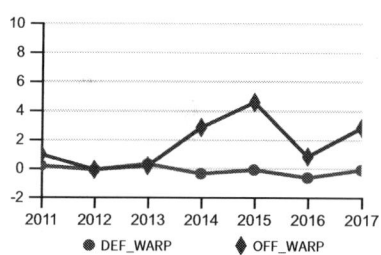

BRR (Relative to Position)

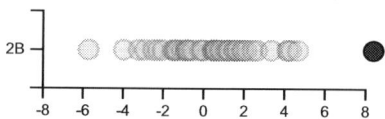

Rank		Player	BRR
1	95°	**Dee Gordon**	8.44
2	93°	Ian Kinsler	4.72
3	90°	Javier Baez	4.36
4	88°	Jonathan Schoop	4.21
5	84°	Cesar Hernandez	4.20

BRR (Relative to Team)

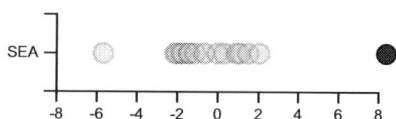

Rank		Player	BRR
1	100°	**Dee Gordon**	8.44
2	99°	Jean Segura	2.09
3	95°	Taylor Motter	1.54
4	84°	Benjamin Gamel	1.14
5	76°	Guillermo Heredia	0.99

Base Running Components

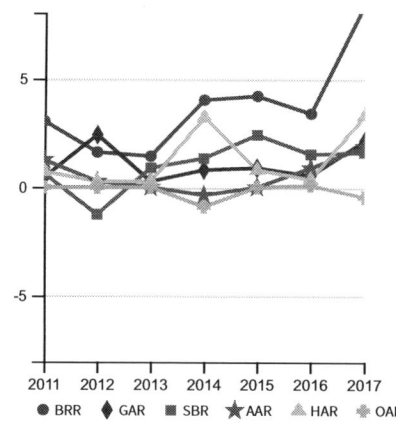

Yasmani Grandal C Los Angeles Dodgers

Born: 11/8/1988 **Age:** 29 **Bats:** B **Throws:** R **Height:** 6' 1" **Weight:** 235 lbs **Draft Info:** Round 1, 2010 Draft (#12 overall)

2017 Daily WARP Profile
4.5 Total WARP

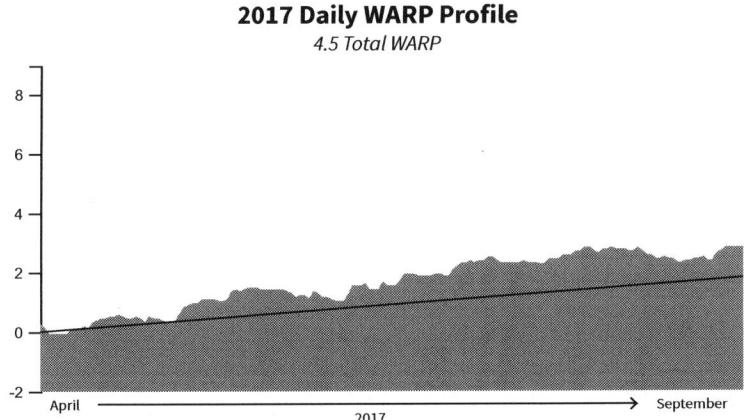

21 Sec/Pit

PACE
45th of 155
71°
Fast

Fantasy Values
2017	2018
$10.39	$11.00

YEAR	TEAM	LVL	AGE	PA	R	2B	3B	HR	RBI	BB	K	SB	AVG/OBP/SLG	TAv	VORP	BABIP	WARP
2017	LAN	MLB	28	482	50	27	0	22	58	40	130	0	.247/.308/.459	.272	25.8	.298	4.5

At the beginning of last year Grandal traded walks for contact, resulting in a higher average but not as many homers as his fantasy buyers were accustomed to. Grandal went back to his pre-2017 ways over the last few months of the season. His power and position make him worth using despite the low batting average, but Grandal lost playing time to teammate Austin Barnes in the postseason. Grandal's framing skills ensure he will start somewhere, but he's been in the majors long enough that it is unlikely he will ever reach the lofty offensive heights some were hoping for from the former first-round pick. — Mike G.

2017 Batting Percentages

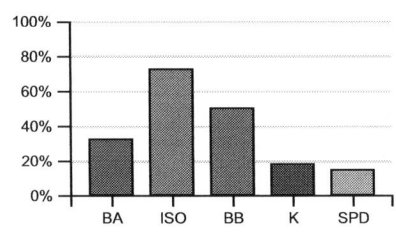

Batting PECOTA Percentiles

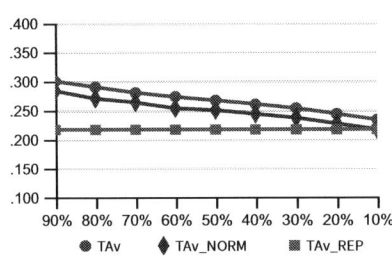

Batting WARP History

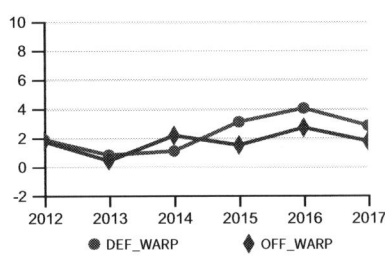

BRR (Relative to Position)

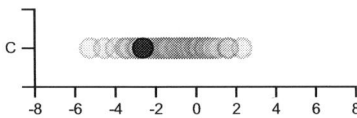

Rank		Player	BRR
64	22°	Travis d'Arnaud	-2.25
65	19°	Martin Maldonado	-2.37
66	17°	**Yasmani Grandal**	**-2.58**
67	16°	Nick Hundley	-2.80
68	15°	Rene Rivera	-2.83

BRR (Relative to Team)

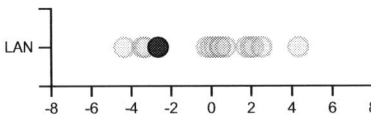

Rank		Player	BRR
10	40°	Travis Taijeron	0.03
11	31°	Cody Bellinger	-0.17
12	25°	**Yasmani Grandal**	**-2.58**
13	16°	Justin Turner	-3.24
14	10°	Matt Kemp	-3.37

Base Running Components

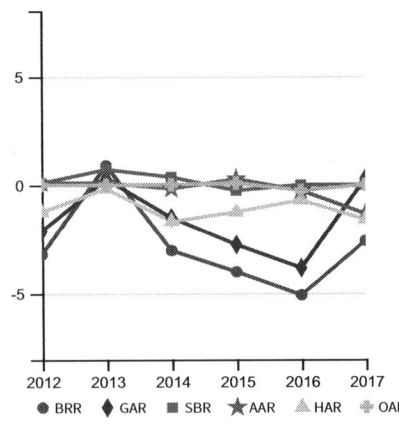

Curtis Granderson OF Toronto Blue Jays

Born: 3/16/1981 **Age:** 37 **Bats:** L **Throws:** R **Height:** 6' 1" **Weight:** 200 lbs **Draft Info:** Round 3, 2002 Draft (#80 overall)

2017 Daily WARP Profile
2.0 Total WARP

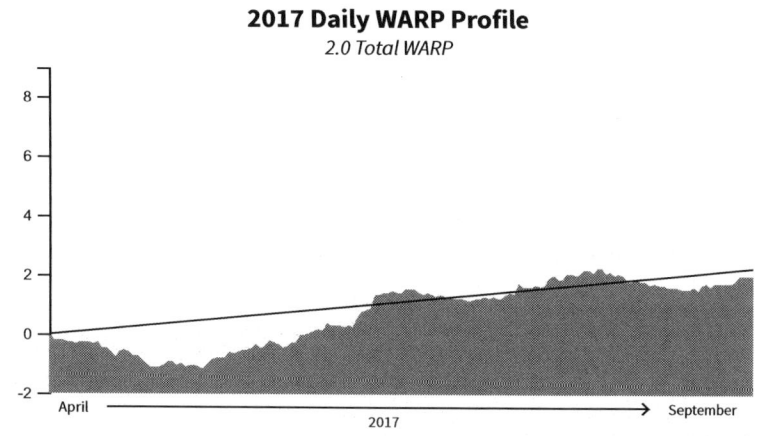

PACE
19 Sec/Pit
4th of 155
97°
Very Fast

Fantasy Values
2017	2018
$11.61	$3.00

YEAR	TEAM	LVL	AGE	PA	R	2B	3B	HR	RBI	BB	K	SB	AVG/OBP/SLG	TAv	VORP	BABIP	WARP
2017	NYN	MLB	36	395	58	22	3	19	52	53	90	4	.228/.334/.481	.294	26.4	.251	2.0
2017	LAN	MLB	36	132	16	2	0	7	12	18	33	2	.161/.288/.366	.258	2.9	.153	-.0

Granderson is an oddity: a streaky hitter whose seasonal numbers are consistent. Granderson's batting average plummeted (in part due to an abysmal .228 BABIP), but his power remained consistent despite long stretches where it appeared the veteran outfielder was done. A late-season trade to the Dodgers briefly revived Grandy, but he started struggling again late in the season and was left off Los Angeles' World Series roster. Granderson has a little more left in the tank, but at his age and as a nonelite performer he shouldn't be counted on as an everyday player in mixed, and could find himself in a platoon or job-sharing arrangement. — Mike G.

2017 Batting Percentages

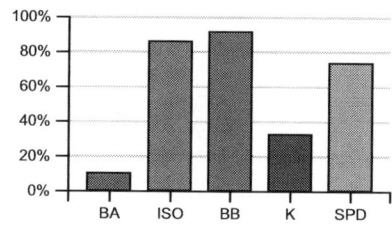

Batting PECOTA Percentiles

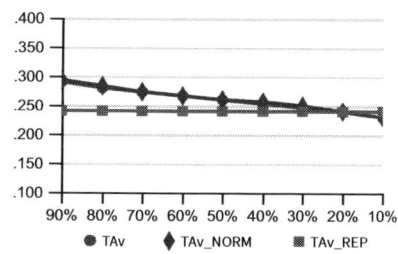

Batting WARP History

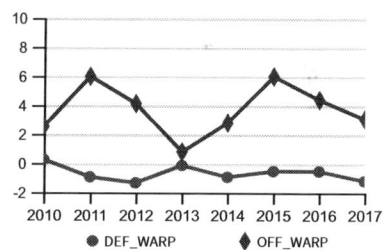

BRR (Relative to Position)

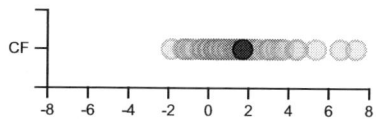

Rank		Player	BRR
18	59°	Joc Pederson	1.80
19	58°	Boog Powell	1.74
20	56°	**Curtis Granderson**	**1.74**
21	54°	Mikie Mahtook	1.63
22	52°	Bradley Zimmer	1.62

BRR (Relative to Team)

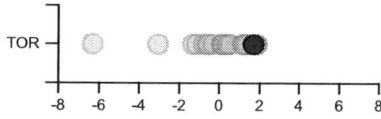

Rank		Player	BRR
2	100°	Ezequiel Carrera	1.88
3	100°	Teoscar Hernandez	1.88
4	99°	**Curtis Granderson**	**1.74**
5	97°	Richard Urena	1.43
6	95°	Michael Saunders	1.29

Base Running Components

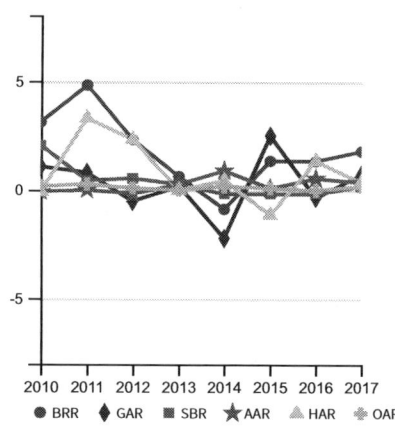

Kendall Graveman   RHP   Oakland Athletics

Born: 12/21/1990   **Age:** 27   **Bats:** R   **Throws:** R   **Height:** 6' 2"   **Weight:** 200 lbs   **Draft Info:** Round 8, 2013 Draft (#235 overall)

2017 Daily WARP Profile
1.7 Total WARP

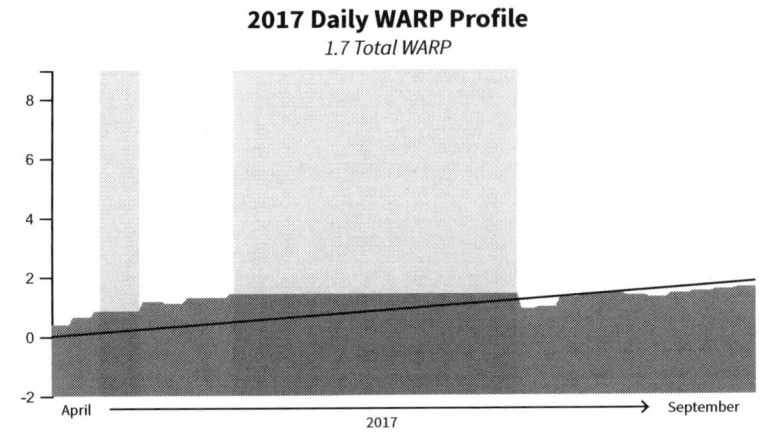

Game 12: DL (shoulder strain), **Game 43:** DL (shoulder strain)

63 PWR — **POWER** 16th of 150

50 STM — **STAMINA** 135th of 150

77 CMD — **COMMAND** 3rd of 150

20 Sec/Pit — **PACE** 37th of 150 / 75° / Fast

Fantasy Values

2017	2018
$4.77	$2.00

YEAR	TEAM	LVL	AGE	W	L	SV	G	GS	IP	H	HR	BB/9	K/9	K	GB%	BABIP	WHIP	ERA	DRA	WARP	MPH 95
2017	OAK	MLB	26	6	4	0	19	19	105.1	114	12	2.7	6.0	70	52%	.313	1.39	4.19	4.16	1.7	95.4

2017 Pitching Percentages

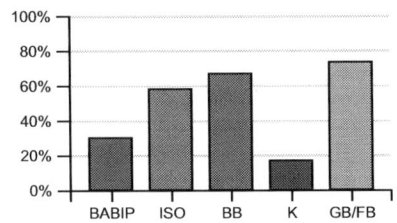

Pitching PECOTA Percentiles

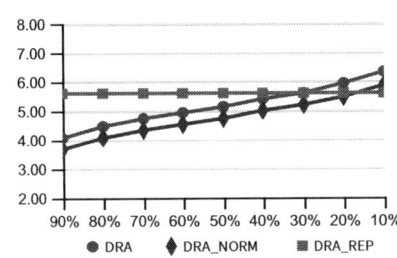

Pitching WARP History

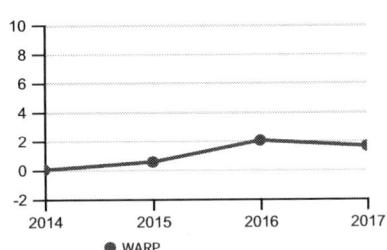

Tunnel vs LHH

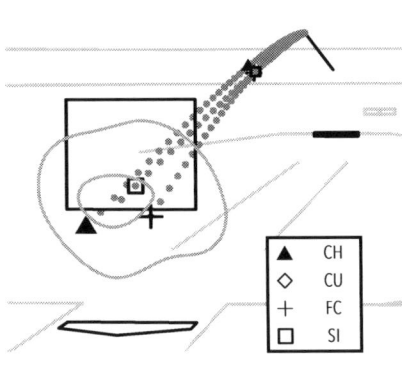

	CH
▲	CH
◇	CU
+	FC
□	SI

Pitch Types

Type	Freq	Velo	H Mov	V Mov
CH	10.4%	86.4 [105]	-12.1 [94]	-28.4 [96]
CU	5.6%	79.5 [104]	11 [113]	-43.7 [109]
FA	2.0%	93.8 [104]	-9.1 [91]	-12.2 [109]
FC	15.1%	90.5 [112]	-0.5 [90]	-21.8 [108]
SI	66.9%	93.8 [109]	-14 [89]	-18.5 [106]

Pitch Tunnel

Pairs	Release Diff	Tunnel Diff	Plate Diff	Speed Changes
1225	24.6	116.6	207.7	0.016

PI Scores

Year	Pitch Ct	Pwr	Cmd	Stm
2015	1870	43	53	66
2016	2817	55	57	74
2017	1666	63	77	50

Tunnel vs RHH

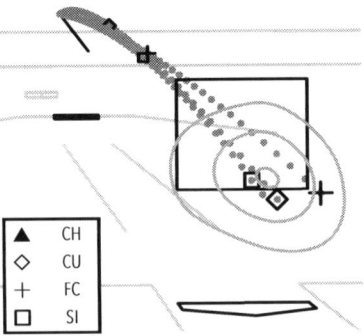

	CH
▲	CH
◇	CU
+	FC
□	SI

Jon Gray   RHP   Colorado Rockies

Born: 11/5/1991   **Age:** 26   **Bats:** R   **Throws:** R   **Height:** 6' 4"   **Weight:** 235 lbs   **Draft Info:** Round 1, 2013 Draft (#3 overall)

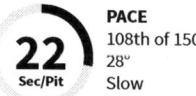

2017 Daily WARP Profile
2.3 Total WARP

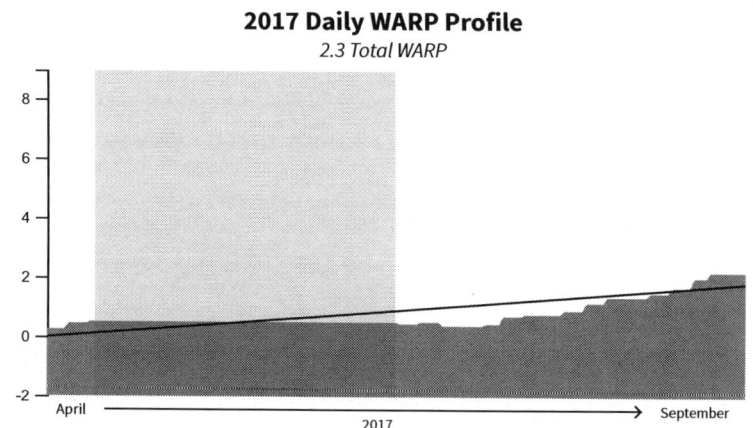

Game 12: DL (foot stress fracture)

POWER 64 — 15th of 150
STAMINA 53 — 121st of 150
COMMAND 60 — 37th of 150
PACE 22 Sec/Pit — 108th of 150 — 28" Slow

Fantasy Values
2017 $12.25 2018 $14.00

YEAR	TEAM	LVL	AGE	W	L	SV	G	GS	IP	H	HR	BB/9	K/9	K	GB%	BABIP	WHIP	ERA	DRA	WARP	MPH 95
2017	COL	MLB	25	10	4	0	20	20	110.1	113	10	2.4	9.1	112	49%	.336	1.30	3.67	3.67	2.3	97.8

Here he is: the starting pitcher who has the ability not only to survive at Coors Field but potentially become an ace. Limited by injuries, Gray nevertheless kept his ERA under 4.00 and even managed to pitch better at home than on the road despite a nonelite whiff rate. Gray moved away from his curve and mostly relied on a fastball/slider combo that was difficult to square up on at any altitude. There is still room for improvement, and while the Coors discount should still apply you also shouldn't be afraid to use Gray in nearly any league. — Mike G.

2017 Pitching Percentages
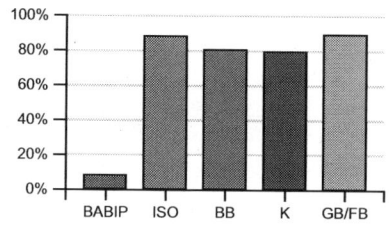

Pitching PECOTA Percentiles
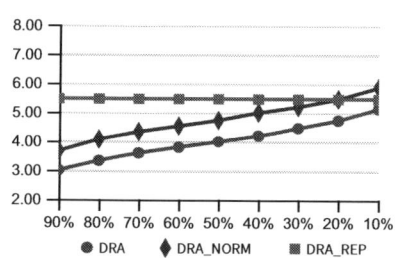

Pitching WARP History
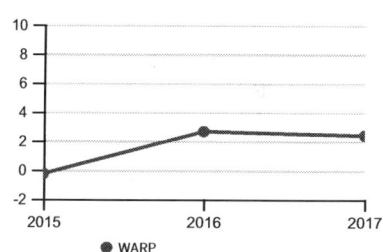

Tunnel vs LHH
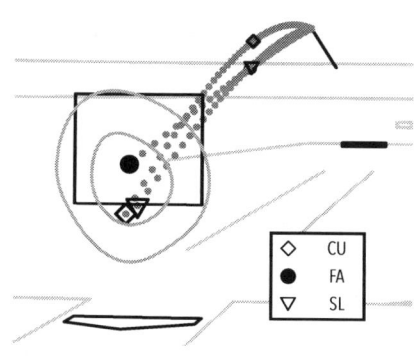

Tunnel vs RHH
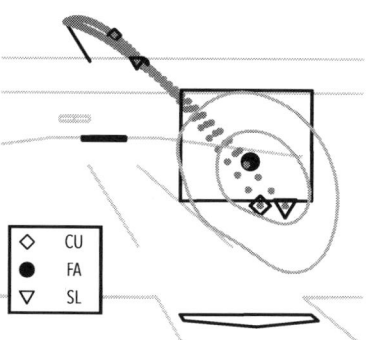

Pitch Types
Type	Freq	Velo	H Mov	V Mov
CH	1.2%	87.3 [109]	-8.4 [114]	-21.4 [116]
CU	13.8%	80.7 [109]	6.7 [96]	-43.8 [109]
FA	57.5%	96.3 [113]	-8.3 [95]	-12.6 [108]
SL	27.5%	90.1 [125]	1.8 [88]	-23.1 [127]

Pitch Tunnel
Pairs	Release Diff	Tunnel Diff	Plate Diff	Speed Changes
1363	31.0	117.7	213.7	0.026

PI Scores
Year	Pitch Ct	Pwr	Cmd	Stm
2015	673	60	55	68
2016	2782	56	35	74
2017	1835	64	60	53

Sonny Gray RHP New York Yankees

Born: 11/7/1989 **Age:** 28 **Bats:** R **Throws:** R **Height:** 5' 10" **Weight:** 190 lbs **Draft Info:** Round 1, 2011 Draft (#18 overall)

PACE

25
Sec/Pit

143rd of 150
5°
Very Slow

2017 Daily WARP Profile
4.2 Total WARP

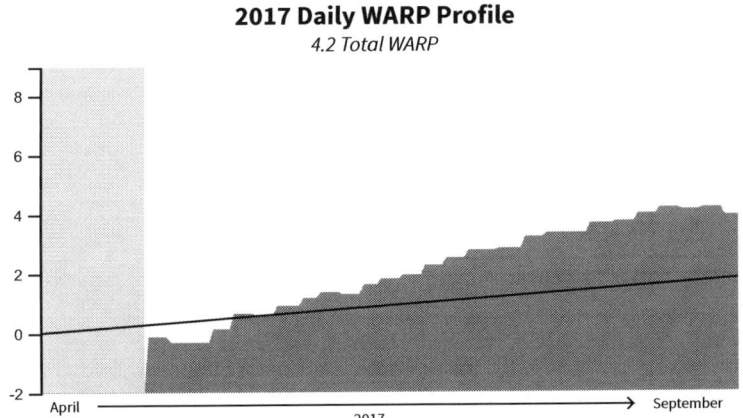

Game 1: DL (shoulder strain)

POWER
53 49th of 150
PWR

STAMINA
74 44th of 150
STM

COMMAND
45 117th of 150
CMD

Fantasy Values

2017	2018
$16.93	$13.00

YEAR	TEAM	LVL	AGE	W	L	SV	G	GS	IP	H	HR	BB/9	K/9	K	GB%	BABIP	WHIP	ERA	DRA	WARP	MPH 95
2017	OAK	MLB	27	6	5	0	16	16	97	84	8	2.8	8.7	94	58%	.285	1.18	3.43	3.49	2.3	94.8
2017	NYA	MLB	27	4	7	0	11	11	65.1	55	11	3.7	8.1	59	48%	.246	1.26	3.72	2.95	1.9	94.6

Gray had a solid season, bouncing back from a miserable 2016. A midseason trade to the Yankees didn't slow him down, and while Gray's home-run rate did spike, his overall numbers otherwise remained solid. The move from Oakland to Yankee Stadium does hamper his value somewhat, but Gray remains a decent contributor who can at least give his fantasy teams SP4 or SP5 value in mixed. — Mike G.

2017 Pitching Percentages

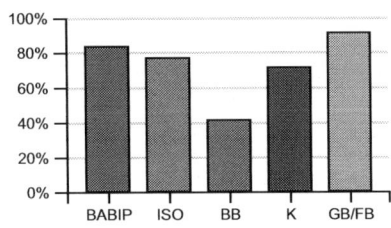

Pitching PECOTA Percentiles

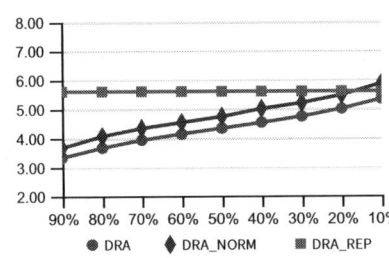

● DRA ◆ DRA_NORM ■ DRA_REP

Pitching WARP History

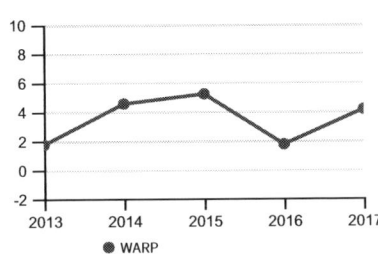

● WARP

Tunnel vs LHH

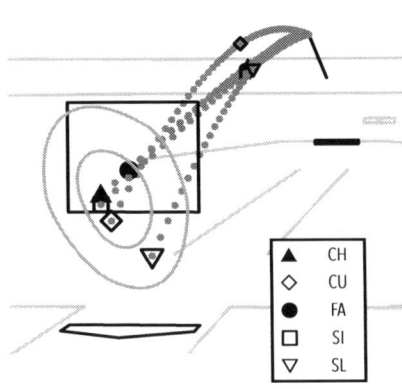

▲	CH
◇	CU
●	FA
□	SI
▽	SL

Pitch Types

Type	Freq	Velo	H Mov	V Mov
CH	5.8%	89.9 [119]	-9 [111]	-23.8 [109]
CU	14.1%	81.5 [112]	13.7 [123]	-47.8 [100]
FA	30.6%	93.8 [104]	-1.9 [124]	-15.4 [99]
FC	0.4%	91.1 [115]	1.5 [100]	-22.5 [105]
SI	33.2%	92 [98]	-9.8 [120]	-21.1 [96]
SL	15.8%	85.5 [105]	7.5 [113]	-38.3 [84]

Pitch Tunnel

Pairs	Release Diff	Tunnel Diff	Plate Diff	Speed Changes
1978	30.5	124.6	232.8	0.024

PI Scores

Year	Pitch Ct	Pwr	Cmd	Stm
2013	995	53	65	70
2014	3274	50	42	81
2015	3067	56	42	78
2016	1945	52	55	49
2017	2660	53	45	74

Tunnel vs RHH

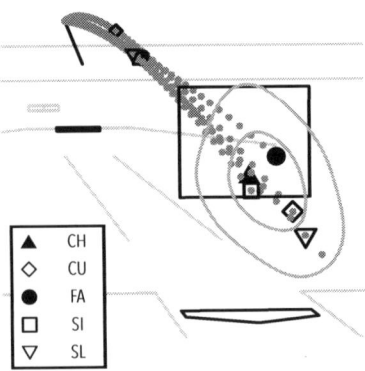

▲	CH
◇	CU
●	FA
□	SI
▽	SL

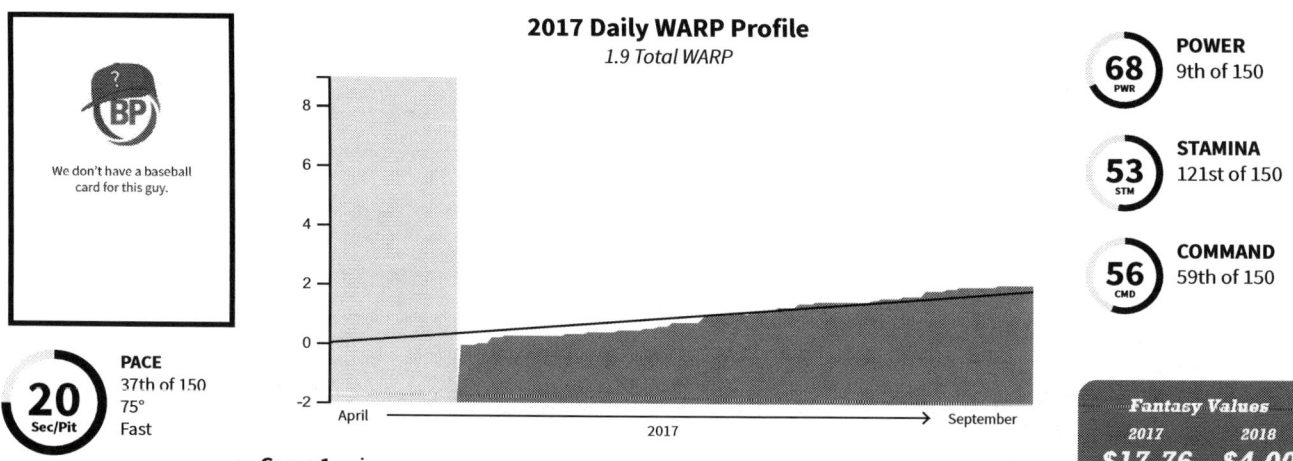

Chad Green   RHP   New York Yankees

Born: 5/24/1991   **Age:** 27   **Bats:** L   **Throws:** R   **Height:** 6' 3"   **Weight:** 210 lbs   **Draft Info:** Round 11, 2013 Draft (#336 overall)

2017 Daily WARP Profile
1.9 Total WARP

We don't have a baseball card for this guy.

POWER 68 PWR 9th of 150

STAMINA 53 STM 121st of 150

COMMAND 56 CMD 59th of 150

PACE 20 Sec/Pit 37th of 150 / 75° / Fast

April — 2017 — September

Game 1: minors

Fantasy Values
2017	2018
$17.76	$4.00

YEAR	TEAM	LVL	AGE	W	L	SV	G	GS	IP	H	HR	BB/9	K/9	K	GB%	BABIP	WHIP	ERA	DRA	WARP	MPH 95
2017	NYA	MLB	26	5	0	0	40	1	69	34	4	2.2	13.4	103	28%	.236	0.74	1.83	2.66	1.9	97.5

2017 Pitching Percentages

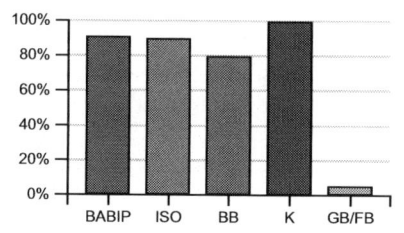

Pitching PECOTA Percentiles

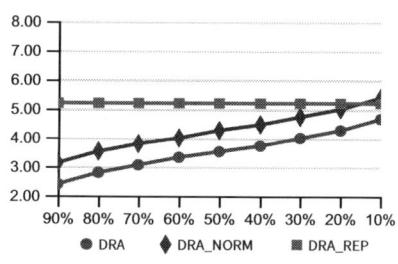

● DRA   ◆ DRA_NORM   ■ DRA_REP

Pitching WARP History

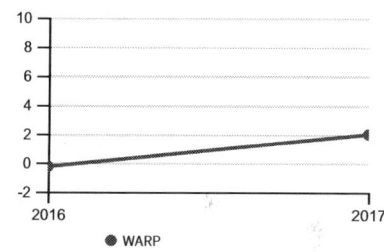

● WARP

Tunnel vs LHH

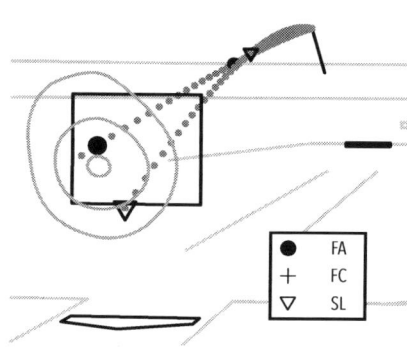

● FA
+ FC
▽ SL

Pitch Types

Type	Freq	Velo	H Mov	V Mov
FA	67.8%	95.9 [112]	-4 [115]	-10.7 [114]
FC	7.4%	90.2 [110]	2.2 [103]	-23.6 [101]
FS	0.7%	85.3 [101]	-8.5 [98]	-22.8 [123]
SI	1.6%	94.2 [111]	-10.2 [117]	-17.8 [108]
SL	22.5%	85.9 [107]	3 [93]	-35.1 [93]

Pitch Tunnel

Pairs	Release Diff	Tunnel Diff	Plate Diff	Speed Changes
879	26.5	114.3	223.2	0.020

PI Scores

Year	Pitch Ct	Pwr	Cmd	Stm
2016	836	50	45	64
2017	1132	68	56	53

Tunnel vs RHH

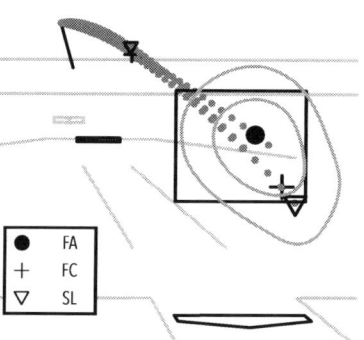

● FA
+ FC
▽ SL

Didi Gregorius   SS   New York Yankees

Born: 2/18/1990   **Age:** 28   **Bats:** L   **Throws:** R   **Height:** 6' 3"   **Weight:** 205 lbs   **Draft Info:** International Free Agent, 2007

22 Sec/Pit

PACE
99th of 155
36°
Slow

2017 Daily WARP Profile
4.4 Total WARP

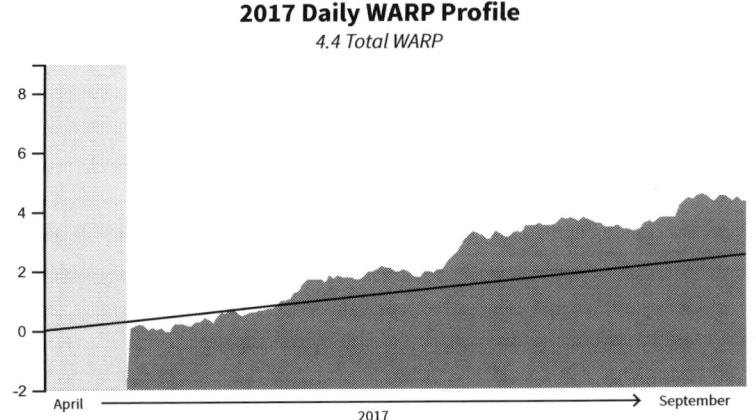

April   2017   September

Game 1: DL (shoulder strain)

Fantasy Values
2017	2018
$20.42	**$17.00**

YEAR	TEAM	LVL	AGE	PA	R	2B	3B	HR	RBI	BB	K	SB	AVG/OBP/SLG	TAv	VORP	BABIP	WARP
2017	NYA	MLB	27	570	73	27	0	25	87	25	70	3	.287/.318/.478	.282	39.0	.287	4.4

Didi put to rest the idea that his 2016 was a fluke by setting yet another career high in home runs and slightly improving on his batting average. Gregorius isn't merely a product of Yankee Stadium. He hit more home runs on the road than at home and with a much higher batting average. His high-contact approach and increased fly-ball rate should keep him at this level, and while 25 home runs aren't as special as they once were, Gregorius is legit. — Mike G.

2017 Batting Percentages

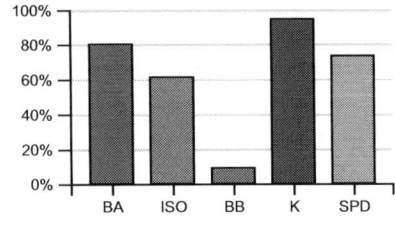

Batting PECOTA Percentiles

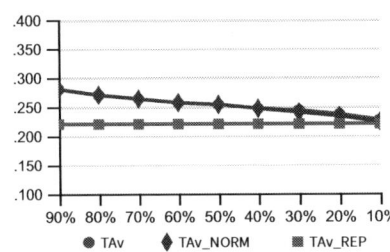

Batting WARP History

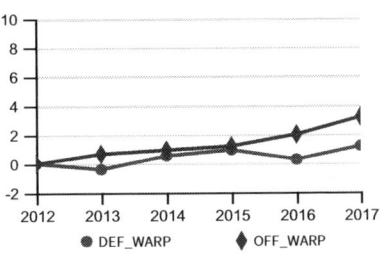

BRR (Relative to Position)

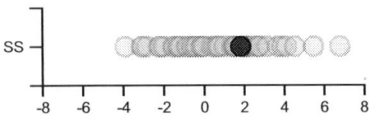

Rank		Player	BRR
15	55°	Orlando Arcia	2.07
16	52°	Tim Anderson	2.06
17	50°	**Didi Gregorius**	**1.87**
18	47°	Freddy Galvis	1.62
19	46°	Ehire Adrianza	1.55

BRR (Relative to Team)

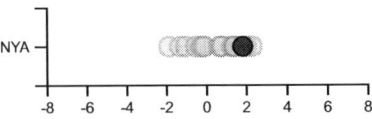

Rank		Player	BRR
1	99°	Gary Sanchez	2.33
2	92°	Aaron Hicks	2.05
3	85°	**Didi Gregorius**	**1.87**
4	70°	Brett Gardner	1.44
5	67°	Jace Peterson	1.44

Base Running Components

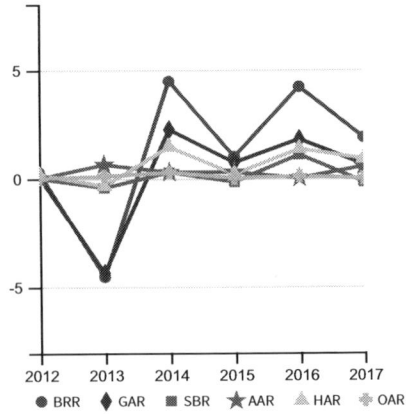

Zack Greinke   RHP   Arizona Diamondbacks

Born: 10/21/1983   **Age:** 34   **Bats:** R   **Throws:** R   **Height:** 6' 2"   **Weight:** 200 lbs   **Draft Info:** Round 1, 2002 Draft (#6 overall)

2017 Daily WARP Profile
5.8 Total WARP

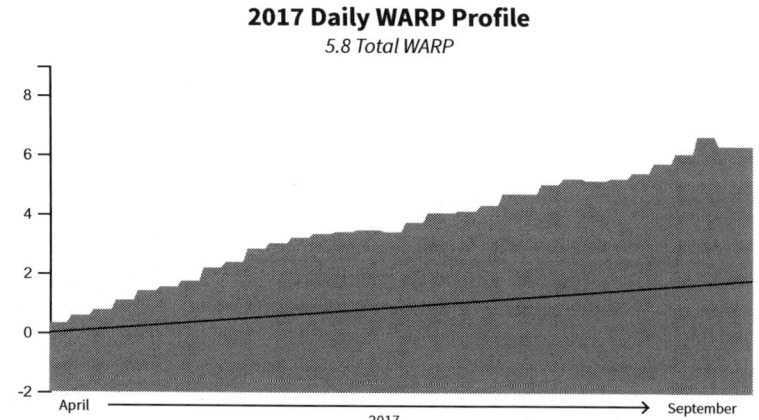

2017

33 PWR   **POWER** 125th of 150

79 STM   **STAMINA** 17th of 150

61 CMD   **COMMAND** 30th of 150

23 Sec/Pit   **PACE** 126th of 150 / 16° / Very Slow

Fantasy Values

2017	2018
$30.63	**$22.00**

YEAR	TEAM	LVL	AGE	W	L	SV	G	GS	IP	H	HR	BB/9	K/9	K	GB%	BABIP	WHIP	ERA	DRA	WARP	MPH 95
2017	ARI	MLB	33	17	7	0	32	32	202.1	172	25	2.0	9.6	215	48%	.285	1.07	3.20	3.00	5.8	92.3

After a disastrous first year in Arizona, Greinke not only bounced back but had one of the stronger campaigns of his already storied career. Greinke worked off his slider more than he ever had in the past, and while his ERA still sat above 3.00, his strikeout rate was the highest it had been since way back in 2011 with the Brewers. Greinke's up-and-down track record will make some reluctant to pay him like an ace, but that just makes him all the better if you can stash him on your team as a top-end SP2. — Mike G.

2017 Pitching Percentages

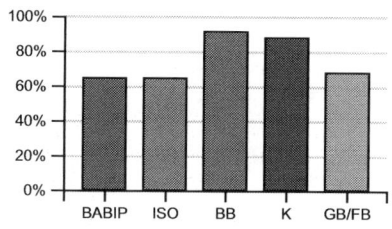

Pitching PECOTA Percentiles

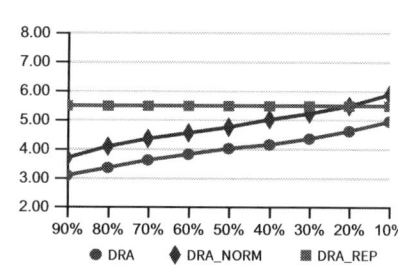

Pitching WARP History

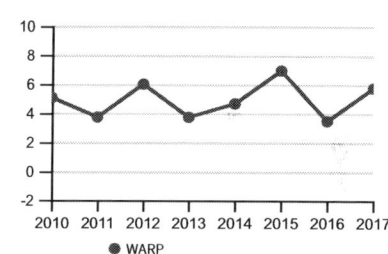

Tunnel vs LHH

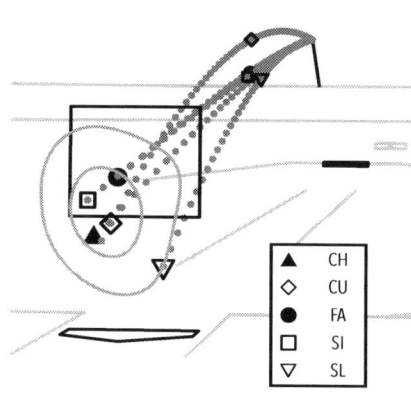

Pitch Types

Type	Freq	Velo	H Mov	V Mov
CH	15.7%	87.4 [109]	-10.5 [103]	-26.9 [100]
CS	0.5%	65.5 [93]	11.8 [104]	-69.3 [91]
CU	13.0%	74.4 [86]	11.6 [115]	-55.1 [85]
FA	42.2%	91 [94]	-1.5 [126]	-14 [104]
SI	6.2%	91 [92]	-9.7 [120]	-17.3 [110]
SL	22.4%	84.2 [99]	6.6 [109]	-31.6 [103]

Pitch Tunnel

Pairs	Release Diff	Tunnel Diff	Plate Diff	Speed Changes
2271	29.9	116.4	220.1	0.034

PI Scores

Year	Pitch Ct	Pwr	Cmd	Stm
2013	2807	47	56	71
2014	3194	45	47	78
2015	3235	45	59	78
2016	2493	42	72	70
2017	3141	33	61	79

Tunnel vs RHH

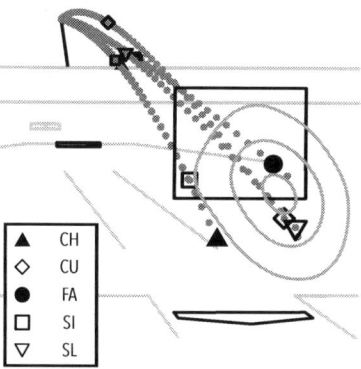

Robert Gsellman   RHP   New York Mets

Born: 7/18/1993 **Age:** 24 **Bats:** R **Throws:** R **Height:** 6' 4" **Weight:** 205 lbs **Draft Info:** Round 13, 2011 Draft (#402 overall)

2017 Daily WARP Profile
-0.9 Total WARP

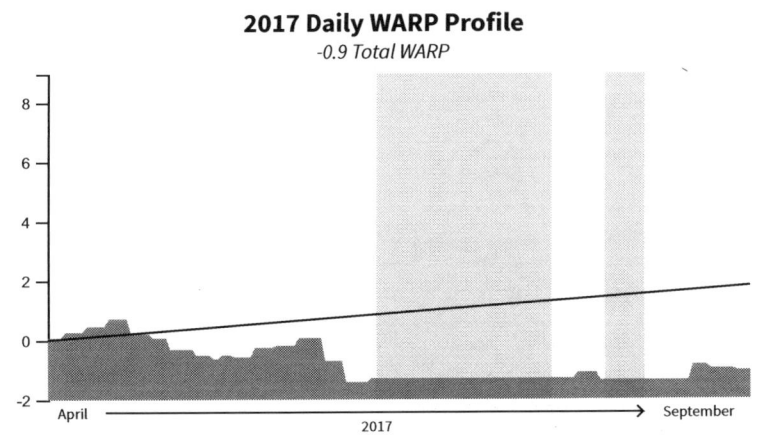

Game 77: DL (hamstring strain), **Game 129:** minors

POWER
55 PWR 43rd of 150

STAMINA
64 STM 89th of 150

COMMAND
55 CMD 62nd of 150

PACE
19 Sec/Pit 16th of 150 89° Very Fast

Fantasy Values
2017	2018
$1.41	$3.00

YEAR	TEAM	LVL	AGE	W	L	SV	G	GS	IP	H	HR	BB/9	K/9	K	GB%	BABIP	WHIP	ERA	DRA	WARP	MPH 95
2017	NYN	MLB	23	8	7	0	25	22	119.2	138	17	3.2	6.2	82	51%	.303	1.50	5.19	6.21	-0.9	94.7

2017 Pitching Percentages

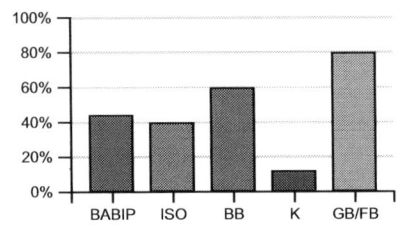

Pitching PECOTA Percentiles

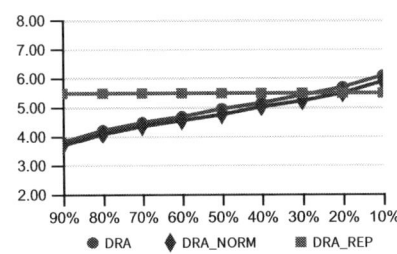

Pitching WARP History

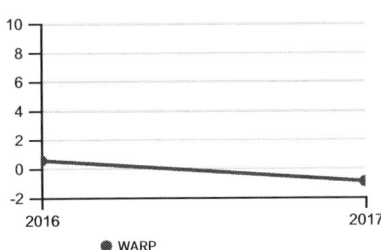

Tunnel vs LHH

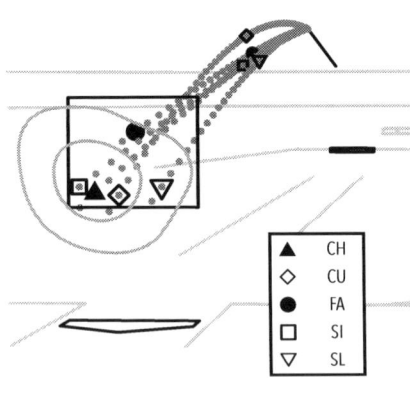

Pitch Types

Type	Freq	Velo	H Mov	V Mov
CH	10.0%	85.9 [103]	-12.4 [93]	-24.5 [107]
CU	11.5%	80.7 [109]	7.9 [101]	-45.2 [106]
FA	18.9%	93.6 [103]	-8.3 [94]	-14.7 [101]
SI	44.5%	93.2 [105]	-15 [82]	-18.7 [105]
SL	15.1%	89.3 [122]	-0.6 [77]	-24.2 [124]

Pitch Tunnel

Pairs	Release Diff	Tunnel Diff	Plate Diff	Speed Changes
1468	22.5	117.5	219.7	0.020

PI Scores

Year	Pitch Ct	Pwr	Cmd	Stm
2016	709	56	42	65
2017	2042	55	55	64

Tunnel vs RHH

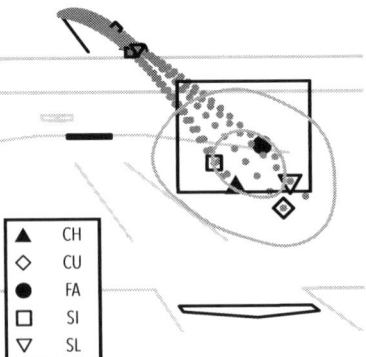

Yulieski Gurriel   1B   Houston Astros

Born: 6/9/1984   **Age:** 34   **Bats:** R   **Throws:** R   **Height:** 6' 0"   **Weight:** 190 lbs   **Draft Info:** International Free Agent, 2016

PACE
20 Sec/Pit
18th of 155
88°
Very Fast

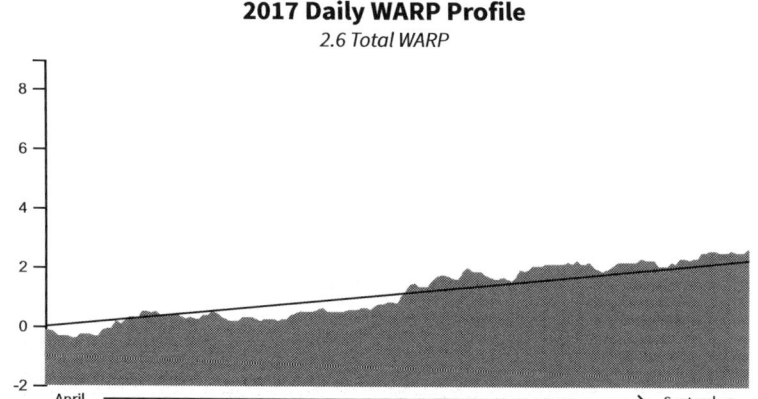

2017 Daily WARP Profile
2.6 Total WARP

April   2017   September

Fantasy Values
2017	2018
$19.48	**$15.00**

YEAR	TEAM	LVL	AGE	PA	R	2B	3B	HR	RBI	BB	K	SB	AVG/OBP/SLG	TAv	VORP	BABIP	WARP
2017	HOU	MLB	33	564	69	43	1	18	75	22	62	3	.299/.332/.486	.282	18.0	.308	2.6

Despite a power output that lagged behind that of many of his first-base counterparts, Gurriel's strong contributions in batting average elevated him above more than a few more prominent sluggers. While Gurriel is unlikely to ever see a spike in home runs, he is enough of a pure hitter that a strong batting average with a decent amount of power should remain part of his portfolio. — Mike G.

2017 Batting Percentages

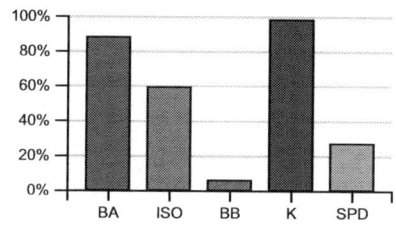

Batting PECOTA Percentiles

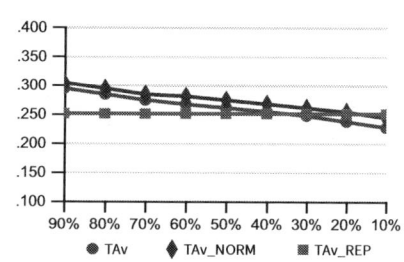

Batting WARP History

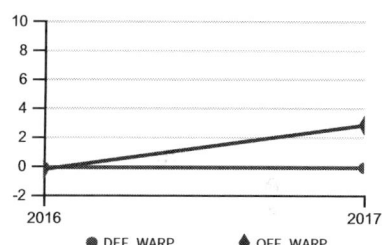

BRR (Relative to Position)

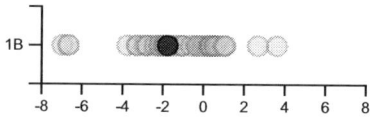

Rank		Player	BRR
26	53°	Tommy Joseph	-1.59
27	51°	Danny Valencia	-1.71
28	48°	**Yulieski Gurriel**	**-1.72**
29	47°	Adrian Gonzalez	-1.82
30	44°	Justin Bour	-1.82

BRR (Relative to Team)

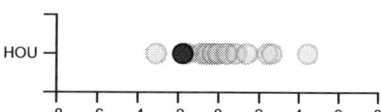

Rank		Player	BRR
13	35°	Carlos Beltran	-0.60
14	27°	Marwin Gonzalez	-0.81
15	16°	Alex Bregman	-1.52
16	7°	**Yulieski Gurriel**	**-1.72**
17	0°	Carlos Correa	-3.04

Base Running Components

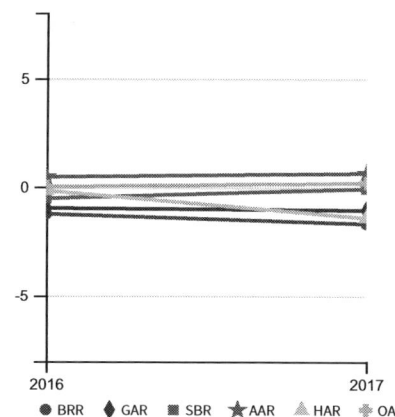

Jedd Gyorko   3B   St. Louis Cardinals

Born: 9/23/1988   **Age:** 29   **Bats:** R   **Throws:** R   **Height:** 5' 10"   **Weight:** 215 lbs   **Draft Info:** Round 2, 2010 Draft (#59 overall)

21 Sec/Pit

PACE
45th of 155
71°
Fast

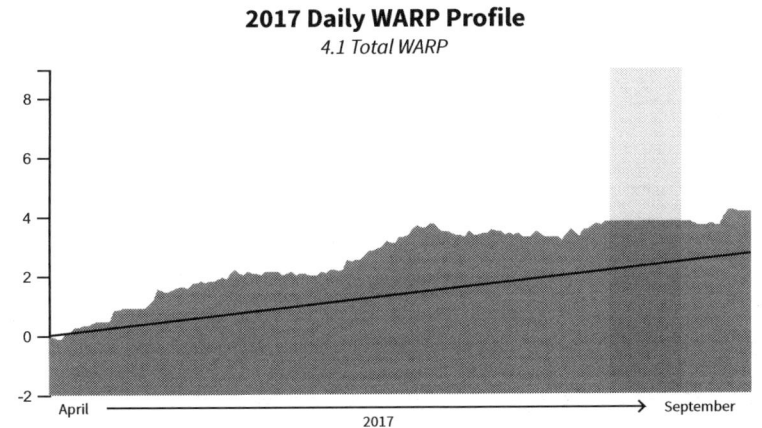

2017 Daily WARP Profile
4.1 Total WARP

April — 2017 — September

Game 130: DL (hamstring strain)

Fantasy Values

2017	2018
$15.68	**$12.00**

YEAR	TEAM	LVL	AGE	PA	R	2B	3B	HR	RBI	BB	K	SB	AVG/OBP/SLG	TAv	VORP	BABIP	WARP
2017	SLN	MLB	28	481	52	21	2	20	67	47	105	6	.272/.341/.472	.287	28.4	.312	4.1

Gyorko is an excellent example of how baseball's power explosion has altered the fantasy landscape. Despite falling from 30 home runs in 2016 to 20 last year, Gyorko jumped up 31 slots in mixed-league rankings thanks to a 30-point spike in batting average and six additional steals. Gyorko isn't a world beater but offers enough power to provide value in any format. — Mike G.

2017 Batting Percentages

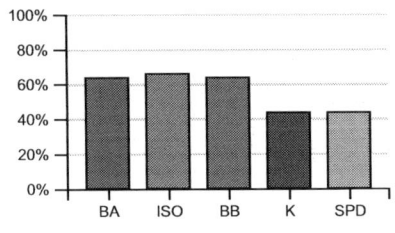

Batting PECOTA Percentiles

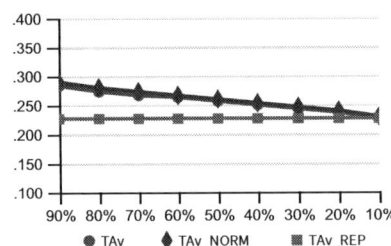

Batting WARP History

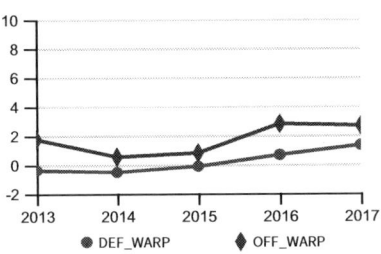

BRR (Relative to Position)

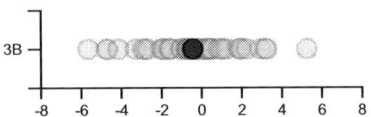

Rank		Player	BRR
29	53°	Marco Hernandez	-0.29
30	52°	Yandy Diaz	-0.39
31	49°	**Jedd Gyorko**	**-0.40**
32	48°	Giovanny Urshela	-0.46
33	45°	Nolan Arenado	-0.47

BRR (Relative to Team)

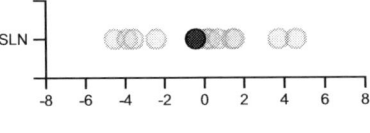

Rank		Player	BRR
7	47°	Jose Martinez	0.14
8	46°	Luke Voit	-0.27
9	38°	**Jedd Gyorko**	**-0.40**
10	25°	Matt Carpenter	-2.37
11	14°	Marcell Ozuna	-3.52

Base Running Components

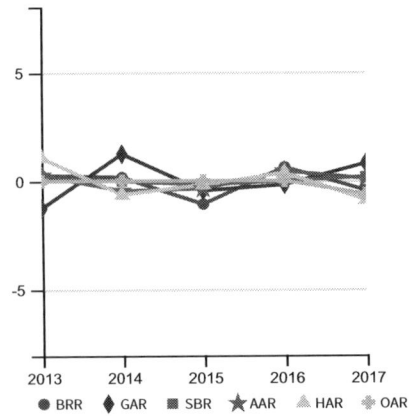

Cole Hamels LHP Texas Rangers

Born: 12/27/1983 **Age:** 34 **Bats:** L **Throws:** L **Height:** 6' 4" **Weight:** 205 lbs **Draft Info:** Round 1, 2002 Draft (#17 overall)

2017 Daily WARP Profile
1.8 Total WARP

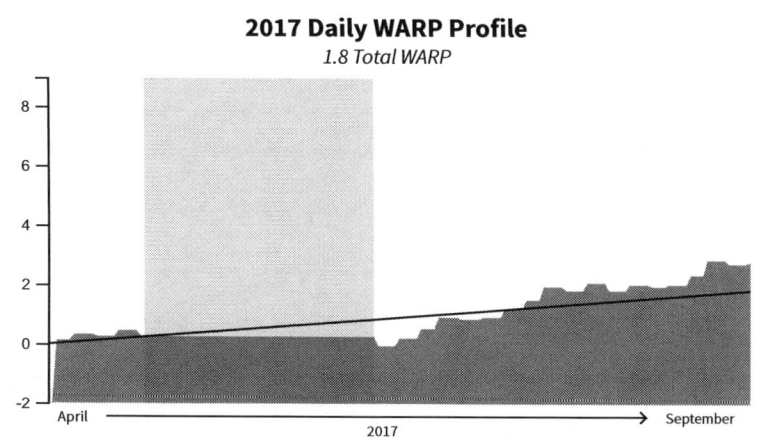

Game 23: DL (oblique strain)

| | POWER | 48 PWR | 66th of 150 |

POWER 48 PWR 66th of 150

STAMINA 63 STM 92nd of 150

COMMAND 47 CMD 102nd of 150

PACE 20 Sec/Pit 37th of 150 75° Fast

Fantasy Values
| 2017 | 2018 |
| $12.34 | $13.00 |

YEAR	TEAM	LVL	AGE	W	L	SV	G	GS	IP	H	HR	BB/9	K/9	K	GB%	BABIP	WHIP	ERA	DRA	WARP	MPH 95
2017	TEX	MLB	33	11	6	0	24	24	148	125	18	3.2	6.4	105	48%	.251	1.20	4.20	4.49	1.8	93.5

By some measures it was the worst season of Hamels' career and it wasn't particularly close. His velocity only dropped off slightly, but he looked far more hittable than he ever had and lacked the ability to finish off hitters that he had in the past. Perhaps 2017 was merely a blip on the radar, but with so many innings under his belt Hamels is a risk you should avoid on draft day unless he is priced based off last year's performance as opposed to past glories. — Mike G.

2017 Pitching Percentages

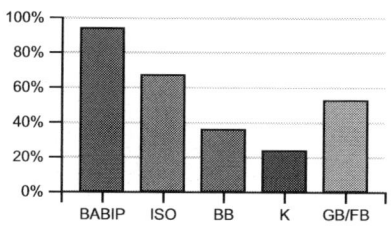

Pitching PECOTA Percentiles

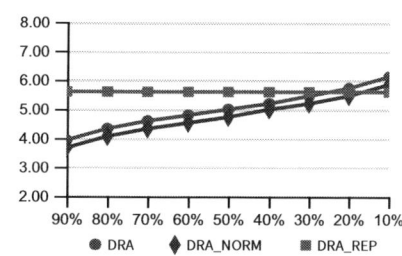

Pitching WARP History

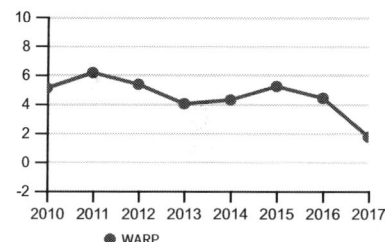

Tunnel vs LHH

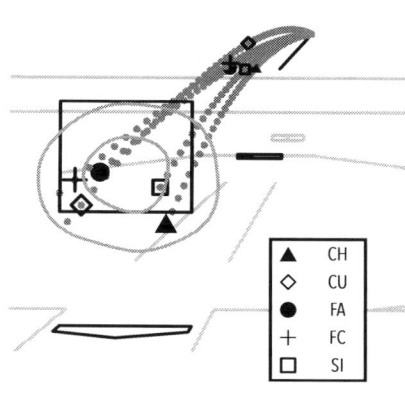

Pitch Types

Type	Freq	Velo	H Mov	V Mov
CH	20.7%	83.4 [93]	13.5 [87]	-26.9 [101]
CU	12.9%	79.4 [104]	-2.5 [79]	-45.6 [105]
FA	26.0%	92.3 [99]	9.3 [90]	-14.5 [102]
FC	18.4%	89.1 [104]	2.3 [80]	-22 [107]
SI	21.9%	92.3 [100]	14.7 [84]	-19 [104]

Pitch Tunnel

Pairs	Release Diff	Tunnel Diff	Plate Diff	Speed Changes
1696	27.4	115.9	231.8	0.025

PI Scores

Year	Pitch Ct	Pwr	Cmd	Stm
2013	3405	52	54	85
2014	3124	55	57	81
2015	3322	54	51	80
2016	3239	53	58	83
2017	2298	48	47	63

Tunnel vs RHH

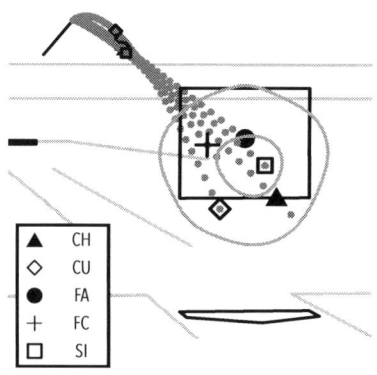

Billy Hamilton   CF   Cincinnati Reds

Born: 9/9/1990   **Age:** 27   **Bats:** B   **Throws:** R   **Height:** 6'0"   **Weight:** 160 lbs   **Draft Info:** Round 2, 2009 Draft (#57 overall)

19 Sec/Pit

PACE
4th of 155
97°
Very Fast

2017 Daily WARP Profile
1.0 Total WARP

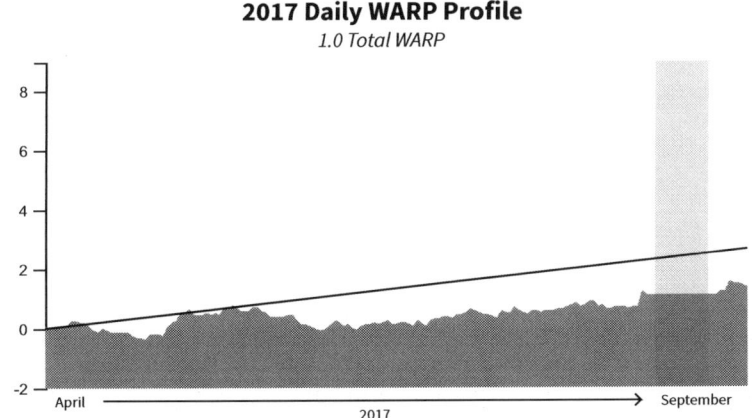

April   2017   September

Game 141: DL (thumb fracture)

Fantasy Values

2017	2018
$28.00	**$27.00**

YEAR	TEAM	LVL	AGE	PA	R	2B	3B	HR	RBI	BB	K	SB	AVG/OBP/SLG	TAv	VORP	BABIP	WARP
2017	CIN	MLB	26	633	85	17	11	4	38	44	133	59	.247/.299/.335	.227	4.7	.313	1.0

He's an offensive liability in real life, but if he's starting Hamilton's ludicrous speed makes him a near-elite asset in fantasy with his steals alone. The idea of Hamilton stealing 100 bases looks more and more like a pipe dream with each passing season, but even with "only" 60 steals Hamilton is a category king in an era when no one else this side of Dee Gordon offers what B-Ham does. — Mike G.

2017 Batting Percentages

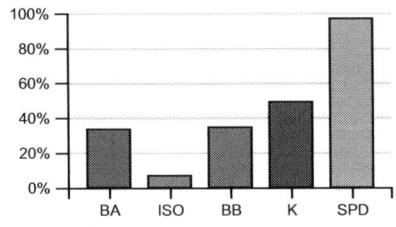

Batting PECOTA Percentiles

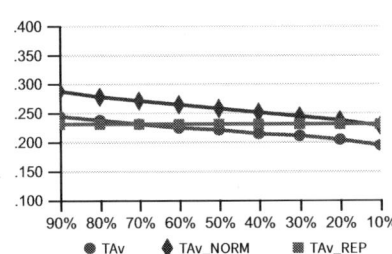

Batting WARP History

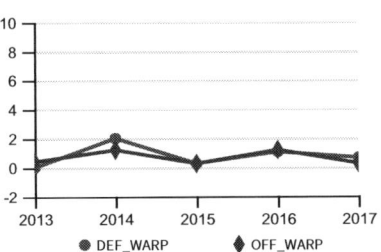

BRR (Relative to Position)

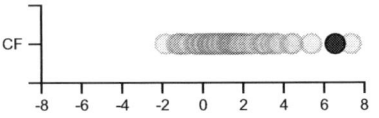

Rank		Player	BRR
1	98°	Byron Buxton	7.39
2	94°	**Billy Hamilton**	**6.60**
3	90°	Ender Inciarte	5.41
4	87°	Cameron Maybin	4.50
5	84°	Chris Taylor	4.37

BRR (Relative to Team)

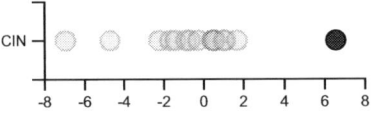

Rank		Player	BRR
1	77°	**Billy Hamilton**	**6.60**
2	75°	Arismendy Alcantara	1.73
3	74°	Phil Gosselin	1.15
4	73°	Phil Ervin	1.06
5	63°	Jose Peraza	0.61

Base Running Components

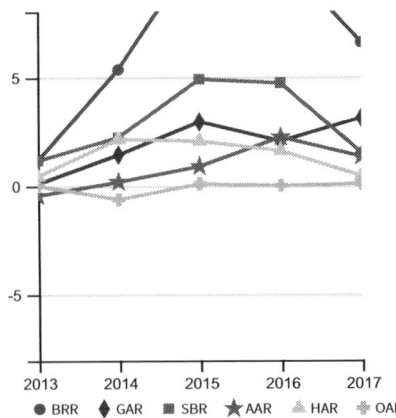

Jason Hammel   RHP   Kansas City Royals

Born: 9/2/1982   **Age:** 35   **Bats:** R   **Throws:** R   **Height:** 6' 6"   **Weight:** 225 lbs   **Draft Info:** Round 10, 2002 Draft (#284 overall)

2017 Daily WARP Profile
1.6 Total WARP

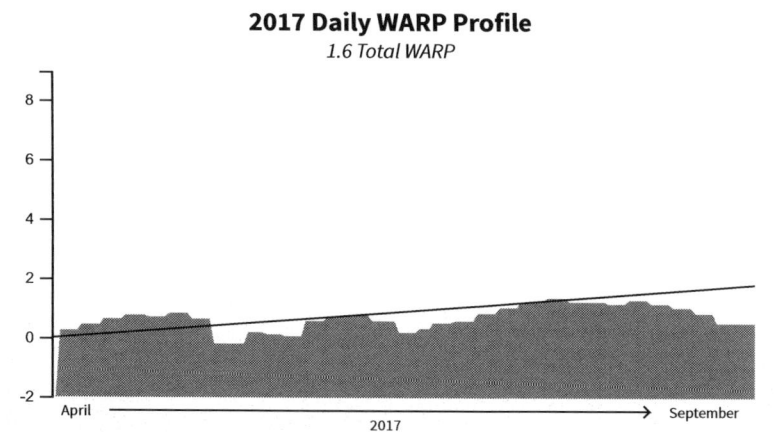

April   2017   September

PACE
23 Sec/Pit
126th of 150
16°
Very Slow

POWER
40 PWR
96th of 150

STAMINA
79 STM
17th of 150

COMMAND
53 CMD
72nd of 150

Fantasy Values

2017	2018
$2.69	**$2.00**

YEAR	TEAM	LVL	AGE	W	L	SV	G	GS	IP	H	HR	BB/9	K/9	K	GB%	BABIP	WHIP	ERA	DRA	WARP	MPH 95
2017	KCA	MLB	34	8	13	0	32	32	180.1	209	26	2.4	7.2	145	38%	.318	1.43	5.29	4.78	1.6	93.5

2017 Pitching Percentages

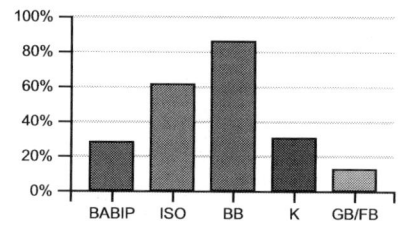

Pitching PECOTA Percentiles

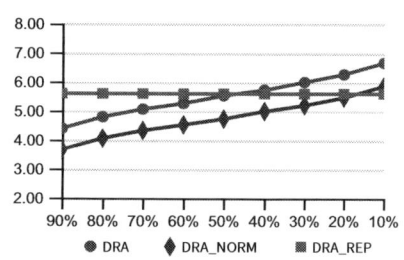

● DRA   ◆ DRA_NORM   ■ DRA_REP

Pitching WARP History

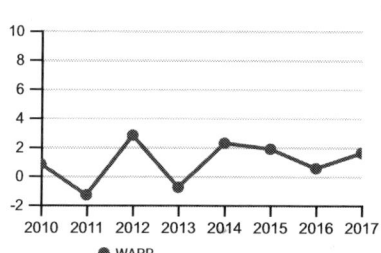

● WARP

Tunnel vs LHH

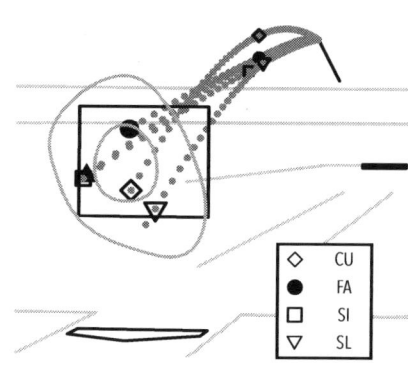

◇ CU
● FA
□ SI
▽ SL

Pitch Types

Type	Freq	Velo	H Mov	V Mov
CH	3.6%	85.5 [102]	-11.7 [97]	-26 [103]
CU	9.5%	77.9 [98]	11.1 [113]	-50.5 [95]
FA	26.6%	92.5 [99]	-6.1 [105]	-13.9 [104]
SI	23.4%	92.7 [102]	-12 [104]	-17.8 [108]
SL	36.9%	85.3 [104]	5 [102]	-33.3 [98]

Pitch Tunnel

Pairs	Release Diff	Tunnel Diff	Plate Diff	Speed Changes
2201	23.9	119.7	230.6	0.025

PI Scores

Year	Pitch Ct	Pwr	Cmd	Stm
2013	2294	52	44	59
2014	2768	49	58	69
2015	2668	43	46	69
2016	2622	43	45	69
2017	3002	40	53	79

Tunnel vs RHH

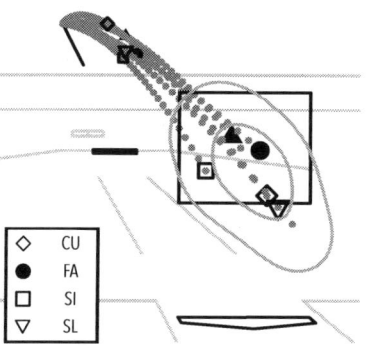

◇ CU
● FA
□ SI
▽ SL

Brad Hand   LHP   San Diego Padres

Born: 3/20/1990   **Age:** 28   **Bats:** L   **Throws:** L   **Height:** 6'3"   **Weight:** 228 lbs   **Draft Info:** Round 2, 2008 Draft (#52 overall)

We don't have a baseball card for this guy.

2017 Daily WARP Profile
1.8 Total WARP

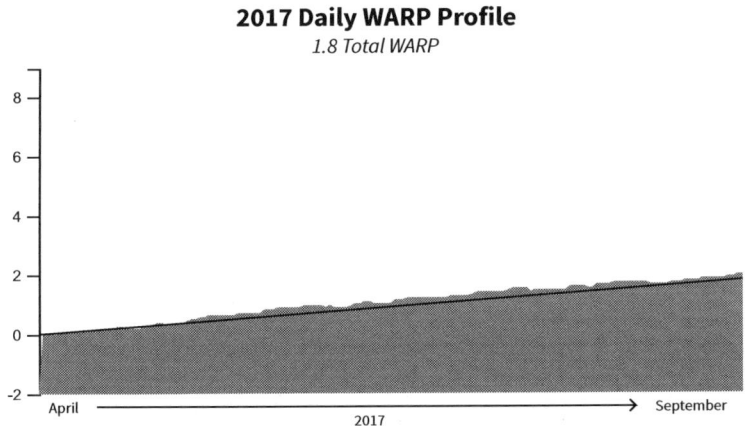

April ——————————————→ September
2017

PACE
27 Sec/Pit
148th of 150
1°
Very Slow

POWER
42 PWR
86th of 150

STAMINA
53 STM
121st of 150

COMMAND
49 CMD
91st of 150

Fantasy Values
	2017	2018
	$21.12	**$17.00**

YEAR	TEAM	LVL	AGE	W	L	SV	G	GS	IP	H	HR	BB/9	K/9	K	GB%	BABIP	WHIP	ERA	DRA	WARP	MPH 95
2017	SDN	MLB	27	3	4	21	72	0	79.1	54	9	2.3	11.8	104	46%	.263	0.93	2.16	3.13	1.8	95.0

A failed starter with the Marlins, Hand was converted to relief with the Padres and the results have been phenomenal. Some added fastball velocity has helped, but most of the improvement has come due to the addition of a slider that has made Hand a first-tier reliever. The Friars locked Hand in with a multi-year deal, locking him as a closer in 2018 and probably beyond. — Mike G.

2017 Pitching Percentages

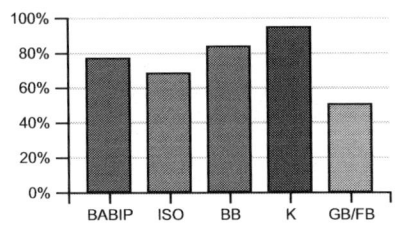

Pitching PECOTA Percentiles

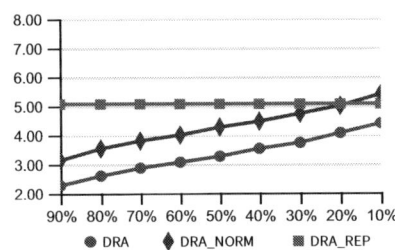

● DRA   ◆ DRA_NORM   ■ DRA_REP

Pitching WARP History

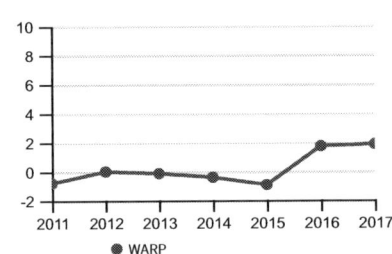

● WARP

Tunnel vs LHH

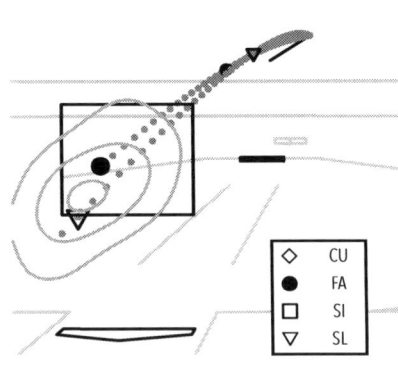

◇	CU
●	FA
□	SI
▽	SL

Pitch Types

Type	Freq	Velo	H Mov	V Mov
CH	0.1%	88.1 [112]	9.3 [110]	-29.5 [93]
CU	4.4%	78.4 [100]	-9.5 [107]	-51.8 [92]
FA	29.2%	93.8 [104]	8.7 [93]	-15.1 [100]
FC	0.5%	93.8 [130]	13.8 [22]	-24.4 [98]
SI	21.4%	93.5 [107]	14.6 [85]	-22.1 [93]
SL	44.4%	82.2 [91]	-13.6 [140]	-39.9 [79]

Pitch Tunnel

Pairs	Release Diff	Tunnel Diff	Plate Diff	Speed Changes
888	30.3	122.6	220.3	0.031

PI Scores

Year	Pitch Ct	Pwr	Cmd	Stm
2013	300	57	35	43
2014	1775	51	39	60
2015	1545	55	47	49
2016	1431	50	40	59
2017	1194	42	49	53

Tunnel vs RHH

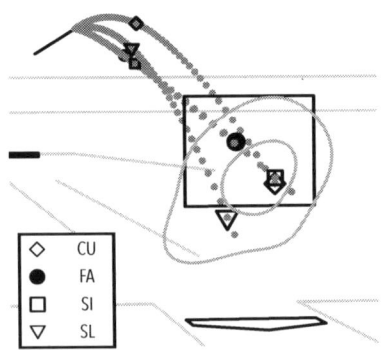

◇	CU
●	FA
□	SI
▽	SL

Mitch Haniger   RF   Seattle Mariners

Born: 12/23/1990   **Age:** 27   **Bats:** R   **Throws:** R   **Height:** 6' 2"   **Weight:** 215 lbs   **Draft Info:** Round 1, 2012 Draft (#38 overall)

PACE
21 Sec/Pit
45th of 155
71°
Fast

2017 Daily WARP Profile
2.2 Total WARP

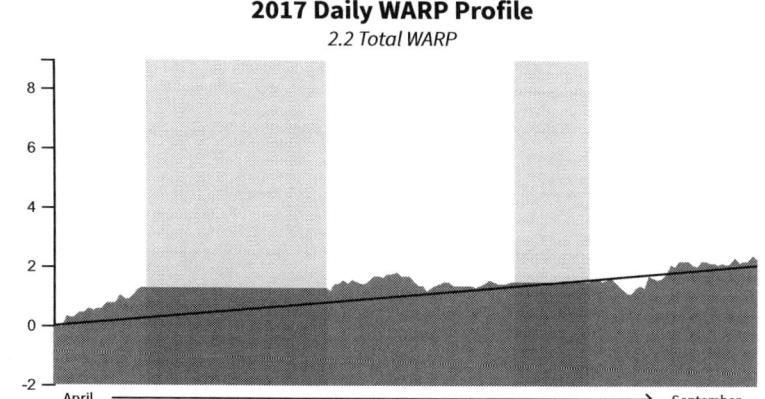

Game 22: DL (oblique strain), **Game 106:** DL (facial laceration)

Fantasy Values
2017	2018
$14.13	$15.00

YEAR	TEAM	LVL	AGE	PA	R	2B	3B	HR	RBI	BB	K	SB	AVG/OBP/SLG	TAv	VORP	BABIP	WARP
2017	SEA	MLB	26	410	58	25	2	16	47	31	93	5	.282/.352/.491	.284	16.8	.338	2.2

2017 Batting Percentages

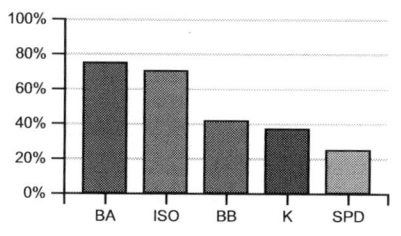

Batting PECOTA Percentiles

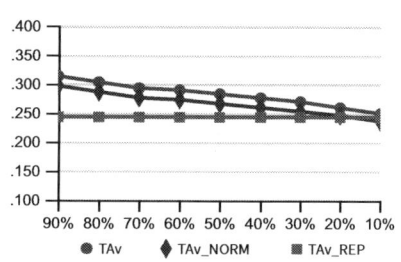

Batting WARP History

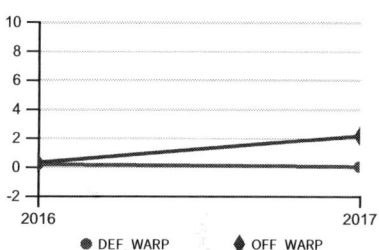

BRR (Relative to Position)

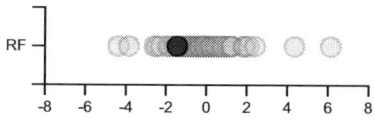

Rank		Player	BRR
45	22°	Bryce Harper	-1.30
46	20°	Seth Smith	-1.39
47	18°	**Mitch Haniger**	**-1.40**
48	16°	Lonnie Chisenhall	-1.55
49	15°	Chad Pinder	-1.76

BRR (Relative to Team)

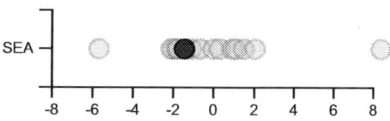

Rank		Player	BRR
9	56°	Cameron Perkins	-1.07
10	49°	Mike Zunino	-1.37
11	42°	**Mitch Haniger**	**-1.40**
12	35°	Danny Valencia	-1.71
13	25°	Nelson Cruz	-1.78

Base Running Components

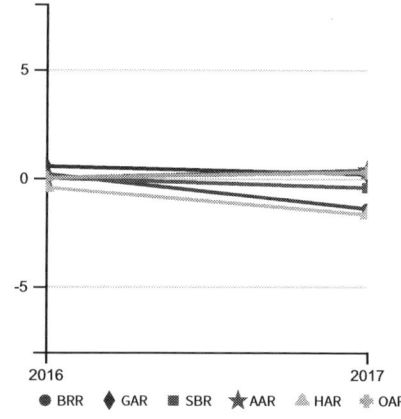

Ian Happ   OF   Chicago Cubs

Born: 8/12/1994   **Age:** 23   **Bats:** B   **Throws:** R   **Height:** 6' 0"   **Weight:** 205 lbs   **Draft Info:** Round 1, 2015 Draft (#9 overall)

21 Sec/Pit

PACE
45th of 155
71°
Fast

2017 Daily WARP Profile
2.1 Total WARP

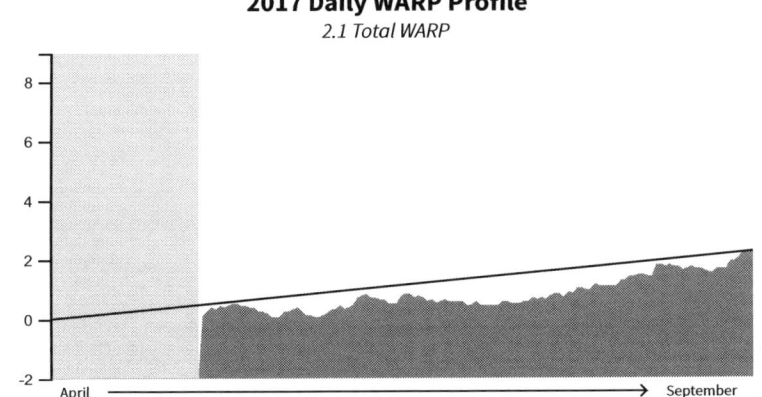

Game 1: minors

Fantasy Values
2017	2018
$16.17	**$18.00**

YEAR	TEAM	LVL	AGE	PA	R	2B	3B	HR	RBI	BB	K	SB	AVG/OBP/SLG	TAv	VORP	BABIP	WARP
2017	CHN	MLB	22	413	62	17	3	24	68	39	129	8	.253/.328/.514	.284	25.2	.316	2.1

Expected to be a quality major leaguer, Happ displayed much more power than anyone would have reasonably expected based on his prior professional stats. His .261 ISO would have tied for 16th in the majors with Nelson Cruz had Happ qualified for the batting title. Happ might not be assured a job in 2018, but his power combined with double-digit stolen-base potential make him a decent target in deeper mixed leagues. — Mike G.

2017 Batting Percentages

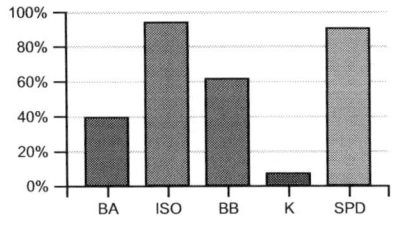

Batting PECOTA Percentiles

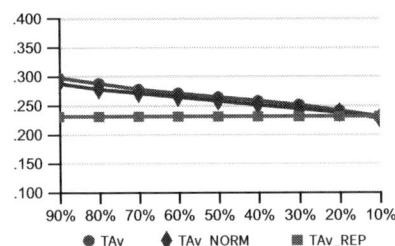

BRR (Relative to Position)

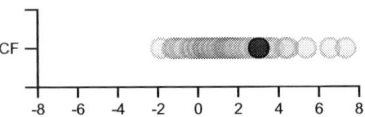

Rank		Player	BRR
8	78°	Adam Jones	3.43
9	76°	Albert Almora	3.17
10	75°	**Ian Happ**	**3.07**
11	73°	Michael Taylor	3.06
12	71°	Kevin Kiermaier	2.89

BRR (Relative to Team)

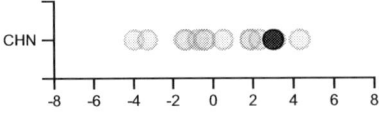

Rank		Player	BRR
1	89°	Javier Baez	4.36
2	83°	Albert Almora	3.17
3	77°	**Ian Happ**	**3.07**
4	68°	Jon Jay	2.37
5	59°	Jason Heyward	1.93

J.A. Happ   LHP   Toronto Blue Jays

Born: 10/19/1982 **Age:** 35 **Bats:** L **Throws:** L **Height:** 6'5" **Weight:** 205 lbs **Draft Info:** Round 3, 2004 Draft (#92 overall)

2017 Daily WARP Profile
3.0 Total WARP

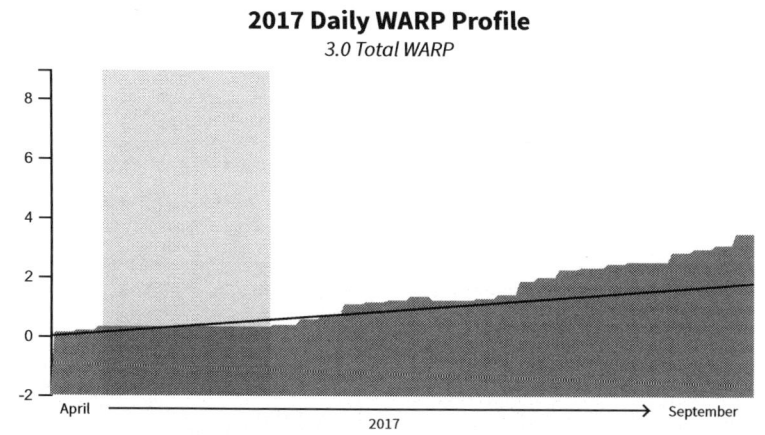

Game 13: DL (elbow inflammation)

POWER 56 PWR 38th of 150
STAMINA 66 STM 84th of 150
COMMAND 58 CMD 49th of 150
PACE 19 Sec/Pit 16th of 150 89° Very Fast

Fantasy Values
2017	2018
$13.87	$12.00

YEAR	TEAM	LVL	AGE	W	L	SV	G	GS	IP	H	HR	BB/9	K/9	K	GB%	BABIP	WHIP	ERA	DRA	WARP	MPH 95
2017	TOR	MLB	34	10	11	0	25	25	145.1	145	18	2.8	8.8	142	48%	.302	1.31	3.53	3.72	3.0	94.0

A late bloomer thanks in part to the work of Pirates' pitching coach Ray Searage in 2015, Happ had the best season of his career to date despite pitching only 145 1/3 innings. Happ works primarily off a low-90s fastball, mixing in his secondary pitches just enough to keep hitters off balance, striking out nearly a batter an inning last year. Happ doesn't look like anything special on the mound, but it is difficult to argue with the results in the last two and a half years, and he continues to pitch like a number 3 starter in mixed who remains a slight bargain. — Mike G.

2017 Pitching Percentages
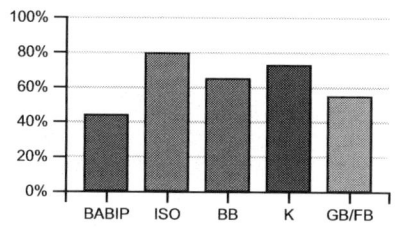

Pitching PECOTA Percentiles
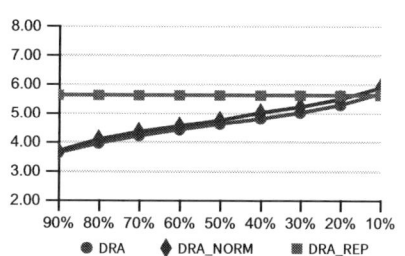

Pitching WARP History
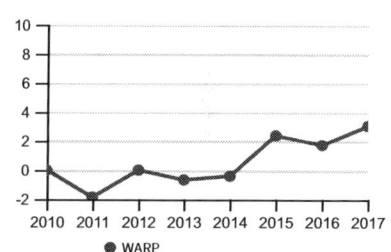

Tunnel vs LHH
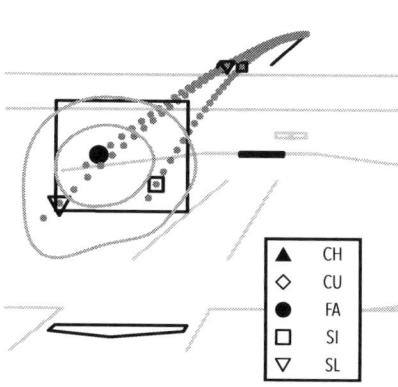

Pitch Types
Type	Freq	Velo	H Mov	V Mov
CH	11.0%	86.7 [107]	12.9 [90]	-25.4 [105]
CU	5.3%	77.2 [96]	-1.6 [76]	-45.8 [105]
FA	42.3%	92.9 [101]	8.2 [95]	-12.9 [107]
SI	29.1%	91 [92]	12.9 [97]	-21.8 [93]
SL	12.4%	86.3 [109]	-1.6 [87]	-27.2 [116]

Pitch Tunnel
Pairs	Release Diff	Tunnel Diff	Plate Diff	Speed Changes
1857	21.6	112.8	222.0	0.018

PI Scores
Year	Pitch Ct	Pwr	Cmd	Stm
2013	1721	47	54	46
2014	2707	54	50	70
2015	2821	50	58	69
2016	3032	56	52	77
2017	2484	56	58	66

Tunnel vs RHH
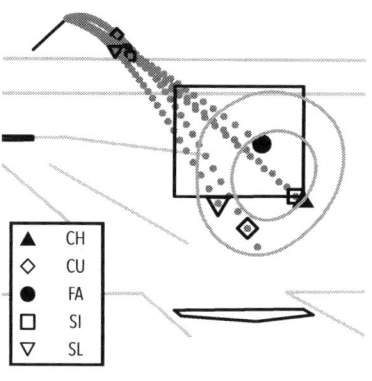

Bryce Harper   RF   Washington Nationals

Born: 10/16/1992   **Age:** 25   **Bats:** L   **Throws:** R   **Height:** 6' 3"   **Weight:** 215 lbs   **Draft Info:** Round 1, 2010 Draft (#1 overall)

2017 Daily WARP Profile
4.4 Total WARP

PACE
24 146th of 155
Sec/Pit 6°
Very Slow

Game 115: DL (knee hyperextension)

Fantasy Values
2017	2018
$26.33	$33.00

YEAR	TEAM	LVL	AGE	PA	R	2B	3B	HR	RBI	BB	K	SB	AVG/OBP/SLG	TAv	VORP	BABIP	WARP
2017	WAS	MLB	24	492	95	27	1	29	87	68	99	4	.319/.413/.595	.336	47.0	.356	4.4

It's tough to label a player with 31 WARP under his belt before his age-25 season as a disappointment, but because he is drafted in the first round every season, this is what Harper has been in fantasy almost every year. He's a really good player, but outside of his stellar 2015 Harper has never returned first-round value. It's okay to take Harper in the back end of the first round for his consistency, but unless he hits 40 bombs or steals bases again, Harper is unlikely to bring back first-round value. — Mike G.

2017 Batting Percentages

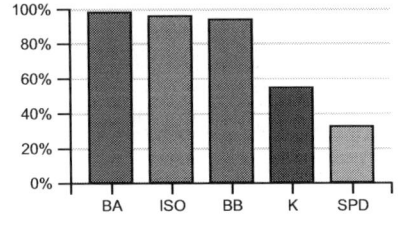

Batting PECOTA Percentiles

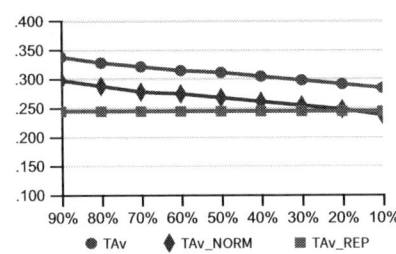

Batting WARP History

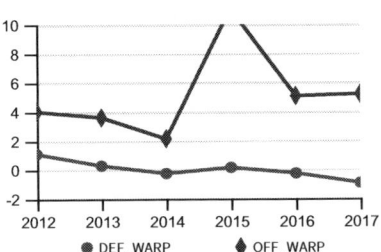

BRR (Relative to Position)

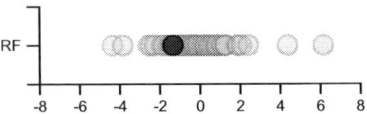

Rank		Player	BRR
43	25°	Daniel Robertson	-1.13
44	24°	Justin Ruggiano	-1.14
45	22°	**Bryce Harper**	**-1.30**
46	20°	Seth Smith	-1.39
47	18°	Mitch Haniger	-1.40

BRR (Relative to Team)

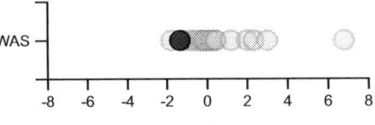

Rank		Player	BRR
14	24°	Matt Adams	-0.56
15	20°	Jayson Werth	-0.79
16	15°	Adam Lind	-1.18
17	6°	**Bryce Harper**	**-1.30**
18	0°	Matt Wieters	-1.75

Base Running Components

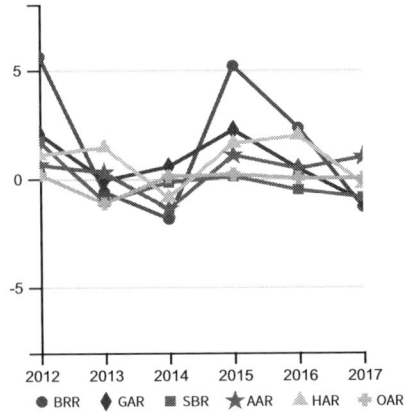

Josh Harrison   INF   Pittsburgh Pirates

Born: 7/8/1987   **Age:** 30   **Bats:** R   **Throws:** R   **Height:** 5' 8"   **Weight:** 180 lbs   **Draft Info:** Round 6, 2008 Draft (#191 overall)

19 Sec/Pit

PACE
4th of 155
97°
Very Fast

2017 Daily WARP Profile
3.2 Total WARP

April — 2017 → September

Game 137: DL (hand fracture)

Fantasy Values
2017	2018
$16.47	$14.00

YEAR	TEAM	LVL	AGE	PA	R	2B	3B	HR	RBI	BB	K	SB	AVG/OBP/SLG	TAv	VORP	BABIP	WARP
2017	PIT	MLB	29	542	66	26	2	16	47	28	90	12	.272/.339/.432	.286	32.6	.303	3.2

2017 Batting Percentages

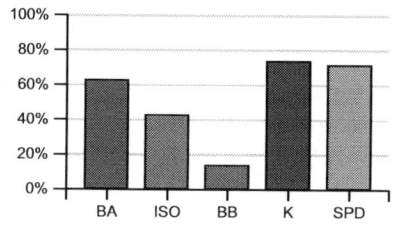

Batting PECOTA Percentiles

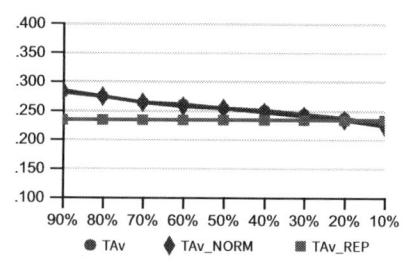

TAv ● TAv_NORM ◆ TAv_REP ■

Batting WARP History

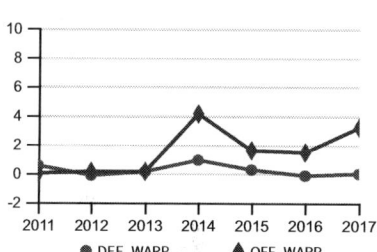

DEF_WARP ● OFF_WARP ◆

BRR (Relative to Position)

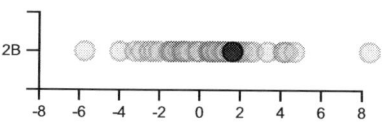

Rank		Player	BRR
11	68°	Cliff Pennington	1.95
12	64°	Whit Merrifield	1.73
13	62°	**Josh Harrison**	**1.68**
14	60°	Jonathan Villar	1.59
15	58°	Kolten Wong	1.56

BRR (Relative to Team)

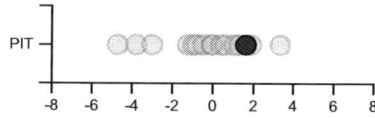

Rank		Player	BRR
1	77°	Starling Marte	3.40
2	73°	John Jaso	1.94
3	62°	**Josh Harrison**	**1.68**
4	53°	Adam Frazier	1.34
5	52°	Sean Rodriguez	1.11

Base Running Components

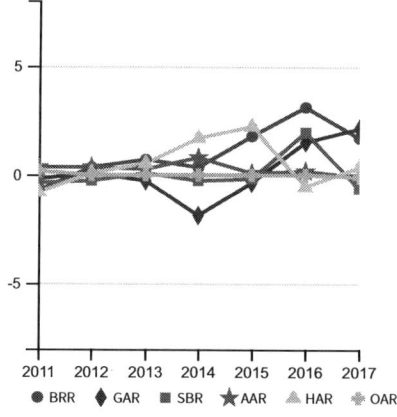

BRR ● GAR ◆ SBR ■ AAR ★ HAR ▲ OAR ✦

Chase Headley   3B   San Diego Padres

Born: 5/9/1984   **Age:** 34   **Bats:** B   **Throws:** R   **Height:** 6'2"   **Weight:** 215 lbs   **Draft Info:** Round 2, 2005 Draft (#66 overall)

21 Sec/Pit

PACE
45th of 155
71°
Fast

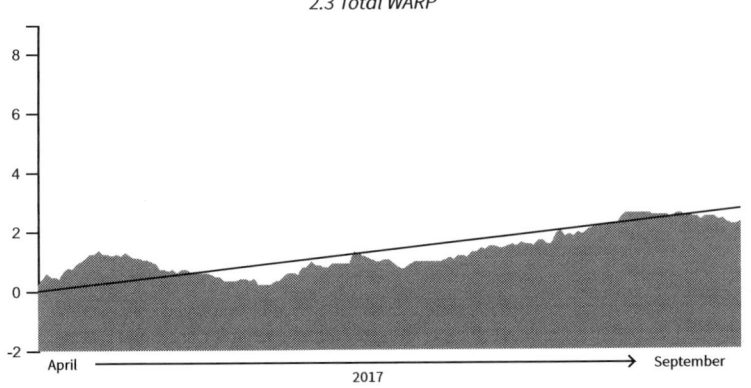

2017 Daily WARP Profile
2.3 Total WARP

April ——————————————→ September
2017

Fantasy Values
2017   2018
$16.71   **$5.00**

YEAR	TEAM	LVL	AGE	PA	R	2B	3B	HR	RBI	BB	K	SB	AVG/OBP/SLG	TAv	VORP	BABIP	WARP
2017	NYA	MLB	33	586	77	30	1	12	61	60	132	9	.273/.352/.406	.272	21.5	.341	2.3

2017 Batting Percentages

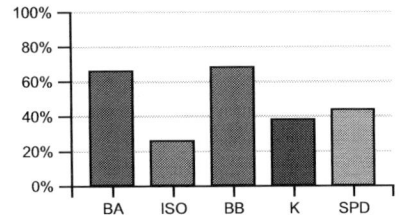

Batting PECOTA Percentiles

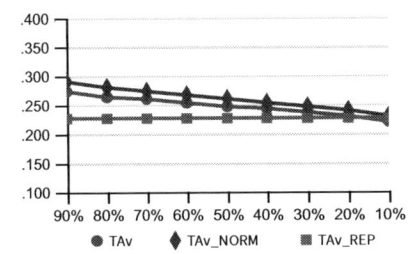

Batting WARP History

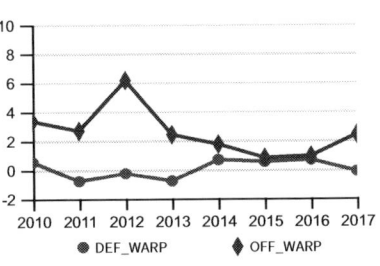

BRR (Relative to Position)

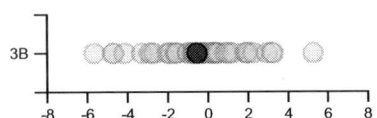

Rank		Player	BRR
32	48°	Giovanny Urshela	-0.46
33	45°	Nolan Arenado	-0.47
34	42°	**Chase Headley**	**-0.50**
35	41°	Wilmer Flores	-0.61
36	39°	Luis Valbuena	-0.62

BRR (Relative to Team)

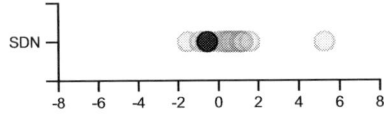

Rank		Player	BRR
13	34°	Dusty Coleman	0.02
14	28°	Erick Aybar	-0.40
15	16°	**Chase Headley**	**-0.50**
16	14°	Shane Peterson	-0.56
17	7°	Hunter Renfroe	-0.87

Base Running Components

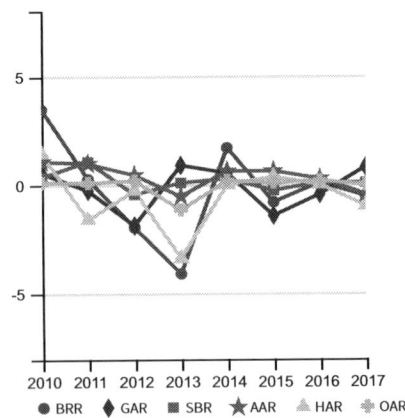

Austin Hedges   C   San Diego Padres

Born: 8/18/1992   **Age:** 25   **Bats:** R   **Throws:** R   **Height:** 6' 1"   **Weight:** 206 lbs   **Draft Info:** Round 2, 2011 Draft (#82 overall)

PACE
45th of 155
71°
Fast

21 Sec/Pit

2017 Daily WARP Profile
3.5 Total WARP

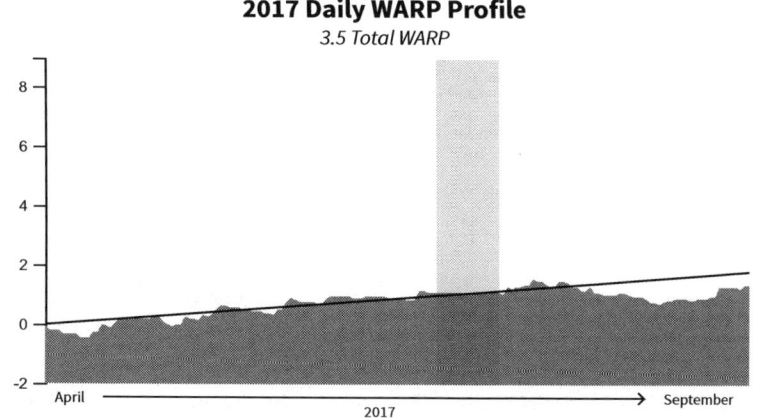

April   2017   September

Game 90: DL (concussion)

Fantasy Values
2017	2018
$6.87	$9.00

YEAR	TEAM	LVL	AGE	PA	R	2B	3B	HR	RBI	BB	K	SB	AVG/OBP/SLG	TAv	VORP	BABIP	WARP
2017	SDN	MLB	24	417	36	17	0	18	55	23	122	4	.214/.262/.398	.233	8.3	.260	3.5

2017 Batting Percentages

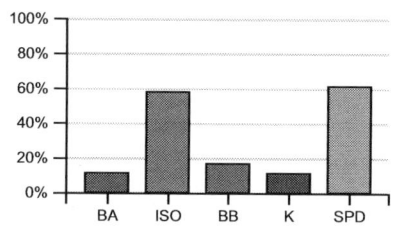

Batting PECOTA Percentiles

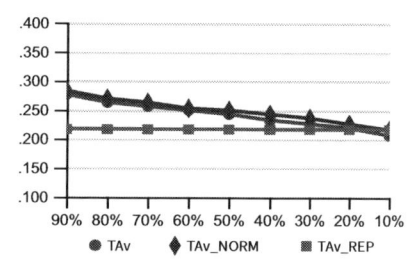

● TAv   ◆ TAv_NORM   ■ TAv_REP

Batting WARP History

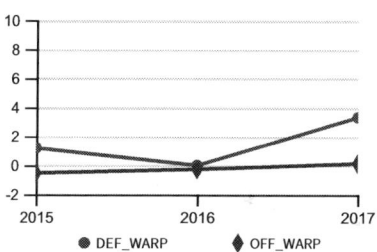

● DEF_WARP   ◆ OFF_WARP

BRR (Relative to Position)

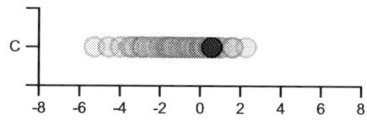

Rank		Player	BRR
9	87°	Carson Kelly	0.74
10	86°	Rafael Lopez	0.70
11	85°	**Austin Hedges**	**0.62**
12	83°	Kevan Smith	0.55
13	83°	Bryan Holaday	0.54

BRR (Relative to Team)

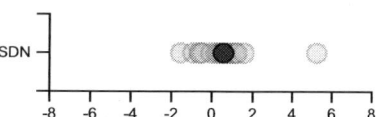

Rank		Player	BRR
7	57°	Travis Jankowski	0.88
8	56°	Rafael Lopez	0.70
9	51°	**Austin Hedges**	**0.62**
10	46°	Matt Szczur	0.52
11	42°	Allen Cordoba	0.40

Base Running Components

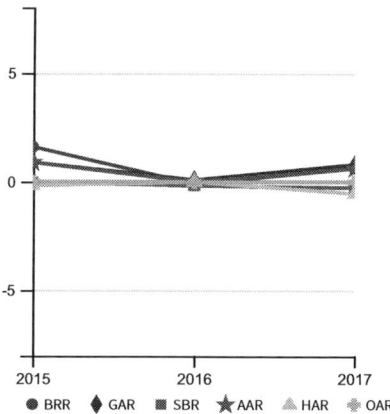

● BRR   ◆ GAR   ■ SBR   ★ AAR   ▲ HAR   ✦ OAR

Jeremy Hellickson   RHP   Baltimore Orioles

Born: 4/8/1987   **Age:** 31   **Bats:** R   **Throws:** R   **Height:** 6'1"   **Weight:** 190 lbs   **Draft Info:** Round 4, 2005 Draft (#118 overall)

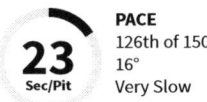

PACE
23
Sec/Pit
126th of 150
16°
Very Slow

2017 Daily WARP Profile
1.7 Total WARP

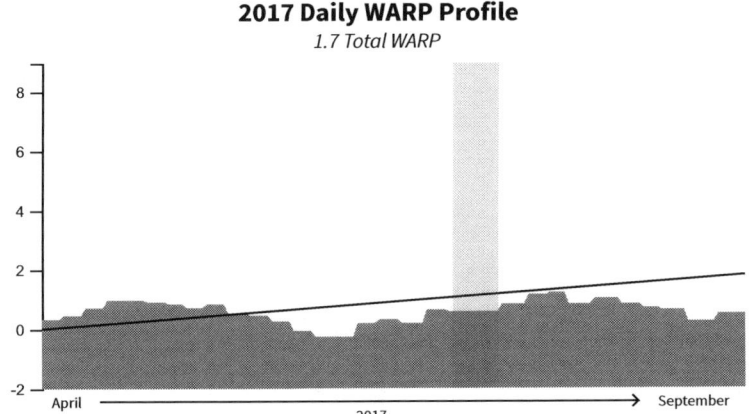

April   2017   September

Game 96: traded

POWER
32
PWR
128th of 150

STAMINA
70
STM
67th of 150

COMMAND
57
CMD
53rd of 150

Fantasy Values

2017	2018
$-1.37	**$4.00**

YEAR	TEAM	LVL	AGE	W	L	SV	G	GS	IP	H	HR	BB/9	K/9	K	GB%	BABIP	WHIP	ERA	DRA	WARP	MPH 95
2017	PHI	MLB	30	6	5	0	20	20	112.1	111	22	2.4	5.2	65	37%	.255	1.26	4.73	4.71	1.1	91.3
2017	BAL	MLB	30	2	6	0	10	10	51.2	49	13	3.0	5.4	31	36%	.225	1.28	6.97	4.45	0.6	91.6

2017 Pitching Percentages

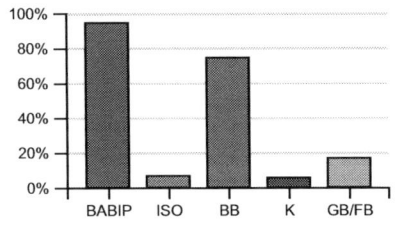

Pitching PECOTA Percentiles

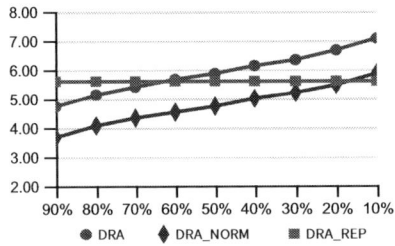

Pitching WARP History

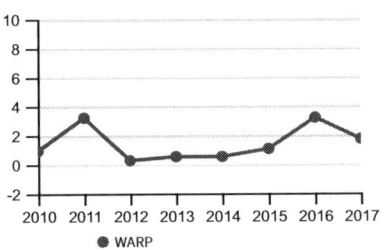

Tunnel vs LHH

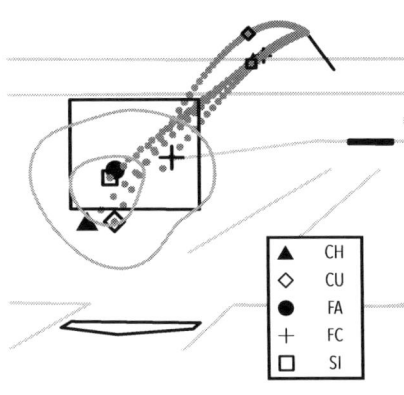

▲	CH
◇	CU
●	FA
+	FC
□	SI

Pitch Types

Type	Freq	Velo	H Mov	V Mov
CH	30.3%	81.5 [86]	-9.2 [110]	-28.4 [96]
CU	12.7%	76.9 [95]	8.7 [104]	-53.8 [88]
FA	19.0%	90.3 [91]	-10.2 [86]	-16.1 [97]
FC	11.9%	87.1 [93]	-1.2 [86]	-19.7 [116]
SI	26.2%	90.2 [88]	-13 [97]	-19.6 [102]

Pitch Tunnel

Pairs	Release Diff	Tunnel Diff	Plate Diff	Speed Changes
1818	29.3	117.6	212.2	0.027

PI Scores

Year	Pitch Ct	Pwr	Cmd	Stm
2013	2885	34	56	72
2014	1175	30	56	54
2015	2446	33	46	63
2016	2900	37	56	75
2017	2565	32	57	70

Tunnel vs RHH

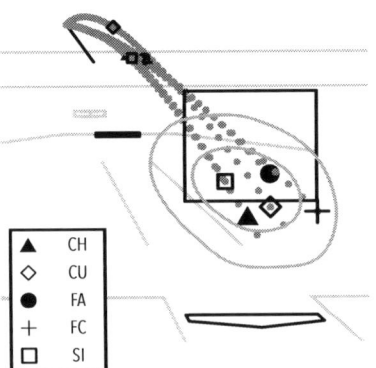

▲	CH
◇	CU
●	FA
+	FC
□	SI

Kyle Hendricks　RHP　Chicago Cubs

Born: 12/7/1989　**Age:** 28　**Bats:** R　**Throws:** R　**Height:** 6' 3"　**Weight:** 190 lbs　**Draft Info:** Round 8, 2011 Draft (#264 overall)

PACE
18
Sec/Pit
5th of 150
97°
Very Fast

2017 Daily WARP Profile
3.5 Total WARP

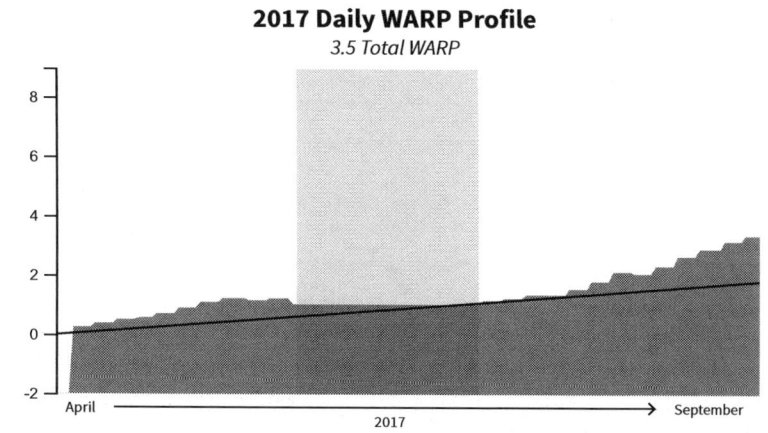

2017

April → September

Game 56: DL (hand tendinitis)

POWER
20
PWR
146th of 150

STAMINA
62
STM
94th of 150

COMMAND
76
CMD
4th of 150

Fantasy Values
2017	2018
$15.90	**$17.00**

YEAR	TEAM	LVL	AGE	W	L	SV	G	GS	IP	H	HR	BB/9	K/9	K	GB%	BABIP	WHIP	ERA	DRA	WARP	MPH 95
2017	CHN	MLB	27	7	5	0	24	24	139.2	126	17	2.6	7.9	123	52%	.281	1.19	3.03	3.31	3.5	87.6

It's always a fine line for pitchers who don't throw hard. Hendricks struggled with his velocity at the beginning of the year and for a time looked like he'd be one of the biggest fantasy busts of 2017. Then he recovered and returned to being one of the best pitchers in the game despite a fastball that doesn't come anywhere close to 90 mph. Hendricks is one of the smartest pitchers in baseball, and while a repeat of 2016 is unlikely a $20+ season in NL-only is quite possible given the underlying skills and pitching smarts. — Mike G.

2017 Pitching Percentages

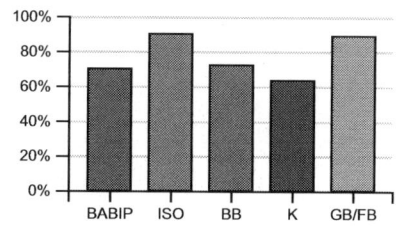

Pitching PECOTA Percentiles

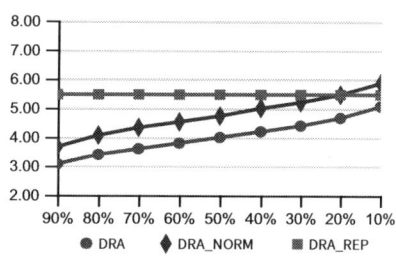

● DRA　◆ DRA_NORM　■ DRA_REP

Pitching WARP History

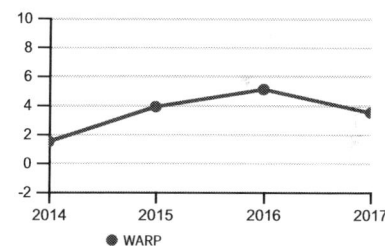

● WARP

Tunnel vs LHH

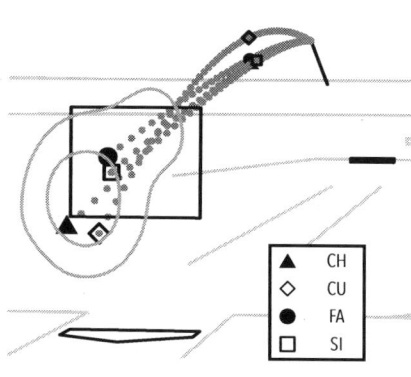

▲	CH
◇	CU
●	FA
□	SI

Pitch Types

Type	Freq	Velo	H Mov	V Mov
CH	27.9%	79.1 [76]	-6.8 [123]	-29.8 [92]
CU	7.9%	72.5 [78]	13.9 [124]	-57.2 [80]
FA	22.1%	86.3 [77]	-1.6 [126]	-18.9 [88]
SI	42.0%	86 [63]	-8.6 [128]	-23.7 [87]

Pitch Tunnel

Pairs	Release Diff	Tunnel Diff	Plate Diff	Speed Changes
1595	21.2	116.8	214.0	0.023

PI Scores

Year	Pitch Ct	Pwr	Cmd	Stm
2014	1144	27	52	70
2015	2788	34	81	70
2016	2843	38	79	72
2017	2231	20	76	62

Tunnel vs RHH

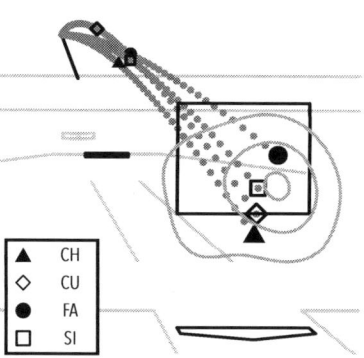

▲	CH
◇	CU
●	FA
□	SI

Cesar Hernandez   2B   Philadelphia Phillies

Born: 5/23/1990   **Age:** 28   **Bats:** B   **Throws:** R   **Height:** 5' 10"   **Weight:** 160 lbs   **Draft Info:** International Free Agent, 2006

PACE
18 Sec/Pit
1st of 155
99°
Very Fast

2017 Daily WARP Profile
3.5 Total WARP

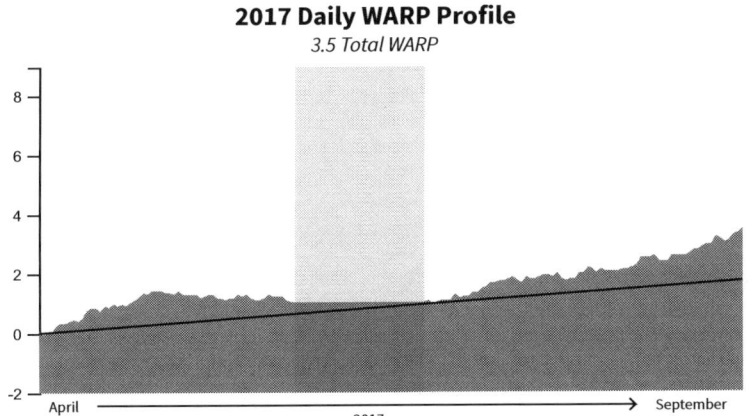

April ————————————— 2017 ————————————→ September

Game 60: DL (oblique strain)

Fantasy Values
2017	2018
$19.22	$15.00

YEAR	TEAM	LVL	AGE	PA	R	2B	3B	HR	RBI	BB	K	SB	AVG/OBP/SLG	TAv	VORP	BABIP	WARP
2017	PHI	MLB	27	577	85	26	6	9	34	61	104	15	.294/.373/.421	.288	37.2	.353	3.5

2017 Batting Percentages

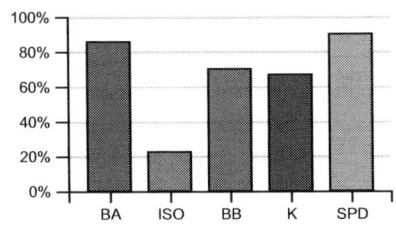

Batting PECOTA Percentiles

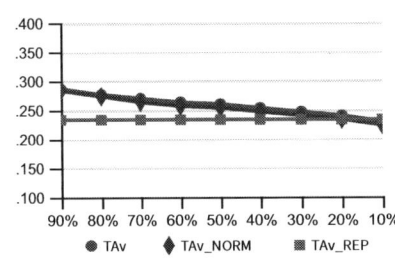

Batting WARP History

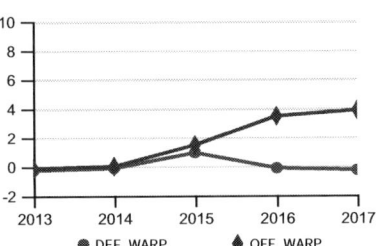

BRR (Relative to Position)

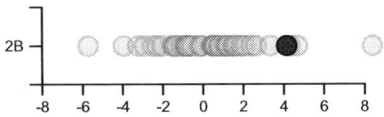

Rank		Player	BRR
3	90°	Javier Baez	4.36
4	88°	Jonathan Schoop	4.21
5	84°	**Cesar Hernandez**	**4.20**
6	81°	DJ LeMahieu	3.38
7	77°	Jose Altuve	2.68

BRR (Relative to Team)

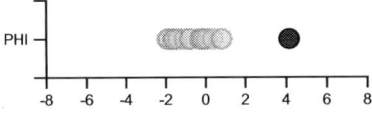

Rank		Player	BRR
1	83°	**Cesar Hernandez**	**4.20**
2	81°	Ty Kelly	0.88
3	80°	Eric Fryer	0.84
4	73°	Aaron Altherr	0.40
5	69°	Andrew Knapp	0.11

Base Running Components

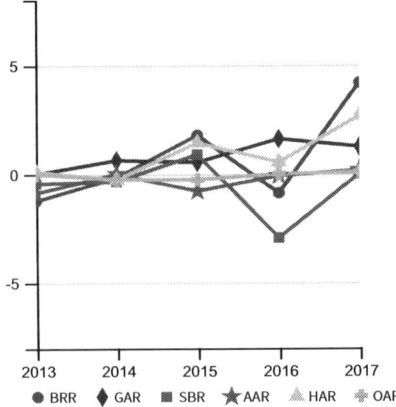

Enrique Hernandez   CF   Los Angeles Dodgers

Born: 8/24/1991   **Age:** 26   **Bats:** R   **Throws:** R   **Height:** 5' 11"   **Weight:** 200 lbs   **Draft Info:** Round 6, 2009 Draft (#191 overall)

21 Sec/Pit

PACE
45th of 155
71°
Fast

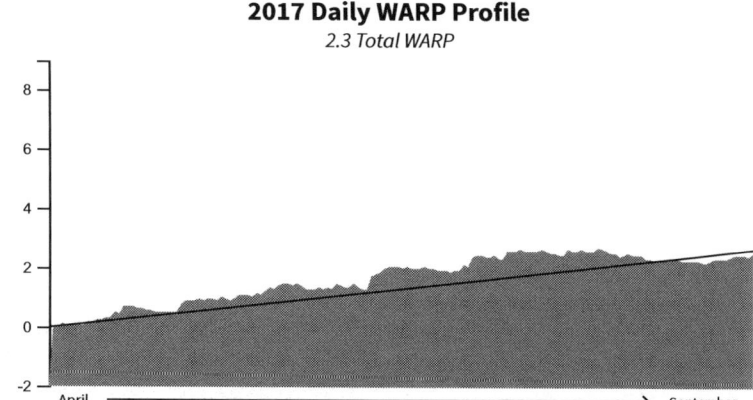

2017 Daily WARP Profile
2.3 Total WARP

Fantasy Values
2017	2018
$5.60	$4.00

YEAR	TEAM	LVL	AGE	PA	R	2B	3B	HR	RBI	BB	K	SB	AVG/OBP/SLG	TAv	VORP	BABIP	WARP
2017	LAN	MLB	25	342	46	24	2	11	37	41	80	3	.215/.308/.421	.265	14.5	.254	2.3

2017 Batting Percentages

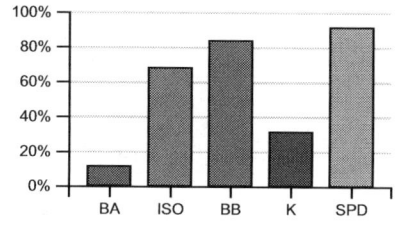

Batting PECOTA Percentiles

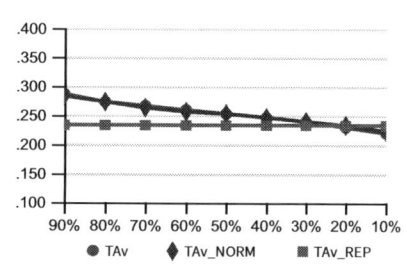

Batting WARP History

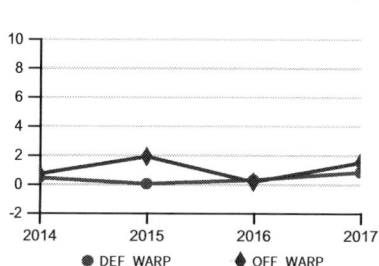

BRR (Relative to Position)

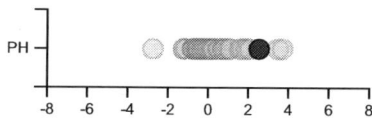

Rank		Player	BRR
1	94°	Greg Garcia	3.75
2	87°	Kelby Tomlinson	3.53
3	82°	**Enrique Hernandez**	**2.58**
4	80°	Patrick Valaika	2.11
5	75°	John Jaso	1.94

BRR (Relative to Team)

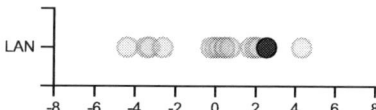

Rank		Player	BRR
1	88°	Chris Taylor	4.37
2	84°	**Enrique Hernandez**	**2.58**
3	70°	Corey Seager	2.17
4	62°	Chase Utley	2.02
5	56°	Joc Pederson	1.80

Base Running Components

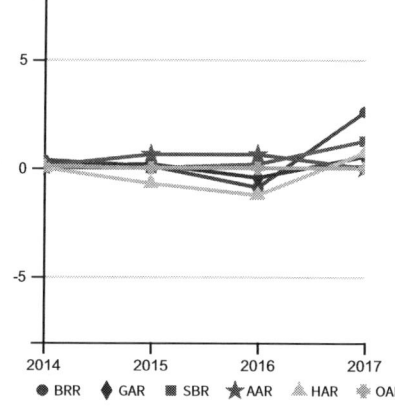

Felix Hernandez   RHP   Seattle Mariners

Born: 4/8/1986   **Age:** 32   **Bats:** R   **Throws:** R   **Height:** 6' 3"   **Weight:** 225 lbs   **Draft Info:** International Free Agent, 2002

2017 Daily WARP Profile
1.6 Total WARP

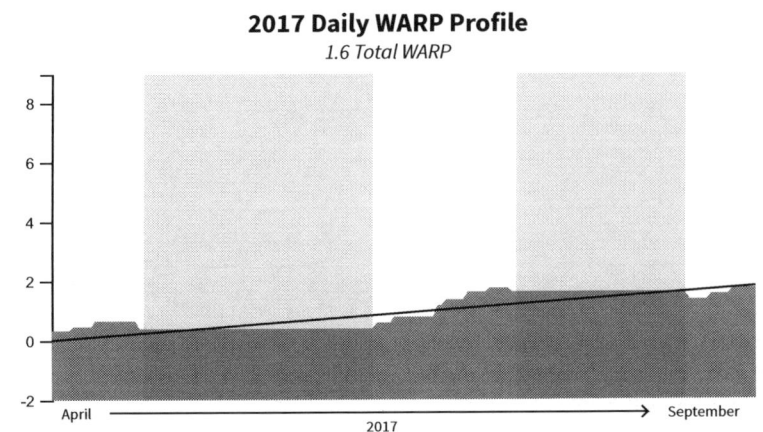

Game 22: DL (shoulder inflammation), **Game 108:** DL (biceps tendinitis)

PACE
21 Sec/Pit
81st of 150
46°
Average

POWER
31 PWR
131st of 150

STAMINA
41 STM
149th of 150

COMMAND
45 CMD
117th of 150

Fantasy Values
2017	2018
$6.37	$5.00

YEAR	TEAM	LVL	AGE	W	L	SV	G	GS	IP	H	HR	BB/9	K/9	K	GB%	BABIP	WHIP	ERA	DRA	WARP	MPH 95
2017	SEA	MLB	31	6	5	0	16	16	86.2	86	17	2.7	8.1	78	49%	.287	1.29	4.36	3.96	1.6	92.2

2017 Pitching Percentages

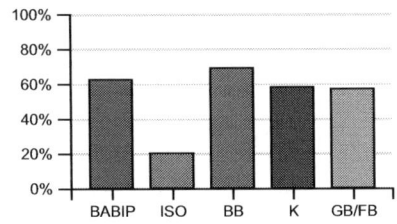

Pitching PECOTA Percentiles

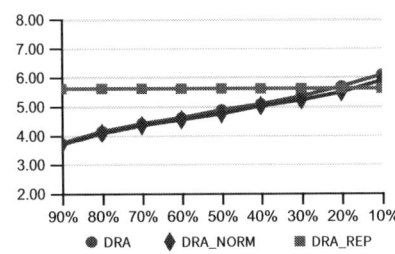

Pitching WARP History

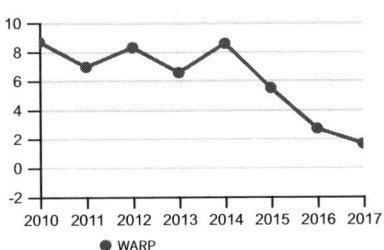

Tunnel vs LHH

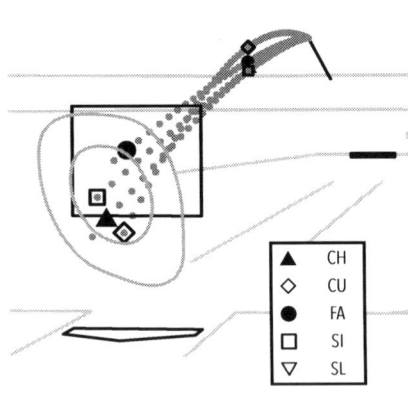

Pitch Types

Type	Freq	Velo	H Mov	V Mov
CH	25.2%	86.8 [107]	-7.9 [118]	-31.9 [86]
CU	21.4%	80.1 [107]	10.8 [112]	-47.8 [100]
FA	21.3%	91.1 [94]	-3.2 [118]	-17.6 [92]
FC	0.7%	87.1 [93]	1.8 [101]	-27.7 [85]
SI	23.1%	90.7 [91]	-10.4 [115]	-21.5 [95]
SL	8.3%	85.1 [103]	4 [97]	-30.5 [106]

Pitch Tunnel

Pairs	Release Diff	Tunnel Diff	Plate Diff	Speed Changes
1009	28.7	112.7	209.5	0.027

PI Scores

Year	Pitch Ct	Pwr	Cmd	Stm
2013	3163	46	51	78
2014	3418	42	51	84
2015	3026	37	46	77
2016	2452	38	45	66
2017	1376	31	45	41

Tunnel vs RHH

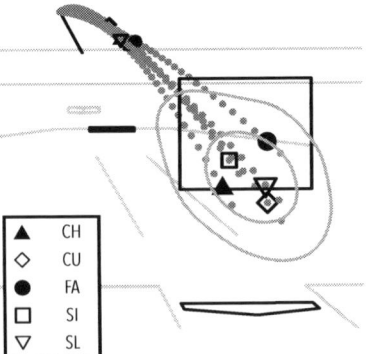

Odubel Herrera CF Philadelphia Phillies

Born: 12/29/1991 **Age:** 26 **Bats:** L **Throws:** R **Height:** 5' 11" **Weight:** 205 lbs **Draft Info:** International Free Agent, 2008

25 Sec/Pit

PACE
151st of 155
3°
Very Slow

2017 Daily WARP Profile
3.3 Total WARP

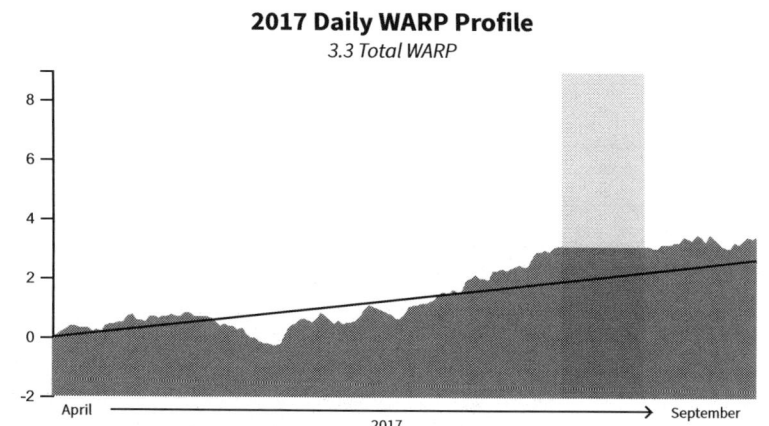

2017

April — September

Game 117: DL (hamstring strain)

Fantasy Values
2017	2018
$16.67	$20.00

YEAR	TEAM	LVL	AGE	PA	R	2B	3B	HR	RBI	BB	K	SB	AVG/OBP/SLG	TAv	VORP	BABIP	WARP
2017	PHI	MLB	25	563	67	42	3	14	56	31	126	8	.281/.325/.452	.271	22.7	.345	3.3

2017 Batting Percentages

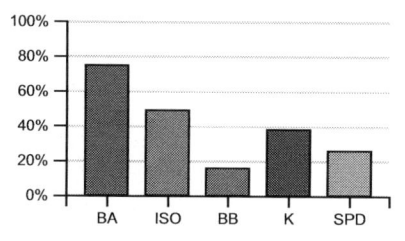

Batting PECOTA Percentiles

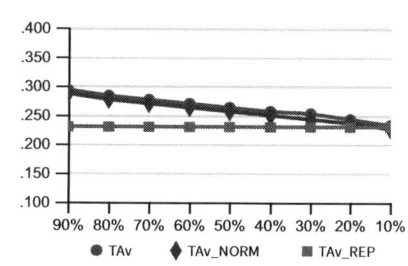

TAv ● TAv_NORM ◆ TAv_REP ■

Batting WARP History

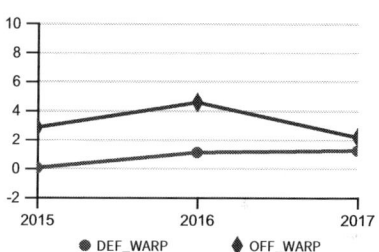

DEF_WARP ● OFF_WARP ◆

BRR (Relative to Position)

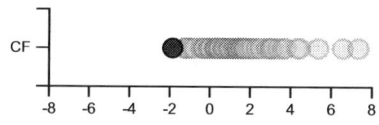

Rank		Player	BRR
54	6°	Tyler Collins	-0.87
55	3°	Kevin Pillar	-1.07
56	3°	Jaff Decker	-1.13
57	2°	Jaycob Brugman	-1.23
58	0°	**Odubel Herrera**	**-1.81**

BRR (Relative to Team)

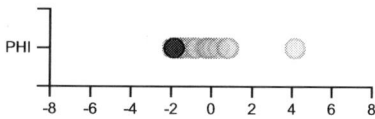

Rank		Player	BRR
15	38°	Jorge Alfaro	-1.54
16	31°	Tommy Joseph	-1.59
17	22°	**Odubel Herrera**	**-1.81**
18	12°	Maikel Franco	-1.82
19	0°	Carlos Santana	-1.88

Base Running Components

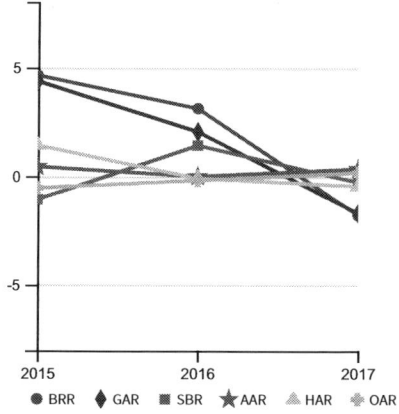

BRR ● GAR ◆ SBR ■ AAR ★ HAR ▲ OAR ✦

Jason Heyward   RF   Chicago Cubs

Born: 8/9/1989   **Age:** 28   **Bats:** L   **Throws:** L   **Height:** 6' 5"   **Weight:** 240 lbs   **Draft Info:** Round 1, 2007 Draft (#14 overall)

PACE
21 Sec/Pit
45th of 155
71°
Fast

2017 Daily WARP Profile
2.0 Total WARP

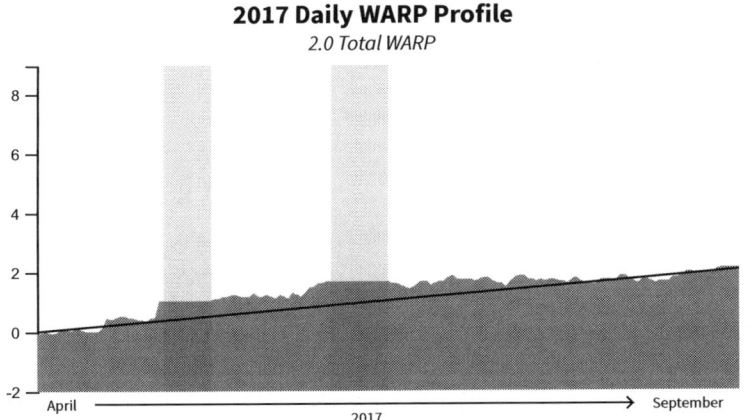

April — 2017 — September

Game 30: DL (finger sprain), **Game 69:** DL (hand abrasion)

Fantasy Values
2017	2018
$11.59	**$7.00**

YEAR	TEAM	LVL	AGE	PA	R	2B	3B	HR	RBI	BB	K	SB	AVG/OBP/SLG	TAv	VORP	BABIP	WARP
2017	CHN	MLB	27	481	59	15	4	11	59	41	67	4	.259/.326/.389	.254	8.6	.284	2.0

2017 Batting Percentages

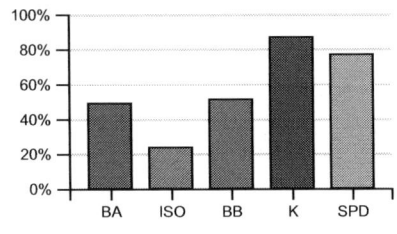

Batting PECOTA Percentiles

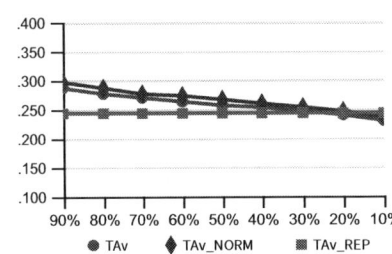

● TAv   ◆ TAv_NORM   ■ TAv_REP

Batting WARP History

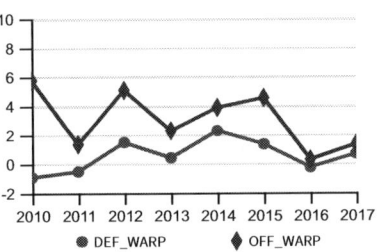

● DEF_WARP   ◆ OFF_WARP

BRR (Relative to Position)

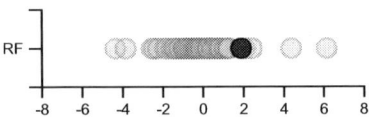

Rank		Player	BRR
3	90°	Josh Reddick	2.45
4	87°	Nick Markakis	2.12
5	85°	**Jason Heyward**	**1.93**
6	82°	Matt Joyce	1.90
7	82°	Shane Robinson	1.31

BRR (Relative to Team)

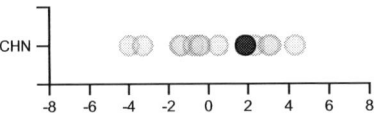

Rank		Player	BRR
3	77°	Ian Happ	3.07
4	68°	Jon Jay	2.37
5	59°	**Jason Heyward**	**1.93**
6	47°	Kris Bryant	1.90
7	40°	Kyle Schwarber	0.55

Base Running Components

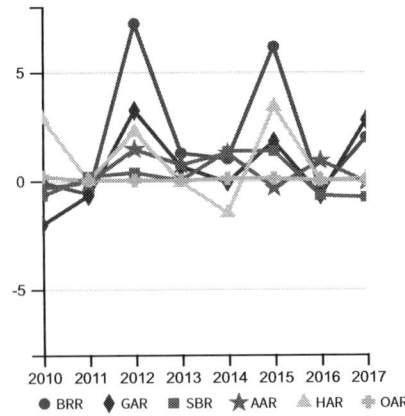

● BRR   ◆ GAR   ■ SBR   ★ AAR   ▲ HAR   ● OAR

Rich Hill   LHP   Los Angeles Dodgers

Born: 3/11/1980   **Age:** 38   **Bats:** L   **Throws:** L   **Height:** 6' 5"   **Weight:** 220 lbs   **Draft Info:** Round 4, 2002 Draft (#112 overall)

2017 Daily WARP Profile
2.1 Total WARP

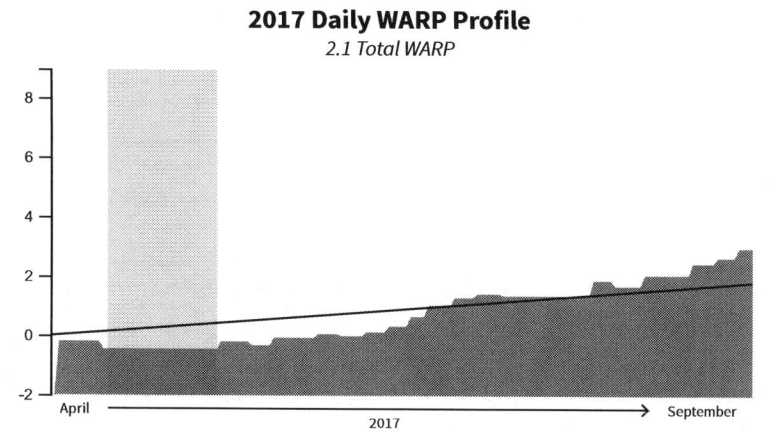

2017   April → September

Game 14: DL (finger blister)

21 PWR — **POWER** 144th of 150

61 STM — **STAMINA** 100th of 150

43 CMD — **COMMAND** 125th of 150

19 Sec/Pit — **PACE** 16th of 150 / 89° / Very Fast

Fantasy Values
2017	2018
$21.62	$17.00

YEAR	TEAM	LVL	AGE	W	L	SV	G	GS	IP	H	HR	BB/9	K/9	K	GB%	BABIP	WHIP	ERA	DRA	WARP	MPH 95
2017	LAN	MLB	37	12	8	0	25	25	135.2	99	18	3.3	11.0	166	39%	.261	1.09	3.32	4.16	2.1	90.7

Hill's second year with the Dodgers wasn't anywhere nearly as dominant as his first, but the one-time reclamation project still managed to increase both his strikeout rate and total number of innings pitched, which nearly made up for the spike in ERA. If you draft Hill remember to account for the fact that he's a poor bet to pitch more than 130-140 innings, but with his potential for an elite performance every time out he's worth the investment. — Mike G.

2017 Pitching Percentages

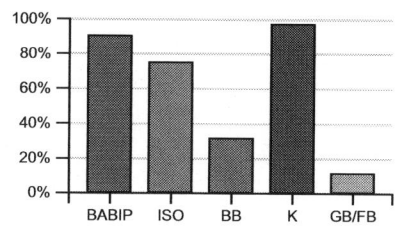

BABIP / ISO / BB / K / GB/FB

Pitching PECOTA Percentiles

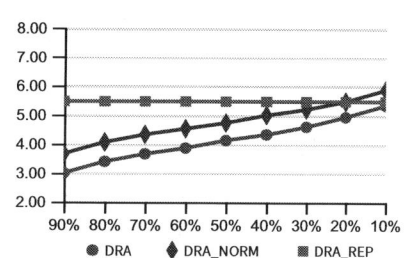

● DRA   ◆ DRA_NORM   ■ DRA_REP

Pitching WARP History

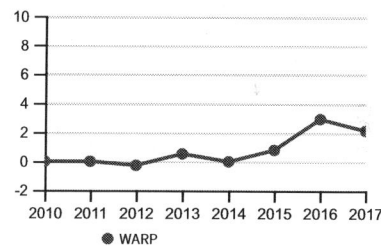

● WARP

Tunnel vs LHH

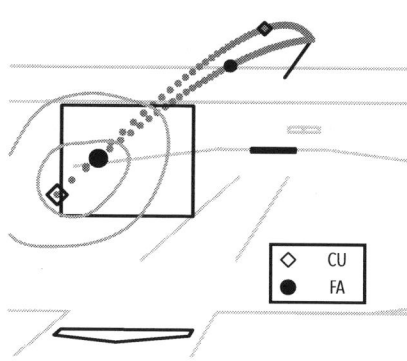

◇ CU
● FA

Pitch Types

Type	Freq	Velo	H Mov	V Mov
CH	0.6%	84 [96]	11.3 [99]	-23.9 [109]
CU	39.3%	74.1 [84]	-15.6 [131]	-57.7 [79]
FA	54.7%	89.3 [87]	10.2 [86]	-15.3 [100]
FC	2.8%	85.4 [83]	0.5 [89]	-23.2 [102]
SI	0.1%	87.3 [71]	16 [74]	-24.9 [82]
SL	2.6%	77 [68]	-10.7 [127]	-45.9 [62]

Pitch Tunnel

Pairs	Release Diff	Tunnel Diff	Plate Diff	Speed Changes
1666	52.7	137.9	217.5	0.046

PI Scores

Year	Pitch Ct	Pwr	Cmd	Stm
2012	347	31	60	27
2013	770	32	61	42
2015	434	21	51	41
2016	1811	28	55	42
2017	2219	21	43	61

Tunnel vs RHH

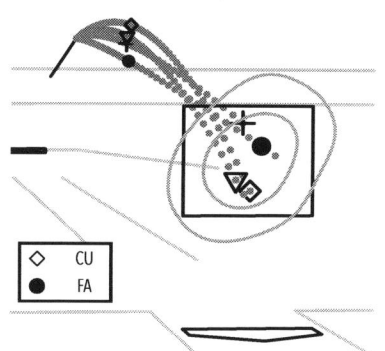

◇ CU
● FA

Jeff Hoffman   RHP   Colorado Rockies

Born: 1/8/1993   **Age:** 25   **Bats:** R   **Throws:** R   **Height:** 6'5"   **Weight:** 225 lbs   **Draft Info:** Round 1, 2014 Draft (#9 overall)

2017 Daily WARP Profile
-0.5 Total WARP

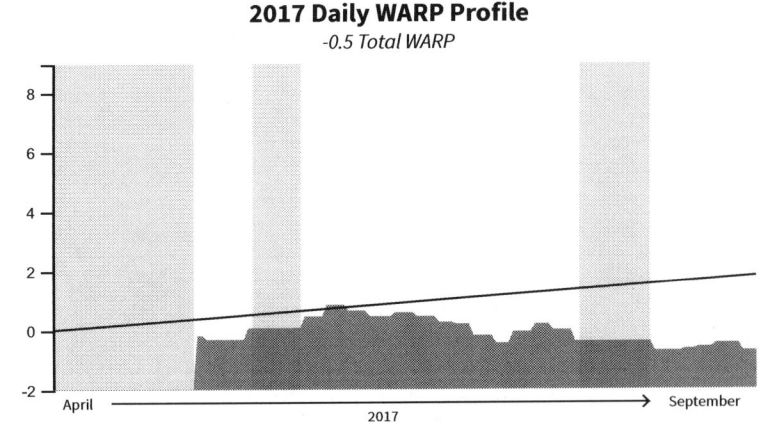

Game 1: minors, **Game 47:** minors, **Game 122:** minors

POWER
57 PWR 35th of 150

STAMINA
66 STM 84th of 150

COMMAND
47 CMD 102nd of 150

PACE
22 Sec/Pit 108th of 150
28°
Slow

Fantasy Values
2017	2018
$0.20	$1.00

YEAR	TEAM	LVL	AGE	W	L	SV	G	GS	IP	H	HR	BB/9	K/9	K	GB%	BABIP	WHIP	ERA	DRA	WARP	MPH 95
2017	COL	MLB	24	6	5	0	23	16	99.1	106	15	3.6	7.4	82	42%	.304	1.47	5.89	5.98	-0.5	96.5

2017 Pitching Percentages

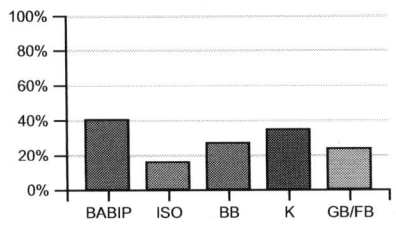

Pitching PECOTA Percentiles

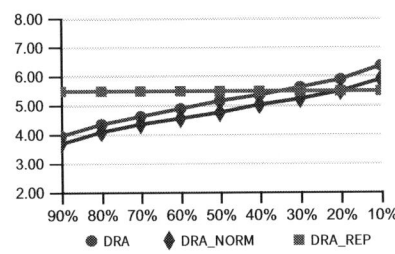

Pitching WARP History

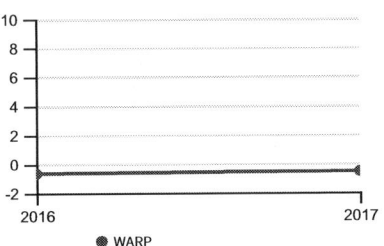

Tunnel vs LHH

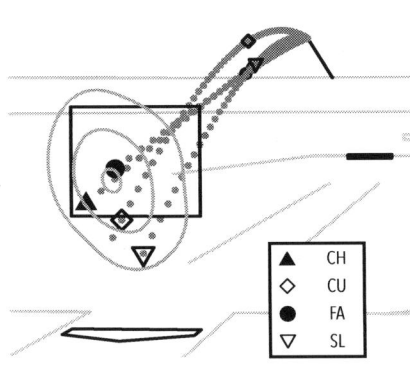

Pitch Types

Type	Freq	Velo	H Mov	V Mov
CH	5.9%	87.1 [108]	-10.8 [101]	-21.1 [117]
CU	18.7%	77.5 [97]	9.2 [105]	-53.6 [88]
FA	67.0%	94.8 [108]	-8.5 [94]	-12.5 [109]
SL	8.4%	83.2 [95]	3.4 [95]	-39.1 [81]

Pitch Tunnel

Pairs	Release Diff	Tunnel Diff	Plate Diff	Speed Changes
1167	29.4	126.9	229.2	0.035

PI Scores

Year	Pitch Ct	Pwr	Cmd	Stm
2016	552	52	42	65
2017	1605	57	47	66

Tunnel vs RHH

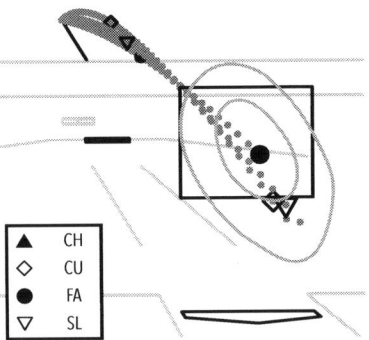

Rhys Hoskins   LF   Philadelphia Phillies

Born: 3/17/1993   **Age:** 25   **Bats:** R   **Throws:** R   **Height:** 6' 4"   **Weight:** 225 lbs   **Draft Info:** Round 5, 2014 Draft (#142 overall)

We don't have a baseball card for this guy.

22 Sec/Pit

PACE
99th of 155
36°
Slow

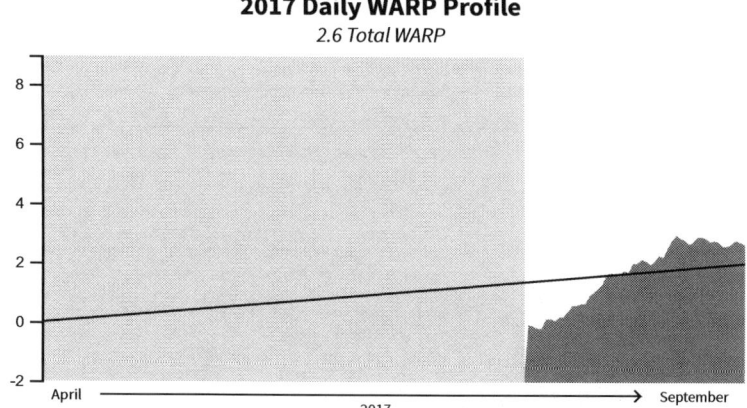

2017 Daily WARP Profile
2.6 Total WARP

Game 1: minors

Fantasy Values

2017	2018
$10.41	$25.00

YEAR	TEAM	LVL	AGE	PA	R	2B	3B	HR	RBI	BB	K	SB	AVG/OBP/SLG	TAv	VORP	BABIP	WARP
2017	PHI	MLB	24	212	37	7	0	18	48	37	46	2	.259/.396/.618	.367	27.4	.241	2.6

Promoted in August after destroying International League pitching while playing in one of the toughest hitters' parks in the minors, Hoskins continued his Babe Ruth impression in Philadelphia before coming down to earth somewhat in September. Even when the batting average crashed, Hoskins kept hitting home runs and refused to give in to pitchers who were no longer challenging him. Hoskins won't duplicate his fast major-league start, but the raw power is legit, and his approach will make him one of the better power bats in the majors even as a sophomore. — Mike G.

2017 Batting Percentages

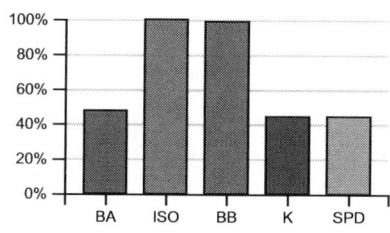

Batting PECOTA Percentiles

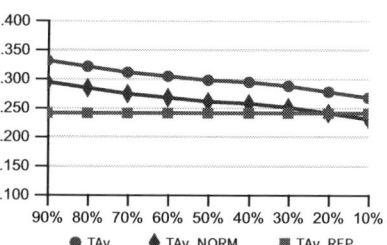

BRR (Relative to Position)

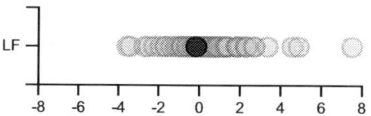

BRR (Relative to Team)

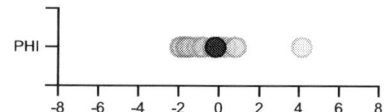

Rank		Player	BRR
43	39°	Cesar Puello	0.13
44	37°	Howie Kendrick	-0.08
45	36°	**Rhys Hoskins**	**-0.11**
46	35°	Chris Young	-0.11
47	32°	Khris Davis	-0.22

Rank		Player	BRR
5	69°	Andrew Knapp	0.11
6	66°	Adam Rosales	-0.07
7	62°	**Rhys Hoskins**	**-0.11**
8	60°	J.P. Crawford	-0.18
9	59°	Pedro Florimon	-0.24

Eric Hosmer   1B   Kansas City Royals

Born: 10/24/1989   **Age:** 28   **Bats:** L   **Throws:** L   **Height:** 6' 4"   **Weight:** 225 lbs   **Draft Info:** Round 1, 2008 Draft (#3 overall)

22 Sec/Pit

PACE
99th of 155
36°
Slow

2017 Daily WARP Profile
3.6 Total WARP

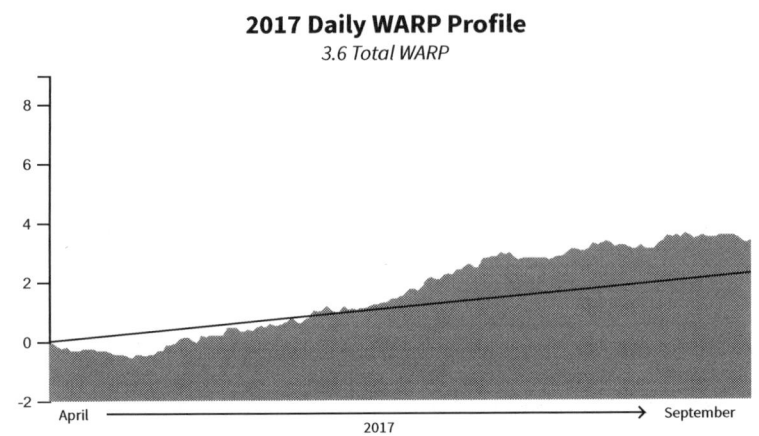

Fantasy Values

2017	2018
$28.72	**$23.00**

YEAR	TEAM	LVL	AGE	PA	R	2B	3B	HR	RBI	BB	K	SB	AVG/OBP/SLG	TAv	VORP	BABIP	WARP
2017	KCA	MLB	27	671	98	31	1	25	94	66	104	6	.318/.385/.498	.302	35.1	.351	3.6

Hosmer had the best offensive year of his career, but you wouldn't know it if you didn't look at his batting average. Nearly all of Hosmer's fantasy gains came in that category; insert Hosmer's 2016 average into his 2017 line and he drops all the way from 16th to 62nd among mixed hitters. This isn't to suggest that Hosmer was lucky. He had a very good season and has now hit .297 or higher in three of the last five years. However, betting on a nonelite hitter repeating in average isn't the best gambit. — Mike G.

2017 Batting Percentages

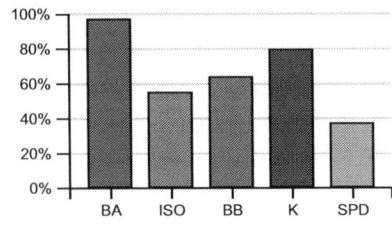

Batting PECOTA Percentiles

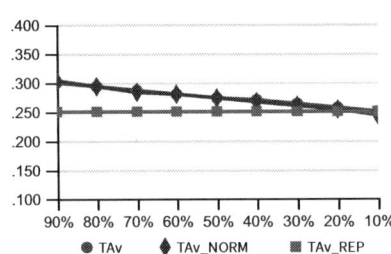

Batting WARP History

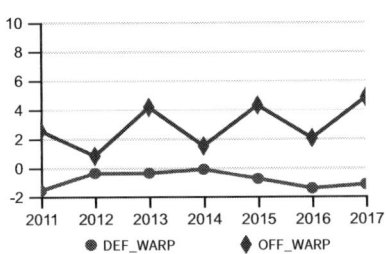

BRR (Relative to Position)

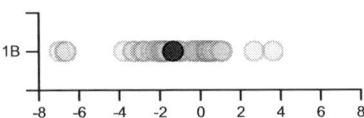

Rank		Player	BRR
23	61°	Greg Bird	-0.98
24	60°	Sam Travis	-1.01
25	56°	**Eric Hosmer**	**-1.31**
26	53°	Tommy Joseph	-1.59
27	51°	Danny Valencia	-1.71

BRR (Relative to Team)

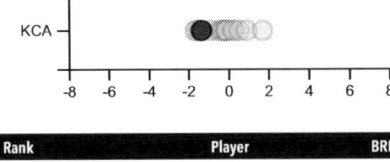

Rank		Player	BRR
11	41°	Cameron Gallagher	-0.44
12	40°	Ramon Torres	-0.83
13	26°	**Eric Hosmer**	**-1.31**
14	21°	Salvador Perez	-1.33
15	20°	Raul Mondesi	-1.41

Base Running Components

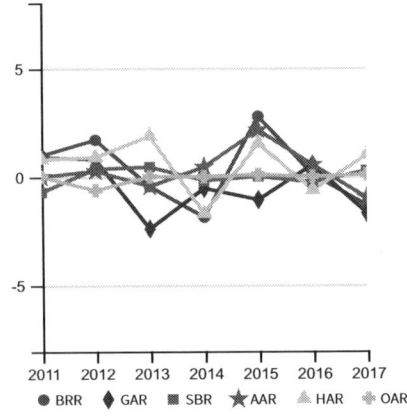

Chris Iannetta C Colorado Rockies

Born: 4/8/1983 **Age:** 35 **Bats:** R **Throws:** R **Height:** 6' 0" **Weight:** 230 lbs **Draft Info:** Round 4, 2004 Draft (#110 overall)

21 Sec/Pit

PACE
45th of 155
71°
Fast

2017 Daily WARP Profile
3.2 Total WARP

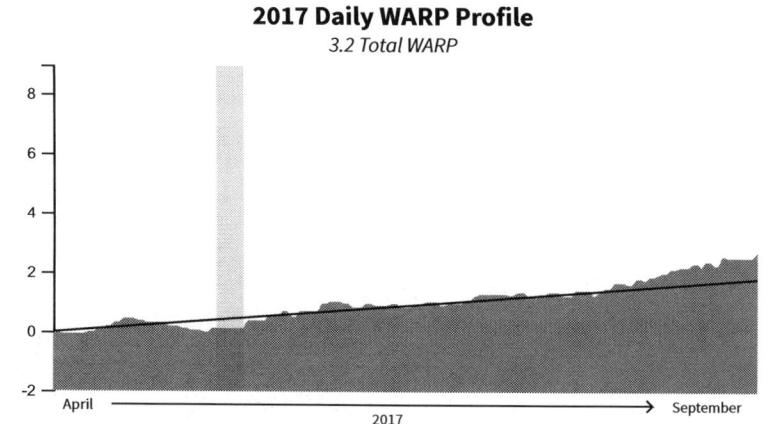

Game 38: DL (concussion)

Fantasy Values
2017	2018
$8.63	**$6.00**

YEAR	TEAM	LVL	AGE	PA	R	2B	3B	HR	RBI	BB	K	SB	AVG/OBP/SLG	TAv	VORP	BABIP	WARP
2017	ARI	MLB	34	316	38	19	0	17	43	37	87	0	.254/.354/.511	.300	25.7	.308	3.2

2017 Batting Percentages

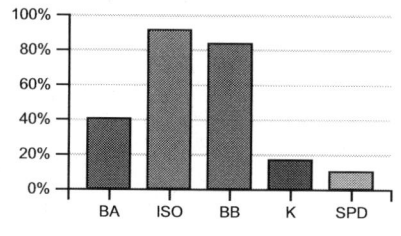

Batting PECOTA Percentiles

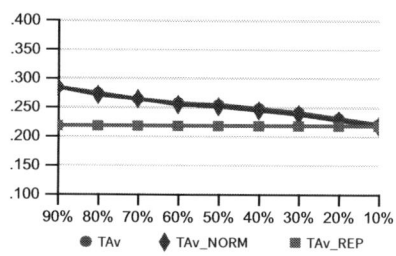

Batting WARP History

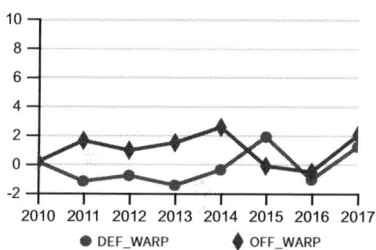

BRR (Relative to Position)

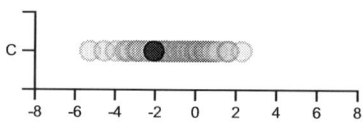

Rank		Player	BRR
61	25°	Austin Romine	-1.82
62	24°	Jett Bandy	-1.95
63	23°	**Chris Iannetta**	**-2.02**
64	22°	Travis d'Arnaud	-2.25
65	19°	Martin Maldonado	-2.37

BRR (Relative to Team)

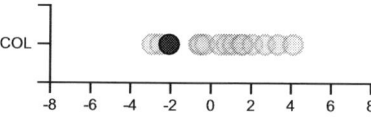

Rank		Player	BRR
11	21°	Nolan Arenado	-0.47
12	21°	Michael Tauchman	-0.53
13	17°	**Chris Iannetta**	**-2.02**
14	10°	Gerardo Parra	-2.47
15	0°	Mark Reynolds	-2.86

Base Running Components

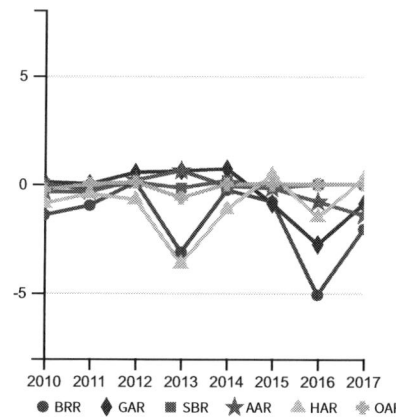

Ender Inciarte   CF   Atlanta Braves

Born: 10/29/1990   **Age:** 27   **Bats:** L   **Throws:** L   **Height:** 5' 11"   **Weight:** 190 lbs   **Draft Info:** International Free Agent, 2008

PACE
19 Sec/Pit
4th of 155
97°
Very Fast

2017 Daily WARP Profile
4.6 Total WARP

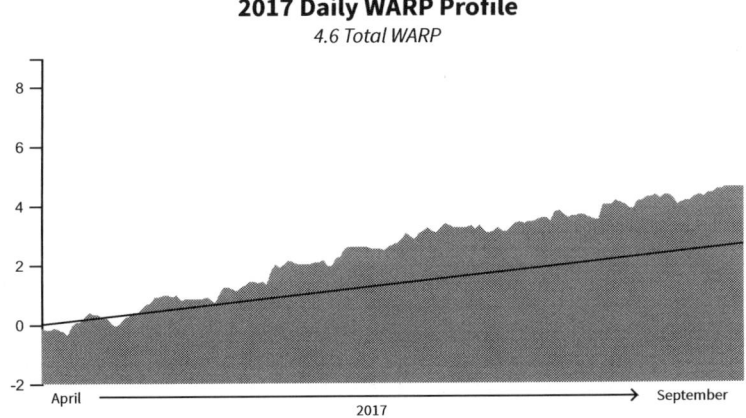

Fantasy Values
2017	2018
$26.89	$19.00

YEAR	TEAM	LVL	AGE	PA	R	2B	3B	HR	RBI	BB	K	SB	AVG/OBP/SLG	TAv	VORP	BABIP	WARP
2017	ATL	MLB	26	718	93	27	5	11	57	49	94	22	.304/.350/.409	.270	35.6	.339	4.6

A boost in playing time along with a jump in home runs quietly boosted Inciarte's value. Speedsters aren't properly valued, and this is particularly true for hitters like Inciarte who aren't elite basestealers but who run enough to contribute significantly in the category. Inciarte isn't dominant in any facet of his fantasy game. This makes him a volume play, but given his youth and defensive value Inciarte is a decent bet to repeat most of his 2017 line even if the home runs dip slightly. — Mike G.

2017 Batting Percentages

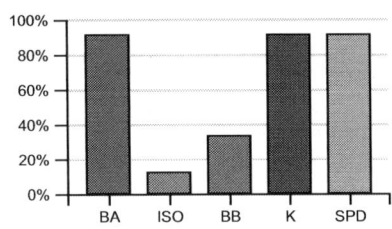

Batting PECOTA Percentiles

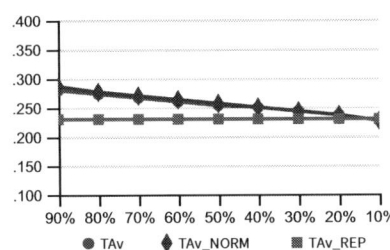

Batting WARP History

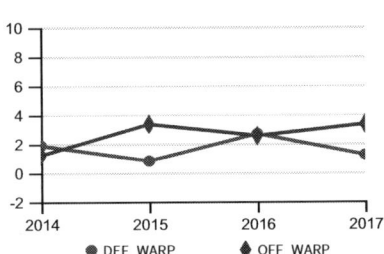

BRR (Relative to Position)

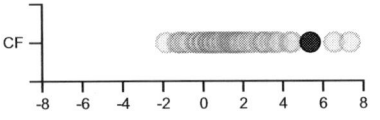

Rank		Player	BRR
1	98°	Byron Buxton	7.39
2	94°	Billy Hamilton	6.60
3	90°	**Ender Inciarte**	5.41
4	87°	Cameron Maybin	4.50
5	84°	Chris Taylor	4.37

BRR (Relative to Team)

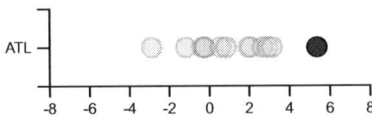

Rank		Player	BRR
1	61°	**Ender Inciarte**	5.41
2	52°	Dansby Swanson	3.19
3	47°	Johan Camargo	2.97
4	39°	Freddie Freeman	2.72
5	28°	Nick Markakis	2.12

Base Running Components

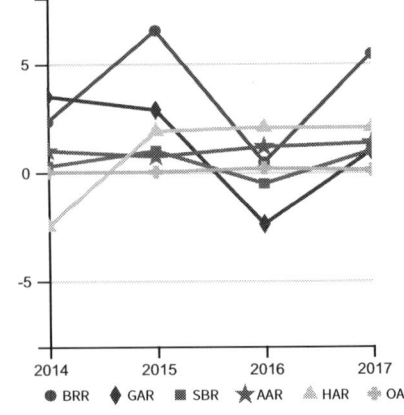

Kenley Jansen   RHP   Los Angeles Dodgers

Born: 9/30/1987 **Age:** 30 **Bats:** B **Throws:** R **Height:** 6' 5" **Weight:** 275 lbs **Draft Info:** International Free Agent, 2004

2017 Daily WARP Profile
2.2 Total WARP

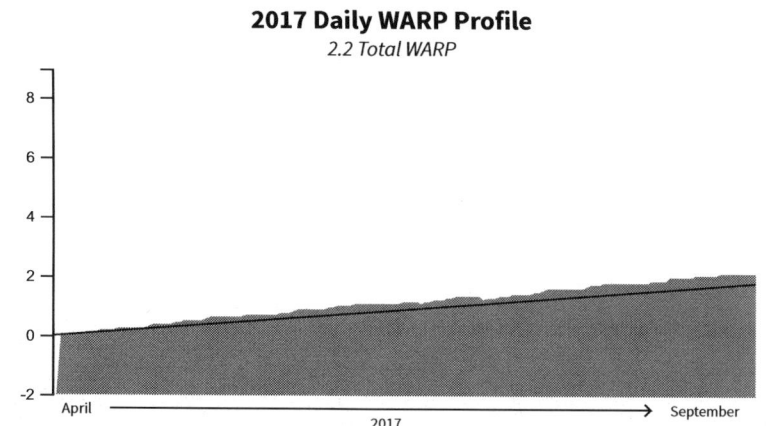

POWER 73 PWR 5th of 150

STAMINA 48 STM 140th of 150

COMMAND 64 CMD 18th of 150

PACE 26 Sec/Pit 146th of 150 3° Very Slow

Fantasy Values
2017	2018
$30.29	$24.00

YEAR	TEAM	LVL	AGE	W	L	SV	G	GS	IP	H	HR	BB/9	K/9	K	GB%	BABIP	WHIP	ERA	DRA	WARP	MPH 95
2017	LAN	MLB	29	5	0	41	65	0	68.1	44	5	0.9	14.4	109	40%	.291	0.75	1.32	2.34	2.2	95.7

You can count the number of relievers you want to make a big investment on with one hand and have some fingers left over, but Jansen is one of them. He put up his best season to date, which is no small feat given his already illustrious career. Conventional wisdom is always reluctant to draft a closer in the Top 50 overall but if you're going to take the plunge with a closer, Jansen is the one to do it with. — Mike G.

2017 Pitching Percentages
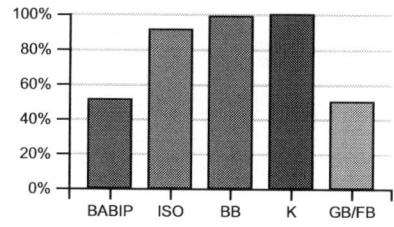

Pitching PECOTA Percentiles
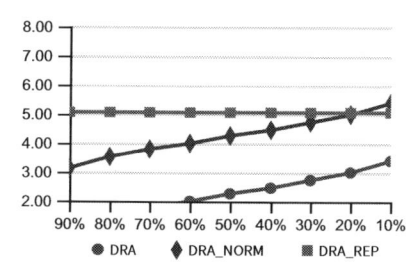

Pitching WARP History
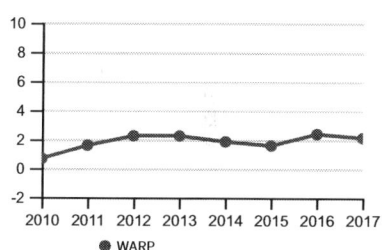

Tunnel vs LHH
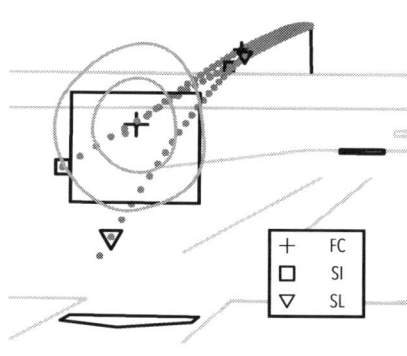

Pitch Types
Type	Freq	Velo	H Mov	V Mov
FC	86.1%	93.6 [129]	5.7 [121]	-13.5 [140]
SI	5.9%	95.3 [117]	-7.4 [137]	-10.4 [136]
SL	8.0%	83.6 [96]	5.3 [103]	-38.1 [84]

Pitch Tunnel
Pairs	Release Diff	Tunnel Diff	Plate Diff	Speed Changes
695	30.1	100.4	198.2	0.012

PI Scores
Year	Pitch Ct	Pwr	Cmd	Stm
2013	1239	73	46	53
2014	1027	79	47	47
2015	788	67	49	48
2016	994	73	52	49
2017	997	73	64	48

Tunnel vs RHH
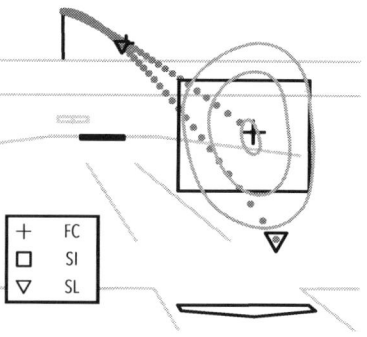

Ubaldo Jimenez RHP Baltimore Orioles

Born: 1/22/1984 **Age:** 34 **Bats:** R **Throws:** R **Height:** 6' 5" **Weight:** 210 lbs **Draft Info:** International Free Agent, 2001

We don't have a baseball card for this guy.

2017 Daily WARP Profile
-1.8 Total WARP

April — 2017 — September

POWER
37 PWR
110th of 150

STAMINA
69 STM
73rd of 150

COMMAND
37 CMD
144th of 150

PACE
19 Sec/Pit
16th of 150
89°
Very Fast

Fantasy Values

2017	2018
$-5.78	$1.00

YEAR	TEAM	LVL	AGE	W	L	SV	G	GS	IP	H	HR	BB/9	K/9	K	GB%	BABIP	WHIP	ERA	DRA	WARP	MPH 95
2017	BAL	MLB	33	6	11	0	31	25	142.2	169	33	3.7	8.8	139	44%	.329	1.59	6.81	6.68	-1.8	92.7

2017 Pitching Percentages

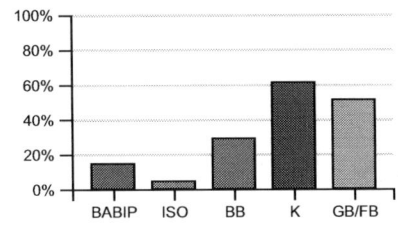

Pitching PECOTA Percentiles

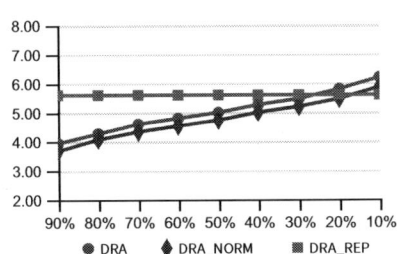

● DRA ◆ DRA_NORM ■ DRA_REP

Pitching WARP History

● WARP

Tunnel vs LHH

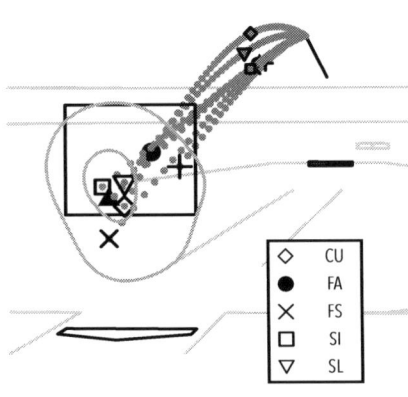

◇ CU
● FA
✕ FS
□ SI
▽ SL

Pitch Types

Type	Freq	Velo	H Mov	V Mov
CH	2.9%	82.6 [90]	-12.4 [93]	-24.5 [107]
CU	4.4%	75.3 [89]	11.3 [114]	-51.3 [93]
FA	11.7%	91.5 [96]	-7 [101]	-14.3 [103]
FC	2.8%	90.3 [111]	-1.8 [83]	-16.8 [128]
FS	17.4%	84.6 [97]	-8.6 [98]	-29.8 [100]
SI	41.8%	90.7 [91]	-12.5 [100]	-17.7 [109]
SL	19.0%	82.6 [92]	7.7 [114]	-32.5 [101]

Pitch Tunnel

Pairs	Release Diff	Tunnel Diff	Plate Diff	Speed Changes
1871	48.5	132.6	236.8	0.025

PI Scores

Year	Pitch Ct	Pwr	Cmd	Stm
2013	3151	46	50	76
2014	2297	44	41	57
2015	3041	45	59	74
2016	2488	42	50	64
2017	2568	37	37	69

Tunnel vs RHH

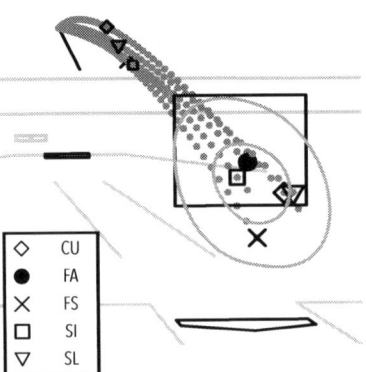

◇ CU
● FA
✕ FS
□ SI
▽ SL

Adam Jones CF Baltimore Orioles

Born: 8/1/1985 **Age:** 32 **Bats:** R **Throws:** R **Height:** 6' 2" **Weight:** 215 lbs **Draft Info:** Round 1, 2003 Draft (#37 overall)

21 Sec/Pit

PACE
45th of 155
71°
Fast

2017 Daily WARP Profile
2.3 Total WARP

Game 158: leg soreness

Fantasy Values
| 2017 | 2018 |
| $20.00 | $19.00 |

YEAR	TEAM	LVL	AGE	PA	R	2B	3B	HR	RBI	BB	K	SB	AVG/OBP/SLG	TAv	VORP	BABIP	WARP
2017	BAL	MLB	31	635	82	28	1	26	73	27	113	2	.285/.322/.466	.266	28.0	.312	2.3

2017 Batting Percentages

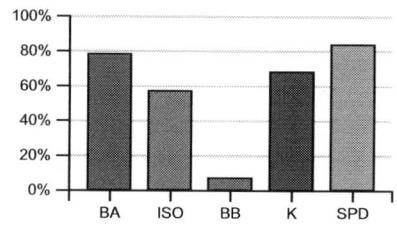

Batting PECOTA Percentiles

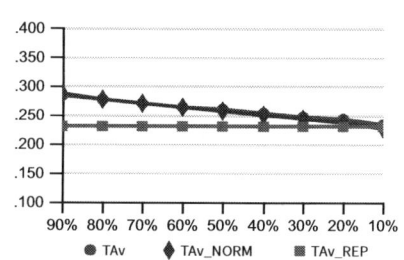

Batting WARP History

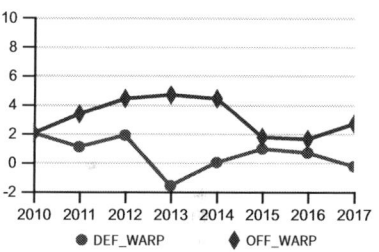

BRR (Relative to Position)

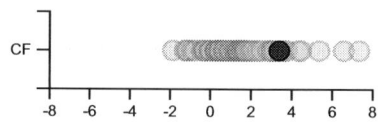

Rank		Player	BRR
6	82°	Jackie Bradley	3.79
7	80°	Keon Broxton	3.64
8	78°	**Adam Jones**	**3.43**
9	76°	Albert Almora	3.17
10	75°	Ian Happ	3.07

BRR (Relative to Team)

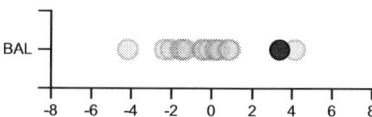

Rank		Player	BRR
1	89°	Jonathan Schoop	4.21
2	78°	**Adam Jones**	**3.43**
3	69°	Trey Mancini	0.95
4	63°	Joey Rickard	0.88
5	53°	Tim Beckham	0.41

Base Running Components

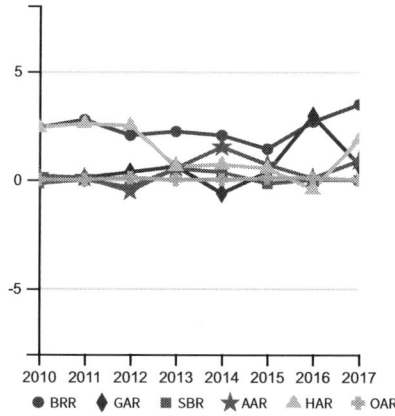

Aaron Judge   RF   New York Yankees

Born: 4/26/1992   **Age:** 26   **Bats:** R   **Throws:** R   **Height:** 6' 7"   **Weight:** 282 lbs   **Draft Info:** Round 1, 2013 Draft (#32 overall)

2017 Daily WARP Profile
7.3 Total WARP

PACE
21 Sec/Pit
45th of 155
71°
Fast

Fantasy Values

2017	2018
$33.20	**$27.00**

YEAR	TEAM	LVL	AGE	PA	R	2B	3B	HR	RBI	BB	K	SB	AVG/OBP/SLG	TAv	VORP	BABIP	WARP
2017	NYA	MLB	25	678	128	24	3	52	114	127	208	9	.284/.422/.627	.339	68.5	.357	7.3

The long swing Judge displayed in 2016 disappeared in 2017, as he started the season with a monster first half and looked like he might supplant every Yankees great in his first full season. But then the book started circulating on Judge and he struggled mightily, striking out in every game for over a month before bouncing back with a big September. Judge is a legitimate player, but the batting average should slip even as the power remains elite. Judge shouldn't get paid for his rookie campaign, but he is worth a second-round pick for another shot at 50 dongs. — Mike G.

2017 Batting Percentages

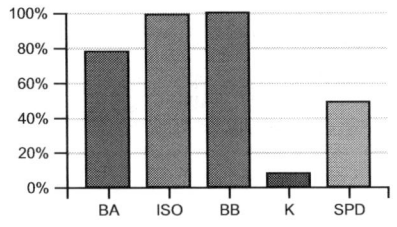

Batting PECOTA Percentiles

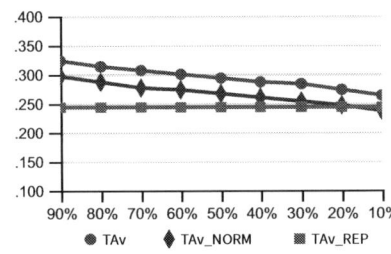

Batting WARP History

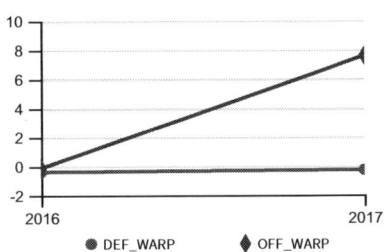

BRR (Relative to Position)

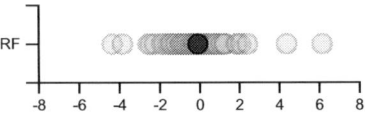

Rank		Player	BRR
24	58°	Alejandro De Aza	0.14
25	58°	Travis Taijeron	0.03
26	54°	**Aaron Judge**	**-0.06**
27	52°	Jorge Bonifacio	-0.06
28	49°	Giancarlo Stanton	-0.14

BRR (Relative to Team)

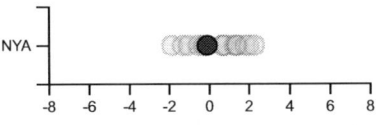

Rank		Player	BRR
9	47°	Clint Frazier	0.75
10	46°	Tyler Wade	0.67
11	34°	**Aaron Judge**	**-0.06**
12	22°	Giancarlo Stanton	-0.14
13	13°	Todd Frazier	-0.24

Base Running Components

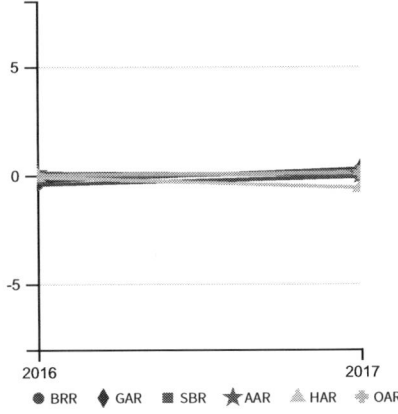

Tommy Kahnle   RHP   New York Yankees

Born: 8/7/1989   **Age:** 28   **Bats:** R   **Throws:** R   **Height:** 6' 1"   **Weight:** 235 lbs   **Draft Info:** Round 5, 2010 Draft (#175 overall)

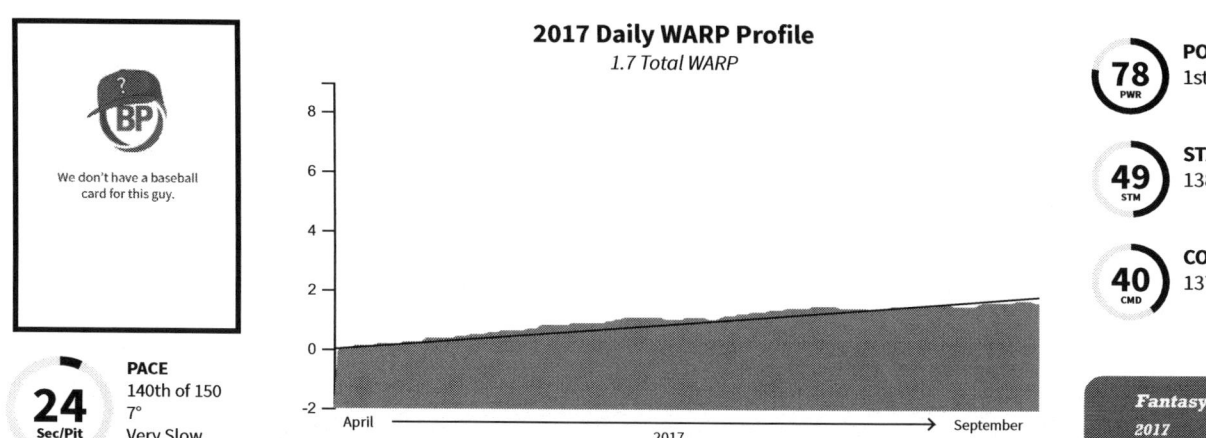

We don't have a baseball card for this guy.

2017 Daily WARP Profile
1.7 Total WARP

PACE
24 Sec/Pit
140th of 150
7°
Very Slow

POWER
78 PWR
1st of 150

STAMINA
49 STM
138th of 150

COMMAND
40 CMD
137th of 150

Fantasy Values

2017	2018
$10.10	$2.00

YEAR	TEAM	LVL	AGE	W	L	SV	G	GS	IP	H	HR	BB/9	K/9	K	GB%	BABIP	WHIP	ERA	DRA	WARP	MPH 95
2017	CHA	MLB	27	1	3	0	37	0	36	28	3	1.8	15.0	60	43%	.352	0.97	2.50	2.91	0.9	99.7
2017	NYA	MLB	27	1	1	0	32	0	26.2	25	1	3.4	12.1	36	40%	.364	1.31	2.70	2.62	0.8	99.3

2017 Pitching Percentages

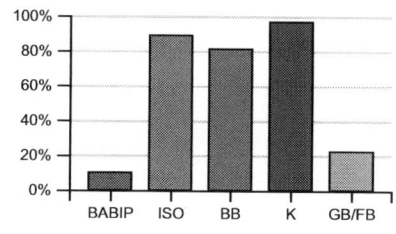

Pitching PECOTA Percentiles

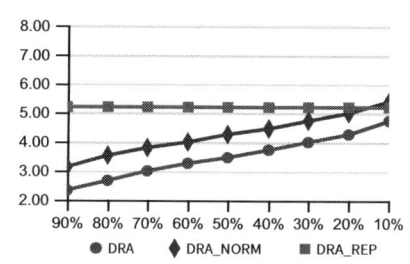

Pitching WARP History

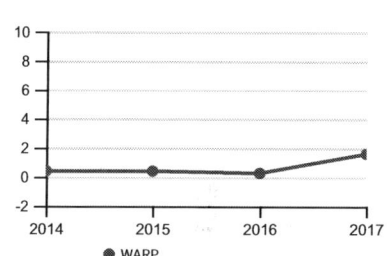

Tunnel vs LHH

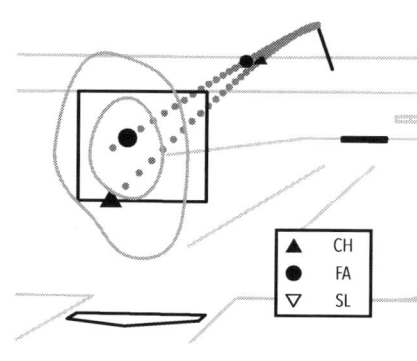

Pitch Types

Type	Freq	Velo	H Mov	V Mov
CH	22.0%	90.7 [122]	-12.4 [93]	-25 [106]
FA	66.4%	98.1 [120]	-4.9 [110]	-10.2 [116]
SL	11.6%	86.5 [109]	7.5 [113]	-30.7 [105]

Pitch Tunnel

Pairs	Release Diff	Tunnel Diff	Plate Diff	Speed Changes
758	41.6	111.2	209.6	0.018

PI Scores

Year	Pitch Ct	Pwr	Cmd	Stm
2014	1070	69	46	45
2015	650	65	38	51
2016	488	69	34	41
2017	1015	78	40	49

Tunnel vs RHH

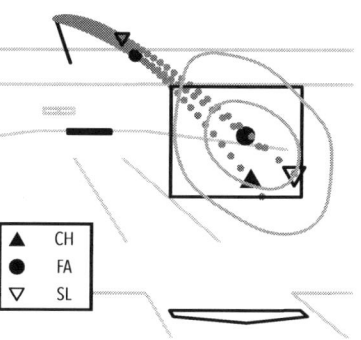

Ian Kennedy   RHP   Kansas City Royals

Born: 12/19/1984   **Age:** 33   **Bats:** R   **Throws:** R   **Height:** 6' 0"   **Weight:** 200 lbs   **Draft Info:** Round 1, 2006 Draft (#21 overall)

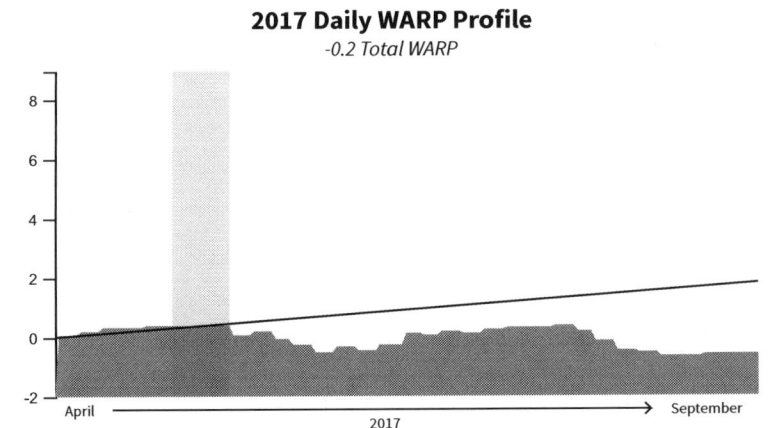

2017 Daily WARP Profile
-0.2 Total WARP

Game 28: DL (hamstring strain)

PACE
21 Sec/Pit
81st of 150
46°
Average

POWER
48 PWR
66th of 150

STAMINA
68 STM
77th of 150

COMMAND
55 CMD
62nd of 150

Fantasy Values
2017	2018
$3.43	**$2.00**

YEAR	TEAM	LVL	AGE	W	L	SV	G	GS	IP	H	HR	BB/9	K/9	K	GB%	BABIP	WHIP	ERA	DRA	WARP	MPH 95
2017	KCA	MLB	32	5	13	0	30	30	154	143	34	3.6	7.7	131	36%	.257	1.32	5.38	5.68	-0.2	93.6

2017 Pitching Percentages

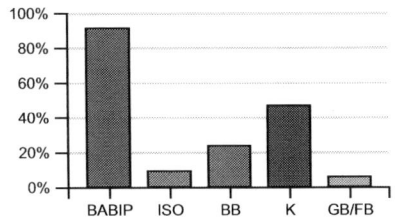

Pitching PECOTA Percentiles

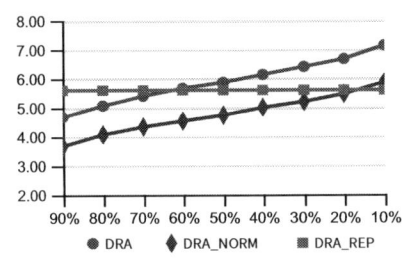

● DRA   ◆ DRA_NORM   ■ DRA_REP

Pitching WARP History

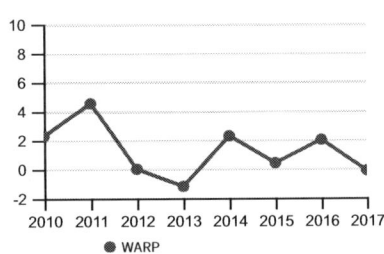

● WARP

Tunnel vs LHH

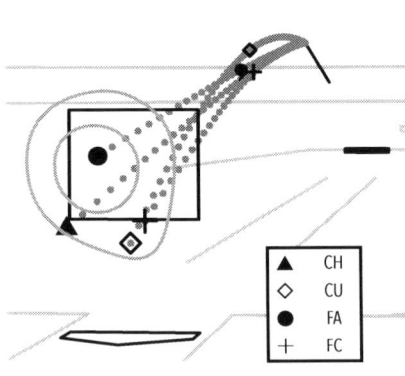

▲	CH
◇	CU
●	FA
+	FC

Pitch Types

Type	Freq	Velo	H Mov	V Mov
CH	10.7%	85.3 [101]	-11.6 [97]	-22.7 [112]
CU	15.7%	78.3 [100]	9.7 [108]	-51.2 [93]
FA	61.7%	92.4 [99]	-8.6 [93]	-13.3 [106]
FC	11.9%	86.3 [88]	1.5 [100]	-28.2 [83]

Pitch Tunnel

Pairs	Release Diff	Tunnel Diff	Plate Diff	Speed Changes
1937	25.6	108.1	220.0	0.028

PI Scores

Year	Pitch Ct	Pwr	Cmd	Stm
2013	3087	41	55	77
2014	3366	47	54	82
2015	2877	46	58	70
2016	3371	51	59	81
2017	2637	48	55	68

Tunnel vs RHH

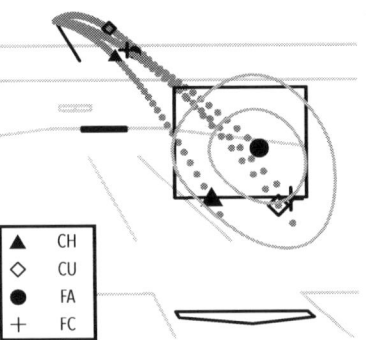

▲	CH
◇	CU
●	FA
+	FC

Max Kepler   RF   Minnesota Twins

Born: 2/10/1993   **Age:** 25   **Bats:** L   **Throws:** L   **Height:** 6' 4"   **Weight:** 205 lbs   **Draft Info:** International Free Agent, 2009

2017 Daily WARP Profile
0.7 Total WARP

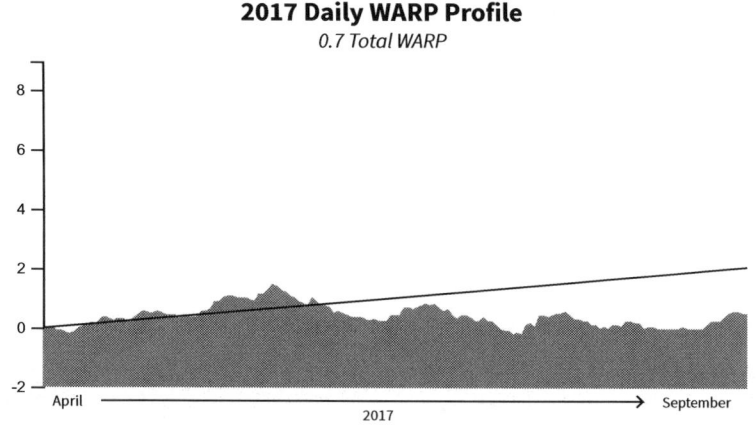

PACE
21 Sec/Pit
45th of 155
71°
Fast

Fantasy Values
2017	2018
$13.03	**$12.00**

YEAR	TEAM	LVL	AGE	PA	R	2B	3B	HR	RBI	BB	K	SB	AVG/OBP/SLG	TAv	VORP	BABIP	WARP
2017	MIN	MLB	24	568	67	32	2	19	69	47	114	6	.243/.312/.425	.247	1.2	.276	.7

2017 Batting Percentages

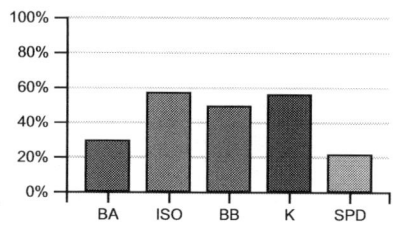

Batting PECOTA Percentiles

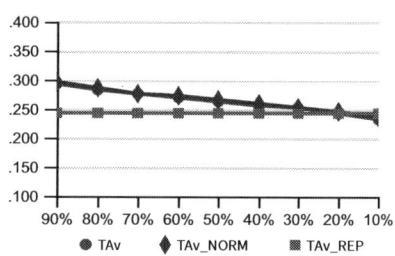

Batting WARP History

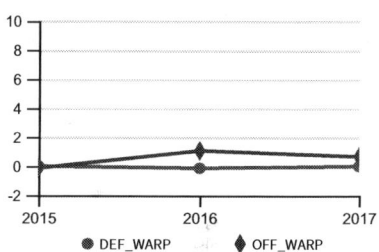

BRR (Relative to Position)

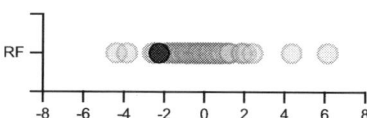

Rank		Player	BRR
49	15°	Chad Pinder	-1.76
50	12°	Steven Souza	-1.85
51	9°	**Max Kepler**	**-2.21**
52	7°	Nomar Mazara	-2.41
53	5°	Stephen Piscotty	-2.54

BRR (Relative to Team)

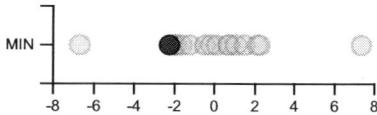

Rank		Player	BRR
12	35°	Eddie Rosario	-1.60
13	28°	Robbie Grossman	-1.86
14	21°	Miguel Sano	-1.98
15	12°	**Max Kepler**	**-2.21**
16	0°	Joe Mauer	-6.63

Base Running Components

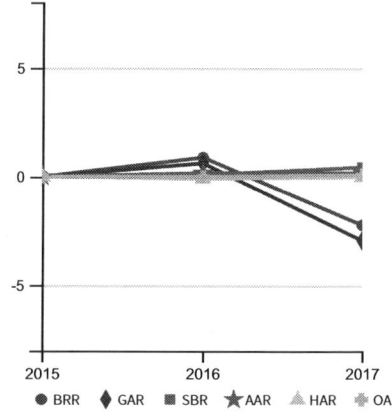

Clayton Kershaw   LHP   Los Angeles Dodgers

Born: 3/19/1988   **Age:** 30   **Bats:** L   **Throws:** L   **Height:** 6' 4"   **Weight:** 228 lbs   **Draft Info:** Round 1, 2006 Draft (#7 overall)

2017 Daily WARP Profile
4.4 Total WARP

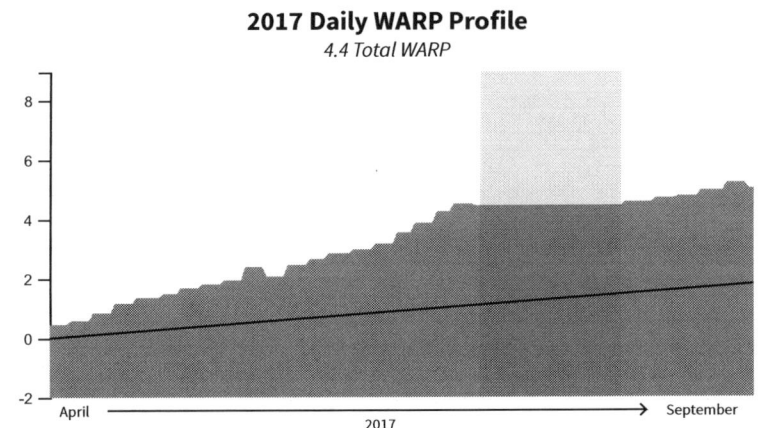

Game 100: DL (back strain)

POWER
45 **PWR**
73rd of 150

STAMINA
68 **STM**
77th of 150

COMMAND
63 **CMD**
20th of 150

PACE
21 **Sec/Pit**
81st of 150
46°
Average

Fantasy Values
2017	2018
$36.09	$34.00

YEAR	TEAM	LVL	AGE	W	L	SV	G	GS	IP	H	HR	BB/9	K/9	K	GB%	BABIP	WHIP	ERA	DRA	WARP	MPH 95
2017	LAN	MLB	29	18	4	0	27	27	175	136	23	1.5	10.4	202	49%	.267	0.95	2.31	3.30	4.4	94.3

Kershaw remains one of the best pitchers in baseball, but it would be foolish to ignore the spike in home runs and the fact that he wasn't quite the off-the-charts arm he had been in the past. His repertoire and stuff remain top tier, but he makes more mistakes than he used to and for the second consecutive season didn't reach 200 innings. Kershaw remains a potential anchor for any fantasy staff, but for the first time in years it is forgivable if you want to consider someone else the best fantasy pitcher in baseball. — Mike G.

2017 Pitching Percentages

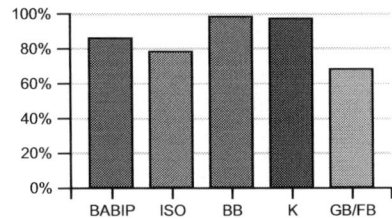

Pitching PECOTA Percentiles

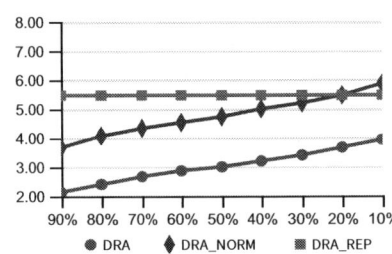

Pitching WARP History

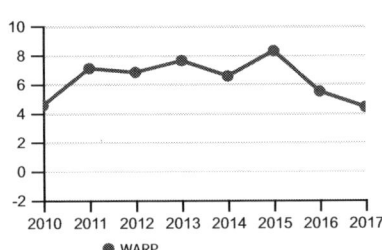

Tunnel vs LHH

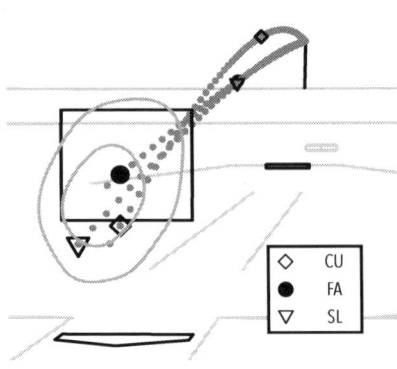

Pitch Types

Type	Freq	Velo	H Mov	V Mov
CH	1.2%	86.2 [105]	7.6 [119]	-17 [129]
CU	16.7%	73.7 [83]	-2.4 [79]	-61.5 [71]
FA	46.6%	93.1 [101]	-0.5 [136]	-10.5 [115]
SI	1.2%	94.9 [115]	9.5 [122]	-12 [130]
SL	34.3%	88.9 [120]	-4.3 [99]	-23 [128]

Pitch Tunnel

Pairs	Release Diff	Tunnel Diff	Plate Diff	Speed Changes
1769	38.7	130.8	217.5	0.042

PI Scores

Year	Pitch Ct	Pwr	Cmd	Stm
2013	3424	48	60	85
2014	2608	51	54	72
2015	3382	51	55	81
2016	2057	47	51	52
2017	2427	45	63	68

Tunnel vs RHH

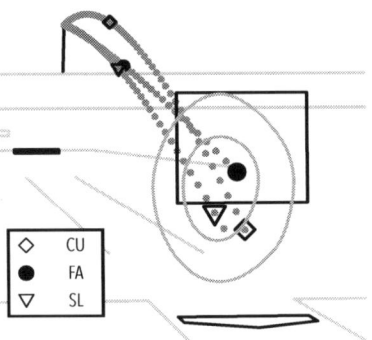

Dallas Keuchel   LHP   Houston Astros

Born: 1/1/1988   **Age:** 30   **Bats:** L   **Throws:** L   **Height:** 6' 3"   **Weight:** 205 lbs   **Draft Info:** Round 7, 2009 Draft (#221 overall)

2017 Daily WARP Profile
4.7 Total WARP

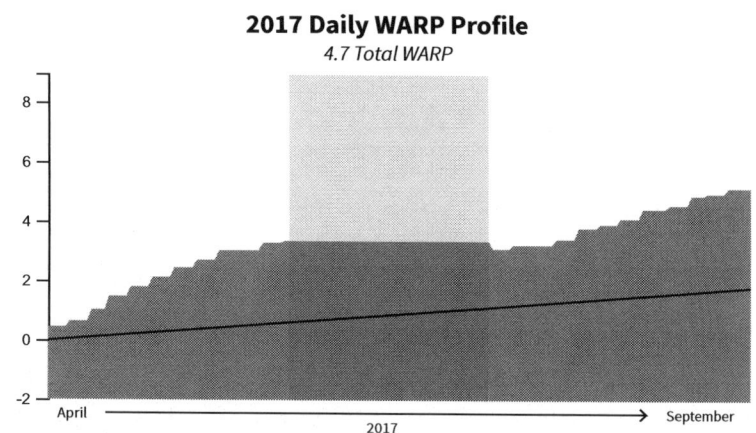

April — 2017 — September

Game 56: DL (neck soreness)

34 PWR **POWER** 120th of 150

62 STM **STAMINA** 94th of 150

74 CMD **COMMAND** 6th of 150

21 Sec/Pit **PACE** 81st of 150 46° Average

Fantasy Values
2017	2018
$21.41	$21.00

YEAR	TEAM	LVL	AGE	W	L	SV	G	GS	IP	H	HR	BB/9	K/9	K	GB%	BABIP	WHIP	ERA	DRA	WARP	MPH 95
2017	HOU	MLB	29	14	5	0	23	23	145.2	116	15	2.9	7.7	125	68%	.256	1.12	2.90	2.65	4.7	90.4

It's a fine line for Keuchel, who relies on a severe GB/FB rate and pinpoint control as opposed to a dominant strikeout pitch, but excluding a poor 2016 campaign the formula has worked well for the hirsute Astro. In 2017 Keuchel delivered a 68 percent ground-ball rate, which will play for nearly any major-league pitcher even without dominant strikeout stuff. Nonelite strikeout totals do make it challenging to price Keuchel too aggressively, but otherwise there is no reason not to push him into at least the low $20s in AL-only and to the top 15 in mixed drafts. — Mike G.

2017 Pitching Percentages

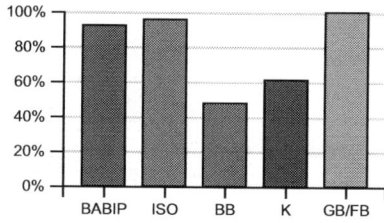

Pitching PECOTA Percentiles

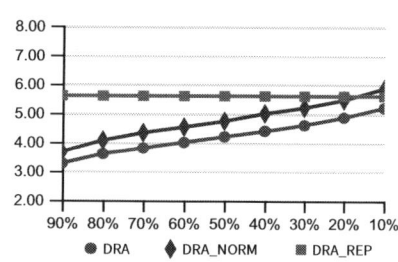

Pitching WARP History

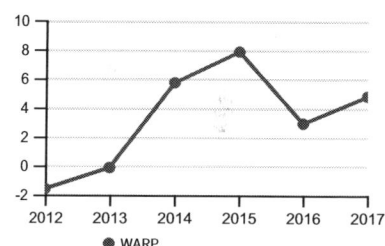

Tunnel vs LHH

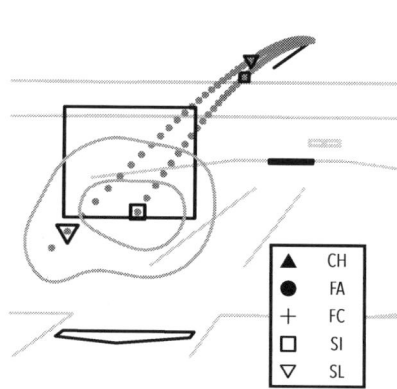

	CH
▲	CH
●	FA
+	FC
□	SI
▽	SL

Pitch Types

Type	Freq	Velo	H Mov	V Mov
CH	13.0%	79.1 [76]	12 [95]	-31.1 [88]
CU	0.6%	78.7 [102]	-9.2 [105]	-41.4 [114]
FA	6.9%	89.6 [88]	3.2 [119]	-18.8 [88]
FC	10.3%	86.9 [92]	-1.8 [101]	-25.5 [93]
SI	51.1%	89.1 [81]	10.2 [117]	-23 [89]
SL	18.1%	78.9 [76]	-10.4 [125]	-42 [73]

Pitch Tunnel

Pairs	Release Diff	Tunnel Diff	Plate Diff	Speed Changes
1523	25.0	112.7	214.8	0.025

PI Scores

Year	Pitch Ct	Pwr	Cmd	Stm
2013	2495	34	60	67
2014	3004	36	76	78
2015	3478	36	81	83
2016	2645	38	65	76
2017	2187	34	74	62

Tunnel vs RHH

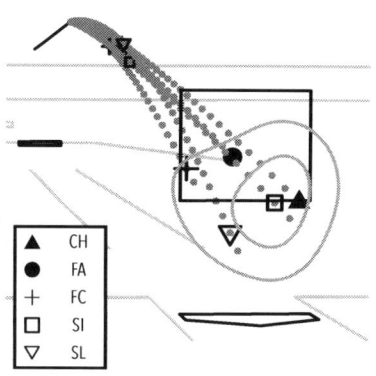

	CH
▲	CH
●	FA
+	FC
□	SI
▽	SL

Kevin Kiermaier   CF   Tampa Bay Rays

Born: 4/22/1990   **Age:** 28   **Bats:** L   **Throws:** R   **Height:** 6' 1"   **Weight:** 215 lbs   **Draft Info:** Round 31, 2010 Draft (#941 overall)

20 Sec/Pit

PACE
18th of 155
88°
Very Fast

2017 Daily WARP Profile
3.2 Total WARP

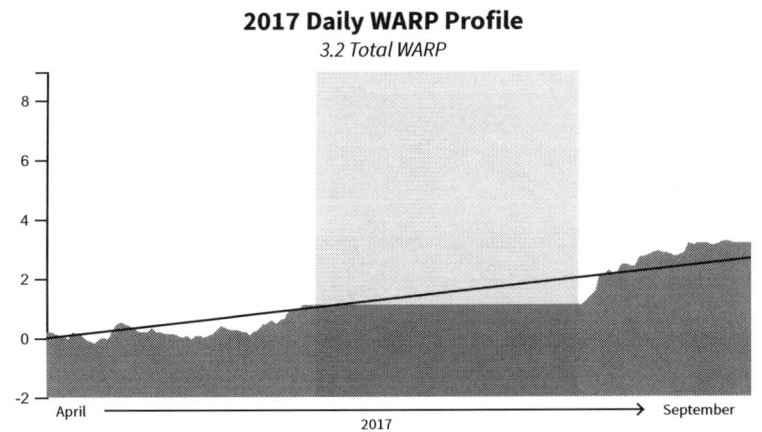

Game 63: DL (hip fracture)

Fantasy Values
2017	2018
$16.66	**$21.00**

YEAR	TEAM	LVL	AGE	PA	R	2B	3B	HR	RBI	BB	K	SB	AVG/OBP/SLG	TAv	VORP	BABIP	WARP
2017	TBA	MLB	27	421	56	15	3	15	39	31	99	16	.276/.338/.450	.279	24.6	.337	3.2

"If only Kevin Kiermaier could stay healthy" you say to yourself in late March, drafting or purchasing him as if this is the year he'll play 150 games, hit 20 home runs, and steal 30 bases. Alas, he has done all three of those things as often as you have. While the final numbers are fine on a per-at-bat basis, Kiermaier's absence from your lineup for long stretches is rough, particularly in deeper leagues where replacements are virtually nonexistent. Kiermaier's power/speed combo is a rarity, but he should be pushed down a couple of rounds based on the spotty health history. — Mike G.

2017 Batting Percentages

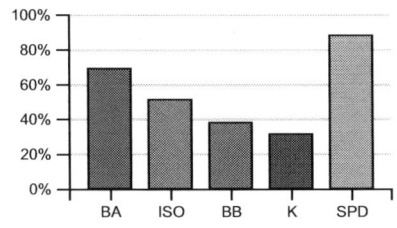

Batting PECOTA Percentiles

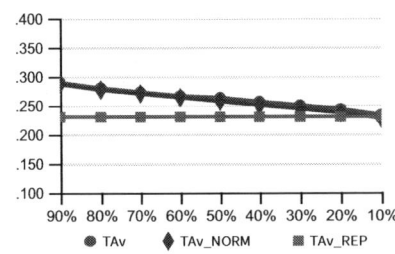

Batting WARP History

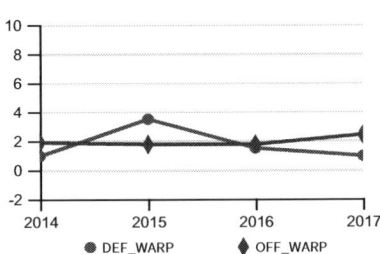

BRR (Relative to Position)

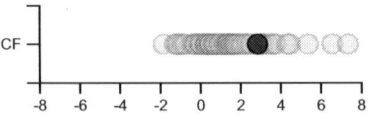

Rank		Player	BRR
10	75°	Ian Happ	3.07
11	73°	Michael Taylor	3.06
12	71°	**Kevin Kiermaier**	**2.89**
13	69°	Rajai Davis	2.55
14	65°	Lorenzo Cain	2.36

BRR (Relative to Team)

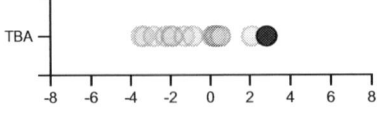

Rank		Player	BRR
1	98°	**Kevin Kiermaier**	**2.89**
2	90°	Mallex Smith	2.15
3	88°	Ryan Schimpf	0.57
4	87°	Colby Rasmus	0.55
5	79°	Logan Morrison	0.39

Base Running Components

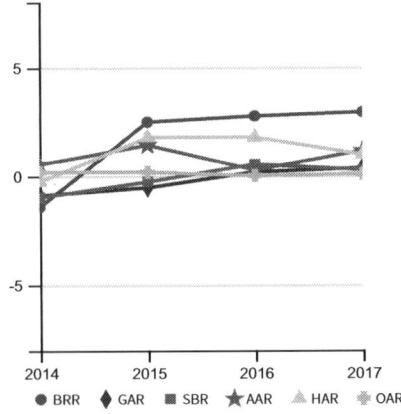

Craig Kimbrel RHP Boston Red Sox

Born: 5/28/1988 **Age:** 30 **Bats:** R **Throws:** R **Height:** 6'0" **Weight:** 210 lbs **Draft Info:** Round 3, 2008 Draft (#96 overall)

2017 Daily WARP Profile
2.5 Total WARP

PACE
25 Sec/Pit
143rd of 150
5°
Very Slow

POWER **78** PWR 1st of 150
STAMINA **50** STM 135th of 150
COMMAND **59** CMD 43rd of 150

Fantasy Values
2017 **$29.89** 2018 **$22.00**

YEAR	TEAM	LVL	AGE	W	L	SV	G	GS	IP	H	HR	BB/9	K/9	K	GB%	BABIP	WHIP	ERA	DRA	WARP	MPH 95
2017	BOS	MLB	29	5	0	35	67	0	69	33	6	1.8	16.4	126	37%	.260	0.68	1.43	1.89	2.5	99.8

After a slightly off year in 2016, Kimbrel returned to his usual dominant self, with a DRA under 2.00 for the fifth time in his career. Kimbrel is an all-or-nothing proposition. He gets hit hard when he leaves the ball in the fat part of the zone, but thankfully that seldom happens, resulting in plenty of saves and lots of strikeouts. He was the best reliever in baseball this side of Kenley Jansen, and while some of the metrics say Kimbrel is "unclutch" that doesn't matter in fantasy. — Mike G.

2017 Pitching Percentages

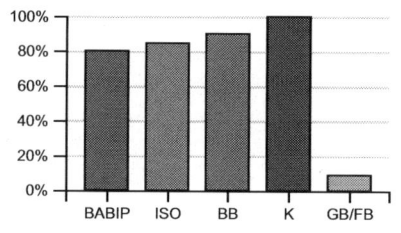

Pitching PECOTA Percentiles

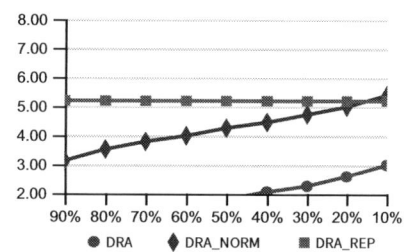

Pitching WARP History

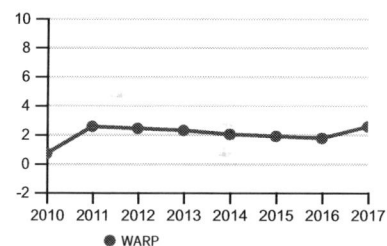

Tunnel vs LHH

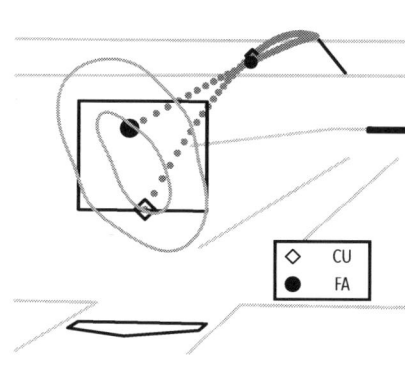

Pitch Types

Type	Freq	Velo	H Mov	V Mov
CU	31.5%	87.7 [135]	8.9 [104]	-40.6 [116]
FA	68.5%	98.7 [122]	-9.6 [88]	-11.6 [111]

Pitch Tunnel

Pairs	Release Diff	Tunnel Diff	Plate Diff	Speed Changes
895	27.7	104.3	209.8	0.020

PI Scores

Year	Pitch Ct	Pwr	Cmd	Stm
2013	1031	77	37	47
2014	1036	80	52	46
2015	1001	77	43	47
2016	934	67	43	43
2017	1150	78	59	50

Tunnel vs RHH

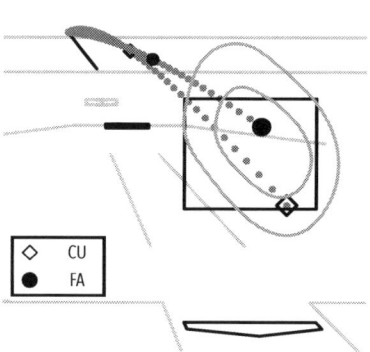

Ian Kinsler 2B Los Angeles Angels

Born: 6/22/1982 **Age:** 36 **Bats:** R **Throws:** R **Height:** 6' 0" **Weight:** 200 lbs **Draft Info:** Round 17, 2003 Draft (#496 overall)

20 Sec/Pit

PACE
18th of 155
88°
Very Fast

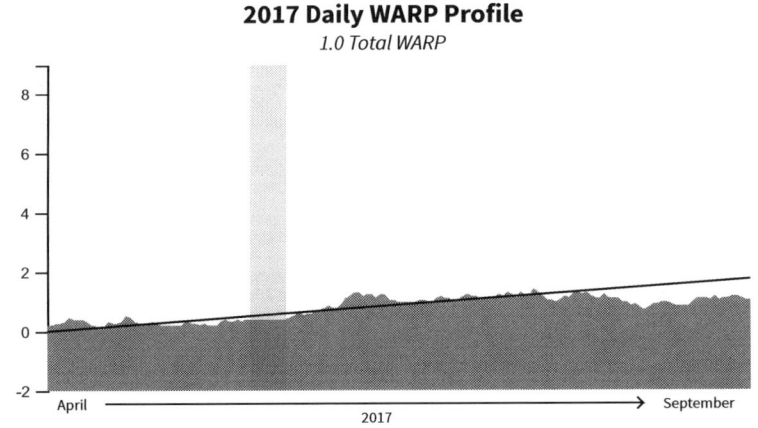

2017 Daily WARP Profile
1.0 Total WARP

April — 2017 — September

Game 48: DL (hamstring strain)

Fantasy Values
2017	2018
$15.78	$15.00

YEAR	TEAM	LVL	AGE	PA	R	2B	3B	HR	RBI	BB	K	SB	AVG/OBP/SLG	TAv	VORP	BABIP	WARP
2017	DET	MLB	35	613	90	25	3	22	52	55	86	14	.236/.313/.412	.240	9.0	.244	1.0

A subpar batting average combined with a lack of RBI opportunities because of the Tigers' awful bottom of the lineup led to one of the worst seasons of Kinsler's career. Twenty-two home runs and 14 stolen bases did give Kinsler value, but it is difficult to know if his BABIP drop was a fluke or due to a sharp decline in hard-hit balls. Traded to the Angels, Kinsler will benefit from a stronger lineup but be wary of overbidding on a hitter clearly in the decline phase of his career. — Mike G.

2017 Batting Percentages

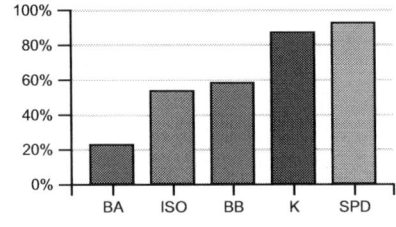

Batting PECOTA Percentiles

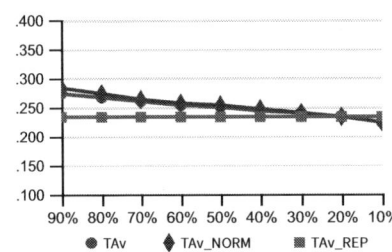

Batting WARP History

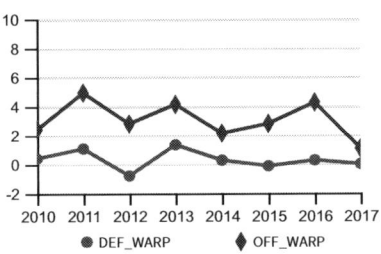

BRR (Relative to Position)

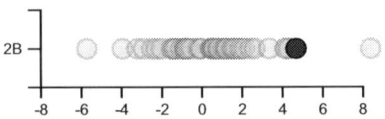

Rank		Player	BRR
1	95°	Dee Gordon	8.44
2	93°	**Ian Kinsler**	**4.72**
3	90°	Javier Baez	4.36
4	88°	Jonathan Schoop	4.21
5	84°	Cesar Hernandez	4.20

BRR (Relative to Team)

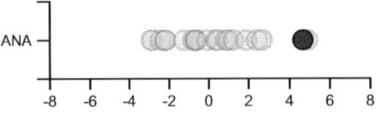

Rank		Player	BRR
1	100°	Ben Revere	4.94
2	100°	**Ian Kinsler**	**4.72**
3	100°	Andrelton Simmons	2.71
4	89°	Brandon Phillips	2.46
5	85°	Cliff Pennington	1.95

Base Running Components

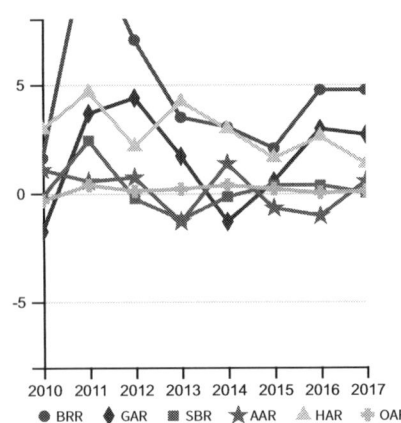

Corey Kluber RHP Cleveland Indians

Born: 4/10/1986 **Age:** 32 **Bats:** R **Throws:** R **Height:** 6' 4" **Weight:** 215 lbs **Draft Info:** Round 4, 2007 Draft (#134 overall)

PACE
20 37th of 150
Sec/Pit 75°
Fast

2017 Daily WARP Profile
8.0 Total WARP

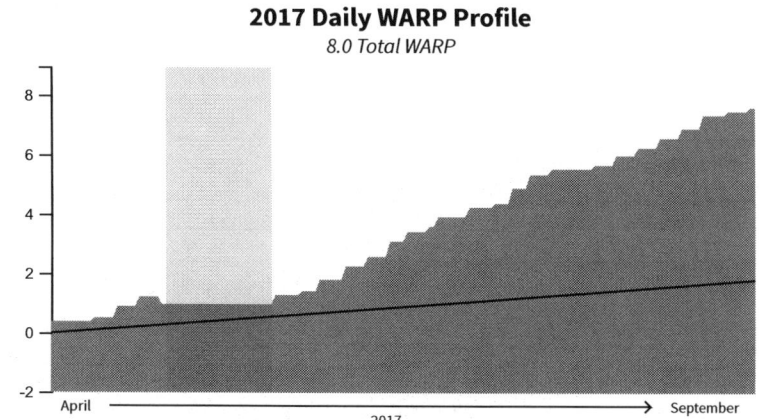

2017

April ——————————————————→ September

Game 27: DL (back strain)

38 **POWER**
PWR 104th of 150

77 **STAMINA**
STM 32nd of 150

60 **COMMAND**
CMD 37th of 150

Fantasy Values
| *2017* | *2018* |
| **$43.61** | **$35.00** |

YEAR	TEAM	LVL	AGE	W	L	SV	G	GS	IP	H	HR	BB/9	K/9	K	GB%	BABIP	WHIP	ERA	DRA	WARP	MPH 95
2017	CLE	MLB	31	18	4	0	29	29	203.2	141	21	1.6	11.7	265	46%	.267	0.87	2.25	2.05	8.0	94.0

Kluber started the year poorly, a mystery that was quickly solved when a back ailment was diagnosed. Once he returned from the injury he was his same old dominant self, making up for lost time to become the number 1 fantasy pitcher in 2017. There's no reason to doubt the Klubot outside of another injury, and given how great he was returning from the back malady Kluber should easily a Top 3 starter once again in 2018. — Mike G.

2017 Pitching Percentages

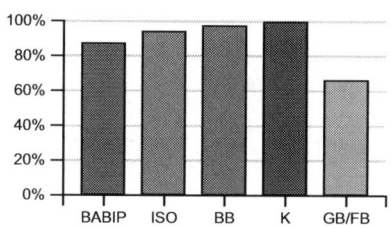

Pitching PECOTA Percentiles

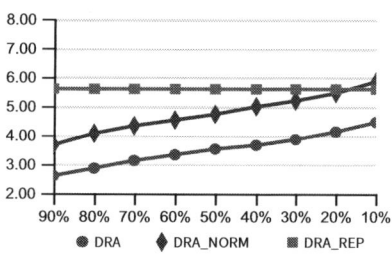

● DRA ◆ DRA_NORM ■ DRA_REP

Pitching WARP History

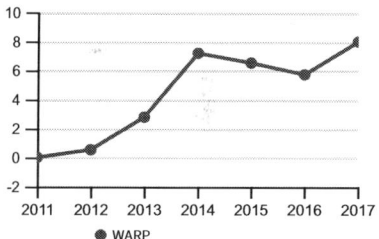

● WARP

Tunnel vs LHH

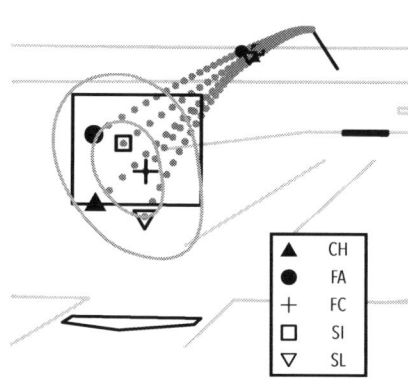

▲ CH
● FA
+ FC
□ SI
▽ SL

Pitch Types

Type	Freq	Velo	H Mov	V Mov
CH	6.3%	86.2 [104]	-9.7 [107]	-28.3 [96]
FA	14.5%	93.1 [101]	-4.6 [112]	-14.8 [101]
FC	24.2%	89.2 [105]	3.9 [112]	-25.4 [94]
SI	27.9%	93 [104]	-11.6 [106]	-19.8 [101]
SL	27.1%	84.7 [101]	13.4 [139]	-31.8 [102]

Pitch Tunnel

Pairs	Release Diff	Tunnel Diff	Plate Diff	Speed Changes
2097	23.9	118.3	225.7	0.020

PI Scores

Year	Pitch Ct	Pwr	Cmd	Stm
2013	2287	51	48	62
2014	3486	53	55	88
2015	3262	49	56	80
2016	3172	48	51	83
2017	2931	38	60	77

Tunnel vs RHH

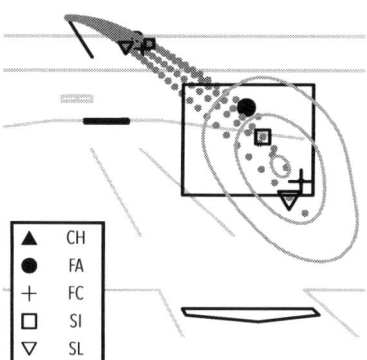

▲ CH
● FA
+ FC
□ SI
▽ SL

Corey Knebel   RHP   Milwaukee Brewers

Born: 11/26/1991   **Age:** 26   **Bats:** R   **Throws:** R   **Height:** 6' 4"   **Weight:** 220 lbs   **Draft Info:** Round 1, 2013 Draft (#39 overall)

2017 Daily WARP Profile
2.3 Total WARP

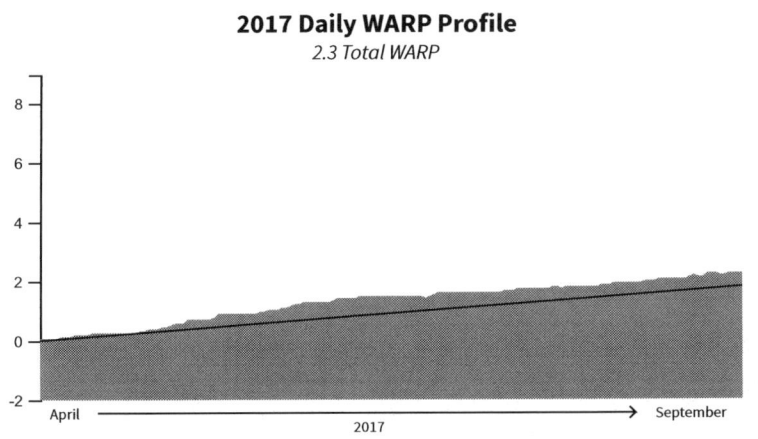

POWER
70 PWR
7th of 150

STAMINA
56 STM
112th of 150

COMMAND
59 CMD
43rd of 150

PACE
23 Sec/Pit
126th of 150
16°
Very Slow

Fantasy Values

2017	2018
$24.04	$17.00

YEAR	TEAM	LVL	AGE	W	L	SV	G	GS	IP	H	HR	BB/9	K/9	K	GB%	BABIP	WHIP	ERA	DRA	WARP	MPH 95
2017	MIL	MLB	25	1	4	4	39	76	0	76	48	6	4.7	14.9	126	39%	.311	1.16	1.78	2.44	2.3	98.9

Slated to set up behind Neftali Feliz to start the year, Knebel quickly found his way into the closer's role in Milwaukee and never looked back. The control is a problem at times, but Knebel is so difficult to hit and get a read on that it seldom matters. The WHIP is the only thing keeping Knebel from having the same lofty price tag as a handful of relievers ahead of him, but there is little reason to fear drafting him if you need a closer and the big dogs in your league have already been nabbed. — Mike G.

2017 Pitching Percentages

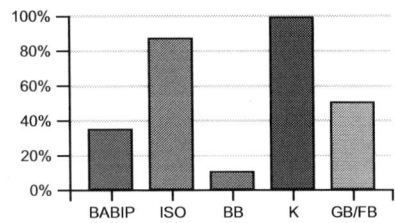

Pitching PECOTA Percentiles

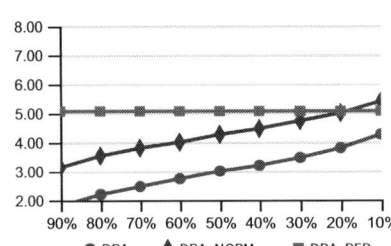

● DRA   ◆ DRA_NORM   ■ DRA_REP

Pitching WARP History

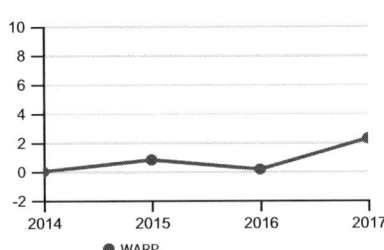

● WARP

Tunnel vs LHH

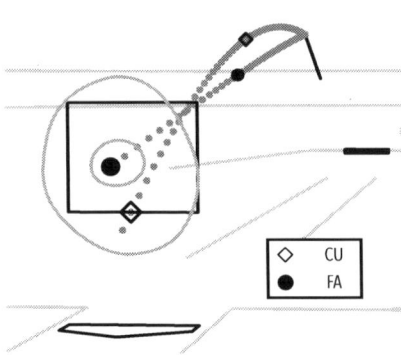

◇ CU
● FA

Pitch Types

Type	Freq	Velo	H Mov	V Mov
CU	28.2%	81 [110]	10.3 [110]	-51.8 [92]
FA	71.8%	97.8 [118]	-5 [110]	-9.3 [119]

Pitch Tunnel

Pairs	Release Diff	Tunnel Diff	Plate Diff	Speed Changes
1050	32.8	123.4	224.9	0.033

PI Scores

Year	Pitch Ct	Pwr	Cmd	Stm
2015	819	60	44	50
2016	603	60	60	46
2017	1357	70	59	56

Tunnel vs RHH

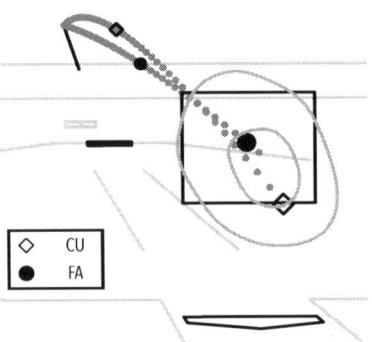

◇ CU
● FA

Chad Kuhl RHP Pittsburgh Pirates

Born: 9/10/1992 **Age:** 25 **Bats:** R **Throws:** R **Height:** 6' 3" **Weight:** 216 lbs **Draft Info:** Round 9, 2013 Draft (#269 overall)

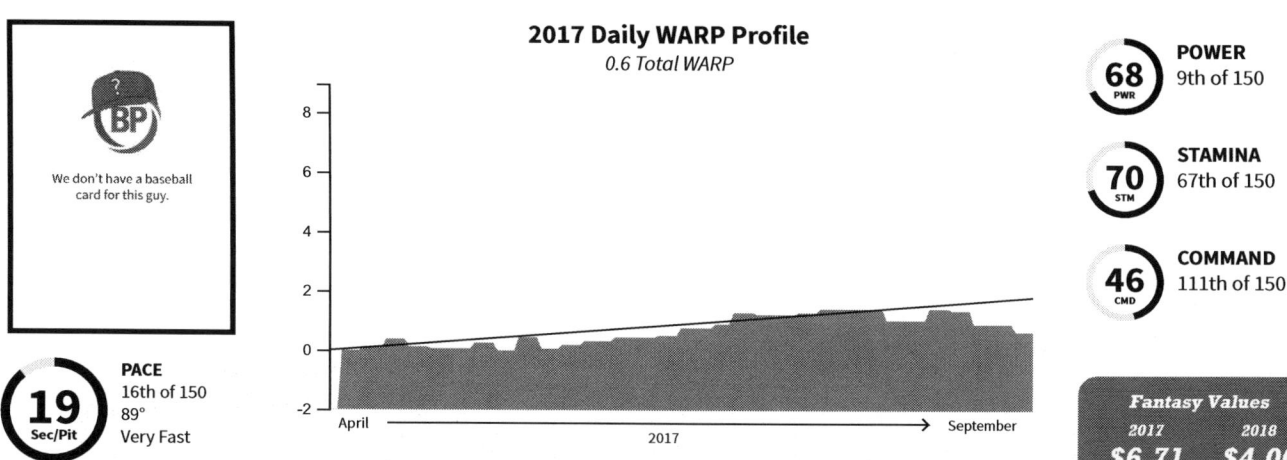

2017 Daily WARP Profile
0.6 Total WARP

POWER 68 PWR 9th of 150

STAMINA 70 STM 67th of 150

COMMAND 46 CMD 111th of 150

PACE 19 Sec/Pit 16th of 150 89° Very Fast

Fantasy Values
2017 **$6.71** 2018 **$4.00**

We don't have a baseball card for this guy.

YEAR	TEAM	LVL	AGE	W	L	SV	G	GS	IP	H	HR	BB/9	K/9	K	GB%	BABIP	WHIP	ERA	DRA	WARP	MPH 95
2017	PIT	MLB	24	8	11	0	31	31	157.1	159	17	4.1	8.1	142	43%	.321	1.47	4.35	5.24	0.6	97.8

2017 Pitching Percentages
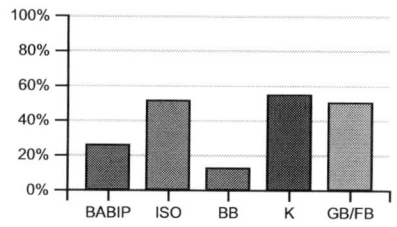

Pitching PECOTA Percentiles
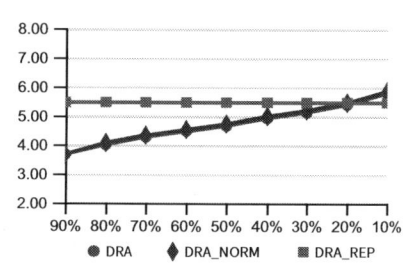

Pitching WARP History
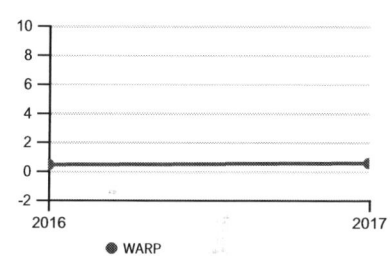

Tunnel vs LHH
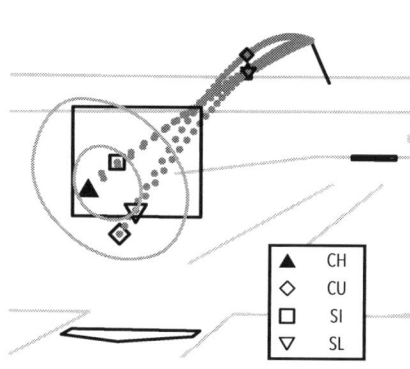

Pitch Types

Type	Freq	Velo	H Mov	V Mov
CH	9.7%	89.2 [117]	-13.4 [88]	-24.5 [107]
CU	6.3%	82.9 [117]	8.9 [104]	-46 [104]
SI	63.5%	95.9 [121]	-11.2 [110]	-13.8 [123]
SL	20.5%	88.9 [120]	3.5 [95]	-29 [110]

Pitch Tunnel

Pairs	Release Diff	Tunnel Diff	Plate Diff	Speed Changes
1992	34.1	127.2	235.8	0.019

PI Scores

Year	Pitch Ct	Pwr	Cmd	Stm
2016	1138	55	53	64
2017	2679	68	46	70

Tunnel vs RHH
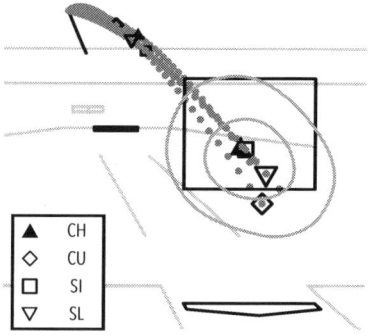

John Lackey RHP Chicago Cubs

Born: 10/23/1978 **Age:** 39 **Bats:** R **Throws:** R **Height:** 6' 6" **Weight:** 235 lbs **Draft Info:** Round 2, 1999 Draft (#68 overall)

PACE
20 37th of 150
Sec/Pit 75°
Fast

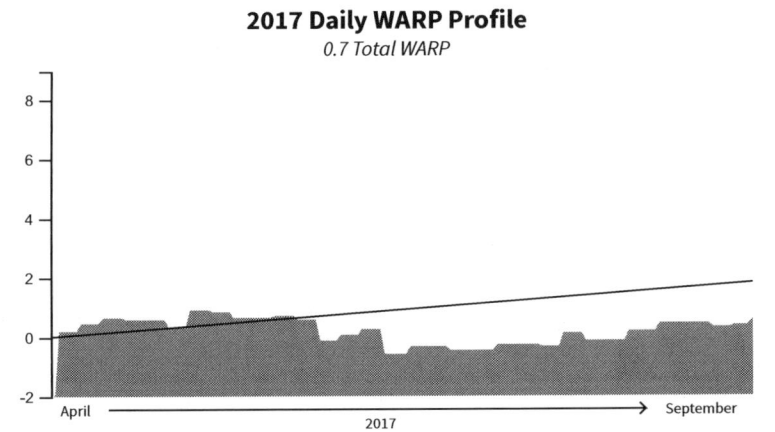
2017 Daily WARP Profile
0.7 Total WARP

POWER
35 117th of 150
PWR

STAMINA
72 59th of 150
STM

COMMAND
53 72nd of 150
CMD

Fantasy Values
2017	2018
$12.37	$2.00

YEAR	TEAM	LVL	AGE	W	L	SV	G	GS	IP	H	HR	BB/9	K/9	K	GB%	BABIP	WHIP	ERA	DRA	WARP	MPH 95
2017	CHN	MLB	38	12	12	0	31	30	170.2	165	36	2.8	7.9	149	43%	.268	1.28	4.59	5.20	0.7	92.8

2017 Pitching Percentages

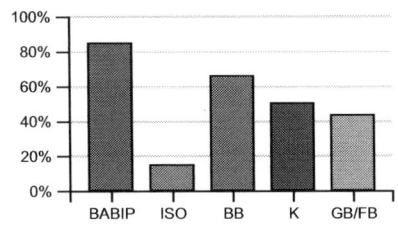

Pitching PECOTA Percentiles

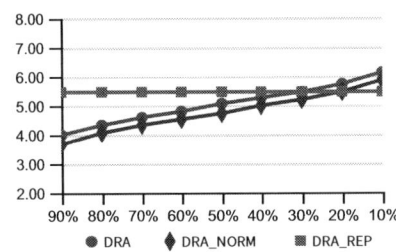

Pitching WARP History

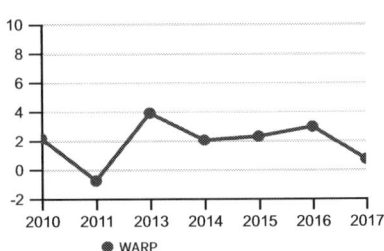

Tunnel vs LHH

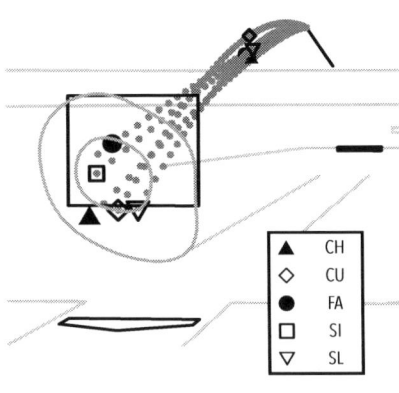

▲	CH
◇	CU
●	FA
□	SI
▽	SL

Pitch Types

Type	Freq	Velo	H Mov	V Mov
CH	4.7%	83.8 [95]	-11.4 [98]	-29 [94]
CU	7.2%	77.8 [98]	8 [101]	-45.6 [105]
FA	35.6%	91.4 [95]	-6.6 [102]	-16.2 [97]
SI	16.5%	91 [92]	-13.1 [96]	-23 [89]
SL	35.9%	82.7 [93]	5.1 [102]	-35 [93]

Pitch Tunnel

Pairs	Release Diff	Tunnel Diff	Plate Diff	Speed Changes
2017	52.8	119.1	226.6	0.023

PI Scores

Year	Pitch Ct	Pwr	Cmd	Stm
2013	2864	48	57	75
2014	3068	50	56	78
2015	3096	51	50	79
2016	2823	46	57	74
2017	2739	35	53	72

Tunnel vs RHH

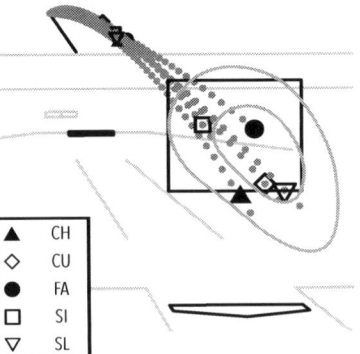

▲	CH
◇	CU
●	FA
□	SI
▽	SL

Jake Lamb 3B Arizona Diamondbacks

Born: 10/9/1990 **Age:** 27 **Bats:** L **Throws:** R **Height:** 6' 3" **Weight:** 215 lbs **Draft Info:** Round 6, 2012 Draft (#213 overall)

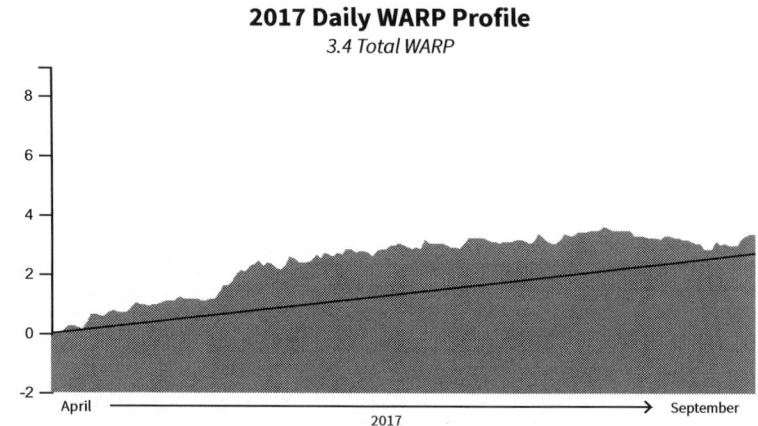

2017 Daily WARP Profile
3.4 Total WARP

PACE
21
Sec/Pit
45th of 155
71°
Fast

Fantasy Values
2017	2018
$20.28	$19.00

YEAR	TEAM	LVL	AGE	PA	R	2B	3B	HR	RBI	BB	K	SB	AVG/OBP/SLG	TAv	VORP	BABIP	WARP
2017	ARI	MLB	26	635	89	30	4	30	105	87	152	6	.248/.357/.487	.293	44.8	.287	3.4

2017 Batting Percentages

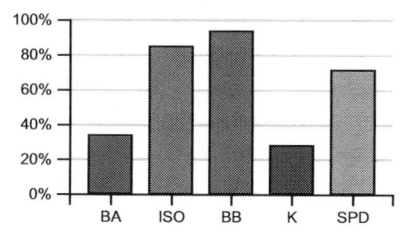

Batting PECOTA Percentiles

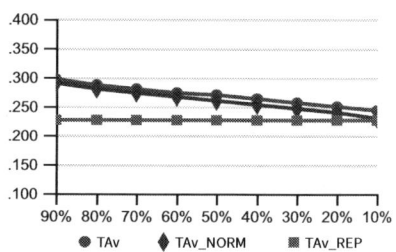

Batting WARP History

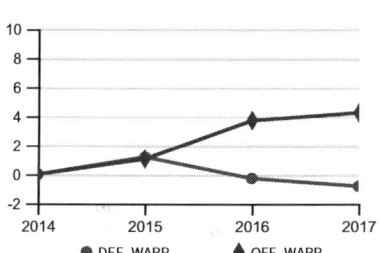

BRR (Relative to Position)

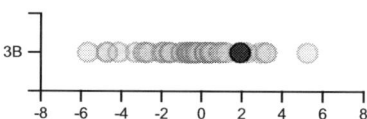

Rank		Player	BRR
5	87°	Eduardo Escobar	2.30
6	84°	Anthony Rendon	2.04
7	81°	**Jake Lamb**	**1.96**
8	77°	Kris Bryant	1.90
9	75°	Josh Donaldson	1.27

BRR (Relative to Team)

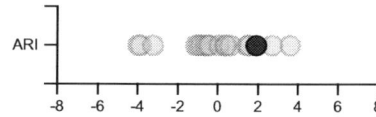

Rank		Player	BRR
1	91°	Paul Goldschmidt	3.66
2	84°	Gregor Blanco	2.75
3	74°	**Jake Lamb**	**1.96**
4	70°	Chris Herrmann	1.62
5	65°	Ketel Marte	1.53

Base Running Components

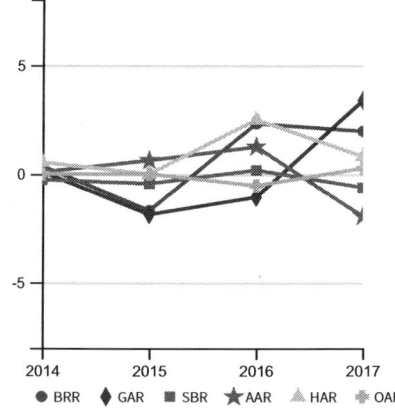

Dinelson Lamet RHP San Diego Padres

Born: 7/18/1992 **Age:** 25 **Bats:** R **Throws:** R **Height:** 6' 4" **Weight:** 187 lbs **Draft Info:** International Free Agent, 2014

2017 Daily WARP Profile
2.2 Total WARP

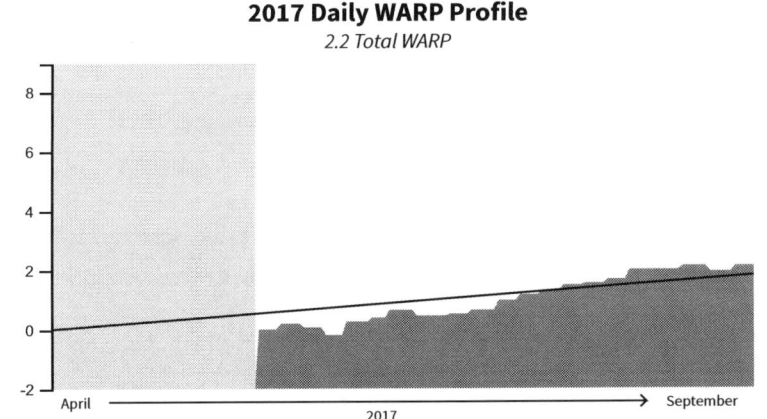

POWER 57 PWR 35th of 150

STAMINA 68 STM 77th of 150

COMMAND 41 CMD 135th of 150

PACE 21 Sec/Pit 81st of 150 46° Average

Game 1: minors

Fantasy Values
| 2017 | 2018 |
| $10.45 | $12.00 |

YEAR	TEAM	LVL	AGE	W	L	SV	G	GS	IP	H	HR	BB/9	K/9	K	GB%	BABIP	WHIP	ERA	DRA	WARP	MPH 95
2017	SDN	MLB	24	7	8	0	21	21	114.1	88	18	4.3	10.9	139	37%	.261	1.24	4.57	3.85	2.2	96.8

It was an up-and-down season for Lamet, who looked dominant at times but was inconsistent, as many rookie pitchers often are. Lamet's two-pitch repertoire was good enough on occasion, but when the slider was missing it allowed experienced hitters to sit on the fastball. Command was also a problem, as the walk rate jumped in the second half. Lamet's prodigious whiff rate alone makes him worth a roster spot, but there is enough risk that he should be considered more of a back-end arm in mixed than a mid-tier arm, at least for now. — Mike G.

2017 Pitching Percentages

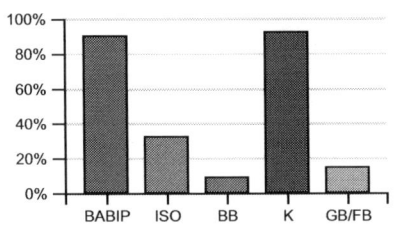

Pitching PECOTA Percentiles

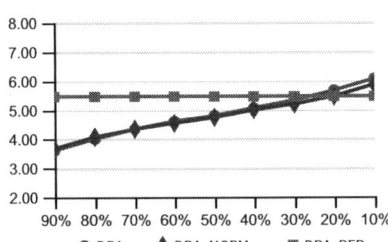

Tunnel vs LHH

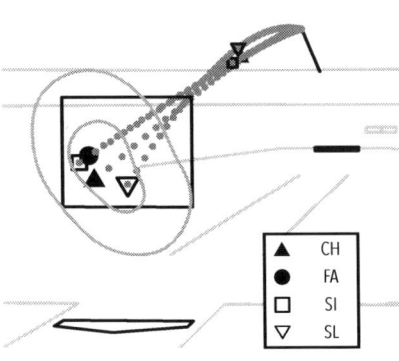

Pitch Types
Type	Freq	Velo	H Mov	V Mov
CH	4.6%	90.1 [120]	-11 [101]	-22.2 [114]
FA	48.7%	95.2 [109]	-6.4 [104]	-11.6 [111]
SI	7.0%	94.7 [114]	-11.9 [104]	-15 [119]
SL	39.7%	86 [107]	9.2 [120]	-32.1 [102]

Pitch Tunnel
Pairs	Release Diff	Tunnel Diff	Plate Diff	Speed Changes
1370	28.6	128.3	236.4	0.026

PI Scores
Year	Pitch Ct	Pwr	Cmd	Stm
2017	1829	57	41	68

Tunnel vs RHH

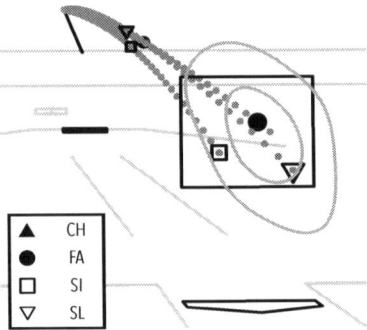

Mike Leake RHP Seattle Mariners

Born: 11/12/1987 **Age:** 30 **Bats:** R **Throws:** R **Height:** 5' 10" **Weight:** 170 lbs **Draft Info:** Round 1, 2009 Draft (#8 overall)

We don't have a baseball card for this guy.

2017 Daily WARP Profile
2.7 Total WARP

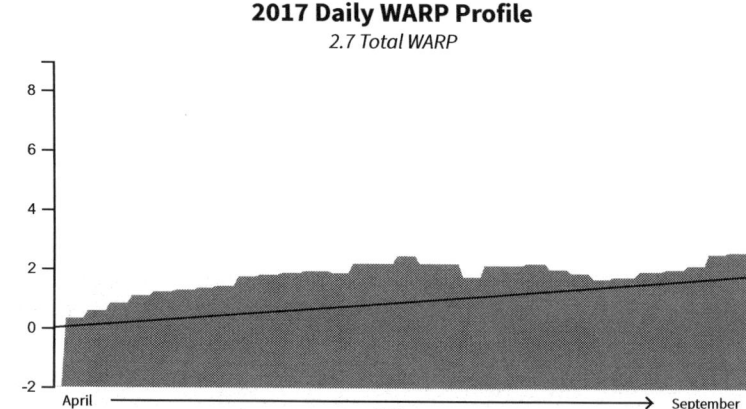

POWER
42 PWR
86th of 150

STAMINA
76 STM
36th of 150

COMMAND
61 CMD
30th of 150

17 Sec/Pit
PACE
2nd of 150
99°
Very Fast

Fantasy Values
2017	2018
$5.40	$8.00

YEAR	TEAM	LVL	AGE	W	L	SV	G	GS	IP	H	HR	BB/9	K/9	K	GB%	BABIP	WHIP	ERA	DRA	WARP	MPH 95
2017	SLN	MLB	29	7	12	0	26	26	154	169	19	2.0	6.0	103	55%	.306	1.32	4.21	4.23	2.3	91.6
2017	SEA	MLB	29	3	1	0	5	5	32	32	1	0.6	7.6	27	50%	.323	1.06	2.53	4.32	0.4	92.1

2017 Pitching Percentages

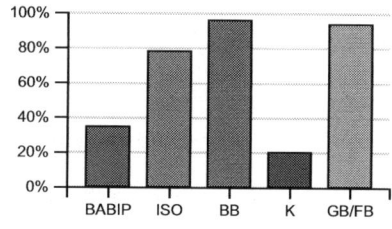

Pitching PECOTA Percentiles

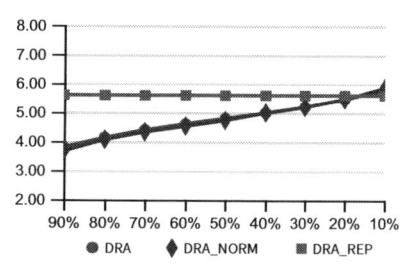

Pitching WARP History

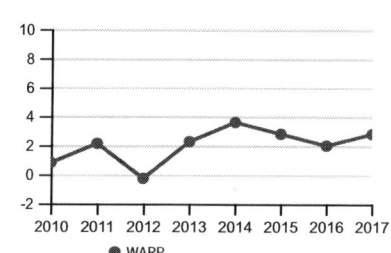

Tunnel vs LHH

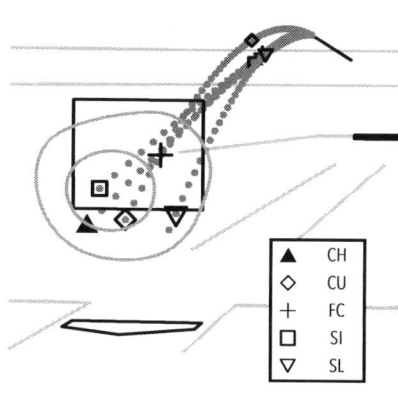

▲	CH
◇	CU
+	FC
□	SI
▽	SL

Pitch Types

Type	Freq	Velo	H Mov	V Mov
CH	10.9%	84.6 [98]	-12.6 [92]	-33.7 [81]
CU	7.3%	78.6 [101]	12.1 [117]	-48.1 [100]
FA	1.5%	91.4 [95]	-7.2 [99]	-19.7 [86]
FC	22.7%	89.2 [105]	-1.2 [86]	-23.9 [100]
SI	44.5%	90.4 [89]	-12.8 [98]	-26.4 [77]
SL	13.1%	81.3 [86]	7 [111]	-39 [82]

Pitch Tunnel

Pairs	Release Diff	Tunnel Diff	Plate Diff	Speed Changes
1959	25.9	108.0	208.7	0.022

PI Scores

Year	Pitch Ct	Pwr	Cmd	Stm
2013	2893	43	60	75
2014	3112	48	58	82
2015	2733	46	67	71
2016	2645	53	80	71
2017	2723	42	61	76

Tunnel vs RHH

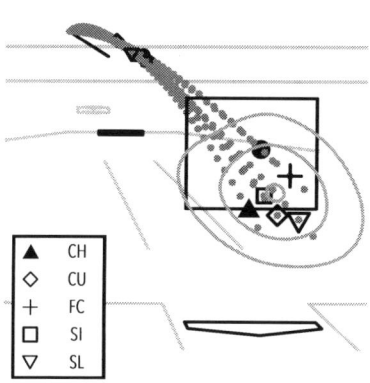

▲	CH
◇	CU
+	FC
□	SI
▽	SL

Mark Leiter RHP Philadelphia Phillies

Born: 3/13/1991 **Age:** 27 **Bats:** R **Throws:** R **Height:** 6' 0" **Weight:** 195 lbs **Draft Info:** Round 22, 2013 Draft (#661 overall)

PACE
37th of 150
75°
20 Sec/Pit Fast

2017 Daily WARP Profile
1.5 Total WARP

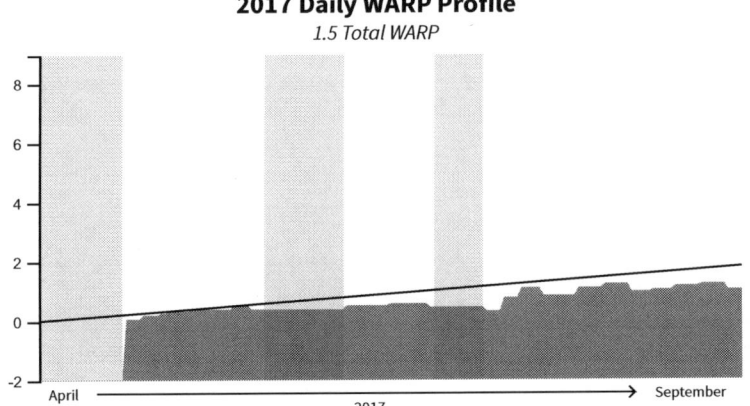

Game 1: minors, Game 53: minors, Game 92: minors

POWER
38 PWR 104th of 150

STAMINA
56 STM 112th of 150

COMMAND
56 CMD 59th of 150

Fantasy Values
2017	2018
$3.34	$1.00

YEAR	TEAM	LVL	AGE	W	L	SV	G	GS	IP	H	HR	BB/9	K/9	K	GB%	BABIP	WHIP	ERA	DRA	WARP	MPH 95
2017	PHI	MLB	26	3	6	0	27	11	90.2	90	18	3.1	8.3	84	50%	.282	1.33	4.96	3.91	1.5	92.5

2017 Pitching Percentages

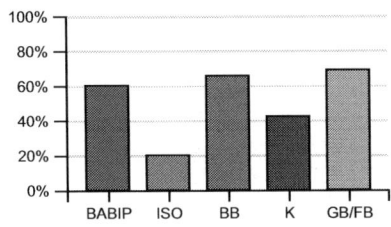

Pitching PECOTA Percentiles

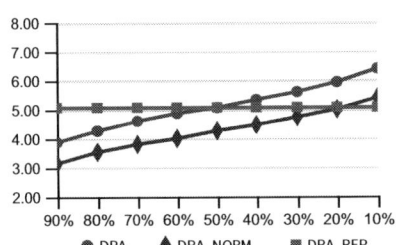

Tunnel vs LHH

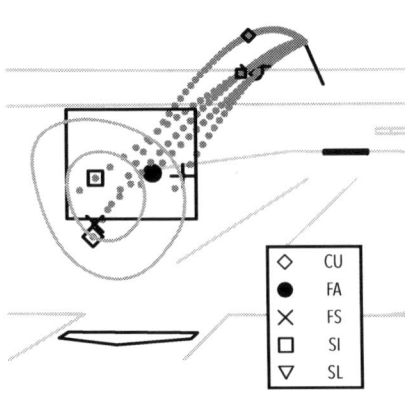

◇	CU
●	FA
✕	FS
□	SI
▽	SL

Pitch Types

Type	Freq	Velo	H Mov	V Mov
CH	0.1%	83.6 [94]	-8.4 [114]	-33.8 [81]
CU	8.6%	72.6 [79]	6.4 [95]	-61.2 [72]
FA	31.5%	91.4 [95]	-5.1 [109]	-14 [104]
FC	3.3%	89 [103]	0.7 [96]	-22.6 [105]
FS	27.8%	84.2 [95]	-5.3 [110]	-29.3 [102]
SI	24.1%	91 [92]	-11.1 [110]	-17.9 [108]
SL	4.5%	82.9 [94]	3 [93]	-37.1 [87]

Pitch Tunnel

Pairs	Release Diff	Tunnel Diff	Plate Diff	Speed Changes
1120	40.4	123.5	227.5	0.030

PI Scores

Year	Pitch Ct	Pwr	Cmd	Stm
2017	1505	38	56	56

Tunnel vs RHH

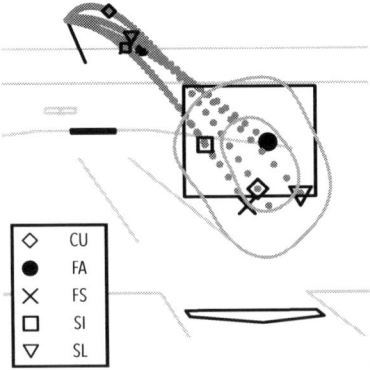

◇	CU
●	FA
✕	FS
□	SI
▽	SL

DJ LeMahieu   2B   Colorado Rockies

Born: 7/13/1988   **Age:** 29   **Bats:** R   **Throws:** R   **Height:** 6' 4"   **Weight:** 215 lbs   **Draft Info:** Round 2, 2009 Draft (#79 overall)

2017 Daily WARP Profile
4.8 Total WARP

PACE
21 Sec/Pit
45th of 155
71°
Fast

Fantasy Values
2017 **$21.82**   2018 **$18.00**

YEAR	TEAM	LVL	AGE	PA	R	2B	3B	HR	RBI	BB	K	SB	AVG/OBP/SLG	TAv	VORP	BABIP	WARP
2017	COL	MLB	28	682	95	28	4	8	64	59	90	6	.310/.374/.409	.268	27.9	.351	4.8

LeMahieu is an oddity: a Coors-aided hitter who is somehow underrated in fantasy. In his case, it is because batting average is an underappreciated category, as few appreciate the nearly automatic .300 average LeMahieu delivers thanks to a .346 average at Coors since 2015. It would be nice if he stole more bases or cleared the fences occasionally, but the average alone made him one of the more valuable second basemen in fantasy, and someone you can easily draft three or four rounds under value. — Mike G.

2017 Batting Percentages

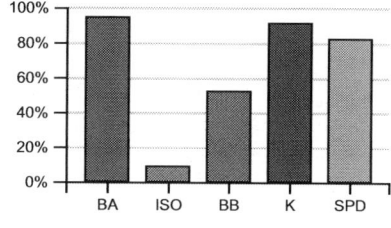

Batting PECOTA Percentiles

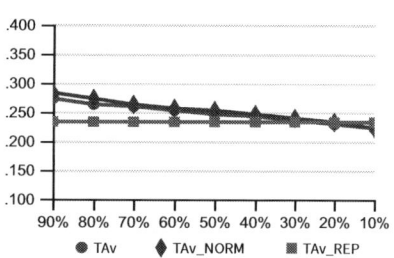

Batting WARP History

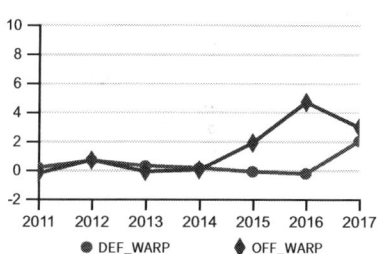

BRR (Relative to Position)

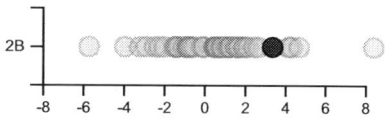

Rank	Player	BRR
4	88° Jonathan Schoop	4.21
5	84° Cesar Hernandez	4.20
6	81° **DJ LeMahieu**	**3.38**
7	77° Jose Altuve	2.68
8	74° Brandon Phillips	2.46

BRR (Relative to Team)

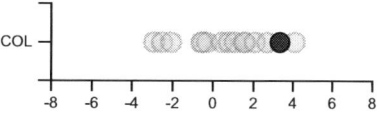

Rank	Player	BRR
1	96° Trevor Story	4.16
2	83° **DJ LeMahieu**	**3.38**
3	76° Ian Desmond	2.73
4	74° Patrick Valaika	2.11
5	70° Raimel Tapia	1.62

Base Running Components

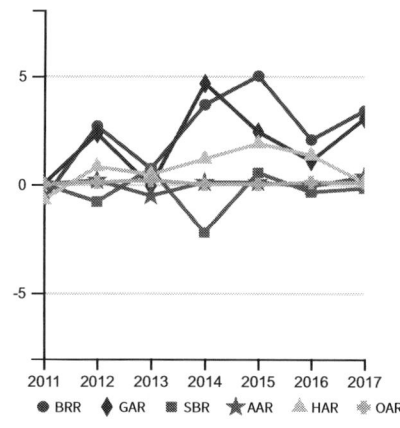

Dominic Leone RHP St. Louis Cardinals

Born: 10/26/1991 **Age:** 26 **Bats:** R **Throws:** R **Height:** 5' 11" **Weight:** 210 lbs **Draft Info:** Round 16, 2012 Draft (#491 overall)

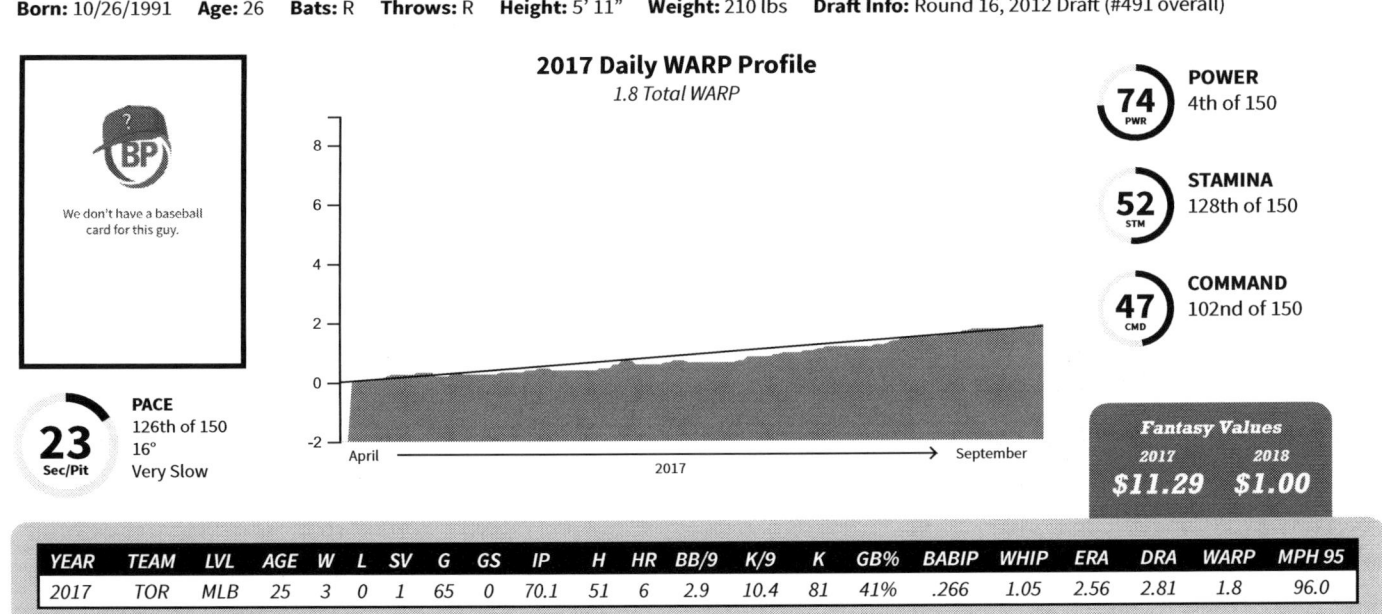

2017 Daily WARP Profile
1.8 Total WARP

POWER 74 PWR 4th of 150

STAMINA 52 STM 128th of 150

COMMAND 47 CMD 102nd of 150

PACE 23 Sec/Pit 126th of 150 / 16° / Very Slow

Fantasy Values
2017 $11.29 2018 $1.00

YEAR	TEAM	LVL	AGE	W	L	SV	G	GS	IP	H	HR	BB/9	K/9	K	GB%	BABIP	WHIP	ERA	DRA	WARP	MPH 95
2017	TOR	MLB	25	3	0	1	65	0	70.1	51	6	2.9	10.4	81	41%	.266	1.05	2.56	2.81	1.8	96.0

2017 Pitching Percentages
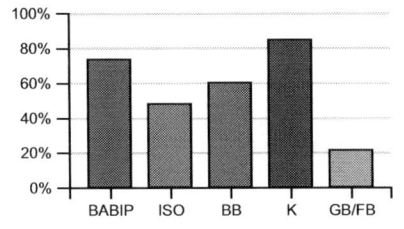

Pitching PECOTA Percentiles
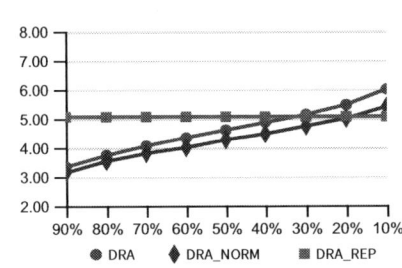

Pitching WARP History
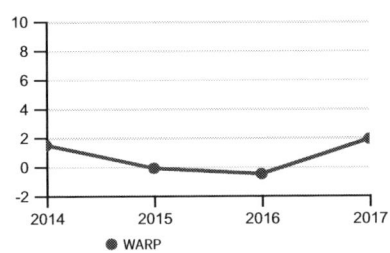

Tunnel vs LHH
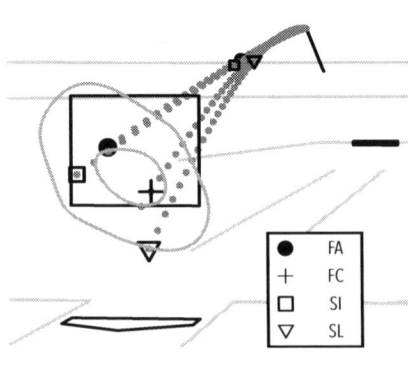

Tunnel vs RHH
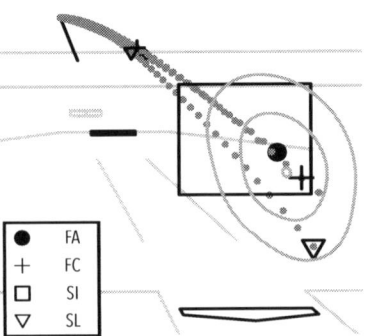

Pitch Types
Type	Freq	Velo	H Mov	V Mov
FA	45.0%	94.9 [108]	-5.3 [109]	-12.2 [110]
FC	35.2%	89 [103]	4.5 [115]	-26 [91]
SI	9.1%	94.5 [112]	-11.9 [105]	-16.8 [112]
SL	10.6%	84.3 [99]	4.8 [101]	-37 [87]

Pitch Tunnel
Pairs	Release Diff	Tunnel Diff	Plate Diff	Speed Changes
787	21.2	107.5	216.9	0.016

PI Scores
Year	Pitch Ct	Pwr	Cmd	Stm
2014	1067	69	49	46
2015	279	59	31	46
2016	473	63	37	47
2017	1082	74	47	52

Jon Lester LHP Chicago Cubs

Born: 1/7/1984 **Age:** 34 **Bats:** L **Throws:** L **Height:** 6' 4" **Weight:** 240 lbs **Draft Info:** Round 2, 2002 Draft (#57 overall)

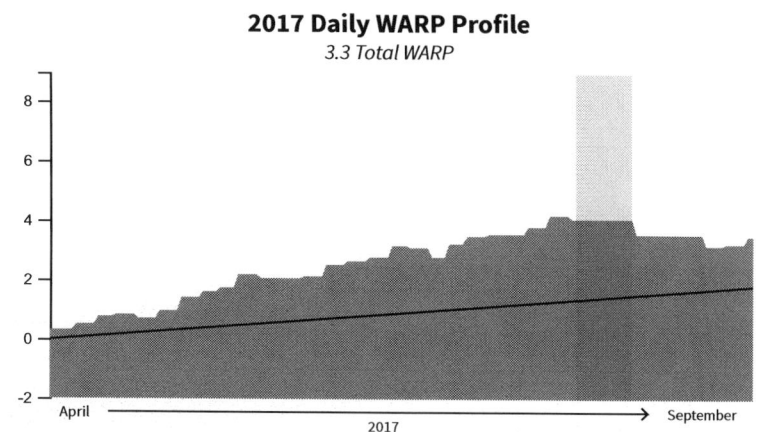

2017 Daily WARP Profile
3.3 Total WARP

2017

Game 121: DL (lat tightness)

 POWER 38 PWR 104th of 150

 STAMINA 78 STM 25th of 150

COMMAND 69 CMD 12th of 150

PACE 20 Sec/Pit 37th of 150 75° Fast

Fantasy Values
2017	2018
$14.44	$19.00

YEAR	TEAM	LVL	AGE	W	L	SV	G	GS	IP	H	HR	BB/9	K/9	K	GB%	BABIP	WHIP	ERA	DRA	WARP	MPH 95
2017	CHN	MLB	33	13	8	0	32	32	180.2	179	26	3.0	9.0	180	48%	.310	1.32	4.33	3.94	3.3	92.7

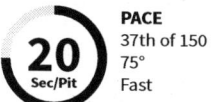 *Year three of Lester's Cubs tenure was his rockiest to date, as the veteran lefty struggled with maintaining his velocity just as every other Cub starter did. The results were good, but nowhere close to the near-ace level of performance he had shown previously. There was no sign of injury, so Lester is a good bet to bounce back and give his fantasy owners an SP2 performance. — Mike G.*

2017 Pitching Percentages
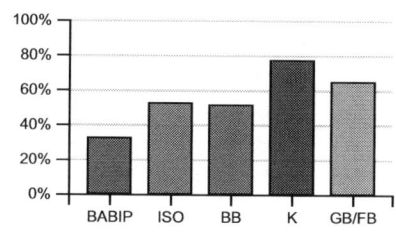

Pitching PECOTA Percentiles
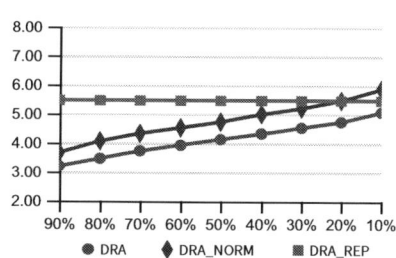

Pitching WARP History
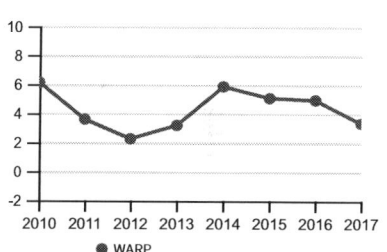

Tunnel vs LHH
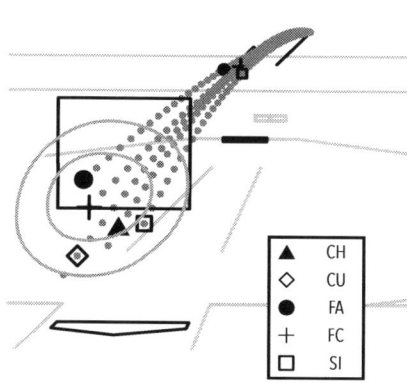

Tunnel vs RHH
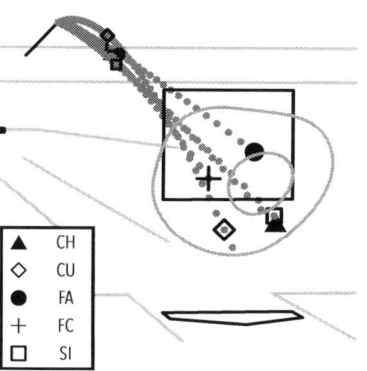

Pitch Types
Type	Freq	Velo	H Mov	V Mov
CH	8.4%	84.9 [99]	13.4 [88]	-28.8 [95]
CU	13.1%	75.8 [91]	-7.1 [97]	-47.7 [101]
FA	38.4%	91.7 [96]	8.1 [96]	-15.4 [99]
FC	27.8%	87.9 [97]	-1.1 [98]	-23.3 [102]
SI	12.3%	90.5 [90]	13.7 [91]	-23.5 [87]

Pitch Tunnel
Pairs	Release Diff	Tunnel Diff	Plate Diff	Speed Changes
2298	19.3	114.0	222.9	0.026

PI Scores
Year	Pitch Ct	Pwr	Cmd	Stm
2013	3555	50	58	86
2014	3480	47	75	85
2015	3204	45	81	78
2016	3149	51	67	78
2017	3091	38	69	78

Francisco Lindor   SS   Cleveland Indians   ⚓

Born: 11/14/1993   **Age:** 24   **Bats:** B   **Throws:** R   **Height:** 5' 11"   **Weight:** 190 lbs   **Draft Info:** Round 1, 2011 Draft (#8 overall)

PACE
4th of 155
97°
Very Fast

19 Sec/Pit

2017 Daily WARP Profile
5.2 Total WARP

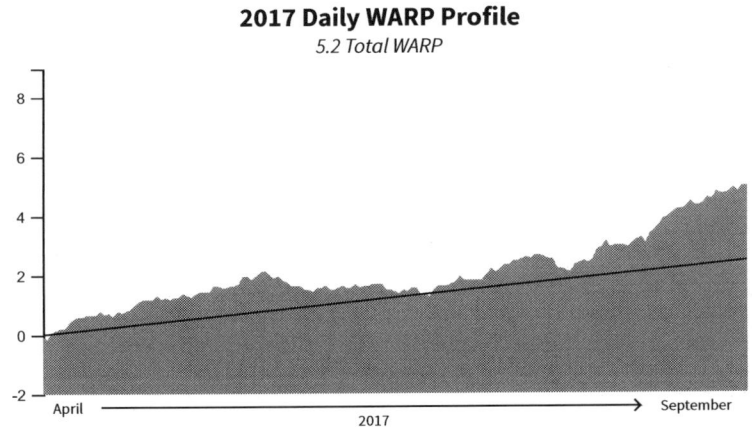

April → 2017 → September

Fantasy Values

2017	2018
$26.78	$31.00

YEAR	TEAM	LVL	AGE	PA	R	2B	3B	HR	RBI	BB	K	SB	AVG/OBP/SLG	TAv	VORP	BABIP	WARP
2017	CLE	MLB	23	723	99	44	4	33	89	60	93	15	.273/.337/.505	.280	48.4	.275	5.2

The last thing anyone expected from Lindor was a power outburst, but that's exactly what he provided, more than doubling his previous major-league home-run total with 33. But because his batting average dropped by almost 30 points Lindor's earnings remained static. Entering his age-24 season, it makes sense to bet on improvement and the concept that Lindor could be a first-round earner as soon as this year. If he isn't, the stolen bases and all-around categorical contributions mean he won't be a disappointment even if he stands still. — Mike G.

2017 Batting Percentages

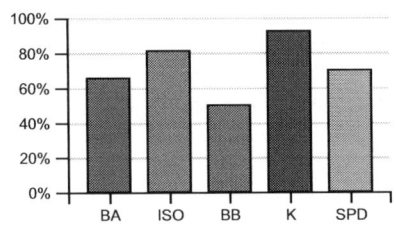

Batting PECOTA Percentiles

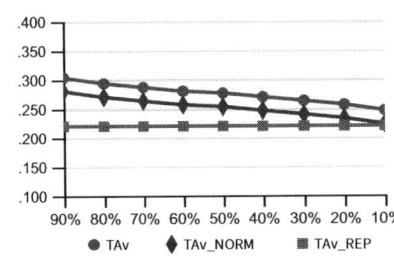

Batting WARP History

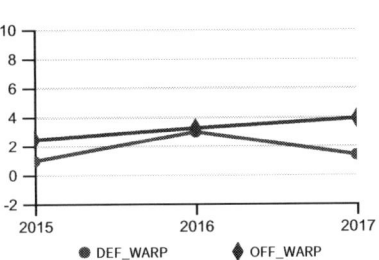

BRR (Relative to Position)

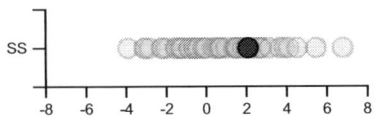

Rank		Player	BRR
11	69°	Wilmer Difo	2.38
12	66°	Corey Seager	2.17
13	62°	**Francisco Lindor**	**2.14**
14	58°	Jean Segura	2.09
15	55°	Orlando Arcia	2.07

BRR (Relative to Team)

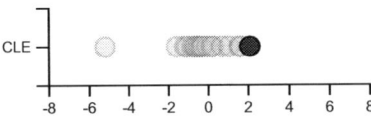

Rank		Player	BRR
1	77°	**Francisco Lindor**	**2.14**
2	72°	Yan Gomes	1.67
3	66°	Bradley Zimmer	1.62
4	63°	Abraham Almonte	1.10
5	62°	Greg Allen	0.74

Base Running Components

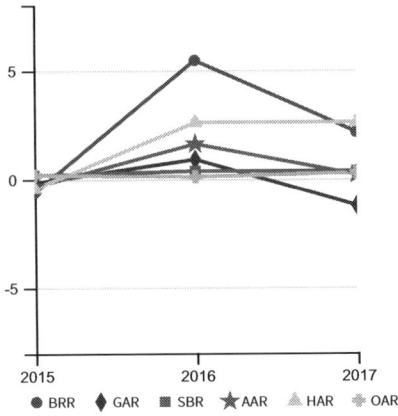

Francisco Liriano   LHP   Houston Astros

Born: 10/26/1983 **Age:** 34 **Bats:** L **Throws:** L **Height:** 6' 2" **Weight:** 225 lbs **Draft Info:** International Free Agent, 2000

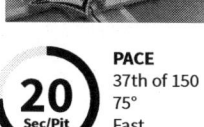

2017 Daily WARP Profile
0.1 Total WARP

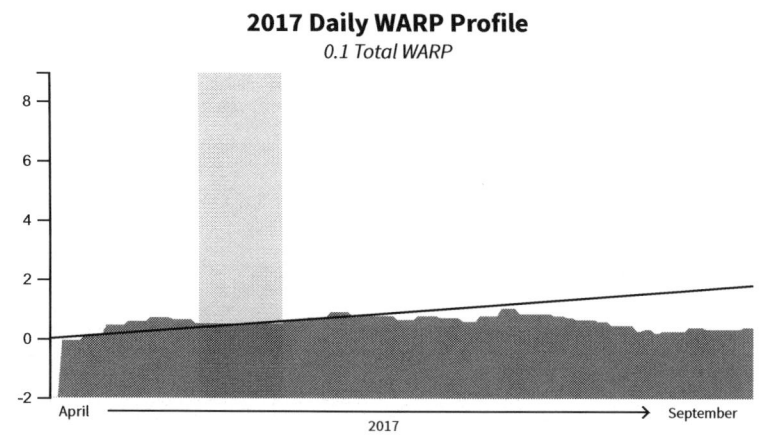

Game 35: DL (shoulder inflammation)

POWER 46 PWR — 69th of 150

STAMINA 54 STM — 118th of 150

COMMAND 49 CMD — 91st of 150

PACE 20 Sec/Pit — 37th of 150 / 75° / Fast

Fantasy Values

2017	2018
$-1.46	$2.00

YEAR	TEAM	LVL	AGE	W	L	SV	G	GS	IP	H	HR	BB/9	K/9	K	GB%	BABIP	WHIP	ERA	DRA	WARP	MPH 95
2017	TOR	MLB	33	6	5	0	18	18	82.2	91	11	4.7	8.1	74	44%	.327	1.62	5.88	5.58	-0.1	94.5
2017	HOU	MLB	33	0	2	0	20	0	14.1	14	0	6.3	6.9	11	54%	.341	1.67	4.40	4.25	0.2	96.1

2017 Pitching Percentages

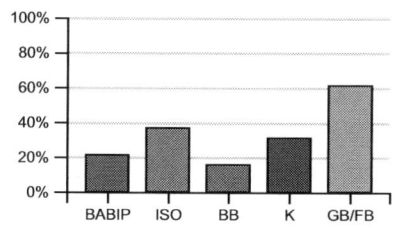

Pitching PECOTA Percentiles

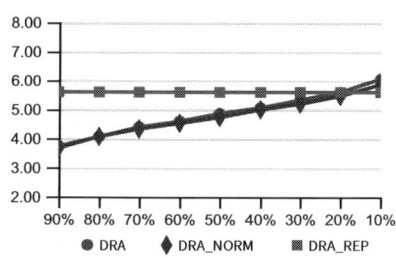

Pitching WARP History

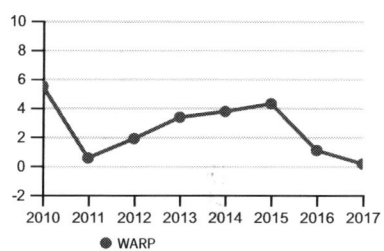

Tunnel vs LHH

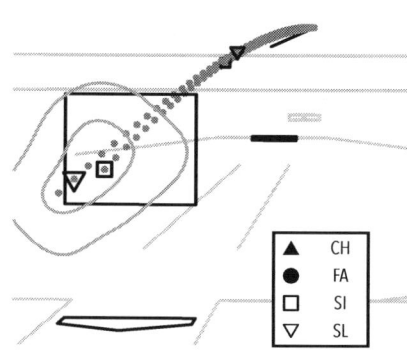

Type	Freq	Velo	H Mov	V Mov
CH	16.8%	85.9 [103]	14.3 [83]	-25.7 [104]
CU	0.1%	74.9 [87]	-4.6 [88]	-45 [106]
FA	7.3%	93.7 [103]	11.1 [81]	-15.5 [99]
SI	42.8%	93.3 [106]	13 [96]	-17.8 [108]
SL	33.0%	85.9 [107]	-1.4 [86]	-28.8 [111]

Pitch Tunnel

Pairs	Release Diff	Tunnel Diff	Plate Diff	Speed Changes
1286	33.1	127.7	231.6	0.020

PI Scores

Year	Pitch Ct	Pwr	Cmd	Stm
2013	2493	44	40	74
2014	2665	44	40	67
2015	2999	43	53	73
2016	2770	47	55	72
2017	1737	46	49	54

Tunnel vs RHH

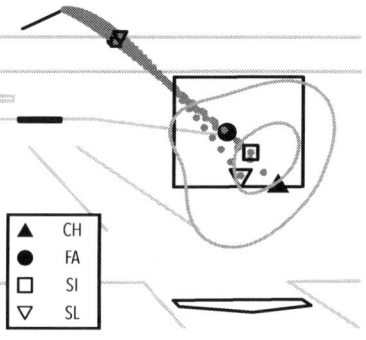

Evan Longoria   3B   San Francisco Giants

Born: 10/7/1985   **Age:** 32   **Bats:** R   **Throws:** R   **Height:** 6' 2"   **Weight:** 210 lbs   **Draft Info:** Round 1, 2006 Draft (#3 overall)

2017 Daily WARP Profile
2.6 Total WARP

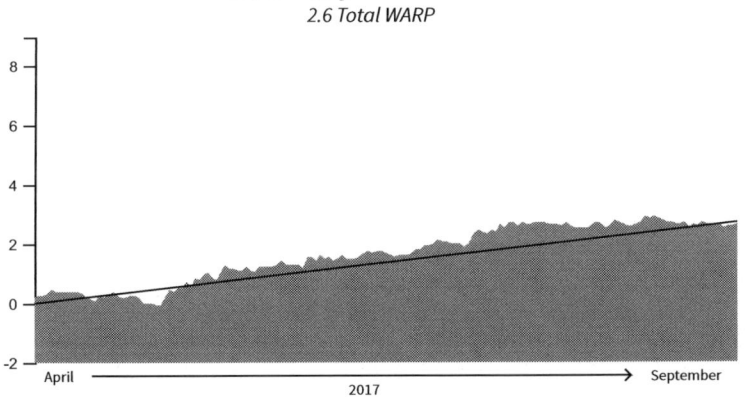

PACE
20 Sec/Pit
18th of 155
88°
Very Fast

Fantasy Values

2017	2018
$17.00	**$18.00**

YEAR	TEAM	LVL	AGE	PA	R	2B	3B	HR	RBI	BB	K	SB	AVG/OBP/SLG	TAv	VORP	BABIP	WARP
2017	TBA	MLB	31	677	71	36	2	20	86	46	109	6	.261/.313/.424	.264	22.4	.282	2.6

2017 Batting Percentages

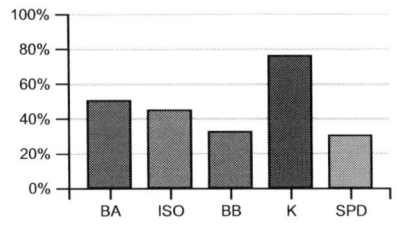

Batting PECOTA Percentiles

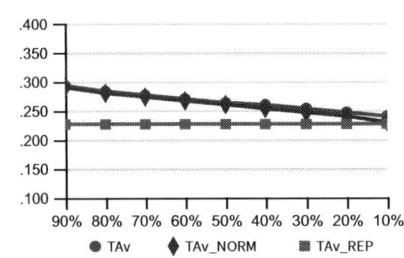

Batting WARP History

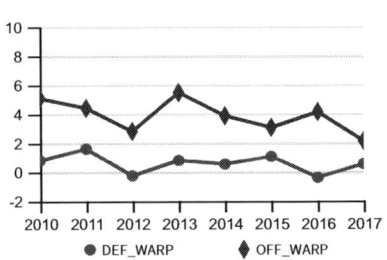

BRR (Relative to Position)

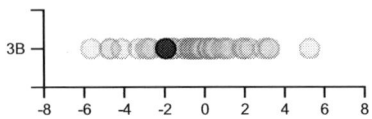

Rank		Player	BRR
45	26°	Mike Moustakas	-1.59
46	23°	Maikel Franco	-1.82
47	20°	**Evan Longoria**	**-1.90**
48	18°	Miguel Sano	-1.98
49	16°	Nick Castellanos	-2.63

BRR (Relative to Team)

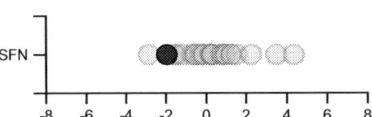

Rank		Player	BRR
21	31°	Justin Ruggiano	-1.14
22	22°	Brandon Crawford	-1.44
23	12°	Buster Posey	-1.49
24	4°	**Evan Longoria**	**-1.90**
25	0°	Nick Hundley	-2.80

Base Running Components

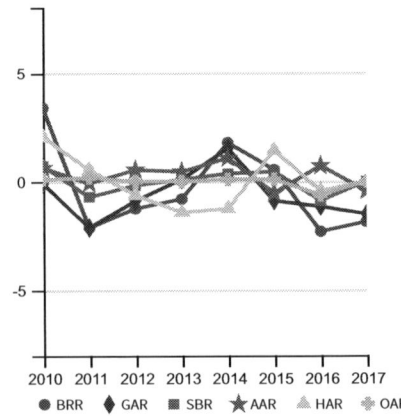

Reynaldo Lopez   RHP   Chicago White Sox

Born: 1/4/1994   **Age:** 24   **Bats:** R   **Throws:** R   **Height:** 6' 0"   **Weight:** 185 lbs   **Draft Info:** International Free Agent, 2012

2017 Daily WARP Profile
-0.9 Total WARP

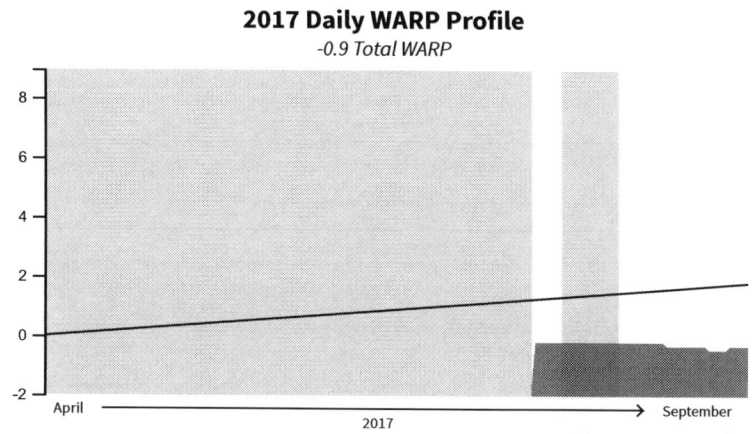

Game 1: minors, **Game 119:** DL (back strain)

59 PWR	**POWER**	27th of 150
73 STM	**STAMINA**	53rd of 150
59 CMD	**COMMAND**	43rd of 150

20 Sec/Pit — **PACE** 37th of 150 — 75° Fast

Fantasy Values

2017	2018
$1.97	$3.00

YEAR	TEAM	LVL	AGE	W	L	SV	G	GS	IP	H	HR	BB/9	K/9	K	GB%	BABIP	WHIP	ERA	DRA	WARP	MPH 95
2017	CHA	MLB	23	3	3	0	8	8	47.2	49	7	2.6	5.7	30	30%	.271	1.32	4.72	7.34	-0.9	97.6

Lopez pitched well in the minors but struggled after his late-season promotion to the White Sox. Acquired as part of the Adam Eaton deal with the Nationals, Lopez has good stuff but remains a work-in-progress, particularly regarding command within the strike zone. Lopez is a high-risk/moderate-reward pitcher who should be nabbed in AL-only but is more of a matchup play in mixed, particularly since he lacks the upside of other, more highly touted prospects. — Mike G.

2017 Pitching Percentages

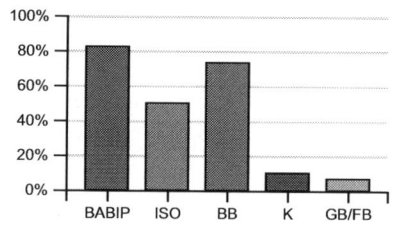

Pitching PECOTA Percentiles

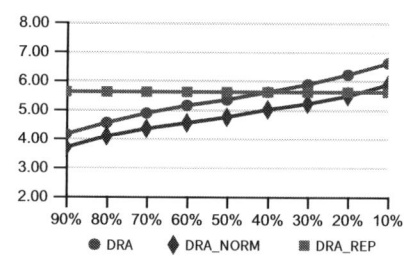

Pitching WARP History

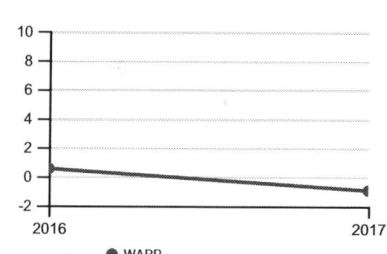

Tunnel vs LHH

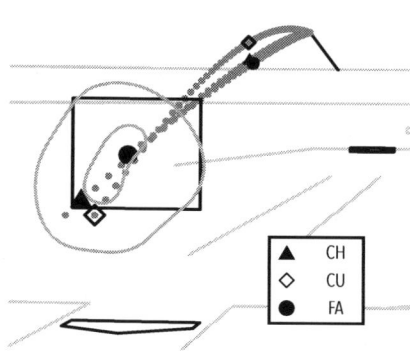

▲	CH
◇	CU
●	FA

Pitch Types

Type	Freq	Velo	H Mov	V Mov
CH	23.6%	83.7 [94]	-10.1 [105]	-26.4 [102]
CU	12.7%	78.3 [100]	5 [89]	-43.1 [110]
FA	61.2%	94.8 [108]	-9 [91]	-14.7 [101]
FC	2.5%	86.5 [89]	-0.4 [90]	-24.1 [99]

Pitch Tunnel

Pairs	Release Diff	Tunnel Diff	Plate Diff	Speed Changes
635	34.5	123.1	224.5	0.038

PI Scores

Year	Pitch Ct	Pwr	Cmd	Stm
2016	799	55	47	65
2017	788	59	59	73

Tunnel vs RHH

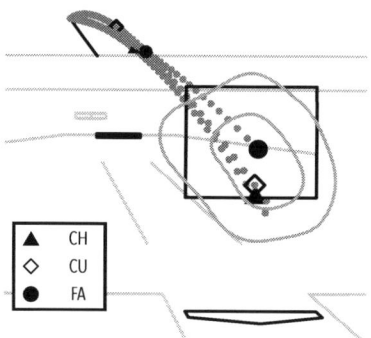

▲	CH
◇	CU
●	FA

Jed Lowrie   2B   Oakland Athletics

Born: 4/17/1984   **Age:** 34   **Bats:** B   **Throws:** R   **Height:** 6' 0"   **Weight:** 180 lbs   **Draft Info:** Round 1, 2005 Draft (#45 overall)

22 Sec/Pit

PACE
99th of 155
36°
Slow

2017 Daily WARP Profile
2.2 Total WARP

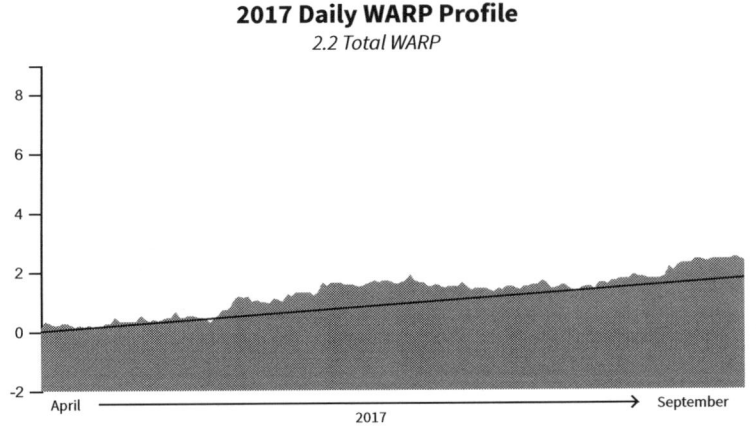

Fantasy Values

2017	2018
$15.72	$9.00

YEAR	TEAM	LVL	AGE	PA	R	2B	3B	HR	RBI	BB	K	SB	AVG/OBP/SLG	TAv	VORP	BABIP	WARP
2017	OAK	MLB	33	645	86	49	3	14	69	73	100	0	.277/.360/.448	.276	25.7	.314	2.2

2017 Batting Percentages

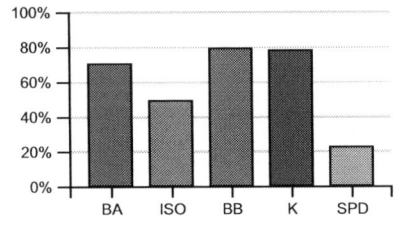

Batting PECOTA Percentiles

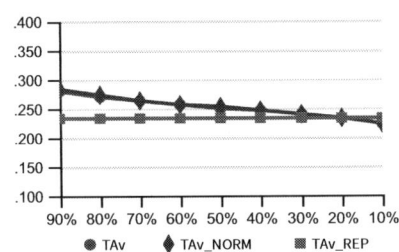

Batting WARP History

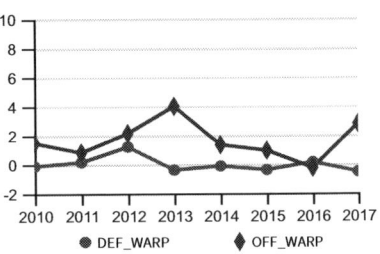

BRR (Relative to Position)

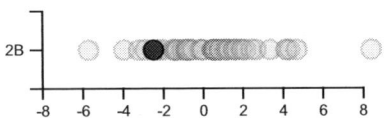

Rank		Player	BRR
50	12°	Robinson Cano	-1.98
51	10°	Neil Walker	-2.22
52	7°	**Jed Lowrie**	**-2.45**
53	5°	Eric Sogard	-2.86
54	4°	Daniel Descalso	-3.18

BRR (Relative to Team)

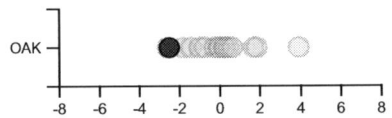

Rank		Player	BRR
12	29°	Matt Chapman	-0.97
13	24°	Bruce Maxwell	-1.37
14	19°	Chad Pinder	-1.76
15	8°	**Jed Lowrie**	**-2.45**
16	0°	Stephen Piscotty	-2.54

Base Running Components

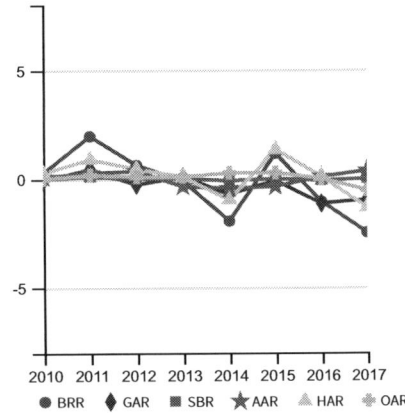

Jonathan Lucroy C Colorado Rockies

Born: 6/13/1986 **Age:** 32 **Bats:** R **Throws:** R **Height:** 6' 0" **Weight:** 200 lbs **Draft Info:** Round 3, 2007 Draft (#101 overall)

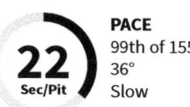

PACE
22 Sec/Pit
99th of 155
36°
Slow

2017 Daily WARP Profile
-0.6 Total WARP

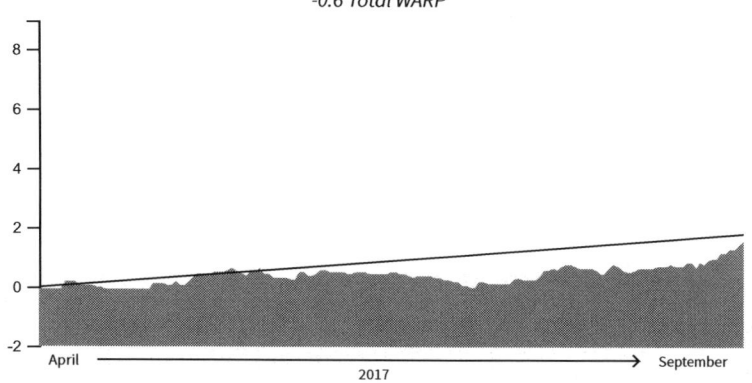

Fantasy Values

2017	2018
$3.56	**$8.00**

YEAR	TEAM	LVL	AGE	PA	R	2B	3B	HR	RBI	BB	K	SB	AVG/OBP/SLG	TAv	VORP	BABIP	WARP
2017	TEX	MLB	31	306	27	15	0	4	27	19	32	1	.242/.297/.338	.217	.0	.259	-1.4
2017	COL	MLB	31	175	18	6	3	2	13	27	19	0	.310/.429/.437	.292	13.9	.341	.8

2017 Batting Percentages

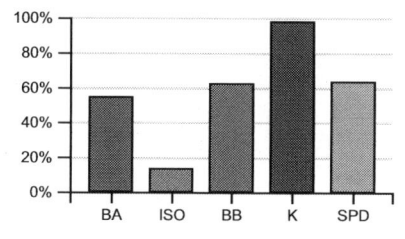

Batting PECOTA Percentiles

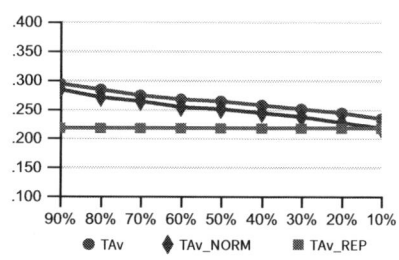

Batting WARP History

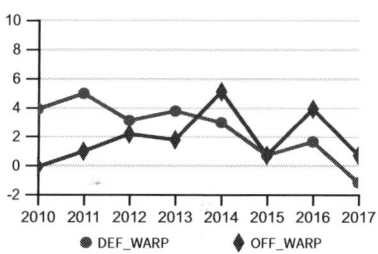

BRR (Relative to Position)

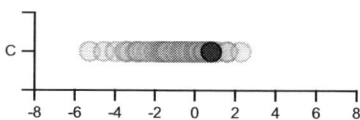

BRR (Relative to Team)

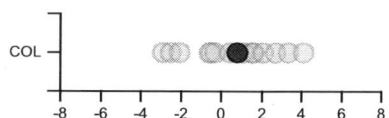

Base Running Components

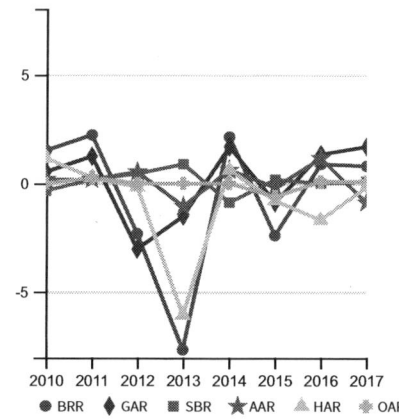

Rank		Player	BRR
5	93°	Luis Torrens	1.14
6	90°	J.T. Realmuto	1.03
7	87°	**Jonathan Lucroy**	**0.84**
8	87°	Eric Fryer	0.84
9	87°	Carson Kelly	0.74

Rank		Player	BRR
6	53°	Charlie Blackmon	1.57
7	44°	Carlos Gonzalez	1.14
8	37°	**Jonathan Lucroy**	**0.84**
9	32°	Tony Wolters	0.50
10	31°	Ryan Hanigan	-0.24

Lance Lynn   RHP   St. Louis Cardinals

Born: 5/12/1987   **Age:** 31   **Bats:** B   **Throws:** R   **Height:** 6' 5"   **Weight:** 280 lbs   **Draft Info:** Round 1, 2008 Draft (#39 overall)

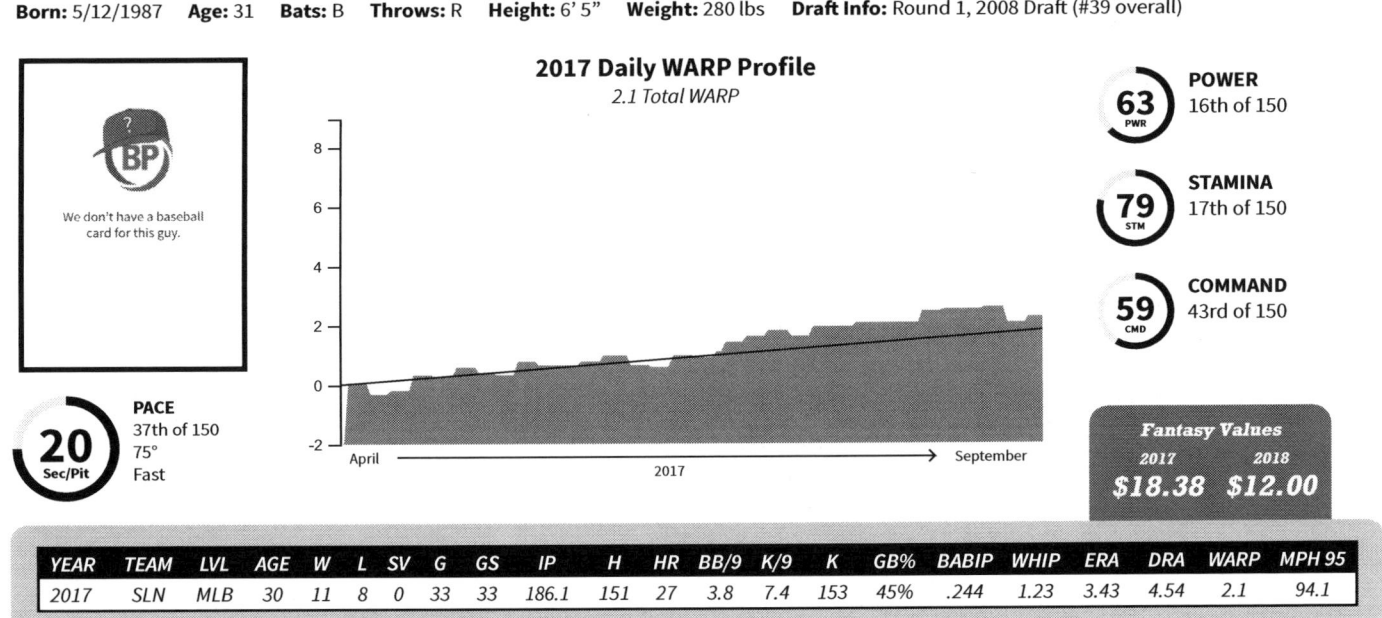

2017 Daily WARP Profile
2.1 Total WARP

POWER 63 PWR 16th of 150

STAMINA 79 STM 17th of 150

COMMAND 59 CMD 43rd of 150

PACE 20 Sec/Pit 37th of 150 75° Fast

We don't have a baseball card for this guy.

Fantasy Values
2017	2018
$18.38	$12.00

YEAR	TEAM	LVL	AGE	W	L	SV	G	GS	IP	H	HR	BB/9	K/9	K	GB%	BABIP	WHIP	ERA	DRA	WARP	MPH 95
2017	SLN	MLB	30	11	8	0	33	33	186.1	151	27	3.8	7.4	153	45%	.244	1.23	3.43	4.54	2.1	94.1

2017 Pitching Percentages

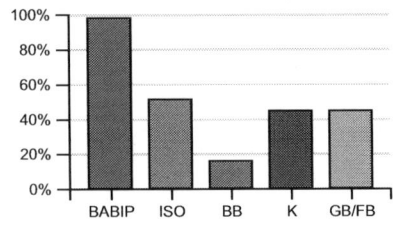

Pitching PECOTA Percentiles

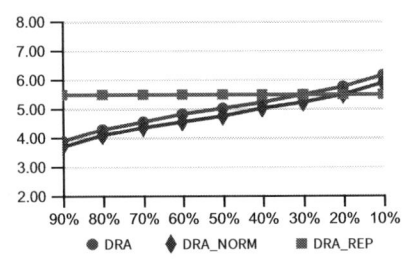

● DRA   ◆ DRA_NORM   ■ DRA_REP

Pitching WARP History

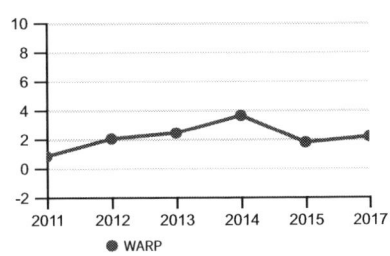

● WARP

Tunnel vs LHH

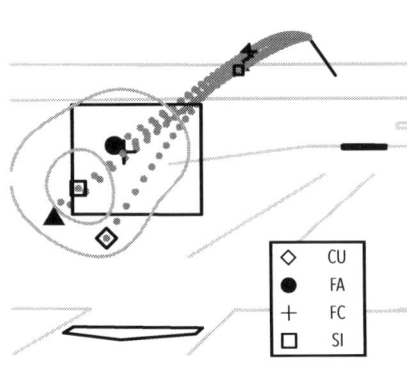

◇	CU
●	FA
+	FC
□	SI

Pitch Types

Type	Freq	Velo	H Mov	V Mov
CH	2.6%	84.7 [98]	-11.3 [99]	-26.7 [101]
CU	4.6%	79.2 [103]	6.2 [94]	-45.7 [105]
FA	39.9%	92.6 [100]	-7.4 [99]	-15.2 [100]
FC	11.3%	87.5 [95]	1.5 [100]	-24.8 [96]
SI	41.1%	91.6 [96]	-11.8 [105]	-21.8 [93]
SL	0.6%	84.9 [102]	1.8 [87]	-30.7 [106]

Pitch Tunnel

Pairs	Release Diff	Tunnel Diff	Plate Diff	Speed Changes
2370	25.0	114.9	222.4	0.013

PI Scores

Year	Pitch Ct	Pwr	Cmd	Stm
2012	2985	56	49	71
2013	3351	59	50	82
2014	3443	65	63	83
2015	3026	66	58	72
2017	3146	63	59	79

Tunnel vs RHH

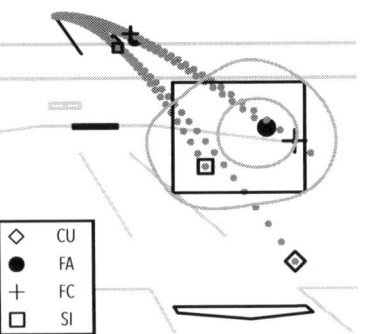

◇	CU
●	FA
+	FC
□	SI

Manny Machado 3B Baltimore Orioles

Born: 7/6/1992 **Age:** 25 **Bats:** R **Throws:** R **Height:** 6' 3" **Weight:** 185 lbs **Draft Info:** Round 1, 2010 Draft (#3 overall)

PACE
20 Sec/Pit
18th of 155
88°
Very Fast

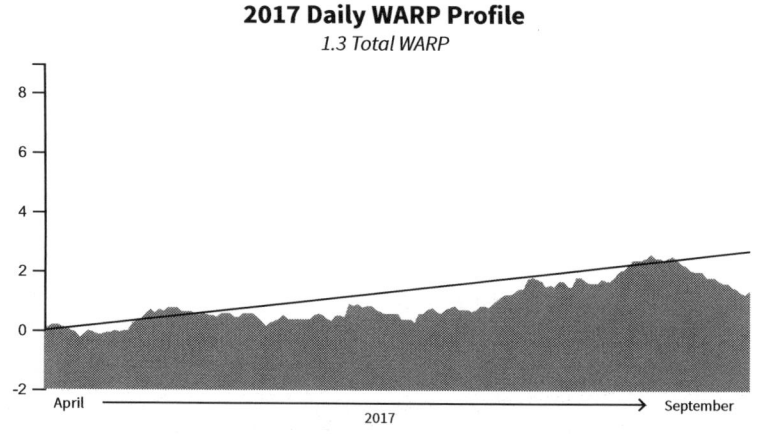

2017 Daily WARP Profile
1.3 Total WARP

Fantasy Values	
2017	2018
$21.56	**$29.00**

YEAR	TEAM	LVL	AGE	PA	R	2B	3B	HR	RBI	BB	K	SB	AVG/OBP/SLG	TAv	VORP	BABIP	WARP
2017	BAL	MLB	24	690	81	33	1	33	95	50	115	9	.259/.310/.471	.261	19.4	.265	1.3

 For the second consecutive season, Machado's fantasy earnings fell. Where the culprit in 2016 was the disappearance of his steals, in 2017 it was a big drop in batting average that contributed to Manny's decline. He's entering his prime, and it's more likely that last year was a blip on the radar and not the start of a new normal. It will be tempting to bet on a complete revival, but given how commonplace power is, it will be safer to leave Machado until at least the end of the second round, if not the beginning of the third. — Mike G.

2017 Batting Percentages

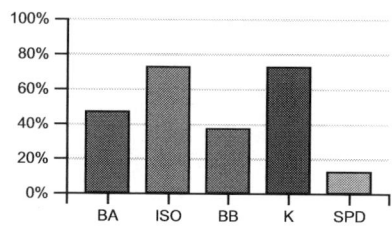

Batting PECOTA Percentiles

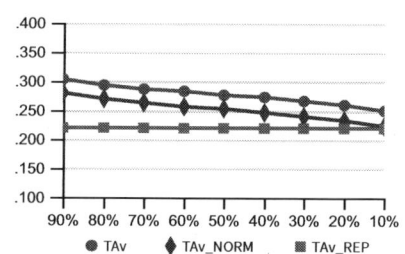

Batting WARP History

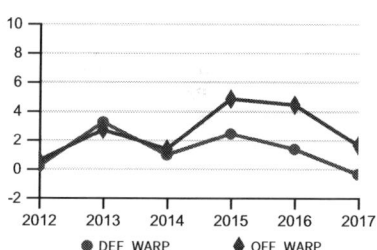

BRR (Relative to Position)

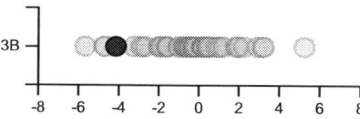

Rank		Player	BRR
51	13°	Adrian Beltre	-2.87
52	11°	Justin Turner	-3.24
53	8°	**Manny Machado**	**-4.10**
54	6°	David Freese	-4.66
55	3°	Eugenio Suarez	-4.67

BRR (Relative to Team)

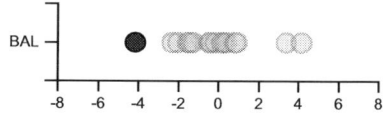

Rank		Player	BRR
12	32°	Seth Smith	-1.39
13	28°	J.J. Hardy	-1.50
14	21°	Chris Davis	-1.98
15	10°	Mark Trumbo	-2.28
16	0°	**Manny Machado**	**-4.10**

Base Running Components

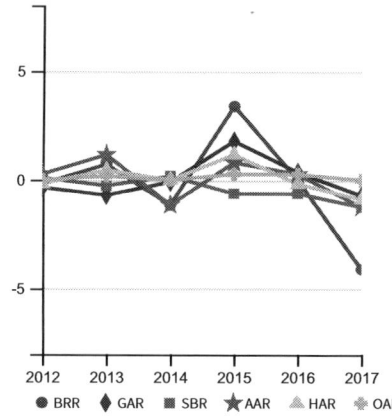

Kenta Maeda   RHP   Los Angeles Dodgers

Born: 4/11/1988   **Age:** 30   **Bats:** R   **Throws:** R   **Height:** 6' 1"   **Weight:** 175 lbs   **Draft Info:** International Free Agent, 2016

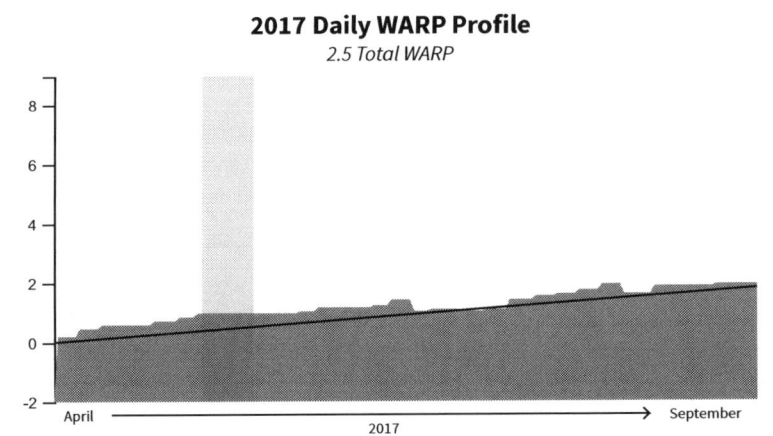

2017 Daily WARP Profile
2.5 Total WARP

Game 35: DL (hamstring tightness)

POWER
33 125th of 150
PWR

STAMINA
60 102nd of 150
STM

COMMAND
62 24th of 150
CMD

PACE
22 108th of 150
Sec/Pit 28°
Slow

Fantasy Values
2017	2018
$16.69	**$10.00**

YEAR	TEAM	LVL	AGE	W	L	SV	G	GS	IP	H	HR	BB/9	K/9	K	GB%	BABIP	WHIP	ERA	DRA	WARP	MPH 95
2017	LAN	MLB	29	13	6	1	29	25	134.1	121	22	2.3	9.4	140	40%	.278	1.15	4.22	3.89	2.5	93.3

2017 Pitching Percentages

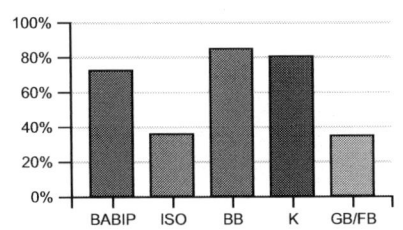

Pitching PECOTA Percentiles

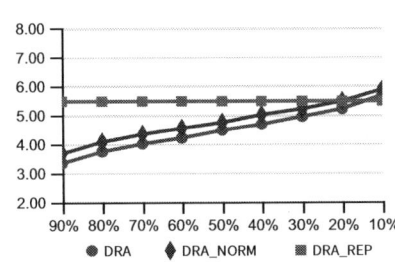

Pitching WARP History

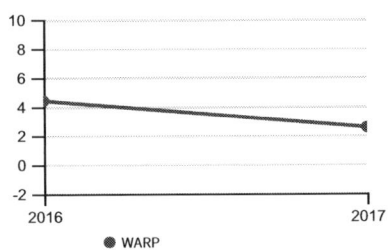

Tunnel vs LHH

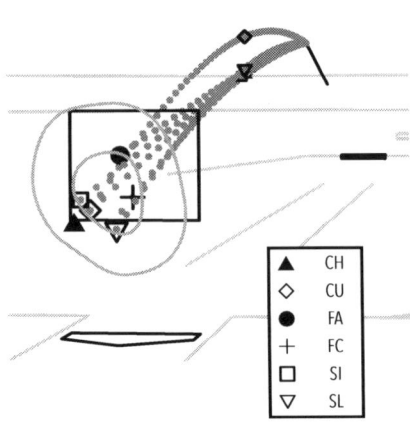

Pitch Types

Type	Freq	Velo	H Mov	V Mov
CH	9.3%	83.9 [95]	-11 [101]	-25.9 [103]
CU	14.1%	75.4 [89]	7.6 [99]	-54.8 [85]
FA	32.7%	92.2 [98]	-6.5 [103]	-13.1 [106]
FC	24.1%	85.9 [86]	1.6 [100]	-25.3 [94]
SI	10.7%	90.6 [90]	-12.2 [102]	-19.9 [101]
SL	9.1%	83.1 [94]	4.7 [100]	-29.2 [110]

Pitch Tunnel

Pairs	Release Diff	Tunnel Diff	Plate Diff	Speed Changes
1613	30.8	123.4	221.1	0.033

PI Scores

Year	Pitch Ct	Pwr	Cmd	Stm
2016	2902	30	62	72
2017	2174	33	62	60

Tunnel vs RHH

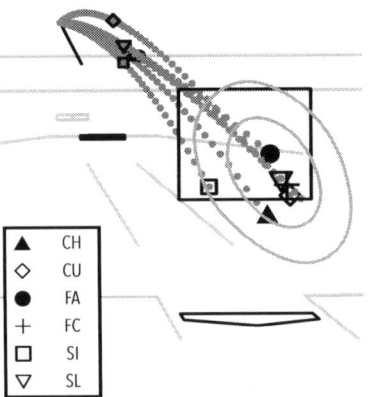

Sean Manaea   LHP   Oakland Athletics

Born: 2/1/1992   **Age:** 26   **Bats:** R   **Throws:** L   **Height:** 6' 5"   **Weight:** 245 lbs   **Draft Info:** Round 1, 2013 Draft (#34 overall)

PACE
20 Sec/Pit
37th of 150
75°
Fast

2017 Daily WARP Profile
1.7 Total WARP

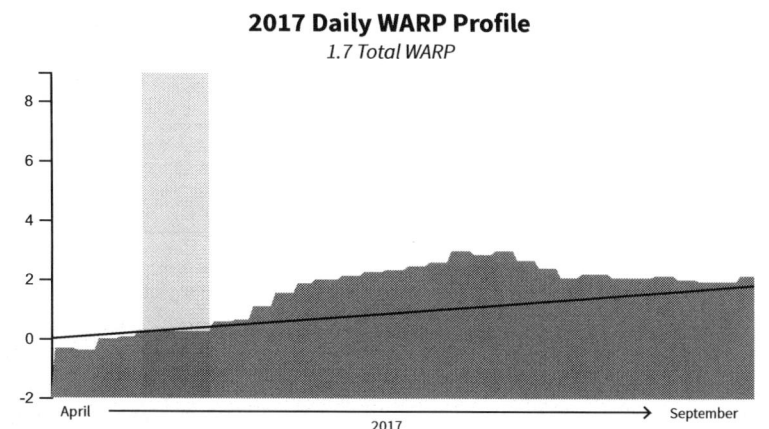

Game 22: DL (shoulder strain)

POWER 44 PWR 80th of 150

STAMINA 71 STM 63rd of 150

COMMAND 38 CMD 139th of 150

Fantasy Values

2017	2018
$9.71	$7.00

YEAR	TEAM	LVL	AGE	W	L	SV	G	GS	IP	H	HR	BB/9	K/9	K	GB%	BABIP	WHIP	ERA	DRA	WARP	MPH 95
2017	OAK	MLB	25	12	10	0	29	29	158.2	167	18	3.1	7.9	140	44%	.318	1.40	4.37	4.61	1.7	93.7

2017 Pitching Percentages

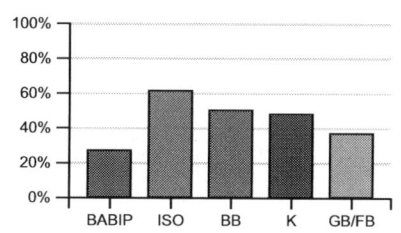

Pitching PECOTA Percentiles

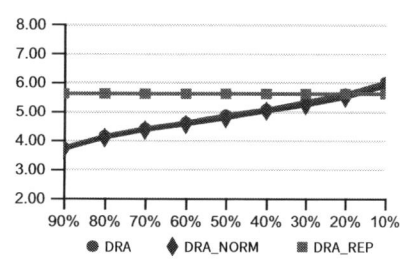

Pitching WARP History

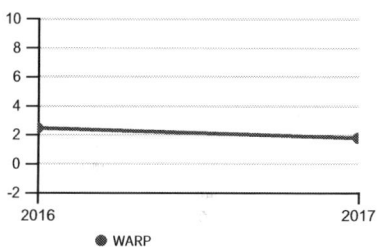

Tunnel vs LHH

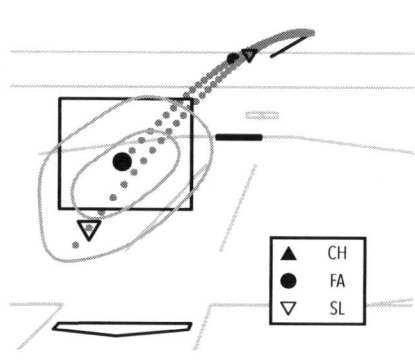

Pitch Types

Type	Freq	Velo	H Mov	V Mov
CH	24.3%	83.8 [95]	8.7 [113]	-35.1 [77]
FA	58.3%	92.1 [98]	13.5 [70]	-20 [84]
SL	17.4%	80.4 [82]	-0.8 [83]	-38.8 [82]

Pitch Tunnel

Pairs	Release Diff	Tunnel Diff	Plate Diff	Speed Changes
1916	31.3	112.5	230.1	0.030

PI Scores

Year	Pitch Ct	Pwr	Cmd	Stm
2016	2165	49	53	65
2017	2680	44	38	71

Tunnel vs RHH

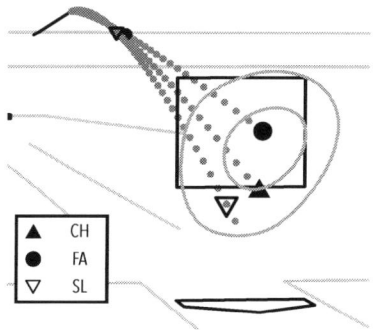

Trey Mancini LF Baltimore Orioles

Born: 3/18/1992 **Age:** 26 **Bats:** R **Throws:** R **Height:** 6' 4" **Weight:** 215 lbs **Draft Info:** Round 8, 2013 Draft (#249 overall)

2017 Daily WARP Profile
2.0 Total WARP

PACE
19 Sec/Pit
4th of 155
97°
Very Fast

Fantasy Values
2017	2018
$19.21	**$16.00**

YEAR	TEAM	LVL	AGE	PA	R	2B	3B	HR	RBI	BB	K	SB	AVG/OBP/SLG	TAv	VORP	BABIP	WARP
2017	BAL	MLB	25	586	65	26	4	24	78	33	139	1	.293/.338/.488	.277	21.7	.352	2.0

2017 Batting Percentages

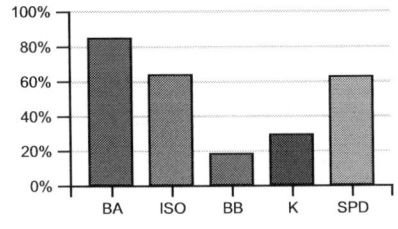

Batting PECOTA Percentiles

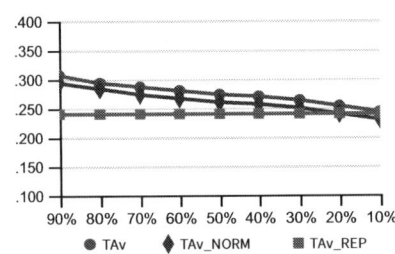

Batting WARP History

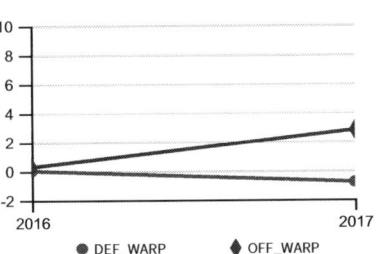

BRR (Relative to Position)

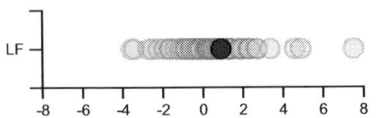

Rank		Player	BRR
20	60°	Benjamin Gamel	1.14
21	59°	Eric Young	1.04
22	57°	**Trey Mancini**	**0.95**
23	57°	Tony Kemp	0.90
24	56°	Travis Jankowski	0.88

BRR (Relative to Team)

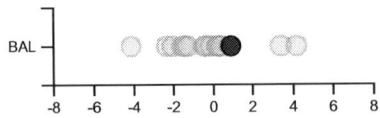

Rank		Player	BRR
1	89°	Jonathan Schoop	4.21
2	78°	Adam Jones	3.43
3	69°	**Trey Mancini**	**0.95**
4	63°	Joey Rickard	0.88
5	53°	Tim Beckham	0.41

Base Running Components

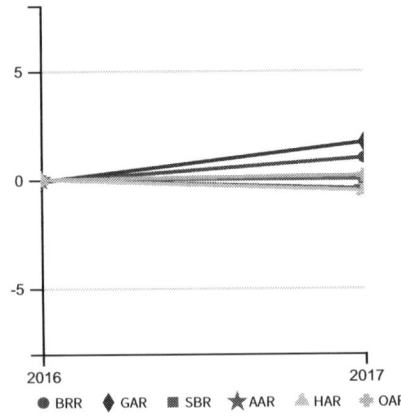

Manuel Margot   CF   San Diego Padres

Born: 9/28/1994   **Age:** 23   **Bats:** R   **Throws:** R   **Height:** 5' 11"   **Weight:** 180 lbs   **Draft Info:** International Free Agent, 2011

PACE
18 Sec/Pit
1st of 155
99°
Very Fast

2017 Daily WARP Profile
2.3 Total WARP

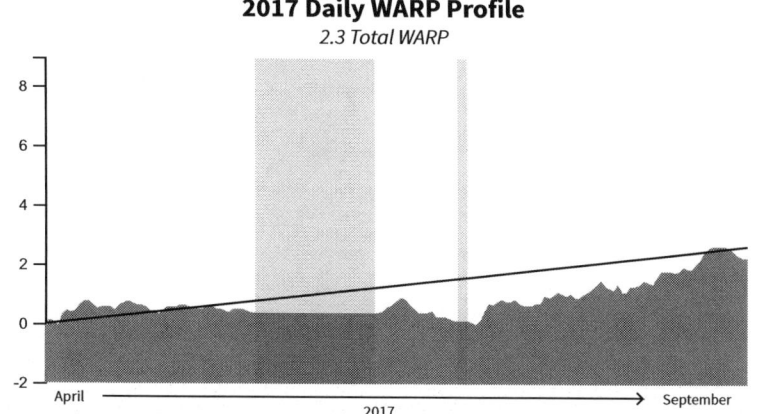

Game 49: DL (calf sprain), **Game 95:** paternity

Fantasy Values
2017	2018
$15.03	$17.00

YEAR	TEAM	LVL	AGE	PA	R	2B	3B	HR	RBI	BB	K	SB	AVG/OBP/SLG	TAv	VORP	BABIP	WARP
2017	SDN	MLB	22	529	53	18	7	13	39	35	106	17	.263/.313/.409	.270	23.6	.309	2.3

2017 Batting Percentages

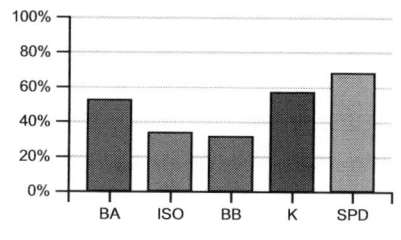

Batting PECOTA Percentiles

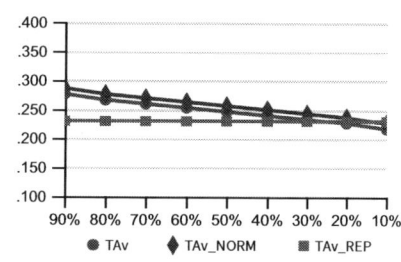

Batting WARP History

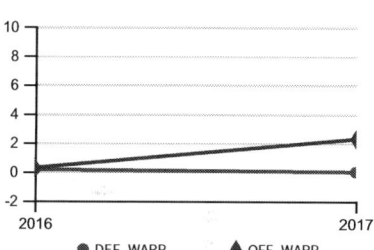

BRR (Relative to Position)

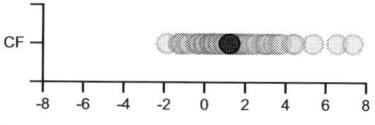

Rank		Player	BRR
28	40°	Adam Engel	1.37
29	39°	Jared Hoying	1.36
30	37°	**Manuel Margot**	**1.26**
31	36°	Franchy Cordero	1.24
32	36°	Jacoby Jones	1.06

BRR (Relative to Team)

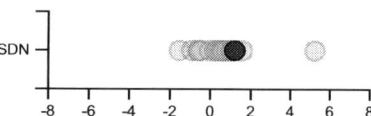

Rank		Player	BRR
1	98°	Cory Spangenberg	5.29
2	87°	Freddy Galvis	1.62
3	75°	**Manuel Margot**	**1.26**
4	73°	Franchy Cordero	1.24
5	71°	Luis Torrens	1.14

Base Running Components

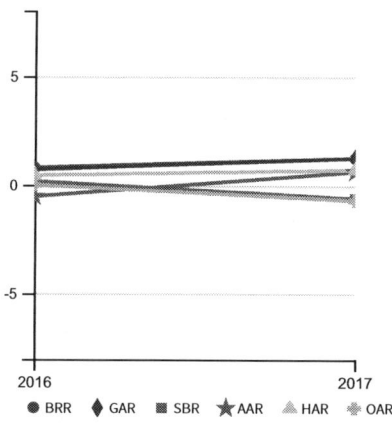

German Marquez RHP Colorado Rockies

Born: 2/22/1995 **Age:** 23 **Bats:** R **Throws:** R **Height:** 6'1" **Weight:** 185 lbs **Draft Info:** International Free Agent, 2011

PACE
18 5th of 150
Sec/Pit 97°
Very Fast

2017 Daily WARP Profile
-0.5 Total WARP

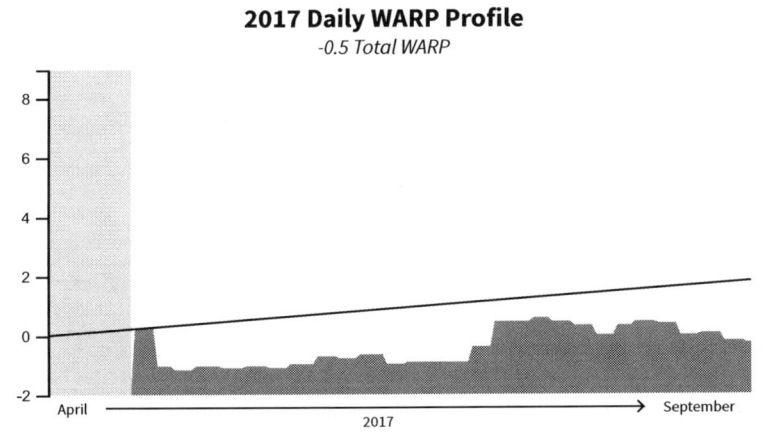

Game 1: minors

POWER
60 26th of 150
PWR

STAMINA
73 53rd of 150
STM

COMMAND
33 149th of 150
CMD

Fantasy Values
| 2017 | 2018 |
| $10.35 | $2.00 |

YEAR	TEAM	LVL	AGE	W	L	SV	G	GS	IP	H	HR	BB/9	K/9	K	GB%	BABIP	WHIP	ERA	DRA	WARP	MPH 95
2017	COL	MLB	22	11	7	0	29	29	162	174	25	2.7	8.2	147	47%	.316	1.38	4.39	5.88	-0.5	97.5

2017 Pitching Percentages

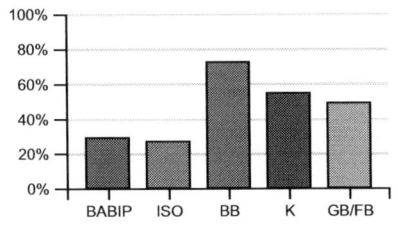

Pitching PECOTA Percentiles

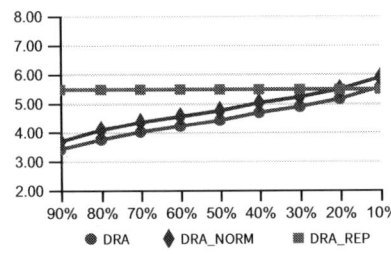

Pitching WARP History

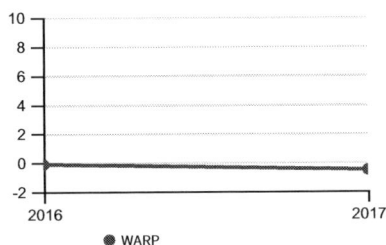

Tunnel vs LHH

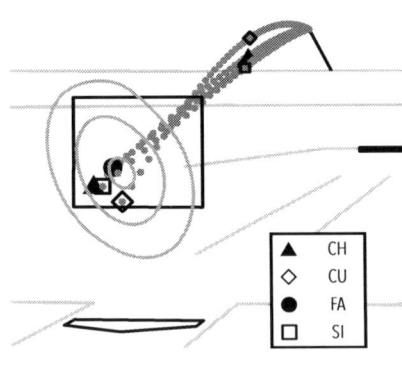

Pitch Types

Type	Freq	Velo	H Mov	V Mov
CH	5.5%	85.9 [103]	-6.9 [123]	-24.7 [107]
CU	25.0%	80.8 [110]	6.4 [95]	-44.5 [107]
FA	56.0%	95.3 [109]	-5.9 [105]	-13.4 [106]
SI	9.6%	94.2 [111]	-11.6 [107]	-19 [104]
SL	4.0%	86.9 [111]	1.4 [86]	-26 [119]

Pitch Tunnel

Pairs	Release Diff	Tunnel Diff	Plate Diff	Speed Changes
1956	28.4	126.2	222.0	0.033

PI Scores

Year	Pitch Ct	Pwr	Cmd	Stm
2016	348	50	46	73
2017	2655	60	33	73

Tunnel vs RHH

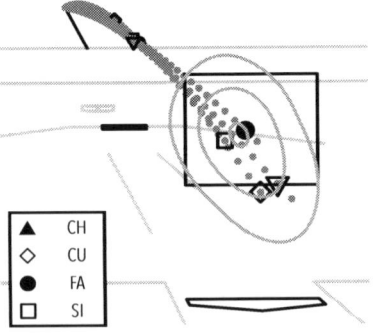

Russell Martin   C   Toronto Blue Jays

Born: 2/15/1983   **Age:** 35   **Bats:** R   **Throws:** R   **Height:** 5' 10"   **Weight:** 205 lbs   **Draft Info:** Round 17, 2002 Draft (#511 overall)

PACE
22 99th of 155
Sec/Pit 36°
Slow

2017 Daily WARP Profile
1.3 Total WARP

Game 32: DL (shoulder nerve irritation), **Game 116:** DL (oblique strain)

Fantasy Values
2017	2018
$5.67	$11.00

YEAR	TEAM	LVL	AGE	PA	R	2B	3B	HR	RBI	BB	K	SB	AVG/OBP/SLG	TAv	VORP	BABIP	WARP
2017	TOR	MLB	34	365	49	12	0	13	35	50	83	1	.221/.343/.388	.250	12.8	.261	1.3

2017 Batting Percentages

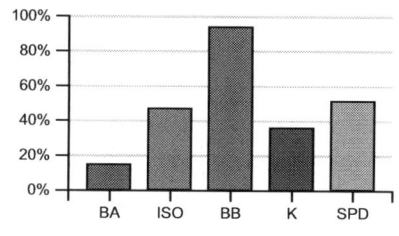

Batting PECOTA Percentiles

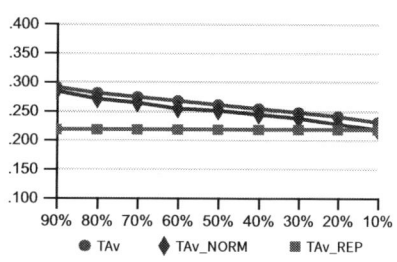

Batting WARP History

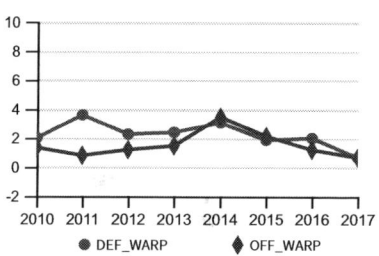

BRR (Relative to Position)

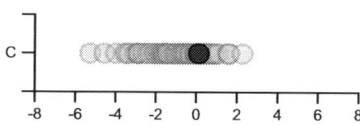

Rank		Player	BRR
22	75°	Luke Maile	0.20
23	75°	Mitch Garver	0.18
24	73°	**Russell Martin**	**0.17**
25	72°	Jesus Sucre	0.15
26	71°	Andrew Knapp	0.11

BRR (Relative to Team)

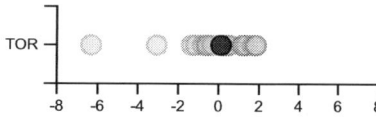

Rank		Player	BRR
12	62°	Steve Pearce	0.28
13	59°	Luke Maile	0.20
14	53°	**Russell Martin**	**0.17**
15	41°	Jose Bautista	-0.25
16	37°	Miguel Montero	-0.49

Base Running Components

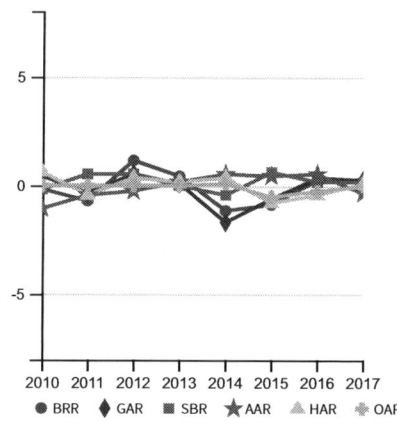

Carlos Martinez RHP St. Louis Cardinals

Born: 9/21/1991 **Age:** 26 **Bats:** R **Throws:** R **Height:** 6' 0" **Weight:** 190 lbs **Draft Info:** International Free Agent, 2009

2017 Daily WARP Profile
4.1 Total WARP

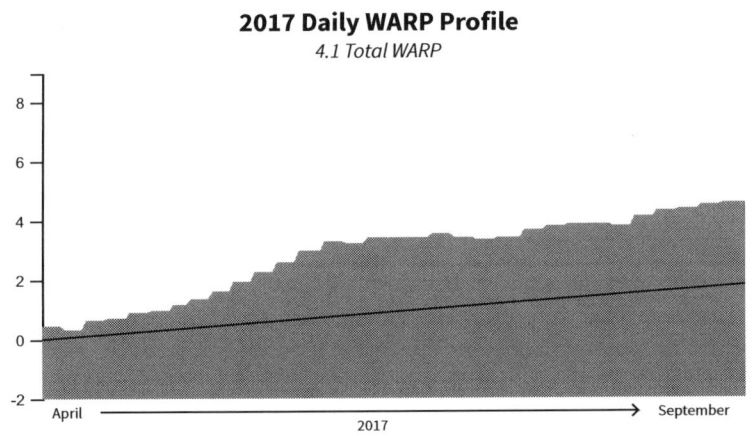

April — 2017 — September

63 PWR — **POWER** 16th of 150

82 STM — **STAMINA** 7th of 150

43 CMD — **COMMAND** 125th of 150

17 Sec/Pit — **PACE** 2nd of 150 / 99° / Very Fast

Fantasy Values
2017	2018
$21.94	$18.00

YEAR	TEAM	LVL	AGE	W	L	SV	G	GS	IP	H	HR	BB/9	K/9	K	GB%	BABIP	WHIP	ERA	DRA	WARP	MPH 95
2017	SLN	MLB	25	12	11	0	32	32	205	179	27	3.1	9.5	217	52%	.285	1.22	3.64	3.76	4.1	98.8

Martinez is one of those pitchers who have the arsenal of an ace yet can never quite seem to deliver at that level. The Cardinals hurler threw 200 innings and struck out more than 200 batters for the first time in his career yet finished with an ERA over 3.50 for the first time since 2014. He also allowed more than a home run per nine innings for the first time ever and had a DRA over 3.50 for the third consecutive season. Martinez is very good, but if you pay a premium for his services you're reaching for a ceiling he has never quite achieved. — Mike G.

2017 Pitching Percentages

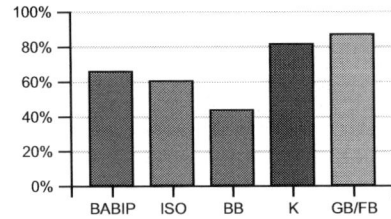

Pitching PECOTA Percentiles

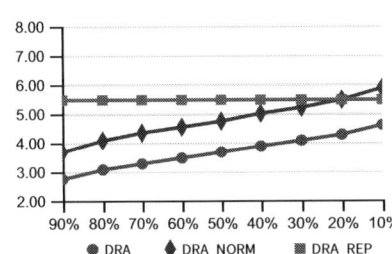

● DRA ◆ DRA_NORM ■ DRA_REP

Pitching WARP History

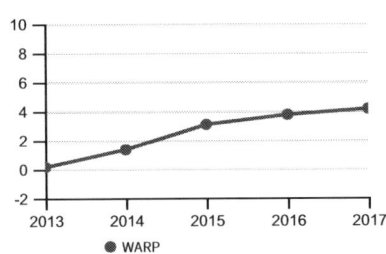

● WARP

Tunnel vs LHH

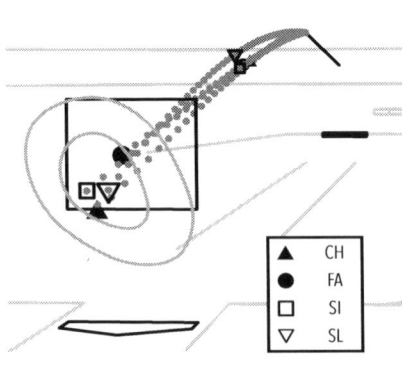

▲ CH
● FA
□ SI
▽ SL

Pitch Types

Type	Freq	Velo	H Mov	V Mov
CH	16.2%	88 [111]	-13.5 [87]	-30.7 [90]
CU	0.5%	79.2 [103]	9.6 [107]	-40.5 [116]
FA	27.3%	96.7 [115]	-7.8 [97]	-14.9 [101]
SI	28.9%	95.1 [116]	-14.2 [88]	-22.4 [91]
SL	27.1%	85.4 [104]	8.8 [119]	-30.8 [105]

Pitch Tunnel

Pairs	Release Diff	Tunnel Diff	Plate Diff	Speed Changes
2255	36.5	121.4	218.9	0.024

PI Scores

Year	Pitch Ct	Pwr	Cmd	Stm
2013	470	81	39	52
2014	1350	77	31	54
2015	2821	65	39	72
2016	3000	59	42	77
2017	3112	63	43	82

Tunnel vs RHH

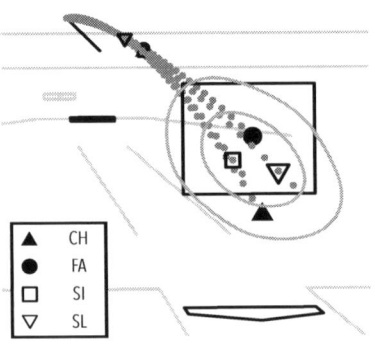

▲ CH
● FA
□ SI
▽ SL

J.D. Martinez   RF   Arizona Diamondbacks

Born: 8/21/1987   **Age:** 30   **Bats:** R   **Throws:** R   **Height:** 6' 3"   **Weight:** 220 lbs   **Draft Info:** Round 20, 2009 Draft (#611 overall)

2017 Daily WARP Profile
3.5 Total WARP

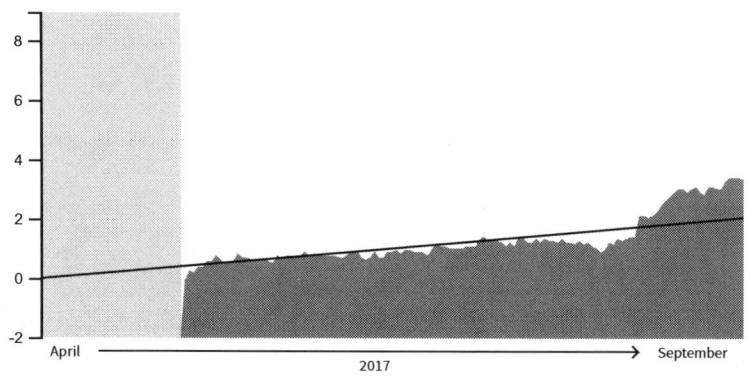

PACE
22 Sec/Pit
99th of 155
36°
Slow

Game 1: DL (foot sprain)

Fantasy Values
2017	2018
$11.46	**$31.00**

YEAR	TEAM	LVL	AGE	PA	R	2B	3B	HR	RBI	BB	K	SB	AVG/OBP/SLG	TAv	VORP	BABIP	WARP
2017	DET	MLB	29	232	38	13	2	16	39	29	54	2	.305/.388/.630	.322	17.9	.338	1.2
2017	ARI	MLB	29	257	47	13	1	29	65	24	74	2	.302/.366/.741	.350	26.6	.315	2.3

Martinez was having a good season in Detroit, but turned on the after jets after a midseason trade to the Diamondbacks. Always a strong hitter, Martinez found the desert air in Arizona to his liking, hitting an absurd 29 homers in 257 plate appearances. Freed from the cavernous confines of Comerica Park, Martinez should hit wherever he goes and will be one of the rare elite power bats in fantasy who will have top-tier value no matter how many home runs are hit in the majors. — Mike G.

2017 Batting Percentages

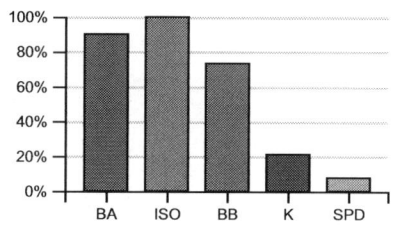

Batting PECOTA Percentiles

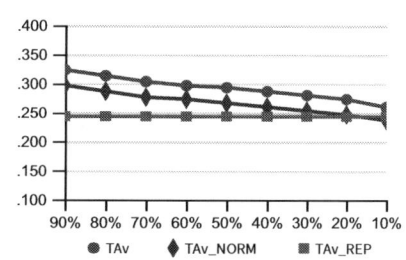

Batting WARP History

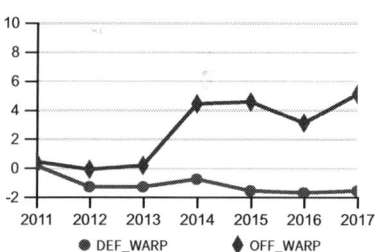

BRR (Relative to Position)

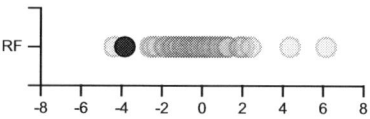

Rank		Player	BRR
51	9°	Max Kepler	-2.21
52	7°	Nomar Mazara	-2.41
53	5°	Stephen Piscotty	-2.54
54	3°	**J.D. Martinez**	**-3.80**
55	0°	Yasiel Puig	-4.33

BRR (Relative to Team)

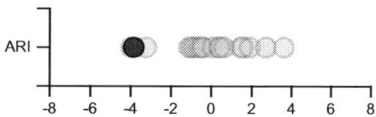

Rank		Player	BRR
14	25°	David Peralta	-0.91
15	20°	Alex Avila	-1.05
16	14°	Daniel Descalso	-3.18
17	8°	**J.D. Martinez**	**-3.80**
18	0°	Brandon Drury	-3.92

Base Running Components

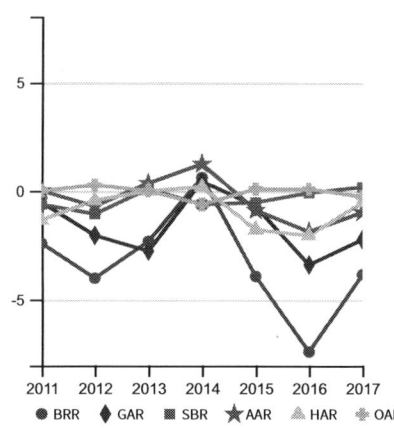

Steven Matz   LHP   New York Mets

Born: 5/29/1991   **Age:** 27   **Bats:** R   **Throws:** L   **Height:** 6' 2"   **Weight:** 200 lbs   **Draft Info:** Round 2, 2009 Draft (#72 overall)

2017 Daily WARP Profile
0.0 Total WARP

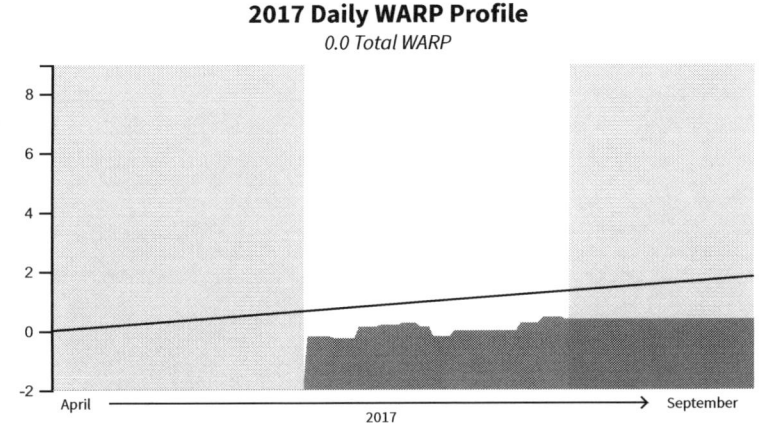

Game 1: DL (elbow inflammation), **Game 120:** DL (elbow irritation)

44 PWR — **POWER** 80th of 150

55 STM — **STAMINA** 115th of 150

53 CMD — **COMMAND** 72nd of 150

18 Sec/Pit — **PACE** 5th of 150 / 97° / Very Fast

Fantasy Values
2017	2018
$-2.38	$6.00

YEAR	TEAM	LVL	AGE	W	L	SV	G	GS	IP	H	HR	BB/9	K/9	K	GB%	BABIP	WHIP	ERA	DRA	WARP	MPH 95
2017	NYN	MLB	26	2	7	0	13	13	66.2	83	12	2.6	6.5	48	49%	.329	1.53	6.07	5.55	0.0	94.5

2017 Pitching Percentages

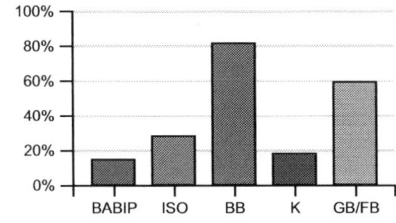

Pitching PECOTA Percentiles

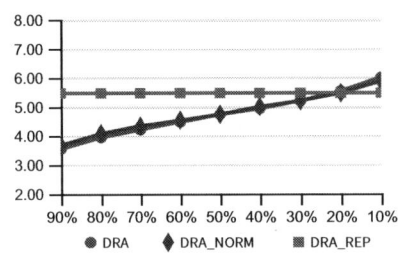

Pitching WARP History

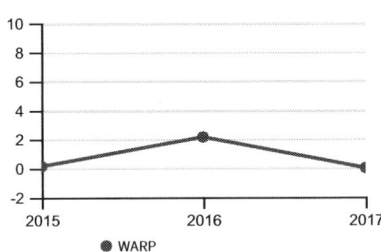

Tunnel vs LHH

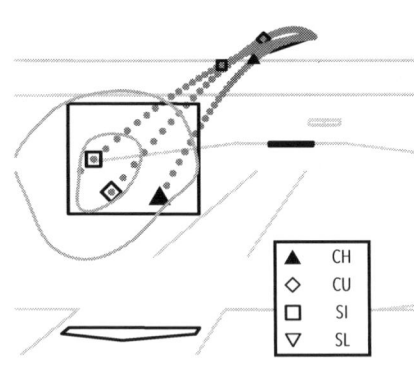

▲	CH
◇	CU
□	SI
▽	SL

Pitch Types

Type	Freq	Velo	H Mov	V Mov
CH	13.4%	84 [96]	15.1 [78]	-28.6 [96]
CU	23.3%	78.7 [101]	-6.5 [95]	-46.6 [103]
SI	59.1%	93.5 [107]	12.8 [98]	-18.1 [107]
SL	4.2%	86.1 [108]	-0.5 [82]	-30 [108]

Pitch Tunnel

Pairs	Release Diff	Tunnel Diff	Plate Diff	Speed Changes
873	27.4	120.0	224.4	0.035

PI Scores

Year	Pitch Ct	Pwr	Cmd	Stm
2015	576	54	50	56
2016	2145	51	55	65
2017	1170	44	53	55

Tunnel vs RHH

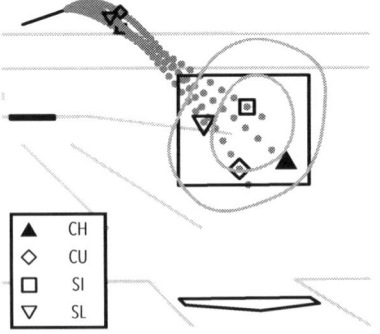

▲	CH
◇	CU
□	SI
▽	SL

Joe Mauer   1B   Minnesota Twins

Born: 4/19/1983   **Age:** 35   **Bats:** L   **Throws:** R   **Height:** 6' 5"   **Weight:** 225 lbs   **Draft Info:** Round 1, 2001 Draft (#1 overall)

2017 Daily WARP Profile
1.0 Total WARP

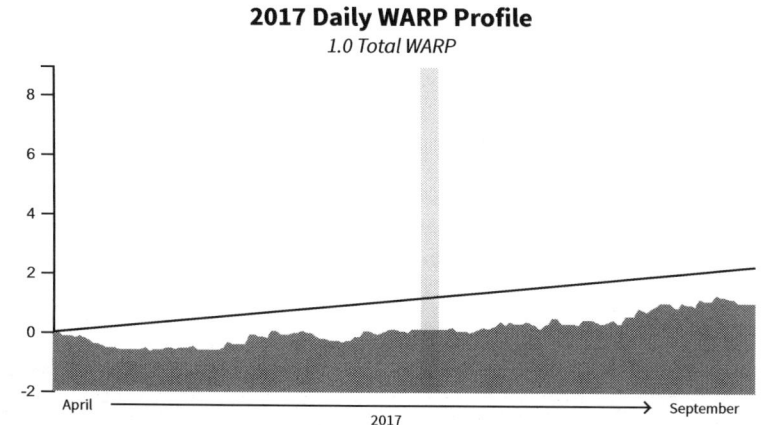

23 Sec/Pit

PACE
135th of 155
13°
Very Slow

Game 85: DL (back strain)

Fantasy Values
2017	2018
$17.46	$10.00

YEAR	TEAM	LVL	AGE	PA	R	2B	3B	HR	RBI	BB	K	SB	AVG/OBP/SLG	TAv	VORP	BABIP	WARP
2017	MIN	MLB	34	597	69	36	1	7	71	66	83	2	.305/.384/.417	.274	8.5	.349	1.0

2017 Batting Percentages

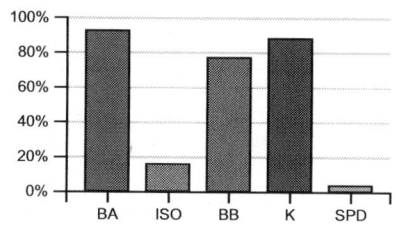

Batting PECOTA Percentiles

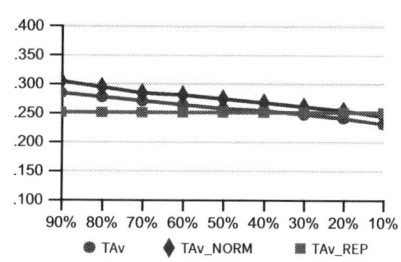

Batting WARP History

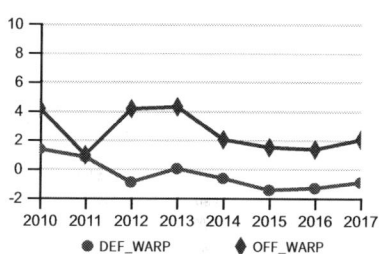

BRR (Relative to Position)

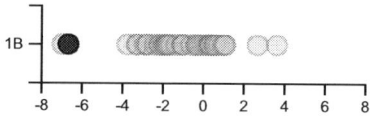

Rank		Player	BRR
41	14°	Lucas Duda	-3.26
42	11°	Josh Bell	-3.73
43	9°	Miguel Cabrera	-6.61
44	4°	**Joe Mauer**	**-6.63**
45	0°	Joey Votto	-6.92

BRR (Relative to Team)

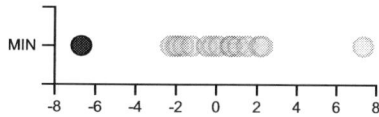

Rank		Player	BRR
12	35°	Eddie Rosario	-1.60
13	28°	Robbie Grossman	-1.86
14	21°	Miguel Sano	-1.98
15	12°	Max Kepler	-2.21
16	0°	**Joe Mauer**	**-6.63**

Base Running Components

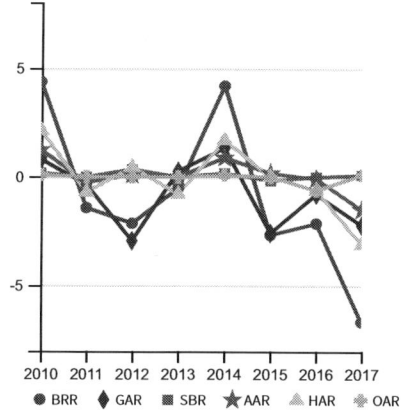

Nomar Mazara RF Texas Rangers

Born: 4/26/1995 **Age:** 23 **Bats:** L **Throws:** L **Height:** 6' 4" **Weight:** 215 lbs **Draft Info:** International Free Agent, 2011

2017 Daily WARP Profile
-0.5 Total WARP

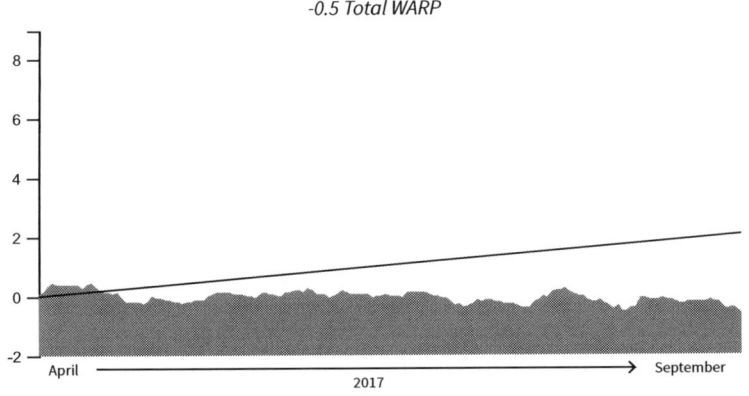

PACE
22 Sec/Pit
99th of 155
36°
Slow

	Fantasy Values	
	2017	2018
	$15.03	$19.00

YEAR	TEAM	LVL	AGE	PA	R	2B	3B	HR	RBI	BB	K	SB	AVG/OBP/SLG	TAv	VORP	BABIP	WARP
2017	TEX	MLB	22	616	64	30	2	20	101	55	127	2	.253/.323/.422	.247	.8	.293	-.5

2017 Batting Percentages

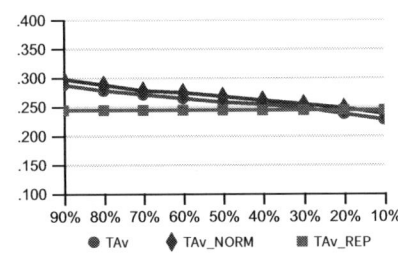

Batting PECOTA Percentiles

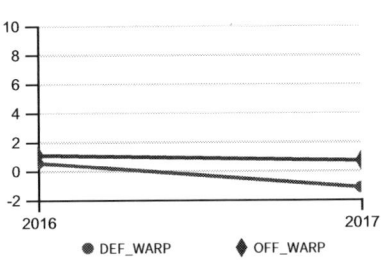

Batting WARP History

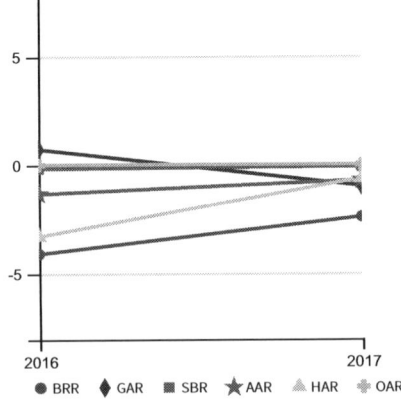

BRR (Relative to Position)

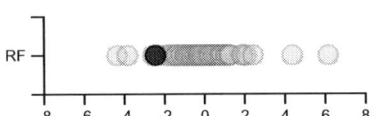

Rank		Player	BRR
50	12°	Steven Souza	-1.85
51	9°	Max Kepler	-2.21
52	7°	**Nomar Mazara**	**-2.41**
53	5°	Stephen Piscotty	-2.54
54	3°	J.D. Martinez	-3.80

BRR (Relative to Team)

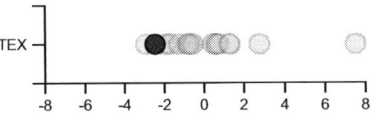

Rank		Player	BRR
13	27°	Brett Nicholas	-1.22
14	21°	Robinson Chirinos	-1.67
15	14°	Mike Napoli	-1.90
16	6°	**Nomar Mazara**	**-2.41**
17	0°	Adrian Beltre	-2.87

Base Running Components

Lance McCullers RHP Houston Astros

Born: 10/2/1993 **Age:** 24 **Bats:** L **Throws:** R **Height:** 6' 1" **Weight:** 205 lbs **Draft Info:** Round 1, 2012 Draft (#41 overall)

2017 Daily WARP Profile
2.7 Total WARP

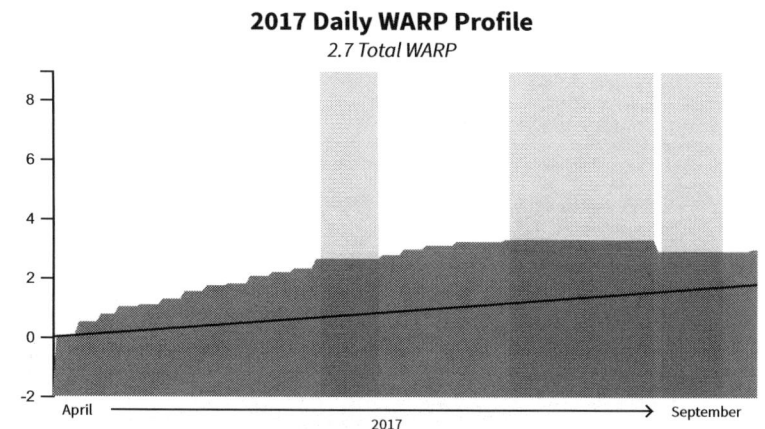

Game 62: DL (back discomfort), **Game 105:** DL (back discomfort), **Game 140:** arm fatigue

PACE	21 Sec/Pit	81st of 150 / 46° / Average

POWER 46 PWR 69th of 150

STAMINA 55 STM 115th of 150

COMMAND 36 CMD 146th of 150

Fantasy Values

2017	2018
$9.70	$14.00

YEAR	TEAM	LVL	AGE	W	L	SV	G	GS	IP	H	HR	BB/9	K/9	K	GB%	BABIP	WHIP	ERA	DRA	WARP	MPH 95
2017	HOU	MLB	23	7	4	0	22	22	118.2	114	8	3.0	10.0	132	62%	.330	1.30	4.25	3.52	2.7	96.5

As he showed in the postseason, when he is on his game McCullers can be one of the best pitchers in baseball. Heck, even his raw results haven't been too shabby. Inconsistency and injury have been McCullers' biggest limitations so far, but he is both young enough and talented enough to put all this behind him with one big season. McCullers is a pitcher it is okay to reach for a little bit in drafts, if you don't push him into the top tier. — Mike G.

2017 Pitching Percentages
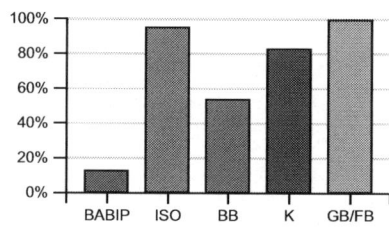

Pitching PECOTA Percentiles
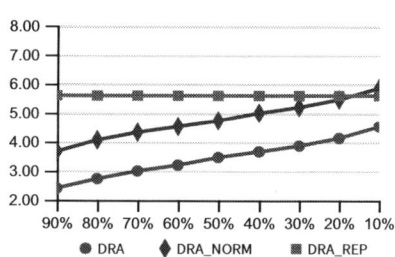

Pitching WARP History
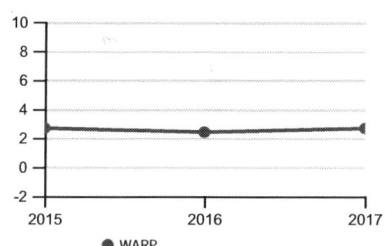

Tunnel vs LHH
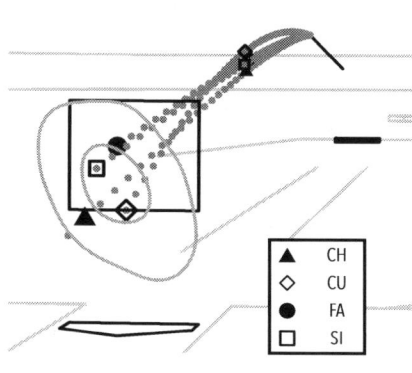

Pitch Types

Type	Freq	Velo	H Mov	V Mov
CH	12.0%	89.2 [117]	-13.8 [86]	-28.2 [97]
CU	47.2%	86 [129]	7.9 [101]	-41.9 [113]
FA	20.4%	94.5 [106]	-9.7 [88]	-18 [91]
FC	0.1%	92.3 [122]	-2.6 [79]	-21 [111]
SI	19.9%	94.5 [113]	-12.2 [102]	-19.9 [101]
SL	0.4%	86 [107]	7.6 [113]	-34.5 [95]

Pitch Tunnel

Pairs	Release Diff	Tunnel Diff	Plate Diff	Speed Changes
1485	26.2	121.8	224.6	0.021

PI Scores

Year	Pitch Ct	Pwr	Cmd	Stm
2015	2098	54	40	63
2016	1335	45	46	47
2017	2003	46	36	55

Tunnel vs RHH
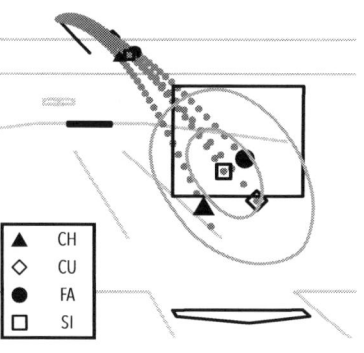

Andrew McCutchen   CF   San Francisco Giants

Born: 10/10/1986   **Age:** 31   **Bats:** R   **Throws:** R   **Height:** 5' 10"   **Weight:** 195 lbs   **Draft Info:** Round 1, 2005 Draft (#11 overall)

2017 Daily WARP Profile
3.9 Total WARP

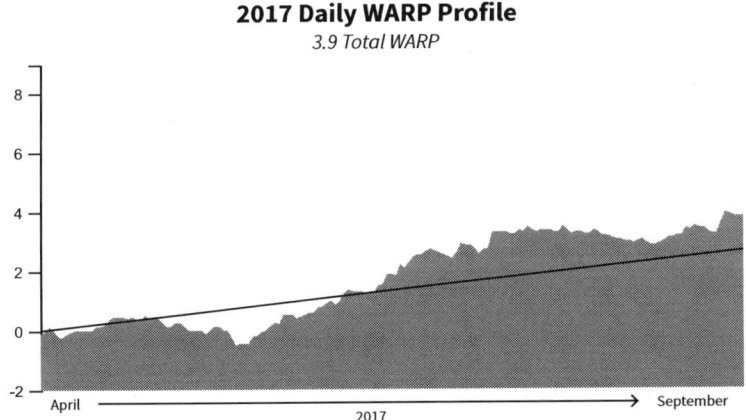

21 Sec/Pit

PACE
45th of 155
71°
Fast

Fantasy Values

2017	2018
$24.83	$24.00

YEAR	TEAM	LVL	AGE	PA	R	2B	3B	HR	RBI	BB	K	SB	AVG/OBP/SLG	TAv	VORP	BABIP	WARP
2017	PIT	MLB	30	650	94	30	2	28	88	73	116	11	.279/.363/.486	.303	50.2	.305	3.9

For the first few weeks of 2017, Cutch looked finished, a shell of his former self struggling to produce. Then he turned on the jets, a hot streak making him look once again like the elite hitter he had been for the Pirates from 2012 to 2015. The final product was something in the middle: a very good hitter who wasn't anything close to the guy who was a first-round mainstay in his heyday. Cutch's resurgence makes him a worthy second outfielder in mixed, but the drop in steals and batting average prevent Cutch from realizing more than a third-round ceiling. — Mike G.

2017 Batting Percentages

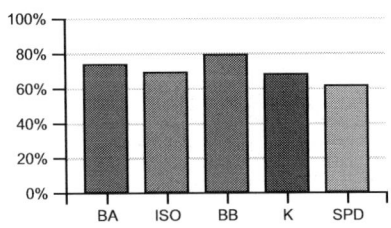

Batting PECOTA Percentiles

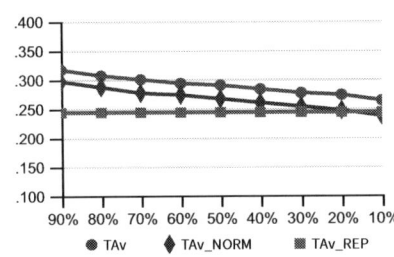

Batting WARP History

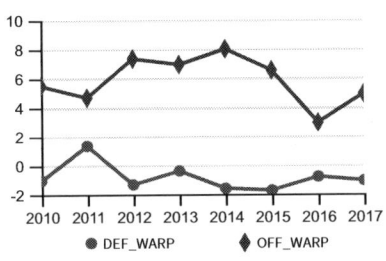

BRR (Relative to Position)

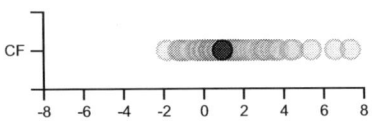

Rank		Player	BRR
32	36°	Jacoby Jones	1.06
33	34°	Guillermo Heredia	0.99
34	31°	**Andrew McCutchen**	**0.98**
35	28°	Christian Yelich	0.81
36	28°	Zach Granite	0.75

BRR (Relative to Team)

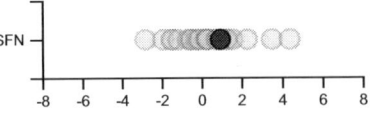

Rank		Player	BRR
6	84°	Mac Williamson	1.30
7	82°	Ryder Jones	1.00
8	71°	**Andrew McCutchen**	**0.98**
9	60°	Joe Panik	0.85
10	55°	Alen Hanson	0.78

Base Running Components

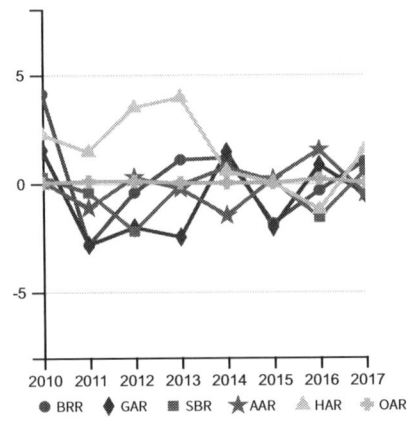

Wade Miley LHP Baltimore Orioles

Born: 11/13/1986 **Age:** 31 **Bats:** L **Throws:** L **Height:** 6'0" **Weight:** 220 lbs **Draft Info:** Round 1, 2008 Draft (#43 overall)

2017 Daily WARP Profile
0.6 Total WARP

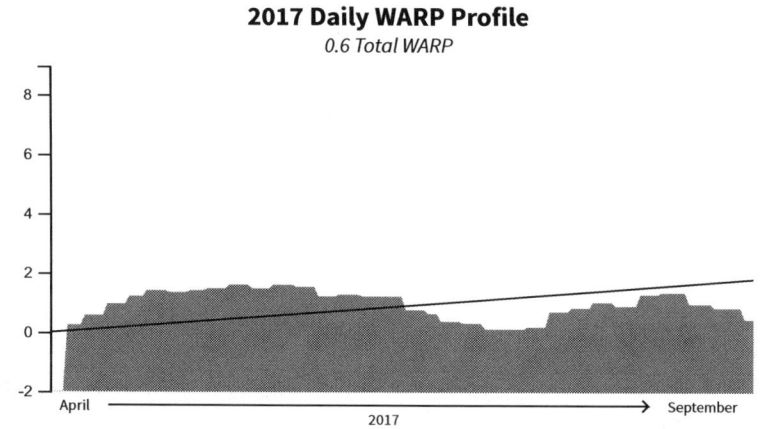

 POWER 40 PWR 96th of 150

 STAMINA 76 STM 36th of 150

 COMMAND 61 CMD 30th of 150

PACE 18 Sec/Pit 5th of 150 97° Very Fast

Fantasy Values 2017 $-4.43 2018 $2.00

YEAR	TEAM	LVL	AGE	W	L	SV	G	GS	IP	H	HR	BB/9	K/9	K	GB%	BABIP	WHIP	ERA	DRA	WARP	MPH 95
2017	BAL	MLB	30	8	15	0	32	32	157.1	179	25	5.3	8.1	142	51%	.332	1.73	5.61	5.23	0.6	93.3

2017 Pitching Percentages
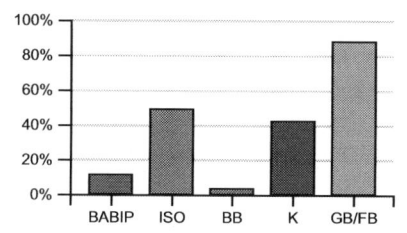

Pitching PECOTA Percentiles
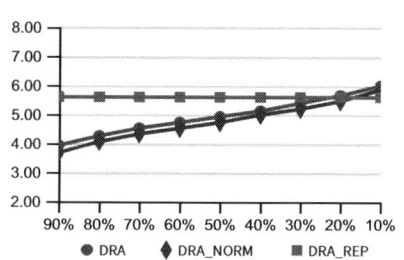

Pitching WARP History
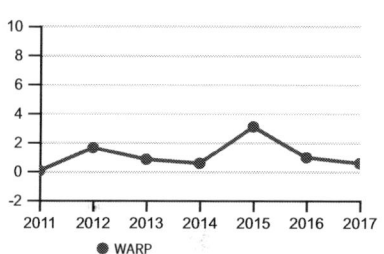

Tunnel vs LHH
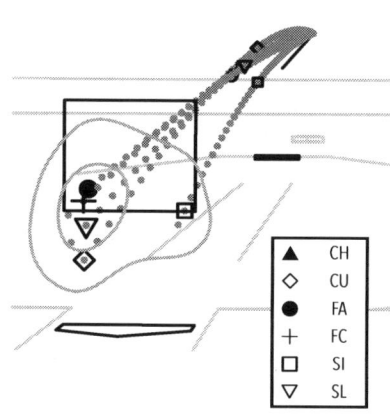

Pitch Types

Type	Freq	Velo	H Mov	V Mov
CH	10.7%	83.3 [93]	13.3 [88]	-24.4 [108]
CU	10.3%	77.3 [96]	-5 [89]	-51.9 [92]
FA	21.9%	91.8 [97]	4.4 [113]	-12.7 [108]
FC	11.9%	88.7 [101]	-2.4 [104]	-22 [107]
SI	31.5%	90.9 [92]	11.9 [104]	-15.2 [118]
SL	13.7%	84.4 [100]	-2.7 [92]	-33.3 [98]

Pitch Tunnel

Pairs	Release Diff	Tunnel Diff	Plate Diff	Speed Changes
2321	38.6	112.6	222.4	0.025

PI Scores

Year	Pitch Ct	Pwr	Cmd	Stm
2013	3224	51	47	79
2014	3117	47	59	79
2015	3193	42	59	78
2016	2714	38	59	70
2017	3049	40	61	76

Tunnel vs RHH
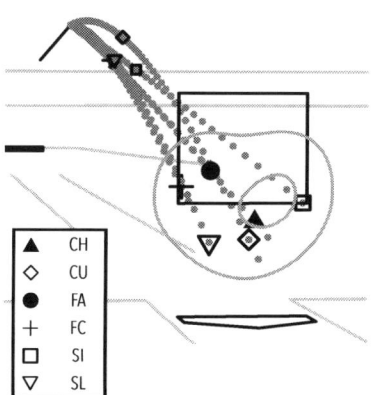

Andrew Miller   LHP   Cleveland Indians

Born: 5/21/1985   **Age:** 33   **Bats:** L   **Throws:** L   **Height:** 6' 7"   **Weight:** 205 lbs   **Draft Info:** Round 1, 2006 Draft (#6 overall)

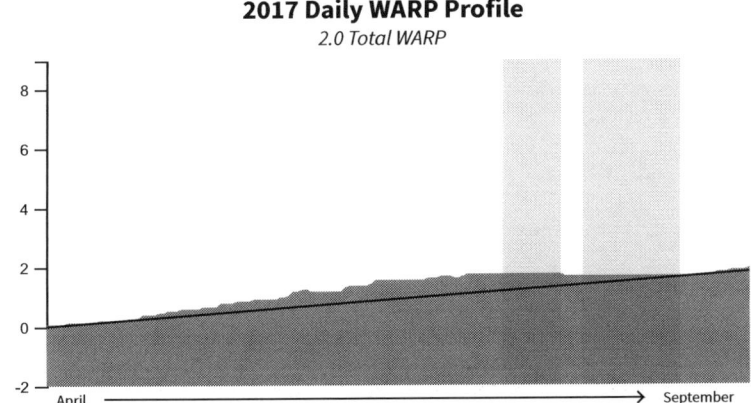

2017 Daily WARP Profile
2.0 Total WARP

45 PWR **POWER** 73rd of 150

45 STM **STAMINA** 145th of 150

57 CMD **COMMAND** 53rd of 150

20 Sec/Pit **PACE** 37th of 150 75° Fast

Game 106: DL (knee tendinitis), **Game 124:** DL (knee tendinitis)

Fantasy Values
2017	2018
$16.30	$9.00

YEAR	TEAM	LVL	AGE	W	L	SV	G	GS	IP	H	HR	BB/9	K/9	K	GB%	BABIP	WHIP	ERA	DRA	WARP	MPH 95
2017	CLE	MLB	32	4	3	2	57	0	62.2	31	3	3.0	13.6	95	42%	.233	0.83	1.44	2.32	2.0	96.9

Miller dropped from 12 saves to two, but otherwise it was another elite season for arguably the best middle reliever in baseball. It typically doesn't pay to shell out more than a buck or two for a noncloser, but Miller is the rare exception, a set-up man who is virtually guaranteed to post an ERA under 1.50 and strike out well over a batter an inning. He's an $8-10 buy in AL-only and someone who should be on your radar in the middle rounds in mixed. — Mike G.

2017 Pitching Percentages

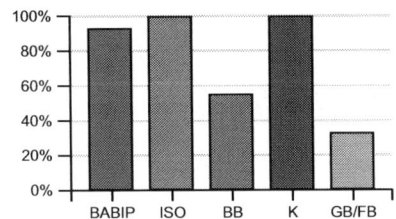

Pitching PECOTA Percentiles

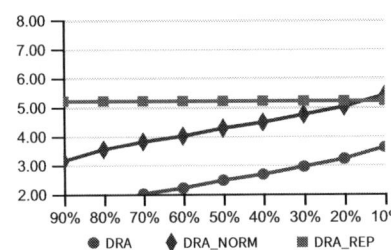

Pitching WARP History

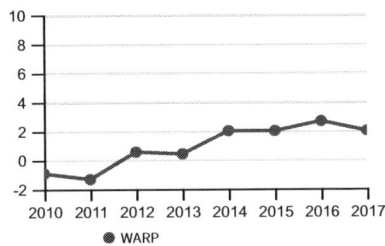

Tunnel vs LHH

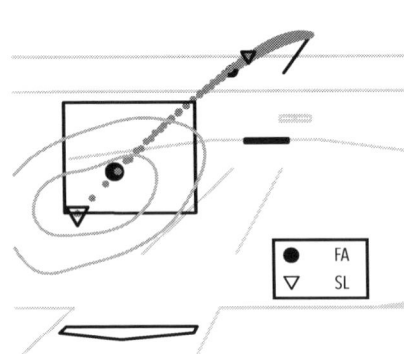

Tunnel vs RHH

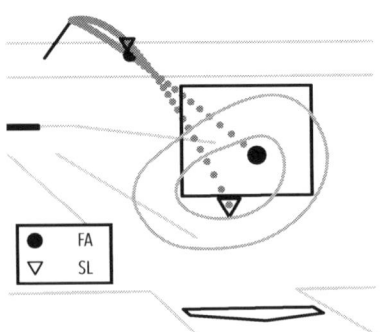

Pitch Types

Type	Freq	Velo	H Mov	V Mov
CH	0.2%	90.3 [121]	6.3 [126]	-16.9 [129]
FA	41.8%	94.5 [107]	8.6 [93]	-14.4 [102]
SL	57.9%	84.2 [99]	-9.4 [121]	-36.1 [90]

Pitch Tunnel

Pairs	Release Diff	Tunnel Diff	Plate Diff	Speed Changes
719	41.8	108.2	206.5	0.028

PI Scores

Year	Pitch Ct	Pwr	Cmd	Stm
2013	554	62	43	42
2014	980	57	44	50
2015	953	49	57	47
2016	1104	43	52	50
2017	975	45	57	45

Mike Minor   LHP   Texas Rangers

Born: 12/26/1987 **Age:** 30 **Bats:** R **Throws:** L **Height:** 6' 4" **Weight:** 210 lbs **Draft Info:** Round 1, 2009 Draft (#7 overall)

We don't have a baseball card for this guy.

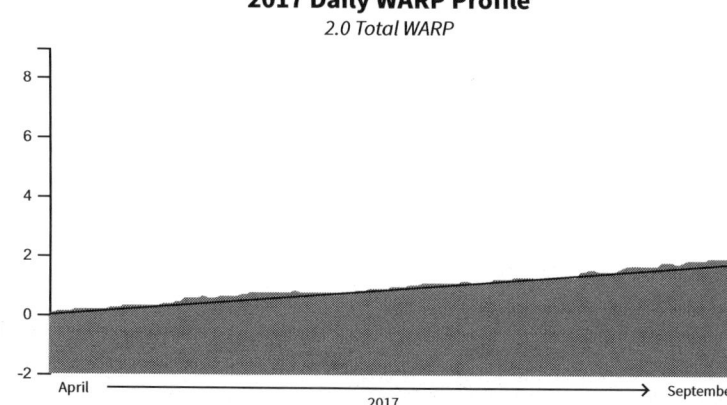

2017 Daily WARP Profile
2.0 Total WARP

POWER
50 PWR   59th of 150

STAMINA
51 STM   133rd of 150

COMMAND
61 CMD   30th of 150

PACE
20 Sec/Pit   37th of 150
75°
Fast

Fantasy Values
2017	2018
$15.55	$4.00

YEAR	TEAM	LVL	AGE	W	L	SV	G	GS	IP	H	HR	BB/9	K/9	K	GB%	BABIP	WHIP	ERA	DRA	WARP	MPH 95
2017	KCA	MLB	29	6	6	6	65	0	77.2	57	5	2.5	10.2	88	43%	.272	1.02	2.55	2.86	2.0	96.1

2017 Pitching Percentages

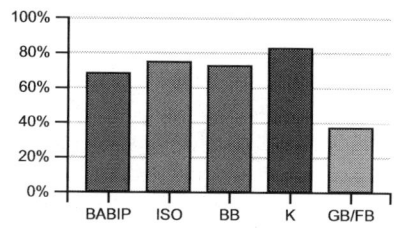

Pitching PECOTA Percentiles

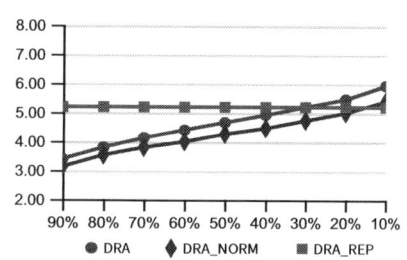

Pitching WARP History

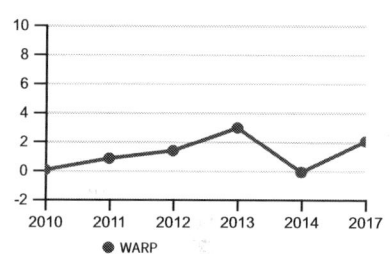

Tunnel vs LHH

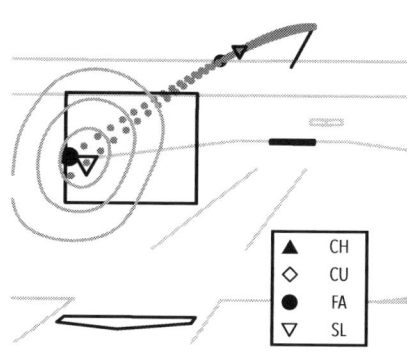

▲	CH
◇	CU
●	FA
▽	SL

Tunnel vs RHH

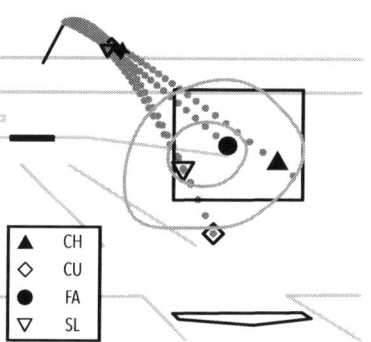

▲	CH
◇	CU
●	FA
▽	SL

Pitch Types

Type	Freq	Velo	H Mov	V Mov
CH	10.9%	87.3 [109]	13.4 [87]	-20.9 [118]
CU	7.9%	82.9 [117]	-4 [85]	-41.8 [113]
FA	43.5%	94.9 [108]	6.2 [105]	-12.9 [107]
FC	0.3%	87.8 [97]	-2.2 [103]	-24.6 [97]
SI	2.1%	92.5 [101]	11.8 [105]	-20.2 [99]
SL	35.4%	88.9 [120]	-2.8 [92]	-24.2 [124]

Pitch Tunnel

Pairs	Release Diff	Tunnel Diff	Plate Diff	Speed Changes
899	23.1	111.7	212.3	0.020

PI Scores

Year	Pitch Ct	Pwr	Cmd	Stm
2011	1358	47	65	75
2012	2835	42	61	68
2013	3119	40	63	77
2014	2418	43	63	70
2017	1197	50	61	51

Yadier Molina   C   St. Louis Cardinals

Born: 7/13/1982   **Age:** 35   **Bats:** R   **Throws:** R   **Height:** 5' 11"   **Weight:** 205 lbs   **Draft Info:** Round 4, 2000 Draft (#113 overall)

20 Sec/Pit

PACE
18th of 155
88°
Very Fast

2017 Daily WARP Profile
2.6 Total WARP

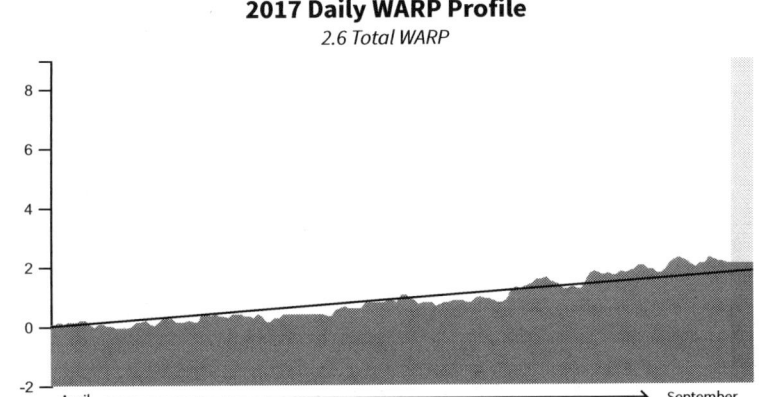

April   2017   September

Game 157: concussion

Fantasy Values
2017   2018
$18.25 $12.00

YEAR	TEAM	LVL	AGE	PA	R	2B	3B	HR	RBI	BB	K	SB	AVG/OBP/SLG	TAv	VORP	BABIP	WARP
2017	SLN	MLB	34	543	60	27	1	18	82	28	74	9	.273/.312/.439	.260	21.0	.285	2.6

2017 Batting Percentages

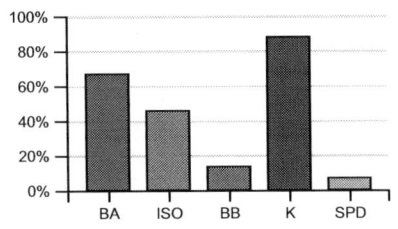

Batting PECOTA Percentiles

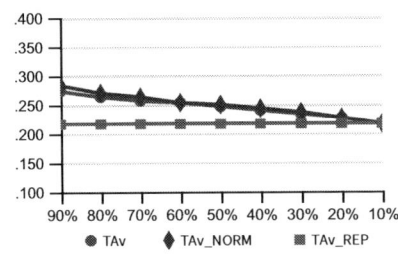

Batting WARP History

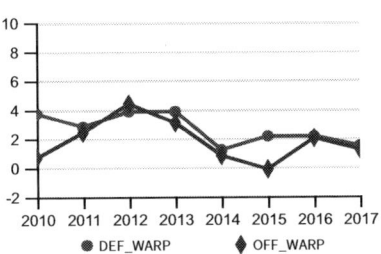

BRR (Relative to Position)

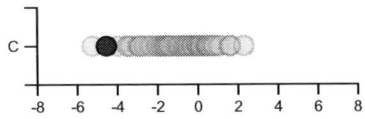

Rank		Player	BRR
72	8°	Wilson Ramos	-3.42
73	7°	Stephen Vogt	-3.45
74	4°	Willson Contreras	-3.93
75	2°	**Yadier Molina**	**-4.51**
76	0°	Sandy Leon	-5.21

BRR (Relative to Team)

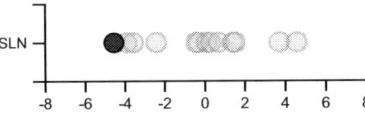

Rank		Player	BRR
9	38°	Jedd Gyorko	-0.40
10	25°	Matt Carpenter	-2.37
11	14°	Marcell Ozuna	-3.52
12	8°	Paul DeJong	-3.86
13	0°	**Yadier Molina**	**-4.51**

Base Running Components

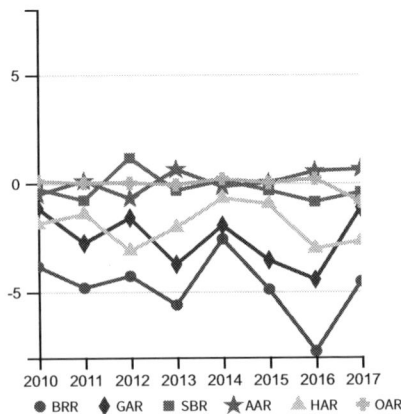

Yoan Moncada   2B   Chicago White Sox

Born: 5/27/1995   **Age:** 23   **Bats:** B   **Throws:** R   **Height:** 6'2"   **Weight:** 205 lbs   **Draft Info:** International Free Agent, 2015

PACE
19 Sec/Pit
4th of 155
97°
Very Fast

2017 Daily WARP Profile
1.0 Total WARP

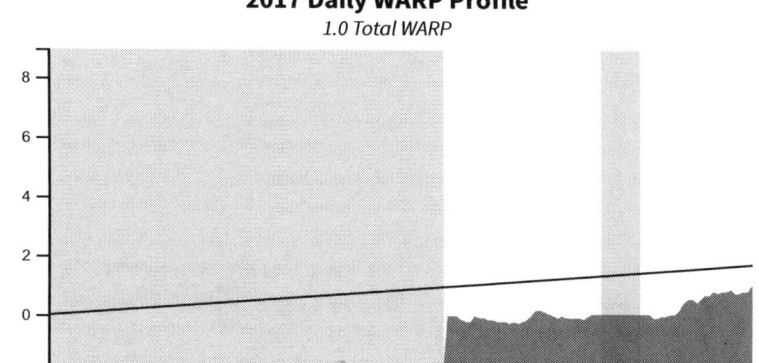

Game 1: minors, **Game 127:** DL (shin contusion)

Fantasy Values
2017	2018
$4.78	**$17.00**

YEAR	TEAM	LVL	AGE	PA	R	2B	3B	HR	RBI	BB	K	SB	AVG/OBP/SLG	TAv	VORP	BABIP	WARP
2017	CHA	MLB	22	231	31	8	2	8	22	29	74	3	.231/.338/.412	.254	4.2	.325	1.0

In a year where seemingly every rookie thrived right out of the gate, Moncada's major-league debut was especially disappointing. Lost in the poor overall numbers was a month-by-month improvement that perhaps presages a future star in the making. The biggest disappointment for Moncada buyers was the fact that he didn't run, stealing only three bases (and getting caught twice) after stealing 111 in two-and-a-half minor-league seasons. Moncada was only 22 years old, which should be taken into consideration. He was a 20/20 player between Triple-A and Chicago, and there is still considerable potential in fantasy. — Mike G.

2017 Batting Percentages

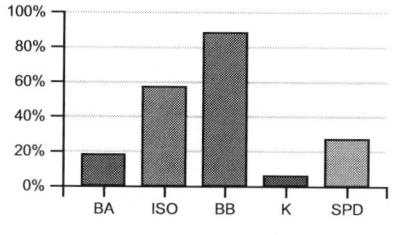

Batting PECOTA Percentiles

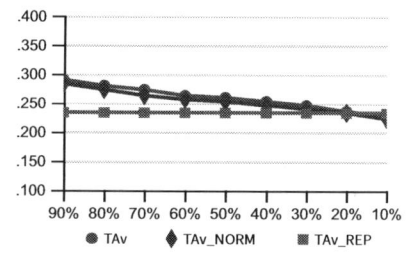

Batting WARP History

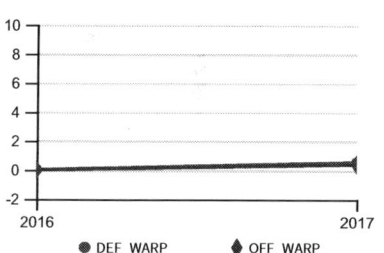

BRR (Relative to Position)

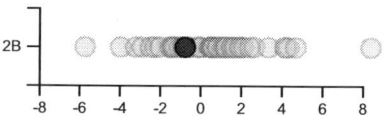

Rank		Player	BRR
37	29°	Andrew Romine	-0.61
38	28°	Gift Ngoepe	-0.72
39	27°	**Yoan Moncada**	**-0.72**
40	26°	Jason Kipnis	-0.75
41	24°	Darwin Barney	-0.81

BRR (Relative to Team)

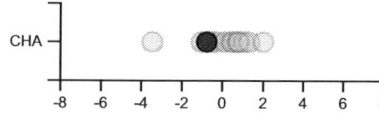

Rank		Player	BRR
11	21°	Avisail Garcia	-0.50
12	15°	Welington Castillo	-0.67
13	11°	**Yoan Moncada**	**-0.72**
14	5°	Omar Narvaez	-0.98
15	0°	Matt Davidson	-3.40

Base Running Components

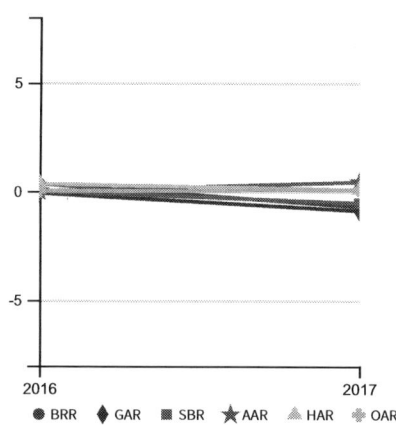

Rafael Montero   RHP   New York Mets

Born: 10/17/1990   **Age:** 27   **Bats:** R   **Throws:** R   **Height:** 6' 0"   **Weight:** 185 lbs   **Draft Info:** International Free Agent, 2011

We don't have a baseball card for this guy.

2017 Daily WARP Profile
0.6 Total WARP

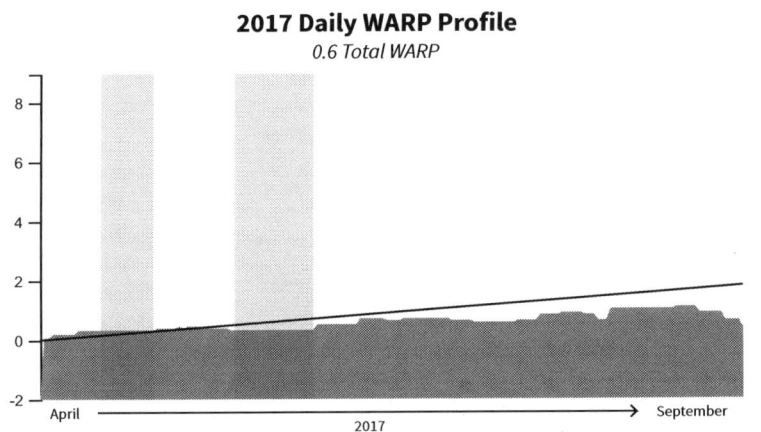

Game 15: minors, **Game 46:** minors

	POWER
51 PWR	56th of 150
69 STM	STAMINA 73rd of 150
60 CMD	COMMAND 37th of 150

21 Sec/Pit	PACE 81st of 150 46° Average

Fantasy Values

2017	2018
$-3.64	**$1.00**

YEAR	TEAM	LVL	AGE	W	L	SV	G	GS	IP	H	HR	BB/9	K/9	K	GB%	BABIP	WHIP	ERA	DRA	WARP	MPH 95
2017	NYN	MLB	26	5	11	0	34	18	119	141	12	5.1	8.6	114	50%	.366	1.75	5.52	5.02	0.6	95.3

2017 Pitching Percentages

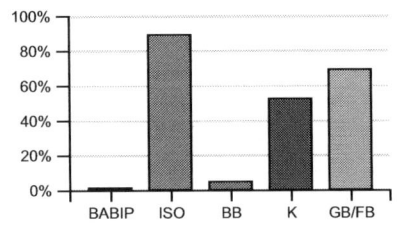

Pitching PECOTA Percentiles

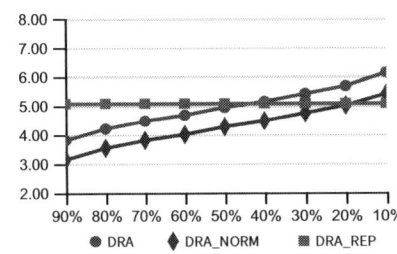

Pitching WARP History

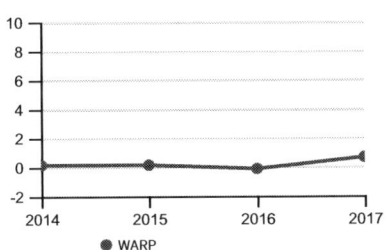

Tunnel vs LHH

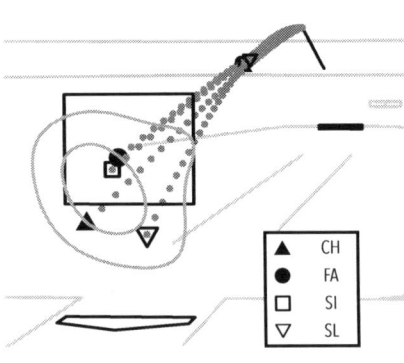

	CH
●	FA
□	SI
▽	SL

Pitch Types

Type	Freq	Velo	H Mov	V Mov
CH	19.6%	88.6 [114]	-13.3 [88]	-23.7 [109]
FA	36.4%	94.3 [106]	-5.8 [106]	-13.6 [105]
SI	19.1%	93.7 [108]	-12.1 [103]	-18.4 [106]
SL	24.9%	84.2 [99]	6.4 [108]	-34.1 [96]

Pitch Tunnel

Pairs	Release Diff	Tunnel Diff	Plate Diff	Speed Changes
1663	35.8	109.5	209.4	0.021

PI Scores

Year	Pitch Ct	Pwr	Cmd	Stm
2014	836	57	54	52
2016	384	47	62	71
2017	2214	51	60	69

Tunnel vs RHH

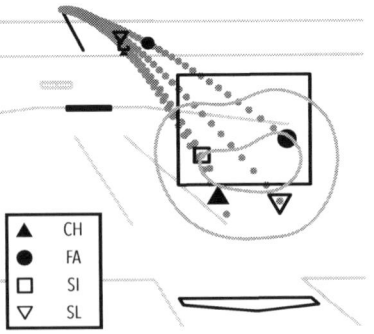

	CH
●	FA
□	SI
▽	SL

Jordan Montgomery   LHP   New York Yankees

Born: 12/27/1992   **Age:** 25   **Bats:** L   **Throws:** L   **Height:** 6' 6"   **Weight:** 225 lbs   **Draft Info:** Round 4, 2014 Draft (#122 overall)

2017 Daily WARP Profile
2.1 Total WARP

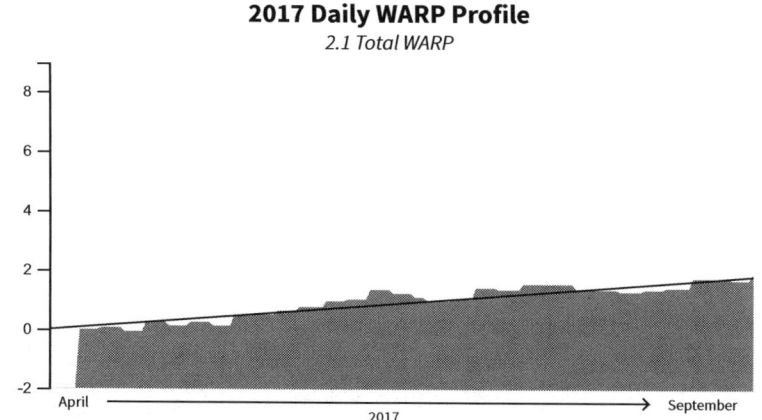

April — 2017 — September

31 PWR	**POWER**	131st of 150
68 STM	**STAMINA**	77th of 150
37 CMD	**COMMAND**	144th of 150

21 Sec/Pit	**PACE**	81st of 150 / 46° / Average

Fantasy Values

2017	2018
$14.02	**$10.00**

YEAR	TEAM	LVL	AGE	W	L	SV	G	GS	IP	H	HR	BB/9	K/9	K	GB%	BABIP	WHIP	ERA	DRA	WARP	MPH 95
2017	NYA	MLB	24	9	7	0	29	29	155.1	140	21	3.0	8.3	144	42%	.275	1.23	3.88	4.36	2.1	93.4

Injuries in the Yankees rotation accelerated Montgomery's timetable, but the tall southpaw held his own in his rookie campaign. The young lefty works off a sweeping curve but effectively mixes in a low-90s fastball and decent change as well. Montgomery's innings were limited last year, but he should have a higher innings cap in 2018. He is a low-end starter in mixed and a $10-12 AL-only arm. — Mike G.

2017 Pitching Percentages

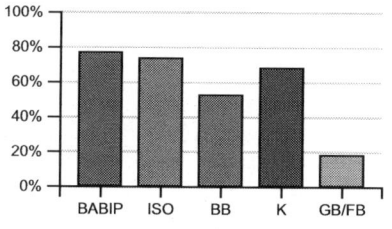

BABIP, ISO, BB, K, GB/FB

Pitching PECOTA Percentiles

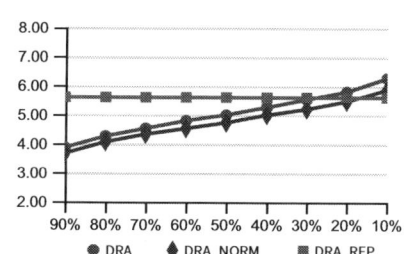

90% 80% 70% 60% 50% 40% 30% 20% 10%
● DRA   ◆ DRA_NORM   ■ DRA_REP

Tunnel vs LHH

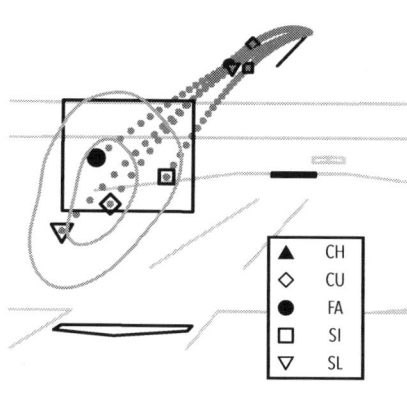

▲	CH
◇	CU
●	FA
□	SI
▽	SL

Pitch Types

Type	Freq	Velo	H Mov	V Mov
CH	19.2%	84.4 [97]	10.1 [106]	-19.8 [121]
CU	26.1%	80.5 [108]	0.7 [67]	-41.5 [114]
FA	17.8%	92.1 [98]	6.1 [105]	-12.5 [109]
SI	24.0%	91.8 [97]	12.8 [98]	-15.7 [116]
SL	12.9%	85.9 [107]	0.5 [77]	-28 [113]

Pitch Tunnel

Pairs	Release Diff	Tunnel Diff	Plate Diff	Speed Changes
1866	22.6	129.3	245.3	0.029

PI Scores

Year	Pitch Ct	Pwr	Cmd	Stm
2017	2512	31	37	68

Tunnel vs RHH

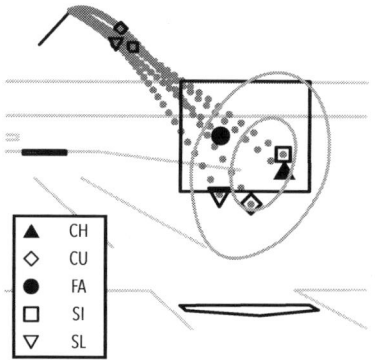

▲	CH
◇	CU
●	FA
□	SI
▽	SL

Mike Montgomery   LHP   Chicago Cubs

Born: 7/1/1989   **Age:** 28   **Bats:** L   **Throws:** L   **Height:** 6'5"   **Weight:** 215 lbs   **Draft Info:** Round 1, 2008 Draft (#36 overall)

We don't have a baseball card for this guy.

2017 Daily WARP Profile
1.6 Total WARP

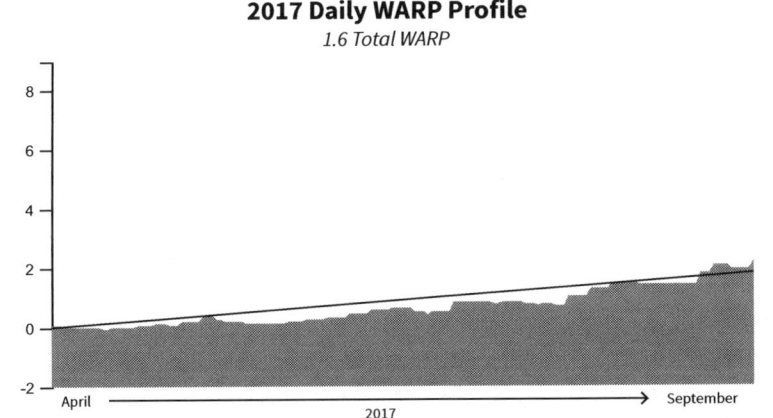

April — 2017 — September

	POWER	
40 PWR	POWER	96th of 150
60 STM	STAMINA	102nd of 150
46 CMD	COMMAND	111th of 150

20 Sec/Pit	PACE	37th of 150 / 75° / Fast

Fantasy Values

2017	2018
$13.63	**$2.00**

YEAR	TEAM	LVL	AGE	W	L	SV	G	GS	IP	H	HR	BB/9	K/9	K	GB%	BABIP	WHIP	ERA	DRA	WARP	MPH 95
2017	CHN	MLB	27	7	8	3	44	14	130.2	103	10	3.8	6.9	100	59%	.253	1.21	3.38	4.29	1.6	94.1

2017 Pitching Percentages

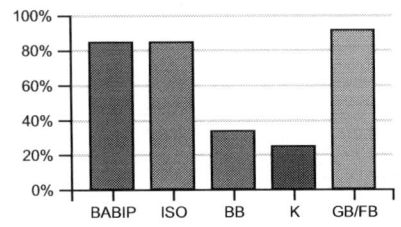

Pitching PECOTA Percentiles

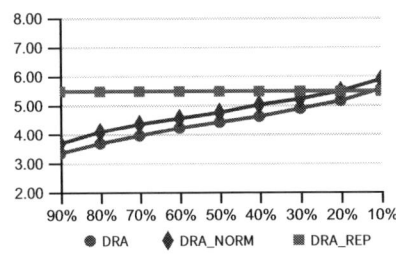

● DRA   ◆ DRA_NORM   ■ DRA_REP

Pitching WARP History

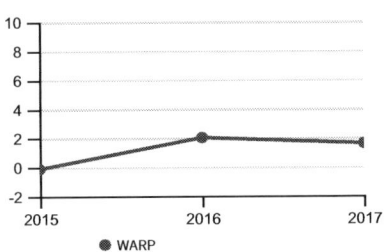

● WARP

Tunnel vs LHH

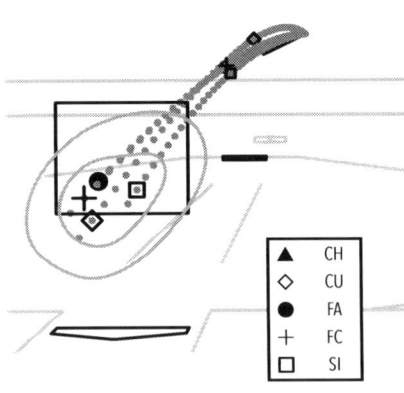

▲	CH
◇	CU
●	FA
+	FC
□	SI

Pitch Types

Type	Freq	Velo	H Mov	V Mov
CH	12.0%	83.6 [94]	16.1 [73]	-30.4 [90]
CU	23.8%	77.5 [97]	-5.9 [93]	-50.6 [94]
FA	22.6%	92.2 [98]	9.5 [89]	-18.5 [89]
FC	11.0%	88.7 [102]	4.6 [69]	-27.1 [87]
SI	30.5%	92.7 [102]	14.4 [86]	-20.1 [100]
SL	0.0%	89.2 [121]	1.5 [73]	-25.6 [120]

Pitch Tunnel

Pairs	Release Diff	Tunnel Diff	Plate Diff	Speed Changes
1480	28.2	130.4	237.3	0.033

PI Scores

Year	Pitch Ct	Pwr	Cmd	Stm
2015	1446	34	45	68
2016	1495	43	37	51
2017	2064	40	46	60

Tunnel vs RHH

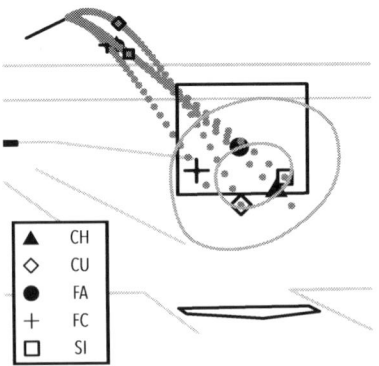

▲	CH
◇	CU
●	FA
+	FC
□	SI

Matt Moore   LHP   Texas Rangers

Born: 6/18/1989   **Age:** 28   **Bats:** L   **Throws:** L   **Height:** 6' 3"   **Weight:** 210 lbs   **Draft Info:** Round 8, 2007 Draft (#245 overall)

2017 Daily WARP Profile
-2.9 Total WARP

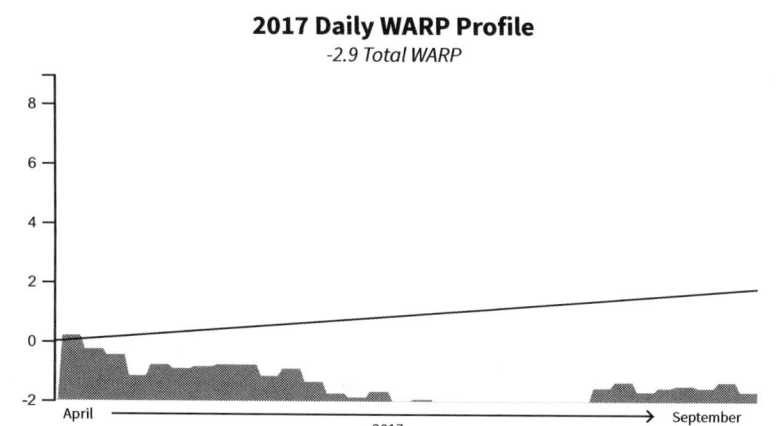

April — 2017 → September

POWER
41 PWR
93rd of 150

STAMINA
77 STM
32nd of 150

COMMAND
44 CMD
121st of 150

PACE
20 Sec/Pit
37th of 150
75°
Fast

Fantasy Values
2017	2018
$-1.06	$5.00

YEAR	TEAM	LVL	AGE	W	L	SV	G	GS	IP	H	HR	BB/9	K/9	K	GB%	BABIP	WHIP	ERA	DRA	WARP	MPH 95
2017	SFN	MLB	28	6	15	0	32	31	174.1	200	27	3.5	7.6	148	39%	.320	1.53	5.52	7.06	-2.9	93.6

2017 Pitching Percentages

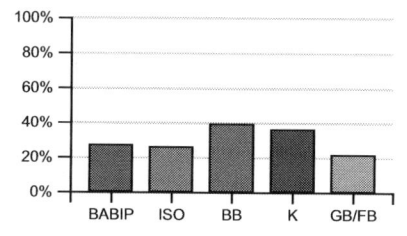

Pitching PECOTA Percentiles

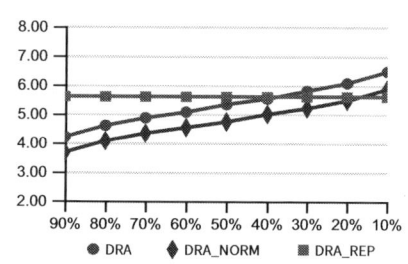

● DRA   ◆ DRA_NORM   ■ DRA_REP

Pitching WARP History

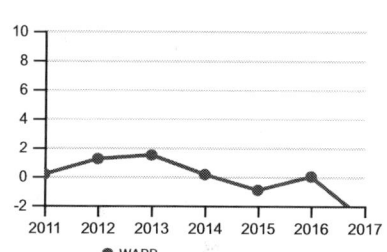

● WARP

Tunnel vs LHH

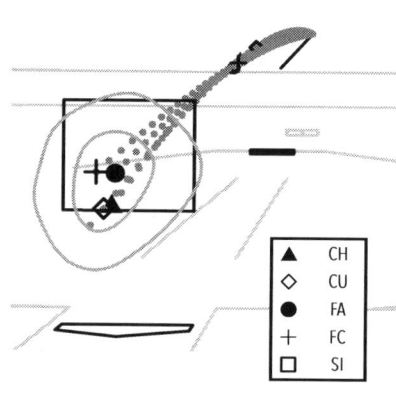

▲	CH
◇	CU
●	FA
+	FC
□	SI

Pitch Types

Type	Freq	Velo	H Mov	V Mov
CH	15.8%	83.5 [94]	13 [90]	-29.8 [92]
CU	17.8%	81.5 [112]	-5.2 [90]	-42.7 [111]
FA	47.7%	92.4 [99]	11.2 [81]	-15.2 [100]
FC	14.5%	89.4 [105]	2.1 [81]	-19.3 [118]
SI	4.1%	91.3 [94]	12.7 [98]	-17.5 [109]

Pitch Tunnel

Pairs	Release Diff	Tunnel Diff	Plate Diff	Speed Changes
1991	28.4	126.2	228.9	0.024

PI Scores

Year	Pitch Ct	Pwr	Cmd	Stm
2012	3007	63	35	72
2013	2617	52	30	64
2015	1053	44	47	56
2016	3279	49	42	81
2017	2862	41	44	77

Tunnel vs RHH

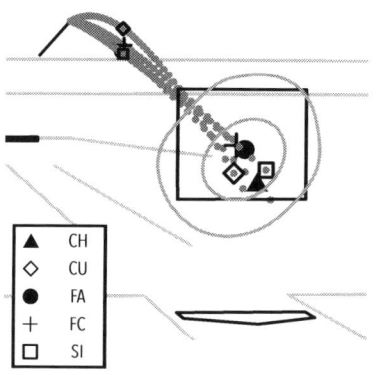

▲	CH
◇	CU
●	FA
+	FC
□	SI

Logan Morrison   1B   Tampa Bay Rays

Born: 8/25/1987   **Age:** 30   **Bats:** L   **Throws:** L   **Height:** 6' 3"   **Weight:** 245 lbs   **Draft Info:** Round 22, 2005 Draft (#666 overall)

25 Sec/Pit

PACE
151st of 155
3°
Very Slow

2017 Daily WARP Profile
2.8 Total WARP

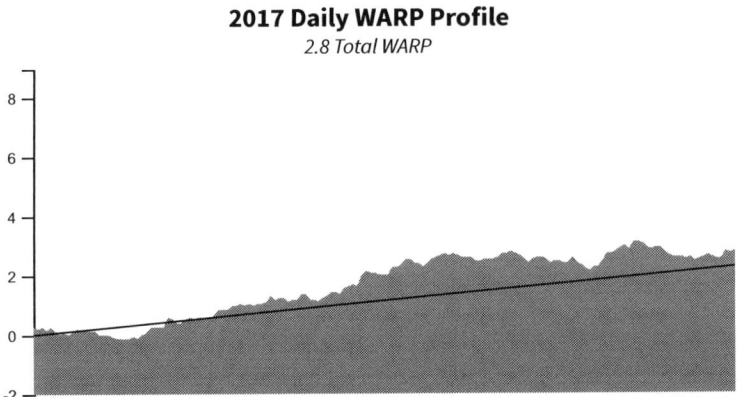

April ——————————————→ September
2017

Fantasy Values
2017	2018
$17.39	$14.00

YEAR	TEAM	LVL	AGE	PA	R	2B	3B	HR	RBI	BB	K	SB	AVG/OBP/SLG	TAv	VORP	BABIP	WARP
2017	TBA	MLB	29	601	75	22	1	38	85	81	149	2	.246/.353/.516	.294	28.3	.268	2.8

2017 Batting Percentages

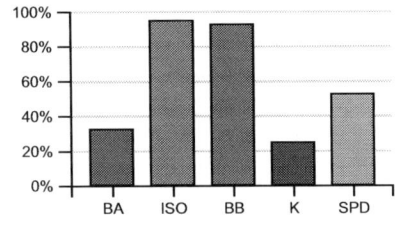

Batting PECOTA Percentiles

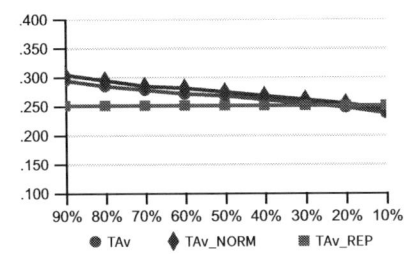

Batting WARP History

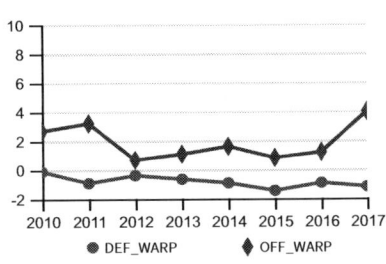

BRR (Relative to Position)

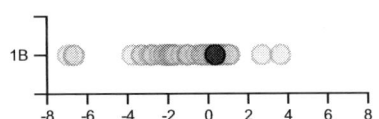

BRR (Relative to Team)

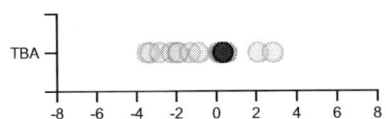

Base Running Components

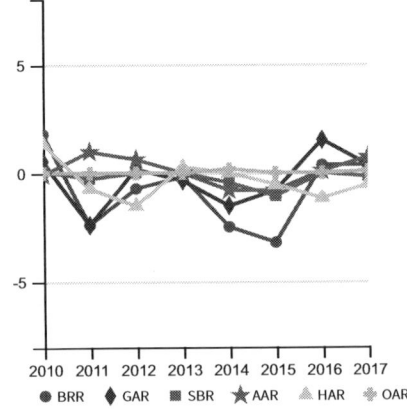

Rank		Player	BRR
9	82°	Tomas Telis	0.55
10	82°	Tyler White	0.43
11	79°	**Logan Morrison**	**0.39**
12	78°	Jesus Aguilar	0.39
13	78°	Dominic Smith	0.35

Rank		Player	BRR
3	88°	Ryan Schimpf	0.57
4	87°	Colby Rasmus	0.55
5	79°	**Logan Morrison**	**0.39**
6	77°	Rickie Weeks	0.31
7	73°	Peter Bourjos	0.30

Charlie Morton   RHP   Houston Astros

Born: 11/12/1983   **Age:** 34   **Bats:** R   **Throws:** R   **Height:** 6' 5"   **Weight:** 235 lbs   **Draft Info:** Round 3, 2002 Draft (#95 overall)

2017 Daily WARP Profile
3.4 Total WARP

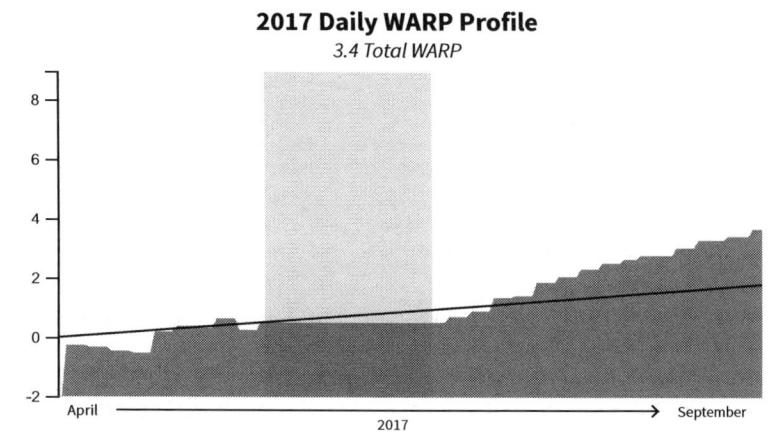

2017

April → September

Game 48: DL (lat strain)

	POWER
58 PWR	32nd of 150

	STAMINA
66 STM	84th of 150

	COMMAND
42 CMD	128th of 150

	PACE
21 Sec/Pit	81st of 150 46° Average

Fantasy Values
2017	2018
$19.30	**$14.00**

YEAR	TEAM	LVL	AGE	W	L	SV	G	GS	IP	H	HR	BB/9	K/9	K	GB%	BABIP	WHIP	ERA	DRA	WARP	MPH 95
2017	HOU	MLB	33	14	7	0	25	25	146.2	125	14	3.1	10.0	163	53%	.295	1.19	3.62	3.46	3.4	96.6

Morton showed signs of turning the corner with the Phillies in 2016, but a season-ending hamstring injury in April masked any progress he made. Morton was healthy enough for long enough last year to show that the gains he made on his fastball were legitimate. He didn't reach 150 innings, but when he was on the mound he looked like a dominant pitcher, striking out more than a batter per nine and putting up the best year of his career. The health and durability risk remain, but there is no reason to doubt that Morton's velocity and stuff will continue to play up in 2018 and beyond. — Mike G.

2017 Pitching Percentages

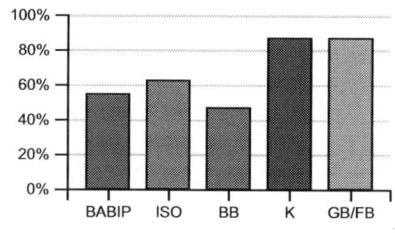

Pitching PECOTA Percentiles

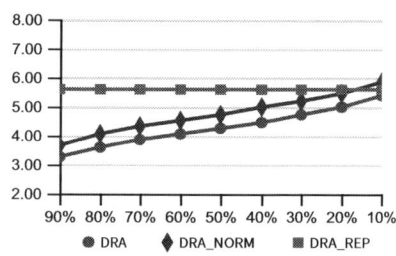

● DRA   ◆ DRA_NORM   ■ DRA_REP

Pitching WARP History

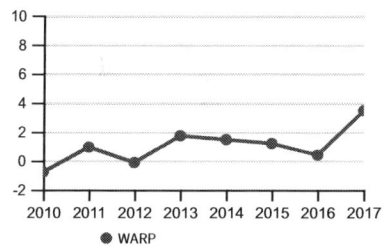

● WARP

Tunnel vs LHH

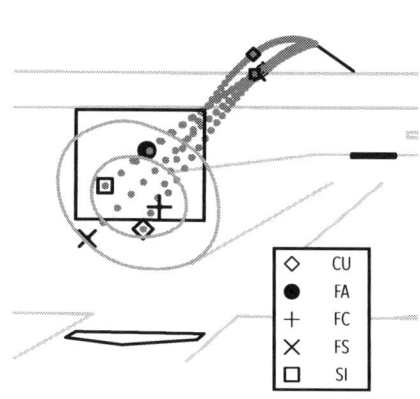

◇ CU
● FA
+ FC
✕ FS
□ SI

Pitch Types

Type	Freq	Velo	H Mov	V Mov
CH	0.2%	86.5 [106]	-15.2 [78]	-27.8 [98]
CU	28.2%	80.9 [110]	14.2 [125]	-47.1 [102]
FA	12.4%	96 [112]	-12.6 [75]	-15.6 [99]
FC	11.3%	88.5 [100]	2.4 [104]	-27.5 [86]
FS	6.0%	86.9 [110]	-16.1 [70]	-31 [97]
SI	41.9%	95.2 [117]	-15.4 [79]	-22.1 [92]

Pitch Tunnel

Pairs	Release Diff	Tunnel Diff	Plate Diff	Speed Changes
1733	25.0	117.8	217.9	0.033

PI Scores

Year	Pitch Ct	Pwr	Cmd	Stm
2013	1707	55	52	63
2014	2476	45	43	66
2015	1970	46	59	66
2016	276	52	53	37
2017	2340	58	42	66

Tunnel vs RHH

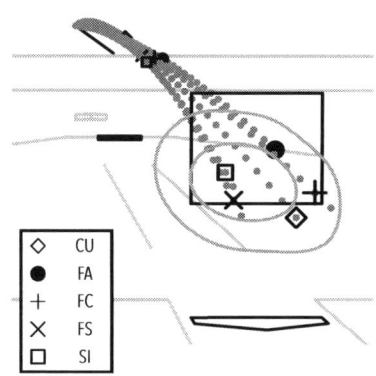

◇ CU
● FA
+ FC
✕ FS
□ SI

Mike Moustakas   3B   Kansas City Royals

Born: 9/11/1988   **Age:** 29   **Bats:** L   **Throws:** R   **Height:** 6' 0"   **Weight:** 215 lbs   **Draft Info:** Round 1, 2007 Draft (#2 overall)

2017 Daily WARP Profile
1.9 Total WARP

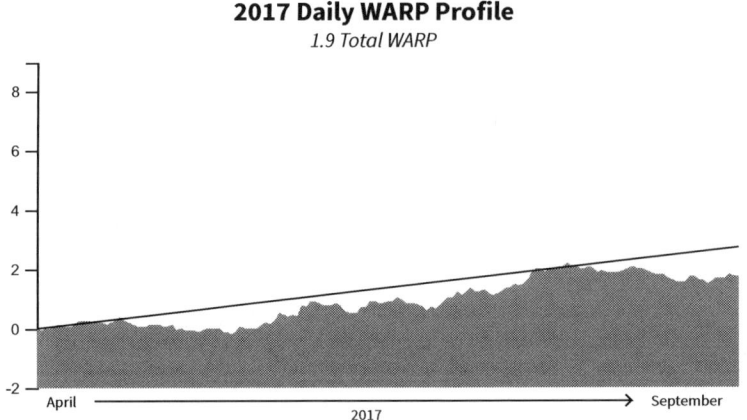

PACE
20 Sec/Pit
18th of 155
88°
Very Fast

Fantasy Values	
2017	*2018*
$20.04	**$18.00**

YEAR	TEAM	LVL	AGE	PA	R	2B	3B	HR	RBI	BB	K	SB	AVG/OBP/SLG	TAv	VORP	BABIP	WARP
2017	KCA	MLB	28	598	75	24	0	38	85	34	94	0	.272/.314/.521	.275	26.3	.263	1.9

2017 Batting Percentages

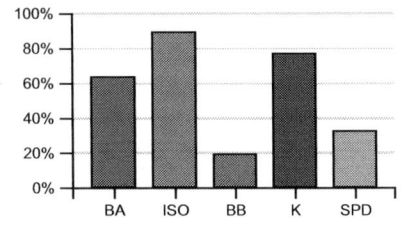

Batting PECOTA Percentiles

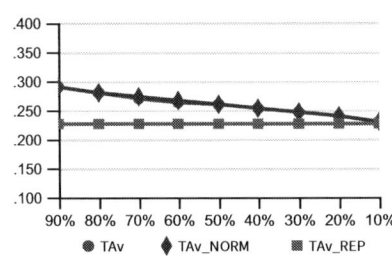

Batting WARP History

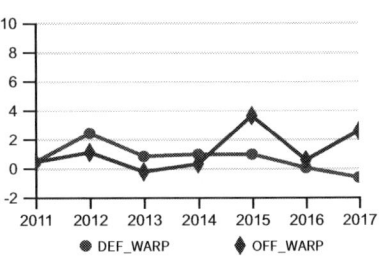

BRR (Relative to Position)

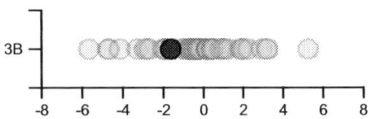

Rank		Player	BRR
43	29°	Alex Bregman	-1.52
44	28°	Jhonny Peralta	-1.53
45	26°	**Mike Moustakas**	**-1.59**
46	23°	Maikel Franco	-1.82
47	20°	Evan Longoria	-1.90

BRR (Relative to Team)

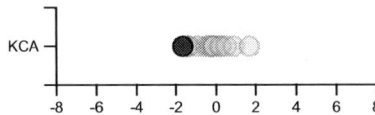

Rank		Player	BRR
13	26°	Eric Hosmer	-1.31
14	21°	Salvador Perez	-1.33
15	20°	Raul Mondesi	-1.41
16	11°	**Mike Moustakas**	**-1.59**
17	0°	Melky Cabrera	-1.60

Base Running Components

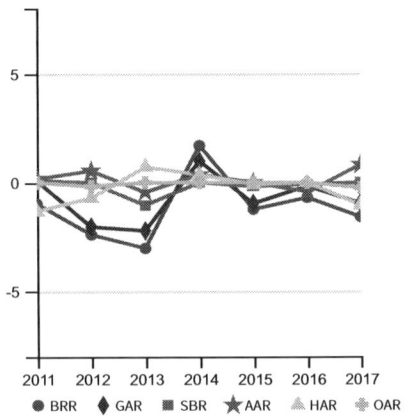

Peter Moylan   RHP   Kansas City Royals

Born: 12/2/1978   **Age:** 39   **Bats:** R   **Throws:** R   **Height:** 6' 2"   **Weight:** 225 lbs   **Draft Info:** International Free Agent, 1996

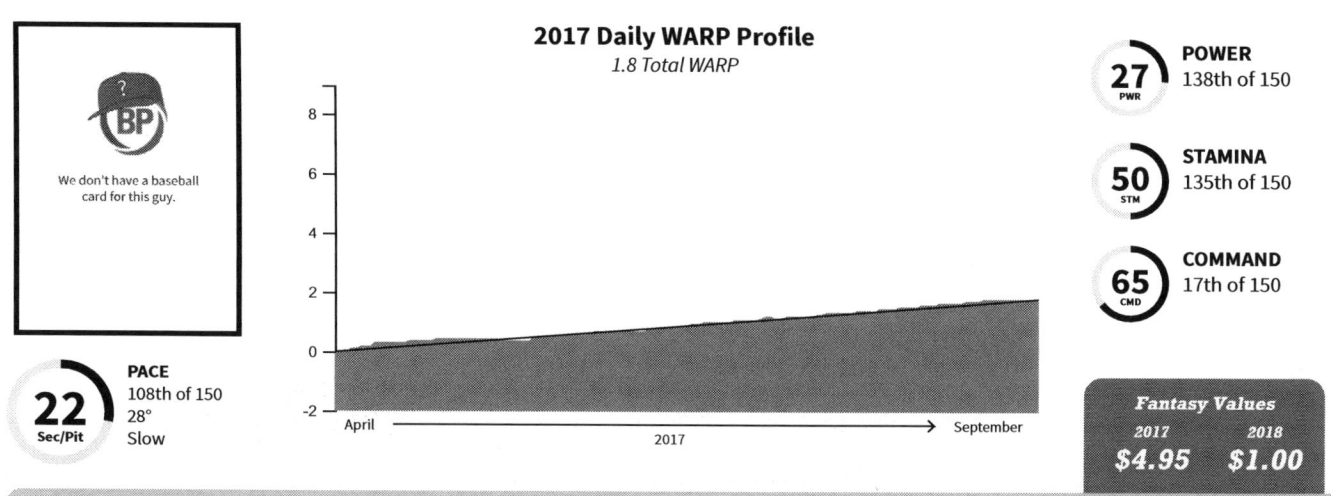

We don't have a baseball card for this guy.

2017 Daily WARP Profile
1.8 Total WARP

PACE
22 Sec/Pit
108th of 150
28°
Slow

POWER
27 PWR
138th of 150

STAMINA
50 STM
135th of 150

COMMAND
65 CMD
17th of 150

Fantasy Values
2017	2018
$4.95	$1.00

YEAR	TEAM	LVL	AGE	W	L	SV	G	GS	IP	H	HR	BB/9	K/9	K	GB%	BABIP	WHIP	ERA	DRA	WARP	MPH 95
2017	KCA	MLB	38	0	0	0	79	0	59.1	40	4	3.8	7.0	46	62%	.221	1.10	3.49	2.52	1.8	91.8

2017 Pitching Percentages

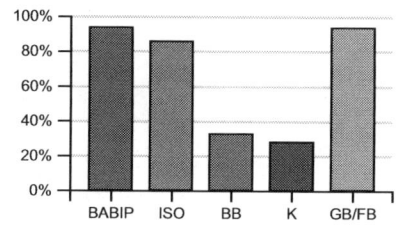

Pitching PECOTA Percentiles

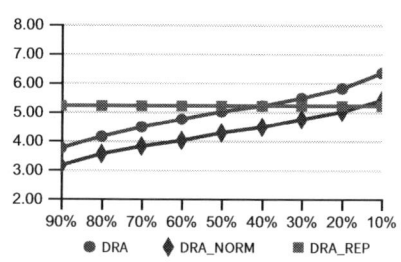

● DRA   ◆ DRA_NORM   ■ DRA_REP

Pitching WARP History

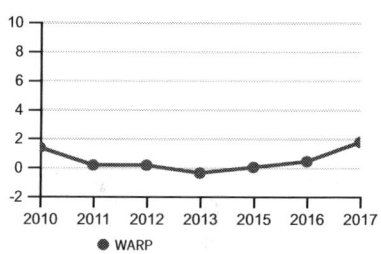

● WARP

Tunnel vs LHH

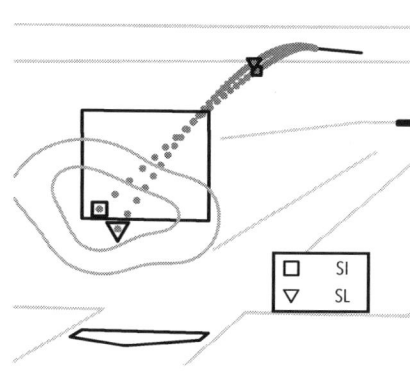

□ SI
▽ SL

Pitch Types

Type	Freq	Velo	H Mov	V Mov
CH	2.9%	84.8 [99]	-11.9 [96]	-37.6 [70]
SI	49.9%	90.7 [91]	-15.6 [77]	-33.8 [49]
SL	47.2%	79.2 [77]	7.7 [114]	-39.6 [80]

Pitch Tunnel

Pairs	Release Diff	Tunnel Diff	Plate Diff	Speed Changes
668	35.3	113.3	206.2	0.029

PI Scores

Year	Pitch Ct	Pwr	Cmd	Stm
2010	1024	44	49	54
2013	243	36	54	42
2016	668	36	50	45
2017	906	27	65	50

Tunnel vs RHH

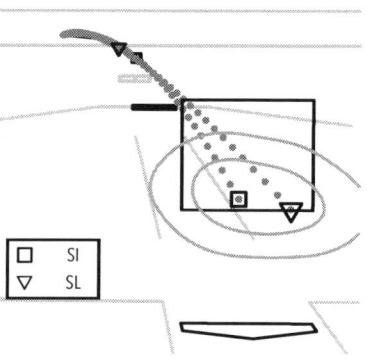

□ SI
▽ SL

Daniel Murphy   2B   Washington Nationals

Born: 4/1/1985   **Age:** 33   **Bats:** L   **Throws:** R   **Height:** 6'1"   **Weight:** 220 lbs   **Draft Info:** Round 13, 2006 Draft (#394 overall)

2017 Daily WARP Profile
5.6 Total WARP

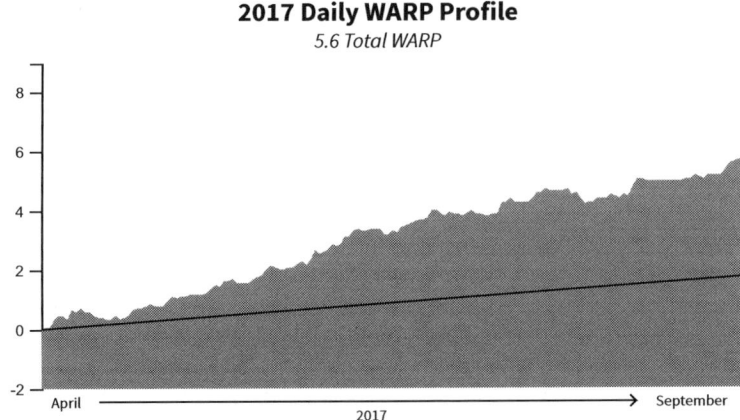

22 Sec/Pit

PACE
99th of 155
36°
Slow

Fantasy Values
2017	2018
$26.47	$24.00

YEAR	TEAM	LVL	AGE	PA	R	2B	3B	HR	RBI	BB	K	SB	AVG/OBP/SLG	TAv	VORP	BABIP	WARP
2017	WAS	MLB	32	593	94	43	3	23	93	52	77	2	.322/.384/.543	.314	51.6	.341	5.6

Year Two of Murphy's Nationals' contract wasn't quite as dominant as his first, but the raw numbers barely budged from what he did in 2016. In an era where so many players hit home runs Murphy's value comes primarily from his batting average. It did slip, but a 25-point drop hardly matters when you hit .322. A knee injury limited Murph in the second half, but he should be ready for Opening Day with no limitations. — Mike G.

2017 Batting Percentages

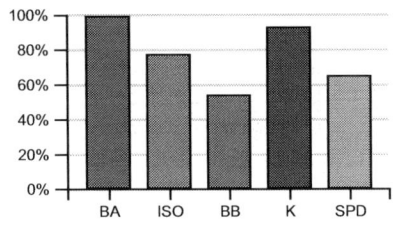

Batting PECOTA Percentiles

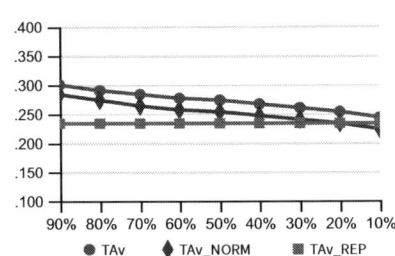

Batting WARP History

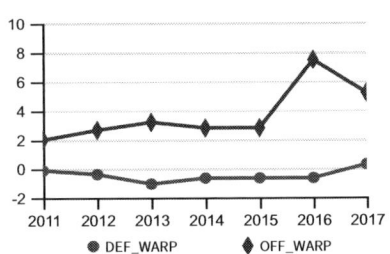

BRR (Relative to Position)

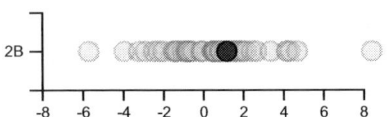

Rank		Player	BRR
17	54°	Ronald Torreyes	1.30
18	54°	Devon Travis	1.23
19	51°	**Daniel Murphy**	**1.22**
20	50°	Tyler Saladino	1.11
21	49°	Kaleb Cowart	0.91

BRR (Relative to Team)

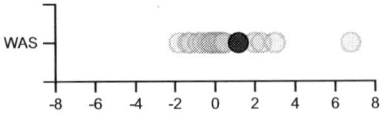

Rank		Player	BRR
3	77°	Wilmer Difo	2.38
4	65°	Anthony Rendon	2.04
5	57°	**Daniel Murphy**	**1.22**
6	56°	Andrew Stevenson	0.49
7	55°	Chris Heisey	0.44

Base Running Components

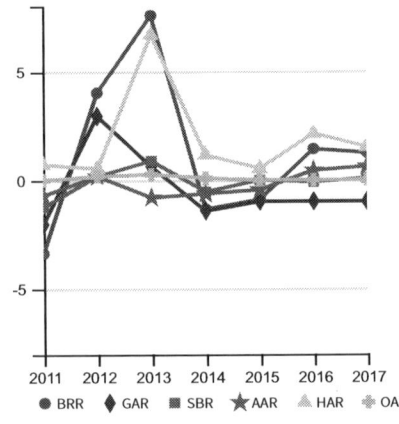

Wil Myers 1B San Diego Padres

🗑

Born: 12/10/1990 **Age:** 27 **Bats:** R **Throws:** R **Height:** 6' 3" **Weight:** 205 lbs **Draft Info:** Round 3, 2009 Draft (#91 overall)

2017 Daily WARP Profile
2.7 Total WARP

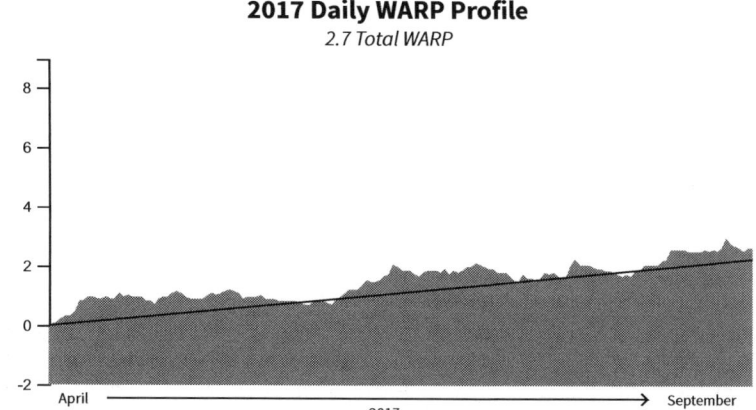

21 Sec/Pit

PACE
45th of 155
71°
Fast

Fantasy Values
2017	2018
$21.50	$25.00

YEAR	TEAM	LVL	AGE	PA	R	2B	3B	HR	RBI	BB	K	SB	AVG/OBP/SLG	TAv	VORP	BABIP	WARP
2017	SDN	MLB	26	649	80	29	3	30	74	70	180	20	.243/.328/.464	.290	28.6	.297	2.7

Myers was one of the quietest 30/20 hitters in fantasy history. The subpar batting average is part of this, but all the top-tier first basemen who are currently available likely play a factor as well. For all the concerns about Myers over the years (health, maintaining the steals, he's not Trea Turner), he has now had two consecutive seasons as a 20/20 player. When the elite first basemen are off the board, Myers should be nabbed for his all-around contributions. — Mike G.

2017 Batting Percentages

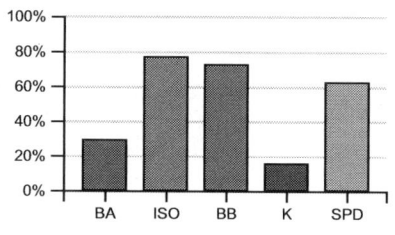

Batting PECOTA Percentiles

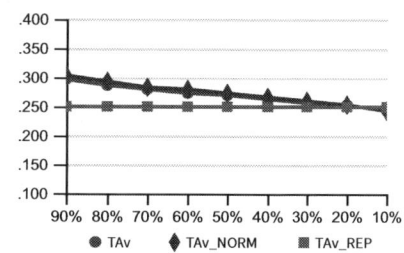

Batting WARP History

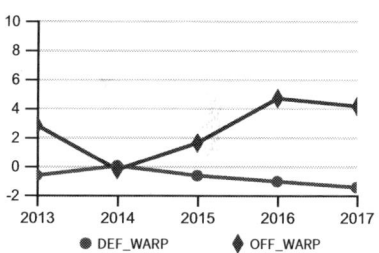

BRR (Relative to Position)

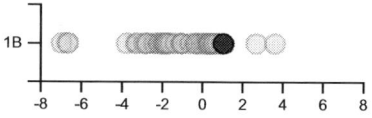

Rank		Player	BRR
2	94°	Freddie Freeman	2.72
3	93°	Kennys Vargas	1.12
4	89°	**Wil Myers**	**1.08**
5	89°	Ryder Jones	1.00
6	86°	Jose Abreu	0.78

BRR (Relative to Team)

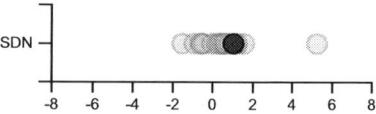

Rank		Player	BRR
4	73°	Franchy Cordero	1.24
5	71°	Luis Torrens	1.14
6	59°	**Wil Myers**	**1.08**
7	57°	Travis Jankowski	0.88
8	56°	Rafael Lopez	0.70

Base Running Components

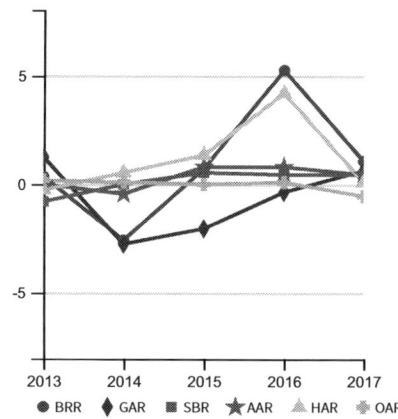

Jimmy Nelson RHP Milwaukee Brewers

Born: 6/5/1989 **Age:** 29 **Bats:** R **Throws:** R **Height:** 6' 6" **Weight:** 250 lbs **Draft Info:** Round 2, 2010 Draft (#64 overall)

PACE
22 108th of 150
Sec/Pit 28°
Slow

2017 Daily WARP Profile
3.9 Total WARP

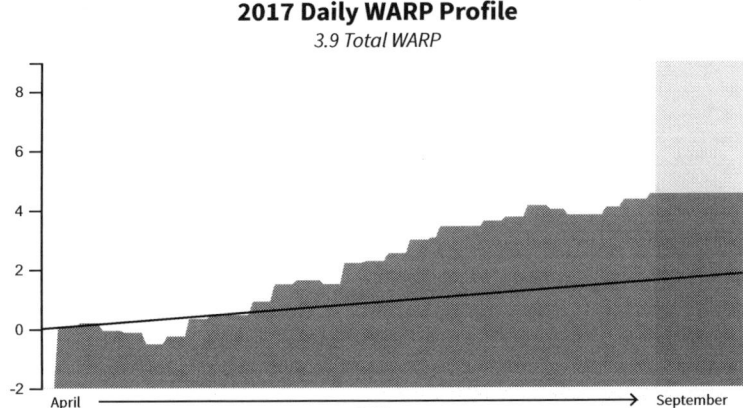

April ——————————— September
2017

Game 142: DL (shoulder impingement)

POWER
56 38th of 150
PWR

STAMINA
76 36th of 150
STM

COMMAND
47 102nd of 150
CMD

Fantasy Values
2017	2018
$20.40	**$5.00**

YEAR	TEAM	LVL	AGE	W	L	SV	G	GS	IP	H	HR	BB/9	K/9	K	GB%	BABIP	WHIP	ERA	DRA	WARP	MPH 95
2017	MIL	MLB	28	12	6	0	29	29	175.1	171	16	2.5	10.2	199	51%	.340	1.25	3.49	3.58	3.9	95.5

2017 Pitching Percentages

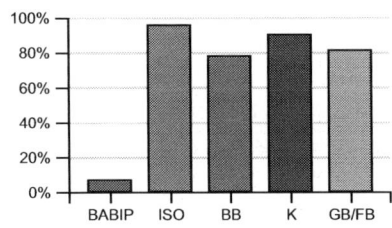

Pitching PECOTA Percentiles

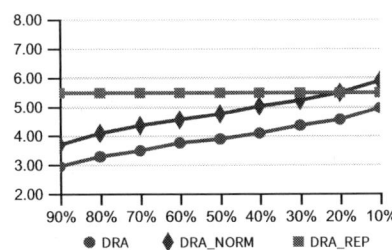

● DRA ◆ DRA_NORM ■ DRA_REP

Pitching WARP History

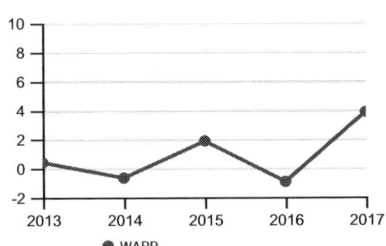

● WARP

Tunnel vs LHH

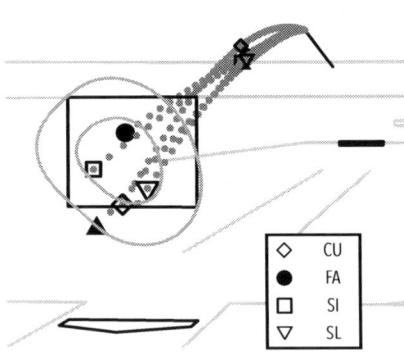

◇	CU
●	FA
□	SI
▽	SL

Pitch Types

Type	Freq	Velo	H Mov	V Mov
CH	2.4%	88.1 [112]	-7 [122]	-30 [92]
CU	20.1%	84.8 [125]	10 [109]	-39.2 [119]
FA	26.1%	94.6 [107]	-6.4 [103]	-13.6 [105]
SI	35.1%	94.3 [111]	-12.4 [101]	-21.3 [95]
SL	16.2%	88.9 [120]	5.5 [104]	-27.3 [115]

Pitch Tunnel

Pairs	Release Diff	Tunnel Diff	Plate Diff	Speed Changes
2021	32.6	116.1	218.9	0.019

PI Scores

Year	Pitch Ct	Pwr	Cmd	Stm
2014	1108	64	39	70
2015	2780	54	39	73
2016	2967	59	30	78
2017	2750	56	47	76

Tunnel vs RHH

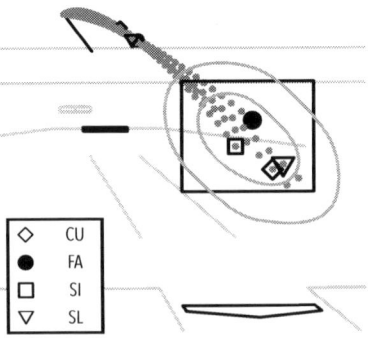

◇	CU
●	FA
□	SI
▽	SL

Pat Neshek RHP Philadelphia Phillies

Born: 9/4/1980   **Age:** 37   **Bats:** B   **Throws:** R   **Height:** 6' 3"   **Weight:** 220 lbs   **Draft Info:** Round 6, 2002 Draft (#182 overall)

PACE
20 Sec/Pit
37th of 150
75°
Fast

2017 Daily WARP Profile
1.8 Total WARP

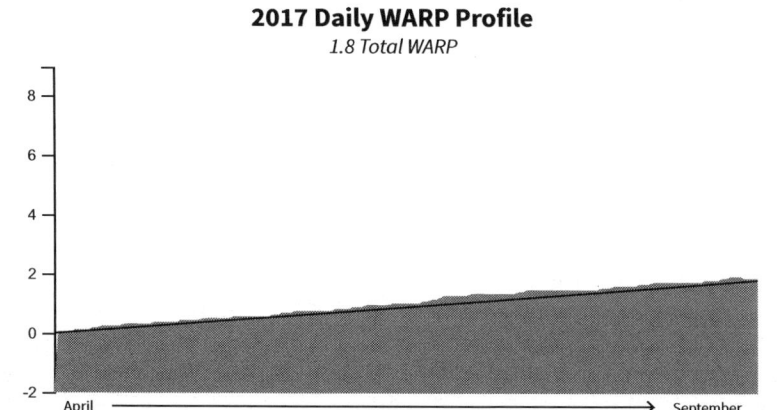

POWER
29 PWR
135th of 150

STAMINA
49 STM
138th of 150

COMMAND
76 CMD
4th of 150

Fantasy Values
2017	2018
$14.71	**$2.00**

YEAR	TEAM	LVL	AGE	W	L	SV	G	GS	IP	H	HR	BB/9	K/9	K	GB%	BABIP	WHIP	ERA	DRA	WARP	MPH 95
2017	PHI	MLB	36	3	2	1	43	0	40.1	28	2	1.1	10.0	45	37%	.271	0.82	1.12	2.39	1.2	92.3
2017	COL	MLB	36	2	1	0	28	0	22	20	1	0.4	9.8	24	36%	.311	0.95	2.45	2.72	0.6	92.2

2017 Pitching Percentages

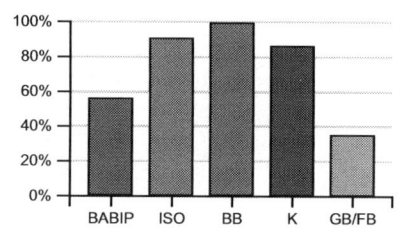

Pitching PECOTA Percentiles

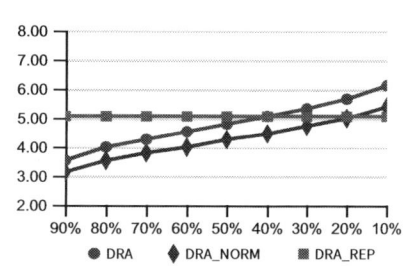

Pitching WARP History

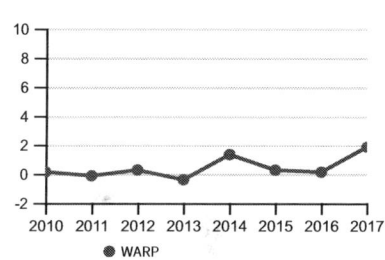

Tunnel vs LHH

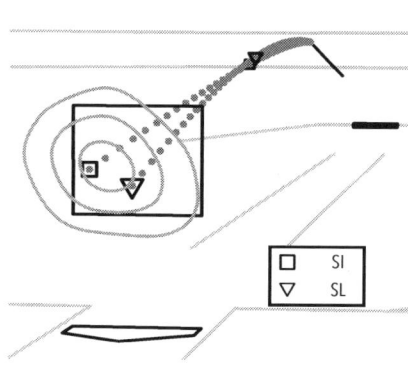

Pitch Types

Type	Freq	Velo	H Mov	V Mov
CH	2.6%	68.1 [32]	-7.3 [121]	-46.4 [45]
SI	45.4%	90.4 [89]	-13.4 [94]	-22.1 [92]
SL	52.1%	83.7 [97]	1.9 [88]	-31.7 [103]

Pitch Tunnel

Pairs	Release Diff	Tunnel Diff	Plate Diff	Speed Changes
701	49.4	101.2	178.8	0.026

PI Scores

Year	Pitch Ct	Pwr	Cmd	Stm
2013	661	9	32	34
2014	973	38	63	49
2015	845	37	61	46
2016	681	29	52	41
2017	939	29	76	49

Tunnel vs RHH

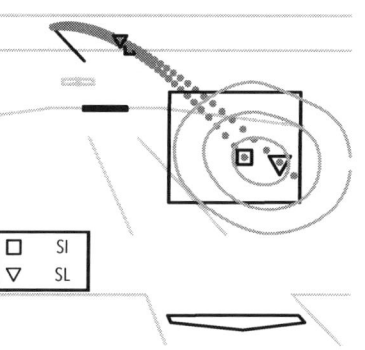

Sean Newcomb LHP Atlanta Braves

Born: 6/12/1993 **Age:** 24 **Bats:** L **Throws:** L **Height:** 6' 5" **Weight:** 255 lbs **Draft Info:** Round 1, 2014 Draft (#15 overall)

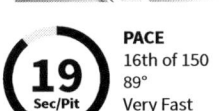

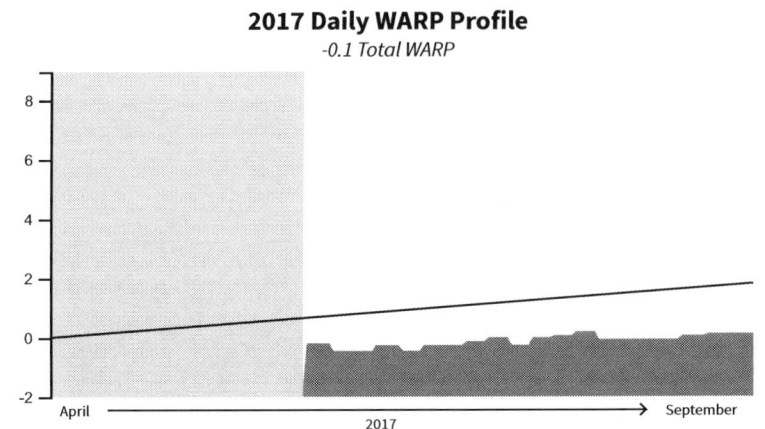

2017 Daily WARP Profile
-0.1 Total WARP

Game 1: minors

POWER
54 PWR 45th of 150

STAMINA
73 STM 53rd of 150

COMMAND
44 CMD 121st of 150

PACE
19 Sec/Pit 16th of 150
89°
Very Fast

Fantasy Values

2017	2018
$3.07	$6.00

YEAR	TEAM	LVL	AGE	W	L	SV	G	GS	IP	H	HR	BB/9	K/9	K	GB%	BABIP	WHIP	ERA	DRA	WARP	MPH 95
2017	ATL	MLB	24	4	9	0	19	19	100	100	10	5.1	9.7	108	46%	.327	1.57	4.32	5.66	-0.1	96.2

2017 Pitching Percentages

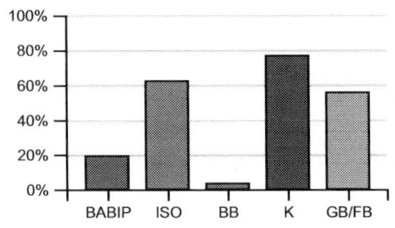

Pitching PECOTA Percentiles

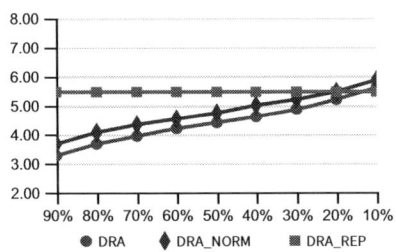

Tunnel vs LHH

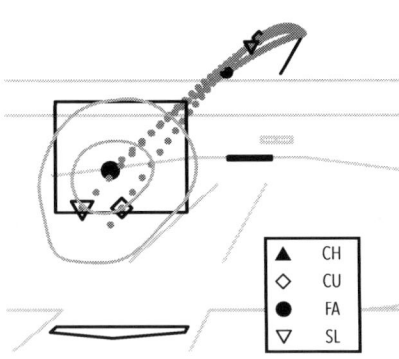

	CH
△	CH
◇	CU
●	FA
▽	SL

Pitch Types

Type	Freq	Velo	H Mov	V Mov
CH	10.6%	86.4 [105]	13 [90]	-23.7 [110]
CU	21.8%	78.8 [102]	-7 [97]	-51.8 [92]
FA	63.4%	94.2 [105]	8.2 [95]	-11.9 [110]
SL	4.2%	81.2 [86]	-11.3 [129]	-41 [76]

Pitch Tunnel

Pairs	Release Diff	Tunnel Diff	Plate Diff	Speed Changes
1309	26.9	132.0	236.3	0.037

PI Scores

Year	Pitch Ct	Pwr	Cmd	Stm
2017	1831	54	44	73

Tunnel vs RHH

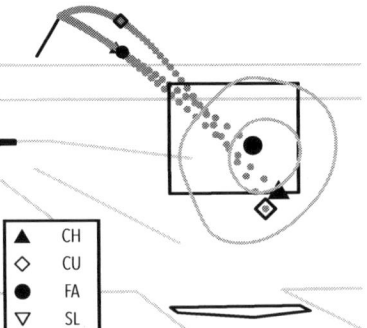

△	CH
◇	CU
●	FA
▽	SL

Aaron Nola   RHP   Philadelphia Phillies

Born: 6/4/1993   **Age:** 25   **Bats:** R   **Throws:** R   **Height:** 6'2"   **Weight:** 195 lbs   **Draft Info:** Round 1, 2014 Draft (#7 overall)

2017 Daily WARP Profile
5.5 Total WARP

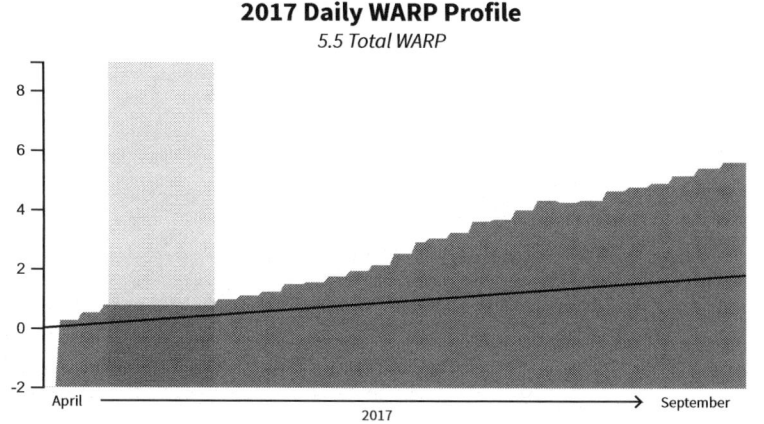

April ← 2017 → September

Game 16: DL (back strain)

PACE
21 Sec/Pit
81st of 150
46°
Average

POWER
37 PWR
110th of 150

STAMINA
74 STM
44th of 150

COMMAND
64 CMD
18th of 150

Fantasy Values
2017	2018
$20.25	$16.00

YEAR	TEAM	LVL	AGE	W	L	SV	G	GS	IP	H	HR	BB/9	K/9	K	GB%	BABIP	WHIP	ERA	DRA	WARP	MPH 95
2017	PHI	MLB	24	12	11	0	27	27	168	154	18	2.6	9.9	184	50%	.309	1.21	3.54	2.64	5.5	94.1

For the second consecutive season, Nola posted a sub-3.00 DRA, but in 2017 the fantasy results came much closer to matching sabermetric ones. Nola thrives off a knee-buckling curve he uses to set up his other offerings, particularly a fastball/sinker combination that keep hitters off balance. Citizens Bank Park doesn't do pitchers any favors, but Nola's stuff is good enough that he should continue to improve and once again inch closer to ace status. — Mike G.

2017 Pitching Percentages

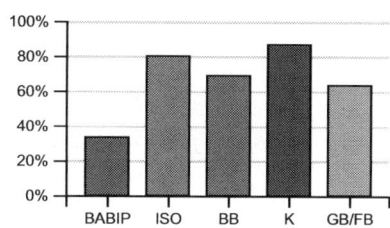

Pitching PECOTA Percentiles

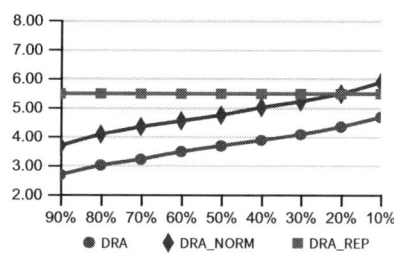

● DRA   ◆ DRA_NORM   ■ DRA_REP

Pitching WARP History

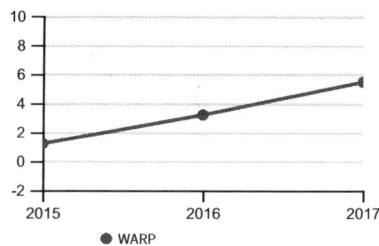

● WARP

Tunnel vs LHH

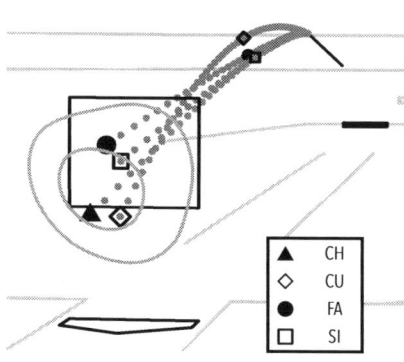

▲ CH
◇ CU
● FA
□ SI

Pitch Types

Type	Freq	Velo	H Mov	V Mov
CH	15.9%	84.2 [96]	-12.4 [93]	-33.7 [81]
CU	30.8%	77.7 [98]	15.8 [131]	-50.7 [94]
FA	27.9%	92.7 [100]	-10.2 [86]	-17.5 [93]
SI	25.4%	91.8 [97]	-13.6 [92]	-22.4 [91]

Pitch Tunnel

Pairs	Release Diff	Tunnel Diff	Plate Diff	Speed Changes
1995	29.3	116.3	206.6	0.037

PI Scores

Year	Pitch Ct	Pwr	Cmd	Stm
2015	1111	39	62	71
2016	1786	36	67	60
2017	2661	37	64	74

Tunnel vs RHH

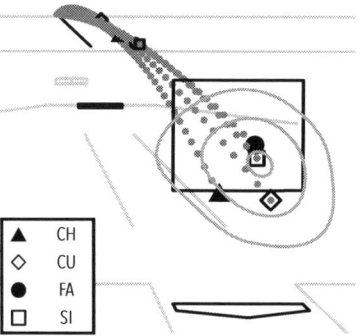

▲ CH
◇ CU
● FA
□ SI

Ricky Nolasco   RHP   Los Angeles Angels

Born: 12/13/1982   **Age:** 35   **Bats:** R   **Throws:** R   **Height:** 6' 2"   **Weight:** 235 lbs   **Draft Info:** Round 4, 2001 Draft (#108 overall)

2017 Daily WARP Profile
-0.9 Total WARP

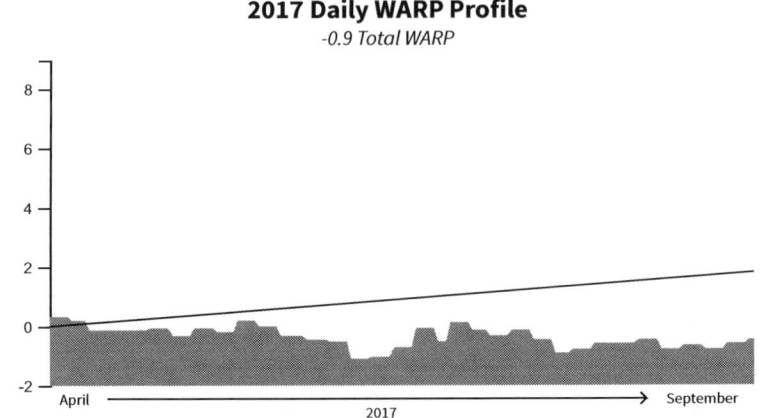

POWER
31 131st of 150
PWR

STAMINA
78 25th of 150
STM

COMMAND
53 72nd of 150
CMD

PACE
21 81st of 150
Sec/Pit 46°
Average

Fantasy Values
2017	2018
$2.42	$2.00

YEAR	TEAM	LVL	AGE	W	L	SV	G	GS	IP	H	HR	BB/9	K/9	K	GB%	BABIP	WHIP	ERA	DRA	WARP	MPH 95
2017	ANA	MLB	34	6	15	0	33	33	181	205	35	2.9	7.1	143	41%	.311	1.45	4.92	6.00	-0.9	92.8

2017 Pitching Percentages

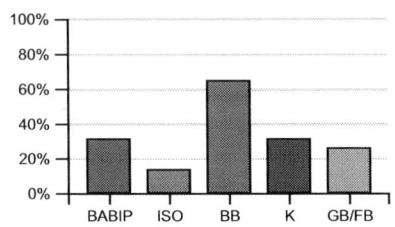

Pitching PECOTA Percentiles

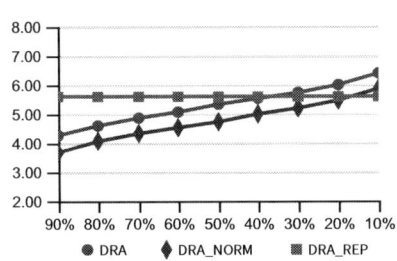

● DRA   ◆ DRA_NORM   ■ DRA_REP

Pitching WARP History

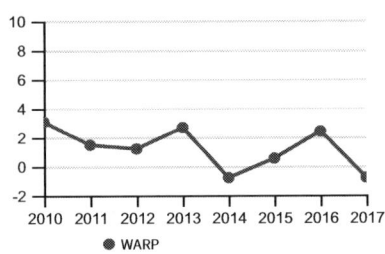

● WARP

Tunnel vs LHH

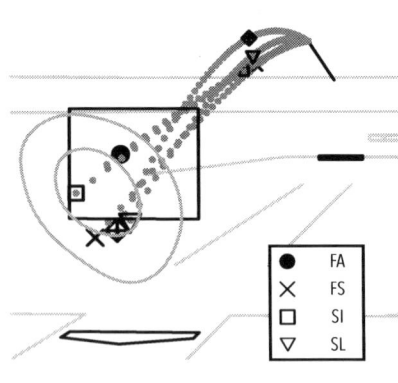

● FA
✕ FS
□ SI
▽ SL

Pitch Types

Type	Freq	Velo	H Mov	V Mov
CS	9.2%	73.9 [114]	14 [113]	-57.7 [116]
FA	20.3%	91.3 [95]	-6.7 [102]	-15.4 [99]
FS	14.9%	81.1 [79]	-9.4 [95]	-33.6 [88]
SI	28.2%	91.1 [93]	-13.3 [94]	-21.1 [96]
SL	27.5%	81.3 [86]	4.6 [100]	-39.8 [80]

Pitch Tunnel

Pairs	Release Diff	Tunnel Diff	Plate Diff	Speed Changes
2211	36.1	123.1	224.5	0.034

PI Scores

Year	Pitch Ct	Pwr	Cmd	Stm
2013	3174	30	47	79
2014	2635	33	52	67
2015	657	34	47	0
2016	3125	35	50	80
2017	3056	31	53	78

Tunnel vs RHH

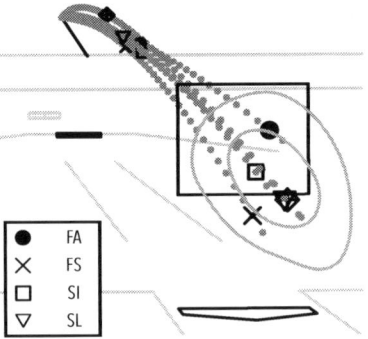

● FA
✕ FS
□ SI
▽ SL

Ivan Nova   RHP   Pittsburgh Pirates

Born: 1/12/1987   **Age:** 31   **Bats:** R   **Throws:** R   **Height:** 6' 5"   **Weight:** 245 lbs   **Draft Info:** International Free Agent, 2004

PACE
20
Sec/Pit
37th of 150
75°
Fast

2017 Daily WARP Profile
0.5 Total WARP

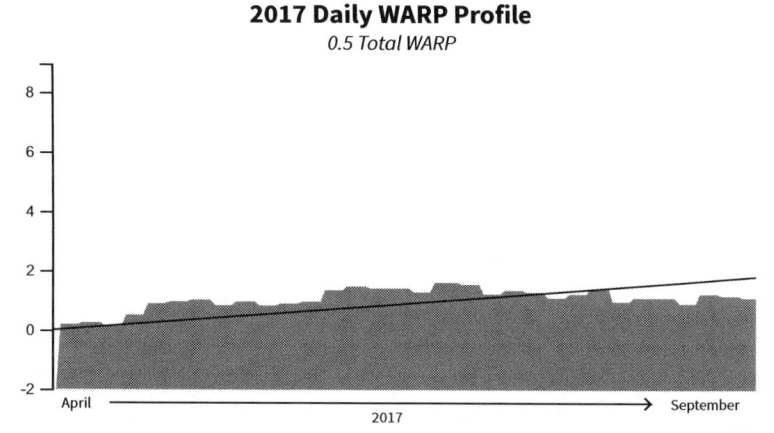

April   September
2017

POWER
52
PWR
52nd of 150

STAMINA
74
STM
44th of 150

COMMAND
52
CMD
79th of 150

Fantasy Values
2017	2018
$12.73	**$6.00**

YEAR	TEAM	LVL	AGE	W	L	SV	G	GS	IP	H	HR	BB/9	K/9	K	GB%	BABIP	WHIP	ERA	DRA	WARP	MPH 95
2017	PIT	MLB	30	11	14	0	31	31	187	203	29	1.7	6.3	131	48%	.299	1.28	4.14	5.33	0.5	94.7

Some of it is because of PNC Park, but Nova's DRA tells us he was lucky his results weren't worse. Nova has always survived plenty of contact due to a decent ground-ball rate, but even this slipped in 2017. The temptation will be to bet on a bounce-back year, but despite the favorable home venue there is significant risk in the profile and the price should be adjusted accordingly. — Mike G.

2017 Pitching Percentages

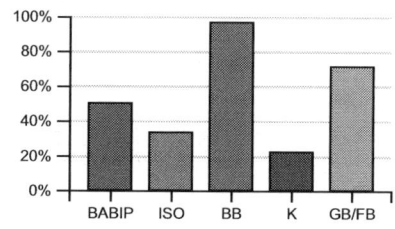

Pitching PECOTA Percentiles

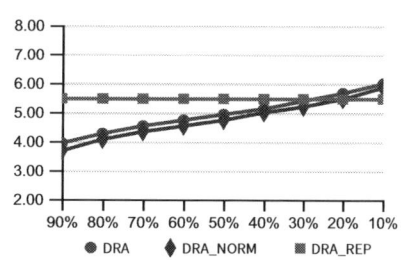

● DRA   ◆ DRA_NORM   ■ DRA_REP

Pitching WARP History

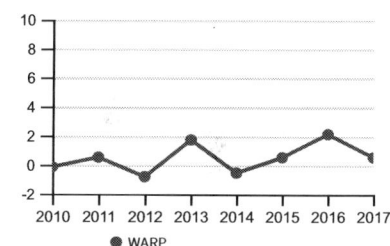

● WARP

Tunnel vs LHH

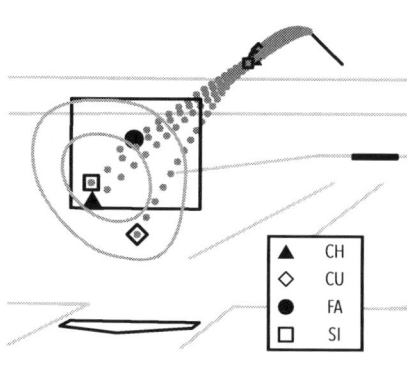

▲	CH
◇	CU
●	FA
□	SI

Pitch Types

Type	Freq	Velo	H Mov	V Mov
CH	9.7%	86.7 [107]	-13.7 [86]	-25.3 [105]
CU	22.1%	80.9 [110]	3 [81]	-43.2 [110]
FA	28.7%	93.5 [103]	-10.6 [84]	-16.7 [95]
SI	39.5%	92.8 [103]	-14.6 [85]	-21.8 [93]

Pitch Tunnel

Pairs	Release Diff	Tunnel Diff	Plate Diff	Speed Changes
1812	24.8	120.3	235.0	0.026

PI Scores

Year	Pitch Ct	Pwr	Cmd	Stm
2013	2079	53	39	60
2014	326	51	51	42
2015	1526	49	35	56
2016	2226	49	46	64
2017	2574	52	52	74

Tunnel vs RHH

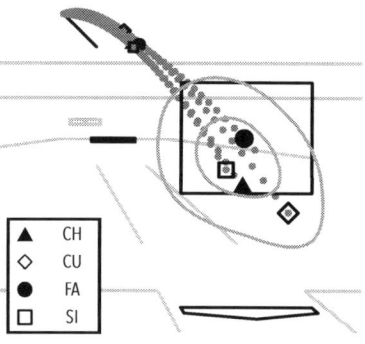

▲	CH
◇	CU
●	FA
□	SI

Eduardo Nunez   UT   Boston Red Sox

Born: 6/15/1987   **Age:** 31   **Bats:** R   **Throws:** R   **Height:** 6' 0"   **Weight:** 195 lbs   **Draft Info:** International Free Agent, 2004

PACE
21 Sec/Pit
45th of 155
71°
Fast

2017 Daily WARP Profile
3.2 Total WARP

April — 2017 — September

Game 73: minors, **Game 143:** minors, **Game 157:** knee sprain

Fantasy Values
2017	2018
$9.75	$23.00

YEAR	TEAM	LVL	AGE	PA	R	2B	3B	HR	RBI	BB	K	SB	AVG/OBP/SLG	TAv	VORP	BABIP	WARP
2017	SFN	MLB	30	318	37	21	0	4	31	12	29	18	.308/.334/.417	.273	18.8	.328	2.0
2017	BOS	MLB	30	173	23	12	0	8	27	6	25	6	.321/.353/.539	.305	12.0	.341	1.2

2017 Batting Percentages

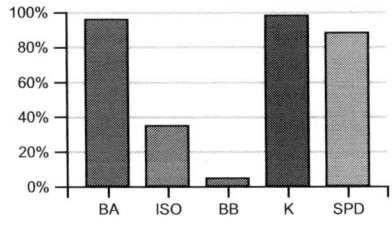

Batting PECOTA Percentiles

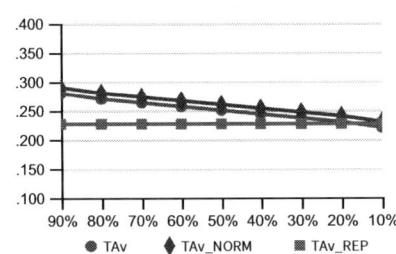

Batting WARP History

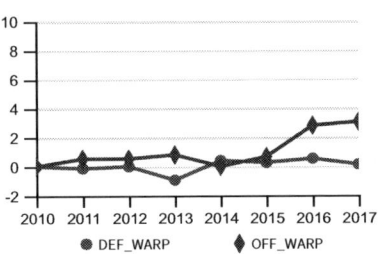

BRR (Relative to Position)

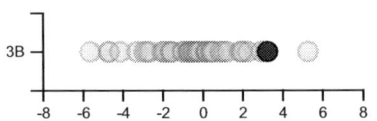

Rank		Player	BRR
1	97°	Cory Spangenberg	5.29
2	94°	**Eduardo Nunez**	**3.28**
3	91°	Travis Shaw	3.21
4	89°	Johan Camargo	2.97
5	87°	Eduardo Escobar	2.30

BRR (Relative to Team)

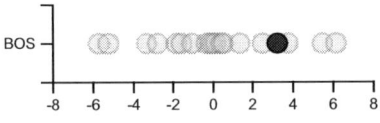

Rank		Player	BRR
2	88°	Xander Bogaerts	5.51
3	81°	Jackie Bradley	3.79
4	72°	**Eduardo Nunez**	**3.28**
5	65°	Rajai Davis	2.55
6	55°	Andrew Benintendi	1.41

Base Running Components

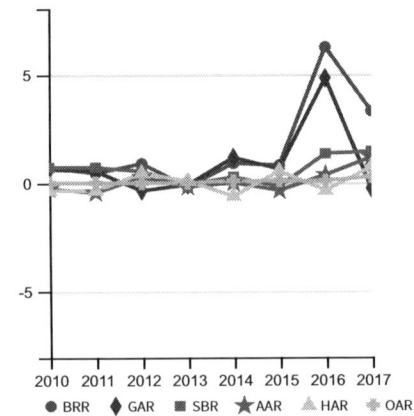

Darren O'Day RHP Baltimore Orioles

Born: 10/22/1982 **Age:** 35 **Bats:** R **Throws:** R **Height:** 6' 4" **Weight:** 220 lbs **Draft Info:** Undrafted Free Agent, 2006

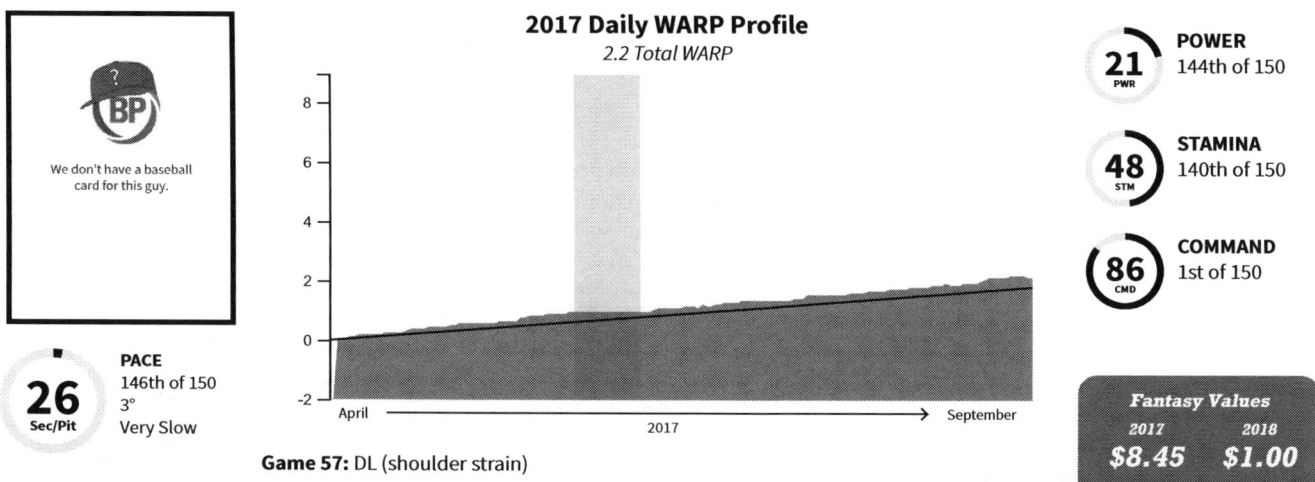

2017 Daily WARP Profile
2.2 Total WARP

PACE
26 146th of 150
Sec/Pit 3°
Very Slow

POWER
21 144th of 150
PWR

STAMINA
48 140th of 150
STM

COMMAND
86 1st of 150
CMD

Game 57: DL (shoulder strain)

Fantasy Values
2017	2018
$8.45	$1.00

We don't have a baseball card for this guy.

YEAR	TEAM	LVL	AGE	W	L	SV	G	GS	IP	H	HR	BB/9	K/9	K	GB%	BABIP	WHIP	ERA	DRA	WARP	MPH 95
2017	BAL	MLB	34	2	3	2	64	0	60.1	41	8	3.6	11.3	76	48%	.256	1.08	3.43	1.94	2.2	89.0

2017 Pitching Percentages

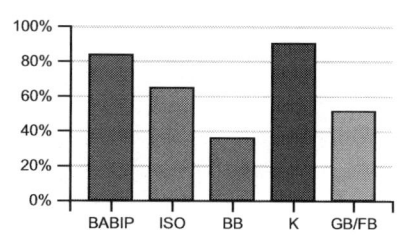

Pitching PECOTA Percentiles

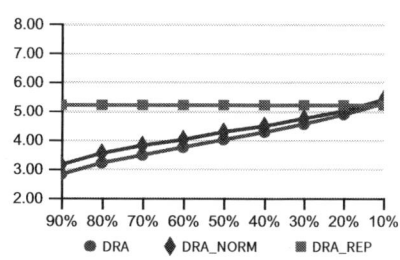

Pitching WARP History

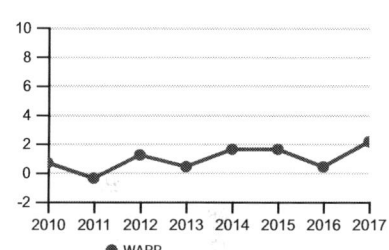

Tunnel vs LHH

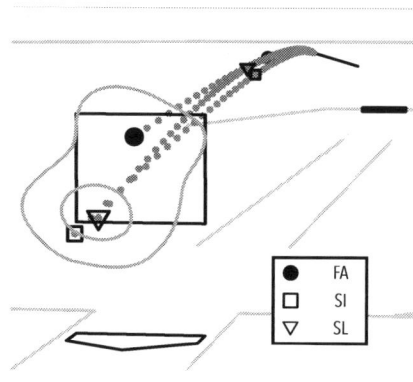

	FA
	SI
	SL

Pitch Types

Type	Freq	Velo	H Mov	V Mov
FA	36.2%	88.3 [84]	-12.5 [75]	-24.3 [71]
SI	17.6%	87.5 [72]	-14.5 [85]	-36 [41]
SL	46.2%	80.6 [83]	6.1 [107]	-35.2 [93]

Pitch Tunnel

Pairs	Release Diff	Tunnel Diff	Plate Diff	Speed Changes
745	30.0	111.8	199.5	0.020

PI Scores

Year	Pitch Ct	Pwr	Cmd	Stm
2013	976	12	72	48
2014	1045	22	67	48
2015	1060	20	78	50
2016	529	30	71	24
2017	1009	21	86	48

Tunnel vs RHH

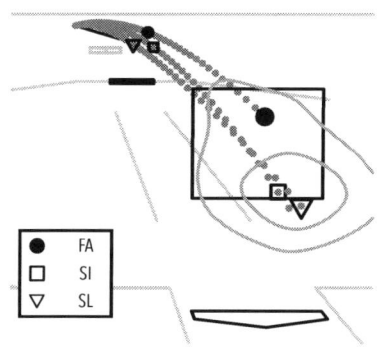

	FA
	SI
	SL

Jake Odorizzi   RHP   Tampa Bay Rays

Born: 3/27/1990   **Age:** 28   **Bats:** R   **Throws:** R   **Height:** 6' 2"   **Weight:** 190 lbs   **Draft Info:** Round 1, 2008 Draft (#32 overall)

2017 Daily WARP Profile
1.4 Total WARP

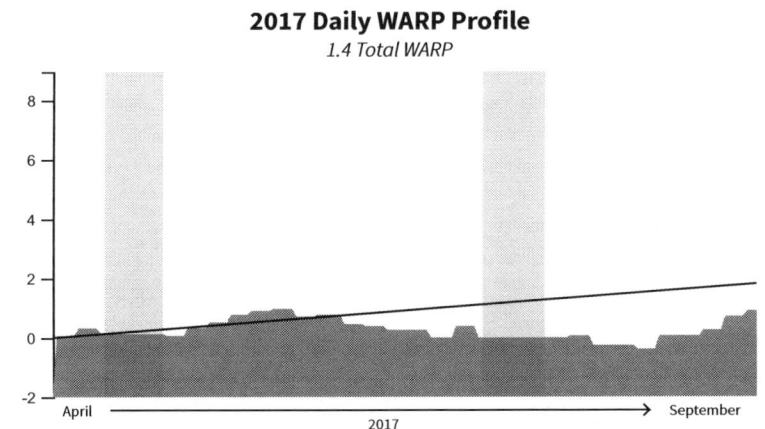

Game 13: DL (hamstring strain), **Game 100:** DL (back strain)

PACE
20 Sec/Pit
37th of 150
75°
Fast

POWER **38** PWR
104th of 150

STAMINA **67** STM
82nd of 150

COMMAND **54** CMD
70th of 150

Fantasy Values

2017	2018
$12.34	$8.00

YEAR	TEAM	LVL	AGE	W	L	SV	G	GS	IP	H	HR	BB/9	K/9	K	GB%	BABIP	WHIP	ERA	DRA	WARP	MPH 95
2017	TBA	MLB	27	10	8	0	28	28	143.1	117	30	3.8	8.0	127	32%	.227	1.24	4.14	4.70	1.4	93.4

It was a bad year for Odorizzi, and it could have been far worse if not for a lucky BABIP. Odorizzi saw his walk and fly-ball rates spike, a bad combination for a pitcher who doesn't generate weak contact. Odorizzi had a few decent outings, but it is difficult to predict a bounce-back without knowing if he can find the location that eluded him last year. — Mike G.

2017 Pitching Percentages

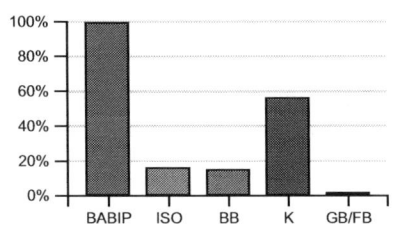

Pitching PECOTA Percentiles

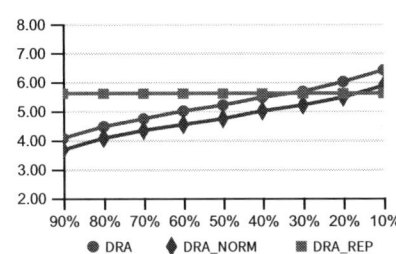

● DRA   ◆ DRA_NORM   ■ DRA_REP

Pitching WARP History

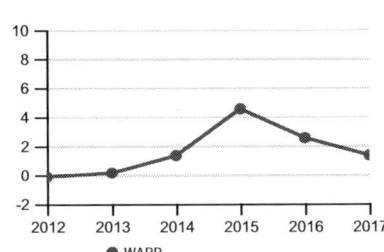

● WARP

Tunnel vs LHH

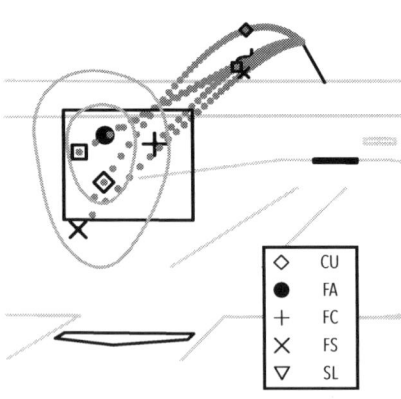

◇	CU
●	FA
+	FC
✕	FS
▽	SL

Pitch Types

Type	Freq	Velo	H Mov	V Mov
CH	0.8%	85.9 [103]	-12.7 [91]	-23.8 [109]
CU	5.8%	72.6 [79]	7.9 [100]	-55.9 [83]
FA	46.0%	91.8 [97]	-8.9 [92]	-13.1 [107]
FC	16.4%	86.2 [87]	3.7 [111]	-21.6 [109]
FS	21.8%	84.3 [96]	-10.2 [92]	-27.3 [108]
SI	2.6%	93.1 [104]	-11.5 [107]	-13.3 [125]
SL	6.5%	81.6 [88]	6.1 [106]	-33 [99]

Pitch Tunnel

Pairs	Release Diff	Tunnel Diff	Plate Diff	Speed Changes
1917	24.2	115.4	227.8	0.026

PI Scores

Year	Pitch Ct	Pwr	Cmd	Stm
2013	534	45	49	64
2014	3015	42	42	73
2015	2752	41	57	70
2016	3298	48	57	80
2017	2590	38	54	67

Tunnel vs RHH

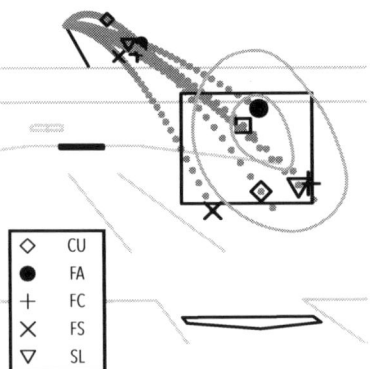

◇	CU
●	FA
+	FC
✕	FS
▽	SL

Matt Olson 1B Oakland Athletics

Born: 3/29/1994　**Age:** 24　**Bats:** L　**Throws:** R　**Height:** 6' 5"　**Weight:** 230 lbs　**Draft Info:** Round 1, 2012 Draft (#47 overall)

PACE
22 99th of 155
Sec/Pit 36°
Slow

2017 Daily WARP Profile
2.3 Total WARP

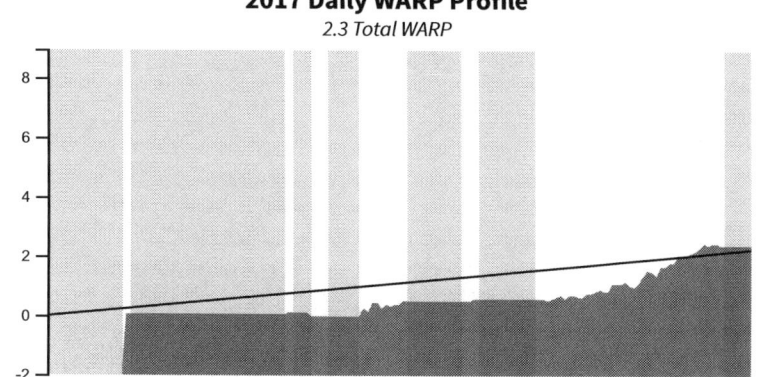

Game 1: minors, **Game 20:** minors, **Game 57:** minors, **Game 65:** minors, **Game 83:** minors, **Game 99:** minors, **Game 156:** hamstring strain

Fantasy Values
2017	2018
$10.02	$23.00

YEAR	TEAM	LVL	AGE	PA	R	2B	3B	HR	RBI	BB	K	SB	AVG/OBP/SLG	TAv	VORP	BABIP	WARP
2017	OAK	MLB	23	216	33	2	0	24	45	22	60	0	.259/.352/.651	.315	15.4	.238	2.3

2017 Batting Percentages
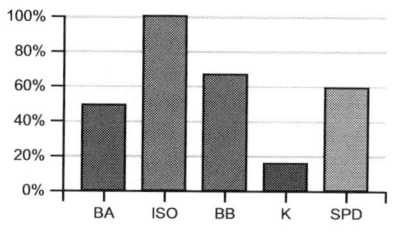

Batting PECOTA Percentiles
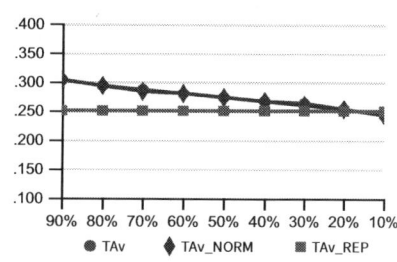

Batting WARP History
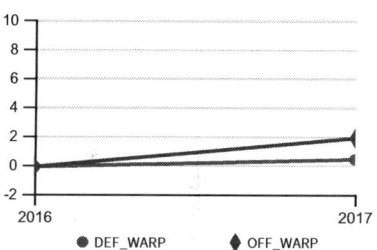

BRR (Relative to Position)
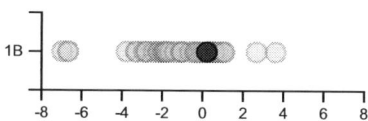

Rank		Player	BRR
13	78°	Dominic Smith	0.35
14	75°	Brandon Belt	0.33
15	74°	**Matt Olson**	**0.26**
16	72°	Jose Martinez	0.14
17	71°	Chris Carter	-0.01

BRR (Relative to Team)
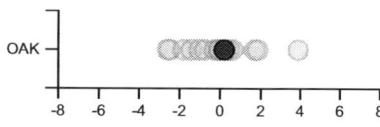

Rank		Player	BRR
5	59°	Dustin Garneau	0.49
6	56°	Mark Canha	0.30
7	54°	**Matt Olson**	**0.26**
8	52°	Josh Phegley	0.02
9	49°	Chris Carter	-0.01

Base Running Components
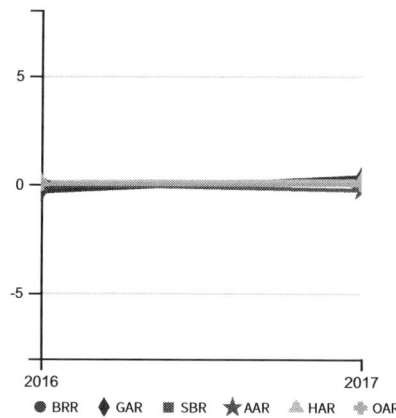

Roberto Osuna RHP Toronto Blue Jays

Born: 2/7/1995 **Age:** 23 **Bats:** R **Throws:** R **Height:** 6' 2" **Weight:** 215 lbs **Draft Info:** International Free Agent, 2011

2017 Daily WARP Profile
2.1 Total WARP

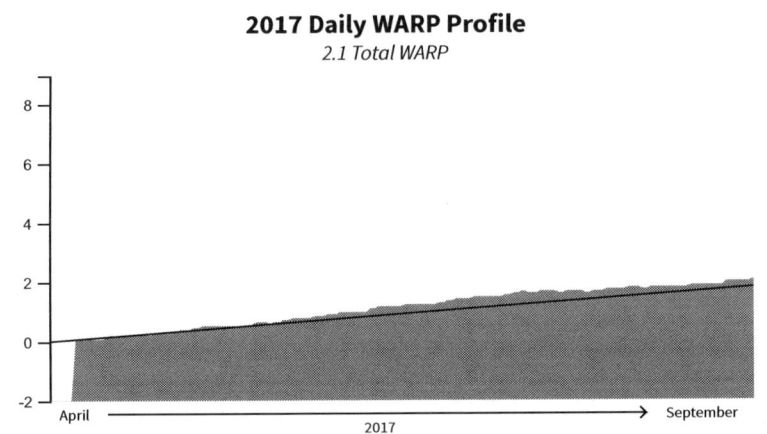

POWER
52 PWR 52nd of 150

STAMINA
48 STM 140th of 150

COMMAND
71 CMD 9th of 150

PACE
23 Sec/Pit 126th of 150
16°
Very Slow

Fantasy Values
2017 2018
$21.86 $16.00

YEAR	TEAM	LVL	AGE	W	L	SV	G	GS	IP	H	HR	BB/9	K/9	K	GB%	BABIP	WHIP	ERA	DRA	WARP	MPH 95
2017	TOR	MLB	22	3	4	4	39	66	0	64	46	3	1.3	11.7	83	47%	.285	0.86	3.38	2.19	2.1	95.9

Ignore the ERA; after a down year in 2016, Osuna bounced back in a big way, posting a 2.17 DRA in his third full season. The young closer continues to have the inside track in Toronto for saves and should continue to be as safe a bet for 35+ saves as any closer can be, relatively speaking. — Mike G.

2017 Pitching Percentages

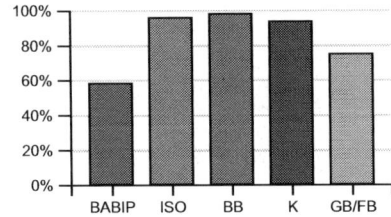

Pitching PECOTA Percentiles

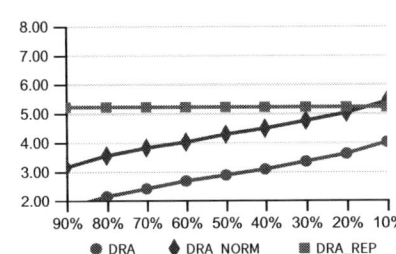

Pitching WARP History

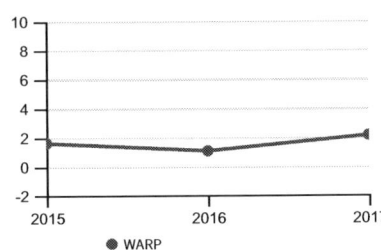

Tunnel vs LHH

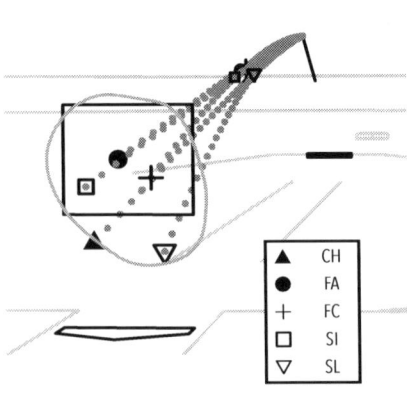

	CH
●	FA
+	FC
□	SI
▽	SL

Pitch Types

Type	Freq	Velo	H Mov	V Mov
CH	4.2%	83.8 [95]	-10.8 [102]	-22.4 [113]
FA	35.2%	95 [108]	-3.9 [115]	-10.9 [114]
FC	28.6%	90.5 [112]	4.5 [115]	-21.2 [110]
SI	12.8%	94.5 [113]	-10.7 [113]	-13.8 [123]
SL	19.2%	86 [107]	5.8 [105]	-31 [105]

Pitch Tunnel

Pairs	Release Diff	Tunnel Diff	Plate Diff	Speed Changes
691	25.0	112.2	225.8	0.018

PI Scores

Year	Pitch Ct	Pwr	Cmd	Stm
2015	1084	70	52	50
2016	1118	63	61	51
2017	954	52	71	48

Tunnel vs RHH

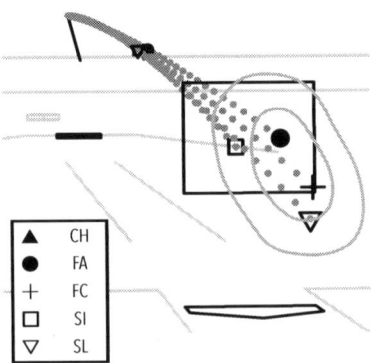

▲	CH
●	FA
+	FC
□	SI
▽	SL

Marcell Ozuna   LF   St. Louis Cardinals

Born: 11/12/1990   **Age:** 27   **Bats:** R   **Throws:** R   **Height:** 6' 1"   **Weight:** 225 lbs   **Draft Info:** International Free Agent, 2008

2017 Daily WARP Profile
6.1 Total WARP

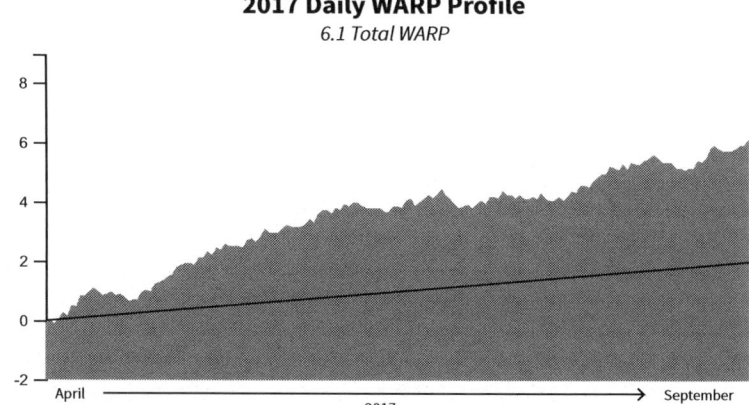

PACE

21 **Sec/Pit**

45th of 155
71°
Fast

Fantasy Values

2017	2018
$30.72	**$27.00**

YEAR	TEAM	LVL	AGE	PA	R	2B	3B	HR	RBI	BB	K	SB	AVG/OBP/SLG	TAv	VORP	BABIP	WARP
2017	MIA	MLB	26	679	93	30	2	37	124	64	144	1	.312/.376/.548	.321	55.4	.355	6.1

It took years, but Ozuna finally blossomed into the superstar hitter the Marlins—and many of his fantasy managers—believed he could be. While teammate Giancarlo Stanton deservedly hogged the spotlight, Ozuna put on a power show of his own. If there was a weakness to Ozuna's game it was his relatively weak performance against southpaws, with only three of his 37 home runs coming against lefties. Traded to the Cardinals, Ozuna gets the benefit of a stronger lineup in his effort to prove '17 was no fluke. — Mike G.

2017 Batting Percentages

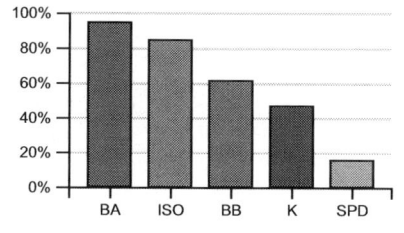

Batting PECOTA Percentiles

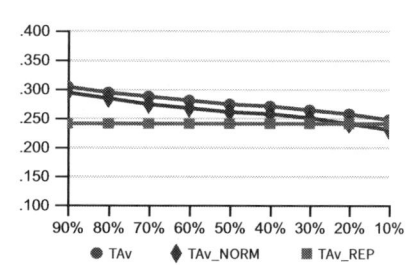

Batting WARP History

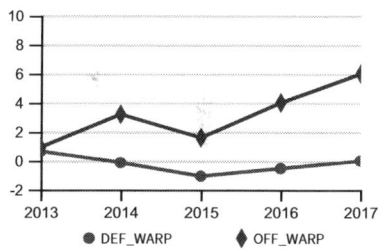

BRR (Relative to Position)

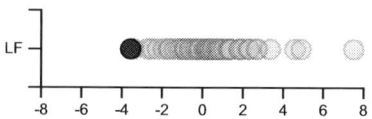

BRR (Relative to Team)

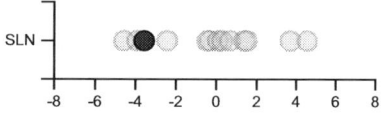

Base Running Components

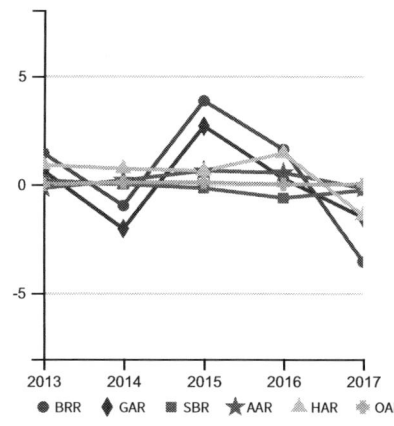

Rank		Player	BRR
62	8°	Adam Duvall	-2.18
63	6°	Gerardo Parra	-2.47
64	4°	Nori Aoki	-2.67
65	3°	Matt Kemp	-3.37
66	0°	**Marcell Ozuna**	**-3.52**

Rank		Player	BRR
9	38°	Jedd Gyorko	-0.40
10	25°	Matt Carpenter	-2.37
11	14°	**Marcell Ozuna**	**-3.52**
12	8°	Paul DeJong	-3.86
13	0°	Yadier Molina	-4.51

Blake Parker   RHP   Los Angeles Angels

Born: 6/19/1985   **Age:** 32   **Bats:** R   **Throws:** R   **Height:** 6' 3"   **Weight:** 225 lbs   **Draft Info:** Round 16, 2006 Draft (#479 overall)

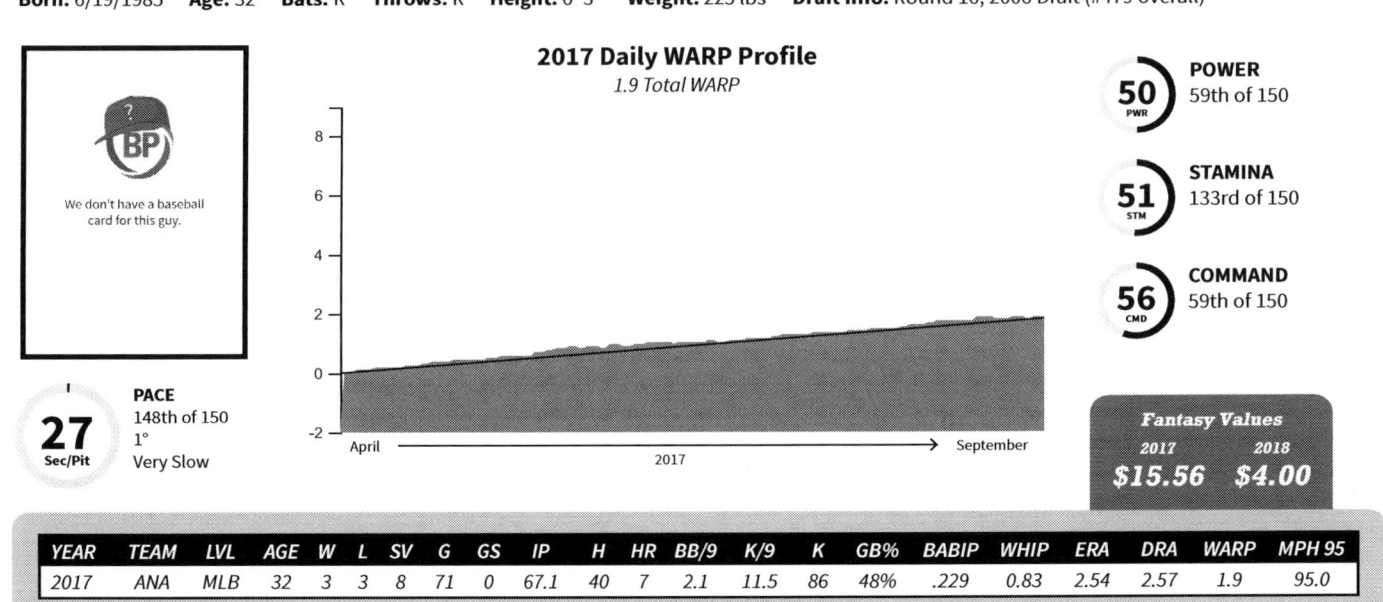

2017 Daily WARP Profile
1.9 Total WARP

We don't have a baseball card for this guy.

PACE
27 148th of 150
Sec/Pit 1°
Very Slow

POWER
50 59th of 150
PWR

STAMINA
51 133rd of 150
STM

COMMAND
56 59th of 150
CMD

Fantasy Values
2017	2018
$15.56	$4.00

YEAR	TEAM	LVL	AGE	W	L	SV	G	GS	IP	H	HR	BB/9	K/9	K	GB%	BABIP	WHIP	ERA	DRA	WARP	MPH 95
2017	ANA	MLB	32	3	3	8	71	0	67.1	40	7	2.1	11.5	86	48%	.229	0.83	2.54	2.57	1.9	95.0

2017 Pitching Percentages

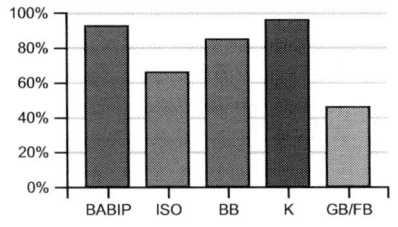

Pitching PECOTA Percentiles

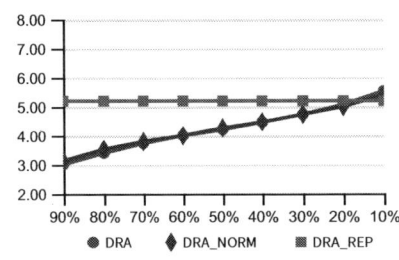

● DRA   ◆ DRA_NORM   ■ DRA_REP

Pitching WARP History

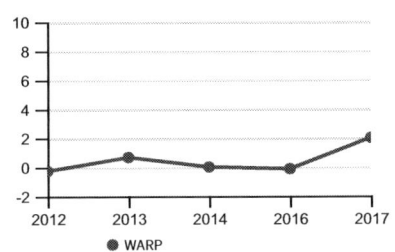

● WARP

Tunnel vs LHH

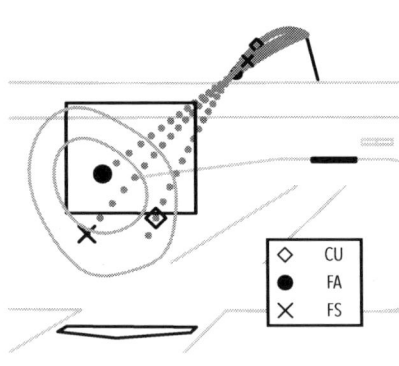

◇ CU
● FA
✕ FS

Pitch Types

Type	Freq	Velo	H Mov	V Mov
CU	7.5%	79.8 [106]	6.9 [97]	-48.3 [99]
FA	60.0%	94 [105]	-3.9 [115]	-12.4 [109]
FS	32.4%	82.7 [87]	-6.3 [106]	-34.8 [84]

Pitch Tunnel

Pairs	Release Diff	Tunnel Diff	Plate Diff	Speed Changes
791	28.2	112.8	226.4	0.027

PI Scores

Year	Pitch Ct	Pwr	Cmd	Stm
2013	808	44	41	48
2014	355	40	44	41
2016	329	40	50	42
2017	1061	50	56	51

Tunnel vs RHH

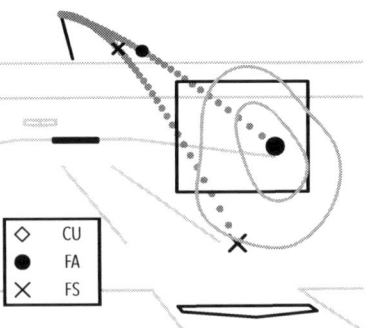

◇ CU
● FA
✕ FS

James Paxton   LHP   Seattle Mariners

Born: 11/6/1988   **Age:** 29   **Bats:** L   **Throws:** L   **Height:** 6'4"   **Weight:** 235 lbs   **Draft Info:** Round 4, 2010 Draft (#132 overall)

2017 Daily WARP Profile
3.7 Total WARP

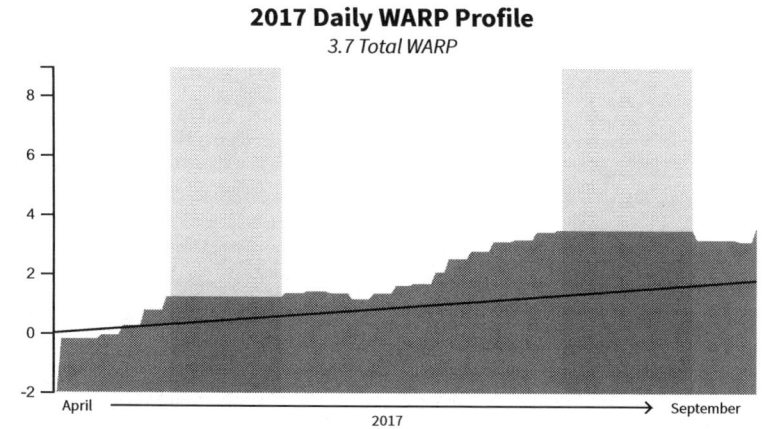

April   2017   September

Game 28: DL (forearm strain), **Game 117:** DL (pectoral strain)

62 PWR — **POWER** 21st of 150

58 STM — **STAMINA** 107th of 150

34 CMD — **COMMAND** 148th of 150

19 Sec/Pit — **PACE** 16th of 150 / 89° / Very Fast

Fantasy Values
2017	2018
$21.62	$23.00

YEAR	TEAM	LVL	AGE	W	L	SV	G	GS	IP	H	HR	BB/9	K/9	K	GB%	BABIP	WHIP	ERA	DRA	WARP	MPH 95
2017	SEA	MLB	28	12	5	0	24	24	136	113	9	2.4	10.3	156	46%	.300	1.10	2.98	3.15	3.7	97.6

After years of tantalizing with glimpses of potential between multiple injuries, Paxton finally showed us what the hype had been all about. His mid-90s fastball and low-80s curve offer plenty of separation, making it difficult to hit him and forcing weak contact when batters do connect. Paxton did miss some time due to injury, which will likely always be part of the package. Even so, 140 innings of Paxton are more valuable than what most of the starting pitcher pool can do, so invest early and worry about the potential for lost time later — Mike G.

2017 Pitching Percentages

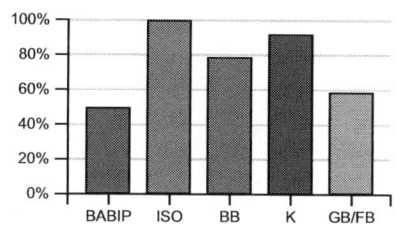

Pitching PECOTA Percentiles

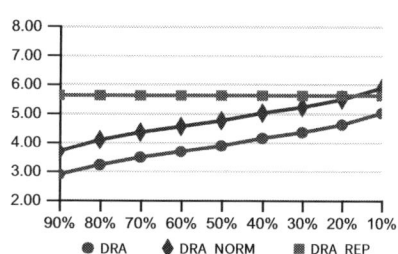

● DRA   ◆ DRA_NORM   ■ DRA_REP

Pitching WARP History

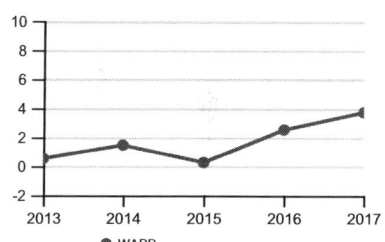

● WARP

Tunnel vs LHH

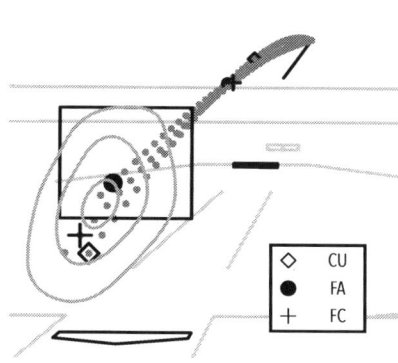

◇ CU
● FA
+ FC

Pitch Types

Type	Freq	Velo	H Mov	V Mov
CH	2.9%	87 [108]	10.2 [105]	-23.2 [111]
CU	21.4%	80.8 [109]	-5.5 [91]	-45.2 [106]
FA	62.6%	95.9 [112]	9.3 [90]	-11.9 [110]
FC	9.5%	89.4 [105]	0.4 [90]	-25.7 [93]
SI	3.0%	95.3 [117]	13.9 [90]	-15.8 [116]
SL	0.6%	87.5 [114]	1 [75]	-26.9 [116]

Pitch Tunnel

Pairs	Release Diff	Tunnel Diff	Plate Diff	Speed Changes
1670	29.3	117.9	225.3	0.033

PI Scores

Year	Pitch Ct	Pwr	Cmd	Stm
2013	367	66	47	73
2014	1177	66	39	21
2015	1106	64	40	27
2016	1940	63	47	71
2017	2222	62	34	58

Tunnel vs RHH

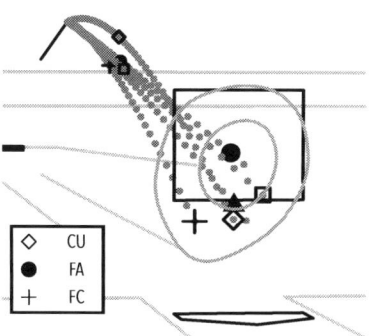

◇ CU
● FA
+ FC

Brad Peacock   RHP   Houston Astros

Born: 2/2/1988   **Age:** 30   **Bats:** R   **Throws:** R   **Height:** 6' 1"   **Weight:** 210 lbs   **Draft Info:** Round 41, 2006 Draft (#1231 overall)

We don't have a baseball card for this guy.

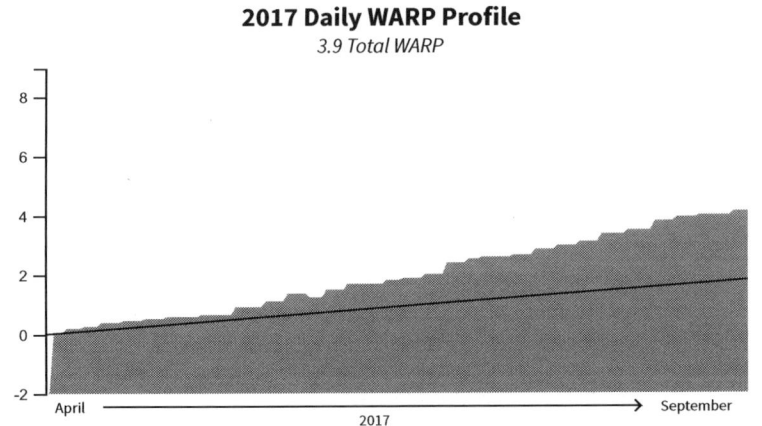

2017 Daily WARP Profile
3.9 Total WARP

POWER
38
PWR
104th of 150

STAMINA
60
STM
102nd of 150

COMMAND
55
CMD
62nd of 150

PACE
21
Sec/Pit
81st of 150
46°
Average

Fantasy Values
2017	2018
$20.51	$14.00

YEAR	TEAM	LVL	AGE	W	L	SV	G	GS	IP	H	HR	BB/9	K/9	K	GB%	BABIP	WHIP	ERA	DRA	WARP	MPH 95
2017	HOU	MLB	29	13	2	0	34	21	132	100	10	3.9	11.0	161	44%	.286	1.19	3.00	2.83	3.9	93.9

Few pitchers thrive in a dual role, but Peacock seemed just as capable for Houston as a starting pitcher as he did as a reliever. For fantasy, Peacock would have more value as a starter, but if the plan once again is to shift him back and forth from the rotation to the 'pen, there is enough upside that it's okay to draft him and shift him to your reserve list in mixed leagues when he is in the 'pen. — Mike G.

2017 Pitching Percentages

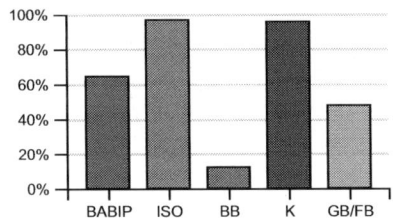

Pitching PECOTA Percentiles

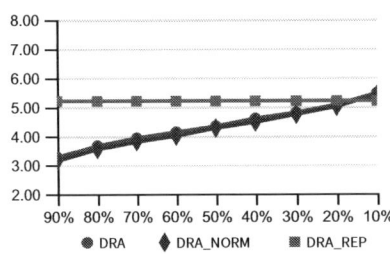

● DRA   ◆ DRA_NORM   ▦ DRA_REP

Pitching WARP History

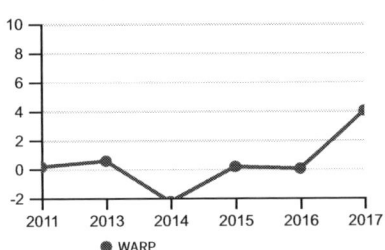

● WARP

Tunnel vs LHH

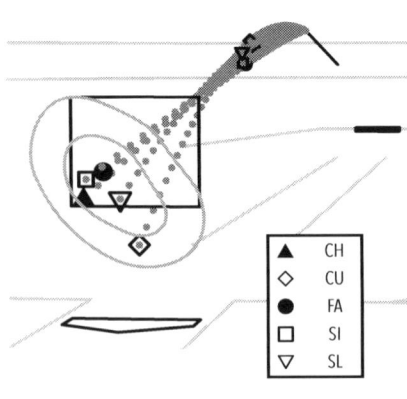

▲	CH
◇	CU
●	FA
□	SI
▽	SL

Pitch Types

Type	Freq	Velo	H Mov	V Mov
CH	4.4%	81.5 [86]	-15.5 [76]	-31.5 [87]
CU	6.8%	77.8 [98]	12.1 [117]	-53.2 [89]
FA	27.9%	93 [101]	-11.2 [81]	-15.1 [100]
SI	23.4%	92.1 [99]	-15.4 [79]	-20.8 [97]
SL	37.5%	81.8 [89]	10.5 [126]	-30.8 [105]

Pitch Tunnel

Pairs	Release Diff	Tunnel Diff	Plate Diff	Speed Changes
1620	36.3	111.2	204.3	0.033

PI Scores

Year	Pitch Ct	Pwr	Cmd	Stm
2011	201	55	56	59
2013	1485	51	47	69
2014	2330	43	45	60
2016	492	39	44	64
2017	2239	38	55	60

Tunnel vs RHH

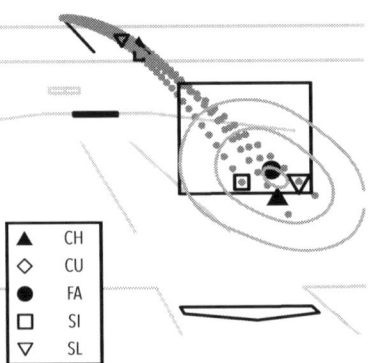

▲	CH
◇	CU
●	FA
□	SI
▽	SL

David Peralta RF Arizona Diamondbacks

Born: 8/14/1987 **Age:** 30 **Bats:** L **Throws:** L **Height:** 6' 1" **Weight:** 210 lbs **Draft Info:** International Free Agent, 2005

PACE
20
Sec/Pit
18th of 155
88°
Very Fast

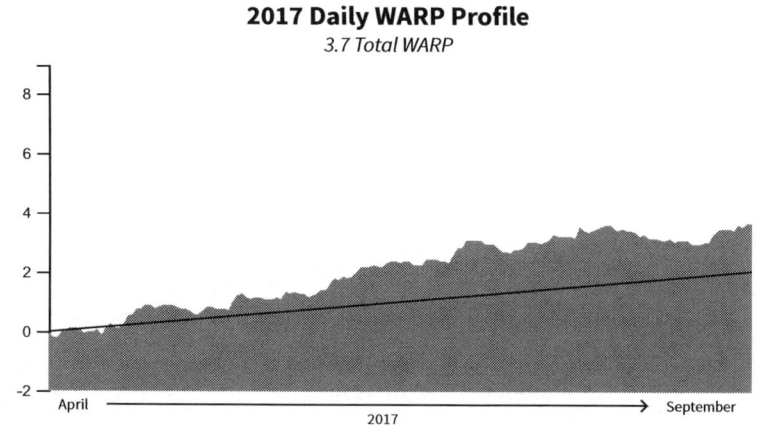

2017 Daily WARP Profile
3.7 Total WARP

April — 2017 — September

Fantasy Values
2017 *2018*
$19.36 $16.00

YEAR	TEAM	LVL	AGE	PA	R	2B	3B	HR	RBI	BB	K	SB	AVG/OBP/SLG	TAv	VORP	BABIP	WARP
2017	ARI	MLB	29	577	82	31	3	14	57	43	94	8	.293/.352/.444	.283	24.6	.333	3.7

2017 Batting Percentages

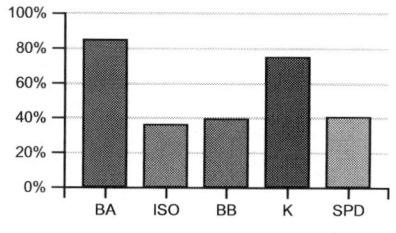

Batting PECOTA Percentiles

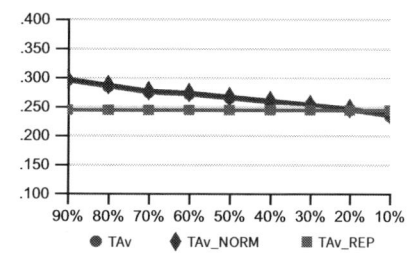

Batting WARP History

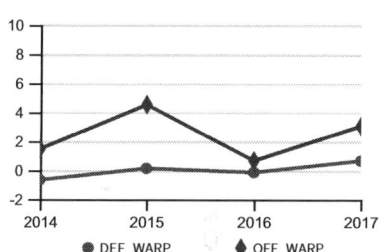

BRR (Relative to Position)

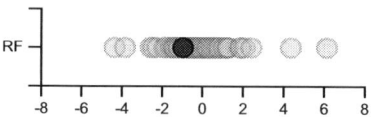

Rank		Player	BRR
39	31°	Alex Presley	-0.78
40	29°	Hunter Renfroe	-0.87
41	26°	**David Peralta**	**-0.91**
42	25°	Jim Adduci	-0.93
43	25°	Daniel Robertson	-1.13

BRR (Relative to Team)

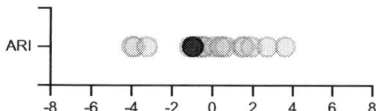

Rank		Player	BRR
12	40°	Chris Owings	-0.58
13	37°	Nick Ahmed	-0.77
14	25°	**David Peralta**	**-0.91**
15	20°	Alex Avila	-1.05
16	14°	Daniel Descalso	-3.18

Base Running Components

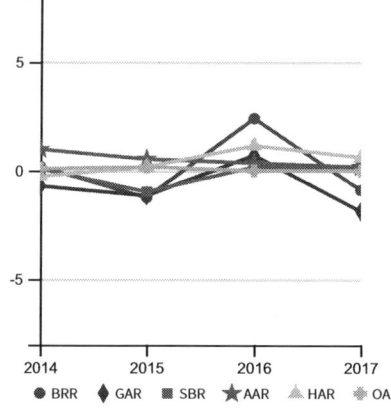

Martin Perez LHP Texas Rangers

Born: 4/4/1991 **Age:** 27 **Bats:** L **Throws:** L **Height:** 6' 0" **Weight:** 200 lbs **Draft Info:** International Free Agent, 2007

2017 Daily WARP Profile
1.6 Total WARP

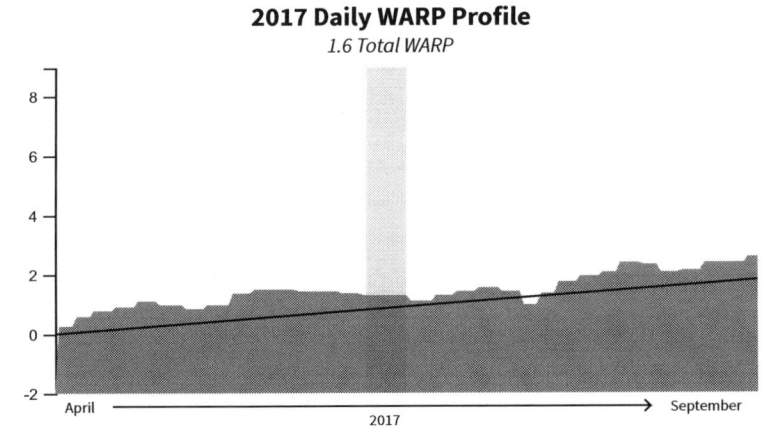

Game 73: DL (thumb fracture)

	POWER
50 PWR	59th of 150
79 STM	STAMINA 17th of 150
62 CMD	COMMAND 24th of 150

20 Sec/Pit	PACE 37th of 150 75° Fast

Fantasy Values
2017	2018
$2.82	**$1.00**

YEAR	TEAM	LVL	AGE	W	L	SV	G	GS	IP	H	HR	BB/9	K/9	K	GB%	BABIP	WHIP	ERA	DRA	WARP	MPH 95
2017	TEX	MLB	26	13	12	0	32	32	185	221	23	3.1	5.6	115	48%	.328	1.54	4.82	4.80	1.6	95.0

2017 Pitching Percentages

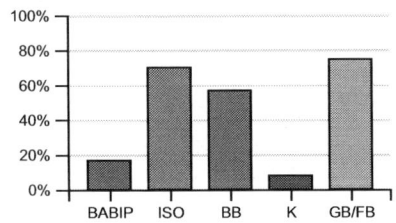

Pitching PECOTA Percentiles

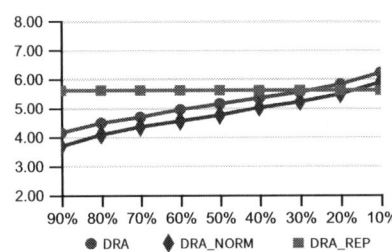

● DRA ◆ DRA_NORM ■ DRA_REP

Pitching WARP History

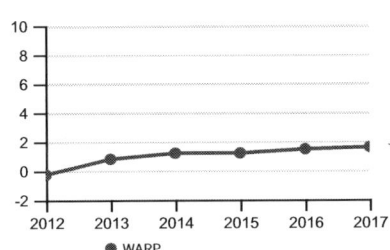

● WARP

Tunnel vs LHH

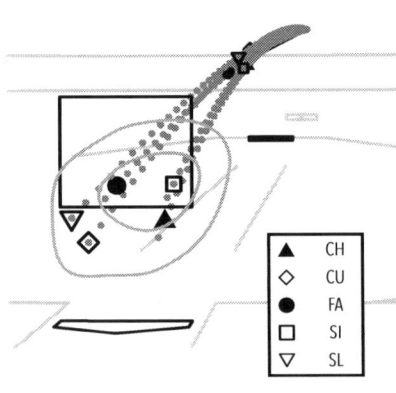

▲	CH
◇	CU
●	FA
□	SI
▽	SL

Pitch Types

Type	Freq	Velo	H Mov	V Mov
CH	20.4%	84.9 [99]	14.7 [80]	-25.4 [105]
CU	10.1%	79.1 [103]	-3.2 [82]	-43 [110]
FA	22.0%	93.5 [103]	9.8 [87]	-14.3 [103]
SI	36.7%	93.2 [105]	15.6 [77]	-19.2 [103]
SL	10.8%	84.2 [99]	-2.5 [91]	-31.5 [103]

Pitch Tunnel

Pairs	Release Diff	Tunnel Diff	Plate Diff	Speed Changes
2120	27.1	112.5	218.8	0.025

PI Scores

Year	Pitch Ct	Pwr	Cmd	Stm
2013	1854	52	41	69
2014	771	48	55	49
2015	1213	46	59	54
2016	3070	52	53	79
2017	3075	50	62	79

Tunnel vs RHH

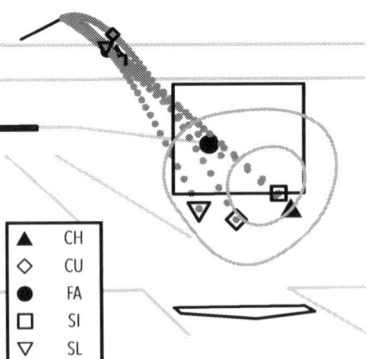

▲	CH
◇	CU
●	FA
□	SI
▽	SL

Yusmeiro Petit   RHP   Oakland Athletics

Born: 11/22/1984   **Age:** 33   **Bats:** R   **Throws:** R   **Height:** 6' 1"   **Weight:** 255 lbs   **Draft Info:** International Free Agent, 2001

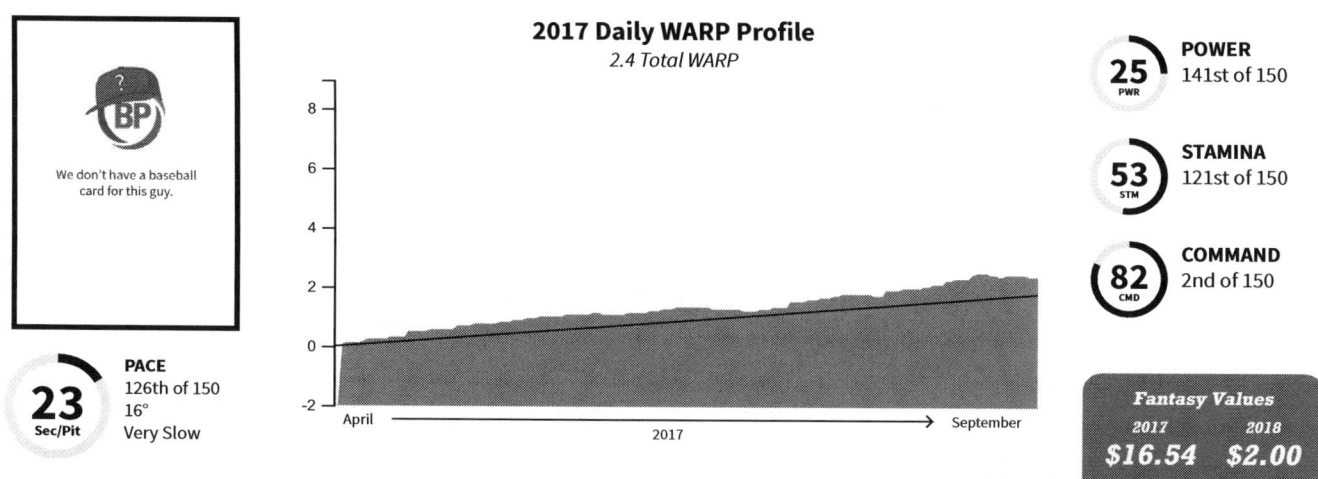

2017 Daily WARP Profile
2.4 Total WARP

April — 2017 — September

POWER 25 PWR — 141st of 150
STAMINA 53 STM — 121st of 150
COMMAND 82 CMD — 2nd of 150

PACE 23 Sec/Pit — 126th of 150 — 16° — Very Slow

Fantasy Values
2017	2018
$16.54	$2.00

YEAR	TEAM	LVL	AGE	W	L	SV	G	GS	IP	H	HR	BB/9	K/9	K	GB%	BABIP	WHIP	ERA	DRA	WARP	MPH 95
2017	ANA	MLB	32	5	2	4	60	1	91.1	69	9	1.8	10.0	101	34%	.267	0.95	2.76	2.84	2.4	91.2

Petit's stuff appears underwhelming at first glance, but he throws four pitches for strikes and does a great job with deception, making it difficult for hitters to guess which pitch is coming on any given count. It would be difficult to anticipate a repeat performance, though, so while Petit's 2017 is worth a tip of the cap it likely isn't worth more than a $2-3 bid in AL-only. Petit's value doesn't change much if at all with his move to the Athletics. — Mike G.

2017 Pitching Percentages

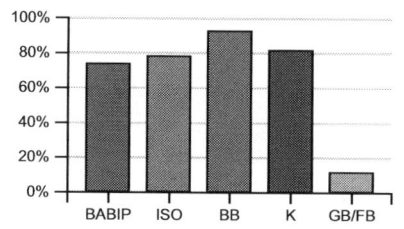

BABIP, ISO, BB, K, GB/FB

Pitching PECOTA Percentiles

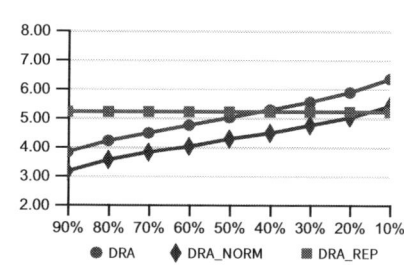

● DRA   ◆ DRA_NORM   ■ DRA_REP

Pitching WARP History

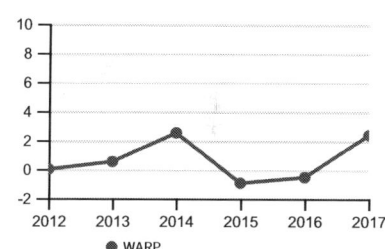

● WARP

Tunnel vs LHH

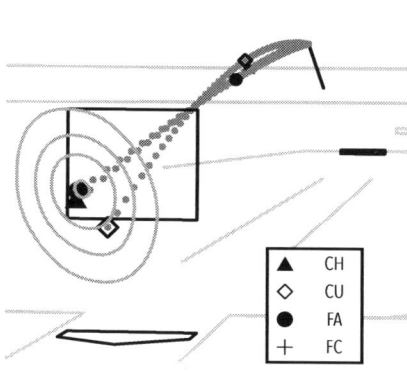

▲ CH   ◇ CU   ● FA   + FC

Pitch Types

Type	Freq	Velo	H Mov	V Mov
CH	17.0%	82.5 [90]	-8.1 [116]	-22.2 [114]
CU	20.3%	77.5 [97]	11.9 [116]	-36.3 [125]
FA	47.8%	90 [90]	-4.9 [111]	-14.6 [102]
FC	14.8%	86 [87]	0.9 [97]	-19.1 [119]

Pitch Tunnel

Pairs	Release Diff	Tunnel Diff	Plate Diff	Speed Changes
967	26.7	101.7	182.0	0.032

PI Scores

Year	Pitch Ct	Pwr	Cmd	Stm
2013	725	24	82	51
2014	1617	25	68	49
2015	1104	25	55	42
2016	954	33	68	35
2017	1342	25	82	53

Tunnel vs RHH

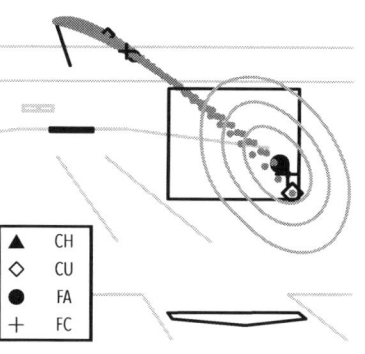

▲ CH   ◇ CU   ● FA   + FC

Tommy Pham   OF   St. Louis Cardinals

Born: 3/8/1988   **Age:** 30   **Bats:** R   **Throws:** R   **Height:** 6' 1"   **Weight:** 210 lbs   **Draft Info:** Round 16, 2006 Draft (#496 overall)

PACE
18th of 155
88°
Very Fast

20 Sec/Pit

2017 Daily WARP Profile
5.6 Total WARP

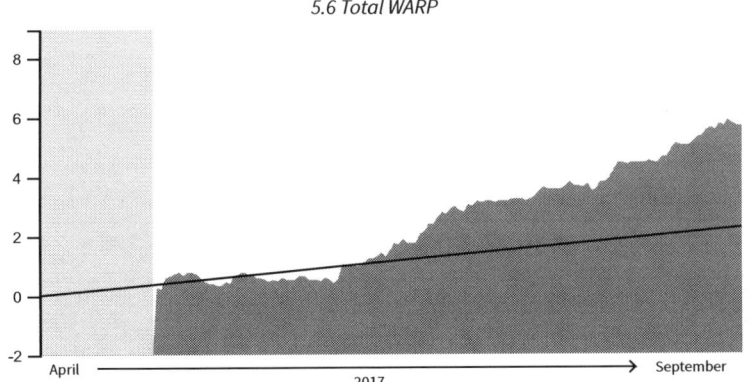

April   2017   September

Game 1: minors

Fantasy Values
2017	2018
$30.35	$26.00

YEAR	TEAM	LVL	AGE	PA	R	2B	3B	HR	RBI	BB	K	SB	AVG/OBP/SLG	TAv	VORP	BABIP	WARP
2017	SLN	MLB	29	530	95	22	2	23	73	71	117	25	.306/.411/.520	.332	58.0	.368	5.6

After years of fighting injuries and then hoping just to nab a spot as a backup in a crowded Cardinals outfield rotation, Pham not only secured a starting job but was one of the best fantasy outfielders in baseball. At age 29, Pham finally put all the tools together and provided a devastating power/speed combo that was not only consistent all season long but even improved in the second half. Despite his relatively advanced age there is little if any reason to doubt Pham can deliver a repeat performance and be a top-tier fantasy outfielder yet again. — Mike G.

2017 Batting Percentages

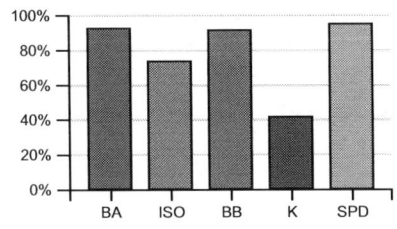

Batting PECOTA Percentiles

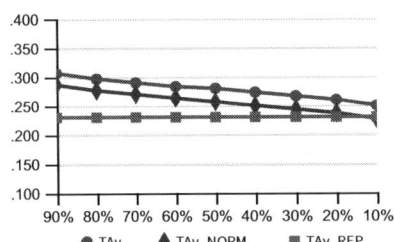

Batting WARP History

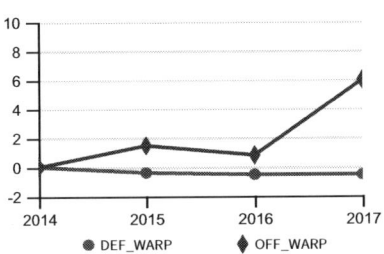

BRR (Relative to Position)

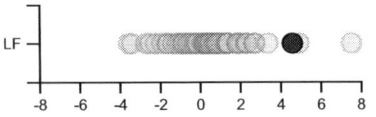

Rank		Player	BRR
1	97°	Delino DeShields	7.56
2	95°	Ben Revere	4.94
3	92°	**Tommy Pham**	**4.62**
4	90°	Starling Marte	3.40
5	88°	Gregor Blanco	2.75

BRR (Relative to Team)

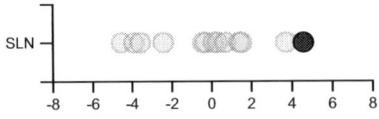

Rank		Player	BRR
1	77°	**Tommy Pham**	**4.62**
2	72°	Greg Garcia	3.75
3	64°	Kolten Wong	1.56
4	56°	Dexter Fowler	1.44
5	55°	Carson Kelly	0.74

Base Running Components

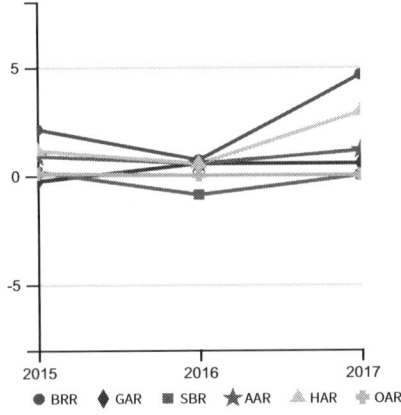

Jose Pirela   LF   San Diego Padres

Born: 11/21/1989   **Age:** 28   **Bats:** R   **Throws:** R   **Height:** 6' 0"   **Weight:** 220 lbs   **Draft Info:** Undrafted Free Agent, 2006

We don't have a baseball card for this guy.

2017 Daily WARP Profile
2.8 Total WARP

Game 1: minors, **Game 150:** jammed finger

21 Sec/Pit

PACE
45th of 155
71°
Fast

Fantasy Values
2017	2018
$11.32	$9.00

YEAR	TEAM	LVL	AGE	PA	R	2B	3B	HR	RBI	BB	K	SB	AVG/OBP/SLG	TAv	VORP	BABIP	WARP
2017	SDN	MLB	27	344	43	25	4	10	40	27	71	4	.288/.347/.490	.302	22.8	.343	2.8

2017 Batting Percentages

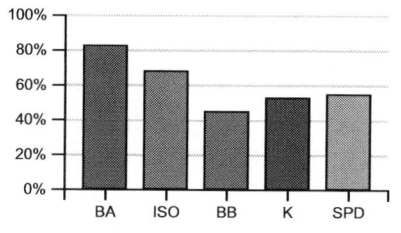

Batting PECOTA Percentiles

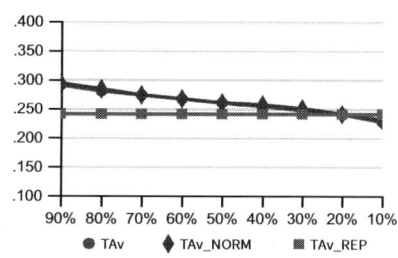

Batting WARP History

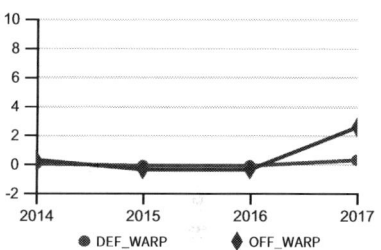

BRR (Relative to Position)

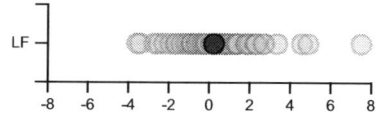

BRR (Relative to Team)

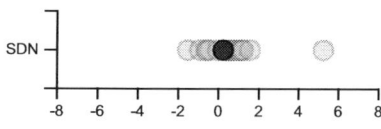

Base Running Components

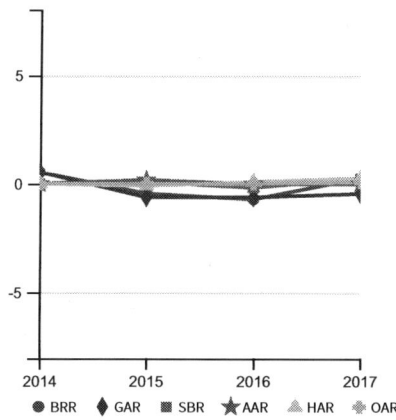

Rank		Player	BRR
36	44°	Orlando Calixte	0.31
37	43°	Peter Bourjos	0.30
38	42°	**Jose Pirela**	**0.28**
39	41°	Steve Pearce	0.28
40	40°	Austin Slater	0.25

Rank		Player	BRR
10	46°	Matt Szczur	0.52
11	42°	Allen Cordoba	0.40
12	35°	**Jose Pirela**	**0.28**
13	34°	Dusty Coleman	0.02
14	28°	Erick Aybar	-0.40

Nick Pivetta RHP Philadelphia Phillies

Born: 2/14/1993 **Age:** 25 **Bats:** R **Throws:** R **Height:** 6' 5" **Weight:** 220 lbs **Draft Info:** Round 4, 2013 Draft (#136 overall)

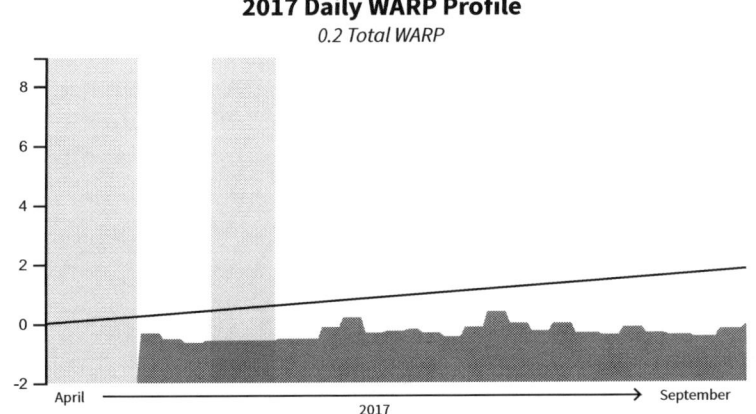

2017 Daily WARP Profile
0.2 Total WARP

April — 2017 — September

Game 1: minors, **Game 39:** minors

POWER 58 PWR — 32nd of 150

STAMINA 72 STM — 59th of 150

COMMAND 47 CMD — 102nd of 150

PACE 19 Sec/Pit — 16th of 150 / 89° / Very Fast

Fantasy Values

2017	2018
$0.88	$1.00

YEAR	TEAM	LVL	AGE	W	L	SV	G	GS	IP	H	HR	BB/9	K/9	K	GB%	BABIP	WHIP	ERA	DRA	WARP	MPH 95
2017	PHI	MLB	24	8	10	0	26	26	133	144	25	3.9	9.5	140	45%	.332	1.51	6.02	5.41	0.2	96.5

2017 Pitching Percentages

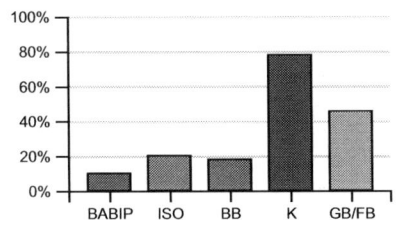

Pitching PECOTA Percentiles

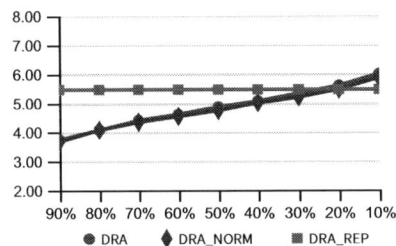

Tunnel vs LHH

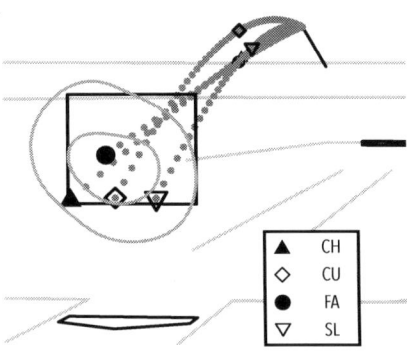

	CH
▲	CH
◇	CU
●	FA
▽	SL

Pitch Types

Type	Freq	Velo	H Mov	V Mov
CH	4.2%	86.9 [107]	-11.4 [98]	-23.5 [110]
CU	15.5%	79.8 [106]	12.2 [117]	-48 [100]
FA	66.0%	94.7 [107]	-7.9 [96]	-11.9 [111]
SL	14.3%	83.8 [97]	6.6 [109]	-34.3 [95]

Pitch Tunnel

Pairs	Release Diff	Tunnel Diff	Plate Diff	Speed Changes
1791	39.8	122.6	220.7	0.030

PI Scores

Year	Pitch Ct	Pwr	Cmd	Stm
2017	2428	58	47	72

Tunnel vs RHH

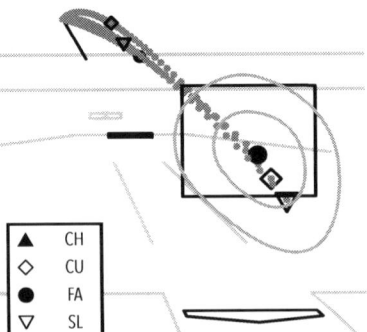

▲	CH
◇	CU
●	FA
▽	SL

Jorge Polanco   SS   Minnesota Twins

Born: 7/5/1993   **Age:** 24   **Bats:** B   **Throws:** R   **Height:** 5' 11"   **Weight:** 200 lbs   **Draft Info:** International Free Agent, 2009

21
Sec/Pit

PACE
45th of 155
71°
Fast

2017 Daily WARP Profile
0.8 Total WARP

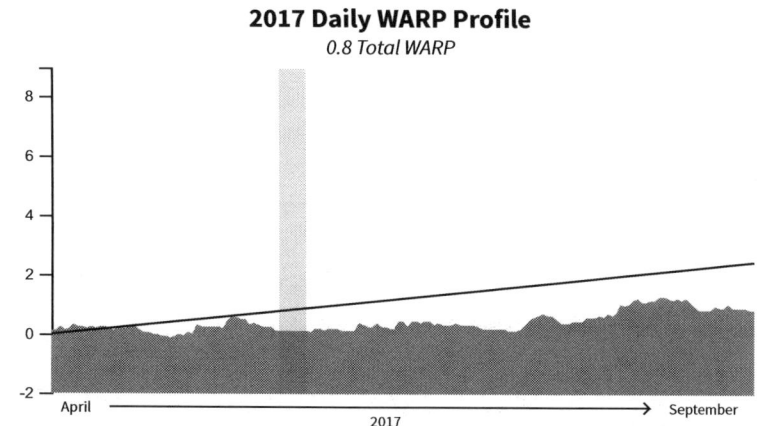

Game 53: bereavement

Fantasy Values

2017	2018
$15.93	**$14.00**

YEAR	TEAM	LVL	AGE	PA	R	2B	3B	HR	RBI	BB	K	SB	AVG/OBP/SLG	TAv	VORP	BABIP	WARP
2017	MIN	MLB	23	544	60	30	3	13	74	41	78	13	.256/.313/.410	.248	17.1	.278	.8

2017 Batting Percentages

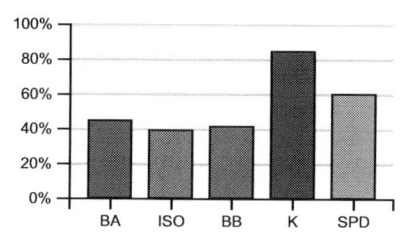

Batting PECOTA Percentiles

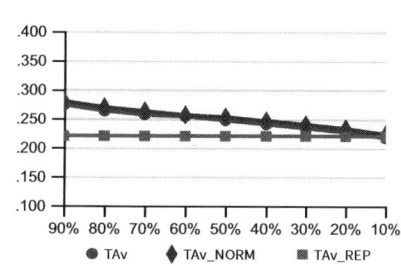

Batting WARP History

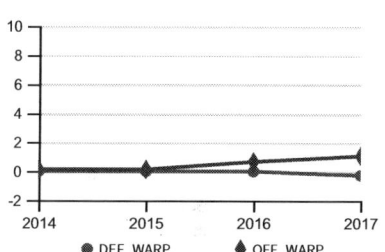

BRR (Relative to Position)

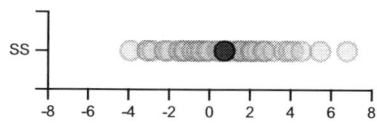

Rank		Player	BRR
22	43°	Richard Urena	1.43
23	42°	Amed Rosario	1.05
24	40°	**Jorge Polanco**	**0.78**
25	38°	Joshua Riddle	0.74
26	38°	Franklin Barreto	0.68

BRR (Relative to Team)

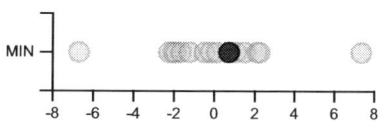

Rank		Player	BRR
4	67°	Ehire Adrianza	1.55
5	64°	Kennys Vargas	1.12
6	56°	**Jorge Polanco**	**0.78**
7	54°	Zach Granite	0.75
8	53°	Mitch Garver	0.18

Base Running Components

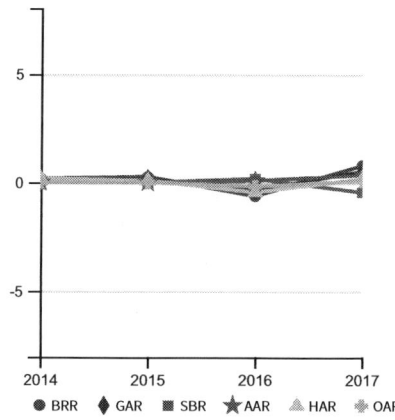

A.J. Pollock   CF   Arizona Diamondbacks

Born: 12/5/1987   **Age:** 30   **Bats:** R   **Throws:** R   **Height:** 6' 1"   **Weight:** 195 lbs   **Draft Info:** Round 1, 2009 Draft (#17 overall)

PACE
146th of 155
6°
24 Sec/Pit   Very Slow

2017 Daily WARP Profile
2.9 Total WARP

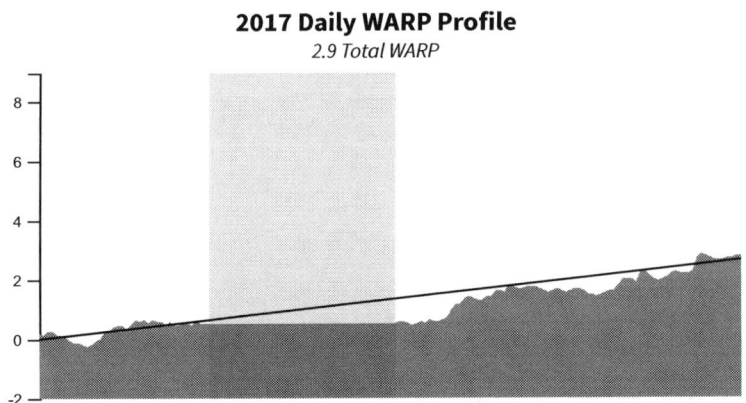

April — 2017 — September

Game 40: DL (groin strain)

Fantasy Values
2017   2018
$18.87 $22.00

YEAR	TEAM	LVL	AGE	PA	R	2B	3B	HR	RBI	BB	K	SB	AVG/OBP/SLG	TAv	VORP	BABIP	WARP
2017	ARI	MLB	29	466	73	33	6	14	49	35	71	20	.266/.330/.471	.286	28.1	.291	2.9

2017 Batting Percentages

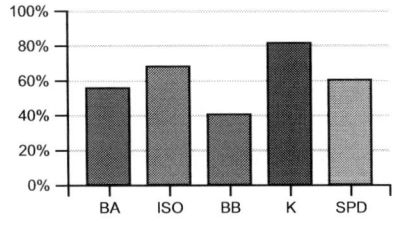

Batting PECOTA Percentiles

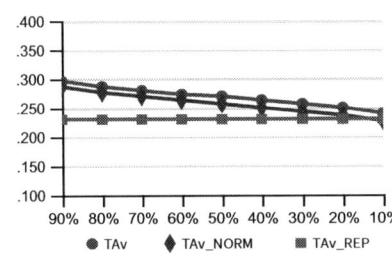

Batting WARP History

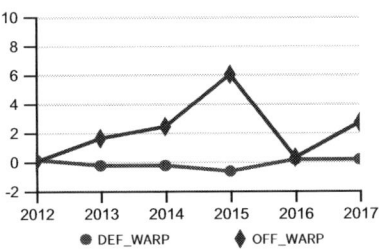

BRR (Relative to Position)

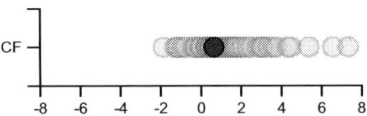

Rank		Player	BRR
36	28°	Zach Granite	0.75
37	27°	Greg Allen	0.74
38	25°	**A.J. Pollock**	**0.68**
39	24°	Leury Garcia	0.50
40	20°	George Springer	0.50

BRR (Relative to Team)

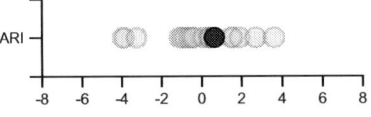

Rank		Player	BRR
4	70°	Chris Herrmann	1.62
5	65°	Ketel Marte	1.53
6	56°	**A.J. Pollock**	**0.68**
7	53°	Reymond Fuentes	0.48
8	50°	Jeff Mathis	0.43

Base Running Components

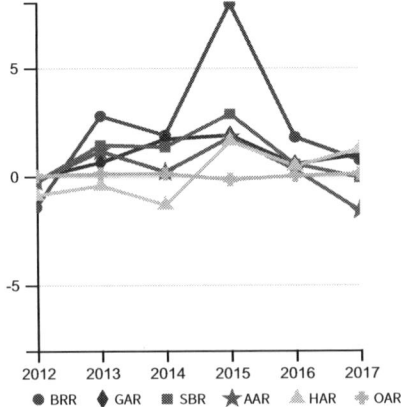

Drew Pomeranz   LHP   Boston Red Sox

Born: 11/22/1988   **Age:** 29   **Bats:** R   **Throws:** L   **Height:** 6' 6"   **Weight:** 240 lbs   **Draft Info:** Round 1, 2010 Draft (#5 overall)

2017 Daily WARP Profile
3.3 Total WARP

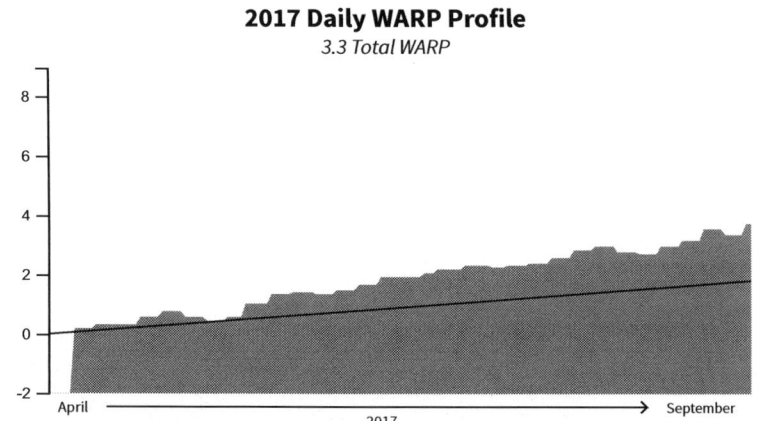

2017

41 PWR **POWER** 93rd of 150

76 STM **STAMINA** 36th of 150

43 CMD **COMMAND** 125th of 150

22 Sec/Pit **PACE** 108th of 150 / 28° / Slow

Fantasy Values

2017	2018
$19.39	$13.00

YEAR	TEAM	LVL	AGE	W	L	SV	G	GS	IP	H	HR	BB/9	K/9	K	GB%	BABIP	WHIP	ERA	DRA	WARP	MPH 95
2017	BOS	MLB	28	17	6	0	32	32	173.2	166	19	3.6	9.0	174	45%	.310	1.35	3.32	3.86	3.3	93.5

2017 Pitching Percentages

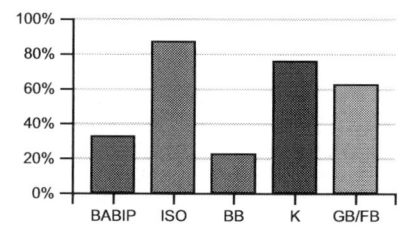

Pitching PECOTA Percentiles

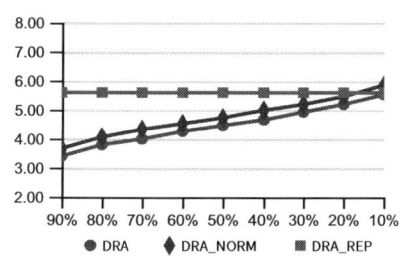

Pitching WARP History

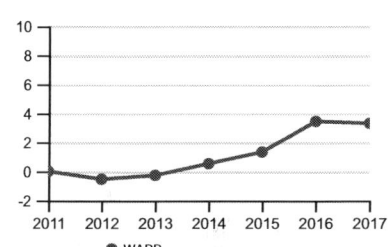

Tunnel vs LHH

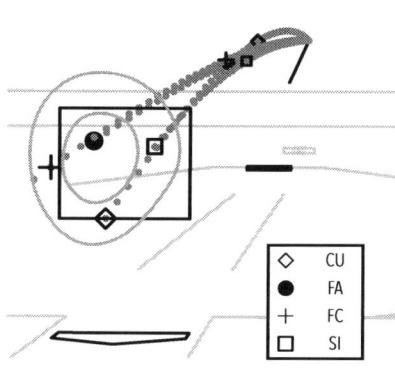

◇	CU
●	FA
+	FC
□	SI

Tunnel vs RHH

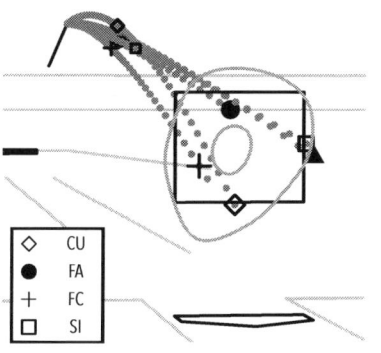

◇	CU
●	FA
+	FC
□	SI

Pitch Types

Type	Freq	Velo	H Mov	V Mov
CH	1.5%	81.3 [85]	11.5 [98]	-26.2 [102]
CU	36.9%	79.6 [105]	-4.8 [88]	-53.6 [88]
FA	46.1%	91.7 [96]	5.4 [108]	-13.1 [107]
FC	6.5%	86.9 [91]	-1.6 [100]	-24.5 [97]
SI	8.9%	90.4 [89]	11.9 [105]	-16.6 [113]

Pitch Tunnel

Pairs	Release Diff	Tunnel Diff	Plate Diff	Speed Changes
2298	29.6	131.9	256.8	0.031

PI Scores

Year	Pitch Ct	Pwr	Cmd	Stm
2013	413	47	44	48
2014	1121	52	57	47
2015	1429	49	51	53
2016	2824	38	43	71
2017	3043	41	43	76

Rick Porcello   RHP   Boston Red Sox

Born: 12/27/1988   **Age:** 29   **Bats:** R   **Throws:** R   **Height:** 6' 5"   **Weight:** 205 lbs   **Draft Info:** Round 1, 2007 Draft (#27 overall)

2017 Daily WARP Profile
0.1 Total WARP

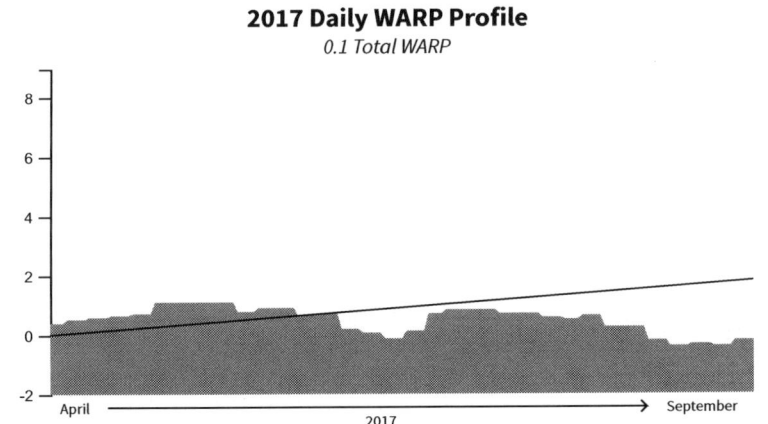

POWER
43 **PWR** 84th of 150

STAMINA
86 **STM** 1st of 150

COMMAND
61 **CMD** 30th of 150

PACE
20 **Sec/Pit** 37th of 150
75°
Fast

Fantasy Values

2017	2018
$9.09	$12.00

YEAR	TEAM	LVL	AGE	W	L	SV	G	GS	IP	H	HR	BB/9	K/9	K	GB%	BABIP	WHIP	ERA	DRA	WARP	MPH 95
2017	BOS	MLB	28	11	17	0	33	33	203.1	236	38	2.1	8.0	181	40%	.322	1.40	4.65	5.51	0.1	93.9

2017 Pitching Percentages

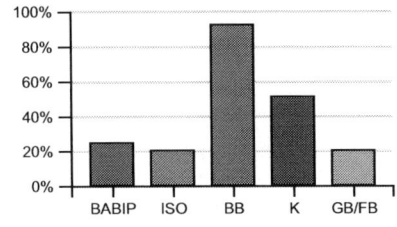

Pitching PECOTA Percentiles

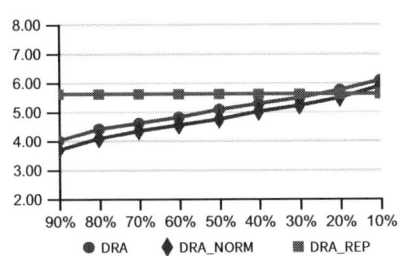

● DRA   ◆ DRA_NORM   ■ DRA_REP

Pitching WARP History

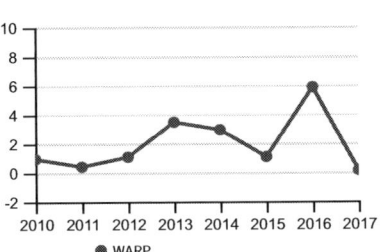

● WARP

Tunnel vs LHH

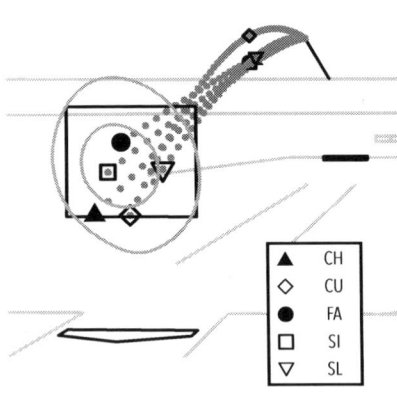

▲	CH
◇	CU
●	FA
□	SI
▽	SL

Pitch Types

Type	Freq	Velo	H Mov	V Mov
CH	8.3%	80.7 [82]	-11.9 [96]	-30.3 [91]
CU	15.5%	75 [88]	13.4 [122]	-54.7 [86]
FA	29.0%	92.7 [100]	-7.1 [100]	-13.9 [104]
SI	30.4%	90.3 [88]	-13 [96]	-20.1 [100]
SL	16.8%	85.9 [106]	3.5 [95]	-28.5 [112]

Pitch Tunnel

Pairs	Release Diff	Tunnel Diff	Plate Diff	Speed Changes
2474	32.5	124.7	231.0	0.031

PI Scores

Year	Pitch Ct	Pwr	Cmd	Stm
2013	2819	47	57	71
2014	3036	41	52	78
2015	2732	47	58	70
2016	3391	43	61	85
2017	3358	43	61	86

Tunnel vs RHH

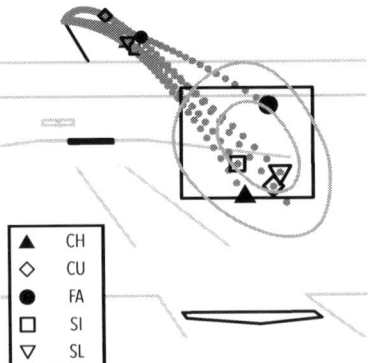

▲	CH
◇	CU
●	FA
□	SI
▽	SL

Buster Posey   C   San Francisco Giants

Born: 3/27/1987   **Age:** 31   **Bats:** R   **Throws:** R   **Height:** 6' 1"   **Weight:** 215 lbs   **Draft Info:** Round 1, 2008 Draft (#5 overall)

2017 Daily WARP Profile
5.8 Total WARP

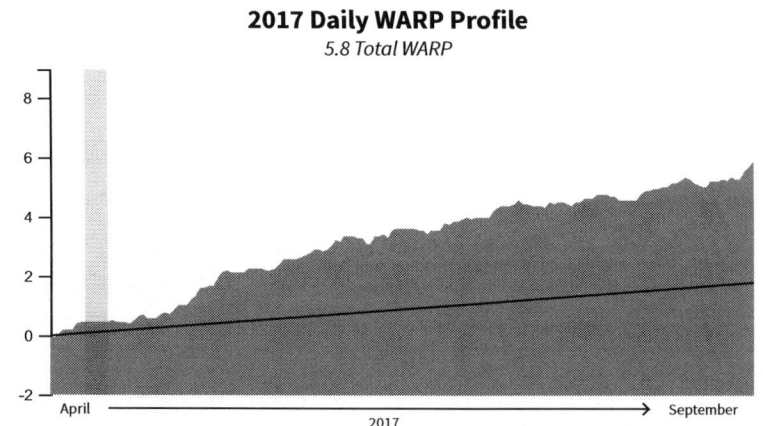

Game 9: DL (concussion)

PACE
21 Sec/Pit
45th of 155
71°
Fast

Fantasy Values
2017	2018
$20.55	$20.00

YEAR	TEAM	LVL	AGE	PA	R	2B	3B	HR	RBI	BB	K	SB	AVG/OBP/SLG	TAv	VORP	BABIP	WARP
2017	SFN	MLB	30	568	62	34	0	12	67	61	66	6	.320/.400/.462	.312	50.3	.347	5.8

Despite a slow but steady decline in power, Posey was once again a top-tier catcher thanks to an elite batting average at a position where most hitters struggle to even get to .250. Brandon Belt's concussion allowed Posey to rack up plenty of games at first base and keep Posey's bat in the field, further boosting his value. If your lineup has enough power elsewhere, locking up Posey's elite hit tool and batting average is a good use of a roster spot. — Mike G.

2017 Batting Percentages

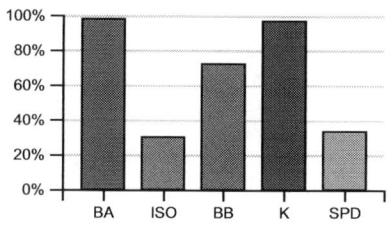

Batting PECOTA Percentiles

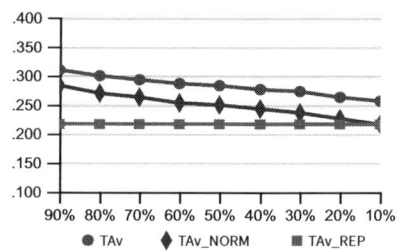

Batting WARP History

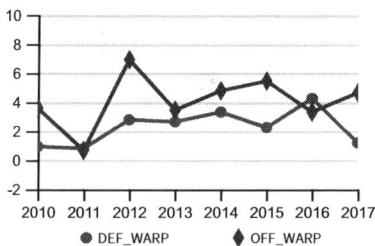

BRR (Relative to Position)

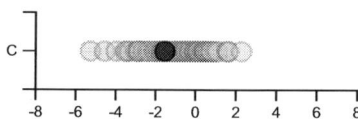

Rank		Player	BRR
52	39°	Mike Zunino	-1.37
53	38°	Chris Gimenez	-1.39
54	35°	**Buster Posey**	**-1.49**
55	33°	Cameron Rupp	-1.51
56	33°	Jorge Alfaro	-1.54

BRR (Relative to Team)

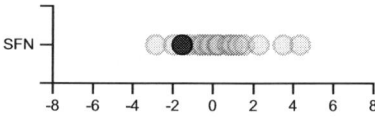

Rank		Player	BRR
21	31°	Justin Ruggiano	-1.14
22	22°	Brandon Crawford	-1.44
23	12°	**Buster Posey**	**-1.49**
24	4°	Evan Longoria	-1.90
25	0°	Nick Hundley	-2.80

Base Running Components

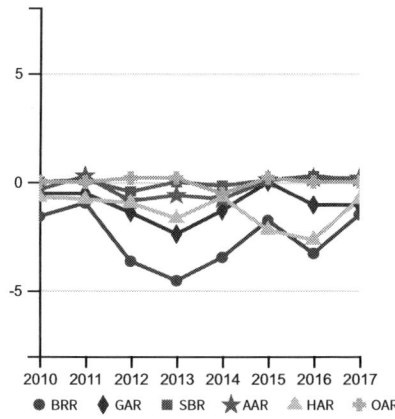

Yasiel Puig   RF   Los Angeles Dodgers

Born: 12/7/1990   **Age:** 27   **Bats:** R   **Throws:** R   **Height:** 6' 2"   **Weight:** 240 lbs   **Draft Info:** International Free Agent, 2012

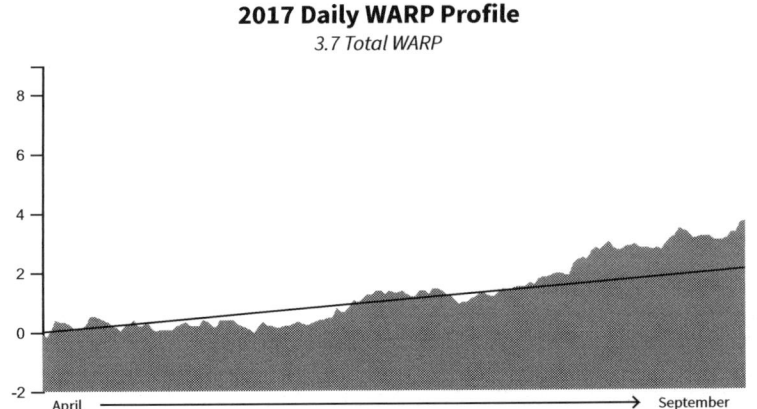

2017 Daily WARP Profile
3.7 Total WARP

PACE

21 Sec/Pit

45th of 155
71°
Fast

Fantasy Values
2017	2018
$21.42	$18.00

YEAR	TEAM	LVL	AGE	PA	R	2B	3B	HR	RBI	BB	K	SB	AVG/OBP/SLG	TAv	VORP	BABIP	WARP
2017	LAN	MLB	26	570	72	24	2	28	74	64	100	15	.263/.346/.487	.296	27.8	.274	3.7

2017 Batting Percentages

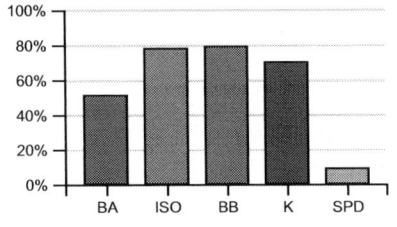

Batting PECOTA Percentiles

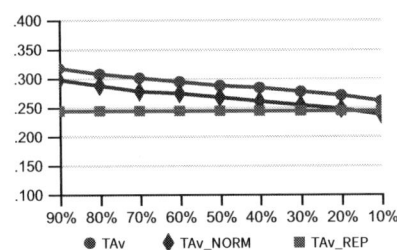

Batting WARP History

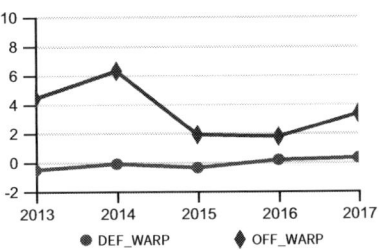

BRR (Relative to Position)

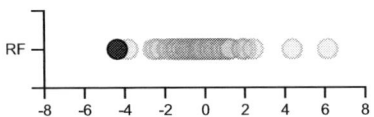

Rank		Player	BRR
51	9°	Max Kepler	-2.21
52	7°	Nomar Mazara	-2.41
53	5°	Stephen Piscotty	-2.54
54	3°	J.D. Martinez	-3.80
55	0°	**Yasiel Puig**	**-4.33**

BRR (Relative to Team)

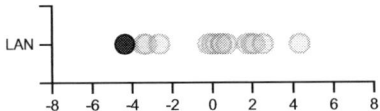

Rank		Player	BRR
11	31°	Cody Bellinger	-0.17
12	25°	Yasmani Grandal	-2.58
13	16°	Justin Turner	-3.24
14	10°	Matt Kemp	-3.37
15	0°	**Yasiel Puig**	**-4.33**

Base Running Components

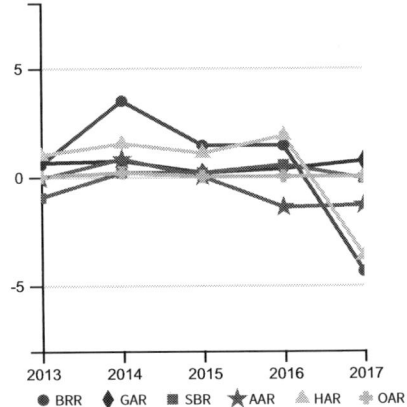

Albert Pujols   DH   Los Angeles Angels

Born: 1/16/1980   **Age:** 38   **Bats:** R   **Throws:** R   **Height:** 6' 3"   **Weight:** 240 lbs   **Draft Info:** Round 13, 1999 Draft (#402 overall)

2017 Daily WARP Profile
-1.8 Total WARP

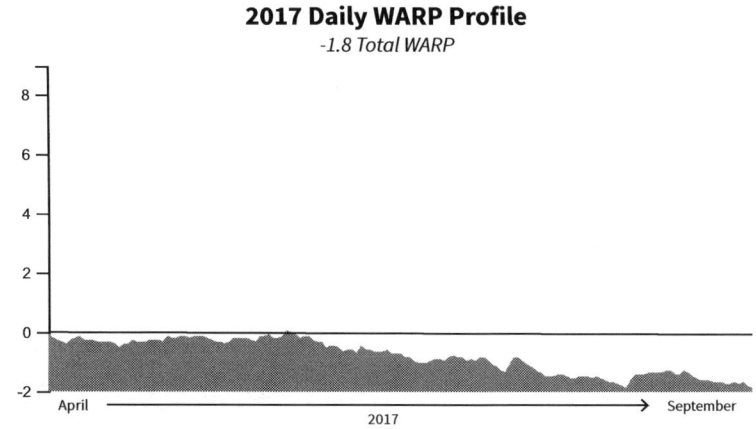

PACE
22 Sec/Pit
99th of 155
36°
Slow

Fantasy Values
2017	2018
$13.49	$12.00

YEAR	TEAM	LVL	AGE	PA	R	2B	3B	HR	RBI	BB	K	SB	AVG/OBP/SLG	TAv	VORP	BABIP	WARP
2017	ANA	MLB	37	636	53	17	0	23	101	37	93	3	.241/.286/.386	.225	-17.8	.249	-1.8

2017 Batting Percentages

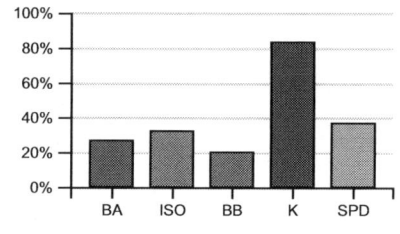

Batting PECOTA Percentiles

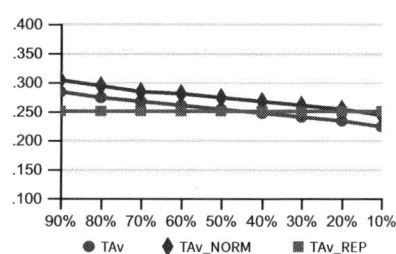

● TAv   ◆ TAv_NORM   ■ TAv_REP

Batting WARP History

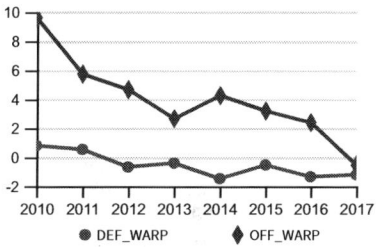

● DEF_WARP   ◆ OFF_WARP

BRR (Relative to Position)

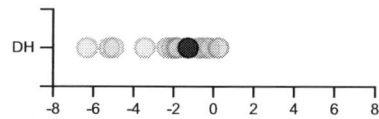

Rank		Player	BRR
5	89°	Carlos Beltran	-0.60
6	84°	Brandon Moss	-0.69
7	77°	**Albert Pujols**	**-1.22**
8	73°	Matt Holliday	-1.27
9	65°	Hanley Ramirez	-1.78

BRR (Relative to Team)

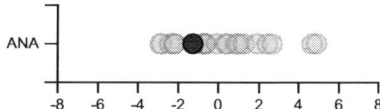

Rank		Player	BRR
14	40°	Luis Valbuena	-0.62
15	34°	Yunel Escobar	-0.75
16	27°	**Albert Pujols**	**-1.22**
17	24°	Jefry Marte	-2.13
18	19°	C.J. Cron	-2.15

Base Running Components

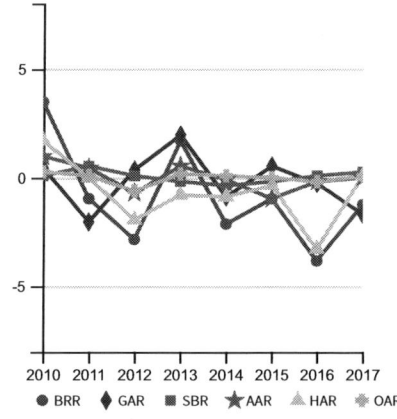

● BRR   ◆ GAR   ■ SBR   ★ AAR   ▲ HAR   ✳ OAR

Jose Quintana LHP Chicago Cubs

Born: 1/24/1989 **Age:** 29 **Bats:** R **Throws:** L **Height:** 6' 1" **Weight:** 220 lbs **Draft Info:** International Free Agent, 2006

2017 Daily WARP Profile
3.6 Total WARP

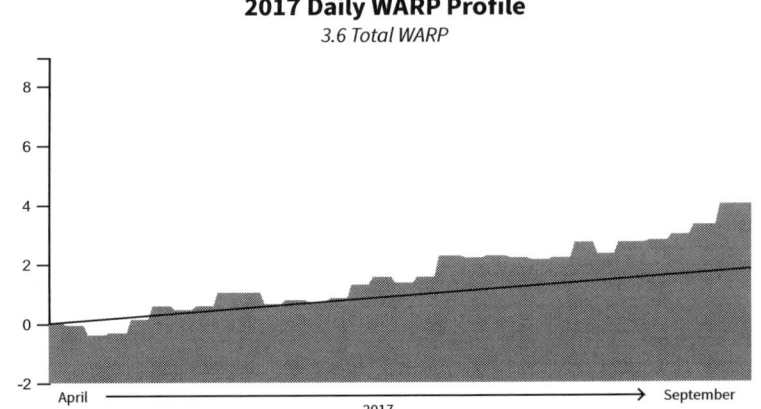

April ⟶ September
2017

POWER
42 86th of 150
PWR

STAMINA
79 17th of 150
STM

COMMAND
50 86th of 150
CMD

PACE
21 81st of 150
Sec/Pit 46°
Average

Fantasy Values
2017	2018
$5.99	**$17.00**

YEAR	TEAM	LVL	AGE	W	L	SV	G	GS	IP	H	HR	BB/9	K/9	K	GB%	BABIP	WHIP	ERA	DRA	WARP	MPH 95
2017	CHA	MLB	28	4	8	0	18	18	104.1	98	14	3.5	9.4	109	45%	.301	1.32	4.49	3.83	2.0	93.3
2017	CHN	MLB	28	7	3	0	14	14	84.1	72	9	2.2	10.5	98	48%	.300	1.10	3.74	3.90	1.6	94.0

On the surface, Quintana had a down year, with the highest ERA of his major-league career and plenty of rides on the struggle bus. However, a deeper look reveals a higher strikeout rate than usual and a pitcher who improved once he was traded across town to the National League. Quintana remains solidly in the second tier: probably not good enough to ever pitch like an ace but not the mid-tier arm he is miscast as at times. — Mike G.

2017 Pitching Percentages

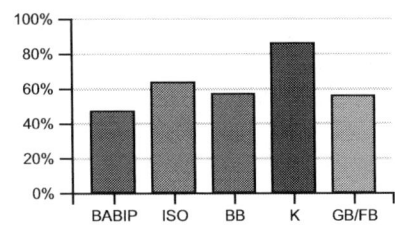

Pitching PECOTA Percentiles

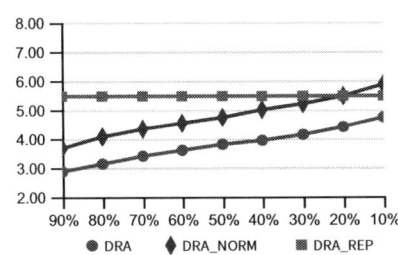

Pitching WARP History

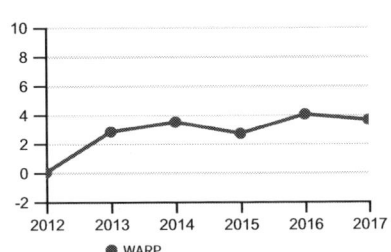

Tunnel vs LHH

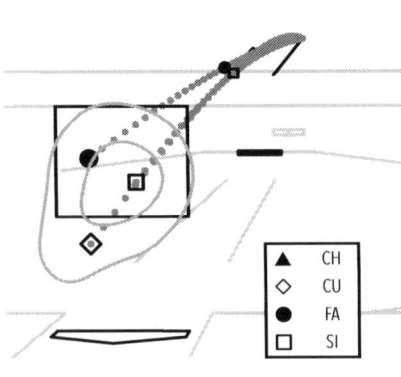

	CH
▲	CH
◇	CU
●	FA
□	SI

Pitch Types

Type	Freq	Velo	H Mov	V Mov
CH	9.0%	86.5 [105]	10.2 [105]	-24.5 [107]
CU	28.2%	77.4 [97]	-7.5 [99]	-45 [106]
FA	35.5%	92.6 [99]	4.7 [112]	-13.4 [106]
SI	27.3%	92.4 [100]	11.4 [108]	-15.9 [115]

Pitch Tunnel

Pairs	Release Diff	Tunnel Diff	Plate Diff	Speed Changes
2297	23.3	118.8	239.1	0.037

PI Scores

Year	Pitch Ct	Pwr	Cmd	Stm
2013	3324	49	61	80
2014	3321	45	56	81
2015	3349	40	52	81
2016	3271	46	64	82
2017	3163	42	50	79

Tunnel vs RHH

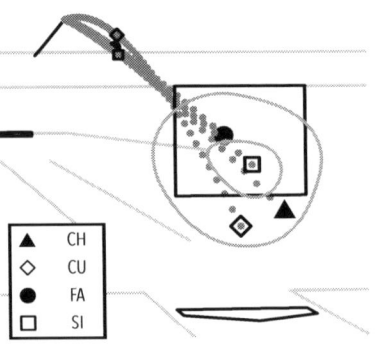

	CH
▲	CH
◇	CU
●	FA
□	SI

Erasmo Ramirez RHP Seattle Mariners

Born: 5/2/1990 **Age:** 28 **Bats:** R **Throws:** R **Height:** 5' 10" **Weight:** 215 lbs **Draft Info:** International Free Agent, 2007

We don't have a baseball card for this guy.

2017 Daily WARP Profile
2.2 Total WARP

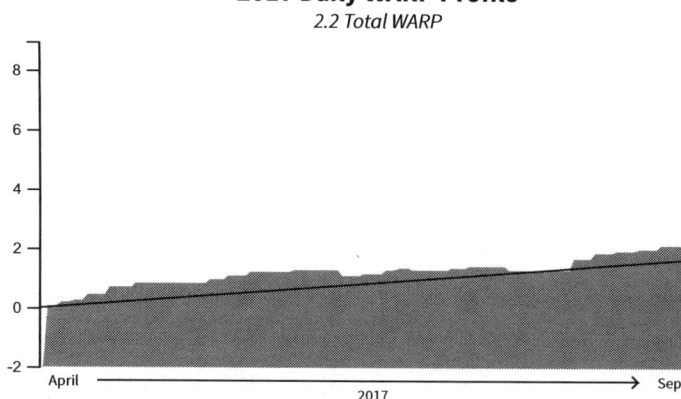

PACE 21 Sec/Pit — 81st of 150 — 46° Average

POWER 36 PWR — 113th of 150

STAMINA 58 STM — 107th of 150

COMMAND 67 CMD — 15th of 150

Fantasy Values

2017	2018
$9.52	$3.00

YEAR	TEAM	LVL	AGE	W	L	SV	G	GS	IP	H	HR	BB/9	K/9	K	GB%	BABIP	WHIP	ERA	DRA	WARP	MPH 95
2017	TBA	MLB	27	4	3	1	26	8	69.1	66	10	2.1	7.1	55	49%	.280	1.18	4.80	3.80	1.3	93.2
2017	SEA	MLB	27	1	3	0	11	11	62	57	12	2.2	7.8	54	39%	.257	1.16	3.92	4.18	0.9	93.4

2017 Pitching Percentages

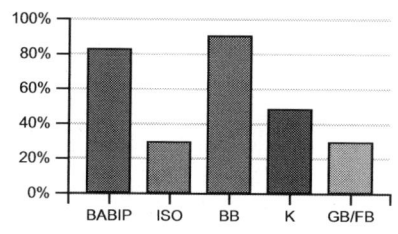

Pitching PECOTA Percentiles

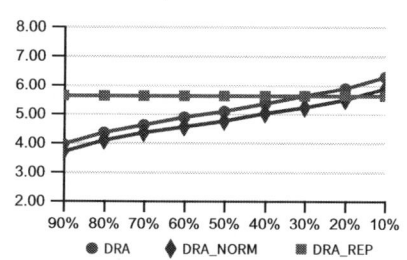

Pitching WARP History

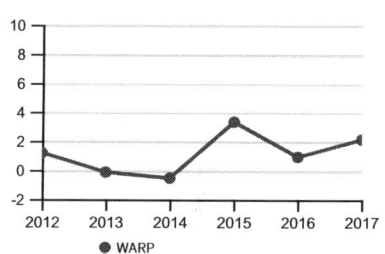

Tunnel vs LHH

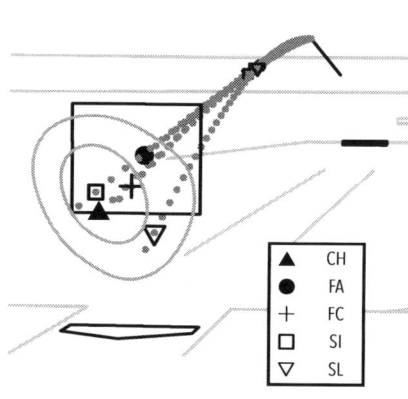

▲	CH
●	FA
+	FC
□	SI
▽	SL

Pitch Types

Type	Freq	Velo	H Mov	V Mov
CH	20.6%	84 [96]	-11.7 [97]	-26.9 [101]
CU	0.4%	77 [95]	8.6 [103]	-44.5 [107]
FA	11.5%	92.3 [99]	-7.5 [98]	-14.6 [102]
FC	25.0%	89 [104]	0.7 [95]	-19.6 [116]
SI	32.9%	91.9 [97]	-14.1 [88]	-20.7 [97]
SL	9.6%	84.2 [99]	5.9 [106]	-32.4 [101]

Pitch Tunnel

Pairs	Release Diff	Tunnel Diff	Plate Diff	Speed Changes
1387	29.6	110.7	213.3	0.020

PI Scores

Year	Pitch Ct	Pwr	Cmd	Stm
2013	1275	47	41	62
2014	1282	38	45	69
2015	2405	41	53	64
2016	1336	50	38	53
2017	1996	36	67	58

Tunnel vs RHH

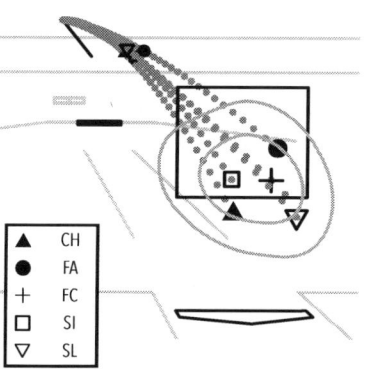

▲	CH
●	FA
+	FC
□	SI
▽	SL

Hanley Ramirez   DH   Boston Red Sox

Born: 12/23/1983   **Age:** 34   **Bats:** R   **Throws:** R   **Height:** 6' 2"   **Weight:** 235 lbs   **Draft Info:** International Free Agent, 2000

PACE
25 Sec/Pit
151st of 155
3°
Very Slow

2017 Daily WARP Profile
-0.1 Total WARP

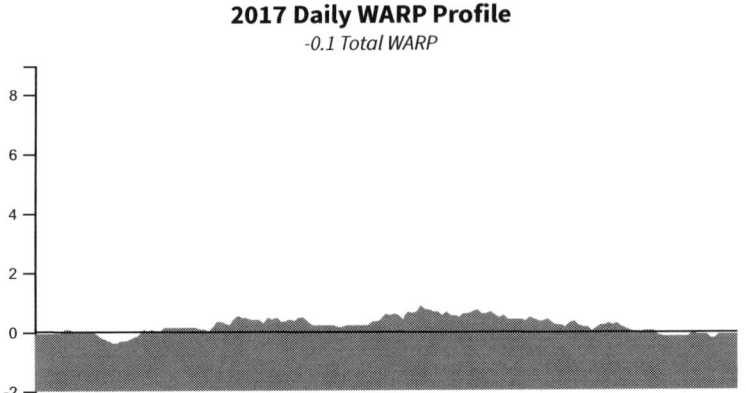

April → September
2017

Fantasy Values
2017	2018
$10.89	$12.00

YEAR	TEAM	LVL	AGE	PA	R	2B	3B	HR	RBI	BB	K	SB	AVG/OBP/SLG	TAv	VORP	BABIP	WARP
2017	BOS	MLB	33	553	58	24	0	23	62	51	116	1	.242/.320/.429	.253	-.2	.272	-.1

2017 Batting Percentages

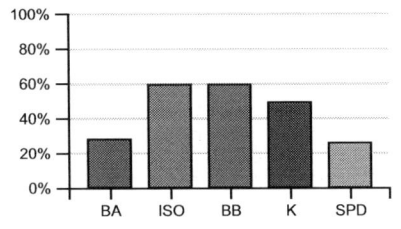

Batting PECOTA Percentiles

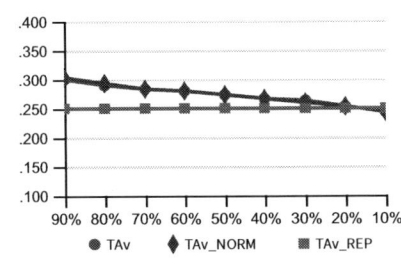

Batting WARP History

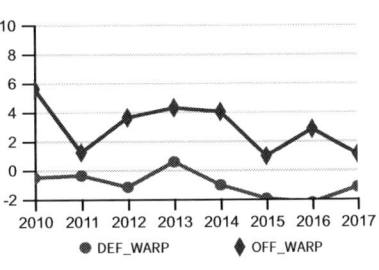

BRR (Relative to Position)

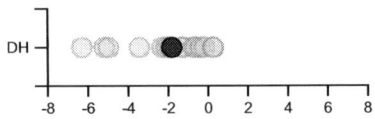

Rank		Player	BRR
7	77°	Albert Pujols	-1.22
8	73°	Matt Holliday	-1.27
9	65°	**Hanley Ramirez**	**-1.78**
10	55°	Nelson Cruz	-1.78
11	48°	Robbie Grossman	-1.86

BRR (Relative to Team)

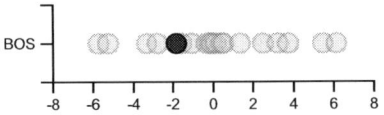

Rank		Player	BRR
13	34°	Sam Travis	-1.01
14	34°	Jhonny Peralta	-1.53
15	27°	**Hanley Ramirez**	**-1.78**
16	19°	Mitch Moreland	-2.72
17	12°	Christian Vazquez	-3.29

Base Running Components

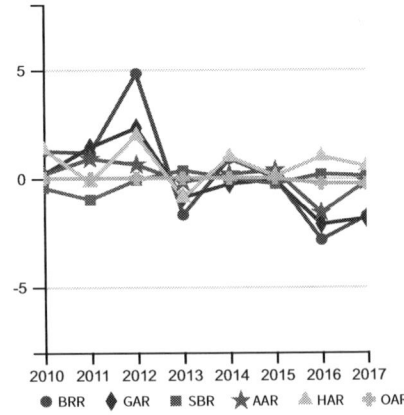

Jose Ramirez 3B Cleveland Indians

Born: 9/17/1992 **Age:** 25 **Bats:** B **Throws:** R **Height:** 5' 9" **Weight:** 165 lbs **Draft Info:** International Free Agent, 2009

2017 Daily WARP Profile
6.3 Total WARP

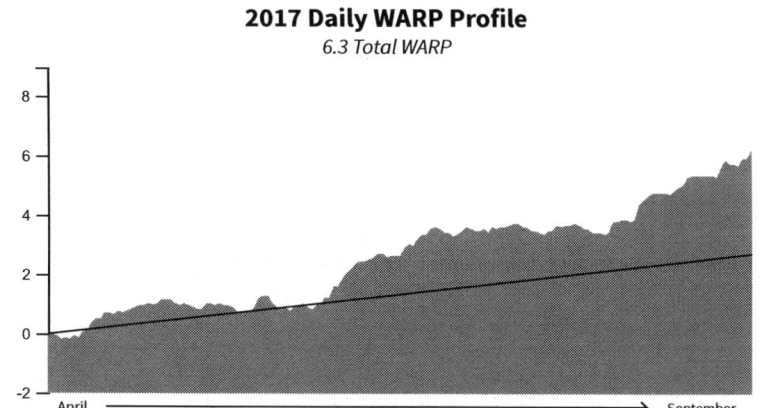

19 Sec/Pit

PACE
4th of 155
97°
Very Fast

Fantasy Values
2017	2018
$32.95	**$28.00**

YEAR	TEAM	LVL	AGE	PA	R	2B	3B	HR	RBI	BB	K	SB	AVG/OBP/SLG	TAv	VORP	BABIP	WARP
2017	CLE	MLB	24	645	107	56	6	29	83	52	69	17	.318/.374/.583	.315	57.2	.319	6.3

Ramirez not only put aside any questions about whether he was a legitimate starter but also turned himself into an elite player, adding power to his already impressive game and making himself a first-round talent in fantasy. It's rare to find a hitter with 30/ 20 potential who can hit over .300 with ease, but that's what Ramirez did in 2017. Doubting Ramirez is something that you do at your own peril at this point; he is a great hitter who is about to enter his prime as part of one of the strongest offenses in baseball. — Mike G.

2017 Batting Percentages

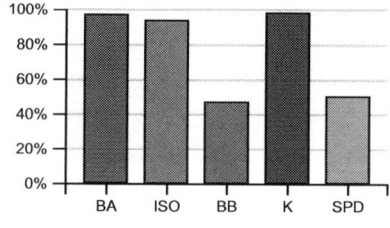

Batting PECOTA Percentiles

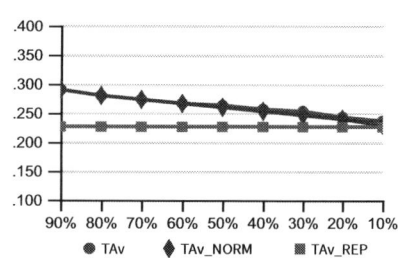

Batting WARP History

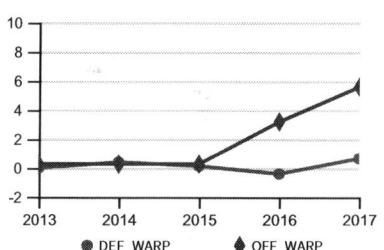

BRR (Relative to Position)

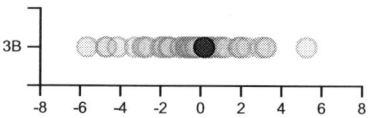

Rank		Player	BRR
20	65°	Jeimer Candelario	0.24
21	64°	Matt Reynolds	0.22
22	60°	**Jose Ramirez**	**0.21**
23	59°	Rafael Devers	0.17
24	58°	Josh Rutledge	-0.09

BRR (Relative to Team)

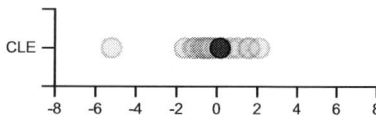

Rank		Player	BRR
5	62°	Greg Allen	0.74
6	59°	Brandon Guyer	0.29
7	48°	**Jose Ramirez**	**0.21**
8	47°	Rob Refsnyder	-0.02
9	46°	Tyler Naquin	-0.24

Base Running Components

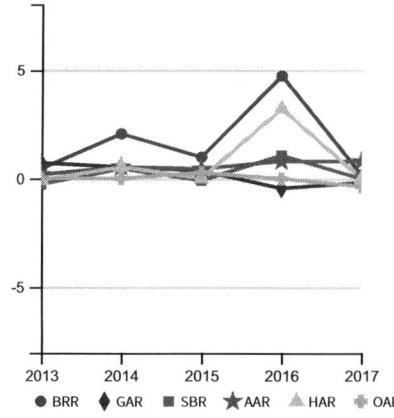

A.J. Ramos   RHP   New York Mets

Born: 9/20/1986   **Age:** 31   **Bats:** R   **Throws:** R   **Height:** 5' 10"   **Weight:** 200 lbs   **Draft Info:** Round 21, 2009 Draft (#638 overall)

2017 Daily WARP Profile
1.5 Total WARP

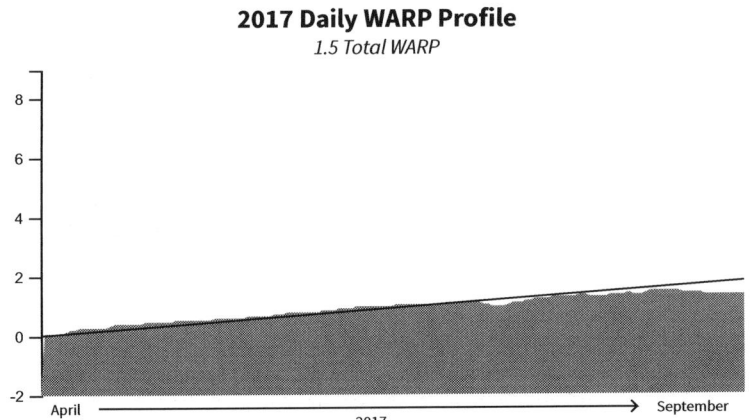

April   2017   September

POWER 32 PWR — 128th of 150

STAMINA 48 STM — 140th of 150

COMMAND 47 CMD — 102nd of 150

PACE 23 Sec/Pit — 126th of 150 / 16° / Very Slow

Fantasy Values	
2017	2018
$11.29	$9.00

YEAR	TEAM	LVL	AGE	W	L	SV	G	GS	IP	H	HR	BB/9	K/9	K	GB%	BABIP	WHIP	ERA	DRA	WARP	MPH 95
2017	MIA	MLB	30	2	4	20	40	0	39.2	30	4	5.0	10.7	47	42%	.271	1.31	3.63	3.23	0.9	94.5
2017	NYN	MLB	30	0	0	7	21	0	19	19	3	5.7	11.8	25	40%	.340	1.63	4.74	2.11	0.6	94.7

A dominant Marlins reliever for years, Ramos was flipped to the Mets midseason. New York continued to use Ramos as its closer, but new manager Mickey Callaway floated the idea of a job share in 2018. Even if Ramos stays on in the ninth, the high walk rate and spike in home runs make him very risky as a fantasy closer going forward. If he hangs on to the job, a low double-digit bid is the safe play. — Mike G.

2017 Pitching Percentages

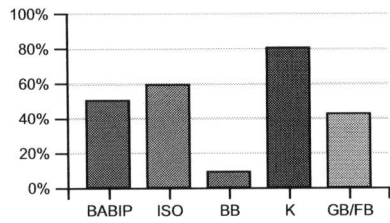

Pitching PECOTA Percentiles

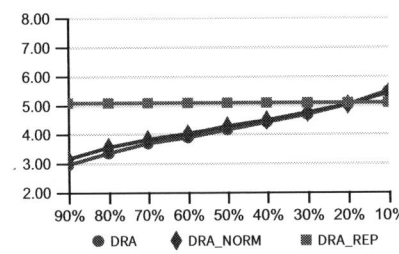

● DRA   ◆ DRA_NORM   ■ DRA_REP

Pitching WARP History

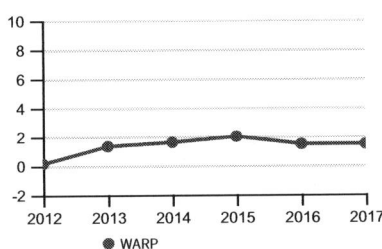

● WARP

Tunnel vs LHH

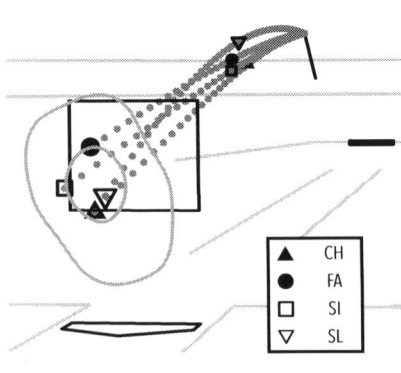

▲ CH
● FA
□ SI
▽ SL

Pitch Types

Type	Freq	Velo	H Mov	V Mov
CH	17.6%	85.8 [103]	-10.3 [104]	-27.6 [99]
CU	2.0%	75.4 [89]	10.7 [111]	-57.1 [80]
FA	29.0%	92.7 [100]	-1.5 [126]	-13.6 [105]
FC	0.2%	88.3 [99]	2.8 [106]	-19.8 [116]
SI	8.1%	92.6 [102]	-10.9 [112]	-17.3 [110]
SL	43.1%	80.4 [83]	9.8 [123]	-43.2 [70]

Pitch Tunnel

Pairs	Release Diff	Tunnel Diff	Plate Diff	Speed Changes
833	25.7	134.6	239.5	0.034

PI Scores

Year	Pitch Ct	Pwr	Cmd	Stm
2013	1331	54	44	53
2014	1071	39	50	50
2015	1084	42	49	51
2016	1103	35	51	50
2017	1090	32	47	48

Tunnel vs RHH

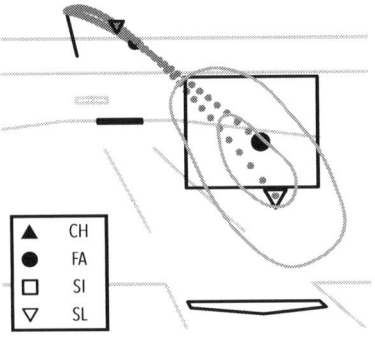

▲ CH
● FA
□ SI
▽ SL

Robbie Ray   LHP   Arizona Diamondbacks

Born: 10/1/1991   **Age:** 26   **Bats:** L   **Throws:** L   **Height:** 6'2"   **Weight:** 195 lbs   **Draft Info:** Round 12, 2010 Draft (#356 overall)

PACE
20 37th of 150
Sec/Pit 75°
Fast

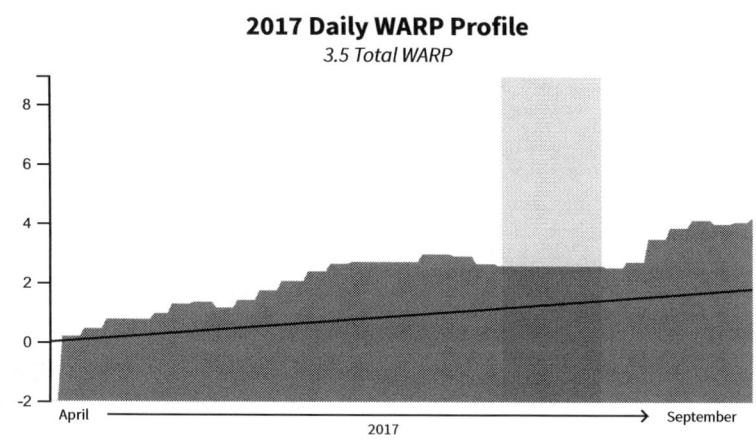

2017 Daily WARP Profile
3.5 Total WARP

April — 2017 — September

Game 104: DL (concussion)

54 POWER
PWR 45th of 150

70 STAMINA
STM 67th of 150

44 COMMAND
CMD 121st of 150

Fantasy Values
2017	2018
$27.34	$17.00

YEAR	TEAM	LVL	AGE	W	L	SV	G	GS	IP	H	HR	BB/9	K/9	K	GB%	BABIP	WHIP	ERA	DRA	WARP	MPH 95
2017	ARI	MLB	25	15	5	0	28	28	162	116	23	3.9	12.1	218	42%	.267	1.15	2.89	3.61	3.5	96.3

The hard-contact and high-strikeout rates are difficult to reconcile, but the results last year are difficult to argue against. Those strikeouts were valuable and even if some of those loud fly-ball outs from last year turn into extra-base hits this year, Ray still should produce next-to-top-tier value. There's nothing in his profile to suggest that the swing-and-miss stuff isn't repeatable. — Mike G.

2017 Pitching Percentages

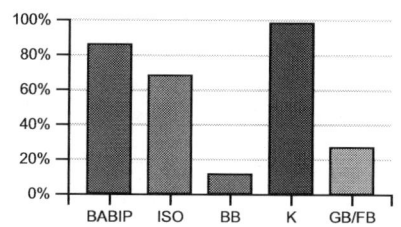

Pitching PECOTA Percentiles

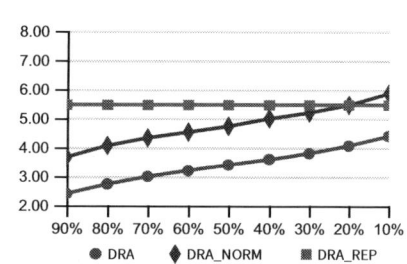

● DRA   ◆ DRA_NORM   ■ DRA_REP

Pitching WARP History

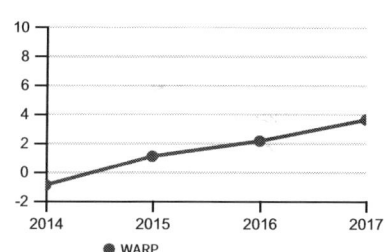

● WARP

Tunnel vs LHH

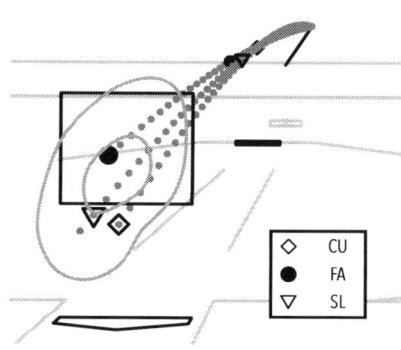

◇ CU
● FA
▽ SL

Pitch Types

Type	Freq	Velo	H Mov	V Mov
CH	0.9%	85.4 [101]	10.3 [104]	-25.1 [105]
CU	20.5%	81.8 [113]	-1 [74]	-40.4 [116]
FA	55.7%	94.5 [106]	8.4 [94]	-12.1 [110]
SI	3.5%	93.6 [107]	15.3 [80]	-17.2 [111]
SL	19.3%	85.1 [103]	0.7 [77]	-30.2 [107]

Pitch Tunnel

Pairs	Release Diff	Tunnel Diff	Plate Diff	Speed Changes
2039	35.8	124.3	240.3	0.030

PI Scores

Year	Pitch Ct	Pwr	Cmd	Stm
2014	547	53	51	56
2015	2249	62	44	72
2016	3159	63	57	79
2017	2705	54	44	70

Tunnel vs RHH

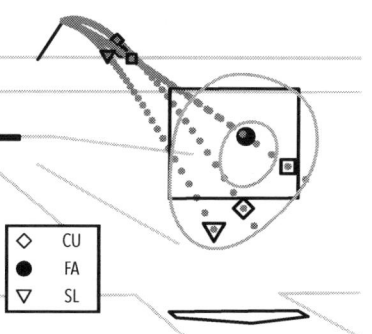

◇ CU
● FA
▽ SL

J.T. Realmuto   C   Miami Marlins

Born: 3/18/1991   **Age:** 27   **Bats:** R   **Throws:** R   **Height:** 6' 1"   **Weight:** 210 lbs   **Draft Info:** Round 3, 2010 Draft (#104 overall)

22 Sec/Pit

PACE
99th of 155
36°
Slow

2017 Daily WARP Profile
5.2 Total WARP

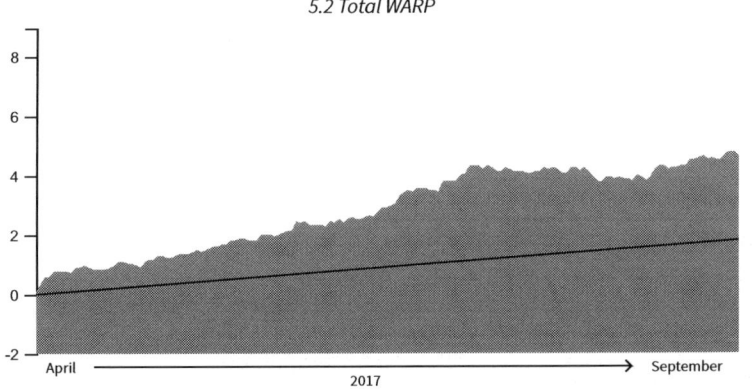

April — 2017 — September

Fantasy Values

2017	2018
$17.66	**$16.00**

YEAR	TEAM	LVL	AGE	PA	R	2B	3B	HR	RBI	BB	K	SB	AVG/OBP/SLG	TAv	VORP	BABIP	WARP
2017	MIA	MLB	26	579	68	31	5	17	65	36	106	8	.278/.332/.451	.279	37.8	.318	5.2

2017 Batting Percentages

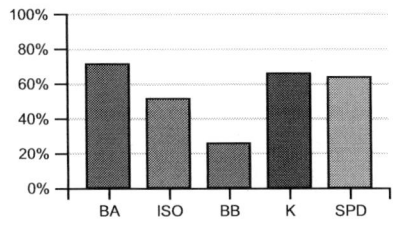

Batting PECOTA Percentiles

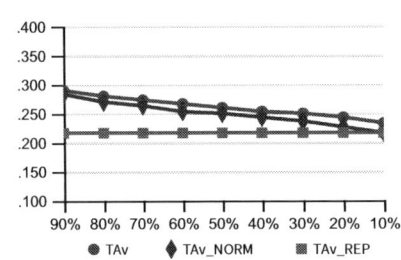

Batting WARP History

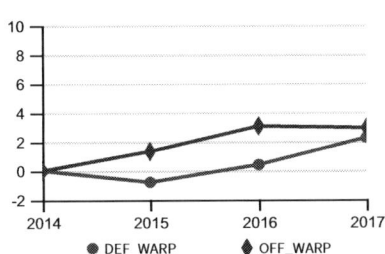

BRR (Relative to Position)

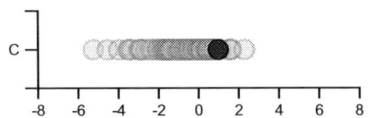

Rank		Player	BRR
4	94°	Chris Herrmann	1.62
5	93°	Luis Torrens	1.14
6	90°	**J.T. Realmuto**	**1.03**
7	87°	Jonathan Lucroy	0.84
8	87°	Eric Fryer	0.84

BRR (Relative to Team)

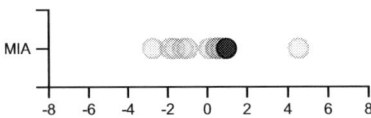

Rank		Player	BRR
1	52°	Miguel Rojas	4.57
2	42°	**J.T. Realmuto**	**1.03**
3	40°	Brian Anderson	0.98
4	38°	Magneuris Sierra	0.78
5	34°	Joshua Riddle	0.74

Base Running Components

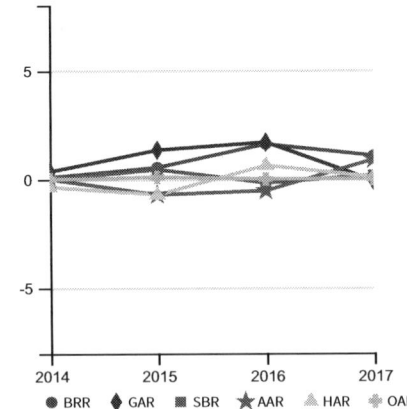

Josh Reddick RF Houston Astros

Born: 2/19/1987 **Age:** 31 **Bats:** L **Throws:** R **Height:** 6' 2" **Weight:** 195 lbs **Draft Info:** Round 17, 2006 Draft (#523 overall)

PACE
18th of 155
88°
Very Fast

20 Sec/Pit

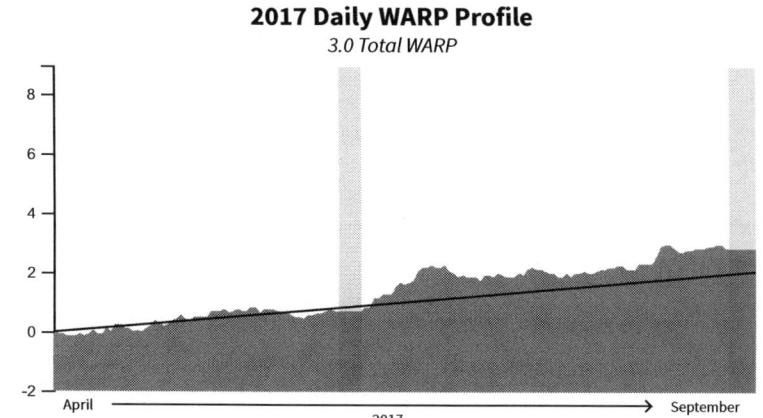

2017 Daily WARP Profile
3.0 Total WARP

Game 66: DL (concussion), **Game 156:** sore back

Fantasy Values
2017 **$22.39** 2018 **$16.00**

YEAR	TEAM	LVL	AGE	PA	R	2B	3B	HR	RBI	BB	K	SB	AVG/OBP/SLG	TAv	VORP	BABIP	WARP
2017	HOU	MLB	30	540	77	34	4	13	82	43	72	7	.314/.363/.484	.296	33.4	.339	3.0

2017 Batting Percentages
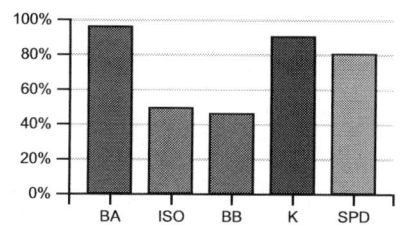

Batting PECOTA Percentiles
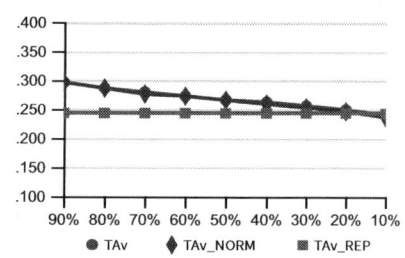

Batting WARP History
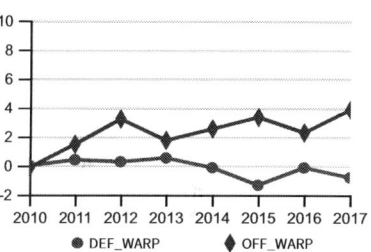

BRR (Relative to Position)
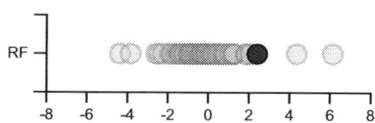

Rank		Player	BRR
1	96°	Mookie Betts	6.19
2	93°	Hunter Pence	4.40
3	90°	**Josh Reddick**	**2.45**
4	87°	Nick Markakis	2.12
5	85°	Jason Heyward	1.93

BRR (Relative to Team)
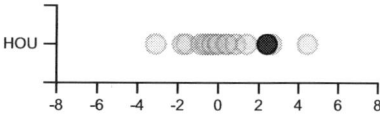

Rank		Player	BRR
1	95°	Cameron Maybin	4.50
2	82°	Jose Altuve	2.68
3	73°	**Josh Reddick**	**2.45**
4	69°	Jake Marisnick	1.44
5	68°	Tony Kemp	0.90

Base Running Components
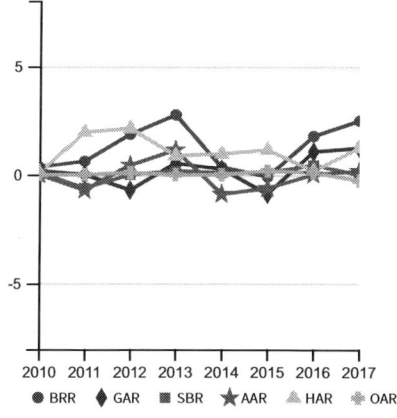

Anthony Rendon 3B Washington Nationals

Born: 6/6/1990 **Age:** 28 **Bats:** R **Throws:** R **Height:** 6' 1" **Weight:** 210 lbs **Draft Info:** Round 1, 2011 Draft (#6 overall)

2017 Daily WARP Profile
6.2 Total WARP

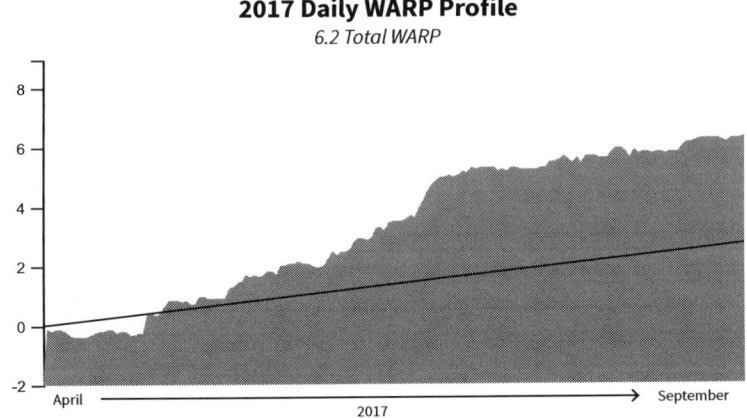

22
Sec/Pit

PACE
99th of 155
36°
Slow

Fantasy Values

2017	2018
$25.33	**$23.00**

YEAR	TEAM	LVL	AGE	PA	R	2B	3B	HR	RBI	BB	K	SB	AVG/OBP/SLG	TAv	VORP	BABIP	WARP
2017	WAS	MLB	27	605	81	41	1	25	100	84	82	7	.301/.403/.533	.325	63.4	.314	6.2

Rendon had an excellent season, but some of this did not translate to fantasy, particularly in leagues that use average instead of OBP. He is a solid citizen, but without 30+ home runs and/or 10+ stolen bases Rendon will be more of a third-round selection in mixed or a $25-30 player in only as opposed to an elite talent who is a first-round buy. There's nothing wrong with that, but don't overpay based on how great he is in real life. — Mike G.

2017 Batting Percentages

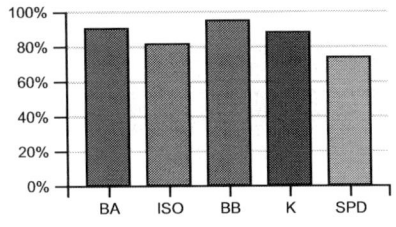

Batting PECOTA Percentiles

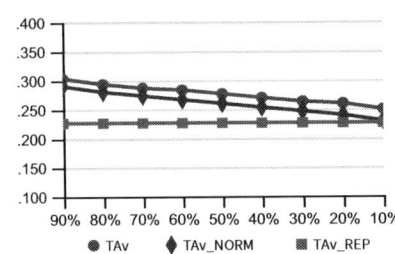

Batting WARP History

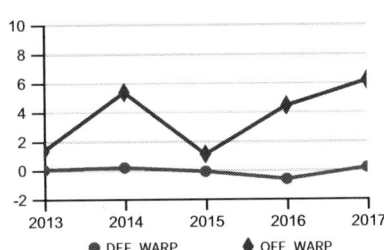

BRR (Relative to Position)

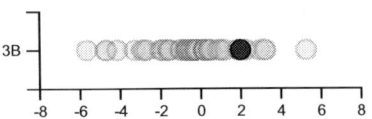

Rank	Player	BRR
4	89° Johan Camargo	2.97
5	87° Eduardo Escobar	2.30
6	84° **Anthony Rendon**	**2.04**
7	81° Jake Lamb	1.96
8	77° Kris Bryant	1.90

BRR (Relative to Team)

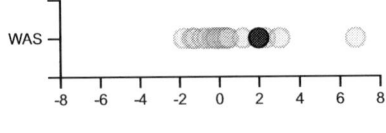

Rank	Player	BRR
2	84° Michael Taylor	3.06
3	77° Wilmer Difo	2.38
4	65° **Anthony Rendon**	**2.04**
5	57° Daniel Murphy	1.22
6	56° Andrew Stevenson	0.49

Base Running Components

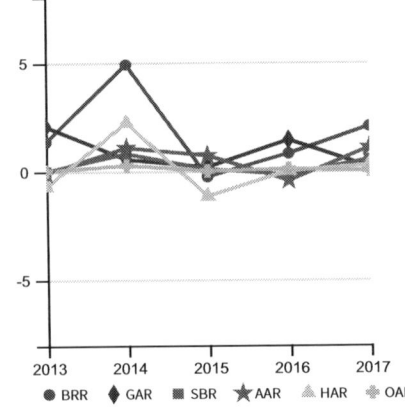

Mark Reynolds 1B Colorado Rockies

Born: 8/3/1983 **Age:** 34 **Bats:** R **Throws:** R **Height:** 6' 2" **Weight:** 220 lbs **Draft Info:** Round 16, 2004 Draft (#476 overall)

PACE
45th of 155
71°
Fast

21 Sec/Pit

2017 Daily WARP Profile
0.6 Total WARP

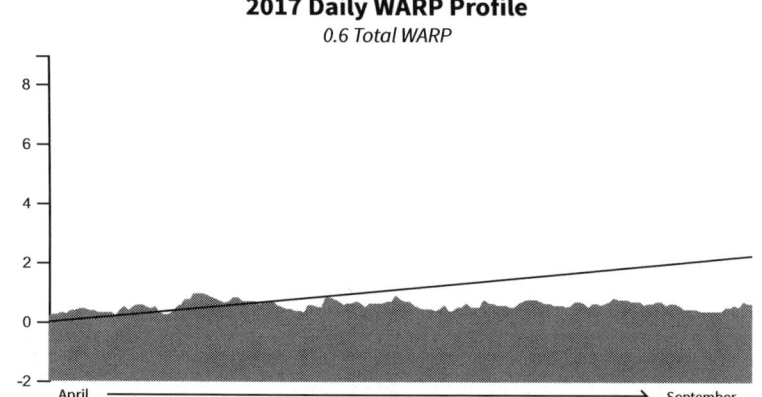

April 2017 September

Fantasy Values
2017	2018
$20.26	$3.00

YEAR	TEAM	LVL	AGE	PA	R	2B	3B	HR	RBI	BB	K	SB	AVG/OBP/SLG	TAv	VORP	BABIP	WARP
2017	COL	MLB	33	593	82	22	1	30	97	69	175	2	.267/.352/.487	.284	18.3	.343	.6

2017 Batting Percentages

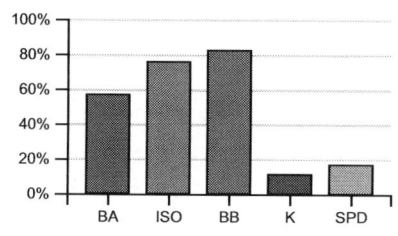

Batting PECOTA Percentiles

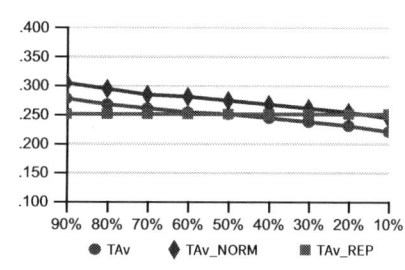

Batting WARP History

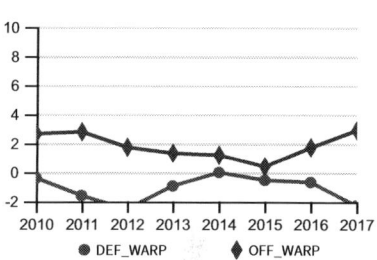

BRR (Relative to Position)

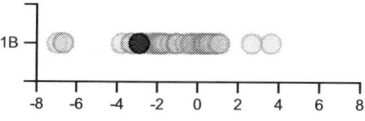

Rank		Player	BRR
37	26°	Mitch Moreland	-2.72
38	23°	Eric Thames	-2.73
39	20°	**Mark Reynolds**	**-2.86**
40	16°	Anthony Rizzo	-3.23
41	14°	Lucas Duda	-3.26

BRR (Relative to Team)

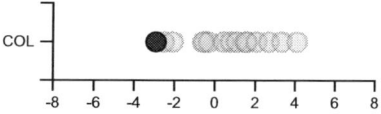

Rank		Player	BRR
11	21°	Nolan Arenado	-0.47
12	21°	Michael Tauchman	-0.53
13	17°	Chris Iannetta	-2.02
14	10°	Gerardo Parra	-2.47
15	0°	**Mark Reynolds**	**-2.86**

Base Running Components

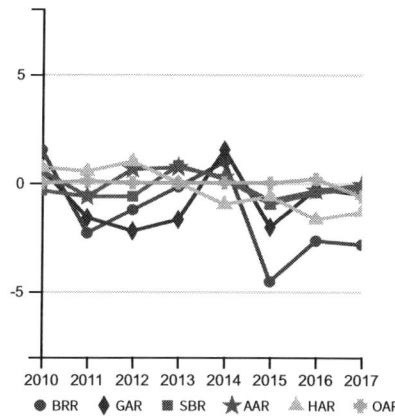

Clayton Richard   LHP   San Diego Padres

Born: 9/12/1983   **Age:** 34   **Bats:** L   **Throws:** L   **Height:** 6'5"   **Weight:** 240 lbs   **Draft Info:** Round 8, 2005 Draft (#245 overall)

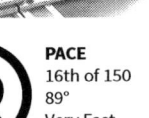

2017 Daily WARP Profile
-0.7 Total WARP

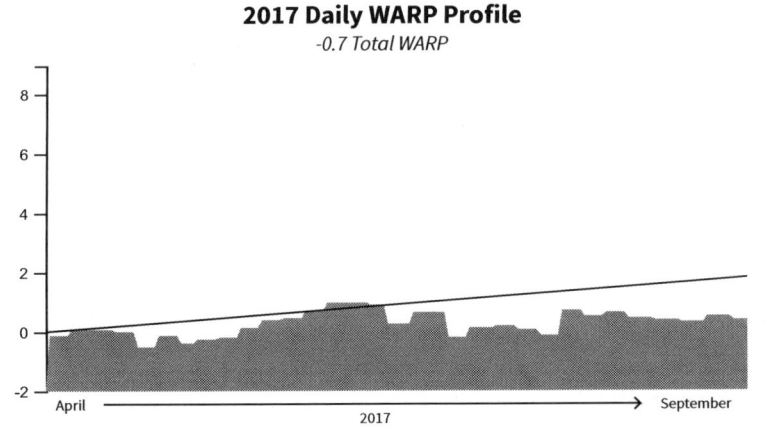

PACE
19 Sec/Pit
16th of 150
89°
Very Fast

POWER **45** PWR
73rd of 150

STAMINA **81** STM
11th of 150

COMMAND **44** CMD
121st of 150

Fantasy Values
2017	2018
$2.70	$1.00

YEAR	TEAM	LVL	AGE	W	L	SV	G	GS	IP	H	HR	BB/9	K/9	K	GB%	BABIP	WHIP	ERA	DRA	WARP	MPH 95
2017	SDN	MLB	33	8	15	0	32	32	197.1	240	24	2.7	6.9	151	60%	.351	1.52	4.79	5.90	-0.7	92.4

2017 Pitching Percentages

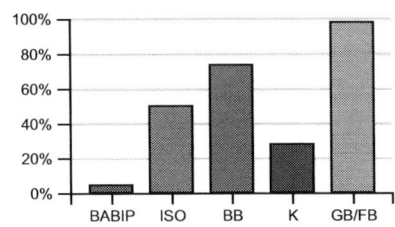

Pitching PECOTA Percentiles

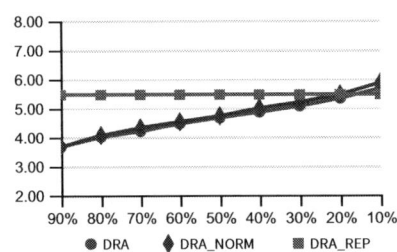

Pitching WARP History

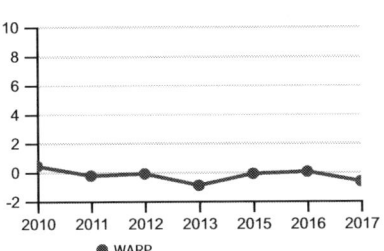

Tunnel vs LHH

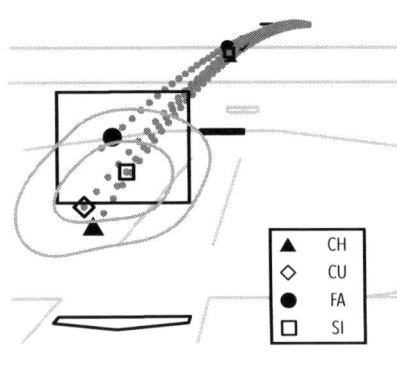

▲	CH
◇	CU
●	FA
□	SI

Pitch Types

Type	Freq	Velo	H Mov	V Mov
CH	10.7%	84 [96]	15.5 [76]	-31.9 [86]
CU	18.6%	81.5 [112]	1.3 [65]	-38.8 [120]
FA	10.1%	91.7 [96]	13.3 [71]	-19.4 [86]
FC	1.4%	85.7 [85]	4.4 [69]	-28.6 [81]
SI	59.2%	90.6 [90]	15.9 [75]	-26.8 [75]

Pitch Tunnel

Pairs	Release Diff	Tunnel Diff	Plate Diff	Speed Changes
2133	33.4	114.7	212.6	0.020

PI Scores

Year	Pitch Ct	Pwr	Cmd	Stm
2012	3151	50	47	78
2013	844	47	36	44
2015	611	58	61	53
2016	1074	54	50	43
2017	2993	45	44	81

Tunnel vs RHH

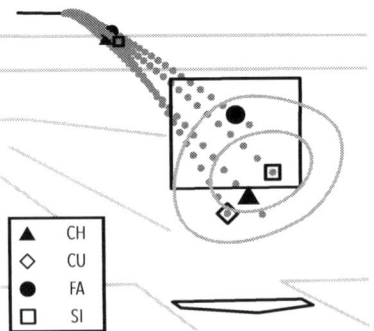

▲	CH
◇	CU
●	FA
□	SI

Felipe Rivero   LHP   Pittsburgh Pirates

Born: 7/5/1991   **Age:** 26   **Bats:** L   **Throws:** L   **Height:** 6' 2"   **Weight:** 210 lbs   **Draft Info:** International Free Agent, 2008

PACE
21 Sec/Pit
81st of 150
46°
Average

2017 Daily WARP Profile
1.9 Total WARP

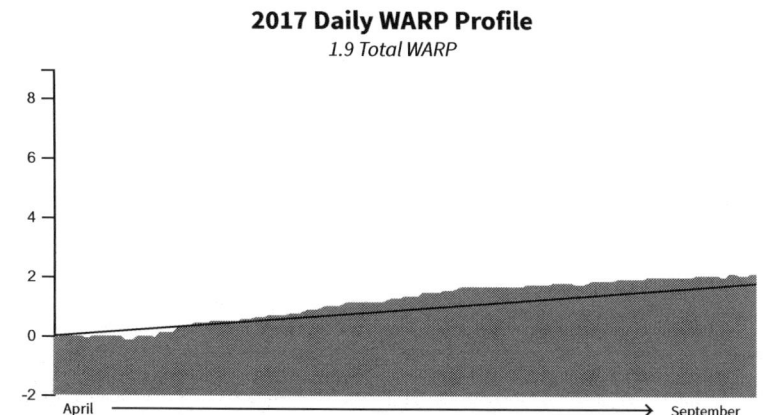

POWER
76 PWR
3rd of 150

STAMINA
53 STM
121st of 150

COMMAND
46 CMD
111th of 150

Fantasy Values
2017	2018
$22.38	$18.00

YEAR	TEAM	LVL	AGE	W	L	SV	G	GS	IP	H	HR	BB/9	K/9	K	GB%	BABIP	WHIP	ERA	DRA	WARP	MPH 95
2017	PIT	MLB	25	5	3	21	73	0	75.1	47	4	2.4	10.5	88	53%	.234	0.89	1.67	2.94	1.9	100.7

Cast as a set-up man to start the season, Rivero quickly supplanted Tony Watson before the latter was traded to the Dodgers. Rivero was one of the hardest throwers in baseball, averaging nearly 99 mph on his fastball, which makes his 88-mph change seem slow by comparison. No closer is a certainty, but Rivero's raw stuff gives him a leg up on most of the competition. — Mike G.

2017 Pitching Percentages

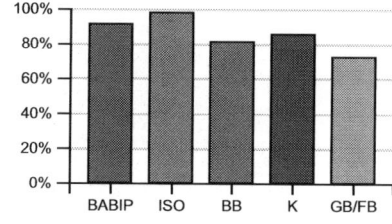

Pitching PECOTA Percentiles

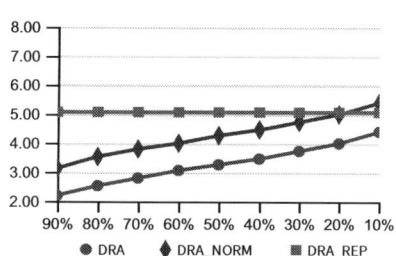

Pitching WARP History

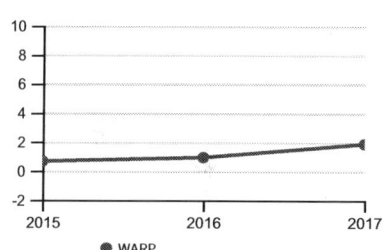

Tunnel vs LHH

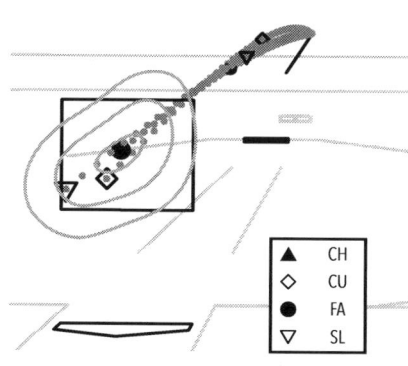

▲	CH
◇	CU
●	FA
▽	SL

Pitch Types

Type	Freq	Velo	H Mov	V Mov
CH	20.3%	88.8 [115]	12.4 [93]	-29.2 [94]
CU	9.9%	82.3 [115]	-10.9 [112]	-41.1 [115]
FA	61.0%	98.8 [122]	7 [100]	-12.2 [109]
SL	8.9%	86.2 [108]	-11.5 [130]	-28.5 [112]

Pitch Tunnel

Pairs	Release Diff	Tunnel Diff	Plate Diff	Speed Changes
849	39.3	110.7	204.3	0.031

PI Scores

Year	Pitch Ct	Pwr	Cmd	Stm
2015	752	67	51	44
2016	1281	61	41	55
2017	1145	76	46	53

Tunnel vs RHH

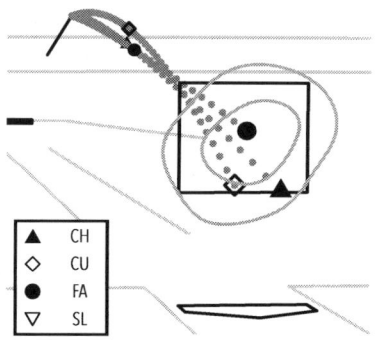

▲	CH
◇	CU
●	FA
▽	SL

Anthony Rizzo   1B   Chicago Cubs

Born: 8/8/1989   **Age:** 28   **Bats:** L   **Throws:** L   **Height:** 6' 3"   **Weight:** 240 lbs   **Draft Info:** Round 6, 2007 Draft (#204 overall)

2017 Daily WARP Profile
5.1 Total WARP

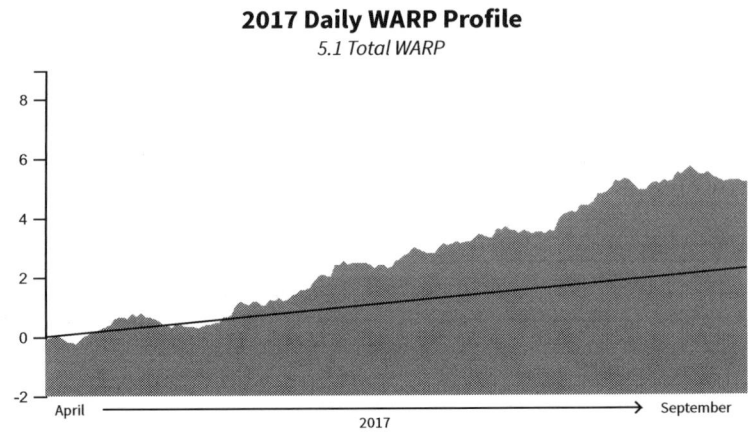

22 Sec/Pit

PACE
99th of 155
36°
Slow

Fantasy Values

2017	2018
$26.39	$29.00

YEAR	TEAM	LVL	AGE	PA	R	2B	3B	HR	RBI	BB	K	SB	AVG/OBP/SLG	TAv	VORP	BABIP	WARP
2017	CHN	MLB	27	691	99	32	3	32	109	91	90	10	.273/.392/.507	.304	36.3	.273	5.1

Rizzo isn't the best first baseman in fantasy, but when you buy him you're purchasing an extremely consistent player. For the third consecutive season Rizzo was good for at least 31 home runs, 94 runs, and 101 RBI. His fantasy value mostly fluctuates depending on how much he decides he will or won't run in any given year. Rizzo isn't quite up there in the stratosphere with Joey Votto and Paul Goldschmidt, but he's one of the next best things. — Mike G.

2017 Batting Percentages

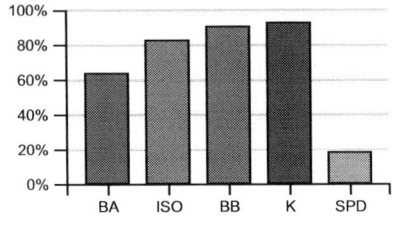

Batting PECOTA Percentiles

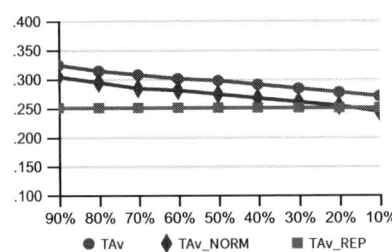

Batting WARP History

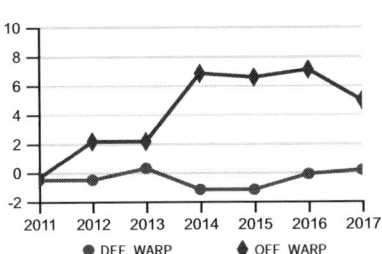

BRR (Relative to Position)

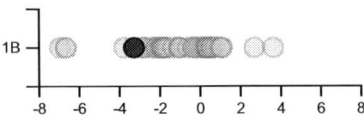

Rank		Player	BRR
38	23°	Eric Thames	-2.73
39	20°	Mark Reynolds	-2.86
40	16°	**Anthony Rizzo**	**-3.23**
41	14°	Lucas Duda	-3.26
42	11°	Josh Bell	-3.73

BRR (Relative to Team)

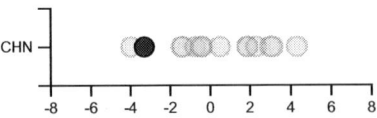

Rank		Player	BRR
10	30°	Tommy La Stella	-0.70
11	22°	Ben Zobrist	-1.32
12	18°	Chris Gimenez	-1.39
13	7°	**Anthony Rizzo**	**-3.23**
14	0°	Willson Contreras	-3.93

Base Running Components

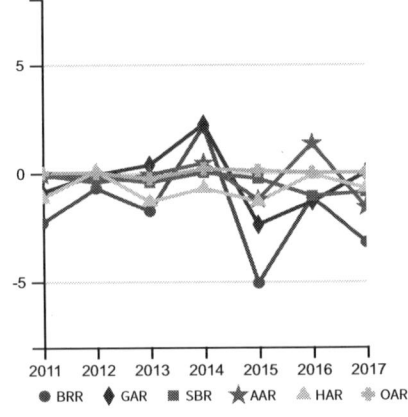

Tanner Roark   RHP   Washington Nationals

Born: 10/5/1986   **Age:** 31   **Bats:** R   **Throws:** R   **Height:** 6' 2"   **Weight:** 235 lbs   **Draft Info:** Round 25, 2008 Draft (#753 overall)

2017 Daily WARP Profile
2.9 Total WARP

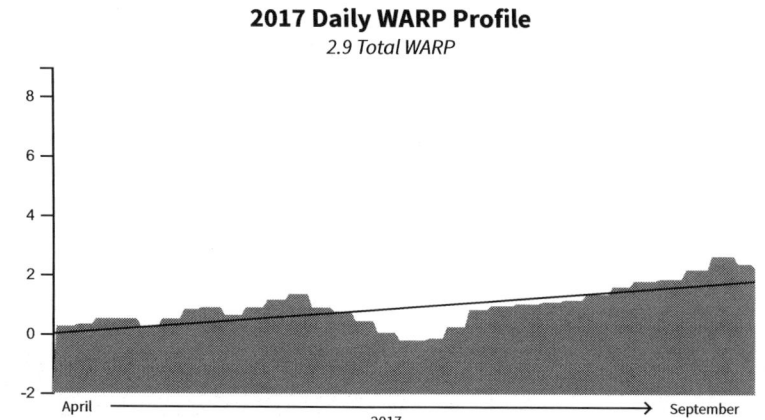

April — 2017 — September

POWER **45** PWR — 73rd of 150

STAMINA **79** STM — 17th of 150

COMMAND **62** CMD — 24th of 150

PACE **20** Sec/Pit — 37th of 150, 75°, Fast

Fantasy Values
2017	2018
$11.92	$10.00

YEAR	TEAM	LVL	AGE	W	L	SV	G	GS	IP	H	HR	BB/9	K/9	K	GB%	BABIP	WHIP	ERA	DRA	WARP	MPH 95
2017	WAS	MLB	30	13	11	0	32	30	181.1	178	23	3.2	8.2	166	49%	.300	1.33	4.67	4.10	2.9	94.3

2017 Pitching Percentages
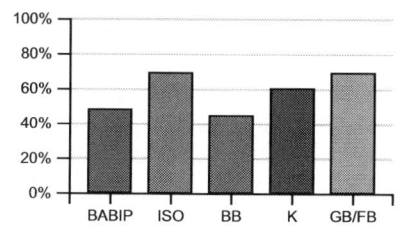

Pitching PECOTA Percentiles
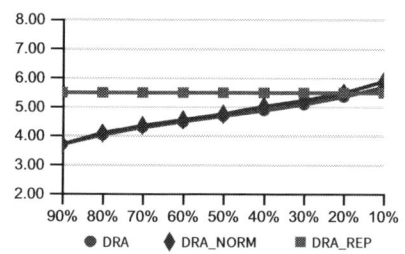
● DRA   ◆ DRA_NORM   ■ DRA_REP

Pitching WARP History
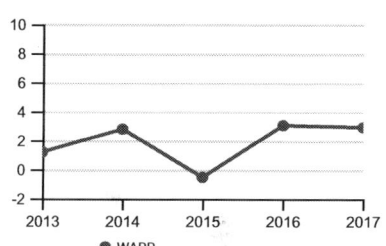
● WARP

Tunnel vs LHH
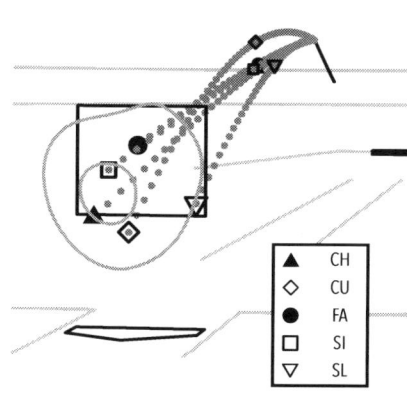

▲	CH
◇	CU
●	FA
□	SI
▽	SL

Pitch Types
Type	Freq	Velo	H Mov	V Mov
CH	12.2%	84 [96]	-10.7 [102]	-26.8 [101]
CU	15.1%	76.1 [92]	12.6 [119]	-55.6 [84]
FA	20.2%	92.8 [100]	-4.7 [111]	-13.6 [105]
FC	1.7%	89.1 [104]	2.2 [103]	-21.2 [110]
SI	36.1%	92.5 [101]	-10.8 [112]	-17 [111]
SL	14.8%	85.9 [107]	3.7 [96]	-28.3 [112]

Pitch Tunnel
Pairs	Release Diff	Tunnel Diff	Plate Diff	Speed Changes
2411	38.1	121.9	226.0	0.033

PI Scores
Year	Pitch Ct	Pwr	Cmd	Stm
2013	759	52	58	63
2014	2984	48	52	76
2015	1776	54	48	54
2016	3337	50	57	83
2017	3181	45	62	79

Tunnel vs RHH
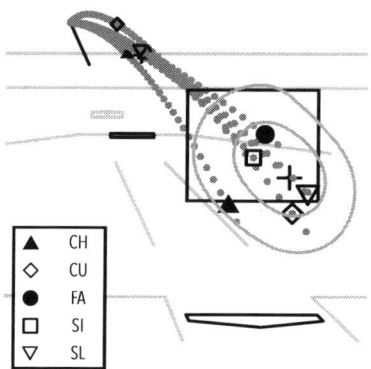

▲	CH
◇	CU
●	FA
□	SI
▽	SL

David Robertson   RHP   New York Yankees

Born: 4/9/1985   **Age:** 33   **Bats:** R   **Throws:** R   **Height:** 5'11"   **Weight:** 195 lbs   **Draft Info:** Round 17, 2006 Draft (#524 overall)

22 Sec/Pit   **PACE** 108th of 150   28°   Slow

2017 Daily WARP Profile
2.2 Total WARP

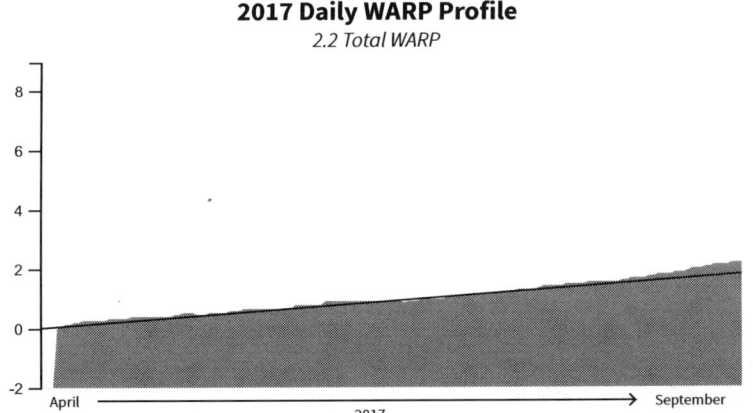

38 PWR   **POWER** 104th of 150

48 STM   **STAMINA** 140th of 150

40 CMD   **COMMAND** 137th of 150

Fantasy Values
2017	2018
$22.18	$5.00

YEAR	TEAM	LVL	AGE	W	L	SV	G	GS	IP	H	HR	BB/9	K/9	K	GB%	BABIP	WHIP	ERA	DRA	WARP	MPH 95
2017	CHA	MLB	32	4	2	13	31	0	33.1	21	4	3.0	12.7	47	43%	.250	0.96	2.70	2.14	1.1	93.2
2017	NYA	MLB	32	5	0	1	30	0	35	14	2	3.1	13.1	51	56%	.182	0.74	1.03	2.30	1.1	93.7

Middle relievers are generally poor fantasy investments, not because they can't earn but rather because so many useful nonclosers are available in the free agent pool. The exception is a pitcher like Robertson, who gets the opportunity to vulture multiple wins on a strong Yankees team in a bullpen where roles frequently fluctuate. Robertson will nab few if any saves behind Aroldis Chapman and Dellin Betances, but he puts up so many quality innings that he should be ranked ahead of the lowest tier of fungible starting pitchers. — Mike G.

2017 Pitching Percentages

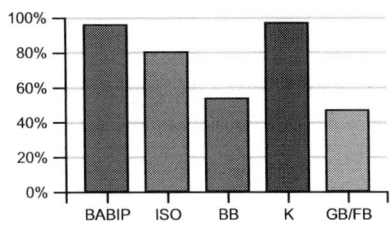

Pitching PECOTA Percentiles

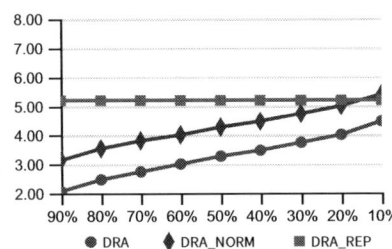

Pitching WARP History

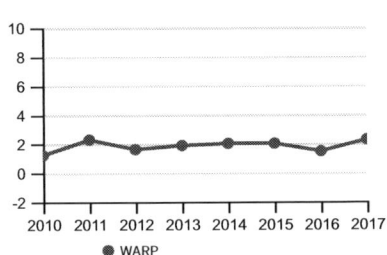

Tunnel vs LHH

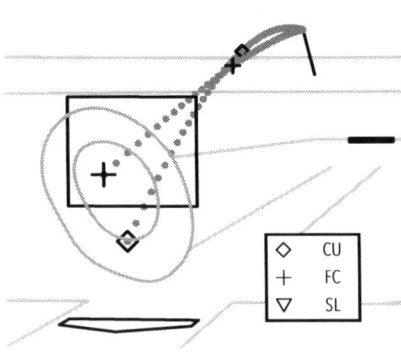

◇	CU
+	FC
▽	SL

Pitch Types

Type	Freq	Velo	H Mov	V Mov
CH	1.2%	87.7 [110]	-10.3 [104]	-22.8 [112]
CU	39.3%	82.7 [116]	10.7 [111]	-44.5 [107]
FC	51.5%	91.9 [120]	2.1 [103]	-15.6 [132]
SI	1.0%	92.3 [100]	-11.8 [105]	-16.3 [114]
SL	7.1%	83.7 [97]	8.9 [119]	-34.6 [94]

Pitch Tunnel

Pairs	Release Diff	Tunnel Diff	Plate Diff	Speed Changes
778	25.9	113.2	225.1	0.024

PI Scores

Year	Pitch Ct	Pwr	Cmd	Stm
2013	1049	55	48	49
2014	1072	50	44	48
2015	972	51	60	47
2016	1032	51	57	47
2017	1032	38	40	48

Tunnel vs RHH

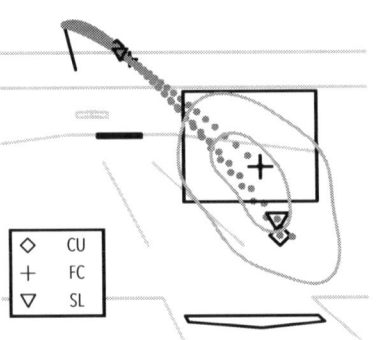

◇	CU
+	FC
▽	SL

Carlos Rodon   LHP   Chicago White Sox

Born: 12/10/1992   **Age:** 25   **Bats:** L   **Throws:** L   **Height:** 6' 3"   **Weight:** 235 lbs   **Draft Info:** Round 1, 2014 Draft (#3 overall)

PACE
20 Sec/Pit
37th of 150
75°
Fast

2017 Daily WARP Profile
0.3 Total WARP

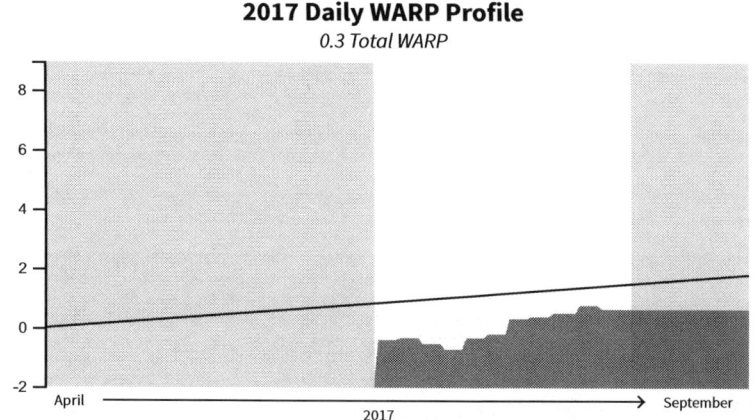

April — 2017 — September

Game 1: DL (biceps bursitis), **Game 135:** DL (shoulder inflammation)

POWER
55 PWR
43rd of 150

STAMINA
58 STM
107th of 150

COMMAND
42 CMD
128th of 150

Fantasy Values
2017	2018
$3.90	$2.00

YEAR	TEAM	LVL	AGE	W	L	SV	G	GS	IP	H	HR	BB/9	K/9	K	GB%	BABIP	WHIP	ERA	DRA	WARP	MPH 95
2017	CHA	MLB	24	2	5	0	12	12	69.1	64	12	4.0	9.9	76	45%	.297	1.37	4.15	5.22	0.3	96.4

For the second consecutive year Rodon showed flashes of brilliance but was erratic and ineffective. Shoulder surgery in September puts Rodon's status for Opening Day in doubt. Even if he is ready to answer the bell, his mediocre career stats make him a low-end play in most leagues and someone to stay away from in formats with limited reserve and/or DL slots. — Mike G.

2017 Pitching Percentages

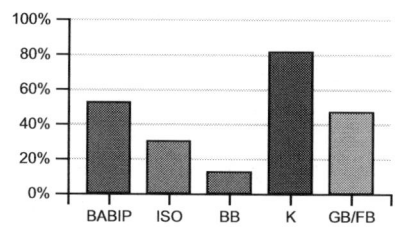

Pitching PECOTA Percentiles

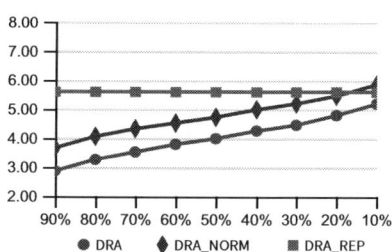

● DRA   ◆ DRA_NORM   ■ DRA_REP

Pitching WARP History

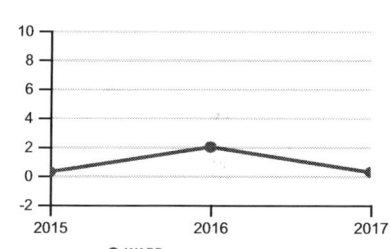

● WARP

Tunnel vs LHH

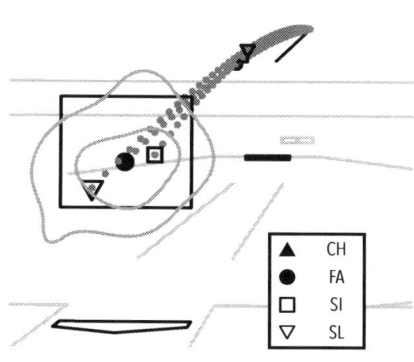

▲	CH
●	FA
□	SI
▽	SL

Pitch Types

Type	Freq	Velo	H Mov	V Mov
CH	12.2%	83.4 [93]	12.9 [90]	-30.2 [91]
FA	37.1%	93.6 [103]	7.5 [98]	-14.2 [103]
SI	24.1%	93.2 [105]	12.4 [100]	-18.3 [106]
SL	26.6%	85.3 [104]	-5.9 [106]	-33.1 [99]

Pitch Tunnel

Pairs	Release Diff	Tunnel Diff	Plate Diff	Speed Changes
880	26.6	122.5	239.2	0.024

PI Scores

Year	Pitch Ct	Pwr	Cmd	Stm
2015	2441	59	32	66
2016	2786	57	41	72
2017	1179	55	42	58

Tunnel vs RHH

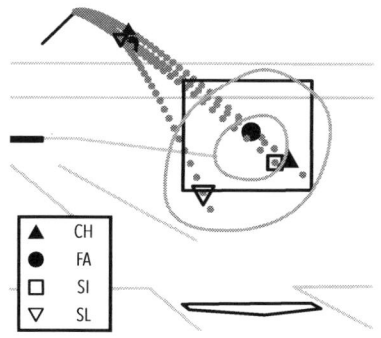

▲	CH
●	FA
□	SI
▽	SL

Eduardo Rodriguez   LHP   Boston Red Sox

Born: 4/7/1993   **Age:** 25   **Bats:** L   **Throws:** L   **Height:** 6'2"   **Weight:** 220 lbs   **Draft Info:** International Free Agent, 2010

2017 Daily WARP Profile
3.0 Total WARP

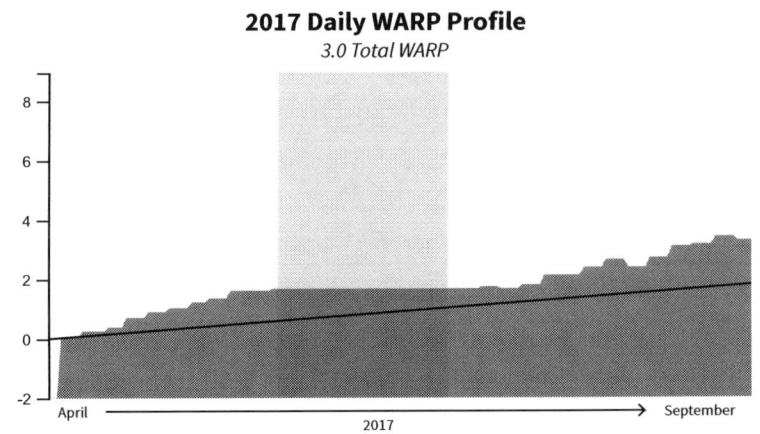

April — 2017 — September

Game 54: DL (knee subluxation)

57 PWR — POWER — 35th of 150

68 STM — STAMINA — 77th of 150

55 CMD — COMMAND — 62nd of 150

22 Sec/Pit — PACE — 108th of 150 — 28° — Slow

Fantasy Values

2017	2018
$10.49	$7.00

YEAR	TEAM	LVL	AGE	W	L	SV	G	GS	IP	H	HR	BB/9	K/9	K	GB%	BABIP	WHIP	ERA	DRA	WARP	MPH 95
2017	BOS	MLB	24	6	7	0	25	24	137.1	126	19	3.3	9.8	150	36%	.299	1.28	4.19	3.61	3.0	95.0

2017 Pitching Percentages

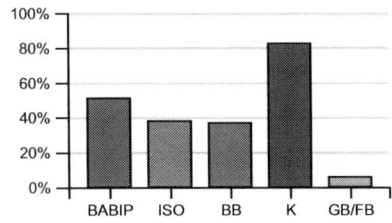

Pitching PECOTA Percentiles

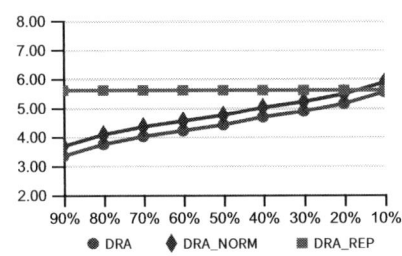

Pitching WARP History

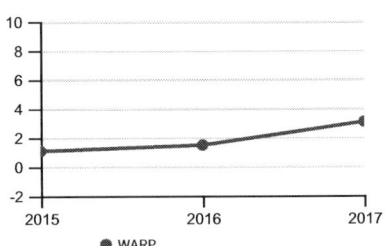

Tunnel vs LHH

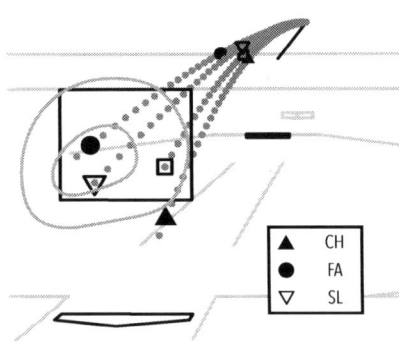

▲	CH
●	FA
▽	SL

Pitch Types

Type	Freq	Velo	H Mov	V Mov
CH	18.0%	86.6 [106]	15.7 [75]	-26.3 [102]
FA	61.4%	93.6 [103]	8.5 [94]	-14.8 [101]
SI	3.9%	92.9 [103]	14.7 [84]	-19.4 [102]
SL	16.7%	85.7 [106]	-1.2 [85]	-28.1 [113]

Pitch Tunnel

Pairs	Release Diff	Tunnel Diff	Plate Diff	Speed Changes
1878	34.2	118.3	227.6	0.017

PI Scores

Year	Pitch Ct	Pwr	Cmd	Stm
2015	2004	64	54	69
2016	1839	58	51	65
2017	2460	57	55	68

Tunnel vs RHH

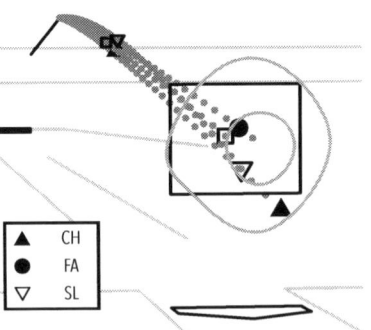

▲	CH
●	FA
▽	SL

Sergio Romo RHP Tampa Bay Rays

Born: 3/4/1983 **Age:** 35 **Bats:** R **Throws:** R **Height:** 5' 11" **Weight:** 185 lbs **Draft Info:** Round 28, 2005 Draft (#852 overall)

2017 Daily WARP Profile
1.5 Total WARP

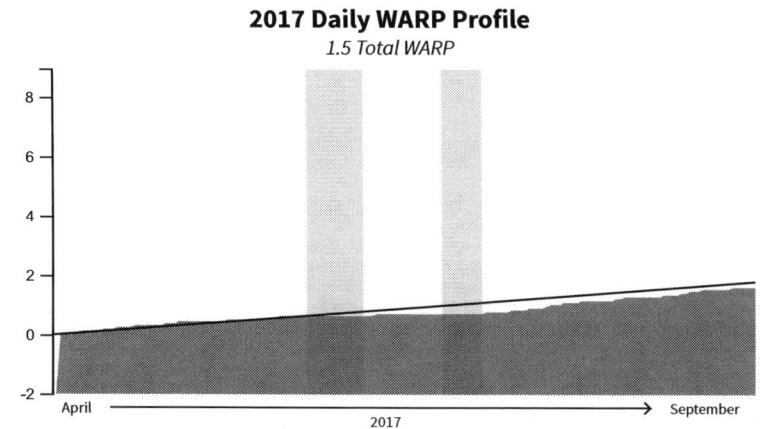

PACE
25 Sec/Pit
143rd of 150
5°
Very Slow

Game 59: DL (ankle sprain), **Game 90:** traded

POWER
0 PWR
149th of 150

STAMINA
45 STM
145th of 150

COMMAND
59 CMD
43rd of 150

Fantasy Values
2017	2018
$6.74	$1.00

YEAR	TEAM	LVL	AGE	W	L	SV	G	GS	IP	H	HR	BB/9	K/9	K	GB%	BABIP	WHIP	ERA	DRA	WARP	MPH 95
2017	LAN	MLB	34	1	1	0	30	0	25	23	7	4.3	11.2	31	35%	.276	1.40	6.12	2.80	0.7	87.9
2017	TBA	MLB	34	2	0	0	25	0	30.2	19	2	2.1	8.2	28	40%	.218	0.85	1.47	2.68	0.8	87.4

2017 Pitching Percentages

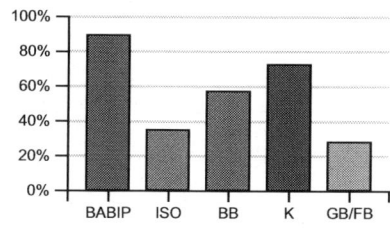

Pitching PECOTA Percentiles

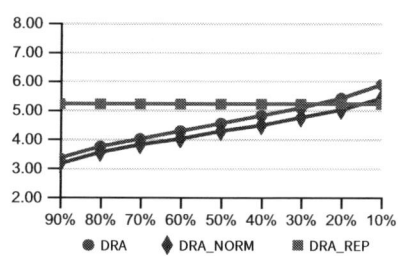

Pitching WARP History

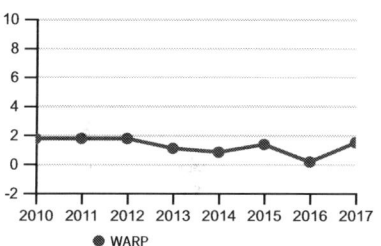

Tunnel vs LHH

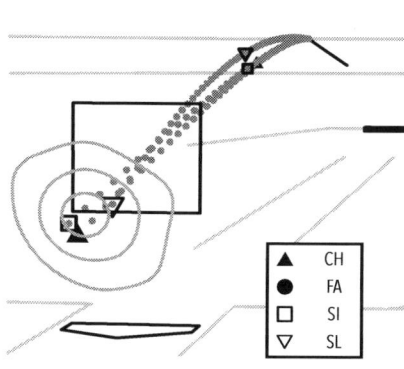

Pitch Types

Type	Freq	Velo	H Mov	V Mov
CH	7.3%	81 [84]	-15.3 [77]	-34.1 [80]
CU	0.1%	74 [84]	17 [136]	-51.6 [92]
FA	19.1%	86.8 [78]	-11 [82]	-21.9 [78]
SI	15.2%	86.1 [64]	-15.8 [76]	-30.5 [61]
SL	58.3%	77.3 [69]	14.1 [142]	-35.5 [92]

Pitch Tunnel

Pairs	Release Diff	Tunnel Diff	Plate Diff	Speed Changes
679	36.6	118.7	208.8	0.028

PI Scores

Year	Pitch Ct	Pwr	Cmd	Stm
2013	960	16	76	46
2014	840	11	73	44
2015	850	8	78	48
2016	465	10	63	35
2017	906	0	59	45

Tunnel vs RHH

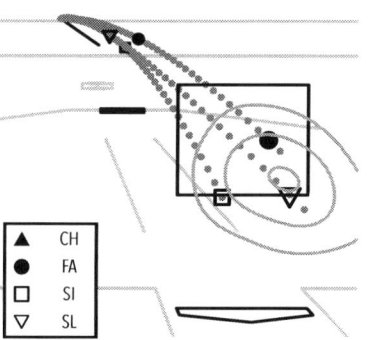

Eddie Rosario LF Minnesota Twins

Born: 9/28/1991 **Age:** 26 **Bats:** L **Throws:** R **Height:** 6' 1" **Weight:** 180 lbs **Draft Info:** Round 4, 2010 Draft (#135 overall)

2017 Daily WARP Profile
1.3 Total WARP

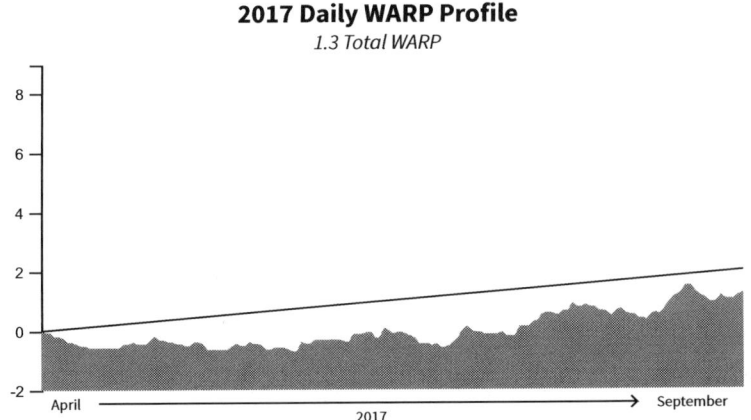

PACE
99th of 155
36°
Slow

22 Sec/Pit

Fantasy Values
2017 | 2018
$23.17 | **$17.00**

YEAR	TEAM	LVL	AGE	PA	R	2B	3B	HR	RBI	BB	K	SB	AVG/OBP/SLG	TAv	VORP	BABIP	WARP
2017	MIN	MLB	25	589	79	33	2	27	78	35	106	9	.290/.328/.507	.271	18.1	.312	1.3

2017 Batting Percentages

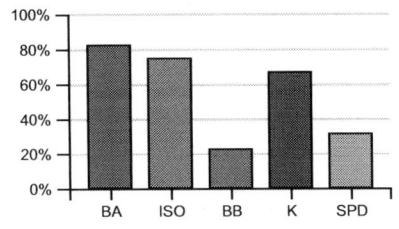

Batting PECOTA Percentiles

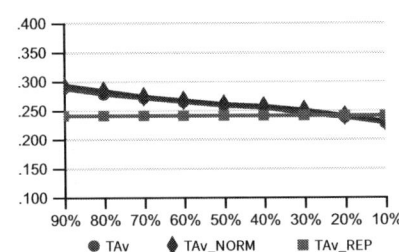

Batting WARP History

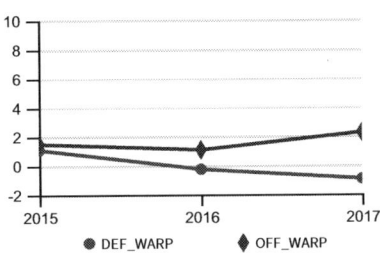

BRR (Relative to Position)

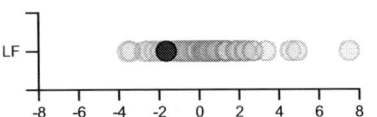

Rank		Player	BRR
57	20°	Yoenis Cespedes	-1.12
58	19°	Hyun-Soo Kim	-1.33
59	16°	**Eddie Rosario**	**-1.60**
60	13°	Melky Cabrera	-1.60
61	10°	Corey Dickerson	-1.88

BRR (Relative to Team)

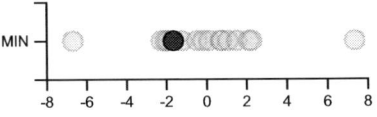

Rank		Player	BRR
10	46°	Jason Castro	-0.43
11	44°	Brock Stassi	-1.18
12	35°	**Eddie Rosario**	**-1.60**
13	28°	Robbie Grossman	-1.86
14	21°	Miguel Sano	-1.98

Base Running Components

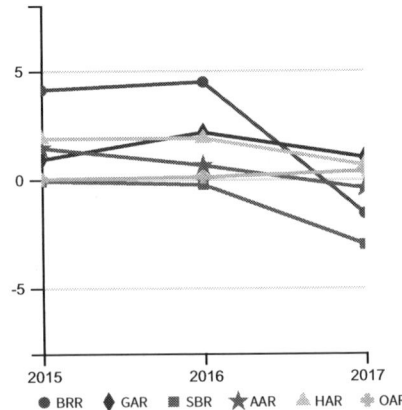

Hyun-jin Ryu   LHP   Los Angeles Dodgers

Born: 3/25/1987   **Age:** 31   **Bats:** R   **Throws:** L   **Height:** 6' 3"   **Weight:** 250 lbs   **Draft Info:** International Free Agent, 2013

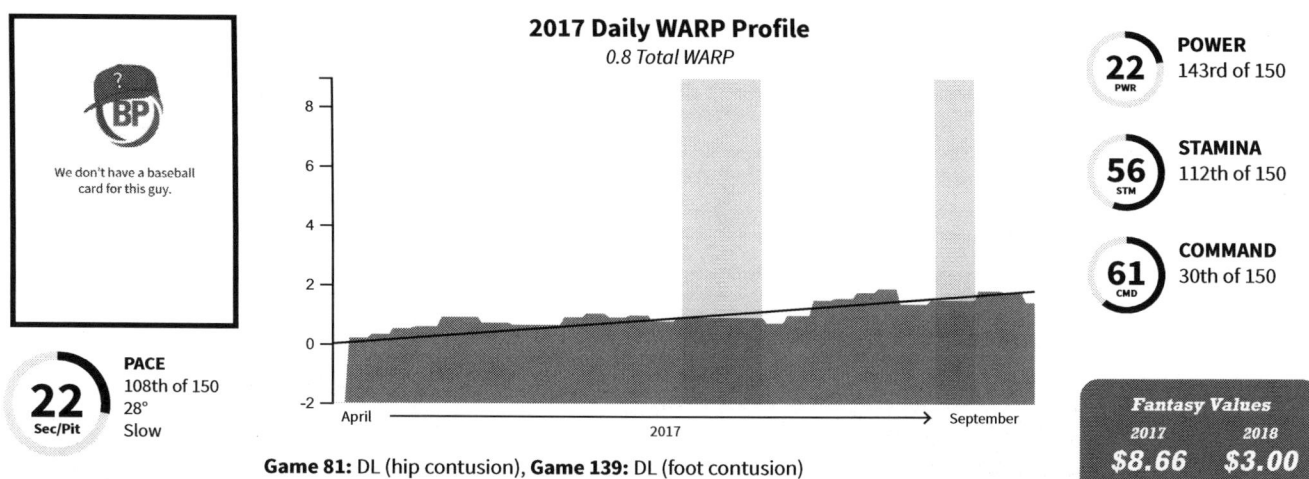

2017 Daily WARP Profile
0.8 Total WARP

Game 81: DL (hip contusion), **Game 139:** DL (foot contusion)

We don't have a baseball card for this guy.

PACE
22 Sec/Pit
108th of 150
28°
Slow

POWER
22 PWR
143rd of 150

STAMINA
56 STM
112th of 150

COMMAND
61 CMD
30th of 150

Fantasy Values
2017	2018
$8.66	$3.00

YEAR	TEAM	LVL	AGE	W	L	SV	G	GS	IP	H	HR	BB/9	K/9	K	GB%	BABIP	WHIP	ERA	DRA	WARP	MPH 95
2017	LAN	MLB	30	5	9	1	25	24	126.2	128	22	3.2	8.2	116	48%	.299	1.37	3.77	4.99	0.8	92.3

2017 Pitching Percentages

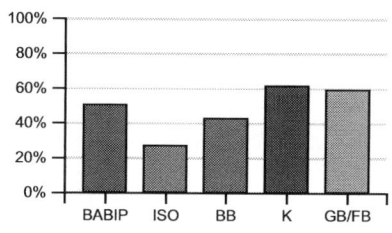

Pitching PECOTA Percentiles

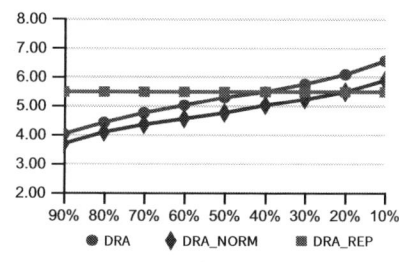

● DRA   ◆ DRA_NORM   ■ DRA_REP

Pitching WARP History

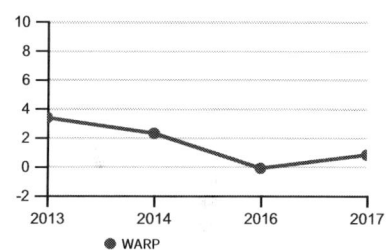

● WARP

Tunnel vs LHH

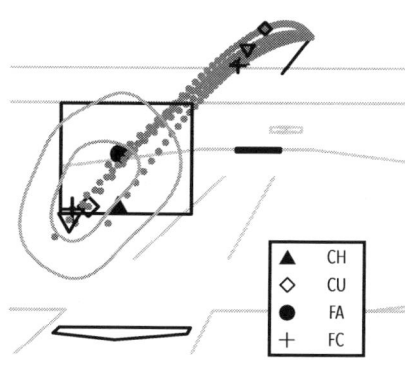

▲ CH
◇ CU
● FA
+ FC

Pitch Types

Type	Freq	Velo	H Mov	V Mov
CH	25.3%	81.2 [85]	11.8 [96]	-29.5 [93]
CU	16.0%	72.1 [77]	-10.6 [111]	-61 [72]
FA	36.7%	90.6 [92]	9 [91]	-17.1 [94]
FC	18.1%	86.8 [91]	-0.9 [96]	-26 [92]
SL	3.8%	78.4 [74]	-3.9 [97]	-44.1 [67]

Pitch Tunnel

Pairs	Release Diff	Tunnel Diff	Plate Diff	Speed Changes
1495	39.3	132.0	238.4	0.043

PI Scores

Year	Pitch Ct	Pwr	Cmd	Stm
2013	3052	37	75	75
2014	2330	39	71	61
2017	2108	22	61	56

Tunnel vs RHH

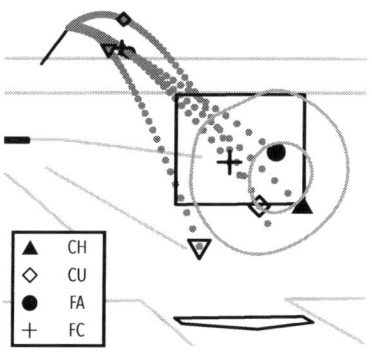

▲ CH
◇ CU
● FA
+ FC

CC Sabathia LHP New York Yankees

Born: 7/21/1980 **Age:** 37 **Bats:** L **Throws:** L **Height:** 6'6" **Weight:** 300 lbs **Draft Info:** Round 1, 1998 Draft (#20 overall)

21 Sec/Pit
PACE
81st of 150
46°
Average

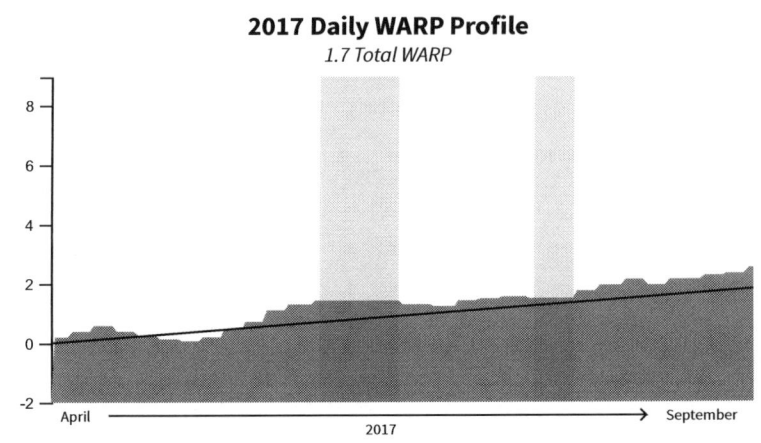

2017 Daily WARP Profile
1.7 Total WARP

Game 63: DL (hamstring strain), **Game 112:** DL (knee inflammation)

34 PWR
POWER
120th of 150

62 STM
STAMINA
94th of 150

58 CMD
COMMAND
49th of 150

Fantasy Values
2017	2018
$15.13	**$5.00**

YEAR	TEAM	LVL	AGE	W	L	SV	G	GS	IP	H	HR	BB/9	K/9	K	GB%	BABIP	WHIP	ERA	DRA	WARP	MPH 95
2017	NYA	MLB	36	14	5	0	27	27	148.2	139	21	3.0	7.3	120	51%	.276	1.27	3.69	4.52	1.7	92.9

2017 Pitching Percentages

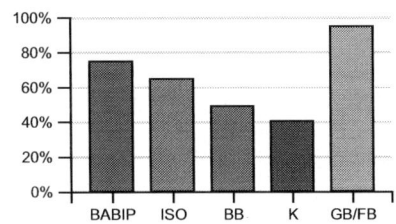

Pitching PECOTA Percentiles

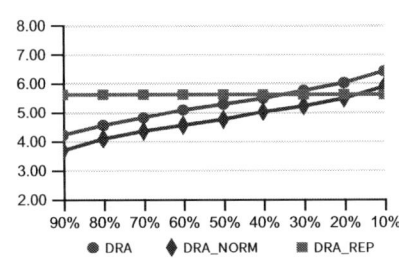

Pitching WARP History

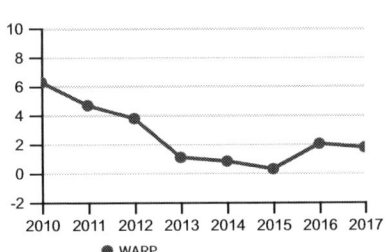

Tunnel vs LHH

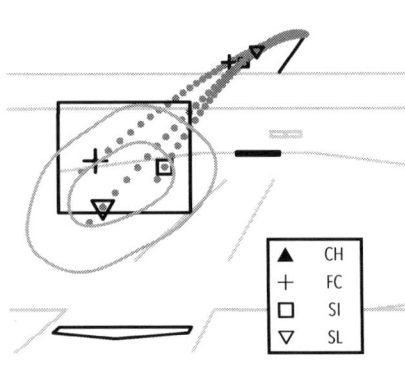

	CH
▲	CH
+	FC
□	SI
▽	SL

Pitch Types

Type	Freq	Velo	H Mov	V Mov
CH	15.4%	84.1 [96]	11.1 [100]	-27 [100]
FC	31.5%	90.1 [110]	2.4 [80]	-19.2 [118]
SI	21.8%	91 [92]	14.3 [87]	-20.4 [99]
SL	31.4%	79.8 [80]	-10.4 [125]	-38.2 [84]

Pitch Tunnel

Pairs	Release Diff	Tunnel Diff	Plate Diff	Speed Changes
1694	30.1	136.6	241.8	0.032

PI Scores

Year	Pitch Ct	Pwr	Cmd	Stm
2013	3319	44	50	86
2014	796	34	69	22
2015	2682	37	65	68
2016	2902	45	66	75
2017	2312	34	58	62

Tunnel vs RHH

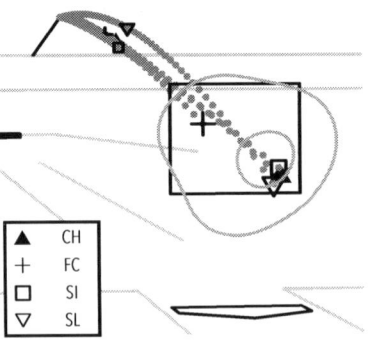

	CH
▲	CH
+	FC
□	SI
▽	SL

Danny Salazar   RHP   Cleveland Indians

Born: 1/11/1990   **Age:** 28   **Bats:** R   **Throws:** R   **Height:** 6'0"   **Weight:** 195 lbs   **Draft Info:** International Free Agent, 2006

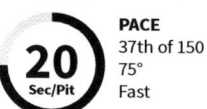

2017 Daily WARP Profile
2.3 Total WARP

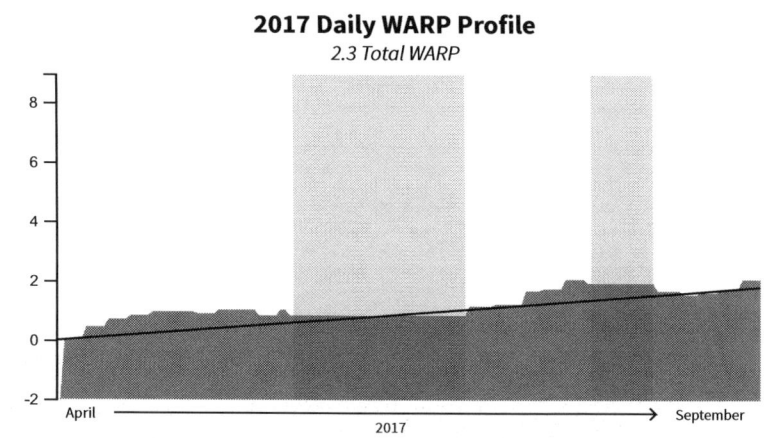

Game 55: DL (shoulder soreness), **Game 123:** DL (elbow inflammation)

POWER
61 PWR
23rd of 150

STAMINA
55 STM
115th of 150

COMMAND
48 CMD
97th of 150

PACE
20 Sec/Pit
37th of 150
75°
Fast

Fantasy Values
2017	2018
$8.73	$11.00

YEAR	TEAM	LVL	AGE	W	L	SV	G	GS	IP	H	HR	BB/9	K/9	K	GB%	BABIP	WHIP	ERA	DRA	WARP	MPH 95
2017	CLE	MLB	27	5	6	0	23	19	103	94	14	3.8	12.7	145	39%	.343	1.34	4.28	3.55	2.3	97.2

Arguably the most maddening pitcher in baseball, Salazar will string together innings where he looks like the most dominant pitcher in the game but will then follow this up with stretches where he is extremely hittable. High pitch counts and limited durability push his strikeout totals up but knock him out of the game before he can get the win. There's a chance that Salazar rattles off a Cy Young caliber campaign one of these seasons, but it's just as likely that he never makes it as a starting pitcher. The bet in fantasy rests somewhere in the middle of these two radical outcomes. — Mike G.

2017 Pitching Percentages

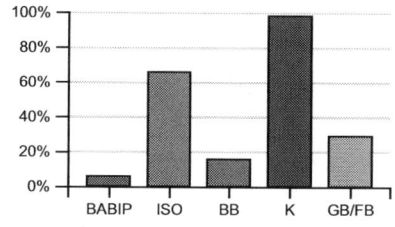

Pitching PECOTA Percentiles

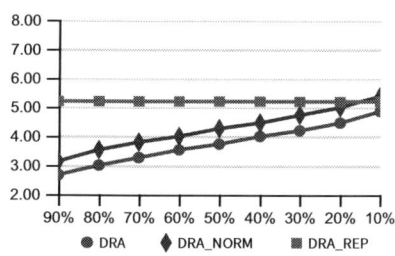

Pitching WARP History

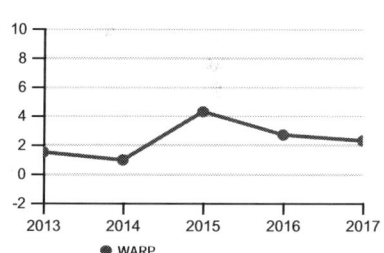

Tunnel vs LHH

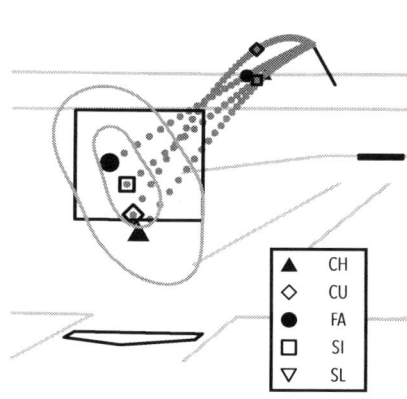

Pitch Types

Type	Freq	Velo	H Mov	V Mov
CH	26.5%	86.8 [107]	-6.7 [124]	-29 [94]
CU	5.9%	81.3 [111]	5.8 [92]	-46.6 [103]
FA	44.1%	95.6 [111]	-7.5 [98]	-11.4 [112]
SI	15.6%	94.6 [113]	-12.8 [98]	-16.3 [114]
SL	7.9%	86.4 [109]	3.5 [95]	-30 [108]

Pitch Tunnel

Pairs	Release Diff	Tunnel Diff	Plate Diff	Speed Changes
1358	25.0	123.6	235.2	0.023

PI Scores

Year	Pitch Ct	Pwr	Cmd	Stm
2013	820	75	44	58
2014	1856	73	44	73
2015	3043	66	44	74
2016	2369	61	47	64
2017	1811	61	48	55

Tunnel vs RHH

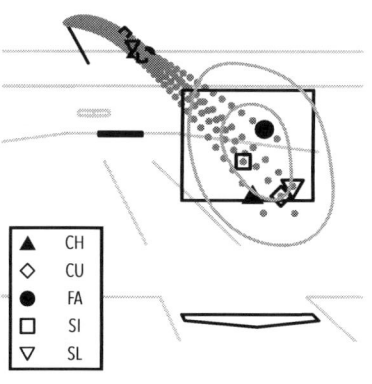

Chris Sale LHP Boston Red Sox

Born: 3/30/1989 **Age:** 29 **Bats:** L **Throws:** L **Height:** 6'6" **Weight:** 180 lbs **Draft Info:** Round 1, 2010 Draft (#13 overall)

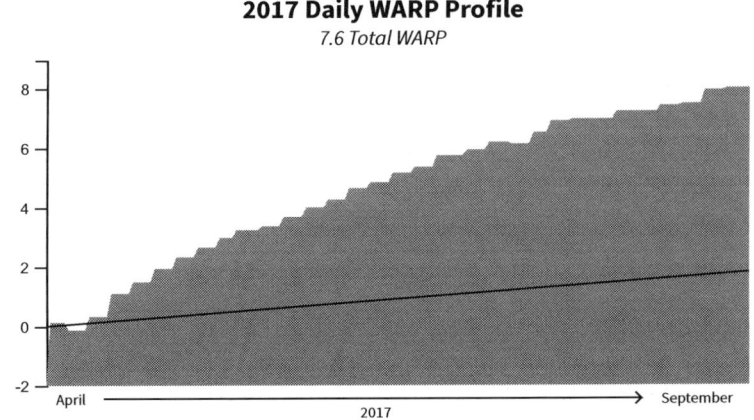

2017 Daily WARP Profile
7.6 Total WARP

POWER 51 PWR 56th of 150

STAMINA 85 STM 3rd of 150

COMMAND 42 CMD 128th of 150

PACE 18 Sec/Pit 5th of 150 97° Very Fast

Fantasy Values
2017	2018
$40.03	$32.00

YEAR	TEAM	LVL	AGE	W	L	SV	G	GS	IP	H	HR	BB/9	K/9	K	GB%	BABIP	WHIP	ERA	DRA	WARP	MPH 95
2017	BOS	MLB	28	17	8	0	32	32	214.1	165	24	1.8	12.9	308	40%	.301	0.97	2.90	2.37	7.6	97.4

In his first year with the Red Sox, Sale didn't miss a beat, posting the highest WARP of his career and striking out over 300 batters for the first time. The only minor blemish on Sale's season is that he faded down the stretch, earning "only" $40 in AL-only and getting passed by Corey Kluber in the last month of the season. Despite this, Sale should be treated like a top-five pitcher in every fantasy format, and a case could easily be made to draft him second or third among hurlers. — Mike G.

2017 Pitching Percentages

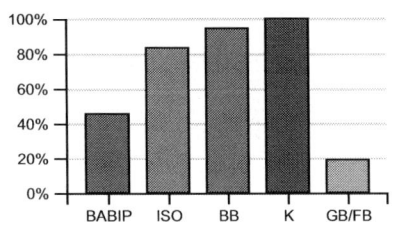

Pitching PECOTA Percentiles

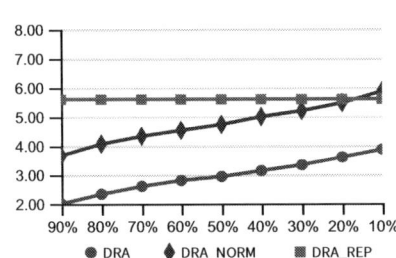

Pitching WARP History

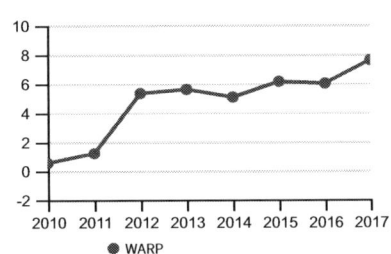

Tunnel vs LHH

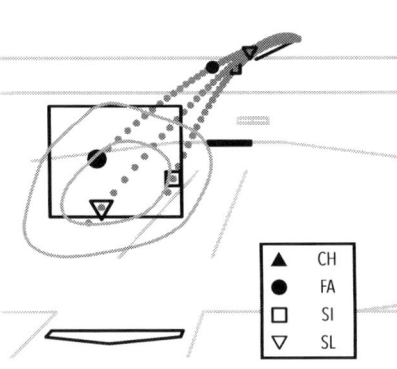

	CH
●	FA
□	SI
▽	SL

Pitch Types

Type	Freq	Velo	H Mov	V Mov
CH	16.6%	86.9 [107]	17.2 [67]	-28.3 [97]
FA	37.4%	95 [108]	13.9 [68]	-16.2 [97]
SI	13.1%	93.1 [104]	17.5 [64]	-23.7 [86]
SL	32.9%	80 [81]	-10 [124]	-41.7 [74]

Pitch Tunnel

Pairs	Release Diff	Tunnel Diff	Plate Diff	Speed Changes
2563	33.0	118.4	214.4	0.036

PI Scores

Year	Pitch Ct	Pwr	Cmd	Stm
2013	3279	49	53	81
2014	2747	54	53	68
2015	3316	56	61	80
2016	3417	50	65	85
2017	3418	51	42	85

Tunnel vs RHH

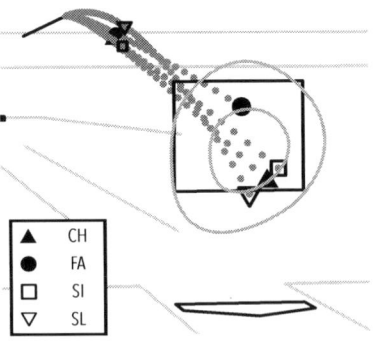

▲	CH
●	FA
□	SI
▽	SL

Jeff Samardzija   RHP   San Francisco Giants

Born: 1/23/1985   **Age:** 33   **Bats:** R   **Throws:** R   **Height:** 6' 5"   **Weight:** 225 lbs   **Draft Info:** Round 5, 2006 Draft (#149 overall)

2017 Daily WARP Profile
4.5 Total WARP

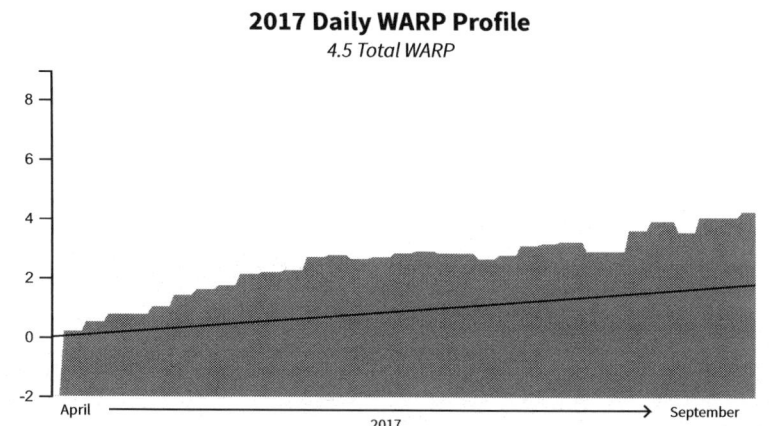

April — 2017 — September

56 PWR	**POWER**	38th of 150
83 STM	**STAMINA**	5th of 150
62 CMD	**COMMAND**	24th of 150

20 Sec/Pit	**PACE** 37th of 150 75° Fast

Fantasy Values

2017	2018
$18.27	**$15.00**

YEAR	TEAM	LVL	AGE	W	L	SV	G	GS	IP	H	HR	BB/9	K/9	K	GB%	BABIP	WHIP	ERA	DRA	WARP	MPH 95
2017	SFN	MLB	32	9	15	0	32	32	207.2	204	30	1.4	8.9	205	43%	.303	1.14	4.42	3.63	4.5	96.3

In an era when most starters can't even reach 180 innings, the best thing about Samardzija is his durability. He tossed 200+ innings and had at least 32 starts for the fifth consecutive season. While he has been able to stay healthy the results have been erratic. Shark's DRA is almost always better than his ERA, but he has been around long enough that it is difficult to label this an aberration. The durability combined with the strikeouts do make Shark a category anchor, particularly in deeper formats, but a return to his ace-like form of 2014 is highly unlikely. — Mike G.

2017 Pitching Percentages

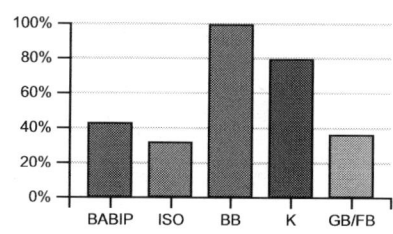

Pitching PECOTA Percentiles

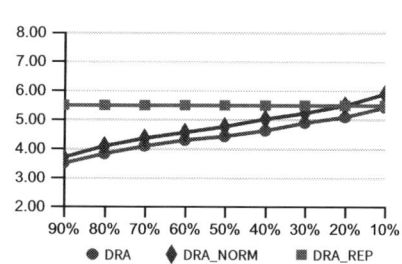

Pitching WARP History

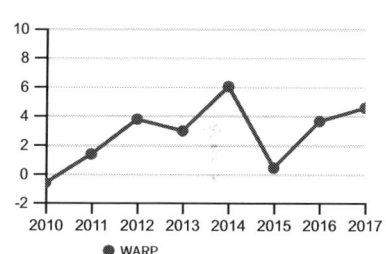

Tunnel vs LHH

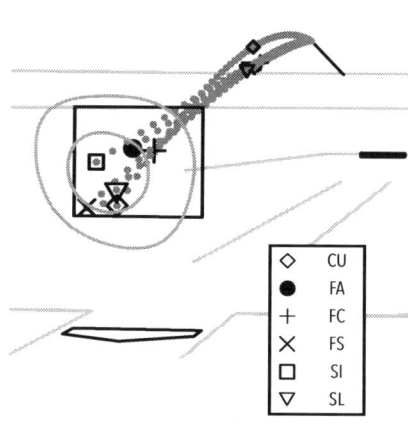

◇	CU
●	FA
+	FC
×	FS
□	SI
▽	SL

Pitch Types

Type	Freq	Velo	H Mov	V Mov
CH	0.1%	87.5 [110]	-11.3 [99]	-21.9 [115]
CU	14.7%	81.2 [111]	4 [85]	-44.1 [108]
FA	19.4%	94.5 [106]	-9.9 [87]	-15 [101]
FC	9.0%	92.7 [124]	-3.3 [75]	-17.3 [126]
FS	10.5%	86.8 [109]	-7.6 [102]	-25.7 [114]
SI	28.5%	94.8 [115]	-14.2 [87]	-19 [104]
SL	17.8%	88.8 [120]	-0.9 [76]	-24.6 [123]

Pitch Tunnel

Pairs	Release Diff	Tunnel Diff	Plate Diff	Speed Changes
2402	28.3	119.3	219.4	0.025

PI Scores

Year	Pitch Ct	Pwr	Cmd	Stm
2013	3418	63	51	85
2014	3301	66	52	82
2015	3334	58	46	83
2016	3166	59	51	81
2017	3247	56	62	83

Tunnel vs RHH

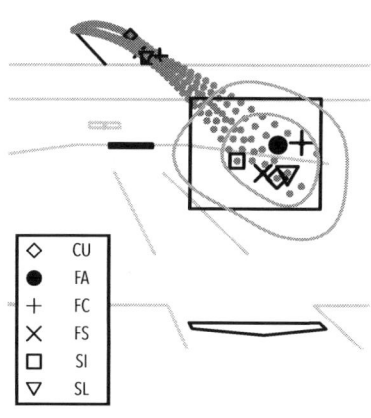

◇	CU
●	FA
+	FC
×	FS
□	SI
▽	SL

Gary Sanchez   C   New York Yankees

Born: 12/2/1992 **Age:** 25 **Bats:** R **Throws:** R **Height:** 6' 2" **Weight:** 230 lbs **Draft Info:** International Free Agent, 2009

PACE
146th of 155
6°
Very Slow

24 Sec/Pit

2017 Daily WARP Profile
4.7 Total WARP

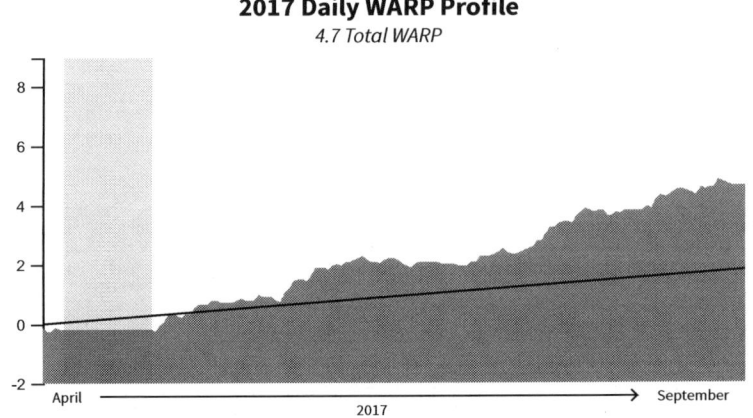

April — 2017 — September

Game 6: DL (biceps strain)

Fantasy Values
2017 **$20.90** 2018 **$24.00**

YEAR	TEAM	LVL	AGE	PA	R	2B	3B	HR	RBI	BB	K	SB	AVG/OBP/SLG	TAv	VORP	BABIP	WARP
2017	NYA	MLB	24	525	79	20	0	33	90	40	120	2	.278/.345/.531	.297	44.8	.304	4.7

Any lingering doubts about Sanchez's ability or staying power were erased with a terrific season that propelled him past every catcher in baseball in fantasy. Sanchez did have difficulties with passed balls and game calling, but this had no impact on his bat, as the young phenom had more home runs and RBI than any backstop in baseball. While Sanchez's defensive woes might eventually lead to a move to another position, in 2018 feel free to enjoy the positional eligibility for one more year from one of the most exciting bats in the game at any position. — Mike G.

2017 Batting Percentages

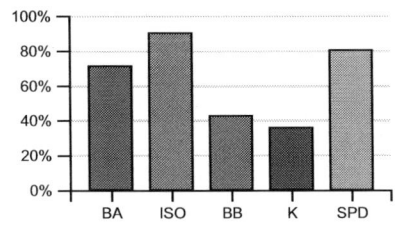

Batting PECOTA Percentiles

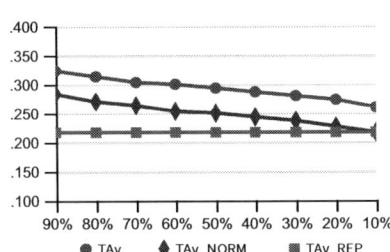

Batting WARP History

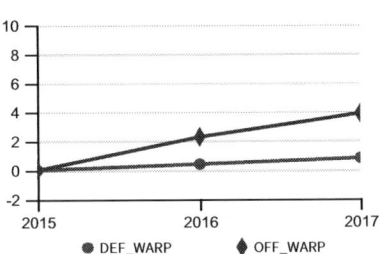

BRR (Relative to Position)

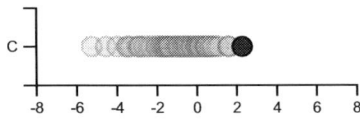

Rank	Player	BRR
1	98° Gary Sanchez	2.33
2	96° Yan Gomes	1.67
3	95° Jose Lobaton	1.65
4	94° Chris Herrmann	1.62
5	93° Luis Torrens	1.14

BRR (Relative to Team)

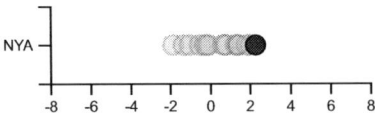

Rank	Player	BRR
1	99° Gary Sanchez	2.33
2	92° Aaron Hicks	2.05
3	85° Didi Gregorius	1.87
4	70° Brett Gardner	1.44
5	67° Jace Peterson	1.44

Base Running Components

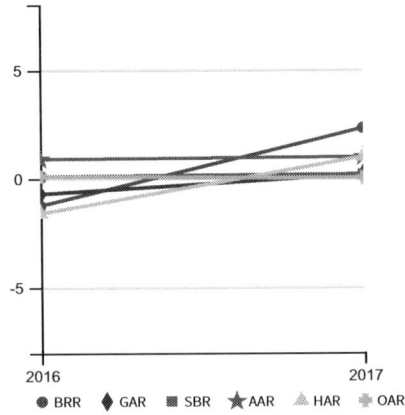

Carlos Santana 1B Philadelphia Phillies

Born: 4/8/1986 **Age:** 32 **Bats:** B **Throws:** R **Height:** 5' 11" **Weight:** 210 lbs **Draft Info:** International Free Agent, 2004

PACE

22 99th of 155
Sec/Pit 36°
Slow

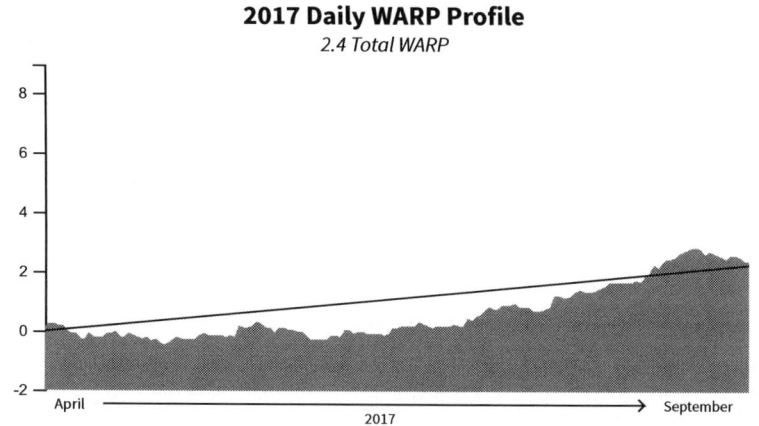

2017 Daily WARP Profile
2.4 Total WARP

Fantasy Values
2017	2018
$17.79	**$18.00**

YEAR	TEAM	LVL	AGE	PA	R	2B	3B	HR	RBI	BB	K	SB	AVG/OBP/SLG	TAv	VORP	BABIP	WARP
2017	CLE	MLB	31	667	90	37	3	23	79	88	94	5	.259/.363/.455	.277	17.6	.274	2.4

2017 Batting Percentages

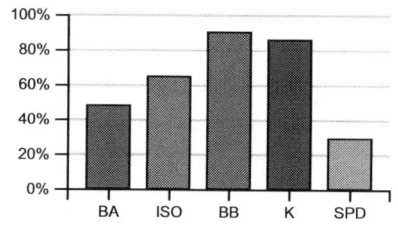

Batting PECOTA Percentiles

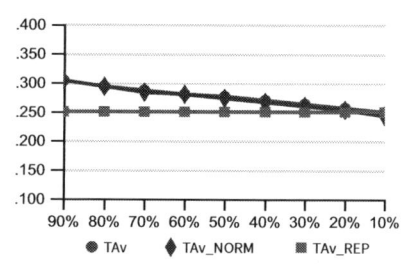

Batting WARP History

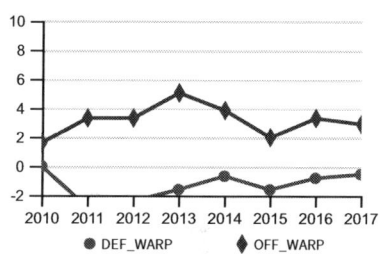

BRR (Relative to Position)

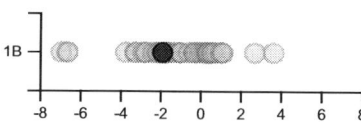

Rank		Player	BRR
29	47°	Adrian Gonzalez	-1.82
30	44°	Justin Bour	-1.82
31	41°	**Carlos Santana**	**-1.88**
32	38°	Mike Napoli	-1.90
33	36°	Chris Davis	-1.98

BRR (Relative to Team)

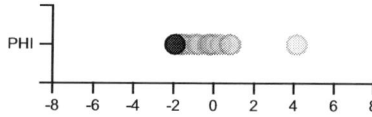

Rank		Player	BRR
15	38°	Jorge Alfaro	-1.54
16	31°	Tommy Joseph	-1.59
17	22°	Odubel Herrera	-1.81
18	12°	Maikel Franco	-1.82
19	0°	**Carlos Santana**	**-1.88**

Base Running Components

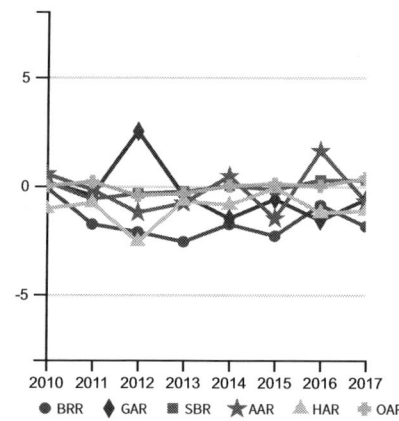

Domingo Santana RF Milwaukee Brewers

Born: 8/5/1992 **Age:** 25 **Bats:** R **Throws:** R **Height:** 6' 5" **Weight:** 220 lbs **Draft Info:** International Free Agent, 2009

19 Sec/Pit

PACE
4th of 155
97°
Very Fast

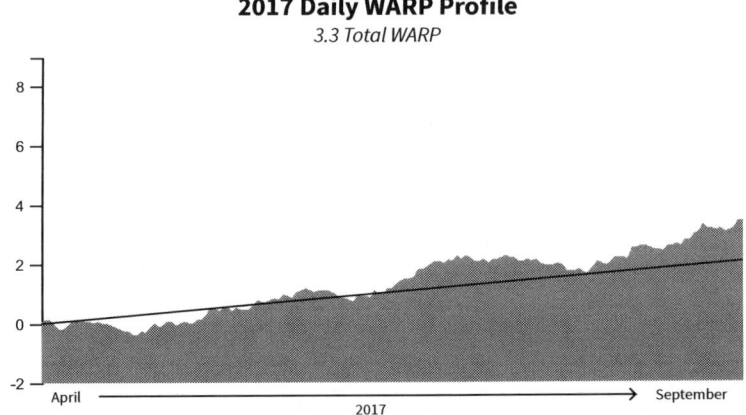

2017 Daily WARP Profile
3.3 Total WARP

Fantasy Values

2017	2018
$25.78	$23.00

YEAR	TEAM	LVL	AGE	PA	R	2B	3B	HR	RBI	BB	K	SB	AVG/OBP/SLG	TAv	VORP	BABIP	WARP
2017	MIL	MLB	24	607	88	29	0	30	85	73	178	15	.278/.371/.505	.306	40.5	.363	3.3

For a time, Santana was one of those toolsy outfielders who showed flashes of greatness but never lived up to his potential. Then everything came together in 2017. Despite a high strikeout rate, Santana still made enough punishing contact to reach the 30-home-run plateau and was finally able to translate some of his above-average speed to the basepaths. Except for the batting average, Santana is an elite talent and is young enough where he could even see some slight improvement. — Mike G.

2017 Batting Percentages
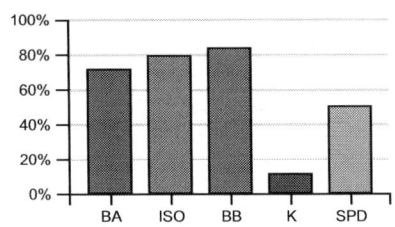

Batting PECOTA Percentiles
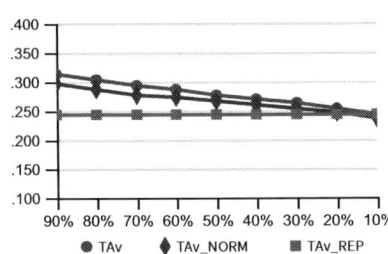

Batting WARP History
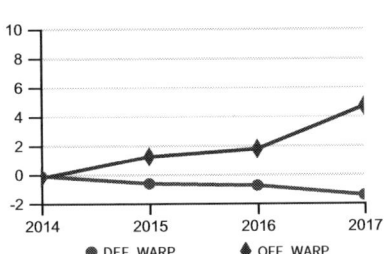

BRR (Relative to Position)
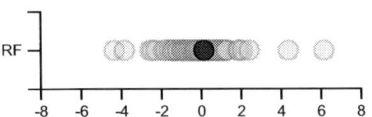

Rank		Player	BRR
21	63°	Craig Gentry	0.30
22	62°	Brandon Guyer	0.29
23	59°	**Domingo Santana**	0.17
24	58°	Alejandro De Aza	0.14
25	58°	Travis Taijeron	0.03

BRR (Relative to Team)
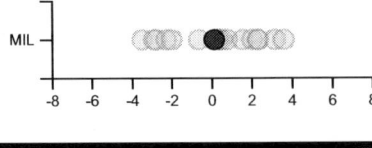

Rank		Player	BRR
9	50°	Jesus Aguilar	0.39
10	48°	Brett Phillips	0.34
11	37°	**Domingo Santana**	0.17
12	31°	Manny Pina	-0.60
13	28°	Jett Bandy	-1.95

Base Running Components
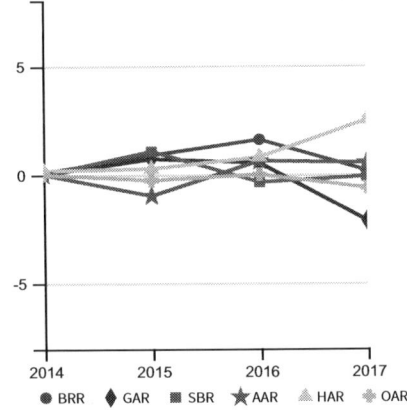

Ervin Santana   RHP   Minnesota Twins

Born: 12/12/1982   **Age:** 35   **Bats:** R   **Throws:** R   **Height:** 6' 2"   **Weight:** 175 lbs   **Draft Info:** International Free Agent, 2000

2017 Daily WARP Profile
4.3 Total WARP

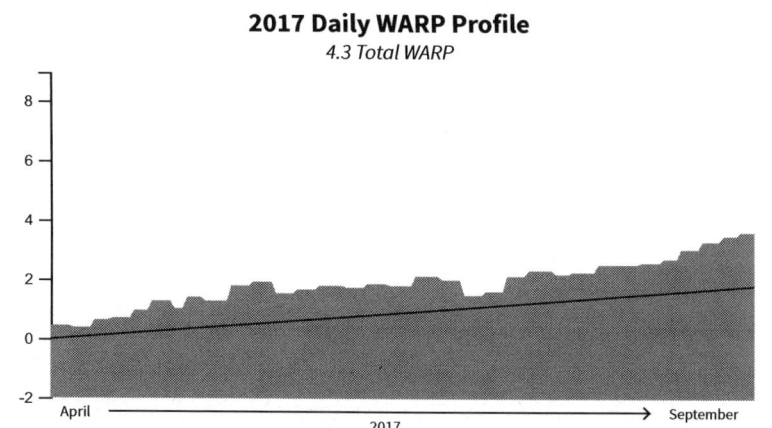

POWER 46 PWR 69th of 150

STAMINA 83 STM 5th of 150

COMMAND 52 CMD 79th of 150

PACE 20 Sec/Pit 37th of 150 75° Fast

Fantasy Values
2017	2018
$25.43	$14.00

YEAR	TEAM	LVL	AGE	W	L	SV	G	GS	IP	H	HR	BB/9	K/9	K	GB%	BABIP	WHIP	ERA	DRA	WARP	MPH 95
2017	MIN	MLB	34	16	8	0	33	33	211.1	177	31	2.6	7.1	167	43%	.245	1.13	3.28	3.74	4.3	95.0

Santana is a great example of a pitcher whose FIP doesn't do him justice. The quality of contact against Santana is below average, so while he's unlikely to ever have a big strikeout year the overall numbers are generally solid. The low whiff rate caps Big Erv's fantasy value, but this is offset by his durability and reliability. Minnesota's strong outfield defense behind him—and Byron Buxton in particular—helps. — Mike G.

2017 Pitching Percentages

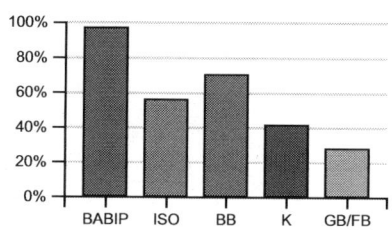

Pitching PECOTA Percentiles

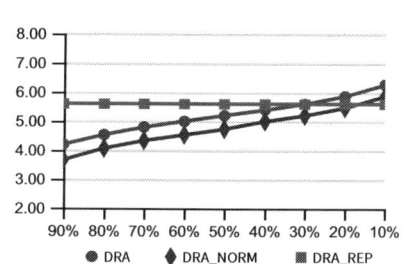

Pitching WARP History

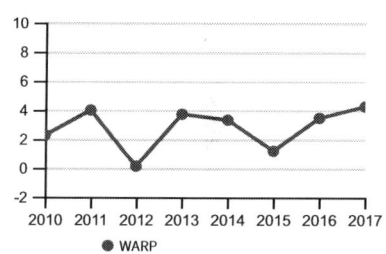

Tunnel vs LHH

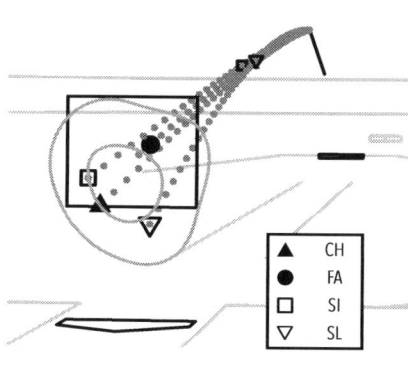

Pitch Types

Type	Freq	Velo	H Mov	V Mov
CH	10.7%	86.1 [104]	-8.9 [112]	-21.6 [115]
FA	39.1%	93.3 [102]	-4.4 [113]	-13.5 [105]
SI	13.6%	92.2 [99]	-9.9 [119]	-17.4 [110]
SL	36.6%	84.6 [101]	5.5 [104]	-29.8 [108]

Pitch Tunnel

Pairs	Release Diff	Tunnel Diff	Plate Diff	Speed Changes
2331	23.5	117.4	240.4	0.024

PI Scores

Year	Pitch Ct	Pwr	Cmd	Stm
2013	3238	49	41	81
2014	2968	49	53	78
2015	1561	47	51	65
2016	2921	46	46	74
2017	3187	46	52	83

Tunnel vs RHH

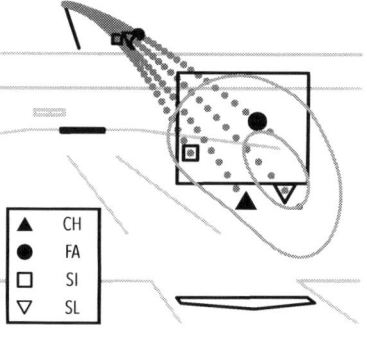

Scott Schebler   RF   Cincinnati Reds

Born: 10/6/1990   **Age:** 27   **Bats:** L   **Throws:** R   **Height:** 6' 0"   **Weight:** 228 lbs   **Draft Info:** Round 26, 2010 Draft (#802 overall)

PACE
45th of 155
71°
Fast

21 Sec/Pit

2017 Daily WARP Profile
1.7 Total WARP

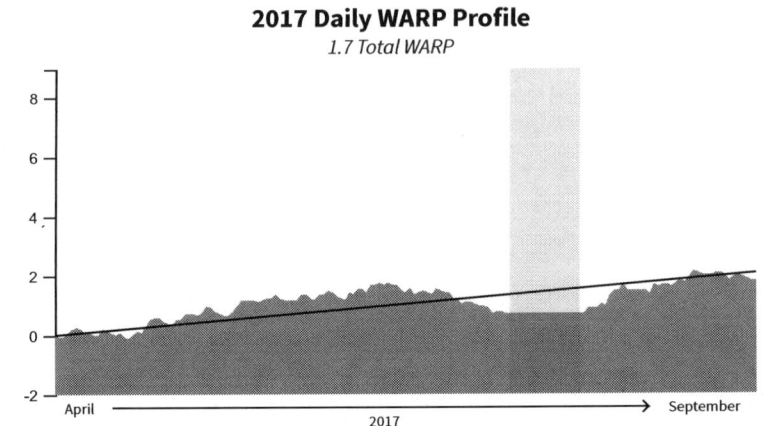

Game 106: DL (shoulder strain)

Fantasy Values

2017	2018
$13.66	$11.00

YEAR	TEAM	LVL	AGE	PA	R	2B	3B	HR	RBI	BB	K	SB	AVG/OBP/SLG	TAv	VORP	BABIP	WARP
2017	CIN	MLB	26	531	63	25	2	30	67	39	125	5	.233/.307/.484	.278	20.6	.248	1.7

2017 Batting Percentages

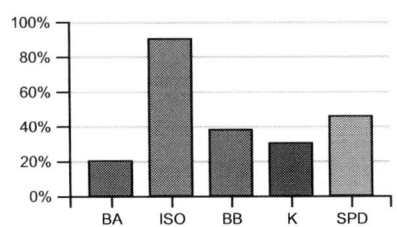

Batting PECOTA Percentiles

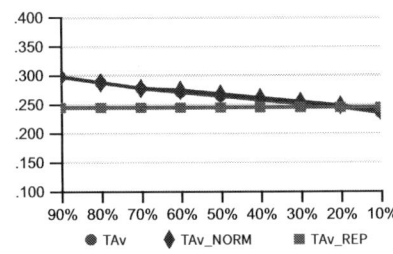

Batting WARP History

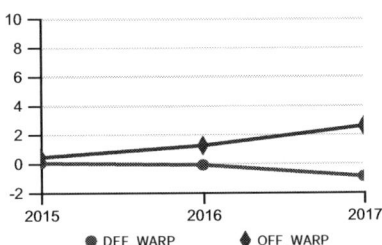

BRR (Relative to Position)

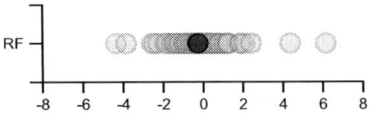

Rank		Player	BRR
27	52°	Jorge Bonifacio	-0.06
28	49°	Giancarlo Stanton	-0.14
29	46°	**Scott Schebler**	**-0.22**
30	43°	Jose Bautista	-0.25
31	42°	Jorge Soler	-0.28

BRR (Relative to Team)

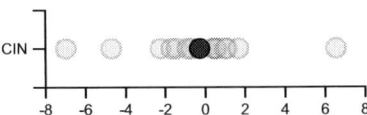

Rank		Player	BRR
7	59°	Mason Williams	0.49
8	58°	Stuart Turner	0.48
9	50°	**Scott Schebler**	**-0.22**
10	48°	Jesse Winker	-0.63
11	45°	Devin Mesoraco	-0.82

Base Running Components

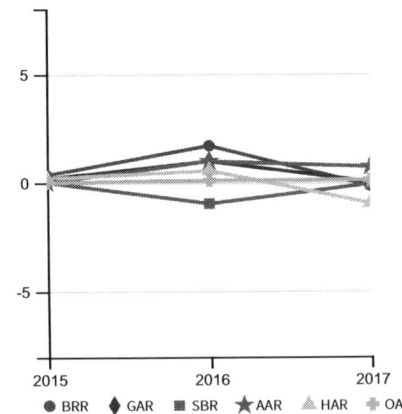

Max Scherzer RHP Washington Nationals

Born: 7/27/1984 **Age:** 33 **Bats:** R **Throws:** R **Height:** 6' 3" **Weight:** 210 lbs **Draft Info:** Round 1, 2006 Draft (#11 overall)

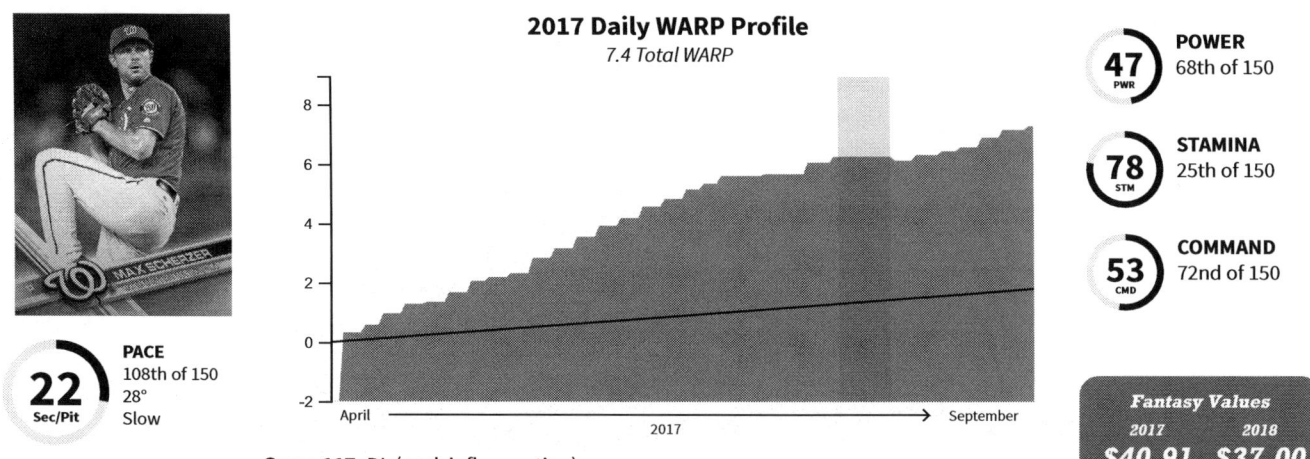

2017 Daily WARP Profile
7.4 Total WARP

PACE
22 Sec/Pit
108th of 150
28°
Slow

POWER
47 PWR
68th of 150

STAMINA
78 STM
25th of 150

COMMAND
53 CMD
72nd of 150

Game 117: DL (neck inflammation)

Fantasy Values
2017	2018
$40.91	**$37.00**

YEAR	TEAM	LVL	AGE	W	L	SV	G	GS	IP	H	HR	BB/9	K/9	K	GB%	BABIP	WHIP	ERA	DRA	WARP	MPH 95
2017	WAS	MLB	32	16	6	0	31	31	200.2	126	22	2.5	12.0	268	38%	.245	0.90	2.51	2.26	7.4	95.7

Once upon a time it would have been radical to suggest Scherzer would supplant Clayton Kershaw as the best pitcher in baseball, but Scherzer's combined durability and high whiff rate mean that's exactly what has happened the last two seasons. Scherzer does go through slumps where he gives up hard contact, but these slumps are never prolonged and the high strikeout totals more than make up for it. There's a case to be made for drafting Scherzer as the top dog before any pitcher off the board. — Mike G.

2017 Pitching Percentages

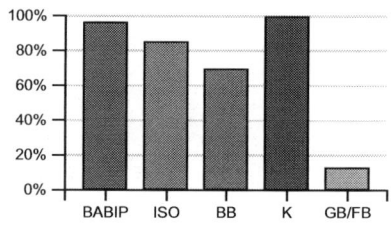

Pitching PECOTA Percentiles

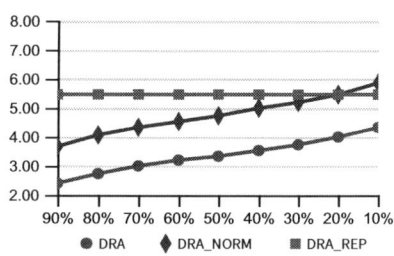

Pitching WARP History

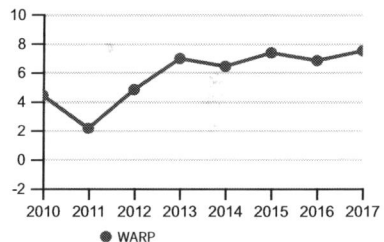

Tunnel vs LHH

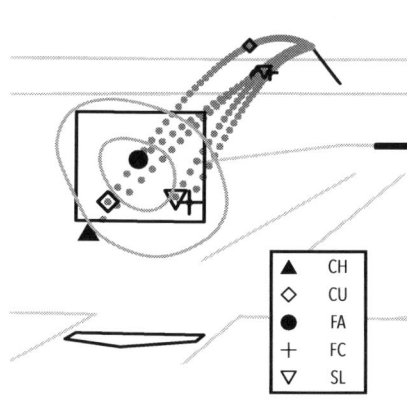

▲	CH
◇	CU
●	FA
+	FC
▽	SL

Pitch Types

Type	Freq	Velo	H Mov	V Mov
CH	14.0%	84.9 [99]	-12 [95]	-32.4 [85]
CU	8.3%	77.7 [98]	9.1 [105]	-47.9 [100]
FA	48.7%	94.3 [106]	-8.6 [93]	-14.3 [103]
FC	4.2%	88.3 [99]	3.1 [108]	-26.3 [90]
SL	24.8%	86 [107]	3.9 [97]	-31.2 [104]

Pitch Tunnel

Pairs	Release Diff	Tunnel Diff	Plate Diff	Speed Changes
2305	34.2	120.1	221.3	0.030

PI Scores

Year	Pitch Ct	Pwr	Cmd	Stm
2013	3387	55	50	82
2014	3616	52	52	88
2015	3348	57	50	81
2016	3553	52	39	87
2017	3083	47	53	78

Tunnel vs RHH

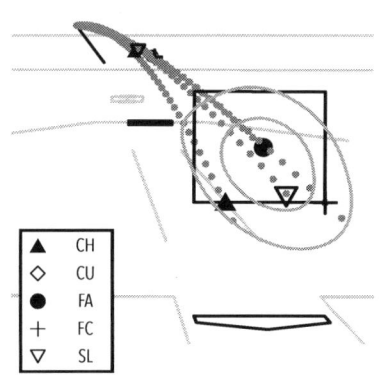

▲	CH
◇	CU
●	FA
+	FC
▽	SL

Jonathan Schoop 2B Baltimore Orioles

Born: 10/16/1991 **Age:** 26 **Bats:** R **Throws:** R **Height:** 6' 1" **Weight:** 225 lbs **Draft Info:** International Free Agent, 2008

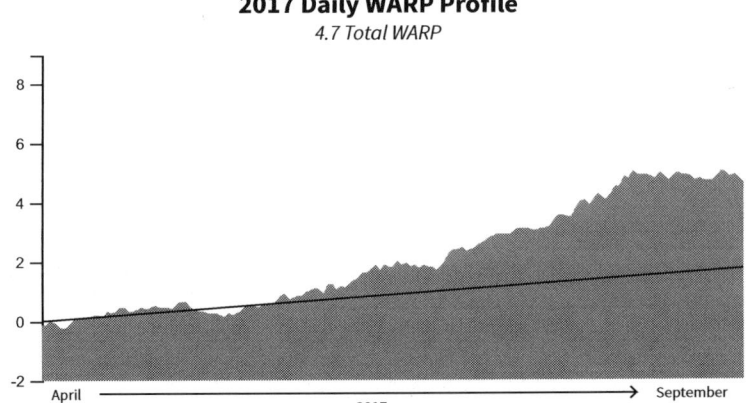

2017 Daily WARP Profile
4.7 Total WARP

PACE
21 Sec/Pit
45th of 155
71°
Fast

Fantasy Values

2017	2018
$25.05	$23.00

YEAR	TEAM	LVL	AGE	PA	R	2B	3B	HR	RBI	BB	K	SB	AVG/OBP/SLG	TAv	VORP	BABIP	WARP
2017	BAL	MLB	25	675	92	35	0	32	105	35	142	1	.293/.338/.503	.280	37.5	.330	4.7

Once considered an offensively challenged second baseman with a good glove, Schoop has flipped the script, morphing into a 30+ home-run hitter who can do everything in fantasy except steal bases. The average could slip back into the .270 range, but the rest of the profile is solid and Schoop enters his prime in a great hitters' ballpark. He isn't quite an elite second baseman but slots in easily in the next tier. — Mike G.

2017 Batting Percentages

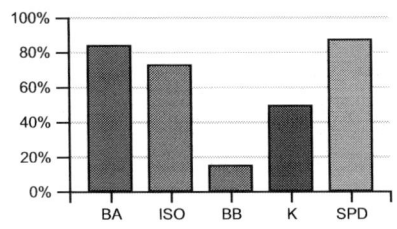

Batting PECOTA Percentiles

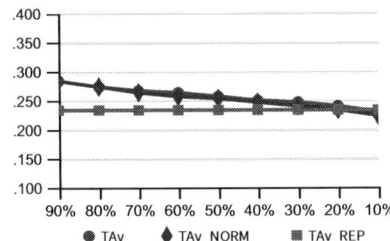

Batting WARP History

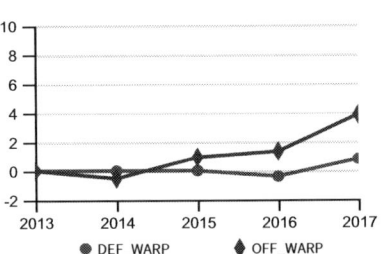

BRR (Relative to Position)

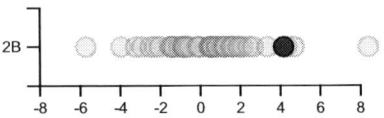

Rank		Player	BRR
2	93°	Ian Kinsler	4.72
3	90°	Javier Baez	4.36
4	88°	**Jonathan Schoop**	**4.21**
5	84°	Cesar Hernandez	4.20
6	81°	DJ LeMahieu	3.38

BRR (Relative to Team)

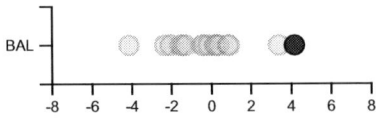

Rank		Player	BRR
1	89°	**Jonathan Schoop**	**4.21**
2	78°	Adam Jones	3.43
3	69°	Trey Mancini	0.95
4	63°	Joey Rickard	0.88
5	53°	Tim Beckham	0.41

Base Running Components

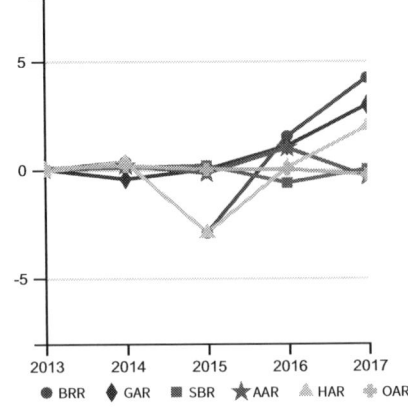

Corey Seager   SS   Los Angeles Dodgers

Born: 4/27/1994   **Age:** 24   **Bats:** L   **Throws:** R   **Height:** 6' 4"   **Weight:** 220 lbs   **Draft Info:** Round 1, 2012 Draft (#18 overall)

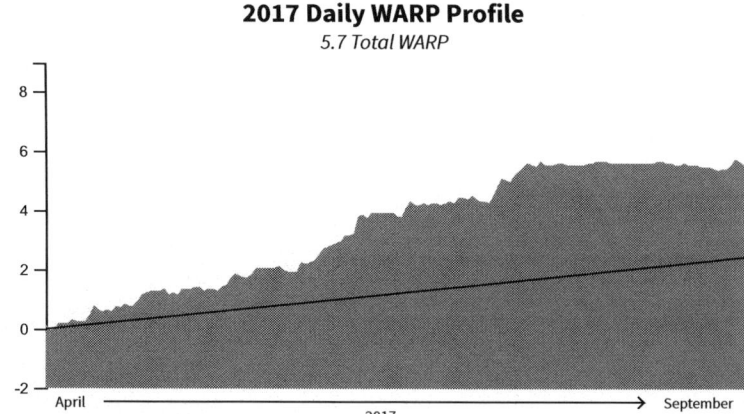

2017 Daily WARP Profile
5.7 Total WARP

PACE
20 Sec/Pit
18th of 155
88°
Very Fast

Fantasy Values
2017	2018
$21.63	$25.00

YEAR	TEAM	LVL	AGE	PA	R	2B	3B	HR	RBI	BB	K	SB	AVG/OBP/SLG	TAv	VORP	BABIP	WARP
2017	LAN	MLB	23	613	85	33	0	22	77	67	131	4	.295/.375/.479	.307	58.5	.352	5.7

Already one of the baseball's brightest stars after only two seasons, Seager possesses an excellent all-around game that doesn't seamlessly translate to fantasy. He isn't elite in any category and the lack of stolen bases pushes him back as well. Seager is young enough and talented enough that the counting categories should continue to grow, but fantasy managers should be wary of paying a first-round price for what thus far has been a fourth- or fifth-round talent. — Mike G.

2017 Batting Percentages

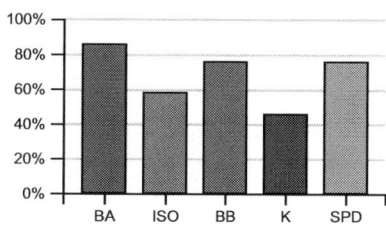

Batting PECOTA Percentiles

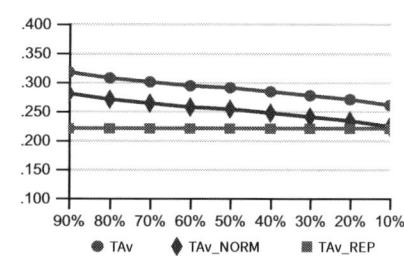

Batting WARP History

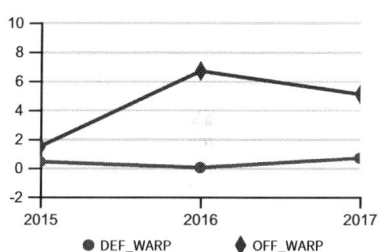

BRR (Relative to Position)

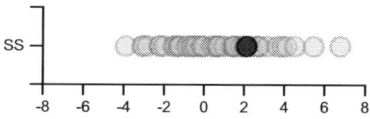

Rank		Player	BRR
10	71°	Andrelton Simmons	2.71
11	69°	Wilmer Difo	2.38
12	66°	**Corey Seager**	**2.17**
13	62°	Francisco Lindor	2.14
14	58°	Jean Segura	2.09

BRR (Relative to Team)

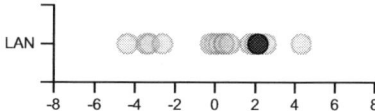

Rank		Player	BRR
1	88°	Chris Taylor	4.37
2	84°	Enrique Hernandez	2.58
3	70°	**Corey Seager**	**2.17**
4	62°	Chase Utley	2.02
5	56°	Joc Pederson	1.80

Base Running Components

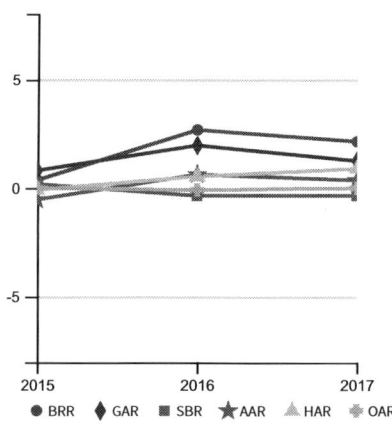

Kyle Seager   3B   Seattle Mariners

Born: 11/3/1987   **Age:** 30   **Bats:** L   **Throws:** R   **Height:** 6' 0"   **Weight:** 210 lbs   **Draft Info:** Round 3, 2009 Draft (#82 overall)

PACE

22 Sec/Pit

99th of 155
36°
Slow

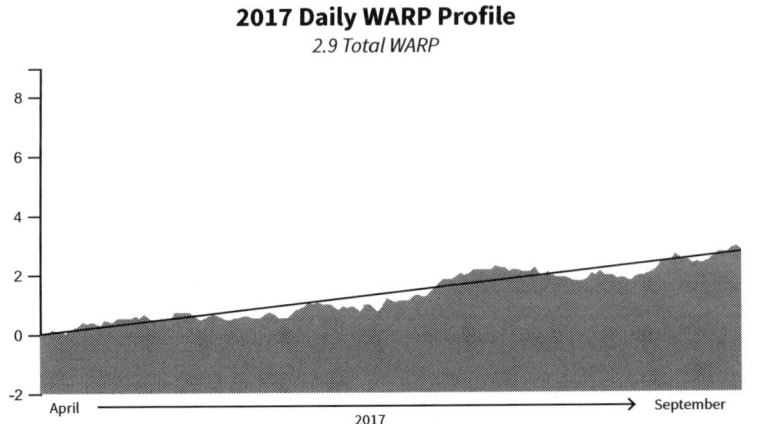

2017 Daily WARP Profile
2.9 Total WARP

Fantasy Values

2017	2018
$15.48	**$22.00**

YEAR	TEAM	LVL	AGE	PA	R	2B	3B	HR	RBI	BB	K	SB	AVG/OBP/SLG	TAv	VORP	BABIP	WARP
2017	SEA	MLB	29	650	72	33	1	27	88	58	110	2	.249/.323/.450	.268	21.2	.262	2.9

2017 Batting Percentages

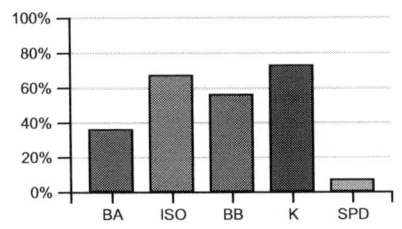

Batting PECOTA Percentiles

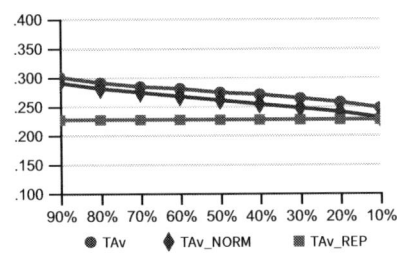

Batting WARP History

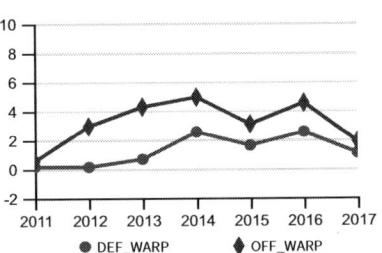

BRR (Relative to Position)

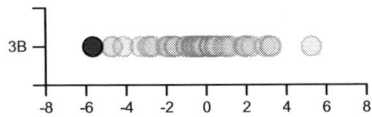

Rank		Player	BRR
52	11°	Justin Turner	-3.24
53	8°	Manny Machado	-4.10
54	6°	David Freese	-4.66
55	3°	Eugenio Suarez	-4.67
56	0°	**Kyle Seager**	**-5.62**

BRR (Relative to Team)

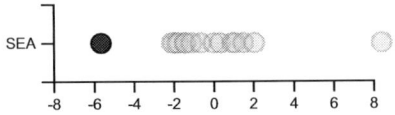

Rank		Player	BRR
12	35°	Danny Valencia	-1.71
13	25°	Nelson Cruz	-1.78
14	17°	Robinson Cano	-1.98
15	9°	Ryon Healy	-2.05
16	0°	**Kyle Seager**	**-5.62**

Base Running Components

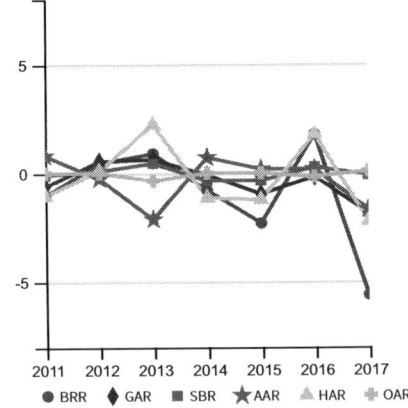

Jean Segura   SS   Seattle Mariners

Born: 3/17/1990   **Age:** 28   **Bats:** R   **Throws:** R   **Height:** 5' 10"   **Weight:** 205 lbs   **Draft Info:** International Free Agent, 2007

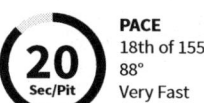

2017 Daily WARP Profile
1.9 Total WARP

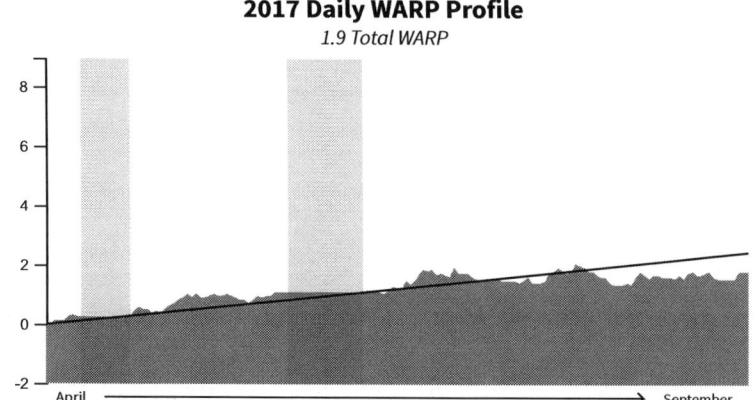

PACE
20 Sec/Pit
18th of 155
88°
Very Fast

Game 9: DL (hamstring strain), **Game 56:** DL (ankle sprain)

Fantasy Values
2017	2018
$23.59	$25.00

YEAR	TEAM	LVL	AGE	PA	R	2B	3B	HR	RBI	BB	K	SB	AVG/OBP/SLG	TAv	VORP	BABIP	WARP
2017	SEA	MLB	27	566	80	30	2	11	45	34	83	22	.300/.349/.427	.262	27.6	.339	1.9

2017 Batting Percentages

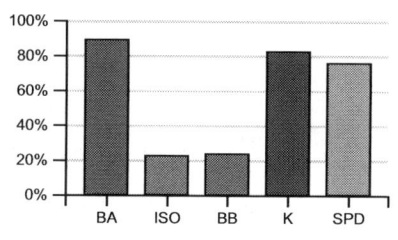

Batting PECOTA Percentiles

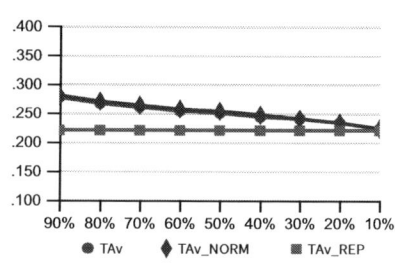

Batting WARP History

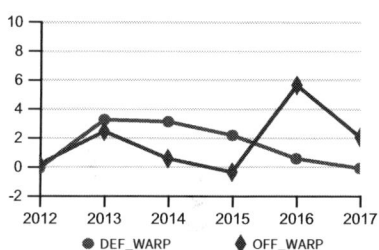

BRR (Relative to Position)

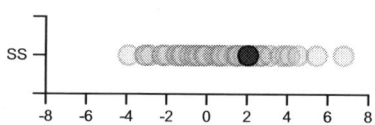

Rank		Player	BRR
12	66°	Corey Seager	2.17
13	62°	Francisco Lindor	2.14
14	58°	**Jean Segura**	**2.09**
15	55°	Orlando Arcia	2.07
16	52°	Tim Anderson	2.06

BRR (Relative to Team)

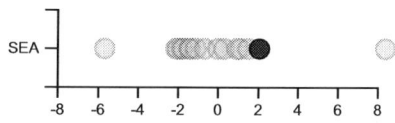

Rank		Player	BRR
1	100°	Dee Gordon	8.44
2	99°	**Jean Segura**	**2.09**
3	95°	Taylor Motter	1.54
4	84°	Benjamin Gamel	1.14
5	76°	Guillermo Heredia	0.99

Base Running Components

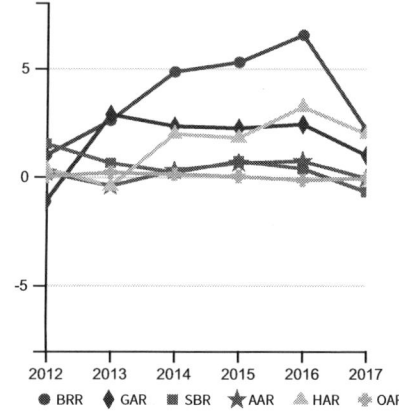

Antonio Senzatela   RHP   Colorado Rockies

Born: 1/21/1995   **Age:** 23   **Bats:** R   **Throws:** R   **Height:** 6' 1"   **Weight:** 180 lbs   **Draft Info:** International Free Agent, 2011

2017 Daily WARP Profile
-0.4 Total WARP

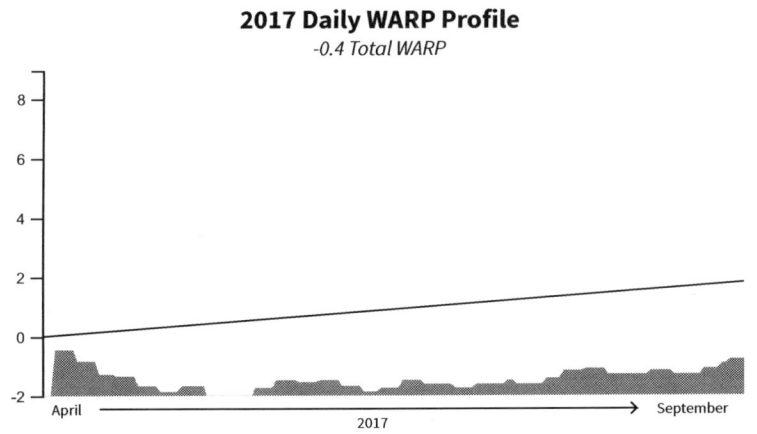

April — 2017 — September

POWER 12th of 150 — 65 PWR

STAMINA 94th of 150 — 62 STM

COMMAND 139th of 150 — 38 CMD

PACE 37th of 150 — 20 Sec/Pit — 75° Fast

Fantasy Values
2017	2018
$8.43	$1.00

YEAR	TEAM	LVL	AGE	W	L	SV	G	GS	IP	H	HR	BB/9	K/9	K	GB%	BABIP	WHIP	ERA	DRA	WARP	MPH 95
2017	COL	MLB	22	10	5	0	36	20	134.2	128	18	3.1	6.8	102	50%	.280	1.30	4.68	5.77	-0.4	96.9

2017 Pitching Percentages
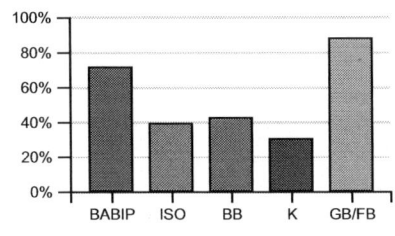

Pitching PECOTA Percentiles
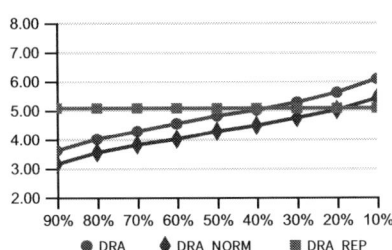

Tunnel vs LHH
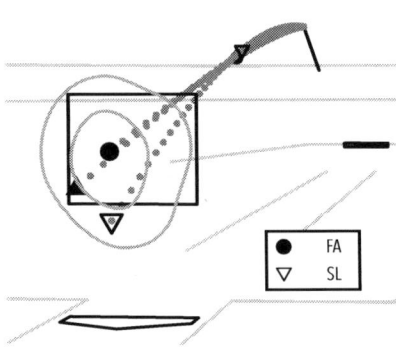

Pitch Types
Type	Freq	Velo	H Mov	V Mov
CH	3.9%	86 [103]	-4.4 [136]	-23.3 [111]
CU	2.2%	77.8 [98]	10.5 [110]	-44.8 [107]
FA	71.8%	94.9 [108]	-3.5 [117]	-14.3 [103]
SL	22.1%	83 [94]	5.7 [105]	-36 [90]

Pitch Tunnel
Pairs	Release Diff	Tunnel Diff	Plate Diff	Speed Changes
1650	44.9	119.8	223.6	0.025

PI Scores
Year	Pitch Ct	Pwr	Cmd	Stm
2017	2213	65	38	62

Tunnel vs RHH
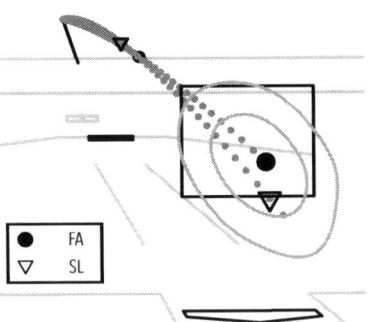

Luis Severino RHP New York Yankees

Born: 2/20/1994 **Age:** 24 **Bats:** R **Throws:** R **Height:** 6' 2" **Weight:** 215 lbs **Draft Info:** International Free Agent, 2011

2017 Daily WARP Profile
5.4 Total WARP

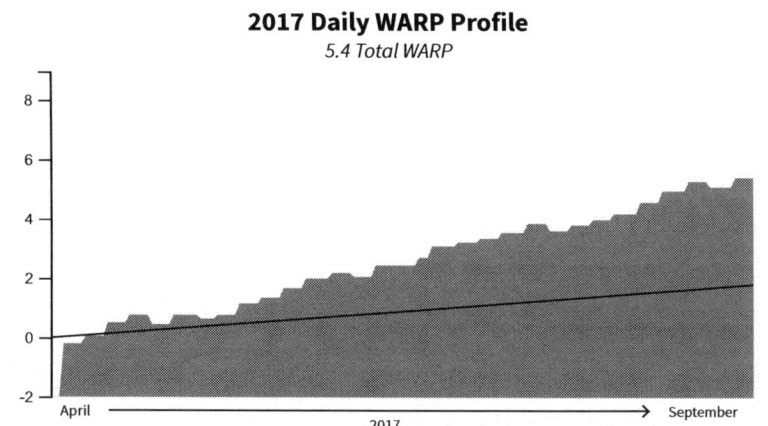

April — 2017 — September

PACE
19 Sec/Pit
16th of 150
89°
Very Fast

POWER
65 PWR
12th of 150

STAMINA
78 STM
25th of 150

COMMAND
48 CMD
97th of 150

Fantasy Values
2017	2018
$30.84	$19.00

YEAR	TEAM	LVL	AGE	W	L	SV	G	GS	IP	H	HR	BB/9	K/9	K	GB%	BABIP	WHIP	ERA	DRA	WARP	MPH 95
2017	NYA	MLB	23	14	6	0	31	31	193.1	150	21	2.4	10.7	230	50%	.272	1.04	2.98	3.05	5.4	99.5

Offseason work with fellow Dominican Pedro Martinez turned Severino from a pitcher with potential to a staff ace. A deep sleeper who delivered, Severino will be one of the more sought-after pitchers this year. If there is a concern, it is that he vastly exceeded his career high in innings thanks to a long stint in the postseason, but assuming the Yankees continue to be judicious with his game-to-game workload, Severino should continue to thrive in the Bronx. — Mike G.

2017 Pitching Percentages

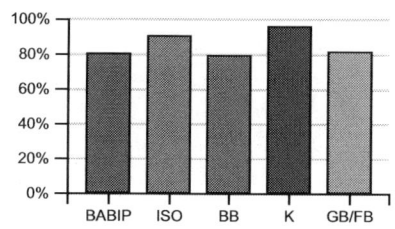

Pitching PECOTA Percentiles

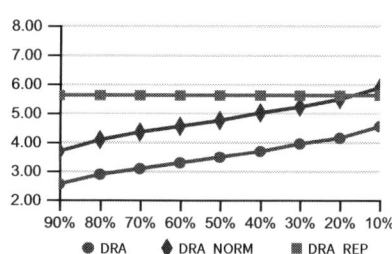

Pitching WARP History

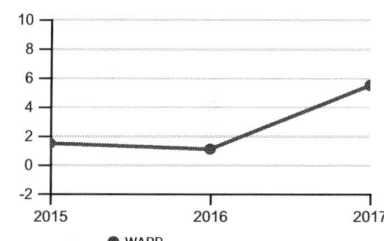

Tunnel vs LHH

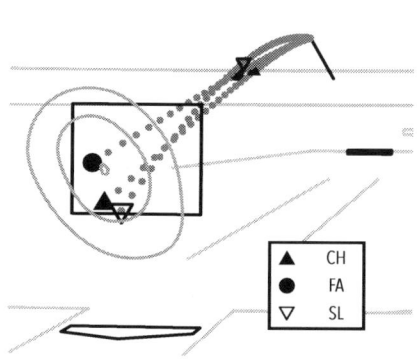

	CH
	FA
	SL

Pitch Types

Type	Freq	Velo	H Mov	V Mov
CH	13.5%	87.4 [109]	-10.4 [104]	-22.5 [113]
FA	51.3%	97.7 [118]	-7.7 [98]	-11.2 [113]
SL	35.1%	88.5 [118]	6.9 [110]	-33.6 [97]

Pitch Tunnel

Pairs	Release Diff	Tunnel Diff	Plate Diff	Speed Changes
2293	37.6	116.3	220.1	0.026

PI Scores

Year	Pitch Ct	Pwr	Cmd	Stm
2015	1022	59	45	65
2016	1259	60	43	65
2017	3077	65	48	78

Tunnel vs RHH

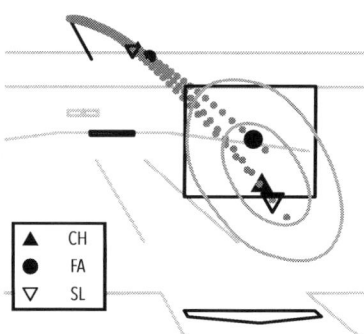

	CH
	FA
	SL

Travis Shaw 3B Milwaukee Brewers

Born: 4/16/1990 **Age:** 28 **Bats:** L **Throws:** R **Height:** 6' 4" **Weight:** 230 lbs **Draft Info:** Round 9, 2011 Draft (#292 overall)

PACE
18th of 155
88°
Very Fast

20 Sec/Pit

2017 Daily WARP Profile
4.2 Total WARP

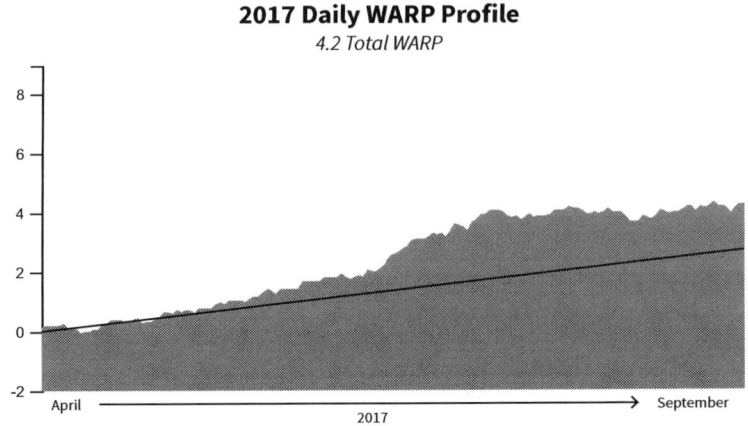

Fantasy Values

2017	2018
$24.53	$20.00

YEAR	TEAM	LVL	AGE	PA	R	2B	3B	HR	RBI	BB	K	SB	AVG/OBP/SLG	TAv	VORP	BABIP	WARP
2017	MIL	MLB	27	606	84	34	1	31	101	60	138	10	.273/.349/.513	.289	41.5	.312	4.2

2017 Batting Percentages

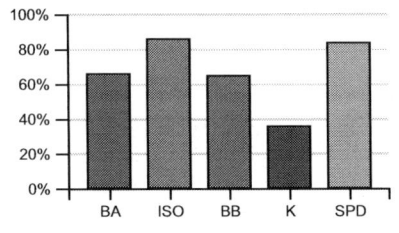

Batting PECOTA Percentiles

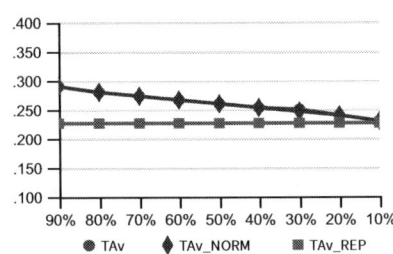

Batting WARP History

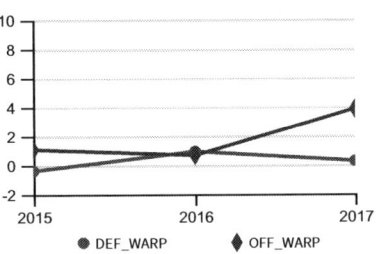

BRR (Relative to Position)

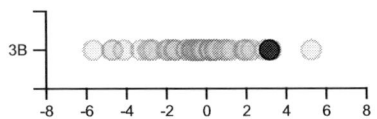

Rank		Player	BRR
1	97°	Cory Spangenberg	5.29
2	94°	Eduardo Nunez	3.28
3	91°	**Travis Shaw**	**3.21**
4	89°	Johan Camargo	2.97
5	87°	Eduardo Escobar	2.30

BRR (Relative to Team)

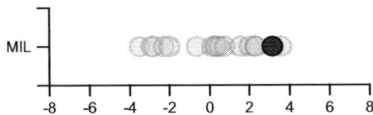

Rank		Player	BRR
1	100°	Keon Broxton	3.64
2	100°	**Travis Shaw**	**3.21**
3	96°	Lorenzo Cain	2.36
4	89°	Hernan Perez	2.36
5	80°	Orlando Arcia	2.07

Base Running Components

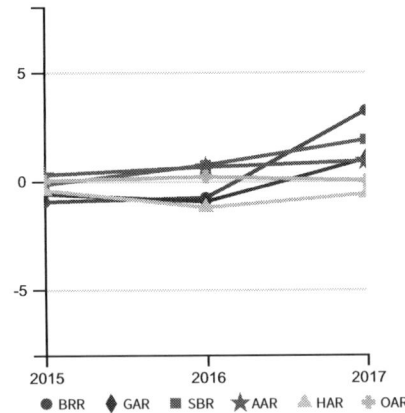

James Shields   RHP   Chicago White Sox

Born: 12/20/1981   **Age:** 36   **Bats:** R   **Throws:** R   **Height:** 6' 3"   **Weight:** 215 lbs   **Draft Info:** Round 16, 2000 Draft (#466 overall)

2017 Daily WARP Profile
1.1 Total WARP

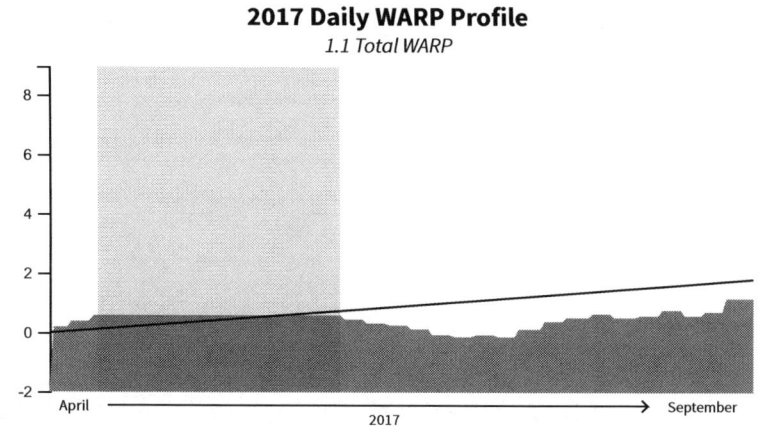

April   2017   September

Game 12: DL (lat strain)

POWER
24 PWR   142nd of 150

STAMINA
60 STM   102nd of 150

COMMAND
48 CMD   97th of 150

PACE
22 Sec/Pit   108th of 150
28°
Slow

Fantasy Values
2017	2018
$1.68	**$1.00**

YEAR	TEAM	LVL	AGE	W	L	SV	G	GS	IP	H	HR	BB/9	K/9	K	GB%	BABIP	WHIP	ERA	DRA	WARP	MPH 95
2017	CHA	MLB	35	5	7	0	21	21	117	116	27	4.1	7.9	103	40%	.270	1.44	5.23	4.72	1.1	91.9

2017 Pitching Percentages

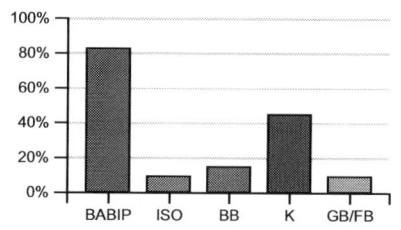

Pitching PECOTA Percentiles

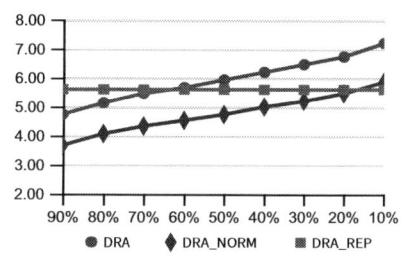

● DRA   ◆ DRA_NORM   ■ DRA_REP

Pitching WARP History

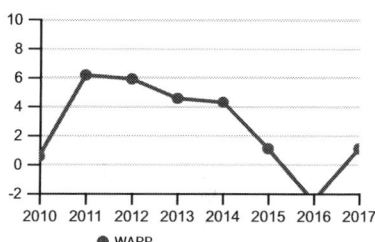

● WARP

Tunnel vs LHH

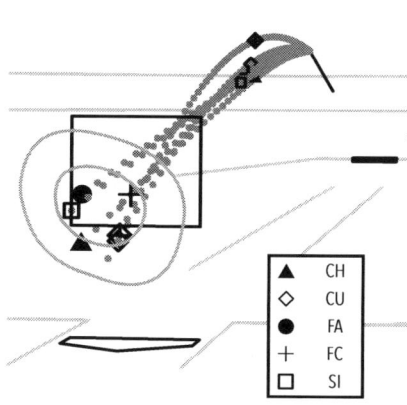

▲ CH
◇ CU
● FA
+ FC
□ SI

Pitch Types

Type	Freq	Velo	H Mov	V Mov
CH	10.8%	83 [92]	-11.9 [96]	-30.9 [89]
CS	4.6%	69.6 [103]	14 [113]	-63.4 [104]
CU	20.1%	78.5 [101]	7.5 [99]	-45.1 [106]
FA	33.4%	90.5 [92]	-5.9 [106]	-17.7 [92]
FC	26.0%	86.4 [88]	4.8 [117]	-27.6 [85]
SI	5.0%	90.1 [87]	-11.2 [109]	-23.2 [88]

Pitch Tunnel

Pairs	Release Diff	Tunnel Diff	Plate Diff	Speed Changes
1498	44.4	122.7	218.5	0.034

PI Scores

Year	Pitch Ct	Pwr	Cmd	Stm
2013	3655	39	52	89
2014	3624	42	61	89
2015	3313	35	48	81
2016	3114	35	49	79
2017	2011	24	48	60

Tunnel vs RHH

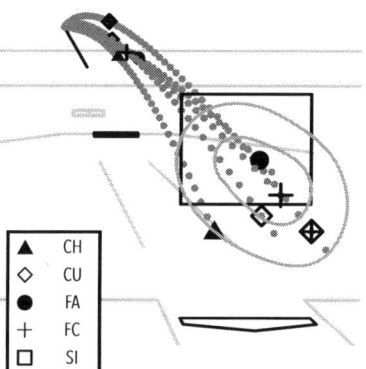

▲ CH
◇ CU
● FA
+ FC
□ SI

Andrelton Simmons   SS   Los Angeles Angels

Born: 9/4/1989   **Age:** 28   **Bats:** R   **Throws:** R   **Height:** 6'2"   **Weight:** 200 lbs   **Draft Info:** Round 2, 2010 Draft (#70 overall)

22 Sec/Pit

PACE
99th of 155
36°
Slow

2017 Daily WARP Profile
4.8 Total WARP

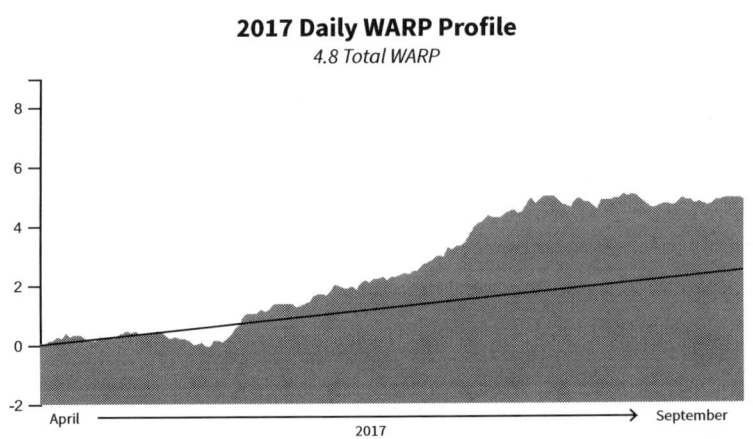

Fantasy Values

2017	2018
$22.13	$15.00

YEAR	TEAM	LVL	AGE	PA	R	2B	3B	HR	RBI	BB	K	SB	AVG/OBP/SLG	TAv	VORP	BABIP	WARP
2017	ANA	MLB	27	647	77	38	2	14	69	47	67	19	.278/.331/.421	.262	31.8	.291	4.8

Simmons' TAv didn't improve all that much, but his fantasy value spiked significantly due to jumps in both home runs and RBI and more games played than ever. There is danger in paying the full sticker price for a hitter like Simmons, but in deeper leagues it makes sense to believe in the gains and lock in the playing time. In mixed leagues there likely isn't much more upside, and if Simmons loses even a little ground he falls to a third middle infielder. — Mike G.

2017 Batting Percentages

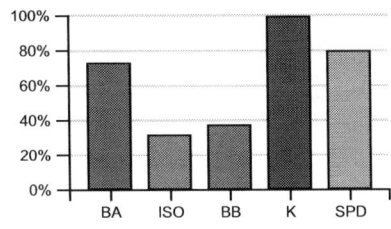

Batting PECOTA Percentiles

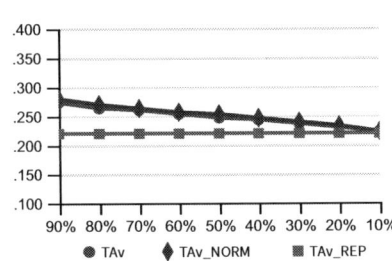

Batting WARP History

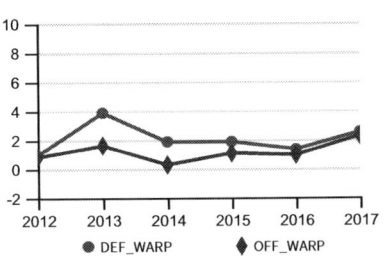

BRR (Relative to Position)

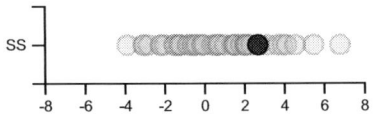

Rank		Player	BRR
8	77°	Elvis Andrus	2.81
9	75°	Jose Reyes	2.71
10	71°	**Andrelton Simmons**	**2.71**
11	69°	Wilmer Difo	2.38
12	66°	Corey Seager	2.17

BRR (Relative to Team)

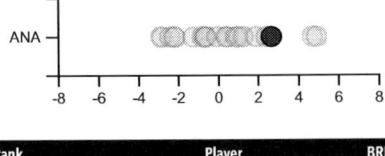

Rank		Player	BRR
1	100°	Ben Revere	4.94
2	100°	Ian Kinsler	4.72
3	100°	**Andrelton Simmons**	**2.71**
4	89°	Brandon Phillips	2.46
5	85°	Cliff Pennington	1.95

Base Running Components

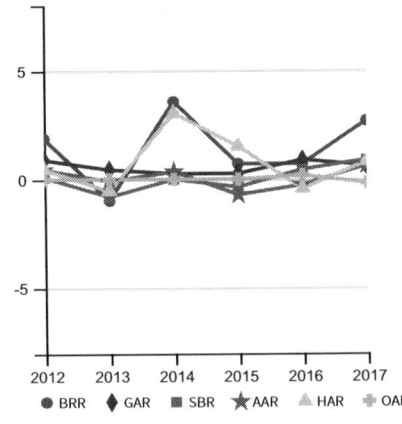

Joe Smith   RHP   Houston Astros

Born: 3/22/1984   **Age:** 34   **Bats:** R   **Throws:** R   **Height:** 6' 2"   **Weight:** 205 lbs   **Draft Info:** Round 3, 2006 Draft (#94 overall)

We don't have a baseball card for this guy.

2017 Daily WARP Profile
1.8 Total WARP

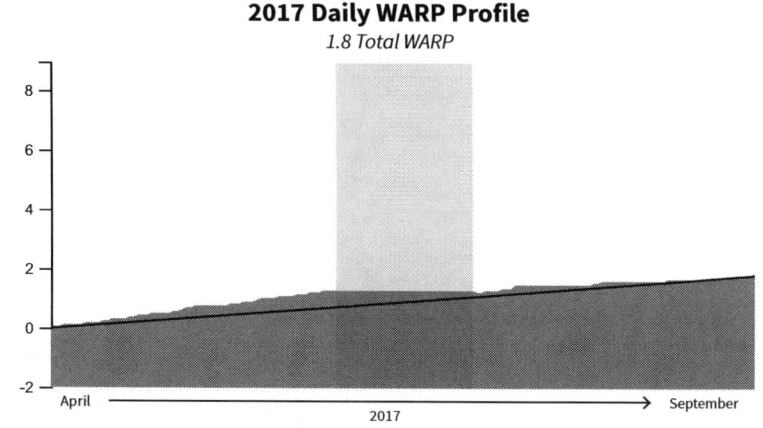

2017

Game 66: DL (shoulder inflammation)

35 PWR — **POWER** 117th of 150

44 STM — **STAMINA** 147th of 150

50 CMD — **COMMAND** 86th of 150

19 Sec/Pit — **PACE** 16th of 150 / 89° / Very Fast

Fantasy Values
2017	2018
$8.63	$1.00

YEAR	TEAM	LVL	AGE	W	L	SV	G	GS	IP	H	HR	BB/9	K/9	K	GB%	BABIP	WHIP	ERA	DRA	WARP	MPH 95
2017	TOR	MLB	33	3	0	0	38	0	35.2	30	3	2.5	12.9	51	44%	.342	1.12	3.28	1.98	1.3	90.6
2017	CLE	MLB	33	0	0	1	21	0	18.1	16	1	0.0	9.8	20	60%	.306	0.87	3.44	2.73	0.5	90.1

2017 Pitching Percentages

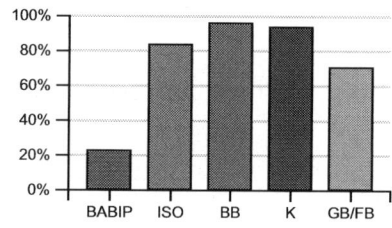

Pitching PECOTA Percentiles

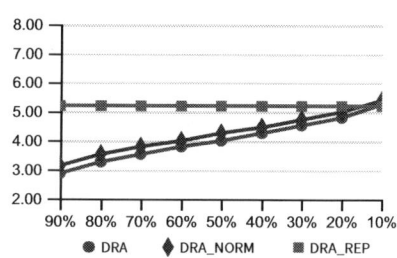

● DRA   ◆ DRA_NORM   ■ DRA_REP

Pitching WARP History

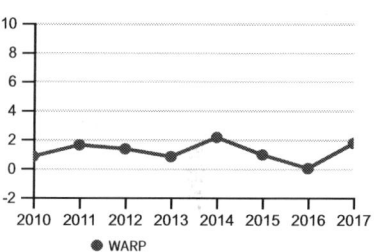

● WARP

Tunnel vs LHH

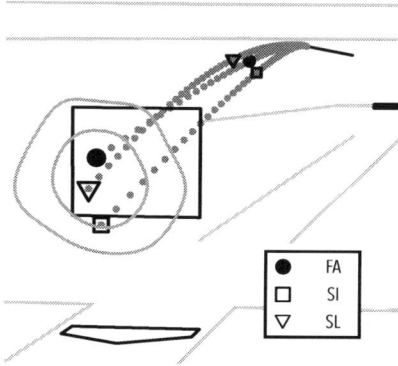

●	FA
□	SI
▽	SL

Pitch Types

Type	Freq	Velo	H Mov	V Mov
CH	0.6%	79.4 [77]	-10.9 [101]	-44.1 [51]
FA	29.4%	89.8 [89]	-15.1 [63]	-25.3 [68]
SI	37.3%	89.1 [81]	-15.6 [77]	-33.9 [49]
SL	32.8%	81.1 [85]	13.1 [137]	-30.3 [107]

Pitch Tunnel

Pairs	Release Diff	Tunnel Diff	Plate Diff	Speed Changes
590	20.6	108.0	198.0	0.023

PI Scores

Year	Pitch Ct	Pwr	Cmd	Stm
2013	985	42	67	48
2014	1087	37	60	52
2015	978	35	72	50
2016	802	37	63	42
2017	800	35	50	44

Tunnel vs RHH

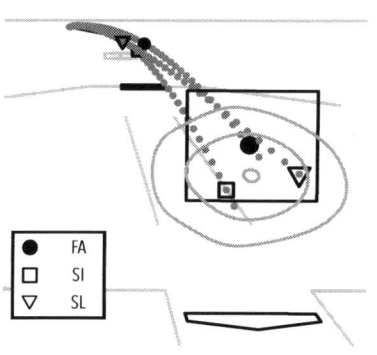

●	FA
□	SI
▽	SL

Justin Smoak 1B Toronto Blue Jays

Born: 12/5/1986 **Age:** 31 **Bats:** B **Throws:** L **Height:** 6' 4" **Weight:** 220 lbs **Draft Info:** Round 1, 2008 Draft (#11 overall)

21 Sec/Pit

PACE
45th of 155
71°
Fast

2017 Daily WARP Profile
2.6 Total WARP

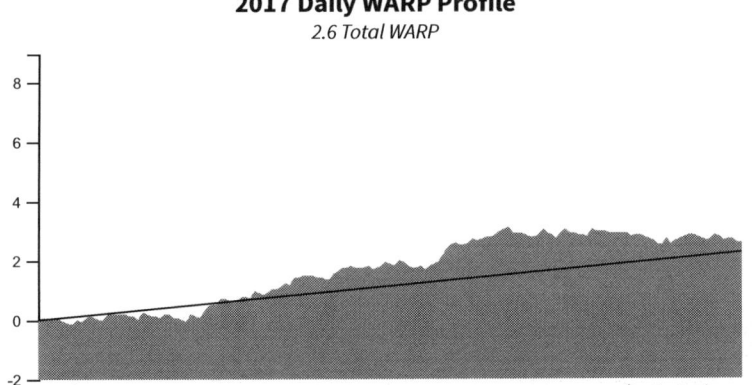

April — 2017 — September

Fantasy Values
2017 *2018*
$20.77 $17.00

YEAR	TEAM	LVL	AGE	PA	R	2B	3B	HR	RBI	BB	K	SB	AVG/OBP/SLG	TAv	VORP	BABIP	WARP
2017	TOR	MLB	30	637	85	29	1	38	90	73	128	0	.270/.355/.529	.289	26.6	.285	2.6

2017 Batting Percentages

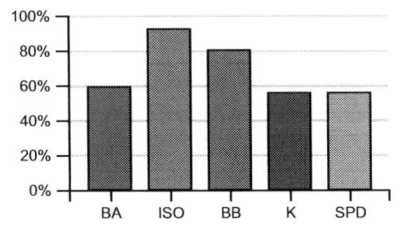

Batting PECOTA Percentiles

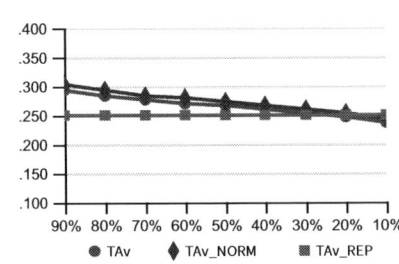

Batting WARP History

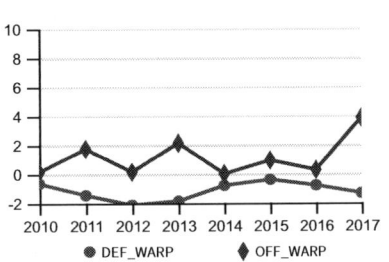

BRR (Relative to Position)

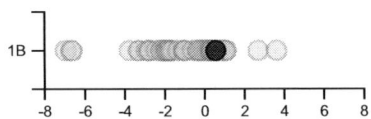

Rank		Player	BRR
6	86°	Jose Abreu	0.78
7	85°	Efren Navarro	0.63
8	82°	**Justin Smoak**	**0.60**
9	82°	Tomas Telis	0.55
10	82°	Tyler White	0.43

BRR (Relative to Team)

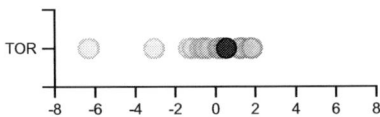

Rank		Player	BRR
7	88°	Josh Donaldson	1.27
8	84°	Devon Travis	1.23
9	74°	**Justin Smoak**	**0.60**
10	68°	Yangervis Solarte	0.52
11	66°	Chris Coghlan	0.44

Base Running Components

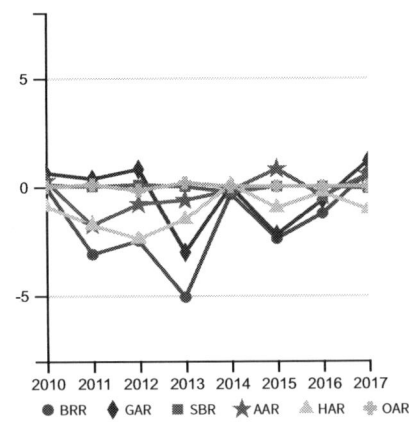

Blake Snell   LHP   Tampa Bay Rays

Born: 12/4/1992   **Age:** 25   **Bats:** L   **Throws:** L   **Height:** 6' 4"   **Weight:** 200 lbs   **Draft Info:** Round 1, 2011 Draft (#52 overall)

PACE
21 Sec/Pit
81st of 150
46°
Average

2017 Daily WARP Profile
2.6 Total WARP

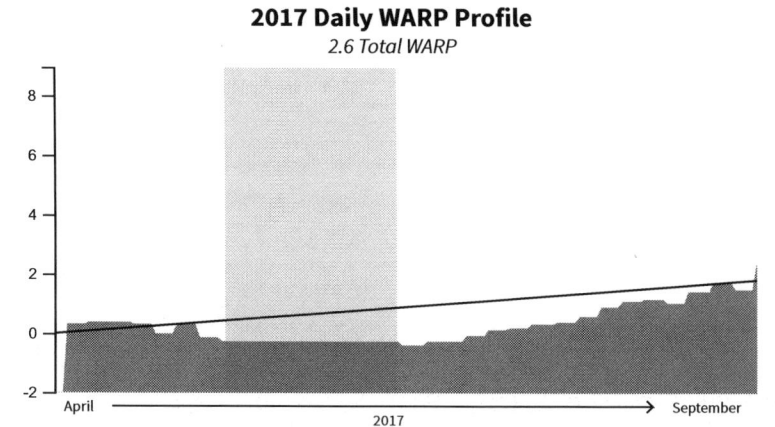

Game 40: minors

POWER
53 PWR
49th of 150

STAMINA
74 STM
44th of 150

COMMAND
50 CMD
86th of 150

Fantasy Values
2017	2018
$7.96	$8.00

YEAR	TEAM	LVL	AGE	W	L	SV	G	GS	IP	H	HR	BB/9	K/9	K	GB%	BABIP	WHIP	ERA	DRA	WARP	MPH 95
2017	TBA	MLB	24	5	7	0	24	24	129.1	113	15	4.1	8.3	119	45%	.278	1.33	4.04	3.80	2.6	96.0

2017 Pitching Percentages

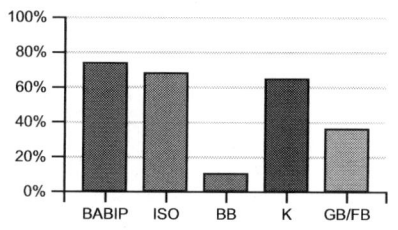

Pitching PECOTA Percentiles

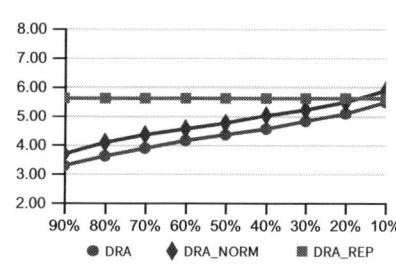

● DRA   ◆ DRA_NORM   ■ DRA_REP

Pitching WARP History

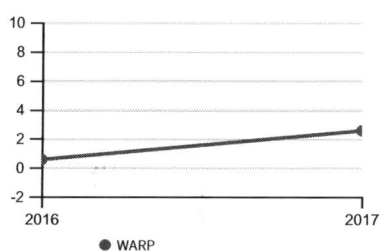

● WARP

Tunnel vs LHH

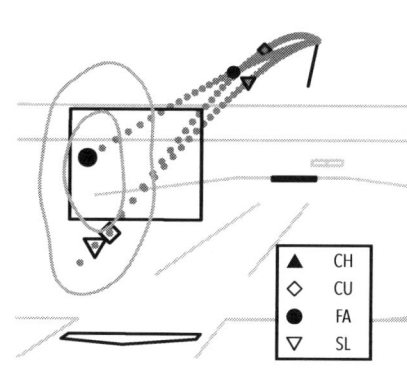

▲ CH
◇ CU
● FA
▽ SL

Pitch Types

Type	Freq	Velo	H Mov	V Mov
CH	21.1%	86.8 [107]	10.3 [105]	-18.7 [124]
CU	10.3%	79.5 [105]	-3.6 [84]	-47.7 [101]
FA	55.1%	94.7 [107]	2.9 [120]	-10.5 [115]
SL	13.5%	86.4 [109]	-3.2 [94]	-29.4 [109]

Pitch Tunnel

Pairs	Release Diff	Tunnel Diff	Plate Diff	Speed Changes
1725	33.4	120.8	243.4	0.028

PI Scores

Year	Pitch Ct	Pwr	Cmd	Stm
2016	1716	49	44	70
2017	2271	53	50	74

Tunnel vs RHH

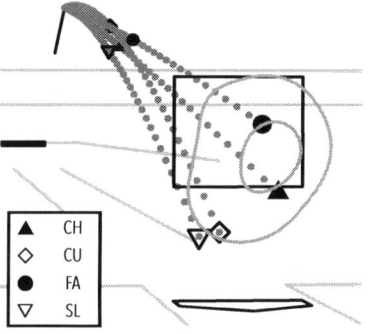

▲ CH
◇ CU
● FA
▽ SL

Steven Souza   RF   Tampa Bay Rays

Born: 4/24/1989   **Age:** 29   **Bats:** R   **Throws:** R   **Height:** 6' 4"   **Weight:** 225 lbs   **Draft Info:** Round 3, 2007 Draft (#100 overall)

PACE

22 Sec/Pit

99th of 155
36°
Slow

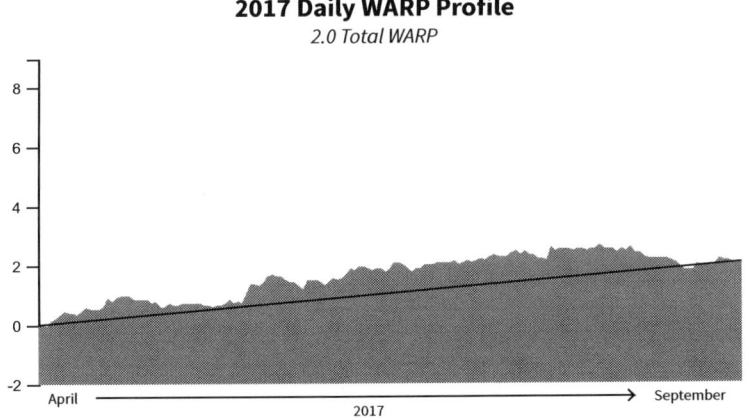

2017 Daily WARP Profile
2.0 Total WARP

Fantasy Values

2017	2018
$19.58	$17.00

YEAR	TEAM	LVL	AGE	PA	R	2B	3B	HR	RBI	BB	K	SB	AVG/OBP/SLG	TAv	VORP	BABIP	WARP
2017	TBA	MLB	28	617	78	21	2	30	78	84	179	16	.239/.351/.459	.287	27.3	.302	2.0

2017 Batting Percentages

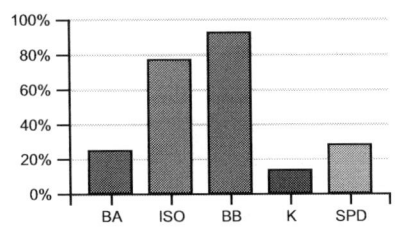

Batting PECOTA Percentiles

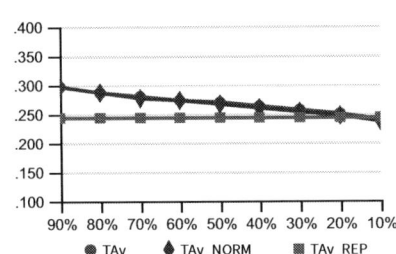

Batting WARP History

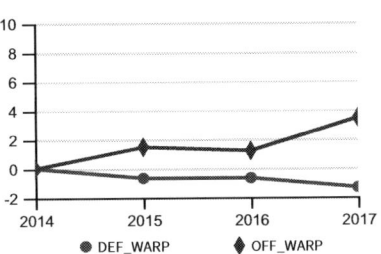

BRR (Relative to Position)

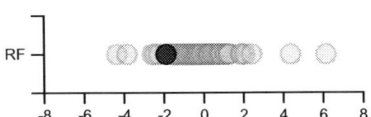

Rank		Player	BRR
48	16°	Lonnie Chisenhall	-1.55
49	15°	Chad Pinder	-1.76
50	12°	**Steven Souza**	**-1.85**
51	9°	Max Kepler	-2.21
52	7°	Nomar Mazara	-2.41

BRR (Relative to Team)

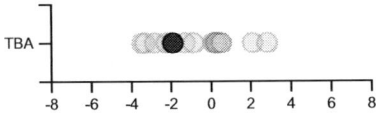

Rank		Player	BRR
11	49°	Daniel Robertson	-0.83
12	41°	Brad Miller	-1.26
13	29°	**Steven Souza**	**-1.85**
14	18°	Corey Dickerson	-1.88
15	13°	Adeiny Hechavarria	-2.18

Base Running Components

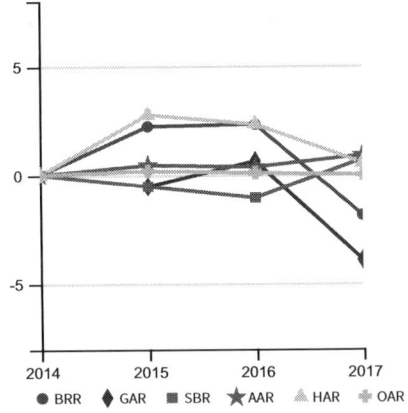

George Springer RF Houston Astros

Born: 9/19/1989 **Age:** 28 **Bats:** R **Throws:** R **Height:** 6' 3" **Weight:** 215 lbs **Draft Info:** Round 1, 2011 Draft (#11 overall)

PACE
21 45th of 155
Sec/Pit 71°
Fast

2017 Daily WARP Profile
4.4 Total WARP

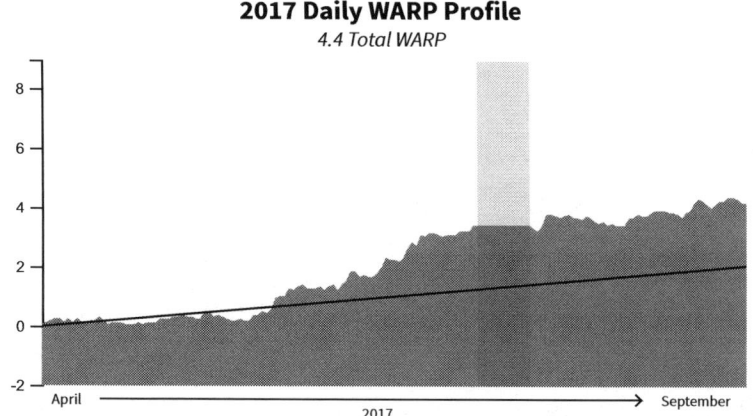

Game 100: DL (quad soreness)

Fantasy Values
2017 | 2018
$25.01 | **$29.00**

YEAR	TEAM	LVL	AGE	PA	R	2B	3B	HR	RBI	BB	K	SB	AVG/OBP/SLG	TAv	VORP	BABIP	WARP
2017	HOU	MLB	27	629	112	29	0	34	85	64	111	5	.283/.367/.522	.297	40.7	.297	4.4

Springer took his power to another level and likely would have topped 40 home runs had he played a full season. The speed some were hoping would make Springer into a 40/25 player likely won't materialize in the majors, but Springer offers a top flight power bat in a solid Astros' lineup that gives him plenty of run and RBI opportunities. He isn't an elite fantasy player but is comfortably ensconced at the top of the second tier. — Mike G.

2017 Batting Percentages

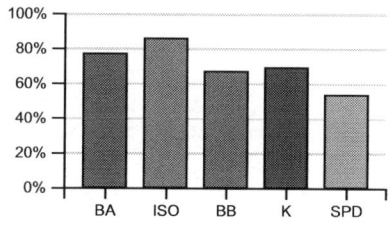

Batting PECOTA Percentiles

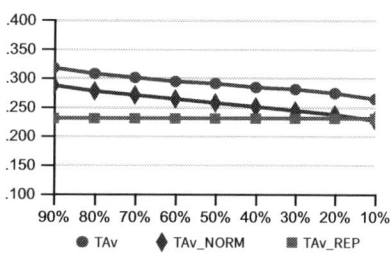

Batting WARP History

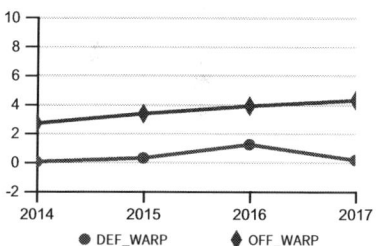

BRR (Relative to Position)

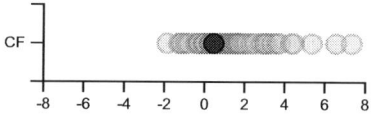

Rank		Player	BRR
38	25°	A.J. Pollock	0.68
39	24°	Leury Garcia	0.50
40	20°	**George Springer**	**0.50**
41	20°	Mason Williams	0.49
42	19°	Reymond Fuentes	0.48

BRR (Relative to Team)

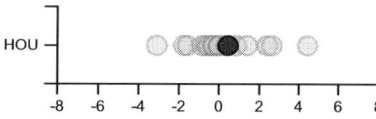

Rank		Player	BRR
4	69°	Jake Marisnick	1.44
5	68°	Tony Kemp	0.90
6	55°	**George Springer**	**0.50**
7	54°	Tyler White	0.43
8	51°	Evan Gattis	0.04

Base Running Components

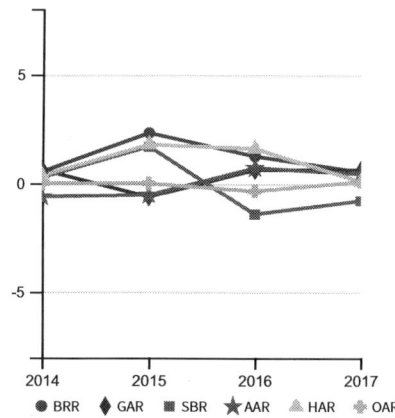

Giancarlo Stanton   RF   New York Yankees

Born: 11/8/1989   **Age:** 28   **Bats:** R   **Throws:** R   **Height:** 6' 6"   **Weight:** 245 lbs   **Draft Info:** Round 2, 2007 Draft (#76 overall)

19 Sec/Pit

PACE
4th of 155
97°
Very Fast

2017 Daily WARP Profile
8.5 Total WARP

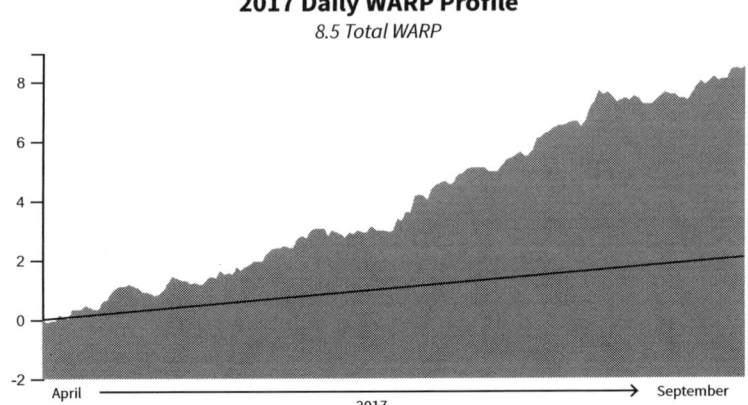

Fantasy Values

2017	2018
$33.98	$32.00

YEAR	TEAM	LVL	AGE	PA	R	2B	3B	HR	RBI	BB	K	SB	AVG/OBP/SLG	TAv	VORP	BABIP	WARP
2017	MIA	MLB	27	692	123	32	0	59	132	85	163	2	.281/.376/.631	.348	76.7	.288	8.5

After years of freak injuries and chunks of missed games, Stanton finally put together the signature power season that his raw power made a seeming inevitability. As three-category players go, there isn't anyone in baseball with a higher ceiling, and the move away from cavernous Marlins Park to cozy Yankee Stadium could make Stanton a threat to Barry Bonds' single-season home-run record. Some will discount Stanton because of the injuries, but since they aren't chronic feel free to bid with confidence. — Mike G.

2017 Batting Percentages

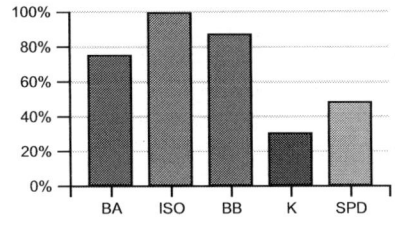

Batting PECOTA Percentiles

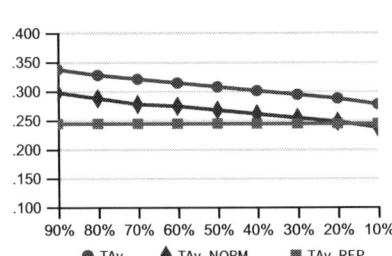

Batting WARP History

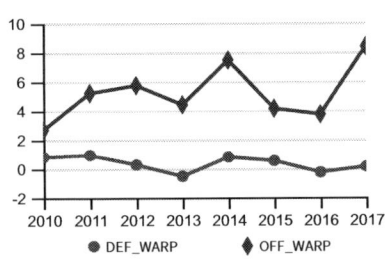

BRR (Relative to Position)

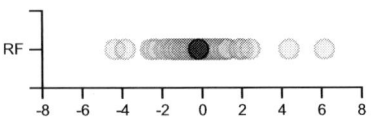

Rank		Player	BRR
26	54°	Aaron Judge	-0.06
27	52°	Jorge Bonifacio	-0.06
28	49°	**Giancarlo Stanton**	**-0.14**
29	46°	Scott Schebler	-0.22
30	43°	Jose Bautista	-0.25

BRR (Relative to Team)

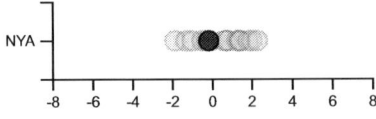

Rank		Player	BRR
10	46°	Tyler Wade	0.67
11	34°	Aaron Judge	-0.06
12	22°	**Giancarlo Stanton**	**-0.14**
13	13°	Todd Frazier	-0.24
14	10°	Danny Espinosa	-0.48

Base Running Components

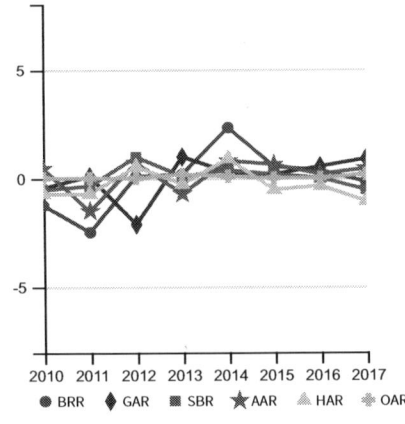

Trevor Story   SS   Colorado Rockies

Born: 11/15/1992   **Age:** 25   **Bats:** R   **Throws:** R   **Height:** 6' 1"   **Weight:** 210 lbs   **Draft Info:** Round 1, 2011 Draft (#45 overall)

PACE
135th of 155
13°
Very Slow

23 Sec/Pit

2017 Daily WARP Profile
2.8 Total WARP

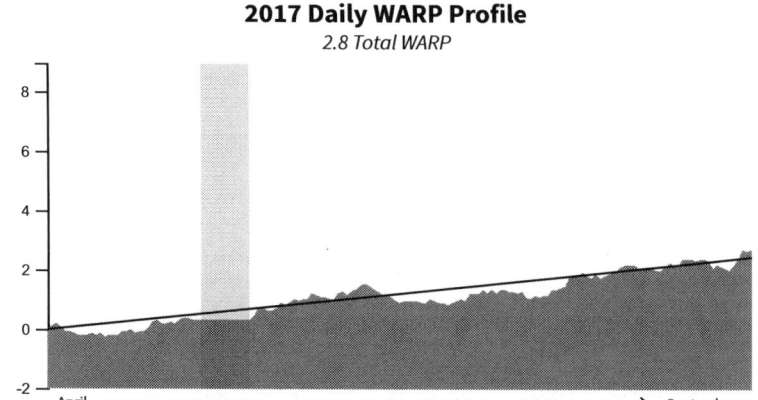

Game 36: DL (shoulder strain)

Fantasy Values
2017 2018
$15.10 $18.00

YEAR	TEAM	LVL	AGE	PA	R	2B	3B	HR	RBI	BB	K	SB	AVG/OBP/SLG	TAv	VORP	BABIP	WARP
2017	COL	MLB	24	555	68	32	3	24	82	49	191	7	.239/.308/.457	.261	28.6	.332	2.8

It was obvious that Story wouldn't duplicate his strong rookie campaign, but no one anticipated he would take such a fall from grace. The sophomore shortstop struggled at home and against righties and saw his strikeout rate spike, but mostly suffered because his batted ball distance dropped. Story is young, plays in Coors, and is a good bounce-back candidate simply because it can't get much worse, but his price tag has to drop by at least a third of what it was in 2018 to make him worth our time. — Mike G.

2017 Batting Percentages

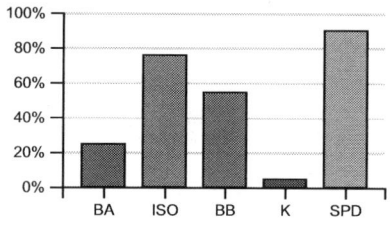

Batting PECOTA Percentiles

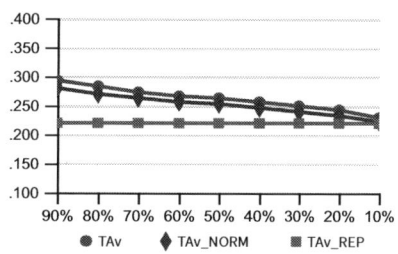

Batting WARP History

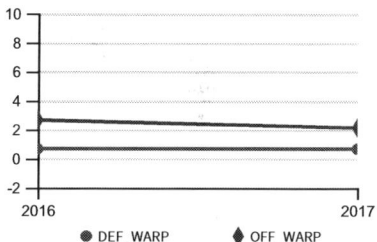

BRR (Relative to Position)

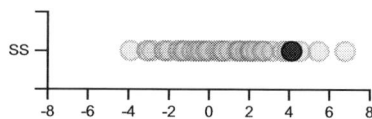

BRR (Relative to Team)

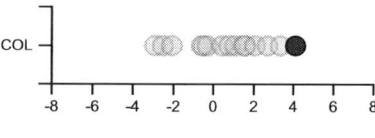

Base Running Components

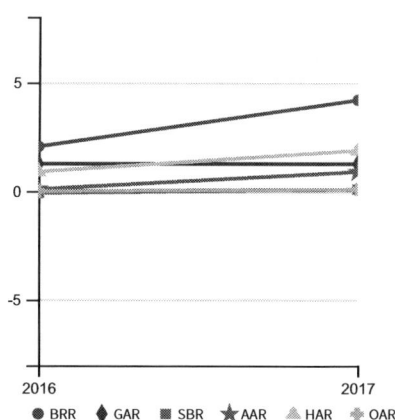

Rank	Player	BRR
2	Xander Bogaerts (93°)	5.51
3	Miguel Rojas (91°)	4.57
4	**Trevor Story** (88°)	**4.16**
5	Marcus Semien (86°)	3.94
6	Jose Iglesias (83°)	3.72

Rank	Player	BRR
1	**Trevor Story** (96°)	**4.16**
2	DJ LeMahieu (83°)	3.38
3	Ian Desmond (76°)	2.73
4	Patrick Valaika (74°)	2.11
5	Raimel Tapia (70°)	1.62

Dan Straily RHP Miami Marlins

Born: 12/1/1988 **Age:** 29 **Bats:** R **Throws:** R **Height:** 6' 2" **Weight:** 220 lbs **Draft Info:** Round 24, 2009 Draft (#723 overall)

We don't have a baseball card for this guy.

2017 Daily WARP Profile
2.2 Total WARP

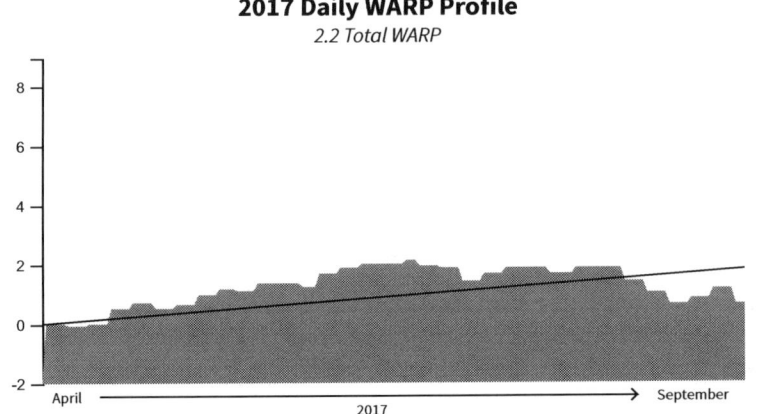

April 2017 September

POWER
33 PWR
125th of 150

STAMINA
77 STM
32nd of 150

COMMAND
48 CMD
97th of 150

18 Sec/Pit
PACE
5th of 150
97°
Very Fast

Fantasy Values
2017	2018
$13.24	$9.00

YEAR	TEAM	LVL	AGE	W	L	SV	G	GS	IP	H	HR	BB/9	K/9	K	GB%	BABIP	WHIP	ERA	DRA	WARP	MPH 95
2017	MIA	MLB	28	10	9	0	33	33	181.2	176	31	3.0	8.4	170	36%	.288	1.30	4.26	4.51	2.2	92.1

2017 Pitching Percentages

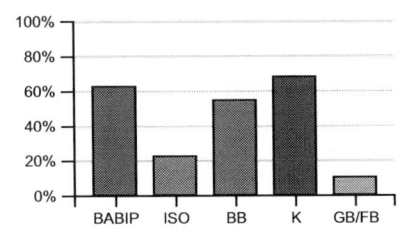

Pitching PECOTA Percentiles

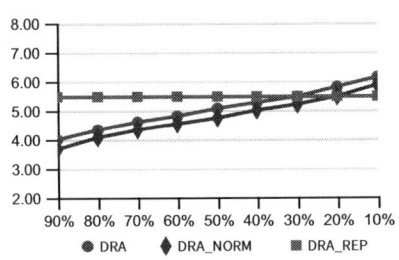

Pitching WARP History

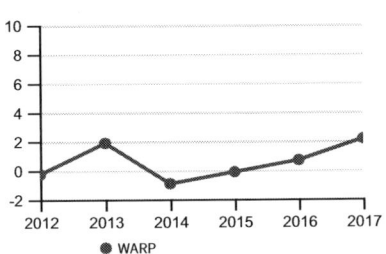

Tunnel vs LHH

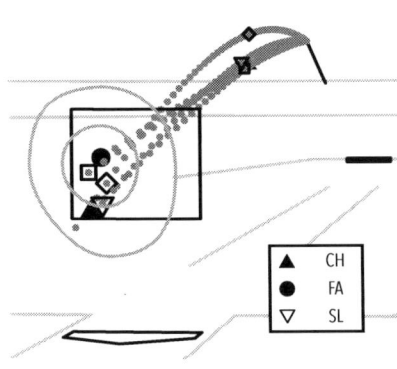

▲ CH
● FA
▽ SL

Pitch Types

Type	Freq	Velo	H Mov	V Mov
CH	16.9%	83.7 [94]	-10.8 [101]	-31.2 [88]
CU	3.0%	73.9 [83]	8 [101]	-50.9 [94]
FA	48.6%	90.8 [93]	-6.7 [102]	-12.9 [107]
SI	1.8%	90.4 [89]	-10.8 [112]	-17.1 [111]
SL	29.7%	84.1 [99]	4.5 [99]	-30.4 [107]

Pitch Tunnel

Pairs	Release Diff	Tunnel Diff	Plate Diff	Speed Changes
2305	37.3	119.8	224.8	0.022

PI Scores

Year	Pitch Ct	Pwr	Cmd	Stm
2013	2462	42	46	74
2014	876	34	41	72
2015	290	28	45	61
2016	3033	36	49	78
2017	3072	33	48	77

Tunnel vs RHH

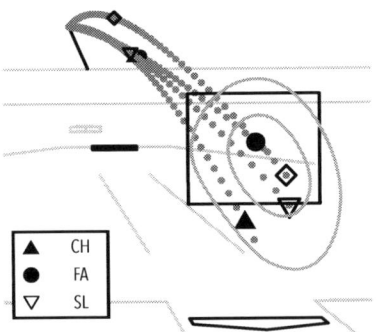

▲ CH
● FA
▽ SL

Stephen Strasburg   RHP   Washington Nationals

Born: 7/20/1988   **Age:** 29   **Bats:** R   **Throws:** R   **Height:** 6' 4"   **Weight:** 235 lbs   **Draft Info:** Round 1, 2009 Draft (#1 overall)

22 Sec/Pit

PACE
108th of 150
28°
Slow

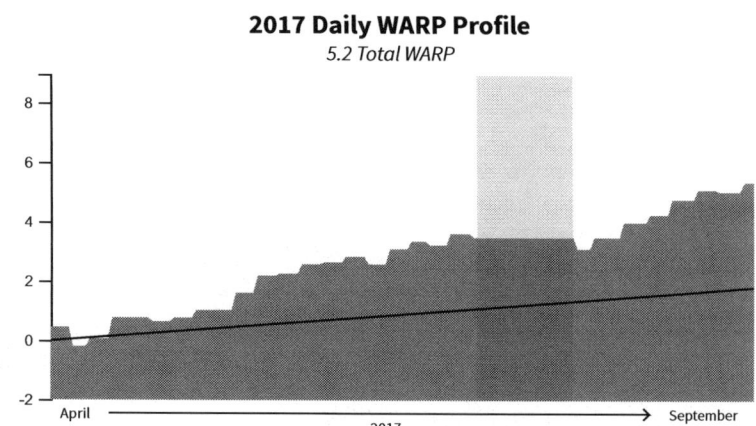

2017 Daily WARP Profile
5.2 Total WARP

April   2017   September

Game 98: DL (elbow impingement)

56 PWR — **POWER** 38th of 150

72 STM — **STAMINA** 59th of 150

50 CMD — **COMMAND** 86th of 150

Fantasy Values
| 2017 | 2018 |
| **$32.16** | **$26.00** |

YEAR	TEAM	LVL	AGE	W	L	SV	G	GS	IP	H	HR	BB/9	K/9	K	GB%	BABIP	WHIP	ERA	DRA	WARP	MPH 95
2017	WAS	MLB	28	15	4	0	28	28	175.1	131	13	2.4	10.5	204	48%	.274	1.02	2.52	2.93	5.2	97.4

2017 Pitching Percentages

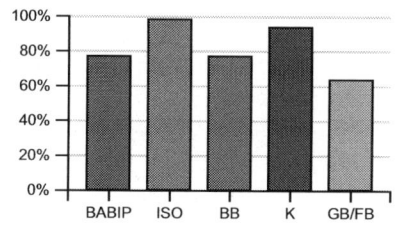

Pitching PECOTA Percentiles

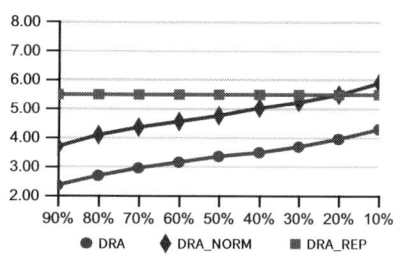

● DRA   ◆ DRA_NORM   ■ DRA_REP

Pitching WARP History

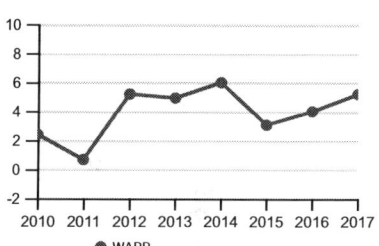

● WARP

Tunnel vs LHH

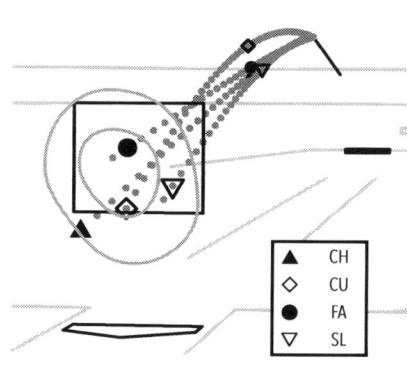

▲ CH
◇ CU
● FA
▽ SL

Pitch Types

Type	Freq	Velo	H Mov	V Mov
CH	18.8%	89.1 [116]	-13.6 [87]	-26.4 [102]
CU	22.7%	82.8 [117]	12.1 [117]	-44.6 [107]
FA	51.6%	96 [112]	-9.4 [89]	-12.6 [108]
SI	0.3%	94.7 [114]	-13.7 [91]	-18.7 [105]
SL	6.6%	90.6 [127]	2.5 [91]	-22 [130]

Pitch Tunnel

Pairs	Release Diff	Tunnel Diff	Plate Diff	Speed Changes
1983	21.1	108.9	213.0	0.026

PI Scores

Year	Pitch Ct	Pwr	Cmd	Stm
2013	2844	61	46	70
2014	3266	63	56	81
2015	2037	61	46	57
2016	2378	57	54	64
2017	2666	56	50	72

Tunnel vs RHH

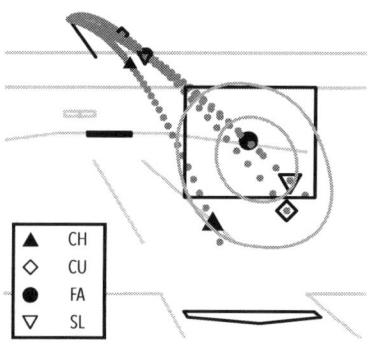

▲ CH
◇ CU
● FA
▽ SL

Marcus Stroman   RHP   Toronto Blue Jays

Born: 5/1/1991   **Age:** 27   **Bats:** R   **Throws:** R   **Height:** 5'8"   **Weight:** 180 lbs   **Draft Info:** Round 1, 2012 Draft (#22 overall)

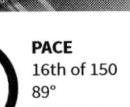

PACE
19 16th of 150
Sec/Pit 89°
Very Fast

2017 Daily WARP Profile
4.4 Total WARP

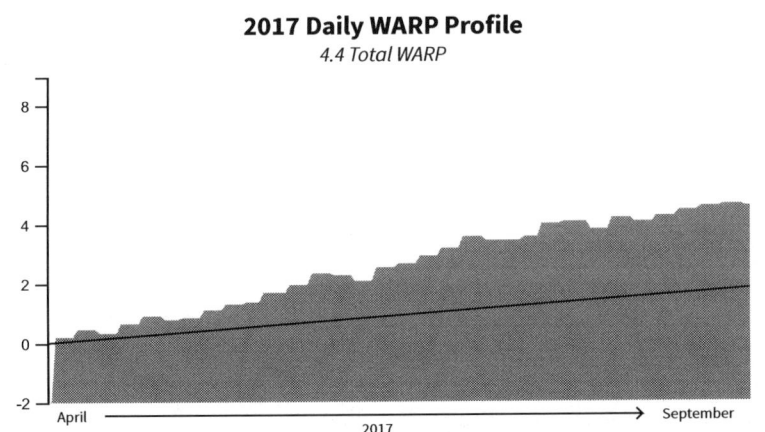

April   2017   September

POWER
54 45th of 150
PWR

STAMINA
80 14th of 150
STM

COMMAND
52 79th of 150
CMD

Fantasy Values
2017   2018
$19.24 $15.00

YEAR	TEAM	LVL	AGE	W	L	SV	G	GS	IP	H	HR	BB/9	K/9	K	GB%	BABIP	WHIP	ERA	DRA	WARP	MPH 95
2017	TOR	MLB	26	13	9	0	33	33	201	201	21	2.8	7.3	164	63%	.310	1.31	3.09	3.60	4.4	94.9

2017 Pitching Percentages

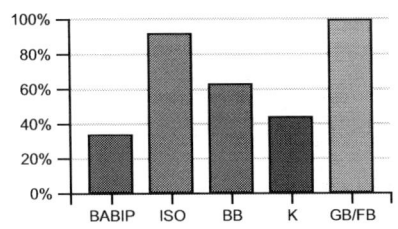

Pitching PECOTA Percentiles

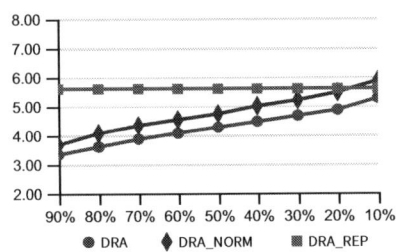

● DRA   ◆ DRA_NORM   ■ DRA_REP

Pitching WARP History

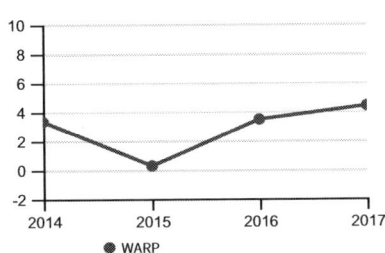

● WARP

Tunnel vs LHH

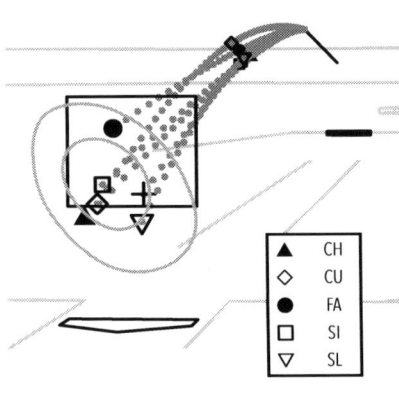

▲ CH
◇ CU
● FA
□ SI
▽ SL

Pitch Types

Type	Freq	Velo	H Mov	V Mov
CH	5.9%	82.9 [91]	-11.3 [99]	-29.6 [93]
CU	4.9%	82.8 [117]	14.3 [125]	-40.3 [116]
FA	6.2%	94.2 [105]	-4 [114]	-16.6 [95]
FC	4.0%	89.6 [107]	4.6 [115]	-28.2 [83]
SI	55.9%	93.7 [108]	-8.8 [127]	-23.7 [87]
SL	23.0%	86.8 [111]	10.6 [126]	-33.5 [98]

Pitch Tunnel

Pairs	Release Diff	Tunnel Diff	Plate Diff	Speed Changes
2296	26.6	117.5	221.6	0.020

PI Scores

Year	Pitch Ct	Pwr	Cmd	Stm
2014	2077	53	53	67
2015	370	39	55	45
2016	3102	50	49	81
2017	3134	54	52	80

Tunnel vs RHH

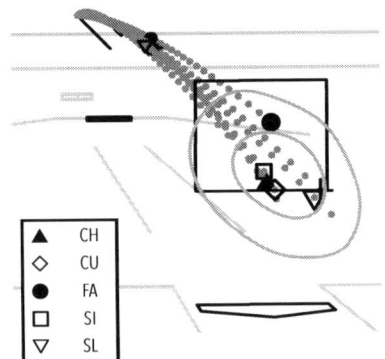

▲ CH
◇ CU
● FA
□ SI
▽ SL

Eugenio Suarez 3B Cincinnati Reds

Born: 7/18/1991 **Age:** 26 **Bats:** R **Throws:** R **Height:** 5' 11" **Weight:** 213 lbs **Draft Info:** International Free Agent, 2008

PACE
21 Sec/Pit
45th of 155
71°
Fast

2017 Daily WARP Profile
3.7 Total WARP

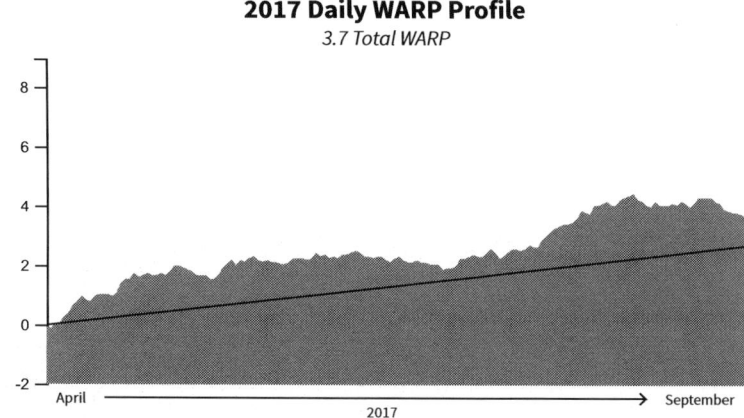

Fantasy Values
2017 2018
$18.46 $15.00

YEAR	TEAM	LVL	AGE	PA	R	2B	3B	HR	RBI	BB	K	SB	AVG/OBP/SLG	TAv	VORP	BABIP	WARP
2017	CIN	MLB	25	632	87	25	2	26	82	84	147	4	.260/.367/.461	.294	38.8	.309	3.7

2017 Batting Percentages
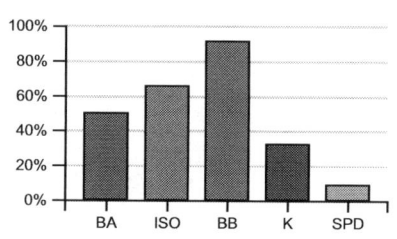

Batting PECOTA Percentiles
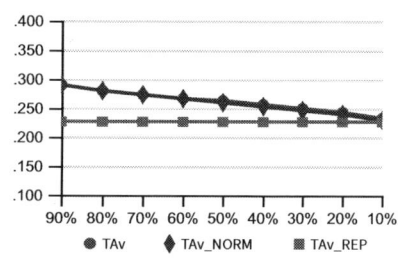

Batting WARP History
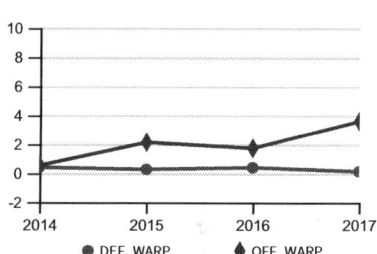

BRR (Relative to Position)
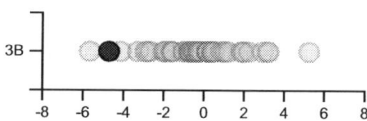

Rank		Player	BRR
52	11°	Justin Turner	-3.24
53	8°	Manny Machado	-4.10
54	6°	David Freese	-4.66
55	3°	Eugenio Suarez	-4.67
56	0°	Kyle Seager	-5.62

BRR (Relative to Team)
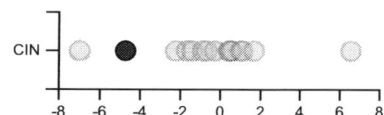

Rank		Player	BRR
12	37°	Scooter Gennett	-1.36
13	31°	Tucker Barnhart	-1.63
14	23°	Adam Duvall	-2.18
15	13°	Eugenio Suarez	-4.67
16	0°	Joey Votto	-6.92

Base Running Components
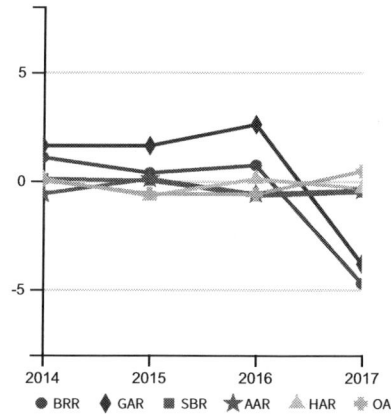

Kurt Suzuki C Atlanta Braves

Born: 10/4/1983 **Age:** 34 **Bats:** R **Throws:** R **Height:** 5' 11" **Weight:** 205 lbs **Draft Info:** Round 2, 2004 Draft (#67 overall)

2017 Daily WARP Profile
2.6 Total WARP

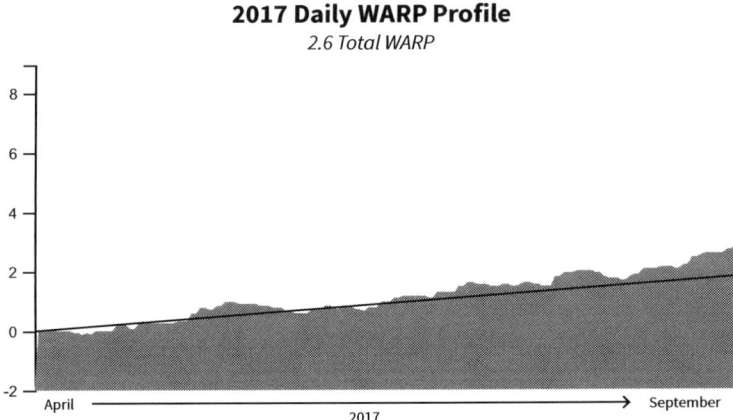

23 Sec/Pit

PACE
135th of 155
13°
Very Slow

Fantasy Values
2017	2018
$11.59	$10.00

YEAR	TEAM	LVL	AGE	PA	R	2B	3B	HR	RBI	BB	K	SB	AVG/OBP/SLG	TAv	VORP	BABIP	WARP
2017	ATL	MLB	33	309	38	13	0	19	50	17	39	0	.283/.351/.536	.308	27.3	.268	2.6

2017 Batting Percentages

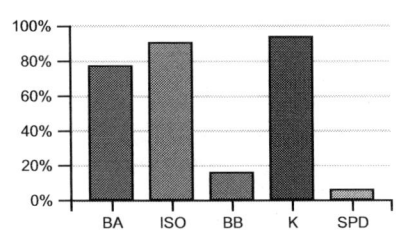

Batting PECOTA Percentiles

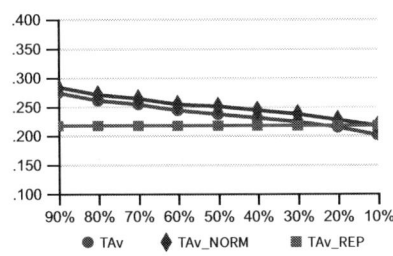

Batting WARP History

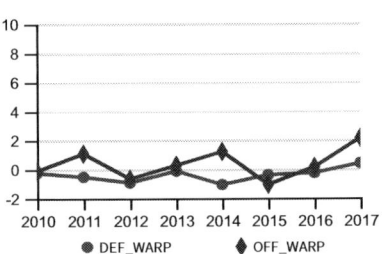

BRR (Relative to Position)

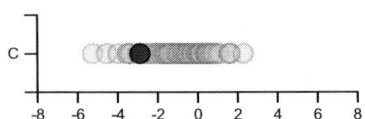

Rank		Player	BRR
67	16°	Nick Hundley	-2.80
68	15°	Rene Rivera	-2.83
69	13°	**Kurt Suzuki**	**-2.84**
70	11°	Francisco Cervelli	-2.94
71	9°	Christian Vazquez	-3.29

BRR (Relative to Team)

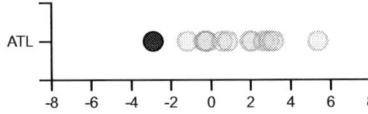

Rank		Player	BRR
9	11°	Tyler Flowers	-0.18
10	8°	Adonis Garcia	-0.21
11	5°	Lane Adams	-0.29
12	4°	Jaff Decker	-1.13
13	0°	**Kurt Suzuki**	**-2.84**

Base Running Components

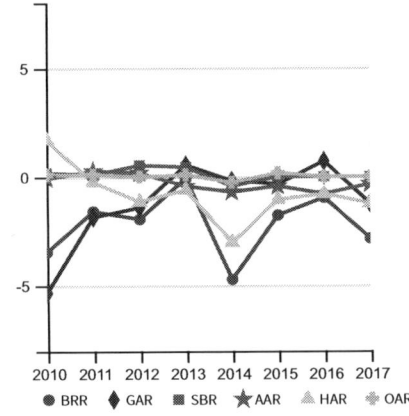

Dansby Swanson   SS   Atlanta Braves

Born: 2/11/1994   **Age:** 24   **Bats:** R   **Throws:** R   **Height:** 6' 1"   **Weight:** 190 lbs   **Draft Info:** Round 1, 2015 Draft (#1 overall)

23 Sec/Pit

PACE
135th of 155
13°
Very Slow

Game 101: minors

2017 Daily WARP Profile
0.3 Total WARP

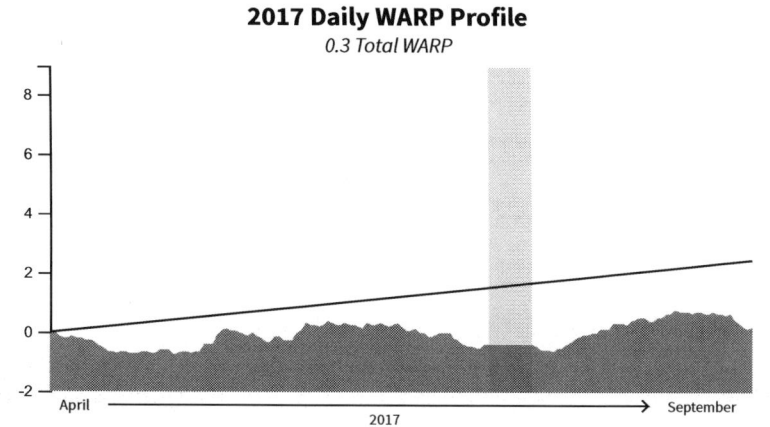

April   2017   September

Fantasy Values

2017	2018
$6.18	**$11.00**

YEAR	TEAM	LVL	AGE	PA	R	2B	3B	HR	RBI	BB	K	SB	AVG/OBP/SLG	TAv	VORP	BABIP	WARP
2017	ATL	MLB	23	551	59	23	2	6	51	59	120	3	.232/.312/.324	.237	13.3	.292	.3

2017 Batting Percentages

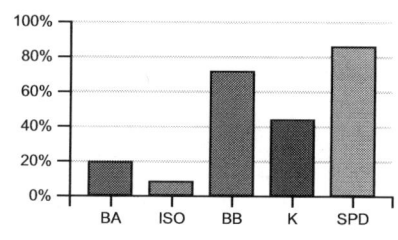

Batting PECOTA Percentiles

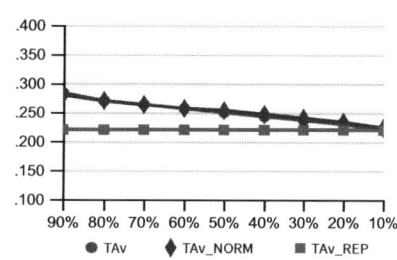

Batting WARP History

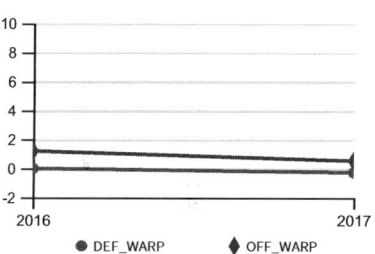

BRR (Relative to Position)

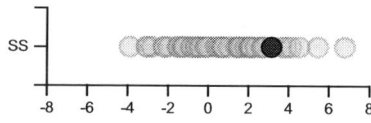

Rank		Player	BRR
5	86°	Marcus Semien	3.94
6	83°	Jose Iglesias	3.72
7	81°	**Dansby Swanson**	**3.19**
8	77°	Elvis Andrus	2.81
9	75°	Jose Reyes	2.71

BRR (Relative to Team)

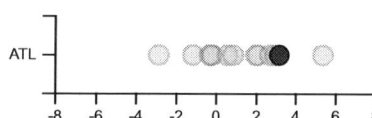

Rank		Player	BRR
1	61°	Ender Inciarte	5.41
2	52°	**Dansby Swanson**	**3.19**
3	47°	Johan Camargo	2.97
4	39°	Freddie Freeman	2.72
5	28°	Nick Markakis	2.12

Base Running Components

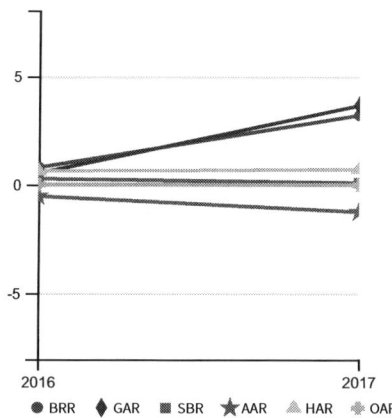

Anthony Swarzak   RHP   New York Mets

Born: 9/10/1985   **Age:** 32   **Bats:** R   **Throws:** R   **Height:** 6' 4"   **Weight:** 215 lbs   **Draft Info:** Round 2, 2004 Draft (#61 overall)

We don't have a baseball card for this guy.

2017 Daily WARP Profile
1.7 Total WARP

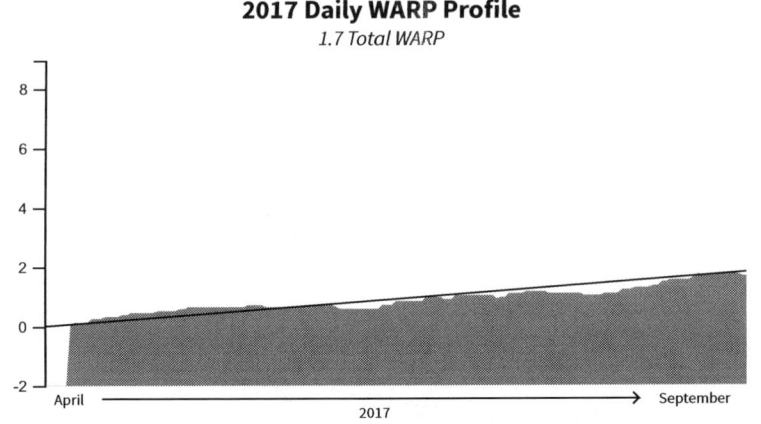

PACE
24 Sec/Pit
140th of 150
7°
Very Slow

50 PWR **POWER** 59th of 150

54 STM **STAMINA** 118th of 150

63 CMD **COMMAND** 20th of 150

Fantasy Values
2017	2018
$9.29	$3.00

YEAR	TEAM	LVL	AGE	W	L	SV	G	GS	IP	H	HR	BB/9	K/9	K	GB%	BABIP	WHIP	ERA	DRA	WARP	MPH 95
2017	CHA	MLB	31	4	3	1	41	0	48.1	37	2	2.4	9.7	52	40%	.294	1.03	2.23	3.09	1.1	95.9
2017	MIL	MLB	31	2	1	1	29	0	29	21	4	2.8	12.1	39	51%	.270	1.03	2.48	3.32	0.6	96.3

2017 Pitching Percentages

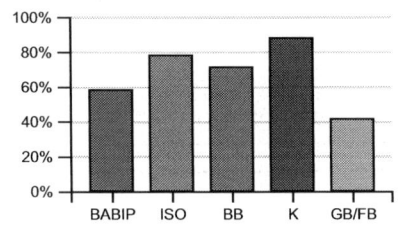

Pitching PECOTA Percentiles

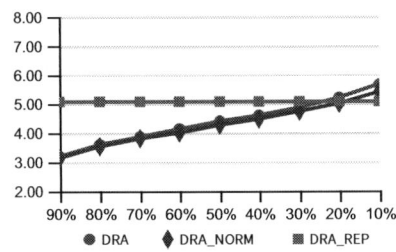

Pitching WARP History

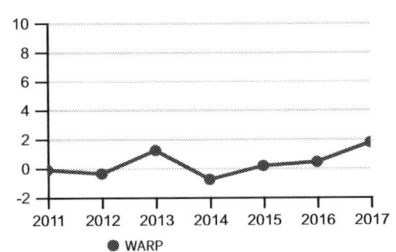

Tunnel vs LHH

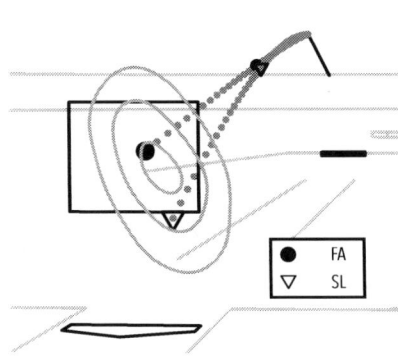

Pitch Types

Type	Freq	Velo	H Mov	V Mov
FA	48.6%	95 [108]	-7.8 [97]	-11.2 [113]
SL	51.4%	87.5 [114]	3.2 [94]	-28.1 [113]

Pitch Tunnel

Pairs	Release Diff	Tunnel Diff	Plate Diff	Speed Changes
953	22.0	98.2	196.9	0.016

PI Scores

Year	Pitch Ct	Pwr	Cmd	Stm
2012	1426	53	61	47
2013	1492	53	66	49
2014	1383	57	59	48
2016	488	46	65	42
2017	1255	50	63	54

Tunnel vs RHH

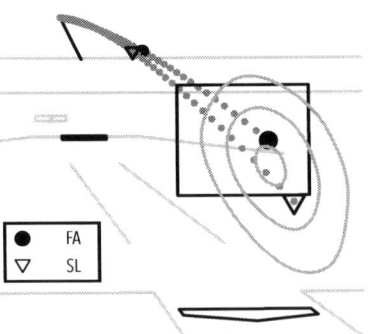

Jameson Taillon   RHP   Pittsburgh Pirates

Born: 11/18/1991   **Age:** 26   **Bats:** R   **Throws:** R   **Height:** 6' 5"   **Weight:** 225 lbs   **Draft Info:** Round 1, 2010 Draft (#2 overall)

2017 Daily WARP Profile
1.6 Total WARP

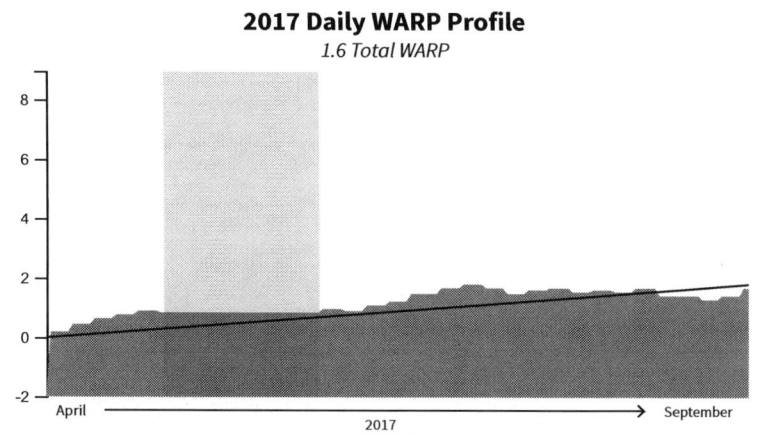

Game 28: DL (cancer treatment)

PACE — 19 Sec/Pit — 16th of 150 — 89° — Very Fast

POWER — 59 PWR — 27th of 150

STAMINA — 65 STM — 88th of 150

COMMAND — 49 CMD — 91st of 150

Fantasy Values

2017	2018
$5.91	$12.00

YEAR	TEAM	LVL	AGE	W	L	SV	G	GS	IP	H	HR	BB/9	K/9	K	GB%	BABIP	WHIP	ERA	DRA	WARP	MPH 95
2017	PIT	MLB	25	8	7	0	25	25	133.2	152	11	3.1	8.4	125	49%	.352	1.48	4.44	4.51	1.6	96.7

 It's difficult to judge Taillon's 2017 due to a cancer diagnosis in early May that led to surgery and a six-week absence. He struggled throughout the year but there is too much talent to write him off, and the fact that he pitched at all last year is a triumph. Taillon remains one of the more promising young arms in baseball, and there is plenty of room for improvement now that he is one year removed from his diagnosis. — Mike G.

2017 Pitching Percentages

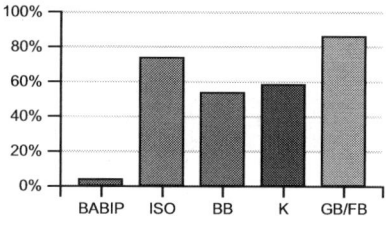

Pitching PECOTA Percentiles

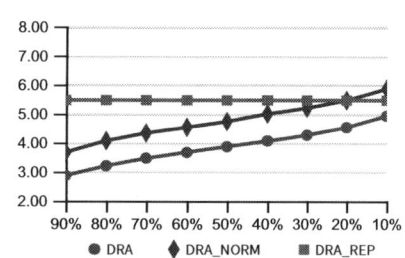

Pitching WARP History

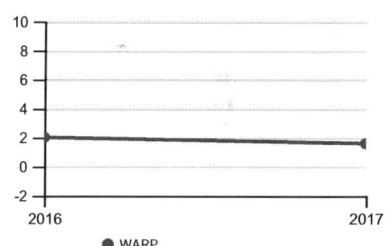

Tunnel vs LHH

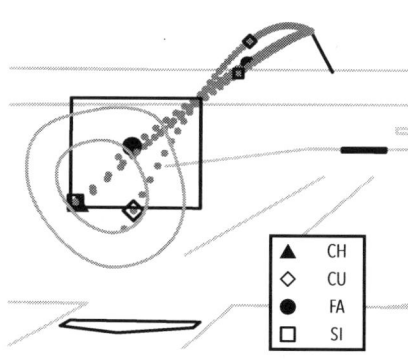

Pitch Types

Type	Freq	Velo	H Mov	V Mov
CH	9.9%	88.6 [114]	-7.1 [122]	-22.6 [113]
CU	26.0%	81.9 [113]	10.4 [110]	-48.6 [99]
FA	29.7%	95.8 [111]	-3.9 [115]	-13.3 [106]
SI	34.4%	95.5 [119]	-11.3 [109]	-18.8 [105]

Pitch Tunnel

Pairs	Release Diff	Tunnel Diff	Plate Diff	Speed Changes
1654	27.5	116.5	221.8	0.032

PI Scores

Year	Pitch Ct	Pwr	Cmd	Stm
2016	1535	50	54	65
2017	2312	59	49	65

Tunnel vs RHH

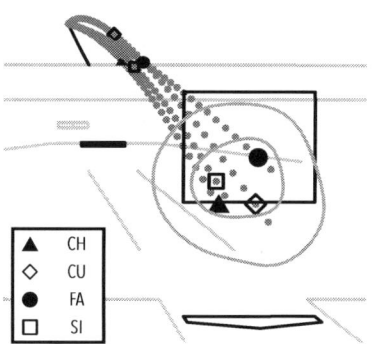

Masahiro Tanaka　RHP　New York Yankees

Born: 11/1/1988　**Age:** 29　**Bats:** R　**Throws:** R　**Height:** 6' 3"　**Weight:** 215 lbs　**Draft Info:** International Free Agent, 2014

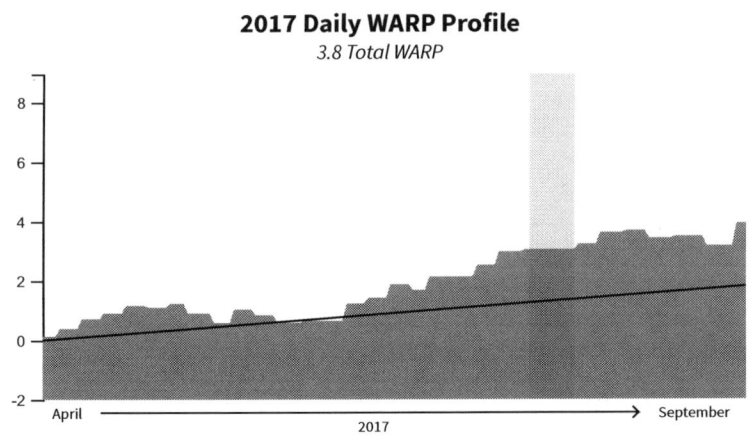

2017 Daily WARP Profile
3.8 Total WARP

April — 2017 — September

Game 113: DL (shoulder inflammation)

	POWER
32 PWR	128th of 150
73 STM	STAMINA 53rd of 150
55 CMD	COMMAND 62nd of 150
23 Sec/Pit	PACE 126th of 150 16° Very Slow

Fantasy Values

2017	2018
$15.01	$16.00

YEAR	TEAM	LVL	AGE	W	L	SV	G	GS	IP	H	HR	BB/9	K/9	K	GB%	BABIP	WHIP	ERA	DRA	WARP	MPH 95
2017	NYA	MLB	28	13	12	0	30	30	178.1	180	35	2.1	9.8	194	50%	.306	1.24	4.74	3.66	3.8	94.0

Tanaka struggled mightily in the first half before recovering and putting together a strong finish. Some of his struggles were blamed on pitching in day games as well as to batterymate Gary Sanchez, but once Tanaka got back on track none of these reasons seemed to matter. Tanaka is a good candidate to carry over his second half success into 2018, although a partially torn UCL that was never operated on always leaves him with some level of risk. — Mike G.

2017 Pitching Percentages

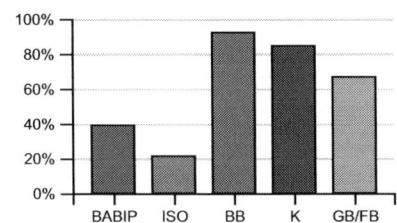

Pitching PECOTA Percentiles

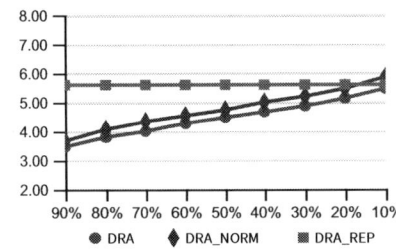

● DRA　◆ DRA_NORM　■ DRA_REP

Pitching WARP History

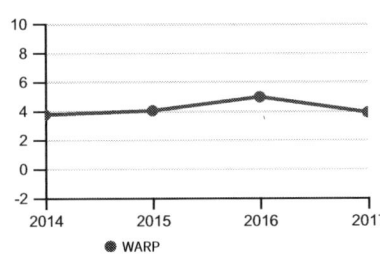

● WARP

Tunnel vs LHH

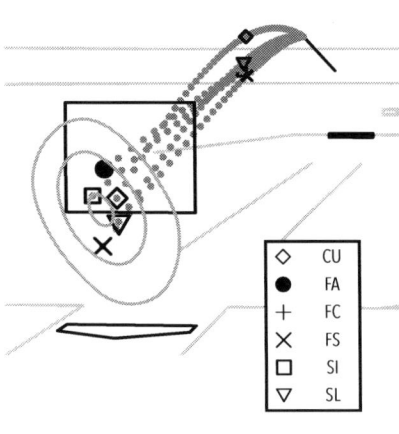

◇	CU
●	FA
+	FC
✕	FS
□	SI
▽	SL

Pitch Types

Type	Freq	Velo	H Mov	V Mov
CU	6.2%	77.2 [96]	8.7 [104]	-49.7 [96]
FA	11.0%	92.9 [101]	-8.3 [94]	-15 [101]
FC	8.7%	89.8 [108]	-2 [82]	-21.9 [107]
FS	24.9%	87.7 [114]	-9.4 [95]	-30.5 [98]
SI	17.9%	91.4 [95]	-13.3 [94]	-22.2 [92]
SL	31.2%	84.7 [101]	4.7 [101]	-33 [99]

Pitch Tunnel

Pairs	Release Diff	Tunnel Diff	Plate Diff	Speed Changes
1980	27.1	111.8	208.6	0.024

PI Scores

Year	Pitch Ct	Pwr	Cmd	Stm
2014	1996	40	57	45
2015	2287	37	57	61
2016	2925	38	59	79
2017	2721	32	55	73

Tunnel vs RHH

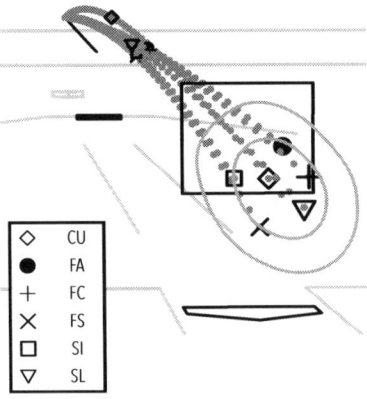

◇	CU
●	FA
+	FC
✕	FS
□	SI
▽	SL

Chris Taylor   UT   Los Angeles Dodgers

Born: 8/29/1990   **Age:** 27   **Bats:** R   **Throws:** R   **Height:** 6' 1"   **Weight:** 195 lbs   **Draft Info:** Round 5, 2012 Draft (#161 overall)

We don't have a baseball card for this guy.

21 Sec/Pit

PACE
45th of 155
71°
Fast

2017 Daily WARP Profile
5.7 Total WARP

Game 1: minors

Fantasy Values
2017	2018
$24.62	$19.00

YEAR	TEAM	LVL	AGE	PA	R	2B	3B	HR	RBI	BB	K	SB	AVG/OBP/SLG	TAv	VORP	BABIP	WARP
2017	LAN	MLB	26	568	85	34	5	21	72	50	142	17	.288/.354/.496	.309	50.3	.361	5.7

2017 Batting Percentages

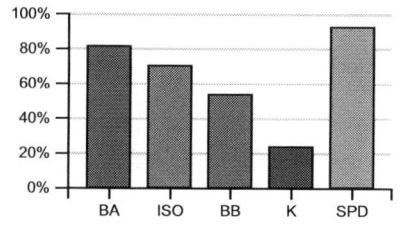

Batting PECOTA Percentiles

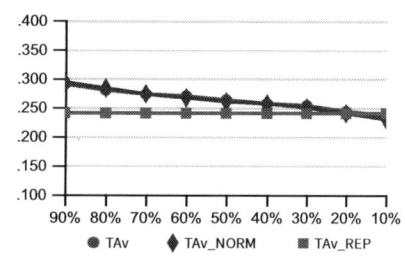

Batting WARP History

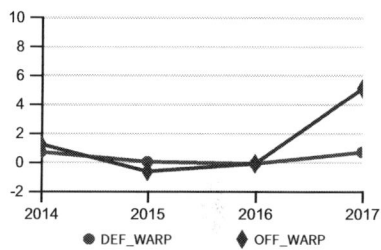

BRR (Relative to Position)

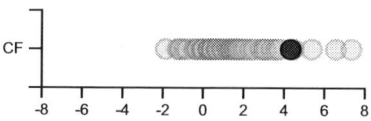

Rank		Player	BRR
3	90°	Ender Inciarte	5.41
4	87°	Cameron Maybin	4.50
5	84°	**Chris Taylor**	**4.37**
6	82°	Jackie Bradley	3.79
7	80°	Keon Broxton	3.64

BRR (Relative to Team)

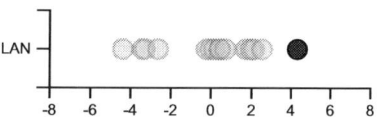

Rank		Player	BRR
1	88°	**Chris Taylor**	**4.37**
2	84°	Enrique Hernandez	2.58
3	70°	Corey Seager	2.17
4	62°	Chase Utley	2.02
5	56°	Joc Pederson	1.80

Base Running Components

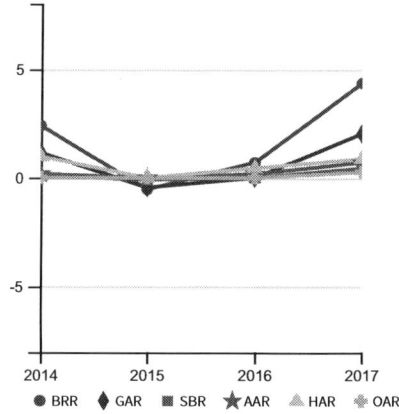

Michael Taylor   CF   Washington Nationals

Born: 3/26/1991   **Age:** 27   **Bats:** R   **Throws:** R   **Height:** 6' 3"   **Weight:** 210 lbs.   **Draft Info:** Round 6, 2009 Draft (#172 overall)

2017 Daily WARP Profile
3.9 Total WARP

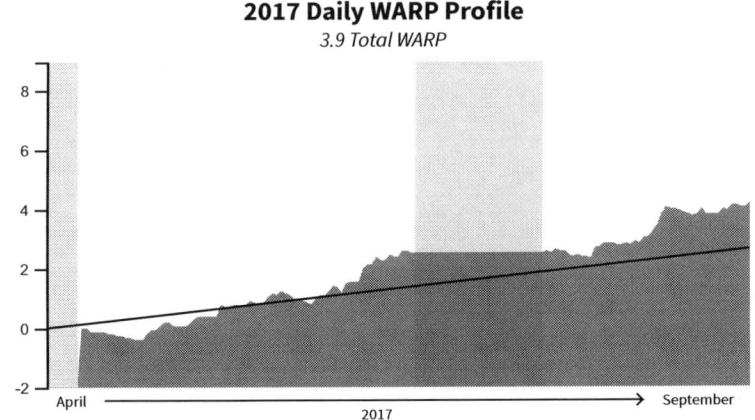

21 Sec/Pit

PACE
45th of 155
71°
Fast

Game 1: minors, **Game 86:** DL (oblique strain)

Fantasy Values
2017	2018
$18.34	**$12.00**

YEAR	TEAM	LVL	AGE	PA	R	2B	3B	HR	RBI	BB	K	SB	AVG/OBP/SLG	TAv	VORP	BABIP	WARP
2017	WAS	MLB	26	432	55	23	3	19	53	29	137	17	.271/.320/.486	.281	26.5	.363	3.9

2017 Batting Percentages

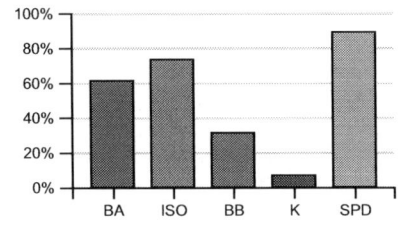

Batting PECOTA Percentiles

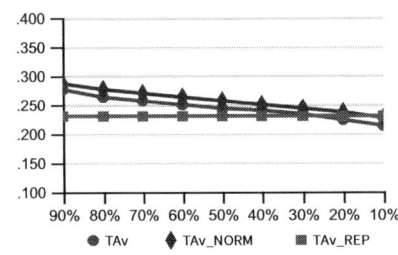

Batting WARP History

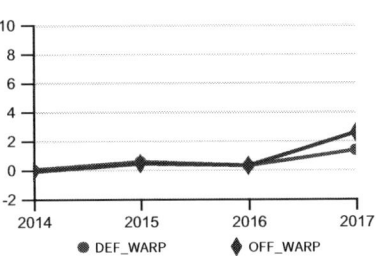

BRR (Relative to Position)

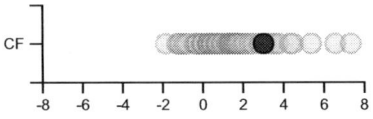

Rank		Player	BRR
9	76°	Albert Almora	3.17
10	75°	Ian Happ	3.07
11	73°	**Michael Taylor**	**3.06**
12	71°	Kevin Kiermaier	2.89
13	69°	Rajai Davis	2.55

BRR (Relative to Team)

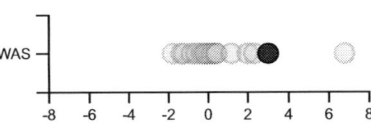

Rank		Player	BRR
1	91°	Trea Turner	6.83
2	84°	**Michael Taylor**	**3.06**
3	77°	Wilmer Difo	2.38
4	65°	Anthony Rendon	2.04
5	57°	Daniel Murphy	1.22

Base Running Components

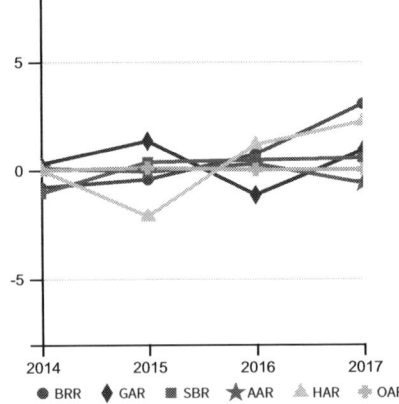

Julio Teheran   RHP   Atlanta Braves

Born: 1/27/1991 **Age:** 27 **Bats:** R **Throws:** R **Height:** 6' 2" **Weight:** 205 lbs **Draft Info:** International Free Agent, 2007

2017 Daily WARP Profile
3.8 Total WARP

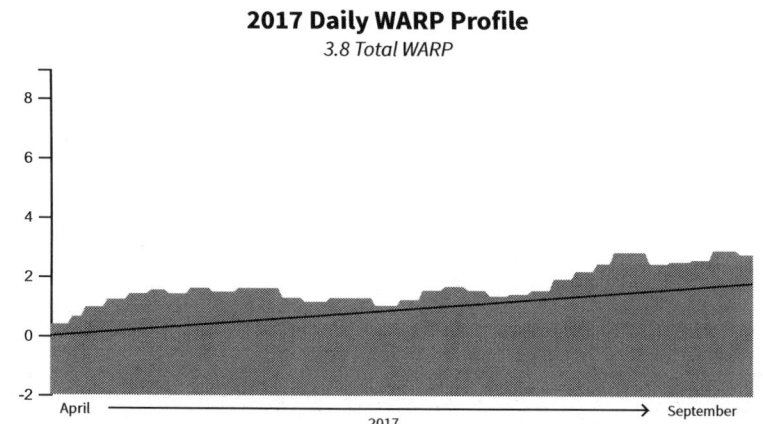

POWER
46 PWR 69th of 150

STAMINA
79 STM 17th of 150

COMMAND
70 CMD 10th of 150

PACE
21 Sec/Pit 81st of 150
46°
Average

Fantasy Values
2017	2018
$9.80	**$10.00**

YEAR	TEAM	LVL	AGE	W	L	SV	G	GS	IP	H	HR	BB/9	K/9	K	GB%	BABIP	WHIP	ERA	DRA	WARP	MPH 95
2017	ATL	MLB	26	11	13	0	32	32	188.1	186	31	3.4	7.2	151	41%	.281	1.37	4.49	3.74	3.8	93.7

2017 Pitching Percentages

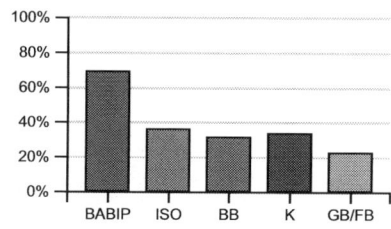

Pitching PECOTA Percentiles

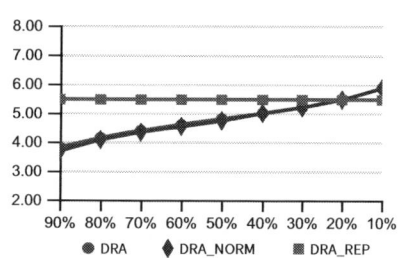

- ● DRA ◆ DRA_NORM ▦ DRA_REP

Pitching WARP History

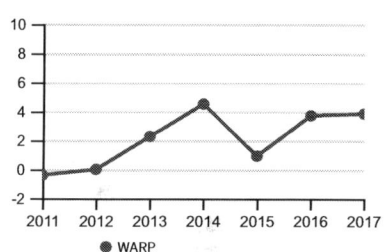

- ● WARP

Tunnel vs LHH

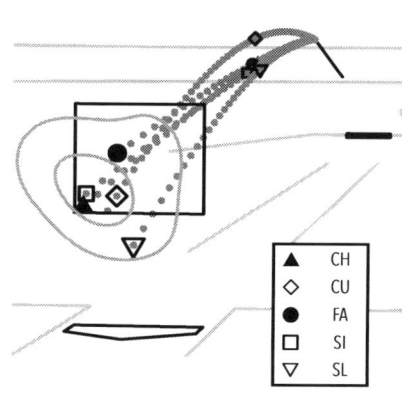

▲	CH
◇	CU
●	FA
□	SI
▽	SL

Pitch Types

Type	Freq	Velo	H Mov	V Mov
CH	7.7%	82.8 [91]	-10.6 [103]	-26.8 [101]
CU	9.0%	73.8 [83]	11 [113]	-48.5 [99]
FA	42.6%	92 [97]	-6.5 [103]	-16.3 [96]
SI	21.7%	91.8 [97]	-13.5 [93]	-22.4 [91]
SL	19.0%	83.1 [94]	3.1 [93]	-31.7 [103]

Pitch Tunnel

Pairs	Release Diff	Tunnel Diff	Plate Diff	Speed Changes
2241	30.5	117.3	218.5	0.029

PI Scores

Year	Pitch Ct	Pwr	Cmd	Stm
2013	2866	49	52	72
2014	3246	43	49	83
2015	3256	44	61	79
2016	2959	42	53	75
2017	3060	46	70	79

Tunnel vs RHH

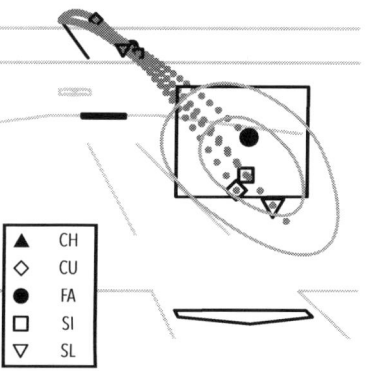

▲	CH
◇	CU
●	FA
□	SI
▽	SL

Eric Thames 1B Milwaukee Brewers

Born: 11/10/1986 **Age:** 31 **Bats:** L **Throws:** R **Height:** 6' 0" **Weight:** 210 lbs **Draft Info:** Round 7, 2008 Draft (#219 overall)

2017 Daily WARP Profile
2.5 Total WARP

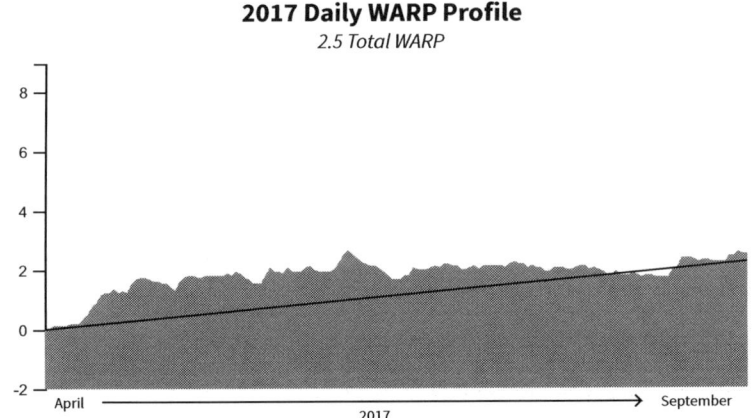

PACE
20 Sec/Pit
18th of 155
88°
Very Fast

Fantasy Values
2017	2018
$16.40	$13.00

YEAR	TEAM	LVL	AGE	PA	R	2B	3B	HR	RBI	BB	K	SB	AVG/OBP/SLG	TAv	VORP	BABIP	WARP
2017	MIL	MLB	30	551	83	26	4	31	63	75	163	4	.247/.359/.518	.304	29.4	.309	2.5

April stats have a way of distorting our perceptions. Had Thames hit 11 home runs in August and finished with the same line his season would have been seen as far more of a success. Instead, many believed the league quickly caught up to him, even though he rallied in both July and September and finished as a well-above-average hitter. The talk of Thames as a potential 50+ home-run hitter seems silly now, but another 30+ home-run year is a reasonable baseline. — Mike G.

2017 Batting Percentages
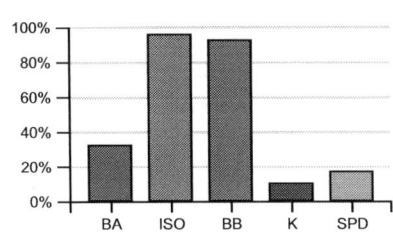

Batting PECOTA Percentiles
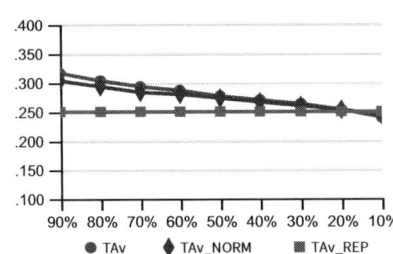

Batting WARP History
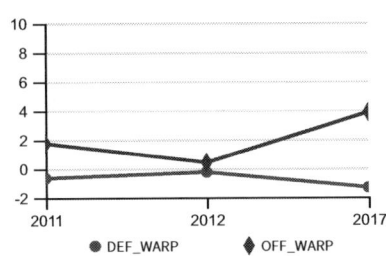

BRR (Relative to Position)
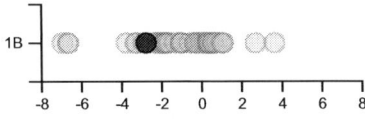

Rank	Player	BRR
36	29° Matt Carpenter	-2.37
37	26° Mitch Moreland	-2.72
38	23° **Eric Thames**	**-2.73**
39	20° Mark Reynolds	-2.86
40	16° Anthony Rizzo	-3.23

BRR (Relative to Team)
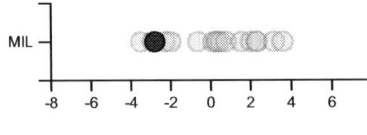

Rank	Player	BRR
13	28° Jett Bandy	-1.95
14	20° Neil Walker	-2.22
15	12° **Eric Thames**	**-2.73**
16	4° Eric Sogard	-2.86
17	0° Stephen Vogt	-3.45

Base Running Components
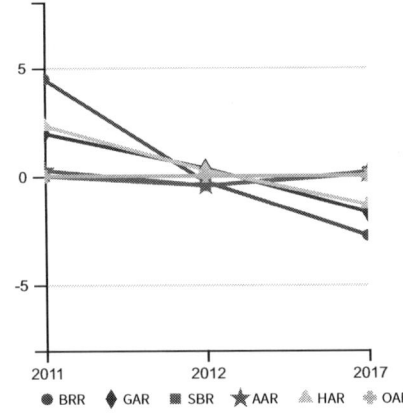

Mike Trout   CF   Los Angeles Angels

Born: 8/7/1991   **Age:** 26   **Bats:** R   **Throws:** R   **Height:** 6' 2"   **Weight:** 235 lbs   **Draft Info:** Round 1, 2009 Draft (#25 overall)

PACE
21 Sec/Pit
45th of 155
71°
Fast

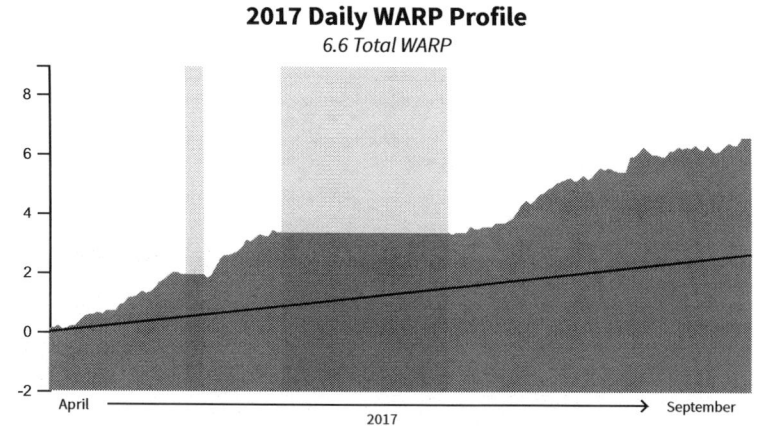

2017 Daily WARP Profile
6.6 Total WARP

Game 32: hamstring tightness, **Game 54:** DL (thumb ligament tear)

Fantasy Values
2017	2018
$30.13	$43.00

YEAR	TEAM	LVL	AGE	PA	R	2B	3B	HR	RBI	BB	K	SB	AVG/OBP/SLG	TAv	VORP	BABIP	WARP
2017	ANA	MLB	25	507	92	25	3	33	72	94	90	22	.306/.442/.629	.360	69.0	.318	6.6

Despite missing significant time due to injury for the first time in his career, Trout still managed to finish in the Top 15 among hitters while logging only 402 plate appearances. On a per-plate-appearance basis, Trout had the finest year of his already illustrious career, and now he enters his prime. While Jose Altuve has outperformed Trout the last couple of seasons, it is completely understandable if you prefer Trout to Altuve if you have the number 1 overall pick. — Mike G.

2017 Batting Percentages

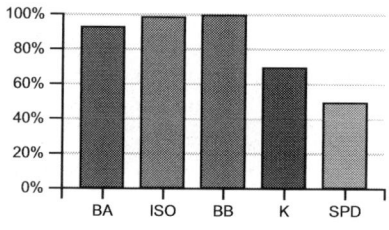

Batting PECOTA Percentiles

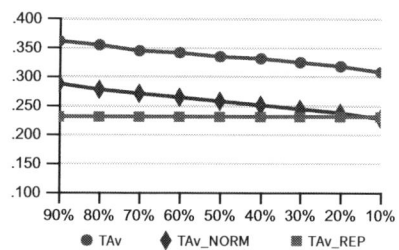

Batting WARP History

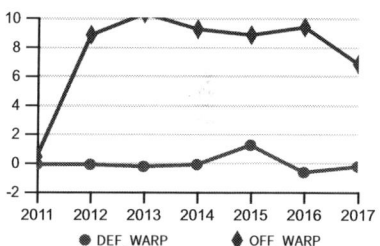

BRR (Relative to Position)

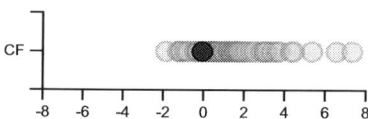

Rank		Player	BRR
47	13°	Brian Goodwin	0.06
48	11°	Jarrod Dyson	0.04
49	9°	**Mike Trout**	**-0.03**
50	9°	Tyler Naquin	-0.24
51	8°	Pedro Florimon	-0.24

BRR (Relative to Team)

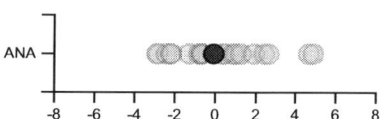

Rank		Player	BRR
9	77°	Juan Graterol	0.50
10	67°	Justin Upton	0.44
11	57°	**Mike Trout**	**-0.03**
12	46°	Kole Calhoun	-0.59
13	45°	Nick Franklin	-0.61

Base Running Components

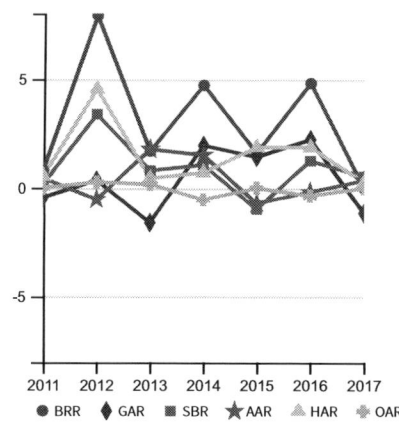

Justin Turner 3B   Los Angeles Dodgers

Born: 11/23/1984 **Age:** 33 **Bats:** R **Throws:** R **Height:** 5' 11" **Weight:** 205 lbs **Draft Info:** Round 7, 2006 Draft (#204 overall)

PACE
22 Sec/Pit
99th of 155
36°
Slow

2017 Daily WARP Profile
5.9 Total WARP

Game 43: DL (hamstring strain)

Fantasy Values
2017	2018
$23.59	$21.00

YEAR	TEAM	LVL	AGE	PA	R	2B	3B	HR	RBI	BB	K	SB	AVG/OBP/SLG	TAv	VORP	BABIP	WARP
2017	LAN	MLB	32	543	72	32	0	21	71	59	56	7	.322/.415/.530	.347	63.9	.326	5.9

2017 Batting Percentages

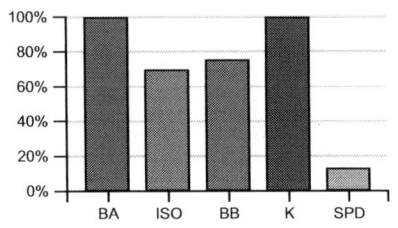

Batting PECOTA Percentiles

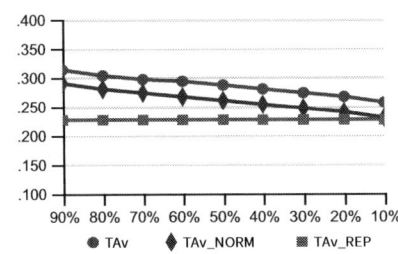

Batting WARP History

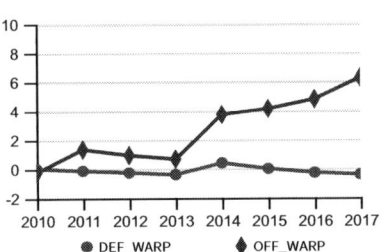

BRR (Relative to Position)

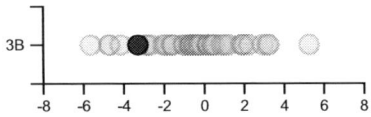

Rank		Player	BRR
50	15°	Christian Arroyo	-2.77
51	13°	Adrian Beltre	-2.87
52	11°	**Justin Turner**	**-3.24**
53	8°	Manny Machado	-4.10
54	6°	David Freese	-4.66

BRR (Relative to Team)

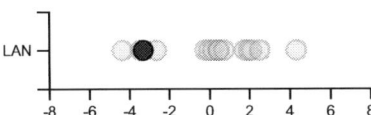

Rank		Player	BRR
11	31°	Cody Bellinger	-0.17
12	25°	Yasmani Grandal	-2.58
13	16°	**Justin Turner**	**-3.24**
14	10°	Matt Kemp	-3.37
15	0°	Yasiel Puig	-4.33

Base Running Components

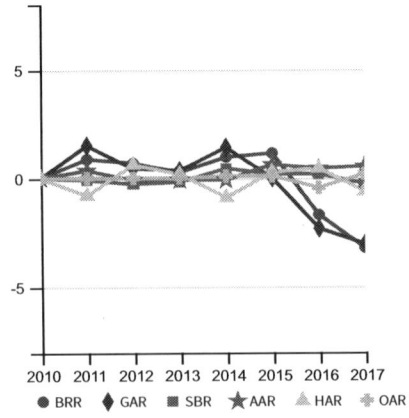

Trea Turner   SS   Washington Nationals

Born: 6/30/1993   **Age:** 25   **Bats:** R   **Throws:** R   **Height:** 6' 1"   **Weight:** 185 lbs   **Draft Info:** Round 1, 2014 Draft (#13 overall)

19 Sec/Pit

PACE
4th of 155
97°
Very Fast

2017 Daily WARP Profile
3.7 Total WARP

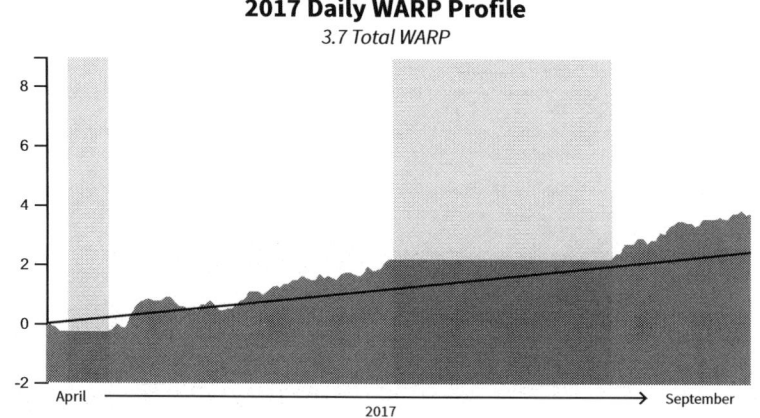

Game 6: DL (hamstring strain), **Game 80:** DL (wrist fracture)

Fantasy Values
| 2017 | 2018 |
| $29.15 | $34.00 |

YEAR	TEAM	LVL	AGE	PA	R	2B	3B	HR	RBI	BB	K	SB	AVG/OBP/SLG	TAv	VORP	BABIP	WARP
2017	WAS	MLB	24	447	75	24	6	11	45	30	80	46	.284/.338/.451	.283	36.6	.329	3.7

An injury quietly dampened how valuable Turner was in fantasy last year. In only 412 plate appearances, Turner was the 16th best hitter, thanks mostly to his 46 stolen bases, although his modest power contributions and solid batting average certainly helped. Even if Turner cannot maintain this aggressive steal pace over the course of a full season, he will be first-round material easily if he can stay on the field. — Mike G.

2017 Batting Percentages

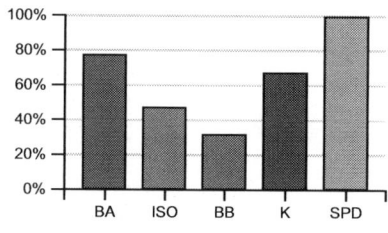

Batting PECOTA Percentiles

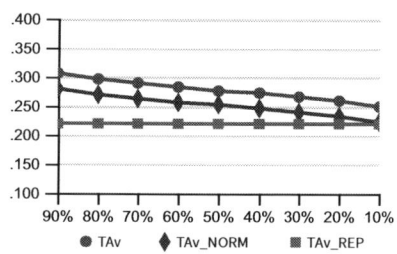

Batting WARP History

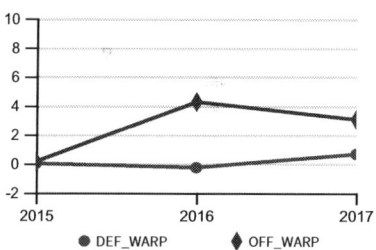

BRR (Relative to Position)

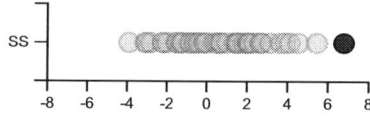

Rank		Player	BRR
1	96°	**Trea Turner**	**6.83**
2	93°	Xander Bogaerts	5.51
3	91°	Miguel Rojas	4.57
4	98°	Trevor Story	4.16
5	86°	Marcus Semien	3.94

BRR (Relative to Team)

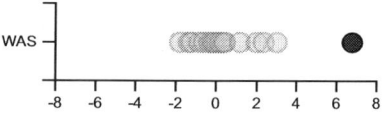

Rank		Player	BRR
1	91°	**Trea Turner**	**6.83**
2	84°	Michael Taylor	3.06
3	77°	Wilmer Difo	2.38
4	65°	Anthony Rendon	2.04
5	57°	Daniel Murphy	1.22

Base Running Components

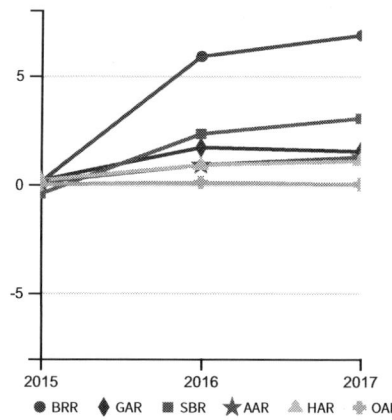

Justin Upton   LF   Los Angeles Angels

Born: 8/25/1987   **Age:** 30   **Bats:** R   **Throws:** R   **Height:** 6' 2"   **Weight:** 205 lbs   **Draft Info:** Round 1, 2005 Draft (#1 overall)

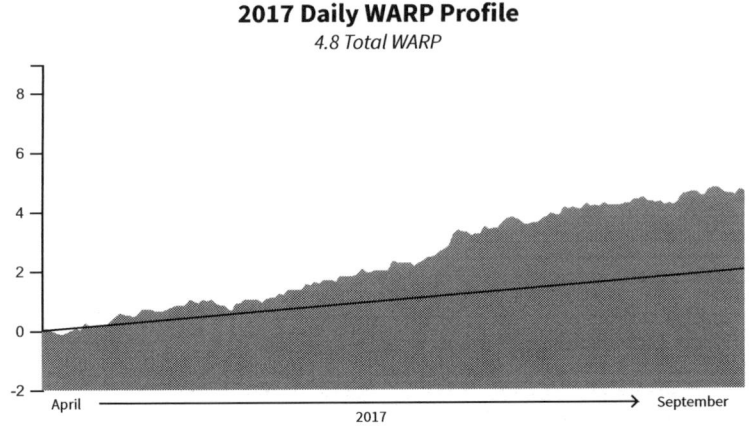

2017 Daily WARP Profile
4.8 Total WARP

PACE
23 Sec/Pit
135th of 155
13°
Very Slow

Fantasy Values
2017	2018
$27.96	$25.00

YEAR	TEAM	LVL	AGE	PA	R	2B	3B	HR	RBI	BB	K	SB	AVG/OBP/SLG	TAv	VORP	BABIP	WARP
2017	DET	MLB	29	520	81	37	0	28	94	57	147	10	.279/.362/.542	.297	31.4	.351	4.3
2017	ANA	MLB	29	115	19	7	0	7	15	17	33	4	.245/.357/.531	.292	7.6	.293	.5

Despite playing in two pitchers' parks, Upton quietly put up one of the best seasons of his career. Even in his "down" years, the veteran outfielder always manages to hit at least 25 home runs and steal a few bases. Now that the Angels have locked him down with a long-term deal, Upton is one of the safer bets to produce at least sixth-round value with considerably more upside than that if he stays locked in at his 2017 level. — Mike G.

2017 Batting Percentages

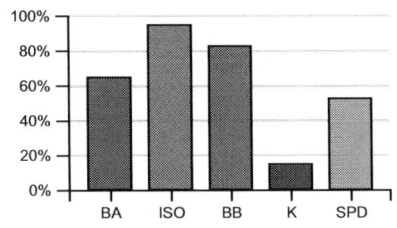

Batting PECOTA Percentiles

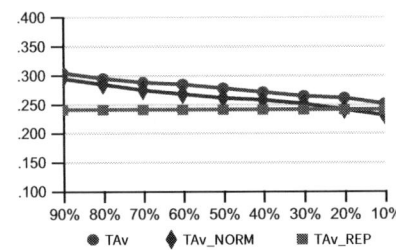

Batting WARP History

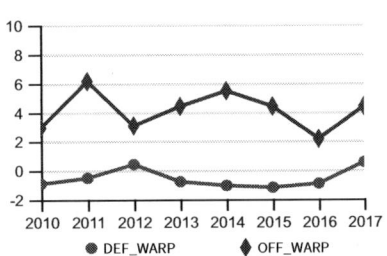

BRR (Relative to Position)

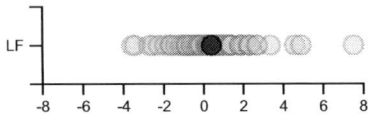

Rank		Player	BRR
30	52°	Colby Rasmus	0.55
31	50°	Ryan Braun	0.54
32	48°	**Justin Upton**	**0.44**
33	47°	Chris Heisey	0.44
34	46°	Allen Cordoba	0.40

BRR (Relative to Team)

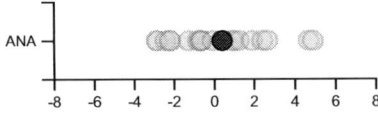

Rank		Player	BRR
8	78°	Kaleb Cowart	0.91
9	77°	Juan Graterol	0.50
10	67°	**Justin Upton**	**0.44**
11	57°	Mike Trout	-0.03
12	46°	Kole Calhoun	-0.59

Base Running Components

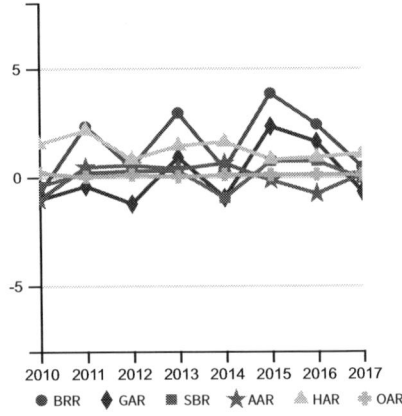

Jason Vargas   LHP   Kansas City Royals

Born: 2/2/1983   **Age:** 35   **Bats:** L   **Throws:** L   **Height:** 6' 0"   **Weight:** 215 lbs   **Draft Info:** Round 2, 2004 Draft (#68 overall)

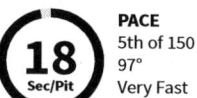

2017 Daily WARP Profile
3.5 Total WARP

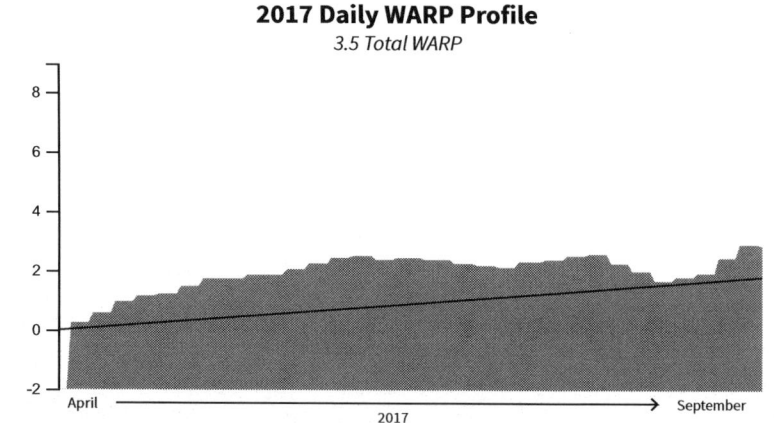

2017

April   September

POWER
9 PWR   148th of 150

STAMINA
74 STM   44th of 150

COMMAND
55 CMD   62nd of 150

PACE
18 Sec/Pit   5th of 150
97°
Very Fast

Fantasy Values
2017	2018
$14.72	$6.00

YEAR	TEAM	LVL	AGE	W	L	SV	G	GS	IP	H	HR	BB/9	K/9	K	GB%	BABIP	WHIP	ERA	DRA	WARP	MPH 95
2017	KCA	MLB	34	18	11	0	32	32	179.2	181	27	2.9	6.7	134	41%	.289	1.33	4.16	3.83	3.5	87.5

2017 Pitching Percentages

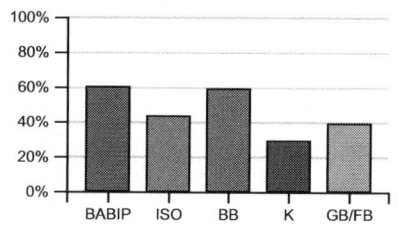

BABIP ISO BB K GB/FB

Pitching PECOTA Percentiles

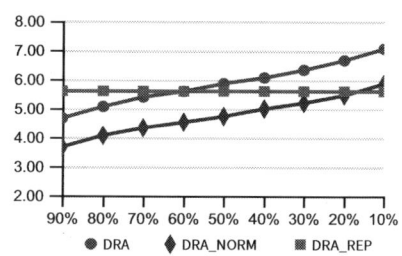

90% 80% 70% 60% 50% 40% 30% 20% 10%

● DRA   ◆ DRA_NORM   ■ DRA_REP

Pitching WARP History

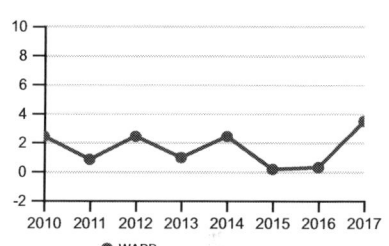

2010 2011 2012 2013 2014 2015 2016 2017

● WARP

Tunnel vs LHH

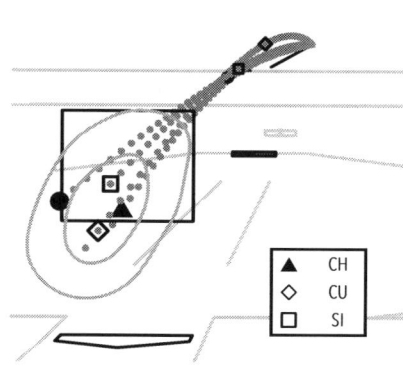

▲ CH
◇ CU
□ SI

Pitch Types

Type	Freq	Velo	H Mov	V Mov
CH	32.8%	80 [80]	14.8 [80]	-27.4 [99]
CU	20.4%	72.5 [78]	-7.1 [97]	-55.7 [83]
FA	3.7%	86.5 [77]	7.8 [97]	-16.6 [95]
SI	43.1%	86 [63]	12.1 [103]	-20.3 [99]

Pitch Tunnel

Pairs	Release Diff	Tunnel Diff	Plate Diff	Speed Changes
2154	27.9	127.9	232.8	0.034

PI Scores

Year	Pitch Ct	Pwr	Cmd	Stm
2013	2376	25	66	60
2014	2986	24	70	75
2015	683	25	68	22
2016	209	25	62	29
2017	2906	9	55	74

Tunnel vs RHH

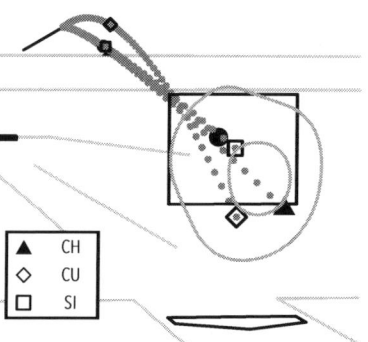

▲ CH
◇ CU
□ SI

Justin Verlander   RHP   Houston Astros

Born: 2/20/1983   **Age:** 35   **Bats:** R   **Throws:** R   **Height:** 6' 5"   **Weight:** 225 lbs   **Draft Info:** Round 1, 2004 Draft (#2 overall)

2017 Daily WARP Profile
5.3 Total WARP

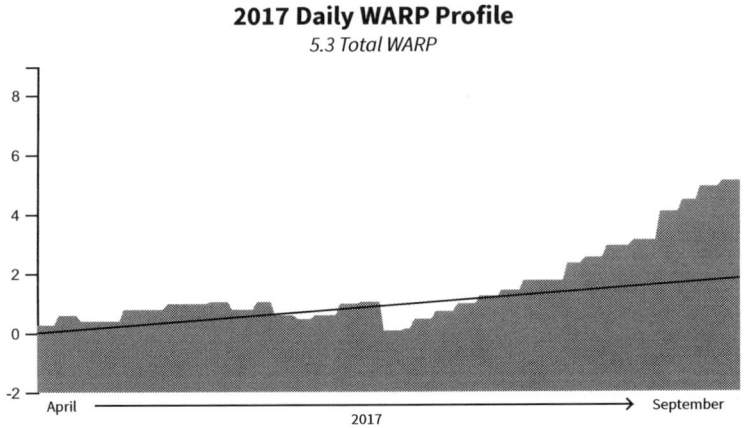

POWER
61 PWR 23rd of 150

STAMINA
86 STM 1st of 150

COMMAND
62 CMD 24th of 150

PACE
23 Sec/Pit 126th of 150
16°
Very Slow

Fantasy Values

2017	2018
$25.71	$21.00

YEAR	TEAM	LVL	AGE	W	L	SV	G	GS	IP	H	HR	BB/9	K/9	K	GB%	BABIP	WHIP	ERA	DRA	WARP	MPH 95
2017	DET	MLB	34	10	8	0	28	28	172	153	23	3.5	9.2	176	34%	.283	1.28	3.82	3.10	4.7	97.3
2017	HOU	MLB	34	5	0	0	5	5	34	17	4	1.3	11.4	43	32%	.194	0.65	1.06	3.97	0.6	97.3

He isn't the same pitcher he was during his halcyon days with the Tigers, but he's close enough that it doesn't really matter. Verlander upped his game after he was traded to the Astros, dominating down the stretch. At his age and with all the mileage on his arm it's probably wise to discount him somewhat, but he remains a safe SP2 in mixed and a high teens auction value in AL-only. — Mike G.

2017 Pitching Percentages

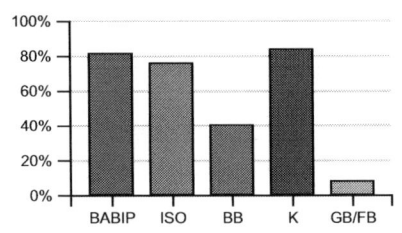

Pitching PECOTA Percentiles

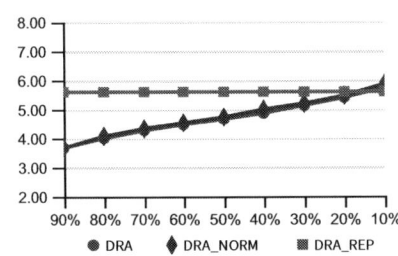

Pitching WARP History

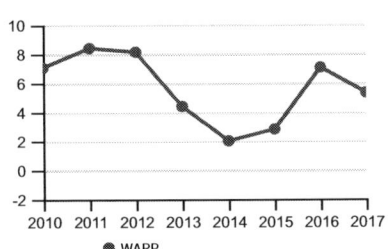

Tunnel vs LHH

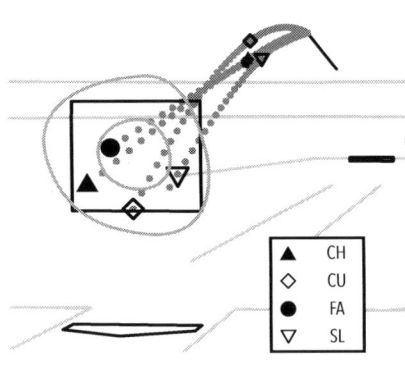

▲	CH
◇	CU
●	FA
▽	SL

Pitch Types

Type	Freq	Velo	H Mov	V Mov
CH	4.0%	87.8 [111]	-13.4 [87]	-25.4 [105]
CU	15.9%	80.8 [110]	8.6 [103]	-46.7 [103]
FA	57.8%	95.6 [110]	-11.3 [81]	-12.4 [109]
FC	0.3%	90.8 [113]	0.6 [95]	-21.3 [110]
SI	0.4%	95.1 [116]	-15.1 [81]	-15.3 [117]
SL	21.6%	88.5 [118]	1.9 [88]	-26.1 [119]

Pitch Tunnel

Pairs	Release Diff	Tunnel Diff	Plate Diff	Speed Changes
2681	26.8	112.3	213.4	0.023

PI Scores

Year	Pitch Ct	Pwr	Cmd	Stm
2013	3681	60	64	88
2014	3396	53	56	85
2015	2146	54	63	66
2016	3662	53	65	88
2017	3530	61	62	86

Tunnel vs RHH

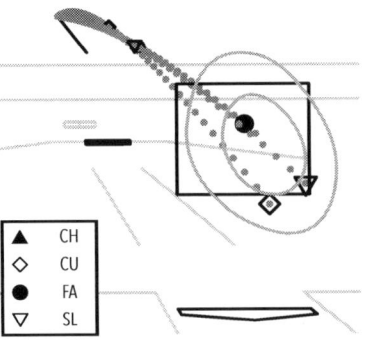

▲	CH
◇	CU
●	FA
▽	SL

Edinson Volquez RHP Miami Marlins

Born: 7/3/1983 **Age:** 34 **Bats:** R **Throws:** R **Height:** 6' 0" **Weight:** 220 lbs **Draft Info:** International Free Agent, 2001

2017 Daily WARP Profile
1.9 Total WARP

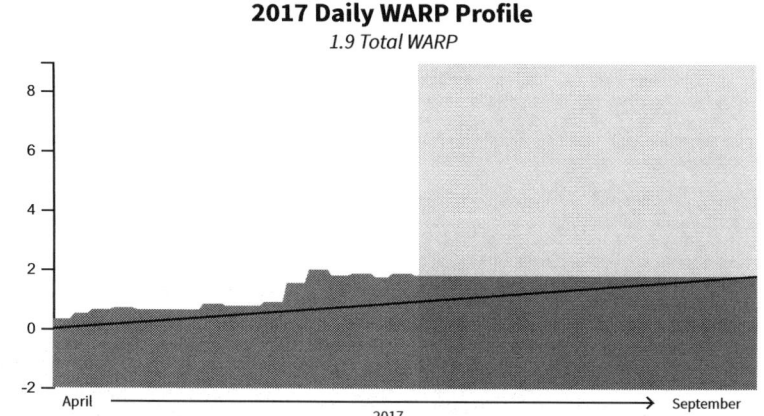

Game 84: DL (knee tendinitis)

49 PWR — **POWER** 64th of 150

58 STM — **STAMINA** 107th of 150

46 CMD — **COMMAND** 111th of 150

22 Sec/Pit — **PACE** 108th of 150 / 28° / Slow

Fantasy Values
2017	2018
$4.35	$0.00

YEAR	TEAM	LVL	AGE	W	L	SV	G	GS	IP	H	HR	BB/9	K/9	K	GB%	BABIP	WHIP	ERA	DRA	WARP	MPH 95
2017	MIA	MLB	33	4	8	0	17	17	92.1	78	8	5.2	7.9	81	49%	.278	1.42	4.19	3.76	1.9	95.0

Volquez had Tommy John surgery in August and will likely miss all of 2018. You can forget about him in redraft leagues. — Mike G.

2017 Pitching Percentages
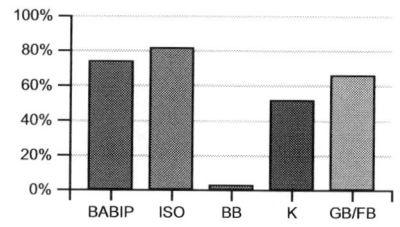

Pitching PECOTA Percentiles
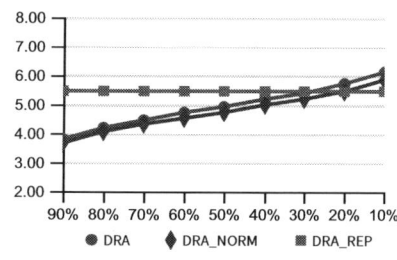

Pitching WARP History
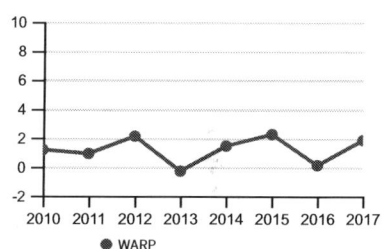

Tunnel vs LHH
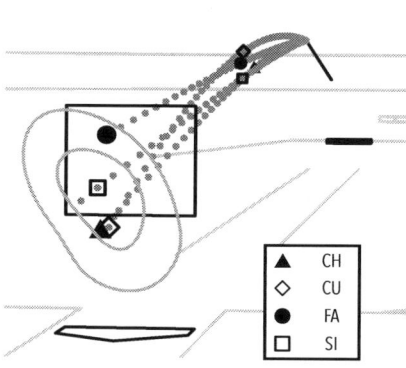

Pitch Types
Type	Freq	Velo	H Mov	V Mov
CH	25.5%	84.3 [97]	-10.3 [104]	-31.4 [88]
CU	17.7%	81.5 [112]	8.3 [102]	-44.8 [107]
FA	6.4%	93.9 [104]	-7.1 [100]	-12.7 [108]
SI	50.4%	93.6 [108]	-13 [97]	-17.7 [109]

Pitch Tunnel
Pairs	Release Diff	Tunnel Diff	Plate Diff	Speed Changes
1110	33.8	119.6	215.6	0.027

PI Scores
Year	Pitch Ct	Pwr	Cmd	Stm
2013	3001	47	43	75
2014	2939	49	43	76
2015	3293	47	49	79
2016	3225	45	44	82
2017	1510	49	46	58

Tunnel vs RHH
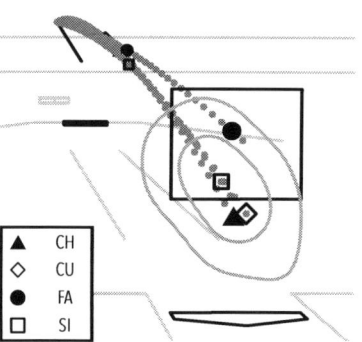

Joey Votto   1B   Cincinnati Reds

Born: 9/10/1983   **Age:** 34   **Bats:** L   **Throws:** R   **Height:** 6' 2"   **Weight:** 220 lbs   **Draft Info:** Round 2, 2002 Draft (#44 overall)

21 Sec/Pit

PACE
45th of 155
71°
Fast

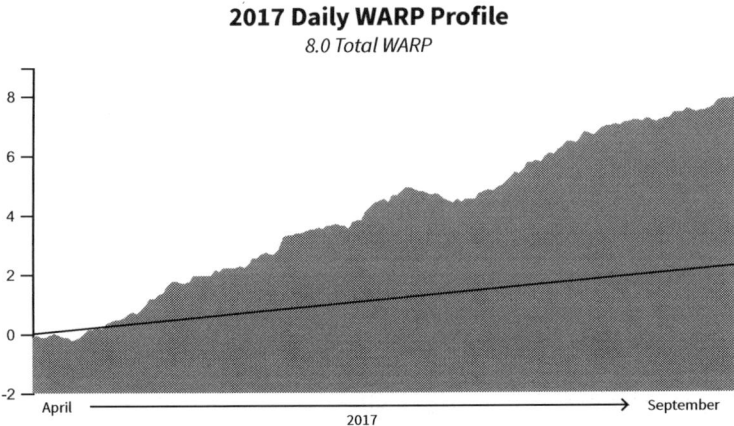

2017 Daily WARP Profile
8.0 Total WARP

Fantasy Values

2017	2018
$31.72	**$33.00**

YEAR	TEAM	LVL	AGE	PA	R	2B	3B	HR	RBI	BB	K	SB	AVG/OBP/SLG	TAv	VORP	BABIP	WARP
2017	CIN	MLB	33	707	106	34	1	36	100	134	83	5	.320/.454/.578	.354	70.1	.321	8.0

Miscast as a suboptimal fantasy asset early in his career because of low RBI totals, since 2015 Votto has been no worse than a Top 15 hitter. His batting average combined with strong power numbers makes him second to only Paul Goldschmidt in fantasy at first base, although Votto is good for a handful of steals as well. The days of hoping to sneak Votto in the third round are long past, but there's nothing wrong with paying the premium in the middle or back of the first round and locking in a strong performance in four categories. — Mike G.

2017 Batting Percentages

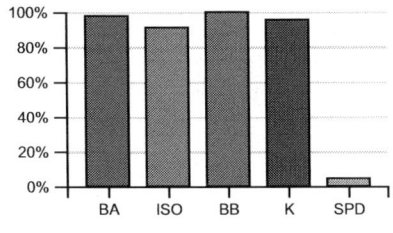

Batting PECOTA Percentiles

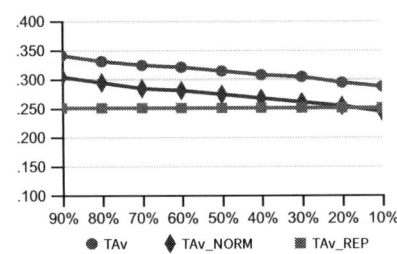

Batting WARP History

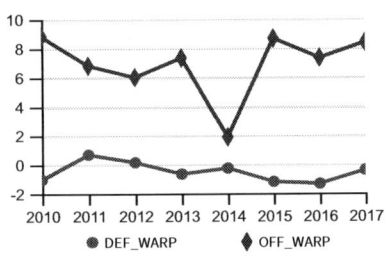

BRR (Relative to Position)

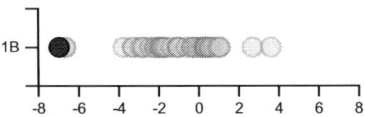

BRR (Relative to Team)

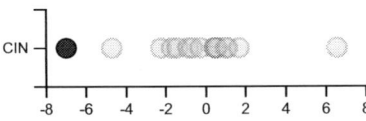

Base Running Components

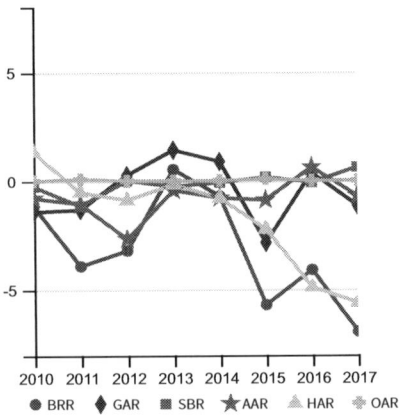

Rank		Player	BRR
41	14°	Lucas Duda	-3.26
42	11°	Josh Bell	-3.73
43	9°	Miguel Cabrera	-6.61
44	4°	Joe Mauer	-6.63
45	0°	**Joey Votto**	**-6.92**

Rank		Player	BRR
12	37°	Scooter Gennett	-1.36
13	31°	Tucker Barnhart	-1.63
14	23°	Adam Duvall	-2.18
15	13°	Eugenio Suarez	-4.67
16	0°	**Joey Votto**	**-6.92**

Michael Wacha   RHP   St. Louis Cardinals

Born: 7/1/1991   **Age:** 26   **Bats:** R   **Throws:** R   **Height:** 6' 6"   **Weight:** 215 lbs   **Draft Info:** Round 1, 2012 Draft (#19 overall)

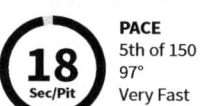

2017 Daily WARP Profile
0.7 Total WARP

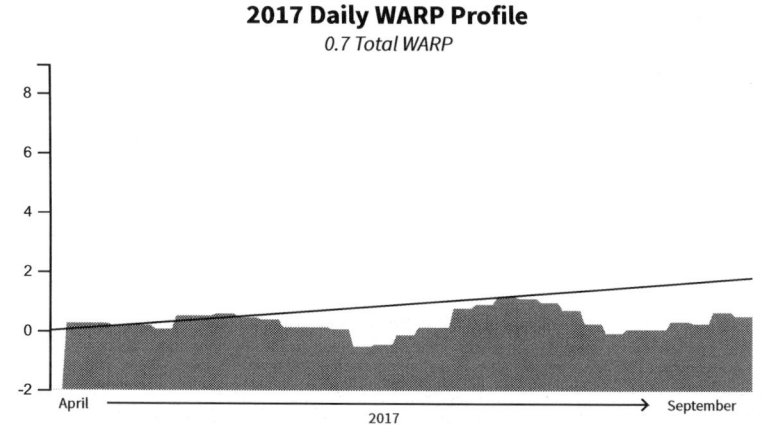

POWER 27th of 150 — **59** PWR

STAMINA 63rd of 150 — **71** STM

COMMAND 53rd of 150 — **57** CMD

PACE — **18** Sec/Pit — 5th of 150 — 97° — Very Fast

Fantasy Values
2017	2018
$12.89	$10.00

YEAR	TEAM	LVL	AGE	W	L	SV	G	GS	IP	H	HR	BB/9	K/9	K	GB%	BABIP	WHIP	ERA	DRA	WARP	MPH 95
2017	SLN	MLB	25	12	9	0	30	30	165.2	170	17	3.0	8.6	158	50%	.327	1.36	4.13	5.21	0.7	97.2

Wacha is a pitcher who seems like he should get great results based on raw stuff but who frequently doesn't. His ERA improved last year, but his DRA said it was more of the same for a pitcher whose mid-90s heater catches too much of the plate at times with not enough movement. The raw talent and youth make it difficult to completely abandon Wacha, but it is time to start pricing him more as a fourth or fifth starter in mixed rather than a mid-tier option. — Mike G.

2017 Pitching Percentages
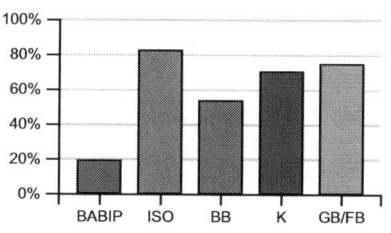

Pitching PECOTA Percentiles
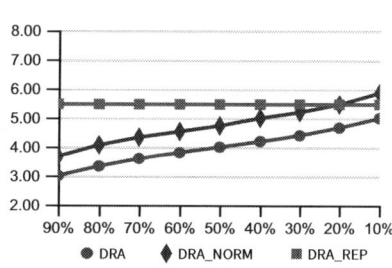

Pitching WARP History
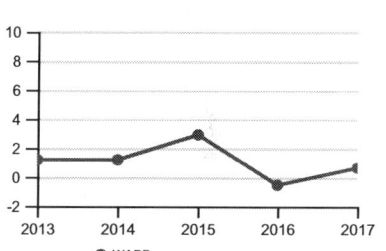

Tunnel vs LHH
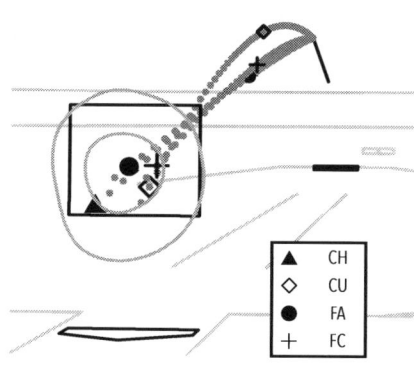

Pitch Types

Type	Freq	Velo	H Mov	V Mov
CH	18.2%	88.2 [112]	-8.3 [115]	-22.1 [114]
CU	11.4%	76.9 [95]	7.1 [97]	-54.1 [87]
FA	52.1%	95.6 [110]	-5.9 [106]	-11.2 [113]
FC	17.6%	91.2 [116]	2.1 [103]	-19.7 [116]
SI	0.7%	94.4 [112]	-8.4 [130]	-12.9 [127]

Pitch Tunnel

Pairs	Release Diff	Tunnel Diff	Plate Diff	Speed Changes
1988	34.9	125.1	223.6	0.030

PI Scores

Year	Pitch Ct	Pwr	Cmd	Stm
2013	1033	59	56	60
2014	1688	57	52	35
2015	2912	59	47	73
2016	2301	49	45	60
2017	2678	59	57	71

Tunnel vs RHH
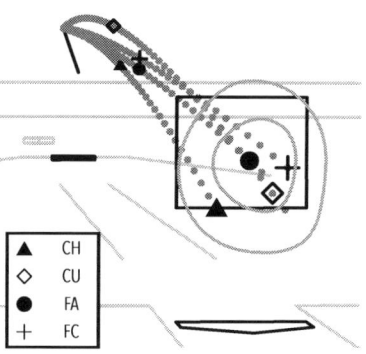

Taijuan Walker   RHP   Arizona Diamondbacks

Born: 8/13/1992   **Age:** 25   **Bats:** R   **Throws:** R   **Height:** 6' 4"   **Weight:** 235 lbs   **Draft Info:** Round 1, 2010 Draft (#43 overall)

19 Sec/Pit

PACE
16th of 150
89°
Very Fast

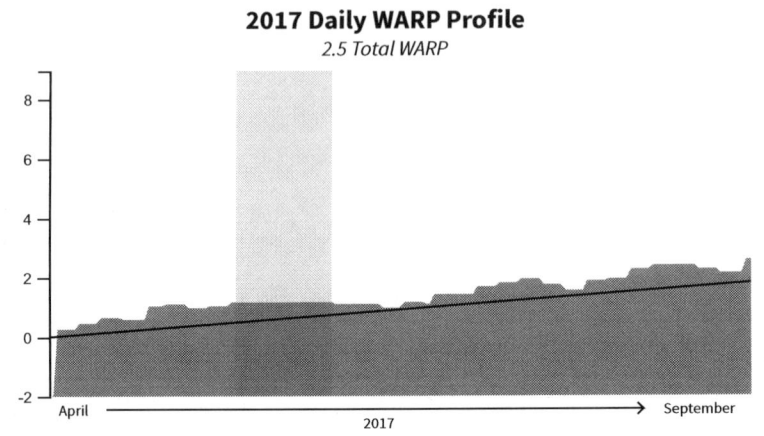

2017 Daily WARP Profile
2.5 Total WARP

Game 44: DL (finger blister)

54 PWR — **POWER** 45th of 150

70 STM — **STAMINA** 67th of 150

51 CMD — **COMMAND** 84th of 150

Fantasy Values
2017	2018
$13.91	$12.00

YEAR	TEAM	LVL	AGE	W	L	SV	G	GS	IP	H	HR	BB/9	K/9	K	GB%	BABIP	WHIP	ERA	DRA	WARP	MPH 95
2017	ARI	MLB	24	9	9	0	28	28	157.1	148	17	3.5	8.4	146	50%	.291	1.33	3.49	4.17	2.5	95.6

It was an odd year for Walker. He generated more groundballs but in exchange gave up for more hard-hit balls than he had in 2016. The result was a better ERA, thanks in part to a Diamondbacks defense that was in the top third in the league in ground-ball defensive efficiency. Walker is a solid pitcher and young enough to grow, but he still hasn't taken the big step necessary to live up to his first-round billing from way back in 2010. — Mike G.

2017 Pitching Percentages

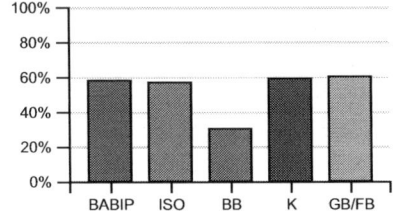

Pitching PECOTA Percentiles

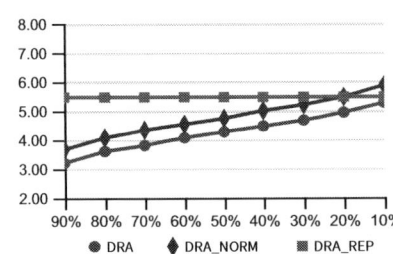

● DRA   ◆ DRA_NORM   ■ DRA_REP

Pitching WARP History

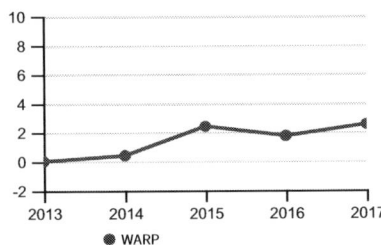

● WARP

Tunnel vs LHH

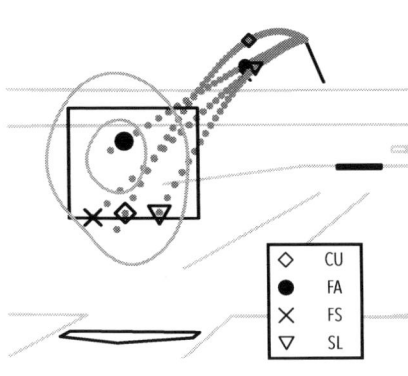

◇ CU
● FA
✕ FS
▽ SL

Pitch Types

Type	Freq	Velo	H Mov	V Mov
CU	12.5%	75.9 [91]	10.3 [110]	-51.3 [93]
FA	57.2%	93.9 [104]	-6.2 [104]	-12.2 [110]
FS	13.6%	88.4 [118]	-9.3 [96]	-22.9 [123]
SI	1.9%	93.1 [105]	-11.5 [107]	-16.7 [112]
SL	14.7%	86.7 [110]	5 [102]	-26.9 [117]

Pitch Tunnel

Pairs	Release Diff	Tunnel Diff	Plate Diff	Speed Changes
2058	25.4	123.6	232.0	0.029

PI Scores

Year	Pitch Ct	Pwr	Cmd	Stm
2013	233	67	31	67
2014	617	69	37	47
2015	2618	70	52	70
2016	2302	60	59	64
2017	2741	54	51	70

Tunnel vs RHH

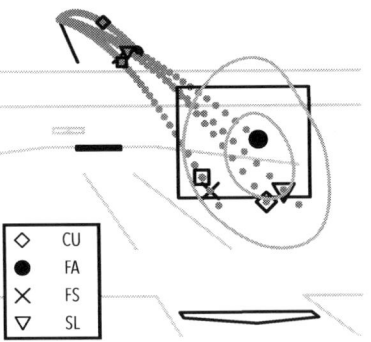

◇ CU
● FA
✕ FS
▽ SL

Adam Warren   RHP   New York Yankees

Born: 8/25/1987   **Age:** 30   **Bats:** R   **Throws:** R   **Height:** 6' 1"   **Weight:** 224 lbs   **Draft Info:** Round 4, 2009 Draft (#135 overall)

We don't have a baseball card for this guy.

2017 Daily WARP Profile
1.7 Total WARP

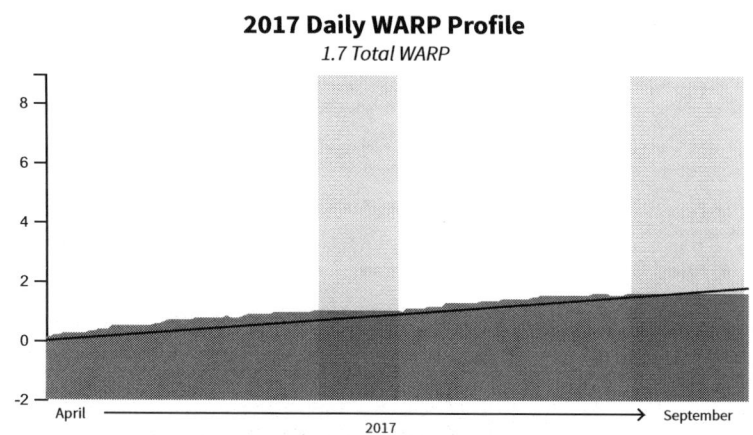

April — 2017 — September

Game 63: DL (shoulder inflammation), **Game 135:** DL (back spasm)

34 PWR — **POWER** 120th of 150

40 STM — **STAMINA** 150th of 150

70 CMD — **COMMAND** 10th of 150

23 Sec/Pit — **PACE** 126th of 150 — 16° — Very Slow

Fantasy Values
2017	2018
$10.84	$2.00

YEAR	TEAM	LVL	AGE	W	L	SV	G	GS	IP	H	HR	BB/9	K/9	K	GB%	BABIP	WHIP	ERA	DRA	WARP	MPH 95
2017	NYA	MLB	29	3	2	1	46	0	57.1	35	4	2.4	8.5	54	44%	.208	0.87	2.35	2.53	1.7	94.1

2017 Pitching Percentages

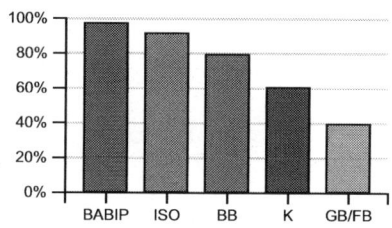

Pitching PECOTA Percentiles

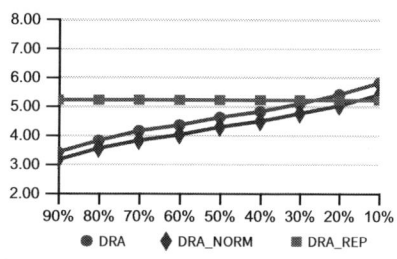

● DRA   ◆ DRA_NORM   ■ DRA_REP

Pitching WARP History

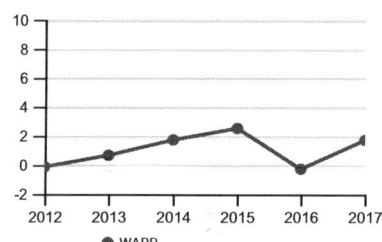

● WARP

Tunnel vs LHH

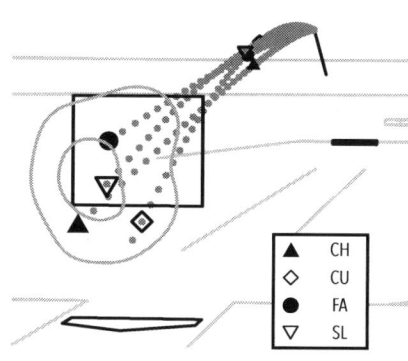

▲ CH
◇ CU
● FA
▽ SL

Pitch Types

Type	Freq	Velo	H Mov	V Mov
CH	10.1%	85.6 [102]	-14.2 [83]	-28.4 [96]
CU	7.5%	80.2 [107]	6.7 [96]	-48.7 [99]
FA	38.6%	93 [101]	-3.6 [116]	-13.5 [105]
SI	0.3%	93.9 [109]	-11.5 [107]	-18.2 [107]
SL	43.5%	86.5 [109]	6 [106]	-29 [111]

Pitch Tunnel

Pairs	Release Diff	Tunnel Diff	Plate Diff	Speed Changes
716	27.6	119.2	232.8	0.022

PI Scores

Year	Pitch Ct	Pwr	Cmd	Stm
2013	1291	46	49	37
2014	1322	47	52	54
2015	2154	43	58	60
2016	1161	41	51	50
2017	938	34	70	40

Tunnel vs RHH

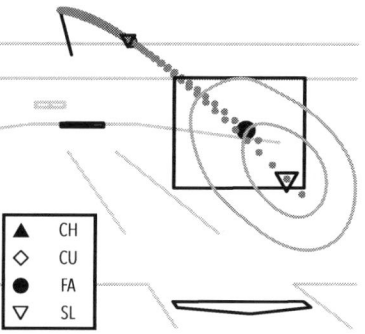

▲ CH
◇ CU
● FA
▽ SL

Matt Wieters   C   Washington Nationals

Born: 5/21/1986   **Age:** 32   **Bats:** B   **Throws:** R   **Height:** 6'5"   **Weight:** 230 lbs   **Draft Info:** Round 1, 2007 Draft (#5 overall)

PACE
20 18th of 155
Sec/Pit 88°
Very Fast

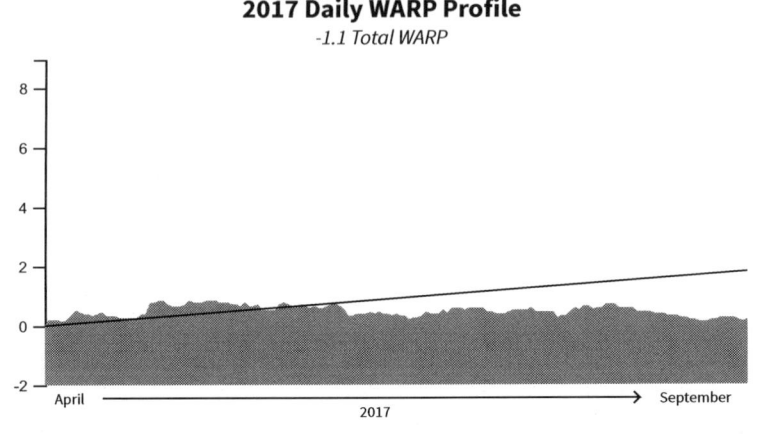

2017 Daily WARP Profile
-1.1 Total WARP

Fantasy Values
2017	2018
$5.09	**$6.00**

YEAR	TEAM	LVL	AGE	PA	R	2B	3B	HR	RBI	BB	K	SB	AVG/OBP/SLG	TAv	VORP	BABIP	WARP
2017	WAS	MLB	31	465	43	20	0	10	52	38	94	1	.225/.288/.344	.223	2.0	.264	-1.1

2017 Batting Percentages

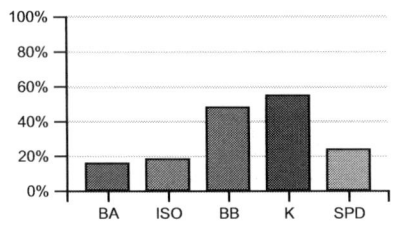

Batting PECOTA Percentiles

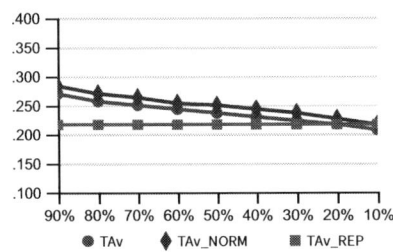

Batting WARP History

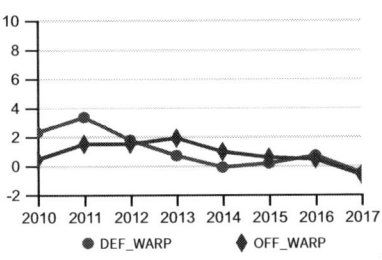

BRR (Relative to Position)

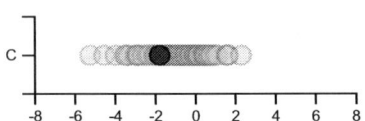

Rank		Player	BRR
58	30°	Tucker Barnhart	-1.63
59	28°	Robinson Chirinos	-1.67
60	26°	**Matt Wieters**	**-1.75**
61	25°	Austin Romine	-1.82
62	24°	Jett Bandy	-1.95

BRR (Relative to Team)

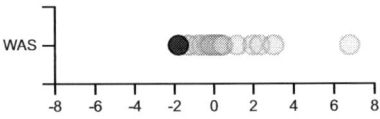

Rank		Player	BRR
14	24°	Matt Adams	-0.56
15	20°	Jayson Werth	-0.79
16	15°	Adam Lind	-1.18
17	6°	Bryce Harper	-1.30
18	0°	**Matt Wieters**	**-1.75**

Base Running Components

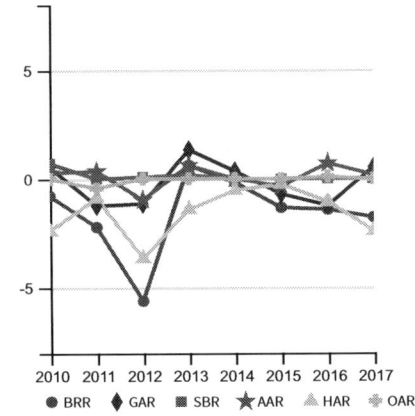

Trevor Williams RHP Pittsburgh Pirates

Born: 4/25/1992 **Age:** 26 **Bats:** R **Throws:** R **Height:** 6' 3" **Weight:** 230 lbs **Draft Info:** Round 2, 2013 Draft (#44 overall)

We don't have a baseball card for this guy.

2017 Daily WARP Profile
2.7 Total WARP

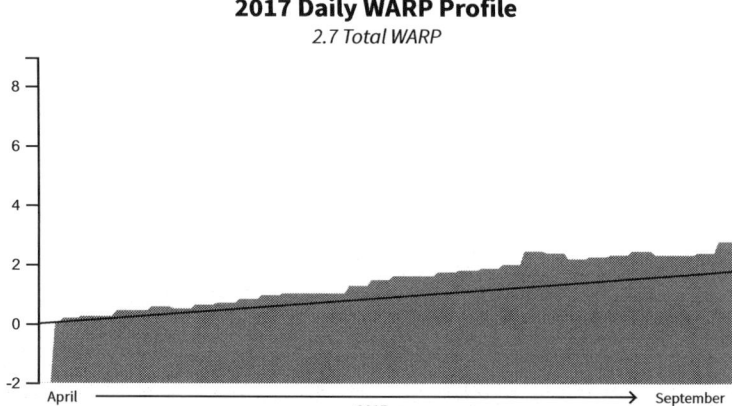

PACE
20 Sec/Pit
37th of 150
75°
Fast

POWER
58 PWR
32nd of 150

STAMINA
66 STM
84th of 150

COMMAND
69 CMD
12th of 150

Fantasy Values
2017	2018
$9.45	$6.00

YEAR	TEAM	LVL	AGE	W	L	SV	G	GS	IP	H	HR	BB/9	K/9	K	GB%	BABIP	WHIP	ERA	DRA	WARP	MPH 95
2017	PIT	MLB	25	7	9	0	31	25	150.1	145	14	3.1	7.0	117	50%	.292	1.31	4.07	3.95	2.7	94.6

2017 Pitching Percentages

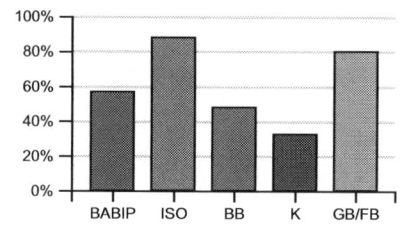

Pitching PECOTA Percentiles

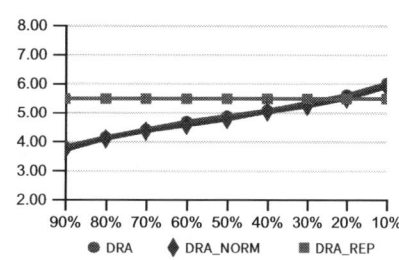

Pitching WARP History

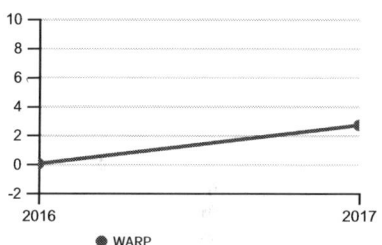

Tunnel vs LHH

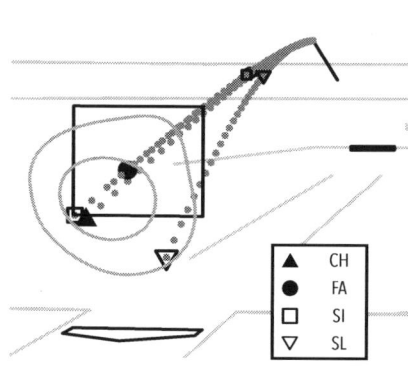

▲	CH
●	FA
□	SI
▽	SL

Pitch Types

Type	Freq	Velo	H Mov	V Mov
CH	10.1%	85.7 [102]	-12.3 [94]	-26.2 [102]
CU	2.0%	77.2 [96]	8.6 [103]	-45.3 [106]
FA	49.2%	93.2 [102]	-4.6 [112]	-16 [97]
SI	22.4%	90.8 [91]	-12.5 [100]	-24.5 [84]
SL	16.3%	84.5 [100]	6.4 [108]	-31.6 [103]

Pitch Tunnel

Pairs	Release Diff	Tunnel Diff	Plate Diff	Speed Changes
1765	36.1	111.3	221.3	0.021

PI Scores

Year	Pitch Ct	Pwr	Cmd	Stm
2016	224	54	49	52
2017	2410	58	69	66

Tunnel vs RHH

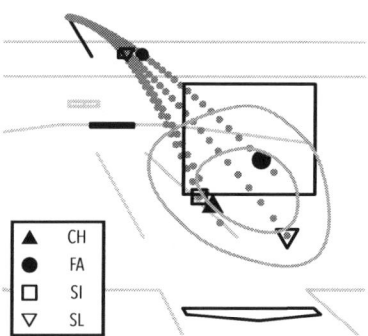

▲	CH
●	FA
□	SI
▽	SL

Alex Wood   LHP   Los Angeles Dodgers

Born: 1/12/1991   **Age:** 27   **Bats:** R   **Throws:** L   **Height:** 6' 4"   **Weight:** 215 lbs   **Draft Info:** Round 2, 2012 Draft (#85 overall)

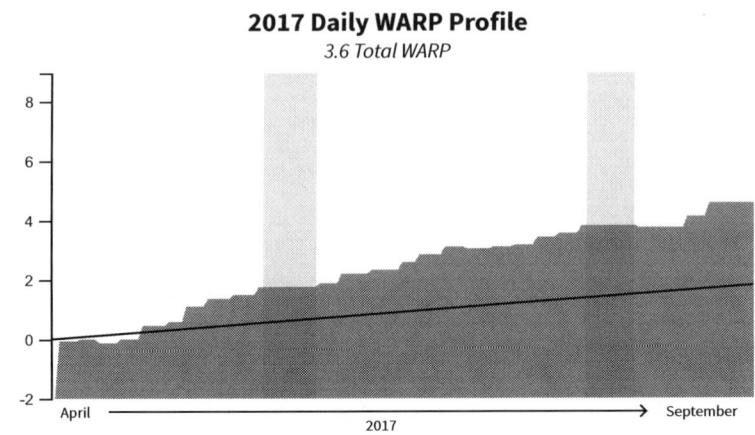

2017 Daily WARP Profile
3.6 Total WARP

Game 50: DL (SC joint inflammation), **Game 124:** DL (SC joint inflammation)

40 PWR	**POWER**	96th of 150
62 STM	**STAMINA**	94th of 150
57 CMD	**COMMAND**	53rd of 150

21 Sec/Pit	**PACE** 81st of 150 46° Average

Fantasy Values

2017	2018
$26.62	$17.00

YEAR	TEAM	LVL	AGE	W	L	SV	G	GS	IP	H	HR	BB/9	K/9	K	GB%	BABIP	WHIP	ERA	DRA	WARP	MPH 95
2017	LAN	MLB	26	16	3	0	27	25	152.1	123	15	2.2	8.9	151	54%	.267	1.06	2.72	3.44	3.6	94.0

Although 2017 was perceived to be a breakout year for Wood, it was more a return to his 2014 form. This is the challenge with putting a price tag on Wood, a pitcher who has the potential to return Top 15 mixed earnings at his best but has difficulty staying healthy. Paying for 200 strong innings for Wood is folly, but someone is going to bet on a repeat of Wood's 152 1/3 from last year. Given his erratic track record, it is probably wise to let someone else make that bet. — Mike G.

2017 Pitching Percentages

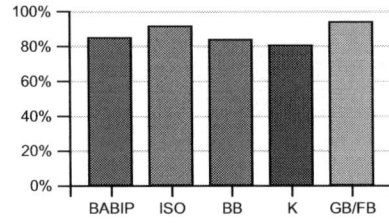

Pitching PECOTA Percentiles

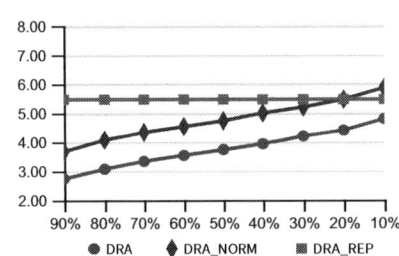

Pitching WARP History

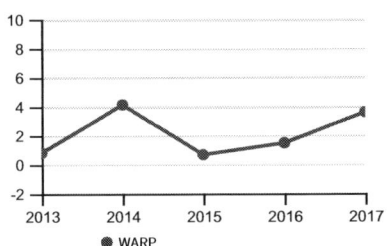

Tunnel vs LHH

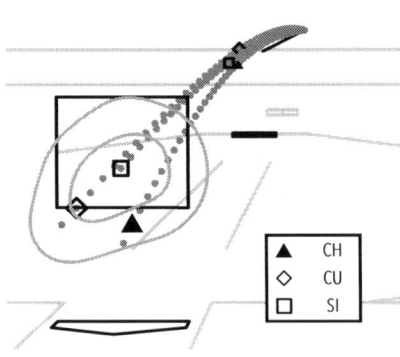

▲	CH
◇	CU
□	SI

Tunnel vs RHH

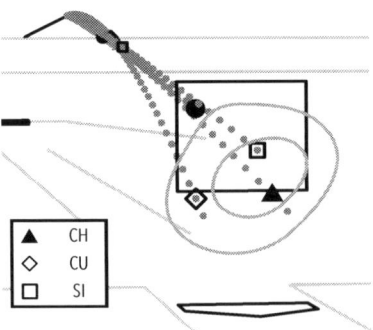

▲	CH
◇	CU
□	SI

Pitch Types

Type	Freq	Velo	H Mov	V Mov
CH	25.6%	85.4 [101]	14.5 [82]	-29.4 [93]
CU	24.0%	83.7 [120]	-4.9 [89]	-38.1 [121]
FA	1.8%	92.6 [100]	9.5 [89]	-11.5 [112]
SI	48.7%	92.2 [99]	12 [103]	-16.7 [112]

Pitch Tunnel

Pairs	Release Diff	Tunnel Diff	Plate Diff	Speed Changes
1522	42.6	114.9	232.0	0.023

PI Scores

Year	Pitch Ct	Pwr	Cmd	Stm
2013	1305	51	47	60
2014	2667	38	57	72
2015	2894	36	59	73
2016	981	39	66	9
2017	2258	40	57	62

Travis Wood LHP Detroit Tigers

Born: 2/6/1987 **Age:** 31 **Bats:** R **Throws:** L **Height:** 5' 11" **Weight:** 175 lbs **Draft Info:** Round 2, 2005 Draft (#60 overall)

We don't have a baseball card for this guy.

2017 Daily WARP Profile
-3.4 Total WARP

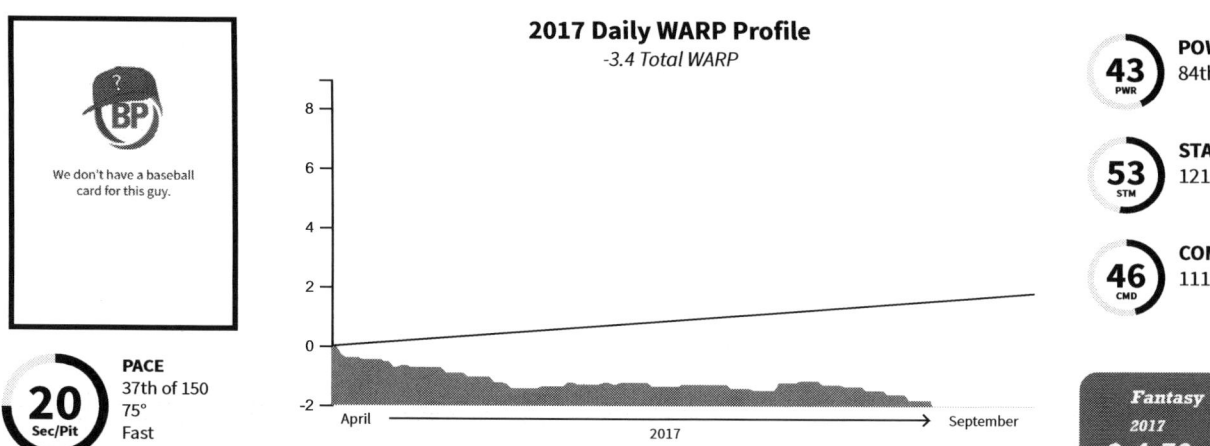

PACE
20 Sec/Pit
37th of 150
75°
Fast

43 PWR **POWER** 84th of 150

53 STM **STAMINA** 121st of 150

46 CMD **COMMAND** 111th of 150

Fantasy Values
2017	2018
$-4.70	$1.00

YEAR	TEAM	LVL	AGE	W	L	SV	G	GS	IP	H	HR	BB/9	K/9	K	GB%	BABIP	WHIP	ERA	DRA	WARP	MPH 95
2017	KCA	MLB	30	1	3	0	28	3	41.2	56	4	4.3	6.3	29	43%	.369	1.82	6.91	8.84	-1.6	91.7
2017	SDN	MLB	30	3	4	0	11	11	52.1	62	15	4.3	6.2	36	34%	.287	1.66	6.71	8.46	-1.8	90.0

2017 Pitching Percentages

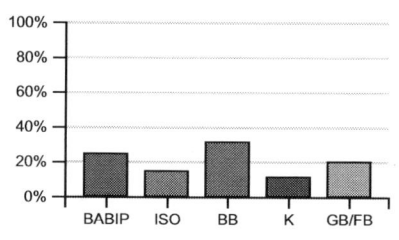

Pitching PECOTA Percentiles

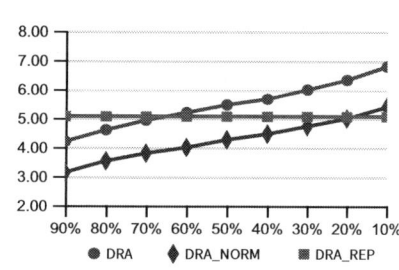

Pitching WARP History

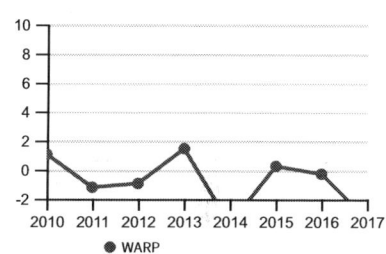

Tunnel vs LHH

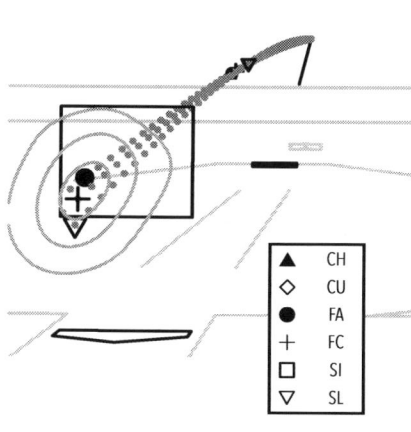

▲	CH
◇	CU
●	FA
+	FC
□	SI
▽	SL

Pitch Types

Type	Freq	Velo	H Mov	V Mov
CH	8.5%	81.1 [84]	11.5 [98]	-25.6 [104]
CU	4.8%	72.3 [78]	-2.2 [78]	-57.7 [79]
FA	38.0%	89.5 [88]	3.4 [117]	-14 [104]
FC	21.7%	86.8 [91]	-1.2 [98]	-21.9 [107]
SI	17.0%	88.4 [77]	9.1 [125]	-17.1 [111]
SL	10.2%	80.3 [82]	-3.6 [95]	-32.3 [101]

Pitch Tunnel

Pairs	Release Diff	Tunnel Diff	Plate Diff	Speed Changes
1271	25.9	118.1	223.1	0.025

PI Scores

Year	Pitch Ct	Pwr	Cmd	Stm
2013	3082	44	56	78
2014	3040	43	52	77
2015	1725	51	62	56
2016	1008	57	64	50
2017	1702	43	46	53

Tunnel vs RHH

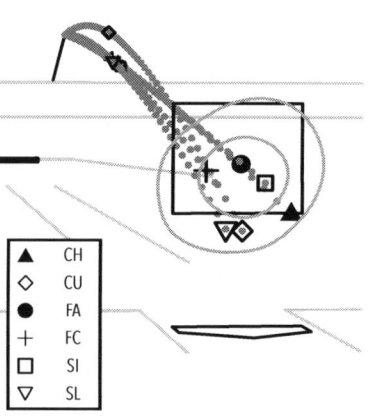

▲	CH
◇	CU
●	FA
+	FC
□	SI
▽	SL

Christian Yelich LF Milwaukee Brewers

Born: 12/5/1991 **Age:** 26 **Bats:** L **Throws:** R **Height:** 6' 3" **Weight:** 195 lbs **Draft Info:** Round 1, 2010 Draft (#23 overall)

2017 Daily WARP Profile
2.9 Total WARP

21 Sec/Pit

PACE
45th of 155
71°
Fast

Fantasy Values

2017	2018
$24.99	**$24.00**

YEAR	TEAM	LVL	AGE	PA	R	2B	3B	HR	RBI	BB	K	SB	AVG/OBP/SLG	TAv	VORP	BABIP	WARP
2017	MIA	MLB	25	695	100	36	2	18	81	80	137	16	.282/.369/.439	.292	46.4	.336	2.9

Yelich isn't a fantasy superstar, but he provided a solid baseline across all five categories. He slipped somewhat in batting average but was still strong enough across the board to return third-round value despite lacking a strong contribution in any particular category. Yelich is entering his prime and could see a power burst, but even if he stands still Yelich is a solid pick as an OF2 in mixed and a low- to mid-$20s buy in only. — Mike G.

2017 Batting Percentages

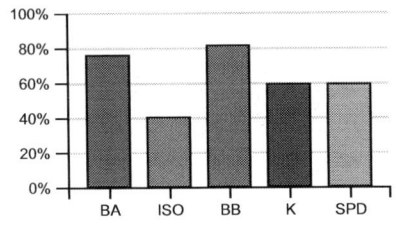

Batting PECOTA Percentiles

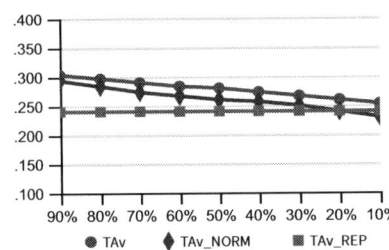

Batting WARP History

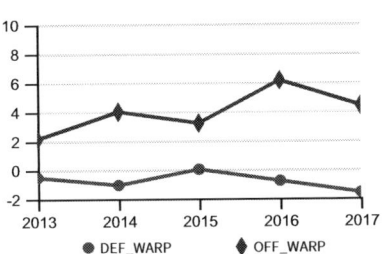

BRR (Relative to Position)

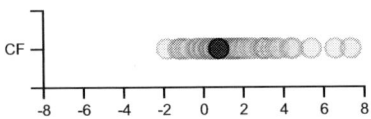

Rank		Player	BRR
33	34°	Guillermo Heredia	0.99
34	31°	Andrew McCutchen	0.98
35	28°	**Christian Yelich**	**0.81**
36	28°	Zach Granite	0.75
37	27°	Greg Allen	0.74

BRR (Relative to Team)

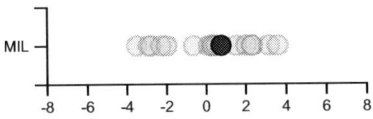

Rank		Player	BRR
5	80°	Orlando Arcia	2.07
6	72°	Jonathan Villar	1.59
7	60°	**Christian Yelich**	**0.81**
8	54°	Ryan Braun	0.54
9	50°	Jesus Aguilar	0.39

Base Running Components

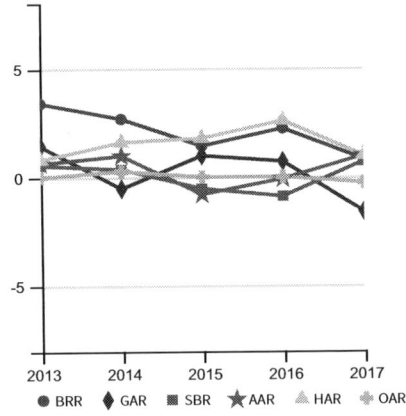

Ryan Zimmerman　1B　Washington Nationals

Born: 9/28/1984　**Age:** 33　**Bats:** R　**Throws:** R　**Height:** 6' 3"　**Weight:** 225 lbs　**Draft Info:** Round 1, 2005 Draft (#4 overall)

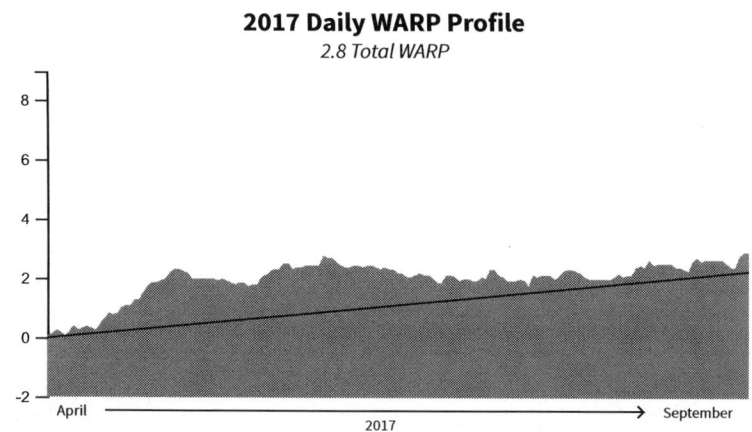

2017 Daily WARP Profile
2.8 Total WARP

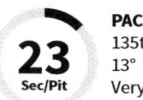

23 Sec/Pit

PACE
135th of 155
13°
Very Slow

Fantasy Values

2017	2018
$27.18	$18.00

YEAR	TEAM	LVL	AGE	PA	R	2B	3B	HR	RBI	BB	K	SB	AVG/OBP/SLG	TAv	VORP	BABIP	WARP
2017	WAS	MLB	32	576	90	33	0	36	108	44	126	1	.303/.358/.573	.315	39.3	.335	2.8

2017 Batting Percentages

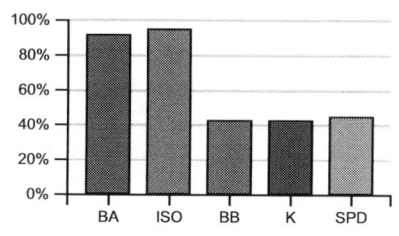

Batting PECOTA Percentiles

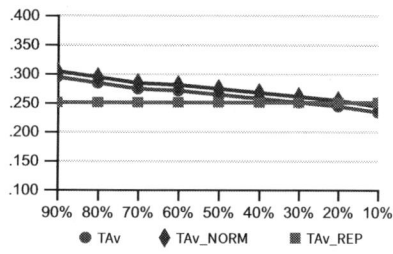

Batting WARP History

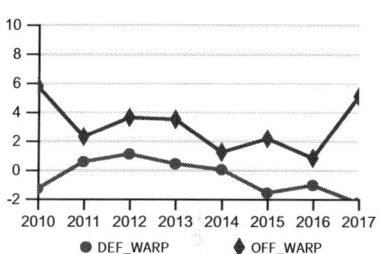

BRR (Relative to Position)

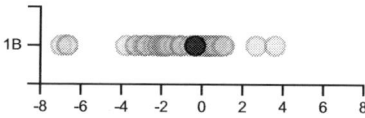

Rank		Player	BRR
18	69°	Cody Bellinger	-0.17
19	66°	Yonder Alonso	-0.29
20	64°	**Ryan Zimmerman**	**-0.29**
21	62°	Matt Adams	-0.56
22	61°	John Hicks	-0.97

BRR (Relative to Team)

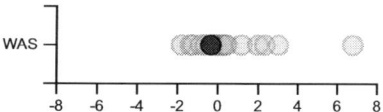

Rank		Player	BRR
11	38°	Howie Kendrick	-0.08
12	37°	Stephen Drew	-0.14
13	29°	**Ryan Zimmerman**	**-0.29**
14	24°	Matt Adams	-0.56
15	20°	Jayson Werth	-0.79

Base Running Components

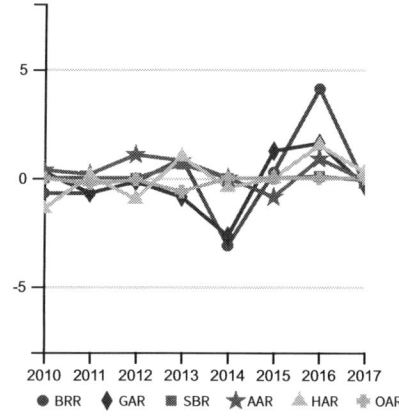

Jordan Zimmermann   RHP   Detroit Tigers

Born: 5/23/1986   **Age:** 32   **Bats:** R   **Throws:** R   **Height:** 6' 2"   **Weight:** 225 lbs   **Draft Info:** Round 2, 2007 Draft (#67 overall)

We don't have a baseball card for this guy.

2017 Daily WARP Profile
-1.3 Total WARP

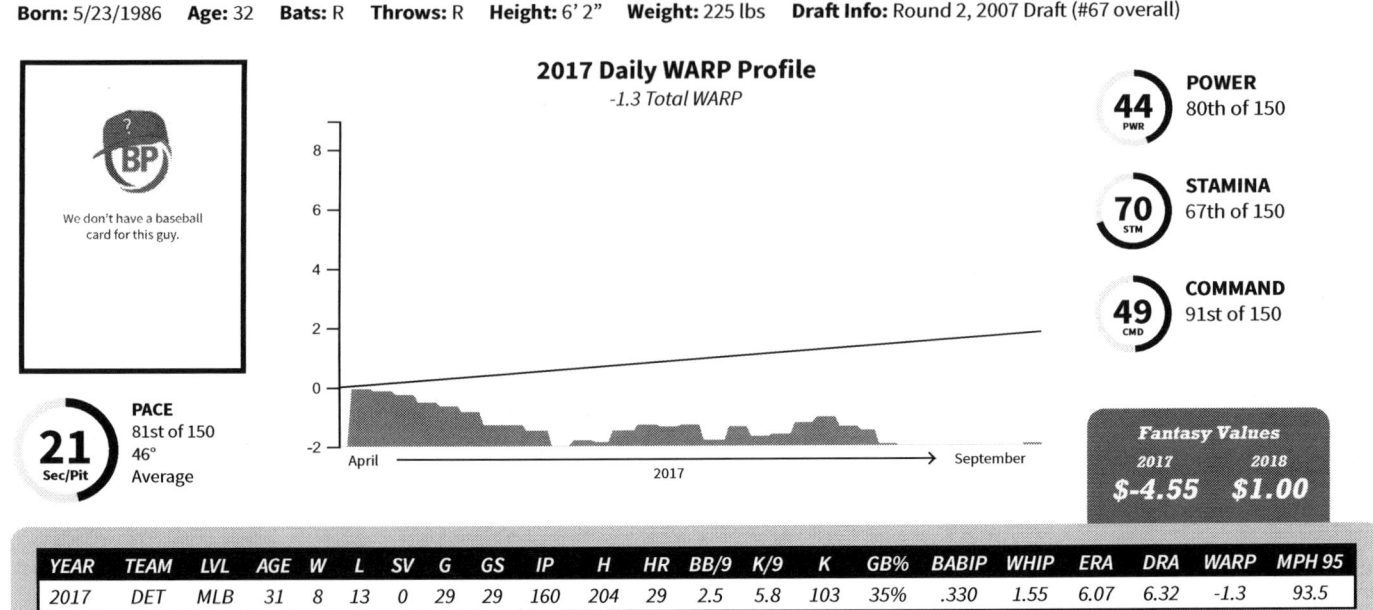

	POWER	44 PWR	80th of 150
STAMINA	70 STM	67th of 150
COMMAND	49 CMD	91st of 150

PACE 21 Sec/Pit — 81st of 150, 46°, Average

Fantasy Values

2017	2018
$-4.55	$1.00

YEAR	TEAM	LVL	AGE	W	L	SV	G	GS	IP	H	HR	BB/9	K/9	K	GB%	BABIP	WHIP	ERA	DRA	WARP	MPH 95
2017	DET	MLB	31	8	13	0	29	29	160	204	29	2.5	5.8	103	35%	.330	1.55	6.07	6.32	-1.3	93.5

2017 Pitching Percentages

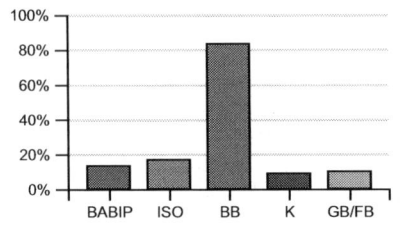

Pitching PECOTA Percentiles

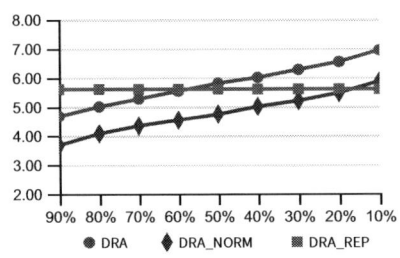

● DRA   ◆ DRA_NORM   ■ DRA_REP

Pitching WARP History

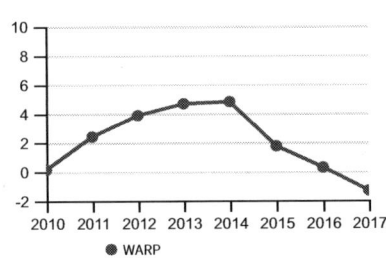

● WARP

Tunnel vs LHH

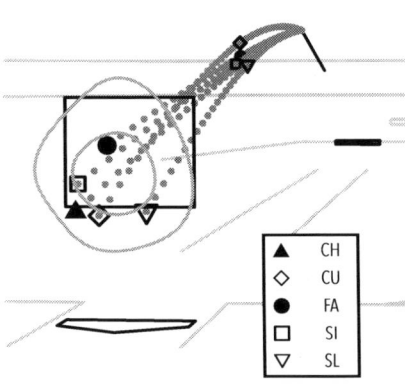

▲ CH
◇ CU
● FA
□ SI
▽ SL

Pitch Types

Type	Freq	Velo	H Mov	V Mov
CH	5.9%	86.8 [107]	-12.9 [90]	-25.5 [104]
CU	15.6%	81.3 [111]	5 [89]	-42.7 [111]
FA	48.4%	92.7 [100]	-6.7 [102]	-14.5 [102]
SI	5.8%	92.5 [101]	-13 [97]	-20 [100]
SL	24.3%	87.4 [113]	3.1 [94]	-26.5 [118]

Pitch Tunnel

Pairs	Release Diff	Tunnel Diff	Plate Diff	Speed Changes
1900	22.9	112.9	219.8	0.021

PI Scores

Year	Pitch Ct	Pwr	Cmd	Stm
2013	3078	59	56	80
2014	2912	63	57	74
2015	3085	53	57	77
2016	1704	46	54	50
2017	2607	44	49	70

Tunnel vs RHH

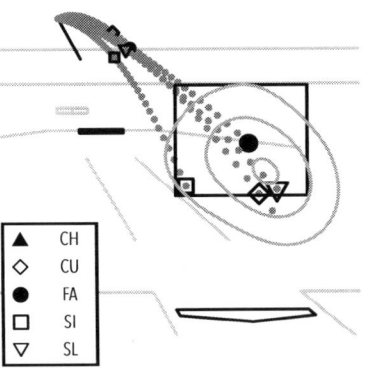

▲ CH
◇ CU
● FA
□ SI
▽ SL

Mike Zunino   C   Seattle Mariners

Born: 3/25/1991   **Age:** 27   **Bats:** R   **Throws:** R   **Height:** 6' 2"   **Weight:** 220 lbs   **Draft Info:** Round 1, 2012 Draft (#3 overall)

PACE
45th of 155
71°
Fast

21 Sec/Pit

2017 Daily WARP Profile
2.9 Total WARP

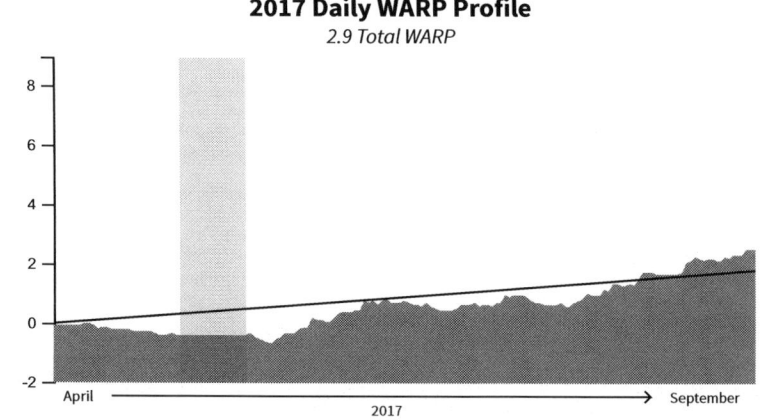

Game 30: minors

Fantasy Values

2017	2018
$12.31	$9.00

YEAR	TEAM	LVL	AGE	PA	R	2B	3B	HR	RBI	BB	K	SB	AVG/OBP/SLG	TAv	VORP	BABIP	WARP
2017	SEA	MLB	26	435	52	25	0	25	64	39	160	1	.251/.331/.509	.279	27.8	.355	2.9

2017 Batting Percentages

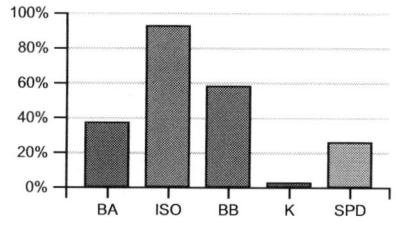

Batting PECOTA Percentiles

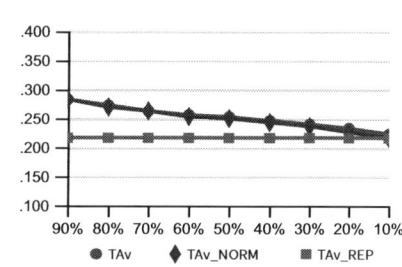

Batting WARP History

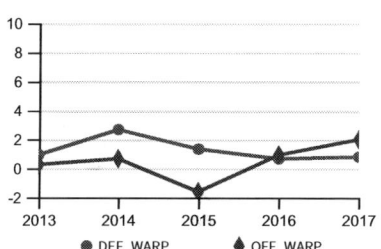

BRR (Relative to Position)

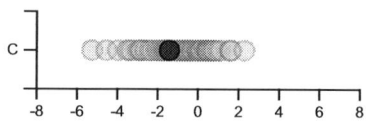

Rank		Player	BRR
50	43°	Salvador Perez	-1.33
51	42°	Bruce Maxwell	-1.37
52	39°	**Mike Zunino**	**-1.37**
53	38°	Chris Gimenez	-1.39
54	35°	Buster Posey	-1.49

BRR (Relative to Team)

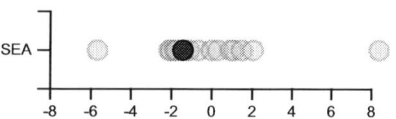

Rank		Player	BRR
8	57°	Andrew Romine	-0.61
9	56°	Cameron Perkins	-1.07
10	49°	**Mike Zunino**	**-1.37**
11	42°	Mitch Haniger	-1.40
12	35°	Danny Valencia	-1.71

Base Running Components

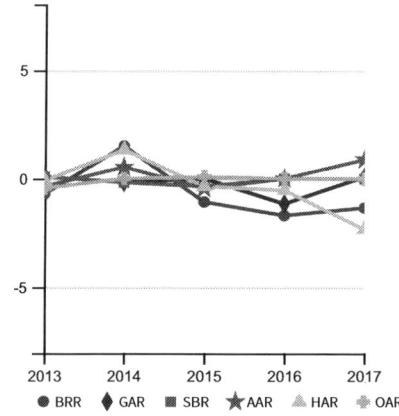

Contributors

David Brown is an author of Baseball Prospectus.

Russell A. Carleton is an author of Baseball Prospectus and has been writing about the Gory Mathematical Details of baseball for more than a decade. He is the author of the forthcoming book *The Shift: The Next Evolution in Baseball Thinking* and lives in Atlanta with his wife and five (!!!) kids.

A native of the Bay Area, **Dennis Cleary** received a degree in Literature from UC Davis. An Athletics fan since the Mustache Gang days, Dennis still hasn't gotten over the pain of the Kirk Gibson home run, the Canseco trade, or the Giambi non-slide (but he's not bitter). He lives in San Lorenzo, CA, with his wife Susan and three dogs.

Mary Craig is a political theory and American political thought scholar and baseball history enthusiast. In her spare time, when she's not tweeting bad puns, she seeks to dispel the myth that baseball is apolitical.

Zach Crizer is a writer for Baseball Prospectus. His Internet baseball writing career began at Beyond the Box Score after he left the newspaper business, where he covered politics and local government for the *Roanoke Times*. He lives in New York City, regularly fending off questions about whether so-and-so is "clutch."

Patrick Dubuque is a wastrel and a general layabout. He has written nominally about baseball for Baseball Prospectus, Lookout Landing, NotGraphs, and other fine websites, most of them dead. He resides in Edmonds, WA, with his wife Kjersten, and his two children, Sylvie and Felix. He devotes his time to instilling a love of baseball in the latter, but for now he settles for soothing them after he changes the channel away from *Octonauts*.

An avid fantasy baseball player for over 20 years, **Mike Gianella** has been a Senior Fantasy Baseball writer for Baseball Prospectus since 2013. Prior to this, Mike was the founder of Roto Think Tank, a blog specifically dedicated to fantasy baseball strategy and tactics. He lives in a Philadelphia suburb with his wife Colleen, his daughters Lucy and Elise, and their three cats.

Craig Goldstein is an author and editor at Baseball Prospectus. His work has appeared in Vice Sports, Fox Sports MLB/JABO, and SB Nation MLB. He lives and works in Washington DC, where he spends just the right amount of time thinking about baseball's large adult sons.

Bryan Grosnick is an author of Baseball Prospectus, a contributor to several Baseball Prospectus Annuals, and the host of the DFA Podcast. Over the years, he has appeared on television as an analyst on MLB Network; over the airwaves on terrestrial and satellite radio broadcasts; and in writing for publishing verticals operated by MLB, Fox, and Vox Media. He currently resides in New England with his two favorite people: his wife and son.

Jonathan Judge is a trial and regulatory lawyer who specializes in consumer products claims and regulation. He is a member of the BP Stats team and focuses on new modeling strategies.

Jeff Long is a member of the Baseball Prospectus stats team who primarily focuses on pitching research and development. His work has appeared at Baseball Prospectus, Sports on Earth, Fox Sports, and Beyond the Box Score. In addition to his statistical work, Jeff has explored and written about player development, roster construction, and scouting. He currently lives with his girlfriend Sarah and their dog Alton in Louisville, where he works for an advertising agency.

Rob Mains is a former Wall Street equities analyst who now writes the "Flu-Like Symptoms" column for Baseball Prospectus. He lives in upstate New York with his wife, dog, and too much Finger Lakes wine. On a personal level he considers 2017 to have been his best year of the Statcast Era.

Kate Morrison is a baseball writer and analyst for publications including Baseball Prospectus, as well as a social and digital media specialist hailing from the Dallas area. Additionally, as a research assistant for Pitch Info, she works to ensure the quality of pitch tagging on BrooksBaseball.net. Kate owes her passion for baseball to her mother, who made sure she understood the game.

Rob Neyer has been obsessed with baseball since before you were born, so please forgive him any signs of encroaching senility. He has written at great length for ESPN, SB Nation, and Fox Sports, and at less length for almost everybody else. In 2018, HarperCollins has promised to publish Rob's seventh book, which might be titled *POWER BALL: Nine Innings of Brains, Brawn, and Post-Modern Baseball*. He lives in Oregon with his wife and daughter.

A former river guide, ranch hand, farm hand, and, most unlikely, editor-in-chief of a magazine, **John Paschal** has written sports and opinion for the *Dallas Morning News*, the *(Memphis) Commercial Appeal*, the *Corpus Christi Caller-Times*, and other dead-tree publications. Online, he has scribbled graffiti across Baseball Prospectus, The Hardball

Times, FanGraphs, NotGraphs, Deadspin, and The Good Men Project. He lives in Austin with his wife, Syboney, and believes there is a global conspiracy against the Rangers.

Harry Pavlidis is the founder of Pitch Info and the Director of Technology for Baseball Prospectus.

Jarrett Seidler is a staff writer for Baseball Prospectus, focusing on player development and the minors, and a member of the BP prospect team. He also cohosts "For All You Kids Out There," the weekly BP Mets podcast. As a lifelong New Jersey resident, he is required to express support for Bruce Springsteen at all times.

Holly M. Wendt is Assistant Professor of English at Lebanon Valley College and teaches creative writing, medieval studies, and baseball literature. Their fiction and nonfiction have appeared in *Baseball Prospectus*, *Barrelhouse*, *The Classical*, *Memorious*, *Sport Literate*, and elsewhere.

Geoff Young founded Ducksnorts, one of the world's first baseball blogs, in 1997. He has written for The Hardball Times, Baseball Prospectus, and ESPN.com, and contributed to many books. He lives in San Diego with his wife Sandra and their pug Charlie, and dreams of a universe in which Sean Burroughs became a superstar.

Index of Names

Made in the USA
San Bernardino, CA
25 April 2018